Modern China

Graham Hutchings studied Chinese history, politics and language at Hatfield Poly-technic, Ealing College of Higher Education and the School of Oriental and African Studies at the University of London. For more than ten years he was China Correspon-dent of London's *The Daily Telegraph*, during which time he lived in Beijing and Hong Kong. He reported on the rise and fall of the Tiananmen Square Democracy Movement, China's economic 'take-off', the first direct presidential elections in Taiwan, the death of Deng Xiaoping and China's recovery of Hong Kong. He has travelled through more than twenty of China's provinces. He is currently a senior editor and China analyst with Oxford Analytica, the international consultancy company.

Modern China

A Guide to a Century of Change

Graham Hutchings

Harvard University Press
Cambridge, Massachusetts
2001

Printed in the United States of America

First United Kingdom publication 2000 by Penguin Books

Library of Congress Cataloging-in-Publication Data

Hutchings, Graham.
Modern China : a guide to a century of change / Graham Hutchings.
p.cm.
Includes bibliographical references and index.
ISBN 0-674-00658-5 (alk. paper)
1. China--History--20th century. I. Title.

DS774 .H796 2001
951.05--dc21
2001024386

For Lizzie, Nick and Annie –
China Companions

Contents

List of Maps   ix
List of Illustrations   xi
Note to the Reader   xiii
Preface   xix

Introduction: Middle Kingdom to Modern State   I
Companion to Modern China   25

Chronology   499
Selected Recommended Reading   509
Index   516

List of Maps

Physical China   xiv–xv
Political China   xvi–xvii
Major crop areas   26
Major ethnic minorities   128
Hong Kong Special Administrative Region   195
China–India disputed borders   222
The Long March   284
Macau Special Administrative Region   289
Manchuguo and China   293
First stage of the Northern Expedition – 1926   318
Chinese overseas   323
China's military regions   339
Urban population   342
South China Sea   392
Republic of China on Taiwan   406
Three Gorges Dam   420
Tibet   434
Treaty ports and foreign territories   437
Tumen River Economic Zone   440
Weihaiwei and neighbouring foreign territories   463
Yangtze River   478

List of Illustrations

(Photographic acknowledgements are given in parentheses)

1. The Empress Dowager Ci Xi (Corbis/Bettmann)
2. Yuan Shi-kai (Popperfoto)
3. Sun Yat-sen (Corbis/Bettmann)
4. Chiang Kai-shek (Corbis)
5. Mao Zedong (Corbis/Bettmann)
6. Deng Xiaoping (Corbis/Bettmann)
7. Jiang Zemin (Corbis/AFP)
8. Chen Shui-bian (Camera Press)
9. Tung Chee-hwa (Corbis/AFP)
10. Edmund Ho Hau-wah (Corbis/AFP)
11. The Politburo Standing Committee (Camera Press)
12. Execution of Boxer rebel (Corbis/Hulton Getty)
13. Armed picket searching a suspected revolutionary (Popperfoto)
14. Japanese soldiers in Hangzhou (Magnum Photos)
15. Mao addresses party members at Yanan (Camera Press)
16. Mao declaring the foundation of the People's Republic of China (Magnum Photos/ New China Pictures)
17. Production Brigade marches to work (Magnum Photos/René Burri)
18. Propaganda poster from the Cultural Revolution (Vintage Magazine Archive)
19. 'Class enemies' being paraded before the masses (Corbis/Bettman)
20. Democracy Wall, Beijing (Colorific)
21. Demonstrations in Tibet (Katz Pictures/Steve Lehman)
22. Pro-democracy demonstrations in Tiananmen Square (Topham Picturepoint)
23. Celebrating fifty years of Communist rule (Camera Press)
24. Traditional farming, Hainan (Popperfoto/Reuters)
25. Volkswagen plant, Shanghai (Magnum/Stuart Franklin)
26. The National People's Congress in session (Corbis/AFP)
27. Nanjing Road, Shanghai (Corbis/Keren Su)
28. Shoppers in Beijing (Popperfoto/Reuters)

Note to the Reader

- Entries are arranged in alphabetical order.
- Cross references are indicated by the use of small capitals and/or the use of the word 'See' in brackets followed by the entry in small capitals.
- Cross references are designed to enhance understanding of the topic(s) and draw attention to related subjects.
- On occasion 'See also' is used in brackets to identify related subjects.
- Most of the few statistics in this book are drawn from official Chinese sources unless otherwise stated. Population figures are given to the nearest million.
- The *pinyin* system of transliterating Chinese names is used for places, people and events concerned primarily with the Mainland. The Taiwanese version of the Wade–Giles system is used for places and proper names concerned mainly with Taiwan. Exceptions include 'Chiang Kai-shek' and 'Sun Yat-sen' which appear in these, their most common dialect forms, complete with hyphenated given names.

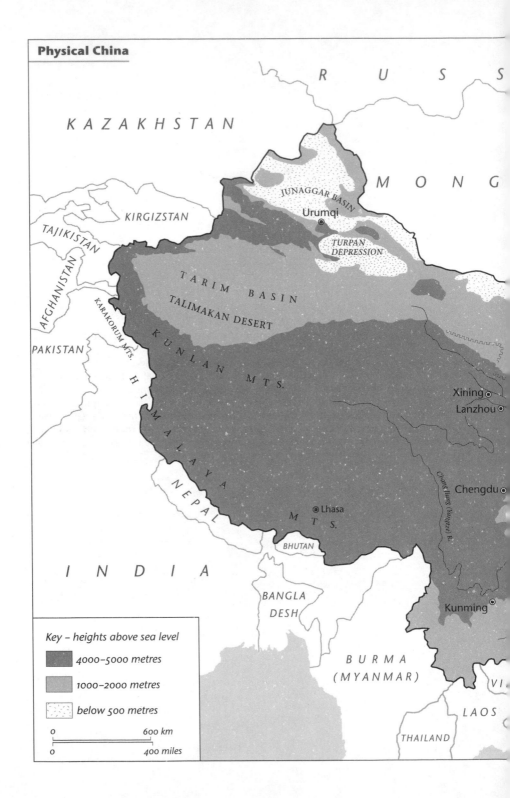

Physical China

KAZAKHSTAN

R U S S

M O N G

KIRGIZSTAN

JUNAGGAR BASIN

Urumqi

TURPAN
DEPRESSION

TAJIKISTAN

AFGHANISTAN

TARIM   BASIN

TALIMAKAN DESERT

KARAKORUM Mts.

PAKISTAN

K U N L A N   M T S.

Xining

Lanzhou

H I M A L A Y A

NEPAL

M T S.

Chengdu

Lhasa

Chung Jiang (Yangtze) R.

BHUTAN

I N D I A

BANGLA
DESH

Kunming

B U R M A
(MYANMAR)

V I

LAOS

THAILAND

Key – heights above sea level

4000–5000 metres

1000–2000 metres

below 500 metres

| 0 | 600 km |

| 0 | 400 miles |

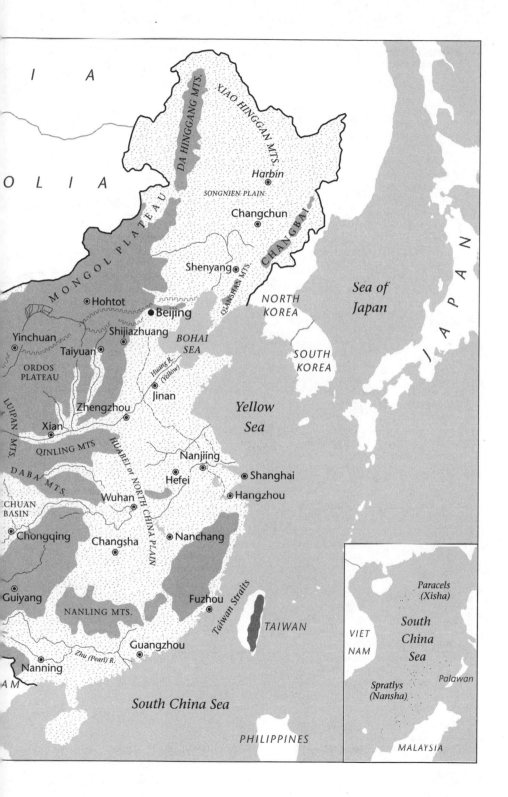

Political China

KAZAKHSTAN

R U S S

M O N G

KIRGIZSTAN

Urumqi ◉

•Turfan

TAJIKISTAN

•Kashgar

AFGHANISTAN

Xinjiang

Gansu

PAKISTAN

Qinghai

Xining ◉

Lanzhou ◉

Xizang
(Tibet)

Chengdu ◉

Sichuan

NEPAL

Chang Jiang (Yangtze) R.

•Lhasa

Thimphu

Kathmandu •

BHUTAN

I N D I A

Kunming ◉

BANGLA
DESH

Mekong

Hunnan

Dacca •

Key

● National capital(s)

◉ Provincial or Autonomous
Region capitals

• Other places

BURMA
(MYANMAR)

VIE

LAOS

Bay of
Bengal

THAILAND

0 ———————— 600 km

0 ———————— 400 miles

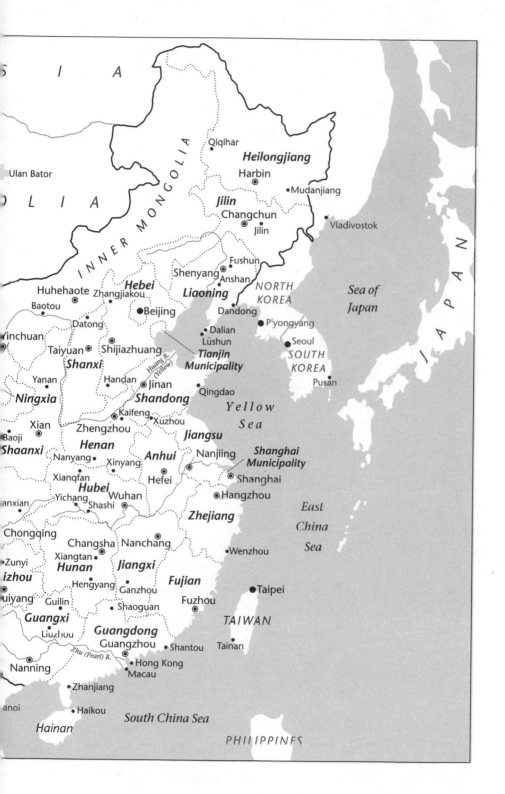

Preface

China is the world's most populous state as well as one of its largest. It is a nuclear power and a permanent member of the United Nations Security Council. According to some estimates its GDP does not need to grow very fast for very long before it overtakes that of the United States and China becomes the world's largest economy.[1] Its history and culture, as rich as they are distinctive, are among the oldest in the world, and yet they cast a long shadow over the future. These are grounds enough for an examination of the kind attempted here of the rise of modern China, its meaning for the Chinese people and the rest of the world.

There are several more. China, defined in this instance, but not invariably in this book, as the People's Republic of China, is ruled by the Chinese Communist Party, an unstable entity which espouses a moribund ideology and presides over powerful social forces unleashed by rapid economic growth. The Party's future – assuming it has one – and the shape of Chinese politics in the new century, are far from clear.

So are many of the consequences of China's extraordinary economic growth. They include the traditional problem of overpopulation, and more recent ones of environmental damage and strains on food and energy supplies of a kind not encountered elsewhere. Little more than twenty years ago, these issues could be regarded as 'internal problems', even though they affected about one quarter of humanity. There is no such luxury in an era of globalization: many of China's problems are those of humanity at large.

To some extent this is true even of China's quest for national unity, a main theme in its modern history and an obsession of its Communist leaders. Military power has secured – at least for the time being – firm control of all but the ethnic fringes of the Mainland such as Tibet and Xinjiang. Diplomacy has wrought the return of Hong Kong and Macau. But Taiwan, half confident in its new democratic identity and 'unofficial' support from the United States and, since the landmark election of 2000, led by a president from the pro-independence Democratic Progressive Party, remains beyond Beijing's grasp.

The Republic of China on Taiwan, or 'Taiwan Province' – depending on whether one views it from Taipei or Beijing – is contested territory. It is as difficult to forecast the outcome of a possible 'war of Chinese unification' as it is to be sure other countries – particularly the United States but possibly also Japan – would not get involved, with disastrous consequences for the Asia-Pacific region and beyond.

Chinese irredentism in the South China Sea is another source of concern. Control over

---

1 For example, Angus Maddison, *Chinese Economic Performance in the Long Run* (OECD, Paris, 1998).

the resources and shipping lanes of this huge expanse of ocean and its islands is contested by several nations. It sometimes seems that diplomacy might settle the dispute between them. At least as often it appears that only war will decide the issue – probably in Beijing's favour.

What is clear is that China's policies in almost every area – from the South China Sea to the Taiwan Straits; from the economy to military spending; from foreign affairs to stewardship of the environment – will have an ever larger impact on the rest of the world. China is a rising power – one that demands accommodation within an international system that is not of its making and many of whose values it does not share. The outcome of this demand cannot confidently be foretold. But its historical background, and the key issues at stake, can at least be understood.

That is the object of this book. Its subject is China's evolution from a decaying empire in 1900 into a rapidly modernizing state more than a century later. Its purpose is to introduce the major aspects of this transition and explain their significance. Its approach is to examine the people, places, events, movements, organizations and ideas that have shaped China's destiny over the past hundred years in a series of short, critical essays. And its aim is to provide general readers and students, government officials and media professionals, business people and non-specialist academics with a comprehensive, accessible, *companionable* source of information about a country whose growing importance calls for still greater understanding.

It seeks to be a reliable and instructive aid to learning as well as an encouragement to learn more. It tries to be authoritative rather than academic; comprehensive rather than exhaustive; enjoyable as well as enlightening. The fact that it is entitled 'a' companion rather than the definite article reflects that it does not claim to be the last word.

These are bold ambitions, not easily realized. Perhaps it is as well, then, to state what this book is not. It is neither a dictionary nor an encyclopedia of modern China. And it does not claim to be exhaustive or definitive. Readers will find no reference to many of the exotic subjects J. Dyer Ball included in his *Things Chinese* or Samuel Couling in *The Encyclopaedia Sinica*.[1] Both of these fine, now dated works are to some extent ancestors of this volume, but the lineage is long and indirect.

The present work concentrates on modern China's politics, society and economy, and the impact on them of individuals, places, organizations and ideas, both Chinese and non-Chinese. In this context, 'modern' generally refers to the period between 1900 and the present day; 'China' includes the Mainland, Taiwan, Hong Kong and Macau, all of which are discussed individually and, on occasion, together.

Realpolitik has persuaded all but about thirty countries in the world, most of them small, to establish diplomatic relations with the People's Republic of China, and maintain only unofficial ties with the Republic of China on Taiwan. The Communist government insists there is only one China, that Taiwan is part of it, and Beijing is its capital. There can be no question of 'two Chinas' or 'one China, one Taiwan'. This book, free of the conventions of diplomacy, takes a different approach: it not only recognizes 'two Chinas', or 'one China, one Taiwan', it exults in their existence as a source of diversity and, ultimately, of benefit to China as a whole.

In form, this book is a work of reference. After an opening essay which provides a narrative 'spine' and introduces key themes, topics are presented alphabetically and cross referenced. There is a chronology at the end. To some extent, then, it is a handbook.

Yet in 'feel' – defined as the style and nature of the more than two hundred essays that

---

1 J. Dyer Ball, *Things Chinese* (1903) (Graham Brash, Singapore, 1989 [reprint of the fifth edn of 1925]). Samuel Couling, *The Encyclopaedia Sinica* (1917) (Oxford University Press Reprint: 1983). 'Exotica' include, in Dyer Ball, 'Beds and Bedsteads', p. 68; and in Couling, 'Bats' (the flying variety), p. 45.

make up the bulk of its content – the book hopes to be something more. Unlike the entries in many dictionaries and encyclopedias, those that appear here present a point of view as well as the principal facts and significance of the issues discussed. In this sense they are better thought of as essays than 'entries'. They take the form of 'soundings': explorations of events, peoples, places, themes and organizations, their role in China's twentieth-century history and, where appropriate, their importance for China's future.

Many of them are quite long. Most begin with an introduction or executive summary explaining the overall significance of what is being discussed. Several contain 'capsules' in which important sub-themes or associated issues are addressed. All are designed to be read in their entirety rather than mined for nuggets of fact, which in any case appear in the context of themes rather than as isolated packages of data.

The same goes for the book as a whole. Each of the essays is self-contained and designed to stand alone, but I hope readers will not let the alphabetic format in which they appear deter them from reading this book as they would any other work of history or politics: from cover to cover. Equally, having opened it to look up a subject of particular interest, either by referring to the individual entries or searching first in the index at the back, I hope readers will read on and discover themselves in new territory.

Whether this is the case will depend on their view of the topics selected for discussion. In a book of this kind selection is hazardous. The extremes of trying to be exhaustive (perhaps at the risk of being undiscriminating), and ending up simply arbitrary are both to be avoided. The first approach would produce a book of enormous size and potential boredom; the second, fewer words but more polemic. I hope I have avoided both extremes, and that the genuinely important people, places, events, political parties, ideas, institutions and international organizations in the history of modern China all find a place.

Among them, for reasons worth stating immediately, are all thirty-one provincial units of the People's Republic of China. China's provinces are larger and more populous than many countries. During the first half of the twentieth century, and again during its final twenty years or so in particular, many of them enjoyed high profiles as distinct political, economic and social units within a broader national canvas. Yet they are not equally important in China's national development. Neither is an equal amount known about them. This goes some way to explaining the different lengths at which they are treated here.

Another required subject in a book of this kind is some treatment of the current leadership line-up in Beijing. China's senior leaders are defined here as the seven members of the Standing Committee of the Politburo of the Central Committee elected at the 15th National Party Congress in 1997; and the premier (also a member of the Standing Committee) and four (one of them also a member of the Standing Committee) vice-premiers of the State Council elected at the First Session of the 9th National People's Congress in March 1998. These ten men – Jiang Zemin, Li Peng, Zhu Rongji, Li Ruihuan, Hu Jintao, Wei Jianxing, Li Lanqing, Qian Qichen, Wu Bangguo and Wen Jiabao – are key decision-makers in the People's Republic. Their names crop up regularly in media coverage and other discussion of contemporary China. One or more among the younger of them is likely to emerge as paramount leader in the next few years.

There is little difficulty justifying the exclusion from a book of this nature of the flora and fauna, customs and cuisines, dialects and diseases treated so abundantly by Messrs Dyer Ball and Couling. The decision to devote relatively little space to the arts and sciences, on the other hand, might seem more controversial.

'Might', though, is the appropriate word. Though interesting and important, China's artists have played a less decisive role in their country's modern history than its militarists, revolutionaries and reformers. China's scientists have played a larger role, notably in the development of atomic and nuclear weapons. Yet even their work is eclipsed in significance by China's remarkable economic growth and its effects on the country's politics, society and environment. China's impact on the rest of the world derives from its wares, weapons and geopolitical weighting rather than its letters and sciences. There is no question that

China is a rising power. There is little evidence that it is undergoing a *cultural* revival of a kind likely to make much of an impression beyond its borders.[1]

Despite these attempted justifications, I have no doubt some people will find certain inclusions in this book unwelcome – just as they will find various exclusions unforgivable. Still others will find their pleasure over the presence of some topics marred by what they consider to be scanty treatment.

Those most likely to do so are China specialists who have laboured long and hard on the study of an individual person, place, or event in China's modern history which they feel is treated inadequately here. To them, I apologize. To others, and perhaps particularly to the general reader, I can say that while some topics have indeed been discussed briefly or excluded altogether, they are, in the overall scheme of things, interesting rather than important.

This is a work of synthesis and interpretation rather than original scholarship. As such it relies much on published materials in both English and Chinese. My debt to academic and journalistic specialists of modern China will be clear to both communities. To those for whom it is not clear, I am happy to acknowledge the debt. Many of the English-language works I have consulted are listed in the recommendations for further reading found at the rear of this book.

Yet there is another important source of this book and its occasionally strong opinions. After an academic training in Chinese studies I spent more than ten years writing about China for London's *The Daily Telegraph*, firstly based in the UK and travelling to China on a regular basis, and then running the paper's bureau in Beijing and finally Hong Kong. I worked and lived in China (in the enlarged sense of the term) for more than eight years, reading the Chinese press on a daily basis, travelling and reporting from more than twenty provinces, and covering events such as the Tiananmen Square Democracy Movement; China's 'economic take-off' of the early 1990s; the first direct presidential elections in Taiwan; the death of Deng Xiaoping; and China's resumption of sovereignty over Hong Kong.

This is not a book about those experiences: the personal pronoun does not crop up outside this preface. Neither do the names of the many contacts and friends – Chinese and non-Chinese, officials and otherwise – I spoke to in and about China. But my encounters with them, and my direct experience of China's often frustrating, sometimes tragic, always absorbing complexity, have made a contribution to the way I have approached many of the events discussed in this book.

Many people and one particular institution helped make this book possible. The institution is *The Daily Telegraph* whose editors allowed me to live in, travel throughout and write about China during more than ten dramatic years in the life of that country. I owe a special debt to Nigel Wade, former foreign editor and before that a distinguished *Telegraph* correspondent in Beijing. His enthusiasm for China, his experience and support were invaluable. They were reinforced by encouragement from Max Hastings and Charles Moore, successive editors of the paper; and Patrick Bishop, Nigel's successor as foreign editor, and all who worked on the foreign desk between 1987 and 1998. Looking back I realize that they often indulged my passion for China and how to cover it. I am grateful that they did.

My encounter with things Chinese began in the unlikely setting of Hatfield Polytechnic

---

1 Chinese complaints, heard at either end of the twentieth century and often in between, over the failure of its artists and scientists to win Nobel prizes tend to say more about the patriotism of those that made them than their discrimination. One complainant was the great reformer Liang Qichao (see page 277); another was the Communist Party's *People's Daily* newspaper (Reuters, Beijing, *China Says Nobel Literature Prize Discriminatory*, 24 January 1997). In the 1980s and 1990s Taiwan and Hong Kong made more significant contributions to global culture than Mainland China, especially in film, literature and fine arts.

during the mid-1970s. I am grateful to my principal tutors in Asian studies there, Dr Jonathan Mirsky (later a fellow newsman) and Dr Alastair Lamb. Jonathan, in particular, encouraged me to pursue Chinese studies and provided advice and friendship along the way. Dr Beverley Southgate, tutor in European history, did more than he knows by way of communicating the joy of history.

In Beijing, Hong Kong and beyond over the years I have been able to draw upon the wisdom and experience of many involved in the task of understanding China and/or writing about it. Most, but not all, are journalists. Others are diplomats, bankers or Chinese friends. They include Zorana Bakovic, Chen Ziqiang, David Coates, Geoffrey Crothall, Ed Gargan, David Holley, Lincoln Kaye, Willem van Kemenade, Henry Li, Simon Long, Floris-Jan van Luyn, Jan van De Made, Eric Meyer, James Miles, Yvonne Preston, Song Gang, Neil Tait, Ashok Tiku, Hans Vriens, Wu Wei and Zhang Dawo. Jurgen and Susie Kremb provided friendship, hospitality – and opportunities to interview Wei Jingsheng and Wang Dan during the few weeks these dissidents were allowed some freedom in Beijing. Adam Brookes, then at Harvard's Fairbank Center, offered helpful comments on Zhou Enlai. Simon Scott Plummer, Jonathan Manthorpe, Nick Rufford, my agent Christopher Sinclair-Stevenson and my editor at Penguin, Nigel Wilcockson, and his colleague Jenny Rayner, were sources of encouragement and wise counsel. Myrna Blumberg copy edited with great care, rescuing me from errors and suggesting improvements. I would have learned less about China had I not been able to spend long hours in the company of two elderly and distinguished Chinese friends in their apartment in Beijing. They would not wish me to name them, but I would like to record the debt I owe 'L' and 'Y'. Always with patience and often with passion, they explained the perils of pursuing the intellectual life in Communist China to someone who, unlike them, has been spared the pains of doing so. My greatest debt is to the principal dedicatee of this book. Liz readily left friends and family in the UK to live first in Beijing and then Hong Kong with Nick and Annie – and a husband too often on the road or seated in front of a keyboard and monitor.

Graham Hutchings
St Albans, Hertfordshire
2000

Introduction

Middle Kingdom to Modern State: China's Unfulfilled Quest for Power and Prestige[1]

China entered the twentieth century in decline. Its territorial fringes – and, thanks to the Boxer Rebellion, its capital – were occupied by the powers, its sovereignty impaired by Unequal Treaties. The country's ideology and institutions, founded in the previous millennium to serve a timeless, universal empire, were in crisis, its Manchu, Qing Dynasty rulers unable or unwilling to reform. Dissent stalked the capital; regional governors resisted re-centralization. Hardly a province was untouched by rebellion. Outside half a dozen major urban centres, the economy remained stubbornly, overwhelmingly, agrarian. Most Chinese were illiterate and conducted their lives according to customs little changed down the centuries. In almost every respect China was ill prepared for the struggle between industrialized nations destined to shape the new century. In 1900, China's very existence seemed under threat.

China enters the twenty-first century in stronger shape. It has regained much of its lost territory and is determined to recover more. Beijing cannot always get its way in adjacent provinces let alone distant frontiers. But neither rich nor remote regions dare defy the central government when the national interest is at stake. China's nuclear weapons, military modernization and above all its recent rapid economic growth have secured it a seat at the world's top table. Agriculture now accounts for about one quarter of GDP, industry for almost one half. China is far indeed from the 'superpower' status forecast by several Western commentators during the 1990s, but the reality and implications of its rise are no less profound for that.[2]

Yet in examining these implications it is important not to exaggerate the contrast between China at the start of the twentieth and twenty-first centuries. Its transformation is no less remarkable for being incomplete. China's leaders are aware of their country's weaknesses and potential instability, the gap between its real and reputed power, even if foreigners sometimes overlook them. Undoubtedly China is stronger and richer than it was in 1900. Just as certainly, it remains a fragile power, dogged by issues that are identical, or closely related to those it confronted more than a century ago. For if, in common with most other parts of the world, China changed dramatically during the hundred years that began in 1900, it did not, in several important respects, do so beyond recognition.

1 The footnotes which follow identify sources to which readers may turn for fuller discussion of the issues addressed in this introduction. Many are included in the list of recommended reading found at the rear of this book.

2 See William H. Overholt, *China: The Next Economic Superpower* (Weidenfeld & Nicolson, London, 1993) and Geoffrey Murray, *China the Next Superpower: Dilemmas in Change and Continuity* (Curzon Press, Richmond, Surrey, 1998).

Much of the past has been discredited but much of it is still lived in. Indeed, the past is less a 'foreign country' in China than a prison. For if it is a matter of pride that China is the world's oldest centre of continuous civilization, its modern history is one of largely unsuccessful attempts to escape the consequences of this extraordinary pedigree. During the twentieth century, conscious thought and constitutions changed more than mindsets; institutions and ideologies more than instincts. The twentieth century was a period of patent, potent change: millions of Chinese have been dislodged from their culture and community by decades of revolution and reform. Yet even bouts of intense iconoclasm have failed to eradicate profound continuities. They include the ideal of the centralized, unitary state, at once a repository of moral wisdom and source of security for a huge population; traditional, often compliant attitudes towards authority – tempered by a desire to be free of it; a feeling that to be Chinese is, in some often undefinable way, to be unique; and the importance of family values and primacy of personal relations. All these are deep-seated sentiments. All continue to be expressed in a unique spoken language and written script that is even older than the ideas it conveys.

In other words China is a highly distinct and complex as well as an increasingly powerful country. Its rise involves much more than expanding frontiers, growing economic power and military might – important though these are. No less significant are questions of cultural identity, of China's 'Chineseness', of how this is to be defined, developed and preserved in an increasingly open, competitive, interdependent, yet, in the view of Communist leaders, still predatory world. The way in which the Chinese people deal with these issues will determine the success – or otherwise – of their country's rise and integration with the wider world. It will have a bearing on whether this is to be a peaceful, if occasionally disruptive, process, or a violent and essentially destructive one.

Ultimately these are matters for speculation. Yet when accompanied by an understanding of the main issues at stake in China during the upheavals of the twentieth century, such speculation can be informed. That is why this introduction to the exploration of individual themes, people and places that follows begins around 1900 – the nadir of Chinese fortunes, but also the birth of powerful new forces of change, many of them still at work more than a century later.

The Lie of the Land

Including Taiwan, Hong Kong and Macau, China occupies an area of approximately 3.7 million square miles (9.6 million sq kms), making it the second-largest country in the world after Canada. A journey from the most northerly point, in Heilongjiang, to the most southerly, a contested reef in the South China Sea, passes through 49 degrees of latitude. An east–west odyssey, from Heilongjiang to Xinjiang, encompasses 62 degrees of longitude. China shares land and/or sea boundaries, some of them contested, with 18 countries: North Korea, Russia, Mongolia, Kazakhstan, Kirghizstan, Tajikistan, Afghanistan, Pakistan, India, Nepal, Bhutan, Burma, Laos, Vietnam, Indonesia, Malaysia, Brunei, and the Philippines.

China's topography is best defined as a three-step staircase, descending from west to east. The top step, the 'roof of the world', is the Qinghai–Tibet plateau, where the highlands average 12,000–15,000 feet (4,000–5,000 metres) above sea level. The Junggar, Tarim and Sichuan basins, together with the Inner Mongolian and Yunnan–Guizhou plateaux form the middle step with an elevation of 3,000–6,000 feet (1,000–2,000 metres) above sea level. The bottom step, generally less than 1,500 feet (500 metres), is made up of a belt of plains in Manchuria, north China, the middle and lower reaches of the Yangtze, and other major rivers such as the Yellow River, the Huai, and the Pearl River – all of which run west to east. Most of China's people, and the majority of its important cities, are crowded into this region, the longest settled and most densely populated in the country.

Size and varied terrain make for a diverse climate. China includes tropical and cold-temperate zones, a moist south and an arid northwest. The average temperature in Haikou, capital of Hainan Island, is 24 degrees centigrade. In Urumqi, capital of Xinjiang, it is 7 degrees centigrade. The central highlands of Taiwan enjoy an annual average rainfall of 218 inches (5,600 millimetres), the middle and lower reaches of the Yangtze, 39–78 inches (1,000–2,000 mm) and the western part of Inner Mongolia, the northern part of the Qinghai–Tibet plateau and most of Xinjiang less than 8 inches (200 mm).

Old World, New World: 1900–1911

Few of these forces were evident in the immediate aftermath of the Boxer Rebellion. The rebels, who had erupted from Shandong, occupied Beijing and laid seige to the International Legations, emerged from the 'dark world' of secret societies. Leading Manchus, beset by the growing foreign presence and pressure to reform at home, had set the millenarian beliefs and xenophobic rage at the heart of the Boxer movement loose on their foes. Perhaps irrational racism and primeval peasant anger could save a dynasty in distress? Perhaps 'old forces' would stave off the advance of the 'new'?

The Eight-Power occupation of Beijing, the flight of the Empress Dowager to Xian in distant Shaanxi, severe punishments for Boxer leaders, and a financial indemnity quite beyond the capacity of the meagre Qing treasury provided grim answers to these questions. The Boxer Rebellion proved less of a defeat for the Qing dynasty than a debacle: it was a wholly inadequate response to the challenges facing the country and its rulers.[1]

Though of longer standing, these challenges had been brought into focus by China's defeat at the hands of Japan in 1894–5. Not only did this result in the loss of Taiwan, it demonstrated the success of Japan's modernization drive and the utter failure of China's. Defeat sparked a movement for *fundamental* reform: the One Hundred Days Reform of 1898, sponsored by the Guangxu Emperor and led, among others, by Kang Youwei and Liang Qichao. The movement was important for two reasons: it championed modern political ideas – including the transformation of the Manchu monarchy into constitutional democracy; and it arose from pressure for change *outside* government. The new study societies, newspapers and magazines of the late 1890s challenged the monopoly over politics exercised by the Qing administration – a monopoly traditionally enjoyed by Chinese governments, and guarded jealously by the present one in Beijing.[2]

Conservative officials proved more adept at crushing the reform movement than coping with another major consequence of the war against Japan: the 'scramble for concessions' by other powers. This 'slicing of the Chinese melon', as Kang Youwei described it, reinforced the sense of national crisis. China was at risk physically, politically and culturally. Unless something was done, the social Darwinism believed to govern the destiny of nations, and introduced to alarmed Chinese readers by Yan Fu, the great apostle of change, would consign China to the margins of history. In the face of such a threat, the Boxer Rebellion – more of a traditional peasant rebellion than a modern political movement, however fondly nationalists might regard its anti-foreign sentiments – could only make things worse. It was the last gasp of the old order rather than a harbinger of the new.

Once the occupying armies had left Beijing and the dust settled in the capital, it was surprising how quickly others, including many Manchus, came round to this view. More surprising still was the way in which fear of national extinction bred determination to avoid it. Patriots of all persuasions, in Beijing and the provinces, where the Boxer fiasco had bred a sense of independence, struggled to revive their country's fortunes.

There was no doubt that China needed to be re-made. But there was much over how it was to be done. The issues at stake seemed impossibly large for a generation to contemplate let alone confront. They were the very ideas and institutions that had defined China for centuries and, until fairly recently, accounted for its extraordinary vigour and success: imperial rule, Confucianism, the agrarian economy, a family-centred social system, and the traditional feelings of superiority and self-sufficiency that each of these concepts, in different

---

1 Two authoritative examinations of the Boxer movement are Joseph Esherick, *The Origins of the Boxer Uprising* (University of California Press, Berkeley, 1987) and Paul Cohen, *History in Three Keys: The Boxers as Events, Experience and Myth* (Columbia University Press, New York, 1997).

2 Andrew J. Nathan discusses this movement and compares it with the Democracy Wall Movement of the late 1970s in *Chinese Democracy: The Individual and the State in Twentieth Century China* (I. B. Tauris, London, 1986).

ways, bred. Ultimately it was a question of overhauling a civilization rather than reforming a state; a case of rejecting overpowering tradition and searching for new forms of legitimacy outside it – and therefore outside China. No wonder, more than a century later, much of this work remains undone.

And yet during the first decade of the twentieth century, reforms touched almost every aspect of China's political, economic and even social life. They did so in varying degrees and with unpredicted, often unsought consequences. But in the final years of Manchu rule the pace – and the purpose – of change increased in extraordinary, unexpected ways.[1]

Reform of education was one of the earliest and most obvious examples. In 1905 the Imperial Court abolished the traditional examination system which had trained the elite in the arts of Confucianism for centuries. Rarely can a single act have done so much to undermine a civilization. It raised questions about an appropriate national ideology for China and the purpose and nature of education which had never been at issue before. Men and, increasingly, women sought answers in new Western-style schools, and at colleges and universities overseas. Many did so in Japan where they learnt the rudiments of every form of radicalism – constitutional democracy, republicanism, anarchism and socialism – and campaigned for them with fervour among the growing ranks of overseas Chinese students and sojourners.

Others concentrated on modern military arts, another major area of innovation and reform at home. China needed no reminding of the importance of modern armies: its history of humiliations in the nineteenth century owed much to the lack of latest weapons and well-trained men. Accordingly, the Manchus reorganized their existing military forces and founded new, Western- and Japanese-style armies the better to defend themselves from internal and external foes.

The Court, under growing pressure, was equally energetic in administrative and constitutional reform. The great 'Boards', the chief institutions of centralized administration under almost every dynasty, gave way to modern ministries which took a proactive role in their areas of responsibility, encouraging the development of industry, trade and railways. Constitutional change followed. In 1908 provincial assemblies were formed, and plans made for a National Assembly in Beijing. Barely a decade after they had crushed the '100 Days' and sponsored the Boxers, the Manchus seemed to be moving towards power sharing.

They were, but only involuntarily, sporadically and inconsistently. The reforms were real but designed to save the dynasty rather than destroy it. And they were accompanied by attempts to reassert central control over the provinces and concentrate power in the hands of a Manchu minority in Beijing. These moves antagonized a broad cross section of society whose members had been empowered by the reforms but were determined to see the end of Manchu rule. They included merchants and new army men in the provincial assemblies; secret societies who combined current peasant grievances with longstanding racial opposition to the 'alien' Manchus; and a determined if sometimes disorganized republican revolutionary movement whose adherents believed there was little hope for China as long as there was a dragon throne in Beijing and a Manchu sitting upon it.

The republicans were led by Sun Yat-sen.[2] A doctor turned itinerant professional revolutionary who had been brought up among the Overseas Chinese, Sun united those who shared his determination to overthrow the Qing in the *Tong Meng Hui*, or United League, which he founded in Tokyo in 1905. Small groups of revolutionaries had staged anti-Manchu uprisings before that date. Larger groups, often acting under Sun's direction, did so for several years afterwards. But it was not until 1911, by which time battles over railway rights

---

1 One of the best sources on the 'new' China of the early 1900s is still Mary Clabaugh Wright (ed.), *China In Revolution: The First Phase, 1900–1913* (Yale University Press, New Haven, 1968).

2 On Sun see Marie-Claire Bergère and Janet Lloyd, *Sun Yat-sen* (Cambridge University Press, Cambridge, 1998); C. Martin Wilbur, *Sun Yat-sen: Frustrated Patriot* (Columbia University Press, New York, 1976); Harold Z. Schiffrin, *Sun Yat-sen and the Origins of the Chinese Revolution* (University of California Press, Berkeley, 1968).

and general disenchantment had weakened Qing rule in several provinces, that rebellion took firm hold. The Republican Revolution began with a minor mutiny in Wuhan, capital of Hubei. It ended a few weeks later with the complete collapse of imperial rule and the abdication of Pu Yi, China's 'last emperor'.

Reaction, Reform, Revolution: 1912–28

With the mixture of conceit and idealism characteristic of many revolutionaries, China's republicans adopted a new calendar in 1912. At the birth of the Chinese Republic, history had begun again: China now had a president – at first Sun Yat-sen – and a parliament of sorts, which met first in Nanjing, capital of Jiangsu, heartland of the Yangtze delta. The Manchus had gone. The revolutionaries had returned from exile. China's future could be debated freely inside the country rather than on its periphery or overseas.[1]

Yet creating new institutions – and securing understanding, loyalty and respect for the novel ideas on which they were based – were just two items on the republican agenda. Huge tasks lay ahead in developing industry and trade, improving transport and communications, and extending education. The Manchus had made progress in some of these areas: modern schools and universities, though few in number, were turning out graduates of high quality; and in Shanghai, Tianjin, Wuhan and the Manchurian provinces of the northeast an industrial infrastructure was taking shape together with a modest network of railways, roads, modern shipping and telecommunications to serve it. Though small, these were the beginnings on which Sun hoped to build his grandiose vision of an industrialized China.

Since these plans required foreign capital, they raised the 'international question': the much less agreeable Qing legacy of Unequal Treaties, extraterritoriality and lack of tariff autonomy which allowed the powers a major say in many areas of China's national life. Worse, the young republic faced new foreign menaces: Russia's expansion in Mongolia, Britain's interference in Tibet, and Russian and Japanese rivalry in Manchuria. China's fringes were far from secure.

For nationalists there could be no question of China becoming strong as long as the network of foreign privileges remained in place. For the powers, such privileges could only be relinquished when China was deemed strong enough to meet its debts and fulfil its 'responsibilities'. This recipe for Chinese frustration and foreign self-interest endured until the abolition of extraterritoriality in 1943 amid the special circumstances of the Second World War.

China's 'new era' had not been under way long before it became clear that the Republican government was too weak to deliver much of its internal or external agenda. The forms and theories of power changed in 1912; the realities did not. These were that mastery of the state depended not on civil sanction or an ideology so much as military power of the kind derived from control over the modern, regional armies which, though founded to defend the Qing, were responsible for its downfall. The chief agent of this power was Yuan Shikai, the northern militarist to whom Sun yielded the presidency in the early months of 1912.[2]

Yuan earned much of the infamy he rapidly incurred in the nationalist history of China. He crushed the newly formed Kuomintang following its electoral success in 1913, had its leader, Song Jiaoren, assassinated, and drove Song's comrades, including Sun, into exile. He yielded to foreign, particularly Japanese, demands for new privileges in exchange for loans. And he tried to unite his divided countrymen by reviving the political idea he thought suited them best: imperial rule with himself as emperor. Yuan's dynasty did not endure: the southern provinces rose in revolt and Yuan died in 1916, his methods detested, his reputation in disgrace.

1 The Republican Revolution of 1911 is examined from many angles in Eto Shinkichi and Harold Z. Schiffrin (eds.), *China's Republican Revolution* (University of Tokyo Press, Tokyo, 1994).
2 On Yuan Shikai, see Ernest P. Young, *The Presidency of Yuan Shi-k'ai: Liberalism and Dictatorship in Early Republican China* (University of Michigan, Ann Arbor, 1977).

Yet Yuan's *goals*, forging unity at home and warding off the powers abroad, were less easy to condemn. They were the concern of every Chinese leader in the twentieth century, despite important differences in the abilities, resources and methods of those who held this position. In one form or another each of Yuan's successors as paramount leader – Sun Yat-sen, Chiang Kai-shek, Mao Zedong, Deng Xiaoping and Jiang Zemin – had to wrestle with issues of democracy versus national unity, regional autonomy versus central control. Each was obliged to address the question of constraints on leadership, how they should be exercised, and by whom. Each saw himself as the custodian of distinct, Chinese values which needed defending in a hostile international and troubled domestic environment. And each, with the exception of Jiang Zemin, shared with Yuan the fact that he owed his rise to close association with, and often control over, the military.

The militarization of politics, a major theme of China's modern history, reached its height in the years after Yuan's death. Presidents, premiers and parliaments came and went in Beijing but warlords called the shots in the capital as they did the provinces.[1] They did not blight every piece of territory they controlled: local militarists such as Yan Xishan of Shanxi, and, later, Li Zongren and his fellow leaders in Guangxi, brought development to areas long unused to such. But warlords, as their derogatory title suggests, fought battles for land, revenue and power. And these not only brought death and destruction to millions, they testified to the crisis of central authority that made national rejuvenation impossible. China needed unity – and the strong government armed with powerful ideas and popular support required to impose it.

These yearnings were at the heart of the May Fourth Movement of 1919, the date of student protests in Beijing against the powers' refusal to hand back to China the former German concessions in Shandong seized by Japan.[2] It was no coincidence that the birth of modern Chinese nationalism was part of a broader movement advocating a 'new culture': the two went in hand in hand. Chinese civilization and society had to be re-fashioned, and this required new, mainly Western ideas and a plain language – bai hua – to propagate them. 'Mr De' (democracy) and 'Mr Sai' (science) featured prominently in literary debates among the intellectuals at the heart of the movement. So did Marxism, a creed stunningly vindicated by the Bolshevik Revolution in Russia, whose size and underdevelopment suggested interesting parallels with China. These and other ideas captivated the mind of 'young' China, challenging, at least in the cities, almost every manifestation of the old order, from politics to patriarchy.

China appealed to foreign Marxists as well as Marxism to China. Soviet Communists saw in China's chaotic search for unity and a new identity the chance to protect the eastern flank of their revolution from imperialism. Moscow's emissaries established contacts with small groups of Chinese Communists in Shanghai and other cities, and with Sun Yat-sen, by now head of a separatist military government in Guangdong. The former led, in 1921, to the founding of the Chinese Communist Party; the latter, in 1923, to the reorganization of the Kuomintang into a revolutionary movement supported by its own army, Soviet money, munitions and advice, and an alliance with the Communist Party known as the United Front. In the space of a few years, China acquired a modern political machine backed by a

---

1 On warlord politics in Beijing, see Andrew J. Nathan, *Peking Politics, 1918–23: Factionalism and the Failure of Constitutionalism* (University of California Press, Berkeley, 1976). Studies of the warlord phenomenon and of individual warlords include Edward A. McCord, *The Power of the Gun: The Emergence of Chinese Warlordism* (University of California Press, Berkeley, 1993); Donald G. Gillin, *Warlord: Yen Hsi-shan in Shansi Province, 1911–49* (Princeton University Press, Princeton, 1967); Diana Lary, *Region and Nation: The Kwangsi Clique in Chinese Politics, 1925–1937* (Cambridge University Press, Cambridge, 1974).

2 Chow Tse-tsung surveyed the May Fourth Movement in *The May Fourth Movement: Intellectual Revolution in Modern China* (Harvard University Press, Cambridge, Mass., 1960). See also Vera Schwartz, *The Chinese Enlightenment: Intellectuals and the Legacy of the May Fourth Movement of 1919* (University of California Press, Berkeley, 1986); Merle Goldman (ed.), *Modern Chinese Literature in the May Fourth Era* (Harvard University Press, Cambridge, Mass., 1977).

powerful military and motivated by a revolutionary mission: overthrowing the warlords, unifying China and ending foreign privilege.[1]

Implementing this mission fell largely to Chiang Kai-shek, who succeeded Sun as leader of the National Revolutionary Army on the latter's death.[2] In 1926 the Nationalist revolution swept north from Guangdong to the Yangtze in a matter of weeks thanks to the mobilization of workers and peasants, much of it the work of Communists; a surge in anti-foreign sentiment; and stunning military victories against warlord foes.

While Nationalist Party leaders struggled to digest these successes, conservatives among them, including Chiang, fought to keep the revolution within bounds. Much was at stake. The anti-foreign movement – fuelled by massacres of Chinese protestors in Shanghai and Guangzhou in 1925 at the hands of foreign police and soldiers – threatened to slip the leash of its organizers and to invite international intervention. Strikes paralysed business in Shanghai and other commercial centres. The peasant movement plunged the countryside into chaos. Class warfare might have been what the Communists and Nationalist Left wing had in mind for their country, but it had no place in Chiang's philosophy.

In 1927 he dealt with these menaces to his authority by curbing the anti-foreign movement and crushing Communist insurrections in Shanghai, Wuhan and Guangzhou. By the end of the year he had driven the demoralized Communist Party into the countryside and its fateful encounter with the Chinese peasantry. When Nationalist troops entered Beijing in 1928, Chiang declared the Northern Expedition at an end and established a new central government in Nanjing.

Fragile Unity: the Era of Chiang Kai-shek

For more than twenty years Chiang Kai-shek struggled to impose his will on a country plagued by weakness, division, Communist insurrection and Japanese invasion. For more than twenty years his efforts met with only mixed success outside a few core provinces where proximity to Nanjing, personal ties with local leaders, and the presence of his own military units made him too powerful to defy.[3] Beyond this Nationalist heartland, which consisted of the lower Yangtze provinces until the Sino-Japanese War forced him to abandon them, Chiang's rule was nominal and China's new unity something of a mirage. In Manchuria; in the vast northwest; in the southwest; even at first in Guangdong, where the National Revolution was born, local militarists counted for more than the newly established central government, even though most of them had pledged loyalty to it. And in Communist-controlled areas, of which there were soon several, Chiang confronted a state within a state. With the creation in 1932 of Manchuguo, he confronted a *foreign* state within a state.

While these were unfavourable circumstances for reconstruction, Chiang's difficulties owed much to his methods and personality. His control of Shanghai and other major cities – many of them sources of much needed revenue – depended on alliances with secret societies and the criminal underworld. His control over the countryside, in so far as it existed, depended on not challenging the social order – and therefore achieving little in the way of rural modernization.

Chiang spoke the language of modern republicanism and professed loyalty to the 'Three

1 C. Martin Wilbur's thorough overview of the origins and development of the National Revolution forms Chapter 11 of John K. Fairbank (ed.), *The Cambridge History of China Vol. 12: Republican China 1912–1949*, Part 1 (Cambridge University Press, Cambridge, 1983).

2 There is as yet no comprehensive study in English of Chiang Kai-shek that uses the abundant archival material. In its absence see Brian Crozier, *The Man Who Lost China: The First Full Biography of Chiang Kai-shek* (Scribner, New York, 1976).

3 The Nationalists' 'Nanjing Decade' (1927–37) is examined in Lloyd Eastman, *The Abortive Revolution: China Under Nationalist Rule, 1927–1937* (Harvard University Press, Cambridge, 1974). See also the special issue of *The China Quarterly* entitled *Reappraising Republican China*, No. 150, June 1997 (School of Oriental and African Studies, London).

Principles of the People' espoused by Sun.[1] He became a Christian on marriage to Soong Mei-ling and seemed to many in the West a modern, enlightened leader. But he brooked no rivals within the Nationalist Party, and demanded absolute obedience. Ultimately he was a soldier politician. His ideology was a mixture of Confucianism and martial nationalism, and he believed little could be accomplished until he had defeated his foes, inside and outside the Party, on the battlefield, or outmanoeuvred them through political manipulation. Since he never managed to do either of these things completely, or for very long, Chiang's weaknesses were often more apparent than his strengths.

This made some of his achievements during the 1930s more remarkable. They included the construction of railways, roads and telecommunications, and the creation or reform of schools and universities. Growing government intervention in the modern economy sometimes resulted in corruption but also produced a trained managerial elite. Tariff autonomy, secured in 1928, boosted revenues and ended foreign control over the maritime customs, the salt tax administration and the Post Office. The end of the era of Unequal Treaties was still some way off, but the Nationalist government did all it could to hasten it.

Yet the 1930s was a time of foreign aggression and internal rebellion rather than genuine revival. And Chiang chose to tackle the second – Communist insurrection in the countryside – first. The Party's flight to the rural hinterland, far from the proletariat and even further from Moscow, headquarters of the world revolution, might have marked the end of Chinese Communism. Instead, thanks largely to the tenacity and resourcefulness of its leaders, notably Mao Zedong, it was reborn as a rural movement in which modern techniques of class war were applied to the traditional world of peasant hardship and discontent. This alchemy occurred in some of the poorest, most remote parts of China: firstly in the impoverished mountain districts of Jiangxi; later in the barren loess of northern Shaanxi. The Communists' passage from one to the other took the form of the Long March, the result of Chiang's fifth 'bandit extermination' campaign of 1934, but also the occasion for a defining myth of Party invincibility, and the ascendancy of Mao and his methods.[2]

Again this might not have amounted to much had Chiang not failed to deliver a fifth and possibly final 'extermination campaign', this time in north China using troops commanded by Zhang Xueliang, former master of Manchuria. The Xian Incident, in which Chiang was kidnapped by his own generals in 1936, and forced to abandon the struggle against the Communists in exchange for leading national resistance against the Japanese, brought the civil war to a temporary halt. Republican China – a patchwork of semi-autonomous provinces, a powerful but far from paramount central government, and a Communist movement of increasingly nationalist hue – faced the industrial and military might of expansionist Japan.

Military conflict began in earnest in 1937 and, despite occasional heroic resistance, resulted in spectacular victories for Japan.[3] Chiang lost control of north China and the Yangtze delta in a matter of weeks, the Yangtze as far as Wuhan within a year, and by the end of 1939, every major port from the Gulf of Bohai to the Gulf of Tonkin. His government was secure in its new capital of Chongqing but isolated and far from its traditional sources of support. In Yanan, which Chiang blockaded with some of his best troops, the Communists concen-

---

1 Sun's 'three principles' were nationalism, democracy and people's livelihood. See SUN YAT-SEN.

2 Analysis and documents on the rise of Chinese Communism can be found in Tony Saich (ed., with a contribution by Benjamin Yang), *The Rise to Power of the Chinese Communist Party: Documents and Analysis* (M. E. Sharpe, Armonk, New York, 1996). Revisionist examinations include Tony Saich and H. Van de Ven (eds.), *New Perspectives on the Chinese Communist Revolution* (M. E. Sharpe, Armonk, New York, 1995).

3 On the Sino-Japanese War and its consequences see Lloyd E. Eastman, *Seeds of Destruction: Nationalist China in War and Revolution, 1937–1949* (Stanford University Press, Stanford, 1974); and Lloyd E. Eastman, Jerome Ch'en, Suzanne Pepper and Lyman P. van Slyke, *The Nationalist Era in China, 1927–1949* (Cambridge University Press, Cambridge, 1991).

trated on perfecting the political and military techniques which enabled them to extend their influence across the North China Plain and eventually would sweep them to national power.

Pear Harbor and the Allied involvement in the struggle against Japan boosted Chiang's prestige but did little to improve his weakening military position relative to the Communists. Nor did it do much for the Chinese war effort. Neither American aid nor advice, provided most vigorously by Joseph Stilwell, Chiang's US-appointed chief of staff, succeeded in improving China's military contribution to the defeat of Japan. American attempts to bring government and Communist forces together in the same cause also came to naught. The two rivals harboured their best resources on the assumption that, with the Americans in the war, the Japanese were bound to be defeated – probably outside China. When that happened, the domestic struggle for China, probably in the form of civil war, would resume.

The impact of Allied participation on China's *international* position was much greater. In 1943 Britain and the United States relinquished their extraterritorial privileges and agreed to surrender the international settlement in Shanghai, which Japan had occupied in December 1941, along with other concessions. Britain declined to restore Hong Kong to China, leaving at least one legacy of the Opium Wars intact. But on the Mainland at least, the era of unequal treaties was a thing of the past.

China's new status was confirmed later in 1943 when President Roosevelt and Prime Minister Churchill met Chiang at the Cairo Conference, the first Sino-Western summit. The principals agreed that Manchuria and Taiwan would return to China after Japan's defeat, restoring yet more lost dignity. Then, in the dying weeks of the war, China became a founder member of the United Nations, with a permanent seat on the Security Council. The Republic of China was cast as a 'Great Power' with an important role to play in the post-war world. It was a respected and (almost) fully sovereign member of the international community, a goal Chinese nationalists had pursued since the forced opening by the West a century earlier.

Yet China's mid-century 'greatness' was thrust upon it by Allied sentiment and realpolitik rather than earned. The accolade was premature. In 1945 China was still weak, poor and divided. A long, bitter domestic struggle was underway to determine what kind of power the country would be. It was settled, with surprising speed and even more striking consequences, in the civil war of 1946–9.[1]

Neither a popular yearning for peace nor American mediation could prevent a resumption of military conflict between the Kuomintang and the Communists. Neither sporadic American assistance for Chiang nor Stalin's reluctance to aid his Chinese comrades could affect the outcome. The result was determined domestically, on the battlefield, and in the minds of many of the men and women over whose future it was fought.

The Civil War was a struggle between an exhausted, ineffective government whose mismanagement of the economy was matched by its lack of vision, and a Communist movement whose control over the countryside made it all but indestructible, and whose discipline, ruthlessness and vision at least promised a jaded nation a new start. The government's incompetence and the Communists' brilliance on the battlefield, first in Manchuria, then in north China and finally in the provinces just north of the Yangtze, decided the speed rather than the nature of the outcome. In October 1949, Mao proclaimed the foundation of the People's Republic of China. By the end of the year the People's Liberation Army had moved into every Mainland province save Tibet, and Chiang had shifted the remnants of his demoralized army and government to Taiwan. The great Chinese Civil War was not quite over but it looked as though it soon might be.

The Great Chinese Revolution – defined by the Communist Party, and an integral part of

---

1 The military campaigns of the Civil War are discussed in Edward L. Dreyer, *China at War, 1901–1949*, Chapter 8 (Longman, London, 1995). The politics of the war are analysed by Suzanne Pepper, *Civil War in China: The Political Struggle, 1945–1949* (University of California Press, Berkeley, 1978).

the Civil War – made rapid progress, too.[1] Though the Party practised 'new democracy', and sought to include as many former Nationalist personnel as deemed compatible with 'people's China', change came quickly to almost every area of life. Its chief expressions were land reform, a new marriage law, the expulsion of foreigners and nationalization of their assets, alliance with and assistance from the Soviet Union, and the ideological reorientation of the entire population to ensure compliance with the Party's methods and goals.

The outbreak of the Korean War in June 1950 intensified these processes – chiefly by reintroducing an international dimension into the Chinese Revolution. With Communists on the attack in Korea, the United States decided it could not afford to abandon Taiwan to its fate. President Truman moved the Seventh Fleet into the Taiwan Straits and pledged military as well as diplomatic support for Chiang's government as the sole representative of China. This was a shot in the arm for a regime whose suppression of an uprising in 1947 had made it unpopular in its new home, and which was braced for Communist attack. In November, American-led United Nations forces clashed with Chinese 'volunteers' in Korea. For the West, China was now less of a 'Great Power' than a threatening one. Support for Taiwan and the containment of Chinese Communism were principal aims of American foreign policy for the next twenty years.

New China, New Terror: 1949–76

That the Cold War polarization of East Asia had a huge impact on China's Revolution is beyond question. That it was the sole or even major determinant of Mao Zedong's long, tortuous, ultimately disastrous pursuit of ideological purity is a matter for debate. What is clear is that, with the passage of time, the Chairman sought to transform the very nature of his people, and that millions of Chinese assented to, connived at, or participated in his repeated attempts to do so. Many of those who did not, and almost all of those who resisted, suffered terribly.[2]

The Korean War contributed to this process by intensifying the struggle between the 'people' and their 'enemies'. In the early 1950s, mass campaigns ferreted out opponents of all kinds, creating a climate of fear and hysteria as well as class and national solidarity. Freedom of worship and of the press, and autonomy in academic and creative life came to an end. The Party established itself wherever organized social activity took place. Millions of ordinary Chinese acquired their first experience of a state that was not only determined to reshape their lives but had the modern, technological means to do so.

The experience was not wholly negative. For all its revolutionary fervour, the new regime satisfied traditional longings for national unity, moral purpose and strong personal leadership. This last was met by Mao, by the mid-1950s almost beyond reproach and, soon, beyond control. More tangible factors were also at work. The achievements of the early years of Communism included rapid industrialization, largely along Soviet lines with an emphasis on heavy industry; a dramatic improvement in communications, which helped the new government integrate remote regions and improve frontier defence; and energetic attempts to wipe out illiteracy and improve health care. In terms of foreign policy, Beijing managed to combine loyalty to the socialist bloc with attempts to lead the Third World, notably at

---

1 The early years of Communist rule are the subject of Roderick MacFarquhar and John K. Fairbank (eds.), *The Cambridge History of China, Vol. 14, Part 1: The Emergence of Revolutionary China, 1949–1965* (Cambridge University Press, Cambridge, 1987).

2 A short biography of Mao is Delia Davin, *Mao Zedong* (Sutton Publishing, Stroud, 1997). Colourful and revealing accounts are provided by Li Zhisui (with Anne F. Thurston), *The Private Life of Chairman Mao* (Random House, New York, 1994). Stuart Schram discusses Mao's Thought up to 1949 in Chapter 14 of John K. Fairbank and Albert Feuerwerker (eds.), *The Cambridge History of China*, Vol. 13, Part 2 (Cambridge University Press, Cambridge, 1986); and from 1949 to 1976 in Chapter 1 of Roderick MacFarquhar and John K. Fairbank (eds.), the *Cambridge History of China, Vol. 15*, Part 2: *Revolutions Within the Chinese Revolution, 1966–1982* (Cambridge University Press, Cambridge, 1991).

the Bandung Conference of 1955. In all these respects as in others, China was much stronger and more united towards the end of the first Five Year Plan (1953–7) than it had been under the Kuomintang.

For Mao, though, it was neither strong nor united enough. Worse, there was a danger China might adhere to 'incorrect' policies. His attempts to avoid this led to the collectivization of agriculture and nationalization of industry in 1956, and – in the belief intellectuals had been 'remoulded' by their experience of Communist rule – a campaign the same year to loosen control over the world of ideas. Liberalization did not last long: the One Hundred Flowers Movement gave way to an 'anti-Rightist' purge which depleted the ranks of intellectuals for two decades.[1]

Still Mao pressed on with his radical agenda. The Great Leap Forward combined his desire for a complete political, social and economic transformation with a belief that it could be accomplished at once and by sheer will. A leap into Communism would not only establish China's superiority to most of the capitalist world, it would take China even further along the socialist road than the Soviet Union. Quite apart from anything else, this would remove the stigma, always hard for Chinese to bear, of being Moscow's socialist 'little brother'.

In the event, the wholesale communization of life did none of these things. Instead it provoked a split in China's Communist leadership, contributed to the ruin of relations with the Soviet Union, and caused a famine that cost twenty to thirty million lives.[2] And while these events were underway, rebellion in Tibet threatened Beijing's grip on one of its most wayward frontier regions.[3] Mao was forced – temporarily – to temper his revolutionary impetuosity, and the Party to concentrate on economic recovery. But there was no reversing the Sino-Soviet split.[4] Neither, following war with India in 1962, was it possible to halt China's drift towards international isolation.

Between 1966 and 1970 China – an atomic power from 1964 – shut its doors on the world to pursue a vision of revolutionary purity at home. The idea of a Cultural Revolution was conjured up by Mao, Lin Biao, his chief Leftist ally, Jiang Qing, his wife, and others who felt the Revolution to be in peril.[5] But it was carried out by ordinary Chinese, many of them Red Guards, whose campaign to wipe out every vestige of the old society and establish the supremacy of Mao's 'Thought' began in the world of ideas and culminated with the purge, arrest, torture and death of hundreds of thousands of people. Liu Shaoqi and Deng Xiaoping, 'capitalist roaders', were among the celebrated victims in the Party. Professionals of every persuasion, religious believers, those with connections overseas, leaders of ethnic minorities and countless others were the unsung casualties of a conflict which often involved armed clashes between rival factions.

Much about the Cultural Revolution was novel, including the barbaric behaviour it often

1 See Roderick MacFarquhar, *The Origins of the Cultural Revolution*, Vol. 1: *Contradictions Among the People, 1956–57* (Columbia University Press, New York, 1974).

2 Roderick MacFarquhar, *The Origins of the Cultural Revolution*, Vol. 2: *The Great Leap Forward* (Columbia University Press, New York, 1983); Jasper Becker, *Hungry Ghosts: China's Secret Famine* (John Murray, London, 1996).

3 Accounts of Tibet's travails during the twentieth century can be found in Melvyn C. Goldstein, *China, Tibet and the Dalai Lama* (University of California Press, Berkeley, 1997) and Tsering Shakya, *The Dragon in the Land of Snows: A History of Modern Tibet Since 1947* (Pimlico, London, 1999).

4 On the Sino-Soviet Split see Odd Arne Westad (ed.), *Brothers in Arms: The Rise and Fall of the Sino-Soviet Alliance, 1945–1963* (Woodrow Wilson Center Press and Stanford University Press, Washington, 1998).

5 The 'high politics' of the Cultural Revolution are examined in Roderick MacFarquhar, *The Origins of the Cultural Revolution*, Vol. 3: *The Coming of the Cataclysm, 1961–1966* (Oxford University Press, Oxford, 1997). Personal accounts are provided by Nien Chang, *Life and Death in Shanghai* (Grove Press, New York, 1986), and Jung Chang, *Wild Swans: Three Daughters of China* (HarperCollins, London, 1991). Zheng Yi unearths cases of cannibalism in *Scarlet Memorial: Tales of Cannibalism in Modern China* (ed. and trans. T. P. Sym), (Westview Press, Boulder, Colorado, 1996).

inspired in otherwise sophisticated people. Much was an apotheosis of revolutionary goals and methods established in Yanan almost twenty-five years earlier. Yet some was a new manifestation of traditional Chinese approaches to politics and the outside world. During the Cultural Revolution, China was isolated but, in its own terms, self-sufficient. Courtesy of its 'Great Sage', Mao Zedong, it was the self-absorbed custodian of ideological purity. If imperial China was at the centre of the civilized world, China in the late 1960s was the centre of world revolution. There was a smugness and superiority about both of these 'Chinas'. Both had something to teach the world. Both had something to fear from contact with it.

At the close of the 1960s, China's greatest fear was the Soviet Union, whose troops confronted those of the People's Liberation Army along the border from Xinjiang in the west to Heilongjiang in the east. Soviet influence in Southeast Asia added to Beijing's fear of encirclement. Waging revolution *and* defending long, vulnerable frontiers were risky. Revolution would have to be wound down; new alliances forged to enhance national security. The mysterious death of Lin Biao in 1971 made these tasks easier. Turmoil in the provinces diminished. Beijing assumed China's seat in the United Nations. And in 1972 President Nixon visited Beijing to inaugurate a new era in Sino-American relations.[1] Cautiously but convincingly, China began to re-enter the world.

These changes had little impact on China's domestic politics until Mao died in September 1976 and members of the 'Gang of Four' were arrested a few weeks later. Then, with the return to power of Deng Xiaoping, they had a very big impact indeed. Between 1978–81, Deng and his allies condemned most of Mao's policies – while leaving the Chairman's reputation generally unscathed – and launched China on the course of reform and opening that remains at the heart of its national agenda at the start of the new century.

Reform, Rejuvenation: Deng and the Limits of Liberty, 1978–97

The revolutionary nature of this undertaking was clear from the start. After decades of condemning the capitalist world, China decided to tap its financial and technological resources. After years of stamping out every vestige of enterprise at home, it encouraged the profit motive – first in agriculture, then in industry, and finally in almost every area of life. After repeated crackdowns, the Party rehabilitated intellectuals and recruited them to the cause of national rejuvenation. And, after thirty years of ignoring its swelling population, Beijing introduced a drastic, one-child-per-family policy to control it.[2]

As a result of these policy shifts, the early 1980s saw a repetition – in much more agreeable circumstances – of the 'great encounter' between China and the outside world that began with the Opium Wars. Beijing made its presence felt in international organizations, largely as a result of establishing full diplomatic relations with the United States in 1979. It welcomed foreign investors, long barred from a promising market, to newly established Special Economic Zones. It encouraged tourists to explore an intriguing country. Overseas Chinese renewed links with their Motherland, and Mainlanders, at first in small numbers, travelled abroad. Military hostilities – though not the war of words – ceased between the Mainland and a Taiwan suddenly deprived of diplomatic allies. Britain agreed to restore Hong Kong to China in 1997 on the understanding that its capitalist economy and personal freedoms would survive. And Portugal did the same for Macau with effect from 1999.[3]

---

1 Relations between China and the United States from the late 1960s to 1998 are examined by James Mann in *About Face: A History of America's Curious Relationship With China From Nixon to Clinton* (Knopf, New York, 1999).
2 Domestic aspects of the early years of reform are discussed by Harry Harding in *China's Second Revolution: Reform After Mao* (Brookings Institution, Washington, 1987).
3 These developments, and their consequences through into the 1990s, are examined by Willem van Kemenade, *China, Hong Kong, Taiwan Inc. The Dynamics of a New Empire* (Knopf, New York, 1997); and Dick Wilson, *China, The Big Tiger: A Nation Awakes* (Abacus, London, 1996).

These mighty changes involved myriad personal encounters. Those who experienced them found them unsettling as well as rewarding, for they showed the price China had paid for its long devotion to revolution. They also spoke of the ambiguities surrounding the new policy of engagement with the world and change at home.

The roots of the reform policy lay in the Communist Party's recognition of China's national weakness. Constant revolution had exhausted the country. It also threatened the Party's grip on power. Without a radical change of direction national strength and political stability would remain illusory. Reform and the Open Door seemed the best route to both. The wonder of free markets and export-led growth had been on display on China's doorstep: by the late 1970s Hong Kong and Taiwan had begun to grow rich on them. The capitalist nations of Southeast Asia and, further north, South Korea, were doing likewise. Communist China, with its unmatched mix of market, resources and manpower, would do the same. The Party renewed its pact with the people: revolutionary goals were redefined in terms of national – and, increasingly, personal – enrichment.

This break with the past was as real as that arising from the Communist victory in 1949. It was similarly incomplete. China would engage the rest of the world, but it would be something less than an embrace. The Open Door was a matter of strategy not affection, utility not emotion. There was no question of China 'going capitalist'. China would be *in* the world of international trade, finance and diplomacy. It would not, indeed, could not, be *of* it. China would retain its identity, its 'Chineseness', the product of centuries of imperial and more than thirty years of Communist rule. Ideologically, Deng defined this identity as 'socialism with Chinese characteristics'. One of its features was the continued political dominance of the Communist Party. Another was a determination to defend 'core values' from attack by 'Western' or 'bourgeois' rivals. This new language conveyed an ancient yet, at the start of the twenty-first century, still current sentiment: the desire to bend foreign ways to Chinese purposes.

Questions of identity aside, Deng's reforms brought tension as well as opportunities to Chinese society. Overseas competition and market forces spurred economic growth but sapped the foundations of state socialism. Egalitarianism was an early casualty, stable prices another. A job for life, free housing and health care came under attack as reform of state-owned enterprises gathered pace. In social and economic life, the old verities were everywhere under attack.

And not only in social and economic life. During the 1980s and 1990s most people became better off and enjoyed more say over their lives than at any time under Communist rule. Thousands of urban Chinese studied abroad in the West. Millions of rural Chinese left the land, now farmed by households again following the dismantling of communes, and flooded into the cities whose appearance they transformed with their labour and simple presence. Many young people, dismissive of the ideals of the Red Guard generation, found their voice in Western fashions, rock music and other manifestations of a popular culture at odds with much of what their parents stood for. Activists, artists, poets and film-makers explored themes of freedom and personal development that probed the frontiers of what was permissible.

Often they crossed them, ensuring that nowhere were the tensions of the reform era more apparent than in the relationship between the Communist Party and China's intellectuals. Deng lacked a clear vision for China: he said conducting reform was 'like feeling for stones when crossing a river'. But political liberalization was never on offer. China was too big, too diverse, too populous, too backward – and Deng too much the emperor for that.[1] If, in most areas of life, rationing was a thing of the past, in self-expression it certainly was not. At best, political freedom was for the very distant future.

In the reform era Wei Jingsheng and other leaders of the Democracy Wall Movement

---

1 Deng's career is examined in Richard Evans, *Deng Xiaoping and the Making of Modern China* (Hamish Hamilton, London, 1993); and David S. G. Goodman, *Deng Xiaoping and the Chinese Revolution* (Routledge, London, 1994).

were the first to discover this.[1] As the 1980s wore on, intellectuals, students and ordinary people who chafed at Party rule, attacked corruption and criticized Marxism, discovered it, too. Deng and his fellow veterans kept dissent in check with campaigns against 'spiritual pollution' and other unwanted byproducts of the Open Door. These were dangerous times – too dangerous, said the old guard, to hand power over to the young generation. When Hu Yaobang, the reform-minded Party leader, took a soft line towards student protests in 1986–7, the Long March veterans promptly sacked him.[2]

This precipitated an even greater crisis. Hu's death, in 1989, sparked an upheaval that, more than any other event, testified to the tensions between growing economic freedom and tight political control, the bankruptcy of China's institutions, and the incompetence of many of its leaders. The Tiananmen Square Democracy Movement was only loosely about democracy: opposition to corruption was an important theme; workers' demands for better pay and conditions was another. But the millions of protestors, students, intellectuals, workers, and civil servants, who filled Tiananmen Square and the streets of other cities, rallied to a cry of freedom which challenged the foundations of Communist Party rule. After weeks of dithering and division – Zhao Ziyang, Hu's successor as Party leader, was the chief casualty this time – Deng ordered the People's Liberation Army to crush the demonstrations. They did so in forty-eight hours of violence and mayhem, conducted in front of the international press corps, and at the cost of several hundred lives.[3]

China's recovery from this debacle in the centre of Beijing was rapid, despite the collapse of socialism abroad that followed it. It was largely the work of Deng Xiaoping. Still paramount despite his years, formal retirement in 1990, and the accession of Jiang Zemin as Party leader, Deng insisted that only economic growth could save socialism. Everything that contributed to this was to be encouraged – as long as it did not challenge Party rule.

Everything soon was. With hopes of political change suffocated in Tiananmen Square, the Chinese people dedicated themselves to making money with the kind of zeal an earlier generation had devoted to building utopia. The results were almost as spectacular. Growth soared. Cities were engulfed by construction. The performance of stock and futures markets, and the antics of China's *nouveaux riches* supplanted politics as subjects of official and personal discourse. Foreign investment spread the economic boom that appeared first in Guangdong and Fujian north to Shanghai, west along the Yangtze valley, further north still to Shandong, and to the provinces and cities around the Gulf of Bohai: Liaoning, Hebei, Beijing and Tianjin. Improved ties with Russia, the newly independent states of central Asia, Mongolia, and Vietnam (with whom China had fought a war in 1979) allowed border trade to enliven once dormant frontier economies. The myth of the great untapped China market acquired new dimensions, especially in the West. So did some of the forecasts concerning China's future as an economic superpower.[4]

Yet inside and outside the Mainland during the 1990s, the mood was not wholly sanguine.[5] At home, rapid economic growth tore at the fabric of society as well as the natural environment. Symptoms included rising crime, particularly violent crime, drug trafficking and prostitution, and corruption, notably on the part of the sons and daughters of Party

---

1 On Democracy Wall see Andrew J. Nathan, *Chinese Democracy: The Individual and the State in Twentieth Century China* (I. B. Tauris, London, 1986).

2 The abortive struggle for greater political freedom in the era of economic reform is the subject of Merle Goldman, *Sowing the Seeds of Democracy in China: Political Reform in the Era of Deng Xiaoping* (Harvard University Press, Cambridge, 1994).

3 An 'instant' account of Tiananmen is Michael Fathers and Andrew Higgins, *Tiananmen: The Rape of Peking* (*The Independent*/Doubleday, London, 1989). A more comprehensive, later one is Timothy Brook, *Quelling the People: The Military Suppression of the Beijing Democracy Movement* (Stanford University Press, Stanford, 1998).

4 William Overholt's account was the most euphoric. See footnote 2, p. 1. Willem van Kemenade and Dick Wilson (see footnote 3, p. 12) were more restrained but generally optimistic.

5 James Miles, *The Legacy of Tiananmen: China in Disarray* (Michigan University Press, Ann Arbor, 1996) is a good antidote to the euphoria of some commentators.

leaders, the so-called 'princelings'. Inequalities between town and countryside, the hinter-land and the coastal provinces, predominantly Han Chinese and non-Han areas, grew. In Beijing neither political fiat nor financial penalty could restrain wayward regions, raising questions in some minds about the fiscal and even the political integrity of the People's Republic: decentralization seemed to be leading to disintegration. The effects of dramatic economic growth on the environment – loss of farmland, atmospheric pollution, acute water shortages, deforestation and desertification – were equally troubling. Clearly, there was a heavy price to pay for the rapid transformation of so large and populous a country as China.

Alarmed by these developments, the Communist Party clung ever more grimly to its mono-poly of power on the grounds that it alone stood between the Chinese people and chaos. The alternative, according to orthodoxy in Beijing, was to see the nation divided and gladden China's enemies, of whom Party leaders said there were many. In 1997 Jiang Zemin, paramount leader following Deng's death earlier in the year, paved the way for the denationalization of state enterprises, consigning the last great shibboleth of the socialist economy to the grave.[1] But he ruled out the possibility of anything but the most cautious of political reforms. The market might have got the better of Marx at the close of the 1990s, but there was no question of China abandoning the Leninist one-party state, despite the introduction of village-level elections and talk of the need for rule by law. Dissent – whether in the form of Tibetan national-ism, the allegiance of Chinese Catholics to Rome, demands for academic freedom, or calls for multi-party democracy – was stifled just as it had been in the 1980s. Communist China was stronger and richer than ever, but its rulers were no kinder to their critics.

The Mainland's rejuvenation raised a host of questions for those beyond its frontiers. The six million people of Hong Kong were in the frontline in more ways than one.[2] Much of the money that fuelled the Mainland boom flowed in from the British colony, where Chris Patten's attempts to increase democracy derailed Sino-British relations but failed to dampen enthusiasm for the China market, or sap the growth that derived from it. To considerable alarm, Beijing pledged to undo Patten's reforms and curb civil liberties when it resumed sovereignty over the territory on 1 July 1997.

Hong Kong's democrats protested but with few exceptions local businessmen remained silent. And in Tung Chee-hwa China found a chief executive for the new Special Administrat-ive Region who was respected, reliable and *pliable* enough to marry the demands of 'one country' with 'two systems', the formula Deng devised for preserving Hong Kong's freedoms and autonomy after 1997. The handover passed without incident, save for the undoing of Patten's reforms. During the first two years of Chinese sovereignty, Hong Kong's economy suffered from the effects of the Asian financial crisis. Politically the period was less eventful – until Beijing overruled a decision of the territory's Court of Final Appeal in 1999. The issue was the sensitive one of Mainland immigration to Hong Kong; the consequence was diminished authority for the rule of law, a serious matter for an international business centre. Macau's transition in December 1999 – a much less momentous matter for all parties, save Portugal – ended the era of European settlement on the coast of China.[3]

Beijing's relations with Taiwan, the largest and most important of its 'lost territories', ended the century on a less satisfactory note. The principal reason for this was Taiwan's transforma-

---

1 On Jiang Zemin see Bruce Gilley, *Tiger on the Brink: Jiang Zemin and China's New Élite* (University of California Press, Berkeley, 1998); and Willy Wo-Lap Lam, *The Era of Jiang Zemin* (Prentice Hall, Singapore, 1998).
2 Hong Kong's transition from Crown Colony to Special Administrative Region is the subject of Robert Cottrell, *The End of Hong Kong: The Secret Diplomacy of Imperial Retreat* (John Murray, London, 1993), and Michael Yahuda, *Hong Kong: China's Challenge* (Routledge, London, 1996).
3 On Macau see Jonathan Porter, *Macau the Imaginary City: Culture and Society, 1557 to the Present Day* (Westview Press, Boulder, Colorado, 1996); and Lo Shiu Hing, *Political Development in Macau* (Chinese University Press, Hong Kong, 1995).

tion from military dictatorship to vibrant democracy – as rapid and significant in its way as anything that had happened on the Mainland since the death of Mao.[1] The desire of Taiwanese people to distinguish themselves from the Mainland was both cause and consequence of this largely peaceful revolution in 'offshore' China. One, minority, expression of the new 'Taiwanese-ness' took the form of growing support for the Democratic Progressive Party, which sought independence for the island. The more moderate, majority view during the 1990s was that of the Kuomintang, which, under Lee Teng-hui, was thoroughly at home in Taiwan despite its Mainland origins. The Nationalists favoured unification – but not until the rest of China became a democracy. Until then the *status quo* would do very nicely.

Beijing had no time for any of these views. It warned that attempts to make Taiwan independent would be met by force. At best democracy was an adjunct to the imperative of national unification, which should take place under a version of the 'one country, two systems' model adopted in Hong Kong and Macau. In 1996, when these issues were addressed in the island's first direct presidential elections, China staged war games and missile tests in Taiwan waters. The voters rallied to Lee and the United States navy to the Taiwan Straits. The first was confirmation of Taiwan's *de facto* independence; the second a telling reminder of Washington's continued involvement in China's unfinished civil war.

High level, but 'unofficial', talks between the 'two Chinas' did not resume until 1998. When they did, Taipei's desire to restrict discussions to practical issues arising from the existence of two governments (or as Lee Teng-hui affirmed in 1999, two 'states') on Chinese soil, and Beijing's insistence that there was only one legitimate government, the People's Republic, and that the purpose of dialogue was to secure Taipei's subjection to it, showed the two sides were far apart. More than a decade of cross-Straits trade and investment had achieved much, but not for the cause of political unification. This goal receded still further in March 2000, when a split in the Kuomintang and the simple desire for a change of government in Taipei resulted in the election of Chen Shui-bian, the leading figure in the Democratic Progressive Party, as president.

The theme of unfinished business was also apparent at the close of the century in the South China Sea, location of China's other major territorial claim. In the mid-1970s China's modest navy drove its even smaller Vietnamese counterpart out of the Paracel Islands, the northern of the two contested archipelagos. In the following two decades it pushed south to the Spratlys, where skirmishes with rival claimants, including Vietnam and the Philippines, and China's erection of military structures on isolated atolls, raised concerns throughout Southeast Asia about Chinese expansionism. Chinese pledges at meetings of the Association of Southeast Nations (ASEAN) not to settle the matter by force were accompanied by reaffirmations of 'indisputable ownership', and a quiet naval build up.

Territorial issues aside, the closing months of the century saw the Mainland grappling with two crises of equal importance for China's future: stubborn deflation, and a downturn in relations with the United States caused by NATO's bombing of the Chinese embassy in Belgrade during the war in Kosovo. The first stemmed from the Asian financial crisis which began with Thailand's sudden devaluation of the baht in the summer of 1997. Other Asian countries, prey to the same or even worse levels of debt, followed suit. Growth collapsed across the region. Beijing, sensing diplomatic advantage and protected by huge foreign exchange reserves and a non-convertible currency, declined to devalue the *yuan*. For a few months China was seen as a pillar of a global economy under stress. This flattered China's leaders but was no defence against the flagging exports, contraction in foreign investment and general economic slowdown that afflicted the rest of East Asia.

In 1998 China's foreign trade failed to increase on the year before – the first time this had happened since 1983. Officially GDP grew by 7.8 per cent, by far the best performance in the

---

1   Taiwan's transformation is discussed in Steve Tsang (ed.), *In the Shadow of China: Political Development in Taiwan since 1949* (Hong Kong University Press, Hong Kong, 1993); and Jaushieh Joseph Wu, *Taiwan's Democratisation: Forces Behind the New Momentum* (Oxford University Press, Hong Kong, 1995).

region. But the true figure was probably closer to half this, and fiscal expansion failed to stimulate the economy. Deflation, an unwelcome novelty in China's recent economic history, made the mass unemployment certain to arise from the reform of state-owned enterprises economically unpalatable and politically dangerous. It made the connected and no less pressing task of restructuring China's indebted state banks difficult, too. The slowdown raised doubts about Beijing's willingness to press on with reforms vital for the health of the economy – and the prospects that China's GDP, as forecast, would overtake that of the United States in the first quarter of the new century. Amid the downturn, discussion of the 'Asian values' said to have accounted for the region's rapid growth and justified opposition to 'Western-style' individual freedoms, fell silent.

The crisis in Sino-American relations originated in an accident in a third country but inflamed the suspicions, misunderstandings and rivalry at the heart of the two countries' relationship since the 1950s. Three Chinese journalists were killed and several diplomats injured when NATO planes mistook the Chinese embassy in Belgrade for a Yugoslav military target. Popular outrage in China was genuine but quickly channelled by the government into protests and attacks against American and British diplomatic missions. This was a convenient distraction on the eve of the tenth anniversary of the suppression of the Tiananmen Square Democracy Movement.

Yet reaction to the bombing also testified to the ambivalent attitude of many urban Chinese towards the West that recalled the stance of an earlier generation of Chinese nationalists towards Japan. Neither the Politburo nor many ordinary people could believe the bombing was accidental: to do so implied that China was unimportant and did not count in world affairs. It was much more acceptable to view the incident as part of an American plot to humiliate and contain China. Were not Washington's policy towards Taiwan, its attacks on China's human rights record, its refusal to let China join the World Trade Organization until Beijing agreed to open its economy to US multinationals, directed to the same end?

China suspended talks with the United States on a range of issues, including membership of the World Trade Organization, pending an apology, explanation and compensation. There was no doubt diplomats would be able to devise a form of words to defuse the crisis; indeed, in the final weeks of 1999 China and America reached an accord on Beijing's entry into the world trade body. Equally, there was no doubt that neither this deal in particular nor diplomacy in general would do much to challenge the underlying assumptions, grievances and mutual mistrust governing relations between the world's most powerful and its most populous nation.

China at the Millennium: a Fragile, Frustrated Power

The extent to which the most populous state is capable of narrowing the gap with the most powerful is among the more interesting questions of international politics at the start of the new millennium. That China has made a start, that it is a rising power, is incontestable: it is one of the main themes to emerge from a survey of its tempestuous history during the twentieth century. China's national power and geopolitical weighting are increasing, with implications for international politics, security, business and the environment. But to suggest that China, at least as presently constituted, is destined to become a 'great power' seems more doubtful. This is so for three reasons.

First, China's continuing fragility is scarcely less apparent than its power. There are many sources of instability within the People's Republic, and several arising from relations with its neighbours and the established powers. Whether judged in economic or in military terms, China remains, as an observer of its fortunes declared almost exactly a century ago, a country whose 'gigantic possibilities are dwarfed by its present realities'.[1]

---

1 Waldo Browne, *China: The Country and its People* (Dana Estates, Boston, 1901), p. 462. Similar sentiments were at work in Gerald Segal's essay 'Does China Matter?' in *Foreign Affairs*, September/October 1999, pp. 24–36.

Second, in the new century, the nature of international politics and society is such that China must undertake further sweeping reforms if it is to realize its potential as a great economic, political and military power. 'Chinese-ness' – defined as insistence on a unitary state, authoritarian nationalism, rule by a supposedly moral elite, intense secrecy, an unaccountable military, a weak sense of law, and the other 'special characteristics' deemed to reflect the uniqueness of the Chinese people, will not serve in an age of global information, technological innovation and economic interdependence.

Third, although China in its present form might strive, and some extent succeed, in becoming a stronger power, it is unlikely to become a 'great' one in the more positive, beneficial sense of the term. For who would gain if China became significantly more powerful in the absence of an overhaul of politics and society in Beijing? The answer is hardly anyone apart from those connected with the Communist Party, and probably not too many of them.

In its present form, Mainland China has little to offer the world save the fading glories of a distant past and the promise of a large but partly mythical future market. Its current leaders, its contemporary political, social and economic institutions and policies invite study and understanding. They even exert a grim fascination. But for the most part they do not inspire, still less encourage emulation – whether in the developing world or elsewhere. The continued rise of this 'unreconstructed' China would be a matter of concern.

An examination of China's domestic and international situation at the start of the new century sheds some light on these themes. China is pursuing rapid economic development while trying to preserve national sovereignty and political stability in a vast, overpopulated country. Two transformations are underway: from an agricultural to an industrial economy; and from a planned to a mostly market economy. Neither geography nor history has left much room for manoeuvre to those caught up in these almost cosmic processes.

China's frontiers filled out long ago. There is some scope for population transfer into the northwest but not much. China does not have the option Britain enjoyed during *its* industrial revolution: 'exporting' surplus population overseas; or that of the United States a century later: settlement of a largely uninhabited west. Instead China's millions must rub shoulders in an environment which has always been precarious, and which is now suffering the effects of rapid industrialization. Food and energy, once sourced comfortably within the country's frontiers, are no longer sufficient and must be bought in larger quantities overseas.

History, as suggested throughout this essay, has set frontiers of its own. The past still informs the instincts of government, even though the forms of administration seem to have broken free. It still reinforces traditional *mentalities*, despite the apparent triumph of modern outlooks on life. History, as one writer has observed, exercises a tyranny over China.[1]

These constraints operate at many levels. They are particularly apparent in China's pursuit of territorial integrity, the holy grail of Chinese nationalism since its inception in the late Qing dynasty. In military terms, continental China is more secure than at any time during the past century. Border disputes with Russia and the Soviet successor states of Central Asia have yielded to diplomacy. And while the same is not true of arguments with India, the chances of Sino-Indian military conflict over disputed territory are small.

The situation is less satisfactory on the Chinese side of these huge 'inner' frontiers. In Xinjiang, secessionist movements led by Uigurs, Kazakhs and others opposed to Beijing's rule pose a threat to security. In Tibet, resistance to Chinese rule is less violent but equally prevalent. The activities of the exiled Dalai Lama complicate matters by keeping Tibet in the international limelight. Even in Inner Mongolia, where Han Chinese far outnumber Mongolians, pro-independence sentiment survives.

In each of these regions, Beijing practises regional autonomy in which local ethnic

---

1 This is a theme of W. J. F. Jenner, *The Tyranny of History: The Roots of China's Crisis* (Penguin, London, 1994).

minorities supposedly run their own affairs. In each of them, it has difficulty commanding the loyalty of local elites and must rely on massive Chinese immigration and a strong military presence to retain control. If there is little chance of Uigurs, Tibetans or Mongolians ending Chinese rule in their homelands, there are few prospects of stability along China's northern and western edges until Beijing changes the way it governs them. As in imperial times, the subjection of distant non-Chinese peoples to rule by a unified, centralized Chinese state makes for fragile frontiers.

The insistence on unity makes for even greater problems along China's 'outer' frontiers. These include Hong Kong, where the territory's promised legal autonomy endured for just two years before Beijing curbed it with a constitutional ruling and public criticism; the South China Sea, whose islands and waters are contested by several countries apart from China; the Diaoyutai Islands, disputed by China and Japan; and, most significant of all, Taiwan.

Political, cultural and economic rather than ethnic differences divide Taiwan from continental China. The gap is no less fundamental for that. Taiwan's determination to preserve its own identity – the origins of its dynamic democracy – and its informal military reliance on the United States, make ending the division of China dangerous as well as difficult. The fact that the People's Liberation Army is strong enough to mount a naval blockade and shower the island with missiles, but too weak to undertake full-scale invasion in the face of determined resistance – stiffened by probable US intervention – adds to the frustrations (in Beijing) and uncertainties (in Taipei and elsewhere) of the situation. Beijing's insistence that Taiwan accept unity on *its* terms, slightly more favourable than those offered to Hong Kong and Macau, but no more acceptable to Taipei, is a major source of regional instability.

Beijing is so obsessed with imposing control over its 'renegade province' that Taiwan has become the prism through which it views and conducts much of its foreign policy. One manifestation of this is the fact that on the rare occasions China has exercised its veto in the United Nations Security Council it has usually done so over Taiwan issues. Another is that Beijing faces potentially hostile alliances designed to thwart its ambitions towards Taiwan on the grounds that they threaten the security of Japan and the United States, as well as the freedoms of the Taiwanese people.

Japan and the United States strengthened their defence relationship in the late 1990s mainly because of concern over North Korea, over whom China exercises only marginal influence. But Beijing was justified in interpreting Tokyo's decision to play a larger military role in its 'surrounding territory' as a partial if oblique reaction to China's policy towards Taiwan. Talk, which began about the same time and has continued ever since, of including Taiwan in an American theatre missile defence system, contains no such ambiguities. It points to a new security axis between Washington and Taipei. Given its approach to these matters, Beijing is right to feel hemmed in along its southeastern frontier – whether Taiwan gets its missile shield or not.

The feeling is not confined to the southeast. Like imperial China, Communist China fears threats to its cultural and political as well as its territorial integrity. These stem from an invasion of 'alien', 'Western' values spread mainly by their most powerful representative: the United States. They include values Beijing deems positively harmful, such as human rights and democracy; those which, with caution, China can use to great effect, such as free markets and economic competition; and those with huge popular appeal but less profound implications, such as Western fashions, food and music. In one form or another, and to a greater or lesser extent, they all constitute an assault on the 'special' nature of China and its people as defined by history and, in political terms, by the Chinese Communist Party.

The Party recognized more than twenty years ago that China would have to engage the outside world if it wished to modernize and strengthen its economy. No other roads led to national power; no other routes to rejuvenation. Ever since, the task has been to engage the capitalist world but preserve the Chinese Communist 'essence'; to modify Marx but cling to Lenin and Mao; to employ international practices but not embrace the values behind them.

For more than twenty years this policy, though it led to crises of the kind that took place in Tiananmen Square in 1989, worked better than many predicted, including some in the Communist Party. China *is* richer and stronger; the Party *is* still in power. Yet the formula of open economy, opaque politics; a free market in everything save ideas; individual enterprise but collective ideals; token autonomy amid tribal nationalism, is coming under increasing strain. So is the belief at the heart of it: that the dictatorship of the Communist Party is the sole guarantee of China's national sovereignty, wealth and well-being.

This is because the world is becoming increasingly interdependent and open; and because the Chinese people, particularly those in the cities, are not immune to these processes. In many areas of life frontiers are falling. This does not spell the end of diversity, still less the birth of a world state; there is no shortage of people around the world determined to defend their 'national essence'. But the ramifications of globalization and the information age are particularly troublesome for China because its political culture consists of a moribund twentieth-century ideology and an outdated nineteenth-century notion of national sovereignty grafted on to an indigenous foundation of feudal authoritarianism. In the twenty-first century these are not the attributes of a major power, let alone a 'great' one. They are those of a fragile one, whose leaders feel at the mercy of revolutionary events – both abroad and at home.

NATO's war against Yugoslavia of 1999 falls into the first category. It does so for reasons which have little to do with the mistaken bombing of the Chinese embassy in Belgrade. The significance of the war lies in NATO's military intervention, without United Nations' approval, in the affairs of a sovereign state on humanitarian – that is, human rights – grounds. NATO went to war in a third country to stop the persecution of a national minority. This was a profound development for China given Beijing's generally poor treatment of the ethnic minorities within its own frontiers, and its ambitions towards a minority of another kind just beyond them: the Taiwanese.

At the start of the twentieth century, Beijing had to abandon the idea that China represented an all-embracing cultural entity to which other nations, to a greater or lesser extent, would conform. Late Qing, Republican and Communist governments sought to protect China's sovereignty by embracing the then alien, Western notion of the nation state. At the start of the twenty-first century, these defences are looking increasingly shaky as the West establishes new diplomatic principles in which human rights and humanitarianism sometimes take precedence over national sovereignty and, in certain circumstances, become grounds for intervention in other countries.

Beijing views 'humanitarianism' of this kind as hegemonism. Rightly, it sees it as a threat to the Communist Party's freedom to dispose of China's sovereignty as it thinks fit. The new diplomatic agenda challenges the Party's freedom of action as well as its monopoly of values. No wonder Beijing is resisting it as vigorously as it can.

But it is fighting a losing battle with few allies. It is true that Russia shares China's fear and resentment over a world in which the United States is supreme. Such sentiments are reflected in Russian weapons sales to China and Sino-Russian pledges to pursue a strategic, cooperative partnership. But the unanimity does not go very far: Sino-Russian relations are a matter of realpolitik and little more. The same is true of China's foreign relations generally. Indeed, with the possible exception of Pakistan, Cambodia, Burma and North Korea, China has no friends and few allies. Even its ties to these countries (Communist North Korea included) are grounded on interests rather than ideology. In some respects, then, the People's Republic, though growing powerful, is alone in the world.

But only in some respects. For the forces of economic globalization and interdependence are at work in China as they are elsewhere, however hard Beijing might try and resist some of them on the grounds of defending its sovereignty. Billions of dollars have flooded into the Mainland in pursuit of comparative advantage, mostly in the manufacturing sector. Together with indigenous township enterprises, foreign funds and technology are the source of much of the country's rapid growth and its vigorous trade performance. The state-owned sector of the economy, a provider of welfare as well as products, cannot begin to generate such dynamism until it, and the indebted state banks which fund it, are thoroughly reformed or, ideally, abolished.

China is so big, its people so numerous, and parts of it so undeveloped that there is still much to be gained from developing the country's vibrant, largely low-end manufacturing economy. Membership of the World Trade Organization will secure fresh sources of capital and new markets, even though it will intensify competition at home. It will bind China still more closely to the global economy. But even if China becomes the workshop of the world during the course of the new century, it will remain far behind developed countries as well as many of its Asian competitors. For the route to national wealth and power now lies in the development of the innovation and information industries, not the production of textiles or transformers. It depends upon the emergence of a mature, competitive service economy (including a convertible currency), and the legal system, individual liberties and educated population needed to sustain it.

In this sense, then, an 'unreconstructed' China will encounter a glass ceiling in its economic trajectory as it has in its quest for territorial unity, international power and prestige. In the new era, an authoritarian state, where a secretive elite divides its time between suppressing political dissent and sponsoring economic initiative, is an encumbrance to economic development, power and prestige because it curbs the individual liberties on which, increasingly, these attributes are based.

This means that a true Chinese renaissance – a genuine realization of the goals of national unification, wealth and power – and China's transformation from a rising yet frustrated power into a major or even 'great' one, depend upon a thorough political and cultural overhaul. This was envisaged on several occasions during the twentieth century. It was what those who led the abortive 'One Hundred Days' of 1898 and the more modest yet more successful Qing reforms that followed had in mind. It was behind the drive to create a republic in 1911, furnish it with new values during the May Fourth Movement, and infuse it with revolutionary nationalism in the Northern Expedition. It was at work, in different ways, in the foundation of the People's Republic, and Chairman Mao's repeated, generally disastrous attempts to re-make his country and people after 1949.

Each of these upheavals changed China profoundly. Each of them left much unchanged. In particular they failed to break the hold of the past and allow China's long history merely to inform the present rather than control it – notably by closing off policy options in the way China is governed and the relationship between the state and the individual.

Thus, while China except for Taiwan is in a host of ways a different country from that of the late Qing a century ago, its politics are still dominated by an elite devoted to restricting popular participation in public life. It is a 'people's republic' whose leaders largely elect themselves even though, in the age of civilian politicians such as Jiang Zemin and Zhu Rongji, this involves more in the way of bargaining than it did in the era of the military or military-related strongmen: Yuan Shikai, Chiang Kai-shek, Mao Zedong and Deng Xiaoping. It is a country where the government claims mastery of an official ideology, insists on shackling the media, the arts, academic and intellectual life to enforce it, and routinely crushes all popular attempts to challenge it. It is a nation in which the military, though under civilian control, is effectively a state within a state, its operations conducted in secrecy, its activities beyond the scrutiny of a tame National People's Congress.

Fortunately, China is also much more than this. It is a country whose cities are bustling centres of economic activity, despite the turn-of-century deflation. It is a place where innumerable contacts with the wider world are extending the intellectual horizons of all those party to them. It is a land where, outside the worlds of politics, creativity and intellectual inquiry, the reach of the state is on the wane, the scope for individual initiative on the rise. Hukou and danwei are everywhere losing their hold: the market is making, and breaking, social communities in China as it is elsewhere. It is challenging assumptions, promoting pluralism, fostering inequalities, and creating winners and losers as well as those who cannot easily be categorized save for the fact that they have in common much greater control over their lives than they have enjoyed before.

Mainly – but far from exclusively – in the countryside, these developments have fostered new interest in religions, clans and secret societies. The old gods offer comfort in times of change and distress. In the cities they are encouraging the growth of civil society; a recourse to law rather than personal relationships to achieve objectives; a hunger for information and the freedom it brings; and, in the case of a brave and determined few, outright political dissent.[1]

This domestic pressure for change presents a challenge to the Communist Party every bit as serious as that posed by the new diplomatic agenda of the West and the onward march of economic globalization. The distinction to some extent is erroneous: these forces, too, are a fruit of globalization, a legacy of the Party's decision in 1978 to engage the world economy. They testify to the fact that, even in a country the size and complexity of China, distinctions between internal and external pressures for change will hardly hold.

The same is true of the Communist Party's grip on a rising yet still unreconstructed China. The Party insists on retaining its grip on power on the grounds that there is no alternative given the nature and history of the Chinese people and the tasks confronting them. Greater political liberty, in other words, is for others – at least for the time being.

The idea that Mainland Chinese are congenitally or culturally unsuited to living in a political system *at least* as free as any in Asia is calumnious as well as contemptuous. Not only is it self-serving, it is a symptom of the very malaise it is supposed to cure. The modern history of Taiwan, though a product of special circumstances, is a powerful refutation of the idea that Chinese 'exceptionalism' is an insurmountable obstacle to the development of individual liberty and political democracy. It suggests rather that these attributes enhance the freedom, dignity and power of those Chinese who possess them. Beijing could yet crush democracy in Taiwan by military force, so this argument may seem premature. But if it did, it would demonstrate that liberties can be snuffed out, not that they cannot emerge within a given cultural context or, having done so once, will not do so again.

None of this is to downplay the obstacles or difficulties involved in governing China in the more open, liberal, accountable way necessary to realize its ambitions and potential. China's population is overwhelmingly agricultural. This is not an excuse to disenfranchise the majority in China any more than it is in India. But it is a reminder that the rhythms and preoccupations of life of most Chinese are not those often found displayed so ostentatiously in cities such as Shanghai and Shenzhen. In many parts of the countryside standards of education are low; levels of illiteracy and poverty stubbornly high.

Neither can Chinese 'exceptionalism' be dismissed entirely out of hand. It is a curse as well as an excuse – and one compounded rather than created by the Communist Party whose insistence on leadership and obedience based on its alleged mastery of an official ideology still strikes a chord, if an increasingly faint one, with many Mainland Chinese. Opposition to authority is as old as China itself. So is violent rebellion against it. The instinctive questioning of authority as a right, as a 'normal' activity of benefit to the whole community, is more of a novelty. The same is true of the notion that authority should be subject to restraint, open to redress and at the mercy of recall.

A novelty but also a necessity for China's development. Mainland Chinese self-evidently are no exception to the pattern established elsewhere in Asia and beyond that greater economic freedoms lead to demands for political liberties, too. It is true of the predominantly Chinese communities of Taiwan, Hong Kong and Singapore. Why should it be different in Shanghai, Beijing, Tianjin and Wuhan? Even the hundreds of millions of Chinese who live far from the lights of these mighty cities should not have to wait indefinitely before they cast off the remaining shackles of bureaucratic feudalism and acquire a greater say over their lives.

---

1   The role of civil society in the downfall of Communism in eastern Europe is discussed by Michael Ignatieff in 'On Civil Society: Why Eastern Europe's Revolutions Could Succeed' in *Foreign Affairs*, March/April 1995, pp. 128–36. A more detailed treatment of its appearance in China is Timothy Brook and B. Michael Frolic (eds.), *Civil Society in China* (M. E. Sharpe, Armonk, New York, 1997).

China's transformation into a modern, powerful, prestigious nation, though sought for well over a century, remains incomplete. It requires more than the establishment of a strong central government, the development of nuclear weapons, recovery of a few lost territories, a few decades of dramatic economic growth and the remarkable social changes they have generated – important though all these developments are for national power and pride. It requires the political and cultural renewal that alone will enable the Chinese to realize their potential in a rapidly changing domestic environment and an increasingly open, interdependent world. It requires the political liberty and social transparency that alone can enable them to live securely, and comfortably, with their Chinese and non-Chinese neighbours. Above all it must have the leadership, vision and determination needed to identify, pursue and deliver these objectives.

Such forces are not yet in prospect. Neither Hu Jintao nor any of the other men tipped to succeed Jiang Zemin as China's paramount leader seems likely to re-shape the world around them. The preservation of Party rule at all costs, continued economic reforms, and strident nationalism is the preferred formula. Pressures for change in society are mounting but they remain disorganized, leaderless and easily suppressed. It is still difficult to envisage *how* China might change let alone speculate how long it might take to change. What is clear is that only when China does change will it be possible to speak of the country as a great power rather than one which, though rising at the start of the century, remains fragile and frustrated, a burden to many of its own people, and a problem for much of the rest of the world.

A

agriculture

China remains an agricultural country, despite recent rapid growth, industrialization and social change. The shiny office towers, luxury hotels and shopping malls of SHANGHAI helped fashion a new image for the country in the 1990s as an industrial giant in waiting. Yet the reality of China is one in which the rhythms and requirements of farming – often carried out by methods, and amid landscapes and social settings, little changed through the centuries – remain the defining characteristics of life for most people. At the start of the new century rapid industrialization has driven agriculture's share of GDP down below 28 per cent, compared with about 65 per cent a century earlier. Yet agriculture remains the foundation of the economy in the obvious sense that it has to support the world's largest POPULATION, and also because the overwhelming majority of Chinese are either peasants themselves, or have had their lives fashioned by birth or residency in the countryside – that locus of tradition and resistance to change, but also of Communist Revolution, SECRET SOCIETIES, popular RELIGIONS and, until recently, considerable POVERTY.

rural revolution

For all these reasons agricultural policy has been high on the revolutionary agenda in China. Revolutionaries have sought to improve the lot of hundreds of millions of peasants for whom physical restraints arising from population pressure, soil erosion, natural disasters, poor communications and primitive technology; and exploitative systems of land-tenure, usury and high taxation, usually made life difficult and often made it desperate. Since 1949 farming has been restructured time and again in an effort to eradicate these problems, achieve social equality, increase production, realize communism and facilitate technical modernization. Some of these goals have been attained. Some have been abandoned amid disaster. All testify to the fact that the Chinese Revolution has been conducted in an agrarian country in which peasants form the overwhelming majority of the population.

Sun Yat-sen's solution to China's agricultural problems began with rent and tax reductions and graduated to the equalization of land rights (see SUN YAT-SEN). The UNITED LEAGUE, China's first alliance of modern revolutionaries, championed Sun's policy of 'land to the tiller'. So did the KUOMINTANG, much of whose revolutionary zeal in the mid-1920s derived from the presence of CHINESE COMMUNIST PARTY activists among its ranks. During the NORTHERN EXPEDITION, peasant revolutionaries helped turn large parts of the countryside in south China upside down by mobilizing farmers to settle old scores with landlords, demand rent reductions, and build a new rural order.

Chiang Kai-shek's purge of the Left in 1927 ended the Kuomintang involvement in rural revolution, but not the Party's commitment to change in the countryside: 'land to the tiller' remained official policy. Yet the Party showed more interest in technological modernization than social change, agronomy than rural sociology. It was too weak to tax agriculture effectively, failing to raise enough revenue to meet government expenditures let alone achieve its vague redistributionist aims. Rural reconstruction was hampered by military campaigns against WARLORDS and Communists, the SINO-JAPANESE WAR and, finally, the CIVIL WAR. These struggles required forced conscription, high taxes and compulsory grain purchases, policies which made the government deeply unpopular with farmers. Not until the Kuomintang fled to TAIWAN was it able to conduct thorough-going land reform where, under the guidance of United States experts, it did so peacefully and to great effect.

productivity vs politics

By that time, the Communist Party's determination to usher in a new, just, revolutionary order in the countryside had helped it to victory on the Mainland. The party was set on sweeping changes in land ownership almost from its inception in 1921. But often there was disagreement over how to achieve them. Rural policies could be divisive and, when they were implemented, the occasion of much cruelty: thousands of landlords and rich peasants were executed in areas under Communist control during the 1930s. The Party moderated its agrarian policies during the war against Japan in the interests of national solidarity against the invader.

After 1949, it fulfilled its pledge to the peasantry by conducting LAND REFORM everywhere on the Mainland save TIBET. This was an extraordinary accomplishment: not for many centuries had there been a Chinese government powerful enough to transform the established rural order so swiftly and completely. It was also an exercise in political violence: as many as 2 million landlords and others who had sustained centuries-old traditions of land ownership and tenancy in the countryside were killed, tortured, or publicly hounded. All were dispossessed.

Land reform boosted agricultural production and contributed to a general economic recovery during the early 1950s. But private farming was never the Party's goal. For one thing it perpetuated inequalities between rich and poor peasants. For another, the division of farmland into tiny plots made agriculture inefficient and unlikely to deliver the surpluses needed to finance an ambitious industrialization programme.

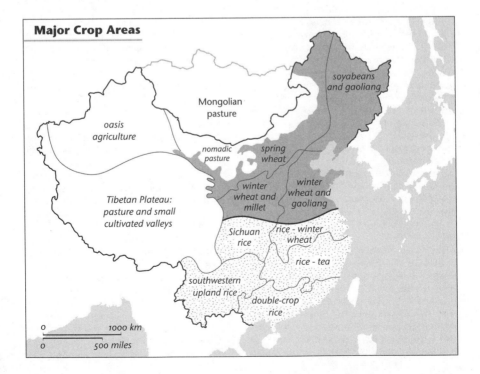

Major Crop Areas

Mongolian pasture

oasis agriculture

soyabeans and gaoliang

nomadic pasture

spring wheat

Tibetan Plateau: pasture and small cultivated valleys

winter wheat and millet

winter wheat and gaoliang

Sichuan rice

rice - winter wheat

rice - tea

southwestern upland rice

double-crop rice

0   1000 km

0   500 miles

Family farming came to a rapid end. The first step was voluntary cooperative farming; the second, thinly disguised forced collectivization. By the end of 1956 private ownership of land was a thing of the past. So was private marketing. For most of the following 25 years, the state planned, planted, bought and sold all main crops. The HUKOU system of household registration tied farmers to their new collectives.

Output suffered almost immediately. The population grew faster than grain production, dashing hopes that a surplus would be produced to fund urban investment. For these and other reasons, MAO ZEDONG believed the Chinese revolution to be failing. In 1958 he launched the GREAT LEAP FORWARD, which saw the transformation of cooperatives into people's communes and radicalized the entire country in an attempt to thrust China into communism.

At the height of the Leap there were about 25,000 communes across the country, each of them supposedly self-sufficient units of production and administration. They were divided into production brigades and production teams whose members ate, worked and relaxed together rather as Marx had suggested would be the case with the advent of a Communist Utopia. But despite unprecedented displays of popular dedication and energy, Mao's vision foundered on the very neglect of agriculture it was designed to reverse. While armies of peasants dug reservoirs, reclaimed land, and built backyard furnaces to produce steel for factories, grain output slumped, creating one of the worst famines of the twentieth century. Between 1959 and 1962, the Chairman's revolutionary caprice, and his Party's neglect of the most basic means of sustenance, cost the lives of 20–30 million people.

As the famine worsened, the idealism of the Great Leap gave way to emergency measures designed to rescue agricultural production and keep people alive. Private plots and other incentives were quietly reinstated, though they remained a matter of controversy. By the mid-1960s the worst of the crisis had passed.

The same could not be said of Mao's radical vision. He refashioned it in the form of the Socialist Education Movement, which called for continuing class struggle in the countryside; and by championing Dazhai, the production brigade in SHANXI whose members were said to combine exemplary class attitudes with staggering productive abilities. 'In agriculture, learn from Dazhai!' was the radicals' cry as they imposed the Dazhai model on the rest of the country. These battles over rural policy were the prelude to the CULTURAL REVOLUTION, a movement whose violent struggles had little physical impact in the countryside but whose political ideals precluded much-needed changes in rural policy.

reform and return of family farming

Change eventually came with the death of Mao and return to power of DENG XIAOPING. The centrepiece of Deng's first round of reforms was the 'agricultural responsibility system', pioneered in ANHUI and SICHUAN, which provided for the return of family farming and the profit motive. Farmers contracted land from the state (initially for a minimum of 15 years; subsequently for much longer periods) and undertook to sell the state a proportion of their output. Once they had fulfilled these obligations, they were free to dispose of the rest of their crops as they thought fit. Private marketing returned, too. And in the early 1980s the communes finally disappeared as units of administration as well as a source of collectivist ideals. Chinese agriculture had been transformed again.

A surge in grain production was one of the most striking consequences of these changes: output increased by a third between 1978 and 1984. Pockets of rural prosperity emerged as farmers were given free rein to develop sidelines ranging from fruit trees to fishponds. In JIANGSU, ZHEJIANG and other provinces of the southeast, small-scale 'township industries' appeared in which peasants no longer needed on the land transformed themselves into factory hands. By the late 1980s township enterprises had spread to other parts of the country and become the mainspring of China's national economic growth. They remained so for much of the 1990s.

Successes on this scale created problems to match: problems that provoked bitter argument within the Communist Party and raised questions about social stability in the countryside. Farmers abandoned grain – soon the only commodity subject to regulation – in favour of commercial crops; investment in communal facilities such as reservoirs, dykes and aqueducts suffered in the rural rush to get rich; and divisions between rich and poor, coast and interior grew.

The government's need to control food prices to appease urban residents meant it could not afford to pay farmers a commercial price for grain. Often the government could not afford to pay them at all: in the mid-1990s it resorted to issuing IOUs, prompting protests and rural unrest in many parts of the country, notably the densely populated 'grain baskets' of the south, Sichuan and HUNAN. Also by the mid-1990s, the government struggled to cope with the 'floating population' – the mass exodus of labour from the countryside to the cities in search of work and a better life (see POPULATION). Some observers, notably Wang Shan (1952–), author of *Looking at China Through a Third Eye*, a controversial polemic, warned that the fragile fabric of urban life would collapse under the weight of rural immigration.

At the start of the new century farming still divides China into traditional agrarian and modern industrial sectors; town and countryside; the richer coastal provinces of the east, and the vast, generally poorer interior. The differences between these worlds are enormous, and the gap between rural and urban incomes is merely one aspect of them. There are millions of prosperous farmers, just as there are many poor city dwellers. But China's cities, though numerous and overcrowded, remain a world apart from the countryside, where most people live and work.

finding enough food

The fact that industry has grown much faster than agriculture during the reform era has raised questions, not only about China's ability to feed itself, but about the capacity of the rest of the world to satisfy growing Chinese demands. Lester Brown, President of Worldwatch Institute, warned in the mid-

1990s that China's inability to grow enough grain had cast the shadow of global scarcity over human history. Rapid economic growth and continued increases in China's population were creating ever higher demands for food at a time when productive farmland was either being turned over to industrialization or falling out of production because of soil erosion and other environmental problems. China had enough foreign exchange to import grain to make up the shortfall, but other countries lacked the capacity to supply it.

The trends Brown identified were indisputable. The extent to which China can escape the fate he predicted, and how far it will have to rely on the world grain market to do so, remain matters of debate.

China's dependence on imports grew in the mid-1990s, when the government quietly abandoned self-sufficiency in grain, a policy most of its predecessors regarded as essential for national security. At first imports generally amounted to a tiny proportion of China's own harvest, and could be justified as the pursuit of comparative advantage. But they also reflected the limitations of Chinese agriculture and have made pursuit of food security an important issue in Beijing's FOREIGN POLICY.

Some of the limits on Chinese farming can be overcome through increased investment, wider application of science and technology, wiser use of fertilizers, reclamation and, perhaps above all, abolition of the irrational price structure that deprives farmers of incentives in the interests of providing cheap grain for urban residents. There is also room for mechanization to replace excessive reliance on human and animal power. However the issue of property rights – one that touches on politics and ideology and therefore the credibility of the Communist Party – remains to be resolved. The difference between private *use* of land and private *ownership* of land use is an important one for an otherwise ideologically bereft Party. But it is no less important for China's farmers who, in common with their counterparts elsewhere in the world, tend to produce most when they are certain that the means of production will remain their own. Thus in the oldest form of economic activity in China, as in more recent forms (see, for example, TELECOMMUNICATIONS), an inadequate, opaque and arbitrary legal system and weak sense of individual rights continue to cloud the future (see LAW).

Amethyst Incident (April to July 1949)

The Amethyst affair marked the end of a century of gunboat diplomacy along the YANGTZE and, what amounted to the same thing, the eclipse of BRITAIN's power in China. It also provided the West with a foretaste of the negotiating style of China's new Communist masters.

On 19 April 1949, the Royal Navy frigate HMS *Amethyst* (*Zishiying* in Chinese) attempted to sail up the Yangtze from Shanghai to relieve another vessel on guard duty at Nanking and re-supply the British embassy there. Since Communist forces were on the point of crossing the Yangtze as part of their campaign to finish off the Nationalists in the CIVIL WAR, the ship sailed directly into a military zone. Communist batteries fired on *Amethyst*, damaging it and causing heavy loss of life. When the *Consort*, the ship due to be relieved, sought to help, it, too, was badly hit and eight of its crew killed. A similar fate met the 10,000-ton cruiser *London* which also tried to assist *Amethyst*.

Lieutenant-Commander John Kerans, Assistant Naval Attaché at the British embassy in Nanking, managed to reach the stricken ship by an overland route. But the Communist crossing of the Yangtze meant *Amethyst's* escape route was cut off, and an RAF Sunderland flying boat, arriving with a doctor and medicines from HONG KONG, was forced to leave the scene before it could offload all its supplies.

As the ship's crew sweltered in the Yangtze summer, Kerans began weeks of fruitless negotiations with the Communists, who wanted Britain to apologize for infringing Chinese sovereignty, and pay compensation as the price of safe passage to Shanghai. He refused to do either and, at the end of July, decided to break out, aided by high waters caused by a typhoon. *Amethyst's* daring escape added to the Royal Navy's annals of bravery and derring-do. It also went down well among the British residents of SHANGHAI who were having an unhappy time under the city's new Communist authorities.

But the affair could not disguise the fact that the balance of power between China and the West had shifted irreversibly. The days when the Royal Navy – indeed any foreign navy – could sail China's inland waterways at will were gone. The door forced open by British gunboats more than a century earlier had been firmly shut.

anarchism

With its call for 'propaganda by deeds', direct action, terrorism, and even martyrdom in the revolutionary cause, anarchism cast a powerful spell over Chinese revolutionaries in the first two decades of the twentieth century. It offered a philosophy of angry protest well suited to the need to transform a decaying, oppressive China. The fact that it promised personal liberation *and* political revolution made it even more compelling for a tempestuous, troubled generation.

Chinese anarchists, like their counterparts in Europe, believed they were in the vanguard of historical change. Their particular task was to throw off the fetters of Confucian society, break through the barriers holding up change, and bring China into the worldwide 'age of revolution'. In this sense, anarchism appealed to the 'voluntarist' tendency in Chinese revolutionary thought: it provided theoretical justification for the desire to wipe out the forces of reaction overnight – a characteristic of Chinese revolutionaries throughout the century.

Such was the doctrine's appeal that, until the founding of the CHINESE COMMUNIST PARTY in July 1921, anarchism, rather than socialism or MARXISM was the dominant creed of China's revolutionary Left. Early in his revolutionary career, MAO ZEDONG acknowledged his debt to anarchist thought.

The sources of Chinese anarchism were Paris and Tokyo, both of them host to large numbers of Chinese students and intellectuals in the dying years of the QING DYNASTY. Anarchist groups emerged in these cities about 1907. Their members saw themselves as part of an international movement that drew inspiration from the Russian nihilists and associated terrorist groups led by Mikhail Bakunin (1814–76), and Peter Kropotkin (1842–1921).

Among the leading Chinese activists in Tokyo were Liu Shifu (1881–1915) and He Zhen (1884–1919), a husband and wife team. They developed anarchist ideas in magazines such as *New Century* and *New Morality*, which found their way back to China. The REPUBLICAN REVOLUTION OF 1911 made dissemination much easier. During the first years of the Republic, anarchism was championed by, among others, Jiang Kanghu (1883–1954), founder of the Chinese Socialist Party, and Liu Shifu, leader of the Conscience Society.

Anarchism's hold over the revolutionary mind in China weakened for the same reasons that it did in Europe: the crushing of inter-nationalist sentiment on the battlefields of the First World War, and the success of Marxism in the form of the Bolshevik Revolution. Yet the influence of anarchism was apparent in the varieties of Chinese Marxism that followed it. The Chinese Communist Party's stress on the re-moulding and rectifying of the individual, on self-reliance, and on human energy as the engine of revolutionary change all owe something to the anarchist doctrines that gave shape to China's first revolutionary Left.

Anhui Province

Diverse terrain, frequent natural disasters, and poor communications have made Anhui the poor cousin among the lower Yangtze provinces. Rapid growth in the early 1990s challenged but failed to alter this state of affairs: Anhui enters the new era far behind its eastern neighbours in the race to get rich. Yet in the broader scheme of things the province has been a pacesetter. It pioneered the return to family farming that revolutionized AGRICULTURE in the early 1980s and, later in the decade, gave birth to the first pro-democracy student protests of the reform era. Anhui's status as an economic backwater belies its larger role in China's modern evolution.

rivalry under the Republic

An early, somewhat unlikely, example of this was the triumph of the 'Anhui Clique' in central politics during the early years of the Republic. The leader of the clique was Duan Qirui (1865–1936). Born in Hefei, Anhui's post-1949 capital, Duan relied on a pool of politicians from his province, and subordinates in the northern, Beiyang Army, to dominate affairs in Beijing during the years after Yuan Shikai's death. His supporters formed the 'Anfu Club' – from the Beijing street of the same name – to lobby politicians and buy the votes needed to legitimize his rule.

In 1920, the 'Zhili Clique' (based in the modern province of HEBEI) defeated the 'Anhui Clique' in one of the first major battles of the warlord era (see WARLORDS). But Duan survived the catastrophe. He went on to hold several important positions in the central government. When at last forced into retirement in 1926, he was the 'provisional chief executive' of the Republic. The only Anhui native to have risen to such a powerful position in national politics since Duan is HU JINTAO, a strong contender to succeed JIANG ZEMIN as China's paramount leader in the new century.

Anhui's proximity to Nanjing made it relatively easy for CHIANG KAI-SHEK to bring the province to heel when he established his new regime in the city in the late 1920s. Communist insurrection in the Dabie mountains area, along the borders with HENAN and HUBEI, was a problem for a while, but not for long: in 1932 Nationalist 'bandit suppression' forces evicted the rebels from their stronghold. During the early 1930s Anhui was gradually integrated into the wider economy of the lower Yangtze. It paid taxes to the new central government and, thanks to a programme of road building, became less isolated.

The SINO-JAPANESE WAR halted this process. This was not simply because Japanese troops occupied the lower Yangtze, though that was important. It was because Anhui fell under the control of the GUANGXI faction of the KUOMINTANG, led by LI ZONGREN and Bai Chongxi (1893–1966). Both men were at odds with Chiang for much of the Republican era; and while their position in Anhui was less secure than in Guangxi itself, their control over the province was a valuable asset in the bitter struggle for control over the Nationalist party.

Anhui also featured in the even more intense wartime struggle between the Kuomintang and the CHINESE COMMUNIST PARTY. In January 1941, at Jingxian, south of the Yangtze, Nationalist forces almost annihilated the headquarters section of the Communist's New Fourth Army. The 'New Fourth Army' or 'Southern Anhui' Incident marked the end of the United Front between the Nationalists and the Communists in the struggle against Japan. Relations between the two domestic rivals for control over China never recovered; and for the next seven years there was no significant Communist Party activity south of the Yangtze.

Yet perhaps fittingly, the Party's route back to south China lay via Anhui. It was made possible by victory in the battle of Huai-Hai in 1948–9 named after the stretch of territory between the east–west railway that runs through north Anhui and JIANGSU, and the Huai river to the south in which it was fought. It was one of three decisive campaigns during the CIVIL WAR. Victory gave the People's Liberation Army control of the north bank of the Yangtze and put an end to effective government resistance to the Communist advance.

hunger and plenty

Little more than a decade after 'liberation', Anhui was among a handful of provinces said to be suffering 'abnormal deaths' because of the famine caused by Mao Zedong's GREAT LEAP FORWARD. As in neighbouring Henan, Mao loyalists kept a tight grip on Anhui, driving its traditionally poor farmers to starvation in an effort to deliver the plenty promised by the Chairman's vision. Deprivation and desperation stalked much of the province from the late 1950s; cruelties on a horrific scale and even cannibalism followed. According to some estimates, the Leap claimed the lives of 8 million in Anhui, about one quarter of the population.

In the late 1970s the province acquired an altogether happier, if again somewhat surprising reputation as a model of agricultural reform. Rarely had Anhui been the subject of such close national attention. The attention focused on Fengyang, a poverty-stricken region in the Huai valley southeast of Bengbu, a key railway junction and industrial centre in north Anhui.

Fengyang had suffered terribly during the famine of the early 1960s. Local farmers had good reason to abandon collective farming and wanted no prompting when the death of Mao in 1976 seemed to make this possible. But the Party's attitude to this spontaneous return to household farming in the region was unclear. The death of the communes would mean the death of much of what the Communist revolution stood for. A lot was at stake.

That is why the decision by Wan Li (1916–), the Anhui Party leader, to encourage and extend the 'Fengyang experiment' was so important. No less crucial was the fact that Wan enjoyed support from DENG XIAOPING,

then easing his way back into power in Beijing. Wan and, about the same time, ZHAO ZIYANG, Party boss of SICHUAN, championed the 'production responsibility system' as the new policy was called. It meant dismantling the communes in favour of private control of land. The state contracted land out to families, and even individuals who agreed to sell a portion of what they grew to the government. They were free to do what they wished with the surplus (see AGRICULTURE).

The success of these reforms gave rise to a popular rhyme: 'If you want grain, ask for Ziyang; if you want rice, look out for Wan Li.' Anhui and Sichuan set the pattern for the rest of the country. Almost everywhere the 'responsibility system' was implemented, productivity and farmers' incomes soared. The same was true of the careers of Wan and Zhao, both of whom were promoted to senior positions in Beijing, and both of whom made a lasting impact on national affairs during the 1980s.

The Lie of the Land

The Yangtze in the south, and the Huai and its tributaries to the north, divide Anhui's 50,200 square miles (130,000 sq kms) into three roughly equal parts. The land north of the Huai belongs to the north China plain; it is rich farming country but subject to floods because of the lack of a natural watershed between the Huai and the Yellow River further to the north. Middle Anhui, between the Huai and the Yangtze, is hilly. There is a large lake almost exactly in the centre of the province called the Chao Hu, or 'nest' lake, because of its shape. Anhui south of the Yangtze is home of some of China's most spectacular mountain scenery, including Huangshan, one of the country's holy mountains. The Dabie Shan mountain range in the southwest is a key strategic area in south China which divides Anhui from Hubei, and commands Wuhan and the middle Yangtze. Anhui's main crops are wheat, sweet potatoes and cotton in the north, and rice, much of it cultivated intensively, in the south around the Yangtze. At the close of the century Anhui had a population of 61 million.

dissent in the 1980s

Anhui was to make its mark again, too. This time the drama centred on the University of Science and Technology in Hefei, where Professor Fang Lizhi (1936–), an outstanding scientist, struggled to foster a spirit of academic freedom (see DISSIDENTS). Fang openly denounced MARXISM in the mid-1980s and called on Chinese intellectuals to shake off their traditional subservience to the state. His appeals found a ready audience among students and intellectuals disappointed over the Party's failure to implement political as well as economic reforms.

In November 1986, Hefei students took matters into their own hands. They went on to the streets to demand less corruption and more democracy. The protests soon spread to a score of other cities across the country, including Beijing. Deng joined his fellow veteran revolutionaries in opposing the unrest, which eventually fizzled out in January 1987. But there were serious consequences and several casualties. Chief of them was the reformist Party leader HU YAOBANG who was dismissed and disgraced. Fang was denounced and expelled from the Party. It was another step along the road that would lead to his exile following the suppression of the TIANANMEN SQUARE DEMOCRACY MOVEMENT.

laggard of the Yangtze: the 1990s

Anhui's pioneering role in bringing relative prosperity to the Chinese countryside tended to be forgotten amid the rapid development of the coastal and lower Yangtze provinces during the late 1980s and 1990s. Natural disasters and poor communications continued to blight the province. Serious flooding along the Huai was a regular occurrence, bringing devastation to much of northern Anhui. In the south, the lack of either a rail or road bridge across the Yangtze impeded development.

Nor did FOREIGN TRADE AND INVESTMENT come to the rescue. In the late 1990s Anhui occupied a middle-ranking position among the 31 provincial units engaged in foreign trade. It fared worse in terms of attracting foreign capital: of the Yangtze provinces only Sichuan put less foreign funds into use than Anhui. These developments made the province a byword for the seemingly intractable problems of development and reform in a country the size of China – despite its location in a region of growing prosperity.

One indication of these difficulties was the high proportion of Anhui people among the 'floating population': the vast army of peasants who have left the countryside for the towns and cities in search of work and better pay (see POPULATION). Anhui labourers can be found on construction sites across China, and the province has long been a chief source of maids for wealthy families in Beijing and other major cities.

This is not to say Anhui has proved immune to the economic changes sweeping through China. Following the opening of the Yangtze Economic Zone in the early 1990s, it grew faster than any other province in terms of GDP, industrial and agricultural output value, fiscal revenue and farmer's per capita income. Prosperity has made inroads in the province's cities, particularly those along the Yangtze and the towns in the north served by the railway. The completion in 1996 of the new Beijing–Kowloon line, which passes through Fuyang, northeast Anhui, will help spread wealth.

Yet this growth is taking place in the context of a much lower base than that of its wealthy neighbours to the east – ZHEJIANG, SHANGHAI and Jiangsu. Urban incomes in Anhui remain stubbornly low compared with other Yangtze provinces, and the gap between town and countryside is as sharp as in some of the poorest parts of the country. In the longer term a tax-sharing scheme introduced in 1994 under which Beijing extracts more from the richer provinces should ease Anhui's standing relative to its neighbours. The government's growing fondness for redistributive policies in favour of the poor interior will have the same effect. But it will be many years before Anhui can shake off its justified reputation as a large, persistent pocket of poverty amid plenty.

armies

The survival of Chinese civilization owes much to the mastering of military technologies and the victory, on countless battlefields, of its armies. The rise and fall of dynasties was likewise decided by military battles. Military conflict was as much the handmaiden of history in China as in other great civilizations. But China differed, at least until the start of the twentieth century, in the store it set on military life. Traditional Chinese society was primarily civilian in ethos: the soldier was not esteemed as a 'social ideal' in the way the Confucian scholar-official was, even though soldiers were often called upon to save the state. The adage 'good iron is not used to make nails; good men do not become soldiers' was a popular expression of this view. Just as emperors and officials were supposed to rule by moral example and not military force, so only scoundrels became soldiers.

This attitude was fine when – as was sometimes the case for long periods of time – China faced no military threats. But when such a threat emerged in the form of the newly industrialized West in the mid-nineteenth century, and at a time of traditional dynastic decline, it made China vulnerable.

As invasions and 'UNEQUAL TREATIES' weakened the country, reformers sought to rebuild China's armed forces and modernize them. Not only did this mean equipping them with the latest weapons and tactics, it meant finding a place for the military man in society and politics. With the breakdown of civil authority in the early twentieth century, that place was found to be at the very centre of life: soldiers dominated and armies determined the course of Chinese politics from the collapse of the QING DYNASTY until the Communist revolution and occasionally beyond.

At the close of the nineteenth century, the government had three main armies at its disposal. The Banner Forces were descendants of the original Manchu conquerors who founded the Qing dynasty. The Army of the Green Standard traced its origins to the Chinese commanders who surrendered to the new dynasty in the mid-seventeenth century. More recent and modern were the provincial armies founded to fight the Taiping Rebellion of the 1850s. These forces tended to be better equipped and disciplined than the first two, but they were of dubious political loyalty so far as the Court was concerned. All of them were unequal to the task of defending the dynasty against its foreign foes and domestic enemies – as China's performance in the Sino-Japanese War of 1894–5 and the BOXER REBELLION showed.

China needed 'new armies'. It acquired them during the early 1900s as a result of government military reforms. Beijing and the provinces set up military academies. Many hired instructors from JAPAN whose progress since the Meiji Restoration, defeat of China itself, and of Russia in 1904, won many admirers. Hundreds of young Chinese officers were sent to Japan for training. While there, they not only learned modern military science but came under the influence of the anti-Qing, pro-republican movement nurtured among overseas Chinese by SUN YAT-SEN and others.

On their return to China these officers helped redefine the role of the military in society. Soldiery was not just for those who could not do anything else. It was for patriots who wanted to serve, modernize and reform China. The new armies were rapidly politicized, their officers to the fore in the REPUBLICAN REVOLUTION of 1911.

military politics to political military

The most powerful military force in the new Republic was the Beiyang Army (named after the 'northern ocean' around whose shores, now included in the province of HEBEI, it first operated). Its commander, YUAN SHIKAI, combined modern military methods with traditional political views and rare cunning. But it was his control of an army rather than his political skills that made him the master of the Republic until his death in 1916. Yuan's attempt to restore dynastic rule by declaring himself emperor was designed to re-establish credibility in traditional institutions and *civilian* authority. It failed and China succumbed to rule by WARLORDS.

The warlord era was the antithesis of almost every Chinese political ideal. Scores of armies – most of their ranks made up of poorly trained infantrymen and armed, for the most part, with rifles – waged battles for territory and other advantages. Some of these conflicts involved hundreds of thousands of troops, lasted for months and caused heavy casualties. Others amounted to little more than threats, feints and skirmishes: the last thing a warlord could afford to do was to lose his army. But looting, violence and cruelty were widespread and, whether they were real or imaginary, warlord battles took a heavy toll. They consumed vast amounts of money and manpower in a backward country that could ill afford them.

The counterpart to this social and economic disruption was political fragmentation. Not only were warlords unable to reunite China, they made it impossible for non-military groups to do so. Warlord rule showed that the collapse of the traditional Confucian order, and the lack of agreement over what to replace it with, meant political solutions had to be imposed by force. Political success was inseparable from prior military success; nationalists and revolutionaries without battalions were doomed to impotence.

This militarisation of politics was not lost on Sun Yat-sen. In the early 1920s he abandoned his attempt to reunite China with the help of 'friendly' southern warlords in exchange for an alliance with the SOVIET UNION. The most important result was the birth of the National Revolutionary Army, China's first modern, revolutionary armed force. Disciplined, well equipped and controlled by powerful political commissars, it was loyal to the newly reorganised KUOMINTANG and committed to that Party's revolutionary goals of reuniting and reforming China. It carried these out with remarkable success during the NORTHERN EXPEDITION.

Yet the Northern Expedition changed the National Revolutionary Army as much as it changed China. CHIANG KAI-SHEK's purge of the Communists in 1927 deprived his troops of much of their revolutionary mission while his tactical alliance with warlords who rallied to the Nationalist cause swelled its ranks with men of often doubtful quality and questionable loyalty. Attempts to disband these forces once China had been reunified led to wars and constant infighting among rival militarists. 'Residual warlordism', as this phenomenon is sometimes called, dogged the Nationalist government from its founding in Nanjing and helped bring its life on the Mainland to an ignominious end in 1949.

rise of the Red Army

By mid-1927 MAO ZEDONG and other Communist leaders were in a similar position to the one Sun had faced in the early 1920s: their party's revolutionary goals could not be realized without an army of its own. China's Communist military history began on 1 August – Army Day in the People's Republic ever since – when a small force known as the Red Army seized and then lost Nanchang, capital of JIANGXI province.

The subsequent development of the Red Army was related to the broader struggles over leadership and line that characterize Communist Party history. In the late 1920s there were more attacks on major cities, all of them failures, until the triumph of Mao's view that the Party could survive and eventually come to power only by building rural bases, or soviets, and relying on the peasantry. What later became known as 'people's war' – in which the Red Army was the 'fish' and the peasantry the 'ocean' – enabled the Party, then headquartered in the Central Soviet of Jiangxi, to withstand the first four of Chiang Kai-shek's five annihilation campaigns.

Nationalist military incompetence helped Communism survive. So did Chiang's preoccupation with rival militarists and Japanese aggression. But the Party's policies of land reform, which won over many farmers in some of China's poorest areas, played an important part, too. Here was a revolutionary

formula that, if unchecked, could spread rapidly. It was not that the Chinese countryside was necessarily crying out for revolution. Conditions, customs and social relations varied widely. And there were solutions to China's agrarian problems other than that of class warfare for a government committed and in control of the countryside. Yet Chiang's regime was neither while the Communists were both – at least within the soviets they set up in isolated parts of south China during the early 1930s.

For Chiang, Japan's occupation of Manchuria in 1931 and attack on Shanghai the following year could be dealt with when the time was ripe. Communism, on the other hand, was a 'disease of the vitals' that had to be eradicated by military means before national defence and reconstruction could begin. The government's fifth annihilation campaign of 1934 finally dislodged the Communists from south China and sent them north on their LONG MARCH. This took a heavy toll on the Party as a fighting force, but failed to wipe it out. Chiang's plans to deliver a knock-out blow in league with the exiled Manchurian armies under ZHANG XUELIANG were thwarted by the XIAN INCIDENT of 1936 which made the Nationalist and Communist rivals allies again – this time in the fight against Japan.

China at war with Japan

The SINO-JAPANESE WAR subjected the Chinese people to full-scale invasion by a truly modern, disciplined, well-equipped fighting machine that enjoyed control of the air and sea as well as large stretches of territory. It also subjected them to outrages, of which the Nanjing Massacre was the most infamous. Despite a programme of military modernization that had seen German officers train elite Nationalist units, mainly for use against the Communists, Chiang's forces crumbled before the assault. There were several heroic stands and, at Taierzhuang in SHANDONG, a genuine victory under general LI ZONGREN. But by the start of 1940 the Nationalist government had lost all of the densely populated, urbanized centres of the east and south, and sought refuge in the isolated 'temporary' capital of CHONGQING, then in SICHUAN. Moral and material support trickled in from the West and the Soviet Union, but China was essentially alone – a fact that made its determination to resist, despite the odds, losses and defection of WANG JINGWEI, all the more remarkable.

Exhaustion, domestic political realities and

the start of the Pacific war in December 1941 sapped this spirit of unity and determination. The front against Japan had stabilized. Chiang believed that victory over Tokyo was inevitable now that the United States had joined the war. There seemed little sense in wasting men and resources fighting the invaders. Far better to conserve military strength for use against the Communists, who had waged guerrilla warfare against the Japanese from their headquarters in YANAN and elsewhere in north China, and rival militarists, whose semi-independent armies still presented a challenge to Chiang's rule. The Communists, contrary to their propaganda, also concentrated on building up resources for the postwar struggle.

By 1942 the Nationalist military effort had become desultory – much to the fury of the US General JOSEPH STILWELL whose faith in the Chinese fighting man was greater than his grasp of the realities of local politics. Corruption, black marketeering, and open trading with the enemy were common. Famine struck. Peasants resented heavy-handed conscription and rampant taxation. In the eyes of many, the Nationalist armies were even worse than those of their warlord predecessors. The idealism of the 'new armies' of the late Qing, and the patriotic, revolutionary fervour of the National Revolutionary Army were things of the past. Soldiery sank again in public esteem.

The popular mood alternated between grim endurance and demoralization. It swung towards the latter in 1944 when a final Japanese offensive cut a swathe through central and southern China, before briefly threatening Chongqing. The end of the war came not, as once seemed likely, through a US-led assault on Japanese troops in China, but by means of the Allied strategy of 'island hopping' towards the Japanese homeland and the dropping of atomic bombs.

China at war with itself

China was a victor in 1945 and, at least in American eyes, a 'Great Power'. The scourge of military conflict – against both domestic and foreign foes – was surely over. China's swollen armies, both Nationalist and Communist, could demobilize. It was time to seek political solutions to China's problems.

These hopes of a war-weary population were premature. Victory, despite its costs, had little effect on China's domestic politics. The country was still divided into armed camps and every effort, including one led by the United States, failed to prevent the outbreak of a further, and this time decisive, military conflict between the protagonists.

The CIVIL WAR between the Nationalists and the Communists saw fighting as intense and extensive as that during the struggle against Japan, if over a shorter period of time. An offensive in 1946 gave the government the upper hand and briefly hinted at the possibility of total victory. It proved illusory. Nationalist armies, still plagued by the rivalry, incompetence, corruption and seeming lack of purpose that characterized Chiang's regime before and after the defeat of Japan, overestimated their own strength as well as the imagined weakness of their opponents. The government's military tactics were as uninspiring as its political appeal.

Communist armies, by contrast, were often brilliantly led, united and committed to their Party's revolutionary cause. They deployed weapons captured first from Japanese troops in Manchuria and later from the defeated Nationalists, and won public support as a result of the Party's policy of land reform and other popular measures. Victory came through a series of set-piece military battles involving hundreds of thousands of men rather than the 'people's war' of earlier (and later) propaganda. But Communist forces – renamed the PEOPLE'S LIBERATION ARMY (PLA) in 1946 – did much to salvage the reputation of the Chinese soldier in many eyes. In propaganda, but also to a large extent in reality, the Communist soldier was dedicated to patriotism and revolutionary change rather than the preservation of self-interest, and the local loyalties that often seemed primary concerns of his opponents.

The Communist victory in 1949 marked the end of almost 50 years of uninterrupted warfare across China. Few parts of the country had been subjected to constant battles throughout this period. Some, most of them remote, escaped completely. But armies, whether those of warlords, Nationalists, Communists or the Japanese, traipsed backwards and forwards across almost every province causing death and destruction on a massive scale. Military power had escaped the civilian constraints that generally kept it in check in traditional society and ensured that the soldier, and much of what he stood for, was held in low esteem. The establishment of a strong central government after the Communist military victory re-established the primacy of civilian authority over the armed forces.

It was not the end of military involvement in Chinese politics. The PLA's function is to support Party leadership as well as defend China's borders. This has required spectacular interventions in domestic politics on two occasions. The first occurred during the CUL-TURAL REVOLUTION, when the army had to 'hold the ring' as Red Guard factions battled for power across the country. The second took place in 1989 when troops suppressed the TIANANMEN SQUARE DEMOCRACY MOVEMENT. The PLA returned to barracks after both interventions; there was no question of China being ruled by generals. Both in theory and (generally) in practice under Communism, the Chinese army is the servant of civilian rule rather than its master.

Yet above all it is the servant of the Party: the Communist Party controls the gun (see PEOPLE'S LIBERATION ARMY). Both constitutionally and in practice, the PLA belongs to the Party rather than the state. The fact that the military owes allegiance to a political party rather than the nation or the state is a reminder of the troubled relations between civilian and military power that have dogged China.

arms sales

China derives substantial, undeclared earnings from arms sales, which help fund the PEOPLE'S LIBERATION ARMY (PLA) and afford Beijing extra leverage abroad, especially in the Third World. The sale in 1988 of *Dong Feng 3* intermediate-range ballistic missiles to Saudi Arabia was an example: China earned valuable hard currency from the exercise and two years later persuaded Riyadh to switch diplomatic relations from TAIWAN to Beijing.

Yet China's arms sales incur diplomatic costs. They are an irritant in relations with the UNITED STATES and a cause of concern elsewhere. This is because of China's choice of customers as well as the kind of weapons it sells them.

Washington regards Beijing's major clients – BURMA, North Korea, Iran and Syria – as 'rogue states' (later 'states of concern') because of their alleged support of terrorism. Moreover the military ambitions of these countries threaten the balance of power in their vicinities. China's weapons sales to another major customer, PAKISTAN, is of concern to rival INDIA because it fuels the arms race in South Asia.

The fact that China has sold missiles and nuclear technology to Iran and Pakistan as well as conventional weapons, adds to the unease. In the early 1990s Washington vigorously opposed the sale of Chinese-made M11 missiles to these countries. Only after tough negotiations did China agree in 1994 to abide by the terms of the Missile Technology Control Regime (MTCR). This forbids the sale of equipment and technology for missiles with a range of 300 kms (187.5 miles) and a payload of 500 kgs (1,100 pounds) of the kind that would enable them to carry nuclear warheads. However, Beijing declined to sign up formally to the MTCR.

As for nuclear exports, China acceded to the Nuclear Non-proliferation Treaty in 1991 and its extension in 1995. But prior to 1991, it transferred equipment and/or nuclear know-how of various kinds to Algeria, Argentina, Brazil, India, Iran, Iraq, North Korea, Pakistan and South Africa. Again Pakistan was the principal beneficiary – so much so that the nuclear device Islamabad tested in 1998, shortly after India conducted a test of its own, might more accurately be described as a 'Chinese', rather than a 'Muslim' bomb. Beijing supplied Pakistan with a design for a bomb, enough enriched uranium for two bombs, tritium gas capable of boosting the yield of fission bombs, magnets for the centrifuges used at a nuclear fuel plant, and a 300MW nuclear power station. China is believed to have conducted a nuclear test on behalf of Pakistan at its Lop Nor testing site in XINJIANG.

Concern in Washington over China's nuclear proliferation continued beyond 1995, when Beijing signed the extension to the non-proliferation accord. The threat of US sanctions against China over the issue was lifted only when Beijing promised, in 1996, not to supply nuclear facilities to any country that refused to accept supervision and monitoring by the International Atomic Energy Agency (IAEA). In the following year it passed its first piece of domestic legislation governing the control of nuclear exports.

None of these developments has removed the threat that China will proliferate nuclear technology, still less cease the sale of conventional weapons. Money, influence and power are at stake, as they are for every country engaged in arms sales. Beijing has often hinted to the United States that its willingness to arm 'rogue states' such as North Korea is a form of retaliation for Washington's weapons sale to Taiwan.

China produces a full range of weapons, from side arms to missiles, in a huge military industrial complex, much of it dating from the early 1960s when Beijing's diplomatic isolation forced the PLA to make its own arms. Since the start of the reform era many military-owned factories have switched to producing civilian goods in a search for profits and efficiency.

During the 1980s and 1990s China's arms sales were conducted by large military-affiliated conglomerates whose connections with the Communist leadership afforded them flexibility, protection and secrecy. The two best known were Polytechnologies Incorporated and Northern Industries Corporation (NORINCO). Both engaged in the production and sale of weapons as part of their diversified business interests. Both became managerial training grounds for the offspring of the Party elite.

In 1998 President JIANG ZEMIN ordered the PLA to relinquish control over most of its commercial operations. As a result, the Commission on Science and Technology for National Defence assumed responsibility for arms sales, which it exercises on behalf of a new organization within the PLA: the General Equipment Department.

Asia-Pacific Economic Cooperation (APEC)

This 21-member body, formed in 1989 to promote trade liberalization, is one of the few major international organizations outside sport to include China and TAIWAN. Another is the Asian Development Bank.

Taiwan and HONG KONG joined APEC at the same time as China, in 1991, but as 'regional economies' rather than states. Rivalry between the 'two Chinas', an obstacle to their joint membership of other international bodies, has for the most part been subdued in APEC – though Beijing, venue of the 13th regional forum in 2001, has opposed Taipei's attempts to host it in future.

APEC provides a useful forum for Mainland diplomacy. JIANG ZEMIN attended the meetings of APEC political leaders that began in Seattle in 1993. They allowed him to meet his counterpart from the UNITED STATES at a time when poor relations between Washington and Beijing made a Sino-US summit impossible. At the 1996 APEC meeting in Manila, China and the US agreed that Jiang would make an official visit to Washington the following year.

Likewise, after China's resumption of sovereignty over Hong Kong, APEC meetings provided valuable international exposure for TUNG CHEE-HWA, the former businessman who became the territory's first Chief Executive. Prior to the handover, Hong Kong's Financial Secretary represented the territory.

Beijing's enthusiasm for good relations with APEC members is grounded in economic necessity: member states and 'regional economies' account for more than 75 per cent of China's foreign trade and more than 80 per cent of inward investment. Its commitment to APEC's goals – free trade for economically developed members by 2010 and for all by 2020 – is more restrained. Chinese leaders have stressed the need for economic and technological cooperation between members rather than the liberalization of trade and investment regimes pursued by the United States.

Founded on an Australian initiative, APEC includes Australia, Brunei, Canada, Chile, China, Hong Kong, INDONESIA, JAPAN, Malaysia, Mexico, New Zealand, Papua New Guinea, Peru, the Philippines, Russia, SINGAPORE, South Korea, Taiwan, Thailand, the United States and VIETNAM.

'Asian values'

The term 'Asian values' acquired a vogue in the 1990s as an *explanation* of the outstanding economic performance of certain Asian states; a *description* of indigenous social and cultural traditions; a *justification* of the social and political status quo; and a *defence* against Western criticism of HUMAN RIGHTS abuses in Asia generally and China in particular. The term lost its appeal with the Asian financial crisis that began in 1997: the supposedly 'Asian' variety of capitalism was a cause of the disaster.

A classic expression of the 'Asian values'

argument was set out in the 'Bangkok Declaration' – the fruit of the World Conference on Human Rights of April 1993. This meeting of representatives from Asian states produced a relativist interpretation of human rights in which as much emphasis was placed on the need for countries to oppose interference in their internal affairs and maintain 'national sovereignty' as on the need to champion human freedom. Human rights were universal in nature, the declaration said, but 'they must be considered in the context of a dynamic and evolving process of international norm setting, bearing in mind the significance of national and regional particularities and various historical, cultural and religious backgrounds.'

The debate on 'Asian values' was a late twentieth-century version of a much older argument among Chinese officials and intellectuals about the relevance of 'national conditions' (*guoqing*). These were the specific conditions, said to be unique to China, which allegedly rendered Western forms of liberalism and democracy at best unsuitable and at worst potentially damaging to the country.

Several Asian leaders rallied to the theme at the end of the twentieth century. Far from such Western concepts being 'universal' in nature, the 'highest' of their kind, or values that were 'bound' to take root in developing Asian states, they were held to be culture-specific, and potentially harmful to the alleged natural social harmony of Asian societies. Thrift, discipline, filial loyalty, hard work and honesty were what counted, not 'Western' notions of press freedom, individual liberty and multi-party politics.

Few exponents of these views – who included TUNG CHEE-HWA in Hong Kong, Communist leaders in Beijing, and Lee Kuan Yew in SINGAPORE – cared to specify what they meant by 'Western' values. More often than not, they referred to 'Western problems' such as crime, drug abuse and prostitution. Also targeted for attack was the alleged tendency of Western governments to engage in excessive spending on welfare, and press freedom of the kind that tolerated the ridiculing of national leaders. There was even less clarity about exactly what constituted 'Asian' values. It was implied that they held sway right across Asia or at the very least, across the scarcely less diverse region of south and east Asia.

In Beijing, the 'Asian values' argument was a supplement to the 'five principles of peaceful coexistence' laid down during the BANDUNG CONFERENCE of 1955 in that it offered a defence against international criticism of China's human rights record. The criticism intensified after the suppression of the TIANANMEN SQUARE DEMOCRACY MOVEMENT, necessitating a vigorous defence on China's part. Protagonists of 'Asian values' tended to be those in positions of power and influence rather than ordinary Asians themselves. Critics, in both East and West, pointed out that the doctrine could too easily be used to disguise unacceptable political behaviour as 'cultural differences'. Indeed, the vigorous growth of democracy in TAIWAN, South Korea, the Philippines and Thailand, and the collapse of the Suharto regime in INDONESIA in 1998, suggested that many Asians liked 'Asian values' rather less than many Asian leaders.

Association of Southeast Asian Nations (ASEAN)

A desire to promote interregional cooperation and oppose outside interference, not least from revolutionary China, was behind the decision of Indonesia, Malaysia, the Philippines, Singapore and Thailand to form ASEAN in 1967. More than 30 years later, the inclusion of all ten Southeast Asian nations has fostered a sense of community within ASEAN but failed to remove anxieties over China, which now centre on Beijing's claim to sovereignty over the SOUTH CHINA SEA.

Prior to the 1980s, non-Communist Southeast Asia had more to fear from Beijing's claims on the allegiance of OVERSEAS CHINESE in the region than ownership of an ocean and

its largely uninhabited islands. Ethnicity and Mao Zedong's revolutionary message afforded China unwelcome leverage in the area. The 1965 coup in INDONESIA, in which Beijing was implicated, was the most striking but not the only example.

Such adventures died with Chairman Mao; China's commitment to economic reforms and search for foreign investment required good relations with its neighbours. ASEAN's opposition, shared by Beijing, to Vietnam's invasion of Cambodia in 1978 helped the process of *rapprochement*. Growing investment opportunities in China for Southeast Asia's largely Chinese business leaders encouraged it. Indonesia and Singapore established diplomatic relations with Beijing in 1990. Brunei, an ASEAN member from 1984, followed in 1991.

Territorial disputes tarnished the new amity almost as soon as it began. The Philippines, Malaysia and Brunei all contested China's claims to ownership of the islands or waters of the South China Sea closest to their own shores. In 1992 ASEAN issued a 'Declaration on the South China Sea' which called on all parties to settle their disputes in the region peacefully. The following year it formed the ASEAN Regional Forum, of which China is a member, to defuse tensions and establish a dialogue on regional security with the South China Sea much in mind.

This was something of a diplomatic setback for Beijing, which dislikes discussing territorial disputes with multilateral bodies where it can be hard to play one party off against another. However, it did nothing to curb China's claims in the region, or its push south to enforce them. The construction in 1995 of military facilities on Mischief Reef, a speck of land in the south of the Spratlys, sparked a row with the Philippines almost as intense – though not of such long standing – as that with VIETNAM, an ASEAN member from 1995, and, like China, a claimant to *all* the islands in the Spratly chain.

In 1997 and 1999 respectively, BURMA and CAMBODIA, China's closest allies in Southeast Asia, joined ASEAN. Both countries – and ASEAN itself – had powerful reasons of their own for becoming members. But some within the association hoped an expanded membership might lessen Beijing's influence in the region. Whether or not this is the case, ASEAN's ability to stand up to China on territorial questions is weakened by competing claims to the same territory within its own ranks, and the association's inability – and unwillingness – to undertake a joint defence role in the region.

ASEAN's members are Brunei, Burma, Cambodia, Indonesia, Laos, Malaysia, the Philippines, Singapore, Thailand and Vietnam.

bai hua (plain speech)

The use of *bai hua* – 'plain speech', or the vernacular – instead of literary Chinese as the primary written form dates from the MAY FOURTH MOVEMENT of 1919 and ranks alongside the abolition of the civil service examination system in 1905, and the REPUBLICAN REVOLUTION of 1911 in significance (see EDUCATION). These three developments felled the pillars of traditional Chinese civilization.

The abolition of classical Chinese was equivalent to the abandonment of Latin in favour of the vernacular in early modern Europe. Both made communication, whether in the form of government circulars, novels, plays, or, later, magazines and newspapers more accessible to the public. Both made written culture the subject of information and enjoyment across lines of class that had previously been reinforced by language, education and training. They also facilitated the transmission of new ideas. In early twentieth-century China, just as in renaissance Europe, this meant the transmission of *revolutionary* ideas which led to the making of a new intellectual order.

Reform of the Chinese language had been championed since at least the late nineteenth century. Scholars were concerned that while written and spoken languages in the West and Japan were close to each other, Chinese was divided into *wenyan* (literary Chinese) – in which most higher learning and ideas were conveyed – and numerous, often incomprehensible local dialects. There was no standard pronunciation for *wenyan*; and many local dialects, although understood by millions, could not become genuine koines. There was therefore a need for a standard form of verbal communication across the empire. Mandarin (*guanhua*, later *bai hua*), based on Beijing dialect, gradually became the *lingua franca* linking the official and popular Chinese worlds.

Promotion of *bai hua* as the main literary form was a key aim of the May Fourth Movement of 1919. It was part of the campaign to 'save' China; to end the nation's cultural weaknesses which were no less apparent than the political, social, economic and military shortcomings exposed by foreign aggression. For the champions of *bai hua*, elitist terms, decrepit expressions, unnecessarily complex arguments and redundant literary forms preserved an old world of Chinese culture which stifled individual initiative and national renewal. Plain thinking and plain speech were needed to break the hold of antiquity.

HU SHI was the leading exponent of *bai hua* as a written form. He argued that the mainstream of Chinese literature was to be found, not in the 'higher' poetry and prose written in *wenyan*, but in that written in the vernacular. Classical Chinese was a dead language. Nothing valuable could come from it – and certainly nothing new. Since contemporary writers, whatever their subjects, should not try to feel, behave and think like the ancients, it followed that they should not try to write like them either. LU XUN, the literary giant of the early twentieth century and exponent of a kind of 'literary' *bai hua*, owed much of his impact to the fact that he did neither.

The point about language for the new generation of radical intellectuals was that it should be used to *change* the world, not just *describe* it. *Bai hua* aided this by unifying speech and word, thought and action, instincts and ideas. It gave ready expression to the new language of politics, philosophy and revolution, with its notions of equality, nationalism, realism, participation; and acted as a unifying force in Chinese culture by facilitating the communication of ideas once the preserve of a minority with the time (and money) to master classical Chinese.

Numerous ideas were advocated, analysed and attacked during the May Fourth era. But they were practically all expressed in books, pamphlets and magazines written in the vernacular. The 'new' language was so successful that the Ministry of Education announced in 1921 that *bai hua* would henceforth be used in all primary school text books. Classical Chinese, once the highest expression of a living civilization, quickly became an academic specialism.

bandits

In China, as elsewhere, one person's 'bandit' was another's 'rebel' or 'revolutionary'. SUN YAT-SEN and his fellow revolutionaries were 'bandits' in the eyes of the late Qing rulers; the Nationalists branded their Communist foes 'bandits'; and after 1949, when the Communists seized power and sought to wipe out the vestiges of Nationalist resistance, they returned the compliment. Yet pejoratives aside, 'pure' bandit behaviour – theft, kidnapping, violence and murder carried out by gangs, and undertaken for survival or personal gain rather than broader political aims – was widespread during the first half of the twentieth century. Vast areas of China became a 'bandit's world' in which gangs of outlaws roamed the countryside, alarming the authorities but sometimes winning the admiration of local peasants from whose ranks they were drawn.

A prominent bandit leader was the man known as 'White Wolf' (Bai Lang, 1873–1914). Between 1911 and 1914 he and thousands of his followers drifted backwards and forwards across the North China Plain, occupying and pillaging cities. His activities occasionally sparked concern for the safety of major centres such as Beijing and Wuhan. Bai's ranks were swollen by revolutionaries fleeing YUAN SHI-KAI's persecution of their movement. This lent a political dimension to Bai's 'ordinary' bandit activity which made the authorities even more determined to suppress it. To escape the pressure, his forces moved west into SICHUAN pursued by 200,000 government troops. When they turned north into GANSU the bandits encountered even more hostility. Most of the gang, including White Wolf himself, returned to HENAN where they were wiped out.

An even more spectacular example of

banditry, mainly because foreigners were involved, was the Lincheng Incident of May 1923. More than 3,000 outlaws attacked the luxury Blue Express of the Tianjin–Pukou railway at Lincheng in southern SHANDONG and carried off 300 passengers, 30 of them foreigners, one of whom was killed. The bandits, led by Sun Meiyao (c 1898–1923), demanded a huge ransom, free pardons for the kidnappers, and the right to enrol in the regular army. With the powers threatening reprisals, the ransom was paid and the foreigners, together with most other captives, released.

Banditry in China was usually less dramatic and more desperate than these examples suggest. Its growth was a reflection of the precarious nature of life in the countryside during the late Qing and Republican eras. After the 1911 Revolution, civilian government gave way to rule by militarists anxious to expand their influence and fend off intrusion by Beijing. Warlord infighting added to the distress caused by rural indebtedness, heavy taxes, and natural disasters. Society became militarized. Millions turned to banditry as a solution. For the most part they were driven to do so by distress: those who could find other ways to survive in an unstable, unequal society rather than engage in kidnapping, murdering, looting and stealing on a massive scale tended to do so.

Banditry did not end with the birth of the People's Republic, though it decreased in scale. In the late 1990s, reports of the criminal activities of rural gangs, some of them, as in the past, linked with SECRET SOCIETIES, still featured in the official media. Life in the margins – geographic, social, economic or political – continues to be hard in China, and recourse to banditry is still a way of softening it. The persistence of banditry is also a reminder of the limits of state power in a large country with long, remote frontiers and isolated 'intermediate' zones running across provincial and other administrative boundaries.

Bandung Conference (18–24 April 1955)

The People's Republic of China sat down with the Powers for the first time at the GENEVA CONFERENCE ON KOREA AND INDOCHINA in 1954. At Bandung, in Indonesia, the Communist government made its mark among the Third World, spelling out the principles of 'peaceful coexistence' to an audience of Asian and African leaders keen to chart a path in a world polarized by Cold War rivalry. As at Geneva, the 'personal' diplomacy of ZHOU ENLAI – the target of an unsuccessful assassination attempt in Hong Kong immediately before the conference – helped China's cause by presenting Beijing as a 'reasonable' diplomatic partner.

China's moderate foreign policy, subsequently known as the 'Bandung Line', was made possible by a rare outbreak of stability at home, the easing of the first Taiwan Straits Crisis a year before, and good relations between Beijing and Moscow. The Communist leadership appeared more confident than at any time since the foundation of the People's Republic in 1949.

The chief diplomatic legacy of Bandung was the 'five principles of peaceful coexistence': mutual respect for territorial integrity and sovereignty; non-aggression; non-interference; mutual equality and benefit; and peaceful coexistence. They were not born at the conference, having appeared first in a Sino-Indian agreement the year before, in which New Delhi agreed to give up the remaining extra-territorial privileges in TIBET it had inherited from Britain. But the principles were well received by the 29 Asian and African leaders who had gathered in Indonesia: they pointed to the existence of a 'middle way' in the struggle between the Communist and non-Communist blocs. The 'Bandung Spirit' suggested that the Cold War need not become a hot one, and gave impetus to the Non-Aligned Movement.

Until the upheavals of the GREAT LEAP FORWARD and CULTURAL REVOLUTION, the 'five principles' were the official cornerstone of China's FOREIGN POLICY. They became so again from the late 1970s and have remained so ever since, during which time, in keeping with the imperial Chinese tradition, Beijing has suggested that they form the basis of relations between *all* states.

Yet the principles must be seen in the context of the United Front adopted by the Chinese Communists to weaken and divide those deemed to be enemies. As far as the Third World is concerned the Five Principles were designed to frustrate the emergence of blocs and alliances potentially hostile to Beijing. They have since acquired additional value: Beijing evokes the sanctity of the 'non-interference' clause to reject Western criticism of its HUMAN RIGHTS record.

Beijing

China's capital for most of the twentieth century, save for the years 1928–49 when the honour went to Nanjing and, briefly, CHONGQING, Beijing has witnessed imperial decay, foreign occupation and republican revolution, as well as the mass rallies, political struggles and killing of unarmed pro-democracy demonstrators that have accompanied Communist rule. In the course of these great upheavals, the city and its people have been neglected, brutalized and, occasionally, inspired. They have also been transformed: fifty years of Communism have changed the city's physical appearance as drastically as its politics – the first time this has happened in its long history as China's premier political, administrative, cultural and military centre. Attempts during the 1990s to turn Beijing into a modern, 'clean', cosmopolitan capital have yet to overcome its unhappy, latter-day image as a typical Third World metropolis marred by grim architectural tributes to its current rulers and a construction boom funded by foreigners.

'Northern Capital', 'Northern Peace'

On the eve of the twentieth century Chinese politics began to depart from the customs and ideals embodied in the timeless celestial geometry of imperial Beijing. Inspired by KANG YOUWEI, the radical reformer, a new generation of intellectuals argued that China's fate could no longer be decided by emperors and officials isolated within the Forbidden City. It had to be discussed with ordinary, educated people outside the city's towering walls. Politics was the business of the people, not the preserve of the palace. And imperial benevolence, deemed to radiate out from the Forbidden City by virtue of its majestic design to the rest of Beijing and the vast empire beyond, was no longer enough. Kang's '100 Days Reform Movement' of 1898 proved an abortive attempt at constitutional change (see GUANGXU EMPEROR; EMPRESS DOWAGER). But it showed the extent to which the modern politics of public discussion and protest had impinged upon the old order. In this sense it challenged the architecture as well as the politics of the imperial capital.

Another challenge soon followed. The Court's decision in 1899 to recruit the BOXER REBELLION to the cause of dynastic survival subjected the centre of Beijing to an orgy of violence. With the siege of the Legations, the foreign settlement just inside the city walls, it made China the focus of an international crisis. The rebels looted the capital at will – though less systematically than soldiers of the eight-power Allied Expeditionary Army who in 1900 lifted the siege and drove the Court west to Xian. Palaces and libraries were plundered. Books and booty were shipped home. Yet the physical fabric of Beijing, the essential shape and purpose of the imperial capital, survived such depredations relatively unscathed.

Even the final collapse of imperial rule in 1911 did not deprive Beijing of its political potency (see QING DYNASTY; REPUBLICAN REVOLUTION). At first it was unclear what part the capital of discredited Manchu rule would play in the new republican order. SUN YAT-SEN and his fellow revolutionaries envisaged a secondary role for the metropolis: they made a point of establishing their new government in Nanjing, JIANGSU province. Yet the spell of a city synonymous with power and authority for centuries could not be broken so easily. Neither could the revolutionaries ignore the presence in Beijing of YUAN SHIKAI, commander of the country's most powerful military forces, and the strongman whom even the most radical of them felt China needed at such a crucial time. Thus within weeks of the Republic's founding in January 1912, Beijing

became China's capital again and Yuan its president. Both developments reflected the tenacity of the imperial idea, which Yuan tried, and failed, to revive in person in 1916 (see YUAN SHIKAI). A further, even more farcical attempt followed at the hands of warlord Zhang Xun (1854–1923) (see QING DYNASTY). Neither of these abortive restorations could disguise the fact that the last tragic scenes of imperial rule had been played out earlier in the secluded palaces and courtyards of the Forbidden City where, under an agreement of 1912, the self-absorbed 'last emperor', PU YI, and his retinue were allowed to live in isolation. They were not finally evicted until the armies of FENG YUXIANG occupied Beijing in 1924.

Control over Beijing was a principal objective for many of the WARLORDS and politicians who contended for power after Yuan's death in 1916. Command of the capital brought prestige, recognition from the powers, and entitlement to customs revenues and foreign loans – all of them valuable assets in China's fragmented domestic politics. Yet Chinese politics were so fragmented in the early Republic that the 'national' government was known, often pejoratively, as 'the Beijing Government' – a reflection of the fact that it was run by the warlord of the day, was essentially a local administration, and probably a temporary one. Grand-sounding presidents, premiers and cabinets came and went, but their writ ran only as far as the network of personal allegiances enjoyed by the warlords who backed them. Beijing was the capital in name only, and in 1928, when troops of the Nationalist Revolutionary Army loyal to CHIANG KAI-SHEK occupied the city in the final stage of the NORTHERN EXPEDITION, it lost even that status in favour of Nanjing. Beijing – the 'northern capital' – was renamed 'Beiping', 'northern peace'.

Not that Beijing played a passive role in the nation's affairs following the collapse of empire, or that the city was no more than a warlords' plaything. Indeed, it was a source of national renewal, a function of its continuing importance as a cultural centre and home for some of China's most prestigious colleges and universities. In May 1919, public despair over national weakness turned to popular rage in Beijing when, at the Paris Peace Conference, the Allies transferred areas of SHANDONG leased to Germany before the First World War to Japan rather than restoring them to China. The city became the birthplace of modern protest in China as students, many of them from Beijing University, intellectuals and businessmen demonstrated against their weak, vacillating government. The protests, known as the MAY FOURTH MOVEMENT, spread to almost every other major city, producing China's first national movement of urban dissent.

The significance of May Fourth lies in the wider movement of cultural renewal associated with it as much as in the political protests that took place on that day. But the Beijing demonstrations quickly became an icon of Chinese nationalism from which both Nationalist and Communist Chinese governments still draw inspiration, and which both claim as part of their revolutionary pedigree. The 1919 protests were unequalled in scale and significance until the massive outpouring of dissent of 1989 in Tiananmen Square, which ended in military suppression and heavy loss of life.

Beijing in the 1930s, free of the burden of national politics, was able to bask in its past glories relatively undisturbed. The former capital had seen better times, and was destined to see worse; but neither the arrival of Japanese troops following the Marco Polo Bridge Incident of 1937, nor its recovery by the Nationalist government in 1945 seemed to stir the city from its slumbers. (See SINO-JAPANESE WAR.) Even the violence and tumult of the CIVIL WAR appeared to pass Beijing by – despite the fact that its inhabitants were inconvenienced by a Communist encirclement from late 1948 that amounted to the last siege of a major walled city in Chinese history. In January 1949, the Nationalist General Fu Zuoyi (1895–1974) agreed to vacate the city peacefully in favour of the PEOPLE'S LIBERATION ARMY waiting in the suburbs. Beijing, its grandeur much faded but its imperial form still essentially intact despite the ravages of revolution, occupation and modernization, quietly received its new rulers.

lost harmonies: Communist Beijing

Nine months later, amid the staged fanfare, popular curiosity and cautious enthusiasm that marked the start of the Communist era elsewhere in China, Mao Zedong and his senior comrades mounted the Gate of Heavenly Peace and proclaimed the establishment of the People's Republic of China before huge crowds in Tiananmen Square. Beijing was declared the capital again. And after some debate the rulers of 'New' China moved into Zhongnanhai, the complex of buildings near

The Lie of the Land

Beijing is situated at the northern limit of China 'proper', close to the old nomad border between steppe and sown. The city has been a frontier capital, both for Chinese dynasties and for the northern invaders for whom it was comfortably near home. It is protected to the north and west by serried mountain ranges, while to the south, the great North China Plain stretches for hundreds of miles. The municipality of Beijing covers an area of more than 16,800 sq kms (6,486 square miles), of which the city proper forms 87 sq kms (34 square miles). At the close of the 1990s Beijing had a population of 12 million, plus a 'floating population' of about one million transients.

the heart of the Forbidden City where, like Chinese rulers before them, they decided the nation's fate in secret compounds behind high walls and closed doors.

The Communists had less use for other architectural legacies of empire, and quickly set about transforming Beijing in accordance with their vision of a modern socialist capital. This meant converting what was essentially an administrative and cultural centre into a partly self-sufficient political, military, and industrial base set in a rural hinterland and invested with the powers of a province. In the 1950s Beijing expanded its territorial reach deep into HEBEI and became home for the numerous ministries, government departments and other bureaucratic networks inseparable from Communist rule.

A frenzy of destruction and construction accompanied these developments. In the 1950s Beijing's city walls, and in the 1960s all but a few of the massive gates that once breached them, were torn down because they were deemed obstacles to modern transport and remnants of a feudal past. The capital's second ring road is built on their foundations. Many temples and churches disappeared, too, casualties of the need for space to accommodate a swelling population and the government's determination to replace old gods with new. Courtyard houses and stately mansions once home for the city's wealthy, cultured elite, were sequestered by government departments, taken over by the new Communist elite or turned into homes for scores of poor families rather than the one or two wealthy owners for whom they had been built. The old Legation Quarter, a cruel symbol of China's humiliation by the powers, suffered a similar fate. Many architectural tokens of the foreign presence have survived the twentieth century but, until the 1990s, the majority were in poor repair. Most are still occupied by government departments. Many remain closed to the public.

New monuments soon replaced the old. The Great Hall of the People, which dominates the western flank of Tiananmen Square, is chief among them. It was built in 1959 as a suitably imposing venue for the great set pieces of Communist political theatre: national meetings of the Party itself, and gatherings of the NATIONAL PEOPLE'S CONGRESS and the CHINESE PEOPLE'S POLITICAL CONSULTATIVE CONFERENCE. In the centre of the Square the 'monument to the people's heroes' is a proletarian architectural dagger thrust into the heart of the otherwise open southern approaches to the Forbidden City. In 1977, the Party administered the *coup de grace* to the grand imperial design by building the giant mausoleum which houses the sarcophagus of MAO ZEDONG. Long before then the construction of coal-burning factories in the urban area had added to the smog which all too often blotted out Beijing's blue skies and deprived the city of anything but the occasional glimpse of the majestic Western Hills.

The Forbidden City itself, the Temple of Heaven, and a handful of lesser temples and ancillary buildings escaped this devastation. At the start of the twenty-first century they remain the treasures they have always been. Yet, isolated and sundered from the network of buildings that once gave them meaning and form, they offer only muted, disjointed testimony to a city whose stones, tiles, walls, roofs and arches, and the strict grid pattern according to which they were constructed, embodied one of the world's great civilizations. Less than a century after the collapse of the last dynasty, the architectural legacy of imperial Beijing is modest in the extreme.

street politics

Political as well as architectural dramas unfolded on the streets of Beijing under Communism. The most spectacular was the CULTURAL REVOLUTION. In 1966 hundreds of thousands of Red Guards thronged Tiananmen Square in adoration of Chairman Mao and his new revolutionary line. Together with the dwindling band of comrades who remained in his favour, the Chairman hailed the sons and daughters of his revolution from the Gate of Heavenly Peace. The marches, parades and mass rallies of that summer were the most dramatic expressions of revolution-

ary ardour ever seen in Beijing – and indeed the whole of China. Their first major political victim was PENG ZHEN, mayor of the capital, whom radicals accused of running an independent 'bourgeois' kingdom in the very heart of the nation. Peng's fall, and the public criticism and psychological cruelties which accompanied it, marked the start of open season on the 'revisionists' whom Mao said had sneaked into the Party.

Almost ten exhausting years after Red Guards filled Tiananmen, a different kind of protest erupted in the Square, one which unnerved the Maoist radicals known as the 'GANG OF FOUR' then at the top of the Party. In April 1976 thousands of people placed flowers around the monument to the people's heroes to mourn the death, the previous month, of ZHOU ENLAI. It was as much a protest against present leaders, Mao included, as an expression of grief over one who had departed, and the radicals crushed the movement, branding it 'counter-revolutionary'. They then, for the second time in 10 years, secured the dismissal and disgrace of DENG XIAOPING, Zhou's ally, and, following Mao's death in September, plotted to secure the succession. The 'Gang' lacked the military, political and popular support to do so. In October security forces loyal to HUA GUOFENG, the Chairman's own choice as successor, arrested JIANG QING, Mao's widow and the other members of the 'Gang'. It was a palace coup almost worthy of Beijing in its warlord days, and it paved the way for Deng's return and, in 1978, the start of the reform era.

Deng's return to power owed something to renewed street protests. The DEMOCRACY WALL MOVEMENT of 1978–9, named after the wall in Xidan district, west of Tiananmen Square, where ordinary citizens displayed posters criticizing the excesses of the Cultural Revolution, helped reformers gain the upper hand over their Maoist opponents in the Party. For a few brief months, the streets of Beijing crackled with political debate as people dared to make their voices heard. But only for a few months. Activists such as WEI JINGSHENG crossed forbidden frontiers by raising questions about the legality of Party rule, branding Deng a dictator, and demanding a 'fifth modernization': democracy (see FOUR MODERNIZATIONS). In 1979 Deng had Wei and other leaders arrested and sealed off Democracy Wall. Reform was confined to the economy; politics was for the Politburo, not ordinary people.

Generally speaking, this formula endured in Beijing until the massive pro-democracy protests in Tiananmen Square of April to June 1989. (See TIANANMEN SQUARE DEMOCRACY MOVEMENT.) The movement that, in the outside world at least, has come to be known simply as 'Tiananmen' demoralized and divided Communist leaders, forcing them to declare martial law in their own capital and then 'reconquer' it by means of a bloody, heavy-handed armoured assault. For several days after the People's Liberation Army cleared the Square of demonstrators, soldiers terrorized Beijing, killing curious onlookers at will, and shooting randomly at buildings. The scale – and the death toll – of the suppression exceeded anything undertaken by the warlords, the Kuomintang or the Japanese during their tenure of Beijing.

in search of new Beijing

Rapid economic growth and social change in the 1990s erased the physical but not the psychological scars of Tiananmen. Beijing hosted the Asian Games in September 1990, and staged a narrowly unsuccessful bid in 1993 to host the year 2000 Olympics. In 1995 it was the venue for the United Nations' Women's Conference. (See WOMEN.) By this time high-rise buildings dominated the cityscape, overshadowing historic thoroughfares, parks, and quieter quarters once immune to the ravages of change and time. Once a sprawling 'horizontal' city, whose buildings dared not pierce a skyline defined by the stunning roofs of the Forbidden City, Beijing is now a predominantly 'vertical' capital, like its counterparts elsewhere in Asia.

A principal casualty of all this change, of the ceaseless construction of new ringroads, expressways, shopping centres, offices and apartment complexes, and of the traffic and pollution that go with them, are the *hutongs* – the narrow lanes or alleys – that for centuries served as arteries of the community. Once one of Beijing's most distinctive features, they

have been all but obliterated by the onward march of concrete, steel and glass. China's capital has not quite succumbed to commercialism on the scale of SHANGHAI, Guangzhou and scores of other cities. But neither has it put up much of a fight against the all-consuming creed of the 1990s.

Certainly the city's rapid development in the decade following Tiananmen offered temptations enough for CHEN XITONG, the longserving mayor and then Party secretary of Beijing. Chen was a principal advocate of the use of force against the students in 1989 and the author of the official report into the 'counter-revolutionary rebellion' issued after the suppression. In 1992 he was promoted to the Politburo. But he was sacked three years later following the suicide of Wang Baosen (1935–95), one of his deputies, who was said to have killed himself as officials investigating CORRUPTION in the municipal administration closed in. Chen's crimes, which earned him a 16-year jail sentence in 1998, were compounded by his opposition to JIANG ZEMIN, whom he apparently felt was unqualified to lead the Communist Party.

At the start of the new century, the physical appearance of Beijing speaks eloquently of China's fate during the past 50 years and also says something about its future. The architectural emblems of Communism – the Great Hall and the equally Stalinesque Museum of the Revolution on the opposite side of Tiananmen Square; the drab office blocks and apartments that can be found almost everywhere; and even the garish office towers, hotels, shopping and entertainment centres of the reform era – all seem to speak of Beijing's, and therefore China's, unease with itself and its past, and its quest for an ill-defined identity. Neglect, iconoclasm, and 'modernization' have destroyed the fabric of a 'unified', 'integral' history. Unfortunately recent attempts at city planning and preservation have yet to produce much in the way of a national style, vision or sense of purpose to replace it.

Bo Yang (1920–   )

Bo Yang, a writer based in Taiwan, is author of *The Ugly Chinaman* (1985), perhaps the most negative critique of Chinese civilization produced by one of its representatives since the works of LU XUN. Its message is simple: Chinese civilization, of which virtually all Chinese people are so proud, is riddled with

shortcomings and properly a source of shame. It is a 'soy paste vat': a stagnant pond, he wrote, which drowns every trace of decency, honesty, initiative and love of freedom. In the series of lectures and essays that make up the book Bo attributes China's problems to the stifling effect of CONFUCIANISM and the corrosive influence of socialism. Both have 'infected people with a virus . . . This huge country, with one quarter of the world's population, is a pit of quicksand filled with poverty, ignorance, strife and bloodshed, a pit from which it cannot extricate itself,' he wrote.

Born in the Mainland, Bo fled to Taiwan in the late 1940s to escape Communism. He became highly prolific, producing fiction, poetry and history as well as criticism, but fell foul of the island's authoritarian government. In 1968 he was jailed as a Communist spy. He remained in prison until 1977.

Bo's iconoclasm, his merciless dissection of the sloppiness, selfishness, envy, infighting and boastfulness that sometimes characterizes Chinese personal behaviour, hit particularly hard. *The Ugly Chinaman* went down badly among hardline Marxists in Beijing who succeeded in banning the book a year after it was published but not before it had won quiet acclaim among students and intellectuals.

A Mainland work in similar, critical vein to Bo's appeared in 1988, firstly in the form of a television series, *River Elegy*. Written by Su Xiaokang (1949–) and other collaborators, it, too, condemned traditional Chinese civilization and praised the dynamic, developing, open cultures of the West. It, too, was banned by a government keen to stress the glory of China's past as a means of fostering nationalism and boosting Communist Party rule.

The Ugly Chinaman can induce a sense of hopelessness about China's future that accounts for its hostile reception in Beijing. Bo called upon foreigners to help China change but warned that only the Chinese can reform themselves. He wrote that it would 'take the re-establishment of a market economy, the institution of a democratic system of government, and a long period of political and economic stability before the Chinese people can begin to live normal, healthy lives'.

Boxer Rebellion

The Boxer Rebellion of 1899–1900 was a spectacular, violent, and above all tragic manifestation of much that was wrong with China at the beginning of the twentieth century. Its origins lay in oppression and rural superstition. Its course involved killing and destruction on a massive scale. And its consequences included foreign occupation, harsh reprisals, and the utter humiliation of the QING DYNASTY. The Boxer Rebellion marked the nadir of Manchu fortunes, from which the dynasty rallied only briefly before it was swept away by the REPUBLICAN REVOLUTION of 1911.

Small bands of men and women known in English as 'Boxers' (in Chinese they were called *yihetuan*: 'united in righteousness and harmony') made their appearance first in SHANDONG in the late 1890s. They acquired the name because of the elaborate martial arts rituals that allegedly made their members immune to bullets and capable of other supernatural acts. In many ways, the Boxers were another of the many SECRET SOCIETIES that have flourished in rural China since ancient times.

What lifted them out of obscurity was the general malaise of Chinese society at the close of the nineteenth century, brought on by weak government and the growing foreign presence. The 'scramble for concessions' of 1897–8, in which the powers competed to partition China, created panic in the Court and fear among officials elsewhere. On the ground, new inroads by MISSIONARIES and foreign businesses threatened the traditional social order and disrupted established patterns of trade. Drought across north China and a general breakdown of authority contributed to a popular feeling that disaster would befall unless the people rose up against their oppressors. The Boxers of Shandong, where there was a growing, generally unwelcome, German presence in the late 1890s, did exactly that, slaughtering hundreds of Christians and other Chinese believed to have connections with foreigners in a whirlwind of violence that startled the authorities and enraged the foreign community.

What transformed a peasant rebellion of a familiar if highly focused kind into something quite different was a decision by powerful figures at Court, including the EMPRESS DOWAGER, to recruit the Boxers to the cause of the dynasty. By the summer of 1900, thousands of Boxer rebels had arrived in BEIJING and TIANJIN, where they attacked and killed hundreds of Chinese they branded 'foreign slaves'. They then cut the railway and telegraph lines between the two cities, creating panic among the capital's foreign community, which was now isolated in the Legation Quarter and subject to regular attack.

On 21 June, the Court declared war on *all* the powers in the hope of ridding China of her foreign tormentors once and for all. Decades of reform – sometimes sponsored by the Court, sometimes crushed by it – had failed to make China strong in the face of aggression. Perhaps violent rebellion would rid her of her enemies?

It did not. The Siege of the Legations created outrage in the West of the kind generated by the military suppression of the TIANANMEN SQUARE DEMOCRACY MOVEMENT nearly 90 years later. It proved equally productive of myths and misunderstandings. For the roughly 1,000 foreigners present, it was a terrifying experience to be besieged in a quarter of a city where many of them had grown used to being treated with deference and respect. Boxer savagery outside Beijing, notably in SHANXI, included the murder of missionaries as well as their children. With the Court behind them, there was no telling what the rebels might do were they to breach the Legation walls. Relief, in the form of foreign armies stationed off Tianjin, seemed far away. The 2,300 Chinese Christians who sought refuge in the diplomatic quarter had even more to fear: the Boxers were bound to turn on 'traitors' first.

Yet the threat to the Legations was more apparent than real. The Court was divided over support for the rebels, generals were reluctant to mount a full-scale offensive against the diplomatic quarter, and reformist officials in the south refused to join the war. Practically the whole of southeast China was free of the Boxer menace, and outside Beijing's control. To make matters worse for the Manchus, in August 1900 an eight-power expeditionary army, made up chiefly of troops from Japan, Russia, Britain, the United States and France, battled its way into the capital and raised the siege. It was time to exact revenge.

Vengeance was two-fold. The expeditionary forces pillaged central Beijing with the kind of enthusiasm the Boxers had shown for the destruction of *their* enemies. Not even the Hanlin Academy, the repository of Qing dynasty scholarship, just south of the British Legation, was spared. Thousands of priceless books and documents were stolen or destroyed.

The occupation of Beijing by such powerful and savage armies was an enormous blow to Chinese self-confidence. China was exposed as 'backward' and 'barbaric', and foreigners as 'modern' and above all invincible. The gulf between China and the industrialized world was shown to be painfully large.

The episode was a particular disaster for the government, which having cast its lot with the rebels now faced nemesis at the hands of both foreign and domestic foes. The court fled to the safety of Xian, capital of SHAANXI, entrusting the unenviable task of negotiating a peace settlement with the invaders to Li Hongzhang (1823–1901).

This took the form of the Boxer Protocol, the most vengeful treaty in the history of Sino-Western diplomacy. Its main stipulations were the punishment – by execution or orders to commit suicide – of officials deemed responsible for encouraging the Boxers; the stationing of foreign troops along the road from Beijing to Tianjin; suspension of the examination system in Shandong as a means of punishing literati in the province; and a ban on arms imports. The sting in the Protocol's tail was a huge indemnity imposed on the Court both as a punishment and to compensate for foreign losses sustained during the rebellion.

The indemnity was a burden, secured against customs and other domestic revenues, that the Qing government could not afford to bear. It contributed to the growing indebtedness and declining revenues that weakened the central government and played a large part in its fall in 1911. Moreover, the debt was inherited by the new Republican government, adding to its financial woes at a time when civil wars and an inefficient bureaucracy deprived it of much needed cash. In 1908, the US agreed to return that part of the Boxer indemnity in excess of certified claims for actual losses. The surplus was used for educating Chinese in the United States. China cancelled indemnity payments to Germany and Austria-Hungary in 1917 when it declared war on the two powers. In 1924, the US agreed to return the remaining portion of the Boxer indemnity, then amounting to US$12.5 million, for the development of education and cultural enterprises in China.

At the political level, the Boxer catastrophe marks a division between 'old' China and the 'new'. It was the last truly large-scale traditional peasant rebellion to threaten the entire political order – a threat made more real by patronage from a Court desperate to resist foreign aggression and preserve its decrepit rule. Its failure was thus a failure of tradition.

Yet the Qing dynasty survived and went on to carry out a series of reforms that were a world away from the Boxer agenda. The powers also played a part in the Manchu's post-Boxer revival. Each of the countries that made up the expeditionary army had its own agenda in China, despite an ability to make common cause in defending the Legations. Fear of the harm open rivalry might inflict on their respective positions encouraged them to accept the principles of the 'Open Door Notes' set out by the United States in 1900 (see UNITED STATES). These spoke of the need to preserve China's territorial and administrative integrity. Yet the disaffection of the southern provinces during the rebellion had shown how fragile this integrity was. And events during the next few years demonstrated that neither the central government nor the foreign powers were able to preserve it.

Britain

Britain's involvement in the evolution of modern China has been profound but largely pragmatic; intimate but far from idealistic. Britain pioneered China's forced opening to the West in the mid-nineteenth century, remained the dominant power there until at least the First World War and a major one until the defeat of Japan in 1945. Its continued occupation of HONG KONG made for greater contact (though little closeness) with the Communist government after 1949 than other Western countries enjoyed. Indirectly, the colony was also responsible for the destruction of Britain's mission in Beijing during the CULTURAL REVOLUTION. A 'parting shot' in terms of British influence over China came towards the end of the century: the Sino-British Joint Declaration of 1984, under which Hong Kong returned to Chinese rule in 1997, requires Beijing to practise a 'hands off' policy in its own territory.

treaties and territories

The most obvious expression of Britain's presence in China at the start of the twentieth century was its occupation of Chinese territory. The colony of Hong Kong was expanded in 1898 with the acquisition of a 99-year lease on the New Territories, north of the Kowloon Peninsula. A second leased territory, WEIHAIWEI, was acquired the same year. The Younghusband Expedition of 1903–4 extended British influence into TIBET. Britain's interests were predominant in foreign SHANGHAI, whose 'International' Settlement was controlled by Britons, as well as in many other TREATY PORTS. For decades the Royal Navy was the dominant foreign force along China's coast and its inland waterways. Britain had a cumulative total of more than 40 consulates in China, some of them deep in the interior.

Britons were the most numerous and influential group within the three Chinese government agencies that employed foreign nationals: the Maritime Customs Service, the Post Office and, from 1913, the Salt Administration. Most MISSIONARIES came from the British empire until the 1920s, when Americans formed the largest single group within the Protestant community.

In the first three decades of the century British firms dominated sectors of China's modern economy. Jardine Matheson and Butterfield & Swire – two of the best-known *hongs*, or trading houses – handled much of China's foreign trade along with the shipping lines that kept it afloat. They also contributed to foreign domination of China's domestic shipping. Hong Kong and Shanghai Bank and the Chartered Bank helped ensure foreign control over China's foreign exchange market and trade finance. Companies linked to British banks held rights for mining and to build railways which they subsequently controlled. Imperial Chemical Industries, British American Tobacco and the Asiatic Petroleum Company (a subsidiary of the Anglo-Dutch consortium, Royal Dutch Shell) were among the large British companies involved in manufacturing or distribution in China.

imperialism and nationalism

A symbol of Britain's pre-eminent position in China was the leading role of its legation in Beijing during the BOXER REBELLION. It was both a principal target and a source of resistance against the rebels who laid siege to the foreign quarter of the city in 1900. British troops, many of them Indians, were among the eight-power army that rescued the besieged and went on to ransack the capital.

British imperialism became the target of a new generation of Chinese nationalists in the mid-1920s: the revolutionaries of the reorganized KUOMINTANG. Hatred of foreign privilege, in particular of EXTRATERRITORIALITY, was behind their campaign – waged in league with the COMMUNIST PARTY and under the guidance of the SOVIET UNION – to unify China and shed its semi-colonial status. British crimes were compounded in Chinese eyes by the May Thirtieth Incident of 1925 in Shanghai, when police opened fire on unarmed protestors. The National Revolutionary Government, based in Guangzhou, retaliated with a strike-boycott against Hong Kong. A few days later, British and French troops killed more than 50 people among a crowd of demonstrators opposite Shamian Island, the site of Guangzhou's international concession. The strike-boycott lasted a year and almost brought Hong Kong to its knees. It also crippled British interests in south China. Many merchants and missionaries fled to Shanghai. Some were maltreated. Much foreign property was destroyed.

This outpouring of revolutionary nationalism was extended throughout south China by the NORTHERN EXPEDITION. Britain was hurt most because its interests were the greatest and most prominent. The rise to power of CHIANG KAI-SHEK curbed the radicalism, and anti-foreign activism subsided in 1927 following his purge of the Communists and other Left-wingers in the Nationalist Party. But by then anti-imperialist protestors had attained a symbolic victory: they forced Britain to restore the international concessions in Hankou (modern Wuhan, capital of HUBEI) and Jiujiang, further down the Yangtze. London abandoned these trinkets of the nineteenth-century treaties in the interests of defending the much bigger prize of Shanghai, which was rapidly reinforced by British troops.

The new Nationalist government in Nanjing made abolition of the UNEQUAL TREATIES a principal aim of its diplomacy with the West. It was only partly successful. TARIFF AUTONOMY was secured in 1928, but the treaty system itself endured until 1943, when Britain and the United States surrendered their extraterritorial rights to their wartime ally. Nevertheless, the strains of a 'last post' for Britain were heard in China before then: in 1929 Britain voluntarily abandoned its concessions in Amoy (Xiamen, in FUJIAN) and Zhenjiang (in JIANGSU) and, a year later, restored Weihaiwei, having no further need for a naval base that had not fulfilled the role expected of it.

Despite the scale and intensity of the British imperial experience in China its temper was practical, perhaps even prosaic. Sentiment and sympathy, morality and mission are important themes in relations between the UNITED STATES and China. In the history of China's encounter with Britain they are less

evident. While successive generations of Britons wanted to 'change' China by dragging it into the modern world, many had low expectations of the country and little of the instinctive sympathy and close identity with its people Americans seemed to find so natural. There were exceptions – important ones in the case of some people at certain times. But, as exemplified in the treaty port life most Britons enjoyed in China between 1842 and 1943, the two nations lived side by side yet apart.

Not that the British presence was simply swallowed up and exerted no influence. It patently did. But the Sino-British encounter was predicated on British power and Chinese weakness – and this was not a recipe for goodwill on the part of a proud yet humiliated nation.

relations with the new regime, 1949–72

Questions as to the kind of relations Britain and other Western powers could expect with the Nationalist government after the abolition of the treaties soon became academic. The Communist victory in the CIVIL WAR presented a very different prospect: that of dealing with a revolutionary Marxist government which added an obsession with class to the traditional hatred of foreign privilege. Britain acquired an early taste of the obstinacy and self-righteousness that soon came to be identified as Chinese Communist negotiating style during the AMETHYST INCIDENT of 1949. It marked the end of the days when the Royal Navy could sail at will along China's inland waterways. British power in the Chinese interior was a thing of the past.

Britain's occupation of Chinese territory, however, was not. Although many officials feared Communist troops would cross into Hong Kong when they 'liberated' south China at the close of 1949, no such incursions took place. The new government in Beijing, already at odds with the United States over its support for Chiang Kai-shek, then newly located in Taiwan, had enough on its plate. There was no reason to antagonize Britain by forcing it out of Hong Kong. On the contrary, once the KOREAN WAR started and the Americans launched a trade embargo against the People's Republic, it was useful to have a Western colony on the doorstep. Hong Kong was a source of information and intelligence. Thanks to its 'patriotic' citizens, it was also a conduit for vital supplies.

To protect its position in Hong Kong, and

try to salvage several hundred million pounds' worth of investment in China, Britain recognized the People's Republic in January 1950, the first major Western country to do so. Relations were anything but normal. Britain and China were adversaries in the Korean War. British businesses in Shanghai were squeezed dry and, with few exceptions, forced to close. There were a few Sino-British trade deals in the 1950s, but Britain's closeness to the United States and Mao Zedong's obsession with revolution, made dialogue with Beijing all but impossible. Britain's few diplomats at the Office of the Charge d'Affaires in Beijing (from 1954) and the shell of the great consulate general building in Shanghai twiddled their thumbs.

That changed in the mid-1960s: Britain became one of the chief victims of the breakdown of diplomatic immunity that was part of the general lawlessness of the Cultural Revolution. Its roots lay in Chairman Mao's determination to radicalize a revolution he believed was turning 'revisionist'. The source of the trouble for British diplomats in China was Hong Kong, where in 1967 the authorities arrested Leftists, Communists and Mainland journalists as part of a crackdown against labour unrest, demonstrations and, soon, a bombing campaign.

The reaction in China, where Red Guards had taken over the foreign ministry as well as most other government departments, was violent and chaotic. Crowds broke into the British office in Shanghai and assaulted the few British staff. Anthony Grey, Reuters correspondent in Beijing, disappeared into house arrest. In August 1967 protestors burnt down the British Mission in Beijing and beat up many of its personnel. A few days later, staff of the Chinese Mission in London poured out of their building to attack British police guarding them. It was an attempt, characteristic in its crudity, to claim that worse outrages had been committed against Chinese diplomats in Britain than against their British counterparts in China. British subjects in China, both diplomats and ordinary citizens, became hostages. Their misery dragged on until the Cultural Revolution lost some of its fervour and a semblance of normality – defined as the absence of threats and restrictions on individual movements – returned to Britain's relations with China.

Normalization of a more genuine kind came in 1972, the year of China's opening to the West, symbolized by the visit to Beijing of President Richard Nixon. Britain was one of several Western countries to expand relations with the People's Republic as a result. Ambassadors were exchanged and Britain closed its Consulate at Tamshui in Taiwan, long an obstacle, though a minor one, to better relations with Beijing. By then China was a member of the UNITED NATIONS and a strategic counterweight to the Soviet Union. Soon, it would abandon the pursuit of revolution for economic modernization, providing new opportunities for Sino-British diplomacy.

handing over Hong Kong

From the early 1980s, China's relations with Britain centred on the issue of Hong Kong. The catalyst here was the approaching expiry of the lease on the New Territories. China's longstanding desire to recover sovereignty over its lost territories was reinforced by Hong Kong's growing economic importance for the country's modernization drive. Somehow, sovereignty had to be reasserted *and* the territory's success maintained. For Beijing the stakes were high: national pride, economic benefit and the need to lure Taiwan back to the fold by handling Hong Kong properly were all at issue. However, the first of these, that of recovering Hong Kong and burying a last legacy of the UNEQUAL TREATIES was foremost.

For Britain, once it had abandoned attempts to exchange sovereignty for continued British administration of Hong Kong, the aim was to ensure that Chinese promises to leave the territory's way of life intact after 1997 were codified as unambiguously as possible in a detailed agreement. The agreement, which took the form of the Sino-British Joint Declaration on the Question of Hong Kong, was reached in 1984.

At the time and since, Beijing has been quick to attribute to Chinese genius the 'one country, two systems' formula whereby Hong Kong returned to China as a highly autonomous Special Administrative Region with its capitalist way of life intact and guaranteed for 50 years. Certainly the concept, designed originally for Taiwan and then applied to Hong Kong, was China's. Just as certainly it was an imaginative stroke of pragmatism on the part of political leaders who had only just emerged from a period in which politics and 'principles' came before everything. Yet the 'system' to be preserved in Hong Kong was British rather than Chinese. The territory's free press, rule of law, transparent government, generally free-market economy and, in the later 1990s, lively democratic politics were things China's leaders opposed vehemently at home long after the signing of the Joint Declaration and, in some cases, well after Hong Kong's restoration. They were obliged to tolerate them in Hong Kong as the price of maintaining the territory's economic success, and securing the acquiescence of its people to Chinese rule.

The fact that the Joint Declaration was registered at the United Nations made it an international agreement – one in which, perhaps by default, perhaps not, Britain had obliged China to behave in a certain way in its own territory, albeit a tiny part of it. There was an element of irony here for, in a different way, in different circumstances and on a different scale, this was what Britain had in mind 150 years earlier when it 'opened' China by force, and occupied Hong Kong in the first place.

China's relations with Britain were a prisoner of the Hong Kong issue until the territory's rendition on 1 July 1997. The moderate amity of the early years of the transition evaporated with the suppression in 1989 of the TIANANMEN SQUARE DEMOCRACY MOVEMENT. Attempts to repair the damage were largely undone by the row over the political reforms of CHRIS PATTEN, Hong Kong's last governor. Britain occasionally sought to compartmentalize the Hong Kong issue in its dealings with Beijing. It vigorously pursued trade relations with China in the mid-1990s, becom-

ing the largest European investor in the People's Republic – at the cost of frequent complaints from Hong Kong's democratic politicians that profits were getting the better of principles. Beijing confirmed such assumptions with hints that British companies were bound to suffer in the world's largest market from the 'mistaken' policies of the governor of Hong Kong.

Yet the bad odour between China and Britain created by the row over Hong Kong disappeared with the transfer of sovereignty. Partly this was because Beijing at first adhered more closely than many had dared expect to its promise not to interfere in the territory. Partly it was simply because, for both sides, a burden of history had been laid aside. In Hong Kong, Britain shed its last major colony. Its future relations with Beijing would therefore be 'uncluttered'. They would be those between a major, though not *the* major, European power and a rapidly modernizing power, both in the region and beyond. This was not a recipe for smooth sailing: the protests and attacks on British diplomatic property in China following NATO's accidental destruction of the Chinese embassy in Belgrade in 1999 showed that. But while some of these actions recalled earlier dramas, their cause was quite different from the great Sino-British conflicts that punctuated the earlier years of the twentieth century.

Burma

Burma was the unlikely theatre for China's first significant overseas military operation of the modern era: participation in the Allied expedition of 1944–5 against Japan. More than half a century later Beijing maintains close relations with Rangoon, selling arms to the Burmese military, and sharing its concern over the growing power of INDIA (see ARMS SALES). China and Burma are united in opposing international criticism of their HUMAN RIGHTS record.

Burma was a vassal of China before its annexation by Britain in 1886. Japan's swift occupation of the British colony in 1942 isolated China from the outside world by severing the Burma Road, the 350-mile-long supply road hacked through rough terrain in 1938 by 200,000 Chinese labourers. In an attempt to keep the road open, Chinese forces had moved as far south in Burma as Toungoo

to help the British resistance. They were routed but managed to escape to the west and re-form in India.

By the end of 1942, more than 30,000 Chinese soldiers were under training in the Indian town of Ramgarh. Led by generals Sun Liren (1900–1990) and Liao Yaoxiang (1903–68), they came under the operational command of the United States, an unprecedented development for a purely Chinese force, and one which ensured that CHIANG KAI-SHEK trusted neither of the two men or their armies again.

General JOSEPH STILWELL was in overall command of the Chinese forces in India. Stilwell believed that when properly trained, equipped and led, Chinese Nationalist armies could match the best in the world. He went some way towards proving the point in the campaign to recover Burma, in which both 'X-force' – the Chinese forces based in India –

and 'Y-force' – Chinese forces in southwest China – played important roles.

Victory in Burma reopened the overland supply route to China. But Chinese military involvement was regarded as a mixed blessing by Chiang, for whom, even in wartime, armies were best subjected to personal control rather than modern forms of 'impartial' command that might weaken their loyalty when it came to settling domestic disputes with the Communists and other rivals.

Thousands of Nationalist troops returned to Burma in 1949–50 – this time in chaos and in order to avoid capture by the People's Liberation Army. For the next few years, from bases inside Burma, the exiles harassed Communist forces across the border in YUNNAN, home of many of China's ETHNIC MINORITIES.

The new Communist government in Beijing lent moral support to the Burmese Communist Party which opposed the government in post-independence Rangoon. In Burma as elsewhere in Southeast Asia, China's backing for insurgency provoked a crisis in its relations with governments in the region. They did not improve until the late 1970s when China abandoned revolution for reform at home.

Since the late 1980s Beijing has looked upon Rangoon as one of its most reliable allies, though it has often expressed concern over its failure to suppress the local drug trade, much of which is routed east through China to international markets. This became a serious problem in the early 1990s with the formal opening of several Chinese border towns to trade and investment.

On occasion the similarity between political values in Rangoon and Beijing, both of whose governments oppose liberalism and internationalism, has pointed to the existence of an informal, anti-Western alliance. Yet military cooperation is at the heart of the relationship. Rangoon not only purchases arms from Beijing, it has granted China access to 'listening stations' on islands in the Indian Ocean that enable it to keep watch on the Indian navy. These developments have worried members of the ASSOCIATION OF SOUTHEAST ASIAN NATIONS (ASEAN) – as well as India. Partly with a view to weakening the Beijing–Rangoon axis, ASEAN in 1997 accepted Burma as a member.

Cairo Conference (22–6 November 1943)

Egypt was the unlikely venue for what amounted to the first formal recognition during the twentieth century that China was a 'great power' and for the first meeting between a Chinese national leader and his American and British counterparts. These developments occurred towards the end of the Second World War, and shortly after the UNITED STATES and BRITAIN gave up their extraterritorial privileges (see EXTRATERRITORIALITY), freeing China of the burden of the UNEQUAL TREATIES in every important respect save that of Britain's occupation of HONG KONG.

The Cairo Declaration of 1 December 1943 specified that the Allies would pursue the war against JAPAN until Tokyo surrendered unconditionally, and that when that happened, Manchuria (northeast China), TAIWAN and the Pescadores Islands would be returned to China. The conference thus marked a turning point in China's international standing – one that the CHINESE COMMUNIST PARTY has since preferred to play down for the simple reason that it was not in power at the time.

Yet the recognition of China as the 'fourth power' (alongside the United States, Britain and the SOVIET UNION), and the summit between CHIANG KAI-SHEK, President Franklin Roosevelt and Prime Minister Winston Churchill, stemmed from the exigences of the war against Japan rather than China's geopolitical weighting (see SINO-JAPANESE WAR). Both events were stronger on symbolism than substance, and spoke of the Allies', mainly America's, unrealistic view of Nationalist China as a key military and political player, both during the war and after. China *did* become a 'big player' shortly after the war, but not in the form the Allies expected at Cairo.

The military imperative for convening the conference was to find the best way of reconquering BURMA, aiding China and defeating Japan. Little progress was made in any of these areas. One reason for this was the difficulty the principals found in dealing with Chiang. Early fascination with the Chinese leader gave way to despair at what were deemed his stubborn, unrealistic demands for more aid and a massive amphibious assault on Rangoon. Those of his generals present had little to offer when asked about China's contribution to the reconquest of Burma and overall defeat of Japan. 'Big power' or not, the United States and Britain found China a frustrating partner when it came to mounting a coordinated effort at a common goal.

The Cairo conference showed that China could not play a major role in the defeat of Japan. The Allies realized this would be better achieved by the Soviet Union's entry into the Far Eastern War. China's new international status thus proved fleeting: it remained a military sideshow for the remainder of the war.

Cambodia

A desire to contain the influence of the United States, curb the ambitions of Vietnam and compete with TAIWAN have made for greater Chinese interest in Cambodia than in most other countries in the region. The longstanding relationship between China's leaders and King Norodom Sihanouk, the Cambodian king; Beijing's past support for the murderous Khmer Rouge; and its unprecedented involvement in the country through the auspices of the UNITED NATIONS all testify to the People's Republic of China's closeness to the Southeast Asian kingdom.

Sihanouk first met Mao Zedong in Beijing in 1956, the beginning of a series of royal visits and several protracted stays in the Chinese capital during the following 40 years. The king pleased his hosts by keeping newly independent Cambodia out of the South East Asian Treaty Organization (SEATO), which was formed to contain Communism in Southeast Asia. Beijing responded by granting Cambodia US$22 million in aid, the first time the Communist government offered financial assistance to a non-Communist country. Yet the largesse was partly designed to wean Cambodia's ethnic Chinese away from Taiwan; and Phnom Penh, angered by what it took to be interference in its internal affairs, fought back by expelling Chinese 'Leftists' from the country (see OVERSEAS CHINESE). The government did so again in the CULTURAL REVOLUTION when the Chinese embassy in Phnom Penh encouraged Cambodian Chinese to emulate the Red Guards in Beijing.

During the Vietnam War, China accepted that the Vietcong must pass through Cambodia in order to carry the fight from North Vietnam to the US-backed government of South Vietnam. This was an imperative of geography. But Beijing was not ready to let a growth of Vietnamese influence bring Cambodia into Moscow's orbit. It was keen to check Soviet as well as American influence in Southeast Asia. Thus China aided the Khmer Rouge, which grew strong, both on the back of military victories in the field, and from its association with Sihanouk, temporarily exiled in Beijing after the US-backed Cambodia coup of 1970. Cambodian king and Cambodian Communists seized power in Phnom Penh in April 1975.

The murderous experiment in utopianism that followed owed much to Chinese inspiration and support. Pol Pot, the Khmer Rouge leader, was a devotee of Mao's revolutionary methods and sought to replicate the GREAT LEAP FORWARD and the Cultural Revolution simultaneously on Cambodian soil. More important for a China whose leaders were by then growing weary of revolution themselves, he shared their dislike of Vietnam's ambition to dominate Indochina. Pol Pot's presence at the rear of a newly united Vietnam was a strategic gift.

The Vietnamese invasion of 1978 ended Cambodia's utopian nightmare, but upset the regional balance of power. China, King Sihanouk, several ASEAN countries and the West saw the invasion as a dramatic extension of Soviet influence. For the next 10 years they kept the Khmer Rouge alive as part of the opposition to the Vietnamese government in Phnom Penh – in China's case by supplying it with weapons.

Vietnam's withdrawal at the end of 1989 left Cambodia divided and ready for full-scale civil war. A United Nations-administered Peace Plan avoided this fate and facilitated the generally peaceful elections of 1993. China played an important part in the peace process: it stopped arming the Khmer Rouge and sent military observers and military engineers to Cambodia to support the United Nations Transitional Authority.

This first involvement of substantial numbers (a total of 800 personnel was sent in two batches) of Chinese troops in an overseas UN operation showed the importance Beijing attached to stability in Cambodia. It did not make China keen to bring Pol Pot and other Khmer Rouge leaders before an international tribunal to account for their crimes. Beijing resisted UN-led attempts to achieve this up to and beyond Pol's death in April 1998.

However, in the same year, a desire to keep Cambodia diplomatically neutral, politically stable and free of unwelcome influence from Hanoi prompted another unprecedented Chinese move. In response to a Cambodian request, Beijing dispatched observers to monitor the elections of July 1998. The aim, in the words of a Chinese spokesman, was to ensure the elections were 'free, just and transparent' – characteristics not usually associated with elections in China itself (see DEMOCRACY; NATIONAL PEOPLE'S CONGRESS).

Chen Duxiu (1879–1942)

The first leader of the CHINESE COMMUNIST PARTY was eventually expelled as a 'Right Opportunist' and branded a 'Trotskyite renegade'. But Chen, a life-long rebel against shifting orthodoxy, played a major role in the spread of MARXISM during the MAY FOURTH MOVEMENT of 1919 and after.

He came to prominence as editor of *New Youth*, founded in 1915 and soon a vehicle for the energy and iconoclasm of the young intellectuals of the May Fourth generation. As Dean of Letters at Beijing University he encouraged the use of BAI HUA – plain speech – in literary works, and championed Western liberalism. The First World War sank his faith in Western values which, following the Bolshevik Revolution, were replaced by those of Marx, Lenin and Trotsky. Like LI DAZHAO, a fellow pioneer of Marxism, Chen was inspired by the way the Russian revolutionaries appeared to have propelled their huge, backward, agrarian country into the vanguard of

history. The lesson for China seemed clear. Chen was made secretary (*in absentia*) of the first central committee of the Chinese Communist Party, which met in SHANGHAI in 1921. A few years later he was required by the Communist International in Moscow to cooperate with the KUOMINTANG under SUN YAT-SEN. He was unhappy with the policy and spoke out against it. When CHIANG KAI-SHEK succeeded Sun and purged the Kuomintang of its Communist and Left-wing allies in 1927, Chen's comrades blamed him for the disaster. He was expelled from the Party and formed a Trotskyite splinter group.

The Kuomintang government arrested Chen in 1932 and sentenced him to 15 years in prison on charges of subversion. He was released as a result of an amnesty connected with the outbreak of the SINO-JAPANESE WAR, and died in obscurity, his faith in Western-style democracy apparently restored.

Chen Shui-bian (1951–   )

The election as president of TAIWAN in March 2000 of Chen Shui-bian, a leading figure in the pro-independence DEMOCRATIC PROGRESSIVE PARTY, was a defining moment in the island's history as well as that of Chinese politics generally. It ended 55 years of rule by the KUOMINTANG, whose defeat left a once unassailable party divided and facing demise as a major political force. It was a rebuff for Beijing, whose leaders had repeatedly warned the people of Taiwan that a vote for Chen would risk war because of his proclivity for independence. And it challenged the political, military and diplomatic status quo concerning Taiwan under which its people were deemed by almost everybody but themselves to have no political future outside the People's Republic of China. Amid such weighty, almost alarming implications it was easy to overlook something equally profound: Chen's victory marked the first occasion in which Chinese people changed their government by popular consent, through the ballot box (see DEMOCRACY).

modest victory

These are grand conclusions to draw from the narrow election victory of a 49-year-old lawyer

from a numerically insignificant opposition party who owed his success to a fatal split in the Kuomintang rather than the appeal of the DPP. Chen won just over 39 per cent of the vote compared with 36 per cent for James Soong Chu-yu (1942–), the former KMT heavyweight who ran as an independent, and the much less impressive 23 per cent secured by Lien Chan (1936–), the official ruling-party candidate.

His victory also owed much to his 'moderation'. Stung by its defeat in the 1996 presidential elections, the DPP dropped a promise to declare Taiwan an independent republic the moment it was elected. It even distanced itself from the principle that a plebiscite on the matter would be held shortly after it came to power. Instead, the party took a line similar to that of the Kuomintang under president LEE TENG-HUI: the 'Republic of China on Taiwan' was already a sovereign state, even though few countries recognized it as such and Beijing promised to invade the moment too many did. The fact that Chen's administration was a minority one; that the DPP lacked the talent and experience to staff more than a few ministries from its own ranks; and that recklessness on the independence issue promised to sabotage the party's drive to curb corruption and reform government in Taiwan, let alone provoke Beijing and incur the ire of the UNITED STATES, were powerful grounds for restraint.

Following his inauguration as president in May 2000, Chen strove to maintain this prudence. He formed a cabinet drawn from political parties other than the DPP (Chen chose Tang Fei (1932–), the former Kuomintang defence minister, as his first premier) as well as those from none; pledged a new era of reconciliation with the Mainland; and emphasized that there was no need to change Taiwan's official name, flag or constitution. Difficulties lay ahead in terms of taming a bureaucracy and a military and security apparatus which had been at least as loyal to the KMT as to the state, but to some extent it was to be business as usual.

three obstacles to power

To a large extent, however, it patently was not. There were implications of the DPP's triumph that simply could not be finessed. One of them was the fact that a man from humble origins had risen to be the youngest president of Taiwan as well as the first from an opposition party. This involved victory over three main forces, each of them formidable, and each of them capable of confounding a less determined, resourceful politician than Chen Shui-bian.

The first was the Kuomintang's dominance of Taiwanese politics and, until the 1980s, of many other areas of life. The KMT old guard, Mainlanders virtually to a man, shared with their Communist counterparts across the Straits a belief that there was only one China, of which Taiwan was an inseparable part. They also shared with Beijing the view that the most appropriate form of politics was one-party rule. They differed only over which party should rule. In the context of 'one China, one party' it was dangerous for Taiwanese to speak out. Theirs was the voice of sedition as well as dissent. It had to be suppressed.

It was in a spectacular fashion during the 'Formosa Incident' of 1979, when a rally in Kaohsiung by pro-independence activists linked to the magazine of the same name turned into a riot. Close to 50 of those associated with the embryonic opposition, then known as the *dangwai* – 'outside the (KMT) party' – were jailed. One of them was Annette Lu Hsiu-lian (1944–), elected vice-president in 2000. Among those defending the accused

was Chen Shui-bian, who graduated in law from the National Taiwan University in 1974.

During the 1980s Chen's fortunes fluctuated with the struggle of Taiwanese to make their voice heard in a one-party system maintained until 1987 by martial law and fortified by bans on political parties, controls on the press and harsh laws against sedition. There were some modest successes: Chen served on Taipei City Council from 1981 to 1985, and in 1987 joined the newly formed Democratic Progressive Party where he soon became a leading figure. There was also one particular tragedy: in 1985 Chen's wife, Wu Shu-jen, was run over by a van in what was believed to be a politically motivated attempt on Chen's life. She has been confined to a wheelchair ever since.

Chen was elected to the Legislative Yuan (see TAIWAN/GOVERNANCE) in 1989 and retained his seat until 1994. In that year he went on to confirm his reputation as the DPP's most impressive, popular politician, winning the first direct elections (in recent times) for the mayor of Taipei. The DPP acquired a formidable platform, and one of its most accomplished leaders a powerful voice.

As mayor, Chen made his mark by cracking down on Taipei's red-light district, cutting red tape in city hall and easing the traffic congestion that had made Taiwan's capital famous the world over, and life miserable for most of those who lived or worked in the city. A tough line on corruption also endeared him to voters. However, an apparent authoritarian streak made him less popular and, in 1998, the Kuomintang mounted a huge campaign to secure his replacement by the equally charismatic and energetic Ma Ying-jeou (1950–). Chen sought consolation by preparing himself and his party for the presidential elections in 2000.

This involved taking on a second foe, a formidable one determined to thwart the DPP's designs on Taiwan: the Communist leadership in Beijing. During the 1990s China's leaders watched the democratization of Taiwanese politics with dismay. They believed, correctly, that it made the prospects for reunification in accordance with the 'one country, two systems' principle adopted in HONG KONG and MACAU more remote. Much of this they blamed on Lee Teng-hui, whom they abused unreservedly at every turn. But their most violent threats and warnings of dire consequences were directed at the DPP which, even after its defeat in the 1996 presidential elections, retained a commitment to turn Taiwan into an independent republic when it gained power. This, China stated at regular intervals throughout the late 1990s, would mean war.

After his failure to be re-elected mayor of Taipei, Chen and his colleagues brooded on these matters. Beijing's opposition to Taiwanese independence was implacable. So, for that matter, was America's: Washington made it clear that while the United States had a moral and, thanks to the Taiwan Relations Act of 1979 (see TAIWAN), a legal obligation to help defend Taiwan from attack, there could be no question of Taipei provoking Beijing and hoping to get away with it with outside help.

Neither was that the end of the matter. It was clear that, at most, 30 per cent of the electorate in Taiwan favoured formal independence for the island. The overwhelming majority did not. And while most people were uninterested in reunification with China, at least on Beijing's terms, they were likely to be even cooler towards a party whose triumph at the polls could threaten the status quo in which Taiwan enjoyed independence in everything but name. Public anxiety that a DPP government would upset the delicate balance in the triangular relationship between Taipei, Washington and Beijing was the third great obstacle Chen had to overcome to win the presidency.

in search of the 'centre'

A softening of the DPP's stance on independence helped this cause. Chen campaigned for the presidency in 2000 on the understanding that since Taiwan was already an independent state, there was no need to insist on it in the narrow legal sense that would require a change of name and flag and a new constitution. On the contrary, he would serve happily as the '10th President of the Republic of China'. The new president coupled these affirmations of loyalty to an entity he had spent much of his early career opposing with peace overtures towards the Mainland, including an offer to establish direct trade and transport links long opposed by the Kuomintang. At least at first, this seemed to disarm Beijing, though it did not remove deep-seated anxieties about the consequences of the DPP's victory or weaken the determination of the Communist Party to crush separatism in 'Taiwan Province'.

In the event Chen's electoral triumph had less to do with questions of Taiwan's international identity than with a profound split within the Kuomintang and the simple desire for change. After 55 years in power incumbency offered few automatic advantages to the KMT. Even the party's formidable business empire, size and organization could not overcome public disaffection in the face of the challenge from James Soong and Chen's young, wholesome, Taiwan-first image.

As with leaders elsewhere in the democratic world, Chen Shui-bian was elected president of Taiwan because more people voted for him than for any other single candidate, not because he won a majority of votes. As with many political parties obliged to compete in elections, victory was possible because the Democratic Progressive Party shifted towards the 'centre ground' in an effort to win power and, having done so, pursued 'moderate' policies to stay there. Finally, Chen's victory marked the start in Taiwan of an era of alternate party rule – again in keeping with democracies worthy of the name elsewhere, and again marking a fundamental break with China's past.

Chen Xitong (1930–)

The only member of the CHINESE COMMUNIST PARTY's Politburo to be sacked and jailed for corruption owed his downfall in 1995 to political rivalry with JIANG ZEMIN as well as a fondness for the luxuries available to corrupt officials during the Mainland's economic boom.

Chen rose to national and even international fame twice during a long career in the Beijing bureaucracy. He was mayor (chief government official) of BEIJING during the TIANANMEN SQUARE DEMOCRACY MOVEMENT of 1989 which he opposed vigorously and took the lead in suppressing. Once troops secured the capital, he delivered the official *Report on Checking the Turmoil and Quelling the Counter-Revolutionary Rebellion*, whose condemnation of the largest urban uprising in China's history survived his own political demise.

This came six years later, by which time he was Party boss of the capital, one of the most powerful positions in the country. Chen's fall was presaged by the death in April 1995 of Wang Baosen (1935–95), a vice-mayor of Beijing. Wang allegedly shot himself during a visit to the suburbs to escape investigation on charges of corruption. The case against Wang suggested that the entire leadership of Beijing – host to a building boom since the early 1990s – had grown fat on bribes and commissions. Chen was then forced to resign and his son and allies were detained. It was a sensational development for a man who had seemed politically invulnerable.

It was also an advantageous one for Jiang Zemin, whom Chen believed unqualified to lead the Communist Party, a position Chen had hoped to fill himself. Chen was stripped of membership of the Politburo and Central Committee, kept under house arrest and sub-

jected to investigation. A catalogue of excesses emerged, most of them doubtless accurate, but many of them probably presented in an attempt to assuage public anger over CORRUP-TION. Chen was accused of accepting bribes and building luxurious villas in the suburbs. An ordinary person would have been executed for such crimes. Chen was far from ordinary. He threatened to expose other senior figures said to have lined their pockets. Details of his detention and trial remained obscure, and more than three years passed before he was sentenced, in July 1998, to 16 years in jail for corruption and dereliction of duty.

Chen Yun (1905–95)

A cautious economic planner who enjoyed immense authority in the CHINESE COMMU-NIST PARTY from the 1950s until his death, Chen was the only senior leader to be at odds with MAO ZEDONG over the GREAT LEAP FOR-WARD yet escape criticism at the time and during the subsequent CULTURAL REVOLUTION. He survived to bicker with DENG XIAOPING in the 1980s over the consequences of free-market reforms, which Chen said weakened Party rule and threatened the production of staple foods.

Chen, born in Shanghai and a typesetter by training, had a pedigree in the Communist Party at least as long as that of Deng. He joined in 1926 and played an important, though often unspectacular, part in the Party's victory of 1949. He concentrated on economic work and was in charge of China's first five-year plan (1953–7). Chen favoured rapid growth but insisted that it be pursued in a disciplined, organized manner. He opposed what he saw as Mao's revolutionary, romantic approach. His expertise and studied low profile spared him persecution, though he did lose some of his posts in the Cultural Revolution.

Chen and Deng were at one on the need to revive China's economy after the death of Mao, and both favoured the introduction of free-market reforms. However, Chen was far more cautious than Deng and soon sought to slow the pace of change. At a Party conference in 1985, he made his misgivings public. Agri-

cultural reforms, he complained, were encouraging farmers to switch from grain to cash crops. China would sink into chaos if grain production was neglected. He also insisted that China's reforms remain socialist in nature. For Chen, the proper relationship between the planned and market economies was best expressed in the 'birdcage theory'. The 'cage' was the planned, state-owned sector of the economy within which the 'bird' of private enterprise was allowed some, but only some, freedom.

During the 1980s high politics in Beijing often amounted to a struggle over the pace of reform between Deng and Chen and their respective younger allies. Deng's men were HU YAOBANG and ZHAO ZIYANG; Chen's were LI PENG, Yao Yilin (1917–94) and Song Ping (1917–). The see-saw battle between the two veterans continued through the suppression of the 1989 democracy protests in Tiananmen Square, when Chen and his fellow conservatives gained the upper hand.

Their triumph was shortlived. Deng's landmark tour of southern China in 1992, during which he called for faster reforms, swept caution of the kind associated with Chen Yun away. Ill health and then death removed the 'brake' for good. However, it did not end the appeal for a certain section of the leadership of the steady, planned approach towards development Chen Yun made his own.

Chiang Ching-kuo (1910–88)

CHIANG KAI-SHEK had long groomed his eldest son to take over the reins in TAIWAN, so there was little surprise when Ching-kuo replaced Yen Chia-kan (1905–), the Generalissimo's nominal successor, as president of the Republic of China in 1978. Much more remarkable was the way in which the junior partner in this only son-and-father team to rule part of modern China destroyed the foundations of the one-party state he inherited, and set Taiwan on the path to become the first genuine democracy in Chinese history.

There was little in Chiang's career before he became president to hint of the revolution to come. True, he was more personable and less aloof than his father, and he possessed a common touch that endeared him to many who felt no such attachment to the older man. But Ching-kuo – born of Mao Fumei, his father's first wife – was bred in a political environment that, first on the Mainland and later in Taiwan, showed little tolerance towards dissent.

His political life began at the age of 15, when he was sent to study in the Soviet Union, then a keen backer of the National Revolution led by SUN YAT-SEN. His father's bloody purge of the Communists in 1927 prompted the Soviet authorities to keep Ching-kuo as a hostage: he was not allowed to return to China until after the XIAN INCIDENT of 1936, which he did, with his Russian wife and two children.

It was the economic crisis of 1948 that first brought Ching-kuo to prominence. As Special Economic Commissioner for SHANGHAI, he became the hammer of inflation, overseeing the introduction of a new currency which the residents of China's wealthiest city were forced to buy on pain of severe punishment. Although well intentioned, the plan amounted to sequestration. It exhausted what was left of public support for the KUOMINTANG government, and forced Ching-kuo to apologize and resign.

In Taiwan, he held a variety of political and security posts that helped his father keep a grip on power. That power passed down the family line in 1972, when the elder Chiang's health deteriorated and his son became premier. At first, the only change was that of political style. But Ching-kuo sensed that genuine change would have to come if the government was not to become dangerously out of step with Taiwan's increasingly pros-

perous, educated, diverse and politically demanding population. He sought to reduce the potential for conflict by promoting native Taiwanese in the government, among whom was LEE TENG-HUI, his successor.

Yet a government and ruling party still dominated by the Mainlanders who had fled to the island 30 years ago, and one that still relied on martial law, a ban on opposition parties and tight control over the media to stay in power, needed a new institutional basis, not just new faces. Chiang appeared to recognize this in the 1970s, when opposition activities, mostly designed to secure greater freedom for native Taiwanese, were first tolerated. (See DEMOCRATIC PROGRESSIVE PARTY.) The process was interrupted by the Kaohsiung Incident of December 1979 – an opposition rally that police repression turned into a riot. Hardliners in the Kuomintang used fears about the island's security arising from the United States' decision to recognize Beijing as an excuse to crack down on the infant opposition, most of whose leaders were jailed for sedition.

Yet pressures for change mounted, partly because of government blunders. Prominent among these was the murder in October 1984 by Nationalist agents in California of Henry Liu, author of a biography of Chiang Ching-kuo banned in Taiwan. Exactly who was responsible for an outrage that jeopardized US–Taiwan relations remains unclear. But it appears to have helped persuade Ching-kuo of the need for genuine political reform.

Within two years beginning in 1986, and against formidable opposition, he secured the lifting of martial law, revoked the ban on the formation of political parties, and allowed new newspapers to start publication. These measures weakened the Leninist organizational structure of the Kuomintang that dated back to the days of Sun Yat-sen and his Soviet advisers. They also cleared the way for the reforms championed by Lee Teng-hui, culminating in his re-election in the first direct presidential polls of March 1996.

Political liberalization in Taiwan coincided with Communist peace overtures towards the government in Taipei. Beijing offered the island a high degree of autonomy within a unified China of the kind eventually agreed for Hong Kong after 1997. Chiang Ching-kuo was unimpressed. However, in the last year of his life he helped reduce tension across the Straits by allowing local residents to visit family members on the Mainland, a move that, for better or worse, brought citizens of the 'two Chinas' into contact with each other after decades of estrangement.

Chiang Kai-shek (1887–1975)

Chiang was the first leader of modern China to secure genuine international stature – for himself and his country. In this regard he eclipsed SUN YAT-SEN, his revolutionary mentor, and became the dominant figure in Chinese politics for a quarter of a century before he was driven to TAIWAN in 1949 by MAO ZEDONG. Even then, he retained the status of an elder statesman, and was seen by the West as a valuable ally in the fight against Communism in Asia. Yet Chiang had few genuine admirers outside China, at least over any length of time, and at home many regarded him with respect rather than affection. Lean and ascetic, aloof and autocratic, he was not a popular leader in any sense of the term. And unlike some of China's Communist leaders, he had neither the power nor the will to stamp his image in the hearts and minds of his citizens. This helped ensure that there was little popular sympathy when his KUOMINTANG government collapsed on the Mainland. His death, at the age of 87 in Taiwan, where his rule coincided with growing prosperity, produced more in the way of popular sentiment. But his reputation fell sharply in the 1980s as democracy took root in the island.

revolutionary soldier, 1911–28

Chiang, the son of a wealthy salt merchant from ZHEJIANG, owed his rise, rule and often uncanny survival to control of some of the best trained and equipped ARMIES within the constellation of military forces that made up the Republic of China. The collapse of political institutions at the start of the century, and the frailty of those set up to replace them, meant that political consensus had to be established on the battlefield. Chiang's first experience of this came in 1911 when he returned from military training in JAPAN to fight on the Republican side during the revolution (see REPUBLICAN REVOLUTION). The lesson was rubbed in by the failure of Sun Yat-sen to make any headway against his warlord foes until the Kuomintang had an army of its own. This was developed and trained by the SOVIET UNION which saw in Sun and his party a means of extending the world revolution. Moscow ordered the young CHINESE COMMUNIST PARTY

to join Sun's ranks, which in 1923–4 were rapidly reorganized and radicalized.

The training ground of the National Revolutionary Army was the Whampoa Military Academy in Guangzhou, of which Chiang was made commandant in 1924. Here he built the ties of personal loyalty to future commanders that were to stand him in good stead for the rest of his career. With key sections of the army on his side, he was able to succeed Sun in 1925, despite the presence of senior rivals within the Party. The following year he commanded the NORTHERN EXPEDITION, the generally successful military campaign to crush the warlords, unite the country and end foreign privileges.

Chiang's ascendancy also owed much to the fact that, following the Northern Expedition, he enjoyed control over SHANGHAI and the rich provinces of the Yangtze Delta. His armies marched into China's largest city in 1927 and quickly won the gratitude of the local and foreign business communities by crushing a workers' insurrection and wiping out the Kuomintang's Left wing and its Communist Party allies. Chiang's bloody purge of April 1927 divided China into two armed, hostile, Kuomintang and Communist camps. Almost 80 years later they have yet to settle their differences.

Chiang's fortunes fluctuated wildly in the years that followed his occupation of Shanghai. But the fact that he could usually tap the wealth of the city provided him with the military resources needed to crush other rivals in the Kuomintang and curb resistance in the provinces.

unity of a sort, 1928–37

In the summer of 1928, Chiang's forces completed the final stage of the Northern Expedition and occupied BEIJING. Nominally, China was now unified under a Kuomintang government of which Chiang was head. The new regime worked hard to re-build China's national dignity, securing TARIFF AUTONOMY in 1928, and freeing the maritime customs, salt tax administration and Post Office of foreign influence or control. The end of EXTRATERRI-TORIALITY had to wait until the middle of the

Second World War. Other achievements included road building, some railway construction, the founding of schools and colleges, and moves to create a public health network (see HEALTH).

Yet wars, rebellion and the threat of invasion were the dominant themes of the 1930s rather than reconstruction. And Chiang was determined to deal with what he perceived to be the menace of Communism before trying to eliminate challenges from within his own regime or engage Japan. In the late 1920s groups of Communists had fled to various remote spots in south China to escape suppression and advance the revolution among poor peasants. Under the leadership of Mao and others, they created rural soviets and formed Red Armies to defend them. Chiang vowed to wipe them out. In JIANGXI and elsewhere during the early 1930s he ordered 'bandit suppression' campaigns to be conducted against his foes. The first four were unsuccessful. But the fifth, in which Chiang employed blockade tactics recommended by his German military advisers, drove the Communists out of south China in 1934 and on to the LONG MARCH. Central government troops gave chase but failed to catch up with the rebels. However the fact that they pursued them doggedly across provinces where Chiang's authority previously held little sway effected national unity of a sort.

But only of a sort. In 1935, the Communists, their ranks decimated by losses sustained en route, nevertheless managed to establish a new base in SHAANXI in north China, which the following year Chiang also moved to destroy. By this time, however, there was little popular appetite for civil war. Japan had occupied Manchuria (northeast China), attacked Shanghai and was making ever deeper inroads in north China. Students and intellectuals protested against Chiang's unwillingness to resist the invaders and criticized his government for being unrepresentative. Though politically embarrassing this was hardly a serious challenge. The real threat came in December 1936, when ZHANG XUELIANG, the 'Young Marshal' of Manchuria, arrested Chiang in Xian, and insisted that he abandon the war against the Communists and fight the Japanese (see XIAN INCIDENT).

Shaken by such insubordination, Chiang conceded Zhang's demands. After complex negotiations involving the Communists and even distant Moscow, where Stalin wanted the Chinese government to be a bulwark against

Japan, Chiang agreed that the Kuomintang would fight *with* the Communists and *against* the Japanese in the context of a new United Front. On his release and return to Nanjing, he was greeted as a national hero. Past errors were forgiven in the light of his new determination to stand up to China's gravest foe.

war, diplomacy, defeat, 1937–49

In July 1937, the Japanese struck again, quickly overwhelming Shanghai and Nanjing (see SINO-JAPANESE WAR). Chiang was forced to move inland, hundreds of miles away from his traditional base of support. By 1940, the 'Generalissimo', as he was then known, was leading the badly bruised armies and government of 'Free China' from CHONGQING, a remote city but not remote enough to escape Japanese bombs. In these difficult circumstances, he fell back on military luck to survive the Japanese invasion and mastery of factional politics to defeat the rivals in his own ranks.

This last was necessary because China was not only at war with Japan from 1937–45. It was also at war with itself. The United Front with the Communists, and a reconciliation between Nanjing and the southern provinces of GUANGDONG and GUANGXI the same year suggested a degree of national unity that was rarely apparent on the ground. Wartime China consisted of a constellation of forces: Chiang's central government and its armies; provincially controlled forces of varying degrees of loyalty; Communist troops; and 'quisling' Chinese regimes of the kind led by WANG JINGWEI. This gave the lie to foreign, chiefly American, expectations that China would prove a valued ally and 'great power' in the struggle against Japan. General JOSEPH STILWELL, the senior US officer in China and chief of staff to Chiang, was given the impossible, frustrating task of turning such expectations into realities. His attempt to do so was the cause of bitter conflict between the two men.

Chiang sought and generally managed to get the better of the complex forces that threatened him by dint of sheer cunning, personal manipulation of foes, a policy of bribing and sowing disaffection among adversaries, and the ultimate accusation that, as he was national leader at a time of desperate crisis, anyone who defied him defied the Chinese nation. He was a zealous protector of what he believed to be China's interests. Unfortunately, he was unable to distinguish between such interests and his own. His view of Chinese sovereignty was a highly personalized one; something shared by his Communist successors.

Chiang's vision

Chiang was a man of narrow education, and one for whom leadership did not require familiarity with the way in which governments worked or close cooperation with other talented individuals. Often inaccessible for weeks at a time, he preferred to have mediocrities around him than potential rivals. His ideals were those of the militarized life, reinforced by the revolutionary teachings of Sun Yat-sen and tempered by the moral strictures of CONFUCIANISM. Chiang's politics were thus a curious mix of traditional Chinese authoritarianism and Sun's 'Three Principles of the People': nationalism, democracy and an ill-defined form of socialism.

Supposedly these ideals were embodied in the Leninist structure, discipline and purpose of the Kuomintang, the vanguard of change. In Chiang's view the Kuomintang's role was to unite China, modernize it, educate its people and provide them with a say in government. These were revolutionary tasks by any standards, but as far as Chiang was concerned they did not require violent revolutionary upheavals – either in town or countryside. Rather they called for discipline and self-sacrifice on the part of all social classes. Unfortunately these aims and values were poorly served by a regime best known for its weakness, inefficiency, military incompetence and pervasive CORRUPTION.

There is little evidence that the Generalissimo was himself corrupt but some to suggest he had a more colourful personal life than his code strictly called for. He was married three times, and appears to have sent his second wife, Jenny Chieh-ju Chen (d. 1971), to the UNITED STATES simply to clear the way for a politically advantageous union in 1927 with SOONG MEI-LING, sister-in-law of Sun Yat-sen. The new Madame Chiang travelled to the United States during the Sino-Japanese War. Her charm, beauty and fluent English did much to win support for her embattled husband and his government.

Though Chiang was keen to see the defeat of Japan, he was at least equally keen to dominate domestic politics. Throughout the Sino-Japanese War, therefore, he sought to monopolize the best resources – whatever their form, and from wherever they came –

for the forthcoming struggle with his arch rivals, the Communists. The uneasy truce between China's two main contenders for power broke down almost immediately following Japan's surrender in 1945. So did the prospects for rapid post-war reconstruction. This was unfortunate because Chiang, fêted as a victorious war leader in 1945, seemed to have been given another chance to build and unify his battered nation. There was a distinct yearning for this at home coupled with goodwill and support from the United States, whose leaders still saw Chiang as China's best bet, and who, fatefully, remained committed to his regime.

Such illusions soon lost their lustre yet managed to linger on until 1948, by which time US attempts at mediation between the Nationalists and the Communists had ended in acrimony, Chiang's government had all but disintegrated, and the reputation of its leader had sunk with it. Corruption, inflation, demoralization and utter weariness with war engulfed the country (see CIVIL WAR). Communist military assaults, the work of a well-organized, disciplined, committed, and ruthless enemy, shattered Chiang's best forces and led to the capture of most of his key towns. In the summer of 1949, the Generalissimo dispatched what remained of his troops, the shell of a civilian administration, and much of China's gold and art treasures to Taipei, capital of Taiwan.

Taiwan years, 1949–75

The speed of the Communist triumph stunned many and led to agonizing debates in the United States over 'Who lost China?' The question had more to do with American Cold War politics than events in China where, in essence, Chiang's rule had collapsed rather than been overthrown. His long attempt to bind the country together during a time of political, social and economic decay, invasion, and civil war was over. China had not been 'lost', and certainly not by Americans. It had, however, been convulsed by a dramatic political change whose consequences would not be clear for some time.

Chiang had resigned the presidency of China in January 1949, when the Nationalist government still retained a tenuous hold on Beijing and most of the important centres in the south. When he resumed it again in Taipei in March 1950, the Communists had conquered virtually the whole of the mainland and were preparing to 'liberate' his island redoubt. In the meantime, vice-president LI ZONGREN became acting president. He failed to stem the Communist advance and prevent Chiang interfering in decision-making. At this crucial juncture, Washington reluctantly washed its hands of Chiang: the US maintained diplomatic relations with the Nationalist government, but regarded its chances of survival in Taipei as slim. Such expectations were confounded by North Korea's Soviet-backed invasion of South Korea in June 1950. President Truman decided Taiwan could not be allowed to fall into Communist hands. He ordered the US Seventh Fleet into the Straits of Formosa to deter an expected attack from the Mainland.

America's protection of Taiwan – which came to be regarded as an 'unsinkable aircraft carrier' – did not stop the Chinese Communists from attacking Nationalist-held outlying islands. Neither did it remove the threat of force, which Beijing still holds over the island at the start of the new century in an attempt to prevent it from seeking formal independence. But it did raise the stakes involved in an attack to a level that allowed Chiang's regime to survive until his death in office in 1975, and Taiwan's de facto independence long thereafter.

Generally speaking Chiang's record in Taiwan, though far from unmixed, compared favourably with his rule on the Mainland. One reason for this was that Taiwan was a province rather than a 'continent': its problems, though many, were less severe than those of the Mainland during the 1920s and 1930s. The island had inherited a high level of literacy, and well-developed industries from its Japanese masters. Agriculture, though in need of reform, was highly developed. There were few opportunities for Communist insurgency. The most serious social conflict was that between the native Taiwanese and the roughly two million refugees and soldiers who arrived from the Mainland. In February 1947, tension between these groups had spilt over into protests and violent suppression in an incident that left deep wounds (see FEBRUARY TWENTY-EIGHTH INCIDENT). The scars were not

healed until the 1990s, and even then not completely.

In the last few years of his life, Chiang saw the island backwater from which he had hoped to stage the reconquest of the Mainland undergo an economic 'take off'. A surge in the export of manufactured goods generated high growth and set Taiwan on the road that would turn it into one of the world's most dynamic trading economies. Political development was less rapid: the government remained repressive and the island under martial law until 1987, when CHIANG CHING-KUO, Chiang Kai-shek's son, who also became president, yielded to mounting pressures for liberalization.

Taiwan's diplomatic status deteriorated in Chiang's last years. In 1971, Beijing finally eased itself into China's seat in the UNITED NATIONS and Taiwan – the Republic of China – withdrew. The following year, Washington took the first of the steps that would lead to a switch in recognition from Taipei to Beijing. Chiang Kai-shek was mercifully unaware of this last development, which occurred in 1979. But the drift of American policy in the early 1970s must have been clear to him, and it must have been hard to bear for a man once fêted as the leader of a 'great power'.

History may be kinder to Chiang Kai-shek in the new century than it was in the old, for his achievements were considerable. He established significant veneers of modernity, national unity and social cohesion over a country long accustomed to being governed as an empire and unused to the methods of the modern nation state. Prior to his ascendancy in 1927–8, the Republic had degenerated into warlordism, banditry, Communist rebellion, and continuing weakness in the face of foreign aggression. Chiang's Nationalist government failed to root out these problems, and very often the 'veneer' of modernity was no more than that. But, particularly during the ten years before the outbreak of the Sino-Japanese War, it went some way towards tackling China's ills, despite worldwide economic depression, dissension within its own ranks, and the gathering clouds of war.

Chinese Communist Party

Founded by a cabal of urban intellectuals in 1921, but matured in the violence of war and peasant revolution that followed, China's Communist Party managed to destroy its enemies in 1949 and seize power. This was

an extraordinary achievement, one that ranks among the key events of the twentieth century. No less extraordinary – but far more tragic – was the fact that, under MAO ZEDONG, the Party continually found new foes after

1949, plunging the country into a maelstrom of purges, famine, and social upheavals that cost millions of lives. Only with Mao's death in 1976 did the tumult subside, leaving his successors to rescue the country from the excesses of his rule. They did so by preserving the Party's stranglehold on political life while promoting rapid economic growth. The consequences have been momentous. They include a dramatic rise in living standards and the suppression of massive political dissent in Tiananmen Square in 1989. At the start of the new era, the Party's power, prestige, and ideological appeal are waning, but it shows no sign of adjusting to growing pressures for change from an increasingly sophisticated society. Indeed, if anything, the defeat of the Kuomintang, the Communists' great rival, in Taiwan's fiercely contested presidential polls of 2000, reinforced the feeling that the Communist Party must never place itself at the mercy of genuine elections or allow multi-party politics at home.

proletarians, peasants and purges

Much of the cruelty, violence and repression of the Party's first three decades in power were foreshadowed in its tortuous pre-1949 history. It spent much of the time fighting for its life. It was also prey to constant struggles over leadership and 'line'. Sudden changes in both were usually followed by rectification campaigns, violence, the re-writing of history, and the hounding of those who failed to keep up with ever changing orthodoxy.

These problems grew out of the complexity of making a modern revolution in a deeply traditional country. Many of the dozen or so intellectuals who, guided by agents of the Comintern (the Communist International, headquartered in Moscow), gathered in SHANGHAI to found the Party in July 1921, were as international in their outlook as the city in which they met. Inspired by the Bolshevik Revolution, and exhilarated by the great debates of the MAY FOURTH MOVEMENT, their attraction to MARXISM stemmed both from its promise to make China strong, and its potential to save the oppressed of the world from the crisis of capitalism. Marxism was then the most modern of creeds. Where better might it be expected to make its mark in China than Shanghai, the country's most modern city, the one in closest touch with the rest of the world, and the home of China's infant proletariat?

Yet the Chinese revolution could not be sparked by workers alone. Peasants had to be mobilized. So did the 'bourgeois nationalists', whom Moscow deemed to be a revolutionary class in semi-colonial, feudal China. This meant a special role for the KUOMINTANG, whose leader, SUN YAT-SEN, was desperate to end warlord rule and to unify and modernize China. Sun eagerly accepted Soviet aid and advice to achieve these ends. One piece of advice from Moscow was that Communist Party members enter the ranks of the KUOMINTANG to strengthen the revolution.

The consequences were spectacular. Strikes, anti-foreign boycotts and protests broke out throughout southern China as agitators played on nationalist and class grievances, and the foreign powers, their position under threat, responded with heavy-handed repression. By mid-1926 – five years after the Communist Party's birth, and only two years after the reorganization of the Kuomintang – the National Revolutionary Army set out on its NORTHERN EXPEDITION from Guangzhou. Scarcely six months later, much of China south of the Yangtze was in revolutionary hands. The great prizes of Shanghai, Nanjing and Wuhan loomed.

Such rapid success placed the alliance between the Kuomintang and the Communists under intense strain. Both parties wanted to overthrow the WARLORDS, unify China, modernize the country and abolish the UNEQUAL TREATIES undermining Chinese sovereignty. But they could not agree how this should be done. Though there were differences within both camps, the Communists and the Kuomintang Left favoured a redistribution of power in town and countryside in favour of workers and peasants. They were under no illusions that this could be achieved without violence. Mao Zedong, then observing revolution in the countryside, was among them. On the other hand, many in the Kuomintang, and particularly CHIANG KAI-SHEK, whom the rapid progress of the Northern Expedition had made one of the most powerful military figures in the revolutionary alliance, put national unification and political reform before social revolution. It was necessary to re-make China, but not by waging class war. That was the 'Bolshevist' not the Chinese way. It also threatened Chiang's grip on military and political power, which depended on a tacit alliance with moderate nationalists and merchants in the cities and the status quo in the countryside (see AGRICULTURE).

Chiang tried to settle the future of the revol-

Leaders of the Chinese Communist Party and their Fate
(Note: Party leaders were variously called 'general secretary' or 'chairman')

Name	Dates in office	Reasons for dismissal	Circumstances of death
Chen Duxiu (1879–1943)	1921–7	'Right opportunism'	Expelled from the Party. Died of illness in 1943, a convert to Western democracy.
Qu Qiubai (1899–1935)	1927–8	'Left adventurism'	Caught and executed by the Nationalists.
Xiang Zhongfa (1880–1931)	1928–31	Xiang leader only in name; real power was exercised by Li Lisan (see below)	Caught and executed by the Nationalists.
Li Lisan (1899–1967)	1930–31	'Leftist adventurism'	Tortured to death in the Cultural Revolution.
Wang Ming aka Chen Shaoyu (1904–47)	1931	Assigned to work in Comintern; later accused of 'new surrenderism' and 'dogmatism'	Left China for the Soviet Union in 1946, where he died, a fierce critic of Mao Zedong.
Bo Gu aka Qin Bangxian (1907–46)	1931–5	Military defeats that had forced the Communists on to the Long March	Killed in a plane crash.
Zhang Wentian (1900–1976)	1935–45 (formally)	Growing supremacy of Mao	Persecuted during the Cultural Revolution; died of illness in 1976; posthumously rehabilitated in 1979.
Mao Zedong (1893–1976)	1945–76	Not applicable	Party leader, but manipulated by his wife, Jiang Qing, and others.
Hua Guofeng (1921–)	1976–80	Perpetuating 'Leftist errors'	
Hu Yaobang (1919–89)	1980–87	Committing 'political mistakes' (in handling student protests)	Retained his Politburo seat; death, caused by heart attack, sparked Tiananmen democracy protests.
Zhao Ziyang (1919–)	1987–9	'Supporting the turmoil and splitting the Party' (a reference to Tiananmen)	
Jiang Zemin (1926–)	1989–		

ution in April 1927 with a bloody purge of his radical opponents. Thousands were killed in towns and cities across south China. Amid recriminations in the Communist ranks, CHEN DUXIU, one of the Party's founders and its first leader, was deposed and disgraced. (See table above.) Survivors of the purge fled to the countryside, leaving Chiang to unify China in 1928 by force of arms rather than social upheaval. As he did so small bands of Communists, including those led by Mao and ZHU DE, scattered across south China where they regrouped and struggled to redefine the Chinese Revolution.

rural revolution and the role of Mao

Mao was not the first Chinese Communist to lead a peasant movement. Peng Pai (1896–1929), leader of the Haifeng rural soviet in GUANGDONG, could claim that title. But in his *Report on an Investigation of the Peasant Movement in Hunan* of 1927, Mao identified the central role of the peasantry in overthrowing the old order. He also argued that the Party could never defend the revolution without its own army. First in Jinggangshan, a mountainous area of JIANGXI, then in Ruijin, capital of the Central Soviet, in the same province, Mao and his comrades conducted rural insurrection according to these precepts. Revolutionary bases, defended by the infant Red Army, were created, Soviet governments set up. Landlords and merchants were dispossessed, persecuted or killed. Land was redistributed to those who tilled it.

Moscow looked askance at many of these activities. So did the formal leadership of the Chinese Communist Party, then operating underground in Shanghai under Qu Qiubai (1899–1935). Qu was succeeded by other Party leaders equally unhappy over events in distinct Jiangxi during the early 1930s. On more than one occasion, Mao, one of the chief architects of these events, fell under a political cloud. On more than one occasion, the formal Party hierarchy ordered Communist troops to forsake the 'base areas', of which there were soon several, in order to attack cities where a 'high tide' of workers' revolt was expected. The failure of all such attempts – in Nanchang (1927 and 1930), Guangzhou (1927) and Changsha (1930) – was as costly as it was fateful. Physically, politically – even psychologically – the Party was driven ever deeper into the Chinese countryside. Twenty years would pass before its leaders and their armies emerged into the lights of China's big cities.

Rural China in the first half of the century was a world away from the cities and coastal fringe. Its ancient rhythms were not unaffected by the upheavals arising from China's encounter with the outside world: all too often they were interrupted by banditry, warlord depredations and foreign invasion. And the worldwide economic depression of the 1930s could sometimes make its effects felt in the remotest of hamlets. Yet the countryside still remained immune to many of the wider changes engulfing China. In many parts of the country, the peasant's world was one of POVERTY, indebtedness, natural calamities, landlord oppression, cruelty and superstition.

It was also a world of relative simplicity, earthy humour and tradition of the kind that sometimes appeals to revolutionary intellectuals – especially those, like Mao, who were prey to 'voluntarism': the belief that will alone (supplemented by force and cruelty when necessary), can change the world. The Chairman said that China's peasants were 'poor and blank'. They were both political victims and political virgins, and beautiful, revolutionary things could be written on their souls. The Communists wrote much into the hearts of those they were forced to live with for so many years. Peasant mentalities made a lasting impression on the Party, too.

retreat, revival, supremacy: 1927–49

First in south China, and later in the north, Mao and his comrades grafted modern techniques of mass mobilization, class consciousness, land reform, and the violent overthrow of landlords on to the explosive base of traditional peasant discontent. The rural revolution encountered many setbacks. For ten years after 1927, the Communists had to fight off Chiang's 'bandit-suppression campaigns', most of them huge military operations which took a heavy toll of life. For several, the Moscow-inclined leadership opposed Mao's military tactics of drawing the 'bandit suppression' forces into the Central Soviet in order to destroy them, and his apparent reluctance to wipe out the rich peasants as a class. The Party soon regretted abandoning such methods and demoting their author: in 1934 Chiang's fifth suppression campaign forced the Communists on to the LONG MARCH out of south China, through some of the country's most inhospitable terrain, and into the backwaters of SHAANXI. There they faced a future as bleak as the landscape until Japanese aggression compelled Chiang to abandon further efforts at suppression and form a new United Front with his old foes against the invaders (see XIAN INCIDENT; SINO-JAPANESE WAR).

The Party never looked back. As Japan's armies occupied ever larger tracts of the country, wrecked Chiang's government and destroyed many of his best forces, the Communists engaged in guerrilla war and rapidly built up new base areas, subsequently known as border regions. The most important – and the most secure – was the Shaanxi–Gansu–Ningxia (Shaan–Gan–Ning) border region. Its capital, YANAN, was the Party's wartime headquarters. Three other major centres of Communist influence were located further east in SHANXI: the Shanxi–Suiyuan (now part of Inner Mongolia) base; the Shanxi–Chahaer (also part of Inner Mongolia) base; and, further south, the Shanxi–Hebei–Shandong–Hebei base. Each of these three was subject to Japanese attack. Each was led by political and/or military leaders who went on to wield great influence after 1949. Each, by virtue of its different terrain, social and economic conditions, presented different problems for a Party committed to organizing revolution and stiffening national resistance. And, in each, the Party adopted different but generally successful strategies to win popular support.

This owed much to the fact that Mao – his authority in the Party restored at the Zunyi Conference held in GUIZHOU during the Long March and his tactics vindicated – redefined the revolution in nationalist terms. The Party was saving China from its foreign foes by defending the 'people', a broad category which included those deemed 'class enemies' in the past but whose new-found patriotism made them part of the United Front. The Communists' apparent moderation, described by Mao as 'new democracy', won many admirers: thousands travelled to Yanan to cast in their lot with the Communists. They believed they were creating a new China, a very different one from that symbolized by the corruption, sloth and low morale in CHONGQING, the Kuomintang capital.

Certainly Mao was creating a new Party. The expansion in membership, growth of the Eighth Route Army (as the Red Army was then known), and enlargement of the area under Communist control (which extended east into SHANXI, HENAN, HEBEI and SHANDONG in the form of 'border regions') were accompanied by mass movements, campaigns and purges of those in the Party deemed to have incorrect views, leaving Mao and his 'Thought' supreme. There was a good deal of heady excitement about this process: it was designed to reshape men and women, as well as the poor, unpromising environment around them. Plain living became a virtue as well as a necessity. The pursuit of self-sufficiency turned infertile Yanan hillsides into farmland. Unity, selflessness, and hatred for the enemy and love of labour were watchwords in the border regions, and Yanan especially. Visitors could not fail to be impressed by such spirit, determination and diligence.

But there were darker sides to wartime Communism. The freedom and independence of artists and intellectuals were derided and destroyed in Yanan – a grim prelude of their fate throughout China. Even well-meaning criticism was stifled in 'rectification movements' and 'study sessions', most of them based around the numerous speeches and essays Mao produced during this time. A formidable security apparatus, run by KANG SHENG who learnt his skills from the Soviet secret police, screened out 'spies' and 'counter-revolutionaries'. Casualties of these campaigns included Ding Ling (1904–85), a writer whose boldness soon made her a target, and Wang Shiwei (1900–1947), whose collections of essays, *Wild Lilies*, had criticized the luxurious lifestyles of Party leaders at a time when ordinary Chinese were suffering the hardships of war. Wang was purged as a Trotskyite and secret agent, and later executed.

By 1945 Mao had ditched his major rivals in the leadership, Wang Ming (1904–47) and Bo Gu (1907–46), and distanced his Party from the ideological dependence on Moscow which had sustained them. In his view it was precisely slavish adherence to Soviet tactics that had led to so many disasters during the previous twenty years. He himself had become the source of orthodoxy whose 'correct line', based upon Chinese conditions, required obedience. The Chairman still consulted key leaders: ZHOU ENLAI, LIU SHAOQI, ZHU DE, PENG DEHUAI were among those who had their say. Collective leadership was not entirely a myth – as Mao found, to his occasional discomfort, in the late 1950s and early 1960s. But at Yanan, Mao Zedong became both philosopher and king. And it was not long before the price of criticism and differences of opinion became, not just political ruin, but persecution and even death.

Orthodoxy in China holds that the Communist Party's success in Yanan and elsewhere derived from Mao's adaptation of Marxism to Chinese conditions. Another way to put it would be to say that the Party grounded its revolution in Chinese experience, tapping the resentments and grievances created by an unjust, decaying agricultural society at a time of national crisis, and mobilizing them for change. The Party did not ride to power on a wave of popular support. Rather, it remained flexible, tailoring its policies to circumstances and making strategic compromises with local interests. Inevitably, this meant shedding what little remained of the Party's cosmopolitan intellectual heritage dating back to the May Fourth Movement. The Communists opposed feudalism as a system. But to seize and then retain power they drew on its deep roots, acceptance of authority, isolation and tendency towards self-sufficiency as well as the narrow, factional interests it often generated. At Yanan and elsewhere, feudalism informed revolutionary politics, creating a deadly mix that would soon lead to disasters, many of which haunt China still.

The Party's policies won enthusiastic acceptance among many. Others merely tolerated them. What is clear is that during the 12 years of invasion and civil war that scarred China between 1937 and 1949, the Communists alienated far fewer people than did the Nationalists. No less important, they performed better on the battlefield. By 1945, protected by an army and militia close to 2 million-strong, the Party was beyond suppression, at least by troops of the kind led by Chiang Kai-shek. It was also able to resist attempts led by the UNITED STATES to lure it into a coalition government with the Kuomintang that would have forced it to give up many of its wartime territorial gains. Instead, at a speed which astonished Mao as much as it did the rest of the world, Communist troops swept into Manchuria (northeast China) in the wake of Japan's surrender. Chiang's costly attempts to oust them failed. Soon, they were in a position to move south and engage the main Nationalist armies in a series of set-piece battles that, by early 1949, secured them victory in the CIVIL WAR. The revolutionary party of peasants returned to the cities – this time as the ruling party.

'New China': construction, control

The 'New China' of the People's Republic was born on 1 October 1949. There was a degree of genuine enthusiasm for 'Liberation', tempered by caution and, in some cases, fear. If corruption, inflation and inefficiency had sapped support for Chiang's regime, a yearning for peace, reconstruction and a new start for the country supplied a measure of goodwill for its replacement.

The Communist Party's seizure of power marked a turning point in a host of ways. It brought the world's most populous state into the Communist camp, and close alliance (despite past misgivings) with the SOVIET UNION under Beijing's policy of 'leaning to

one side' in the great post-war ideological divide. This was a serious matter for the United States and the other Western powers, as well as for China's neighbours, some of whom appeared ripe for Communist insurgency themselves.

At home, the new Communist government engineered an economic recovery after years of war. It did so by carrying out a Common Programme said to reflect the interests of the workers, peasants, petty bourgeoisie and national bourgeoisie who supported the 'new democracy'. AGRICULTURE was transformed with a programme of LAND REFORM that wiped out the gentry class – a true revolution that altered the structure of power in the countryside for ever. With surprising speed (and Soviet help), the government built an industrial base that quickly eclipsed earlier Nationalist and Japanese efforts on Chinese soil. It also brought rudimentary education, health care and, above all, a sense of modern nationhood to a people long unfamiliar with such. Here, indeed, was a 'new' China. The sense of purpose, unity and public honesty many people remembered to have accompanied these endeavours led, in the very different climate of the 1990s, to a nostalgia among the older generation for the Party's early years in power.

Yet these triumphs were just half the story. After 1949, China's political history, indeed its entire national life, became inseparable from that of the Communist Party. Any distinction between the Party and the state was more apparent to Western political scientists in retrospect than to Chinese citizens at the time. The Party penetrated every sphere of life, soon establishing a tyranny without equal in China's long history of authoritarian rule.

People were classified according to their class. DANGAN (dossiers) were opened on them to record their obedience, or otherwise, to the Party line. Movement from the countryside to the city was prohibited. The urban population was monitored by an extensive security network that began with local 'residents committees' and continued all the way up, through Party committees at every workplace, to central organizations in Beijing charged with ensuring Party discipline.

In farms and factories, and schools and universities; in churches and temples, and newspaper offices and radio stations; in distant provinces inhabited by non-Chinese peoples and government departments in the heart of the capital, the Party rooted out representa-

Members and Leaders, Congresses and Committees

At the start of the new century the Party claims a membership of more than 61 million, or about 5.1 per cent of the Mainland's population. There is no reliable evidence showing why people join. Factors that draw people to political parties elsewhere in the world – principles, idealism, a desire to do something for their country – must be at work in China. As important is the fact that nothing can be accomplished in Chinese politics, and little in public life generally by those without access to the connections, power and privilege that go with Party membership. A few senior government posts are occupied by people who, at least in name, are not Party members. An example in the mid-1990s was Rong Yiren (1916–), the 'red capitalist', who served as vice-president. But the role of 'non-Party personages', as they are known, is almost always ornamental: compliance with Party policies and doctrine is enjoined on Party members and non-members alike (see GOVERNMENT AND ADMINISTRATION).

The Party functions according to the principles of 'democratic centralism'. Individual Party members are subordinate to the organization, the minority to the majority, lower levels to the Central Committee. The 'centralism' of this scheme is more apparent than its 'democracy'. Discussion in the Party is often fierce; in Chairman Mao's day, murderously so. But it is usually confined to the senior leadership, whose decisions are transmitted to lower levels for implementation.

The Party's leading body is the Central Committee whose members (following election at the 15th National Party Congress in 1997) number just short of 200. In ordinary circumstances a new Central Committee is elected at the end of each national congress, held every five years. The Central Committee *approves*, but the Politburo, and in particular its powerful Standing Committee, *decides* all major questions of policy. The Politburo Standing Committee is the apex of formal power in the Party and thus in China. Only marginally less powerful is the Party's Central Military Commission, the command organ of the People's Liberation Army. Historically, the commission was the main source of both Mao's and Deng's personal political power. Its chairman – at the start of the century, the militarily untested Jiang Zemin – is commander in chief (see PEOPLE'S LIBERATION ARMY).

The formal organizational structure says only so much about the distribution of power within the Party. During the Cultural Revolution power resided in the person of Mao Zedong. In the 1980s and early 1990s, Deng ruled in conjunction with a handful of Party veterans whose revolutionary credentials placed them beyond contradiction. They exercised a decisive role even though, as members of the Central Advisory Commission, they were supposed only to advise the younger, formal leadership. The era of the strongman in Party politics is over but not that of personal relationships. Senior leaders enjoy patron–client networks, based on shared professional backgrounds and policy preferences, which extend deep into the formal bureaucracy. The Party polices its own members through a Central Disciplinary Inspection Committee. This body generally takes precedence over the national legal system – both in the sense that it deals with the illegal activities of senior Party members *before* the courts, and because it has greater power in deciding their fate.

tives of the old order. Depending on the time and the circumstances, they were branded 'landlords', 'counter-revolutionaries', 'Rightists', 'local nationalists', 'revisionists' and 'capitalist roaders'. Such labels made sense only in terms of the Party's prevailing orthodoxy. But that did not make them any less deadly for those to whom they were assigned. On the contrary, in campaign after campaign they were singled out for humiliation, persecution, imprisonment, torture and death. No wonder genuine expressions of individuality – sometimes cannily encouraged by a Party apparently keen to listen to its critics before silencing them, as was the case during the ONE HUNDRED FLOWERS MOVEMENT of 1956 – disappeared amid a welter of denunciations and criticism at the workplace and in the official media.

This grim culture of control was lubricated by the tension and fear that always accompany totalitarianism. In China's case it was fuelled by Mao's mercurial, often murderous quest for ideological purity, and his growing struggles against erstwhile comrades. The latter began with the ousting in 1954 of Gao Gang (1895–1954) and Rao Shushi (1903–75), two senior Party leaders said to have engaged in 'conspiratorial activities'. It continued with the disgrace of Peng Dehuai in 1959 over his opposition to the GREAT LEAP FORWARD. It culminated in the CULTURAL REVOLUTION, when, at one time or another, Mao turned on the remainder of the top Party leadership, with the exception (though sometimes only just) of Zhou Enlai.

the Leap and the Cultural Revolution

The Chairman's pursuit of ideological breakthroughs plunged China first into a 'Great Leap' into Communism. In 1958–9, a Communist wind swept through China. The PEOPLE'S LIBERATION ARMY became a 'politically sound' rural militia. Agriculture, subjected to increasing collectivization in the mid-1950s in an attempt to boost productivity, was suddenly communized. Just as suddenly, farmers neglected the fields in favour of 'backyard furnaces' in which they sought to make steel for industry. Mass mobilization and, with it, the hold of the Party over society, intensified.

The official media praised the Leap's economic achievements and extolled the appearance of a new form of society, which Mao compared favourably with that of the Soviet Union. Yet as Peng pointed out at the Lushan Plenum, a crucial Party meeting in 1959, the Great Leap was a disaster. The evidence for this was not hard to find. But it was either kept from Mao or, like the other leaders who feared him, he chose to ignore it. Between 1959 and 1962 starvation stalked many parts of China with a ferocity that outstripped the darkest days of Nationalist and imperial rule.

Relations between the Chinese Communist Party and its Soviet counterpart were another casualty of the Leap. Mao maintained a lower profile during the early 1960s, but he was active polemically, fashioning new theories to explain how Moscow had allowed socialism to degenerate into 'revisionism', and warning that the Chinese Party was taking the same, capitalist, road. Bitter polemics were exchanged as the dispute hardened into the Sino-Soviet split (see SOVIET UNION).

As the work of government and life in general gradually returned to normal after the Leap, Mao detected complacency and careerism everywhere. He attributed this to the rise of a 'new bourgeoisie' within the Party itself. Its representatives regarded material incentives, old-fashioned Party discipline and modern bureaucratic methods as the keys to development and modernization. If such tendencies were not checked, the revolution would be for naught. Capitalism would stage a comeback, perhaps with Moscow's help. So, too, might Chiang Kai-shek.

To avoid this, China needed a cultural revolution. In 1966, backed by radical allies including his wife, JIANG QING, Lin Biao, the defence minister, and those soon to be denigrated as the 'GANG OF FOUR' – the Chairman declared open season on the Party he had brought to power. The traumas and frustrations of a people who had been subject to the strictest controls since 1949 came to the surface in massive, violent outpourings of support for what was believed to be the Chairman's 'revolutionary line'. It was accompanied by bitter hatred for those said to be against it. Red Guards staged huge parades in Tiananmen Square and celebrated their new liberty by terrorizing those who represented old or new manifestations of 'bourgeois', 'capitalist', or 'revisionist' behaviour.

The personal cult of Mao, a feature of Party life since the 7th Party Congress of 1945, reached extraordinary heights. Many Chinese, not so revolutionary that they could shake off ancient yearnings for a 'great leader', regarded their Chairman as omniscient. His former comrades, but now enemies, were 'struggled' against, humiliated and toppled. In the case of the already disgraced Peng Dehuai, and President Liu Shaoqi, the number two in the party hierarchy, they were imprisoned and left to die. DENG XIAOPING, then Party General Secretary, was declared the 'number two person taking the capitalist road' (after Liu) and sent into internal exile.

The violence and upheavals in Beijing spread quickly, leaving few parts of the country untouched. In some places violence between Red Guard factions took on the characteristics of civil war. In others cruelties on an almost unimaginable scale occurred, including politically motivated cannibalism. Within months, the formal apparatus of Party and government broke down, forcing Mao to order the People's Liberation Army, now under the command of Lin Biao, to hold the ring. 'Revolutionary Committees' appeared across the country, backed up by local militia and the military. Education came to a virtual halt. So, in some areas of China, did production.

By 1969 exhaustion, confusion and stalemate between various factions in the provinces had induced a degree of stability. But it was fragile and the struggle for power in Beijing acute. This became apparent two years later when, in a still unresolved mystery, Lin Biao died, allegedly in a plane he was travelling in, which crashed in Mongolia while he tried to flee to the Soviet Union following an unsuccessful attempt to assassinate the Chairman. With Lin removed, Zhou Enlai fought to keep in check the 'Gang of Four' and other radicals who wanted to pursue Cultural Revolution goals; he also engineered the return of Deng. Such moves helped the process of rapprochement with the United States whose leaders, while perturbed at China's messianic brand of Communism and its evident instability, valued Beijing as a strategic counterweight to the Soviet Union.

Zhou's death in January 1976, and that of Mao in September of the same year, gave radicals among the leadership, now led by Jiang Qing and the three other members of the 'Gang', a chance to consolidate their gains and keep China on the road of 'perpetual revolution'. At first things went their way: in April 1976 they crushed a large gathering in Tiananmen Square ostensibly designed to commemorate Zhou but in fact a protest against the Gang's own rule. But the victory was shortlived. Within weeks of Mao's death, the 'Gang' and their allies were arrested by security forces loyal to HUA GUOFENG, a nondescript leader who none the less had the best claim to be considered Mao's heir. It was time for the Party to clear up the chaos it had created, but without jeopardizing its hold on power.

the Party under Deng

That it was able to accomplish this owed much to the political genius of Deng Xiaoping. Against strong opposition, Deng regained his former influence and re-rooted the Party's legitimacy in the liberation of productive forces – the pursuit of wealth and national power – rather than the liberation of the proletariat. The Party's purpose was not to make China ever more 'revolutionary'; the seizure of power in 1949 and the remaking of society that followed was enough in the way of revolution. Now it was time to make China rich and strong, the goal of Chinese nationalists since the mid-nineteenth century. This meant opening the country to the capitalist world and carrying out free market reforms at home.

Given all that had gone before, this was a revolutionary move. The Party had to reverse the entire thrust of its policies. It meant admitting that, despite 'Liberation' and everything that had followed, China was still backward, still poor and still far behind the developed world. And it led to a cultural revolution of a different kind: one that brought the Chinese people – heirs to millennia of self-satisfied isolation and superiority cruelly reinforced by the chimera of ideological purity – into contact with the 'real world' of international economic competition and modernization. It was the start of a historic re-engagement between China and the rest of the world that, more than 20 years later, has transformed the country and brought it within the ambit of the international community.

In terms of domestic politics, the Communist Party's pursuit of economic reform has proved as complex as its earlier quest for revolutionary purity. Deng, the dominant figure from 1978 until incapacitated by ill health in 1994, had to perform a constant balancing act between warring 'conservatives' and

---

'History' and 'Mistakes'

Since the Party bases its claim to legitimacy largely on history, the past and the present are closely linked in Chinese politics. This means that when present policies change, 'history' is often required to change, too. The Party has reinvented the past several times during its own history. The most recent and celebrated occasion occurred in 1981, after Deng had consolidated his power and sought historical justification for ending class struggle and pursuing free market reforms. The *Resolution on Certain Questions in the History of Our Party Since the Founding of the People's Republic of China* tried to rid China of the shadow of the Cultural Revolution and debunk the myth of Chairman Mao's revolutionary infallibility. This was in keeping with popular aspirations, for while the Cultural Revolution was dead it had yet to be buried. At the same time, the Resolution had to exclude from the indictment the political system that gave birth to the Chairman and many of his works or risk undermining Party rule. Mao was blamed for the Cultural Revolution, but his errors were those of 'a great proletarian revolutionary', and his contributions were said to far outweigh his mistakes. This cut and paste job on the past was presented as a great achievement. It showed that the Communist Party could correct its own mistakes and needed no supervisory body, such as parliament or the electorate, to oversee it. The Resolution insisted that the fact that the Party had made mistakes did not justify opposition to its rule for this would lead to 'even greater mistakes and court grievous disasters'. The 1981 Resolution remains the touchstone of China's official history.

'reformers' in order to keep his policies on track. Sometimes he made concessions to 'conservatives' such as CHEN YUN by arresting DISSIDENTS and staging campaigns against the 'bourgeois liberalization' that accompanied capitalist-style reforms. Sometimes he launched stunning assaults – such as his calls for political reform in 1986 and his whirlwind tour of south China in 1992 when he called for faster economic reforms. Always he had to stay ahead of his rivals, nurture his successors and, when necessary, as was the case with HU YAOBANG and ZHAO ZIYANG, be prepared to sack them when divisions over their policies threatened to split the Party. These methods, though savage, were free of the bloodshed and cruelty of Mao's day. Deng treated dissidents such as WEI JINGSHENG without mercy; but he engineered 'soft landings' for leaders whom he ousted over policy or personal differences.

As Deng's reforms took effect – they began in AGRICULTURE, where farmers were once again allowed to practise private farming in everything but name, and continued in

Socialism: A Retreating Goal?

Is China a *socialist* country? This is an important issue for the Communist Party because it concerns the question of political legitimacy. The constitution describes China as a 'socialist state under the people's democratic dictatorship led by the working class and based on the alliance of workers and peasants'. Citizens are required to adhere to the 'four cardinal principles': Communist Party leadership; Marxism-Leninism and Mao Zedong Thought; the people's democratic dictatorship; and the socialist road. Since these principles are found in the preamble to the constitution, they fetter the individual freedoms that follow. But *if* China is a socialist state, what is Chinese socialism? The Party has never been able to make up its mind – at least for very long. In the 1960s Mao's growing radicalism taxed his ideological apologists, while in the 1980s and 1990s, problems of definition became even more complex as Communism collapsed abroad and capitalist-style policies generated an economic boom in which some were encouraged to get rich before the others.

Deng's reforms, inaugurated at the Third Plenum of the Party's 11th Central Committee in December 1978, were justified on the grounds that 'practice is the sole criterion of truth'. This boiled down to saying that whatever policies contributed to the task of 'socialist modernization' were acceptable, provided they did not challenge Party rule. At the 12th National Congress in 1982, Deng said the Party's task was to build 'socialism with Chinese characteristics', a further example of his pragmatism and one that defined socialism in *Chinese* terms – the appropriate order of things for a patriot whose country has traditionally 'Sinified' the foreign creeds it adopted. But 'socialism with Chinese characteristics' soon began to look like capitalism with Chinese characteristics, and the Party fine tuned its theories at the 13th Congress in 1987 by saying China was in the 'initial stage of socialism'. This was predicted to last for a century, during which the central task was eliminating poverty and backwardness by developing productive forces.

The Tiananmen rebellion in 1989 made the Party realize it must tighten political control and ideological discipline while pursuing economic reform or risk losing power. For a while, modernization took a back seat to the need to oppose 'peaceful evolution': the alleged plot by Western powers to undermine Chinese socialism. Deng's celebrated tour of the south in 1992 reordered priorities again, forcing the leadership to embrace economic reform with greater vigour and build what the 14th Party Congress of that year described as the 'socialist market economy'. This required a much reduced role for state planning, but the continued dominance of a public sector, albeit one subjected to reform and made responsive to the market. Again, there was no question of changing the Party's leading role in politics, which was described as the 'political guarantee of socialist construction'.

The 15th Party Congress of 1997, the first after the death of Deng, came up with yet other, novel theoretical formulations. Deng's 'theories' were written into the Party's constitution where they joined Mao's 'thought' and Marxism and Leninism as the 'guiding ideology'. China was again said to be in the 'initial stage' of socialism and thus susceptible neither to utopian flights into Communism favoured by the Left nor a vigorous, if transient, stage of capitalism advocated by the Right. Jiang Zemin said, rather bleakly: 'The task we are undertaking is a new one. Marx did not speak of it, our predecessors did not do it, other socialist countries have not done it. There is no ready made model to be studied.'

The notion of public ownership was redefined. It was expanded to include every part of the economy in which there was a state interest, including every joint venture with a foreign partner. Ownership was less important than *control*. Thus, state enterprises, the economically unsuccessful Behemoths of socialism, could be invigorated by turning them into joint stock companies – providing the state controlled the process and retained a key stake in their development.

This justification of the mixed economy amounted to a thinly disguised retreat from any kind of socialism worth the name. In the 1950s socialism was deemed to have been imminent. In the Cultural Revolution it was alleged to have been attained. It has since become elusive. The only genuinely socialist thing about China at the start of the new century is the continued existence of an ailing state sector and the political monopoly of a Party that calls itself Communist. China's economic reforms may have provided a lesson in how to develop a vast, backward, traditional country whose economy was once stifled by the dead hand of state planning. They have yet to show that the results can, in any meaningful sense, be described as 'socialism'.

INDUSTRY, where private, collective and township enterprises began to eclipse the lumbering state sector – the Party's hold over society weakened. This brought problems of its own. For, if the real question under Chairman Mao was which faction of the Party was to rule, the issue under Deng was whether the Party itself would be able to survive the social and economic changes, including greater freedom of thought, it had unleashed. At Tiananmen Square in 1989, the leadership had to settle the matter with troops and tanks, snuffing out massive protests in favour of more democracy with heavy loss of life. Talk of political reform disappeared from the Party's agenda.

nationalism and authoritarianism

Rapid economic growth and further cautious liberalization have continued under JIANG ZEMIN, Deng's third chosen successor who survived his mentor to lead China into the new century. Jiang cemented his hold on power at the Party's 15th National Congress in 1997. As Party General Secretary, he leads a seven-man Politburo Standing Committee composed (in

The 'Fourth Generation': Rising Stars

Dynastic thinking dies hard in China: identifying suitable successors has dogged China's Communist leaders no less than their imperial and republican predecessors. Current orthodoxy holds that Mao Zedong was the 'core of the first generation of Party leaders'; Deng Xiaoping the 'core of the second'; and Jiang Zemin the 'core of the third'. Under this schema, each generation is associated with a major historical experience or event – though in some cases different generations underwent the same experience. The first generation is usually defined by its participation in the Long March; the second by its role in the Sino-Japanese War. The third attained political maturity during the Civil War and the transformation of Chinese society that followed. The third generation leaders, men in their late sixties and early seventies, led China into the new century. Its members were expected to give way to the 'fourth generation' in the early years of the new millennium, particularly at the Party's 16th National Congress, scheduled for the autumn of 2002. At the turn of the century it was unclear whether Jiang, Li Peng and Zhu Rongji would indeed retire or seek to exercise power behind the scenes, much as Deng Xiaoping did during the 1980s and early 1990s. Jiang, in particular, was believed to have set his sights on becoming head of a 'new' old guard. This did not augur well for Hu Jintao, whom the Party earmarked as the 'core of the fourth generation leadership' in the early 1990s and promoted accordingly.

Nevertheless, there is no doubt that a large number of younger men (accompanied by a tiny number of women) will enter the upper ranks of the Party during and after the 16th Congress. This 'fourth generation' might not eclipse the third at the very apex of power for some time, but its members are bound to infuse the Party with a different ethos and, quite possibly, new aspirations. The effect of the transition is hard to forecast, but the background, qualifications and experience of fourth-generation leaders provide a few clues. For the most part, China's new leaders will be between their late forties and early sixties when they reach the pinnacles of power. The formative period of their lives was the Cultural Revolution, which interrupted their education and left many of them disillusioned with politics and ideology. Most are well educated and schooled in different disciplines, and a different political environment, from their immediate predecessors, many of whom studied engineering in the Soviet Union. They are a diverse group, both in education and career experience. While many studied engineering, notably at Beijing's Qinghua University, now a finishing school for the elite, others studied economics, finance, management and law. Expertise in these subjects is essential for China's economic reforms. Some of the fourth generation owe their rise to family background: they are 'princelings', offspring of the great Communist 'families'. However, personal affiliations generally count for less among the rising stars than among those who came before them. The same is true of politics *per se*: few have come up through the Party's ideological or propaganda organizations, fewer still through the military. Many gained experience – and exhibited skill – administering key provinces or 'open cities' where they have pioneered reforms and, sometimes, won international acclaim.

The political outlook of the new elite, its attitude towards Party rule, ideology, nationalism and human rights, is even harder to forecast. It would certainly be rash to assume a preference for political liberalization on the part of the fourth generation. For one

order of rank) of LI PENG, ZHU RONGJI, LI RUIHUAN, HU JINTAO, WEI JIANXING and LI LANQING. It has stuck to the old formula of economic reform coupled with tight political control. Thus, Jiang has called for the dismantling of state factories but silenced demands for a reassessment of Tiananmen. He has repeated Deng's calls for the liberation of productive forces but continued to imprison dissidents. He has insisted on the rule of LAW, but largely as an instrument of the Party rather than its master.

Jiang has shown no interest in political reforms that would subject the Party to restraint, still less to recall. Instead he has preferred to rely on control of the military, the MEDIA, the judiciary and intellectual life to pursue the Party's goals by waging 'mass' campaigns. Examples, at the turn of the century, included propaganda offensives to whip up support for enterprise reform; building on the resentment caused by NATO's accidental bombing in 1999 of the Chinese embassy in Belgrade; and rooting out the religion-cum-health cult known as Fa Lun Gong.

These measures have exposed the gap between the Party's aspirations to mobilize and control society and its decreasing ability to do so. They have emphasized the discrepancy between the vibrant, increasingly sophisticated society of China's cities and the Party's crude, if fragmented authoritarianism. The contrast with the Kuomintang in Taiwan, which conducted political reforms, retained power through elections, and then in the presidential polls of 2000 was driven from office, could hardly be clearer. Neither, as far as the Communist Party was concerned, could there be a more powerful argument against introducing genuine elections in China.

Accustomed, like most previous Chinese governments, to rule on the basis of its mastery of a powerful, all-encompassing ideology, the Party has found Marxism, even in Chinese form, to be a minority interest among the thing, democracy could spell an end to the power its members have coveted so long. For another, it is likely to be seen as an obstacle to the rapid economic development and growth of national power China's future leaders are keen to deliver. The only certainty is that political power in China is changing hands, and that during the first decade of the twenty-first century, a younger, more diverse, better-educated, more 'professional' team will have to grapple with some of the most difficult questions confronting political leadership anywhere in the world. Among those likely to do so, in addition to established candidates such as Hu Jintao, Wu Bangguo and Wen Jiabao, are:

Zeng Qinghong (1939–) Perhaps Jiang Zemin's closest political ally, Zeng was appointed head of the Central Committee's Organization Department in 1997, the body which chooses leaders at central and provincial levels. Born in Jiangxi, both his parents were senior figures in the Party. He studied engineering and rose to prominence in the Party apparatus in Shanghai where, in the mid-1980s, he began a long association with Jiang, who transferred him to Beijing in 1989 when he became Party general secretary.

Li Changchun (1944–) Li, a graduate in electrical engineering, is an innovative administrator. In 1983, when he was 39, he became the youngest mayor of Shenyang. Three years later, he was the youngest provincial governor of Liaoning, where he applied radical remedies, including experiments in bankruptcy, to the ailing state-owned factories of his home province. He was no less ambitious as Party chief and governor of Henan, and in 1997 became the youngest member of the newly selected Politburo. The following year he was transferred to Guangdong to lead

the Party in China's richest, most reform-minded province.

Huang Ju (1938–) Another graduate in engineering, this time from Qinghua University, Huang Ju worked in the Party apparatus in Shanghai for 15 years before he was appointed Party secretary, the city's principal official, in 1995. He joined the Politburo in 1997. Close association with Jiang Zemin suggested further promotion would follow, but opposition in Beijing to the ascendancy of a 'Shanghai Gang' (Huang is from Zhejiang, close to Shanghai) proved an obstacle. However, Huang's ascendancy appeared to have been delayed rather than thwarted.

Xu Kuangdi (1937–) Xu, also a Zhejiang man, is an academic turned administrator who joined the Party relatively late, at the age of 46. He is a specialist in metallurgy. In the late 1980s he exchanged the laboratory and lecture hall for the Shanghai education bureaucracy. He was appointed vice-mayor in 1992 and mayor three years later, and was responsible for the smooth running and rapid development of China's flagship city.

Bo Xilai (1949–) In 1993, Bo was made mayor of Dalian, the leading port city of northeast China, which he helped turn into a major centre of international trade, investment and tourism known for its environmentally friendly approach to construction. He owes his position to an impeccable family political background (he is the son of Bo Yibo (1908–), a Long Marcher and close ally of Deng Xiaoping), relative youthfulness, high standard of education (he specialized in media studies), administrative competence and zeal for economic reform. Such attributes provide a springboard into the ruling elite.

public. It has fallen back on nationalism, economic development and securing greater international standing for a China the Party says is beset by potential foes abroad. These are not unworthy goals. But, for an educated public seeking greater freedoms, and in an era of economic globalization, innovation and interdependence, they are not compelling grounds for the preservation of authoritarian

rule. Instead the Party's continuing secrecy and conspiratorial approach to politics, its determination to curb the growth of civil society, neuter even nominally representative institutions, and insist upon the first – and last – word in deciding China's fate, reflect the hold of the feudal past, despite decades of revolution, and point to an uncertain, potentially unstable political future.

Chinese People's Political Consultative Conference (CPPCC)

This body brings together representatives of the DEMOCRATIC PARTIES, independent political figures, religious leaders and other social worthies, and members of the COMMUNIST PARTY for 'political consultation'. Its function is to give form to the 'United Front', the Party's strategy of maximizing political support and marginalizing opponents. The extent to which it provides a forum for genuine discussion must be questioned: its public debates

amount to orchestrated expressions of support for the Communist Party. And if livelier discussions take place behind closed doors, news of them rarely leaks out. The post of Chairman of the CPPCC has been monopolized by senior Communist Party leaders, including ZHOU ENLAI, DENG XIAOPING and, from 1993 until 2003, LI RUIHUAN.

The present CPPCC traces its origins to an organ of a similar name formed in 1946 to pave

Party Power

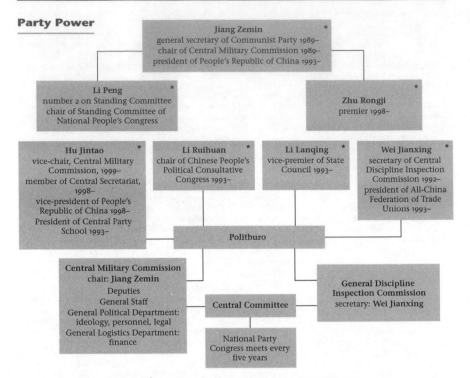

Jiang Zemin *
general secretary of Communist Party 1989–
chair of Central Military Commission 1989–
president of People's Republic of China 1993–

Li Peng *
number 2 on Standing Committee
chair of Standing Committee of
National People's Congress

Zhu Rongji *
premier 1998–

Hu Jintao *
vice-chair, Central Military
Commission, 1999–
member of Central Secretariat,
1998–
vice-president of People's
Republic of China 1998–
President of Central Party
School 1993–

Li Ruihuan *
chair of Chinese People's
Political Consultative
Congress 1993–

Li Lanqing *
vice-premier of State
Council 1993–

Wei Jianxing *
secretary of Central
Discipline Inspection
Commission 1992–
president of All-China
Federation of Trade
Unions 1993–

Politburo

Central Military Commission
chair: Jiang Zemin
Deputies
General Staff
General Political Department:
ideology, personnel, legal
General Logistics Department:
finance

Central Committee

General Discipline
Inspection Commission
secretary: Wei Jianxing

National Party
Congress meets every
five years

* Members of the seven-man Politburo Standing Committee

the way for a coalition government between the KUOMINTANG and the Communists. Agreements were reached in principle on this issue but subsequently altered by the Nationalists.

The Communist-controlled successor organization met in 1949 as People's Liberation Army troops were putting the finishing touches to their victory in the CIVIL WAR. As the highest organ of state power, the CPPCC proclaimed the establishment of the People's Republic of China on 1 October 1949, and passed the Common Programme – a proto-constitution which laid down the 'new democracy' that was to govern China prior to

the transition to socialism (see DEMOCRACY). The NATIONAL PEOPLE'S CONGRESS (NPC) assumed the legislative functions of the CPPCC on its foundation in 1954.

The CPPCC failed to meet during the Cultural Revolution. It was revived as a talking shop in 1978. The closest it has come to openly challenging Party policy was in the mid-1980s, when several elderly scientists among its ranks led opposition to construction of the THREE GORGES DAM. National congresses of the CPPCC are held every five years and coincide with those of the NPC.

Chongqing

That this former backwater and warlord redoubt, once part of SICHUAN, became the home of China's central government between 1939 and 1945 was remarkable enough. That it has risen to prominence again as the country's largest province-level city easily secures Chongqing a place in China's modern history.

The 30 million people, large industrial base and, before long, the upper reaches of the Three Gorges reservoir that fall within its administrative reach make it a city unlike any other – in China or elsewhere. Chongqing is a huge inland metropolis.

stronghold of the southwest

The city is built on the narrow promontory that divides the Jialing and the Yangtze rivers, some 1,250 miles (2,000 kms) upstream from Shanghai. It was, and remains, a key transshipment point for transporting the riches of Sichuan out of the province and far beyond. The rivers over whose confluence it presides provide its life blood, while the mountains into whose folds the modern city has spread make it the most visually stunning urban centre in China – seasonal fog and perpetual pollution permitting.

For most of the century, Chongqing's economic and strategic importance was unaccompanied by administrative and political clout. Chengdu, a city of a different stamp in a different geographical setting, 156 miles (250 kms) to the northwest, was the capital of Sichuan before Chongqing's elevation to provincial status in 1997. It remains the capital of the downsized province. Chongqing (unlike Chengdu) was opened as a TREATY PORT in 1890, but remoteness and a poor climate made it an unattractive posting for foreigners. Western MISSIONARIES and merchants exerted little impact – even when steamships began to reach the city regularly in the 1900s after they had learnt to navigate the Three Gorges. Central governments in Beijing and, later, Nanjing found it no easier to make their influence felt.

Sichuan provided many of the sparks that ignited the REPUBLICAN REVOLUTION of 1911. Local gentry, merchants and modern-minded military officers rose to power on the back of the late Qing constitutional reforms and shook the dynasty by resisting its attempts to gain control of local railway construction. For much of the early Republic, and for several years after Chiang Kai-shek established his government in Nanjing, Sichuan – Chongqing included – was in the grip of WARLORDS whose attachment to the central government was nominal at best. Chief among these satraps was Liu Xiang (1888–1938), who died shortly before Chiang moved his embattled government to Chongqing to escape the advancing Japanese.

The Generalissimo's arrival put the city on the map of national politics for the first time. His armies had sought to bring Sichuan to heel a few years earlier when they entered the province in pursuit of the Communists, then engaged on their LONG MARCH. But it was not until the central government moved into the fastness of Chongqing that the Nationalists were able to secure the strategic heartland of southwest China.

Even then it was not easy. The reasons Chongqing and its environs had been hard to control from the centre were precisely those which made the city an unsuitable, as well as an unlikely site for a capital. It was a world away from Chiang's traditional base of support, which lay in the rich, southeastern provinces. In the late 1930s, the nearest of the country's few railway lines was hundreds of miles away. Japan temporarily controlled most of the shipping on the lower Yangtze. The city was almost untouched by modern economic development and a stranger to modern ideas.

Yet during the war this sleepy, if important, trade centre was catapulted into prominence as the capital of 'Free China'. It was subjected to a vast influx of bureaucrats, ministries, politicians, military chiefs, diplomats, foreign reporters, and other supporters of China's war effort. And it endured devastating, if mercifully brief, Japanese bombing raids designed to bring Chiang's government to its knees.

Morale was sometimes low, corruption rife, and disillusion with Chiang often widespread in China's temporary capital. Contemporary observers, as well as some historians, compared Chongqing and what it stood for unfavourably with YANAN, where the Communists were seen to be building a new type of society. But Chiang's resistance did not crumble, and Chongqing did not fall, despite a dangerous Japanese thrust towards the city from the south in late 1944 (see SINO-JAPANESE WAR).

rapid construction, reluctant reform

Following Japan's defeat, the Nationalist government returned to Nanjing. Shortly beforehand, Chiang and MAO ZEDONG held talks in Chongqing in an effort to prevent renewed civil war and allow China to pursue construction in peace. The Chongqing negotiations bore little fruit: in a little over four years, Chiang was swept from power, and Communist armies 'liberated' his former capital.

Chongqing did not quite return to its former obscurity. That was impossible. But its not always happy moment of national glory had passed, and for political reasons the new rulers treated the episode as a distasteful memory. The city became the headquarters of the Southwest Regional Government which controlled the provinces of GUIZHOU, YUNNAN and Xikang (now incorporated into Sichuan) as well as Sichuan. Chongqing was built up as an important base for heavy industry, all of it state-owned and much of it controlled by the military. The fact that Mao believed China faced a serious security threat arising from the Vietnam War encouraged this process: in 1964 the Chairman called for the construction of a 'third line' of industry deep in southwest China. Chongqing and other Sichuan cities formed a new industrial belt in the interior.

This legacy left the city floundering in the age of reform. Chongqing's remoteness and poor communications were obstacles enough at a time when coastal cities were forging ahead. Its substantial but increasingly creaky industrial base made the task of reform even harder. It is only since the Yangtze was opened up to foreign trade and investment in 1992, and work on the THREE GORGES DAM officially began two years later, that the city has started to make up lost ground.

It has done so by presenting itself as the commercial and industrial hub of southwest China whose spokes extend down into the northern part of Southeast Asia. The idea is that the region's rich resources and cheap labour will lure investors away from the developed coastal cities and spread economic growth into the interior. The fact that ships of 10,000 tonnes will be able to reach Chongqing once the Three Gorges are flooded, should remove another of the city's chief obstacles to rapid development.

However, the dam is something of a mixed blessing for the city. Chongqing is responsible for resettling the bulk of those who must leave their homes as a result of the project – a difficult task administratively and one which carries political risks. And while Chongqing should benefit from the fact that ocean-going ships will have access to it all year round, doubts remain about the effects of silting and other problems on the city once the Gorges are flooded.

In 1997, the city was given the political weight its growing economic importance deserved: it joined Beijing, Tianjin and Shanghai to become China's fourth province-level municipality reporting directly to the central government. Chongqing is easily the biggest such administrative unit in China, in terms of both population and area. Its 32,000 square miles (83,000 sq kms) extend as far east along the Yangtze as the border with HUBEI and southwest to the borders with HUNAN and Guizhou. What remains to be seen is how well it copes with the burdens that accompany its new status: resettling migrants from the Gorges and helping narrow the disparities between the coast and the hinterland that have become such a prominent feature of China's development.

Christianity

The exact number of Christians in Mainland China at the start of the new century is unclear, but it is certainly larger than the figure of about 12 million Protestants and 4 million Catholics claimed by the government. Despite decades of persecution, continuing restrictions and occasional crackdowns, the faith is growing rapidly. On Sundays churches are packed in almost every major city; on feast days they are overflowing. Many churches are relatively wealthy; virtually all are in need of trained clergy. The number of believers remains a tiny percentage of the total population. But Christianity is spreading. Few provinces have proved immune to its influence.

missionaries and mandarins

These are remarkable developments and for a host of reasons. The history of Christianity in China is long but the faith at the heart of it exercised an often tenuous, frequently interrupted hold over society. It made its debut in China under the Tang dynasty (AD 613–907), several of whose emperors tolerated the presence of Nestorian missionaries. Persecutions crushed the movement in the ninth century, though there was a revival under Mongol, Yuan rule (1279–1368). The great Jesuit mission to Beijing of the seventeenth century re-established a connection between Court and Christianity, largely because of the missionaries' mastery of mathematics and mechanics. But once again, imperial favours were withdrawn, leaving Christianity to make an impact next in the context of the Western invasions of the nineteenth century and the UNEQUAL TREATIES.

A startling example of Christianity's renewed influence was its role in inspiring Hong Xiuquan (1813–64), leader of the Taiping Rebellion (1850–64). Hong, the self-declared brother of Jesus Christ, founded the 'Heavenly Kingdom of the Taipings', a dynasty whose radical ideas, popular support and powerful armies nearly toppled the Qing. Following suppression of the revolt, Christian teachings made a less dramatic but often unsettling impact on a people torn between the old gods of tradition and new, largely external forces of change.

The Communist victory in 1949 changed the nature of China's encounter with Christianity by ending more than a century and a half of continuous Western missionary effort. (See MISSIONARIES.) The missionary contribution was mixed: its exponents not only depended on the Unequal Treaties for their presence, but some of them displayed a racial superiority and self-righteousness that Chinese found galling. Yet these qualities were neither universal nor unique to the China mission. Missionaries pioneered the introduction of modern medicine and EDUCATION in addition to harvesting souls. Two of China's major twentieth-century leaders – SUN YAT-SEN and CHIANG KAI-SHEK – were Christians. So is LEE TENG-HUI, former president of Taiwan.

A few missionaries stayed on in China into the early 1950s, but their work was curtailed and some of them were persecuted. The schools, colleges, hospitals and other organizations they founded passed into government hands. Chinese Christians faced a greater dilemma: they were forced to chose between allegiance to the new state and its officially sanctioned versions of Protestantism and Catholicism, or take the more dangerous road of resistance to a secular authority set upon reshaping society.

church and state

Generally, Protestant churches chose the former. They were reorganized within the framework of a 'Three Self Patriotic Movement' (TSPM): self-support, self-government and self-propagation. The aim of the body was – and is, for it remains the leading official Protestant organization – to create a truly Chinese church free of links with 'imperialism'.

There was a Christian case for encouraging the growth of a national church in the early 1950s. But the Communist Party's determination to control every area of life, especially those in which groups linked closely with overseas organizations were active, was an important factor in the TSPM's creation. It was founded at a time of tension and fear

arising from the KOREAN WAR and the intensification of class struggle at home. Despite these pressures, not every Protestant church joined the new body. Several prominent pastors and their followers declined to do so on grounds of conscience. Some of them were persecuted as a result.

The severing of foreign links was a much more serious matter for Chinese Catholics, and most of them at first refused to support a 'patriotic church' set up to disavow the authority of Rome. Part of the problem arose from the Vatican's decision to retain diplomatic relations with the Nationalist government, which had fled to TAIWAN. More than half a century later, official ties between the Holy City and Taiwan (home of about 300,000 Catholics) remain an obstacle to rapprochement between their co-religionists in the Mainland and Rome.

Again, however, the issue for Beijing in the early 1950s was largely one of *control*: the Communist government was determined to break the power of a body that professed a higher allegiance than that due to the state and was subject to overseas authority. It did so by arresting scores of leading Catholics and, in 1957, setting up a Catholic Patriotic Association whose adherents appointed their own bishops and looked to Rome only for the most vague spiritual guidance. The most celebrated victim of this move was Gong Pinmei (1901–2000), Bishop of Shanghai. He was arrested in 1955, and spent the following 30 years in prison, the unyielding conscience of traditional Roman Catholicism in China.

These developments fostered the creation of four streams of Christianity in China by dividing both Protestants and Catholics into official and unofficial churches. Until the mid-1960s members of the latter suffered more for their faith than the former. But during the CULTURAL REVOLUTION, believers of every persuasion – 'official' and 'unofficial'; Christian and otherwise – were persecuted. Almost every church was closed, put to other use or pulled down. Believers were hounded, Bibles destroyed. Christians kept their faith alive by meeting in small groups at home. Even this was risky until the late 1970s, when the Communist Party opened China's doors to the outside world and embarked on reforms at home.

post-revolutionary revival

The new policies affected almost every area of life. Political tensions decreased; individuals began to enjoy more autonomy. Churches reopened, pastors emerged from prison, and the faithful resumed public worship. There was still some risk involved in practising Christianity in the new climate, but at least it was possible.

Greater religious tolerance and rapid economic change soon exposed a crisis of faith in China, especially on the part of the young. Beginning in the late 1980s materialist and competitive values engulfed society, eroding what remained of collective ideals, and fostering individual avarice as much as enterprise. Government attempts to combat these trends by stressing socialist morality have made little headway. MARXISM, though still the creed of the state, is a minority faith among the people.

Christianity, on the other hand, has acquired new appeal as a source of morality and eternal values in a changing world. For some, its very 'foreign-ness' is an attraction: it is a link to a wider, more 'modern' world. Others have sought solace in China's indigenous religions, or exotic varieties of them incorporating elements of Christianity (see RELIGIONS).

trials of faith

At the start of the new era many thousands of Protestants continue to worship outside the confines of the Three Self Patriotic Movement. They do so in 'underground churches' which are deprived of the legal protection enjoyed, at least in principle, by the official church. Their members are subject to government crackdowns, arrests and the confiscation of their property.

Some of these groups fall prey to heresy, a consequence of the rapid spread of faith, and much slower development of institutions and clergy required to ensure orthodoxy. In rural areas, Christian millenarian sects are active. Some of them have encouraged their members to abandon farming and prepare for the imminent coming of Christ. The official church and the government are often at one in opposing these groups. Sometimes they cooperate in breaking them up.

Hundreds of thousands of Catholics also remain at odds with the state by maintaining their loyalty to Rome. They worship semi-secretly. They, too, are subject to bouts of persecution.

A reunion of Chinese Catholicism with Rome seems distant. The Vatican's maintenance of diplomatic relations with Taipei is only one obstacle. The fact that the Chinese Church appoints its own bishops is another. Yet probably neither matters as much to Rome as China's policy on birth control, and the high incidence of abortion, sometimes forced abortion, in the People's Republic.

The Three Self Patriotic Movement and the Catholic Patriotic Association have legitimized Christianity in China even as they have struggled to control it. Their leaders are required to declare their support for the Communist Party, leaving most of their members to get on with the business of practising their faith. Yet the fact that many believers have chosen to worship outside the confines of these two bodies points to their failure to bridge the gulf between church and state. It also suggests they must change. This is unlikely, other than in the context of wider political and social reforms necessary to extend individual liberties. While such trends are apparent, they are far from being institutionalized. Until they are, Christianity in China will continue to coexist uneasily with a secular power which, though weaker than it was, is no less determined to set the agenda when it comes to values, morals and ideology.

civil aviation

Two decades of dramatic economic growth have turned China into an international force in civil aviation, transforming operations at home and luring foreign suppliers with the promise of sales. New domestic airlines, new aircraft, modern airports, and improved service have made flying a happier experience for China's rapidly growing number of air travellers. There have been disappointments along the way: the Mainland is still far from producing a commercially viable airliner; flight safety has often been at issue; and China's leaders, faced with a choice between Boeing of the United States, or Airbus, the European consortium, readily treat aircraft purchases as a tool of foreign policy. Yet if these developments mar China's aviation industry, they do not diminish its growing importance, either for the domestic economy or the wider world.

A struggle for mastery of the air was part of China's wider search for wealth and power during the last century. 'Modern' countries had fighters, bombers and airliners; China wanted the same – for defence and as part of a modern transport system. The first aviation factory was set up in Beijing in 1911. An air force was formed the following year. Certain WARLORDS boosted their military capability by acquiring small fleets of ageing fighters. In the 1930s, China set up small airlines with help from the United States and Germany. It also began small-scale joint operations in aircraft manufacturing.

Air combat on any scale made its debut in China during the SINO-JAPANESE WAR when the 'Flying Tigers' or American Volunteer Group led by Claire Chennault, a retired United States Air Corps officer, tried to blunt Japanese advances. After the war, United States planes ferried Chinese troops to east and northeast China to accept the Japanese surrender and check Communist expansion.

Air power played little or no part in the CIVIL WAR, though Chiang Kai-shek's control over most of China's aircraft enabled him and his senior officials to flee safely to Taiwan in 1949. They left behind a handful of passenger planes on the Mainland, and rather more in Hong Kong, where the British government, after first conceding they belonged to Beijing, bowed to pressure from Washington and handed them over to the United States.

All this was an unpromising basis on which to develop a civil aviation industry: Communist China had few planes and fewer pilots. Airports were rare and rudimentary. Hostility from the United States and its allies meant there could be few international flights.

Yet a powerful stimulus to the development of aviation existed in the form of the military, which was concerned to defend China's long borders and conquer Taiwan. This was impossible in the absence of air power. China needed a fleet of modern military aircraft and, in time, a civilian fleet to meet anticipated passenger demand, too. The military's influence on civil aviation was of long standing: the PEOPLE'S LIBERATION ARMY Air Force supplied most airline pilots and controlled all of China's airspace until the eve of the new century.

In the meantime China built a small civil fleet composed mainly of Soviet planes leased or bought during the era of friendship between Moscow and Beijing. Attempts to produce copies or 'clones' of these models during the secluded years of the Cultural Revolution did not result in commercial success.

Into Space

Advanced missile technology and low labour costs have made China a strong competitor in the commercial space industry. Occasional technical problems and growing American concern that China has acquired military secrets as a result of launching US-made satellites, have made it a controversial one. China's first commercial satellite launch – Asia-Sat-1, manufactured by Hughes of the US, and lifted into orbit by a Long March rocket – took place in 1990. Other successes followed, mainly from launch sites in Xichang, SICHUAN and Taiyuan in SHANXI. But a failed launch in 1995, when a Long March rocket crashed immediately after take-off, claiming several lives; and two more in 1996, one of which put a Hughes satellite into the wrong orbit, raised questions about the reliability of Chinese technology. Successful launches in 1997 and 1998 – the year in which China put a European satellite, Sino-Sat-1, made by Alcatel of France, into orbit for the first time – recovered lost ground. By the end of the decade China had captured almost 10 per cent of the international satellite launching business.

Then disaster of another kind struck: US allegations that China was using its commercial space programme to steal American military secrets. They were contained in the 'Cox Report' (named after Christopher Cox, Republican) to Congress of 1999 which detailed China's alleged theft of nuclear weapons technology. Sino-US cooperation in the space industry, dogged by American anxieties that it might allow Beijing to improve its long-range missile capabilities, entered the new era in the doldrums. The same was not true of China's determination to become the first developing country to launch a manned spacecraft. American allegations that China had 'stolen' space technology rather than 'developed' it only increased Beijing's resolve to put Chinese astronauts into orbit and, perhaps, send them to the moon. The launch and successful recovery of an unmanned spacecraft in November 1999 paved the way for China to become the third nation after the United States and the Soviet Union to put a man into orbit.

China bought Tridents from Britain in the 1970s – a breakthrough in its way. But this did not alter the fact that the development of civil aviation remained secondary to military aviation in government priorities. Air transport was for officials and the military not the public, who lacked either the means or perhaps the purpose to travel very often by air. Ordinary people, like most freight, travelled by rail, ship or road. Aviation was the poor cousin of the Mainland's modern transport system (see RAILWAYS; ROADS).

This changed when China did – when the People's Republic opened its doors to the outside world in the late 1970s and introduced capitalist-style reforms at home. Beijing began buying the latest aircraft, at first mostly Boeings. It also developed the infrastructure needed to service an increasing number of domestic and international destinations. The growing importance of the People's Republic in world affairs demanded this rapid expansion of the route network. So did vigorous economic growth and a burgeoning tourist industry.

It was at first less clear whether, as the government hoped, China's own aviation industry could supply most of these needs. The Communists' strong commitment to aircraft production resulted in many prototypes and several copies but few successes, at least in terms of commercially viable aircraft. Beginning in the late 1970s, numerous specialists in aviation and aeronautics were sent abroad. Much foreign equipment was purchased. China began assembling MD80s and MD90s, so called 'trunkliner' aircraft produced by McDonnell Douglas. It fought hard in the 1990s to win foreign backing for the manufacture of a short-haul 100-seater aircraft. Both of these projects collapsed: the MD operation because even China's own airlines preferred to buy aircraft made abroad rather than those assembled in China; the 100-seater because of arguments with Western partners over technology transfer and concern about the size of the market for this kind of plane.

At the start of the new century it is clear that China will have to content itself with subcontracting operations – the production of parts for leading foreign manufacturers – rather than build complete passenger aircraft on its own. Beijing has not abandoned this larger goal but has reluctantly conceded it cannot be realized soon. Until it is, Boeing and Airbus will compete for China's business with the outcome determined, to some extent, by Beijing's perceived need for good relations with Washington.

If the history of aircraft construction in China is largely one of failure, the growth of civil air traffic is another matter. Since 1986, when the Civil Aviation Administration of China (CAAC) became the regulator rather than the sole owner and operator of all civilian aircraft, the number of airlines has grown, the fleet expanded and the volume of passengers increased dramatically.

There are now dozens of airlines on the Mainland. Many are small regional carriers or tiny 'general purpose' airlines. Others, such as Air China, China Eastern and China Southern, have large, modern fleets of aircraft and operate lucrative domestic and international routes. The last two carriers are listed on the New York and Hong Kong stock exchanges. More are expected to be listed in future. Some will forge links with foreign airlines. Chinese interests control Air Macau, the airline founded to serve the airport in the former Portuguese territory, and have major stakes in Hong Kong-based Cathay Pacific and Dragonair.

Until the 1980s few Chinese travelled by air for leisure purposes. In the 1990s millions did so each year. At the close of the century there were almost 80 million passenger journeys by air compared with 16 million in 1990. Many were made by Taiwanese visiting the Mainland for business or pleasure. In the absence of direct flights, most travelled via Hong Kong or Macau. Airlines in both territories grew fat on revenues from Taiwanese in transit.

Lapses in safety and security accompanied this dramatic growth. A series of crashes in the mid-1990s suggested some Chinese operators were cutting corners on training and maintenance. International organizations advised against air travel on domestic Chinese carriers. A spate of hijacks to Taiwan by disgruntled Mainland passengers, and on one occasion by a Mainland pilot, further harmed China's reputation for safety. Many of these problems arose from the fact that such rapid expansion in air travel outstripped the growth of infrastructure to support it. At the close of the 1990s China improved its safety record and several airlines began to establish reputations for service and efficiency.

Yet the needs of China's civil aviation industry remain as conspicuous as its achievements. Beijing lacks adequate air traffic controllers, pilot training schools, and flight simulators. At the close of the century there were still no direct air routes between Europe or the United States and any of China's interior cities: traffic had to pass through Beijing, Shanghai, Hong Kong or Macau. Despite an economic slowdown caused by the Asian financial crisis, the Mainland needs new and better airports. And, before long, it must purchase new aircraft to satisfy the relentless movement of people – both within China and to and from the world beyond.

Civil War (1946–9)

'Never has a civil war been waged with so many troops over so vast an area. More than five million Nationalist and Communist soldiers have been engaged, and the victorious Communists have ended up thousands of miles from where they started. They have crushed all organized resistance.'

The Chinese Civil War delivered a vast country to an initially out-numbered, out-equipped rebel movement in a remarkably short time, as this contemporary observation by a British military official in Beijing makes clear. The Communist triumph transformed China's political fortunes; it also reshaped the international order, extending the Cold War to East Asia. For much of the following thirty years, China was in turmoil as its new masters pursued the revolution they won first on the battlefield in 1949.

old enmities in a new context

The KUOMINTANG (Nationalist Party or KMT) and the COMMUNIST PARTY had been at war since 1927, when their alliance broke down during the NORTHERN EXPEDITION. The KMT gained the upper hand in the 1930s, but CHIANG KAI-SHEK failed to wipe out his foes during the course of their LONG MARCH. Throughout the SINO-JAPANESE WAR, he devoted some of his best troops to keeping the Communists bottled up in north China. Japan's surrender in 1945 suggested that the time had come to deliver the knock-out blow.

American-led attempts to avoid the resumption of full-scale conflict soon came to naught. Understandings reached during a 1945 meeting in Chongqing between Chiang and MAO ZEDONG, and at a meeting of a Political Consultative Conference a few weeks later, failed to materialize. Neither side could agree terms for the creation of a coalition government or the unification of their respective armies into a national force. Ceasefires brokered by General George C. Marshall, President Truman's special envoy to China, floundered in the face of both sides' pursuit of military advantage.

The consequences of this for relations between China and the UNITED STATES were disastrous. After the Second World War, Washington was keen to see the emergence of a peaceful, unified, democratic China, an aim it is still pursuing at the start of the twenty-first century. In the context of the mid-1940s this was believed to require direct US mediation to stop the KMT-CCP conflict dragging on indefinitely and ruining the prospects for national reconstruction.

Such mediation pleased none of the parties. KMT leaders saw it as a waste of time better used on the battlefield. They resented US demands for sweeping democratic reforms – a feeling shared by their Communist foes years later when they, too, having won the Mainland, came under American pressure to end one-party rule. In the late 1940s the Communists complained that the US was both mediator and major supporter of the Nationalist government.

As indeed it was. The US airlifted government troops to east and north China after the war to allow them to take over from the Japanese. With a brief interruption, America supplied arms, ammunition and finance to the Nationalists throughout the Civil War. Mediation was no more popular in the United States, where its failure led to painful soul-searching and, in the McCarthy era, the pursuit of scapegoats.

Military conflict resumed in earnest in mid-1946 with government offensives to clear Manchuria (China's three northeastern provinces) and north China of Communist troops. Chiang, whose armies were more numerous and better equipped than those of the Communists, believed victory was close at hand. The Americans might be unhappy with his government, but they could hardly fail to give him at least limited backing in a fight against Communism. Moscow, meanwhile, could be discounted as a potential ally of the Chinese Communists by the terms of a treaty of friendship and alliance it had signed with the Nationalist government (see SOVIET UNION).

Chiang was proved wrong on all these counts. He greatly overestimated his own strength and underestimated that of the Communists. Washington proved unwilling to write him a blank cheque – at least until the start of the KOREAN WAR in 1950. And the Soviet Union, while reluctant to believe that the Communists could win, helped make it possible by allowing them into the parts of Manchuria its troops had occupied at the close of the Second World War, and enabling them to acquire supplies of Japanese arms and ammunition.

three decisive battles

Despite these developments, the first full year of the war went Chiang's way. Government troops controlled the railway lines linking Beijing with the major centres of north, northwest and northeast China, and greatly expanded the area under their control, particularly in Manchuria. The symbolic high point of the offensive was the conquest of YANAN, the Communist's headquarters.

From then on, Nationalist fortunes declined precipitously. Tactical ineptitude, factionalism, CORRUPTION, grave economic mismanagement and simple lack of purpose scuppered the war effort on all fronts. The 'Mandate of Heaven', the idea familiar in China that a government depends on broad popular acceptance for its survival, was slipping away.

The Communists, by contrast, had a clear mission: the radical restructuring of society, and the policies of LAND REFORM, redistribution of urban wealth and commitment to revolutionary violence needed to carry it out. For many war-weary Chinese, this lent the Party considerable prestige. Even for sceptics, the Communists had the considerable advantage of not being the KMT.

Yet the Communist Party won power on the battlefield – the arbiter of Chinese politics since the collapse of the Qing dynasty – rather than in the minds of the people. It did so in three massive set-piece battles waged by the PEOPLE'S LIBERATION ARMY that were a world away from the guerrilla tactics deployed earlier against the Japanese and championed later as examples of revolutionary 'people's war'. Superior mobility, communications, command and the recruitment of civilians for transport and other support won the day. So did the rapid assimilation of defecting Nationalist troops dismayed and demoralized by corruption and ineptitude within their own command.

The first of these battles was in Manchuria. Chiang had never ruled this strategic area which, under the Japanese, had been home for some of China's most advanced INDUSTRY. His determination to control it led him to commit, and then lose, some of his best forces to LIN BIAO, the most brilliant of Mao's commanders. Lin's lightning strikes and constant mobility outwitted government commanders whose armies were soon holed up in major cities and deprived of reinforcement and supply. By November 1948, the Communists had conquered all of Manchuria, and Lin was ready to move south to 'choke' BEIJING and TIANJIN into submission. Fierce fighting occurred near Tianjin, as well as northwest and southwest of Beijing, but in January 1949 the Nationalist commander surrendered the former capital without firing a shot.

The battle of Huai-Hai – so called because it took place in an area bounded to the north by the east–west railway known as the Long-Hai line and the Huai River in the south – was joined about the same time. More than one million men were engaged and it resulted in a stunning victory for the Communists. China north of the Yangtze was now in Communist hands and the rest of the country at their mercy.

The final collapse of Nationalist rule on the Mainland took a further year. Chiang resigned the presidency in January 1949, handing over to vice-president LI ZONGREN, who unsuccessfully sued for peace with the Communists. Li's attempts to mount a last-ditch resistance also failed, largely because Chiang kept power in his own hands and moved troops and equipment, along with the government's gold supplies and the treasures of the Forbidden City, to TAIWAN, where he sought to rebuild his government and launch a new campaign to recover the Mainland.

The Communists crossed the Yangtze in April 1949 and took Nanjing and Shanghai. Their armies forged south and southwest, driving the remains of the Nationalist government out of a series of 'temporary' capitals and 'liberating' them just days later. The collapse of Nationalist power was no less sudden in northwest China and TIBET which Chiang had never controlled, but which soon succumbed to the PLA, albeit in special circumstances. With the conquest of HAINAN ISLAND, the second largest of China's islands, in April 1950, it seemed only a matter of time before Taiwan would fall and Nationalist rule would end completely.

China's unfinished Civil War

Chiang was spared this indignity by the outbreak of the Korean War. While the United States had effectively washed its hands of China by this time, it was not prepared to see Communism make further advances – in Asia or in Europe. President Truman ordered the Seventh Fleet into the Taiwan Straits to defend Chiang's redoubt. The US also led a United Nations force to rebuff North Korea's invasion of South Korea. Soon, the US was at war with Chinese 'volunteers' on the Korean Peninsula, and Taiwan was transformed from the last hide-out of a decrepit regime into a valuable ally of the Free World. The Nationalist government was re-supplied with US weapons and aid, and was soon turned, by treaty, into a strategic defence partner.

While these sudden developments saved Chiang's government from having to defend itself against a full-scale invasion from the Mainland, they did not end the Civil War. The Communists subjected Quemoy (Jinmen), the largest offshore island held by Taiwan, to bombardment in 1954 and even more sustained attack in 1958. The two 'Straits Crises', and in particular the second, were important chapters in the Cold War in East Asia as well as further episodes in the Chinese Civil War.

This war remains unfinished, despite Beijing's preference, expressed publicly in 1981, to reunify China peacefully. China's opening to the outside world and the end of authoritarian rule in Taiwan ushered in an era of détente across the Straits. The rapid growth of Taiwanese investment in the Mainland and growing unofficial contacts between the 'two Chinas' at first pointed to an end to hostilities and even possible reunification. Yet rapid democratization in Taiwan has been both cause and consequence of the determination of local people to, at the very least, retain their separate identity. Beijing has tried to prevent Taiwan 'slipping away' by warning that it will crush by force any attempt to make the island independent. An example of its determination to do so occurred in March 1996. China staged missile tests and war games near its 'renegade province' to coincide with the island's first direct presidential elections. In a tense but fortunately only partial replay of the situation in 1950 and 1958, the United States sent two carrier forces to the region to warn Beijing off. While tension quickly subsided, Beijing's determination to bring Taipei to heel – and the island's equally strong resolve to remain free – continue to cast a shadow over security in the region and complicate Sino-US relations (see TAIWAN).

clans

A primary, age-old form of social organization in China, clans have survived Communist Party campaigns to collectivize their land and temples, criticize and persecute their leaders, ban their rituals, and destroy their genealogies. More than that, they have grown in strength with the break-up of agricultural communes and the general weakening of state authority in the countryside that began in the early 1980s. Beijing frets at this revival of 'feudalism' but is unable to do much about so powerful a resurgence of tradition.

Clans are lineage organizations formed of families with the same surname who trace their origins to a common ancestor. They provide a focus for loyalty and the protection of group interests. They also supply a folk memory and sense of belonging reflected in elaborately maintained genealogies. Clan leaders once exercised considerable power. Clan life was celebrated in ancestor worship, marriage rituals, funeral rites and other, often expensive, public ceremonies.

The Communist Party despised clans for the same reasons they did SECRET SOCIETIES: they were closed, conservative organizations which crossed class frontiers and obscured the divide between landlord and peasant. LAND REFORM weakened the hold of both over rural life in the 1950s. The sequestration of clan properties and a ban on 'reactionary' rituals that followed undermined popular religion, too (see RELIGIONS). New units of loyalty – the production team, brigade and commune – were set up, extending state power deep into the countryside.

They endured until communal farming was abandoned in the early 1980s in favour of the 'household responsibility system' (see AGRICULTURE). What happened next showed that clans were not dead but sleeping. As private farming returned in everything but name, 'natural' social organizations gained the upper hand over 'artificial' ones set up by the Party and state. Peasants, free at last from the turbulence of politics, faced the new challenge of market forces and competition, displacement and change. The desire for a sense of community and belonging was as strong as ever. Clan activities revived almost everywhere. Genealogies, including the names of clan members overseas or in Hong Kong, Taiwan and Macau, were rewritten and rituals revived to celebrate the rhythms of rural life. Clans sometimes even managed to 'capture' local Party or state organs, promptly excluding 'outsiders' from the ranks. Clan feuds were also common: they occasionally involved pitched battles between villagers and villages.

Geographic mobility, urbanization, improved education and greater access to the outside world may weaken the hold of clans over time – though this has yet to happen in Taiwan. In the meantime their revival on the Mainland shows they fulfil a need that cannot easily be satisfied by other forms of social organization in China's still traditional and largely fragmented economy.

Confucianism

As an official creed of state, Confucianism collapsed with the QING DYNASTY in 1911. As an intellectual orthodoxy, it was demolished eight years later by the MAY FOURTH MOVEMENT. As a diffuse set of values which frame instincts and govern personal behaviour, it remains embedded in the hearts and minds of almost every Chinese, despite – and perhaps because of – the experience of Communism.

Confucius (Kongzi, 551–479 BC) taught that strict adherence to ceremony and ritual in social and political affairs were the only guarantors of harmony. The cardinal principles were *ren* – 'benevolence' – and *shu* – 'reciprocity' – values exemplified by the ancients. An ideal past was the touchstone for the understanding and interpretation of new knowledge. The purpose of individual development, like that of the polity itself, was to attain, and keep, the values of a 'golden age'. Ultimately, politics, like life itself, was a matter of morality. The golden rule was: do unto others what you would like done to you.

Relations within the family were strictly hierarchical: sons subordinate to fathers, women to men (see FAMILY; WOMEN). Absolute loyalty was enjoined; so was filial piety. Both found expression in ancestor worship, the lifeblood of China's popular RELIGIONS, which Confucianism refined and reinforced.

Thus the orientation of Confucianism was backward-looking and conservative, a fact that led many to jettison it in the early twentieth century as a major cause of China's inability to modernize and keep pace with the West. An exception was KANG YOUWEI, the brilliant if eccentric scholar, who reinterpreted Confucius to show that the Sage was an advocate of reform rather than conservatism. It was a view which found few adherents: Confucianism was the chief intellectual casualty of the May Fourth Movement, despite imaginative attempts by Liang Shuming (1893–1988), a professor of philosophy, to transform it into an 'inner religion'.

Yet the legacy could not be rooted out so easily. Confucianism was much more than an intellectual discipline: it was an approach to life, a way of behaving. And it manifests itself in 'typical Chinese' personal behaviour, including respect for one's family, age and authority, and a tendency to emphasize personal relations rather than rules and regulations in achieving objectives. It had power at the level of policy even in the later republic: Confucianism informed developments such as the 'New Life Movement' sponsored by CHIANG KAI-SHEK in the 1930s to instil self-discipline and civilized behaviour in his subjects.

After 1949, the Communists denounced Confucius and all he stood for as feudal. Certainly MARXISM, the new creed of state, was at odds with the old. It emphasized struggle, conflict and perfection in the future whereas the Sage insisted upon cosmic and social harmony, moderation and the glories of the past. Yet these major differences of principle were not always reflected in political behaviour. The Party's elevation of role models – in this case 'labour heroes' – deemed worthy of emulation, and the obviously related belief that people could improve and cultivate themselves owed something to the Confucian approach. At the very least Chinese Communism shared with Confucianism the idea that education can transform an individual's outlook and behaviour.

However, Confucianism came under savage attack during the CULTURAL REVOLUTION. Red Guards razed every symbol of Confucius in Qufu, the Sage's hometown in SHANDONG, and elsewhere in the country. The offensive later took a bizarre turn. In 1974 the 'GANG OF FOUR' staged a campaign to 'criticize Lin Biao, criticize Confucius'. The real target of this odd pairing was neither the Sage nor LIN BIAO, Mao's former comrade-in-arms. Instead it was the dying ZHOU ENLAI, whom radicals accused of wanting to return to old ways and rehabilitate officials toppled in the Cultural Revolution.

During the late 1980s and 1990s, the Party adopted a more respectful view of Confucius, arguing that some of his doctrines, though expounded in the sixth century BC, still had relevance for contemporary China. As a result the Qufu mansion, temple and burial ground of the Kong family, the Sage's descendants, were restored and opened to the public. The new message of moderation had the additional advantage of bringing in money.

To some extent, the Party's new appraisal of Confucius was related to the growing appeal of ASIAN VALUES. To some extent, it was a reflection of the fact that faith in Marxism and socialism was fading fast. People, and perhaps more particularly their leaders, needed something to believe in and rally round. Confucianism – an indisputably Chinese creation with a magnificent civilization to its credit – seemed a good candidate, if handled carefully. It offered balm to an authoritarian state in ideological crisis. Moreover, as the common inheritance of Chinese everywhere, it could prove useful in pursuing national unity with TAIWAN. After their flight to the island in 1949 the Nationalists were quick to venerate Confucius as an emblem of a great civilization under threat from Communism. The Sage's birthday, 28 September, is still celebrated on the island as Teacher's Day.

More adventurous philosophers on the Mainland have advocated Confucianism as a solution to what they perceive as an intellectual and moral crisis in the West. Participants at a seminar in 1995 were told that the problem with Western culture was that science and religion were no longer compatible. 'If Westerners' morals and their values of life were based on another humanism rather than on CHRISTIANITY, the above contradiction would not arise,' said one of the speakers. 'The right solution is Confucianism, because it is a non-religious humanism that can provide a basis for morals and the value of life. It will thrive particularly well in the next century, and will replace modern and contemporary Western culture.' The implications of these remarks for Marxism, both in China and the West, have yet to be explored in the People's Republic – at least in public.

corruption

The scourge of Chinese public life for centuries, corruption helped sink the QING DYNASTY in 1911 and sped the KUOMINTANG to defeat in the CIVIL WAR. The Communists at first got the better of governance's ancient foe but the victory was shortlived: Deng Xiaoping's free market reforms spawned corruption on a scale that sparked massive protests and threatened Party rule. Corruption still stalks the Mainland, scarring many aspects of life and souring relations between government and people.

power and riches

China's traditional emphasis on personalities rather than institutions, on customary practices rather than 'objective' law, on *guanxi* (personal relationships) rather than merit or free competition, provides fertile ground for corruption. The fact that power tends to be the route to wealth, rather than wealth the route to power, makes the soil richer still. Tight control over the MEDIA and the lack of an independent judiciary, neutralize two powerful weapons against corruption (see LAW).

Under every Chinese regime, public office brought perquisites. Under most, there was no surer route to riches – or, if it was at issue, survival – than cultivating those in office. The effects of all this on the bureaucracy are clear from the tendency of governments, past and present, to make the championing of honest officials a main plank of their propaganda. Leaders and officials who spurn personal advantage in the service of the people are as powerful as popular ideals as they are rare in practice.

This state of affairs has proved surprisingly resistant to political change. Corruption has long been part of the very fibre of Chinese society: a social as well as a political revolution is required to root it out.

This was more than the Kuomintang could accomplish during its years on the Mainland. Corruption blighted the Nationalists the moment they began to rule a newly united China in 1928 after long years of struggle. There was a measure of idealism in Nanjing, the new capital, and there were upright Nationalist officials. But whatever favourable impression they made on the public was outweighed by the recurrence of 'traditional practices' in the provinces and new ones in the capital. The 'four big families' of the Nationalist regime – headed by Song Tzu-wen (T. V. Soong, 1894–1971), Kung Hsiang-hsi (H. H. Kung, 1880–1967), Chen Kuo-fu (1892–1951) and Chen Li-fu (1900–), all of them close to CHIANG KAI-SHEK – amassed personal fortunes thanks to their government positions and control over China's modern banking sector.

Corruption sapped the Nationalists' every endeavour, from state building to resisting Japan; from controlling inflation to fighting the Communists. It shortened Chiang's rule and ensured, at least at the time, that few ordinary people regretted his demise. Many might be apprehensive about some aspects of Communist Party rule, but the prospect of a new, 'clean' government was something to look forward to.

after 1949: curbs and complaints

So it proved. There was less corruption in public life in the early 1950s than the late 1940s. Official graft was a target of one of the new regime's earliest mass campaigns; the 'three-anti movement' of 1951 which attacked corruption, waste and excessive bureaucracy in the cities. The 'five-anti movement' the following year focused on similar ills, though with a view to breaking the capitalists as a class rather than simply correcting their bad ways.

Whatever the effects of these movements, they neither ended corruption nor silenced complaints about it. The public took up the issue during the brief relaxation in political life afforded by the ONE HUNDRED FLOWERS MOVEMENT of 1956, and the Party railed against it constantly in the official media. For Mao Zedong, casting around for a new revolutionary strategy in the early 1960s, corruption was an inevitable product of the bureaucratic socialism China had adopted from the Soviet Union. Only a 'true' revolution – a Cultural Revolution – could change this, along with much else that was wrong with the country under its 'revisionist' leaders.

Mao's obsession with revolution in the 1960s and 1970s cost China dear, not least because his failure to deliver a better society destroyed faith in the Communist ideals that had sustained and *restrained* people during earlier years of his rule. It weakened the moral defences of the public just when China's leaders, officials and ordinary citizens were exposed to new temptations afforded by Deng Xiaoping's free market reforms and the Open Door. Suddenly, personal enrichment was not just possible, it was obligatory. Hard work and personal initiative were the approved routes to wealth, but they were not the only ones. In the harsh new competitive environment of the 1980s, corruption flourished on a scale not seen since the last days of Nationalist rule on the Mainland.

reform era: a world of corruption

Public anger mounted accordingly. The improved living standards generated by reform were welcome; the fact that those with political connections used them to amass fortunes, often through illegal means, was infuriating. Evidence of the abuse of power was legion. It could be found in the SPECIAL ECONOMIC ZONES, where officials took advantage of tax exemptions and weak supervision to earn huge sums of money through trade and other businesses. The illegal sale by the authorities in HAINAN ISLAND in 1985 of thousands of vehicles imported at low duty was merely the most spectacular example. It was found in the new companies run by 'princelings', or offspring of the Party elite, bent on turning their revolutionary lineage to profit. And it was encountered in daily life where dual prices – one set by the state, the other by the market – fuelled inflation *and* corruption. Demands for an end to both were major factors in the rise of the TIANANMEN SQUARE DEMOCRACY MOVEMENT.

Once it had crushed the protests, Beijing took a tougher line against the abuse of power. The children of high officials, though not of the revolutionary elders actually running the country, were banned from engaging in business. Senior leaders abandoned their Mercedes for less ostentatious sedans. A few leading officials were sacked in an apparent attempt to appease the public without unsettling the bureaucracy. At best these were half-hearted measures, and they were soon undermined by Deng's trip through south China in 1992 which gave new impetus to growth and an even bigger one to corrupt means of achieving it. The get-rich-quick mentality that engulfed much of China in the months that followed tore at the fabric of society and corrupted the institutions of state.

This came about because of a remarkable absence of restraint. Government and Party officials at almost every level, tired of low wages and less public esteem, marketed their power, forming companies, running businesses and selling their services to anyone who would pay for them. Often there was little choice in the matter. Genuine entrepreneurs could achieve little without a powerful official on their side; bribes and gifts running into millions of *yuan* were essential business costs for many during the 1990s.

The commercialization and corruption of official life knew few bounds. Numerous ministries, commissions, bureaux and academic institutions formed business arms to which they readily devoted the state's resources. The PEOPLE'S LIBERATION ARMY had done so long before Deng headed south. During the late 1980s and early 1990s it supplemented China's traditional defence industries with military-controlled pharmaceutical factories, real estate companies, luxury hotels, night clubs and discos. The police were not far behind. It sometimes seemed as though fewer resources were dedicated to catching criminals than cooperating with them; less time was spent patrolling the streets than making money.

Many of these commercial activities were illegal. China's flourishing sex industry of the 1990s owed much to police protection and official connivance. It could hardly be otherwise in a world where Tao Siju (1935–), minister of public security, shocked a press conference – and public opinion in Hong Kong – by saying that some Triads, Chinese underworld gangsters, were 'patriotic', and that the Communist government had cooperated with them in the past (see SECRET SOCIETIES). Official propriety seemed to have evaporated. The government could no longer afford to pay the country's overstaffed bureaucracy. Officials, vexed by the climate of materialism enveloping society, had to turn their hands to any activity likely to keep them afloat or, better still, ahead in the race to get rich.

The 'princelings' were particularly unrestrained. Foreign investors, anxious to establish links to the centre of power in Beijing, sought them out as partners. This did not stop many international companies complaining that corruption made life costly and unpleasant for them in the People's Republic (see FOREIGN TRADE AND INVESTMENT).

Ordinary citizens were on the giving rather than the receiving end. Most could not accomplish even commonplace tasks without 'sweetening' the officials who still dispensed most of the services in China's half-reformed economy. For many, the loss of faith in the government appeared total. There was little premium on honesty outside the pages of the *People's Daily*; and though China's rapid growth was remarkable and welcome, much of it came with a stench that attached itself to those who came into contact with it. Suggestions that corruption oiled the wheels of commerce and bureaucracy overlooked the fact this made both less efficient and more costly.

curbing excesses

In the mid-1990s the Party tried to reverse this state of affairs with a new campaign against graft. There were several controversial victims and some prominent ones, including the head of Beijing's giant Capital Iron and Steel Works, and his son, both of whom were close to the family of Deng Xiaoping. The father, Zhou Guanwu (1918–), already in his late seventies, was quietly retired. The son, Zhou Beifang, who had business links with Li Ka-shing, the Hong Kong tycoon, was jailed.

None of the victims was so controversial or prominent as CHEN XITONG, the Party boss of Beijing, who in 1995 became the first member of the Politburo to be sacked for corruption. He was sentenced to 16 years in jail – but only after a three-year interlude that suggested nervousness on the part of the authorities over how to deal with such an important case.

At the end of the century, the Party launched another campaign. The targets were rampant smuggling and the huge business empires run by the army, the police and the judiciary. President Jiang Zemin displayed uncharacteristic boldness by suddenly ordering all three to cease commercial operations and concentrate on their professional duties. The desirability of this was not in doubt. Its feasibility was another matter. The only certainty was that none of the three arms responsible for China's security could afford to lose their extra-budgetary revenues.

If these high-profile campaigns temporarily checked the tide of official graft they have yet to turn it back. Corruption will flourish in the Mainland as long as there is an absence of moral or ethical restraint; as long as personal relationships remain at the heart of society; and as long as the government retains its discretionary power. Political reform, a free media and the creation of a genuinely independent anti-graft body, along the lines of Hong Kong's Independent Commission Against Corruption, would go some way to curbing the last of these problems. They did so in Hong Kong and Taiwan. But they would also constitute an assault on the leadership of the Communist Party, the cardinal principle of politics in Beijing. This is intolerable for a Party which, though threatened by corruption more than any other single problem, still insists on 'correcting its own mistakes'.

Cultural Revolution (1966–76)

The 'Great Proletarian Cultural Revolution', a cataclysmic movement launched by MAO ZEDONG, was not particularly 'proletarian', and was about 'culture' largely in the sense that it sought to destroy much of what existed. But it was truly 'revolutionary' for it toppled many of Mao's comrades and destroyed the institutional base of Communist Party rule (see CHINESE COMMUNIST PARTY). It also marked a departure from the norms of civilized behaviour, producing cruelty and oppression on a horrific scale. Millions of Chinese suffered; many behaved pitifully and disgracefully. Nearly 40 years after it broke out, the movement continues to stain the Party and nation that gave birth to it.

Mao on revolution and revisionism

The origins of the movement lay in Mao's unhappiness with measures taken to recover from the GREAT LEAP FORWARD. The recovery had been swift and effective: by 1963 the worst effects of the famine were over and the economy was responding to the reintroduction of material incentives. Revolutionary goals became more sober. Professionalism and expertise, cast aside during the Leap, came back into vogue. Politics was as ubiquitous as ever, but no longer in command.

Mao looked askance at these developments. While most Party leaders rejoiced in the return of discipline and order, he saw only the growth of bureaucracy and hierarchy. Where intellectuals took comfort from the fact that their skills were valued again, the Chairman could see only the gulf between those who worked with their heads and those who worked with their hands. As rural industry floundered along with the Communes that fostered it, Mao was reminded of the unbridgeable gap between town and countryside. He saw corruption, mediocrity and injustice everywhere. Despite bitter polemics with Moscow, China's version of socialism was uncomfortably close to that of the SOVIET UNION. The purpose of the Revolution was to change mankind, not merely change the economy. Human nature, and particularly the nature of those at the top of the Party, was proving immune to change.

Free of the burdens of state since 1959, when he gave up the presidency to LIU SHAOQI, Mao developed theories to explain what had gone wrong. The Revolution was going into reverse.

The bourgeoisie were staging a comeback. Communist leaders, including his closest comrades, were 'revisionists' and 'capitalists'. Soon they would be declared 'traitors and scabs'.

Post-Leap attempts to radicalize the revolution met with mixed success. The 'Socialist Education Movement' (1963) to inculcate collectivist values in the countryside; campaigns to 'Learn from Daqing' (1963) and 'Learn from Dazhai' (1964), respectively an oil field in HEILONGJIANG, and an agricultural production brigade in SHANXI where success was attributed to hard work and self-reliance; and a movement to 'Learn from the PEOPLE'S LIBERATION ARMY', (1964), which, under LIN BIAO, had become an exemplar of revolutionary purity, all had an impact. But it fell far short of Mao's hopes. Something else was needed. In his early seventies at the time, Mao felt he had to provide it before it was too late.

'bombarding the headquarters'

His response was a frontal assault on the leaders, institutions, and values of the Communist state – a state he had done more than anyone to create. The Chairman needed allies for this cause. He found them in Lin Biao and the army; in Chen Boda (1904–89), the chief interpreter of his 'thought'; in JIANG QING, his third wife, who wanted to reshape the 'dead' world of Chinese culture; and among a small group of literary theorists and ideologues eager to humble the old guard. China's international isolation allowed these factions to concentrate on the revolution at home.

The foot soldiers of the movement were millions of ordinary people, many of them young, who chafed at controls governing almost every aspect of life. Resentment at privilege, frustration with authority, resistance to orthodoxy and convention were widespread. There was a strong desire to speak out, especially on the part of those whose lives had been disadvantaged in the new society by their 'bad class background' in the old. Such people were prominent among the Red Guards, the shock troops of the Cultural Revolution. They saw in Mao a messianic leader, one far above the fray of bureaucratic politics, a great teacher – both of the Chinese and of oppressed peoples everywhere.

The assault began in the world of culture and EDUCATION. Mao and his allies detected the dead hand of tradition, foreign influence – and implied criticism of the Chairman himself – everywhere. Their celebrated first target was a play, *The Dismissal of Hai Rui*, by Wu Han (1909–69), which used the example of a virtuous official in Ming times who scolded his emperor to praise PENG DEHUAI's challenge to Mao over the Great Leap in 1959. Party leaders at first resisted demands for a shake-up. They wanted debate kept within bounds. This was not what Mao had in mind at all. His purpose was to wage a real revolution, one that pitted the people against the Party, whatever the cost.

Mao soon got his way when he returned to Beijing in the summer of 1966 following a celebrated swim in the Yangtze designed to demonstrate his physical prowess. Manoeuvres in the Politburo paved the way for the downfall of PENG ZHEN, mayor and Party boss of Beijing, and then of Liu and DENG XIAO-PING, chief opponents at the top of the Party to Mao's radical approach to revolution. Massive Red Guard rallies in Tiananmen Square signalled the start of attacks on 'enemies of the people' wherever they might hide.

A heady sense of freedom engulfed those who believed they were carrying out the wishes of the Chairman, now elevated to godlike status. Fear, persecution, torture and death were the lot of their targets. Homes were ransacked and property confiscated. Most universities and many schools stopped classes. Teachers were hounded and humiliated. Party officials were made to wear dunces' caps, 'struggled against' and dismissed. Liu Shaoqi, once Mao's successor, was declared a 'traitor, renegade and scab'. He died in prison in 1969. Deng, Party secretary at the time of his fall, escaped physical mistreatment but was banished to the countryside where he tended pigs, repaired tractors and waited for better times.

They were a long time coming. The Cultural Revolution was not a mere protest movement that would soon subside. It was a campaign by the radicals to seize power; an effort to topple those in authority everywhere who favoured the 'bourgeois line' of seeking to make China rich and strong before, or perhaps rather than, making it 'Red'. First in Shanghai and then elsewhere, violence erupted as radical organizations fought each other for control of the formal apparatus of power. In many parts of the country civil administration collapsed. Mao ordered the army to 'support the Left' and end the chaos. Established organs of power were to give way to 'revolutionary committees' formed from the PLA, the radical factions and local Party members.

The army's direct involvement in political administration was a departure from Communist tradition and one that inflamed the political ambitions of Lin Biao, whom Mao now regarded as his number two. More immediately, it added to the confusion and violence because it was by no means clear which of the many factions battling for power in the provinces qualified as the 'Left'. Several local commanders, such as Chen Zaidao (1909–) in Wuhan, tended to support the less radical groups among those claiming to represent Mao's will. But in Beijing, where Lin and the radicals led by Jiang Qing, Zhang Chunqiao and Yao Wenyuan – three members of what would soon become known as the 'GANG OF FOUR' – were in the ascendant, different views prevailed. As a result, Wuhan, in common with other parts of the country, saw skirmishes on a scale worthy of civil war. Other places were even worse hit, GUANGXI among them. There, rival groups armed with artillery destroyed buildings and killed thousands. Years later, even darker goings-on were revealed to have taken place: a Chinese researcher documented scores of cases of cannibalism in Guangxi where the masses joyously killed and consumed the flesh of their enemies to settle old scores.

Behaviour of this kind made the burning and looting by Red Guards in 1967 of Britain's mission in Beijing seem a mild transgression. In fact they were of a piece. They represented different aspects of the breakdown in civilized values, restraint, rationality and human decency which marked the Cultural Revolution. No one was safe – except Mao. Anyone with a Western connection, however remote and insignificant, was at risk. So, too, were those who had followed the Party all their lives, as well as those who had absolutely nothing to do with politics. Mao and the radicals taught that China was besieged by enemies without, and at the mercy of fiends within. Such official paranoia created a perfect environment for the violence of Communist politics, blind worship of a leader, and the petty hatreds of feudalism to do their work.

Lin Biao: the beginning of the end

By 1969, the worst of the violence was over. Mao, ratcheting up and then retreating from radicalism the better to stay in power, demobilized the Red Guards, many of whom were sent to the countryside to temper their enthusiasm for revolution with a little farm work. Urban cadres were rusticated, too. In front of bemused and usually poverty-stricken peasants, they were sent to rural training classes to purify their class outlook. In Beijing, Lin Biao and the radicals were capitalizing on their gains.

Though Lin's were greater than anyone else's, the vice-premier was uneasy. Playing Mao's deputy was dangerous – witness the fate of Liu. Attempts to solidify his position did nothing but increase Mao's suspicions. Few knew it at the time, but tension between the two men over the place of the People's Liberation Army in the new order and the future of the Revolution was growing. It came to a head in September 1971 when Lin and his allies allegedly attempted to assassinate the Chairman. They were killed in a plane crash in Mongolia, apparently while trying to flee to the Soviet Union.

The peculiar circumstances of Lin's death were as difficult to explain to the Chinese people as the reasons why a man long regarded as Mao's closest student was suddenly discovered to have been an even worse traitor than Liu Shaoqi. Many Chinese would recall how this news shattered their faith in the Chairman, just as it did their belief in his Cultural Revolution. However, Mao – glimpses of his own mortality growing stronger with each passing year – had not done with radicalism. Lin, like Liu, had failed him. So be it. He was still determined that power should pass to someone committed to the broad goals of the Cultural Revolution and not a 'revisionist' like Deng.

He settled first on Wang Hongwen (1934–92), a trade unionist from Shanghai who had risen to prominence during the 1967 upheavals, and who would soon become the fourth member of the 'Gang of Four'. Wang was catapulted up the Party hierarchy where he came to rest in the number three position, just below ZHOU ENLAI.

Wang was thus in exalted company as far as experience, prestige and popularity were concerned. In Zhou he also faced a formidable foe. For while the official myth of the 'saintly Zhou', protecting ministers and intellectuals from the violence of the Red Guards, has not survived scholarly analysis outside China, there is no doubt that the premier's methods were different from those of Mao – even if it is not clear that his goals necessarily were. But it was plain that Zhou, like Mao (on occasions)

was at odds with the radicals led by Jiang Qing, and that he wanted a return to political stability and economic development. His reward was to be the target of a bizarre movement launched in 1974 to 'Criticize Lin Biao, Criticize Confucius'. Zhou was said to be a Confucian because of his desire to 'restore old families', that is, bring back disgraced cadres (see CONFUCIANISM).

It was cancer that toppled Zhou, not Confucianism, and this presented another challenge to Mao's attempt to arrange the succession. Wang Hongwen was clearly not up to the job of running the government. Deng Xiaoping, on the other hand, was. Painful though it might be to Mao and others, he would have to be brought back into the apex of power for, in the present situation, he was almost indispensable.

During a year of running the country before Zhou died in January 1976, Deng sought to shift the focus from politics to production and break the spell of class struggle the Chairman had cast over the country. His efforts were premature. Mao appointed HUA GUOFENG, former Party chief of HUNAN, the Chairman's home province, to be Zhou's successor as premier. Faced with growing criticism from the radicals, Deng prepared for another undignified exit from politics. It came in 1976 after a spontaneous outbreak of mourning for Zhou in Tiananmen Square which the government broke up and declared a 'counter-revolutionary riot'. With Zhou gone, Mao dying, and Deng in disgrace, power was divided between the 'Gang of Four' and Hua Guofeng, the Chairman's third heir to whom he famously declared: 'With you in charge, I feel at ease.'

If by that Mao meant that he believed Hua would stop the 'Gang' from seizing power, his faith was justified, albeit posthumously. Within five weeks of the Chairman's death in September 1976, Hua arrested the Gang and their allies before they could mount a coup of their own. But if Mao believed Hua could keep the 'revisionists' at bay, and safeguard the 'key link' of class struggle and the idea of continuous revolution, then his own death was a happy release. Hua Guofeng was no match for Deng Xiaoping in any department. Deng had to be brought back, that was obvious. But so, too, was the only possible outcome of his return: the defeat of Hua and that of the Cultural Revolution.

legacy: condemned but unexamined

So it proved. Deng was as different from Mao in his political beliefs as he was in his tactics, but he rang the curtain down on the Cultural Revolution in much the same way as Mao raised it in 1966: by appealing to popular feeling rather than inner-Party politics. By 1978, there was growing popular demand for a reassessment of the Cultural Revolution. People wanted to know how and why it had happened. They wanted many of its victims rehabilitated. And they wanted assurances that something like it would never happen again. Such demands found their most articulate and public expression during the DEMOCRACY WALL MOVEMENT which Deng turned to his own account before deciding it was too dangerous and imprisoning its leading protagonists. Those who had just returned to power after mistreatment at the hands of the Red Guards were determined to keep politics off the streets.

The Party gave its verdict on the Cultural Revolution and Chairman Mao in a lengthy 'resolution on history' approved in 1981. It remains the official view. The Cultural Revolution was 'responsible for the most severe setback and the heaviest losses suffered by the Party and the people since the founding of the People's Republic', it said. Mao made 'gross mistakes', though his contributions far outweighed them. The formula was carefully chosen: it had to provide for the ditching of the Cultural Revolution yet preserve intact the Chairman's stature as founder of the Communist state and great Marxist. To do otherwise would threaten the legitimacy of Party rule. It was safer to present the Party as a victim of the upheaval rather than the cause.

Resolution of the post-Mao power struggle and the formal jettisoning of the Cultural Revolution's goals fell far short of addressing, let alone repairing, the damage caused by the movement. No exhaustive reckoning has been made. Perhaps none is possible. But HU YAOBANG, successor to Hua as Party leader, said 100 million people had been 'treated unjustly' during the Cultural Revolution. Hundreds of thousands of victims were cited by the prosecution during the show trial of the 'Gang of Four' in 1980–81.

Few corners of the country were untouched by a self-inflicted disaster whose folly was outweighed only by its tragedy. A significant physical chunk of China's cultural heritage was swept away, particularly in TIBET, where all but a handful of monasteries were destroyed. The damage to Chinese scholarship, education, religion, idealism, morals and manners was even greater. Millions of people had their careers disrupted and in many cases ruined. Political innocence died in the Cultural Revolution; and for many, cynicism, materialism and selfishness replaced it, especially when free-market reforms began to change the entire agenda of life.

It is true that those, young and not so young, who travelled to the countryside in the Cultural Revolution acquired a new understanding of China's problems. It is true also that the violence and chaos of the movement created impetus for the political and economic liberalization that followed. But the costs of these 'benefits' was enormous. Among them is the fact that, almost 40 years on, China still lacks the legal framework, free press and independent judiciary necessary to make another Cultural Revolution impossible rather than merely unlikely on the grounds that there is no political constituency for it. Public discussion and academic research into the Cultural Revolution are rare and discouraged, leaving largely unexplained why the Chinese people behaved as they did, and how they have lived since without demanding an investigation, apologies and compensation.

D

Dalai Lama(s)

The biggest obstacle to China's claim to TIBET is the 14th Dalai Lama (1935–), the region's exiled spiritual leader. Revered as a God King at home despite a long absence and repeated campaigns against him, he is also respected in the West as the conscience of his troubled homeland. Thus the Dalai presents a unique challenge to Beijing: he is the only leader of a government in exile who enjoys the allegiance of people under Chinese control, as well as the affection of many beyond.

Dalais and Panchens

Dalai Lamas assumed authority during the seventeenth century and were venerated as the supreme spiritual and temporal rulers of Tibet. They were – and are still – worshipped as incarnations of the Compassionate Buddha, known as Chenrezi in Tibetan. PANCHEN LAMAS, incarnations of Amitabha, or in Tibetan, Opame, the meditative Buddha, are even more spiritual. But their temporal authority, while considerable around the Tashilhunpo Monastery in Xigaze where they were based, was usually secondary to that of the Dalai Lamas in Lhasa. Both lamas are heirs of the 'Yellow Hat' school of Tibetan Buddhism. Both often fell prey to political rivalry which China exploited to extend its influence over Tibet.

So, to some extent, did BRITAIN and RUSSIA during their battle for influence in Central Asia in the early twentieth century. When Britain sent a military expedition to Lhasa in 1903–4, the 13th Dalai Lama (1876–1933) fled to Mongolia. In 1910, he sought sanctuary in British India from a Chinese invasion. He returned home in triumph in 1913 when the REPUBLICAN REVOLUTION exposed China's military weakness in Tibet. Ten years later the Panchen fled to China, leaving the Dalai to worry away the final years of his life over whether the Chinese government would insert a pretender by force of arms.

The travails of the 13th Dalai are as nothing to those of his successor, Tenzin Gyatso, who was born in QINGHAI. His early life spanned the last years of Tibet's relative isolation from the world, China included. Most of the rest of it has been spent in exile while the world, and China in particular, have imposed themselves on his homeland.

This was still some way off when the Dalai, a Mongolian term meaning 'ocean', was installed in Lhasa in 1940. During the following ten years the boy Buddha was tutored in the scriptures and the duties expected of a God King. Impish by nature despite his upbringing, he learned English and everything he could about the outside world from his foreign tutor, Heinrich Harrer, an Austrian mountaineer.

from accord to exile, 1951–9

What seems with hindsight to have been a Tibetan idyll was interrupted in 1950 by the arrival of the People's Liberation Army. The following year Chinese and Tibetan representatives signed a 'Seventeen-point Agreement' providing for Tibet's 'peaceful liberation' and its 'return to the Motherland'. Within the domains ruled by Lhasa, the special positions of the Panchen Lama and Dalai Lama, the local government and the region's traditional way of life were not to be challenged. Reforms would be undertaken only in response to popular demand. But Chinese troops would enter Tibet to 'drive out imperialists' and defend the borders.

Generally speaking, China kept its word as far as the territory ruled by the Dalai was concerned. It was a different story in Tibetan areas to the east, which Lhasa insisted were part of Tibet, even though it had not ruled them for two centuries and they had been incorporated in the provinces of SICHUAN, QINGHAI, GANSU and YUNNAN. There, Tibetans were subjected to LAND REFORM, collectivization and, soon, the more radical policies of the GREAT LEAP FORWARD. By the mid-1950s Tibetans in the east were in revolt against their new masters. They soon gained the sympathy of those in 'Tibet proper'. So much so that when the Dalai visited India in 1956 to celebrate Buddha's birthday, he considered remaining there in protest at what was happening. It took a promise from ZHOU ENLAI that 'democratic' reforms would not be extended into western Tibet before he agreed to go home.

However, the Tibetan revolt – and China's suppression of it – intensified and spread west. By 1958 refugees were pouring into Lhasa. China pressed the Dalai to use Tibetan troops against the rebels. He prevaricated. Tension grew in the Tibetan capital as Chinese military commanders, officials of the Tibetan government, and the Dalai sought to contain the situation. In March 1959, crowds assembled in front of the Norbulingka Palace in Lhasa to protect the Dalai from possible capture by Chinese troops. Chinese orders and requests from the Dalai that the crowd disband went unanswered. On 17 March, the Dalai and his entourage fled under cover of darkness for India. During a dangerous journey made more hazardous by bad weather, he repudiated the Seventeen-point Agreement and announced the formation of his own government. It promptly went into exile and has remained there ever since.

the end of old Tibet

The Dalai's flight opened the way for the destruction of Tibet's traditional way of life. It gave China the chance to crush the rebellion and bring the entire region to heel. As the Panchen Lama, who remained in his homeland, confided in a secret report, thousands of Tibetans were either killed, died of starvation or were persecuted as a result of 'democratic' reforms. Most monasteries were destroyed.

More to the point, the flight of the God King – whose worship was an essential part of being Tibetan – together with thousands of his supporters, lay and religious, meant that 'Tibet' had gone into exile with its spiritual leader. Crushed in the land of its origin, the Tibetan way of life was replicated in the foothills of Dharamsala, northwest India, seat of the Dalai's exiled government.

Resistance to Chinese rule in Tibet, some of it armed and encouraged by the Central Intelligence Agency, continued during the 1960s and 1970s. The Dalai admired the rebels' bravery but disapproved of their violence. When the UNITED STATES sought to improve relations with the Communist government rather than overthrow it, the resistance petered out.

Eventually, the same was true of the Communist Party's revolutionary zeal. Once the CULTURAL REVOLUTION was over the Party sought a new start in Tibet, as elsewhere. It would encourage economic development rather than revolution, modernization rather than class struggle. Beijing hoped to recruit the Dalai to the cause: he was welcome to return, provided he accepted China's ownership of Tibet and spent most of his time in Beijing.

the Dalai's international campaign

In the late 1970s emissaries of the exiled government visited China and Tibet. Their reception in a region that had clearly been ransacked was rapturous: after 30 years of Chinese rule, Tibetans were impoverished, but still devoted to their faith and the Dalai. Many urged him not to return until China relaxed its grip on their homeland. He agreed. In the 1980s and 1990s the Dalai stepped up the pressure on Beijing with an international campaign for Tibet that took him around the world and included meetings with its political leaders.

China's new openness meant that many Tibetans heard about the activities of their exiled leader, and responded accordingly. This became clear in 1987 when Beijing rejected the Dalai's 5-point peace proposal calling for the demilitarization of Tibet and talks about its future: riots and protests broke out in Lhasa. Unrest flared again in 1988. The same year the Dalai gave an address in Strasbourg in which he urged China to grant Tibet autonomy of the kind it had promised HONG KONG. Tibet would run its own affairs in everything save defence and foreign affairs. The question of 'ownership' was sidestepped, to the displeasure of radicals in the Tibetan Youth League who favoured a more combative approach.

There was talk of the possibility of talks but no more. The Dalai declined an invitation to attend the funeral in Beijing of the 10th Panchen Lama, who died in January 1989. Diplomacy of any kind was ruled out by serious anti-Chinese unrest in Lhasa in March and the imposition of martial law. In 1989, the Dalai was awarded the Nobel Peace Prize for his efforts on behalf of his countrymen. Beijing, presumably committed to the view that the Dalai was the first 'Chinese citizen' to be so honoured, mocked the choice as the work of hostile foreign powers.

defeating the Dalai at home

By the early 1990s China had decided to go its own way in Tibet. It began to transform the region by increasing investment and altering Lhasa's ethnic composition by encouraging Chinese migration to the Tibetan capital. Most controversially of all, it presented itself as the custodian of traditional Tibetan customs and religion.

Beijing restored key religious monuments in Tibet, encouraged a limited, controlled revival of monastic life, and in 1995 overrode the Dalai Lama during procedures to select the 11th Panchen Lama. The Dalai's candidate was rejected in favour of another who was chosen according to what Beijing insisted was the traditional method of drawing lots to determine the correct reincarnation. It took many arrests and an intensive campaign in 'patriotic education' in the monasteries before lamas showed much in the way of enthusiasm for the new boy. The Dalai, ritually denounced by those in charge of his homeland as a 'splittist' and 'tool of anti-Chinese forces' declined to endorse 'China's Panchen'.

Controversy over the reincarnation of the Panchen Lama suggests an even larger one may arise when the Dalai dies and the search begins for his successor. China said in the late 1990s that the Dalai would be reborn in China. The Dalai countered that, if the status of his homeland was still in dispute at the time of his death, he would be reborn outside Tibet. Both of these outcomes point to a weakening in the authority of the institution of the Dalai Lama, and a grave loss for Tibetans.

Both point to a loss for the outside world, too. There is an irony in the fact that Communist China's policies in Tibet are opposed from exile by a monk reared as a God King. After 50 years of rule, Beijing can command almost everything in Tibet except the loyalty of its people. This remains focused on a man whose spirituality, though nurtured in a remote, rapidly disappearing culture, has made an impression in the West at a time when new critiques of materialism and concern for the environment are in vogue. The person – and the teachings – of the 14th Dalai Lama offer an antidote to consumerism in the West, as well as to Chinese rule in Tibet.

dangan (personal dossiers)

Along with the HUKOU, the household registration system, and the DANWEI, the work unit, one of the Communist government's most powerful tools of state is the large manila folder it maintains on almost every urban resident. *Dangan* record their subject's political background, profession, educational qualifications and seniority. Without one, an individual cannot be employed by the state, and for most urban residents that means no subsidized housing, health care and other social benefits.

Dangan are updated, in their hundreds of millions, by local Communist Party officials at the workplace. They are closed to scrutiny by those whose lives they record. Black marks in a *dangan*, deserved or otherwise, can blight a career with little possibility of redress.

Economic reforms and increased social mobility have weakened the controls imposed by the dossier system. The *dangan* of Chinese employed by foreigners are 'minded' by the Ministry of Foreign Trade, which has little interest in upgrading them because it has few social and economic obligations towards such personnel. Those who enter the private sector are required to lodge their *dangan* with the local 'talent exchange centre'. When a dossier is lodged there it means that the state has shed most of its responsibilities for the physical well-being of the subject – and lost much of its political control over the person in the process.

danwei (work unit)

The basic unit of individual identity in the People's Republic, even though economic reforms are weakening its hold, is the *danwei* or work unit. Superficially, *danwei* are employers. More profoundly they form the interface between individual and society, supply the material needs of much of the urban population and facilitate government control. They are units of production as well as the lowest level of GOVERNMENT AND ADMINISTRATION. Together with DANGAN (personal dossiers), and HUKOU (household registration system), they afford Beijing a powerful means of disciplining its huge population.

Government departments, hospitals, factories, schools, hotels, shops – every organizational entity in the Mainland is a *danwei*, including foreign-owned enterprises. They are concentrated in urban areas and industrial centres but, before the abolition of communes in the early 1980s and the return to household farming, they dominated rural life, too.

The *danwei* is a socialist concept. The fact that almost every person is attached to one supposedly symbolizes the stake they have in China's socialist system. For many this stake remains large. Despite two decades of economic reform many *danwei* not only provide work, they supply accommodation, medical care, schooling, bonuses in cash and kind, and even holidays for their members. They also afford a means for the government to get its message across in the form of political campaigns, ensure compliance with major policies, such as birth control, and generally monitor people's behaviour.

Nevertheless, the decline of state control over the economy, growth of private enterprise and presence of foreign-invested firms during the 1990s have impaired many of these functions. Social mobility and a rapid turnover in personnel, particularly among young people, have weakened the hold of the *danwei* over society still further. The *obligations* of many *danwei* towards their staff have proved less susceptible to change. A major obstacle to the reform of state-owned enterprises is the fact these huge *danwei* provide living accommodation, health care and education for their underemployed workforce in addition to a modest wage (see INDUSTRY/STATE ENTERPRISES). In the absence of adequate state welfare covering all citizens, it is not proving easy to dismantle a system once said to demonstrate the 'superiority of socialism'.

democracy

For more than a century, Chinese intellectuals, reformers and many ordinary people have yearned for democracy as a means of making their country strong, modern and free. For more than a century, they have been frustrated, oppressed, and sometimes killed for doing so. Democracy has made significant inroads in TAIWAN and lesser ones in HONG KONG and MACAU, but Mainland China remains a dictatorship. Its failure to develop democratic institutions during a century of otherwise dramatic change means that the overwhelming majority of Chinese people are still prisoners of the past. A state whose leaders select themselves is not modern. Neither, as China's unhappy modern history proves, is it stable.

Chinese views on state and society

There are many explanations for the failure of democracy to take root in China. One of the most important concerns the fact that whereas democracy in the West emerged from the conflict between monarchs, the church and new social classes, in China it had to be imposed from the outside. For nationalist reformers such as KANG YOUWEI, LIANG QICHAO and SUN YAT-SEN a democratic political system appeared to be the equivalent of the steam engine: China did not need to invent it, merely *use* it. Its usefulness was precisely what made it so attractive. China was weak and poor. Rich and powerful countries were democratic. So was Japan, whose defeat of China in the mid-1890s made such a deep impression on patriots and sparked the first public debates on politics in China's modern history. Alone among political systems, democracy would 'multiply' China's power by making its people and government subject to a common purpose. It would tap the resources of a vast population which, under the traditional rule of emperors, had been passive, parochial and disorganized. Democratic participation in political life was a prerequisite of national strength and the prelude to economic modernization.

The fact that democracy was valued in China mainly because it promised to make the state strong at a time of crisis invested it with a different role from that performed in the West. There, democracy had emerged as a defensive device to weaken the power of kings and other authorities. One of its main functions was to strengthen the individual or class relative to the state. Partly this was a matter of preserving the material interests of individuals or classes. Partly it was a question of democracy's ability to allow maximum scope for individual freedom and personal development. While it indeed tended to make states stable and powerful, it was often a happy consequence of a system first championed to protect freedom of religious or political conscience, economic interests, or both.

Most Chinese advocates of democracy were more concerned to strengthen the state than strengthen the rights of the individual. The national crisis dictated this. So did the presumed harmony between ruler and ruled in China that was a legacy of CONFUCIANISM. The idea that the individual and the state might be natural adversaries whose conduct towards each other would have to be regulated by strict laws was foreign to Chinese political culture. To a large extent it still is. Mainstream Chinese thought subscribes to a theory of civil rather than natural rights. Individual rights are granted by the state rather than inherent in individuals who enter civil society to strengthen them, as is generally the case in the Western tradition. The state derives its legitimacy from mastery of a moral doctrine or ideology rather than democratic mandate. In this context, democracy is favoured because it promises to make China strong – not so much because it promises to make Chinese *individuals* strong.

democracy in practice before 1949

The democracy inaugurated by the REPUBLICAN REVOLUTION of 1911 made neither the Chinese state nor its people strong. It was the plaything of WARLORDS whose own power testified to the collapse of traditional civilian authority and the failure of new institutions to take its place. There were elections (see p. 101) in the early republic, and parliaments met. SONG JIAOREN, a leader of one of them, sought to curb the powers of President YUAN SHIKAI. He was assassinated for his pains. Yuan became so weary of the democratic experi-

ment that in 1916 he tried to restore the monarchy. Yet democracy did not lose its allure. Personified as 'Mr De' in the outpouring of essays, articles and speeches of the MAY FOURTH MOVEMENT, it was championed as the source of China's national salvation and renewal in the face of warlord rule and foreign aggression.

Another strand of thought associated with the May Fourth Movement promised better solutions than liberal democracy to the problem of state strengthening: Soviet MARXISM. This appealed to many nationalists because its references to the laws of history pointed to a marriage between democracy and science – two of the world's most modern creeds. Moreover it had worked in RUSSIA, a vast, backward agrarian country then being transformed into a modern revolutionary state. The fact that by 1924 the young SOVIET UNION was ready to help an armed alliance between Sun Yat-sen's KUOMINTANG and the infant CHINESE COMMUNIST PARTY overthrow the warlords and unify China increased its appeal.

The NORTHERN EXPEDITION of 1926–7, which introduced the age of mass revolutionary politics in China, delivered unity of a sort, but little democracy. Not much seems to have been expected. Liang Qichao, by this time an old man and no friend of the Kuomintang, had come round to the view that the Chinese people were not ready for democracy. They would be better off, at least for a while, with enlightened despotism. The Kuomintang, first under Sun Yat-sen and then under CHIANG KAI-SHEK, was of similar opinion. It put forward a 3-stage theory of political development. The Chinese people would pass through distinct periods – one of military rule, the other of political tutelage – before the age of constitutional rule could dawn. In the event the sun did not rise on the final era until the late 1980s, by which time the Kuomintang had already been confined to Taiwan for 40 years.

This was long after it first began to contend with the Communists for rule of the Mainland. Following the Northern Expedition, both parties pursued different policies in the various parts of the country they controlled. They differed in the vigour and effectiveness of their rule. But for the next 60 years, the nature of Communist Party and Nationalist Party rule was similar. Both were centralized, disciplined, Leninist parties with a claim over most aspects of their peoples' lives. Both were only prepared to tolerate the existence of other political parties as long as they presented no serious challenge. Both controlled the press, intellectual life and the courts within their jurisdiction, although with different degrees of efficiency. Both made the legislature subordinate to the executive and the executive subject to their whim. Both were led by men who perpetuated their own power and removed, often by illegal means and, in the case of the Communists, by persecution, torture and death, those they believed to threaten it. Both parties, until the 1980s in the case of the Kuomintang, deprived the Chinese people of democracy in any meaningful sense of the term.

Communism and 'new democracy'

Indeed, under Communist rule after 1949, the state became more powerful and the individual weaker than at any time in Chinese history. The Party's determination and ruthlessness, its mastery of the modern techniques of mobilization and propaganda, its use – firstly in YANAN and then elsewhere in China – of political movements, 're-education' campaigns and purges generated a powerful new form of autocracy. The 'New Democracy' championed during the early 1950s and described by MAO ZEDONG as the 'joint dictatorship of all revolutionary classes' did little to disguise this. And in any event, the weak constitutional machinery of the People's Republic of China collapsed when Mao mobilized the entire population in an effort to realize his revolutionary goals. During the GREAT LEAP FORWARD of 1958–60 and the CULTURAL REVOLUTION of 1966–76 every kind of legal restraint was swept aside. The Chairman acquired almost divine status. He commanded absolute obedience. Defiance could mean death. Certainly it would mean persecution.

The calamities of Communist rule could not have happened had millennia of Chinese feudalism not provided fertile soil for tyranny and barren conditions for the growth of democracy. Like Chinese leaders before him, Mao and his Party were beneficiaries of a tradition of obedience to authority that, thanks to the techniques of modern propaganda, could be manipulated into adulation in good times and converted to endurance in bad. They benefited, too, from a tradition of elite politics. In traditional times, the rule of the elite was based on its superior education and presumed virtue. In Mao's day, the elite was made up of those deemed truly revolutionary. Its power was based on mastery of the doc-

trines of Marx, Lenin and, more particularly, of Mao himself. Since politics was a matter of right and wrong rather than opinion, and since almost every aspect of life was politicized, there could be no question of a 'loyal opposition' of the kind found in most democracies. Those who opposed Mao and the Party were either 'class enemies' or traitors. They were treated accordingly.

The death of Mao, the end of the Cultural Revolution, and the economic reforms introduced by DENG XIAOPING curbed some of these excesses and expanded the limits of personal freedom. People could choose where they worked and where they lived. Yet these changes did little to make China more democratic. While the Party was willing to admit it had made mistakes and change its policies, it had no intention of giving up its control over political life. This remains its position at the start of the new century.

democracy and dissent

Many Chinese hold different views and many always have, despite the burdens of history and culture that have enhanced tyranny and made dissent so dangerous. (See DISSIDENTS.) Just as there were those who spoke out against Manchu rule, the warlords and the Kuomintang, so others (sometimes they were the very same people) have opposed the Communist brand of tyranny and privilege in the name of democracy. Early Communist dissenters included Wang Shiwei (1900–1947) and Ding Ling (1904–85), two writers jailed (and in Wang's case killed), for attacking aspects of the new order in Yanan.

Pleas for liberty on a much larger scale were heard periodically after 1949. The ONE HUNDRED FLOWERS MOVEMENT of 1956 unleashed a storm of criticism of Party dictatorship. It was silenced by the 'Anti-Rightist' campaign the following year. The Cultural Revolution at first promised a kind of freedom to those deemed genuinely proletarian. But the fact that it rapidly sank into chaos and a deadly exercise in tyranny gave rise to new calls for legal curbs on the Party and the creation of a democratic political system. They came to the surface in the DEMOCRACY WALL MOVEMENT of 1978–9 which Deng and his allies used to outmanoeuvre their Maoist opponents in the Party, but crushed when some of its advocates, notably WEI JINGSHENG – for whom democracy was the 'fifth modernization' – began to question the very basis of Communist rule (see FOUR MODERNIZATIONS).

For a while, the need to strengthen democracy and the rule of law was advocated within the highest councils of the Party itself. So was 'neo-authoritarianism', another 'three-stage' theory of development advocated, in the mid-1980s, by a young political scientist, Wu Jiaxiang (c 1956–). He and others argued that China needed a strongman to override the interest groups that had emerged during the course of economic reform and which blocked further progress towards freedom and democracy. Democracy was desirable and possible, but it depended on a great leader to bring it into being. HU YAOBANG, Party leader from 1980 to 1987, encouraged discussion of these and other radical ideas. On occasion even Deng spoke in favour of the need for democracy and political reform. He blew cold again in 1986–7 when students took to the streets of several cities to demand change. Together with other members of the old guard he forced Hu from power. Calls for political reform were silenced by a campaign against 'bourgeois liberalism', the Party's term for the Western forms of democracy it still loathes and fears.

The campaign was shortlived and ineffective. The TIANANMEN SQUARE DEMOCRACY MOVEMENT which began after Hu's death in April 1989 was the largest, most spectacular popular movement for democratic political change in Chinese history. It was also further proof that tyranny, old or new, had not overcome the demands of millions of people for a greater say in their lives. The tactics of those who occupied Tiananmen Square for seven weeks can be questioned. So can their strategy. But that they and the millions who supported them glimpsed another kind of political future, however vague and fleeting, than the repressive, dictatorial one in which they had been brought up, is beyond doubt. Many of them might not have had a deep understanding of democracy, or expressed a demand for it in a sophisticated way. But simple experience made the idea that they should select their own leaders (rather than the leaders choosing themselves) more attractive than any amount of political theory.

For Deng and the revolutionary veterans who engineered the military assault on Tiananmen Square, the democracy movement threatened disorder on a massive scale. With its calls for radical change and savage verbal attacks on senior leaders, it was too reminiscent of the Cultural Revolution for comfort. It had to be stamped out. In their view there was no future for China without continued Party rule. It was – and, in the minds of most Party leaders, remains – as simple as that.

democracy and disorder

Yet the idea that democracy in China would spell chaos is not just the special pleading of a threatened elite. It was a widely held view in the 1980s and 1990s, even among urban intellectuals. Some feared the consequences of democracy because it would lead to rule by the peasantry who made up the majority of the Chinese population. A China ruled by peasants would be neither modern, strong nor free. Other arguments, sometimes advanced by the Party, sometimes by those who had no interest in perpetuating Party rule, sought to justify a delay in the introduction of democracy or even deny it altogether.

China was described as too poor for democracy, too big for democracy, too populous for democracy. Its low level of education, and sharp regional and ethnic divisions were said to render democracy unworkable. There were suggestions that 'Western' democratic forms were, by definition, unsuitable for Chinese people. 'ASIAN VALUES' and the political dictatorship, benign or otherwise, that usually went with them, were more appropriate. They included a different notion of HUMAN RIGHTS. The Chinese, being poor, set more store on the 'right to development' – that is, food and clothing – than free speech and genuine elections.

For the Party, 'socialist democracy' – the system of 'multi-party cooperation' said to exist between the Communist and the DEMOCRATIC PARTIES, and the network of local people's congresses culminating in the NATIONAL PEOPLE'S CONGRESS (NPC) – is best for China. As the highest organ of state power, the NPC should have real teeth, and be a forum of real debate, but the Party must still lead all aspects of government. Deng warned that if China adopted the tripartite division of powers between the executive, legislature and judiciary characteristic of Western democracy, nothing would ever get done: the government would be at perpetual war with itself. At the local level, notably in the village elections of the 1990s that some observers saw as the sprouts of Chinese democracy, people can choose their leaders in direct elections. But at every level above that, *indirect* elections, presided over by the Party, are still necessary to secure the 'correct' results.

A Short History of Mainland Elections

Voting is common in contemporary Chinese political life. Free and fair elections of the kind usually associated with democracy are rare. Generally speaking, they are confined to TAIWAN, HONG KONG and MACAU. Most of the few 'real' elections to have taken place on the Mainland occurred before the Communist Party came to power. They were conducted on the basis of an extremely limited franchise and often carried out in times of uncertainty, political tension or civil war. Abuses were common, although the polls, unlike those of the Communist era, were designed to give voters a genuine choice. The earliest example of elections on any scale was in 1909. Voters chose members of the provincial assemblies set up under the late Qing reforms (see QING DYNASTY).

The average rate of enfranchisement was 4 people per 1,000, or less than half of 1 per cent. Polls for the national parliament of 1912–13 were larger: registered voters constituted between 4 and 6 per cent of the population. The Kuomintang, led by Song Jiaoren, won a clear majority. The Party was promptly suppressed. In 1947–8, with the country embroiled in Civil War, the Kuomintang government conducted elections for the National Assembly and Legislative Yuan. It claimed that 20 million people voted out of a population of about 500 million. The 'temporary provisions' of 1948, introduced as the Communists swept to power and the Nationalists fled to Taiwan, allowed those voted into office to retain their seats until free elections could again take place on the Mainland. Forty years later, many of those elected in 1948 were still members of the National Assembly, by then located in Taipei (see TAIWAN).

The role of elections in the People's Republic – and the purpose of voting within the National People's Congress, the national legislature – is to acclaim rather than choose. Voting, at age 18, is direct only for local congresses. At all other levels it is indirect. Thus, members of local congresses elect county congresses; county congresses elect provincial congresses who, finally, select the 2,400 or so delegates to the National People's Congress. All key issues concerning personnel and policies are decided in private by the Party before they are submitted, for validation, to the people or their representatives. A rare exception to

this procedure occurred in 1980 under the first wave of political reforms sponsored by Deng Xiaoping. Genuinely competitive elections were held for local people's congresses. Several pro-democracy activists, frustrated by the clampdown on Democracy Wall a year earlier, took part. They need not have bothered. When a few of them, including Hu Ping (c 1948–) and Chen Ziming (1952–) in Beijing, and Tao Sen (c 1949) and Liang Heng (c 1953) in HUNAN won after campaigns enlivened by fiery speeches, leaflets and wall posters, the Party annulled the results. Elections for local congresses quickly reverted to timid, Communist type.

This began to change during the 1990s. Under a village self-government law passed in 1987, village committees, the lowest level of government organization, were chosen by competitive direct elections. Voters were often given a choice of candidates, many of whom were not members of the Communist Party. There was no question of anyone being allowed to stand on an anti-Party ticket, or to form a new party to contest the elections. Candidates were vetted. But the election campaigns were lively and involved an element of genuine choice. They centred on specific, local issues, primarily those of economic development.

The government's enthusiasm for the democratization of village life is not due to a conversion to the merits of free political choice. It stems from the same desire to strengthen the state – particularly at the local level – that had attracted reformers to democracy and popular political participation in earlier times. By the mid-1990s, Party organizations had all but collapsed in many rural areas. Clans, local mafiosi, and religious groups had taken over. Village elections were a way of re-establishing local authority. However, they have set the stage for the introduction of direct, competitive elections at higher levels of government. In 1998 one of these occurred in a township in SICHUAN. Beijing condemned it as illegal. What remains unclear at the start of the new century is whether the Sichuan experiment will be copied elsewhere, and whether genuine elections will be common in the Mainland within the 50 years Deng Xiaoping had said might be needed in 1987.

democracy in the future

Despite the apparent merit of some of these arguments, there are few signs that educated Chinese accept them as grounds for the indefinite deferral of democracy. Instead, as people have become richer and better educated, interest in democracy and its auxiliary freedoms such as a free press and an independent judiciary, have grown stronger and the Party's reasons for resisting them weaker. In many cities, a nascent middle class has emerged. In several of them at the turn of the century, activists attempted to form a 'China Democratic Party' before they were carted off

to prison. Improved communications and transport have enabled many to become familiar with conditions in Taiwan and Hong Kong – the first a vibrant democracy, the second an often lively one. Both territories have their own special circumstances, but both give the lie to the idea that Chinese people are unable to make democracy work or to benefit from it.

Weak institutions and the determination of the Party to stay in power suggest there are few prospects for the rapid development of democracy in the early years of the century. The moment when politicians on the Mainland can live or die by popular acclaim rather than decisions made in private by the Party few, well away from public scrutiny and possible humiliation, seem far away. ZHU RONGJI, the Chinese politician most admired in the West during the 1990s, said as much when the National People's Congress 'elected' him premier in March 1998.

'The process of democratic election is different in China from that in foreign countries,' he said. 'It is also different in the East and in the West. I think this issue needs further study. As to when such elections [that is, direct elections for the premier and other national leaders] will take place, it is now hard for me to predict.' Zhu was the only candidate for premier, the Party having decided earlier, and in private, that delegates to the NPC should not be given the possibility of choosing anyone else. As long as this remains the case, as long as most Chinese people cannot freely choose who is to rule them, the visions of modernity shared by Liang Qichao and many of those who came after him will remain unfulfilled.

Democracy Wall Movement (1978–9)

The movement refers to the outpouring of complaints, dissent and demands for more democracy that took place in Beijing and elsewhere from late 1978 until the Communist Party stamped it out the following year. The wall itself, and the posters plastered on it; the leading activists and the unofficial magazines they produced, were soon removed from the scene. The ideas they stood for proved more resilient. Many reappeared during the TIANANMEN SQUARE DEMOCRACY MOVEMENT. Many haunt the Communist government still.

There were several 'Democracy Walls' in the Mainland, but the most important was at Xidan, west of the Forbidden City. Chosen because of its size and central location, it became the notice board for a nation in anguish over what had happened during the CULTURAL REVOLUTION, and the drawing board for political change designed to ensure it could never happen again. It drew huge crowds and prompted rare public discussion of China's political future by ordinary people.

The general mood in China was one of relief and anticipation. Tyranny seemed to have died with MAO ZEDONG and the arrest of the 'GANG OF FOUR'. DENG XIAOPING was fighting his way back into power. Many officials and senior Party leaders purged in the Cultural Revolution had been rehabilitated. Thousands of ordinary people sent to the countryside were returning to Beijing and other cities. The national obsession with politics and class struggle was giving way to calls for economic modernization and, perhaps, legal and political change. In November 1978, the Party redesignated as patriotic and revolutionary the gathering in Tiananmen Square of April 1976 to commemorate the death of Zhou Enlai and protest against the 'Gang', which had been broken up by police and declared 'counter-revolutionary'. Change was in the air.

It was certainly apparent in the posters, speeches and magazines on display in Xidan. For the most part, they were the work of former Red Guards, blue-collar workers and educated youths – those unable to use the official media to convey their ideas and who often lacked close connections with the Party hierarchy. Some of the activists courted foreigners, establishing close connections with the then small pool of foreign correspondents based in Beijing. The opinions they expressed varied, but they were at one in their support for Deng, at least at first, and in their desire to understand why China was still poor and backward. Most realized China's ills could not simply be attributed to one man or a small 'gang' of his followers. Such failures were the fault of a decrepit feudal system.

This was argued most forcefully by WEI JINGSHENG, a former Red Guard, and by this time an electrician at Beijing Zoo, who in December 1978 put up a poster declaring that the FOUR MODERNIZATIONS would fail without a 'fifth': DEMOCRACY. He explored the same theme in his magazine *Explorations* (*tansuo*). Wei's ideas were different from those of other activists. As his later writings were to make clear, he sought a fundamental break with China's current political system and ideology of a kind few others envisaged or thought necessary.

For Deng and his allies, Democracy Wall provided useful ammunition in their campaign against conservatives in the Party. It showed the public was on their side and in favour of reform. On more than one occasion, Deng let it be known he thought the airing of different opinions was a good thing. He began to have different ideas once he had consolidated his position. Then, the calls for radical change and increasing public discussion of politics normally confined to stage-managed Party gatherings took on a troublesome, even threatening aspect. The 'great debates' and right to paste up wall posters guaranteed by the Constitution were proving too reminiscent of the start of the Cultural Revolution. They were obstacles to the unity and strong government required for China's modernization.

Deng called a halt to Democracy Wall in March 1979. By that time he had completed his successful visit to the United States, but was under pressure within the Party over the poor performance of China's troops in the war against Vietnam. Instinct and expedience joined hands. He said there would be four modernizations, not five, and that they would be realized in accordance with 'four cardinal principles'. These enforced Party rule, the ideological dominance of Marxism-Leninism-Mao Zedong Thought, proletarian dictatorship and the socialist system (see CHINESE COMMUNIST PARTY).

Wei responded by attacking Deng as a dictator. He was promptly arrested along with several other activists. In October 1979, he was tried and sentenced to 15 years in prison for inciting counter-revolution and 'leaking state secrets'. The last charge referred to Wei's discussion with foreigners of China's performance in the war against VIETNAM. 'State secrets' in China constitute any information that has not been published in the official MEDIA.

Posters continued to appear on Democracy Wall despite Wei's arrest. But some of the fire and much of the hope went out of the movement. Liu Qing (c 1947-), Wei's friend and fellow activist, obtained a transcript of the trial and sold copies at Xidan. He, too, was jailed. So was Ren Wanding (1947-), another leading activist. At the end of 1979, the authorities scraped the posters off the wall and built a large row of billboards in front of it. Those who wanted to put up posters in public could do so in a park in the suburbs – after they had registered their names at a purpose-built office near by. In September 1980, at Deng's instigation, the NATIONAL PEOPLE'S CONGRESS revoked the clause in the Constitution which allowed people to engage in 'great debates' and 'put up big-character posters'.

Some of the unofficial magazines launched at the time of the Democracy Wall Movement survived the crackdown. However, most were closed in 1981 and their editors arrested. They included Xu Wenli (1944-), editor of the influential *April Fifth Forum*, which took its name from the date of the 1976 protests in Tiananmen Square to commemorate Zhou's death. The Party, and Deng in particular, had stifled a rare outbreak of democracy with considerable ease, and almost no international complaint.

democratic parties

The eight 'democratic' parties of the People's Republic do little for Chinese democracy but much for the CHINESE COMMUNIST PARTY'S desire to disguise its one-party rule. Their activities on the fringes of political life sustain the fiction that government in Beijing is the work of 'multi-party cooperation led by the Communist Party', rather than a dictatorship.

Most of the minority parties – the only legal political parties in the People's Republic apart from the Communist Party – were founded by liberals and Left-wingers opposed to the policies of Chiang Kai-shek's Nationalist government during the Civil War. One of them, the Revolutionary Committee of the Kuomintang, claimed to represent the 'true' values of SUN YAT-SEN which Chiang allegedly betrayed. It appealed to members of the established KUOMINTANG. The China Democratic League, founded in 1944, was a grouping of liberal intellectuals who aspired towards Western-style democracy. In 1946 three of its leaders were assassinated by government agents. The League later aligned itself with the Communists. The Jiu San (Nine-Three) Society took its name from the date of its founding – the 3 September 1945, Chinese VJ Day – and brought together politically minded scientists and engineers.

The other parties are: the China Association for Promoting Democracy; the Chinese Peasants and Workers Democratic Party; the Zhi Gong Dang (Public Interest Party); the China Democratic National Construction Association; and the Taiwan Democratic Self-Government League. The last was founded in Hong Kong by exiles who escaped from Taiwan after the FEBRUARY TWENTY-EIGHTH INCIDENT. It claims to represent the interests of Taiwanese and pursues re-unification, on Beijing's terms, with the Mainland.

Representatives of most of the parties took part in the formalities leading to the foundation of the People's Republic on 1 October 1949. They did so in the context of the United Front composed of supposedly 'patriotic' forces. Some members went on to serve as ministers and officials of the new Communist government. It was the era of 'New Democracy', described by Mao Zedong as one of the 'joint dictatorship of the revolutionary classes'.

The dictatorship soon became a Communist monopoly. Democratic parties were among the victims of Mao's swing towards radicalism in the late 1950s. Most of their officials were sacked and purged during the 'Anti-Rightist Movement' (see ONE HUNDRED FLOWERS MOVEMENT). Their rehabilitation was interrupted by the Cultural Revolution. In the new climate of revolutionary purity there was little room for even the pretence of 'multi-party cooperation'.

The reform era brought resurrection of a kind. Elderly Party leaders, many of whom had endured years of persecution, emerged into the modest limelight afforded them by the Communist-controlled media. Communist Party leaders fêted them, advising them of the latest policies and soliciting their opinions, on the understanding such opinions would be expressed privately and not challenge the Communists' monopoly of power. Members of democratic parties are selected as delegates to the legislature, the NATIONAL PEOPLE'S CONGRESS, and the CHINESE PEOPLE'S POLITICAL CONSULTATIVE CONFERENCE, an advisory body. They remain visible, participating in the turgid forms of Communist Chinese political life. Exactly what role they play in these proceedings is unclear. It is hard to detect any substantial difference between their policies and those of the Communist Party.

An exception concerned the controversial THREE GORGES DAM on the Yangtze. In the 1980s prominent members of the Jiu San Society, most of them elderly technical experts, objected to the scheme on environmental and cost grounds. Their opposition played a part in delaying the project for several years but failed to stop it.

If China's democratic parties do not lack influence they certainly lack power. The fact that, together, they probably have a membership of less than half a million partly accounts for this. So does their lack of leadership, authority and legitimacy in the eyes of almost everyone outside the Communist leadership. They are in no position to challenge the Communist Party or reform China's authoritarian politics.

Democratic Progressive Party (DPP)

TAIWAN's first opposition party was formed in 1986 during the dying days of martial law. Fourteen years later, following the victory of CHEN SHUI-BIAN, its candidate in the presidential elections of March 2000, the DPP formed its first administration – and the first in Taiwan's modern history not to be controlled by the KUOMINTANG. Neither the narrowness of Chen's victory, nor his cautious retreat from the DPP's goal of Taiwanese independence, disguised the significance of these events. The party's victory transformed politics in the island, injected a new, potentially destabilizing element into relations with the Mainland, and confronted the UNITED STATES with a fresh challenge in handling ties with Beijing and Taipei. In almost every respect, therefore, the DPP's victory was a defining moment in Chinese history, one whose consequences will test leadership in Taiwan, China and the United States for years to come.

on the 'outside'

Under martial law, it was illegal to form political parties in Taiwan. The only legitimate way to take on the Kuomintang was to stand as an independent in local elections or occasional 'supplementary elections' designed to increase Taiwanese representation in 'national' organs such as the Legislative Yuan and National Assembly (see TAIWAN/GOVERNANCE). *Dangwai* candidates – that is, those 'outside the (Kuomintang) party' – often did well, particularly at the local level, though they were never strong enough to threaten KMT dominance.

It was sometimes a different story on the streets. Forbidden to organize a political party of their own, radicals in 1979 founded a magazine, *Formosa*, the voice of the opposition. In 1979, a rally in Kaohsiung in support of the magazine degenerated into a riot. Most opposition activists, including Shi Ming-teh (1941–), general manager of *Formosa*, were jailed on charges of sedition. Their cause continued at home, where a middle class keen to assert its political rights was taking shape, as well as abroad, where groups of exiled Taiwanese, some of whom sought to keep alive the more radical ideals of the FEBRUARY 28TH INCIDENT, were active.

Despite the risks, representatives from these

groups decided to form a party in time to take part in the legislative elections of 1986. That the founders of the DPP were not arrested, even though many of them advocated independence for Taiwan, was a sign of President CHIANG CHING-KUO's determination to reform the island's authoritarian political system. For many in Taiwan, such tolerance of dissent was a heartening novelty.

the party at the polls

However, the DPP's size, weak organization and lack of resources meant it could not compete fairly at the polls until President LEE TENG-HUI's reforms of 1991 forced those deputies elected on the Mainland in 1947 into retirement and opened their seats to election. Even then, taking on the Kuomintang was difficult. The DPP did not have the advantage of incumbency. More important, it lacked control over the media, and the huge business empire that enabled the Nationalists to make their voices heard and rarely want for funds.

Despite these handicaps, the opposition often performed creditably. A notable triumph came in 1994 with the election of Chen Shui-bian as mayor of Taipei. Another followed in 1997 when the DPP won 12 of 23 constituencies in local elections. It secured 43.47 per cent of the vote compared with the Kuomintang's 42.06 per cent, the first time the opposition won more votes than the ruling party in Taiwan's history.

The DPP's appeal was based on its determination to put Taiwan first and the Mainland second. It opposed almost everything about the Kuomintang's pre-reform record, from the fact that it insisted that Taiwan was part of China to its often brutal attempts to suppress Taiwanese identity. In the DPP view, Taiwanese could only speak their mind, and could only do so in their own language, Taiwanese or *minnanhua*, if they achieved independent statehood or the nearest thing to it. The political hold of ageing Mainlanders had to be broken; the 'one China' principle dumped along with 'one-party' politics.

Political reforms during the late 1980s and early 1990s weakened some of these criticisms. But the Kuomintang's inability to shed its image as a money-making machine that was too tolerant of corruption provided new grist for the DPP mill. The opposition positioned itself as the party of youth, the party of change, the party that was too young to have an unsavoury past. All three factors contributed to its great victory of 2000.

Prior to that, however, support for the DPP tended to fluctuate in accordance with Taiwan's overall political fortunes. These usually revolved around the island's mercurial relationship with the Mainland and popular perceptions of the Kuomintang, whose leaders no longer convinced voters that it was 'dangerous' to vote for the opposition. Throughout the 1990s those who wanted to show their unhappiness with the Kuomintang did so by supporting the DPP, particularly during local elections.

However, voting for the opposition in island-wide polls was a different matter because of the DPP's commitment to Taiwanese independence, a cause Beijing pledged to crush by force. This was a factor in the DPP's relatively poor showing during Taiwan's first direct presidential elections in March 1996. Peng Min-min (1923–), sometimes known as the 'father of the Taiwan independence movement', won 21 per cent of the vote against Lee Teng-hui's 54 per cent. China's military posturing during the polls undoubtedly weakened support for the DPP.

independence, eventually

While independence for Taiwan has always been part of the DPP's platform, how and when to achieve it have been the cause of division in the ranks. Following the electoral setback of 1996, those who favoured the permanent, but perhaps unstated, political separation of Taiwan from the Mainland gained the upper hand over those who wanted an immediate declaration of independence, a new constitution and new national flag the moment the party came to power. This forced a group of radicals to leave the DPP and form the Taiwan Independence Party. They soon found themselves in the political wilderness.

The DPP's drift towards 'moderation' – apparently confirmed by the selection of Lin Yi-hsiung (1941–) as party chairman in 1998 – was matched by that of the KMT under the long tenure of Lee Teng-hui. Both parties seemed to advocate independence for Taiwan in everything but name. Both seemed content to leave it at that in the interests of maximizing popular support at home, declining to antagonize Beijing, and preserving an ambiguous, but generally productive relationship with the United States essential for keeping the peace across the Straits. Thus, the fact that by the late 1990s Lee Teng-hui had stolen many of the DPP's clothes, and President Bill Clinton had made it clear during his visit to

China in 1998 that the United States opposed Taiwanese independence, indicated that Taiwan's two main political parties were less divided than their bitter rivalry might suggest.

enter the DPP

If so, it was not reflected in the intense competition for the presidency in 2000. While little in their approach to the Mainland separated the DPP, the Kuomintang, and James Soong Chu-yu (1942–), the former KMT stalwart who ran as an independent, voters perceived real differences in the candidates' domestic policy. It was a choice between Lien Chan (1936–), the lacklustre but official Kuomintang candidate whose victory would mean more of the same; Soong, the maverick to whom many KMT supporters looked for a new start; and Chen Shui-bian who promised real change tempered by skilful caution on the question of Taiwanese independence, once the DPP's biggest handicap in national elections. They narrowly chose Chen over Soong, awarding them 39 per cent and 36 per cent of the vote respectively. Lien garnered barely 23 per cent. In May 2000, Chen was inaugurated as the tenth president of the Republic of China on Taiwan, and the first to secure the position through victory over the incumbent in genuine elections. The Democratic Progressive Party, almost overnight, had come of age.

The extent to which this was true would become clear in the months following Chen's triumph. The party faced many challenges. One was concern over Beijing's reaction to the DPP's victory. Given the enthusiasm with which Communist Party leaders had demonized the party in previous years, their initial reaction was restrained. However, there was no guarantee it would remain that way, despite Chen's spirited peace overtures to China.

Another problem was the DPP's small membership – about 120,000 compared with the Kuomintang's more than 2 million. The pool of talent and experience was smaller still. It was impossible for Chen to form a confidence-inspiring administration composed solely of his own party members. Moreover, with less than 40 per cent of the vote, the new president headed a minority administration: he and Annette Lu Hsiu-lien, the vice-president, had to cast their nets wide to form a balanced government. This meant turning to those affiliated with other parties as well as those who were members of none. An early result was the appointment as prime minister of Tang Fei (1932–), defence minister in the outgoing Kuomintang government and a former air force general. Among other things Chen valued Tang for his ties to the military, many of whose senior officers were lifelong members of the Kuomintang.

These developments gave few clues as to the future shape of relations between the president and his party. It is true that the DPP had lost some of its yearnings for Taiwanese independence before the polls. It is also true that the narrowness of its election victory, and sustained threats from Beijing, may cause it to lose more. Nevertheless many of the party faithful will look to Chen to 'deliver' – possibly in the form of a formal break with the idea that Taiwan is part of China.

Would Chen be willing to do so? Would his cabinet colleagues, many of them not members of the DPP, allow such a move? What would Beijing's reaction be? Perhaps the president would prefer a break with his party than with the majority of Taiwanese people? These were just a few of the questions that haunted Taiwan's future as Chen Shui-bian began his honeymoon as the first president of the Republic of China on Taiwan from the Democratic Progressive Party.

Deng Liqun (1914–)

DENG XIAOPING's economic reforms inaugurated an informal liberalization in China's political and intellectual life which Deng Liqun, a leading conservative ideologue in the CHINESE COMMUNIST PARTY, did all he could to counter. He was eventually dispatched to the margins of politics but remained the main theoretical opponent of Deng's policies.

'Little Deng', as he was known to distinguish him from his namesake, was determined that China should abandon neither ideological discipline nor Party leadership in the era of economic reform. This placed him at odds with many younger intellectuals in the Party and, periodically, with the elder Deng. At issue throughout the late 1970s and 1980s were the limits of intellectual and political discourse in the People's Republic. In numerous conferences, meetings and workshops 'Little Deng' opposed every conceivable manifestation of liberalism. His position as head of the Party's Propaganda Department and spokesman for the old guard meant he could not easily be defied. He was a leading force in the campaign against 'spiritual pollution' of 1983, and a key figure in the dismissal of HU YAOBANG as Party leader in 1987 for being soft on student protests. Deng revelled in the campaign against 'bourgeois liberalization' which followed Hu's dismissal – until Deng Xiaoping, fearing it might threaten his economic reforms, ordered it stopped. Reformist forces gained the upper hand, and at the 13th National Party Congress of 1987 Deng Liqun lost his seat on the Central Committee.

The suppression of the TIANANMEN SQUARE DEMOCRACY MOVEMENT in 1989 enabled the old guard to stage an ideological comeback. It did not last long: Deng Xiaoping again took the initiative with his call for faster, bolder reforms. 'Leftist' policies of the kind championed by Deng Liqun came under attack. 'Little Deng' refused to be silenced. In a series of long, scathing 'statements' circulated, but rarely published, during the mid-1990s, he and his allies attacked the corruption, materialist excesses, moral degeneracy and breakdown of Party authority unleashed by economic reforms. Private enterprise was taking hold in the People's Republic, the statements warned. It spelt the ruin of socialism and the restoration of capitalism.

Part analysis, part call to action, the 'statements' contained little of appeal to the general public. They were a more serious matter for Party leaders whose authority still depended on their ability to match policies with some form of socialist theory. Above all, the 'statements' were a reminder of Deng Liqun's continuing personal influence, as well as proof that the intellectual legacy of the old guard, if not the old guard itself, had outlived Deng Xiaoping.

Deng Xiaoping (1904–97)

No leader in the twentieth century did more to push China towards its long-sought goals of wealth and power than Deng Xiaoping. He enabled millions of Chinese to escape the poverty imposed upon them by MAO ZEDONG's policies and ended the seemingly endless concern with politics that ruined so many lives. He presided over a great loosening up of society which expressed itself in a multitude of ways – not all of them welcome – from the emergence of sharp regional differences to revivals of folk religion; from a surge in official corruption to the spread of Western fashions and food. Deng exposed China to foreign influence on a scale never seen before. He was the first paramount Chinese leader to visit the West and, during the 1990s, made his country count in the boardrooms and chanceries of the developed world. He secured the return of HONG KONG, though he did not live to see it, and presided over a thaw in relations with TAIWAN. He legitimized the goal of material self-improvement, enabling his people to enter (though not always to flow in) the mainstream of human history and create one of the most sustained periods of rapid economic growth China had ever known.

But if China's economic rejuvenation is inseparable from Deng Xiaoping, so is the massacre of unarmed civilians and pro-democracy demonstrators around Tiananmen Square in June 1989. It was merely the most dramatic example of the distinction Deng insisted on between politics and economics, Party rule and reform, control and freedom. Tiananmen was testimony to failure: the failure of Deng's reforms to accommodate the more fundamental, if sometimes unfocused, aspirations for change his reforms encouraged.

revolutionary apprenticeship

Politics, in particular those of the CHINESE COMMUNIST PARTY, dominated Deng's life from adolescence. The son of a prosperous landlord, he left SICHUAN at the age of 16 to be a 'worker student' in France. He found some work but showed little inclination to study: most of his time he devoted to émigré politics, joining the European branch of the Chinese Communist Party, and establishing an enduring political and personal friendship with ZHOU ENLAI, then also in France. The French authorities soon tired of the Chinese radicals in their midst. In 1926 they raided Deng's house, a day after he and his companions had left for Moscow.

Deng was one of many Chinese students at the Sun Yat-sen University in Moscow set up to train personnel for the revolution in China under the terms of the Soviet-sponsored alliance between the KUOMINTANG and the Communists. He returned to China in 1927 to work briefly as a political instructor in the armies of

FENG YUXIANG, the 'Christian general' of north China. Two years later he was operating in very different circumstances: the Party, struggling to develop rural bases now that the cities were denied them by the Nationalists, sent him to organize peasant insurrections in GUANGXI, close to the border with Vietnam. Two Soviet governments were set up, but quickly crushed. The remnant Communist troops fled to join Mao's base at Ruijin in JIANGXI, but not before Deng, for reasons that remain unclear, left his troops en route and travelled to SHANGHAI.

Deng and Mao: allies, adversaries

Deng began his close, but later strained, relationship with Mao in the early 1930s when he was transferred to Jiangxi. Like Mao, Deng was soon at odds with the Moscow-inclined formal leadership of the Party whose members took a dim view of the Red Army's reliance on guerrilla warfare and what they saw as Mao's 'moderate' policy of land reform. While Mao was too important to be criticized directly, Deng was not: in 1933 he was sacked and briefly imprisoned. Recovery was swift. He took part in the LONG MARCH and was present at the Zunyi Conference of 1935 when Mao triumphed over his 'Bolshevik' foes. With the outbreak of the SINO-JAPANESE WAR in 1937, Deng was made political commissar of what became one of the most successful of the Communist armies: the 129th division of the Eighth Route Army, later known as the Second Field Army of the PEOPLE'S LIBERATION ARMY. For the following 15 years, he was closely involved with military affairs, building connections with army leaders that would stand him in good stead in later life.

Of more immediate importance, he and Liu Bocheng (1892–1986) – the 'one-eyed' commander of the 129th division – played a key role in expanding Communist power behind Japanese lines in north China. They went on to make a major contribution to the defeat of the Nationalists in the CIVIL WAR. In the battle of Huai-Hai, the Second and Third Field Armies surrounded and destroyed some of Chiang Kai-shek's best forces and opened the way for the Communist capture of Nanjing, Chiang's capital. As the Nationalist regime crumbled, Deng and Liu moved their forces into the southwest to complete the Communist victory.

In 1952 Deng was transferred from the southwest to Beijing and made a vice-premier. In 1955 he joined the Politburo, the apex of formal power in the Party, and the following year became Party General Secretary, a position of immense influence within the organization. In this capacity, he oversaw the execution of the 'Anti-Rightist Movement' of 1957 – a vicious purge that ended public criticism of the Communist Party and destroyed hundreds of thousands of careers (see ONE HUNDRED FLOWERS MOVEMENT). Years later Deng admitted that the methods and results of the movement were 'excessive', but neither then, nor since, has there been an official admission that the movement was a mistake. It damaged China enormously, yet still stands as testimony to Deng's unwillingness to allow independent criticism of the Communist Party, an intolerance he displayed throughout his career.

Yet Deng also had little patience for what he regarded as revolutionary romanticism. He declined to side with PENG DEHUAI, the defence minister who in 1959 took issue with Mao over the GREAT LEAP FORWARD, but came to hold different ideas from the Chairman as to how China should recover from the disaster of rapid communization. Together with LIU SHAOQI, he favoured the use of material incentives and private plots to rejuvenate the rural economy. Mao, only marginally humbled by the failure of the Leap, stuck to his radical vision. He grew even more attached to it during the 1960s when he discerned 'revisionism' rather than socialism at work in the Soviet Union. Deng did not take issue with the Chairman over the break with Moscow. Where he differed was over what it meant for dealing with alleged 'revisionism' in the Chinese Party. Deng and Liu, ranked number two in the Party, maintained that any re-radicalizing of the Chinese revolution should take the form of a disciplined, inner-Party rectification movement. Mao and the radicals surrounding him ruled that out: the Cultural Revolution became open season on the Party and its top leaders – Liu and Deng in particular.

Liu suffered the most: he died on a prison floor. Deng, probably on Mao's orders, escaped direct criticism – he was always the 'number two person taking the capitalist road' – though he was stripped of power and sent into internal exile. One of his sons, Pufang, was thrown from the upper storey of a building in Beijing. He has spent his life in a wheelchair ever since.

Deng returned to politics in 1973. Premier Zhou Enlai was dying and Mao, though still in league with the radicals led by JIANG QING, his wife, needed an experienced administrator at the helm. For almost three years, Deng fought the Left from the narrow political ground granted him by the Chairman. Even that disappeared in early 1976 when Zhou died and popular attempts to commemorate him in Tiananmen Square turned into a protest against the 'GANG OF FOUR'. The 'Gang' and their allies, stung by this defiance, turned on Deng again, removing him from office and castigating his emphasis on economic modernization as unrepentant revisionism. He remained in disgrace until the death of Mao in September 1976, and the arrest of the 'Gang' the following month brought the reign of the radicals to an end.

tempestuous ascendancy, 1978–89

Deng reemerged as vice-premier in July 1977. By the end of the following year, he had effectively shoved HUA GUOFENG, Mao's nominal successor, aside and, at the key Third Plenum of the Eleventh Central Committee in 1978, committed the Party to a programme of fundamental economic modernization, reform and engagement with the outside world that violated almost every tenet of the Cultural Revolution. Hua soon sank into complete obscurity. Deng secured the appointment of two key protégés, HU YAOBANG and ZHAO ZIYANG, as Party General Secretary and premier respectively. In 1981, the Party approved a controversial resolution that officially jettisoned most of Mao's policies while leaving intact the Chairman's status as founder and philosopher-king of the People's Republic. Deng's status in the Party, connections with the army, organizational skills and, sometimes, merciless cunning, rendered him all but invincible. The present belonged to him. So, with the approval of the resolution, did the past.

For a while, the people were on his side as well. Deng rode to power on the back of popular exhaustion with the Cultural Revolution and hatred for its perpetrators. There were also those, associated with the DEMOCRACY WALL movement of 1978–9, who wanted far-reaching changes to ensure a Cultural Revolution could never occur again. Deng used their movement to oust his opponents in the Party, but then cracked down on its leaders. The most prominent casualty was WEI JINGSHENG who spent all but a few months of the following 18 years in jail, becoming the most famous of China's DISSIDENTS in the 1980s and 1990s. Deng demanded 'socialist', not 'capital-

Deng the Man: The Enigma of Power

In keeping with mandarin tradition, Deng did not bother to cultivate a personal image of the kind essential to make progress in Western politics. Just as he never held the very highest offices in the Chinese Communist Party or government, so he never sought to rub shoulders with other international statesmen. Everyone, at home and abroad, knew he was the paramount leader, but his was an enigmatic form of power, manifested in the manipulation of events behind the scenes. It could neither be expressed in, nor confined to, formal positions of office. Deng's power was also disproportionate to his physical stature and lack of personal and sartorial finesse. He was barely five feet tall. He spoke in a thick Sichuanese accent. Until the last few years of his life, he was a chain smoker, favouring expensive 'Panda' brand cigarettes. Even while meeting foreign dignitaries, he frequently expectorated into a strategically placed spittoon. After his return from France, he was rarely photographed wearing anything other than a Sun Yat-sen suit (usually, and incorrectly, referred to as a 'Mao suit') or plain shirt, slacks and, often, sandals. He kept his private life private. So far, there have been no revelations about him of the kind that Li Zhisui, Mao's personal doctor, disclosed concerning the Chairman's sexual and other peccadilloes. Deng was married three times. His first wife died in childbirth. The second divorced him in 1933 when he was under a political cloud and married his chief accuser in the Party. His third wife, Zhuo Lin, outlived him. In later life, Deng presented himself as a family man. He was accompanied almost everywhere by one of his daughters, Deng Rong (1950–), who acted as his secretary, biographer and, as her father's hearing deteriorated and his speech slurred, interpreter and spokeswoman. Deng was an enthusiastic player of bridge, a soccer fan and a lover of French cuisine. He was especially fond of croissants.

ist', democracy. Political conduct was to be governed by 'four cardinal principles' he set out whose purpose was to ensure unchallenged Party rule (see below).

Deng, by then paramount leader of a coalition composed of other rehabilitated veterans and their protégés, launched even more profound changes in the economy. AGRICULTURE was decollectivized and households encouraged to contract land. Farmers produced a fixed amount for the state and were allowed to dispose of the surplus as they wished. Control over INDUSTRY was decentralized and factory managers granted decision-making power. Foreign trade and investment were encouraged, joint ventures set up. SPECIAL ECONOMIC ZONES (SEZS) – coastal enclaves where capitalist-style reforms could be conducted without fear of contaminating the socialist body politic – were created. China, soon pursuing what Deng described as 'socialism with Chinese characteristics' in which some people were allowed to get rich quicker than others, came alive after decades of Maoist stagnation.

The United States, which Deng visited in 1979, saw in the Chinese leader a late-flowering liberal. Britain, traditionally less sanguine about anything to do with China, still thought that since the issue of Hong Kong had to be addressed at some point, it was a good idea to start talks with a China under Deng than another, possibly less enlightened leader. The Sino-British agreement that returned the former colony to China in 1997 was signed in 1984. (See HONG KONG.) Other Western countries, concerned about the threat posed by the Soviet Union, saw in Deng's China a far more attractive version of Communism than that practised elsewhere. Mutual fear of Moscow and all-round relief that the Cultural Revolution was over made for friendly relations between Beijing and Western Europe.

Few of the achievements secured by Deng's reforms were free of problems. He had to make tactical reverses as well as bold advances to stay on top. Sometimes he advocated sweeping changes, even calling for significant political reforms. He frequently demanded 'ideological emancipation' yet just as often shifted the focus to strengthening Party discipline and waging war on 'bourgeois liberalism' – Party-speak for Western democracy. Many of these apparent policy swings were a response to complaints from conservatives among the old guard, chief of whom was CHEN YUN, about the Party's weakening grip over society, ideological laxity, corruption, and inflation arising from Deng's reforms. Deng was also genuinely concerned about these things. He was particularly anxious about the growth of 'bourgeois' and 'decadent' ideas – 'flies', he called them – that inevitably entered China when it opened its doors to the West. Like the great reformers and nationalists of the nineteenth century, Deng wanted 'foreign' things to be China's servant not its master. The world had much to teach China about science, technology and economics. When it came to politics, China had all the knowledge and experience it needed in the form of the Communist Party.

The failure of Hu and Zhao, both of whom Deng had been grooming as successors, to swat these 'pests' was responsible for their downfall. Hu was sacked as Party leader in 1987 for not taking a strong line against the 'bourgeois liberalism' manifested in a series of student protests. Deng also drove several liberal intellectuals out of the Party, including Fang Lizhi (1936–), a dissident astrophysicist. Zhao, who took over as general secretary from Hu, was dismissed in 1989 for failing to back the use of force against demonstrators in Tiananmen Square. Deng dumped both men without apparent feeling or regret, despite the fact that they had done much to turn his often vague ideas of reform and modernization into concrete, often striking successes. However, he ensured that neither suffered physically for their 'mistakes': Hu retained his seat on the Politburo after his dismissal, while Zhao, though subjected to a loose form of house arrest after his disgrace, nevertheless fared much better than he would have done had he crossed Mao instead of Deng.

In no area of political life was Deng so clear and consistent than in his determination that the Communist Party should retain its monopoly over political power even as it gave it up over the economy. He believed China needed a 'core', both in terms of ideology and organization, if it was to become a truly modern, powerful, independent nation. China's future was inseparable from that of the Communist Party to which he had devoted his life.

This explains his attitude towards the great pro-democracy protests that engulfed Beijing and scores of other cities across China between April and June 1989 (see TIANANMEN SQUARE DEMOCRACY MOVEMENT). They were sparked by the death of Hu, whom many students and intellectuals regarded as a martyr because he had been sacked two years earlier for not taking a hard line against the smaller protests of that time. In fact, the longer-term causes of the unrest were the results of a decade of Deng's reforms. Economic freedom had increased, but political freedom had hardly done so at all. Incomes had grown, but nowhere near as fast as inflation. CORRUPTION, much of it connected with the Communist leadership, had spread into almost every area of life. The protestors believed improvements were possible in many of these areas because there were strong indications that Party leaders were divided over the issues themselves.

Deng tried to put a stop to that. On 26 April the *People's Daily* published an editorial at his behest which denounced the protests as a

Deng's 'Theories': The Reformer in his Own Words

Deng occupies fourth position in China's official intellectual pantheon behind Marx, Lenin and Mao. The first two are deemed to have contributed *Isms*: complete systems of thought and, in Lenin's case, action, while the Chairman is said to have developed an 'ideology' (in Chinese, *sixiang*) or 'thought'. Deng's contribution took the form of 'theories' (in Chinese, *lilun*) about building 'socialism with Chinese characteristics'. They were written into the charter of the Communist Party shortly after he died.

They might more accurately be described as tips, aphorisms and assertions rather than 'theories'. Although he allowed three volumes of his collected works to be published, Deng made no pretensions to the title of philosopher or ideologue. He was concerned for the most part with practical matters of Party organization and economic performance. He sought to justify certain policies – chiefly those dealing with economic development and modernization – in the context of a political culture that required ideological sanction.

Perhaps the most famous single remark of Deng's was made in a speech in 1962: '*It doesn't matter if a cat is black or white; if it catches mice, it is a good cat.*' He was criticized for this sentiment during the Cultural Revolution when it was seen as proof of his devotion to 'capitalist' methods of economic development. The '*four cardinal principles*' Deng set out in 1979 endure for a different reason. They set the limits of political tolerance in China and have been written into both the Party charter and the state constitution. They are: '*Keep to the socialist road; uphold the dictatorship of the proletariat; uphold the leadership of the Communist Party; uphold Marxism-Leninism and Mao Zedong Thought.*'

Many of the phrases of contemporary Chinese politics can be attributed to Deng or were used by him to describe policies. They include:

● '*Seek truth from facts.*' The sentence was coined by Mao but popularized by Deng as a weapon to attack the earlier emphasis on studying Mao's Thought or other works of Communism rather than basing decisions and actions on experience.

● '*Socialism with Chinese characteristics*'. A phrase used from 1982 to refer to China's free market reforms.

● '*The socialist market economy*'. An extension of the above, that was used after Deng's 'southern journey' in 1992.

● '*One country, two systems*'. The policy under which Hong Kong was reunified with the Mainland in 1997 but allowed to maintain its capitalist system. Beijing has promised Taiwan the same.

Two longer extracts from Deng's speeches stand as testimony to the man and his determination to maintain tight political control – by a massive show of force, if necessary – and encourage rapid economic growth.

Five days after the suppression of the Tiananmen Square Democracy Movement in 1989, Deng said: '*This disturbance would have occurred sooner or later. It was determined by both the international environment and the domestic environment. It was bound to occur, whether one wished it or not; the only question was the time and the scale. That it has occurred now is to our advantage, especially because we have a large number of veteran comrades who are still in good health. They have experienced many disturbances and understand the possible consequences of different ways of dealing with them. They support the resolute action taken against the rebellion. Some comrades do not understand that action for the time being, but they will come to understand it and support the decision of the central authorities.*'

[*Selected Works of Deng Xiaoping, Vol. III (1982–1992)*
Foreign Languages Press, Beijing, 1994, p. 294]

During his 'southern journey' early in 1992, Deng remarked: '*We should be bolder than before in conducting reform and opening to the outside and have courage to experiment. We must not act like women with bound feet. Once we are sure that something should be done, we should dare to experiment and break a new path . . . If we don't have the pioneering spirit, if we're afraid to take risks, if we have no energy and drive, we cannot break a new path, a good path, or accomplish anything new. Who dares claim he is 100 per cent sure of success and that he is taking no risks? No one can ever be 100 per cent sure at the outset that what he is doing is correct. I've never been that sure.*'

[*Selected Works of Deng Xiaoping, Vol. III (1982–1992)*
Foreign Languages Press, Beijing, 1994, p. 360.]

---

conspiracy to plunge China into chaos. The response was even more dramatic: a massive demonstration which raised the stakes in the struggle between the Party and the protestors still higher. The protestors vilified Deng, likening him to the elderly and infirm EMPRESS DOWAGER who still insisted on intervening in everyday politics from 'behind the screen'.

Deng continued to take a hard line, though

his hands were tied by the imminent arrival of Mikhail Gorbachev, the Soviet leader, on a visit that would mark the normalization of relations between Moscow and Beijing. Once that was out of the way, an enlarged meeting of the leadership – including the elders whom Deng had tried to force into retirement two years before – decided to impose martial law on 20 May. By this time, Zhao had been sidelined as Party leader. There was another stalemate as the protestors prevented troops entering the centre of Beijing. It lasted until the night of 3–4 June when the People's Liberation Army mounted an armoured assault on the capital and cleared Tiananmen Square. In the process, they killed hundreds of unarmed civilians and wounded many others. For the next few weeks troops terrorized the people of Beijing. Protests elsewhere in China rapidly subsided.

Deng's exact role during the course of one of the most spectacular events in modern Chinese history is unclear. It is likely to remain so. But there is no doubt that he supported the crackdown, and no clear evidence has surfaced to suggest he believed it had been handled wrongly. If he felt any regret about the loss of life, he kept it to himself or his close confidants. It would have been out of character for a man who had been schooled in political violence since his early twenties to have done otherwise.

Deng in 'retirement', 1990–97

With JIANG ZEMIN, former Party boss of Shanghai, installed as Zhao's successor, Deng retired. He gave up his last formal position, the chairmanship of the state central military commission, in 1990. The paramount leader began to describe himself as an ordinary pensioner.

He was to prove the most powerful pensioner in the world. By the start of 1992, with Communism in ruins almost everywhere outside China, Deng grew dissatisfied with the slow growth of the Chinese economy and, apparently, the lack-lustre performance of Jiang and Premier LI PENG. His response – an extraordinary one given his 87 years and failing health – was to undertake a tour of south China and call for faster, bolder reforms. In remarks which, after a delay attributed to 'conservatives' in Beijing, found their way into the official media, Deng said socialism would succeed only if it made people rich.

Poverty was not socialism, he declared, suggesting that almost any economic system likely to make China and the Chinese people richer, was. Deng said there was still some danger from the 'Right' in China, but that the real task was to oppose the 'Left' – the hardline Marxists who could still sabotage China's modernization.

If Deng's 'southern journey' shocked and galvanized the Party leadership, the effect on ordinary people was even more electric. It released a surge of energy of the kind that had accompanied earlier political movements such as the Great Leap Forward and the Cultural Revolution. This time, however, it was harnessed to a cause – getting rich – which, while it produced problems, did not claim lives or generate waves of persecution. It gave fresh impetus to rapid economic growth already under way in many parts of the country and contributed to a process of dramatic social change whose consequences for China's political future remain unclear.

At first it was also uncertain whether Deng's policies would die with him. His death, the subject of repeated rumour and speculation long before it actually occurred in February 1997, removed the doubts. In a sense this was not the least of Deng's achievements. He had not always been successful in forcing his fellow Long Marchers into retirement, but a combination of his own will and ill health appeared to remove him from the political scene at least three years before he died. Unlike the case with Mao, there was therefore no need for potential successors to hover around Deng's bed waiting for a few croaks from the lips of the dying strongman. His passing was the occasion for neither a power struggle nor a policy change. Jiang Zemin remained in charge, and Deng's 'theories' were made part of the Communist Party's charter – the closest thing to permanence available in the volatile world of Chinese politics Deng had dominated for so long.

dissidents

The cost of dissent has always been high in China, as the careers of KANG YOUWEI, LIANG QICHAO, the GUANGXU EMPEROR, SONG JIAOREN, and those who opposed Chiang Kaishek's rule on the Mainland and then Taiwan testify. The dismissal, persecution, imprisonment and killing of political opponents were commonplace. Sometimes suppression

assumed enormous dimensions, as in the FEBRUARY TWENTY-EIGHTH INCIDENT of 1947 in Taiwan. Yet no Chinese government in the modern era has stamped on criticism so ruthlessly or for so long as that of the People's Republic. More than 50 years after coming to power the CHINESE COMMUNIST PARTY tolerates less formal dissent than the QING DYNASTY did a century ago. It is a telling indictment of Party rule. And it is a grim reminder of China's stunted modernization and poor HUMAN RIGHTS record.

Communism and its critics

Dissent *within* the Party dates almost from its founding. The different views – and the unhappy fate – of some of its early leaders speak of this. So do the fortunes of others who fell foul of the Party's numerous campaigns before it came to power. The largest of these took place in YANAN. Ding Ling (1904–85), a female novelist, and Wang Shiwei (1900–1947), another prominent writer, were merely the most celebrated casualties of the belief that under Mao Zedong the Party could tolerate criticism of its leaders, policies and ideology. It was a lesson the rest of the country learnt after 1949.

Party control of the MEDIA and repeated political movements against enemies, real and imagined, made this possible. Some of these waves of repression could be attributed to the need to deal with genuine foes at home. Some reflected the regime's difficult international position vis-à-vis TAIWAN and the UNITED STATES. But a campaign in 1955 against Hu Feng (1902–85), a prominent writer, showed that the Party would crush even mild criticism by apolitical intellectuals. Hu, a disciple of LU XUN, had complained about the turgid nature of intellectual life in China under its new Marxist orthodoxy. Mao responded by branding him a 'counter-revolutionary' and calling for a nationwide campaign of condemnation. Amid a wave of denunciations from colleagues, friends and family, Hu was sacked, purged and imprisoned.

The often brittle courage of Mainland intellectuals crumbled. In 1956, partly to win support from a section of society whose skills were needed to make China rich and strong, Mao encouraged a mood of political relaxation known as the ONE HUNDRED FLOWERS MOVEMENT. The blooms were more numerous and less fragrant than the Chairman anticipated. When critics began to challenge the very foundations of Party rule, he called a halt. The 'anti-Rightist Movement' that followed, organized by DENG XIAOPING, terrorized intellectuals as a class. Perhaps half a million were sacked, purged and disgraced. Many were sent to prison or LABOUR CAMPS where they remained for the next 20 years.

This neutering of the intellectuals made it easier for Mao to launch the GREAT LEAP FOR-WARD, an attempt to attain Communism overnight. It ended in catastrophe, but the fact that even so senior a figure as PENG DEHUAI was purged for saying so in private hardly encouraged criticism in public. Moreover, the slight increase in tolerance during the early 1960s, occasioned by the need to recover from the excesses of the Leap and Mao's temporary loss of prestige, came to an abrupt end with the CULTURAL REVOLUTION. For the next few years the Party was at war with itself in the pursuit of revolutionary truth; amid the confusion, there was neither interest nor occasion to question the Party's right to rule or the extent of its power.

dissent in the reform era

Yet before long, the destruction, cruelties and chaos of the Chairman's last great experiment in revolution raised precisely these issues. How could China descend into such tyranny? How might such a calamity be avoided again? What were the proper limits of power in a people's state? Some were willing to ask these questions in public. An example was that of the three men who gave their surnames to the 'Li-Yi-Zhe' poster displayed in the streets of Guangzhou in 1974. It called for the creation of a socialist legal system to protect the rights of the individual and, by implication, end one-party rule. Beijing, still in the grip of the radicals, condemned the poster and arrested its authors.

A later example, the DEMOCRACY WALL MOVEMENT of 1978–9, proved much more influential. It raised demands for freedom which have been pursued (unsuccessfully) by dissidents ever since, and it served as a training school, some of whose graduates, tempered by long spells in prison, still challenge the regime long after their movement was crushed. They include WEI JINGSHENG (until he was released from jail and forced into exile in 1997), Ren Wanding (1947–), founder of the Chinese Human Rights League, and Xu Wenli (1944–), editor of *April Fifth Forum*, a magazine of the era. These men, disillusioned Red Guards and educated youths sent to the countryside rather than alienated intellectuals of the kind who became dissidents in the Soviet Union, were unknown to most Chinese people. Neither was their cause championed in the West: Washington's principal interest in China was the cultivation of a diplomatic counterweight to Moscow. Yet the Democracy Wall Movement is the foundation of modern dissent in Communist China. It is the historical source of an alternative political future for China which the Party has sought (also unsuccessfully) to destroy.

An early casualty of its campaign to do so was Bai Hua (1930–), a playwright who became the conscience of the regime in the years of optimism immediately after Mao's death. His 1981 screenplay *Unrequited Love* attacked the persecution of patriotic intellectuals and worship of Mao, including that of the author himself. Party leaders, anxious to turn the page on the past rather than re-examine it, attacked Bai and silenced him. Yet in the new climate of economic reform and cautious condemnation of Mao, the boundary between constructive criticism and dangerous dissent was hard to draw. It shifted constantly during the 1980s as reformers in the Party, many of them influenced by Democracy Wall, fought over China's future with veteran revolutionaries such as CHEN YUN, DENG LIQUN, PENG ZHEN and, very often, Deng himself.

Sometimes the reform faction, protected first by HU YAOBANG, was in the ascendant. Certainly this was the case in 1985–6 when Fang Lizhi (1936–), an astrophysicist, Liu Binyan (1925–), a campaigning journalist, Wang Ruowang (1917–), a writer, and several other prominent intellectuals either publicly denounced MARXISM and/or called for an end to one-party rule, and for genuine democracy, freedom of speech and the rule of law. Partly because of their outspokenness, students took to the streets of several cities at the end of 1986 with calls for more freedom and less corruption. The protests soon ended, but so did the political careers of Hu, Fang, Liu and Wang. Hu was sacked as leader, and Fang, Liu and Wang were dismissed from the Party. They and their ideas were attacked in a campaign against 'bourgeois liberalization'.

Yet dissent grew again under the less enthusiastic protection of ZHAO ZIYANG, Hu's successor as Party leader. One of its more remarkable manifestations was the broadcast, in 1988, of a controversial television series called *River Elegy* (*He Shang*). It criticized China's traditional civilization as backward and a source of shame rather than pride. Party elders were furious.

In the spring of 1989, the tenth anniversary of the suppression of the Democracy Wall Movement, Fang Lizhi and others spoke out with a new boldness. They called for the release of Wei Jingsheng and the retirement of Deng Xiaoping. Such appeals, along with the campus 'democracy salons' they addressed, helped pave the way for the TIANANMEN SQUARE DEMOCRACY MOVEMENT. So did the activities of Wang Juntao (1958–) and Chen Zeming (1950–), both of whom had taken part in the Democracy Wall Movement but both of whom, by the late 1980s, had become dissidents of a different kind. Rather than try to cultivate the Party elite and work from within, they sought a genuinely independent voice based on their position as founders of a non-government social research institute.

This made them particularly dangerous in the eyes of the authorities. And it made them particular targets of attack once troops had suppressed the demonstrations. Wang and Chen were jailed for 13 years, the longest sentences imposed on those deemed to have masterminded the protests. Fang Lizhi might have suffered a similar fate had he and his wife not been able to shelter in the American embassy in Beijing, where they remained for a year before leaving for the United States.

diplomacy and the Party's dilemma

Tiananmen stifled dissent and saved the regime. In the aftermath of the military crackdown even 'apolitical' criticism of Party policies, such as the plan to build the THREE GORGES DAM, was muted. One reason for this was the imprisonment of Dai Qing (1943–), a journalist who campaigned most vigorously against the project. Yet Tiananmen exacted a price on the Party, too. It stifled the personal freedom and initiative required to reinvigorate the economy; and it complicated China's foreign policy towards the West whose governments and people were horrified by the repression. These factors – coupled with a determination to stay in power – governed the Party's attitude towards dissent during the 1990s. Beijing tightened and loosened its grip to suit the demands of the moment, sometimes raising hopes in the West. But it consistently refused to tolerate any political change of the kind that might give its critics a legitimate voice.

Wei Jingsheng and Wang Dan (1965–), a Tiananmen student leader, were beneficiaries and casualties of this new 'human rights diplomacy'. Both men were released in 1993 to secure diplomatic objectives – in Wei's case, success for Beijing in its campaign to host the year 2000 Olympics; in Wang's, an extension of trading privileges with the United States. But when Sydney won the Games, Wei resumed his calls for democracy, and Washington decoupled trade from human rights, both men were sent back to prison. They remained there until 1997 and 1998 respectively, when they were released into exile to improve relations with the United States. Other imprisoned activists, including Wang Juntao, were also allowed to leave China 'for medical reasons'.

Similar factors were at work in Beijing's decision to sign the two main United Nations covenants on human rights at the close of the century. The move was enough to suggest to the outside world that genuine changes were afoot without challenging the Party's dominance at home. Within weeks of China signing the International Covenant on the Protection of Political and Civil Rights, security agents arrested Xu Wenli and several other dissidents who had sought permission to form a China Democratic Party. This party's programme called for direct elections at all levels of government. At the time of the arrests, LI PENG, number two in the Communist Party, warned that groups which advocated a multiparty system or challenged the dominance of the Communist Party would not be tolerated. In December 1998 Xu was sentenced to 13 years in prison. The crackdown against the China Democratic Party continued throughout 1999.

This nipped another political challenge in the bud, but has not resolved the Communist Party's dissident dilemma. Rather, it has highlighted a growing, dangerous disparity between Chinese state and society. China's Communist political system changed little during the last two decades of the twentieth century, while Chinese society, particularly in the developed, urbanized parts of the country, changed much. Thanks to rapid economic growth, society is becoming semi-autonomous, even pluralistic in outlook. China's dissident movement remains numerically weak and sometimes divided. But it refuses to go away. So does the broader, if sometimes unspoken, demand for change sustaining it.

education

For more than 2,000 years China's rulers maintained political and social order through the regimentation of knowledge. When they could no longer do so, at the start of the twentieth century, an entire civilization collapsed along with imperial rule. Modern Chinese governments have been just as concerned to control intellectual life in order to stay in power, realize political goals and discipline the population. As a result, education has become a crucial battleground in the struggle over China's future. There has often been disagreement about what education in China is *for*; there has rarely been any about its importance.

education and the old order

The status of education in China owes much to Confucius (see CONFUCIANISM). The Sage taught that all men could acquire virtue and that the virtuous should rule. For centuries, complex civil service examinations selected those among the tiny, educated minority considered worthy of office. None of them were WOMEN, virtually all of whom were illiterate. Most men were illiterate, too, until the Communist Party introduced mass education in the second half of the twentieth century.

In the sense that education served the state in traditional China, it was utilitarian. In so far as it involved rote learning, mastery of ancient texts and competence in arcane written forms it was impractical and entirely unsuited to China's needs at the close of the nineteenth century. The country was weak, divided and backward, its QING DYNASTY rulers unable to resist foreign invasion or modernize the economy. The traditional education system had trained China's ruling elite for more than 2,000 years. Yet its graduates could teach their country little about the role of a modern army, an industrial economy, constitutional government, and the rule of law. A thorough overhaul was required.

This was envisaged in the 100 Days Reform Movement of 1898 championed by KANG YOUWEI. Most of Kang's ideas fell foul of the EMPRESS DOWAGER, but the Court did establish a new institution to provide modern education. It later became known as Beijing University (abbreviated in Chinese as *Beida*), still one of the Mainland's premier educational institutions.

Many of Kang's ideas were implemented on a grander scale in the early years of the twentieth century when the Qing at last confronted the challenge of reform. Thousands of students studied abroad, many of them in JAPAN. At home, the traditional examination system was abolished and a Ministry of Education established. This dramatic move, in 1905, buried a large part of China's past but left unanswered a series of questions about the future. Chief among them was the purpose of education in the new era. How should the future scholar class be trained? How was China to build the universities, colleges, libraries and research institutions needed for the future? In the Chinese context, merely posing these questions was revolutionary. The fact that attempts were made to answer them showed how much the country had changed.

reform and political change, 1911–49

The process intensified with the REPUBLICAN REVOLUTION of 1911. Higher education grew rapidly as the government, private individuals and missionary organizations founded or expanded institutions. Qinghua, set up as a technical school in Beijing in 1911 and designated a university in 1928, was an example of the first. Nankai University (from 1919) in Tianjin, funded by patriotic Chinese entrepreneurs, was an example of the second. China's well-known Christian colleges included St John's University in Shanghai, and Peking (Beijing) Union Medical College.

Faculty and curricular development were equally striking, nowhere more so than at Beida. Under Chancellor Cai Yuanpei (1868–1940), leading radicals were appointed to the staff, women students admitted and the entire community encouraged to devote itself to learning rather than look upon education as the stepping stone to an official career. The student body was politicized from the start: its members took to the streets in 1919 to protest at China's treatment by the powers at the Versailles Peace Conference. In one form or another Beida was involved in all the great issues of the MAY FOURTH MOVEMENT – from opposition to Japan's occupation of Shandong to wider use of BAI HUA or the vernacular; from calls for an end to warlord rule to the introduction of science, democracy and MARXISM. The university established a tradition of student activism that worried governments at the time and ever since.

Yet if it was often uneasy, the relationship between intellectuals and the state during the Republican era was more relaxed than proved the case under Communism. One reason for this was the absence of a dominant intellectual orthodoxy in the period 1912–49. Another was that governments, whether led by WAR-LORDS or the KUOMINTANG, were rarely powerful enough to impose their will over academic life.

This is not to say that students and intellectuals supported the Kuomintang. In the first half of the century, China's academic community looked towards the West, where many of its members had studied, for inspiration. They were attracted to the liberal ideal of education as an independent pursuit of scholars. Yet they were anxious to serve their country, usually by acting as its conscience. It was on these grounds that students and intellectuals opposed Chiang Kai-shek's appeasement of

Japan in the 1930s and his determination to wipe out the Communists in the 1940s. Many were bitterly opposed to authoritarian Nationalist rule, suffered as a result of it, and welcomed its demise in the Civil War.

controlling the curriculum

When the Communists seized power, China's higher education system was vigorous, diverse but small and confined largely to the coastal cities of the east. Its approximately 120,000 students accounted for about 0.3 per cent of the total age group. Below the modern tertiary sector, old-style schools, some of them charitable foundations, and many of them still teaching the Confucian classics, were common. Perhaps 25 per cent of primary-age children attended school and 3 per cent of those of secondary age. An estimated 80 per cent of the population was illiterate. The Party had much to do, both in extending education, and bending that already in existence to its revolutionary purpose.

Its first move was to nationalize higher education and remould it, along with much of the rest of the society, along Soviet Russian lines. The SOVIET UNION, not the capitalist West, was now the exemplar. China needed less liberal arts students and more engineers to build a modern economy. Many Chinese students, the young JIANG ZEMIN and LI PENG among them, were sent to study in Moscow. China also needed an academic community loyal to the new regime. At first, resistance to the imposition of Marxist dogma and Party control was considerable. It was broken by the political campaigns of the 1950s, particularly the 'Anti-Rightist Movement' of 1958 (see ONE HUNDRED FLOWERS MOVEMENT).

Elementary education expanded with LAND REFORM and the creation of agricultural cooperatives during the early 1950s. It was designed to eradicate illiteracy and win peasants over to the regime. At secondary level, new schools offered shortened courses for workers and peasants with work experience to prepare them for higher education. The idea was to break the stranglehold over college enrolment enjoyed by graduates of regular secondary schools.

Despite this rapid expansion, by 1956 78 per cent of the population remained illiterate and only about 52 per cent of children of school age attended primary school. The gulf between the elite tertiary sector and primary and secondary levels was almost as wide as before 1949. This raised fundamental

Language and Learning

Even in times of political disintegration, China's written language helped bind the country together culturally, unifying meaning and facilitating communication across huge distances and among speakers of mutually incomprehensible dialects. A Chinese character bears the same meaning whether it is pronounced in Cantonese (the dialect spoken mostly in Hong Kong, Guangdong and parts of Guangxi), Shanghainese (the Southern Wu dialect spoken in and around the city of the same name) or Taiwanese (the Southern Min dialect spoken in Taiwan and the province of Fujian opposite). But only the educated can read Chinese characters; and until the second half of the century, the vast majority of Chinese were not educated. In this respect, educators, reformers, and revolutionaries – indeed many of those in the twentieth century who sought to communicate new ideas – viewed China's complex system of writing as an obstacle to progress rather than an object of beauty. Several devised ways of replacing or simplifying it.

One of them, LU XUN, tried in the 1930s to substitute a Latin, alphabetic script for Chinese characters. The system failed other than as a guide to how characters should be pronounced in Standard Chinese. Lu was among those who, rather than writing in literary Chinese, wrote in bai hua, or the vernacular, a profound linguistic break with the past launched by the May Fourth Movement.

The Communists preferred the simplification of characters to their substitution. In 1956 and again in 1964 Beijing issued approved lists of 'simplified' characters, more than 2,000 in all, which reduced the numbers of strokes in the original forms. At the same time, old or redundant characters were eliminated while others, often written in different ways, were standardized. The move was designed to aid the spread of literacy, but some condemned it as an attempt to cut Chinese off from their classical and literary past. Another series of simplified forms, issued in 1977, was later withdrawn. Simplified characters are used in all Mainland materials for domestic consumption, but they have not been adopted in Hong Kong, Taiwan, Macau, or among many Overseas Chinese communities.

Taiwan and the Mainland are also divided by their respective systems of romanization, the transliteration of the sounds of characters, mainly for the purposes of teaching the language and for the benefit of foreigners unable to read Chinese. Jesuit missionaries undertook this task first in the seventeenth century, but the most widely used method until the final decades of the twentieth century was created by Thomas Francis Wade (1818–95) and revised by Herbert Alan Giles (1845–1935), both of them Britons. The Chinese Post Office added a few varieties of its own in 1906 for the spelling of Chinese place names.

In 1928, the Kuomintang government promulgated a new system: the Gwoyeu Romatzyh which incorporates the tone of each character within the romanized spelling. It failed to catch on during the Kuomintang's years on the Mainland, and is now virtually unknown outside Taiwan where, in revised form, it remains the official system of romanization. The equivalent on the Mainland is Hanyu Pinyin, which in the final decades of the century eclipsed Wade-Giles as the most widely used system. All foreign-language publications in the Mainland use pinyin. So do most publications outside the People's Republic, especially when they deal with affairs in the Mainland. Hong Kong continues to use a variety of English equivalents to the Cantonese pronunciation of characters.

Chinese governments have had more success in propagating a national spoken language than in producing a uniform method of romanization. Republican, Nationalist and Communist regimes all made a version of the Beijing dialect, known in English as Mandarin, the national tongue. The Kuomintang call Standard Chinese kuoyu (national language), the Communists, putonghua (common speech). Its purpose is to facilitate communication and strengthen national identity in a country plagued by a diversity of dialects. The northern version of spoken Chinese was made the basis of national language because it is spoken by more people over a wider area than any other. The north is also the traditional centre of political power in China. Linguistic diversity is greatest south of the Yangtze River. At the start of the new century, putonghua has not triumphed over patois despite a clause in the constitution calling for its propagation, and repeated efforts by Beijing to do so.

---

questions about the purpose of education in the new order. Some of them had been foreshadowed in the late Qing and early Republic. Others were rehearsed when the Party ruled large tracts of countryside from YANAN, its wartime capital. But in the circumstances of the mid-1950s, they acquired new urgency.

Among the issues at stake were: how best to use the limited funds available for education; whether education should suit present or future needs; whether it was designed to deliver quality or quantity; and whether it was best used to train highly specialized professionals for economic construction (later known as 'experts') or personnel committed first to the Party and the Revolution (the so-called 'reds'). There was also the question of the nature of the Revolution itself, its goals, and how and when they might be realized. In the late 1950s MAO ZEDONG decided they should be attained sooner rather than later. Education was an important issue during the GREAT LEAP FORWARD, and a central one in the CULTURAL REVOLUTION.

education and revolution

During the Leap, education changed from a breeding ground for intellectual aristocrats into an instrument of mass politicization. Officially at least, the division between mental and manual labour was abolished. So was the idea of education for education's sake. Mass education in the countryside, right down to kindergarten level, was designed to end illiteracy at the same breakneck pace that the new communes were ordered to produce grain and steel. None of these goals was reached. And in 1960 the entire experiment floundered amid famine, economic chaos, rivalry with Moscow and political setbacks for Mao.

It was far from the end of the Chairman's vision. The Socialist Education Movement that began in 1962 sought to reinvigorate the Revolution at a time when 'Soviet revisionism' was said to be making inroads in China. The People's Republic was falling prey to bureaucratism and privilege; it was in the grip of a 'two-line struggle' between genuine revolutionaries and 'Soviet revisionists'. One example of this was the concentration in the best schools and colleges of the offspring of the country's new leaders. 'Experts', discounted during the Leap, were regaining their ascendancy; workers and peasants, supposed beneficiaries of the Revolution, were once again at a disadvantage. Students and intellectuals were sent to labour in the countryside and learn Revolution the hard way.

Yet it was not until 1966, when the Chairman focused his attack on rivals within the Party, that the goals of the Socialist Education Movement were realized. China's students formed the first wave in the assault on 'bourgeois revisionism' known as the Cultural Revolution. They began by attacking the hold 'old ideas' were said to have over their institutions. Then, with Mao's encouragement, they overthrew those said to be responsible for them. Once again, Beida was at the forefront.

Within weeks China's higher education system, and many of its secondary schools, suspended formal operations. Students metamorphosed into Red Guards, attended mass rallies in Tiananmen Square, and spread the message of iconoclasm and revolutionary violence across the country courtesy of free rail travel. Their attacks on traditional learning, and physical assaults on those associated with it, marked a fundamental departure from the respect for knowledge and the elite who sustained it which had defined China for centuries. It was in this respect, as much as the dismissal and disgrace of LIU SHAOQI and DENG XIAOPING, Mao's erstwhile comrades in the Party leadership, that the Cultural Revolution was genuinely revolutionary.

Changes to the educational system were no less radical. The pace at which they were introduced varied in accordance with the ebb and flow of the power struggle in Beijing, but their purpose was clear. It was to produce a new type of worker-peasant intellectual to replace the now politically damned 'bourgeois' kind. New model intellectuals would be as familiar with the 'thought' of Chairman Mao as their own specialism; as much at home engaged in farm or industrial production as in the library or laboratory. Such people would help eradicate the 'three differences' that had dogged China for years: those between town and countryside, worker and peasant, mental and manual labour.

To this end, 'bourgeois examinations' were abolished and entry to higher education made subject to 'recommendations' and class background. 'Key point' secondary schools were closed as manifestations of elitism. Streaming was stopped, and the number of school years shortened to make education more accessible to workers and peasants. Labour was combined with study at every level of education. Red Guards, their revolutionary excesses now curbed by the PEOPLE'S LIBERATION ARMY, were sent to the countryside to enhance and complete their education. Decentralization of control over schools and colleges, an end to the national curriculum, and the production of new textbooks incorporating Mao's teachings accompanied these stunning changes.

The net result of the Cultural Revolution on education was first to paralyse it, then extend and equalize educational opportunity across the country. The effects on quality, especially at the tertiary level, were far less favourable. There was no college intake for four years and the quality of education available once enrolments resumed was poor. Moreover, the violence, excesses, and chaos created by the Cultural Revolution tended to undermine such gains as were made. When Mao died and the 'GANG OF FOUR' were toppled in 1976, the educational policies of the Cultural Revolution were roundly attacked and comprehensively reversed.

training talent, controlling minds

From the late 1970s cramming and competition returned at all levels of the system and were more intense for their long absence. The FOUR MODERNIZATIONS, the Party's new development strategy, required experts of all kinds. China had squandered a generation of talent. Many 'bourgeois' intellectuals disgraced under Mao were rehabilitated and sent back to work. Deng Xiaoping, in charge of the country by 1978, was quick to rehabilitate intellectuals as a whole, describing them as mental labourers in the service of socialism. Thousands of students were sent to study overseas, this time to the West where some of them resumed scholarly contacts established a century earlier but sundered by the Communist Revolution.

The new emphasis on quality and cost effectiveness took a toll on secondary education in urban areas, where many schools were closed, and at both primary and secondary levels in the countryside, where the demise of agricultural communes often meant schools simply disappeared. Many farmers, masters of their land again, preferred their children to work at home than attend school to no very clear purpose. This was particularly true if their children were girls. The long struggle against illiteracy has yet to be won.

The same is true of the battle every Chinese government has waged to control the minds of its people, and in particular the minds of its educated minority. China's opening to the outside world made this task more difficult. A campaign against 'spiritual pollution' in 1983 tried but failed to curb Western influence among urban youth. Three years later students took to the streets to protest against corruption and demand more freedom. Their movement culminated in the fall of HU YAOBANG as Party leader and sparked another anti-Western campaign, this time against 'bourgeois liberalism'.

That this, too, failed to tame China's students was clear from the great outpouring of dissent that unfolded in Tiananmen Square during the spring of 1989 (see TIANANMEN SQUARE DEMOCRACY MOVEMENT). Once again the students and faculty of Beida played an important role in a movement which swept through educational institutions across the Mainland and won support from almost every section of urban society. The imposition of martial law, the military assault on the Square and what amounted to a military occupation of several of Beijing's top universities in the weeks that followed, cast the battle between intellectuals and the state, education and ideological orthodoxy, into sharp relief.

There was no recurrence of student activism in the 1990s, most students and many intellectuals showing more interest in business than politics. Education itself has became more of a business, too. Private schools patronized by the offspring of the urban rich are common.

Less favoured schools run factories and other commercial activities to supplement meagre state funds. Private education has also made inroads at the tertiary level: Shanghai Shanda University, established in 1992, is the first private university founded under Communist rule. Elsewhere university students are charged fees for accommodation and tuition, and then left to find their own jobs on graduation.

the future of education

Old and new problems gnaw away at the Mainland education system at the start of the new era. Perhaps the oldest of them all simply concerns providing enough of it. In the 1990s the government set a target of providing 9 years of compulsory education to 85 per cent of the population by the start of the new millennium. The goal seemed likely to prove elusive, though primary schools claimed to have enrolled nearly 99 per cent of primary-aged children by the end of 1997. Because of the size of its population, China ought to have the largest higher education establishment in the world. The plan was to have enrolled 3.5 million in the formal sector and 2.5 million in the adult education sector by the year 2000. During the first decade of the new century, the People's Republic is likely to reach the threshold of 'mass' higher education, defined as enrolment of 15 per cent of the age cohort.

Delivering *quality* education is proving more difficult than supplying quantity. This is because it involves politics and culture, neither of which encourages the critical spirit essential for genuine development – whether in the classroom or elsewhere. Despite two decades of dramatic change and, in education, rapid commercialization, the Communist Party still sets limits on what can be taught, written and discussed by its brightest citizens. China has mastered the rudiments and, in several cases, much more than the rudiments, of the world's advanced technologies: biotechnology; nuclear power and nuclear weapons; computing and telecommunications. But much Chinese science is conducted in institutes controlled by the military, or modelled on those of the former Soviet Union, or both. Too much knowledge is subject to secrecy and a concern with security. Too many of China's universities resemble technical institutes rather than genuine academies. 'Larger' issues of life, such as the *purpose* of education, science, democracy, politics etc., are rarely examined because they raise too many sensitive questions. In all these respects, therefore, political control in China still relies heavily on the regimentation and restriction of knowledge.

Empress Dowager (Ci Xi) (1835–1908)

Even when cloaked in elaborate imperial finery – as was the case in most turn-of-the-century depictions of her – the Empress Dowager presented an austere image. It was worthy of a woman who dominated Court life for almost half a century and the affairs of her nation for most of its final, troubled years as a monarchy. The Manchu QING DYNASTY she served, sometimes by sponsoring reform, sometimes by crushing it, and in 1900 by backing the violent BOXER REBELLION, survived her by a mere three years. In the end, her capricious, domineering, conservative leadership was regarded by opponents as symptomatic of all that was wrong with Manchu rule and a principal reason for overthrowing it. Both at the time and since Ci Xi attracted an almost universally 'bad press'. Her perceived misdeeds have contributed to a feeling in China – reinforced by the brief supremacy of JIANG QING in the Communist period – that women are best kept out of high politics.

The extent to which the Empress Dowager's poor reputation is justified must be determined in the light of what she had to contend with and what she sought to achieve. Her task was to preserve Manchu rule amid a ferment of change generated by imperial decay, foreign aggression and growing anti-Manchu, pro-Chinese feeling. In the sense that the dynasty outlasted her, Ci Xi's political career might be judged a success. In the sense that through a mixture of foolishness, manipulation, corruption and reaction she managed to defy change until, too late, she was forced to comply with it before it swept her and her ruling house into oblivion, she emerges as a flawed, tragic figure, reminiscent of the last rulers of European monarchies in the twentieth century. More than skills and skulduggery at Court were required to ensure the survival of a system of government which had changed little in the previous 2,000 years.

Ci Xi entered the Court as a concubine of Xian Feng Emperor (ruled 1851–62). She bore his only surviving son who became the Tong Zhi Emperor (ruled 1864–74), and for whom she served as co-regent. When he died in 1874, she secured the succession of her nephew, GUANGXU. This was a violation of the laws of imperial succession which stipulated that power should pass to the next generation. In fact, power remained in her hands and those of her allies in a Court vexed by internal rebellions, calls for reform and growing foreign aggression. Throughout her adult life, Ci Xi presided over a shrinking empire that was also an unstable one.

She gave up her second regency in 1888 when Guangxu married and formally assumed the functions of government. But Ci Xi remained the dominant figure for solid, dynastic reasons. As the mother of the previous emperor she belonged to the elder generation and thus commanded respect and obedience. She saw most of the memorials addressed to the Throne, and had a say in all major appointments. Guangxu knew that he was her creature: she had made him and – as he was soon to find out – she could break him, too.

Contemporary Western observers were almost at one in viewing the Empress Dowager as ignorant, superstitious and susceptible to flattery. She was not so hidebound as to set her face against all attempts at reform, but her overriding aim was to preserve Manchu rule and, in particular, that of a certain Manchu faction she felt she could rely on. One consequence of this was the continued pursuit of public grandeur for a dynasty in desperate straits, and one that needed to devote its last penny to national defence and reform if it was to retain the Mandate of Heaven, the closest thing in imperial China to popular sanction. However, Ci Xi had not forgiven BRITAIN and France for destroying the imperial Summer Palace in 1860. She ordered the construction of another on the same site, northwest of the Forbidden City, using funds earmarked for the development of China's first modern navy. Starved of money and short of leadership, the new Chinese fleet was sent to the bottom of the sea by the Japanese in the war of 1894–5 (see JAPAN).

A few months later, the Empress Dowager crushed an attempt at sweeping reform sponsored by her nephew who, following China's defeat by Japan, had woken up to the need for drastic change. With its call for a comprehensive overhaul that would have transformed Manchu rule into a constitutional monarchy, the '100 Days' reform of 1898 bore the hall-marks of later Chinese attempts at instant renewal. But Guangxu, who had placed himself at the head of the reform movement championed by the scholar KANG YOUWEI, misjudged the resistance to a programme which threatened many at Court and most officials beyond. Ci Xi had the reformers arrested and many of their leaders executed. She then placed Guangxu under 'palace arrest', a fate the bewildered, tragic emperor was to endure until his death, a day before the Empress Dowager's, in 1908.

Ci Xi proceeded to rule China for the remainder of her life from 'behind the curtain'. Propriety meant she could not be *seen* to rule, but she remained the decisive voice in national affairs, manipulating Court factions to get her own way. This pattern of leadership was to be repeated in the different circumstances of the Communist era. Ci Xi, like DENG XIAOPING in the final decade of his life, belonged to the older generation from whom power had supposedly passed to younger, more reform-minded leaders. But neither could refrain from intervening in the conduct of politics, and both 'locked up' or otherwise isolated those deemed their successors. In Ci Xi's case, the prisoner was Guangxu, a rejected symbol of reform. In Deng's, it was first HU YAOBANG, dismissed for 'mistakes', and second, ZHAO ZIYANG, who was sacked and placed under house arrest in Beijing for opposing the use of force against the 1989 TIANAN-MEN SQUARE DEMOCRACY MOVEMENT. At the end of the twentieth century, as at its beginning, China's paramount leaders found it hard to pass on power.

The most tragic example of the Empress Dowager's desperation, folly and, ultimately, failure to shore up the dynasty was her support

for the Boxer Rebellion of 1899–1900. The attempt to turn a violent peasant rebellion fuelled by social discontent, xenophobia, and magical beliefs into a force for resisting the foreign presence in China ended with the Allied occupation and looting of Beijing, and the Court's flight to Xian, capital of SHAANXI. The Boxer Protocol imposed by the Powers did not require China to cede territory, but it was one of the most humiliating treaties the by now painfully weak, demoralized dynasty was required to sign.

Ci Xi's last years in power cast her in a slightly different, but no less comfortable light. Dissatisfaction with the Qing grew rapidly as the dynasty failed to meet the expectations of a society buffeted by change on all fronts, and increasingly subject to the influence of developments beyond China's borders. Reformers and Republicans (among them LIANG QICHAO and SUN YAT-SEN), merchants and militarists, peasants and provincial leaders, and the foreign powers each demanded different – often radically different – things. But they shared the view that little could be accomplished as long as the Manchus remained in power. The Court responded by sponsoring wholesale changes in EDUCATION, the military (see ARMIES), and government and administration of the kind championed by Guangxu almost a decade earlier (see QING DYNASTY). But in the new climate, these reforms, though bold, were too little, too late (see REPUBLICAN REVOLUTION). Neither the hopes of the emperor, nor the fears of the Empress Dowager were realized: they died within 24 hours of each other, allowing Ci Xi, who managed to outlive her nephew, just enough time to stipulate that PU YI, her grand nephew, would become the next, and as it happened, the last, Manchu Emperor.

energy

As with food supplies, so with energy: growth in demand has forced China to abandon its insistence on self-sufficiency and look increasingly to trade for the supply of this most strategic of commodities. Important consequences follow from this striking example of China's growing interdependence with the outside world. One concerns FOREIGN POLICY: the inevitable pursuit of energy security implies greater Chinese interest – and influence – in those parts of the world which supply China's needs. Another has to do with world

energy markets: China's growing hunger for oil may affect prices, and perhaps patterns of production beyond its borders. The global implications of China's energy equation aside, the fact that the People's Republic must supply most of its needs itself points to continuing strain on transport networks, growing use of hydro- and nuclear power, and steady pressure on the ENVIRONMENT.

China is rich in energy resources but, given its huge population, not rich enough. Per capita resources of coal, oil, gas and hydro-power are far below world averages. They need to be far above to ensure industrial and economic growth in the new era matches that in the final years of the old. China is the world's third-largest producer of energy resources after the United States and Russia. But it is also the third-largest *consumer*; and its share of world energy consumption is expected to rise to 20 per cent by 2010, compared with 9 per cent in 1990. China cannot meet such needs despite the fact that its primary energy consumption is growing less quickly than GDP.

Unequal distribution and inaccessibility make the utilization of existing resources difficult. Much of the Mainland's INDUSTRY is concentrated in the east while the best coal is found in the north, northwest and southwest. Hydro-power potential is enormous, but largely confined to the southwest. Several major oil fields – including Daqing, the former Maoist industrial model in HEILONGJIANG, and Shengli in SHANDONG – are closer to industrial centres, but most of them are mature. The best prospects for significant new oil finds are in the Tarim Basin, the most inaccessible part of inaccessible XINJIANG, or offshore where exploitation presents problems of capital, technology and transport all its own. Widespread dispersion of resources causes transport bottlenecks, particularly on the RAILWAYS which struggle to move coal and other commodities across the country to places of need.

Regional imbalance in power supplies is almost as acute as the uneven distribution of resources. In the late 1990s, electricity supply nationwide was about 10 per cent short of demand. Eleven rural counties and 72 million people had no electricity at all. Several inland provinces, including some major cities, suffered from power cuts and/or limited supplies. However, there was a surplus of electricity along the coast as consumption slowed along with economic growth owing to the Asian financial crisis.

Coal dominates China's energy scene. It accounts for three quarters of primary energy consumption and is burnt throughout the Mainland in power stations, industrial boilers, kilns, furnaces and residential homes. It will remain the dominant energy source for decades. China's reserves are enormous yet unsatisfactory: coal quality is generally poor and many burners are inefficient. As a result, ambient levels of particulates and sulphur dioxide in China are among the highest in the world. Heavy investment in coal cleaning and flue-gas desulphurization technologies is required to lessen the environmental impact of coal dependency. Greater residential use of gas – a marginal fuel in China's energy scene – will help.

China became a major oil producer in the last two decades of the twentieth century. In 1970, it produced 0.5 million barrels of oil a day. At the close of the century it produced almost 4 million barrels a day which supplied about 20 per cent of total energy demand. Oil consumption grew faster still. In 1993, China became a net importer of oil for the first time, a major turning point for a country long committed to self-sufficiency in energy, and potentially an important one for the international oil market.

In the absence of major new finds at home, China's oil shortfall – estimated at 28 million tonnes a year in the late 1990s – is set to grow to about one-third of total needs. To meet it, Beijing has entered into a flurry of agreements with foreign countries. This signified a move from spot market purchases of foreign oil to the laying down of guaranteed supplies for the future. In terms of potential, the largest deal involved Kazakhstan. In 1997 China agreed to take a 60 per cent stake in a local producer and build a pipe line to transport oil east, all the way to the People's Republic. Arguments over costs soon cast a cloud over the project. But in Kazakhstan and elsewhere in Central Asia, Beijing is anxious to secure reliable energy supplies. Russia may provide one: Beijing is exploring the possibility of piping gas from Lake Baikal, just north of Mongolia, to east China, and from Siberia to the far western province of Xinjiang. It has also conducted discussions with Thailand, Iraq, Canada, Venezuela, Papua New Guinea, Sudan, Mongolia and Kuwait. In several of these countries Chinese engineers have either prospected or actually drilled for oil and gas.

Beijing's hunger for energy reinforces its claim to sovereignty over the Spratlys and Paracels, the vast collection of islands, islets and atolls scattered across the SOUTH CHINA SEA. The area is believed to be rich in oil and gas as well as fishing resources. Ownership is contested, in whole or in part, by Vietnam, Taiwan, Malaysia, Brunei and the Philippines. Even if the South China Sea delivers fewer energy resources than expected, the region will remain strategically important to the People's Republic. In the new era China is likely to turn increasingly to the Middle East for oil supplies. In common with oil from the same source bound for Japan and Taiwan,

China's purchases will pass through the sea lanes of the South China Sea on the way to the Mainland, increasing the need for a strong Chinese naval presence in the region (see PEOPLE'S LIBERATION ARMY).

Hydro-power met a modest 6 per cent of energy demand at the turn of the century. It will meet more in future. Completion of the controversial THREE GORGES DAM, scheduled for 2009, is one reason for this. The enormous untapped potential of hydro-power is another. Beijing's two nuclear plants – a Sino-French joint venture at Daya Bay in GUANGDONG and Qinshan in ZHEJIANG, built by Chinese engineers but with many imported components – currently generate less than 1 per cent of demand. Plans to expand these facilities and build new ones in Lianyungang, JIANGSU province, with Russian assistance,

should increase the figure to 2.2 per cent by 2015. In the 1990s China matched nuclear development at home with sales abroad, exporting a reactor to Algeria and helping build a nuclear power station in PAKISTAN.

Nuclear power plays a much larger role in Taiwan than in the People's Republic. At the close of the century the island's three nuclear power stations generated almost 30 per cent of total output. In 1999 the government gave the go-ahead for a fourth plant despite a twenty-year opposition campaign by environmental activists. Starved of energy resources, save for hydro-power, Taiwan is heavily dependent on imports of oil and gas. This makes it particularly vulnerable to blockade, the most likely form of pressure to come from the Mainland in the event of increased tension between Beijing and Taipei.

environment

For much of China's history, and for many of its people, existence has been a precarious business. For millions it has proved impossible. Floods, famine and other natural disasters – often the fruits of population pressure on slender resources as well as more blatant human mismanagement – have claimed a huge toll in lives and property. Fresh environmental dangers stalk the Chinese people at the start of the new century. Rapid industrialization has seriously polluted the land, the water and the air, killing hundreds of thousands each year, harming the health of many more, and causing huge economic losses. For Chinese and non-Chinese alike, the environmental impact of China's rejuvenation could prove as significant as its growing economic and military power.

the politics of famines and floods

Managing the environment has been a concern of Chinese governments for centuries. Dynasties depended for their survival on the mastery of water resources and an ability to deliver bumper harvests. Ultimately, famine, floods, earthquakes and other natural disorders were *political* failures. This tradition has survived half a century of Communist rule. The effects of natural disasters tend to be concealed unless, and until, they can be used to demonstrate the Party's ability to organize disaster relief and showcase its concern for the people. This was the case in 1976 when the Tangshan earthquake in HEBEI killed 240,000

people. It was so again during the summer floods of 1998 which killed far fewer. These and other disasters were presented to the public as battles between man and nature. Though the idea is alien to some aspects of China's intellectual tradition, such battles are supreme expressions of politics in the People's Republic.

During the first half of the twentieth century, nature usually won these contests. China was a land of famine and floods. Much of the country had long been denuded by intense settlement. Major disasters scarred every decade as a series of weak governments wrestled with foreign invaders, warlords, rebellions and civil wars. China's traditional agrarian economy could sustain millions, but it could not sustain all. Flood or drought rapidly translated into famine, whose effects international relief agencies struggled to contain. No end to the grim harvest of natural disasters seemed likely without the emergence of a strong central government and the modernization of AGRICULTURE.

famine and despoliation after 1949

In 1949, the Communist victory in the CIVIL WAR promised to deliver both. Serious flooding along the YANGTZE RIVER in 1949 and 1954 claimed hundreds of lives and revived debate in Beijing about the merits of a THREE GORGES DAM. But there was no famine during the early years of Communist rule, and while agriculture was not exactly modernized, LAND

REFORM boosted productivity. The new central government was better organized and more powerful than any of its predecessors in the previous century. It seemed to be in a good position to deal with the vagaries of nature, even in a diverse, continental-sized country.

This view overlooked the fact that the government was led by MAO ZEDONG, a man whose revolutionary vision was as fantastic as his personal authority. The Chairman's GREAT LEAP FORWARD of 1958–60 plunged China in a burst of 'revolutionary productivity' designed to achieve self-sufficiency in grain and industrialization overnight. These spurious goals were based on suspect science and scarcely credible production techniques. Massive deforestation to clear areas for cultivation and provide fuel, close planting, deep ploughing, ill-advised irrigation schemes and arbitrary, mass destruction of pests inflicted lasting damage on the environment. They also helped induce a famine that cost as many as 30 million lives, the Leap's most tragic legacy.

While the Great Leap Forward destroyed much of China's natural habitat, the CULTURAL REVOLUTION, Mao's second great revolutionary experiment, diverted attention from the need to protect what remained. Isolated and at odds with much of the outside world, China was absorbed in political struggle. The search for ideological purity and battle for control of the Communist Party were what mattered, not man's precarious relationship with the material world. This neglect did not begin to change until 1971, when Beijing at last secured China's seat at the UNITED NATIONS and came into contact with mainstream international thinking on the environment. The following year delegates from the People's Republic of China attended the first UN Conference on the Human Environment, held in Sweden. In 1973, Beijing formed a National Environmental Protection Agency and held its first national conference on protecting the environment. It was the start of a slow process of realization that environmental protection would have to accompany economic growth if China was to avoid disaster.

Not only slow but painful. When DENG XIAOPING persuaded the Party to focus on economic development during the late 1970s, China's population was close to one billion – almost twice that when the Communists seized power. Fear that growth would be even faster in future panicked the Party into the draconian one-child-per-family policy (see POPULATION). The spirit of Thomas Malthus, who forecast that food supplies could not keep up with the increase in the population, stalked China's leaders. Not only did Malthus's theories cast doubts on the Party's plans to make people richer, they seemed to threaten mass starvation. Something had to be done.

Yet however successfully birth control might restrain population growth, there could be no question that China's natural resources were finite and, thanks to ignorance, neglect and abuse, under intense strain. The damage was everywhere apparent. Industrialization, whether carried out along Soviet lines in the 1950s, or according to Mao's methods during the Leap, had taken its toll on rivers, land and air. Massive Han Chinese immigration into once lightly populated regions such as TIBET and XINJIANG, and the unrestrained exploitation of natural resources that accompanied it, destroyed much of China's remaining least-spoilt habitat. Growing awareness of these problems in Beijing at the start of the 1980s was an encouraging sign but no more than that. Rapid economic growth in the two decades that followed has turned severe environmental degradation into something close to a crisis.

the environment and economic reform

The People's Republic's environmental problems do not stem from an absolute deficiency in natural resources so much as their low per capita levels, uneven distribution and difficulty of access. China accounts for about 22 per cent of the world's population but only 7 per cent of its arable land. Agricultural land per head is 28 per cent below that of the world average and still shrinking. The amount of range lands available to Chinese is less than half the world average, forests and wilderness about 15 per cent, and water resources less than one-third of world average. Water is abundant in the south where floods are frequent, while in the north, water shortages are acute and worsening. Hydro-power potential tends to be far from industrial centres. Oil and gas reserves are considerable but awkwardly located and insufficient to meet growing energy demands. Coal supplies are abundant but generally of poor quality (see ENERGY).

All this would make for a weak resource base at the best of times. Population growth, urbanization and industrialization conducted at a pace and on a scale unseen elsewhere in the world have made it a decidedly fragile and polluted one. In most of China's large cities, pollution is palpable even to passers-by. It clogs the air and the water in almost every developed part of the country and is particularly serious in Beijing, the Pearl River Delta (see GUANGDONG), the industrial heartland of the northeast, SHANGHAI, CHONGQING, WUHAN, Taipei and HONG KONG. Residents in some of these centres face real risks.

Air pollution is especially serious. Its main causes are coal and cars. No other major economy is so reliant on coal, which is burnt in inefficient boilers and used by households for heating and cooking. Particulate pollution in the north, sulphur dioxide pollution in the south (where coal has a high sulphur content), and indoor pollution (caused by residential use of coal) accounted for almost 300,000 premature deaths a year from chronic pulmonary disease, and billions of dollars in lost work-years and medical treatment, according to a World Bank study in the late 1990s. Acid rain blights large areas of south China and is believed to fall as far away as the Korean Peninsula and Japan. Large-scale investment in coal cleaning and flue-gas desulphurization technologies is required to lessen the damage. Rapid growth in car ownership during the 1990s drove up lead levels in most cities and forced Beijing to announce a nationwide ban on the sale of leaded fuel with effect from July 2000. By 2015 the People's Republic will be the world's largest emitter of carbon monoxide. Emissions aside, China's expanding fleet of vehicles is creating severe problems for its urban transport network (see ROADS).

Water pollution is equally damaging, especially when combined with the traditional water shortages that blight the north. Main pollutants are industrial and municipal waste, and chemical and organic fertilizer run-off. At the close of the century at least 40 per cent of monitored river sections did not meet the government's minimum requirements for water quality. The fact that many rivers went unmonitored disguised the true extent of the problem. Beijing hopes the Three Gorges Dam will end the annual scourge of flooding along the Yangtze, and a new 'grand canal', to channel water from the country's longest river hundreds of miles across country, will relieve the drought-affected north. Both projects are large, expensive and controversial. Both demonstrate that the current Chinese government's concern with water conservancy is as intense as any of its predecessors.

Reduction in vegetation cover and soil erosion – causes *and* consequences of floods and water shortages in the vicious cycle of environmental degradation – are other effects on the environment of China's dramatic encounter with rapid growth. Neither is new. But both have intensified under the impact of commercial logging, over-grazing, slope cultivation, house building and industrialization. Soil fertility has suffered accordingly. Deserts have grown. Lakes have shrunk. Flora and fauna, some of it unique to China, have been lost. Even the Panda, the very symbol of the country, is under threat.

search for sustainable development

Beijing has not sat mute in the face of mounting degradation. It has created institutions, passed laws, and conducted educational campaigns to heighten public awareness of the environment. Detailed ecological goals are set out in most development plans. The People's Republic is an active member of the international environmental community, insisting, on almost every occasion, that rich countries take the lead in controlling pollution rather than use the issue to curb growth in China and the rest of the developing world. Under the Montreal Protocol of 1991, Beijing is committed to phasing out the consumption and production of ozone-depleting substances by 2010.

While these trends augur well for an improvement in China's rapidly deteriorating environment they are not guarantees of such. A week sense of law blunts the government's legislative attack on the problem. Low education levels frustrate attempts to popularize environmental issues. Poverty, both absolute and relative, makes many Chinese, particularly at the local level, put growth and development before environmental protection. The Communist Party's refusal to countenance the existence of powerful independent pressure groups also hinders the cause. The reasons are not hard to find. In Hong Kong and more particularly Taiwan, environmental pressure groups became the focus of political dissent, the pioneers of civil society and midwives of democracy. On all accounts they are anathema to Beijing, regardless of their track record in defending the environment.

Despite Beijing's turn-of-century enthusiasm for 'sustainable development', a feeling persists in Chinese minds that since Europe, the United States and Japan developed first and dealt with pollution later, China should be allowed to do the same. Given the get-rich-quick mentality arising from China's reforms, the idea that it will be Chinese, albeit of the next generation, who suffer most if this policy is pursued, does not always find favour. Thus, the world's most populous nation has yet to solve one of the great dilemmas of development: how to enrich its people rapidly without ruining their environment, and perhaps that of neighbouring countries, permanently.

ethnic minorities

Every Chinese government in the modern era has insisted that China is a unitary, *multi-national* state whose frontiers contain large numbers of non-Chinese peoples. Every government has paid a price in terms of resentment, rebellion and attempted secession on the part of ethnic minorities unreconciled to Chinese rule. So far, the Communist government has proved strong enough to stamp out ethnic revolt in its frontier regions, notably TIBET and XINJIANG – but only at the cost of strained relations between Chinese and non-Chinese, and international criticism of its HUMAN RIGHTS record. A worldwide revival of ethnic consciousness suggests China's relations with some of its 'minority nationalities' will be fraught for years to come.

the republican era: 'five races'

The new Republican government of 1912 abandoned most QING DYNASTY policies but insisted on preserving China's imperial boundaries. These included virtually all the lands inhabited by the Mongols; Manchuria, traditional homeland of the Manchus; the Turkic-speaking, Muslim province of Xinjiang in Central Asia; and Tibet. At the time Chinese control over all these areas save Manchuria was either nebulous or non-existent, but only the Mongols were able to turn this to advantage. With backing from RUSSIA and then the SOVIET UNION, they founded an independent state of MONGOLIA in 1924 and escaped Chinese control.

At the start of the twenty-first century, more than 50 years after it relocated to Taiwan, the KUOMINTANG government still declines to recognize the independence of Mongolia, and continues to staff a 'Commission for Mongolian and Tibetan Affairs' whose purpose is to serve members of both nationalities worldwide. Taipei recognizes nine major indigenous peoples in Taiwan who have a total population of almost 400,000. The most numerous are the Ami.

During Republican rule on the Mainland the government recognized five nationalities: the numerically and politically dominant Han, or Chinese; the Mongols; the Manchus; the Tibetans; and the Hui, or Chinese Muslims. SUN YAT-SEN was prepared to grant these groups a degree of self-determination, but his successor, CHIANG KAI-SHEK, was less keen. For him a unified, rejuvenated China meant control over, and the allegiance of, ethnic minorities traditionally subject to Chinese rule. Otherwise national frontiers might have to be redrawn, perhaps reducing China's total land area by up to a half.

However, Chiang's authority was constrained by WARLORDS, Communist rebellion and Japanese invasion: he could not control large parts of the Chinese homeland, let alone the vastness of Mongolia, Central Asia and Tibet. For the most part, the predominantly non-Chinese people in these areas were left to their own devices. Where local Chinese leaders did seek to impose their will, as in Xinjiang under Governor Sheng Shicai (1896–1961), there were massive revolts. On two occasions during the Republican era, Xinjiang Muslims tried to set up a 'Republic of East Turkestan' (see XINJIANG).

Communism and 'minority peoples'

In the early history of Chinese Communism, ethnicity was a minor issue but not a neglected one. During the late 1920s the Party assigned DENG XIAOPING to lead a revolt among the predominantly Zhuang people of west GUANGXI. The 1931 constitution of the Chinese Soviet Republic promised national independence to those ethnic minorities who wanted it. During the LONG MARCH the Party encountered several minority peoples and won some of them over to the Communist cause.

But with Japan nibbling at China's periphery in Manchuria and Mongolia, ethnic secession soon lost its appeal for an aspirant *national* government. The Constitution of the embryonic Communist state was revised: independence for national minorities gave way to 'autonomy'. MAO ZEDONG was as keen as Chiang had been to inherit the great Manchu 'dependencies' of Mongolia, Tibet and Xinjiang. He wanted to transform them – along with other areas inhabited by ethnic minorities – through revolution. This task

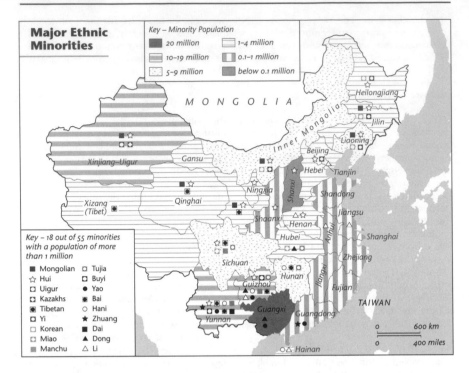

Major Ethnic Minorities

Key – Minority Population

- ■ 20 million
- ▤ 10–19 million
- ⬚ 5–9 million
- ▥ 1–4 million
- ▯ 0.1–1 million
- ▨ below 0.1 million

MONGOLIA

Inner Mongolia

Heilongjiang

Jilin

Liaoning

Beijing

Hebei   *Tianjin*

Shanxi   *Shandong*

Ningxia

Gansu

Qinghai

Xinjiang–Uigur

Xizang (Tibet)

Shaanxi   *Henan*   *Jiangsu*

Hubei   *Shanghai*

Anhui

Zhejiang

Sichuan

Hunan   *Jiangxi*

Guizhou   *Fujian*

Yunnan   *Guangxi*   *Guangdong*

TAIWAN

Hainan

0   600 km
0   400 miles

Key – 18 out of 55 minorities with a population of more than 1 million

- ■ Mongolian
- ☆ Hui
- ▢ Uigur
- ⬖ Kazakhs
- ◉ Tibetan
- ▢ Yi
- ▯ Korean
- ▢ Miao
- ■ Manchu
- ▢ Tujia
- ▢ Buyi
- ● Yao
- ⬢ Bai
- ○ Hani
- ★ Zhuang
- ■ Dai
- ▲ Dong
- △ Li

would be led by Han cadres, the vanguard of Chinese socialism.

With the foundation of the People's Republic in 1949 Chinese power was projected deep into areas that had long paid only lip service to the central government. Many of them were inhabited by ethnic minorities grown accustomed to running their own affairs during decades of ineffectual Qing and Republican rule. The Communists soon awoke them from their slumbers.

Ethnologists got to work as well as revolutionaries. During the 1950s dozens of *shaozu minzu* (minority nationalities) were identified, usually on the basis of their linguistic and cultural differences from the Han. They included less well-known but often more numerous groups than the Tibetans and the Mongols, such as the Zhuang, the Miao and the Yi of southwest China. Beijing eventually recognized 56 nationalities (including the Han). At the time of the 1990 census the 55 national *minorities* had a total population of more than 90 million, or just over 8 per cent of China's total. Eighteen of them had a population of more than one million. The smallest group, the Luoba of Tibet, numbered 2,322. Though small in number compared with the total population, ethnic minorities inhabit about 60 per cent of China's total land area. Their homelands are far less densely populated than Han areas.

China's minorities are as diverse as they are numerous. The largest group, the Zhuang, are among those most like the Han. They are concentrated in Guangxi. The Hui, the only ethnic minority without a language of its own, are found in number in NINGXIA but are widely scattered throughout north China. They are different from the Han only in the sense that they are Muslims. The Manchus, the second most numerous group, have their own language but by the late 1990s only a few elderly men could speak it, the remainder having adopted Chinese.

If many minorities are hard to distinguish from the Chinese, some are not. The Tibetans, the Uigurs, Kazakhs and Kirghiz of Xinjiang, and, to a lesser extent, the Mongols are very unlike the Han and, in many cases, unhappy with Chinese rule. History, language – and especially religion – distinguish them both from the Chinese and from each other. Several of these groups are nomads or pastoralists pursuing a fundamentally different lifestyle from the Han; their homelands do not support Chinese-style settled agriculture. The problem for Beijing is that these homelands constitute strategic border regions containing valuable natural resources. The central government's determination to control such territories, coupled with the militant atheism at the heart of its ideology, has often made a powder keg of relations between the Han and non-Han in west China.

minorities policy in practice

China's constitution defines the People's Republic as a unitary, multi-national state which practises racial equality and regional autonomy in areas where ethnic minorities form a compact presence. This finds expression in the five province-level 'autonomous regions' of INNER MONGOLIA (established 1947); Xinjiang Uigur Autonomous Region (1955); Guangxi Zhuang Autonomous Region (1958); Ningxia Hui Autonomous Region (1958); and the Tibet Autonomous Region (1965). Although each region takes the name of a particular ethnic group, these groups do not themselves form the majority of the local population except in Tibet. Only in Tibet and Xinjiang, home to other ethnic groups apart from Uigurs, are the Han in the minority. In Inner Mongolia, Mongolians account for less than 20 per cent of the population. Outside the autonomous regions, numerous autonomous prefectures and counties – lower levels of administration – have been set up in provinces containing ethnic minorities.

'Autonomy' generally amounts to (but does not always ensure) the preservation of the language and customs of the local minority. Autonomous Regions are sometimes exempted from key state policies, such as the strict birth control measures enforced among the Han population in most Chinese cities. However, certain ethnic minorities whose birth rates are increasing rapidly are also encouraged to have smaller families, a move which occasionally sparks resistance.

The constitution requires representatives of the local minority to head autonomous regional governments. They are generally less conspicuous among the more powerful regional branches of the Communist Party. Under all circumstances, national unity takes precedence over regional autonomy. The cultures and aspirations of ethnic minorities are tolerated, sometimes even encouraged, but only as long as they do not challenge national unity, socialism and Party rule.

Generally speaking the Communist government has conducted social and economic revolution later and at a slower pace in regions inhabited by ethnic minorities compared with those of the Han. Nevertheless, in the 1950s and 1960s China's rulers regarded the rapid eradication of differences between the Han and the minorities as a measure of social progress. This meant the promised autonomy barely disguised an imminent assault on the minorities' identity, particularly if that identity was centred on religion and bolstered by a politically powerful social order of monks, imams, monasteries and mosques. This was the case with the Tibetans, many Muslims in Xinjiang and, to a lesser extent, the Mongolians.

Revolution rapidly made an impact. Revolt flared inside Tibet in 1959 in response to the introduction of LAND REFORM and then collectivization among Tibetans who lived outside the domain traditionally ruled by the DALAI LAMA. It was soon suppressed but with damaging, long-term consequences. They included the flight of more than 100,000 Tibetans to India, led by their spiritual leader, who remains in exile, a focus of loyalty in his homeland as well as a force for change.

Elsewhere, the persecution and starvation arising from the GREAT LEAP FORWARD drove thousands of Dai people in YUNNAN across the border into Burma. In Xinjiang, even greater numbers of Kazakhs fled to the Soviet Republic of Kazakhstan. A breathing space provided by the more moderate policies Beijing pursued in the early 1960s to recover from the Leap soon gave way to the CULTURAL REVOLUTION, when every aspect of life was subjected to class struggle. Religion and 'feudal' traditions were particular targets for attack. Since these characteristics tended to define the way of life of ethnic minorities more than that of the Han, the damage inflicted on them was sometimes greater.

reforms and racial tensions

Den Xiaoping's economic reforms brought a degree of relaxation to the lives of ethnic minorities, as they did to people everywhere in China. Provinces and regions acquired more power at the expense of Beijing. The market intruded where cadres and the command

Eighteen of China's Most Numerous
Ethnic Minorities with a Population
Over a Million

Name	Population	Primary Location(s)
1. Zhuang	15.55m	Guangxi Zhuang AR*
2. Manchu	9.84m	Jilin, Liaoning, Heilongjiang
3. Hui	8.61m	Ningxia AR, but scattered throughout north China
4. Miao	7.38m	Southwest China
5. Uigur	7.20m	Xinjiang AR
6. Yi	6.57m	Yunnan, Sichuan, Guizhou
7. Tujia	5.72m	Hubei, Hunan, Sichuan
8. Mongol	4.80m	Inner Mongolian AR
9. Tibetan	4.59m	Tibet AR, Gansu, Yunnan, Qinghai, Sichuan
10. Buyi	2.54m	Guizhou
11. Dong	2.50m	Guizhou, Hunan, Guangxi AR
12. Yao	2.13m	Southwest China
13. Korean	1.92m	Jilin, Heilongjiang, Liaoning
14. Bai	1.59m	Yunnan
15. Hani	1.25m	Yunnan
16. Li	1.112m	Guangdong
17. Kazakhs	1.110m	Xinjiang AR
18. Dai	1.02m	Yunnan

[Figures from China's 1990 Census]
* AR = autonomous region

tion in minority languages and sponsor a renaissance of local customs. These moves, though welcomed, have not disguised the fact that, whatever the language of instruction, the school curriculum is much the same across China. Its ultimate purpose is to make people of *all* nationalities accept the prevailing ideology of socialism and the state (see EDUCATION).

China's opening to the outside world has often had a double meaning for the minorities. In their homelands, international influence has been eclipsed by massive Han in-migration. Population balances in west China have been shifting against the minorities for decades as a result of campaigns to encourage Chinese settlers to move into remote regions. The idea has been to make outlying regions 'safe' for Communism and develop their economies. Since the 1980s road and railway construction, new airports and telecommunication links, and a large military presence have afforded the Communist Chinese state far greater power over frontier areas than its predecessors.

Power but not always control – and sometimes little in the way of affection. The Chinese government might insist on the unity of nationalities, but its officials, and many ordinary Chinese, rarely show much genuine regard for minority cultures. Pejorative terms for non-Han peoples disappeared from China's dictionaries long ago; some of the attitudes that kept them there for centuries endure.

Xinjiang and Tibet are frequently restive. In both regions, Han migration has diluted the ethnic component of the population while large-scale investment and development have improved material life. A kind of pincer operation is thus at work, designed to end resistance to Chinese rule through weight of numbers and provide compelling evidence that the minorities' economic future lies in rule by Beijing.

At best, it has been only a partial success. Anti-Chinese protests became so serious in Tibet in 1989 that the authorities imposed martial law in Lhasa, the capital. In Xinjiang, troops had to suppress an armed uprising by local Muslims in 1990. At the close of the century, a campaign of bombings and assassinations by local separatists, many of them inspired by the creation of independent republics across the border in Kazakhstan and Kirghizstan, made Xinjiang the least secure province in China. In Tibet, Xinjiang and

economy once held sway. Communism weakened as an ideal as well as a system of organization: among some of the minorities, as among many Han, old gods and customs regained something of their appeal. Muslim pilgrims visited Mecca and Middle East money was used to rebuild mosques in northwest China. Exiled Tibetans revisited their homeland. Monasteries reopened.

Other forces, and other challenges, were at work as China reformed its economy and opened to the outside world. In the ethnic homelands, standards of life improved, though at a slower rate than in the traditionally Han areas of the east and south. In so far as minorities tended to inhabit remote inland parts of China, they were often victims of the sharp regional disparities in wealth and opportunity that characterized the 1990s.

At the start of the new century ethnic minorities are on average less well educated than the Han, and more likely to be illiterate. Attempts have been made to step up instruc-

Inner Mongolia, the official media rail constantly against 'handfuls of national separatists' whose 'reactionary feudal religious ideas' are designed to 'split the country' – usually 'in league with hostile foreign forces'.

There are no such conflicts between Chinese and ethnic groups elsewhere in the country. Friction is not uncommon, but the minorities concerned are either small in number or, if larger, usually assimilated to Chinese ways. Above all, matters of religion and national security, an explosive combination, are not at stake as they always have been in Tibet, Xinjiang and, to some extent, Mongolia. Tibetan Buddhism and Islam are defining characteristics of life for many people in these regions. Deprived of them, Tibetans, Uigurs, Kazakhs and Mongols could be said to have lost their identity as nationalities: religious freedom amounts to 'national' freedom. At the same time, Beijing believes that failure on the part of the predominantly secular Han to 'tame' these minority religions means that control over those who adhere to them will remain a chimera.

This is the dilemma at the heart of Chinese control over the ethnic minorities of Tibet and northwest China in particular. During the Cultural Revolution, Beijing sought to deal with it by eradicating all trace of religion. It was a recipe for misery all round. The reform era has made possible a religious revival that has often challenged the central government in new ways. Above all, it has required Beijing to compromise: in many Muslim parts of China, the government turns a blind eye to non-Han Party members who attend the mosque or otherwise keep up their faith.

Beijing has gone further, presenting itself as the true protector of minority faiths rather than their persecutor. One example of this was the prompt ban in 1989 of a book entitled *Sexual Customs*, published in Shanghai, that offended Muslims and brought thousands of them out on to the streets in protest. Another was Beijing's intervention in 1995 in the process to choose the 11th PANCHEN LAMA of Tibet. The aim was to oppose the candidate chosen by the Dalai Lama. But the approach Beijing took was unusual: it posed as custodian of traditions allegedly violated by the exiled Tibetan spiritual leader. In both Xinjiang and Tibet, these and similar moves have been accompanied by campaigns to educate local religious leaders in patriotism, socialism and the unity of the nationalities.

The prospects for genuine accord between Han and some of China's more restless ethnic minorities during the early years of the new century seem slim. The insistence of a virtually mono-ethnic Communist Party on ruling a multi-ethnic state will ensure this. Ethnic minorities will find it hard to preserve a meaningful sense of national identity within the context of an authoritarian nation-state, more than 90 per cent of whose population is composed of members of another nationality. Continued unrest and racial friction, especially on the western periphery of the Chinese 'empire', are inevitable.

Yet the prospects that one or more of China's ethnic minorities – such as the Tibetans or the Uigurs of Xinjiang – will be able to break away and form their own state are slimmer still. However strong their resistance to Chinese rule, secession is unlikely without a collapse of central authority in Beijing or severe economic recession. And if either of these were to happen, Han people in a number of provinces might prove as keen as ethnic minorities to pursue a form of independence, or at least genuine autonomy.

extraterritoriality

Superior fire power was usually enough for the foreign powers to crush China's armies, sink its infant navies and force its frightened governments into submission during the nineteenth and early twentieth centuries. Something more was needed if the invaders were to remain on Chinese soil, conduct trade, convert or otherwise change the vast country they had humbled for such purposes. This something was extraterritoriality: the right of foreigners to be tried in their own courts and not be subject to China's legal system.

Extraterritoriality underpinned the entire foreign presence in China from 1842 – when BRITAIN forced China to concede it in the Treaty of Nanjing – to January 1943, when both Britain and the UNITED STATES relinquished it out of respect for a wartime ally. In the intervening century, most foreigners – whether resident in SHANGHAI, home to the largest congregation of them, or remote mission stations, where they might be the only non-Chinese for hundreds of miles – were essentially beyond Chinese jurisdiction. They had the right to be tried by consular officials in the ports, or, if appropriate, by the British Supreme Court in China (set up in 1904) or the United States Court for China (founded two years later).

Not only were the penalties imposed by such courts lighter than defendants would have received at the hands of Chinese magistrates, they tended to be less severe than those administered by courts dealing with similar cases at home. Foreign nationals whose governments had not signed treaties with China usually enjoyed the protection of treaty powers, an abuse that tended to remove *all* foreigners from Chinese judicial control.

Extraterritoriality ensured more than personal immunity from Chinese laws for foreigners. It made it impossible for the Chinese government to register, tax or regulate foreign firms or banks and even to exercise much of a say in schools established by missionary societies deep in the interior. Such endeavours were operated by foreign 'legal persons' to whom the laws of their own country applied, rather than those of their hosts. The foreign commercial presence in China was thus founded on valuable privileges of a kind not available to domestic rivals.

Chinese nationalists of every persuasion found the injustice at the heart of the extraterritoriality system offensive. They longed and campaigned for the day when the powers would either be forced or persuaded to give up such privileges. A minor victory came in 1917, when the treaty rights of Austria-Hungary were abolished as a result of China's participation in the First World War on the Allied side. Two years later, the newly established SOVIET UNION renounced all the territory seized from China by the Tsars, gave up its share of the Boxer Indemnity and abandoned extraterri-

toriality. At the WASHINGTON CONFERENCE of 1921–2, Britain and the United States pledged to work towards giving up extraterritoriality, but did not do so for another 21 years. In TIBET, extraterritoriality survived until 1954 when India abandoned the privileges it had inherited from the days of the Raj.

Despite their opposition to extraterritoriality, many nationalists recognized that sweeping changes were needed to China's legal system, whose inadequacies and cruel punishments were such that foreigners insisted on being exempt from them. The progress of reform was slow. Not until 1905 were 'slicing' (death of a thousand cuts), the public exhibition of severed heads, beheading of corpses, punitive tattooing and torture abolished. Even then, abolition from the statute book did not end such practices. Unease about the consequences of being subject to China's legal system endured among resident Britons and Americans up to and beyond their governments' relinquishment of extraterritoriality in 1943.

Similar feelings have prevailed in the foreign community under Communism. The age of extraterritoriality has long passed, but its spirit lingers on in the perception – among Chinese and foreigners alike – that non-Chinese nationals, while far from legally and physically untouchable in the People's Republic, should nevertheless generally be spared some features of the local judicial system such as confinement to LABOUR CAMPS, show trials, public sentencing rallies and peremptory execution. To the Western mind, there is something unsatisfactory about a legal system in which judgments practically always favour the state (see LAW). This was precisely one of the grounds on which extraterritoriality had been asserted in the 1840s.

F

family, the

The basic unit of Chinese society survived attacks on it during the twentieth century by reformers, who saw its traditions as the main source of their country's weakness; and Communists, who wanted people to identify with class and state rather than family. Both groups succeeded in making the state less like the family and the family less like the state. Neither managed to subordinate the family permanently to the state as a focus of loyalty and obedience.

the old order: family and clan
In traditional China, the family towered over individual and community. Only the CLAN, a lineage association formed of family members with the same surnames, could claim some direct authority over it. For most people, the family was the state writ small, and the state was an idealized family. Three of the five 'primary relationships' central to CONFUCIANISM concerned those between family members. Ancestor worship was one of China's major RELIGIONS. Filial piety was the greatest of the pieties. A person deemed to have wronged his parents was a social outcast.

Ideally, and usually in practice, the father was all-powerful, his sons dutiful and obedient. WOMEN of the household mattered much less. Their birth was not always a cause for joy, their younger lives merely a preparation for an arranged marriage and removal to their husband's home. There, the new bride was expected to obey her husband and his father, and serve her mother-in-law. Her main duty was to produce sons to sustain the family line, inherit the property and provide for the parents' old age.

The family was a unit of production as well as society, loyalty and religion. AGRICULTURE was conducted by families in their capacities as landlords, tenants or labourers. The ideal was for three generations to live under one roof, but this was less common than imagined. Lack of land needed to support so many family members was one reason. A high infant mortality rate and low life expectancy were others. Such data as is available for the early twentieth century suggest the average family size was 4.5–6 persons, and that nuclear families were the majority.

the family under attack
If the traditional family did much to preserve the continuity of Chinese society, reformers bitterly attacked it in the early twentieth century as a cause of their country's decay. Its tyranny of old over young, men over women, and emphasis on conformity with custom and tradition were principal targets of the May Fourth Movement of 1919. There was no place for 'Mr De' (democracy) and 'Mr Sai' (science), the creeds of the future, in such a hidebound institution. (See MAY FOURTH MOVEMENT.) For the new generation of reformers and revolutionaries, the REPUBLICAN REVOLUTION of 1911 was unfinished: it had succeeded in ending Qing dynasty rule, but the real task, that of remaking society, depended on abolishing the traditional family and all it stood for.

These forces of change made some impact on urban families during the Republican period but left the countryside virtually untouched. This did not change until the arrival of the CHINESE COMMUNIST PARTY in the rural areas. Land reform and the associated breakup of powerful families were central elements of Mao Zedong's revolution from the late 1920s. Two decades later, following the Party's victory in the CIVIL WAR, they were applied throughout China.

The effects were dramatic. LAND REFORM in the early 1950s redistributed property on an enormous scale and marked the end of significant private rural wealth. Most large families split up. For growing numbers of people, work, education and other aspects of life were conducted in new social contexts. The Marriage Law of 1950 contributed to the process, freeing women from arranged unions and allowing them to acquire and work property of their own.

But if these moves trimmed family sizes, changed the balance of power within them and destroyed some of their customary functions, they also reinforced the family as a unit of production and, hence, loyalty. The Party had broken the power of landlord families. It had not weakened the family itself, still less supplanted it with a 'higher' source of allegiance such as the community or the state.

Mao hoped the communes set up during the GREAT LEAP FORWARD of 1958 would accomplish this task. For a while they seemed to do so. Officials and team leaders became more decisive in production than family heads. Women, engaged in the nationwide production drive, handed over their traditional household chores to kindergartens and canteens. The Chinese people submitted themselves to a new, larger, 'revolutionary' entity.

They did not do so for long. There were signs of discontent over communal life long before the Leap ended in chaos and famine. And rapid recovery of the country's ills owed much to the cautious return to incentives and household farming of the early 1960s.

The respite proved temporary. The CULTURAL REVOLUTION was an attack on expressions of individuality of every kind, and was highly destructive of family life, particularly in the cities. It was a revolt of the young against the old; of children against parents; of students against teachers. Re-education, rustication, persecution and imprisonment split families up, often for years at a time. Families of officials and intellectuals suffered particularly badly, often falling victim to collective guilt characteristic of the feudal era rather than the People's Republic.

freedom and fertility under Deng

Yet family life in China overcame the Cultural Revolution and outlived the communes, which were rapidly dissolved during the late 1970s and early 1980s as a result of Deng Xiaoping's agricultural reforms. The household again became the unit of production. Under the 'household responsibility system' the state contracted land to families and undertook to buy a share of their output. Farmers were free to dispose of the surplus as they thought best, a policy which soon led to the revival of private markets. After years of trying to control and even abolish the family, the Communist state was forced to yield to it as the only means of rescuing the economy, boosting living standards and, it hoped, making the country strong.

But to some extent the state's withdrawal from family life was illusory. Even as the Party freed up the economy it imposed controls that touched upon the most private area of family life: reproduction. The one-child policy, and the abuses that sometimes accompanied it, was among the most hated of all the Party's measures in the reform era. It led to abhorrent behaviour such as female infanticide, and to forced sterilization and abortion. It created a generation of single children whose consequences for the future of Chinese society can only be guessed at. And it fostered a sharp imbalance in the sex ratio that will make it impossible for many men to find wives. (See POPULATION.)

It also had a major impact in reducing family size across the People's Republic. Falling fertility rates ensured smaller families, despite lengthening life expectancy. What was unforeseen was the 'ageing' of China's population fostered by draconian birth controls. The number of elderly people as a proportion of the total population will increase dramatically in the new century. How they are cared for will do much to determine the future of the Chinese family. If the state is able to deliver a comprehensive welfare scheme to retirees, the size of rural families will decrease. If not, as seems likely given the costs of such schemes, parents will continue to live with their children.

Different, but no less significant changes were under way in urban areas, where one child was the norm. One of them was an increase in the divorce rate. Mainland divorces lagged behind those in Taiwan; the island closed the century with the highest divorce rate in Asia. Yet officials worried just the same. A new marriage law promised to make infidelity illegal and divorce harder to obtain. Many opposed it on the grounds that it intruded into people's private lives – a striking sign of their determination to keep family business in the family and out of government.

Another striking development was the emergence of professional couples who chose not to have children, preferring to spend their time and money on themselves. The growth of marriages between partners from different areas and, on a tiny, but increasing scale, between Chinese and foreigners, were other signs of change at the close of the century.

In China's rapidly modernizing society, there is no doubt that the family has lost the hold over community and individual it once enjoyed. It is equally clear that the family has not surrendered to them. Even in urban China, where the family is one unit among many that socializes an increasingly prosperous population, family-orientated activities and loyalties live on, adapting to new situations, and still restricting the scope for extreme forms of individualism, as well as what, these days, are the much less grandiose ambitions of the state.

February 28th Incident (Taiwan 1947)

For more than 40 years, the 1947 revolt against Kuomintang rule in TAIWAN and its bloody suppression was the most sensitive issue in Taiwanese politics. The *er erba* incident, (Chinese for the numerals 28) was rarely referred to in public; it was too wounding and inflammatory. It was the great unspoken psychological burden of political life, a tragic symbol of the struggle between Mainlanders and Taiwanese to impose their will on the island. Allowing the silence to be broken was a central part of the reforms undertaken by LEE TENG-HUI in the early 1990s. Publication of an official report into the incident, a government apology, compensation for the families of victims and the erection of monuments in their honour helped lay the ghosts of *er erba*. They also set an example of the kind the Communist Party might follow should it choose to defuse the more recent but more sensitive suppression of the TIANANMEN SQUARE DEMOCRACY MOVEMENT.

Taiwan had been reunited with China less than two years when the uprising broke out. It had been a colony of Japan during the previous five decades and enjoyed a standard of living well above that of the Mainland. A generation of Taiwanese grew up appreciative of Japan's modernization efforts and, in many cases, enamoured of Japanese culture. At the same time, many Taiwanese retained an attachment to the Mainland and resented laws excluding them from key positions in the colonial administration. When Japanese rule came to an end in 1945 and Taiwan was reincorporated as a province of China, they had high hopes of running their own affairs and recovering from the damage inflicted by the Sino-Japanese War.

They were disappointed on both counts. Under Chen Yi (1883–1950), the new provincial governor, Mainlanders dominated the administration, sequestered property that had belonged to the Japanese and made no concessions to the local mores that distinguished Taiwan from every other part of the country. Nationalist troops mistreated civilians. Shortages, inflation and corruption blighted many aspects of life. Taiwan's return to the motherland got off to an unhappy start.

The uprising began on the evening of 27 February 1947. Police and officials of the Monopoly Bureau beat up a woman selling cigarettes on the black market in Taipei, and shot and killed a bystander who intervened. This raised the curtain on three weeks of rioting, protests, beatings and killings in almost every major Taiwan city. Taiwanese beat numerous Mainlanders to death on the streets. Nationalist soldiers killed scores of Taiwanese civilians, sometimes at random, sometimes after rounding them up. Such cruelties testified to the tension, misunderstandings and hatred that existed between the two communities, one of them local, the other 'foreign' and imposed.

Attempts to reach a consensus on handling the early stages of the revolt broke down as various Taiwanese groups moved beyond calls for compensation to demands for political reform and even self-rule. Chen Yi introduced and then suspended martial law in Taipei in an effort to reduce tension. He tried to meet some of the demands put forward by the 'Resolution Committees' formed of local leaders, but events on the streets made this impossible. There were limits beyond which he could not go if Nationalist rule on the island was to mean anything. The limits were well understood on the Mainland, where CHIANG KAI-SHEK was engaged in an increasingly bitter Civil War with Communist forces. The revolt in Taiwan had to be crushed.

The beginning of the end came on 8 March when Nationalist reinforcements arrived in Keelung, the main port in northern Taiwan. During the following ten days troops restored order in Taipei, Kaohsiung, Tainan, Taichung and other centres, often with great brutality. By 21 March fighting had ceased. Chen Yi was replaced as governor by Wei Tao-ming (1901–78), a former ambassador to the United States. More than fifty years later the number of those killed during the uprising is still unclear. Estimates ranged from 1,000 to 100,000 with several authorities settling for a figure of 10,000–30,000.

There was less dispute about the consequences of the affair. Suppression of the revolt wiped out Taiwan's urban elite and facilitated Mainland domination of the island. This was reinforced by the arrival of Chiang Kai-shek's defeated government and army in 1949. The 'White Terror' that followed kept resentment of the Nationalist regime alive among local people and, among some, nurtured a desire to see Taiwan become independent. Exiled activists worked towards the same cause, sometimes by conducting terrorist attacks against Nationalist officials in the United States. A riot in Kaohsiung in 1979 following a rally by leading pro-independence figures showed the incendiary nature of the situation in Taiwan. There could be no resol-ution of the Mainland–Taiwanese conflict without political reform and an official reappraisal of *er erba*.

The Nationalist government took steps towards both in the late 1980s. It tolerated the formation in 1986 of an opposition, the DEMOCRATIC PROGRESSIVE PARTY (DPP), many of whose members demanded a thorough investigation of the February 28th Incident as well as an end to the Kuomintang dictatorship. Martial law was rescinded the following year. By 1992 the main organs of the central government were opened to genuine elections.

One of the consequences of liberalization was a flood of publications, conferences and public discussion of the uprising. In 1991 President Lee Teng-hui ordered an eight-person study group to examine the origins and outcome of the incident. Its report, published in 1992, partly blamed the government for causing the revolt and then using excessive force to suppress it. Lee publicly apologized and received the relatives of victims. His government allocated US$71 million to compensate them and build several monuments to commemorate the tragedy.

These moves did not erase the legacy of *er erba*. It was a defining moment in Taiwan's history, one whose consequences outlived those who took part in it. But the government went a long way towards neutralizing it politically. More important, it created democratic institutions of the kind that should make repetition of the tragedy avoidable.

Feng Yuxiang (1882–1948)

Feng's military power, muscular Christianity, and rivalry with Chiang Kai-shek made him one of the most important, and interesting, of the WARLORDS who sought to dominate China in the 1920s. The 'Christian General' led his 'National Army' in religious observances and hymn-singing. Moral indoctrination was accompanied by modern methods of military training. Officers were encouraged to share the rigours of life with their men – a novelty in a warlord army.

In the early 1920s, Feng battled for control of north China, and in particular HENAN, SHAANXI AND GANSU, with Zhang Zuolin (1875–1928), warlord of Manchuria, WU PEIFU, and their various allies. At first Feng was a subordinate of Wu's. But in 1924 he showed an independent streak by suddenly seizing Beijing. During his brief hold on the capital, Feng expelled PU YI, the last Manchu emperor, from the Forbidden City. Wu later extracted revenge and Feng was forced into temporary retirement to the Soviet Union, whose agents had advised and partially equipped the National Army. In 1927, DENG XIAOPING served briefly as a political instructor in Feng's forces.

Feng returned from Moscow to make a decisive intervention in Chinese politics. During the battle for control of the NORTHERN EXPEDITION Feng backed CHIANG KAI-SHEK in Nanjing rather than Chiang's rival, WANG JINGWEI, in Wuhan. The Left-wing government in Wuhan collapsed, ending – at least for a while – the Communist Party's presence in China's cities, and the alliance between the Kuomintang and the Soviet Union. Chiang re-launched the Northern Expedition and captured Beijing in 1928. But he was soon at odds with Feng over the question of troop demobilization in the newly unified China. In 1930, Chiang broke Feng's military power on the battlefield and thus ended his political career. The Christian General remained powerless and a stern critic of the Nationalist leader for the rest of his life.

This came to an end in 1948 when the ship on which he was travelling caught fire as it approached the Soviet port of Odessa. Feng was returning to China from the United States, and seemed about to side with the Communists in the CIVIL WAR. Largely for this reason, Communist historians have refrained from bracketing Feng Yuxiang with other warlords, preferring to describe him as a 'patriot'.

finance

Successive governments in the twentieth century regarded the ability to administer the Chinese state financially – to extract resources and reallocate them according to national priorities – as a key demonstration of power and modernity. Successive governments found it difficult to do so, and some found it impossible. Only the Communists have managed to tax and invest on any scale over any length of time. Yet, operating in a half-reformed economy at the start of the new century, Beijing's ability to raise enough revenues for future development is again in doubt. So are its chances of avoiding a collapse in the archaic banking sector.

tax troubles under the old order

China's size and huge population bedevil governance, financial or otherwise. Regional disparities and cultural diversity make it more difficult still. That there were not more periods of disunity in the long sweep of Chinese history has much to do with the unifying power of a common, 'higher' culture, the presence of powerful emperors, a stable economy – and an efficient bureaucracy to tax it. Hardly any of these conditions obtained during the final years of the Qing Dynasty: China itself was under attack along with its traditional culture. The Court was divided in Beijing and hostage to reform in the provinces. There was no greater sign of the dynasty's weakness than its inability to bring the regions to heel, financially as well as militarily. It was no coincidence that the REPUBLICAN REVOLUTION first swept the Manchus into oblivion in the provinces.

It was no coincidence either that the short lives of successive Republican governments in Beijing owed much to their failure to impose fiscal authority outside the capital. Even YUAN SHIKAI, the military strongman, managed to force only a few provinces to turn taxes over to his 'central' government. His political survival owed as much to foreign loans as it did to domestic revenues. Yuan's other sources of funds included receipts from the Maritime Customs and the Salt Gabelle, both of them managed by foreigners, and both of them pledged first to repayment of foreign loans.

China's finances improved under Chiang Kai-shek's KUOMINTANG government based in Nanjing, but not by very much. TARIFF AUTONOMY, won in the years 1928–30, boosted revenues from trade and, at least until the Sino-Japanese War, the government avoided much in the way of foreign borrowing. The currency was unified and paper money issued, backed by foreign exchange reserves. But this was less than half the story. Throughout its years on the Mainland, the Kuomintang found it impossible to impose direct taxes on agriculture, easily the most important part of the national economy. Since it managed to direct only a tiny portion of total national income into the government treasury it was entirely without the means to promote economic growth of the kind needed to solve China's many problems.

Nanjing's fiscal weakness owed much to continued warlord rule, Communist rebellion, and Japanese aggression. All three created vast 'no-go' zones for the central government from HEILONGJIANG to YUNNAN. Chiang could not defeat his opponents on the battlefield let alone subject their people to taxes. He was determined to crush them nevertheless. This required enormous additional sums of money, particularly after the loss of the 'home' provinces of the Yangtze Delta to Japan during the war. The United States and Britain, keen to support an ally, helped out with lend-lease; the rest was extracted from China's tiny modern banking system, much of it controlled by leading government figures. The banks printed money to cover the growing debt, sparking hyper-inflation which destroyed wealth, sapped morale and proved a major cause of the government's defeat in the CIVIL WAR. The Kuomintang made many mistakes during its unhappy tenure on the Mainland; acute financial mismanagement was among the most serious and costly of them.

triumph of Communist central control

The Communists certainly thought so. Controlling inflation and raising revenues were primary concerns of the new regime in 1949. Both were accomplished with surprising speed. Skilful administrative arrangements helped, including joint political-military rule over groups of provinces long used to ignoring the central government. So did the sheer vigour of a government whose leaders were flushed with victory and united (for a while) by the desire to make a new China. A dramatic broadening of the tax base was among the consequences. At their height, revenues accruing to the Nationalist government amounted to 5–7 per cent of GDP. In 1952, after barely three years of Communist rule, taxation's share of output was 24 per cent. Five years later it was 30 per cent. After a long interlude, China had a powerful central government again.

The use to which that power was put was another matter. China's tax and investment regime changed with shifting political priorities. This was particularly true during Mao Zedong's GREAT LEAP FORWARD, when Soviet-style development based on heavy industry was abandoned for an approach that placed more emphasis on agriculture. The Leap and the CULTURAL REVOLUTION, Mao's other great experiment in revolution, disrupted economic development and created widespread misery. But neither raised fundamental questions about Beijing's ability to raise enough revenue and redistribute it effectively in the pursuit of national goals, however irrational they might seem. That did not become an issue until the late 1980s, almost a decade after DENG XIAOPING launched his free market reforms and opened the economy to the outside world.

The new policies soon delivered higher living standards and greater political stability than China had seen under Mao. But they did so at the expense of the financial power of the state. Decentralization accounted for this: Beijing delegated to farmers, factories, cities, provinces and SPECIAL ECONOMIC ZONES the right to make investment decisions, set prices and retain earnings. This massive release of power by the centre to the regions triggered a burst of growth that, though welcome at first, soon threatened to swamp the country in inflation and excessive investment. Such was the situation in 1987–8 when popular concern over rising prices and corruption forced the government to backpedal on price reforms – only to disappoint many urban residents who saw it as a defeat for the cause of reform and a victory for hardliners in Beijing. Their discontent was a factor in the rise of the TIANANMEN SQUARE DEMOCRACY MOVEMENT. In fact, the government's policy partly reflected a lack of financial instruments to control the economy other than those of 'stop' and 'go'. Trying to control the economy by curbing the provinces has proved a difficult matter in the age of reform.

revenue crisis: China in the 1990s

The same can be said of preserving the financial integrity of the Chinese state. This became clear during the great burst of growth triggered by Deng's trip through south China in 1992 when he called for faster reforms. Coastal provinces shook off Beijing's attempts to rein them in and set their own economic agenda. Foreign and domestic investment flooded in. Central government revenue dried up. Inflation soared. Longstanding disparities between the cities and the countryside, and between the coast and the interior, intensified, leading some observers to speculate on the imminent 'breakup' of China. This seemed to be the message of an alarming report published in 1993 by Hu Angang and Wang Shaoguang, two prominent economists. It moved from the premise that state revenues were declining rapidly as a proportion of GDP to a 'worst case' conclusion that China might soon disintegrate.

It was more than a simple scare. And it was more than a new national tax system designed to boost central government finances seemed likely to rectify when it was introduced in 1994. Between 1978 and 1995 budgetary revenue fell from 35 per cent to 11 per cent of GDP, largely because of the failure of state enterprises, faced with falling or non-existent profits, to pay taxes. (See INDUSTRY.) Government expenditure at the close of the century was about 12 per cent of GDP, compared with a developing country average of 32 per cent. Investment fell from 16 per cent of GDP in 1978 to less than 3 per cent in 1995. The budgetary gaps these figures left behind were filled by 'fees' – a catch-all for local levies, often of an arbitrary nature – growing tax contributions from the private-, collective-, and foreign-owned sectors of the economy, the issuing of 'IOUs' rather than cash to farmers (see AGRICULTURE), and bank lending.

There was so much lending that three of China's four major state-owned banks – the Industrial and Commercial Bank of China, China Construction Bank and the Agricultural Bank of China – ended the century technically insolvent. Bad loans, most of them to state enterprises, were put at 30–40 per cent of GDP. The banks' survival owed much to China's high rate of domestic savings which, despite the modest development of capital markets in the 1990s, had few other places to go.

Bonds were one alternative, securities another. At the close of the 1990s more than 800 firms were listed on the Mainland's two stock exchanges, one in Shanghai, the other in Shenzhen. On both, 'A-shares' were reserved for domestic investors, 'B-shares' for foreigners. If this dual tracking provided a 'cut out' to protect China from instability in global markets, the markets' limited liquidity and high turnover created volatilities of their own. Much of this had to do with their immaturity. But the relatively small role of capital markets, their limited disclosure and uncertain legal status, coupled with the doggedly cautious welcome extended to foreign banks and the non-convertibility of China's currency, the *renminbi* (on the capital account), constrained development of the financial sector. This was a particularly frustrating matter for the authorities in SHANGHAI, whose ambitions to turn their city into a major international financial centre were as well known as they were to remain disappointed, at least during the 1990s. The 1999 agreement on China's entry to the World Trade Organization, which called for liberalization of the financial sector, promised an improvement.

The government's reluctance to rapidly deepen capital markets stemmed from fear that they might drain resources from the banks. The concern was well founded. China's reforms beached its banks. It was not until 1995 that the People's Bank of China, the central bank, acquired an experienced professional as president. He was ZHU RONGJI, concurrently vice-premier in charge of the economy. He subsequently vacated the bank chair for Dai Xianglong (1944–), a close ally and genuine banker.

Many new non-bank financial institutions were set up in the reform era, but at the close of the century four big state banks still accounted for two-thirds of the assets of the financial sector and 90 per cent of total bank assets. Four-fifths of their lending went to state enterprises, loans they would never get back. Their own profit performances were lamentable, returning only a tiny fraction on their assets. Despite attempts to make them behave according to commercial principles, and to let new 'policy' banks take responsibility for government-directed lending, they closed the century at the mercy of the State Planning Commission in Beijing, local governments in the provinces, and the millions of depositors on whose confidence they depended to avoid catastrophe.

The threat of a run on the banks still stalks Beijing at the dawn of the new century. Potentially it is a more serious menace than the possibility of rural unrest or a new outbreak of protests in the cities. The government could probably muster the resources to deal with both of the last two. Controlling the consequences of a massive loss of faith in the banking system would be a different matter – one that revived images of the collapse of Chiang Kai-shek's government in 1948–9.

the fiscal agenda

The Asian financial crisis of the late 1990s aggravated China's woes. FOREIGN TRADE AND INVESTMENT declined. Economic growth slowed. Several international trade and investment corporations – the 'ITICS' founded in the reform era to recruit foreign capital – ran into difficulties with debt. One of them, Guangdong International Trust and Investment Corporation, collapsed: Communist China's biggest financial failure. The fact that Beijing escaped the financial damage sustained by several of its neighbours owed much to its large foreign exchange reserves (almost US$150 billion at the close of the century) and its non-convertible currency.

Yet China has more to do than 'merely' avoid the demise of one or more of its banks and financial institutions to make China's financial system modern, efficient and the true servant of its policy goals. It has to ensure much higher rates of compliance for existing taxes and develop new ones to tap the wealth of the rapidly growing non-state sector. It must develop mechanisms to provide fiscal transfers from rich to poorer provinces. And it must practise transparent budgetary procedures that explain exactly what is being spent where and why. This will require an army of accountants and tax inspectors, and a much greater culture of compliance than enterprises and individuals have displayed in the past. More important, it will require a much greater understanding of where government functions stop and commercial ones start; where the market rules and the government complies. Though these issues dog other aspects of Mainland life, nowhere is their resolution so critical for China's well-being and future as a modern nation than in the financial sector.

'foreign experts' and 'foreign friends'

Late Ming and early Qing emperors turned to Jesuits for advice. Their successors sought out foreign scientists and adventurers. China's Communists have had their resident foreigners, too. The term 'foreign experts' or 'foreign friends' refers to the coterie of Soviet advisers, Marxists, fellow travellers and others who, for personal reasons, preferred life in the People's Republic to that at home.

Until the reform era, and in some cases after, 'foreign experts' and 'friends' lived in China on the government's terms and at its expense. The chief requirement was that they supported its ideological goals. With the exception of the Soviet advisers, all of whom were recalled in 1960 during the Sino-Soviet split, the professional contribution of the 'friends' to China's modernization was negligible. Politically, however, they were useful: they formed the vanguard of 'people's', or unofficial, diplomacy, enabling the Communist government to demonstrate that it enjoyed international support, despite the fact that many countries in the West declined to have full diplomatic relations with it.

From the 1950s to the late 1970s the 'friends' were friends of the Chinese government rather than of ordinary Chinese people. The guests enjoyed much better living conditions than ordinary citizens, from whom they were often isolated. However, they were not spared involvement in political campaigns: some were persecuted and imprisoned during the Cultural Revolution, regardless of their earlier loyalty.

Prominent members of the first generation of 'friends' included George Hatem, Rewi Alley, Wilfred Burchett, Alan Winnington, Sidney Rittenberg, Israel Epstein, Elsie Fairfax-Cholmeley and Sidney Shapiro. Several acquired Chinese citizenship and joined the Chinese Communist Party. A number continued to live in Beijing in the late 1990s.

But if the loyalties of this first generation rarely changed, the meaning of the term 'foreign friends' did. When China opened to the world following the death of Mao, a new generation of foreigners went to live and work in the People's Republic. Most were genuine experts with little ideological attachment to Communism or Beijing. By the mid-1990s China had received more than 500,000 such people.

Meanwhile, Chinese leaders began to use the term 'friends' to refer to prominent foreigners who had never lived in the country and who held distinctly anti-Communist views. They included Richard Nixon, former United States president, Edward Heath, former British prime minister, and Pierre Trudeau, former Canadian prime minister. These men were 'friends' because of the part they played in upgrading relations between China and their own countries. The nature of 'friendship' had changed, but it was still conferred on the basis of, at best, compliance with or at least recognition of, the Communist regime.

foreign policy

There is hardly an aspect of China's rapid modernization more important to its own people, or more troubling for the established powers, than its meaning for the country's relations with the wider world. The issues at stake are easily stated but less easily resolved. They arise from the fact that, in the recent past, a huge country long used to viewing itself as the centre of the world has been humiliated, occupied and divided, and compelled to fit into a world order made in the West. In turn subjugated by, accommodated to, and isolated from, this order, Beijing decided to rejoin it in the 1970s. Thirty years later, an increasingly powerful China is contending with the UNITED STATES for regional dominance, and grappling with the implications of interdependence and globalization. They are matters for which history, culture and politics have left it ill prepared.

middle kingdom to marginal state

China's journey from the 'centre of the civilized world' to the 'sick man of Asia' began with the Opium Wars in 1839–42 and ended in the BOXER REBELLION of 1899–1900. The first required China to come to terms with the new international order created by free trade and industrial revolution in the West. The second, leading to the occupation and ransack of Beijing, the flight of the Qing Court to Xian, and the imposition of a huge indemnity, exposed its failure to do so. At the close of the nineteenth century China was easy prey in a predatory world. Its sovereignty, already impaired by the UNEQUAL TREATIES, was diminished further by the lease of territories, spheres of influence, and Japan's occupation of TAIWAN. In these circumstances, the presence in Beijing in 1900 of an 8-power occupation force was a profound symbol of China's national distress. The recovery of national sovereignty and territorial integrity, along with the modernization required to achieve both, have been principal aims of Chinese foreign policy ever since – save, perhaps, during the revolutionary digression of the CULTURAL REVOLUTION.

This consistency of purpose did not extend to agreement over how to achieve it. Neither did it disguise the difficulty of doing so. This became clear after the REPUBLICAN REVOLUTION of 1911. In terms of foreign policy, the revolution jettisoned the official legacy of China-centrism along with Manchu rule. But it did not make it easy for the new Republic of China to find a place in the community of nations. One reason for this was that, in an age of nationalism and imperialism, the idea of the equality of nations was itself alien. Another was China's continuing weakness and division.

The TWENTY-ONE DEMANDS Japan made of China in 1915, which threatened to turn the country into a client state of Tokyo, emphasized both these realities. So did the Versailles Peace Conference in 1919 when the victors in the First World War divided the spoils arising from Germany's defeat. Despite Chinese objections, JAPAN was rewarded with continued occupation of the parts of SHANDONG seized from Germany at the outbreak of the war. Student protests over this issue, first in Beijing, then elsewhere, sparked the outbreak of modern nationalism and intellectual renewal known as the MAY FOURTH MOVEMENT. The episode demonstrated the close link in the minds of many nationalists between China's internal and external crises; between backward, divisive warlord rule at home, and national shame overseas.

A desire to end both was behind the revolutionary upheavals of the 1920s. Inspiration came from two sources, both of which pointed to ways in which China might regain its lost dignity and power. The most radical was the Bolshevik Revolution and the creation of the SOVIET UNION. The sudden victory of MARXISM in a vast, relatively undeveloped country inspired some Chinese to believe their country could follow a similar course. When Moscow unilaterally relinquished nearly all the rights the Tsars secured in China through unequal treaties, Marxism seemed even more attractive. Practical help in the form of Soviet advisers, arms, and a tactical alliance between the CHINESE COMMUNIST PARTY and a reorganized KUOMINTANG soon confirmed the value of revolution. The NORTHERN EXPEDITION of the National Revolutionary Army overturned the traditional social order and threatened the powers' privileges throughout south China – until CHIANG KAI-SHEK purged the Communists in 1927 and adopted a more moderate line.

The new conciliatory approach was more in keeping with another option for China's recovery which had been sketched out by the powers at the WASHINGTON CONFERENCE of 1921–2. During the proceedings, Japan agreed to return Shandong, and Britain WEIHAIWEI. The participants, who did not include the Soviet Union, pledged to respect China's territorial integrity in what amounted to a reprise of the Open Door policy first put forward by the United States in 1899 (see UNITED STATES). They also hinted at relinquishing their privileges in the country should China undertake legal reforms (see LAW). In the event, such measures were a long time coming: they materialized only after Japan, whose power the conference tried to constrain, had usurped the West as China's main enemy.

the making of a 'great power'

The Kuomintang government secured TARIFF AUTONOMY in 1928 and argued vigorously for an end to EXTRATERRITORIALITY. But by the early 1930s new dangers outweighed the old. China's helplessness in the face of them was underlined by the failure of the League of Nations to punish Japan for its aggression in Manchuria and creation of the puppet state of MANCHUGUO. Worse was to come. During the

SINO-JAPANESE WAR, Japan occupied more territory and inflicted more damage on China than had the other powers in almost a century of imperialism. In the early stages of the war, China's very survival was at stake.

It was ensured by the need of Britain and the United States to defeat Japan as well as Nazi Germany in the Second World War. China became a necessary ally in this cause and, at least in the eyes of Washington, a 'great power' – the fourth member of the wartime coalition alongside the United States, Britain and the Soviet Union. In deference to China's new status, the US and Britain relinquished extraterritoriality at the start of 1943. At the end of the same year, they invited Chiang to the CAIRO CONFERENCE where he met Winston Churchill and Franklin Roosevelt for talks on the war in the Far East. It was agreed that Taiwan and Manchuria would return to China following Japan's defeat.

These developments transformed China's international status. Save for HONG KONG, which Britain declined to return, even to an ally, Chiang's regime recovered most of the privileges conceded in the unequal treaties of the Qing era. Thanks to its role in the war and status as a founder member of the UNITED NATIONS, China had a seat at the world's top table.

'leaning to one side': the Cold War

China's domestic situation was much less impressive. And Chiang's failures at home soon swept his foreign policy gains – and the West's hopes for China – into oblivion. The Communist victory in the CIVIL WAR of 1949 and the Nationalists' flight to Taiwan perpetuated the territorial division that the defeat of Japan was supposed to end. More important, it placed a revolutionary Marxist government in power in Beijing at a time of growing hostility between the Soviet Union and the West.

In Mao Zedong's words, the 'new' China would 'lean to one side', the side of the Soviet Union, with which Beijing signed a Treaty of Friendship, Alliance and Mutual Assistance in 1950. Within the Chinese Communist Party, revolutionary zeal inflamed the sense of wounded nationalism that the end of foreign privilege had failed to heal, and continued Western support for Chiang (and his government's occupation of China's seat in the UN) aggravated. Verbal and ideological hostility between China and the United States was intense.

As far as territorial claims were concerned,

however, the 'new' China was rather like the old – with the important difference that Beijing now had the military power to enforce more of them. In the quest for national security, China went to war in Korea in 1950–53 (see KOREAN WAR); attacked the Taiwan-controlled island of Quemoy in 1954–5 and 1958; subjugated TIBET in 1959; defeated INDIA in a border war in 1962; and checked American power in VIETNAM by supporting the Communist North in 1964–5. In all these encounters, save the last against Taiwan, Beijing strengthened its control over outlying regions and checked the ambitions of external foes. In 1964, despite Moscow's refusal to supply the help it had promised, China became only the fifth country in the world to build an atomic bomb (see PEOPLE'S LIBERATION ARMY/CHINA BUILDS THE BOMB).

Yet all this was less than half the story. Mao's quest for revolution, the main item on China's agenda from the late 1950s, created foreign policy and security problems of its own. With the GREAT LEAP FORWARD China embarked on its own distinctive road to socialism and came to regard the Soviet Union as an even bigger foe than the United States. After almost a decade of fraternity, the two socialist states fell out publicly and profoundly. (See SOVIET UNION.) The Cultural Revolution plunged China into chaos at home and even greater isolation. Both weakened the economy and made the country vulnerable to attack. Both delayed Beijing's chance of occupying China's seat at the United Nations.

In so far as the People's Republic had a foreign policy during the later 1960s, it involved attacks on foreign diplomats in China, and support for insurrectionaries in the Third World. This included countries such as CAMBODIA and INDONESIA, which Beijing had courted since the BANDUNG CONFERENCE of 1954 when the personal diplomacy of ZHOU ENLAI did much to win support for China's then moderate stance of mutual non-interference and peaceful coexistence. The 'Five Principles of Peaceful Coexistence' (see BANDUNG CONFERENCE), an expression of Beijing's identity with the developing world and its supposed neutrality in the Cold War, were abandoned as Red Guards seized control of the Foreign Ministry and recalled China's ambassadors. By the close of the 1960s China was almost as isolated and self-absorbed as it had been at any time in its long history. It was almost as complacent, too. China's emperors believed they ruled all the civilized world;

China's Communists thought they were at the centre of world revolution.

strategic opening to the West

This illusion endured until DENG XIAOPING returned to power shortly after Mao's death in 1976. But the need to seek rapprochement with the West became apparent much earlier. It was brought home by a military standoff between Chinese and Soviet troops along the Sino-Soviet border in 1969. Several years of 'revolutionary diplomacy' left China facing this crisis vulnerable and alone. In such circumstances, continued isolation was not an option. Ultimately, China's *national* interests were more important than its *revolutionary* ones. And these were best served by joining the international order rather than trying to overthrow it.

The door to relations with the United States had never been quite shut since Zhou prised it open at the GENEVA CONFERENCE ON KOREA AND INDOCHINA in 1954. In 1971 it opened wide enough to allow US National Security Adviser Henry Kissinger to make a secret visit to Beijing, and opened wider still a year later when President Nixon followed in his footsteps. In between the visits, the US dropped its objections to Beijing's occupation of China's seat at the UN; and in October 1971 the People's Republic of China finally supplanted the Republic of China in the world body. Also in the same year, LIN BIAO, Mao's erstwhile successor, died in a plane crash, allegedly after trying to assassinate his mentor. The struggle for power in Beijing appeared to stabilize. So, during the 1970s, did the 'strategic triangle' formed by Washington, Moscow and Beijing which governed international relations for the remainder of the Cold War.

Rapprochement with the United States (and soon with Japan and Western Europe) reaped immediate gains for Beijing. It checked the Soviet threat in the north, reduced US support for Taiwan and, eventually, facilitated American withdrawal from Vietnam – though only in the context of defeat. It also held out the prospect of access to finance and technology from the capitalist world. For much of the 1970s, Beijing was hesitant to seek either: as long as the Chairman lived, neither economic self-sufficiency nor ideological purity could be abandoned. But both were sacrificed in 1978 when Deng overcame his rivals in the post-Mao leadership and steered China on a course of engagement with the outside world.

opening to the world

This opening to the world, though momentous, proceeded slowly. It was driven first by the search for security. Under Mao and the 'GANG OF FOUR', the new diplomacy had few implications for domestic policy. The United States was valued as a strategic counterweight to Moscow, not as a model for China's own development. Beijing still opposed US capitalism and 'imperialism'. It was just that it opposed Soviet 'revisionism', which mocked Marxism *and* threatened China's national security, rather more.

Engagement with the outside world intensified once Deng launched his economic reforms at the close of the 1970s. Beijing opened its doors to capital and expertise from every quarter in the search for economic modernization and national power. FOREIGN TRADE AND INVESTMENT rejuvenated the economy. Free market reforms penetrated almost every aspect of life. Educational and cultural exchanges opened minds long closed by ideology and isolation. The People's Republic made its presence felt in a host of multilateral organizations it had previously spurned. War was deemed necessary at the start of the reform era to tame Vietnam's ambitions in Southeast Asia (see VIETNAM). But diplomacy secured the eventual return of Hong Kong and MACAU, and, at least for a while, eased tensions with Taiwan. Throughout this period, Beijing benefited from the willingness of the West to play the 'China card' in its rivalry with the Soviet bloc.

This changed with the suppression of the TIANANMEN SQUARE DEMOCRACY MOVEMENT in 1989, and the collapse of the Soviet Union two years later. The first was a serious setback for China's foreign policy. It revealed a side of the People's Republic very different from that of the reforming, liberalizing state cherished by governments in the West. However, no Western country abandoned the pursuit of amicable relations with Beijing, and none imposed comprehensive economic sanctions because of the crackdown. The collapse of the Soviet Union presented different problems. It raised ideological and international complications. Beijing sought to overcome them by establishing 'strategic partnerships' with the RUSSIAN FEDERATION and the Soviet successor states in central Asia. This was an urgent matter because of the strong pro-independence sentiment among the Turkic-speaking Muslims of XINJIANG, the autonomous region which shares a border with Kazakhstan, Kirgizstan and Tajikistan. One of the conditions binding China to its new partners includes a pledge not to encourage secession in each other's territory. Nevertheless, the extent to which the people of central Asia, as opposed to their governments, will refrain from helping their fellow Muslims under Chinese rule is unclear – worryingly so for Beijing, which needs the oil of central Asia but not the Islamic-based nationalism (see ENERGY).

China's rapid economic growth in the 1990s made Beijing a favoured destination for chief executives of multi-national companies eager to tap into the 'world's largest market'; and statesmen from the developed world anxious to build good relations with the 'next superpower'. Despite Tiananmen, many of them believed that since China was so evidently joining the world, it seemed inevitable that the country would become more *like* the world, usually defined as the liberal, capitalist West. Yet few Communist leaders in Beijing, where the nature and purpose of China's engagement with the world have long been controversial, shared this view. Like the Qing dynasty reformers before them, Communist reformers opened the doors to the West to let in vital resources, not introduce 'alien' political and cultural values. And whenever this policy seemed to be failing, whenever society appeared to be spinning out of control, they tried to curb the influence of foreign values. An early example was the campaign against 'spiritual pollution' of 1983; a later one the struggle against 'peaceful evolution' – the alleged plot of the West to undermine socialism in China following the 1989 crackdown in Tiananmen Square.

in *the world or* of *the world?*

The successors of Deng Xiaoping share their mentor's view that engagement with the outside world is an economic imperative and one that conditions foreign policy. Isolation is not an option, and a sharp deterioration in relations with the West and Japan is to be avoided for fear of losing export markets and access to capital and technology. But none of this, in Beijing's view, implies limitations on Chinese sovereignty, defined as the Communist Party's right to dominate political life at home and pursue China's territorial claims however it thinks fit. It is true that in the 1990s, Beijing reluctantly agreed to discuss its HUMAN RIGHTS record with other countries, a move which seemed like a breakthrough, and a dim-

inution of jealously guarded sovereignty. But there have been few indications that discussion of human rights at the diplomatic level is anything other than a substitute for the significant changes in domestic policy which alone can enlarge individual freedoms. Thus, China ended the century by signing two key United Nations covenants on human rights *and* jailing DISSIDENTS who sought to benefit from them.

Beijing's attitude towards its disputed territories of Taiwan and the SOUTH CHINA SEA provide further evidence of its 'engagement, but without prejudice' approach to the world, in this case the world of its near neighbours. In 1996, the People's Liberation Army test-fired missiles and staged military exercises near Taiwan to curb pro-independence sentiment during the island's first direct presidential polls. It was a vivid expression of China's determination either to absorb Taiwan or isolate it. This obsession governs much of China's foreign policy at the start of the new century, long years after it expelled the island from the United Nations and, in effect, the international community; and despite the fact that parts of the Mainland have grown rich due to an influx of Taiwanese investment.

In the South China Sea, where China's search for energy has reinforced its claims to territory, Beijing has steadily built up quasi-military facilities on disputed islands in the Spratly chain. This is despite an agreement with the ASSOCIATION OF SOUTHEAST ASIAN NATIONS (ASEAN) not to settle questions of ownership over the area by force, and Beijing's participation in the ASEAN Regional Forum, an exercise in cooperative security which the People's Republic signed up to in 1994. Rival claimants have cause to wonder if China is not concerned simply to buy their goodwill on the issue until such time as the Chinese navy is in a position to settle it by force (see PEOPLE'S LIBERATION ARMY/CHINESE SEAPOWER). Taiwan and the South China Sea are two 'foreign policy' areas (though Beijing regards them as domestic affairs) where the Chinese military often makes the running.

realpolitik and insecurity

Realpolitik drives China's foreign policy at the start of the new era. China's leaders speak of their country's 'independent foreign policy of peace' and have signed 'strategic partnerships' with the world's major countries, including the United States. But lofty sentiments aside, there are no over-arching moral principles at work in Beijing's approach to the international community. At home and abroad, China's revolutionary mission died with Mao. Under Deng, its identity with the Third World became a matter of strategy rather than sympathy. In most of the major international disputes of the 1990s, save that of Cambodia, Beijing adopted a reactive rather than proactive stance, both inside and outside the United Nations. It has sought maximum room for manoeuvre to pursue its own interests.

Chief among these is opposing the United States in its role as the world's sole superpower. Beijing describes this as fighting 'hegemonism' and pursuing a 'multi-polar' world. It reflects growing tension between an established and an emerging power, one whose leaders believe Washington and its allies are bent on creating obstacles to China's rejuvenation. One such 'obstacle' is the new US–Japan security doctrine agreed in 1999 which allows Japanese forces to play a greater role in 'areas surrounding' Japan, possibly including Taiwan (see JAPAN). Another is the proposal for a US-led theatre missile defence (TMD) system in East Asia, again possibly including Taiwan. If implemented, TMD could degrade Beijing's missile capability and lessen fears in Taiwan about a Mainland attack.

NATO's war against Serbia in 1999 added to the sense of insecurity in Beijing. It did so partly because of the implications of a successful high-tech air war for China's own defences (see PEOPLE'S LIBERATION ARMY). Few of China's foreign policy goals can be accomplished in the absence of genuine military power. The strictly foreign policy lessons of the conflict were even more significant: NATO attacked a sovereign country on humanitarian grounds to protect the Kosovar Albanian ethnic minority without United Nations sanction. This raised the spectre of US military intervention in China on behalf of Tibetans and Taiwanese. The Kosovo conflict was a psychological blow for a government wedded to the notion that national sovereignty takes precedence over other considerations in foreign affairs and international law. NATO's mistaken bombing of the Chinese embassy in Belgrade rubbed the message in.

Beijing has sought comfort in closer relations with Russia, similarly discomfited by US power and an important source of arms; with North Korea, a dangerously unpredictable country but an important anti-American buffer state adjoining China's industrialized northeast; and with India, but without prejudicing traditionally close ties to Pakistan. None of these countries can supply the markets, technology, capital and expertise China requires. Only Pyongyang and Pakistan are bound by ties of sentiment to Beijing. But they all have an interest, to a greater or lesser extent, in curbing American power.

from engagement to interdependence

If countering the global reach of the United States is a major item on China's foreign policy agenda, contending with the related issues of globalization and economic interdependence is no less important. Despite more than two decades of growing engagement with the wider world, the instinct of China's leaders is still to recoil from interdependence and resist globalization where these powerful forces threaten to diminish Beijing's exaggerated, nineteenth-century conception of sovereignty. Given the tortuous history of their country's foreign relations, China's leaders found it easy, during the late 1990s, to view American demands that they open their economy further to international competition in order to join the World Trade Organization as merely the West's latest attempt to colonize the People's Republic. It is little wonder that negotiations on China's entry were painful and protracted. And it is far from clear that the agreement on China's membership eventually reached in 1999 signalled the end of such worries.

However in an age of cross-frontier innovation and global information industries, interdependence cannot be avoided. During the first decade of the twenty-first century China must turn increasingly to the rest of the world for supplies of food (see AGRICULTURE) and energy if it is to sustain its rapid economic growth. And it must be party to binding international accords if it is not to destroy much of its own, and some of its neighbours', ENVIRONMENT in the pursuit of growth. These are merely the more conspicuous examples of China's growing dependency and, due to the ceaseless search for comparative advantage in the international economy, *inter*dependency with the rest of the world. Foreign policy goals and policies will have to be reshaped accordingly.

It is no surprise that China is finding it hard to adjust to a world not of its own making. China is proud yet still wounded by past humiliations, sophisticated but often startled by progress in the developed world; a nuclear power but still a poor one; an enormous country but not yet a united one; and a secretive, centralized, authoritarian state whose political culture sets it apart from the rest of the world. These attributes make it difficult for China to reconcile itself to becoming 'just another member' of the world community. This is particularly true given that Beijing views the laws of that community as alien, designed to preserve the status quo and discriminate against a powerful newcomer. Partly because Beijing's analysis of this situation is correct, it is just as difficult for the world to accommodate China and its agenda. This is why devising policies to secure China's place in the world on terms acceptable to all parties is one of the most complex tasks facing statesmen in Beijing and beyond.

foreign trade and investment

China's rapid integration in the world economy since the late 1970s is the single most dramatic sign of its growing wealth and power. It has sparked foreign predictions of economic superpowerdom that revived Western desires to exploit the 'world's largest untapped market'. It has excited fears of a 'China threat' first to international trade, then to world peace, that harked back to the 'Yellow Peril' school of China-watching. And – for a while – it breathed new life into the view, still lingering in Beijing, that China is the centre of the world, albeit the new, unpredictable one of global growth. Each of these views is wrong. Each reflects China's growing impact on the world economy, and points to the challenges and conflicts arising from it.

trade under the treaties

Trade and foreign investment are hardly strangers to China. The forced opening of China in the mid-nineteenth century was founded on the Western demand to conduct trade and diplomacy with Beijing on equal terms. QING DYNASTY rulers resisted the idea so strongly that the West had to batter them into submission and establish a trading system of its own. Its chief features were TREATY PORTS, EXTRATERRITORIALITY, and a fixed tariff on imports (see TARIFF AUTONOMY). It took Chinese governments a full century to rescind the first of these two handicaps and almost 90 years to abolish the last of them. Foreign trade and investment flourished in the meantime, but under conditions many Chinese found humiliating.

In late Qing and Republican times the foreign sector of the economy was small yet significant. Foreign trade was equal to about 10 per cent of GDP in the late 1920s. The Great Depression, the loss of Manchuria to JAPAN, and the wars and revolution that toppled Chiang Kai-shek's KUOMINTANG government in the late 1940s, soon made the late 1920s something of a golden age. Yet linkages between the foreign and domestic economies were always weak. Whatever China's trade fortunes, the effects on the wider economy were negligible.

The same pattern was repeated with foreign investment. BRITAIN was the largest investor in China until 1930 when Japan assumed this position. Little foreign capital went into export-oriented agricultural, mining or plantation businesses of the kind seen elsewhere in 'colonial' economies. Most of it was concentrated in foreign trade, RAILWAYS, INDUSTRY, property and FINANCE. It was confined to the treaty ports, coastal provinces and, in the case of Japan, MANCHUGUO. To the extent that they enjoyed privileges of the kind not available to domestic concerns, foreign businesses were at an advantage. But it is not clear that domestic Chinese industry would have flourished in the absence of the external stimuli provided by foreign firms. And if foreigners held a prominent stake in the modern sector of the economy, that sector itself was tiny compared with the economy as a whole.

China's early experience of foreign loans was less ambiguous. Qing, early Republican, and Nationalist governments were all forced to rely on new foreign loans to service old ones, pay outstanding indemnities or finance military campaigns. Railway loans were more productive, but arguments between provinces over ownership, and widespread social unrest characteristic of the era, undermined potential returns. A more constant and valuable source of funds were the OVERSEAS CHINESE: their remittances enabled China to sustain a surplus of imports over exports throughout the Republican period.

isolation to international economy

Extraterritoriality and treaty ports were things of the past when the CHINESE COMMUNIST PARTY seized power in 1949, but that did not stop the new government creating a trade and investment regime of its own. Beijing's bureaucratic approach rapidly drove all but a handful of Western businesses away, a process aided by the KOREAN WAR and the United Nations embargo against the People's Republic. Trade became a monopoly of the state and soon fell victim to politics. In the early 1950s ideology made the SOVIET UNION and Eastern Europe more acceptable trade partners than the West. A few years later, Moscow fell out of favour, too. Mao Zedong's GREAT LEAP FORWARD and, from the mid-1960s, the CULTURAL REVOLUTION, were experiments in self-reliance. The domestic market was isolated from international competition. There was no foreign investment and no foreign loans.

China did not forsake trade. Neither did it stop doing business with the West. Rather, foreign trade became a strategic adjunct to autarchy. During Mao's later years, China exhibited an attitude towards the outside world similar to that of the Qing Dynasty in the late eighteenth century: it needed nothing foreigners might produce, and could produce everything it needed.

In this context, Deng Xiaoping's Open Door policy of the late 1970s was a second 'great awakening' – one scarcely less significant than that begun by the Opium Wars more than a century earlier. At the close of the 1970s, China's trade accounted for about 13 per cent of GDP and the People's Republic ranked 32nd in the league of world traders. Most of its exports were primary products. Most of its imports were producer's goods. Twenty years later the World Bank put Mainland trade, much of it carried in Chinese ships, by now part of one of the world's largest merchant marines, at 30 per cent of GDP (though others thought it less) and ranked China the tenth-largest trading nation, responsible for 4 per cent of world trade. In two decades China's trade had grown more than tenfold. At the close of the century 80 per cent of China's exports were manufactured products.

Decentralization, a reduction in tariffs, an end to export planning, repeated devaluations of the *renminbi*, China's currency, and the general withdrawal of the state from the economy in favour of the market sparked this boom. The long suppressed entrepreneurial flair of the Chinese played a large part, too. There were many aspects to this. One was the creation of the China International Trust and Investment Corporation (CITIC), Communist China's first multinational, whose

founding chief executive, Rong Yiren (1916–), was a former Shanghai capitalist and later vice-president of the People's Republic.

Foreign investment, which poured into the newly created SPECIAL ECONOMIC ZONES and other 'open' areas of the country, played an even bigger role. Much of it was utilized in processing operations, fuelling export-oriented growth of the kind that had already turned the economies of TAIWAN, HONG KONG, South Korea (see KOREA) and SINGAPORE into star performers.

At the close of the century, China accounted for 40 per cent of all foreign direct investment (FDI) in developing countries and was the single largest recipient of FDI after the UNITED STATES. The Mainland's 300,000 foreign enterprises had absorbed close to US$300 billion and employed 17.5 million people. Sino-foreign joint ventures accounted for one-third of China's exports and half of its imports. Portfolio investment, though modest by comparison, moved in to purchase the 'B-shares' reserved for foreign investors on the Shanghai and Shenzhen stock exchanges. Others bought their way into China at a distance, snapping up the shares People's Republic companies listed in Hong Kong ('H-shares' or 'Red Chips') and New York ('N-shares').

This was an extraordinary performance though in some ways a deceptive one. The lion's share of China's 'foreign' investment was not foreign at all but Chinese: it was the capital, technology and expertise of the diaspora returning home in search of profits in the guise of patriotism. At least two-thirds of all investment during the boom years of the mid-1990s originated in Hong Kong, Taiwan and among the Chinese of Southeast Asia. Even some of that sourced from the United States could be attributed to Americans of Chinese extraction. There was no clearer testimony of the value to the People's Republic of the Overseas Chinese – a numerous, wealthy, industrious group of people whose attachment to their homeland survives long years of separation and, in many cases, Communist persecution.

The role in this process of Hong Kong and Taiwan, both of them Chinese territories rather than overseas ones, was fundamental. They were, and remain, conduits for the capital and commitment required to modernize the Mainland. In the late 1980s, Hong Kong virtually abandoned manufacturing and shifted its labour-intensive operations into Pearl River Delta in GUANGDONG, where both land and labour were cheaper. A decade later Hong Kong factories had helped turn the Delta into something approaching a giant industrial park. Similar processes were at work in FUJIAN – host to hundreds of Taiwanese-owned factories, even though politics dictated that contacts between the 'two Chinas' had to take place via third parties, chiefly Hong Kong. Hong Kong's role in trade was no less important than in investment: much of the People's Republic's trade with its principal partners – Japan, the United States, Europe and Taiwan – passed through the territory. The opening of the YANGTZE valley in 1992 shifted the focus of some of this investment north and west.

All this activity breathed new life into the Mainland's *national* economy, helping it become the fastest-growing in the world. It also sparked controversy among Communist leaders who opposed the foreign values, or 'spiritual pollution', which accompanied the influx of foreign trade and investment. They pursued an Open Door policy to augment China's national strength, not facilitate the long march of global capitalism.

markets and myths in the 1990s

That trade and investment, together with free market reforms in the domestic economy, particularly agriculture, transformed the Chinese economy, was not in doubt. That the transformation was complete, would continue at the same pace until it was, or that it had turned the People's Republic into an El Dorado for foreign investors, ought to have been inconceivable. There was plenty of evidence that doing business in China was difficult, especially for Western firms; and there was some to suggest that, while trade and investment had transformed much, there was much it had not even touched. 'New' China in many ways resembled the old.

One aspect of this was the difficulty many Western companies found making money in the People's Republic. The traditional 'lure' of China, long a factor in the Western approach to the country, was reinforced by exaggerated talk of market opportunities amid the rush to get rich. Some firms, famously hard-headed when operating in their own environment, appeared to suspend cherished accounting principles in China. They were there 'for the long term', enduring complaints at home about China's HUMAN RIGHTS record, and CORRUPTION and frustrations on the ground of the kind they would not put up with elsewhere.

There were more prosaic considerations, too. Trade disputes, breaches of copyright, and ill-defined property rights reflected China's lack of transparency and weak sense of LAW. It was no accident that the Communists revived China's legal profession at the same time as they sought capital from the outside world: even they did not expect foreign investors to sink money in the country on the strength of a promise. But revival was not the same as the articulation of legal principles; articulation different from compliance.

And if foreign investment enjoyed superior status under the pre-1949 *ancien regime* it was often at a disadvantage under the new. Not only were there legal uncertainties to contend with, but a host of problems arose from conflicting cultural attitudes. A prominent one – a stereotype but no less important for that – concerned 'face': Chinese joint venture partners were not always ready to be instructed about 'new' things in terms that suggested they were ignorant. For foreigners, on the other hand, ignorance was often all too apparent and best corrected sooner rather than later.

Occasionally Chinese attitudes took a more nationalistic turn. China's growing dependency on the outside world, and particularly the United States, went down badly among some younger nationalists. There was considerable frustration over Washington's decision each year from the late 1980s to the mid-1990s to make extension of China's status as a Most Favoured Trading Nation (MFN) (redesignated 'Normal Trade Relations' in 1999) dependent on improvements in Beijing's human rights record. Extension was always granted, even though human rights rarely improved, ensuring displeasure in Beijing *and* the West. Chinese anger was reflected in a 1996 bestseller, *China Can Say No*, which attacked American 'bullying' of the People's Republic. The authors promised revenge once China was strong. It was an isolated outburst of primitive nationalism, but a no less striking one for that. Shortly after publication, Beijing disassociated itself from the book, claiming its authors were 'inexperienced in foreign affairs'.

perils of engagement

As in the 1930s so in the 1990s: foreign trade and investment in China made most impression in the eastern provinces and coastal cities. In the first half of the century the beneficiaries were called treaty ports; at the end of the second they were known as Special Economic Zones and open cities. The inland provinces of the north and west knew less of foreign capital's transforming power. Attempts by Beijing to entice investors deeper into the country by identifying money-making projects in the interior proved only a limited success. Speculation in coastal real estate was more attractive. So much so that Shanghai and other major cities began the new century with empty office blocks and depressed rentals.

Throughout the 1990s Beijing tried to curb wasteful projects, control foreign debt, and check capital flight, all of which became common in the Mainland's immature investment environment. It became even more important to do so in 1998 when the effects of the Asian financial crisis hit home. The fact that China's currency, the *renminbi*, was not fully convertible; that portfolio investment was a tiny proportion of direct foreign investment; and that foreign debt was covered by foreign reserves, sheltered Beijing from problems of the kind experienced by some of its neighbours. There were no crises in China like those that plagued Latin America and, at the close of the century, Russia.

There was no room for complacency, either. Several non-bank financial institutions – the '-ITICS': international trust and investment corporations – ran into difficulties because of corruption, mismanagement and foreign loans. Some defaulted. One, Guangdong International Trust and Investment Corporation (GITIC), sought bankruptcy. In 1998 foreign trade decreased on the year before – for the first time since 1983. Foreign investors became less enthusiastic as demand in China and the region slumped. The 1990s ended less happily than they had begun.

Moreover, if the Mainland's half-reformed financial sector and partially open trade and investment regime saved it from the worst effects of the crisis, they were also reminders of how far Beijing had to go to line them up with international norms. Even in the late 1990s, at least 50 per cent of China's exports involved the processing of imports. Such activity, though lucrative, had little impact on the domestic economy. Certainly it did not challenge the hold over the national economy of state enterprises, whose reform was an essential but, at the start of the new century, a still unfulfilled task (see INDUSTRY).

The Mainland's attempt to become a member of the World Trade Organization (WTO) proved equally frustrating It began in 1986 when Beijing applied to re-join the Gen-

---

China and the World Bank

The People's Republic joined the World Bank and the International Monetary Fund in 1980 – a striking development for a state better known as a champion of Third World revolution than as a supporter of the global financial order. It rapidly became the Bank's largest borrower, deploying funds in scores of projects across the country. There was a pause in Bank lending following the suppression of the Tiananmen Square Democracy Movement, but it lasted only eighteen months. Beijing valued World Bank expertise as much as its money: a stream of data, reports and recommendations poured out of the Bank's Washington headquarters covering almost every sector of the Chinese economy. The World Bank trained a generation of Chinese managers, officials and economists in the arts of international finance. Beijing went some way to return the favour in 1997 when financial crisis struck Asia. It lent the International Monetary Fund, the World Bank's sister organization, US$4 billion to help bail out the first, worst-hit countries – another striking development for a supposedly Marxist state. Though generally harmonious, the relationship between China and the Bank has not been free of controversy. In 1999, largely because of United States objections, the Bank said it would not go ahead with a loan for the resettlement of poor, mostly Han, Chinese farmers in a predominantly Tibetan and Mongol region of QINGHAI until it had satisfied itself that the identity and culture of these ETHNIC MINORITIES would not suffer as a result of the scheme. China, piqued, withdrew its request for funds.

---

eral Agreement on Tariffs and Trade (GATT), WTO's predecessor. Until 1998 monopolies, restrictive practices and selected high tariffs kept the People's Republic (excluding Hong Kong and Macau) out of the world traders' club, even though it had become a trade giant. In 1999, NATO's accidental bombing of the Chinese embassy in Belgrade during the war against Serbia provoked a crisis in China's relations with the United States, the lead negotiator on Beijing's entry into WTO. Communist hardliners were in no mood to liberalize the economy in favour of international capital. For some of them, the entire WTO issue became a reprise of the West's nineteenth-century campaign to force open the Chinese economy. Sino-US trade talks did not resume until late in the year, when an agreement securing China's membership of WTO was at last signed.

None of these problems disguise the reality of China's growing engagement in the world economy. None hide the fact that, though Beijing seeks to protect strategic areas of the economy such as TELECOMMUNICATIONS, and remains attached to ideals of self-sufficiency in ENERGY and food supplies (see AGRICULTURE), interdependency is becoming a norm in its relations with the outside world – in trade as in other areas of life. This is a momentous development, especially in the context of China's modern history. Statistics alone cannot do it justice. It is part of a 'great encounter' between China and a world that generations of Chinese, both rulers and ruled, have long found it difficult to live with. At the start of the new century the process of engagement is incomplete and likely to prove troublesome. It is, however, irreversible.

Four Modernizations

The CHINESE COMMUNIST PARTY called for the modernization of AGRICULTURE, INDUSTRY, defence, and science and technology first in 1964, when ZHOU ENLAI, then premier, made them the core of a reform programme. The CULTURAL REVOLUTION, more concerned with politics than productivity, ended discussion of the subject. Zhou tried again in 1975, this time with the help of DENG XIAOPING, recently rehabilitated following his dismissal almost ten years earlier for favouring capitalist-style reforms. Radicals at the top of the Party, notably the 'GANG OF FOUR' led by JIANG QING, Chairman Mao's wife, criticized the two men's plans as a prelude to a 'capitalist restoration'. The policies were abandoned again.

However, in 1976 the 'Gang' were arrested and first HUA GUOFENG, the Chairman's designated successor, and then Deng, who soon shoved Hua aside, made the four modernizations the basic policy of the People's Republic. They were incorporated into both the state and the Communist Party constitutions. Before long plans for the rapid transformation of each of the four areas proved too expensive and over-ambitious. They were promptly scaled down.

In 1978, WEI JINGSHENG, one of the leading figures of the DEMOCRACY WALL MOVEMENT, wrote a poster stating that the four modernizations could not be achieved without a fifth: democracy. He spent 18 years in jail for his temerity. As a propaganda slogan, the 'four modernizations' fell out of favour during the early 1980s. As a policy of fundamental economic reform, they remain at the core of China's development strategy in the new century.

Fujian Province

Poor overland communications, a rugged interior and a long coastline have made Fujian one of the most outward-looking of China's provinces. Only GUANGDONG can match its history of contact with the outside world. In Fujian's case, this world begins in TAIWAN, most of whose people trace their origins to the province and speak its language, *minnan hua*; continues to the OVERSEAS CHINESE communities of Southeast Asia, where Fujianese are often second only to Cantonese in number; and extends to trade and other forms of contact with Japan and the West. The Communist victory on the Mainland, China's unfinished CIVIL WAR, and the Cold War severed most of these links, turning Fujian into the least developed of the coastal provinces. Renewed opening to the outside world brought prosperity in the 1980s and 1990s. However, fundamental change in Fujian depends upon improved relations between Beijing and Taipei – and direct links across the Taiwan Straits.

maritime tradition

Fujian's maritime and commercial importance was recognized by BRITAIN in the mid-nineteenth century. British negotiators included the province's two major ports, Fuzhou and Xiamen (Amoy), among the five it wanted opened to foreign trade after the Opium War (see TREATY PORTS). Both cities were part of major trade networks serving Taiwan, Southeast Asia and beyond. Both were a source of mass emigration that soon took the form of labour 'exports'.

Many of the émigrés hailed from the isolated clans and communities of the interior. Since at least the seventeenth century, inhabitants of southeast Fujian had forsaken the poverty and clan wars of home for more land and better opportunities in Taiwan. There was an abundance of both thanks to the island's small population, much of it made up of non-Chinese indigenous peoples (see ETHNIC MINORITIES).

In the nineteenth century foreign labour agents turned the 'natural' exodus of Fujianese and Cantonese into big business. Though condemned by the Chinese and several foreign governments, the 'coolie' trade proved highly profitable. It continued in various forms well into the twentieth century, creating substantial Chinese communities in North and South America, and South Africa. The 'voluntary' outflow of people was even greater. The only change in this one-way flow of traffic came with Japan's occupation of Taiwan in 1895: up to a quarter of a million people returned to the Mainland rather than live under Japanese rule.

During the twentieth century, Fujian's exiles saluted their homeland in the form of remittances and, where possible, philanthropy. An outstanding example of the latter was the foundation in 1921 of Xiamen University. It was endowed by Chen Jiageng (Tan Kah Kee) (1874–1961), owner of a Singapore-based rubber, pineapple and shipping empire. Less successful émigrés were no less solicitous: their funds were an important source of local income and their correspondence and home visits valuable links between Fujian and the wider world.

The Western presence, particularly in the form of MISSIONARIES, performed a similar role in a different sphere of life. During the early years of the twentieth century there were more Protestant mission staff at work in Fujian than anywhere else in China save Guangdong. The seed fell on fertile ground; CHRISTIANITY has flourished in the province despite the expulsion of the missionaries in 1949–50 and more than two decades of Communist persecution.

Domestic upheavals during the first half of the twentieth century affected Fujian but did not threaten its customary exposure to the world. The province was not always as firmly under central government control as CHIANG KAI-SHEK, the KUOMINTANG leader, might wish. But it was not particularly rebellious, either, at least compared with the southwestern provinces.

In 1933, rebellious Kuomintang troops under Cai Tingkai (1892–1968) set up a 'People's Revolutionary Government' in Fuzhou, the provincial capital, in opposition to Chiang. It was quickly crushed. The following year Nationalist forces ousted the Communists from their Central Soviet in JIANGXI, part of which had extended into western Fujian. Thereafter there was little serious challenge to the central government's position in the province until Japanese troops occupied Fuzhou and Xiamen during the SINO-JAPANESE WAR.

> ### The Lie of the Land
>
> Fujian's 46,300 square miles (120,000 sq kms), home for more than 33 million people at the close of the century, consist of a mountainous interior and a fertile coastal strip, especially in the southeast. It includes numerous offshore islands, two groups of which – Jinmen and Matsu – are administered by the Fujian Provincial Government of the Republic of China in Taiwan. Mountains dominate Fujian's hinterland. Scores of isolated communities have developed among the narrow valleys that divide them, giving rise to a wide variety of Fujian dialects, some of them mutually incomprehensible. Fujian's main river is the Min which meets the sea just south of Fuzhou. The second is the Jiulong which empties into Xiamen Bay, and the third, the Jinjiang, which serves the ancient port of Quanzhou.

closing the coastline

The post-war period opened up an entirely different prospect – one that saw the PEOPLE'S LIBERATION ARMY drive Chiang from the Mainland and force him to seek refuge in Taiwan under UNITED STATES' protection. This placed Fujian in the frontline of the Chinese Civil War and, by proxy, the much larger ideological and military conflict between East and West. In the course of 1950 the province changed from one of the most open areas in China to one of the most closed.

It was also one of the most contested, chiefly because of Chiang's decision to make a stand on the Jinmen (Kinmen or Quemoy) and Mazu (Matsu) groups of islands just off the Fujian coast. Parts of Jinmen, the most heavily fortified of the two, are little more than a mile from Xiamen. The People's Liberation Army staged an abortive landing on Jinmen in 1949, subjected it to bombardment in 1954 and heavy, sustained shelling in 1958. (See TAIWAN.) None of these offensives achieved their goals. Each of them hardened attitudes in Beijing, Taipei and Washington, and underscored the bitter, unfinished nature of China's Civil War.

For Fujian, the standoff meant long periods of military control that curbed trade, harmed the fishing industry and hampered development. The arrival of the railway from Jiangxi in the 1950s ended the province's traditional isolation from the north. But, like the causeway built to carry it to what had previously been Xiamen Island, the line was constructed to facilitate rapid movement of troops and artillery rather than economic development. Throughout the Maoist era Beijing did not invest in a single major project in Fujian. The province was a major casualty of military tension, economic autarchy and the obsession with ideological rectitude that characterized much of life under MAO ZEDONG.

trade and Taiwan

Rapprochement in the early 1970s between Beijing and the USA, Taiwan's chief ally, brought modest change. The death of Mao, the rise of DENG XIAOPING, and the opening in the late 1970s of China's economy to foreign trade and investment brought a bigger one. Mainland overtures to Taiwan helped. In 1981, Beijing offered the island reunification on terms later applied to HONG KONG: a high degree of autonomy under the formula 'one country, two systems'. Taipei declined. But military tension across the Straits subsided, and Taiwanese businessmen began to look enviously at emerging investment opportunities on the Mainland.

Fujian was encouraged to offer as many of these as Guangdong. It was also given similar incentives to do so, including the right to retain more revenues and foreign exchange earnings than other provinces, which had to pass their gains on to Beijing. In 1980, parts of Xiamen were designated a SPECIAL ECONOMIC ZONE (SEZ), one of the four original, often controversial enclaves earmarked for foreign investment and capitalist experiment. More of the Fujian coast was opened up as the 1980s progressed, and ZHAO ZIYANG, the reformist premier and later Party leader, pursued his coastal strategy of letting the littoral lead national development.

Fujian scored some genuine firsts in its role as pioneer. Xiamen Airlines, founded in 1984, was China's first local airline. (See CIVIL AVIATION.) Two years later the city became the home of China's first joint venture bank. Yet overall, progress was less impressive than in Guangdong. Local officials were less bold and imaginative than their Cantonese counterparts. They also differed in that many were not locals at all. Cantonese ran Guangdong from the mid-1980s; in Fujian the top jobs were occupied by those who had spent most of their careers outside the province.

The gap between Fujian and Guangdong was clear from a comparison of Xiamen and SHENZHEN during the mid-1980s. Xiamen

attracted some investment from Hong Kong and Overseas Chinese, and a little from Japan and the West. But inflows of capital and technology were modest compared with the flood under way further south. By its own standards Fujian's economy grew rapidly. But it hardly did so at the pace of a potential 'tiger'.

Developments in Taiwan helped change this. In 1988 Taipei allowed its citizens to visit the Mainland for pleasure and business, inaugurating a massive movement of capital across the Straits. Much of it ended up in southeast Fujian, the spiritual and cultural homeland of many Taiwanese. As had been the case earlier with Cantonese from Hong Kong and further afield, Taiwanese who visited the Mainland experienced a 'homecoming'. While some of the sentiment associated with this soon wore off, the desire to make the most of China's cheap land and labour did not. Japan and South Korea had already begun to do so. So had companies from the West. Hong Kong was growing fat on the business. Taiwan, its low-end exports under increasing pressure in world markets, sought to do the same.

between Taipei and Beijing

Though late into the China market, Taiwan's timing was fortuitous. Taiwanese investors moved in when others were either moving out or hesitating to reinvest because of the crackdown on the Tiananmen Square Democracy Movement of 1989. The Taiwanese saw no such need for caution, particularly as the Mainland welcomed industries considered outdated at home or too pollutant to meet the island's rigorous new environmental laws.

Taiwanese investment in Fujian surged in 1989–90. It did so again in 1992–3 following Deng Xiaoping's call for coastal regions to enrich themselves by whatever means were to hand. Overall, Hong Kong and Macau were the biggest source of foreign capital, but in Xiamen and elsewhere in the southeast of the province, Taiwan projects, most of them wholly foreign-owned rather than joint ventures, dominated the scene.

They also caused the most controversy. Taiwan entrepreneurs' buccaneering business practices and hedonistic pleasures openly flouted the culture of puritanism Communist officials liked to cultivate in public. The prevalence of small-scale export processing operations, many of them using low-level technology, presented problems of a different kind. Xiamen SEZ was founded to attract high-tech investment, not just low-end processing. It managed to do so as the 1990s wore on but not on the scale once hoped. Intensive efforts to persuade Y. C. Wang (Wang Yung-ching) (1917–), head of Formosa Plastics, to build a large-scale petrochemical plant in the region came to nought.

Wang could not get the deal he wanted in Fujian. But it was no secret that Taipei opposed Mainland investments on the scale he had proposed. They would lead to economic dependency on an old rival that had still not ruled out the use of force against the island. Beijing's decision in 1996 to stage military exercises in Fujian and test-fire missiles close to the island's main harbours was a powerful reminder of Taiwan's vulnerability – one that Washington felt warranted its intervention.

Throughout the 1990s, Taipei sought to limit Taiwanese investment in the Mainland. Sometimes it did so by encouraging a 'go south' policy that directed businessmen towards the politically safer pastures of Southeast Asia. Sometimes it used legislation, outlawing Mainland investments in certain strategic areas such as energy and infrastructure.

Such policies were only a mixed success: Taiwanese investment continued to flow across the Straits to what many of the island's businessmen considered to be its natural home. Yet the generally poor state of relations between Taipei and Beijing prevented genuine social and economic integration between Taiwan and Fujian of the kind that brought Hong Kong and Guangdong together during the 1990s. It could hardly be otherwise given that Taipei refused to allow direct shipping, aviation and other links across the Taiwan Straits, forcing people, money, trade and even telephone calls to pass through a third party, usually Hong Kong, on their way to and from the Mainland.

To a large extent Fujian's fortunes depend upon an improvement in political relations between Beijing and Taipei of the kind that will permit the 'three connections': direct shipping and aviation; direct mail and telecommunications; and direct commercial and financial links. Beijing reopened the province to the outside world in the 1980s with a view to facilitating the broader political goal of reunification with Taiwan. The easing of military tensions and growth of trade and cultural ties have paved the way for this. In 1994 Taipei even lifted martial law on Jinmen, opening the island to international tourism.

But at the opening of the new era, the 'three connections' remain a distant prospect and reunification itself more distant still. In the meantime Taiwanese investors are finding that Shanghai, Tianjin and other parts of the country offer opportunities at least the equal of Fujian, with its relatively poor infrastructure, small market and undeveloped hinterland. Little change is likely until China's Civil War finally ends, ships and aircraft travel directly across the narrow strip of sea that divides the Mainland and Taiwan, and maritime Fujian is reconnected with its island satellite.

G

'Gang of Four'

JIANG QING, Zhang Chunqiao (1917–91[?]), Yao Wenyuan (1931–) and Wang Hongwen (1934–92) were radical leaders of the CHINESE COMMUNIST PARTY whose role in the CULTURAL REVOLUTION (1966–76) made them widely unpopular and an easy target for attack once the movement was over. In 1980–81 they were subjects of the greatest show trial in China's modern history and given long jail sentences. It was the closest thing to an official investigation of the Cultural Revolution that a Communist government, torn between trying to restore its credibility and preserving as much of MAO ZEDONG's reputation as possible, could manage.

The term 'Gang of Four' is a pejorative one used by the group's opponents. It was probably coined by Mao Zedong, who, late in life, saw the four as a threat. Jiang, Mao's third wife, was the most prominent and powerful of the group. Her marriage made her all but invincible – as long as the Chairman breathed. A former actress, she sought to radicalize the arts in the early 1960s by sponsoring revolutionary operas and other 'ideologically correct' works. Her influence grew, and soon she was at least as powerful as the only other woman who managed to shape China's destiny in the twentieth century: Ci Xi, the EMPRESS DOWAGER.

Zhang Chunqiao was a propaganda specialist and theoretician who ran SHANGHAI when the Cultural Revolution was at its most violent during the late 1960s. He rose to the Politburo Standing Committee, the apex of power in the Party, and was seen briefly as a possible successor to Mao. Yao Wenyuan wrote the original polemic against Wu Han (1909–69), the playwright and historian whose indirect attacks on Mao's imperial pretensions led to the fall of the Party leadership in BEIJING – the radicals' first victory in the Cultural Revolution. Wang Hongwen was a labour activist whose enthusiasm for the radical cause and loyalty to Jiang also secured his elevation to the Politburo Standing Committee.

The 'Gang' was a formidable force throughout the Cultural Revolution, defending its aims in the face of occasional opposition from Mao, who often seemed prey to second thoughts, ZHOU ENLAI, the premier, and more consistent resistance from other leaders. LIN BIAO, the defence minister, was an important ally until shortly before his dramatic death in an air crash in 1971 allegedly while trying to flee China following an unsuccessful attempt on the Chairman's life. The 'Gang' might have survived the Chairman's death in 1976 had they made common cause with HUA GUOFENG, his chosen successor, who seemed reluctant to abandon his mentor's fondness for 'permanent revolution'. Instead, they sought to consolidate their hold over the Party by using force against their opponents. They were neither quick nor clever enough: on 6 October 1976, under orders from Hua, the 'palace guard' unit of the PEOPLE'S LIBERATION ARMY arrested all four in a moment of drama rare even by the standards of China's history.

More drama was to come. The four were denounced, accused of numerous crimes and vilified in a flood of anti-'Gang' propaganda that struck deep chords among a population brutalized and exhausted by events of the preceding decade. As the campaign unfolded, DENG XIAOPING, one of the Gang's chief foes, gained the upper hand. In the course of 1978 the remaining radicals among the leadership – Hua included – were dumped or sidelined, and the Party abandoned political struggle for economic reform. Part of this process required passing judgement on the Cultural Revolution. Putting the 'Gang' on trial along with other leaders of the Cultural Revolution, including the deceased Lin Biao, was seen as an ideal way of doing so.

At the close of 1980, in a Chinese version of the Nuremberg trials, members of the 'Gang', their faces pale in the glare of television lights, were placed in the dock and presented with evidence of their crimes. Together with their accomplices they were said to have framed or persecuted more than 700,000 people, almost 35,000 of whom had died as a result. Most of the defendants cooperated with the prosecution. Zhang Chunqiao remained silent throughout. Only Jiang refused to yield – either in the courtroom or later while serving her life sentence. In 1991 she hanged herself while at home on bail receiving treatment for throat cancer. Zhang, like Jiang, given a suspended death sentence that was later changed to life imprisonment, is believed to have died in prison in 1991. Wang, also sentenced to life, died in prison in 1992. Yao was the only member of the 'Gang' to complete his sentence. He was released into obscurity in Shanghai in 1996, having served a 20-year jail term.

Gansu

The Communist government imposed firm control over Gansu, the gateway between China and Central Asia, in the early 1950s and turned Lanzhou, its once sleepy capital, into a major industrial centre. This marked the end of decades of Muslim power in the province, and a break with years of neglect on the part of weak central governments. But Gansu's remoteness, harsh climate, fragile environment and endemic poverty were not so easily overcome. They provided a deadly context in which to conduct revolution: hundreds of thousands starved to death as a result of Mao Zedong's GREAT LEAP FORWARD. The province grew rapidly in the reform era, but chafed under Beijing's policy of allowing coastal areas to get rich first. While large parts of eastern China have prospered, Gansu, by comparison, remains stubbornly poor.

at the end of the Great Wall

The burdens of geography and history have much to do with this. Gansu marks the outer limit of the Chinese cultural area in the northwest. Its symbol is the great fort at Jiayuguan, at the western end of the Great Wall. Beyond lie the vast, often dangerous expanses of Central Asia, which in more recent times China tamed by creating the frontier province of XINJIANG. Behind it is the 'Gansu corridor' – a fertile strip of land, in some places only 10 miles (16 kms) wide, bound by the mountains and grasslands of INNER MONGOLIA, and the Tibet–Qinghai plateau – which affords access to China proper. Every Chinese government has sought to prevent this vital 'choke point' falling into the hands of enemies.

In the final decades of Qing rule, Beijing's greatest enemies in the area were the Hui, or Chinese Muslims. (See ETHNIC MINORITIES.) Stirred by new religious doctrines, and vexed by crippling poverty and oppression, they rose in revolt in the early 1860s. Soon they controlled much of the northwest. The Court sent Zuo Zongtang (1812–85), one of its best generals, to crush them. He did so but at enormous cost: the loss of life, destruction of agriculture, and general ill-will arising from the suppression of the Muslim rebellions scarred Gansu for decades.

Muslim political dominance of the region resumed following the REPUBLICAN REVOLUTION of 1911. It took the form of the Ma family of warlords whose homeland of Hezhou (modern Linxia), southwest of Lanzhou, was one of the most important Muslim centres in China. In the reform era, it has acquired a different kind of fame as a wealthy centre of collective and private enterprise, an Islamic equivalent to Wenzhou, the prosperous coastal city in ZHEJIANG. The two most prominent members of the Ma clan were Ma Bufang (1902–75), who ruled QINGHAI between 1931 and 1949 and Ma Hongkui (1892–1970), the dominant figure in NINGXIA during the same period. Gansu felt the influence of both during the Republican era.

The Mas owed their position to control of a formidable cavalry and fidelity to Islam. The first afforded them a measure of political independence from Chiang Kai-shek's Nationalist government in Nanjing. The second assured them a following in their homeland. Yet the Mas were at one with Chiang in their anti-Communism. It was first demonstrated in late 1935 when a breakaway section of the Communist's Red Army led by Zhang Guotao (1897–1979) entered southern Gansu at the closing stages of the LONG MARCH. Muslim cavalry wiped out the intruders, and ruined Zhang's once promising political career. Yet the Ma clan failed to keep their domains entirely free of Communist influence. As its name implies, the Shen–Gan–Ning Border Region Government, run by the Party from its capital in YANAN, intruded into both Gansu and Ningxia. The Communists found support for their policies of land reform and political change in an area plagued by earthquakes, famine, banditry and warlordism.

However, most of Gansu remained in Nationalist hands, or the hands of those nominally loyal to the government in Nanjing. The importance of this became clear during the early stages of the SINO-JAPANESE WAR. With neither the UNITED STATES nor BRITAIN willing to back China against Japan, it was left to the SOVIET UNION to come to Chiang's aid. Soviet trucks brought weapons and supplies into China along the old Silk Road, through Gansu, to the collection and distribution point at Lanzhou. The city also became the base for the contingent of Soviet fighter planes that engaged the Japanese air force in the skies over China – until 1941, when Moscow and Tokyo signed a neutrality pact.

Lanzhou resumed its role as a military strong point during the CIVIL WAR. It was the headquarters of the Nationalists' Northwest Political and Military Authority, and the key to control of Ningxia in the east, Qinghai to the south, and Xinjiang in the far west. When it fell to troops of the People's Liberation Army's First Field Army commanded by PENG DEHUAI in August 1949, the entire northwest of China fell with it. The Communists made Lanzhou the centre of their own military and political activities in the region; at the start of the new century, it remains the headquarters of the Northwest Military Region under the direct control of Beijing.

reconstruction, rebellion, reform

In the 1950s Gansu benefited from the Communist government's policy of building up industry and communications in the interior. Under the first five-year plan (1953–7), which

> ### The Lie of the Land
>
> Gansu has the most unusual shape of all China's provinces. Its 174,000 square miles (451,000 sq kms) form a dumbbell, which is tilted heavily towards the southeast where it shares borders with Sichuan, Shanxi and Ningxia. Northwest Gansu unfolds into the arid flatlands of Xinjiang. The bar of the dumbbell is the Hexi or Gansu corridor, principal artery of communication in northwest China. Lanzhou, at the southern end of the bar, occupies a narrow valley on the upper reaches of the Yellow River. It is a major railway junction as well as the northwest's key administrative, military and industrial centre. Much of the land south and east of Lanzhou is loess plateau. Erosion has cut deep rifts and gulleys in the region making it unfavourable to farming or development of any kind. There is better agricultural land further south which is drained by rivers that eventually form part of the Yangtze system. Southwestern Gansu is part of the Tibet–Qinghai Plateau. Many of the inhabitants are Tibetans. The region's Labrang (Xiahe) Monastery is one of the four most important Buddhist institutions of its kind in China.

bore the imprint of Moscow, money and manpower flooded in. The railway was extended to Lanzhou, and heavy industries established in the capital. Other cities were built up, notably Tianshui in the southeast, and Wuwei, Zhangye and Yumen along the Gansu corridor. Yumen was an important centre of oil production before 1949; the Communists were quick to develop it and establish petrochemical industries in Lanzhou to serve it.

The new government trod carefully as far as the region's Muslims were concerned. There could be no question of allowing them to return to power; in any event, the two Mas and their followers had fled. But many of their lesser followers were given jobs in the new administration and, later, some of the Muslim and Tibetan areas of Gansu were redesignated 'autonomous' prefectures where the locals were allowed to pursue their traditional way of life under a measure of self-government. There were few signs, then or later, that the Hui resented the curtailing of their political power, or that they pined for past glories.

Yet there were few signs of enthusiasm for the Communists' more radical policies of the late 1950s, either. In 1958, Tibetans in the south of the province, along the border with SICHUAN, rose in revolt against attempts at forced collectivization associated with the Great Leap Forward. It was one of several preludes to the massive revolt inside TIBET itself the following year. The authorities in Lanzhou continued to pursue Chairman Mao's utopia, setting up agricultural communes and conscripting grain for other provinces, despite Gansu's customary food insufficiency and ingrained poverty. During the nationwide famine of the early 1960s, only ANHUI, in southeast China, suffered more than Gansu. In some parts of the province, up to one-third of the population starved to death. Reports of cannibalism were common.

There was a further period of industrial growth in the later 1960s as a result of Mao's 'third line' policy. This called for the development of heavy industry, and particularly military industries, in the interior, well away from possible Soviet or American attack. GUIZHOU and Sichuan in southwest China were the primary locations for new plant, but Qinghai, Ningxia and Gansu were chosen, too. The 'third line' proved a mixed blessing. It brought industry, science and technology and, in some cases, better communications to remote, backward areas. But after Mao's death, when priorities in Beijing switched from self-sufficiency and socialism to productivity and profits, these military-controlled industries proved a burden to their locations. Though many switched to producing civilian goods, they still found profitability elusive. Their inconvenient locations and manifold problems during the 1980s and 1990s illustrated the difficulty of reforming China's state-owned enterprises (see INDUSTRY/STATE ENTERPRISES).

In the same way, but on a larger scale, the entire thrust of the reform era highlighted Gansu's problems. Deng Xiaoping's economic reforms were founded on the decentralization of decision-making, yet Gansu was too important strategically to be allowed much leeway. The reforms depended on attracting FOREIGN TRADE AND INVESTMENT, but distant Gansu had little with which to lure foreign capitalists, and no community of OVERSEAS CHINESE on whom to rely. Above all, particularly during ZHAO ZIYANG's years in power in the 1980s, China pursued a coastal strategy in which the eastern seaboard was encouraged to get rich first in the hope that wealth would trickle down to central and western China. Gansu's position at the bottom of this pecking order, deep in the interior, meant it would benefit last and least. Surrounded by some of China's poorest provinces and dependent on Beijing for financial support, Gansu was on the 'third line' indeed.

narrowing the Gansu 'gap'

During the 1990s, the local authorities sought to remedy the situation by securing domestic sources of capital, technology and expertise. Gansu struck deals with Shanghai, Tianjin and Guangzhou to manufacture products for these regions and sell them raw materials. Beijing encouraged these 'horizontal' solutions which cut across the traditional bureaucratic apparatus created in the 1950s to serve the planned economy. It also pledged to narrow the widening gap between coast and interior. The Ninth Five-Year Plan (1996–2000) and Long-Term Target for the Year 2010 envisaged Gansu as part of a northwest economic zone, exporting cotton and livestock products, petro-chemicals and mineral and energy resources to central Asia and beyond. A US$1.4 billion development programme for the 'Gansu corridor' included water conservancy projects and plans for a grain production base.

Few of these plans could be implemented quickly. None promised a rapid transformation of the POVERTY which stalked Gansu's more than 26 million people, about 10 per cent of them ethnic minorities, at the close of the century. In all of China only Guizhou and Tibet had a lower per capita GDP than Gansu. In Lanzhou, Tianshui, Linxia and the major cities along the corridor to the northwest, standards of life generally were better than they had ever been. In the Gansu countryside, far from the towns, life was harder and, sometimes, highly precarious.

Geneva Conference on Korea and Indochina, 1954

The first occasion on which a foreign minister of the People's Republic of China (ZHOU ENLAI) sat at the same table with counterparts from the Soviet Union, the United States, Britain and France. This made the conference a diplomatic breakthrough for Beijing, despite hostility from the United States delegation under Secretary of State John Foster Dulles, who ensured that members of the Chinese team were denied normal diplomatic civilities. The novelty of the Communist Chinese presence, coupled with Zhou's 'personal' style of diplomacy, made for a valuable propaganda victory. It was reinforced at the BANDUNG CONFERENCE the following year.

The fruits of the Geneva Conference, April

to July 1954 – and their effects on China's relations with Vietnam – were less happy. While Vietnamese Communist forces were routing the French at Dien Bien Phu, Zhou persuaded Ho Chi Minh to accept the division of his country at the 17th parallel. China was unwilling to see a socialist advance of the kind that might attract new US commitment to the region. The conference called for elections to be held in Vietnam within two years to form a unified government. However, America soon gave its full backing to the government in the South, ensuring that unification would have to be won on the battlefield, while delaying it for 21 years. Vietnam was to denounce China's role at Geneva in 1954 when the two sides fought a bitter border war in 1979.

The Geneva Conference saw the start of tentative negotiations between the People's Republic and the United States, specifically on the question of returning nationals detained in each other's country. The talks later moved to Warsaw, where they continued fitfully until the Sino-US rapprochement of 1971. The Geneva conference confirmed the status quo on the Korean Peninsula, where an armistice dividing the country along the 38th parallel had been agreed the year before and ended the KOREAN WAR.

government and administration

Imperial, republican, nationalist, communist – the *forms* of government in China have changed dramatically during the country's quest for rejuvenation. Each has been associated with different leaders and ideologies. Each has offered different solutions to China's ills. The *nature* of government in China has proved more constant. Throughout the twentieth century, leaders mattered more than LAW, individuals more than institutions and, usually, mastery of a 'correct' doctrine more than DEMOCRACY. Opaque decision-making processes and excessive secrecy blight governance at the start of the new era as they did during much of the old.

individuals and institutions

Many of these characteristics are the legacy of centuries of imperial rule and the adoption of Soviet forms of government in the 1950s. Both traditions stressed the centralization of power in the person of great leaders at the head of mighty bureaucracies. Both emphasized obedience to a prevailing ideology and forbade open or organized opposition. And, at the start of the twenty-first century, both make it difficult for government to adapt to China's rapidly changing society and market economy.

'Modern' government organizations made their debut in China during the early years of the twentieth century. In a spate of reforms which undid rather than revived the dynasty, the Qing Court scrapped the six 'Boards' traditionally responsible for the conduct of government and replaced them with ministries. Traditional civil service examinations were abolished (see EDUCATION) and moves made towards constitutional rule. New, 'national' armies were formed. The government produced China's first budget and standardized the country's weights and measures (see QING DYNASTY; EDUCATION; ARMIES).

The aim of these policies was to centralize power in Beijing. Their result was to provoke such resistance in the provinces that the central government collapsed. Lasting, effective centralized control eluded China until the creation of the People's Republic in 1949.

This was not for want of effort. The KUOMINTANG established partially effective central authority in 1928 after the NORTHERN EXPEDITION. By this time the party had lost much of the revolutionary mission it acquired as a result of its former alliance with the Soviet Union and cooperation with the CHINESE COMMUNIST PARTY. However, it remained Leninist in structure, if not in goals, practising 'democratic-centralism': the concentration of power at the top, and the obligation of members, on pain of disciplinary punishment, to accept decisions made. The Kuomintang was also elitist. Under the theory of 'tutelage' laid down by SUN YAT-SEN, its task was to train the people for constitutional rule. In principle, this came into effect in 1948 with the adoption of a new constitution. In practice, it did not materialize for another 40 years, by which time the Kuomintang had lost the Mainland and been confined to TAIWAN for four decades.

On the Mainland, Nationalist rule took the form of the personal, military dictatorship of CHIANG KAI-SHEK. The government set up impressive new central ministries in Nanjing, the capital, but their authority extended only as far as Chiang's military power. This fluctuated as WARLORDS, Communist rebels and Japanese invaders battled for control over all or part of China. The only constant in this shifting scene was Chiang's tight control over the Nationalists' best military resources which secured his own survival and the downfall of some of his opponents.

The clearest sign that Chiang's power owed little to his position in the party or government structure came in January 1949 when, to pave the way for peace talks with the Communists, then on the way to complete victory in the CIVIL WAR, he resigned as state president. He had no difficulty, in 'retirement', scuppering attempts by his deputy, LI ZONGREN, first to broker peace, and then revive the Nationalists' military fortunes. Through his network of loyal subordinates, Chiang moved the best armies, the remnants of the central government and the bulk of China's gold reserves, to Taiwan. Nationalist authority on the Mainland, deprived of its military strongman and exposed to Communist attack, collapsed.

power in the People's Republic

The foundation of the People's Republic in 1949 marked a break with the institutions of the past as well as the policies. According to MAO ZEDONG's theory of 'New Democracy', China's main task was to overthrow feudalism, bureaucratic capitalism and imperialism. Prominent non-Communists and even 'patriotic' members of the Nationalist Party were encouraged to join the CHINESE PEOPLE'S POLITICAL CONSULTATIVE CONFERENCE (CPPCC) – the chief institutional expression of the Communist Party's United Front policy. The CPPCC declared the foundation of the People's Republic and served as the national legislature until 1954, when it was replaced by the NATIONAL PEOPLE'S CONGRESS (NPC).

This change complied with Beijing's desire to secure a 'transition to socialism' – a policy which required institutional arrangements capable of ensuring central control and mobilizing the population for rapid industrialization. The Soviet Union had already done this: China, with Moscow's help, was determined to do the same. The government structures that emerged during this period all but collapsed during the CULTURAL REVOLUTION and went through several exercises in restructuring during the reform era that followed. But they still govern the *form* of politics in the People's Republic at the start of the new century.

Under them, the NPC forms the apex of government with the once powerful CPPCC relegated to an advisory role. Every five years, with occasional interruptions in the past because of political campaigns, NPC delegates meet in plenary session to elect a state president, and members of a State Council, the equivalent of a cabinet. Headed by a premier, and composed of vice-premiers, directors of state commissions and leading ministers, the State Council leads the work of government. In the interests of efficiency it delegates power to an executive, the Standing Committee of the State Council, again headed by the premier.

Beneath the State Council are the commissions – 'super-ministries' responsible for key policy areas such as family planning, education and ethnic minorities – and the ministries themselves. Then there are the 'mass organizations': official bodies created to represent sections of society such as women, trade unions and various professions who, left to organize themselves, might present a challenge to China's all-embracing vision of government.

The number and function of these vast bureaucracies have changed over time in accordance with the government's priorities. But with the limited exception of the Ministry of Foreign Affairs, they all maintain branches at each level of territorial administration. Within each of them, power flows from the top down. And between many, rivalry, infighting and 'turf wars' hamper efficient government, giving rise to what is sometimes described as China's 'fragmented authoritarianism'.

Authority is fragmented in China because it is divided between *xitongs*, a term meaning 'networks' or 'systems'. Far bigger than a single ministry, these groupings unite top Party and government leaders and low-ranking bureaucrats, senior planners and ordinary members of a distant DANWEI, or work unit, in a complex web of functional interests and shared responsibilities.

China remains authoritarian because government is *for* the people rather than *of* them: it is carried out by and on behalf of the Communist Party whose members are deemed to have mastered 'correct' doctrine – in this case China's version of MARXISM – and who are deemed to know the people's interests better than the people themselves. Open, organized opposition to the government is disallowed on the grounds that it is dangerous as well as simply undesirable. Not only does

Government Structure

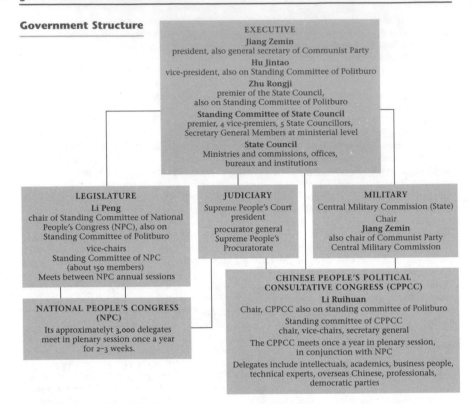

EXECUTIVE
Jiang Zemin
president, also general secretary of Communist Party
Hu Jintao
vice-president, also on Standing Committee of Politburo
Zhu Rongji
premier of the State Council,
also on Standing Committee of Politburo
Standing Committee of State Council
premier, 4 vice-premiers, 5 State Councillors,
Secretary General Members at ministerial level
State Council
Ministries and commissions, offices,
bureaux and institutions

LEGISLATURE
Li Peng
chair of Standing Committee of National
People's Congress (NPC), also on
Standing Committee of Politburo
vice-chairs
Standing Committee of NPC
(about 150 members)
Meets between NPC annual sessions

JUDICIARY
Supreme People's Court
president
procurator general
Supreme People's
Procuratorate

MILITARY
Central Military Commission (State)
Chair
Jiang Zemin
also chair of Communist Party
Central Military Commission

NATIONAL PEOPLE'S CONGRESS (NPC)
Its approximatelyt 3,000 delegates
meet in plenary session once a year
for 2–3 weeks.

CHINESE PEOPLE'S POLITICAL CONSULTATIVE CONGRESS (CPPCC)
Li Ruihuan
Chair, CPPCC also on standing committee of Politburo
Standing committee of CPPCC
chair, vice-chairs, secretary general
The CPPCC meets once a year in plenary session,
in conjunction with NPC
Delegates include intellectuals, academics, business people,
technical experts, overseas Chinese, professionals,
democratic parties

opposition threaten to impair the work of government, its very existence calls into question the regime's monopoly of wisdom – a challenge it could hardly survive in the absence of political reform (see DEMOCRACY).

To keep such a challenge at bay, the government goes to great lengths to demonstrate that it is united. This is a major task of the official MEDIA who celebrate every important political decision as an example of unanimity and wisdom. But they only do so *after* the decisions have been made: beforehand, the public are shielded from even a glimpse of the arguments for or against a policy, or the personalities who champion them. Secrecy, even mystery, surround the actual decision-making process, as well as the personal views of the usually small group of people involved in it. The overriding desire is to present a consensus so as to rally the nation to the government's cause.

In Communist as in Nationalist times, the formal structure of government provides few clues as to how power is *exercised* in China. In both periods, the government has been the weakest of three main administrative entities: government, party and military. And, at various times, to varying degrees, and for different ends, all three have been dominated by powerful individuals, namely Chiang Kai-shek, Mao Zedong and DENG XIAOPING.

The Communist Party and the PEOPLE'S LIBERATION ARMY (PLA) form the locus of power in the People's Republic. This reflects the evolution of the Communist Revolution: the Party was founded first, created an army to defend it, and then, having triumphed over its foes, set up the apparatus of a nation state. Victory did not mean an end to the separate organizational identity of either Party or PLA: both maintain rival or parallel organizations to those of the government which, crucially, controls neither. The Party is supreme, ultimately because it alone controls the military.

Party control of government is secured by a variety of means. On the theoretical level, the constitution provides for Party leadership of the entire nation. On the practical, it makes all key appointments, operates 'leading groups' to handle major policy issues, and is present almost throughout the administration in the form of 'Party Committees' (see CHINESE COMMUNIST PARTY). The fact that leading figures in the Party also hold leading positions in the government, and that only a handful of relatively insignificant posts are filled by non-Communists or members of the tiny DEMOCRATIC PARTIES, seals the Party's institutional dominance.

But the Party does not rule by institutions alone, and, on occasions in the past, not by institutions at all. During the Cultural Revolution, the rule of the Party was replaced by the personal tyranny of Chairman Mao. Determined to overcome his rivals in the leadership, the Chairman encouraged Red Guards to attack Party and government organizations he believed were in the grip of 'revisionists'. The assault on institutions and individual leaders that followed was so disruptive that Mao had to call in the PLA to restore order. Not until the Chairman died did the military withdraw from day-to-day administration and the work of formal government revive.

reform and succession problems

This was largely due to Deng Xiaoping whose style of leadership was as different from Mao's as his policies. Deng wanted to introduce an element of stability, predictability and legality into political life. He also sought to reform the bureaucracy in keeping with the reduced role of planning and the dwindling power of the state arising from his economic reforms.

Neither task was easy. Deng's reforms were controversial. To deliver them he had to win the approval of the revolutionary veterans, most of whom, like him, had returned to power after being ousted by Mao, but many of whom did not share his enthusiasm for free markets and foreign trade. Deng was usually powerful enough to get his way. But he was not powerful enough to prevent serious clashes between his reformist protégés in the formal party and government apparatus, and the old guard. The struggle between the young 'executives', men such as HU YAOBANG and ZHAO ZIYANG, and conservative elders, such as CHEN YUN and PENG ZHEN, marred Chinese politics in the 1980s and early 1990s. The chief, and most tragic, expression of the conflict was the suppression of the TIANANMEN SQUARE DEMOCRACY MOVEMENT, the result, largely, of a seizure of power by the veteran revolutionaries.

The ideological issue at stake at Tiananmen was the future of Chinese socialism. The political issue was one China's institutions had failed to deal with for at least a century: securing the political succession to a strongman, in this case Deng Xiaoping. Like Mao, who designated and then destroyed two 'heirs' in LIU SHAOQI and LIN BIAO, Deng dismissed and disgraced his first protégé, Hu Yaobang (in 1987), and his second, Zhao Ziyang (two years later). But whereas Mao's third heir, HUA GUOFENG, actually succeeded to the throne only to be attacked and sidelined, Deng's third choice, JIANG ZEMIN, survived both his mentor's initial disappointment in him, and the determination of the dwindling band of LONG MARCH veterans to retain their authority. Jiang bowed to these constituencies and managed to outlive them both, securing, in the process, the post of state president to go with his leadership of the Party, and command over the PLA through the Party's Central Military Commission.

Jiang: paramount, not all-powerful

This has made Jiang the most powerful leader in China at the start of the new century. But he is much less powerful than were either Mao or Deng. These men owed their authority to personal achievements – in Mao's case, founding the Communist state; in Deng's, reviving its economy and national power – rather than their occupation of formal positions. There were several indications in the late 1990s that Jiang, aware of his deficiencies, sought achievements of his own to bolster his status. Overseas he invested much effort in improving relations with the United States. Closer to home, he tried to advance the cause of unification with Taiwan, China's one great unsettled territorial issue whose settlement promised a huge political dividend for the leader able to secure it. In the absence of such accomplishments, Jiang seems likely to be remembered as a powerful but rather uninspiring leader compared with his predecessors. A similar fate appears to await HU JINTAO, a man of uncertain credentials, whom Jiang earmarked as his own successor.

reforming the bureaucracy

Reforms in the staffing, structure and role of government accompanied changes at the top of Chinese politics during the last two decades of the century. At all levels of the administration, and in each of its branches – government, Party and military – there was a massive turnover of personnel as older, poorly educated officials gave way to younger, professionally qualified staff. This revitalized the ranks of government and set limits to the system of life tenure that had long blighted it.

Structural reforms proved less easy to accomplish. The diminished role for planning in the 1980s and 1990s required the partial withdrawal of the government from sections of the economy and stricter separation of Party and government. Major efforts to reduce the size of the government bureaucracy, including the abolition and merging of entire

ministries, were conducted in 1988 and 1998. Party officials were told to leave administration to the government and concentrate on 'supervision' and policy matters. These measures were accompanied by attempts to establish 'horizontal' relationships between ministries with a view to ensuring flexibility and meeting pressing local needs in the new China of decentralized decision-making. But, victims of Beijing's determination to remain a unitary, centrally controlled state, the tendency of bureaucrats to defend their own, and the fact that personal relationships, or *guanxi*,

Centre and Region

China's size and diversity make the maintenance of territorial unity and central control – abiding imperatives for Chinese governments of every hue – one of the most intractable problems in national life. The People's Republic is divided into provinces, most of them bigger than many countries; about 2,100 counties; and, beneath them, thousands more townships and/or villages. With certain exceptions, this basic administrative division of the country changed little during the course of the twentieth century despite rapid population growth, long periods of upheaval, and sweeping social and economic change.

In Qing times, formal government stopped at the level of the county: scholar-gentry, the educated elite, ran local affairs on an informal, customary basis. In Communist times, particularly between the GREAT LEAP FORWARD of 1958 and the start of the reform era in the late 1970s, the apparatus of government extended much deeper into rural society in the form of communes, production brigades and production teams. In the cities, quasi-formal authority still extends down to residents' or street committees.

The number and designation of China's provinces has changed over time. At the start of the century there are 31 province-level units in the People's Republic, consisting of 22 conventional provinces, four municipalities – Beijing, Shanghai, Tianjin and Chongqing – and five autonomous regions – Inner Mongolia, Xinjiang, Ningxia, Guangxi and Tibet. These last are a Communist administrative novelty created from provinces or regions with a high concentration of ETHNIC MINORITIES. The same applies to prefectures or counties below the province level which contain large numbers of non-Han: they, too, have been turned into 'autonomous' sub-provincial units. The People's Republic includes two Special Administrative Regions, HONG KONG and MACAU, which, constitutionally, enjoy a high level of autonomy in everything save defence and foreign affairs. The Mainland is divided into seven military regions, each of them containing several provinces or autonomous regions, and all of them subordinate to the Central Military Commission in Beijing rather than the local civilian administration.

Many provinces have natural boundaries defined by terrain. Traditionally, this made communications difficult, fostered a sense of regional identity, and often made it hard for weak central governments to

impose their will. In the twentieth century the rise of warlords was an extreme example of this problem. Since 1949 the Communist government has used a variety of methods to tame the regions and enable the country to function effectively as a unified state. One of them has been the rapid construction of RAILWAYS, ROADS and TELECOMMUNICATIONS. Administratively, the Party first ruled the country by dividing it into Large Administrative Regions which included several provinces and amounted to a form of military control. They were abolished in the mid-1950s. Since then power has shifted backwards and forwards between the centre and the regions, largely in accordance with the national policy agenda pursued in Beijing.

In the reform era, many provinces, cities and other sub-provincial units have grown powerful due to a decentralization of economic decision-making. Communes were abolished in the early 1980s and agricultural production turned over to households. Ten years later, farmers began electing their own village committees, a flawed but sometimes controversial exercise in democracy which gives those involved in it greater say over local affairs (see DEMOCRACY/MAINLAND ELECTIONS). The creation of SPECIAL ECONOMIC ZONES (SEZs) and open cities has sapped the power of provincial capitals as well as Beijing. At every level of administration local officials have been quick to exercise their new authority. Fierce battles with Beijing over domestic and foreign investment, local growth targets, and tax collection are among the results (see FINANCE; FOREIGN TRADE AND INVESTMENT). On several occasions during the 1990s the wayward behaviour of certain provinces – including blockades and embargoes on the products of provincial neighbours; and the resentment of poor, interior provinces towards richer coastal ones – led observers to predict the 'breakup' of China.

This danger is more apparent than real, not least because Beijing continues to control key Party and military appointments at provincial level. But governing China as a unified state in an era of free market reforms and economic decentralization is a difficult matter. Power is diffused across geographical regions and economic sectors; among individuals and corporate entities. Beijing must strike bargains at every level of the administration in order to get its way.

China's Constitutions

Numerous constitutions have been promulgated in China: almost every leader, major political party and government from the late Qing to the People's Republic, fleeting or lasting, has sought to dignify their rule with one. Placed together, these documents would occupy substantial shelf space. Less room is required for accounts of China's *experience* of constitutional rule.

A constitution is the foundation of a democratic political system. Nationalists and reformers saw in constitutional rule a means of linking the raw energy of the Chinese people with the government in the form of a legal bond. Since constitutions also set out the rights and liberties of subjects and prohibit arbitrary rule, they exercised a powerful appeal in a country as misgoverned as China.

The Kuomintang and the Communist Party both promulgated constitutions to govern the areas under their control. In early 1946 they even agreed to draft one together with the help of small minority parties. The Civil War put a stop to that, though the process of constitution-drafting continued. The Nationalist government promulgated its 'five power' constitution – in which the work of government was conducted by five *yuan*, or branches – on 1 January 1947. The following year, many of its provisions were suspended under an emergency decree designed to help the government suppress the 'Communist Rebellion'.

The suppression failed but the decree continued to stifle freedom in Taiwan, home of the Nationalist government from 1949, until 1991 when it was lifted as part of the island's rapid democratization. The addition in 1994 of ten new articles to the constitution entrenched democracy by allowing the people of Taiwan to choose their president in direct elections. The polls were held first in 1996 (see TAIWAN).

The first years of Communist rule on the Mainland were conducted according to a 'common programme' rather than a constitution. It was passed by the Chinese People's Political Consultative Conference (CPPCC), then the highest organ of state power. The first constitution of the People's Republic was promulgated in 1954. It drew heavily on the Soviet Union's constitution of 1936, although it omitted the direct elections provided for in the Soviet document, replacing them with indirect polls.

For most of the following 30 years the constitution was the plaything of the Party. New versions were produced in 1975, 1978 and 1982 to reflect swings in Communist policy, and provide for the return of Hong Kong to Chinese sovereignty as a 'Special Administrative Region'. For much of this time, 'Party line' was more important than constitutional principles, particularly during the Cultural Revolution. This experience strengthened calls for genuine constitutional rule after Mao's death of the kind that would make it impossible for the Party to wreak such havoc again. They went unanswered.

The 1982 constitution was amended in 1988, 1993 and 1999. The changes made room for private enterprise, pursuit of the 'socialist market economy', and a stronger commitment to the rule of LAW. The function of the amendments was to adapt the legal foundation of the state to the latest, and possibly transient, policies of the Communist Party.

Generally speaking the Party views the constitution as a tool rather than the touchstone of the state. It is important for all that. Its preamble legally enshrines the primacy of Party rule and socialism, and sets tight limits on the rights of citizens spelt out in the sections that follow. Yet DISSIDENTS and others have used the fact that these rights are spelt out in the constitution to demand political reforms. Thus the principle of constitutional rule remains a potent element in China's political life. *Fazhi* – the rule of law or constitutional rule – is an appealing alternative to *renzhi* – rule by men – which has inflicted so much harm on China.

---

matter most of all, such structural reforms were at best only a partial success.

The same was true of campaigns to wipe out official CORRUPTION which fed on Deng's free market reforms. Government officials might have *administered* less in the 1980s and 1990s but they were given the right to *approve* more, including lucrative projects involving FOREIGN TRADE AND INVESTMENT. Their monopoly of power, and the absence of a free press and independent judiciary, provided plenty of opportunities for enrichment.

They also spawned a new strain of bureaucratic capitalism. Anxious not to miss out on the economic boom, officials used the authority and sometimes the funds of their government departments to set up powerful commercial enterprises of their own. Many were controlled by the 'princelings', the offspring of senior Party and government leaders, who turned their revolutionary credentials into material assets. Beijing's attempts at the close of the century to make government organs, the courts and the military withdraw from such business operations were trumpeted as a success. Their effect on the battle against corruption remained to be seen.

So did the whole future of government and administration in a country where the state traditionally dominated society. China invented the idea of a civil service bureaucracy, and Chinese governments have been wrestling with the consequences ever since. Rarely have such problems seemed as serious as at the start of the new century, when China must contend with powerful forces of decentralization and corruption, and manage an increasingly complex, sophisticated society unresponsive to traditional bureaucratic solutions.

Great Leap Forward (1958–60)

MAO ZEDONG'S attempt, begun in 1958, to establish Communism overnight proved one of the most catastrophic exercises in utopianism ever conducted. The forced collectivization of AGRICULTURE, and the apparatus of terror needed to keep it in place, created a famine that claimed the lives of at least 30 million people. At the time, China's relative international isolation, and the willingness of a few foreign observers to believe Beijing's propaganda, enabled this man-made disaster to escape the world's attention. Nearly half a century later, the CHINESE COMMUNIST PARTY refuses to acknowledge that a famine took place, and forbids investigation or public discussion of what it calls the 'three difficult years'. This makes the tragedy that swept through almost every part of China between 1958 and 1962 worse. It also exposes a grim reality behind the exercise of power in Communist China: it is based on an ability to suppress the truth, and force people to say, perhaps even believe, things that are evidently untrue.

Mao's search of a strategy

The Leap's origins lay in Mao's search for a development strategy that would allow rapid industrialization of a still backward peasant economy (see MAO ZEDONG). Such a strategy would have to further the gains of the Chinese Revolution. It could not involve a return to capitalism, nor could it continue to rely on the Soviet-style methods adopted up to the late 1950s, which meant extracting huge surpluses from the countryside to finance industrialization. China was an overpopulated, predominantly agrarian economy (see AGRICULTURE). Its Communist Party was made up overwhelmingly of peasants. If there were surpluses in the countryside, the Party that had 'liberated' the farmers by giving them land could hardly be expected to be enthusiastic about appropriating the dividends for the benefit of the cities.

Millenarian zeal, irrationality, obedience to Chairman Mao and simple state terror soon swept all these considerations aside. In 1958, the 'voluntary' collectivization of farmland carried out during the previous three years gave way to rapid communization. First in HENAN and LIAONING, then almost everywhere, huge communes were set up in which peasants pooled their land, animals, tools

and most of their other possessions. Millions were mobilized to construct dams, irrigation schemes and other public works. Farmers built 'backyard furnaces' – small smelters erected in gardens, courtyards and other places – where attempts were made to turn everything from cutlery to bicycles into steel for heavy INDUSTRY. Natural pests were eliminated in campaigns of such intensity that the future of the Chinese race seemed at stake. A Communist wind, fuelled by the Party's official slogan, 'achieve more, faster, better', swept the country.

This was at first gratifying for Mao and other Party leaders. The Chairman believed that dull, cautious socialist planning was not what the Revolution was about. It was about transforming nature as well as man. It was about overcoming what simple farmers, experts, scientists and intellectuals alike said were insurmountable difficulties by means of sheer will and concentrated energy. It was about making a leap in social and economic progress through mass political mobilization. Such romanticism might be at odds with MARXISM as conventionally understood. But it accorded with Mao's 'voluntarism', the creed of impatient revolutionaries everywhere.

Specialist knowledge, and the intellectual class who lived by it, had little place in this scheme of things. The consequences of the ONE HUNDRED FLOWERS MOVEMENT, the ill-fated liberalization of 1956, had reduced the pool of politically acceptable talent and, fatefully, destroyed much of China's ability to collect reliable statistics. Party leaders had little time for timid experts, whether they were academics such as Ma Yinchu (1882–1982), the chancellor of Beijing University, who was sacked and disgraced as a Malthusian after he warned of the consequences of uncontrolled population growth (see POPULATION); or experienced farmers who knew in their hearts that their land could not be persuaded to yield so much more simply by changing techniques and forms of social organization. Mao, on the other hand, believed 'every stomach comes with two hands', and that new seed strains, close planting, deep ploughing and new tools used under the new policy would produce the bumper harvests China needed to leap into the industrial age.

Equally important for the Chairman was the political correctness of the Great Leap strategy. Its chief manifestation was the commune, a new unit of society which pointed to China's progress along the socialist path compared with the SOVIET UNION, until then regarded as the 'elder brother' of socialism. The communes reshaped rural life. They did so by forcing people to eat in communal dining halls rather than as families at home (see FAMILY), replacing wages with work points, and sometimes doing away with money altogether. Differences in status, wealth and education were eradicated, as were most aspects of village custom, tradition and folk religion. The commune, or rather its Communist Party committee, took over virtually all the functions once undertaken by farmers or small villages. China's rural millions were regimented and bound to the state as never before in their country's long history.

disaster and the downfall of Peng

This extraordinary feat of social engineering, a testimony both to Mao's status and power, and the unquestioning obedience of officials and most ordinary people, rapidly led to disaster. Despite a flurry of encouraging 'statistics' compiled by officials anxious to flatter the Chairman and preserve their power, agricultural production slumped. Mass starvation stalked the communes as farmers began to pay the price of obeying the Party's instructions to eat more and grow less, or divert the energy they normally devoted to feeding their families into worthless industrial schemes and ill-considered public works. Just months after the start of the Leap, people began to die in their hundreds of thousands.

Despite the growing crisis in the countryside, only one senior Party leader spoke out against the Leap, and he sought to do so in the form of a private letter to Mao. PENG DEHUAI, the Minister of Defence, could count on a few timid allies in the lower ranks of the Party, but his efforts crumbled before Mao's cunning, and the refusal of other leaders – Premier ZHOU ENLAI included – to face facts rather than remain loyal to the Chairman and his line.

At the Lushan summit meeting of Party leaders in 1959, Mao agreed there were problems with the Communes but insisted they were far less serious than the 'Right Opportunism' and 'attempts to split the Party' represented by Peng's letter. The Chairman chose to regard what could have been tolerated as acceptable criticism within the Party's highest counsels as treachery. Peng was disgraced, and

the fragile unity at the top of the Party shattered. Partly because of what happened at Lushan, China was cast into a cycle of chaos, persecution and violence which lasted almost 20 years.

The immediate effect of Lushan was to inject new zeal into the Leap. Now, though, the stakes were much higher: those who failed to make it work could be regarded as 'Right Opportunists', be arrested, shot or sent to LABOUR CAMPS. An added complication arose from growing enmity over ideological questions between China and the Soviet Union. Mao was worried by the implications of Khrushchev's de-Stalinization campaign, and angered by the Soviet leader's criticism of China's communes. In 1960, Moscow suddenly withdrew its advisers from China, leaving many important projects in limbo, among them Beijing's plans to use Soviet technology to build an atom bomb (see PEOPLE'S LIBERATION ARMY (PLA)/CHINA AND THE BOMB). Mao began to look askance at the direction socialism was taking in the USSR. He set to work on the polemics that would soon shatter the solidarity within the world socialist camp.

famine and retreat

The direction socialism had taken in China led to calamity. The Great Leap and its 'bumper harvests' had to be affirmed, the Chairman's line vindicated and his 'Rightist' opponents rooted out. Thus the Party and its apparatus of control continued to extract grain from desperate peasants who were believed to be hiding it in their homes or beneath the increasingly unproductive soil. Starvation intensified and the death toll soared. People were forced to eat the bark of trees and, in some parts of the country the soil itself, in usually unsuccessful attempts to stave off hunger.

The population of entire villages was wiped out. TIBET – then, as at the start of the twenty-first century, the poorest region of China – was particularly badly hit. So were the provinces of QINGHAI, GANSU, HENAN and ANHUI. In many parts of the country, corpses were a common sight along the roadside. Cannibalism occurred. Millions of starving peasants managed to escape the militia charged with preventing them leaving their home district and fled to the cities where life was marginally better.

Party leaders in Beijing, ensconced within the walls of their Zhongnanhai compound, responded to the nationwide crisis by growing vegetables outside their villas. Mao himself temporarily gave up eating meat. These were insignificant sacrifices in the context of a famine which, unlike many China had suffered in the past due to natural disasters or neglect, was the product of a utopian fantasy on the part of a leader few dared defy.

By 1961, Party leaders realized there would have to be a change of policy or the Communist regime might collapse. Provincial inspection teams disclosed the gravity of the crisis, and Beijing allowed individual provinces to scale back the communes, if it was necessary to produce more food. Some areas, notably Anhui, implemented an early version of the household responsibility system in which peasants grew a fixed amount of grain for the state and sold the rest. Such measures would become the cornerstone of China's first wave of reform in the late 1970s (see AGRICULTURE).

But across China the retreat from the Leap was patchy and subject to bitter disputes in Beijing and beyond. In the capital, LIU SHAOQI and DENG XIAOPING lent their weight to the recovery while seeking to avoid a direct clash with a still defiant Mao and his chief ally LIN BIAO, who had replaced Peng as Minister of Defence. The purchase of grain from Australia and Canada, and the soliciting of food parcels from relatives overseas helped fill empty stomachs. So did the opening of previously closed state granaries, and the arrival of troops bearing emergency supplies to some of the worst-hit areas. By the end of 1962, the immediate crisis was over – but at the cost of an estimated 30 to 40 million lives.

However, the political damage arising from the Leap's failure proved beyond repair. It was to inflict many more years of trauma on the Chinese people. Mao's vision, at first backed by most leaders, had crumbled. The communization of the countryside, his sole major policy initiative since 1949, had failed. China had to be rescued by what he and his increasingly radical allies regarded as essentially bureaucratic, capitalistic methods. The lines of the struggle in the early 1960s were vaguely drawn, and the positions of individual leaders often blurred. But, in the aftermath of the Leap, Mao continued to pursue his revolutionary goals by other means. They culminated in the CULTURAL REVOLUTION, a nationwide attack on the Party leadership the Chairman believed had let him down during the Leap.

Guangdong Province

China's most southerly Mainland province is the country's main engine of economic growth. Almost every year since the reform era began in 1978 it has topped other provinces in terms of GDP, exports, utilization of foreign investment, revenues, investment in fixed assets, the performance of its service sector and retail sales. Guangdong has become a byword for economic power and a symbol of China's potential; its people are among the richest in China. Preferential policies, an independent streak, proximity to HONG KONG, strong representation among the OVERSEAS CHINESE, and local business acumen account for much of this extraordinary success.

revolutionary tradition

Guangdong was once one of China's most revolutionary provinces. It is the home of a distinctive Chinese sub-culture based on dialect (Cantonese), cuisine, and a tradition of contact, some of it violent, with the outside world arising from its position on the country's maritime frontier. Many of its people, notably the Hakkas, who moved into the area from north China, are fiercely independent. Its capital, Guangzhou (Canton), is the historical entry point to China for merchants and MISSIONARIES, invaders and ideas. Guangdong often resisted the new arrivals but usually to little effect. The fact that, like GUANGXI, the other 'Guang' province to the west, it is separated from the rest of China by mountains, reinforced the sense of local identity and independence these experiences fostered.

As far as Qing Dynasty rulers were concerned, Guangdong was a constant headache. Its exposure to the outside world made it a breeding ground for many of the ideas that eventually toppled Manchu rule. Among their advocates during the final years of empire was KANG YOUWEI, a Cantonese, who founded a private academy in Guangzhou at the close of the nineteenth century to spread his radical views. Another was SUN YAT-SEN, also a Cantonese, and an even bigger thorn in Beijing's flesh.

Sun's UNITED LEAGUE, China's first modern revolutionary organization, flourished in Guangdong during the first years of the twentieth century. It drew support from rich merchants, radical intellectuals, disgruntled peasants and SECRET SOCIETIES. When attempts at insurrection failed, as they often did, Sun and his allies sought refuge in Hong Kong. Britain tried to prevent its colony becoming a base for subversion, but the revolutionaries usually managed to recruit funds, weapons and manpower there for the next attempt at insurrection over the border in Guangdong. In the event, it was a revolt in Wuhan that brought the dynasty down, but the Qing cause had been lost in Guangdong several years before the REPUBLICAN REVOLUTION of 1911.

The revolutionary cause, by contrast, went from strength to strength, especially after 1911. In 1916, Sun set up a rival 'national government' in Guangzhou to counter that of YUAN SHIKAI in the north. It soon fell prey to infighting among the southern WARLORDS. But Sun returned in the early 1920s. This time he reinforced his hold over the city, and his claim to rule the rest of China, by reorganizing his party, the KUOMINTANG, accepting aid and advice from the Soviet Union, and agreeing to cooperate with the young CHINESE COMMUNIST PARTY. By the time he died in 1925 Guangzhou was the seat of the 'National Revolutionary Government'.

Revolutionary nationalism engulfed the city. It was aided by outrage over the May Thirtieth Incident of 1925 in Shanghai, when police in the British Settlement opened fire on protestors. (See SHANGHAI.) There was a massacre in Guangzhou a few days later: British and French soldiers based in the city's foreign concession, Shamian Island, shot and killed more than 50 people among a huge crowd of protestors who had gathered near by. This was the spark for the Hong Kong–Guangzhou strike boycott which lasted until September 1926 and all but crippled the colony (see HONG KONG).

The Kuomintang's NORTHERN EXPEDITION of 1926–8 spread the revolutionary upheaval to other parts of China. Communists were particularly active. They always had been in Guangdong. In Haifeng and Lufeng, two towns in the east of the province, Peng Pai (1896–1929) launched China's first Marxist peasant movement. Though occasionally suppressed, by 1927 it was strong enough for Peng to set up a rural soviet in the area – again the first of its kind, and several months before MAO ZEDONG was in a position to do the same in remote JIANGXI. In December 1927, the Communists even attempted to create a commune in Guangzhou. It came to a bloody end as, in 1928, did Peng's Hai-Lu Soviet. By that time CHIANG KAI-SHEK had gained the upper hand and purged the Kuomintang of Communist and Left-wing influence. The revolutionary spirit, nurtured in Guangzhou and disseminated throughout south China, ebbed away.

The province's tradition of independence proved more hardy. Although it gave birth to the movement that culminated in the creation of a new central government, Guangdong remained autonomous in everything but name after the Northern Expedition. Governor Chen Jitang (1890–1954) kept Chiang, then ensconced in Nanjing, China's new capital, at arm's length. During the early 1930s, he linked up with the 'Guangxi Clique' of warlords to create a rival power centre in south China. The two Guang provinces almost went to war with Nanjing in 1936, but their alliance fell apart before a shot was fired. Chiang finally brought Guangdong to heel at the end of the year – only to lose much of it to Japan in the SINO-JAPANESE WAR; Japanese troops occupied Guangzhou and other key areas of the province from 1938 until 1945.

Central government authority in the province was hardly less illusory after the war. Guangdong was a Nationalist rear area for much of the CIVIL WAR against the Communists, and Guangzhou a brief resting place for the central government during its flight, in the course of 1949, from Nanjing to TAIWAN. In October of that year, the People's Liberation Army occupied the city, paving the way for the Communist conquest of south and southwest China. It was time for one of China's most wayward areas to be integrated into the nation state.

a province tamed: the 1950s and 1960s

This was neither an easy nor a particularly productive process. Guangdong's strengths had always been commercialized agriculture, light industry and trade. There was not much room for any of these in the state-owned, centrally planned economy inflicted on the province during the 1950s.

Guangdong suffered from its political history and geographical position, too. In the Cold War, the province's traditional links with the outside world were a source of suspicion. Beijing considered the Cantonese too parochial in outlook and moved northerners in to run the province. At the same time, Guangdong's position on the coast made it vulnerable to 'imperialist' attack. Throughout the Maoist period Beijing invested little in the region relative to other, politically-safe, though economically less promising parts of the country. As a result, Guangdong's rate of economic growth was less than the national average during the first three decades of Communism.

This was a particularly serious matter for local leaders only too familiar with the way Hong Kong had begun to prosper in the 1950s and 1960s. Despite the Cold War, contact between the colony and the province was rarely severed for long: it was impossible to disguise the fact that Cantonese under British rule were doing very much better than those under Communism. It was also impossible to stop many Guangdong people fleeing south across the border, either to escape the famine generated by Mao's GREAT LEAP FORWARD, the political persecution that was part of life in the People's Republic or, simply, to seek a better life.

a province transformed: the 1980s

The solution to some of these problems came in 1978 when DENG XIAOPING launched his free market reforms and Open Door policy. Guangdong could hardly have been better placed to benefit from the change of policy in Beijing. The very factors – proximity to Hong Kong, traditional contacts with the wider world, the commercial flair of its people – which had generated suspicion and held the province in check for 30 years suddenly became its best assets. In China's new drive to follow the export-driven route to economic modernization taken by Hong Kong, Singapore, Taiwan and South Korea, Guangdong was almost perfectly situated.

Almost but not quite. Beijing's decision in 1979 to grant Guangdong preferential policies made up for any deficiencies. Under them, the province could keep more of its local revenues than other regions, retain a bigger share of foreign exchange earnings, and approve investment projects of a certain size without reference to Beijing. Neighbouring FUJIAN was granted similar privileges – with similar economic results. At the same time Beijing kept Shanghai, China's traditional economic powerhouse, on a tight leash, much to the irritation of the city's leaders. For the next 10 years they seethed while the south forged ahead.

Guangdong's success eventually became the foundation for the coastal development strategy advocated in the late 1980s by ZHAO ZIYANG, the reformist premier and later Communist Party leader. Zhao had worked in Guangdong twice before his elevation to Beijing in 1979. Though not a Cantonese himself, he had a wide network of supporters in the region, and was keen to see them make the most of natural and conferred advantages. Deng backed his mentor. The coastal development strategy complied with his own beliefs, later famously expressed in the slogans: 'it is glorious to get rich', and 'some people must get rich before the others'. Guangdong was unleashed: it was opened to foreign capital on a scale unequalled elsewhere in the country with a view to pioneering the development of high-tech industries and allowing it to grow rich through export processing.

At first, though, only parts of it were. In the early 1980s the new policies were confined geographically to SPECIAL ECONOMIC ZONES (SEZs). Of the four founded in 1980, three – Zhuhai (opposite Macau), SHENZHEN (facing Hong Kong) and Shantou (the main port for the Chaozhou region in the east of the province) – are located in Guangdong. The fourth, Xiamen (Amoy), is in Fujian.

Controversies and setbacks surrounded the zones' performance, as they did China's entire reform experiment. Fences between some of the SEZs and the hinterland controlled the flow of people in and out of what rapidly became China's richest regions. But ideas and policies were less easily contained, much to the displeasure of conservatives in Beijing. Zhao and Deng pressed on. In 1984 Guangzhou and Zhanjiang, the main port in southwest Guangdong, were among 14 coastal cities granted similar powers to the Zones. Bending the flexible policies granted them to the limits, Guangdong's leaders, most of them native Cantonese by the mid-1980s, welcomed investment throughout their province and particularly in the Pearl River Delta.

The response to these developments in Hong Kong, Macau and among Chinese communities further afield was enthusiastic. As far as Hong Kong was concerned, the opening of the hinterland to trade and investment could hardly have been better timed. Land and labour in the colony had grown expensive. The territory's future as a centre for manufacturing cheap exports was in doubt. In Guangdong, land and labour were abundant and cheap. Local entrepreneurs seized the chance to relocate manufacturing operations over the border, first in Shenzhen, then further into Guangdong.

For most of them such moves amounted to a 'homecoming': the vast majority of Hong Kong people had family, personal or commercial connections with Guangdong. Virtually every successful local Chinese businessman did. Those without such ties were happy to reinforce their search for profits with latent patriotism. Cultural and linguistic ties overcame worries about the Mainland's opaque legal processes and unpredictable Communist politics. Money poured over the border. Products once made in Hong Kong increasingly were designed and packaged in Hong Kong but made in China. In 1984 the growing economic symbiosis between the two territories was complemented by a political accord: the Sino-British agreement handing sovereignty over Hong Kong to Beijing on 1 July 1997 (see BRITAIN; HONG KONG).

None of the above implies that Hong Kong's economic integration with Guangdong during the 1980s was trouble free. Political conflicts in Beijing often cast a pall over the process. An example was the dismissal of HU YAOBANG as Party leader in 1987 and the brief campaign against 'bourgeois liberalism' that followed. Both developments sent a chill through the region.

Recovery was rapid – the separation of HAINAN ISLAND from Guangdong in 1988 and its designation as a Special Economic Zone was a sign the reformers were briefly back in charge. But recovery was also shortlived. The suppression of the TIANANMEN SQUARE DEMOCRACY MOVEMENT in 1989 threatened a more fundamental setback.

Hong Kong was hurt by the affair because of its manifest support for the student movement and opposition to the use of force against it. Guangdong was harmed because of its close links with the disgraced Zhao Ziyang. In the new hardline atmosphere, Beijing held both territories in disdain. As centres of political liberalism and economic wealth they were at odds with the renewed emphasis on Marxist orthodoxy and opposition to 'peaceful evolution', the supposed plot of the West to undermine Chinese socialism by means of increased trade, investment and ideological infiltration.

They were also at odds with the slowly-slowly approach to economic growth after 1989 favoured by LI PENG, the hardline premier. The preference of JIANG ZEMIN, the new Party leader, and others for the development of Shanghai and the Yangtze valley looked like another blow (see YANGTZE RIVER). It was not a question of Guangdong having

> ### The Lie of the Land
>
> Guangdong lost a strip of coastal territory to Guangxi in 1965 and had its former 'administrative district' of Hainan Island turned into an independent province in 1988. This left it with an area of 68,700 square miles (178,000 sq kms) inhabited, at the end of the century, by just over 70 million people, the overwhelming majority of them Han Chinese. The Nanling mountains separate Guangdong from Hunan to the north and form the watershed of the Yangtze and Pearl River systems. The Pearl River Delta is the largest plain in the province. It includes several 'tributary deltas' that do not flow into the main body of either the West, the North or the East rivers – the main streams of the Pearl River Delta. It is the most densely populated and productive part of the province. Small basins and river valleys are found among the mountainous tableland of southwest Guangdong above the Leizhou peninsula, one of only three of its kind in China. (The others are the SHANDONG peninsula, and the Liaodong peninsula in southern LIAONING). The second-largest plain in the province and another home of fertile land is in the east, around the valley of the Han River. The Han flows into the sea at Shantou, once a TREATY PORT and now a Special Economic Zone.

had its day. But its role as China's economic pacesetter seemed to be in doubt.

a province unleashed: the 1990s

The uncertainty lasted until early 1992 when Deng made his controversial trip to south China. He spent several days in Guangdong, visiting factories and leisure facilities in Guangzhou, Shenzhen and Zhuhai. His message was music to the ears of the provincial officials accompanying him. It was that Guangdong should become East Asia's 'fifth tiger'. The province should tap its advantages and become a mighty export base capable of propelling China's reforms into the next century, enriching its people and, not least, enabling the Communist Party to retain its grip on power. This depended less on obedience to economic strictures laid down in Beijing than emphasis on the 'Guangdong advantage': flexibility, proximity to Hong Kong, and openness to the international economy.

While Deng's message galvanized the economic and social life of the entire nation, nowhere did it do so with such effect as in Guangdong. It gave the green light to officials ready to enrich their region by whatever legitimate (and sometimes illegitimate) means might be at their disposal. During the next few years, foreign investment, again most of it either from, or channelled through, Hong Kong flooded into industrial development, real estate and infrastructure in the province. Most of the money was concentrated in the Pearl River Delta, which by the mid-1990s had become the equivalent of a giant industrial park for Hong Kong and Overseas Chinese investors. Before long it constituted the biggest belt of light industry to be found anywhere in the world.

This was an extraordinary transformation for a region that, until the early 1980s, was characterized by fertile paddy fields and small market towns, where industry on any scale was scarce, roads few, and where meandering rivers were the main arteries of trade and communication. Less than 20 years later grimy factories producing toys, textiles, footwear and electronics line congested roads from Jiangmen in the west to Huizhou in the east; from Guangzhou in the north to Shenzhen in the south. Expressways, ringroads, bridges, power stations, rail links, ports and new airports suffocate the landscape. And urbanization has made major, noisy and sometimes chaotic cities of once quiet country towns such as Dongguan, Zhongshan, Huizhou, Shunde and Panyu.

At the start of the new century the approximately 16,000 square miles (41,440 sq kms) of the Pearl River Delta, including Hong Kong and Macau, contain a population well in excess of 20 million. Most are participants in or beneficiaries of a remarkable burst of rapid economic growth fuelled by injections of capital from the region's many Overseas Chinese. Local incomes are the highest in China. So is consumption. It is illustrated by the rapid development of advertising, the prevalence of pagers and mobile telephones, and the number and variety of leisure facilities spread across the region. The Pearl River Delta is the economic powerhouse of Guangdong, and has a larger GDP than many provinces.

The transformation has not been trouble free. Many of the controversies surrounding development in the Third World have arisen in Guangdong. The effects on the region's ENVIRONMENT have been horrific: water and air pollution blight the entire delta, depositing river-borne toxic algae off the coast of Hong Kong and frequently bathing it and other cities in the region in a grim, artificial, particle-laden light. The aesthetic damage to the landscape caused by endless rows of makeshift factories, warehouses and construction sites, and the giant container trucks ferrying goods between them, is no less striking.

Inside the factories, workers, most of them WOMEN, often labour in conditions that are dangerous, unhealthy or both. Wages are better than those available on the farm but are low by international standards – a key element of the 'Guangdong advantage'. Throughout the 1990s industrial deaths and injuries were high. Many were the result of fires sweeping through buildings in which emergency exits had been locked to prevent theft, or where they simply did not exist. In all these respects, as in the growth of crime and corruption that usually accompany raw capitalism, the dilemmas of development have been writ large during the industrialization of the Pearl River Delta.

In Hong Kong on the other hand it is the advantages of development that have been most apparent. The rise of service and information-based industries more than compensated for the loss of manufacturing across the border. Large firms moved some of their 'back office' operations into Guangdong where costs were lower, and imported graduates from the Mainland to ease local labour shortages. In economic terms the border between the territory and the province lost its meaning: Hong Kong and Guangdong simply performed different roles within one regional economy. Until the Asian financial crisis took its toll in 1998 living standards soared year after year, softening what otherwise might have been damaging blows arising from the Sino-British row over CHRIS PATTEN's political reforms.

losing lustre?: Guangdong's future

At the close of the century the Asian financial crisis took the shine off Guangdong's economic performance. Foreign investment slowed, exports flagged and growth lost something of its earlier dynamism. But the province faced a series of homegrown problems, too, most of them arising from Beijing's reluctance to continue with the 'sweetheart' fiscal deals that had allowed the province to retain much of its revenue since the late 1970s. A challenge to the status quo came in 1994 when the central government implemented a new tax-sharing system. Despite complaints from local leaders and much closed-door bargaining, Guangdong was presented with considerably heavier tax bills than it had faced before (see FINANCE).

The province felt the whip hand of Beijing in other ways. ZHU RONGJI, vice-premier from 1991 to 1998, and then premier, made it his business to tame the regions whose rapid growth had confounded macroeconomic control and whose quasi-independence had starved the treasury of funds. Guangdong was a primary target. Lu Ruihua (1938–), a Cantonese, but a relatively compliant one, was made governor in 1996 in succession to Zhu Senlin (1930–). Two years later, Xie Fei (1932–99), the long-serving provincial Party boss, was replaced by Li Changchun (1944–), an outsider.

When, in 1998, Guangdong International Trust and Investment Corporation (GITIC), a financial arm of the provincial government, announced that it could not pay its foreign debtors, Zhu declined to rescue the company. Instead he forced it to become the first major financial institution to seek bankruptcy in China's Communist history. Whatever the financial merits of the decision it was a blow against provincialism and the incautious local investment policies often associated with it.

Guangdong also faced stronger competition in its role as the 'leading edge' of China's reforms and economic development. The challenge came mainly from Shanghai which in the 1990s enjoyed the kind of political connections with the central leadership in Beijing that Guangdong had enjoyed a decade earlier. Shanghai had other, no less formidable advantages. They included one of the most developed industrial bases in China, a well-educated workforce and, to its rear, the human and material riches of the Yangtze valley. The Pearl River Delta could not match any of them.

At the start of the new millennium Guangdong's chances of staying ahead depend on its ability to offer something new, something other parts of the country either cannot or dare not offer local and foreign investors. In Guangdong's case this means moving away from export processing and casino-like property deals to attracting quality investment in high-tech industries (one of the province's early goals) and the service sector. This in turn requires improved legislation, more information, a sound legal environment and the transparent political processes that usually accompany them. It is a tall order even for China's most go-ahead province.

Guangxi Zhuang Autonomous Region

There is hardly a more striking example of the regional inequalities that have scarred China's rapid development since the 1980s than the wealth gap between Guangxi and GUANGDONG, its neighbour to the east. Both provincial units are part of the same macroeconomic region centred on the Pearl or West River. Both are situated on the coast. Both are predominantly Cantonese-speaking and, to a large extent, culturally homogeneous. Yet Guangxi's per capita GDP at the close of the century was less than half that of Guangdong; and it had attracted less than one-tenth the foreign investment of its neighbour. At the start of the new era, Guangdong is China's richest province while Guangxi, though growing, is among its poorest.

a rebel redoubt

Some of the reasons for this lie in Guangxi's geography, ethnic complexity, and former isolation as a semi-independent region at the southern periphery of the Chinese world. Much of its territory is mountainous with intensive agriculture possible only in the many narrow river valleys and few plains, the largest of them in the southeast. Despite centuries of Han immigration, including the arrival of fiercely independent Hakka people from the north, close to 40 per cent of Guangxi's population is composed of ETHNIC MINORITIES. Most are Zhuang, a Tai-speaking people who are the most numerous of China's recognized minorities. They are also among the most sinicized. But the Communists considered them sufficiently different from the Han Chinese majority to redesignate Guangxi as the Guangxi Zhuang Autonomous Region in 1958. Finally, until 1965, Guangxi was an inland province: Guangdong administered the strip of coastal territory from the border with VIETNAM to the Leizhou peninsula above HAINAN ISLAND.

These factors have made Guangxi's history quite different from that of Guangdong and the other southern provinces. The Taiping Rebellion of the mid-nineteenth century which fatally weakened the Qing Dynasty is an example of this difference. The rebels emerged from the poor, densely populated river valleys of east Guangxi in 1851 and two years later set up a rival capital in Nanjing from which they ruled much of south China. They were eventually suppressed. But in the decades that followed neither Qing nor Republican governments established firm control over the province in which the Taipings first raised their flag. Poor, remote and rebellious, Guangxi was largely left alone.

These were ideal circumstances for the growth of warlordism. Beginning in the early 1920s Guangxi produced a prominent example of this genre of Chinese politics in the form of the 'Guangxi Clique', a triumvirate of military leaders who remained influential until the province fell to the Communists in 1949. LI ZONGREN, Bai Chongxi (1893–1966) and Huang Shaoxiong (1895–1966) (succeeded in 1930 by Huang Xuchu (1892–1975)) did not regard themselves as WARLORDS. They were senior members of the KUOMINTANG whose troops played a leading role in the NORTHERN EXPEDITION of 1926–8 to unite China. They also undertook sweeping reforms within their province in the hope of making it a model for the rest of the country. But all these things they did in the context of bitter opposition to, and often military conflict with, the central government led by CHIANG KAI-SHEK.

In 1929–30, Chiang managed to drive the Clique from their home province, though at the cost of allowing the Communists to stage a rebellion in west Guangxi. With the region in turmoil the Communist Party sent a youthful DENG XIAOPING to Longzhou, close to the border with French Indochina, and Baise, further north, to lead the two soviet governments set up by local Communists, many of them Zhuang. When the Clique returned they crushed the uprisings, forcing the survivors on a grim prelude to the LONG MARCH in the form of a trek to Communist headquarters in JIANGXI while under constant military attack.

In 1936, Guangxi almost went to war with Chiang again – this time over Chiang's appeasement of Japan. The spirit of national resistance was real in Guangxi, as elsewhere. But the Clique tried to use it to ward off central government intrusion in their affairs. They were soon forced to come to terms; and with the outbreak of the SINO-JAPANESE WAR the following year, they had to accept a central government presence in their domain.

They did so with little grace and much covert resistance. Like Kunming in neighbouring YUNNAN, Guangxi's wartime capital, Guilin, became a key rear area in the fight against the Japanese invaders. Refugees flooded into the city along with factory equipment; prominent intellectuals together with businessmen; officials and spies of the 'puppet' government

headed by WANG JINGWEI. Guilin was a bastion of resistance – both to Japan and to the policies of the central government, then based in CHONGQING. Unlike Kunming, however, Guilin and much of southeast Guangxi were occupied by Japanese troops during the closing stages of the war. The fact that they were recovered by armies loyal to the central government rather than the Clique made a return to autonomy in the post-war period difficult.

So did the CIVIL WAR. Li and Bai were as much at odds with Chiang during the struggle against the Communists as they had been in the war against Japan. But they were not clever enough, nor their armies strong enough, to usurp a cunning, skilful leader whose hatred of Communism they shared. Rivalry between the Guangxi and central government factions of the Kuomintang sped the Communists to victory. By November 1949 the People's Liberation Army had occupied most of Guangxi. Li Zongren, at loggerheads with Chiang to the last, left for medical treatment in the United States. He returned to the Mainland and a tumultuous welcome in 1965. Bai Chongxi went straight to Taiwan. Huang Xuchu settled in Hong Kong. The era of the Guangxi Clique was over.

Communism and ethnic minorities

At first the Communists encountered resistance to their rule in Guangxi. The Clique's long hold over the province partly accounted for this. So did the fact that tens of thousands of Nationalist troops fled through Guangxi to escape the PLA advance. Most sailed to Hainan before decamping for TAIWAN. Others crossed the border into French Indochina. Still others took to the hills from where they staged guerrilla raids on the towns below. Guangxi was not fully pacified until the early 1950s.

LAND REFORM, crackdowns on 'counter-revolutionaries' and other campaigns enabled the Party to consolidate its rule in Guangxi as they did in other provinces where there was little Communist influence before the arrival of the PLA. But in Guangxi, the presence of large numbers of ethnic minorities added a new dimension to the situation. Some of these groups, notably the Miao and the Yao, differed sharply from the Han Chinese. Upland peoples, they were often party to the mutual animosity that tends to characterize relations between inhabitants of the plains and the hills. The creation of 'autonomous' counties for such groups complied with the Communist Party's national minority policy.

On the other hand, the Zhuang, by far the

The Lie of the Land

Encircled by mountains save for a natural break along the valley of West River in the east, Guangxi forms the hinterland of neighbouring Guangdong. Little of its 89,000 square miles (231,000 sq kms) is flatland. The exceptions are the stretch of land either side of the West River in the middle of the province; the Right River Plain in the northwest, close to Baise; and the Hepu Plain, north of Beihai. These areas are home for the majority of Guangxi's population which numbered 46 million at the close of the century, about one third of them Zhuang. Distinctive limestone rocks – karst formations – are scattered widely across the province. Most of Guangxi's highest mountains are found in the north and west where they form the periphery of the Yunnan–Guizhou Plateau. This region is the source of the headstreams that form the West River system. Rice is the main crop with southern parts of the province enjoying three harvests a year. Guangxi's most important cash crop is sugarcane.

largest non-Han group in the province, farmed the valleys and inter-married with the Han. Only in the more remote western parts of Guangxi were they able to resist assimilation. For these reasons, the decision to turn the entire western half of Guangxi into a Zhuang Autonomous zhou (prefecture) in 1952 remains something of a mystery. The redesignation in 1958 of the whole of Guangxi as the Guangxi Zhuang Autonomous Region is an even greater one.

Two theories may account for these moves. The first concerns Guangxi's own history. The Zhuang had supported Communist Party activities in their homeland during the late 1920s and early 1930s, and they appear to have been more enthusiastic than the local Han about the prospect of Communist rule after 1949. Perhaps the redesignation of the province as an autonomous region, which allowed the Zhuang to be given positions of at least nominal importance in the new regime, was something of a reward.

The second explanation touches on the new government's overall policy towards ethnic minorities. By treating the Zhuang as they did in 1958, the Party was in a position to deny claims by Tibetans, Uigurs and Mongols for genuine independence on the grounds that these groups could not be given more than China's largest minority – that is, the Zhuang. In this respect, it was fortunate that China's most numerous ethnic minority was among the most assimilated to Han Chinese ways, despite genuine linguistic and other differ-

ences. In any event, there have been no reports of demands from the Zhuang for an end to Chinese rule or even calls for greater autonomy in Guangxi. On the other hand, there has been friction between the dominant Han and Zhuang groups and other ethnic groups in the province.

eating the enemy

Racial friction in Guangxi paled by comparison with that between rival Red Guards during the CULTURAL REVOLUTION. Why fighting in the province should have been so intense compared with other parts of the country is another mystery of Guangxi history. So is a dark secret of those days which only came to light in the 1990s: politically motivated cannibalism. It occurred in 1967–8, a period of violence and chaos created by the struggle for power between Wei Guoqing (1914–89), the Guangxi Party secretary and a local Zhuang, and radicals bent on bringing him down. Both sides raided barracks and hijacked trains passing through Guangxi bearing munitions destined for the Vietcong in Vietnam. In several cities, including Wuzhou, the commercial centre in the east of the region, buildings were razed to the ground by artillery fire. At least 90,000 people died in these conflicts. Corpses from Guangxi were discovered floating down the West River; some finished up as far downstream as Hong Kong.

Cannibalism took place in several of Guangxi's county towns. Chief among them was Wuxuan in the centre of the province, south of Liuzhou. Unlike the outbreaks that occurred in China after the GREAT LEAP FORWARD, cannibalism in Guangxi during the late 1960s had nothing to do with starvation. It was driven by hatred and desire for revenge. People ate the flesh and organs of their rivals or those deemed 'class enemies'. Several hundred people were murdered and consumed. Thousands feasted on their flesh. Nearly 20 years later, Zheng Yi (1947–), a Chinese investigative journalist, pieced together what had happened from interviews and official records. His account, *Scarlet Memorial*, was published in Chinese (in Taiwan) in 1993, and in English in 1996. By that time Zheng had fled to the United States to avoid punishment for his part in the TIANANMEN SQUARE DEMOCRACY MOVEMENT.

slow start: reform in Guangxi

'Leftism' lingered long in Guangxi. Much to Beijing's annoyance, the province was slow to respond to the economic reforms launched by Deng Xiaoping in 1978. The Sino-Vietnamese War of 1979 complicated matters (see VIET-NAM). Much of western Guangxi became a military area. Cross-border shelling persisted long after Chinese troops withdrew from north Vietnam, where they received a drubbing from the defenders. Even when the shelling stopped, at the end of the 1980s, a huge task of mine clearing lay ahead before the border region could be declared safe for travel and trade.

The normalization of relations between Beijing and Hanoi in 1991 helped make this possible. Cross-border trade, at first conducted by human porters who picked their way between the mines laid along narrow mountain paths, flourished. Flights began between Hanoi and Nanning, the provincial capital since 1949, where the Vietnamese opened a consulate. In the mid-1990s, long interrupted rail services resumed via 'Friendship Pass'. Parts of southwest Guangxi, traditionally poor and isolated, experienced a taste of development.

Other parts of the province were less dependent on an improvement in relations with a foreign neighbour for economic change. Guilin, for example, has become an important centre of local and international tourism thanks to the stunning karst topography that surrounds it. Much of the rest of Guangxi looks east to Guangdong and south to Hong Kong for sources of investment, know-how and personnel. Access is still a problem: east Guangxi lacks railways and adequate roads. The main artery of communication remains the West River, with Wuzhou, gateway to eastern Guangxi, almost a day's sailing by jetfoil from Hong Kong. Yet when rapid growth in Guangdong drove up the prices of land and labour in the late 1990s, local and Hong Kong investors cast their eyes west to low-cost Guangxi.

Further south the Guangxi authorities capitalized on the strip of coastal territory acquired in 1965 from Guangdong, apparently to facilitate its defence at a time of tension with the United States, then embroiled in Vietnam. Beihai, once a sleepy treaty port, was one of 14 coastal cities opened in 1984 to foreign trade and investment on preferential terms. Guangxi has only three ports – Beihai, Qinzhou and Fangcheng – and all of them are small. But the completion of a new railway in 1998 between Nanning and Kunming has enabled them to serve as transshipment points for trade to and from landlocked Yunnan.

These developments, though remarkable in many ways, have failed to alter Guangxi's status as the poor sister of Guangdong. Proximity to the richest area in the country undoubtedly has made things better than they might have been. But it also invites comparisons from which Guangxi is bound to suffer. The differences between major cities in the two 'guang' provinces are not obvious, at least to the naked eye. But those between Guangxi's towns and countryside remain profound. Some of the province's border areas, home of ethnic minorities, begin the new era still mired in the poverty and isolation that once characterized most of Guangxi.

Guangxu Emperor (1871–1908)

The penultimate QING DYNASTY emperor spent the last ten years of his life under palace arrest, a tragic, powerless symbol of reform in an age of upheaval and collapse. His fate was echoed almost a century later by that of ZHAO ZIYANG, the Communist Party reformer whose objection to the use of force to crush the 1989 TIANANMEN SQUARE DEMOCRACY MOVEMENT resulted in his house arrest in Beijing. Emperor and Communist both fell foul of the conservatives of their day: their fate was a reminder of the narrow frontiers of Chinese politics at each end of the century – and for most of the time in between.

Guangxu's mistake was to lend his weight to calls for sweeping political change led by KANG YOUWEI and other reformist scholars in the late 1890s. Defeated on the battlefield by Japan and subject to ever greater inroads by the Western powers, China's decay seemed terminal. A complete overhaul was needed. Tradition would have to be scrapped. The rash of decrees Guangxu signed in June 1898 to bring this about struck fear into many at the Manchu Court and troubled those elsewhere for whom change would mean loss of power. If successful, the '100 Days Reform' would have turned China into a constitutional monarchy of the kind Japan had become following the Meiji Restoration 30 years earlier. The reform was brought to an end with a coup.

Conservatives rallied around the EMPRESS DOWAGER who deposed her nephew in everything but name and had the leaders of the movement arrested and executed. Some, such as Kang and LIANG QICHAO, managed to flee into exile, but the reforms, like Guangxu's career as monarch, were in ruins. Abroad, only

Kang Youwei kept the fate of the emperor before the eyes of the public. Guangxu died in mysterious circumstances, one day before the Empress Dowager. He was succeeded by PU YI.

Guizhou Province

Geography has dealt Guizhou a poor hand in the contest for economic development and national integration. History and politics have done much the same. For most of the twentieth century the province, whose name means 'precious land', was a byword for poverty and isolation. The first years of Communist rule challenged this reputation but the reform era, paradoxically, re-established it. So much so that the growing wealth gap between Guizhou and other parts of the country in the 1990s became an indictment of Beijing's entire development strategy.

a place apart

Guizhou rises above GUANGXI, SICHUAN and HUNAN to form part of the Guizhou–Yunnan plateau. Mountains, whose peaks rise to an average of 3,000 feet, account for almost 90 per cent of its 65,600 square miles (170,000 sq kms). Flat land constitutes just 3 per cent, less than in any other Chinese province. Farming is conducted mainly in narrow basins along the Wu, Guizhou's major river. Elsewhere it is mostly confined to terraced hillsides.

Terrain has made trade, transport and communications difficult as well as agriculture. This is true of trade and transport within Guizhou, and between it and its neighbours. Until at least the mid-twentieth century it made little sense to speak of Guizhou as an integrated provincial economy. Links with other parts of the country – with the exception of northeast YUNNAN, of which it forms a geographical part – were just as tenuous. A patchwork of local economies and trading networks, Guizhou looked inward rather than outward. Traditionally it was a secluded, almost self-absorbed province.

It was fragmented ethnically, too. At the close of the twentieth century, about one-third of Guizhou's 36 million people were ETHNIC MINORITIES, the most numerous among them the Miao and the Buyi. Two centuries earlier the Han Chinese component of the population was much smaller. Rapid immigration during the QING DYNASTY sparked constant rebellions by indigenous peoples. The

Miao, themselves often divided into warring groups, were eventually marginalized in their homeland. But they and other minorities resisted excessive sinification, bequeathing Guizhou a complex, sometimes explosive history of race relations.

In so far as it was the backwoods of China, developments in the province short of massive revolt were of little concern to Beijing. The attraction of Guizhou, to past as well as present rulers, was its gold, silver, copper, mercury and, in more recent times, coal. The object was to extract these raw materials with as little trouble as possible. The role of government was similarly unambitious. It was a matter of striking the right compromise with leaders of SECRET SOCIETIES, tribal chieftains, and the thin strata of Chinese officialdom that lay on top. Little was expected of the province before the age of industry and modern communications – either by foreigners, who did not press for the opening of a treaty port in Guizhou, or the central government.

And little was given. Guizhou was second only to Yunnan among the southwestern provinces in supporting the REPUBLICAN REVOLUTION of 1911. It followed Yunnan's lead again in 1916 in the campaign to end the imperial pretensions of YUAN SHIKAI. In the years that followed Guizhou was ruled by warlords, chief of whom was Wang Jialie (1893–1966).

Even the upheavals of the NORTHERN EXPEDITION passed Guizhou by. And though Wang declared his loyalty to Chiang Kai-shek's new KUOMINTANG government, it was no more than a declaration. Nanjing's writ, like Beijing's before it, did not run far in the isolated uplands of southwest China.

Chiang's campaign to wipe out the Communist rebels changed this. Though he failed to crush his foes in JIANGXI, the Nationalist leader managed in 1934 to drive them on to their LONG MARCH, and pursue them in territories formerly beyond his control, Guizhou among them. Wang Jialie's failure to defeat the Communist intruders in 1934–5 brought his career as leader of Guizhou to a sudden end.

There were other more important consequences arising from the Red Army's presence in the province. At the town of Zunyi, about 100 miles (160 kms) north of Guiyang, the provincial capital, the Communists rested and convened a crucial Politburo meeting. It reviewed the predominantly Moscow-influenced tactics that had cost the Party its Jiangxi base and caused the military losses sustained during the first stage of the Long March. MAO ZEDONG, until then eclipsed by ZHOU ENLAI and other Soviet-trained Communists in the leadership, condemned the tactics as departures from the true path – that is, *his* path – of the Chinese Revolution. He carried the day. Another ten years would pass before Mao became the Party's unrivalled leader and chief ideologist. But his ascendancy began in January 1935 in the otherwise undistinguished Guizhou town of Zunyi (see CHINESE COMMUNIST PARTY).

While the Communists soon left Guizhou, the influence of the Central Government remained. It grew stronger when Chiang was forced to move his capital to CHONGQING during the SINO-JAPANESE WAR. Roads were built linking Guizhou with its neighbours. A railway line from Guangxi stopped a few miles short of the provincial border. Chiang controlled senior appointments in the province, and the national rather than local currencies circulated in Wang's old domain, which suddenly became an important if still poor part of the Nationalists' 'rear area'.

These forces of development and national integration were real but shortlived. When the war was over, and Chiang moved his capital back to Nanjing, Guizhou returned to its former isolation. Little changed until Communist troops returned in November 1949 – this time as conquerors.

integration and industrialization

As with most other formerly isolated, semi-autonomous provinces, the Communists brought Guizhou rapidly into the national body politic after 1949. Its people were subjected to *national* policies and mobilized for *national* causes. The construction of RAILWAYS made Guizhou part of the national transport network and opened previously secluded areas within the province to the wider world. Road-building had the same effect. Autonomous prefectures and counties were created for some of its many ethnic minorities with a view to burying ancient enmities. During the first decade of Communist rule Guizhou lost some of its 'backwoods' character.

The same was true of the first years of the second decade, though not before the famine caused by Mao's GREAT LEAP FORWARD took its toll. At least one million of Guizhou's then 16 million people are believed to have died during the early 1960s. Many of the deaths occurred in Zunyi and neighbouring Jinsha county, the result of violent appropriation of grain by officials.

Mao's 'Third Line' policy, which called for the creation of heavy industries deep in the interior, brought a different kind of change to parts of Guizhou during the 1960s. The province was ideal for the Chairman's purpose. It was a long way from the coast and China's land borders and thus was not vulnerable to attack by either of Beijing's main foes: the Soviet Union and the United States. Even if attack came, Guizhou's terrain, and its still rudimentary communications would make conquest and even the destruction of facilities extremely difficult.

'the Guizhou phenomenon'

What was true in the 1960s and 1970s was scarcely relevant in the 1980s. What had been considerable advantages in the Maoist era of self-sufficiency, hostility to the outside world and revolutionary purity proved otherwise in the age of market reform and opening to the international economy championed by DENG XIAOPING. Beijing's dramatic policy shift worked to the disadvantage of many inland provinces, at least at first. But Guizhou – still a predominantly agricultural province, its new heavy industrial base rapidly becoming a burden, and its chances of attracting FOREIGN TRADE AND INVESTMENT impaired by geography and tradition – suffered more than most. The government's decision in the 1980s to abandon the ideal of equal development and allow coastal regions to get rich first made things even worse.

How much worse became clear in the early 1990s. During the period 1978–93, Guizhou's economy grew in both aggregate and per capita terms slightly above the national average of 9 per cent. Yet the province remained stubbornly poor in relation to most of its neighbours, and increasingly so relative to the richest parts of the country such as SHANGHAI and GUANGDONG. Guizhou began the reform era as the poorest province in China in per capita GDP terms. It has remained so ever since. (See POVERTY.)

Relative impoverishment of this kind rang alarm bells among Chinese academics, notably Hu Angang, whose anxiety over China's growing regional inequalities led him to warn that the country faced a Yugoslavia-style breakup. There were two strands to his argument. One was that acute poverty of the kind found in Guizhou and elsewhere might encourage such areas to pursue independence. The other was that the central government's decreasing ability to extract taxes from the provinces prevented it from redistributing funds in the interests of more balanced, equitable national development, and threatened its very survival. Taken together these phenomena presaged financial and political disaster, and possibly the end of China as a unified state.

Critics complained that Hu's argument overlooked a number of vital differences between the situation in southern Europe and China. It did, but was no less shocking for that. Others, some of them foreign observers, were quick to echo his warnings. For a while during the mid-1990s, the prospect that China would disintegrate ran a close second in scholarly and popular debate to the idea that it would soon be the world's largest economy.

Beijing was not blind to the trends Hu described. It sought to remedy the situation in 1994 (earlier than originally planned) by introducing a new tax-sharing scheme designed to raise more revenue from the provinces (see FINANCE). And the new five-year plan, the ninth, introduced in 1996, pledged to narrow regional differences by actively sponsoring development in the inland provinces. At least in policy terms, the coastal provinces could not expect to have everything their own way indefinitely: inland areas such as Guizhou were not forgotten.

Yet if these measures promise to curb what Hu Angang called the 'Guizhou phenomenon' – the province's growing poverty relative to the richest parts of the country – they can only do so in the long term. Some idea of the task ahead was suggested by a number of the province's key indices at the close of the 1990s. Guizhou accounted for a fraction over 1 per cent of national GDP; agriculture generated 34 per cent of provincial GDP (it was higher only in HAINAN and TIBET); and the state-owned sector produced 56 per cent of local industrial output. These figures placed it among the least reformed as well as the least developed of China's provinces.

They also made Guizhou a primary focus of China's national drive to eliminate poverty. In the mid-1990s about one-third of the population were defined as poor according to Beijing's criteria. That made Guizhou home for almost one quarter of the 50 million people said at the time to have trouble finding enough food and clothing. The number has since decreased. But it has not done so to the extent that Guizhou can claim to have escaped from the fact that, in the wider scheme of things, it is something of a casualty of China's race to get rich.

Hainan Province

There are few more dramatic testimonies to China's modern transformation than Hainan Island. There are few more telling examples of the obstacles and frustrations in the way of change. Until the mid-1980s Hainan was a backward, half-forgotten administrative region of GUANGDONG. In 1988 it became China's newest, smallest, province, and its largest SPECIAL ECONOMIC ZONE (SEZ). Money and manpower poured in. The economy grew almost as fast as the ambitions of its leaders. But though Hainan changed, plans to turn it into a separate customs zone and free port, and to conduct experiments in reform deemed impermissible on the Mainland, came to naught. Hainan fell victim to political changes in Beijing and its own ambitions. Its status as the military and administrative nerve centre for the contested islands and waters of the SOUTH CHINA SEA cloud future prospects for change.

the end of the world

A tropical zone and geographically a part of the Southeast Asian rather than the Chinese world, Hainan was formally incorporated into the Chinese empire as early as the first century BC. Steady Chinese settlement led to the growth of a predominantly Han Chinese culture, at least on the coastal fringe. Further inland, what China now defines as its ETHNIC MINORITIES – in this case mainly the Li and the Miao peoples – lived largely separate, undisturbed lives.

From Beijing's point of view, Hainan was the 'end of the world': a remote, barbarous region, not so much ripe for development as a dumping ground for disgraced officials. Neither the REPUBLICAN REVOLUTION of 1911 nor the upheavals associated with the NORTHERN EXPEDITION of 1926–8 did much to change these conceptions. Hainan saw next to no development; even foreigners were not interested. Haikou, the island's capital, was opened as a TREATY PORT in 1876, but Britain closed its consulate there in the late 1920s. The French, within whose 'sphere of influence' Hainan fell, were hardly more active. Thousands of Hainanese continued to leave for Hong Kong and Southeast Asia where they became influential members of the OVERSEAS CHINESE community.

Change came with the SINO-JAPANESE WAR. Japan occupied Hainan in 1939 and used it as a jumping-off point for the conquest of parts of Southeast Asia. The Japanese built factories, roads, a modern port in the south and a stretch of railway in the southwest which still formed part of the island's modest rail network at the close of the century. Much of the interior escaped Japanese control. It was home for ethnic minorities and Hainan's Communist guerrillas who maintained an unbroken tradition of resistance to Nationalist Chinese and Japanese rulers from 1927 until the island's complete 'liberation' in April 1950.

Before that happened Hainan played host to tens of thousands of Nationalist troops who fled to the island to escape defeat in the CIVIL WAR. Most were from GUANGXI and Guangdong. But some hailed from much further north. Turning them into a fighting force capable of resisting the Communist advance proved impossible. Some of the best forces and virtually all the top Nationalist military and civilian officials left at the end of 1949 to join Chiang Kai-shek's beleaguered government in Taiwan. A plan to turn Hainan into a province collapsed with their departure. It was not revived for the best part of 40 years.

During the first decades of Communist rule, Hainan sank back into obscurity. Despite the strong indigenous Communist movement, the island was run largely by Mainlanders as an administrative subdivision of Guangdong. Beijing was concerned to tap the region's valuable resources – rubber, iron and salt – for the development of industry on the Mainland. This was particularly important during the KOREAN WAR when the United States imposed an embargo on strategic exports to the People's Republic. Within Hainan itself, development was as neglected under the new regime as it had been under the old. Inhabitants of an underpopulated as well as undeveloped region, many of the island's 2.5 million people (in 1949) remained in poverty.

This did little for relations between the locals, most of them Hainanese speakers, and the new arrivals, many of whom spoke either Cantonese or Mandarin. Hainanese have a strong sense of identity, a product of their unusual history and geographical position at the southern end of the Chinese world. Rarely, if ever, has this resulted in demands for political independence. But Hainan's quest for provincial identity and, in particular, an end to rule from Guangzhou, the Guangdong capital, was of long standing. It surfaced again in 1957 during the brief period of political tolerance fostered by the ONE HUNDRED FLOWERS MOVEMENT. It was stamped out, and the local officials said to be trying to turn Hainan into an 'independent kingdom' dismissed. Neither the political nor the economic status quo on the island changed until the mid-1980s, by which time the Communist leadership in Beijing began to look upon Hainan as a laboratory to test the country's next round of free market reforms.

Hainan and the coastal strategy

The form this experiment took was unprecedented. So were its results. In the early 1980s the island's leaders were granted special powers to develop the local economy by attracting FOREIGN TRADE AND INVESTMENT on favourable terms. It was part of the strategy favoured by ZHAO ZIYANG, the reformist Party leader, to develop China's coastal areas rapidly in the hope that wealth and the reforms that produced it would trickle into the interior. Hainan was granted the right to import certain goods, including vehicles and electrical products, at next to no duty. At the time, imports of this kind attracted tariffs in excess of 100 per cent on the Mainland. The authorities quickly got to work. By 1985 they had imported close to 90,000 vehicles and hundreds of thousands of television sets and video recorders, many of which they sold on at vast profit to customers on the Mainland. Even the navy was involved, shipping the smuggled goods.

Despite the scale of the scandal, Beijing declined to treat it as CORRUPTION in the generally understood sense of the term. For one thing, much of the money earned through smuggling goods to the Mainland found its way into the Hainan economy rather than disappearing into officials' pockets. For another, Lei Yu (1934–), the man in charge of the island, had powerful backers among the reformist camp in Beijing. He and others were sacked, but in 1988 Lei was made a vice-mayor of Guangzhou, and later still promoted to a senior position in Guangxi. His period of office in Haikou was seen later as something of a golden, pioneering age.

Liang Xiang (1919–), Lei's successor and another acolyte of Zhao Ziyang, sustained the tempo. Zhao continued to push for radical experiments in Hainan and won the rest of the leadership round to the idea of making the island a province and a Special Economic Zone. It was founded as such in April 1988 with the aim of making Hainan another Taiwan, the first, and only slightly larger, of China's by then two coastal provinces.

Once again local leaders got to work making use of the special powers granted them by the central government. Hainan, as the formula of the day put it, was to become a place with 'small government, big society'. It would be more 'special' than the other Special Economic Zones by pursuing innovations such as the long-term leasing of land to foreigners, allowing foreign banks to set up branches, and issuing visas to foreigners on arrival. Economic ownership was to be diversified, ending the dominance of the state sector. The market would rule in Hainan, not the government; the methods of international capitalism, not Communist practice.

Progress was rapid. Mainlanders, many from densely populated SICHUAN, flocked into Hainan to capitalize on the new economic opportunities. Hainanese overseas returned

The Lie of the Land

Hainan province administers a much larger area than the 13,100 square miles (34,000 sq kms) of Hainan Island. It is the seat of government for the scores of usually uninhabited islands, reefs and atolls that make up the Paracel and Spratly Islands in the South China Sea. The task of 'administration' does not amount to much: its chief purpose is to reinforce Beijing's claims, backed up by a strong naval presence in Hainan, to a vast area believed to be rich in minerals and energy resources and the location of important international shipping lanes. The claims are contested, in whole or in part, by Taiwan, VIETNAM, Malaysia, the Philippines and Brunei (see SOUTH CHINA SEA).

Hainan Island lies barely 20 miles (32 kms) south of the Leizhou peninsula of southwestern Guangdong. The middle of the island is mountainous. Peaks rise in the form of an arch with the highest of them in the south-central region. Alluvial plains are found in the north, around Wenchang; the northwest, the Wangwu-Jialei plain; and the southeast, the Qionghai–Wanning Plain. Three main rivers drain the island and they all rise in the Wuzhi – 'five thumb' – mountain range, the highest on the island. The longest of them is the Nandu River, which flows into the sea at Haikou.

Hainan is a base for rubber production and a major source of tropical fruits. It contains China's best reserves of iron ore and is a major source of zirconium and titanium. The northern, eastern and southern coastal fringes are the most developed, while much of the west and parts of the interior remain relatively poor. Of the island's 7.5 million people at the close of the twentieth century about one million were members of the Li ethnic group and about 70,000 Miao.

bringing much-needed capital with them. Hong Kong provided a flood of money. Roads, ports and power plants were built. Hainan secured a portion of revenue from some of the offshore oil and gas fields in its vicinity, and positioned itself to become a base for petrochemicals. Haikou acquired its first tower blocks and, near the golden beaches of Sanya, in the far south, work began on the infrastructure for 'China's Hawaii' – what officials hoped would become one of the region's best holiday destinations.

Yet Liang Xiang and his fellow leaders balked at the prospect of making the new province a separate customs area, as Zhao and others envisaged. To do so would thoroughly internationalize the economy and force Mainland goods, which supplied 80 per cent of the island's needs, to compete with those from abroad. Under Zhao's plan Hainan would also become a free port. Within its confines, China's currency, the *renminbi*, would be fully convertible. These measures carried risks.

Once implemented, prices would rise and so would public discontent. Opportunities for corruption would multiply. Unpredictable political consequences were sure to follow.

On the other hand, the advantages of success – a creation of a new type of privately owned, export-oriented economy – might be larger still. Hainan would no longer be subject to the political and economic rhythms of the Mainland. It would enjoy genuine political autonomy. And it would set an example for other parts of the country to follow.

Liang and many others in Hainan probably came to rue their hesitancy. By the end of 1988, the province was suffering from the austerity drive Beijing launched to cool inflation and excessive investment in the Mainland. In September the following year, Liang was sacked for supporting Zhao's opposition to the military suppression of the TIANANMEN SQUARE DEMOCRACY MOVEMENT and for allowing some of those who escaped the crackdown to shelter in Hainan. In this climate, what had once been 'Hainan fever' cooled rapidly. The new leadership in Beijing preferred to focus on the development of Shanghai where JIANG ZEMIN, Zhao's replacement as Party leader, had served as both mayor and Party boss.

There was particularly strong opposition in Beijing to the creation of the Yangpu Economic Development Area in Hainan. This was a 12 square-mile piece of land about 80 miles (130 kms) northeast of Haikou which had been leased for 70 years to the Hong Kong subsidiary of a Japanese construction company, Kumagai-Gumi. It was the closest thing in Communist China to a foreign concession (see TREATY PORTS). Within the area, the lessee was given a free hand to build a deep-water port, a new city and an industrial park, to sub-let facilities to third parties, and to manage all of them free of Chinese interference. For the post-Tiananmen leaders in Beijing, Yangpu amounted to a return to colonialism. It was worse for being the work of a company owned by JAPAN. They refused to give it the green light.

the early 1990s: boom years

For all these reasons, by 1990, Hainan's attempt to become a second Taiwan appeared to have failed. There was no going back on its status as a province, but the island seemed to have little future as the most 'special' of China's Special Economic Zones. Yet this was to reckon without the intervention of DENG XIAOPING. Deng's celebrated tour through south China in early 1992 transformed Hainan's fortunes just as it did those of almost every other part of the country. The leadership in Haikou, though generally less imaginative than that of the Lei Yu or Liang Xiang era, took the patriarch's statement that it is 'glorious to get rich' at face value.

A particularly virulent form of Chinese-style capitalism developed in Hainan. It was manifest in a boom in real estate, the prevalence of luxury hotels, office blocks, shopping malls, and a raucous night life. Virtually all this activity was financed by money from the Mainland, Hong Kong, Taiwan and Chinese communities further afield. The dividing line between the cut and thrust of commerce and plain illegality was often paper thin. No less often, it was simply non-existent. An example was Haikou's unofficial stock exchange which flourished until the spring of 1992 when ZHU RONGJI flew in and closed it down on the spot, fearful that it would become a source of instability.

In 1992 and 1993 Hainan's GDP grew by 22 per cent. During this period and the years that followed, many Hainanese escaped from poverty. Many of those who moved there from elsewhere in China prospered. Per capita GDP at the close of the decade was higher than in many other southern provinces, Guangdong, ZHEJIANG and FUJIAN excluded. And the ratio of foreign trade to GDP in Hainan was well above the national average.

Yet though its development was both rapid and real, the island failed to perform the trailblazing role first envisaged for it a decade earlier. The slow progress of the Yangpu Economic Development Area symbolized the disappointment. The project was finally approved after Deng's southern journey, but many years later it remained a vehicle for speculation in real estate rather than a centre of construction and production. The idea of escaping from Chinese bureaucracy appeared not to be so attractive to foreign investors after all.

For the rest of the island, there was no escape from policy priorities on the Mainland. In the mid-1990s these were designed to rein in rapid growth in the provinces. Paradoxically they had more effect in Hainan than elsewhere: for three years, beginning in 1995, the island's GDP grew well below the national average. The situation improved slightly as the century came to a close. With it came an apparent rekindling of old ambitions to make Hainan 'special'. Wang Xiaofeng (1944–), the governor, promised to simplify entry procedures for visitors and make it easier for people from Hong Kong, as well as non-Chinese, to buy property in Hainan. It was hardly a return to the idea of a separate customs area, but it suggested that the pioneering spirit had not died out completely in China's maritime frontier zone.

health

A simple comparison of two vital statistics – infant mortality and life expectancy – shows how the health of the Chinese people has improved under Communism. In Republican times estimates of infant mortality ranged from 290 to 500 per 1,000 live births; at the close of the 1990s the figure was 33. Average life expectancy in the 1940s was about 35; half a century later it was 68 for men and 71 for women. Closer inspection suggests that the Communist record, while impressive, is mixed. Health care suffered during the political upheavals of Mao Zedong's years in power. And in the age of reform it has remained underfunded and overburdened. Provision is still inadequate in rural areas while in urban areas the days of free healthcare are over. The number of cases of sexually transmitted diseases is increasing; so are the medical costs of pollution.

the old order

Formidable health-care tasks faced the new regime in 1949. China had undergone decades of war and revolution. The majority of its huge population lacked even a basic understanding of hygiene and sanitation. Finance, physical resources and trained personnel were all in short supply. There was a modern medical legacy of sorts: the KUOMINTANG had founded a national health administration in the 1920s, and MISSIONARIES, secular foreigners, and Western-trained Chinese doctors were at work in modern hospitals, most of them located in coastal areas and major cities. Yet when it came to meeting needs, these efforts barely scratched the surface.

In the countryside they did not even do that. Folk remedies and traditional medicines, some of proven efficacy, some of none, were deployed against a range of infectious, parasitic and endemic diseases, including plague, cholera, smallpox, malaria and tuberculosis. Tetanus – the result of non-sterile birth practices on the part of midwives – was widespread. Schistosomiasis, 'snail fever', affected one in ten south of the Yangtze in the first half of the century. Kala-azar disease, which attacks the liver and spleen and is transmitted by flies that live on dogs, was a common scourge in the north.

health and politics

The CHINESE COMMUNIST PARTY conducted health campaigns among those it ruled long before it conquered the country in 1949. After 1949 it launched a series of nationwide 'patriotic health movements' which stressed the link between sanitation and health; explained – and attacked – the causes of venereal disease; and mobilized millions to wipe out pests such as rats, flies, mosquitoes, and bedbugs. Immunization brought infections such as measles, diphtheria, and polio under control in all but remote regions. Ditches and ponds, breeding grounds for snail fever, were drained and the earth turned over.

As in other areas of life, the Communist government at first valued professionalism and expertise in the medical world. Chinese-, Western- and Soviet-trained practitioners were all esteemed, despite the fact that the length and complexity of their education tended to make them a breed apart. The mood changed with the GREAT LEAP FORWARD, when Mao came to regard 'experts' less reliable builders of socialism than 'reds' – those who lacked professional qualifications but were deemed politically sound. In principle the communal living at the heart of the Leap ought to have made it easier to deliver adequate health care. In fact, potential gains were soon outweighed by the famine, malnourishment and mass starvation that followed the catastrophic neglect of farming.

politics and health

Mao opened a new front against medical 'experts' in the run-up to the CULTURAL REVOLUTION. In 1965 he attacked the urban bias of China's health policies, accusing doctors of concentrating on building an elite, urban-based medical system. He demanded shorter, less sophisticated training programmes, a greater emphasis on practice, and the combination of traditional Chinese and Western medicine. The result was the 'barefoot doctor' movement.

Paramedics with perhaps six months of training, these shock troops of socialist health care fanned out into the countryside. By 1973 about one million of them were at work. Some barefoot doctors could perform quite complicated surgery. But the medical knowledge and diagnostic ability of many left much to be desired.

The demise of the communes and collective ideals made for major changes in health policy. Western practices and institutional forms returned in the new climate created by Deng Xiaoping's reforms. The cornucopia of traditional Chinese medicine was not neglected: its roots in traditional Chinese cosmology and, in many applications, proven efficacy ensured that. It retains its hold in the Chinese medico-scientific and popular minds, as well as a growing number of advocates in the West, because of its holistic, herbalist approach.

old diseases and new: the 1990s

Yet the emphasis of health care in the reform era has shifted from prevention to cure. And greater wealth, improved diets and changing social mores mean there is much to cure: the diseases of 'old' China are being replaced by those of the 'new'.

Or at least some of them are. The eradication of 'snail fever', long trumpeted as one of the Party's greatest feats in the countryside, was found to be illusory in the 1980s and 1990s. Parasites were back at work, stunting the growth and impairing the mental ability of millions whose villages had once been declared 'snail-less'. Outbreaks of hepatitis in Shanghai, bubonic plague in Heilongjiang, and diphtheria in Beijing raised scares of their own even though they were soon confined.

During the 1990s increasing numbers of Chinese caught – and died of – diseases afflicting people in the developed world: cardiovascular disease, cerebrovascular disease, diabetes and cancer. Greater consumption of meat and less of grains and vegetables has resulted in a higher incidence of obesity and an increase in the number of people suffering from high blood pressure.

The situation was, and remains, different in parts of the countryside, especially poverty-stricken areas and those inhabited by ETHNIC MINORITIES. In such regions during the late 1990s the infant mortality rate was found to be more than 50 per 1000 births, millions of children were underweight, and many more below average height. Per capita milk consumption was in the region of 6 per cent of the world average. Low levels of calcium intake led to a high incidence of rickets. Millions lived in areas of iodine deficiency, a deprivation which accounted for perhaps 80 per cent of China's 10 million mentally handicapped. Rural malnutrition, in all its forms, took a heavy toll.

smoking, AIDs and suicide

The same is true, but in this case throughout the country, of smoking. China is the largest producer and consumer of tobacco, and the government obtains about 20 per cent of its revenue from the tobacco tax. The Chinese Smoking and Health Association was formed only in 1990 and is far from an effective pressure group.

Surveys in the 1990s found that 63 per cent of men and 4 per cent of women smoked. The Tenth World Congress on Tobacco and Health, which met in Beijing in 1997, said about 700,000 Chinese died of smoking-related diseases each year, accounting for 14 per cent of the People's Republic's approximately five million annual adult deaths.

Acquired Immune Deficiency Syndrome (AIDS) made only a modest debut due, in part, to the Mainland's sexually conservative climate. But it made greater headway among the growing number of drug users, especially in YUNNAN, close to the border with BURMA. China reported its first case of AIDS in 1985. At the close of the century official figures put the number of confirmed carriers at 10,000 and the number of 'estimated' carriers at 400,000. A figure of 1.5 million was forecast for 2010.

As the 1990s came to a close, more indications emerged that rapid social and economic change was creating health problems of its own. The most obvious arose from serious air and water pollution, a bitter harvest of two decades of rapid economic growth. (See ENVIRONMENT.) Atmospheric pollution contributed to the growing number of deaths from pulmonary disease; the fouling of water supplies aggravated China's shortage of drinking water and increased its cost.

Less easily attributable to social and economic change, though not unconnected with them, was the Mainland's high rate of suicide during the 1990s compared with the world average. Suicide was not uncommon during the earlier years of Communist rule. For many it was a means to escape persecution during political campaigns. But the suicide rate increased in the reform era, a period of relative political relaxation. The World Health Organisation said in 1996 that about 2 million Chinese had committed suicide since 1990 – 40 per cent of all suicides worldwide. Unlike the situation in the West, more women killed themselves than men, and more suicides occurred in the countryside than in the city (see WOMEN).

Depression and various forms of neurosis seemed to be on the rise, too. It was difficult to estimate the size of a problem that carried political as well as cultural stigma. But Chinese experts forecast an increase in the incidence of mental illness as people are forced to cope with the stress of living in a rapidly changing society.

At the start of the new era China's health resources are struggling to meet the needs of the world's largest population, and one that is ageing rapidly (see POPULATION). The government's pledge to provide all of its citizens with preliminary health care from the start of the new century is threatened by figures showing a drop in the number of medical institutes, slow growth in the ranks of medical personnel, and persistent imbalance in urban and rural health services. About 80 per cent of the national health budget is spent in urban areas which account for perhaps one-third of the population.

Partly to rectify this imbalance, the government introduced a new urban medical insurance scheme in 1999. It required citizens to contribute towards the costs of health care once provided free by their DANWEI or socialist work units. Few opposed the allocation of more funds for rural health care. Few doubted that the Mainland's ailing state industries needed to shed their welfare obligations. But at the same time, few denied that a key element of socialism – at least as far as many urban Chinese had understood it – disappeared along with free health care.

Hebei Province

There is hardly a province of greater strategic importance to China than Hebei. It envelops the capital, BEIJING, and the great industrial centre of TIANJIN. It controls the passes to the Mongolian plateau in the north as well as overland access to LIAONING, JILIN, and HEILONGJIANG – the three Manchurian provinces in the northeast. Its coastal location, industry and rich agricultural plains make it one of China's most important economic regions. For all of these reasons, Hebei has been a key battleground in the struggle for China's destiny. For all of them, it will play a major role in the future development of the north and northeast.

the 'metropolitan province'

The KUOMINTANG government created the modern province of Hebei in 1928 after unifying China in the NORTHERN EXPEDITION. In Qing and early Republican times it was known as Zhili – 'direct rule' – a reflection of its status as the metropolitan province. Zhili held the keys to the capital and thus the country: its defence and development were primary concerns of every government in Beijing, imperial and, at least for a while, Republican.

In the late nineteenth century, these tasks fell to Li Hongzhang (1823–1901), the great reforming official. Li was governor-general of the province from 1870 to 1895, and again from 1900 until his death. This made him the chief official responsible for China's troubled relations with the foreign powers and equally troubled introduction of Western technology.

China's weakness meant Li presided over a shrinking empire. For a while he fell out of favour. But in 1900 the Court summoned him from semi-disgrace in the south to rescue it from a disastrous flirtation with the BOXER REBELLION. Back in his former domain, Li negotiated the Boxer Protocol of 1901, the final act in a political career which helped sustain the Manchus through numerous crises.

In Hebei, one of Li Hongzhang's lasting legacies is the coal-mining complex at Kaiping, near Tangshan, which was founded in 1877. Another is the province's first railway line, built to link the colliery with Tianjin. Other railways followed in the late Qing. The Beijing to Mukden (Shenyang), and Beijing to Wuhan lines were built with foreign capital while that from Beijing to Kalgan (Zhangjiakou), the gateway to Mongolia in

northeast Hebei was, unusually for the time, a solely Chinese project (see RAILWAYS).

This late Qing industrialization drive created an axis of communications in Hebei which continues to define the province more than a century later. It is based on the former TREATY PORTS of Tianjin (opened in 1861) and Qinhuangdao (opened 1898) – both of them leading foreign trade ports at the start of the twenty-first century – and the railways radiating out from the capital. Of these, the line heading south to Wuhan (completed in 1905) and on to Guangzhou remains the established artery between north and south China. It meets one of the earliest east–west lines in China proper (to Taiyuan, capital of SHANXI, completed in 1907) at Shijiazhuang, making this once inconsequential settlement, about 120 miles (192 kms) south of Beijing, into a major communications hub. It is Hebei's capital.

Li's successor as governor general of Zhili was YUAN SHIKAI, whose leadership of the Beiyang ('northern ocean') Army, the most powerful of the new military forces founded during the last days of the Qing, made him China's strongman after the REPUBLICAN REVOLUTION (see ARMIES). The army also spawned two of the warlord factions which struggled to control China after Yuan's death. One was the 'Zhili Clique', whose members included Feng Guozhang (1857–1919) and Cao Kun (1862–1938) (both of them, briefly, presidents), WU PEIFU and, on an occasional basis, FENG YUXIANG. The other was the 'Anhui Clique', led by Duan Qirui (1865–1936) (see ANHUI). Together with the 'Fengtian Clique' from Manchuria, these factions fought with and against each other for mastery of the national government in Beijing and the provinces beyond. Their constant infighting finally came to an end in 1928 when the Nationalist army occupied Beijing (see NORTHERN EXPEDITION).

struggle for mastery in 1930s, 1940s

The overriding strategic importance of Zhili came to an end, too, as did its very name. With China's capital relocated to Nanjing there could be no question of a metropolitan province in the north: Zhili became 'Hebei' and Tianjin capital of the new province. Parts of northern Hebei were incorporated into Rehe (Jehol) and Chahaer, two of the three

Mongolian provinces created in the Republican era.

Yet Hebei was still in the frontline, this time in China's deadly contest with Japan. In the early 1930s the Japanese military intervened in the province to eliminate threats to its puppet state of MANCHUGUO. The creation of a supposedly autonomous, but Japanese-controlled Hebei–Chahaer Council sparked protests in China; and the Marco Polo Bridge Incident of July 1937 at Wanping, 15 miles (24 kms) southwest of Beijing, led to full-scale war (see SINO-JAPANESE WAR). The conflict provided the context for a long struggle for control over Hebei between the Japanese, the Chinese Nationalists and the Chinese Communists.

The chief contenders were the first and last of these rivals; generally speaking, Nationalist power crumbled under Japan's initial assault. It left the Japanese in charge of most of Hebei's towns and lines of communications, and the Communists – operating from their newly formed base areas along the Shanxi–Hebei–Shandong–Henan and Shanxi–Chahaer–Hebei border regions – in control of remote country towns and much of the countryside (see CHINESE COMMUNIST PARTY).

The battle lines were fluid and the stakes high. For a few months local Nationalist and Communist forces cooperated against the invaders, and in 1938 Chiang even recognized the Shanxi–Chahaer–Hebei Border Region Government as part of China's formal administrative structure. But clashes within the Chinese camp brought the United Front to an end in Hebei earlier than elsewhere.

As the war continued, the Communists grew in strength, despite setbacks and harsh retaliations. In the mountains of west and north Hebei – and, when Japanese military weakness allowed, on the plains either side of the Beijing–Wuhan railway – they practised the techniques of peasant mobilization, rural administration and guerrilla warfare which made the Party an invincible force by the time of Japan's surrender. Several leading figures in the border region governments became leaders of the People's Republic after 1949. They included Nie Rongzhen (1899–1992) and PENG ZHEN, senior Party officials in the Shanxi–Chahaer–Hebei base area, and Liu Bocheng (1892–1986) and DENG XIAOPING, their counterparts in the Shanxi–Hebei–Shandong–Henan base further to the south.

Chiang managed to curb Communist power in Hebei during the early stages of the CIVIL WAR but could not make the province secure.

The Lie of the Land

Mountainous table land to the north and wide plains to the south: Hebei is divided topographically into two roughly equal parts. The mountainous north leads up to the Mongolian Plateau, an important source of trade but historically an even greater source of threat. The Great Wall snakes across the foothills of north Hebei, just a few miles from central Beijing. It meets the sea at Shanhaiguan on Hebei's border with Liaoning. Mountains define the western border, too: the Taihang range marks the frontier with Shanxi. One of Hebei's counties is sandwiched between Beijing and Tianjin. To the south, about 40 per cent of the province's 69,500 square miles (180,000 sq kms) occupy the great North China Plain which stretches into Shandong, Henan and beyond. The main crops are wheat, millet, maize, gaoliang, tobacco and cotton. At the close of the century Hebei's population was 66 million.

For more than a year he failed to evict his foes from Kalgan where they acquired valuable experience in urban administration. In November 1947 the Communists took Shijiazhuang. This gave them control over the railway, allowed them to create a single 'North China Liberated Area' from the two formerly separated base areas, and provided a home for the 'People's Government of North China', forerunner of the central government of the People's Republic.

In the final year of the Civil War the Party shifted its own nerve centre – which had been on the move since the temporary loss of YANAN in 1947 – into Hebei. MAO ZEDONG and the Party's central committee took up residence in Xibaipo, about 50 miles (80 kms) northwest of Shijiazhuang. There he and his commanders planned the great battles that delivered final victory over Chiang. The Chairman did not leave his enclave in rural Hebei until March 1949, two months after the People's Liberation Army had secured Beijing and made it ready to resume its role as China's capital.

north China heartland

The capital's new status as a province-level municipality directly under the central government meant there was no question of Hebei resuming its role as the metropolitan province. When Tianjin was granted the same rank, the province lost even more territory and prestige. Shijiazhuang, a comfortable distance from both of these much larger urban conglomerations, was made the provincial capital.

It has since become one of Hebei's major industrial centres. Others are Tangshan, the long-established mining and industrial city in the northeast – and site of the disastrous earthquake of 1976 said to have claimed 242,000 lives – Zhangjiakou, Baoding, southwest of Beijing, and Handan, near the border with Henan.

Hebei gained territory to the north of Beijing in the early 1950s when Chahaer and Jehol provinces were abolished. Geographically, this turned the province into a 'collar' around Beijing and Tianjin, the capital's chief outlet to the sea. Administratively, Hebei's writ does not extend to either city, and both municipalities overshadow the province economically as well as politically. As in the days of Zhili, Hebei's location makes it too important to be allowed a free rein.

This proved something of a disadvantage in the early years of the reform era. During the 1980s the provinces which prospered most tended to be those furthest from the capital, and those to whom Beijing granted the most power over foreign trade and finance. At first, Hebei enjoyed little freedom in either area. This was something of an irony in view of the fact that many of the major decisions on the economy during the 1980s were taken in Hebei, at Beidaihe, perhaps China's best-known seaside resort, where Party leaders traditionally hold their annual summer conclave.

However, the opening in 1984 of 14 coastal cities to foreign trade and investment on favourable terms helped spread the focus of economic growth into north China from its source in the southern provinces. Tianjin was one of the port cities, bringing new opportunities to its hinterland of Hebei. Qinhuangdao, Hebei's own port, was another. It has long been one of China's chief coaling ports as well as an important outlet to the sea for western Liao-

ning, INNER MONGOLIA and other parts of north China.

Hebei's long-term potential only became apparent in the 1990s when the central government encouraged the development of regional economies based on groups of provinces and, where appropriate, neighbouring foreign countries. In Hebei's case this means integration within the Bohai Gulf Economic Zone formed of parts of Shandong, Beijing, Tianjin and Liaoning, together with the various provinces that form their respective hinterlands.

One of Hebei's major contributions to this new macro region is ENERGY. Tangshan ranks among China's major coal fields while Dagang, to the south of Tianjin, contains oil fields of similar importance. China's largest offshore gas and oil reserves are found in the Bohai Gulf, off the coasts of Hebei and Tianjin.

Hebei's industry is no less important. At the close of the century, the province ranked sixth in the table of national output, contributing more than 5 per cent of China's total GDP. Less than 20 per cent of this was derived from agriculture, despite Hebei's traditional status as a granary based on its broad southerly plains.

At the start of the new era Hebei, including Beijing and Tianjin, encompasses a population of about 90 million people. They inhabit one of the most resource-rich, heavily industrialized and intensively urbanized parts of China. Communications in the region are almost second to none in the country. Hebei may no longer contain the keys to the capital in the narrow political sense. But it has a decisive role to play in the broader quest for development in and around the seat of Chinese political power.

Heilongjiang Province

Heilongjiang's history reflects 150 years of turmoil in the international politics of northeast Asia as well as the twists and turns of China's own revolution. RUSSIA was the dominant power in the late nineteenth century; JAPAN the master during the first half of the twentieth. Chinese rule was re-established in 1945 – but by the Communist Party, which ended years of rural exile by occupying the city of Harbin. Sino-Soviet cooperation in the 1950s gave way to border clashes in the 1960s. And in the 1990s the Russians returned, this time as traders and entrepreneurs.

foreigners and frontiers

Chinese settlement in the most northerly of three Manchurian provinces (the others are LIAONING and JILIN) during the nineteenth century occurred too little and too late to prevent Russia annexing half of it. Tsarist military adventurers found the cold wilderness of northeast China, which then extended as far east as the Sea of Japan, almost uninhabited. Russian settlers set about making it their own. In China proper Russian diplomats did the same. Both forced the enfeebled QING DYN-

ASTY to acknowledge that Chinese territory stopped at the Amur (the Heilong) and the Ussuri (the Wusuli). Heilongjiang has been truncated and landlocked ever since.

Russian encroachment intensified with the 'scramble for concessions' of the late nineteenth century (see TREATY PORTS). Its symbol was Harbin, present capital of the province. Beginning in 1898 the Russians turned this former fishing village into a railway town. It was the headquarters of the Chinese Eastern Railway, the Russian-owned line which provided the Trans-Siberian with a short cut to Vladivostok. A southern spur, later part of the Japanese-controlled South Manchurian Railway, extended to the port of Dalian in Liaoning (see RAILWAYS).

Russia acquired more than mere railway rights in the region. Tsarist troops guarded the length of the Chinese Eastern Railway as well as the mainly Russian mines and factories founded either side of it. Harbin even became a Russian army base during the Russo-Japanese War of 1904–5, a war whose outcome set limits to Tsarist expansion and inaugurated the era of Japanese control over Northeast Asia.

Japan did not acquire a firm grip on Heilongjiang until it created the 'puppet state' of MANCHUGUO in 1932. Until then, the city of Harbin remained an outpost of Russia – in both Tsarist and Soviet guises. At least 30,000 Russians lived in Harbin in the 1920s, and Russian-style churches and buildings, some of them still intact at the turn of the century, dominated the city. The Bolshevik Revolution brought a fresh flood of émigrés, some of them aristocrats who pursued their extravagant lifestyles on Chinese soil. However, the majority of White Russians were drawn from the opposite end of the social scale; life in their new home was hard.

While Russians formed the largest group among Harbin's foreign community the presence of Japanese, Koreans, Poles, French, Germans and Jews lent the city a cosmopolitan air reminiscent of SHANGHAI and other major treaty ports. There were none the less important differences between these cities. Harbin's location prevented it from exerting the same effect over the rest of China as Shanghai; it was less important economically; and its foreign presence was less obviously a symbol of modernity and object of nationalist resentment.

The creation of Manchuguo extinguished the remnants of Chinese rule over Heilongjiang and brought Soviet influence to an end.

Together with Liaoning and Jilin, the province was developed as a source of raw materials and manufactured goods for Japan's domestic economy. With the outbreak of the SINO-JAPANESE WAR in 1937, the region was geared completely to the Japanese war effort (see MANCHUGUO). There were many aspects to this, but none of them so notorious as Japan's use of Heilongjiang to develop chemical weapons. At 'Unit 731', a complex not far from Harbin, grisly experiments were conducted on human beings with a view to developing bombs capable of disseminating anthrax, tetanus and bubonic plague.

Communism takes hold, 1945–9

Under the terms of the YALTA CONFERENCE, Soviet troops liberated Manchuria in 1945 and garrisoned its major cities until early 1946 when Chiang Kai-shek's troops finally arrived. Two important developments occurred in the meantime. One was the rapid movement into the countryside of Communist forces under LIN BIAO. The other was the Soviet army's dismantling of much of Manchuria's industrial plant and its shipment back to European Russia as war booty.

In Heilongjiang a third, almost equally important event took place: the Chinese Communists occupied Harbin. For the first time since the Party had been forced into the countryside in 1927, it faced the problems of running a large, modern city of some 800,000 people.

Urban administration was not an easy matter. Crime was a problem in Harbin. So was public health. In 1947, 30,000 people died from bubonic plague transmitted by rats which Japanese scientists had infected and then released in 1945. Harbin's population had to be won over to Communist goals, and its labour force mobilized to assist in military campaigns against government forces.

The Party set about these tasks by organizing, disciplining and, where necessary, intimidating residents. Taxes were raised on luxury items and 'contributions' extracted for the war effort. Travel was restricted and other liberties curtailed. Tight control over the MEDIA accompanied these measures, which soon became hallmarks of Communist rule in all of China's great cities.

While the Party learnt the arts of urban rule in Harbin, Lin Biao transformed his guerrilla units into a conventional army and launched large-scale attacks on the Nationalist forces to the south. By the end of 1948, all of Manchuria

The Lie of the Land

The 181,100 square miles (469,000 sq kms) of Hei-longjiang – home to 38 million people at the close of the 1990s – consist of three largely mountainous areas and two extensive plains. The largest of these low-lying, fertile regions is the Song–Nen Plain, named after the two main rivers that run through the province. It is located south of the Greater Xingan mountains, which dominate northwest Heilongjiang, and the Lesser Xingan in the centre of the province. The Song–Nen Plain is part of the great Northeastern or Manchurian plain which stretches south into Liaoning. Main crops are wheat, maize, sorghum and soybeans, most of them produced on large, highly mechanized, state farms. The Three Rivers Plain, in the far east of the province, is where the Amur (Heilong), the Ussuri (Wusuli) and the Songhua meet. Long a border wasteland known as the 'Great Northern Wilderness', it was reclaimed after 1949. Over the years, massive Maoist-style campaigns of labour mobilization – including the use of rusticated Red Guards during the Cultural Revolution – have turned it into an important centre of agricultural production. Southeast Heilongjiang is the province's third mainly mountainous area.

was in his hands. From their nerve centre in Harbin and its surrounding countryside, the Communists won the first – and decisive – large-scale campaign of the CIVIL WAR.

strategic factories and state farms

In common with the other northeastern provinces, Heilongjiang was ripe for rapid development after 1949. It inherited a substantial industrial base and a sophisticated railway network from the Japanese, had abundant coal supplies and, given warm ties between Beijing and Moscow, benefited from Soviet aid and advice. Proximity to the Soviet Union and the zeal of Gao Gang (1895–1954), the leading official in the region until he was purged in 1954, were additional advantages.

By the early 1960s the province had become an important centre nationally for the production of coal, timber, cement, iron and steel, machine tools and precision instruments. Harbin, Qiqihaer (the former provincial capital), and Mudanjiang were major industrial cities. Heilongjiang's agriculture developed rapidly, too. The government built large state farms on the Manchurian plain. Rapid immigration from the rest of China provided the labour to work on them.

One of the most significant developments in the province during the early years of Communist rule was the discovery of a huge oil field at Daqing. The area, northwest of Harbin,

was explored first by Chinese and Soviet experts but the latter were unconvinced of the site's potential. The Chinese pressed on. During the early 1960s, while Beijing and Moscow were at ideological loggerheads, the Chinese discovered enormous reserves and built an oil town, largely from scratch (see ENERGY).

Daqing freed China of reliance on Soviet oil. Almost as important, it provided a political model for the rest of the country. For MAO ZEDONG Daqing embodied the self-sufficiency, mass mobilization and sheer willpower which distinguished Chinese Communism from its 'inferior' counterpart across the border. In 1964 he ordered industry nationwide to emulate its experience. The slogan 'in industry, learn from Daqing!' was the urban counterpart of 'in agriculture, learn from Dazhai!' – the call on farmers to copy the heroic feats of the model agricultural production brigade in SHANXI.

As a model of industrial development which allegedly combined an emphasis on class struggle with egalitarianism and self-sufficiency, Daqing survived until 1981, when the Party conceded it was flawed. It had overlooked the importance of material incentives, the lifeblood of the reform era. As a vital source of much-needed energy, Daqing has endured rather longer. At the start of the new era it is still the main source of China's oil, though an increasingly mature one.

from border clashes to border trade

Heilongjiang responded enthusiastically to Mao's call for a CULTURAL REVOLUTION. It was one of the first provinces to form a revolutionary committee, the new organs of power designed to steer China away from 'Soviet revisionism'. In 1969 the anti-Soviet struggle took a more serious form: Chinese and Soviet troops clashed at Zhenbao Island on the Ussuri (Wusuli), south of the Heilongjiang town of Raohe with heavy loss of life. It was the most serious in a series of confrontations which alerted the principals – and the rest of the world – to the dangers of full-scale war between the great Communist rivals. China's anxiety over security along its long frontier with the Soviet Union led it towards rapprochement with the United States.

Clashes on the scale of 1969, in which hundreds died, most of them Chinese, were not repeated, either in Heilongjiang or other provinces along the frontier. But border tensions endured for the next twenty years. Even in the late 1980s, arguments remained over the demarcation of the boundary and navigation rights along the Amur. They were not settled until the mid-1990s (see RUSSIAN FEDERATION).

By that time the Russians had returned to Heilongjiang. They did so as traders, many of them small-scale and most of them somewhat pale imitations of the Tsarist adventurers, White émigrés and Soviet experts who had preceded them. Many returned to Harbin. But they did not always find a warm welcome in the city built by their forefathers more than a century earlier. For some Chinese there was a certain satisfaction in seeing their erstwhile 'elder brothers' of socialism buying up cheap textiles and other fruits of China's vigorous brand of capitalism.

Trade of a more substantial kind between China and Russia has been conducted at Heihe, on the west bank of the Amur, opposite the Russian city of Blagoveshchensk, and Suifenhe on the Ussuri, about 85 miles (136 kms) north of Vladivostok. Both of these inland entrepôts have brought new sources of growth to previously closed border areas of Heilongjiang and Russia. Both have seen trade fluctuate as the economies of northeast China and the Russian Far East struggle to make the most of their respective comparative advantages. Partly for this reason Beijing expressed dis-appointment at the close of the 1990s over the failure of Sino-Russian trade to match up to the generally healthy state of political ties between the two countries.

During the mid-1990s Heilongjiang at last came to terms with the imperatives of domestic economic reform. This was a difficult matter for the same reasons it had been in Jilin and Liaoning: the province's economy was dominated by state-owned industries, most of them poorly placed to survive in the new climate of competition. Heilongjiang was even slower off the mark than its neighbours. As late as 1994, the state sector accounted for almost 70 per cent of industrial output, and the province's overall growth rate had fallen far behind the national average.

A turnround of sorts began shortly after ZHU RONGJI, then vice-premier, conducted a personnel shake-up when he visited the province in 1994. Heilongjiang's new leadership encouraged rapid growth in the collectively owned sector of the economy. By 1997 the state sector's share of industrial production had fallen to 50 per cent. This was a welcome development in the laggard of the northeast. But it was far from a transformation of the provincial economy. As with the rest of northeast China, this depends on a *fundamental* restructuring of Heilongjiang's state sector.

Henan Province

Few provinces have a better claim to be considered a 'core' area of China than Henan. It sits close to the geographical centre of 'China proper', the area traditionally inhabited by Han Chinese. It is the historic heartland of Chinese civilization. And it was for centuries the home of successive imperial capitals. In the modern era, many of the great dramas of China's modernization – rebellion, banditry, invasion, Communist revolution and the utopian zeal which often accompanied it – have been played out in the province with peculiar, often tragic, intensity.

floods, bandits and warlords

Historically, Henan's fortunes have depended on the Yellow River, which enters the province in the mountainous west and spills on to the North China Plain en route to the sea. Southeast Henan is drained by the Huai, a shorter river but one scarcely less prone to flooding. The vagaries of both rivers, and particularly the longer of the two, have tradition-ally made AGRICULTURE – and therefore life itself – precarious in Henan. Famine has done the same. Deluge and drought have both stalked the vast, fertile plains which make up almost two-thirds of the province, often casting its people into poverty and despair.

SECRET SOCIETIES and banditry flourished in this fragile ecology. For much of the Republican period large areas of Henan escaped formal government authority. Many were bandit lairs. In 'White Wolf' (1873–1914), Henan reared the most feared bandit leader of modern China. He and his forces roamed the plains and mountains of north China almost at will in the years following the Republican Revolution (see BANDITS).

Henan banditry did not die with White Wolf. It was sustained by the militarization of life which accompanied the rise of WARLORDS. Rival militarists fought bitterly for control over the province. They did so because of its traditional importance as a centre of grain production, and its new significance as the locus of a key railway junction. The north-south Beijing–Wuhan line (built in 1905) and the east–west Lianyungang–Xian line (completed in 1916) meet at Zhengzhou, now the provincial capital. Occupation of this once inconsequential town affords control over a vital communications link between north and south China, and between the coast and the hinterland (see RAILWAYS).

WU PEIFU was the first militarist to control the Henan railway network for any length of time. His rise to power in the province owed much to an alliance with the 'Red Spears', a secret society formed to resist taxation and so named because of the red flags its members tied to their spears. Wu later crushed the group. FENG YUXIANG, Wu's ally turned rival, was the second militarist to control the railway. Between them Wu and Feng ruled Henan throughout the 1920s. Their reigns were divided by the NORTHERN EXPEDITION.

In 1927 troops loyal to the Left wing of the KUOMINTANG moved north along the railway line from Wuhan and defeated Wu's forces. The Wuhan leaders then tried to win Feng to their cause. The 'Christian General' promptly demanded – and was given – control over all Henan. But in the great struggle within the Nationalist camp over the future of the Revolution, he sided with CHIANG KAI-SHEK in Nanjing rather than the Left in Wuhan. His decision tipped the scales decisively in Chiang's favour.

It did not lessen the rivalry between the two men. In 1929–30 their armies clashed in west Henan and elsewhere. Chiang emerged victorious but at the cost of yet more death and destruction. Heavy taxes, conscription and consumption of food stocks by the military were common throughout China during the warlord era. In Henan they were particularly severe. The province's merciless cycle of drought and flooding compounded the misery.

Chiang in charge

Chiang soon brought Henan under the control of his new central government in Nanjing. In 1932 his forces crushed the rural soviet the Communist Party had set up in the Da Bie mountains along the border with HUBEI and ANHUI (see CHINESE COMMUNIST PARTY). Its leaders, Zhang Guotao (1897–1979) and Xu Xiangqian (1901–90), escaped into SICHUAN, a prelude to the LONG MARCH of 1934–5. For a few years during the early 1930s, Henan was free of civil war if not of banditry.

The calm was both relative and temporary. In 1938, the second year of the SINO-JAPANESE WAR, Chiang blew up the dykes on the Yellow River at Huayuankou, a few miles north of Zhengzhou, in a desperate attempt to stop the Japanese advance. Militarily the move was a success: the invaders were forced to delay their attack on Wuhan. But diverting the Yellow River south across the province, where it flooded the Huai, caused huge losses. It had little effect on China's prosecution of the war. A more serious disaster struck in 1943: famine. Once again the deadly combination of drought, excessive taxation and official corruption took its toll – this time in the harsh conditions of war.

In 1942 drought killed all prospects of a good harvest in Henan, but had little impact on the desire of landlords for rent and officials for taxes. Starvation soon set in. The central government eventually managed to get supplies into the province via the unoccupied sections of railway, but it was too little too late. At least three million people starved to death in Henan amid reports of cannibalism.

The desperation of local people was clear in 1944: when Japan launched its massive *Ichigo* offensive in Henan, they attacked, robbed and killed fleeing Chinese soldiers. For many Chinese the handling of the famine showed that little could be expected from Chiang Kai-shek's government. Perhaps they would be better off with the Communists when it came to a choice between them and Chiang?

This, of course, was the issue in the CIVIL WAR. The conflict was waged widely and with considerable ferocity across Henan, the crossroads of central China. During the Sino-Japanese War, Communist guerrillas had returned to the Da Bie mountains in the south, and Henan's borders with SHANXI and HEBEI in the north. Nationalist troops cleared both areas in 1946 but not for long. By the end of 1947 the People's Liberation Army had returned in force, taking the nationwide fight against the government deep into the vital region between the Yellow and Yangtze Rivers. In 1948 first Luoyang and then Kaifeng, at the time the provincial capital, fell. By the middle of the year, the strategic heart of Henan was in Communist hands.

home of the Great Leap Forward

In line with other inland provinces, the new government targeted Henan for rapid industrial development after 1949. A new city was built in Luoyang, just west of the old one, to house a number of showcase projects, including the Number One Tractor Works built with Soviet assistance. A steel works at Anyang, served by nearby coalfields, began production in 1958. The coal mines at Pingdingshan, in central Henan, were developed to supply the giant Wuhan Steel works in the south. Zhengzhou, the railway town, was made the provincial capital. Its urban sprawl still blights the north China plain.

Yet agriculture remained the vital issue in this most fertile yet populous of provinces. And agriculture was central to the controversies surrounding China's development during the 1950s. As the decade came to a close MAO ZEDONG became disillusioned with the Soviet strategy pursued under the first Five Year Plan (1953–7). He sought a new, distinctly Chinese approach. It would be labour- rather than capital-intensive. It would depend on popular mobilization and participation rather than a professional bureaucracy and technical expertise. And it would deliver huge gains in production as well as the Communist ideals of equality.

Under Wu Zhifu (1906–67), the Mao loyalist in charge of the province, Henan responded enthusiastically to the Chairman's call for a GREAT LEAP FORWARD. In 1958 an area in the south of the province announced that it had merged several agricultural producers' co-operatives into a 'people's commune'. Henan was not the first province to do so: that accolade went to LIAONING. But Henan's zeal was the better known and, soon, the most disastrous.

The site of this revolutionary breakthrough was Chayashan, just west of Suiping on the Wuhan to Zhengzhou railway line in what was then Xinyang Prefecture. Other regions soon followed. Chief among them was Qiliying, halfway between Zhengzhou and Xinxiang, just north of the Yellow River, which Mao visited in August 1958. Asked to comment on developments in Henan, the Chairman described them as 'good'. It was the green light for the formation of communes throughout the country.

The famine which followed this nationwide pursuit of instant communism hit Henan particularly hard. Starvation, disease and death returned on a scale far exceeding that of the 1940s. Officials extracted almost every ounce of grain from the peasants to meet absurdly high harvest targets. The cruelties that accompanied requisition – many of them orchestrated by local leaders desperate to preserve the myth of plenty and the purity of Mao's

The Lie of the Land

The Yellow River is the dominant physical feature of Henan. It also gives the province its name – 'south of the river' – location of all but about one-sixth of its 64,500 square miles (167,000 sq kms). The river runs a perilous course through the Sanmen Gorges, on the border with Shanxi, and flows through Mengjin, where it enters the North China Plain. There it deposits the loess sediment it has borne from the west, fertilizing the land but also imperilling it. For long stretches, the river banks rise above the surrounding country, compounding the threat of floods with the prospects of a potentially more disastrous, long-lasting change of course: over the centuries, 'China's sorrow' has earned its name. Its recent drying up has brought different but equally serious problems for the parched plains of the north and their harvest of wheat, maize, soybeans, sweet potatoes, cotton and tobacco. Among China's provinces only JIANGSU has more plains as a percentage of total land area than Henan. Henan's mountains are mainly confined to the west, which marks the eastern extension of the Qinling range of southern SHAANXI. To the south is the Nanyang Plain, the second largest in the province. The Taihang mountains, separating Hebei from Shanxi, penetrate into the northern tip of the province, while the Dabie mountains straddle the boundary with Hubei to the south. The alluvial plains between these uplands are home to most of Henan's people, who numbered about 95 million at the close of the century.

vision – were unprecedented, even for Henan.

It took intervention by the military to end the famine in Xinyang. On Mao's order troops arrived in the region in 1961 and organized relief for the starving population. Estimates of the number of deaths range from 1 to 4 million. An investigation into what had gone wrong laid much of the blame on 'counter-revolutionaries' and 'class enemies'. In Henan as a whole, up to 8 million people may have died in the great famine.

The enforced, but cautious, retreat from the goals of the Leap did not mark the end of Maoist experiment in Henan. The CULTURAL REVOLUTION, the Chairman's most grandiose vision, lay ahead. It brought turmoil to the province as it did elsewhere. But Henan acquired particular revolutionary fame as the home of the 'Red Flag Canal'. It made the remote northern corner of the province a place of revolutionary pilgrimage and symbol of the self-sufficiency and transformative power of labour dear to Mao's heart.

Work began on the project, at Linxian, near the border with Shanxi, in 1960. It was designed to bring water from Shanxi's

Zhuozhang river, south to the arid north of Henan. By the time it was completed in 1972, thousands of workers had been mobilized to dig tunnels through mountains and carve canal routes out of rock faces. More than a hundred people lost their lives in the process. The canal was trumpeted as an extraordinary achievement – which it was. Only after Mao's death was it asked whether there might not have been cheaper, quicker and more efficient ways of bringing water into north Henan.

Certainly the community spirit responsible for the canal's construction did not long survive the new, competitive climate inaugurated by Deng Xiaoping's reforms. With the return of household farming, individual farmers rather than the collective had to pay for the water they took from the Red Flag Canal. Some opened sluice gates to avoid payment. Before long the authorities in Henan and Shanxi fell out over water rights. The Red Flag Canal dropped out of the public limelight and disappeared from the list of sites deemed suitable for visitors, Chinese and foreign.

economic reform, religious revival

Henan's rich agricultural resources, improved communications – including the construction of a second north–south rail link to the west of the original Beijing–Guangzhou line – and established, if somewhat outdated, industrial base helped make it one of the better performers among China's provinces during the 1990s. At the close of the decade it had the largest economy of all the inland provinces. Due to the elevation of CHONGQING to provincial status, which reduced the population of Sichuan by 30 million, it had the largest number of people, too. Overpopulation has made it less rich on a per capita basis than the size of its economy suggests.

Henan has been less successful on the FOREIGN TRADE AND INVESTMENT front. Indeed, its middle-ranking position among China's provinces as a source of foreign trade and destination for foreign capital betray the essentially closed nature of the local economy, twenty years after China opened its doors to the outside world. Beijing's plans to build energy and telecommunications projects in the interior, intensify the extraction of natural resources in central and west China, and direct foreign investment away from the coast, are designed to benefit Henan and other inland provinces.

Rapid change has accomplished much in Henan but left many areas of life untouched.

One of them is the apparent predisposition of its people to seek 'idealistic' or unconventional solutions to some of their problems. For many people, these problems remain those of survival and development in an overpopulated, harsh, and now increasingly competitive environment.

In the village of Nanjie, Linying county, the local community has sought refuge in a return to Maoist collectivism. A few families in the district prospered with the return of household farming in the early 1980s, but most did not. In 1986 they decided to pool their assets and resources. Ever since, the local economy has been run as an agricultural-industrial collective under tight Party control. Its inhabitants are richer than their neighbours yet adhere to the Maoist ideals of equality and political discipline of the pre-reform era. Marxist hardliners in Beijing have championed Nanjie as an alternative to the quasi-capitalism sponsored by Deng and his successor, JIANG ZEMIN. Unlike many other 'models' in Communist China, it had yet to be exposed as a fraud as the century came to a close.

Far more Henanese are seeking solace in religion rather than politics. CHRISTIANITY has flourished in parts of the province, particularly in the form of Protestant sects. Overseas church groups have responded by smuggling in religious materials and assigning covert MISSIONARIES to the province. In 1994, the government cracked down on such activities in Henan and elsewhere: new laws required all places of worship to register with the police and banned foreign missionary activity.

The revival of traditional Chinese RELIGIONS in Henan has been more remarkable still and of equal concern to the authorities. Officials and the local media complain about the large sums spent on temples and ancestral halls in the province. In particular they bemoan the fact that some temples honour upright officials from traditional times as well as Communist revolutionaries – a striking testimony to the eclecticism at the heart of Chinese popular religion.

Popular religious fervour and pockets of political idealism say much about the poverty and uncertain nature of life that has been the lot of so many in Henan for decades. The revival of these older 'gods' also reflects the death of more recent ones in the province – gods whose promise that plenty would arise from a new way of life often turned out to be one more disaster.

Hong Kong

Anomalies vie with superlatives, complexity with sensitivities, pragmatism with principle in the story of modern Hong Kong, once Britain's richest colony and, at the start of the new century, still wealthy, still free, despite an economic downturn and renewed embrace by Beijing. As the fruit of the Opium Wars, Britain's long occupation of Hong Kong was a humiliation for every Chinese government, imperial, Republican and Communist. As the richest, most stable, least 'political' part of China, it was admired by many Chinese and envied by more. As a meeting point between East and West, a 'neutral zone', in China yet not of it, Hong Kong was a drive belt for China's modernization during most of its life as a colony. Its fortunes depend on an ability to sustain this role as a Special Administrative Region (SAR) of the People's Republic of China. So do Beijing's: there can be few more important, or visible, tests of China's maturity than the way it treats the most modern, sophisticated part of its territory.

the founding: symbol of shame

The foundation of British Hong Kong occurred in three stages. Possession of Hong Kong Island in 1842 and of Kowloon Peninsula opposite in 1860 (both granted to the Crown in perpetuity) arose from China's defeats in unsavoury wars. Their proximate cause was the opium trade. They might more accurately be described as 'wars of diplomatic recognition': Britain forced a reluctant QING DYN-ASTY to engage in trade and diplomacy with the West according to prevailing *Western* principles of equality (see BRITAIN).

Acquisition of the much larger New Territories in 1898 was a result of the powers' 'scramble for concessions' (see TREATY PORTS; UNEQUAL TREATIES). It added 365 square miles (945 sq kms) of mountains, valleys and islands, and a thriving rural community, to the established possessions, extending the border of British territory a further 20 miles (32 kms) or so north into the province of GUANGDONG. It did so for just 99 years: those engaged in the 'scrambling' doffed their hats to the then fashionable idea that China would soon be strong again by leasing 'concessions' rather than demanding the freehold. When, rather belatedly, China lived up to expectations, the expiry of the New Territories' lease (on 30 June 1997) spelt the end for the *whole* of British Hong Kong.

The territory's unhappy origins scarred the collective psyche across the border. No other foreign power occupied such a large part of China for so long, or as a result of such humiliating circumstances, as Britain did Hong Kong. Every Chinese government during the twentieth century, though preoccupied by wars, reforms and revolutions, clung to the hope of recovering the territory, a goal finally secured by the Sino-British Joint Declaration of 1984.

The circumstances of Hong Kong's foundation mattered less to Chinese inhabitants of the territory. British rule was not welcomed. Occasionally it was resisted. But, over time, it was quietly appreciated. Foreign administration not only protected Hong Kong from continual upheavals across the border, it offered the positive advantages of efficient government and the rule of law. These were especially powerful lures after 1949, when the colony became a haven for casualties of Communist rule.

In the first half of the twentieth century, Hong Kong was closer to the Mainland economically, culturally and even politically than during much of the second. The territory's borders were porous. Trade, funnelled through the fine natural harbour that Britain made a free port, flowed across them. So did people. Hong Kong was not just a frontier town where East met West, it was a staging post for the Chinese diaspora. The desire to escape hardship at home often led through the colony, on to other British dependencies such as Malaya, other parts of Southeast Asia, or even further afield. Money, whether in the form of modest remittances or generous philanthropy, flowed back and forth along the same route (see OVERSEAS CHINESE).

Foreign administration, trade and the diaspora helped make Hong Kong prosperous, but they did not turn it into a great international Chinese city until later in the twentieth century. In the treaty port era, SHANGHAI followed, perhaps, by TIANJIN and Harbin (in HEILONGJIANG) were the great cosmopolitan centres in China. EXTRATERRITORIALITY and international concessions made these cities influential, if sometimes politically vulnerable, sources of modernization. Until the SINO-JAPANESE WAR, they were more important centres of finance and industry than sleepy Hong Kong, which, in the larger scheme of things, was simply the best port city in south China. It served its natural hinterland, Guangdong and GUANGXI, the two culturally homogenous, largely Cantonese-speaking provinces to its north. Hong Kong's most important relationship was with Guangzhou, the economic and political centre of south China.

Hong Kong in Chinese politics

If Britain's possession of Hong Kong grieved Chinese nationalists, the way it administered the territory often inspired them. Late Qing reformers saw in the colony's legal system, schools and colleges, modern civil service, business-friendly government and civil liberties, models for the rest of China. The racism that was part of British rule in Hong Kong, and other parts of the world before the Second World War, hurt and humiliated the Chinese, but it was seen as an inevitable feature of foreign rule. KANG YOUWEI, who escaped to Hong Kong after the failure of the 100 Days Reforms of 1898, was particularly impressed by aspects of British rule. He sought support from Chinese in the territory for his idol, the GUANGXU EMPEROR, a tragic figure whose attempt to transform the Manchu autocracy into a constitutional monarchy earned him the enmity of the EMPRESS DOWAGER and house arrest for the rest of his life.

Late Qing revolutionaries found the territory of more direct practical use. Under the protection of the British flag, they conspired with SECRET SOCIETIES, made bombs, published radical newspapers, and hired mercenaries before heading across the border to conduct insurrection. SUN YAT-SEN, who studied medicine in Hong Kong, was both an admirer of the territory's government and a professional conspirator who sought its protection.

The presence of revolutionaries and reformers in Hong Kong often attracted protests from Beijing and embarrassed the colonial government. In the 1890s, as would be the case almost a century later, China accused Britain of allowing Hong Kong to become a base for subversion against the central government. In both eras – and for much of the time between – the colonial government took the complaints seriously. An 1896 order banishing Sun from the territory (on the grounds that he was conspiring against a 'friendly neighbouring empire') was an early example. The rapid spiriting away to third countries of activists who fled to Hong Kong to escape persecution after the 1989 TIANANMEN SQUARE DEMOCRACY

MOVEMENT was a later one. Even when China was weak, Britain sought to insulate Hong Kong from political controversies across the border to avoid jeopardizing its relationship with Beijing.

Banishing 'subversives' was relatively easy. Preventing Hong Kong people identifying with political causes in the Mainland was impossible. If British administration offered a refuge from the excesses of Chinese rule, it did little to weaken Chinese nationalism in the territory. There was jubilation when the REPUBLICAN REVOLUTION ended Qing rule, even though Hong Kong's – and Sun's – role in the upheaval was less important than once seemed likely. And, if the excitement of the MAY FOURTH MOVEMENT of 1919 passed the territory by, the revolutionary nationalism fostered by the newly reorganized KUOMINTANG a few years later galvanized Hong Kong.

A seaman's strike in 1922, and a strike-boycott in 1925–6 shook the government, by then an object of nationalist attack rather than reformist admiration. Popular sentiment in the colony was outraged by the 'May 30th Incident' of 1925 in which British police in Shanghai shot and killed several protestors. It was incensed by a similar but more serious massacre in Guangzhou a few days later. Anti-British feeling swept through South China. For the first (and last) time, it engulfed Hong Kong. During the strike of 1925–6, up to 250,000 people left for Guangzhou where they enforced a boycott of British goods that wrecked Hong Kong's finances. The fervour subsided only when CHIANG KAI-SHEK clawed his way to the top of the National Revolutionary Government in Guangzhou and directed the revolution along more moderate lines. In 1928, Britain came to terms with the new order, recognizing the national government Chiang established in Nanjing, China's new capital.

conquest and coexistence

Hong Kong escaped the worst effects of Chiang's struggles against recalcitrant WARLORDS and Communist insurrection during the 1930s, but there was no escaping the consequences of Japanese aggression at the end of the decade. Refugees flooded into the colony (see JAPAN; SINO-JAPANESE WAR). China's trade, normally dispersed through mainland ports, concentrated in Hong Kong. For a few months, the territory was a lifeline for the Nationalist government as it fled west to escape the Japanese advance. Japan's occupation of Guangzhou in October 1938 checked

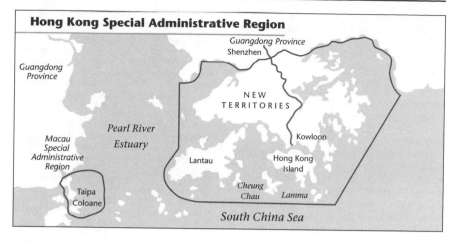

Hong Kong Special Administrative Region

the flow of weapons into the Mainland, and Tokyo's warnings of dire reprisals should it continue stopped supplies of every kind. Britain wanted to help an otherwise isolated China, but not if it meant losing Hong Kong to Japan. This, however, is exactly what happened.

The surrender of Hong Kong in December 1941, after a short, grisly battle, was a humiliation for Britain. Worse, as the United States' fatal attachment to Chiang Kai-shek intensified, it looked as though the territory might be returned to China after the inevitable defeat of Japan. Washington insisted that China was a 'great power'. America's and Britain's relinquishment of extraterritoriality in 1943 appeared to confirm it. The age of empire seemed over. If one key aspect of the Unequal Treaties could be abolished, why not another: British sovereignty over Hong Kong?

It did not happen because Chiang, though determined to recover the territory, was more concerned to defeat the CHINESE COMMUNIST PARTY. This required good relations with the United States whose leaders, tiring of their ally, were more ready to offend China over the future of Hong Kong than Churchill. In August 1945, Admiral Harcourt, commander of Britain's Pacific Fleet, sailed into Hong Kong to accept the Japanese surrender and restore British rule. What local people thought about this was suggested by the fact that only a few Union Jacks were visible among the numerous Chinese flags that fluttered over Hong Kong as the liberators entered the harbour.

If the start of CIVIL WAR in China saved British rule in Hong Kong, the outcome soon threatened it. The Communist victory in 1949 brought a new kind of military and political power up to the colony's borders. More nationalist than the Nationalists, and certainly more powerful, the Communist Party refused to recognize the Unequal Treaties and therefore the legitimacy of Britain's position in Hong Kong. There were some anxious moments in the colony at the end of 1949 as the PEOPLE'S LIBERATION ARMY (PLA) pushed south from Guangzhou. Britain, already concerned about the loss of its commercial interests in the Mainland, was not ready to retreat from Hong Kong.

In the event Communist troops stopped at the Shenzhen River, the established frontier. But that only emphasized the anomaly of British rule to the south – especially as, both then and since, Hong Kong depended on the Mainland for its economic well-being. The KOREAN WAR made Britain's continued presence at the tip of the People's Republic even more sensitive. In 1950, British troops were sent from Hong Kong to fight Chinese forces in Korea, and the colonial government imposed an embargo on much of the trade with China.

Despite this conflict, and the strident anti-imperialism at the heart of 'New China's' ideology, Communist troops did not cross the border into Hong Kong at any time before the restoration of sovereignty in 1997. No less remarkable, Beijing rarely stirred up trouble on the territory's streets during the same period. Even during the riots of 1966 and 1967, which were partly inspired by the CULTURAL REVOLUTION, neither the Communist government nor its supporters in Hong Kong demanded Britain return the colony to China. Rendition was raised first in the early 1980s, in the context of Sino-British diplomacy. Until then, Beijing refused to recognize the legitimacy of Britain's position in Hong Kong but declined to challenge it physically.

There are fewer mysteries about this now than once seemed the case. Had China marched into Hong Kong it would have created diplomatic problems at a time when there were pressing revolutionary tasks at home. It would have deprived Beijing of a valuable window on the outside world. It would have cut the People's Republic off from its most important source of foreign exchange. And it would have gone down badly with Chinese in Hong Kong and elsewhere.

The consequences of Beijing's restraint were even clearer than its causes. They paved the way for an informal *modus operandi* between Crown Colony and revolutionary state. It was reflected in mutual non-recognition of each other's position over the territory, tempered by a desire – despite frequent verbal hostility and minimal formal cooperation – to preserve the status quo until circumstances permitted a more comprehensive resolution. A practical manifestation of this was China's continued supply of food and water essential to the colony's well-being, and Britain's refusal to countenance significant political reforms of the kind that might make Hong Kong a theatre for China's unfinished civil war, or encourage its people to believe they could gain independence. Many of the terms of this unspoken 'deal' did not come under real strain until the mid-1980s.

'made in Hong Kong'

But if British rule survived the emergence of revolutionary China, Hong Kong itself soon changed beyond recognition, particularly in its role and relationship with the Mainland. In the space of a few years, the once sleepy port city, now increasingly cut off from its hinterland, became a manufacturing centre. Later still it became a trade, transport and financial hub for the rest of China on a scale that would have surprised the most imaginative of its nineteenth-century founders. It did all of these things as an outpost of freedom and political stability on the edge of a country

The Lie of the Land

Geography has made a spectacular diversity out of the 423 square miles (1,095 sq kms) of Hong Kong, dividing them into clusters of small islands and several much larger ones; scoring deep channels between them that lead to one of the world's finest harbours; and creating the rugged peninsula of Kowloon and the once rural hinterland of the New Territories stretching up to the border. Man has touched and transformed nearly every piece of this dazzling mosaic, reclaiming more than 23 square miles (60 sq kms) of land in the zeal to accommodate a restless, ever-growing city. The Hong Kong Island skyline, a belt of breathtaking office towers and apartment buildings that march up the steep slopes towards Victoria Peak, speaks of the territory's wealth and modernity.

So, in different ways, do the hundreds of vessels at rest in the roads to the west, and the planes descending into and taking off from Chek Lap Kok airport just north of Lantau, Hong Kong's largest island. On Kowloon side, the peninsula has been reshaped by landfills and reclamation needed to provide road and rail links for the new airport. To the east new buildings are rising on the finger of land that juts into the harbour, location of the former, Kai Tak, airport. Further inland, the rural peace of the New Territories has been shattered by the construction of new towns housing over 21 million people. In the west, container dumps and car-breaking yards disfigure the landscape. Only in the east of the New Territories are there still miles of unspoilt countryside. There, soaring peaks, quiet bays, and even a few hamlets can be found untouched by the ravages of change that have washed over Hong Kong and its almost 7 million people.

convulsed by Mao Zedong's revolutionary excesses. More than ever before, Hong Kong lured Mainlanders south with the promise of freedom from politics and the chance of material improvement – goals sought by millions of Chinese, but realized only rarely in the Mainland during the twentieth century. The journey across tightly guarded borders or shark-infested waters was often dangerous, but the flow was virtually continuous, and almost exclusively one-way.

The first exiles from revolutionary China were the most numerous. About 700,000 arrived in the first half of 1950 alone. A further 1.3 million followed during the course of the decade. So large an immigrant community strained Hong Kong's every resource. Most arrivals lived in appalling physical conditions. The Korean War trade embargo thwarted the colony's recovery. Economic misery seemed set to continue. Many of the new arrivals must have wondered if their journey was worthwhile.

The doubts did not linger. Thanks to the upheavals on the Mainland, Hong Kong received an influx of capital and expertise as well as labour. Much of it came from Shanghai, where the Communists rapidly emasculated private business and drove out the city's commercial elite. Hong Kong was the preferred destination for many of its members, including Y. K. Pao (1918–91) and C. Y. Tung (1912–82) (father of TUNG CHEE-HWA), rival shipping tycoons, and the family heads of the city's great textile firms. Shanghai capital and expertise, combined with local and refugee labour from almost every part of China, made a dynamic economic mix. It was to make millionaires out of many of modest birth, including Li Ka-shing (1928–), from Chaozhou in Guangdong, whose late twentieth-century commercial empire was founded on a factory that produced plastic flowers in the 1950s. Hong Kong became a major manufacturing centre, firstly of textiles, then of artificial flowers, and later of basic electronics. Its products flowed into Southeast Asia, Japan, the United States and Europe. The colony remained a producer of increasingly sophisticated goods until the late 1980s, when businessmen relocated their factories across the border to escape high costs and exploit the cheap labour of their compatriots.

The government's contribution during these years of hardship and growth was to let business take care of business, a philosophy it modified later in the century but declined to abandon. The authorities taxed lightly and spent little: Hong Kong escaped the fascination with social welfarism which captivated Labour and Conservative governments in Britain during the 1960s and 1970s. The watchwords were 'positive non-interventionism' – a doctrine which made Hong Kong a laboratory of free market principles, and confirmed the theorems and prejudices of more than one leading Western economist and politician. The less agreeable aspects of this were the atrocious labour conditions, crude housing, and inadequate provision for health and education which endured until the early 1970s.

Some of these factors were behind the rare outbreaks of unrest in Hong Kong. In 1956, Kuomintang and Communist activists took their war on to the shabby streets of Kowloon and Tsuen Wan. Ten years later, China's supporters in the colony – and many young people inspired by the almost world-wide revolt of youth during the 1960s – took on the authorities in a series of strikes and protests.

Inspired by the Red Guards of Guangzhou, some rebels began a bombing campaign. There were shootings and killings along the border. About 50 people were killed during the unrest. Many more were injured. Scores of activists were arrested, provoking a crisis in relations with Beijing which resulted in the destruction of Britain's diplomatic mission in the capital.

The events of 1956 and 1966–7 were nasty but nowhere near as serious a threat to Britain's position in the territory as the great strike-boycott of 1925–6. One reason for this was China's unwillingness to extend the Cultural Revolution into the colony. The water and food kept flowing, despite the rhetoric of anti-imperialism. Equally important, most Hong Kong people seemed to side with the authorities and, in the first instance, the police. The 'Motherland' was going through its least attractive phase. There was a growing sense of identity with Hong Kong and its peaceful, increasingly prosperous way of life. To rebel might be justified across the border; in Hong Kong, conformity seemed the better option.

This feeling of 'belonging' grew in the 1970s, a crucial decade which reshaped the political, social and economic as well as the physical contours of Hong Kong life. Generational change was one of the factors at work here: by the late 1970s, those born in Hong Kong began to outnumber the immigrants. The new generation were true Hong Kongers with only the weakest of ties to their parents' homeland. New opportunities for education, massive housing provision and the creation of new towns in the New Territories added to the sense of community and identity.

The economy kept growing, too. Manufacturing became ever more sophisticated, its output shipped abroad ever more efficiently thanks to an impressive new network of tunnels, road and rail links at home and improved air and sea communications with partners overseas. China's opening to the United States, followed by an improvement in ties with Britain, banished some of the Cold War atmosphere that had been a natural feature of life in a capitalist outpost on the edge of an unstable Communist empire. The border between Hong Kong and the Mainland remained sealed, save for carefully rationed family visits and occasional 'friendship delegations'. And the colony's economy, like its general approach to life, was still oriented outwards, towards the rest of the world, rather than inwards, towards the People's Republic.

But China, always a heavy if sometimes unspoken presence hovering over Hong Kong, was rapidly becoming a 'factor' in the territory – one that would soon make it rich beyond measure, and determine its political future.

the 1997 issue

After the Second World War, concern over the future of Hong Kong made at first fleeting and then firmer impressions on the British official mind. Almost from the start, the strong possibility that the colony, or at least the New Territories, would have to be returned to China in 1997 was recognized. But it was not certain. Perhaps it could be avoided? Even if it could not, question marks remained over the precise terms of rendition. In Beijing, there seemed less haste, less concern with the details, but more certainty. There was no question that China would take Hong Kong back: it was a matter of when, not whether. As for the terms, they concerned Chinese territory and were for China to dictate.

Decolonization elsewhere in the 1950s emphasized the anomaly of Britain's presence in Hong Kong. The end of the empire in Southeast Asia made the territory a true outpost, one with negligible value to a Britain painfully adjusting to life as a second-rank power. Hints of disengagement came in a series of nationality acts, beginning in the early 1960s, which rescinded the right of abode in Britain once enjoyed by citizens of the British empire. The people of Hong Kong were principal casualties of this and subsequent anti-immigration legislation.

The People's Republic, on the other hand, though still not free of its revolutionary obsessions, seemed destined to make a much bigger mark on Hong Kong and the world beyond. In 1971, Beijing acquired China's seat at the UNITED NATIONS. The following year, it secured the removal of Hong Kong and MACAU from the list of colonial territories maintained by the UN Committee on Decolonisation. Hong Kong and Macau were not 'colonial territories' destined for independence. They were parts of Chinese territory occupied by imperialists. China would settle their fate at an appropriate time.

These developments added to a feeling, at least in some quarters, that the clock had begun to tick for Hong Kong with new urgency. The expiry of the New Territories lease, though still years away, concentrated minds. There was some concern that a time bomb rather than a simple timepiece might be ticking away in the territory. Hong Kong was a 'British Dependent Territory', but it depended increasingly on the Communist Mainland, not Britain, for its economic well-being. The overwhelming majority of its people were not true British subjects, but neither were they true Chinese subjects, even though Beijing regarded them as such. Many were exiles from Communism; all were beneficiaries of British freedoms. It looked increasingly likely that they would have to be handed back to the country from which many had fled and which most still feared. There were rich possibilities for trouble here – for all concerned.

sealing the future

The need to prepare Hong Kong for the future, whatever form it might take, raised questions about the territory's governance – questions which had been avoided since the late 1940s when political survival, economic growth, and coexistence with revolutionary China were foremost in colonial minds. Changes *within* Hong Kong threw up similar challenges to the old order. During the 1970s, local Chinese businessmen competed with and often eclipsed their British counterparts in a series of boardroom coups and canny acquisitions which propelled them to the top of the local elite. Foreign dominance of the economy and society was at an end. The ever-changing skyline of the Central business district testified to this social revolution: the architectural symbols of new money began to tower physically, as well as financially, over old.

For the most part this simply meant new faces at the top: the business sector, Chinese or British, presented little challenge to the established administration. Members of Hong Kong's emerging middle class made more fundamental demands of their rulers. The territory was coming alive politically, both as a result of growing concern over the future and what might be called the natural evolution of society. Hong Kong people were becoming richer and better educated. They lived in a free society, but not a democratic one. Some wanted a greater say in their affairs, and searched for the local leaders and political parties that alone could give them a voice. Such demands vexed both the current and future sovereigns.

With good reason. When Britain and China first broached the subject of Hong Kong's future – during a visit in 1979 to Beijing by Governor Murray MacLehose – the territory was ruled essentially as it had been since the Second World War. Plans by Governor Mark Young in the late 1940s to introduce an element of representative government had fallen foul of the local elite. Power resided in the governor, appointed by London, who exercised his authority in consultation with an executive council, or cabinet. An unelected, but supposedly representative, legislative council turned the wishes of the executive into laws, sometimes after arguments, more often as a result of further consultation. Common Law and civil liberties protected citizens from arbitrary government at home while MPs at Westminster, though rarely exercised by affairs in distant Hong Kong, acted as 'long stop' against colonial misrule.

There was no denying that this system served Hong Kong well during the 1950s and 1960s. And there was little doubt that it needed modifying in the light of the territory's uncertain future and growing demands for change from a section of the community. Where doubt – and soon distrust and division – entered the scene was over the pace, extent and nature of any changes in the government of Hong Kong. This became a principal issue in the Sino-British talks which culminated in the signing of the Joint Declaration in 1984, and in the bitter struggle between Britain and China over the territory that followed.

However, Britain's opening position in the 'talks about talks' that began in 1982 was one of resistance to China's repeated declarations that it would resume sovereignty over Hong Kong on 1 July 1997. Not to resist would make talks about the territory's future pointless. Yet resistance merely made talks impossible, and added to anxieties in Hong Kong. Britain conceded on the question of sovereignty, only to argue that Hong Kong's prosperity after 1997 depended upon continued British *administration*. This was enough to get formal talks started in March 1983 but not enough to stop them becoming bogged down in acrimony six months later. Beijing said sovereignty and administration were inseparable. Confidence in the colony evaporated, driving the value of the Hong Kong dollar down to perilous levels. In October 1983, the government came to the rescue with an imaginative plan pegging the Hong Kong dollar to the US dollar at a fixed rate of HK$7.8:US$1.00. The 'peg' protected the currency throughout the unsettled times that followed, and survived massive speculative attacks during the Asian financial crisis at the end of the century.

Governance

Hong Kong is the first Special Administrative Region (SAR) of the People's Republic of China. It is governed by the Basic Law, whose 160 articles, associated annexes, 'decisions' and 'explanations', promulgated in 1990 after almost five years of carefully controlled consultations, give expression to the principle: 'Hong Kong people ruling Hong Kong'. They grant the territory a 'high degree of autonomy', and the right to manage its own affairs in everything save defence and diplomatic relations. Hong Kong's economic system, laws, freedoms and entire way of life built up under British rule are to remain unchanged for 50 years from 1997 – that is until 1 July 2047. There is no provision for the period after this date. One of Beijing's aims in the Basic Law was to replace British colonial rule with an executive-led system that closely resembled it. The principal change would be that of 'faces' and flags: Hong Kong Chinese would replace Britons in top government posts, and China's national flag and the SAR's regional flag would replace those of the United Kingdom and the Crown Colony of Hong Kong. This is what happened on 1 July 1997 with the change of sovereignty.

But the Basic Law also provides for the development of democracy, if only at a pace designed to keep power in the hands of the executive and, ultimately, Beijing. Whereas British governors were appointed by the Queen on the recommendation of the prime minister, chief executives of Hong Kong are elected by a committee. Its members are drawn from different sections of the community but are essentially Beijing appointees. The Basic Law declares that selection of the chief executive by universal suffrage is an 'ultimate aim', but does not provide for such a development to be considered before the year 2007. Universal suffrage in elections for the legislative council is also an aim but again there is no provision for this in the first ten years of the SAR's life. During that time legislators are to be returned through a mixture of direct and indirect elections of the kind designed to check the power of grassroots politicians in favour of special interest groups and the business elite.

Time constraints aside, there can be no change to the methods of selecting either the chief executive or the legislative councillors unless two-thirds of legislators and the chief executive himself approve. Moreover, the power of interpreting the Basic Law rests, not in Hong Kong, but the Standing Committee of the National People's Congress, the same national parliament in Beijing whose standing committee in 1999 overruled the Hong Kong Court of Final Appeal on the question of Mainland immigration to the SAR.

When Britain agreed, as it soon did, to talk about Hong Kong's future on China's terms, all pretence of a British role after 1997 was abandoned. The task of the British negotiators was to fill in the huge gaps contained in Beijing's blueprint for its future 'Special Administrative Region'. The formation of Special Administrative Regions (SARs) had been provided for in the 1982 Constitution of the People's Republic with a view to unifying the country. Beijing hoped TAIWAN would elect to be China's first SAR, but Hong Kong, though a lesser prize, could be accommodated happily on the same terms. These were encapsulated in the phrase 'one country, two systems', the formula devised by DENG XIAOPING under which Hong Kong people would rule Hong Kong, the territory would enjoy a high degree of autonomy, and its capitalist way of life, basic freedoms and rule of law would remain unchanged for 50 years. Beijing would be responsible solely for the territory's foreign and defence affairs. These principles were fleshed out in the Sino-British Joint Declaration on the Future of Hong Kong, initialled in Beijing in September 1984 after 22 punishing rounds of talks.

economic plenty, delayed democracy

The Joint Declaration satisfied the needs of all parties. For China it promised recovery of a long lost territory on terms that would preserve its enormous wealth and energy – attributes vital to Deng's new reform drive. For most people in the territory, it solved the problem of the future by apparently ignoring it: Hong Kong would have a different flag after 1997 but, under the one country, two systems formula, little else would change. For Britain, the accord secured relief from a colonial burden under conditions far more promising than had once seemed likely. Intriguingly, the Joint Declaration bound China to behave in a certain way in its own territory, principally by ensuring that Beijing's political, legal, social and economic authority stopped at the borders of Hong Kong. The People's Liberation Army would have a garrison in Hong Kong. A local Chinese chief executive, not a British governor, would rule Hong Kong. But in other respects, excluding the issue of sovereignty, the territory would come to resemble a treaty port or international concession of an earlier era.

Of course, there were nagging doubts about whether China would keep its word. The Communist Party was still in charge in Beijing. Marxism remained the dominant ideology, socialism the avowed goal. But economic developments suggested otherwise. Trade between China and the outside world grew rapidly. Foreign investment poured in. Even

before the territory's fate was sealed, Beijing set up SPECIAL ECONOMIC ZONES on the southern coast in an effort to absorb and replicate the Hong Kong experience. The chief of them, SHENZHEN, was just across the border. China seemed irrevocably committed to capitalist ways.

Once a Cold War frontier, the border between the Mainland and Hong Kong opened up on a scale not seen since the early 1950s. People, goods and money flowed into the Mainland, seeding an industrial revolution in the Pearl River Delta and far beyond (see GUANGDONG). Hong Kong life styles and Hong Kong living standards – or at least the pursuit of them – spread far inland. The effects on Hong Kong were as remarkable as those to the north. The territory became the trade, transport and financial centre for a rapidly modernizing China. It was the primary link between the People's Republic and the outside world; and the chief conduit for growing, yet indirect contacts between the Mainland and Taiwan. In both relative and absolute terms Hong Kong eclipsed the Shanghai of the 1930s in its contribution to China's GDP, the amount of China trade it handled, and its contribution to China-bound foreign investment (see FOREIGN TRADE AND INVESTMENT). By the mid-1990s it was the first colony in the history of Britain's empire to grow richer, on a per capita GDP basis, than the metropolitan country. Its wealth, apparent everywhere from skyline to subway, made Hong Kong as mighty an international city as Venice and Amsterdam in their heyday.

Yet for all its abundance, Hong Kong lacked something rather important. Though a prosperous, free international city, history decreed it could never become a city-state. The 'high degree of autonomy' promised in the Joint Declaration was not to be sneezed at, but it fell far short of independence. Moreover, this autonomy had yet to be defined. The Joint Declaration called for a legislature 'constituted by elections'; it did not say how this was to be achieved.

Britain's belated, cautious move towards representative government in Hong Kong began in 1985 with the introduction of indirect elections for 24 of the 57 seats in the legislative council (Legco). The next step was direct elections, possibly in 1988. But this was a step too far, too fast for Beijing and its allies in the territory, who were then drafting the Basic Law, the post-1997 constitution. What China had promised in 1984 to preserve in 1997 was the system Britain had relied on to rule Hong Kong for 150 years: an executive-led government in which 'politics' in any form were kept to a minimum. Sudden conversions to democracy in the twilight of empire were regarded with suspicion and condemned. Hong Kong was gaining autonomy in 1997, not independence. Fatefully, Britain complied: it pledged to confine constitutional development during its last ten years of rule to the pattern set out in the Basic Law. 'Convergence' became the watchword in the interests of a smooth transition.

If this could be justified during one of the phases of optimism about the future of China's great reform experiment, it looked less wise following the suppression of the Tiananmen Square Democracy Movement. The calls for more democracy and less corruption which engulfed nearly all of China's major cities in the spring of 1989 inspired Hong Kong. They reawakened the sense of identity with developments on the Mainland experienced by earlier generations in the territory. Hong Kong people rediscovered they were Chinese, too. Thanks to the Joint Declaration, they were destined to become so in a new sense after 1997. If only some of the cries for change in Tiananmen Square could be answered, the transition would be an even better prospect than many had dared hope. The territory was at one with the protests to the north. Hundreds of thousands took to the streets in their support. They donated money and materials to the cause. And when the cause died on 4 June, Hong Kong's hopes died with it.

So did Beijing's once fairly rosy views of the territory. Humiliated by the students they felt compelled to crush, bruised by the reaction in the West, and worried over the collapse of Communism in Eastern Europe, Party leaders regarded Hong Kong as a source of unwelcome 'subversion' as well as much-needed capital. Like their Qing dynasty predecessors a century earlier, they demanded that Britain curb the activities of those opposed to the central government. They also insisted on modifications in the Basic Law, then going through the final stages of its drafting process. A new clause was added outlawing subversion. MARTIN LEE and Szeto Wah (1931–), a fellow democrat and supporter of the Tiananmen protests, were expelled from the committee preparing the document.

All this was too much for Xu Jiatun (1916–), head of the local branch of the New China News Agency (Xinhua), Beijing's de facto embassy in the colony. He concealed neither his admiration for Hong Kong's way of life, describing capitalism as one of mankind's greatest inventions, nor his support for the protestors in Beijing. When the latter were crushed and the former seemed threatened he fled to the United States, the most senior member of the Chinese Communist Party ever to flee to the West. Xu's replacement, Zhou Nan (1927–), had an almost visceral dislike of the British that did little for his standing in the non-partisan local community but assured him of support in Beijing.

It was left to Britain to try to repair Hong Kong's damaged confidence. Governor David Wilson, an historian of earlier crises in Sino-British relations now obliged to deal with one of his own, persuaded London to offer UK passports to 50,000 heads of households in Hong Kong. The idea was to root them in the colony rather than risk them joining the emigration queues bound for Canada, the United States or Australia. He also announced plans to build a much needed new airport. It would be a highly ambitious, expensive project designed to instil confidence in the future. Finally, Wilson introduced a Bill of Rights in an effort to entrench after 1997 personal freedoms taken for granted under British rule. China condemned all three measures. At best they were unnecessary. At worst they were British plots to weaken China's control over the territory after 1997 and exhaust its financial reserves. The post-Tiananmen pall over Hong Kong endured. Prospects of a breakthrough on the airport were raised by the visit to Beijing in 1991 of John Major, British prime minister. But they were dashed a year later by a much bigger struggle over the political reforms of CHRIS PATTEN, Hong Kong's last and most controversial governor.

Patten, the political governor

Governing Hong Kong during the final phase of its transition from Crown Colony to Special Administrative Region was always going to be difficult. Tiananmen made it tougher still. A host of unsettled issues, including the airport, greeted the new governor when he arrived in 1992. But the most important concerned arrangements for elections in 1995, the last under British rule and the first to return all 60 members of the legislative council, many of them officials or appointees of the governor under the old order. China had promulgated the Basic Law in 1990. The test facing Patten, a senior politician with little experience of China and less admiration for the way British Foreign Office mandarins handled relations with Beijing, was that faced by the previous administration: ensuring that voting arrangements 'converged' with the Basic Law. The new governor said his dramatic widening of the franchise passed the test. Beijing said it failed. Disagreement over this issue cast a cloud over the final five years of British rule in Hong Kong.

A cloud but not darkness. The war of words between Beijing and the governor rattled the stock market and alarmed the business community. Agreement on the airport, commercial contracts, and other issues related to the handover was held up. There were moments when it seemed China's name-calling might escalate into rasher actions. But on the Mainland, much bigger forces were at work than arguments over the pace of democracy in Hong Kong. The new reform drive begun by the ailing Deng Xiaoping at the start of 1992 galvanized China's economy and, with it, the demand for goods, services and expertise Hong Kong alone could provide. However grim relations between Britain and China might be, the territory's economy kept growing.

Sixteen rounds of Sino-British talks failed to secure agreement on Patten's electoral reforms. Essentially, these made fairer and less predictable the outcome of voting in an electoral college and 'functional constituencies' where people voted according to their profession. Patten did not increase the number of seats open to direct elections beyond the 20 provided for in the Basic Law. The issue at the heart of the dispute was control. Beijing wanted elections that would ensure success for the 'right' candidates, principally those other than the Democrats led by Martin Lee. Patten wanted the largest possible electorate because he was a democrat himself, and because he was an admirer of Hong Kong's Democrats, whom previous polls showed to be the territory's most popular party.

So they proved in the 1995 elections. The Democrats and their allies formed a narrow majority in the 60-seat chamber. The Democratic Alliance for the Betterment of Hong Kong, the chief pro-China party, won six seats. Beijing reaffirmed its pledge to scrap the elected legislature on 1 July 1997, and replace it with an appointed body pending the outcome of new elections, conducted on a narrower franchise, after the handover.

Accordingly, Chinese officials spent the final months of the transition forming committees whose task was to select a future chief executive (the post-1997 'governor'), and legislators to replace those elected in 1995. Britain could live with the choice of Tung Chee-hwa as the first leader of 'Chinese' Hong Kong, but it refused to cooperate with the provisional legislature, which was obliged to conduct its business across the border in Shenzhen.

The impasse over the legislature hindered rather than halted settlement of the final issues associated with the change of sovereignty. On 30 June 1997, constant, torrential rain dampened a British farewell pageant and set the mood for a sombre, indoor handover ceremony in the run up to midnight. Martin Lee and the Democrats, their legislative careers temporarily interrupted, protested from the balcony of the Legco building and vowed to return. The People's Liberation Army – damp-looking soldiers standing erect in the backs of open trucks, their faces devoid of emotion – poured across the border at designated checkpoints. Power changed hands smoothly, too smoothly for the assembled international media: the biggest drama was the cancellation of many of the celebrations planned for the next few days because of rain.

China's Hong Kong

Hong Kong emerged from the handover with a chief executive, a new executive council mostly made up of pro-China businessmen, and a selected legislature. Little else seemed to have changed. The existing judiciary pledged allegiance to the new masters. So did leading government officials, all of them by now local Chinese, thanks to a localization policy begun several years earlier. Different flags flew from roof tops. Stamps no longer bore the Queen's head. Quiet descended over Government House, former residence of the governor, now used only for official functions, including receptions for veteran revolutionaries from Beijing keen to see Hong Kong. The PLA disappeared into barracks vacated by British troops. Months after the handover, local people and visitors began to wonder what the fuss had been about. 'Chinese' Hong Kong seemed very much like British Hong Kong.

This was true only up to a point. The first post-handover threat to Hong Kong's established way of life came, not from Beijing, but Southeast Asia. The Asian financial crisis hit the territory hard, driving down the stock market, and draining growth from the economy. A year after the handover Hong Kong was in recession. A few months after that, the government bought millions of dollars of shares to prop up the market and fend off attacks by international speculators convinced that Hong Kong would have to break the peg with the US dollar and devalue its currency. The first round went to the government, but at the cost of damaging Hong Kong's reputation as a place where the market ruled, foul weather or fine.

By the second anniversary of the handover, the economy had improved but high costs and the fixed exchange rate made the territory uncompetitive compared with Singapore and, to some extent, Taipei and Shanghai. Declining margins on China-related trade – the result of better infrastructure and services across the border, which facilitated direct trade – obliged the government to seek a new strategy. One aspect of it was to make Hong Kong a centre for high technology industries as part of a drive to wean the economy away from reliance on property. Such moves, and the way in which they were conducted, pointed to the end of 'positive non-interventionism', the territory's guiding economic principle since at least the 1960s.

Hong Kong's freedoms fared better, at least at first. Reports of media self-censorship did the rounds but, overall, newspapers and radio stations remained as lively and critical as before. The first legislative elections under Chinese sovereignty, held in 1998, were conducted along lines designed to weaken support for the Democrats. This they did, but not sufficiently to block the return of Martin Lee and 8 fellow Democratic Party members. Victories by candidates from several smaller, pro-democratic parties helped keep the closest thing Hong Kong had to an opposition party alive. The Patten reforms had helped Hong Kong find a political voice: it would take much more than an imposed 'provisional legislature' to silence it. In all of these matters, as in others, Beijing exercised restraint. China's leaders seemed keen to enjoy the prestige that accrued from letting Hong Kong run itself.

This changed in 1999, largely as a result of a decision made in Hong Kong rather than Beijing. It arose over a ruling by Hong Kong's Court of Final Appeal that the government's attempts to restrict the right of Mainland children born of one or more parents living in the SAR (Special Administrative Region of Hong Kong) from migrating to the territory were against the Basic Law. The government countered that the true meaning of the Basic Law was that only those born of parents who were themselves permanent residents of the territory had right of abode in Hong Kong. If the court's verdict was allowed to stand, up to 1.5 million people could move to the territory. Hong Kong could not absorb such numbers. The government appealed to the NATIONAL PEOPLE'S CONGRESS in Beijing for an interpretation of the Basic Law, which found in favour of the administration and criticized the Court of Final Appeal. The move was popular in Hong Kong, but the territory's judicial autonomy suffered the first of what some feared would be many blows should the government take exception to rulings against it.

one country, new tensions

By the late 1990s, Hong Kong had become the primary agent of China's modernization in almost every area. By turns it was either China's first- or second-largest trade partner. It was China's biggest foreign investor. It had shifted nearly all its low-end manufacturing across the border into Guangdong, where its factories employed millions of workers. Its financial and legal expertise was an enormous asset to a country without either and in need of both. Hong Kong depended economically on the Mainland, too. It always had. At the start of the new century, the relationship has become one of genuine economic *interdependence*.

As in the past, but now more than ever, Hong Kong's importance derives from its status as a 'meeting point'. It is where China comes into contact with the outside world and where both parties feel comfortable. It is where Overseas Chinese conduct business, tapping their local roots and transforming their homeland with entrepreneurial flair, money and know-how. It is particularly important for Taiwan, nearly all of whose growing commercial and cultural contacts with the Mainland are conducted through Hong Kong in the absence of direct ties between the 'two Chinas'. The territory is bound to suffer if, as CHEN SHUI-BIAN indicated shortly after his election in March 2000 as Taiwan's first non-Kuomintang president, the island was ready to open direct trade and transport links with Beijing. Yet even if that happens Hong Kong will remain the nexus of 'greater China', a huge economic entity which, according to the most modest of several definitions applied to it, includes the Mainland, Taiwan and Macau as well as the SAR itself.

Hong Kong's importance for the modernization of China is much more than a matter of economics. While it is an agent of Chinese modernization, China's recovery of the territory was itself a milestone on the road to modernity. A lost territory had been regained; it was a matter of great national pride. China's unification remains incomplete: Taiwan has yet to be won to the cause. At the start of the century, there are several reasons why this seems likely to remain the case for years to come (see TAIWAN). But it is even more certain that few in Taiwan will welcome Beijing's embrace if Hong Kong's way of life fails to survive reunification.

Yet Hong Kong's importance to China's future, though immense, does not guarantee the territory's survival as a free and prosperous international city. Geography, history, industry and adaptability made Hong Kong what it is. But so did its legal system, non-intrusive government and tradition of civil liberties. These attributes are lacking in the Mainland. Party leaders in Beijing continue to fear aspects of Hong Kong life, particularly its occasionally querulous, often critical, always competitive and restless nature. Its

numerous independent churches, charities and social organizations – part of the rich texture of civil society – are quite outside their experience. So are its independent media and still largely independent judiciary. As long as this is the case, Hong Kong will remain vulnerable. The only guarantee of freedom in Hong Kong is freedom in the Mainland. Until that transpires there is always a danger that the corruption and bureaucratic infighting, the arbitrary rule and overwhelming desire of the Communist Party to control life apparent in the Mainland will swamp – and sink – the SAR.

In the early years of the new century, Hong Kong's survival as a cosmopolitan, free city under the sovereignty of the giant, unstable territory to its north depends on its ability to contribute towards China's modernization in ways other Chinese cities cannot. It also depends on Beijing's restraint. Both of these conditions will be difficult to meet. In the absence of significant political change in Beijing, neither constitutes a very sound basis for the survival of China's only great international centre, one almost as rich in freedoms as it is in material wealth.

Hu Jintao (1942–)

The surprise appointment of a relatively youthful Hu Jintao in 1992 to the Politburo Standing Committee of the CHINESE COMMUNIST PARTY suggested he was being groomed for greatness. His selection as vice-president in 1998 and the higher profile that followed confirmed it. Much less clear is the kind of policies this heir apparent to JIANG ZEMIN as China's paramount leader will champion given his lack of a solid background in the central government bureaucracy and the People's Liberation Army. Hu's almost unfathomable political persona adds to the uncertainty.

The fate of HU YAOBANG and ZHAO ZIYANG illustrates the unhappy experience of heirs apparent in China's Communist history. Yet the political contours of the 1980s have disappeared. Hu, untroubled by the presence of powerful veteran revolutionaries in the wings, has cleaved more closely to the policies of his mentor, Jiang, than the other men did to those of theirs, DENG XIAOPING. Throughout the 1990s Hu's career was a study in caution and restraint, combined with attempts to cultivate the personal dignity and gravitas expected of a future Party leader and state president.

Hu has youth on his side. If Jiang steps down in his favour at the Party's 16th National Congress in 2002, Hu, a native of ANHUI, will still be less than 60 years of age. The People's Republic has not been led by such a young man since HUA GUOFENG briefly succeeded Mao Zedong in 1976. It is less easy to say whether this will translate into new and vigorous policies. A degree in hydraulic engineering from Beijing's elite Qinghua University, and several years as a functionary in the Ministry of Water Resources and Electric Power, have equipped Hu with a similar professional background to Jiang and LI PENG. An important difference is that he is too young to have studied in the SOVIET UNION. However, Hu's support for the controversial THREE GORGES DAM suggests a penchant for large-scale projects of the kind often favoured by technocrats.

Yet it is as an apparatchik rather than as a professional or technical specialist that Hu Jintao has made his mark politically. One aspect of this is his long involvement in the Party's youth work. Another is service in the provinces. He worked first in GANSU and later became Party boss in GUIZHOU. He was also

Party Secretary in TIBET, the most sensitive regional posting in the People's Republic. Though an inability to cope with high altitude kept him away from the region much of the time, Hu was in charge of Tibet in 1989 when the authorities declared martial law in Lhasa to curb anti-Chinese protests. If nothing else this suggests Tibetan independence activists can expect little quarter from the man likely to be China's next leader.

Age, education and experience may make Hu more enthusiastic about economic, and perhaps legal and political reforms, than greater autonomy for Tibet. Nothing in his career points to a willingness to abandon the Party's hold over political life. But the undisputed ascendancy of a man who joined the Party long after it seized power in 1949, and is too young to have been educated in the Soviet Union, would constitute a break with the past, possibly one with implications for the style and substance of politics in Beijing.

Hu Shi (1891–1962)

Hu Shi was one of the great minds of modern China, but his practical, problem-solving approach to China's ills was out of tune with the romantic, revolutionary impulses towards action that marked mainstream Chinese radicalism in the early twentieth century. Many intellectuals, convinced that China could be 'bounced' out of its predicament if the laws of social development could be discerned and accelerated, were visionaries, activists or both. Hu was neither. His solutions were too tame; his remedies seemingly unable to address the pressing crises of national weakness, authoritarianism and warlord rule that marred the Chinese Republic.

Yet if Hu's cautious pragmatism was no match for MARXISM, which emerged as one of the main intellectual legacies of the MAY FOURTH MOVEMENT, he played a profound role in China's intellectual awakening. And his legacy, though long out of favour, is ripe for reassessment.

The precocious son of a minor official, Hu won a scholarship to Cornell University financed by remission of the Boxer Indemnity (see BOXER REBELLION). He became a disciple of the American philosopher John Dewey, obtained a PhD, and returned to China, where he was appointed Professor of Philosophy at Beijing University. Hu then became a leading figure in the May Fourth Movement, writing and speaking on many of the controversies at the heart of the attempt to remake China's culture and cast off the dead hand of Confucianism and convention. Chief among them was the promotion of BAI HUA, the use of the spoken language for literary purposes. Hu was a leading protagonist of this cause which was remarkably successful. An intellectual iconoclast, he wrote on literature, philosophy and politics as well as language. He insisted that China, though the inheritor of a proud, distinct civilization, was not unique, and would have to be brought within the mainstream of historical development as it had unfolded in the West.

But Hu was far from a revolutionary. In a famous essay, he urged the abandonment of various 'isms' in favour of problem-solving. Gradualism would lead to steady progress. Marxism and other ready-made 'systems' could not withstand intellectual criticism, and could lead to disaster – an uncomfortably accurate prediction in China's case. Hu made a virtue of belonging to no party and no faction. He disapproved of the narrow nationalist aims of the National Revolution championed by SUN YAT-SEN, and was a critic of both the KUOMINTANG, and more particularly the CHINESE COMMUNIST PARTY. He spent much of his life out of China, mainly in the United States, where he became Chinese Ambassador to Washington during the early years of the SINO-JAPANESE WAR. He passed his last years in Taiwan where he was president of Academia Sinica.

Hu's association with Chiang Kai-shek's government did little for his reputation among younger, more radical scholars. He also became an early target of the new Communist regime, whose ideologues attacked him for opposing Marxism and insisting that academic research was of value in its own right, apart from any benefit it might bring to politics and society. Yet as pragmatism gained the upper hand over ideology in Beijing during the 1980s and 1990s, Hu's books began to reappear and his ideas were discussed. In the new climate, the methodology and cautious optimism he had advocated during the May Fourth era was seen to have a new relevance.

Hu Yaobang (1915–89)

Hu was the only formal leader of the CHINESE COMMUNIST PARTY to encourage significant reform of China's Leninist political system rather than try to strengthen it or twist it to his own purposes. His period as Party leader (1980–87) was, by Beijing's standards, one of liberalism and experiment. This is precisely why Party elders, led by DENG XIAOPING, sacked him; and why his death, two years later, sparked the TIANANMEN SQUARE DEMOCRACY MOVEMENT.

Hu, born in HUNAN, was a protégé of Deng's from the 1940s. The two men shared a dislike for excessive theorizing and a passion for getting things done, often by using whatever policies were to hand. This practical approach was about all they had in common. Hu joined the Revolution at the age of 13 and took part in the LONG MARCH, but he had a different outlook from many of those in the Party with the same pedigree. His cast of mind was questioning and critical. His temperament was impetuous. He was perhaps the freest spirit to have reached the top of the formal Party apparatus – apart from MAO ZEDONG. None of these characteristics proved advantageous in the tortuous world of elite politics in Beijing.

Hu's political recovery after spending several years in a cow pen during the Cultural Revolution began in 1977. As vice-president of the Central Party School in Beijing and later head of the Party's Propaganda Department, he played a major part in prising off the shackles Mao and his followers had imposed on every aspect of life. He helped secure the defeat of the 'whateverist' policies ('whatever Mao said was right') pursued by HUA GUOFENG, the Chairman's successor, and the victory of Deng's free market reforms. He oversaw the rehabilitation of former Party leaders, lesser officials, and thousands of ordinary people who had been persecuted during the 'Anti-Rightist Movement' (see ONE HUNDRED FLOWERS MOVEMENT) and the Cultural Revolution. He tacitly encouraged the DEMOCRACY WALL activists, inviting two of them to his home. In 1980, during a trip to TIBET, he apologized for Party misrule in the region. These developments contributed to the air of expectation and hope of the late 1970s and early 1980s. They also explain why intellectuals in particular welcomed Hu's elevation to the post of Party General Secretary in 1980, which soon became a more powerful position than that of the Party chairmanship occupied by Hua until it was abolished altogether in 1982.

Hu could not always justify the hope reformers placed in him. Partly this was because of the limited nature of his own radicalism. He was not prepared to abandon Marxism completely – though he publicly conceded it could not solve 'all' mankind's problems – or see the Party give up its leading role in political life. He was not a closet democrat in the Western sense. But he wanted to make the government more responsive, representative and subject to legal checks and balances, despite opposition from Deng and other veterans. Many of the old guard mistrusted Hu from the start. Soon, they grew to fear him.

The battle between the two camps raged throughout Hu's years in power. Under his protection, and often with his encouragement, intellectuals raised sensitive issues in the media. These included radical literary and philosophical theories, and perennial political questions such as DEMOCRACY, HUMAN RIGHTS and the need for institutional limits on the Party's power. The conservatives, sometimes backed by Deng, sometimes not, hit back with campaigns against individual writers and in favour of Communist labour heroes. In 1983, Deng himself launched a broader movement against manifestations of Western values which he described as 'spiritual pollution'. Hu and his allies – together with premier ZHAO ZIYANG who, though often at odds with Hu, was concerned about the consequences of the conservative campaigns for economic reform – managed to blunt these offensives and keep the hopes of political change alive.

With economic reforms biting into every aspect of life, political change was certainly necessary. The days of the state-controlled, planned economy were numbered. Perhaps those of a monolithic, ideologically hidebound, political party ruled by elderly men were, too? By 1986, many intellectuals hoped so. Once again, the narrow frontiers of free discussion expanded a little, and calls for political reform were common in the media. Hu backed this cause and Deng, wavering, as ever, the better to stay on top, also seemed in favour. The Party appeared ready to take the plunge.

It was a false dawn. Talk of political change was overshadowed by the need to oppose 'bourgeois liberalization', the Party's term for Western political ideas. The old guard won Deng round to their agenda. Hu was not exactly humiliated, but he had been unable to carry the day. Clearly, such power as he enjoyed could be exercised only on the sufferance of the elders, and that sufferance was growing thin.

It disappeared three months later when students took demands for political change directly to the streets of at least a dozen Chinese cities. The protests were not only about political issues. They were motivated by concerns common to students the world over: poor facilities, lack of funds, tame student unions. But in China, protests are political acts, whatever the motives. And it was plain that the demands of many participants were sufficiently political in the ordinary sense of that term to make the Party worry.

The unrest began at the University of Science and Technology in Hefei, capital of ANHUI province, where Fang Lizhi (1936–) the controversial scientist, was vice-chancellor. Together with Wang Ruowang (1917–) and Liu Binyan (1925–), two other radical intellectuals, Fang had spoken publicly of the need for thoroughgoing political change of the kind that would spell the demise of the Communist Party as it then was. Deng disliked all three men. He urged Hu to dismiss them from the Party and silence them. Hu refused – just as he refused demands by the old guard to use force against the demonstrators.

By early January 1987 the protests petered out, but the ire of the old guard had not. The demonstrations were a challenge that had to be dealt with. At a Politburo meeting, expanded to include army generals and the elders who made up the 'Central Advisory Commission', Hu was berated for his errors and sacked. He was browbeaten into signing a 'self criticism' for failing to handle the protests firmly and stamp out liberalism. He was also punished for his apparent readiness to take Deng and the other veterans at their word when they spoke, usually insincerely, of retiring. In this sense Hu had presented a double threat: that of abandoning the old guard's policies of tight Party control *and* depriving them of personal power.

Although Hu was publicly condemned, and his policy of tolerance abandoned in favour of a nationwide campaign against 'bourgeois liberalism', he was not humiliated. He retained his seat on the Politburo, and managed to hang on to it after the Party's 13th National Congress in 1987 had put moderate political reform back on the agenda. Yet Hu's biggest political impact was made posthumously. His death of a heart attack on 15 April 1989 provoked an immediate outpouring of public grief, and then anger over his treatment by the old guard. It rapidly developed into a massive popular movement for political change that the veterans had to put down with tanks (see TIANANMEN SQUARE DEMOCRACY MOVEMENT).

Hua Guofeng (1921–)

Hua, the third of MAO ZEDONG's chosen heirs after LIU SHAOQI and LIN BIAO, actually survived to become chairman of the CHINESE COMMUNIST PARTY when Mao died in 1976. But he soon lost power to the infinitely more capable and experienced DENG XIAOPING who promptly dispatched him to the margins of Chinese politics with almost irreverent haste.

Mao got to know Hua, a SHANXI native, during the 1950s when the latter was a senior Party leader in HUNAN, the Chairman's home province. Hua's enthusiasm for the Chairman's radical policies stood him in good stead during the CULTURAL REVOLUTION: he joined the Central Committee in 1969 and the Politburo in 1973. Much greater things lay in store. In 1975 the ailing Mao sought a successor to preserve the 'fruits' of the Cultural Revolution:

policies which placed politics in command but did not neglect economic productivity. He turned to Hua, by then a vice-premier, as the man most likely to oppose the excesses of the radicals, led by the 'GANG OF FOUR', yet prevent a comeback by 'revisionists' such as Deng Xiaoping, who wanted the Party to focus all its energy on economic modernization. 'With you in charge, I'm at ease,' he is supposed to have told his unlikely heir.

Within weeks of Mao's death, Hua had the 'Gang' arrested – a popular move and one which secured his place in Chinese history. But he went on to stress his commitment to the principles laid down by his mentor, including the need for cultural revolutions at regular intervals to keep the Chinese people on their toes. This was much less popular.

Hua's opponents, many of them allies of Deng, accused him of being dogmatic and a 'whateverist': whatever Mao had decided was right; whatever directive Mao had issued must be defended.

Hua held all the formal positions of power: he was Chairman of the Party, Premier of the State Council, and Chairman of the Military Affairs Commission (see GOVERNMENT AND ADMINISTRATION). This made him successor to both Mao *and* ZHOU ENLAI, who also died in 1976. In fact, he was neither. He lacked experience, prestige and military backing – all of which were vital for survival, and all of which Deng, who returned from his second Cultural Revolution purge in 1977, had in abundance.

Deng also had the popular mood on his side. There was growing demand for a reassessment of the Cultural Revolution and a rehabilitation of its victims. At Beijing's DEMOCRACY WALL other, more fundamental, issues were raised, including an end to dictatorship and demands for human rights. Deng turned this to his advantage, until he believed it had outlived its usefulness in his struggle with Hua and threatened the basis of Party rule.

Hua championed the 'FOUR MODERNIZATIONS' put forward by Zhou some years earlier, but the fact that the targets he set were quite beyond China's capacity exposed him to yet more criticism. In 1980 Deng had HU YAOBANG appointed general secretary of the Party and ZHAO ZIYANG made premier. Hua, still Party chairman, was isolated, his ambitious policies abandoned. The Cultural Revolution was condemned and Mao reassessed. Economic reform and the open door were made the foundations of Party policy. The formal end of his career came in 1982 when both Hua and the by then largely figurehead post of Party chairman disappeared from public life. Hua's role in arresting the Gang was acknowledged in his continued, if token, membership of the Central Committee long years after he left the limelight. Since 1982 the senior figure in the Chinese Communist Party has been its general secretary.

Hubei Province

Hubei and in particular Wuhan, its mighty capital, form the strategic heartland of central China. Wuhan is where the Yangtze, the main artery of east–west communication, meets the north–south railway between Beijing and Guangzhou. It is the great gathering place for materials and ideas bound to and from the hinterland. It is a major industrial centre. Hubei has always been crucial to the security and prosperity of the interior; central China's well-being still rides on its fortunes.

modernization of middle China

The YANGTZE RIVER, in whose middle reaches it sits, has made Hubei the crossroads of continental China, though one prone to flooding. The rich agricultural land in the southeast of the province, through which the river flows, has made it rich, if densely populated. Both characteristics have ensured that Hubei is the economic and, on occasion, the political, as well as the geographic, centre of gravity in middle China.

The Western powers were not slow to appreciate this. The fact that ocean-going ships could sail upriver as far as Wuhan lent this established commercial centre new significance. With the QING DYNASTY in decay, a Western presence in the city promised access to the markets and materials of the interior. Accordingly Hankou, on the north bank of the Yangtze, and one of the three cities clustered around the confluence of the Yangtze and the Han, now known collectively as Wuhan, was made a TREATY PORT. Ichang, once the upper limit of steam navigation on the Yangtze followed, and so, at the close of the nineteenth century, did Shashi, two-thirds of the way between Wuhan and Ichang.

The dynasty matched this Western penetration of the middle Yangtze with a modernization drive that soon made Wuhan the most industrialized city in the interior. It was largely the work of Zhang Zhidong (1837–1909), the great reformer and long-serving governor of the region.

Zhang sponsored textile factories, an arsenal and modern schools in Wuhan. But his greatest legacy was the Hanyeping iron and steel works, the first in China, which began production in 1896. Its name reflected the dispersed nature of the enterprise: the foundry was in Hanyang, another of the three Wuhan cities, just across the Han from Hankou; the ore was mined at Daye, southeast of Wuhan; and the coal at Pingxiang, in JIANGXI.

Hanyeping collapsed in the mid-1920s, but provided some of China's first generation of trade unionists and Communist Party members with valuable experience in labour organization.

Republican Revolution

Wuhan's first taste of modern radical politics coincided with the founding of the steel works. Anti-Manchu sentiment was strong in Hubei. SECRET SOCIETIES and officers of the new armies; ardent republicans; conservative yet patriotic merchants and gentry were at one in their opposition to the dynasty. All these groups were active in Wuhan at the start of the twentieth century. Members of all of them participated in the struggle over railway rights in the province (see RAILWAYS).

The arrival of the railway from Beijing in 1905 had boosted Wuhan's importance as a communications centre. Its extension south, eventually to Guangzhou, capital of GUANG-DONG, promised to do so again. It also promised to make those involved in its finance rich and powerful. This is why the Court tried to nationalize China's fledgling railways, even though it had to raise foreign loans to do so. And this, in turn, is why local merchants, gentry, industrialists and a politically aware public insisted that Hubei, not Manchu, interests should finance, build and control the line.

As in neighbouring SICHUAN, the railway protection movement in Hubei forced Beijing to back down: the line south from Wuhan was 'localized' rather than nationalized. But this did little to assuage public anger with the dynasty. Wuhan in particular was a breeding ground for ideas and organizations calling for radical change. It came, partly by default, in October 1911 when a group of conspirators accidentally exploded a bomb in the Russian concession at Hankou. A few hours later, a military revolt in Wuchang, on the south bank of the Yangtze and the third of Wuhan's 'three cities', marked the start of the REPUBLICAN REVOLUTION. Twenty-four hours later most of Wuhan was lost to the dynasty. And so, during the following few weeks, was the rest of China.

revolutionary nationalism in Wuhan

Wuhan sparked the rebellion which ended two millennia of imperial rule. But the political struggle to remake China took place first down river in Nanjing, seat of the 'provisional' Republican government, and then in Beijing, the established capital. Hubei dropped out of the national political limelight. In the early 1920s, the province fell under the control of WU PEIFU, the chief warlord of central China who opposed Sun Yat-sen's reorganized, revolutionary KUOMINTANG and its NORTHERN EXPEDITION to unify the country.

He did not do so for long. In October 1926, the National Revolutionary Army, its advance eased by Communist and Left-wing agitation among peasants and workers en route, occupied Wuhan and pushed Wu north into HENAN. The new regime, led by WANG JINGWEI, and guided by Mikhail Borodin (1884–1952), the Soviet adviser, then presided over a revolutionary upsurge which put the city and the province back on the map of national politics. The Communist Party, including CHEN DUXIU, its leader, played an important part in these proceedings.

One result of the Wuhan revolution was the ransacking of the British concession in Hankou in January 1927 by nationalist demonstrators. The foreign community in China was stunned at this challenge to Western power, but London chose not to resist and the concession was returned. So, a few days later, was that downstream in Jiujiang, Jiangxi.

The strikes which brought Wuhan to a standstill were equally significant: the city was paralysed as its residents reclaimed their radical heritage and carried it to new extremes. More remarkable still was the revolt in the countryside under Wuhan's control. In HUNAN and Hubei the peasants rose up against their oppressors and opponents with a violence that inspired MAO ZEDONG, but troubled some of the more conservative leaders in Wuhan.

Their dilemma deepened once Chiang had crushed the Communists in SHANGHAI and other cities under his control. At times, neither Wang Jingwei, the Communist leaders, or Moscow seemed to know how to advance the revolution or preserve their fragile alliance. The matter was decided – in favour of a conservative, pro-Chiang line – by generals nominally subordinate to Wang and the Kuomintang Left. In mid-1927 they crushed the workers' and peasants' revolution and brought Wuhan's experiment in revolutionary politics to a bloody end. The Communists were driven into the countryside. Almost 20 years would pass before they were able to organize openly in a major city again (see CHINESE COMMUNIST PARTY).

In the interim, Wuhan served briefly as

China's capital during the first stage of the SINO-JAPANESE WAR. Chiang's destruction of the dykes along the Yellow River in Henan halted the Japanese advance on the city from the north but Nationalist resistance to attacks along the Yangtze soon gave way. Japanese troops entered Wuhan in October 1938 almost unmolested. From then until 1945, the Japanese military controlled shipping on the middle Yangtze, depriving CHONGQING, Chiang's new capital, further upstream in SICHUAN, of supplies and subjecting it to fierce bombing.

after 1949: home of heavy industry

Just over a decade after its occupation by Japan, Wuhan fell to another army bent on the conquest of south China: the People's Liberation Army. The Communist victory in the Huai-Hai campaign of late 1948 and early 1949, had opened the Nationalist position on the Yangtze to attack. Between April and May 1949, the PLA occupied all the major cities along the river, effectively sealing the Communist victory in the CIVIL WAR. LIN BIAO's Fourth Field Army took Wuhan, and the city became the seat of the Central-South Military Administrative Committee, the chief organ of Communist rule in the newly 'liberated' provinces of Henan, Hubei, Hunan, Jiangxi, Guangdong and Guangxi.

Hubei's new rulers turned their back on Wuhan's commercial past and built the city into a base for heavy industry. Soviet aid and advice played a part here; they were behind some of the great construction projects of the First Five Year Plan (1953–7): the Wuhan Iron and Steel Plant, the Wuhan Boiler Plant and, most spectacular of all Wuhan projects, the bridge across the Yangtze. Completed in 1957, it was the first to be built over the Long River. Wuhan had to wait almost 20 years for the second.

These developments turned Wuhan into an industrial centre of *national* importance. Hubei became China's third great centre of industry after the Manchurian provinces of the northeast (see LIAONING; JILIN; HEILONGJIANG;) and Shanghai. Industrialization was not confined to the provincial capital: Huangshi, downstream from Wuhan, was also industrialized. So, in a more modest way, was Yichang.

The focus of development switched even further inland in the 1960s, when Communist China entered its greatest period of international isolation. Under Mao Zedong's policy of creating a 'third line' of industries

---

The Lie of the Land

The eastern half of Hubei is a wide alluvial plain, the work of the Yangtze and its longest tributary, the Han. The two rivers meet at Wuhan. Close to two-thirds of the population – in total, 59 million at the close of the century – live around the numerous lakes and lesser rivers of this region, the agricultural heartland of Hubei. The Dabie mountains divide Hubei from Henan in the north and Anhui in the northwest. Another range, the Mufu, straddles the border with Jiangxi in the southeast. The highest and most rugged of Hubei's 69,500 square miles (180,000 sq kms) are in the west. Xiling gorge, one of three famous gorges, is in southwest Hubei. Another, Wu Gorge, extends into Chongqing, which is also the location of the third, the Qutang. All three form the only natural passageway from Hubei into western China. Northwest Hubei is mountainous. It is the eastern extension of the Qinling range which cuts through southern Shaanxi. Intensively cultivated basins in this region are watered by the Han, which is navigable into Shaanxi.

---

deep in the interior, Xiangfan and Shiyan, two cities in mountainous northwest Hubei, were turned into manufacturing centres. Both are bases for vehicle production.

This economic transformation heightened Wuhan's role in national life. And it was no accident that Mao chose the city for his celebrated swim across the Yangtze in July 1966. The episode involved more 'floating' than 'swimming' but its symbolism was no less important for that. It showed that the Chairman was fit enough to tame the torrents and, soon, create some of his own in the form of the CULTURAL REVOLUTION.

It was no accident, either, that events in Wuhan took a particularly dramatic turn as Mao's latest quest for revolutionary purity spread across the country. In 1967, shortly after he ordered the PLA to curb the more radical of the Red Guards in the provinces, the military command in Wuhan waged war on the rebels. Civil war almost engulfed the city and there was heavy loss of life. The victory of the more conservative group, the 'One Million Heroes', backed by Chen Zaidao (1909–), the military commander, over the radical 'Workers' General Headquarters' brought calm of a kind.

Then Beijing intervened. Central leaders sent to the city declared in favour of the radicals. An army unit loyal to Chen responded by kidnapping and beating one of the leaders. Beijing mobilized air, ground and naval forces for an attack on Wuhan. In the event, armed conflict between PLA units was avoided. But, with the possible exception of GUANGXI, nowhere in China did full-scale civil war during the Cultural Revolution seem so likely as in Wuhan during the summer of 1967.

reform era: long road to revival

The new priorities of the reform agenda presented Hubei and its major city with difficult challenges in the early 1980s. For one thing the two jurisdictions tended to be at each other's throats over finance. The provincial government kept Wuhan on as tight a rein as the central government did Shanghai. Both cities suffered from a lack of funds as a result.

Wuhan broke free in 1984 when Beijing granted it province-level powers in economic matters. But that is where central government largesse stopped. While Wuhan was allowed to conduct experiments in domestic banking and enterprise reform, there were no favourable policies to attract FOREIGN TRADE AND INVESTMENT of the kind granted the coastal provinces of the south. The sense of neglect intensified when Shanghai's Pudong project received the go-ahead in 1990. Wuhan, its state industries ailing, its infrastructure in decay, and its officials increasingly disgruntled, seemed to have missed out on the boom.

Or it did until 1992 when DENG XIAOPING made Wuchang the first stop on his celebrated 'southern tour'. Wuchang was the least-developed city on a journey which took China's aged but still paramount leader to the most prosperous parts of the country. Deng acknowledged the region's backwardness by admitting, in the published version of his 'talks' en route, that he had made a mistake in not developing the Yangtze valley earlier.

The remedy was to hand. In mid-1992, the entire Yangtze valley was opened to foreign trade and investment. Almost 30 cities, along the river, from Shanghai to Chongqing, were granted the kind of benefits and privileged policies which had enriched the SPECIAL ECONOMIC ZONES and coastal cities. It was time for the interior to catch up.

In the years that followed there was a minor outbreak of 'Wuhan fever' among the media and foreign investors. Hong Kong companies were afflicted first and most intensely. One or two spoke of conducting a complete 'makeover' of the decrepit yet mighty city in the middle of the country. Wuhan was 'China's Chicago'. It was perfectly positioned midway along the next corridor of global prosperity.

In fact, Wuhan in the mid-1990s was just beginning to tackle the problems which still cloud its future at the start of the new era: reform of state enterprises; funding new infrastructure projects; and educating the city's 7 and a half million people for an era of change and flexibility which almost seemed to have passed middle China by. These tasks defy quick solution at the best of times. They are much more difficult to accomplish in a period of slower growth and failing enthusiasm on the part of investors.

This is not to deny Hubei's and Wuhan's continuing economic importance to the rest of China. In the late 1990s, the province accounted for more than 4.5 per cent of national GDP and was ranked eighth in the league table of provincial output. It remains the powerhouse of the middle Yangtze: a province whose performance will have a major impact on China's attempt to narrow the divide between the coastal regions and the interior generated by two decades of free market reforms.

home of the Three Gorges

The THREE GORGES DAM is supposed to play a key role in this process, generating wealth and energy deep in central China and spreading it along the Yangtze. Once again, Hubei is at the heart of things. Sandouping, the dam site, a few miles upstream from Ichang, is host to the world's largest, most expensive construction project of its kind.

Work began on a 'dry run' for the Three Gorges in 1970 at Ichang. The Gezhouba dam was completed in 1987 after numerous problems and long delays. It has proved less efficient than hoped.

There is no question that the construction of a massive new dam, the relocation of more than a million people and flooding the Three Gorges will have an immense impact on the whole of middle China. Whether the effects will be wholly beneficial is another matter.

Hubei's potential gains appear greater than those of Chongqing, upstream of the dam. Wuhan, in particular, should enjoy two of the main benefits supposed to flow from the project: improved flood control and cheap, abundant power. The main burden of relocating people falls to the new municipality of Chongqing which, with the rise in water level, should benefit from improved communications.

Yet the uncertainties surrounding the Three Gorges are as large as the project itself. They concern security, efficiency, prosperity and the ENVIRONMENT – issues of the utmost importance to Hubei and middle China; and issues likely to hover over the region long after the dam is completed in 2009.

hukou (household registration)

The Communist government introduced its household registration system – the literal meaning of the Chinese term is 'mouths of a family' – to pin its people down geographically, occupationally and to some extent politically. In urban areas it is complemented as a system of social control by the DANGAN system of personal dossiers and the DANWEI, the work unit.

A *hukou* provides a right of residence, usually where a citizen is born. Holders are assigned either 'agricultural' or 'non-agricultural' status. Newborn babies acquire the *hukou* status of their mothers. Introduced in the 1950s, a main purpose of household registration was to stop peasants flooding into cities in search of a better life. It largely achieved this aim until the 1990s, when economic reforms encouraged social mobility and generated a vast 'floating population' (see POPULATION). Even then, a citizen's status and permanent address could only be changed with difficulty and often at great cost. At the start of the new era, members of the 'floating population', deprived of the services and benefits that an urban *hukou* alone can supply, often congregate in shanty towns on the fringes of cities where they provide their own, rudimentary social services, and often incur the dislike of established residents as well as the attentions of the police.

human rights

No single issue has done so much to shape the popular image of contemporary China in the West as human rights. Few single issues have proved so sensitive in Beijing, where the Communist regime has mixed widespread abuse of human rights with attempts to redefine their meaning and sporadic efforts to improve them. The role of human rights in Sino-Western diplomacy, and the extent to which international pressure can be expected improve them, have been no less controversial – as has the nature of China's human rights record itself.

three concepts of human rights

Defined in material terms as the right to food, shelter, clothes, EDUCATION and HEALTH, Communist China's human rights record since the late 1970s is rather impressive. There have been gruesome exceptions, such as the neglect of orphans exposed in the mid-1990s. But since the start of the reform era millions of Chinese have been lifted out of POVERTY, millions more enjoy a much higher standard of living than ever before, and a minority, many of them connected with government, have become genuinely rich.

Defined as liberty, broadly conceived, China's human rights record has also improved. Millions of Chinese can decide themselves where to live and work, travel or study overseas, and start their own businesses. Within bounds, often narrowly drawn, they can practise their religious beliefs (see RELIGIONS; CHRISTIANITY). Tastes in dress, sexual partners, music and many other aspects of life are regarded as the individual's affair. Such 'rights' have long been taken for granted in the West. In China under Communism, where the 'Anti-Rightist Movement' (see ONE HUNDRED FLOWERS CAMPAIGN), the GREAT LEAP FORWARD and the CULTURAL REVOLUTION caused mass persecution, terror and millions of deaths, they are still something of a novelty.

Yet defined *politically*, China's record on human rights remains poor. Harassment, arrest, LABOUR CAMPS, prison and worse await those who advocate political opinions contrary to those of the government, practise religion outside official channels, hold demonstrations, form political parties and independent trade unions, or pursue independence for TIBET, XINJIANG and other areas inhabited by ETHNIC MINORITIES. No one outside the Party elite – and not everyone within it – enjoys absolute freedom from arrest and detention without a trial, or the right to a fair trial should one be held. There is no such thing in China as freedom of the press or academic freedom. Strikes are illegal.

At the start of the new century, nearly all forms of public dissent and criticism have been stamped out and their exponents jailed (see DISSIDENTS). More than 2,000 people are known to be in prison on charges of conducting 'counter-revolutionary' crimes, the legal term for acts, including peaceful ones, opposing the Communist Party or socialism. This was believed to be a fraction of the true figure, and does not include the far larger number of political prisoners confined, often without trial, to labour camps. They include Christian pastors and Catholic priests, Buddhist nuns in Tibet and imams in Xinjiang, labour activists, journalists, and many ordinary people throughout the country whose crime was to speak or act in a way the government disliked.

The situation is made worse by occasionally widespread, though technically illegal, beatings and torture of suspects in police stations and prisons; a coercive birth control policy under which women have been forced to have abortions (see POPULATION); and excessive use of the death penalty, which at times has given rise to a macabre trade in victims' internal organs. Abuses of human rights of this kind disfigured life throughout the rule of Deng Xiaoping and after. The continuing intolerance of the authorities, and the harsh treatment they reserve for critics, show how much China has to change before it can be regarded a genuinely modern nation.

state, society, individual

The fact that almost every Chinese government in the twentieth century persecuted its critics and often did little more than pay lip service to the rights of individuals, reflects the different weight attached to the state and the individual in China compared with the West. Traditionally, individuals in China mattered less than the wider community. Group interests – the FAMILY, CLAN, village, workplace and, in the twentieth century, the state – came first, individuals came second. Individuals derived their value and identities from their participation in communities rather than the other way round. Action directed towards strengthening, improving, or enriching the community or, politically, the state, was desirable. That aimed solely at improving the position of the individual was 'selfish'.

Since the state was seen to create individual worth, individuals had to show they were worthy of the state. Theoretically, this left little room for the idea of legitimate opposition to the state, unless the state was shown to represent the interests of an authoritarian elite rather than the wider community. Even when this was the case, there was a tendency to try and replace 'bad' state leaders with 'good' rather than fundamentally revise the relationship between individual and state in a way that would make the former more important than the latter.

This weak tradition of individual rights helps explain the failure of DEMOCRACY, the guardian of human rights, to take root in China. Both causes had their advocates, notably during the MAY FOURTH MOVEMENT and, intermittently, ever since. But throughout the century, successive Chinese governments, and particularly the Communist one, have had no hesitation about crushing those who opposed their policies. In their own terms, they had the interests of the community, country or, after 1949, the 'revolution' at heart. Moreover, under Communism, people have been perceived even less as individuals than representatives of a *class*. Those who opposed the Party have been stigmatized as representatives of the 'bourgeoisie' – a minority class whose aim is the overthrow of socialism and restoration of capitalism, usually in league with 'anti-China or 'pro-Western' forces abroad. These were precisely the charges levelled at dissidents such as WEI JINGSHENG, those accused of leading the TIANANMEN SQUARE DEMOCRACY MOVEMENT, and all who publicly criticize and oppose the Party or its policies.

The idea that opposition might stem from *conscience*, the grounds of human rights theory and practice in the West, is neither widely accepted nor, perhaps, widely understood by many in the Party. Even if it is, the weight of Chinese tradition and decades of Communist practice mean that little store is set by it. Only in the 1990s did support begin to grow within the Party and even more among ordinary people for the notion that it is the primary duty of the state, and the overriding function of LAW, to strengthen and protect the rights of the individual.

debates, defeats, diplomacy

Three major factors have played a part in this growing awakening to the importance of human rights. One is the experience of the Cultural Revolution whose horrors sparked a debate on the role of the law in curbing tyranny and protecting the individual. Its earliest, most dramatic expression was the

The Dying Rooms

Reports that thousands of orphans, most of them girls, were left to die of starvation, neglect and other cruelties in Victorian-style institutions across China were common in the West during the mid-1990s. The title of a British television programme, *The Dying Rooms*, symbolized the fate of the unloved and unwanted in a heavily overpopulated country where to be a baby girl *and* have no family was the worst possible start in life. Some reports suggested it was as good as a death warrant. *Death by Default*, a 1996 study by Human Rights Watch/Asia of neglect in state orphanages, said that in 1989 the majority of orphans admitted to China's welfare institutions died in care.

In the Shanghai Municipal Children's Welfare Institute, later praised as a 'model institute' by the government, the human rights group said the mortality rate was 90 per cent. In the late 1980s and 1990s well over 1,000 children died there. The manner of many of the deaths was as depressing as their numbers. Based on the testimony of a former doctor at the institute, the report said the authorities developed a technique known as 'summary resolution' in which unwanted, naughty or difficult children were simply left to die of starvation. Many of those assigned to this fate were strapped to their beds and confined to a special room. Others were beaten and sexually abused. Health professionals allegedly played a part in this perversion of medical ethics. The Shanghai government tried to hush it up, and hounded those who wanted the tragedy exposed.

The Chinese government's denials were characteristically swift and emphatic. More surprising were its attempts to disprove the allegations. Foreign journalists were given a guided tour of the Shanghai Municipal Children's Welfare Institute and diplomats allowed to visit a sister institution. No evidence of abuse was found: officials said it had been 'fabricated' in the report, including the photograph of a child tied to a bed. But no satisfactory answers were given to the questions raised in the study which dealt with the period before reforms were undertaken at the two institutes in 1993.

A month later the *People's Daily* published an extensive attack on the ill-treatment of children in the United States. Two months later, the government published a White Paper on child welfare in China, a glowing account of its achievements. While the 'dying rooms' controversy of 1996 focused on the record of the Shanghai institute, it brought to light the widespread neglect of the disadvantaged and those deemed misfits in China's rapidly modernizing, seemingly hard-hearted society. It did not so much demonstrate the want of cash on the part of institutions, though that was sometimes a problem, as something much worse: the want of a culture of care.

DEMOCRACY WALL MOVEMENT of 1978–9. The movement was suppressed, but the debate it sparked survived and occasionally flourished during the 1980s under the unofficial patronage of HU YAOBANG, the most liberal of China's Communist leaders.

The military crackdown on the Tiananmen Square democracy movement dealt a more serious blow to this cause. Leading advocates of human rights either fled into exile or were imprisoned or silenced. Yet domestic discussion of the issue never entirely disappeared. It acquired new momentum in the mid-1990s as a result of China's pursuit of rapid economic modernization. There was a growing realization that this could not be accomplished without adequate legal guarantees. Foreign investors needed a degree of legal protection and so did private individuals if free market economic reforms were to work. These were not the same things as the human rights advocated by Wei Jingsheng at Democracy Wall, the students in Tiananmen Square, or pro-independence monks in Tibet, but they were part of them.

Growing international pressure on China after Tiananmen to improve its human rights record added a new element to these domestic demands for change. Until 1989, the West had been willing to overlook China's human rights abuses in the interests of maintaining good relations with Beijing, then a valued Cold War counterweight to Moscow. If the violent suppression of the democracy movement made this impossible, the collapse of the Soviet Union made it unnecessary. The UNITED STATES, and several Western European countries imposed mild sanctions against China and made lifting them conditional upon an improvement in its human rights record. It became a custom – a ritual, according to the cynics – for Western leaders to present their Chinese counterparts with lists of political prisoners and demands that they be freed. Concern about the situation in Tibet, where anti-Chinese protests had been suppressed and Tibetan culture seemed endangered, also became a staple of Western diplomacy towards Beijing.

China responded by maintaining that human rights were China's domestic affair: third parties had no right to comment, let alone seek changes through sanctions. To do so was 'hegemonism': the practice, led by the United States, of imposing capitalist values on China and other Third World countries the better to control them. This argument from sovereignty remains Beijing's first and final defence against critics of its human rights record at the start of the new era.

Yet it has also fought back in more sophisticated ways by advocating human rights values said to be 'proper' to China and Asia. Among them are the ASIAN VALUES championed by other, mostly authoritarian, governments in the region during the early 1990s. At their heart is the doctrine of sovereignty and the 'right to subsistence', or food and security, said to matter more to many Asians and Chinese than the political and civil rights championed by the West. This is so because China and the West are at different levels of economic development, and their peoples products of different historical traditions and cultures. There can no more be identical conceptions of human rights than there can be identical religions. This denial of the *universal* nature of human rights – to which China had subscribed as a signatory of the United Nations Charter – was enshrined in the Bangkok Declaration of Asian States in 1993. The UN weeded out much of the cultural relativism contained in this document at the World Conference of Human Rights in Vienna the same year. However, Beijing, and several Asian governments remain attached to it.

the language of legality

The fact that China had to discuss and defend its human rights record in the course of diplomacy has forced it to adopt many of the associated *forms* of international protection and discourse. After Tiananmen, Beijing began to publish 'white papers' listing its achievements in human rights. Special issues were produced on Tibet which, unlike Tiananmen, was a running sore which rather than just an open one. It allowed foreign experts to visit prisons and talk to judges, jailers and carefully selected prisoners. It signed up to international conventions outlawing torture and discrimination against women.

In 1996 China carried out changes in the criminal law which strengthened the rights of defendants. In 1997, it redesignated 'counter-revolutionary' crimes – a description which had become outdated and diplomatically embarrassing – as those which 'endangered state security'. This was a happier term all round, particularly as it did not restrict the power of the government to jail its critics. The same year, Beijing signed the United Nations International Covenant on Economic, Social and Cultural Rights. In 1998 it signed the International Covenant on Political and Civil Rights. At the turn of the century both documents remained to be ratified, leaving China outside the fold of the 'international bill of rights', as the Universal Declaration of Human Rights and the two covenants are known collectively.

These legal changes were not accompanied by any significant improvements in China's human rights *practice* other than in the broader senses referred to at the start of this essay. Often during the late 1990s, the apparent legal acceptance of international norms on liberty went hand in hand with renewed crackdowns on dissent. The major difference was that oppression was leavened by the occasional release of celebrated dissidents – usually on condition that they go straight into exile – to secure diplomatic advantage in relations with the West, particularly the United States. This was the fate of Wei Jingsheng and Wang Dan, the Tiananmen student leader, who within the space of a few months, were taken from their cells, driven straight to Beijing airport and put on a plane bound for the US.

Yet China's readiness to move slowly towards internationally accepted legal norms on human rights appeared to count for more with most Western countries than its reluctance to enforce them. Fear that valuable commercial opportunities in China's rapidly growing economy would be lost if too harsh a stand was taken was a factor here – one that Beijing played upon skilfully. There was also a feeling that more might be accomplished if Western leaders took up the issue of human rights with Chinese leaders personally, in private, rather than link it publicly with trade and other issues. In any event it was believed that foreign governments could only accomplish so much: rapid economic and social change in China itself was more likely to deliver improvements than diplomacy. Moreover, some form of relationship had to be built up with China's leaders as their country became richer and more powerful. Beijing's cooperation was needed on a host of international issues from peace on the Korean peninsula, to cooperation over the sale of missiles and nuclear technology. Human rights could not be allowed to dominate the agenda of Sino-Western diplomacy.

Before long it seemed to take a back seat. In 1994, the United States decoupled trade and human rights in its China policy by dropping its insistence that Beijing make substantial improvements to its human rights record to qualify as a 'Most Favoured Nation' – that is, one whose exports could enter the US at preferential tariffs. European leaders travelled

Executions and Organ Transplants

The widespread execution of criminals and the reported 'harvesting' of their corpses for lucrative organ transplants was one of China's more blatant abuses of human rights in the 1990s. Beijing never divulges how many people it executes a year, but Amnesty International said it knew of 2,050 executions in 1994 and 4,367 in 1997. These two figures, taken at random, demonstrate the arbitrary nature of capital punishment in China. It has been administered for publishing pornography as well as murder; for 'hooliganism' as well as trafficking in women and children. An unknown number of political prisoners were executed after the suppression of the Tiananmen Square Democracy Movement. Pro-independence activists are often executed in Xinjiang. The number of executions tends to increase immediately before traditional festivals, special events or as a result of anti-crime campaigns such as the 'strike hard' movement of the late 1990s. Appeals against the death sentence are little more than a formality.

Criminals are often paraded before the public at 'mass sentencing rallies' before execution. On such occasions, shackled and gripped firmly by two or more policemen – most of them, bizarrely, wearing white gloves – offenders are forced to bow their heads and wear placards round their necks specifying their names and crimes. Strings are tied around their trouser bottoms in case fear should cause them to lose control of their bowels. After sentencing, they are paraded through city streets in trucks and driven to the execution grounds – usually a field or open space in the suburbs. A single shot to the back of the neck, or in the back, opposite the heart, is the most common form of execution. But in 1998 China said it was studying the possibility of using lethal injections to carry out capital punishment. The official Xinhua News Agency said lethal injections saved money and helped reduce 'accidents'. The first executions by lethal injection were reported to have been carried out in 1997.

During the 1990s evidence emerged – some of it provided by the human rights activist HARRY WU – that executed prisoners had become the main source of a profitable organ transplant business. It became the custom for some courts to notify health departments and hospitals after they handed down death sentences. Ambulances and other vehicles then appeared at the execution grounds. Once the People's Armed Police had done their work, medical staff quickly removed corpses from the scene. Sometimes kidneys and corneas were removed in the waiting vehicles. More often, the corpses were driven directly to hospitals where organs were extracted for sale to local and overseas customers, many of them Chinese from Hong Kong or the United States.

The Chinese government denied these practices were widespread. It pointed to laws which forbade the use of organs from executed criminals unless prisoners themselves or their families gave prior consent. It did not say these laws were always adhered to. Corroborative, if circumstantial, evidence that most of the raw materials for the transplant business came from executed prisoners was provided by the lack of any system of voluntary organ donation in China.

to Beijing with teams of optimistic businessmen in tow armed with lists of joint ventures rather than stern-faced diplomats bearing the names of political prisoners.

In 1997, several West European governments declined to back a resolution that had been raised (but not passed) every year at the UN Commission on Human Rights since Tiananmen condemning China's human rights record. The following year the United States, sponsor of the resolution, announced that it would abandon the practice, too, given Beijing's willingness to sign up to the two UN international covenants. Criticism of China's human rights record at multilateral forums came to an end, while public criticism by governments was toned down and muted by other concerns. These developments were a triumph for Chinese diplomacy, though in 1999 the United States renewed its censure at the UN, once again without securing majority support.

It would be wrong to conclude from these developments that international pressure accomplished nothing, or that the prospects for improvements in China's human rights record are wholly gloomy at the start of the new century. The weight of tradition and the determination of the Communist Party to stay in power remain powerful impediments to the growth of civil and political liberties. They are likely to do so for some time, and at least until a new generation takes over the reins of power in Beijing. But just as international pressure, however intermittently applied, obliged China to adopt much of the international law and language of the human rights debate, so the social and economic changes wrought by rapid modernization will increase domestic pressures on the government to live up to them. What remains uncertain is when and, indeed, whether the Party will be able to respond to these pressures constructively. In the meantime, improvements in China's human rights record are more likely to arise from the fragmentation of government control over a rapidly changing society than new policy initiatives from a Party determined to hang on to power as long as possible.

Hunan Province

Rice and revolution are among Hunan's most enduring contributions to modern China. The province produces more rice than any other in the country and usually supplies its neighbours with the staple of southern China. Hunan is also where MAO ZEDONG, its most famous son, first observed and then championed the peasant revolution which eventually brought the CHINESE COMMUNIST PARTY to power. The roll call of Hunanese revolutionaries, especially Communists, is particularly long. In the reform era Hunan's importance as a rice producer remains, but its revolutionary past, like that of other provinces, has proved something of a mixed blessing.

resistance and reform under empire

Hunan, a province of 77,200 square miles (200,000 sq kms) and 65 million people at the close of the century, straddles two worlds. Its eastern half, watered by the Yangtze, the Dongting Lake, and the Xiang, which flows in from the south, is a rich rice basket. It is the location of the provincial capital, Changsha, and traditionally the most 'open', modern part of the province.

West Hunan is mountainous, isolated and poor by comparison. Much of it is inhabited by ETHNIC MINORITIES, notably the Miao, Tujia and Dong peoples. Whereas Changsha was linked to the national rail network as early as 1918, railways made no inroads in the west of the province until long after the Communists came to power. Similarly, the province's best roads and its most navigable rivers are concentrated in the east. Much of west Hunan belongs to the relatively closed world of the interior.

In the broader scheme of things, Hunan has a well-earned reputation for resisting the national tide – a reflection of the individual nature of its people and their traditions. Changsha, for example, was almost alone among major cities south of the Yangtze in holding out against the Taiping armies in the mid-nineteenth century as they laid waste to southern China. And in Zeng Guofan (1811–72) and his Hunanese army, Hunan produced one of the chief instruments of Manchu victory over the rebels and their 'Heavenly Kingdom'.

Hunan was unusual, too, in the vehemence of its anti-foreign movement during the final years of the QING DYNASTY. Its targets were MISSIONARIES and the spread of CHRISTIANITY in the province. Sacrilegious materials, described in the missionary literature as 'vile pamphlets', were widespread in Hunan; violence against believers and the destruction of church property were equally common.

During the late 1890s, the province acquired fame as the centre of a more sophisticated movement: the Changsha reform experiment. Between 1896–8 Hunan's capital seethed with new ideas. Many of them owed something to LIANG QICHAO and other luminaries of late Qing radicalism who tried to turn the province into a bastion of anti-Manchu rule. The idea was to force reform on the centre from the provinces, if necessary by declaring independence – much as had happened in Japan during the Meiji Restoration.

At first the omens were encouraging. Hunan fell within the domain of Zhang Zhidong (1837–1909), who pioneered industrialization in central China from his base in HUBEI, and who supported reform in Changsha. The governor of Hunan backed the movement. So did the local gentry. The first fruits of provincial modernization included street lighting in Changsha, the construction of modern roads, a mining bureau and a telegraph line linking the city with Wuhan.

But the movement's main aim was *political* change, a much more sensitive matter. Changsha's new academies, societies and magazines spread this gospel far beyond the world of officialdom to which political debate traditionally had been confined. Notions of individual rights, egalitarianism and other unsettling ideas entered the *public* domain, a departure in China's political history and a benchmark in the quest for modernity. This was too much even for Zhang Zhidong and the 'enlightened' Hunan elite. Partly at the prompting of Beijing, but mainly because the new thinking in Changsha was a threat to their own position, the authorities cracked down on the movement and drove its proponents out of the province.

republicans, federalists, Communists

Revolutionaries as well as reformers looked to Hunan to initiate national change. Huang Xing (1874–1916), a collaborator of SUN YAT-SEN, had particularly high hopes of his home province. Hunanese featured prominently in his 'Society for China's Revival', one of many small revolutionary groups dedicated to destroying the dynasty, as well as the more important UNITED LEAGUE Sun formed in 1905 to topple the Manchus. In the event, army officers played a more important role in the REPUBLICAN REVOLUTION of 1911 than the revolutionaries. But together with SHAANXI, Hunan was quick to rally to the anti-Manchu revolt which broke out in neighbouring Hubei.

The theme of Hunanese independence, of the province's special role in guiding China's destiny, appeared again in the early 1920s – this time in the context of a federalist movement. This was an attempt to remake the young republic from the bottom up by granting the provinces quasi-independent status. The aim was to deliver China from centralized rule by weak governments in Beijing whose main consequence was the rise of WARLORDS. To this end Hunan promulgated a democratic constitution in 1922. Little came of it: WU PEIFU, principal warlord of central China, soon brought Hunan into his domain.

He remained in control until 1926 when Hunan became the first target of the NORTHERN EXPEDITION, the Kuomintang's military campaign to reunify China. The speed of the revolutionaries' victory in the province was startling; the violence and intensity of the peasants' revolts that followed even more so. Class warfare swept along the Xiang valley. Many lives were lost as old scores were settled, landlords attacked and dispossessed, and 'local bullies' dealt with. Both sides resorted to executions and other excesses.

The upheaval inspired Mao Zedong's *Report on an Investigation of the Hunan Peasant Movement*, written in early 1927, and later one of his most famous works. In it Mao identified the untapped revolutionary power of the peasantry and affirmed the violent tactics they waged to overthrow their enemies. Chinese revolutionaries could either march at their head and lead them; follow at their rear criticizing them; or oppose them. Whatever they decided to do, Mao wrote, they had to make up their minds quickly.

Kuomintang military leaders came to share Mao's sense of urgency – though not his delight – at events in the provinces controlled by the Left-wing government in Wuhan. As far as they were concerned, the Wuhan government was ineffective, in thrall to its Soviet advisers, and unwilling to restore order in the towns and countryside. Things were different in east China where in April 1927 CHIANG KAI-SHEK had purged the Communists and brought the anti-foreign movement to heel. It was time for central China to do the same.

First in Changsha, then in the surrounding counties, the militarists nominally loyal to Wuhan executed Communist activists and crushed the peasant revolution in Hunan and Hubei. Communist attempts to reverse the situation by seizing Nanchang, capital of neighbouring JIANGXI, and staging uprisings to coincide with the autumn harvest in Hunan and Hubei, came to naught (see PEOPLE'S LIBERATION ARMY).

So, very nearly, did the Communist movement itself. At the end of 1927 Mao retreated to Jinggangshan, on the border between Hunan and Jiangxi, where he tried to put into practice some of the lessons of his report. It was not the end of armed Communist insurrection in Hunan: in 1930 the Party ordered troops under PENG DEHUAI, another of Hunan's prominent revolutionaries, to occupy Changsha. He managed to hold the city for a few days but was evicted by Nationalist forces. The 'high tide' of revolution that the Soviet-dominated Communist leadership believed would carry the Party to power was by now a myth, in Hunan and elsewhere.

It remained so under He Jian (1887–1956), provincial governor until 1937. He Jian was not one of Chiang's trusted allies, but he was sufficiently opposed to Communism to be left in charge until Hunan was thrust into the frontline of the SINO-JAPANESE WAR. The province's location and food resources made it a key military objective in the conflict.

Twice, first in 1939 and then in 1941, Japanese troops staged massive assaults on Changsha. Twice they were defeated in heroic shows of resistance which counted for much given the generally unimpressive military record of the Nationalists. The heroism did not endure: in 1944 first Changsha and then Hengyang, in the south, on the railway leading to GUANGXI, fell to the Ichigo offensive that brought Japanese power deep into southern China.

Almost exactly five years later, the People's Liberation Army followed the same route through Hunan in their conquest of south China during the CIVIL WAR. Their passage was made easier by the defection of Cheng Qian (1881–1968), governor and military chief of Hunan. Cheng was richly rewarded for changing sides: unusually for a former Kuomintang defector, he was allowed to serve as governor of his home province while the Communists imposed control over it during the early 1950s.

revolutionary test bed

The roll call of revolutionary Hunanese rarely seemed so impressive as during the first years of the People's Republic. It included, most obviously, Mao Zedong, leader of the new regime, and by now the great teacher of the Chinese people; LIU SHAOQI, the second most important figure, and the Chairman's chosen successor; and Peng Dehuai, an outstanding military leader and Politburo member. He Long (1896–1969), Tao Zhu (1908–69) and Wang Zhen (1908–93) were among a host of younger, lesser, but still important Communist leaders with roots in Hunan. Such a revolutionary pedigree lent the province a political cachet, even if it did not produce any favours on the policy front relative to other parts of the country.

It did, however, make Hunan something of a test bed; a place where China's top leaders felt most at home and where they could best observe and understand the effects of the policies they launched in distant Beijing. There was no greater need for this than during the GREAT LEAP FORWARD of 1958, Mao's campaign to attain Communism via instant collectivization and rural industrialization. And there was hardly a greater disaster for modern China than the Chairman's ignorance of, or refusal to listen to, reports of the famine these policies produced during a rare visit to his home town of Shaoshan in June 1959. Mao saw, or pretended to see, no need to change tack.

Another influential Hunan returnee reached very different conclusions about the Leap. Peng Dehuai had visited his home village, close to Shaoshan, in 1958 and turned up at Shaoshan itself early the following year. He drew on both journeys to complain of falsified production figures, widespread lying on the part of local officials and growing peasant distress. Peng warned of disaster unless the Party revised the Leap's strategy and abandoned its more absurd goals.

These two views, partly the result of separate visits by two top leaders to their native province, came out into the open at the Lushan Conference of July–August 1959. Mao prevailed, Peng was purged and the agony of China's peasants prolonged (see GREAT LEAP FORWARD; PENG DEHUAI).

During the first two decades of Communist rule several Hunan towns became important industrial centres. Changsha remained the most populous and important city politically, but Xiangtan and Zhuzhou, just south of the provincial capital, and Hengyang, approximately halfway between Changsha and the border with GUANGDONG, developed into major manufacturing bases. Each of these cities derives its importance from location on the railway network of east Hunan.

In 1970 work began on a railway in the west of the province as part of the Second North–South Trunk Line between Beijing and the south coast. The terrain slowed construction: more than 300 tunnels had to be cut through China's central highlands. But completion of the project in 1979 opened up a huge stretch of southern China that had long been isolated and off the beaten track.

'Leftism' persists

By comparison, Hunan's politics tended to remain locked in the closed world of Mao Zedong. In his final years the Chairman settled on HUA GUOFENG as his successor. Though born in Shaanxi, Hua had spent most of his career in Hunan and served as Party boss of Xiangtan, the administrative centre for Shaoshan. His support for Mao during the Leap resulted in promotion to head of the provincial Party and, in the later stages of the CULTURAL REVOLUTION, transfer to Beijing. Hua's successor in Hunan was Mao Zhiyong (1929–). Mao was unwilling to depart very far from the late Chairman's line, despite Hua's failure to retain power in Beijing and the rise of the reformist faction led by DENG XIAOPING.

Certainly the province was no place for radical political experiments of the kind briefly attempted in Changsha in 1980. The occasion was China's first direct elections for local representative congresses; the venue Hunan Teacher's College (see DEMOCRACY; ELECTIONS). Two candidates, Tao Sen (c 1949–) and Liang Heng (c 1953–), fought a campaign to end bureaucratic privileges that was a thinly disguised assault on the college establishment. In addition Liang made a virtue of declaring his agnosticism as far as MARXISM was concerned. Both men enjoyed broad popular support on campus.

This was too much for the authorities who countered by packing the list of candidates with political cronies. As a result, hundreds of students took to the streets of Changsha and some staged a hunger strike outside the provincial Party headquarters. Beijing intervened, but an investigation failed to condemn the authorities. Tao was sent to labour camp. Liang left China with his American wife. Political reform in Changsha fared no better in 1980–81 than it had in the 1890s.

Far larger protests engulfed the city during the TIANANMEN SQUARE DEMOCRACY MOVEMENT of 1989. HU YAOBANG, the Party leader whose death in April of that year sparked the movement, was a Hunanese; in Changsha grief at his passing lent an edge to the demands for more democracy and an end to corruption at the heart of the movement. Protests brought the city to a standstill in the days after troops cleared the square in Beijing, and the mayor had to appeal for order.

Hunan and the Yangtze strategy

Economic change in the province encountered obstacles, too. Hunan not only had the weight of the past on its shoulders but its inland location ill-prepared it for the engagement with the wider world at the heart of Deng's development strategy. The second trunk railway line improved the situation, but during the 1980s FOREIGN TRADE AND INVESTMENT made few inroads compared with Guangdong to the south. If Hunan fared better than the provinces to its west, it suffered from the growing gap between 'middle' and coastal China.

The opening of the Yangtze valley, including Changsha, to trade and investment on favourable terms in 1992 put the province on the high-speed growth track. And, as the decade came to a close, Hunan's per capita GDP, foreign trade value and use of international capital placed it just below the midway mark in the league table of provincial economic performance. Beijing's efforts to ensure more balanced economic development between the coast and the interior should benefit Hunan in the new century. The THREE GORGES DAM might do the same – though in Hunan as elsewhere, the project's promise of improved flood control and cheap electricity is tempered by concern over environmental and other issues.

India

Frontier disputes, the question of TIBET, and larger rivalries arising from their status as over-populated, undeveloped countries in the midst of modernization have made for uneasy relations between China and India. Beijing and New Delhi co-authored the 'five principles of coexistence' to govern their foreign policy in 1953 (see BANDUNG CONFERENCE), but came to blows over their border. They both aspired to leadership of the Third World, but saw their own relationship sour as part of broader superpower rivalry. In the 1980s and 1990s, they opened their economies to trade, foreign investment and free market reforms, but began to worry about the implications of each other's rejuvenation for their own security, a factor in India's decision to conduct nuclear tests in 1998. China's close relations with PAKISTAN, India's traditional enemy, are a major concern in Delhi.

The Sino-Indian border dispute, unsettled at the start of the new era, is a legacy of British India. Independent India inherited frontiers in the northeast drawn up by McMahon – an imperial administrator – and, in the west, a tract of land, the Aksai Chin, that intruded into what China regarded as XINJIANG and Tibet. Beijing recognized neither boundary. But Jawaharlal Nehru's dream of an Indian-Chinese brotherhood was shared by ZHOU ENLAI, and it seemed conflict might be avoided. The dream turned sour with the 1959 Tibetan revolt, when the DALAI LAMA and his supporters were given refuge in India, and New Delhi's discovery, two years later, of a Chinese-built road in the Aksai Chin linking Xinjiang to Tibet. Skirmishes between Indian and Chinese troops occurred in both the eastern and western sectors of the border. Beijing viewed them against the background of broader security issues, including India's role as a conduit for outside interference in Tibet, and was dismayed by the neutrality of the Soviet Union in a dispute that China felt required solidarity within the socialist camp (see SOVIET UNION). Relations between Beijing and Moscow were coming under strain for a host of reasons; China did not welcome the possibility of tension along its southern *and* northern frontiers.

It eliminated the former by dealing India a crushing blow in a short border war which lasted from October to November 1962. Chinese troops, having made their point, retreated to the 'line of actual control', declining to make territorial gains in either of the two disputed areas. However, as a result of a 1963 treaty with Pakistan, Beijing acquired what India claims to be part of Jammu and Kashmir. Sporadic border clashes continued for years as New Delhi, courtesy of its principal ally the Soviet Union, found itself in the opposite diplomatic camp to a China wracked first by the Cultural Revolution and then the less violent upheavals engendered by reform. Beijing mocked India's anti-colonial pedigree, and its claims to lead or represent the Third World. It worried New Delhi much more by establishing a strategic relationship with Pakistan.

The end of the Cold War and China's recourse to pragmatism at home and abroad made for a thaw in Sino-Indian relations. Ties were 'normalized' in December 1988 with the

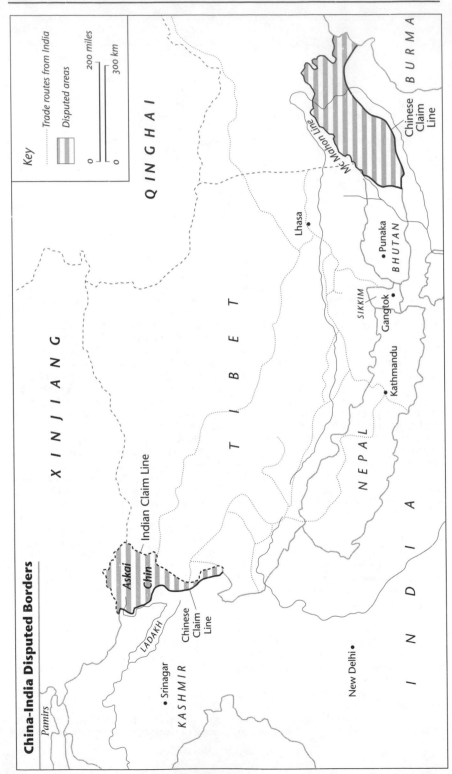

China-India Disputed Borders

Key
- Trade routes from India
- Disputed areas

200 miles
300 km

Pamirs

XINJIANG

QINGHAI

KASHMIR

LADAKH

Srinagar

Askai Chin

Indian Claim Line

Chinese Claim Line

TIBET

Lhasa

NEPAL

Kathmandu

SIKKIM

Gangtok

BHUTAN

Punaka

McMahon Line

Chinese Claim Line

BURMA

INDIA

New Delhi

visit to Beijing of Rajiv Gandhi. In 1993, the two sides agreed 'to maintain peace and tranquillity' along their disputed border. When JIANG ZEMIN became the first Chinese president to visit New Delhi in 1996, both parties undertook not to attack each other across the border, and to reduce their troops in the area.

These moves drew the sting of the border issue in bilateral relations. But they were seen by some in Delhi as lending legitimacy to China's annexation of India's Himalayan territories. There were also broader strategic concerns. China refused to recognize Sikkim as part of India. It supplied missiles and nuclear technology to Pakistan. It armed Bangladesh. It helped bankroll and arm the military government in BURMA, and secured Rangoon's permission to establish observation posts in the Andaman Sea. Beijing's policy seemed to be one of tying India down in the subcontinent, and keeping a watching brief over the Indian Ocean. In this context, the fact that China was also an established nuclear power was a factor in India's refusal in 1996 to join the international ban on nuclear testing. In 1998 George Fernandes, the Indian defence minister, said China, not Pakistan presented the greatest danger to his country. A few days later, India conducted a nuclear explosion. A few days later still, Pakistan followed suit. Beijing expressed concern about both developments but was particularly offended at India's rationale for going nuclear. Tensions of a different kind surfaced in the first months of the new century following the flight to India of the 17th Karmapa Lama –

the third-most-important figure in Tibetan Buddhism after the Dalai Lama and the PANCHEN LAMA – whom Beijing had carefully nurtured with a view to securing greater control over Tibetan religious life (see TIBET).

This strategic and political rivalry occurred against the wider background of competition between China and India – both of them pursuing economic reform – for international capital and multilateral credit. The flow of investment has showed that the world favours China over India when it comes to doing business. But at the close of the century some argued that India's attachment to the rule of law, widespread use of English and democratic political system would help it overcome the ethnic divisions, corruption and bureaucracy which has scarred the country and hampered development. The corollary of this was that China's dictatorial politics and poor human rights record could not be overlooked when making investment decisions, whether for moral or economic reasons.

Naturally, such a view was not shared in China. Until the dawn of the nuclear era in South Asia, India occupied a low priority in the official Chinese mind. It occupied a less important one still in the minds of many ordinary people, who felt comparisons between their country and India were demeaning. India is an Asian country and, like China, the centre of an ancient civilization. But its economic and military performance has not proved so impressive as to make ordinary Chinese raise questions about the potential superiority of India's political or legal system.

Indonesia

Nowhere in Southeast Asia was China's influence so great as in Indonesia during the early 1960s. One reason for this was Beijing's closeness to the minority Indonesian Chinese community. Another was its cultivation of President Sukarno, the mercurial, charismatic Indonesian leader, who favoured an 'anti-imperialist' foreign policy. China's involvement soon spelled disaster for both. Relations were slow to recover and remain fragile at the start of the new century.

Communist China's main concern in developing ties with newly independent Indonesia in the 1950s was to win the loyalty of its OVERSEAS CHINESE and protect them from discrimination. This was a sensitive matter:

Beijing regarded most Indonesian Chinese as citizens of the People's Republic of China, thus tarnishing a community already disliked because of its economic success with the added stigma of alien status. Jakarta was unhappy that so much of the Indonesian economy was in the hands of those under the protection of a foreign power.

Some of the tension arising from this situation was reduced by the Sino-Indonesian Dual Nationality Treaty of 1955. Ethnic Chinese deemed to qualify either for Chinese or Indonesian citizenship could choose one or the other within two years of the treaty's ratification. Those who failed to do so would have the decision made for them on the basis of their father's nationality. The treaty called on those who decided to opt for Chinese citizenship to respect Indonesian customs, and 'not participate in political activities'. It guaranteed their 'lawful rights'.

The treaty was a milestone in Beijing's attitude towards the Overseas Chinese. Previously, the Communist government adhered to the *jus sanguinis* principle of its Qing and Nationalist predecessors according to which anyone born of a Chinese father or a Chinese mother was a Chinese citizen. This was not a recipe for good relations with Southeast Asian countries that included large numbers of Chinese, and whose governments China sought to recruit in its struggle against United States' and Soviet influence. To some extent, blood ties had to be sacrificed for the Revolution.

But to what extent? The question arose because Indonesia at first declined to ratify the nationality treaty on the grounds that it would tie its hands in trying to redistribute wealth away from the Chinese. In 1959, the army ordered all Chinese to vacate rural areas. Beijing protested strongly but quietly for fear of damaging promising relations with Sukarno. Finally, in desperation, it called on the Chinese of Indonesia to 'come home' where a warm welcome was assured.

In the following few months about 120,000 did just that, leaving their wealth behind them. They made the journey across the South China Sea in the few ships available to China's merchant marine. It was the largest exercise in Chinese repatriation in the history of Communist China. The exodus harmed the Indonesian economy, but brought little benefit either to China or those who braved the voyage. Many found life in 'Overseas Chinese Farms' in HAINAN ISLAND or elsewhere in southern China difficult. Some suffered during the CULTURAL REVOLUTION. Others, interviewed almost 40 years after their flight, still seemed unsure why they were in China and regretted lost opportunities in Indonesia, despite the risks.

Indonesia ratified the nationality treaty in 1960. Relations with China soon improved. Beijing developed ties with both President Sukarno and the Indonesian Communist Party (*Partai Komunis Indonesia* – PKI), which it hoped would join the government and, perhaps, eventually take power. That was for the future. China's immediate concern was to counter American influence in Southeast Asia and, as the Sino-Soviet split developed, curb 'revisionism' in the region, too (see SOVIET UNION).

Sukarno shared some of these goals. But he was more interested in achieving dominance in the Malay world. That meant vigorous opposition to the Federation of Malaysia, created in 1963. China lent its support to this campaign, as it did to Indonesia's sudden decision in 1965 to withdraw from the United Nations on the grounds that it was a puppet of the big powers. Sukarno, again with China's backing, founded the Conference of New Emerging Forces to challenge the UN. The idea did not outlive Sukarno's political ascendancy, which came to an abrupt end in the countercoup of October 1965.

The role of the PKI and China in these events is unclear. That they spelt the end of any influence over Indonesian history and politics for both is beyond doubt. The army had long been uneasy over Sukarno's closeness to the PKI at home and Chinese Communism abroad. Most generals opposed requests that the army instal a network of political commissars and work alongside a PKI-controlled militia. When a few Left-leaning military leaders staged a coup against 'anti-Communist forces', retribution was swift. Sukarno was ousted, the PKI crushed and the Chinese community targeted for attack. China's Indonesian policy was in ruins. It had helped sink Sukarno, and exposed both the PKI and the Chinese community to Right-wing, Nationalist resentment.

In 1966 Beijing again announced it would repatriate Indonesian Chinese who wished to escape persecution. Only about 10,000 chose to leave the country, despite often horrific communal violence directed against them.

It took China some time to realize that the generals had a firm grip on power and that Sukarno would not return. Repeated attacks on Chinese diplomatic missions and personnel in Indonesia helped bring the message home. In Beijing groups of Red Guards reciprocated, ransacking the Indonesian embassy. The ritual violence came to an end in October 1967 when Jakarta severed diplomatic relations, inaugurating a 23-year hiatus in Sino-Indonesian ties.

Diplomatic relations were restored in 1990, and President Suharto made his first visit to China the same year. He was a welcome guest at a time when Beijing was fighting off the diplomatic isolation arising from its suppression of the TIANANMEN SQUARE DEMOCRACY MOVEMENT. Both sides agreed to bury the past.

For a while relations were unruffled, though China's claims to ownership over much of the South China Sea appeared to include parts of Indonesia's offshore Natuna gas field. Yet the ghosts of the past were not laid so easily. Violence against the Chinese community was an all-too-regular occurrence in Indonesia, which both China and TAIWAN were quick to condemn. They were particularly outspoken when it emerged that ethnic Chinese women had been raped and killed during the riots that overthrew President Suharto in May 1998. In a mild reprise of the situation in 1960 and 1966, they called on Jakarta to punish the culprits and ensure fair treatment for Indonesia's minority peoples. On Beijing's part, the appeal appeared to risk intervention by third parties on behalf of *its* ethnic minorities, several of whom, notably in TIBET and XIN-JIANG, had cause to complain about Chinese policies towards them.

industry

China's desire to build an industrialized economy dates back to the first generation of modernizers in the mid-nineteenth century. Men such as Zeng Guofan (1811–72), Zhang Zhidong (1837–1909) and Li Hongzhang (1823–1901) saw that industry had made the West and Japan strong, and that China could never become so without it. Then, and for most of the time since, the longstanding dominance of AGRICULTURE, much of it conducted along traditional, labour-intensive lines, made the need to develop industry even more pressing. It was a matter of pride *and* power: the persistent hold of farming over Chinese life was a sign of backwardness and a source of weakness – economically as well as militarily. At the start of the twenty-first century, China is in the midst of transition from an agrarian to an urban, industrialized economy. The process is incomplete, the transition hazardous, especially since China must cope with international competition arising from its membership of the World Trade Organisation. It has also taken longer than imperial reformers, republican revolutionaries or Communist leaders hoped. But it is exerting a profound effect on the country.

the pre-Communist era
Industrialization washed over twentieth-century China in four waves, punctuated by rebellions, wars or equally disastrous Communist political campaigns. The first wave, beginning in the final years of the QING DYNASTY and ending with the flight of Chiang Kaishek's Nationalist government to TAIWAN in 1949, saw the creation of mines, modern utilities, and small-scale factories producing mainly textiles, food stuffs and other consumer goods. For the most part they were concentrated in the TREATY PORTS, especially SHANGHAI, Wuhan (see HUBEI), the coastal provinces and, during the 1930s, in MAN-CHUGUO, the Japanese 'puppet state' in northeast China, where industrial growth was most rapid and industry most advanced. Many of these enterprises were foreign owned. Some, such as those in SHANXI, where a few heavy industries were also established, owed much to the patronage of WARLORDS, in this case YAN XISHAN. In most, equipment was rudimentary, working conditions poor.

Even in the years immediately before the SINO-JAPANESE WAR, when they were at their most developed, these examples of modern production were tiny enclaves within an overwhelmingly agrarian economy. They were responsible for less than 10 per cent of national output – less, even, than that produced by traditional handicraft industries. They also tended to be isolated from the rest of the economy. Japanese rule ensured this in the case of the northeast; elsewhere, weak linkages with the interior and inadequate transportation meant the modern sector of the economy could do little to spur national growth. The wartime relocation of coastal factories in the interior, beyond Japan's reach, checked the pace of industrialization south of the Great Wall; asset-stripping by Soviet troops following the defeat of Japan in 1945 did the same in Manchuria (see LIAONING; JILIN; HEILONGJIANG) These developments, combined with the inflation, destruction and demoralization caused by the CIVIL WAR, ensured that the Communists inherited a weak industrial base when they seized power in 1949. The fact that they went on to sequester most foreign assets and expel foreign personnel made it weaker still.

from Soviet model to self-sufficiency
Weaker but not non-existent. China's second wave of industrialization, inaugurated by the

First Five Year Plan (1953–7), was an extraordinary success; it would not have been had the Communists been forced to start from scratch. Yet there was much that was novel about this concentrated burst of development. A reflection of China's close ties with Moscow, it was based on the Soviet model and emphasized the creation of heavy industries and central planning. (See SOVIET UNION.) At its heart were more than 150 projects, many of them located in interior provinces previously untouched by development of any kind, built with Soviet equipment and assistance. Ten thousand Russian advisers worked in China during the 1950s. Nearly three times that number of Chinese studied in the Soviet Union, among them the young JIANG ZEMIN and LI PENG. With Soviet help China built iron and steel plants, power stations, heavy machinery factories and oil refineries. Some projects were delayed or abandoned in 1960 because of the Sino-Soviet split. But by that time China had collectivized agriculture, nationalized all private industry and created an impressive industrial system which testified to the purpose of the new Communist government and the resourcefulness of its people.

Gains on this scale were not repeated for more than 20 years. Mao Zedong's GREAT LEAP FORWARD, an attempt to establish Communism overnight, collapsed amid chaos and famine. Industry and agriculture both recovered quickly but hostility towards the Soviet bloc as well as the United States meant questions of political ideology and national security infused economic decision-making.

One example of this was the creation in the mid-1960s of a 'third line' of industries deep in the southwest safe from attack by Taiwan or the United States, then engaged in war in Vietnam. In the 1990s the presence of these factories, overstaffed, ill-equipped and with still far from adequate road or rail links, energy supplies and established sources of qualified personnel, troubled a new generation of reformers anxious to make state enterprises profitable.

Another example was the championing of new, self-sufficient industrial models which, it was claimed, delivered record output and fostered political consciousness on the part of workers. Daqing, the giant oil field in HEILONGJIANG, was the favoured Maoist model in the 1960s and 1970s. One of the most common propaganda slogans of the era was 'In industry, learn from Daqing!' – a mantra factories across the country sought to apply to their own operations.

The effects on industry of the CULTURAL REVOLUTION, Mao's final exercise in radicalism, were less marked. There were dips in growth during the most politically chaotic years but they were far from disasters. The real damage lay elsewhere: in the fact that the obsession with politics prevented planners and officials from adopting a new industrial strategy, even though the Soviet-style one they had pursued since the early 1950s was delivering diminishing returns. By the 1970s, given levels of investment were producing smaller increases in output. Incomes were falling. So was consumption. New thinking was required.

the rise of rural industry

It was supplied, after a short period of uncertainty, by DENG XIAOPING, who in 1978 emerged as China's post-Mao strongman. The policy known as the FOUR MODERNIZATIONS, of which industry was the first, ushered in the third, so far most buoyant, wave of Chinese industrialization. It was based on a return to household farming, greater emphasis on material incentives, the decentralization of decision-making, a dramatic expansion in trade, and the opening of the economy to foreign investment (see FOREIGN TRADE AND INVESTMENT). China's role models were now beyond its borders. They were TAIWAN, HONG KONG, South Korea (see KOREA) and SINGAPORE, all of which had launched themselves into sustained, rapid growth by using their low-cost but disciplined labour force to produce light industrial products for export.

Though Deng's policy of reform at home and engagement abroad occasionally faltered and often generated controversy it has never been abandoned. Yet it remains incomplete, chiefly because thousands of state industries, many of them behemoths created during the 1950s and sustained ever since, have yet to submit to the market whose rules govern almost every other area of the Chinese economy. They are concentrated in the northeast, China's 'rust belt', but are found in number in most major cities, particularly in inland centres such as Wuhan, CHONGQING and Lanzhou, capital of GANSU. The third wave of industrialization was therefore largely the work of 'township and village enterprises' (TVEs) or rural enterprises – collectively owned businesses outside the formal state sector.

TVEs appeared during the Leap but they did

not produce consumer goods and were not subject to the market. The agricultural boom generated by Deng's reforms created new conditions in which villages, local governments and private businesses banded together to operate factories for the processing of agricultural products. Lower taxes and fewer restrictions allowed them to produce whatever they wanted – or whatever they could sell. Chinese entrepreneurial flair, temporarily suppressed during the Mao years, surfaced with a vengeance. The People's Republic's first home-grown generation of businessmen and women emerged into riches and fame, often to the accompaniment of praise from the official media, which was keen to counter resistance to the reforms from conservatives in Beijing.

Most rural enterprises are situated near major towns and cities, particularly in the south. JIANGSU province, in the Yangtze Delta, has long been one of their strongholds. Many subcontract production from state enterprises. All have absorbed surplus labour no longer required on the land, driving down the proportion of the national workforce engaged in farming at a faster rate than has occurred anywhere else in the world. In 1978, rural enterprises accounted for 22 per cent of industrial output. In 1984 it rose to 30 per cent, and in 1988 to 36 per cent. The development of rural industries was the key element driving China's rapid economic growth of the 1980s and 1990s. Only at the close of the century did the pace falter, partly because of falling demand caused by the Asian financial crisis.

the 'fourth wave'

China's fourth wave of industrialization built rapidly during the 1990s and will crest early in the new century. It is founded on private enterprise, Sino-foreign joint ventures and wholly foreign-owned businesses. Each has generated controversies in the course of development, and private enterprise in particular has proved sensitive politically.

At the turn of the century, official statistics said there were nearly 1 million private businesses with assets of US$62 billion and 14 million employees. The figure was almost certainly an underestimate. Many private firms are concentrated in ZHEJIANG, where the state sector of the economy has long been on the retreat and individual enterprise has blossomed. The Communist Party amended the Constitution in 1988 and again in 1999 to provide guarantees for private firms, but the title still carries a political stigma. It can also

make it hard for businessmen to obtain credit or operating licences. Many entrepreneurs prefer to designate their firms 'collectives', even though they function as private businesses in everything but name.

This finesses the issue rather than resolves it. Private entrepreneurs face two problems, one of which confronts others engaged in business in China and another that does not. The first concerns the LAW: the right to ownership of private property remains unclear in China, despite more than two decades of free market reforms. The second involves the Party's ambiguous attitude towards the emergence of an independent class of entrepreneurs whose members might raise political demands of their own – and have the independent means to pursue them.

Foreign-funded enterprises have been more visible and less controversial, at least in political terms (see FOREIGN TRADE AND INVESTMENT). They are concentrated mainly, but far from exclusively, in the original SPECIAL ECONOMIC ZONES (SEZS), the open coastal cities set up shortly after the SEZs, and the various development zones established by almost every major city. (See GUANGDONG; FUJIAN; HAINAN ISLAND.) Most of them are funded by OVERSEAS CHINESE from Hong Kong, Taiwan, Southeast Asia and elsewhere. Their preference is for 'wholly foreign-owned' enterprises in which foreign investors enjoy greater control than in joint ventures. Labour-intensive and sometimes requiring little capital, such firms produce the textiles, toys, sportswear and electronics and other goods whose export has helped turn the Mainland into a rapidly industrializing trade giant. Western and Japanese investment, by contrast, tends to be concentrated in larger industries producing high-tech or high-value goods and, increasingly, in the service sector. Western firms usually seek a Chinese partner with whom to found a company, though they, too, turned increasingly to wholly foreign-owned models in the late 1990s.

China's industrialization in the last two decades of the century took place at a speed and on a scale unequalled anywhere in the world. It produced remarkable achievements. The economy grew by an annual average of almost 10 per cent, until the Asian financial crisis sapped demand for Chinese products at home and overseas. Per capita income doubled twice. Millions were lifted out of POVERTY. Urbanization intensified, creating huge new urban and peri-urban areas around estab-

Saving Socialism: The Troubled State Sector

China's flight from Marx to market in the 1980s and 1990s has left only one area of the economy distinctly socialist: the country's approximately 300,000 state-owned enterprises (SOEs) about 100,000 of them industrial concerns. Many of the larger firms date back to the second wave of industrialization of the 1950s. Communities rather than companies, they provide jobs for life, housing, medical services, schools and many other services for their often supernumerary employees. For decades, Beijing treated them as bureaucratic extensions of government, supplying them with credit and demanding repatriation of such funds as they generated. The economics might not always make sense – though for many years SOEs were a primary source of government revenue – but the politics were flawless: state enterprises were what made China socialist. Their existence is grounded in clause seven of the Constitution, still effective at the start of the new century, which describes the state sector of the economy as the 'leading force', and commits the government to ensuring its growth.

Yet in the reform era state enterprises have made China considerably poorer and much less efficient than it might be. Unwieldy, unattuned to the market and plagued by confusion over property rights and financial obligations, they cannot match the stellar performance of rural, private or foreign enterprises. In 1978 they were the mainstay of the economy; two decades later they produced barely one-third of industrial output. Their losses mounted in the 1990s, draining government revenues and dragging the state banks obliged to bankroll them into debt (see FINANCE). The need for reform was, and remains, urgent – so urgent that China's attempts to build a modern, efficient industrial sector depend upon it. So also, until Beijing found the necessary courage in November 1999 to commit itself to change, did China's chance of joining the World Trade Organization (WTO). The obligation to end monopolies, non-tariff barriers and other protective measures that accompany WTO membership will expose even successful state enterprises to intense competition.

Politics is one of many sensitive issues surrounding the revitalization of SOEs. Even as it has sponsored diverse forms of ownership and the rigours of the market, the Communist Party insists that state ownership of the economy is a benchmark of socialism that cannot be abandoned (see CHINESE COMMUNIST PARTY/IN SEARCH OF SOCIALISM). The Party skirted round the issue at its 15th National Congress in 1997

by substituting the term 'public ownership' for state ownership. Public ownership was said to include government stakes in businesses of every kind – state enterprises, rural industries and Sino-foreign joint ventures alike. As long as the 'public' stake was dominant overall, China could still be said to be a socialist country, albeit one in the 'initial' stage of socialism. The Congress accordingly stepped up calls for the restructuring of SOEs, including a programme of mergers, conversion into joint stock enterprises, the sale of factories to private individuals, including foreigners, and bankruptcies.

At this point the ideological gymnastics stopped and the real difficulties began. As the century came to a close SOEs still accounted for two-thirds of employment in the urban areas and more than half of all investment in fixed assets. They could hardly just be closed down. In the absence of national welfare and pension schemes, the livelihoods of millions were at stake. There was a genuine risk of social and political unrest.

A range of solutions was proposed, including the revitalization of about 1,000 large enterprises for conversion into the core of a modern enterprise system. At first, the model was the *chaebol*, or industrial conglomerates, which turned South Korea into an industrial giant. The Asian financial crisis of 1997–9 exposed Seoul's feet of clay and talk of China's own *chaebol* fell silent. Mergers were also undertaken, though sometimes to the disadvantage of the healthier partners involved. The sale of state enterprises, or their conversion into joint stock companies, was the preferred option of radicals. So was bankruptcy for those firms without a future. Both options opened the way for asset stripping by managers, staff and government officials which provoked sharp criticism in Beijing.

Each of these reform options carries risks. Each calls for political courage on the part of the government and, ideally, sustained high growth in the economy to absorb the hundreds of thousands likely to be laid off as a result of the reforms. In the meantime China's state enterprises continue to bleed red ink, which they have tried to stem by laying off employees. Unemployment has risen sharply, sparking strikes and protests in many parts of the country. The situation is particularly severe in the northeast and other major centres where China's industrial base is rusting rapidly, ensuring that enterprise reform remains one of the government's most pressing tasks at the start of the new era.

lished cities (see POPULATION). The market set the price of more than 95 per cent of industrial output. By the close of the century, industry was generating 42 per cent of GDP compared with agriculture's 21 per cent. At least one aspect of the twentieth-century reformist dream had been realized. And plans to close small plants across the country and concentrate the production of textiles, coal, concrete and steel in large centres and to develop 'pillar' industries for the production of

electronics, vehicles, petro-chemicals and building materials sustained the vision of China as a future industrial giant. Agreement on Beijing's membership of the World Trade Organisation, secured at last in 1999, had the same effect, though it raised fears for the future of many large state firms.

the experience of industrialization

Yet some of the problems arising from China's rapid industrialization have proved as staggering as the accomplishments. Record trade figures, the rise of powerful new conglomerates listing shares in New York, or stories of personal achievement and private wealth have been accompanied by CORRUPTION, damage to the ENVIRONMENT, growing income disparities and a central government weakened by the decentralization that made much of the industrial boom possible. Such problems would test the mettle of any government; it is no surprise that they have often proved too much for a Communist regime burdened by weak legitimacy, fading administrative muscle and a determination, above all things, to remain in power.

Then there is the experience of the industrialized. For many workers in the new factories of the 1990s, the majority of whom were often WOMEN, wages were low and living conditions poor. Yet in common with industrial

revolutions elsewhere, incomes in the modern sector of the economy were far higher than those on the farm. In this respect industrialization widened the divide between town and countryside which has always been a feature of Chinese life.

Yet for millions of people it also closed it. Industrialization has scarred China's landscape with ugly factories but subjected those who work in them to urgent new rhythms of life dictated by events overseas and China's reaction to them. The consequences have not always been happy. They are sometimes difficult for those affected by them to understand. Often they prove hard to cope with, at both the personal and community levels. But, indisputably, they are proof that more and more Chinese are living in the modern, industrialized world; and that China's national power is growing accordingly.

Inner Mongolia Autonomous Region

That history and politics have more to do with Inner Mongolia's status as an 'autonomous' region than demography is clear from the size of its Mongol population. At the close of the century Mongols accounted for less than 20 per cent of the region's 23 million people. This made them the most outnumbered of all the ETHNIC MINORITIES Beijing deemed important enough to justify a province-level autonomous region of their own. Such status has not silenced demands for more independence: some of China's Mongols have struggled to preserve a sense of national identity despite the odds and the risks. But the overwhelming presence of Han Chinese, and their domination of the fertile strip of territory in the southwest, close to Huhehaote, the capital, suggest that genuine autonomy for Mongols is even less likely than it is for the Uigurs of XINJIANG and the inhabitants of TIBET.

division and consolidation

Until its collapse, the QING DYNASTY ruled the vast deserts and steppelands of the Mongolian heartland through local nobles and Lamaist prelates. The problems Beijing faced in the area were the same as those it confronted in Tibet, from where the Mongols acquired their Buddhism, and Xinjiang: distance from the capital; the size of the region to be ruled; and the alien, that is non-Chinese, culture of its inhabitants.

What was different about Mongolia was that its leaders could rely on a neighbouring power, RUSSIA, to help them resist Chinese rule (see MONGOLIA). During the REPUBLICAN REVOLUTION of 1911 the tribes of Outer Mongolia, with Russian backing, declared their independence. They subsequently (and briefly) lost it again; and, at least on paper, were obliged to accept Chinese 'suzerainty'.

But in the early 1920s Soviet backing ensured Mongolia's freedom from Chinese rule – though at the cost of making the new Mongolian state a client of Moscow. Chinese governments found both developments unacceptable: the Nationalists did not recognize the Mongolian People's Republic until 1946 (and changed their mind in 1953, having lost the Mainland), while the Communists did so only in 1950, following their victory in the CIVIL WAR.

In the meantime an intense struggle for control over Inner Mongolia took place between Russia, Japan, successive Chinese governments and the Mongols themselves. The first three parties fared better than the last. A secret Russian–Japanese accord of 1913 separated the area into an eastern half, where Japan's interests were dominant, and a western one where Moscow's prevailed. The Chinese government tried to counter the influence of both powers by dividing Inner Mongolia into 'special administrative areas' and then, in 1928, four Chinese-style provincial units: Jehol (*Rehe*), Chahar (*Chahaer*), Sui-yuan and NINGXIA, the so-called Mongolian provinces.

Intensive Han Chinese settlement of the region, begun in the late Qing, accompanied these administrative changes. It was facilitated by railway building. The line from Beijing reached Kalgan (modern Zhangjiakou), capital of Jehol, before the fall of the Qing; and Baotou, in Suiyuan, in the early 1920s (see RAILWAYS). Han Chinese dominated the railway zone, and the fertile valley of the Yellow River, which stretches west from Baotou before it turns south and enters Ningxia. A similar situation unfolded in the plains of southeast Jehol around the modern city of Tongliao. For the most part, the Mongols were confined to the grasslands of the north while the newcomers occupied the plains and valleys in the south of the Mongolian homeland.

puppet state and autonomous region

Mongolian resentment over these developments provided fuel for Japanese ambitions. Shortly after establishing its 'puppet state' of MANCHUGUO in 1932, Japan created a Federated Autonomous Government of Mongolia with its capital in Kalgan. Its leader was De Wang (1902–66), prince of the northern Silingol League of Mongols, who was required to consult with his Japanese 'advisers' before making major decisions. With the outbreak of the SINO-JAPANESE WAR, the new Mongol state expanded to include Chahar, parts of Suiyuan and, until its troops were rebuffed, northern SHANXI. The Nationalist government, stunned by military reverses in China proper, could do little about these setbacks north of the Great Wall. Mongolian nationalism served Japan's purposes, not Chiang's.

It also served the Chinese Communist Party for whom Chiang's difficulties usually amounted to an opportunity. The Party had been active among Mongols for some time. YANAN, its wartime headquarters, was close to Mongol territory. The collapse of Nationalist Chinese power created a vacuum in Inner Mongolia Japan could not fill. One man in particular enabled the Party to spread its message in the region. He was Ulanhu (Wulanfu) (1904–88), a Moscow-trained, sinicized Mongol, who headed the Party's Institute for Nationality Affairs. Ulanhu did much to persuade the Mongols of Inner Mongolia to back the Communists on the grounds that they would have a brighter future under the rule of a revolutionary Chinese government than

under a 'reactionary' one, or a pan-Mongol regime based in Ulan Bator, capital of the Mongolian People's Republic.

The Party's chance to prove this came in 1947 by which time the Japanese had left the region but CHIANG KAI-SHEK had failed to reassert control. It created the Inner Mongolia Autonomous Region led by Ulanhu and based in Chahar. The new regime promised to curb the power of the Mongol princes and preserve the Mongolian way of life. During the following eight years China's first province-level autonomous region expanded to include all of the Mongol lands under Chinese control. Its capital moved from Kalgan to Huhehaote, formerly known as Guisui, capital of the old province of Suiyuan.

remoulding the Mongolians

Mongols were a minority in the new region from its creation, but the Communist Chinese chose not to subject them to LAND REFORM or other forms of revolutionary change. Unusually, Ulanhu was made leader of the local Party apparatus and political commissar of the military as well as chairman of the regional government. It was rare for Beijing to show such trust in a member of an ethnic minority, and an indication that Mongols were more reconciled to Communist rule than had once seemed likely.

The region developed rapidly in the 1950s. Many nomads expanded their herds, some took to farming and a few settled in the cities. Change was fastest in the predominantly Han areas of the south which benefited from an extension of the railway into Ningxia and GANSU, and the spread of INDUSTRY to China's interior. Much of this was the fruit of Sino-Soviet cooperation. The prime example was the creation of a giant iron and steel works in Baotou; it transformed what had once been little more than a caravanserai – if an important one – into a major industrial centre.

Many of these achievements were undone by the GREAT LEAP FORWARD of 1958–60. As the political pace picked up so did tensions between Mongol and Han. Han immigration increased and with it Chinese impatience with the Mongolian way of life. Herders were forced to tend their livestock in communes, reduce the number of animals in private ownership and devote more time to agriculture. Some preferred to kill their animals than do any of these things. As in other minority regions, those who spoke of the need to respect the special characteristics of ethnic minorities

The Lie of the Land

Inner Mongolia's 490,000 square miles (1.28 million sq kms) stretch from the three Manchurian provinces in the east to Central Asia in the West. The region's northern boundary is a 2,600 mile-long (4,160 kms) international frontier dividing China from Russia and the Mongolian Republic. Principal gateways to these two countries are Manzhouli in the northeast, and Erlianhaote in the middle of the region. They give rail access, respectively, to Russia and Mongolia. Northeast Inner Mongolia is home to some of China's remaining forest cover and rare wildlife. The region is sparsely populated. Its defining physical feature is the Greater Hinggan mountain range, which runs north–south and forms the watershed between the Songliao Plain of Manchuria and the Inner Mongolian Plain. The Khorcin Plain in the southeast is a settled agricultural area and forms part of the northeast China Plain. Sandwiched between the bend of the Yellow River and the Great Wall is the Ordos Plateau. The Hetao Plain, to its north, is a densely populated, fertile strip of territory known as Inner Mongolia's granary. The Aalashan Plain is in the northwest of the region. These features account for about half of Inner Mongolia's territory. The remainder, situated in the north, is desert and steppe. Vast and remote, it contains some of China's finest stock-breeding pastureland.

were denounced as 'local nationalists' bent on forming 'independent kingdoms'. The region's difficulties increased with the Sino-Soviet split (see SOVIET UNION). Beijing struggled but failed to maintain friendly relations with Ulan Bator where the government took Moscow's side in the row over revolutionary ideology and international influence. Contacts between Inner Mongolia and the independent republic to its north were suspended.

Ulanhu survived these developments but not the CULTURAL REVOLUTION which followed. As chaos and civil war unfolded in the region in the 1960s he was criticized for encouraging the study of Mongolian language and culture, and plotting to make himself emperor of a new pan-Mongol state. Every manifestation of cultural difference between Han and Mongol was made the object of class struggle. The Mongolian language and lifestyle were ridiculed as feudal and backward. Han Chinese dominated the regional government.

More troops and colonists poured into the region as tension with the Soviet Union turned into armed clashes along the Sino-Soviet, and Sino-Mongolian borders. In 1969 Inner Mongolia was reduced to half its size to forestall any attempt by Mongols to unite in opposition to Chinese rule, and to frustrate 'meddling' in the region on the part of the Soviet Union or the Mongolian People's Republic. A large chunk of eastern Mongolia was absorbed by the three northeastern provinces of JILIN, LIAONING and HEILONGJIANG, while territory in the west was incorporated into Gansu and Ningxia. Inner Mongolia did not regain its pre-Cultural Revolution size until 1978, by which time DENG XIAOPING had set China on a new course of economic reform and contact with the outside world.

in search of development and identity

Ulanhu was among the beneficiaries of the end of political radicalism. He re-emerged to take on a series of senior positions in Beijing, serving as vice-president in the 1980s. At the same time, one of his sons, Buhe (1926–), was chairman of the autonomous region government while another, Wu Jie, was mayor of Baotou.

The rapid development of China's economy meant new demands for the animals and animal products of which Inner Mongolia has long been the major supplier. It meant new demands for its energy resources, too. The region is rich in coal, much of it easily accessible. It is also home to some of the largest deposits of rare earth metals in the world.

While valuable, these endowments hardly made up for the fact that Inner Mongolia was poorly placed to make much of China's open door policy. Only the southeastern corner of its vast territory is close to the sea, and its neighbour to the north is one of the world's largest but least populated and developed countries. This, coupled with a small population of its own and the fact that most of its land consists of desert and steppe, kept the region near the bottom of the provincial league table when it came to utilising FOREIGN TRADE AND INVESTMENT. Per capita GDP in Mongolia in the late 1990s was less than half that of prosperous GUANGDONG.

As far as national security is concerned, the region occupied a more important position. In the reform era relations between Han Chinese and Mongols were never as volatile as those between Chinese and Uigurs or Chinese and Tibetans. Neither were they always harmonious. Han immigration had long since made the Mongols a minority in their homeland, but it had not made the Chinese presence any more popular for that. Protests over the issue occurred in 1981 and sporadic unrest was reported among herdsmen in the east of the region during the early 1990s.

At the same time some Mongolian intellectuals kept the issue of independence alive, albeit at a low level, through clandestine groups such as the 'Southern Mongolian Democratic Alliance' and the 'Inner Mongolian League for the Defence of Human Rights'. Some of the members of these groups seemed inspired by developments in the Mongolian Republic, where the Mongolian People's Revolutionary Party was forced to share power in 1990, and then give it up altogether in favour of multi-party democracy. Pan-Mongolists received no quarter from the authorities in Inner Mongolia: security police broke up their organizations on several occasions during the 1990s and sentenced their leaders to long prison sentences.

Dissent of this kind was a minor theme in the overall scheme of things in Inner Mongolia: the region was far less of a security problem for Beijing than Xinjiang or Tibet. But though China's Mongols are heavily outnumbered and apparently little interested in pan-Mongolism, Beijing knows it must still handle them with caution. Despite decades of Chinese rule, their memories, like the forms of social organization that bound them together in their heyday, remain tribal.

J

Japan

China's relations with Japan have been more tortuous – and more tragic – than those with any other country except TAIWAN during the twentieth century. Tokyo inspired a generation of Chinese nationalists, only to trample over their country and their hopes. Japanese leaders sought to 'save' China from the 'corrupting' influence of the West, yet subjected its people to a form of dominion more abject than any imposed by the Western powers. Japan's soldiers provided a model of Asian invincibility, until they invaded China and inflicted indescribable cruelties on its people. Such calamities have left a legacy of bitterness, suspicion and misunderstanding which sometimes make contacts between individual Chinese and Japanese difficult. Shared economic interests have helped overcome some of these problems: at the start of the century Japan is China's largest trade partner. But rivalry to become the dominant power in Asia, Chinese concern over Japan's security ties with the UNITED STATES, and a small but nagging territorial dispute, make for a volatile relationship.

Japan, catalyst of change

China lost several disastrous wars in the nineteenth century, but none had the impact of defeat at the hands of Japan in 1894–5. One of the reasons for this was that it seemed to reverse the natural order of things. Centuries earlier, Japan had drawn much of its 'higher' culture from China. How, then, could this 'upstart' island nation trounce its giant neighbour so completely on the battlefield? How could it prise Korea – a Chinese tributary

whose complex politics caused the war – away from Beijing, establish a foothold in the Liaodong peninsula of southern Manchuria, (around Dalian in the modern province of LIAONING) and occupy all of Taiwan? These acquisitions and other humiliating conditions were enshrined in the Treaty of Shimonosheki of 1895, the unequal treaty Chinese Nationalists loathed most (see UNEQUAL TREATIES). KANG YOUWEI and other leaders of the '100 Days' reform movement of 1898 sought a thorough overhaul of Qing government and society to ensure such calamities never happened again (see QING DYNASTY).

Yet Japan inspired Chinese admiration as well as fear. The outcome of the war, though unwelcome, demonstrated the success of Japan's modernization programme dating back to the Meiji Restoration of 1868. It showed what a previously 'backward' Asian nation could do. Japan's victory in the Russo-Japanese War of 1904–5 provided even more proof. This, too, was a disaster for China: the conflict was fought on Chinese soil even though Beijing was not a combatant. Victory secured Japan's hold over Korea and brought Japanese power deeper into Manchuria (the modern provinces of JILIN and HEILONGJIANG) which RUSSIA had previously made its own. At the same time, this first defeat of a predominantly European power by an Asian nation underlined the merits of a modernization policy which had created a new Japan while leaving much of its traditional identity intact.

Tokyo attracted and repelled in equal proportions. Much of what China's first generation of Nationalists learnt about Western political and philosophical concepts came from Japanese translations. In the first two decades of the twentieth century, thousands of Chinese students, Nationalists and exiled revolutionaries studied in Japan or lived among its large Overseas Chinese community. Among them were LIANG QICHAO, SUN YAT-SEN, CHIANG KAI-SHEK and others who, depressed by the condition of their own country, sought to shape its destiny through study and activism abroad. Later in the century, the SOVIET UNION and, later still, the United States, performed a similar role as the training ground for China's modernizing elite.

colonization and war, 1919–45

While China's radicals were studying in Tokyo, Chinese officials at home struggled to check Japan's imperial ambitions. They were unequal to the task. Shortly after the outbreak of the First World War, Japan declared war on Germany and seized territory the Kaiser had leased from China in SHANDONG. A few months later Tokyo presented President YUAN SHIKAI with the TWENTY-ONE DEMANDS, a blueprint for turning China into a colony. Though they were not granted in full, Japan's position in China grew stronger as that of the Western powers, locked in mortal combat closer to home, diminished. When Tokyo refused to hand Shandong back to China after the war, and the Versailles Conference of 1919 endorsed its stand, Chinese students took to the streets in the protests known as the MAY FOURTH MOVEMENT. This was a watershed in the development of modern Chinese nationalism – not least because it ended the ambiguities many Chinese radicals felt towards Japan. After May Fourth it became difficult to be a Chinese Nationalist *and* pro-Japanese, as the later career of WANG JINGWEI, head of a 'puppet' Chinese government during the SINO-JAPANESE WAR, made clear.

Diplomatic pressure from the powers restored Shandong to China at the WASHINGTON CONFERENCE of 1921–2, but the meeting reflected Japan's growing power in East Asia rather than its retreat. China felt this in a number of ways – from the growing number of Japanese factories in Shanghai, where working conditions were often atrocious, to the military intervention of 1928 designed to protect Japanese citizens in Jinan, the Shandong city which lay in the path of the final stages of Chiang Kai-shek's NORTHERN EXPEDITION.

Thousands of Chinese soldiers and civilians were killed in clashes around Jinan that inflamed anti-Japanese sentiment across the country.

Worse was to come. Politicians and soldiers in Tokyo began to feel that the destiny of their country was tied to control over China. Japan needed China's resources, particularly those in Manchuria. And it needed to control China strategically if it was to win the anticipated military struggle with the Soviet Union.

These feelings intensified as the international economic and diplomatic order collapsed in the late 1920s and early 1930s. They grew even stronger when Chiang's Nationalists unified China. Tokyo would have to strike soon if it was to fulfil its destiny in the Far East.

Fear that it might not do so encouraged a forward policy in Manchuria, which began with adventurism on the part of Japanese military officers at Mukden (modern Shenyang) – the 'Mukden Incident' – and culminated in 1932 with the creation of the 'puppet state' of MANCHUGUO. Earlier the same year Japanese troops attacked Shanghai. Five years later the Marco Polo Bridge Incident inaugurated full-scale war. Many had long regarded this as inevitable. What they could not have foreseen was how long and destructive it would prove, or how it would transform the political balance of power in China (see SINO-JAPANESE WAR).

The Nationalists committed enough errors during the CIVIL WAR to ensure a Communist triumph in China in 1949. But the fact that after 1945 they were up against a large, disciplined, and highly motivated revolutionary organization which controlled many parts of the country was a consequence of the war with Japan. The length and nature of the conflict provided ample conditions, cleverly exploited by MAO ZEDONG, for the transformation of a small, disorganized, band of rebels into a dedicated fighting force. At the end of the war Soviet intervention in Manchuria, where weapons taken from Japanese troops were handed to local Chinese Communists, strengthened the Nationalists' opponents still further. By the close of 1949, Chiang's government had fled to Taiwan.

rapprochement and rivalry

Japan, effectively under American control, maintained formal diplomatic ties with the Nationalists in Taipei rather than try to forge new ones with the Communists in Beijing. In

1952, Japan and Taiwan signed a peace treaty, formally ending the Sino-Japanese War.

For the new government in Beijing, Japan's history of aggression in China, its rapid recovery under American auspices, and its relations with Taipei made it a principal threat. It was identified as such in the Sino-Soviet Treaty of Friendship, Alliance and Mutual Assistance of 1950. The KOREAN WAR, during which Japan became a major staging area for United States troops, intensified Sino-Japanese antagonism. Yet if China's revolutionary policies and Japan's pro-American alliances kept the two countries apart during the 1950s, trade brought them quietly together in the 1960s. In 1966, Japan became China's principal trade partner. Volumes were small at the time, but a pattern was set that has endured in the reform era.

Diplomacy eventually followed trade. China's opening to the United States in the early 1970s implied an opening to Japan and Western Europe, the two other centres of world economic and industrial strength. Beijing and Tokyo established formal diplomatic relations in 1972 (six years before the United States) and Japan severed official ties with Taiwan. This was a considerable triumph for China's Communist leaders who believed the price of forswearing the right to reparations in respect of damage inflicted during the war worth paying. But it left a hostage to fortune: it made the Party seem impotent during the 1980s and 1990s in the face of popular demands for reparations and a formal apology from Japan. Beijing was happy to see Japan's leaders exposed to such pressures. But it was nervous about the consequences of possible public demonstrations over the issue at home, as well as the effects on Tokyo's generosity with regard to aid and loans.

Issues related to the war frequently inflamed Chinese popular opinion in the 1980s and 1990s and generated tension between Beijing and Tokyo. On some occasions it was caused by the publication of Japanese history books downplaying the country's wartime aggression or glossing over the Nanjing Massacre (see SINO-JAPANESE WAR). On others it was the result of visits by Japanese leaders to Tokyo's Yaksukuni Shrine, where the country's war dead are honoured. Attempts, often unsuccessful, by individual Chinese to seek compensation through Japanese courts in respect of their wartime conscription as 'comfort women', or redress for deaths and injuries caused by Japan's germ warfare experiments

in China, kept the unhappy past alive. Privately, the Chinese government played up Japan's war guilt as a means of extracting diplomatic concessions from Tokyo. In public, it shrank from turning the issue into a political campaign.

It sometimes was more forthcoming on trade matters. Economic complementarity, reinforced by proximity, made China and Japan ideal trade partners: China is rich in resources and has a vast market; Japan has unrivalled technology, marketing skills and capital resources. Yet by the mid-1980s, China saw its massive deficit in trade with Japan and conspicuous absence of either Japanese investment or technology transfer as new forms of old exploitation. On one occasion DENG XIAOPING told a Japanese guest things would have to change. Tokyo had its complaints about Beijing, too. Between 1995 and early 1997, it halted aid in protest against China's nuclear tests.

If the legacy of the war, and trade, nuclear and territorial issues clouded China's relations with Japan at the close of the twentieth century, China's growing power, and nagging economic stagnation in Japan, have added a new element at the start of the twenty-first. For both sides security concerns are foremost. In 1997, Japan and the United States published new guidelines governing their longstanding defensive agreement. These provide for a larger military role for Tokyo. Under certain circumstances, they call on Japan to provide logistic and other non-combatant support functions to US troops in the area in the event of a threat to Japanese security. Search and rescue operations, minesweeping and the evacuation of civilians all fall within the new Japanese remit. The guidelines leave the questions of *where* and *under what circumstances* Japan will engage in these activities unclear: they refer only to Japan's 'surrounding areas'. China concluded that they include Taiwan, and lambasted the new arrangement as 'Cold War thinking designed to contain China'. A combination of Japanese obfuscation and smoothing words about the geographical scope of the accord have failed to dispel Beijing's unease.

In part the guidelines were rewritten to counter a growing military threat from North Korea, whose sabre rattling following the death of Kim Il Sung in 1994 alarmed Tokyo as well as Seoul. In 1998 North Korea test-fired a missile that overflew Japan. Tokyo called on Beijing to use its influence to curb hardliners

Drama over the Diaoyutais

Japan's defeat in the Second World War spelt the end of its occupation of China, and the return to Chinese control of Manchuria and Taiwan. It did not end all territorial disputes between the two countries. Beginning in the early 1970s arguments broke out over a tiny group of uninhabited islands about 90 miles (144 kms) northeast of Taiwan called *Diaoyutai* in Chinese and, in Japanese, *Senkaku*. Ill-feeling over Japan's war record in China infused the row with unwonted passion. These barren, rocky outcrops were not mentioned in the Treaty of Shimonoseki of 1895, under which Japan acquired Taiwan. Nor were they referred to among the possessions Tokyo promised to restore to China after its defeat in 1945. In fact control over them passed in 1945 to the United States along with Japan's Okinawa group of islands. Chinese interest in the matter did not emerge on any scale until 1971, when Washington decided to hand Okinawa back to Japan, again including the Diaoyutai Islands. Even then, objections came mainly from Chinese students in the United States.

Neither was the Diaoyutai issue an obstacle to the establishment of diplomatic relations between Beijing and Tokyo in 1972. Too much was at stake to let what seemed a minor territorial tiff get in the way of normalization. But it was different six years later when the two sides discussed the terms of a Treaty of Peace and Friendship. Deng Xiaoping agreed to defer the islands dispute in order to seal the deal. The calm lasted until 1990, when Japan built a lighthouse on one of the islands, sparking protests from China and Taiwan. It was interrupted again in 1992 by Japanese objections to a law passed in Beijing which placed the Diaoyutais within Chinese jurisdiction.

In 1996, the row intensified into bizarre and dangerous forms of Chinese activism. In the summer of that year, another lighthouse, this time the work of Japanese Rightists, appeared on one of the islands. There was an angry reaction among the public in Hong Kong, Taiwan and to a lesser extent the Mainland. The governments in all three Chinese territories responded less emotionally. In the case of Hong Kong this was because the British colonial government had no fight with Tokyo over the issue. In Taipei and Beijing, the governments were keen not to be upstaged as defenders of Chinese territory, yet anxious not to jeopardize relations with Japan, official or otherwise. For the Communist government there was the added worry that anti-Japanese protests at home might turn into criticism of other aspects of its rule.

Leadership of the 'Protect the Diaoyutai Movement' therefore fell to activists in Taiwan and Hong Kong. This was a striking development so far as Hong Kong was concerned because it occurred at a time when local people might more reasonably be expected to be concerned solely about the future of their own territory, then on the eve of restoration to Chinese sovereignty. Perhaps the Diaoyutai issue presented them with an opportunity to assert their Chinese identity after years of colonial rule. In any event, flotillas of small fishing vessels, many of them supplied and equipped by activists in Taiwan, set sail for the Diaoyutai chain. The aim was to tear down the lighthouse and replace it with Chinese flags.

One expedition ended in tragedy: a Hong Kong man drowned as he sought to land on the islands. The next was more successful. The activists, their vessels bobbing around on the seas, out-manoeuvred the patrol vessels and motorboats of Japan's Maritime Safety Agency, scrambled up one of the outcrops and raised both the Taiwan and Mainland flags. Hong Kong's competitive newspapers sought to outdo each other in the scale and extent of their coverage, but agreed that a great Chinese victory had been won. Japan, naturally, took a different view. In any event, neither lighthouses nor flags, neither claims to history nor the ability to move naval craft into the area, settled the fate of Diaoyutais and the rich energy and fishing resources believed to lie around them. The dispute remains to test the skills of Chinese and Japanese statesmen in the new century.

---

in Pyongyang and backed American plans to establish a Theatre Missile Defence (TMD) system in East Asia. China opposed the scheme on the grounds that it would lead to an arms race in East Asia. Talk in the United States of extending the scheme to Taiwan, to protect the island against a missile build-up on the Mainland, only added to Beijing's concern.

Japan's willingness to take on a larger military role in the region, though modest in scope, is part of its broader campaign to obtain a permanent seat on the United Nations Security Council. China, in common with other countries whose modern history bears the scars of Japanese military adventures, is luke-

warm about the prospect. It revives the spectre of militarism whenever Japan seems to be spending more on defence than its constitution allows or its security strictly warrants. At the same time Beijing half-heartedly complains about the presence of American troops in East Asia, many of them stationed in Japan. Yet on balance it seems to prefer Japan to rely for much of its defence on a third party rather than emerge as a military power in its own right. Above all, China is determined to be strong enough itself – politically, economically and militarily – to survive and triumph in what is likely to be an era of growing rivalry with Japan.

Jiang Qing (1914–91)

A beauty in her youth, Jiang was a film starlet who in the 1930s forsook cosmopolitan SHANG-HAI for the puritanism of Communist-ruled YANAN, married MAO ZEDONG and eventually became one of the two most powerful women in China's modern history. The other was Ci Xi, the EMPRESS DOWAGER. Jiang's career was even more dramatic than that of her predecessor. She was a key figure in the CULTURAL REVOLUTION and, as leader of the 'GANG OF FOUR', became one of the most hated figures in China, was tried and condemned to death. The sentence was changed to life imprisonment but, defiant to the last, she cheated her jailers, taking her own life while undergoing medical treatment at home.

Commitment to revolution drew Jiang to Yanan, as it did many others during the SINO-JAPANESE WAR. But, once there, her poise, sophistication and beauty – characteristics supposedly eschewed by a Party which made a virtue of austerity in virtually every walk of life – enabled her to remain something of a star. Mao found her irresistible. Soon the two of them began sharing one of the caves the Party allocated to its leaders as offices and living quarters. Party leaders looked askance at the Chairman's choice of partner but agreed to the match if Jiang would undertake to leave politics to her husband. KANG SHENG, the security chief and 'grand inquisitor' of Chinese Communism, vouched for his long-time friend, who managed to suppress her political ambitions for the best part of 30 years following her union with Mao in 1938.

In the early 1960s, with Mao and the Party establishment at odds over questions of ideology and much else, she no longer saw the need to do so. The Chairman wanted a Cultural Revolution and she was determined to deliver it. Jiang and other radicals purged the arts of what they considered to be their obsession with kings, princes, beautiful women and feudal subjects. Revolutionary operas and other politically correct works were prescribed instead. This amounted to more than a change of programme: it involved the humiliation, persecution, torture and later the deaths of thousands of artists and intellectuals.

Jiang, whose allies included LIN BIAO until his sudden death in 1971, drove the Cultural Revolution on, sure in the knowledge she could rely on Mao's enthusiastic support or at least benefit from his acquiescence. By 1972, and now a member of the Politburo, she felt powerful enough to 'dissect herself', as she put it, before a foreigner, the American scholar Roxanne Witke. She wished to be regarded as a leader in her own right, not just 'Madame Mao'.

There was no doubt about her power, which increased as Mao's health declined. But it was not absolute. ZHOU ENLAI, the relatively moderate premier, was an obstacle until his death in January 1976; and the 'Gang' had their work cut out dealing with DENG XIAOPING, purged by Mao in 1966 but brought back in desperation in 1973 because of the shortage of administrative talent in Beijing. They managed to oust him again in 1976, but could not stop the Chairman from naming HUA GUOFENG the next leader rather than one of their own. In the weeks following Mao's death in September 1976 they appeared to be planning a coup. Hua beat them to it: on 6 October he had Jiang, her three principal accomplices and various allies arrested; the glory days of the 'Gang' were over; their infamy was about to begin.

Transformed into a monster by cartoonists, Jiang became the principal hate object of a vicious propaganda offensive. The campaign was not contrived: the 'Gang' had persecuted thousands of people and disrupted the lives of millions. The obloquy was deserved. But Jiang and her associates were made the scapegoats for a disaster inflicted on China by Mao and other senior leaders as well as themselves. In a world where the involvement of women in public affairs was regarded as, at best, a mixed blessing, Jiang's gender intensified the indictment (see WOMEN).

Her public career ended as it began: on stage. This time it was a televised courtroom in Beijing, where she and other members of the 'Gang' were tried on charges of 'framing and persecuting to death' thousands of people. She gave the prosecutors as good as she got. 'Fascists!', 'Kuomintang!', she shouted at the judges. On several occasions she had to be removed from the defendants' stand. Jiang refused to acknowledge any guilt. She said: 'I was Chairman Mao's dog. Whom he said bite, I bit.' She was spared death, but languished in prison while the reforms of Deng Xiaoping, her old enemy, transformed the country she had known and, for a while, ruled. Jiang hanged herself in the summer of 1991. Her death went almost unreported in China.

Jiang Zemin (1926–)

The first genuinely non-military figure to establish unrivalled leadership over China since the EMPRESS DOWAGER. The first leader of the CHINESE COMMUNIST PARTY neither to have provoked revolutionary upheavals nor to have suffered from those of his predecessors. The first Chinese leader to admit that the age of 'great leaders' is over, and that a more consensual, collective style of government is required in a rapidly changing society. All these attributes make President Jiang Zemin's current ascendancy in the tempestuous world of Chinese politics remarkable. The fact that they belong to an authoritarian yet pragmatic, avuncular bureaucrat who rose to power amid the suppression of the TIANANMEN SQUARE DEMOCRACY MOVEMENT in 1989, makes it more remarkable still.

the cautious bureaucrat

During the early stages of his career, Jiang, born in Yangzhou, JIANGSU province, suffered little from the turmoil that characterized MAO ZEDONG's China. There were several reasons for this, and they proved important for his later success. One was that he was the adopted son of a 'revolutionary martyr': his uncle was killed while working for the Party during the SINO-JAPANESE WAR, and Jiang's parents agreed to hand over their 13-year-old son to his widowed aunt because there were no males in her family. This was a valuable pedigree for a Communist bureaucrat at the best of times. During the CULTURAL REVOLUTION it proved invaluable; it is probably why he escaped the upheavals of that time with only mild criticism and a suspension from his duties at a nuclear research institute in Wuhan.

Another reason Jiang avoided experiences of the kind that scarred many of his peers was his political caution. This was apparent as early as the late 1940s when, as a student of engineering at Shanghai's Jiaotong University, he joined the Communist Party and took part in protests against KUOMINTANG rule. Jiang's role in the demonstrations was small and discreet. A primary motivation in joining the Party appears to have been patriotism rather than the appeal of MARXISM. His schooling was interrupted by the Japanese invasion, and his university studies by the CIVIL WAR. Both were reminders of China's weakness and humiliation. Jiang was one of many thousands of young intellectuals who

believed things would be different under Communist rule.

A gregarious, out-going if occasionally bombastic personality also proved a political asset. Despite the adoption episode, Jiang had a happy childhood. His was an intellectual family. At home, school and university he acquired a taste for the cultivated pleasures of China and the West, particularly music and languages. Though a scientist by training, he was a roundly educated person by the standards of the day. This also made him different from many of his peers, and very different from those who led the Party before him.

But not so different that he did not prosper in a political organization run by former peasants and hard-bitten veterans of the LONG MARCH. Jiang seemed destined for a role in national politics before he was suddenly elevated to the post of General Secretary of the Communist Party in June 1989. At the time, he was Party boss of SHANGHAI. It was the high point of a career that had included the management of a power plant in a car factory in northeast China; a spell of training in the SOVIET UNION; the directorship of a thermonuclear research institute in Wuhan; a role in establishing China's controversial SPECIAL ECONOMIC ZONES; and the position of vice-minister and then minister of the electronics industry.

Between 1985–7 Jiang was mayor of Shanghai. He led the city government at a time when it was chafing under the tight controls imposed by Beijing, and while GUANGDONG, in the south, prospered under decentralization and free market reforms. When Jiang moved to the slightly more senior position of Communist Party chief of Shanghai in 1987, ZHU RONGJI succeeded him as mayor. It was the beginning of a partnership which, at the start of the twenty-first century, still forms a major axis of national politics.

Jiang could not have become mayor or Party leader of China's largest city without at least a convincing show of adherence to Marxism, a determination to maintain Party control, and an enthusiasm for economic reform. And it was precisely these characteristics that persuaded DENG XIAOPING to select him for even greater things in 1989 as the Party grappled with the crisis provoked by the pro-democracy demonstrations in Tiananmen Square.

called at a time of crisis

At the height of the crisis Deng had grown disillusioned with ZHAO ZIYANG, the reformist Party leader whom he had selected as his second heir apparent after HU YAOBANG. Hu had been dismissed in 1987 for failing to curb an earlier round of student revolt. But his death in April 1989 sparked the much bigger unrest, fuelled by popular anger over inflation, corruption and student-led demands for more democracy now confronting the Party. Neither mediation nor martial law had succeeded in ending the occupation of Tiananmen Square. Deng and his fellow revolutionary veterans decided to crush the protests by force – despite opposition from Zhao, whom they shoved aside and prepared to disgrace.

The old guard settled on Jiang as Zhao's replacement because he had handled student protests in Shanghai firmly, closing the *World Economic Herald*, China's leading liberal newspaper, and supporting the declaration of martial law in Beijing. At the same time, he had not been heavy-handed. Above all he had the advantage of not being involved in planning the military crackdown that began in Beijing on 3 June. This, together with his other attributes, and the fact that while he had been careful to court various revolutionary elders during his career, he was not firmly associated with any one of them, made Jiang a more suitable choice than seemed apparent to observers at the time.

The prospects that Jiang might be a *successful* leader, however, were more remote. For one thing, China's politics, society and economy were in crisis as a result of the military suppression of the democracy movement. For another, the West was outraged, making the crackdown a major FOREIGN POLICY issue. This was more than a highly experienced Chinese Communist leader might be expected to cope with. For Jiang – competent but with limited experience in central government, an indifferent record as an economic manager, only partial familiarity with foreign affairs, and no connections at all with the military – the difficulties promised to be overwhelming.

Jiang's lack of close links with the PEOPLE'S LIBERATION ARMY seemed the most damaging of these weaknesses. The military had just rescued Party rule at the behest of the veteran revolutionaries. Its commanders were likely to want good reasons why they should swear allegiance to a former bureaucrat from Shang-hai who, following Deng's formal retirement in 1989, was made chairman of the Party's powerful Central Military Commission, the high command. The history of Chinese Communism showed that no one had managed to lead the Party very effectively, or for very long, without close ties to the PLA. Jiang's personal history suggested he was ill-prepared to do so.

The new Party secretary was at a disadvantage as far as economic policy was concerned, too. In the post-Tiananmen period the pace was set by Premier LI PENG; and the pace was slow. Li reversed the radical reforms of the Zhao era in an attempt to control inflation and curb investment. With the collapse of international tourism and a fall in FOREIGN TRADE AND INVESTMENT, the economy flagged. So did morale in the Party, government and among the people. Party leaders in particular grew alarmed at developments beyond China's borders. The collapse of Communism in eastern Europe and later in the Soviet Union seemed to presage further upheavals in the sole remaining 'people's dictatorship' of any size. The only answer was to step up the crackdown on dissent at home and place stability above reform and development. Jiang, largely in thrall to the revolutionary elders who feared their world was falling apart, pushed this line with vigour.

But not as much vigour as Deng Xiaoping displayed during the spring of 1992 when he travelled through south China calling for faster reforms. His journey was a decisive event in China's modern history. It inspired an economic revival that shaped the final decade of the twentieth century and beyond. It also invigorated Jiang Zemin, rescuing him from his metaphorical captors in Beijing. Jiang was quick to seize on Deng's message that only reform and development could save Party rule and make China strong. At the Party's 14th National Congress in 1992 this theory became orthodoxy. In the 'socialist market economy', as the Party called it, all forms of economic enterprise were permissible as long as they promised to develop the country's productive capacity.

gaining ground

The rush to growth that followed Deng's intervention generated problems of its own, but not before it had strengthened Jiang's hand. In 1991, he promoted Zhu Rongji from Shanghai to become a vice-premier in Beijing. Two years later Zhu's (and therefore Jiang's) influence grew thanks to an illness that removed

Li Peng from the scene for several weeks. In the summer of 1992, Jiang was able to oust President YANG SHANGKUN and his half brother Yang Baibing (1920–), from the military hierarchy where they had been expanding their influence. In the months that followed Jiang made regular visits to the barracks across the country, and promoted those he trusted to the key levels of command. In 1993, he became state president as well as Party leader and military chief. This gave him the formal status required to represent China on the international stage, something denied him as Party leader alone.

Yet if these developments enabled Jiang to consolidate more power in his own hands than had once seemed likely, they did not answer the question of what he should do with it. As successor to Mao (albeit somewhat removed) and Deng, Jiang stood in the shadow of titans. He made no secret of the fact that China had changed so much as a result of free market reforms that there could not be another great leader of their kind. Power was diffused across institutions, geographical regions and various sectors of the economy; it could not be monopolized by any one individual. Yet Jiang was not coy about wanting to stamp his authority on the era. Mao had brought the Communists to power and built up the country. Deng had rescued it from Mao's excesses, set it on the road to prosperity, and paved the way for reunification with HONG KONG and MACAU. Though these mighty deeds were hard to follow, Jiang was not deterred.

Yet they seemed even mightier given the popular image of China's new leader as something of a lightweight and a clown, particularly when on the international stage. His penchant for breaking into song, wearing outlandish hats, switching to faltering English, Russian or another of the several languages he was said to have mastered, startled his hosts and sometimes prompted mockery at home. What was less often noticed was that these were merely the more extreme manifestations of an avuncular nature which seemed to disarm potential domestic rivals, and therefore help consolidate Jiang's position as, in Deng Xiaoping's phrase, the 'core of the Party's third generation of leaders'. (Mao was leader of the first generation, Deng leader of the second.)

Jiang pushed an agenda of his own in the mid-1990s. He shared his mentor's commitment to radical economic reform in the context of a conservative political dictatorship but was keen to curb what he saw as some of its social excesses. Rising crime, excessive materialism and social disillusionment, especially among the young, ranked high among them. Jiang sought their remedy in campaigns to boost patriotism, 'spiritual civilization' – the Party's catchphrase to describe socialist moral values – and a revival of traditional Chinese culture.

CORRUPTION was another target, and nowhere more so than in BEIJING where the Party boss, CHEN XITONG, had compounded a fondness for bribes and fast living with longstanding political opposition to Jiang, whom he felt unqualified to lead the Party. When Jiang had Chen arrested in 1995 he scored a triple blow, winning popular support in the capital, eliminating a personal rival, and toppling what had become an 'independent kingdom' at the very heart of the country.

At no time during the 1990s did Jiang signal any willingness to weaken the Communist Party's dominance of political life, or expand the frontiers of individual freedom. His attachment to the 'dictatorship of the proletariat' remained undiminished; his commitment to DEMOCRACY perfunctory and always predicated on the supremacy of the Party. There were occasional periods of apparent liberalization in the 1990s but, as DISSIDENTS discovered whenever they stirred, they tended to be more apparent than real. Jiang brooked no political challenge; heavy jail sentences were imposed on those who tried to found an opposition China Democratic Party in 1998–9.

He acted with greater boldness in two other areas where he believed he might be able to make a mark: relations with TAIWAN and the UNITED STATES, the island's main international backer. With Hong Kong and Macau on the road to rendition before he came to power, Jiang began to pursue the most elusive prize in China's quest for reunification: Taiwan. He placed Wang Daohan (1915–), a former mayor of Shanghai, and patron during the first phase of his career, in charge of 'unofficial' talks with the Nationalist-ruled island. The ensuing thaw in relations across the Taiwan Straits was slow but real; in 1993 representatives of the 'two Chinas' started talking at a landmark meeting in Singapore.

Further progress proved difficult, largely because of the dynamics of domestic politics in Taiwan and the United States. In 1995 President LEE TENG-HUI undertook a 'private' but highly controversial visit to America, which appeared to end Washington's ban on official relations with Taiwan. Beijing showed its anger at Taipei's diplomatic breakthrough by staging war games opposite the island. It repeated them on a larger scale in March 1996 to coincide with Taiwan's first direct presidential elections. The United States' navy was ordered to the area to demonstrate support for Taiwan, and Lee won the polls. Jiang's attempt to win Taiwan over with a mixture of diplomacy and displays of force suffered a setback. A second round of high-level talks between Beijing and Taipei had to wait until the end of 1998. Discussions were thwarted the following year by Lee Teng-hui's demand that Beijing treat Taiwan as a separate state. A different kind of obstacle arose in 2000: the victory in Taiwan's second direct presidential elections of CHEN SHUI-BIAN, candidate of the DEMO-CRATIC PROGRESSIVE PARTY which had long campaigned for an independent Taiwan. Paradoxically Chen's victory brought the possibility of talks about practical matters with China nearer yet made the prospects for reunification more remote.

the 'era of Jiang Zemin', 1997–

During the early 1990s an ailing Deng Xiaoping had not always seemed delighted with his protégé, but he was usually willing to defend him against attack. Since the architect of China's reforms lived for almost eight years after appointing his successor, this was a considerable advantage. On the other hand, the fact that Deng was healthy enough to enjoy his retirement but not well enough, or not interested enough, to interfere directly in politics, was an even greater one.

Deng's death in February 1997 enabled Jiang to reap the political benefits arising from China's recovery of sovereignty over Hong Kong on 1 July 1997. His presence in the territory for the occasion was brief. It was no less important for that: Jiang had little direct interest in Hong Kong affairs but had personally selected TUNG CHEE-HWA, whom a pro-Beijing committee then 'elected' to serve as the territory's first Chief Executive or post-colonial governor. He was enthusiastic in his support for Tung during the economic difficulties that marred Hong Kong's birth as a Special Administrative Region of China.

Jiang's formal coronation as China's paramount leader came at the Communist Party's 15th National Congress in October 1997. He secured the retirement of QIAO SHI, the former security chief turned reformer who was a

minor obstacle to an expansion of his authority; and the promotion, confirmed the following year, of Zhu Rongji as premier in place of Li Peng. Li remained number two in the Party, but in many policy areas he was overshadowed by the formidable Jiang–Zhu team.

Jiang also persuaded the Party congress to endorse a new vision of 'socialist shareholding' that enlarged the scope of the 'socialist market economy' established in 1992. Socialism required state ownership of the economy, but according to the new theory, 'ownership' could take many forms. It even included China's stakes in joint venture firms with foreigners, as well as the state enterprises more typical of socialism as it had been understood (see CHINESE COMMUNIST PARTY/IN SEARCH OF SOCIALISM).

If the congress crowned Jiang in the eyes of the Chinese people, his state visit to the United States that followed, and President Bill Clinton's visit to China the following year, established his political dominance for the world. Both occasions were marred by minor controversies. No amount of summitry could mask Sino-US tensions over HUMAN RIGHTS, TIBET, trade and the other issues that made relations between Washington and Beijing so difficult. The suppression of the Tiananmen Square Democracy Movement was particularly sensitive. On one occasion while in the United States, Jiang appeared to admit the military crackdown was a mistake. It was very far from an expression of regret, as his officials were quick to point out. The best that could be said was that, though Jiang often defended the stern measures taken against the protestors in 1989 – as he did in Beijing in 1998 in the presence of President Clinton at a news conference broadcast live across China – he at least had the satisfaction of not being involved in the suppression himself.

In any event, controversies of this kind could not disguise the fact that, almost a decade after he had been appointed, only to be dismissed by many observers as a merely transitional figure, Jiang Zemin was China's paramount leader. Lingering uncertainties as to his authority over the People's Liberation Army were dispelled in 1998 when he ordered the military to disengage from its lucrative commercial activities in exchange for a bigger defence budget. Compliance was less than complete but greater than anticipated.

Nevertheless, the downturn in Sino-US relations caused by NATO's war against Serbia, and Taiwan's continued recalcitrance in 1999, threatened to deprive Jiang of his sought-after legacy as a man who advanced Chinese unification and secured good relations with the world's sole superpower. The 'strategic partnership' Beijing and Washington entered into with such fanfare in 1997 seemed to go up in smoke along with the Chinese embassy in Belgrade, which was destroyed in error by American missiles in May 1999 during the war against Yugoslavia. At home Jiang was preoccupied by the threat arising from the quasi-religious sect, the *Fa Lun Gong*, whose members protested outside the Party and government headquarters in Beijing, and other cities, to demand official recognition of their beliefs. He ordered the movements suppressed and its leaders arrested.

Yet the century closed on a higher note for China's leader than these events had suggested would be the case. In October he presided over celebrations to mark the 50th anniversary of the founding of the People's Republic. It was an occasion of triumph for the Communist Party and for Jiang personally. The following month China and the United States reached agreement on Beijing's entry into the World Trade Organization after years of abortive negotiations. The implications of an accord which promised to open up the entire Chinese economy to reform and international competition were enormous. The same was true of the risks, among them a sharp rise in unemployment. Yet the immediate political advantages of China's entry into the club of world traders, a symbol of its importance and acceptance by the international community, were no less significant. In the immediate aftermath of the accord, many of these advantages accrued to Jiang Zemin. They ensured that his policy of economic reform and closer relations with the outside world – coupled with tight political control – would be carried over into the new century.

Jiangsu Province

Long one of China's richest provinces, Jiangsu owes its prosperity to location at the heart of the YANGTZE delta and proximity to SHANGHAI. It was the site of China's earliest efforts to build a modern economy and, at the start of the new century, leads the country in industrial output. Thus, while GUANGDONG has a larger economy, Jiangsu has a more 'modern' one. Indeed, the performance of Jiangsu's town and village enterprises, most of them collectively owned, is one of the main driving forces of the delta's dramatic growth. Southern Jiangsu is fast becoming an extended suburb of Shanghai – and one of the most urban, industrialized regions in China.

province of culture and commerce

As with ZHEJIANG to the south, Jiangsu grew rich and powerful centuries ago on the back of intensive agriculture, and the manufacture of foodstuffs, textiles and silks. The Yangtze, the Grand Canal, and a host of lesser waterways that pierce the delta's broad plains helped make the region the most developed in China, ending the political and economic dominance of the north. Hangzhou (in Zhejiang), Suzhou, Yangzhou and Nanjing are among the great centres of administration, culture and commerce of the delta. In the pre-modern era some of these cities served as the capitals of national as well as 'southern' dynasties.

By the mid-nineteenth century imperial decline and Western aggression made the Yangtze vulnerable to plunder and occupation. Nanjing, Jiangsu's capital, gave its name to the treaty of 1842 with BRITAIN which symbolized the Qing dynasty's inability to deal with China's problems. The founding of modern Shanghai, and the extension of treaty port status to Zhenjiang, Nanjing and Suzhou, all of them important cities in Jiangsu, rubbed the message in (see TREATY PORTS). Foreigners had forced their way into China's economic heartland; the dynasty's only salvation lay in reform and modernization.

The growth of Shanghai – in the late Qing, as now, China's most important industrial city – spurred economic development in Jiangsu, of which it was then a part. Jiangnan, the strip of territory south of the Yangtze, from Shanghai to Nanjing, formed one of China's first industrial corridors. In 1908 the two cities were linked by rail. In 1911, the year the QING DYNASTY collapsed, work was completed on the Tianjin–Pukou line, China's first north–south trunk route.

This line terminated on the opposite side of the river from the Jiangsu capital. More than half a century would elapse before a bridge was built and trains no longer had to cross the Yangtze from Pukou by ferry. But this did not stop the railway doing its work. It helped bind the embryonic modern economy of the delta together and linked north China with the centre of economic gravity in the south.

Jiangsu in the early Republic

With the REPUBLICAN REVOLUTION China's political centre shifted to the Yangtze. The uprising began in Wuhan on the middle river and most of the battles that determined its outcome were fought in the cities downstream. By the close of 1911 most of the Yangtze valley was in rebel hands and in January 1912 SUN YAT-SEN formed China's first Republican government in Nanjing, China's capital again for the first time since the early 15th century.

Military realities then intervened. In April the government moved to Beijing where YUAN SHIKAI, now won over to the revolution, controlled the country's most powerful military forces. He succeeded Sun as president by agreement, but his rule sparked a bitter contest between north and south which plagued China for more than 15 years. Its outcome hinged on control of the Yangtze delta.

The region was a key target of the NORTHERN EXPEDITION, the Kuomintang's military campaign to end warlord rule, unify China and end foreign privilege. In the spring of 1927, the National Revolutionary Army fought its way into Jiangsu and occupied Nanjing. It was the high tide of revolution in south China. Anti-imperialist demonstrations got out of hand in Nanjing, where rampaging soldiers killed several foreigners. British gunboats shelled the city and evacuated the foreign community.

These events alarmed the powers. It seemed necessary to oppose the Nationalist revolution by force, or accept the loss of privileges in China. CHIANG KAI-SHEK resolved this dilemma: his purge of the Kuomintang's Communist and Left-wing allies in April 1927 drew the anti-imperialist sting of the revolutionary movement. Communist influence lingered in Wuhan, seat of a rival Nationalist faction, but not for very long. The second phase of the Northern Expedition, from the Yangtze to Beijing, was a military campaign rather than an exercise in revolution.

seat of the capital

In 1928 Nanjing became the capital of the newly unified China. The city rapidly acquired the buildings and infrastructure worthy of its status. Imposing central ministries graced spacious, tree lined boulevards. A huge mausoleum was built in the nearby hills

> ### The Lie of the Land
>
> Rivers, canals and lakes dominate the 38,600 square miles (100,000 sq kms) of Jiangsu, China's lowest-lying province and location of its flattest land. At the close of the century its 72 million people made it one of the most densely populated provinces. North Jiangsu is dryer than the south and suffers from flooding. There are a few scattered hills around Xuzhou close to the border with ANHUI in the west. Further south, the Huai flows into the Hongze Lake and on into the Yangtze. The 'long river' dominates the south of the province, meandering across the plain and continually replenishing its numerous lakes and canals. The best known of these waterways is the Grand Canal which leaves the Yangtze near Yangzhou on its journey north to the suburbs of Beijing.

to commemorate Sun. Diplomatic missions moved south from Beijing, which soon became a political backwater.

The central government relied on the riches of the delta for the bulk of its revenue. Beyond the Yangtze valley, provincial militarists and Communist rebels set limits to Chiang's authority. Within it, and particularly in the delta itself, Chiang was supreme. The provinces of Jiangsu and Zhejiang and the city of Shanghai were core areas of financial sustenance and political support for the Nationalist regime.

They helped shape its values, too. Predominantly these were urban in nature and, despite the anti-foreign movement of the late 1920s, increasingly internationalist in tone. Chiang's goals were to restore China's sovereignty, crush domestic opposition, and modernize the economy the better to resist further foreign aggression. His government spent less time thinking about China's rural problems, and less still trying to solve them. In this sense the Nationalists' agenda was very different from that of the Communists, then fomenting revolution in the countryside. The CHINESE COMMUNIST PARTY was a world away, in every sense, from the cities of the delta.

The SINO-JAPANESE WAR broke Chiang's grip on the lower Yangtze. The first stage of the conflict was fought in the Nanjing–Shanghai–Hangzhou triangle and, despite fierce resistance, Japan soon prevailed. As the Nationalists fled, imperial troops occupied Nanjing and in December 1937 carried out the massacre of civilians which still clouds Sino-Japanese relations more than 60 years later (see SINO-JAPANESE WAR; JAPAN). Japan controlled southern Jiangsu and the Yangtze valley for the remainder of the war. One of the instruments of its rule was the 'puppet government' of WANG JINGWEI in Nanjing. The legitimate Nationalist government, evicted from its prosperous coastal base, spent the war in remote, relatively undeveloped CHONGQING.

In 1945 Chiang returned to his old capital but to a very different political situation. Popular relief at the defeat of Japan evaporated in the face of official corruption and incompetence. The national economy was weaker than before the war. So was the ability of the government, now bent on civil war, to manage it.

The Communists, on the other hand, were much stronger. First in Manchuria (northeast China), then in north China, and finally in the stretch of territory between the Yangtze and the Yellow rivers, they inflicted stunning defeats on government forces. The battle of Huai-Hai, the last of these three great CIVIL WAR campaigns, was fought in north Jiangsu around Xuzhou, where China's main east–west and north–south railway lines meet. Victory opened the way for the Communist conquest of the Yangtze valley. It came in April 1949 when the People's Liberation Army crossed the river virtually unopposed and 'liberated' Nanjing. Chiang's regime fled south, en route to exile in Taiwan, leaving the British frigate HMS Amethyst, 60 miles (96 kms) downstream from the capital, grappling with the new military realities along the Yangtze (see CIVIL WAR; AMETHYST INCIDENT).

alien priorities under Communism

Jiangsu was one of the most developed parts of China when the Communists came to power. In 1949, industry accounted for 30 per cent of the province's total output. Only Shanghai and LIAONING, the northeastern province which had benefited from decades of Japanese investment, rivalled Jiangsu. In light industry the province was supreme. Its grain output was often second only to that of SICHUAN.

Yet the priorities of the new regime did not favour further rapid development. Beijing concentrated on developing heavy rather than light industry. It directed investment to the interior rather than the coastal areas. And, as the Cold War intensified and China's isolation grew, Jiangsu's capitalist, pro-Kuomintang past tended to stand it in poor stead.

Nanjing, in particular, was an object of political suspicion. New industries were built in the city, including iron and steel, petrochemical and textile factories. In 1968 a bridge was at last constructed across the Yangtze.

There was no denying the economic importance of the Jiangnan region: it was vital to China's well-being. But much of what it stood for was at odds with Mao Zedong's increasingly radical vision for his country.

Deng Xiaoping's return to power in the late 1970s changed that. The new policies of agricultural reform and engagement with the outside world breathed new life into those provinces best able to implement them. Jiangsu, sandwiched between Shanghai and the resources of central China, and the custodian of a long commercial tradition, was chief among them. It soon emerged as one of the star performers of the reform era, one whose success was copied eagerly elsewhere.

Jiangsu's industrial revolution

The nature of Jiangsu's success was different from that of Guangdong, the other star performer of the early reform period. There, FOREIGN TRADE AND INVESTMENT, much of it conducted with Hong Kong, was the key factor in spurring growth. Jiangsu's development owed more to the domestic than the international economy. It was fuelled by the dramatic expansion of township and village enterprises (TVEs) – collectively-owned but capitalist-run concerns which soon colonized all the major cities of southern Jiangsu – Suzhou, Wuxi, Changzhou, Zhenjiang and Nanjing – and sent output soaring.

In Jiangsu as elsewhere, TVEs predated the reform era. Many dated back to the GREAT LEAP FORWARD. What was new in the early 1980s was that they operated according to free market principles and produced consumer goods. This would have been impossible without Deng's agricultural reforms: the return to household farming freed farm labour to work in factories and created customers by raising incomes. Once again this was the case throughout China. What was special about Jiangsu was its proximity to the enormous market and invaluable expertise of Shanghai.

Faced with new market pressure, state-owned enterprises in Shanghai farmed out many of their operations to smaller, leaner, more competitive township enterprises in Jiangsu. They also assigned experienced staff to run them. Some of these arrangements took the form of joint ventures between state- and collectively-owned firms. Others were less formal, occasionally temporary partnerships. Some did not perform well and closed down. Still others, having failed, changed tack and took on completely new lines of business. But all tended to shift production into smaller units where managerial initiative and the market held sway. They generated profits, productivity and growth on a scale which kept Jiangsu among the country's top performers throughout the 1980s and 1990s.

Much of the growth and most of the output was generated in the south of the province. North Jiangsu generally fared less well. Traditionally much poorer than the delta, the north's strength derives from coal and railways. Most of the former is extracted in the Xuzhou region. The key rail link in northern Jiangsu is the east–west line to Lianyungang, one of the 14 coastal cities opened to the outside world on favourable terms in 1984. This is the eastern terminus of the 'Asia-Europe Land Bridge', the rail link across China, central Asia and Russia and on to Europe. Chinese officials tout it as a rival to the Trans-Siberian Railway and speak of Rotterdam as its western terminus. Improved railway management in China and political stability in central Asia are required before the land-bridge really comes into its own.

In southern Jiangsu, the start of work on Shanghai's Pudong Development Zone in 1990 and the opening of the entire Yangtze valley to foreign investment two years later added a powerful new stimulus to an already vibrant economy. By the end of the decade, much of the province south of the river – from Kunshan on the border with Shanghai, to Nanjing, the revitalized provincial capital and China's biggest inland port – resembled a giant industrial park. It included the high-profile, though not always highly successful, industrial city founded and funded by SINGAPORE in Suzhou; and Zhangjiagang, the model community whose socialist ethics, capitalist incomes and environmental management won praise from President JIANG ZEMIN.

At the start of the new era, Jiangsu's collectively owned sector – the portmanteau term for local government, foreign, and private Chinese enterprise, often in partnership – produces an entire range of products and services. Its output is far greater than that of the non-state sector in any other province, and accounts for more than half of industrial value in Jiangsu. In all these respects, the province is a pacesetter of modernization. And its political economy offers a glimpse of China's future in the event that the rapid development of the 1980s and 1990s can be sustained during the early years of the new century.

Jiangxi Province

As a proving ground of the rural revolution which eventually swept the CHINESE COMMUNIST PARTY to power, Jiangxi ranks close to SHAANXI, seat of YANAN, in importance. As an inland, albeit Yangtze province, in an age of reform and globalization, it still suffers from the relative isolation, poor communications and underdevelopment which once made it a haven for rebels. Jiangxi's status as an 'old revolutionary base area' is a cause of pride for some; for others it is something of an economic stigma.

flood plains and foreigners

The economic heartland of Jiangxi is the great plain in the north of the province. It encompasses the Poyang Lake, a natural flood reservoir for the Yangtze, and stretches deep into the southwest. Watered by the Gan and several lesser rivers, it is the most densely settled part of the province, whose 64,300 square miles (166,500 sq kms) were home for 42 million people at the close of the twentieth century.

Two centuries earlier, the Gan formed part of the main overland communications route between north and south China. Southbound traffic from the Yangtze passed along it as far as the border with GUANGDONG, where the journey was continued via a pass in the mountains leading down to the river system of Guangdong. The arrival of the West in the mid-nineteenth century, the modernization of shipping, and the opening of the TREATY PORTS sent the route into decline.

The foreign presence in Jiangxi centred on the Yangtze port of Jiujiang, opened in 1861. There was an international concession in the city until Nationalist protestors took it over in 1927 at the height of the NORTHERN EXPEDITION. This had little effect on foreigners' fondness for the cool, mountain resort of Guling in Lushan, a few miles south of Jiujiang. Built in the late nineteenth century, it became China's most famous 'hill station' and a great favourite with the expatriate community along the Yangtze. Elsewhere in Jiangxi, MISSIONARIES were active in Nanchang and a few other centres, but for the most part, the area south of the provincial capital remained off the beaten track as far as foreigners were concerned.

Mao in Jiangxi

To an extent the same was true of formal Chinese authority. Save for the extreme north, which forms part of the Yangtze valley, Jiangxi is surrounded by mountains. Towering ranges and isolated valleys dominate much of the south of the province. Before the 1930s few roads penetrated this region, and the modern world, whether in Chinese or foreign guise, made little impact beyond the confines of the Gan.

This was rural China at its least romantic: a land where CLANS and SECRET SOCIETIES provided the main forms of social organization; where banditry was a way of life; where fiercely independent Hakkas sought solidarity in the different dialect and customs which separated them from the majority; and where the often desperate struggle to make a living injected new tension into the inequalities of traditional society. Jiangxi might not have been ripe for revolution in the early decades of the twentieth century. But there is little doubt that it provided promising conditions for professional revolutionaries.

The Communist Party certainly thought so, though not at first. In mid-1927, the Party was reeling from the campaign of terror launched by CHIANG KAI-SHEK following the Nationalists' capture of Shanghai. Its Soviet-controlled leaders conspired to seize an urban centre from which to launch a nationwide revolt. They settled on Nanchang, where several KUO-MINTANG military leaders opposed Chiang, and many of their subordinates seemed well-disposed to Communism.

On 1 August, Party activists launched a military coup and captured the city. They soon abandoned their prize in the face of a superior enemy. But the Nanchang Uprising marked the birth of the Red Army, later the PEOPLE'S LIBERATION ARMY, and then, as now, the Party's *own* army. It has been the key to the Party's survival, seizure and subsequent retention of power. Many of those associated with the Nanchang revolt became senior leaders of China after 1949, among them ZHOU ENLAI, ZHU DE and LIN BIAO.

The failure of the Nanchang Uprising, and the Autumn Harvest Uprisings which followed, forced China's Communists to search for a new strategy. For the most part they did so in Jiangxi under difficult circumstances and against overwhelming odds. In some ways

their efforts were a spectacular failure. But in others, the Party's years in Jiangxi planted the seeds of a mighty victory (see CHINESE COMMUNIST PARTY).

They were sown first in the villages of Jinggangshan in the mountainous southwest of the province, close to the border with HUNAN. MAO ZEDONG retreated there at the end of 1927 with perhaps 1,000 men following the failure of the Autumn Harvest Uprisings. Zhu De, who had more troops and far more military experience at his disposal, joined him a few months later. It was the start of one of the most formidable personal alliances in China's revolutionary history.

Cut off from the outside world, including the Party leadership, Mao and Zhu conducted experiments in land reform, guerrilla warfare, popular mobilization and rural administration. To survive, they struck up relationships with local BANDITS. Survive they did, though at the close of 1928 Mao and Zhu left Jinggangshan for the more promising southwestern part of Jiangxi, close to the border with FUJIAN.

In the early 1930s there were several rural soviets in south China, but the new Jiangxi base soon became the largest and strongest of them. Struggles over leadership and line abounded. In distant Shanghai, the Central Committee often looked askance at Mao's rural revolution. So much so that in 1930, alarmed that the supposed vanguard of the proletariat was becoming a peasants' party, the Party ordered attacks on key cities in the belief that a high tide of worker revolt was imminent. Again Nanchang and Changsha, capital of Hunan, were targeted. Again they proved impossible to hold.

In these circumstances, the rural revolution intensified, if only by default. In November 1931 Mao's base area became the home of the Central Soviet Republic with its capital at Ruijin, just across the border from Fujian. Mao was made president. About the same time the Party Central Committee moved from Shanghai to the relative security of the Jiangxi countryside. The Moscow-trained leadership was now in a position to lead the revolution from the ground.

This was not a happy time, either for Mao personally or the Central Soviet, which began to suffer from Chiang Kai-shek's annihilation campaigns. Chiang's first four attempts at 'bandit suppression' failed, but the fifth, begun in late 1933, proved far more effective. A massive Nationalist military campaign, including intensive road-building and the creation of networks of block houses designed to strangle the revolutionaries, enabled Chiang to project his power deep into the Jiangxi countryside. In October 1934, with the Central Soviet shrinking in size, its leadership in disarray and Mao under a political cloud, the Party evacuated Jiangxi and set out on the LONG MARCH.

Defeat was almost total; a small Communist force left behind tried to keep the revolution alive but was soon broken up. Chiang moved to win over the countryside. He strengthened Nationalist administration in the former 'bandit' areas, and launched his 'New Life Movement', an effort to encourage ordinary people to embrace traditional Confucian values rather than Marxism or other foreign creeds (see CONFUCIANISM). Jiangxi was brought under firm control; during the mid-1930s it was one of the few provinces in which the central government's writ was absolute.

Despite the manner of its exit, the Communist Party learned much during its years in Jiangxi. It had not been possible to perfect the techniques of revolution in the province: the opposition was too strong and the sense of *national* crisis of the kind created by Japan's invasion of China a few years later, and which the Party turned to good account, was lacking. But Mao and other leaders had gained valuable experience in mobilizing the peasantry, creating and administering rural bases, and building the army needed to defend and expand Communist power. They were invaluable lessons, soon put to use in the different circumstances of Yanan.

post-1949 Party battles

Jiangxi's importance in the history of Chinese Communism did not end with the foundation of the People's Republic in 1949. Even as the Party built monuments and museums to mark past struggles in the province, a vital battle over the future took place in 1959 during a leadership conclave in Lushan.

The controversy centred on the GREAT LEAP FORWARD, Mao's attempt to attain Communism overnight which had plunged the country into chaos and, soon, famine. Of the Party's senior leaders, only PENG DEHUAI was ready to criticize the new line. He did so in the form of a private letter to Mao which the Chairman promptly made the basis of an outspoken personal attack on its author. Mao condemned Peng as a 'Right opportunist'. The consequences were immense. Lushan showed

that Mao would not tolerate even 'internal' criticism of his policies. Those who tried it could expect dismissal and disgrace of the kind meted out to the unfortunate Peng. It was a foretaste of the more serious rifts, struggles and upheavals of the CULTURAL REVOLUTION.

These afflicted Jiangxi as they did every other part of China. They also brought a distinguished yet disgraced exile to the province. DENG XIAOPING, a chief target and early casualty of the Cultural Revolution in Beijing, was exiled to Jiangxi in 1969. The 'second most important capitalist roader' (after LIU SHAOQI) went to work in a tractor factory in Xinjian, a few miles northwest of Nanchang. He remained there for the following three years, in the company of his family and in conditions of increasing comfort.

obstacles to development

The same conditions which enabled Jiangxi to play such an important role in the history of Chinese Communism have made the quest for development at the heart of the reform era a difficult task in the province. It has not been easy to overcome the circumstances which fostered rural revolution in the early 1930s. The same is true of the legacies of central planning and emphasis on heavy industry of Mao's years in power. If the first three decades of Communist rule brought change to Jiangxi, the new priorities of Deng's reform programme showed how much remained to be done in what is still a rather poor, isolated province.

After an indifferent performance in the 1980s, the opening of the Yangtze valley to foreign trade and investment in 1992 breathed new life into the provincial economy. For much of the 1990s, Jiangxi's GDP, like that of neighbouring Anhui, grew comfortably faster than the national average. This did not alter the province's modest contribution to the national economy: judged by most indices, including per capita GDP, industrial output, values of foreign trade and foreign capital used, Jiangxi enters the new era firmly in the bottom half of the league table of provincial economic performance.

One possible new source of growth is the Beijing–Kowloon railway, which runs through the heart of southern Jiangxi (see RAILWAYS). Services began in 1996. Beijing's aim in building this new north–south link was to bring prosperity to parts of the country long denied it by geography and history. The vast expanse of southern Jiangxi, where rivers and indifferent roads were the main arteries of communication before the railway arrived, and where Mao and Zhu first made their revolution in the late 1920s, is certainly among them.

Jilin Province

Jilin is the least populous of the three Manchurian provinces (see LIAONING; HEILONGJIANG) and has the smallest economy. This has not saved it from the consequences of location in a historic heartland of Chinese industry: the presence of numerous state-owned industries, many of them ailing. Trade and investment from South Korea and JAPAN have provided new sources of growth; the TUMEN RIVER ECONOMIC ZONE perhaps promises another.

Jilin was settled by Han Chinese later and less intensively than Liaoning during the nineteenth century. Colder, more wooded and more remote, the province was an altogether less hospitable part of Manchuria than its southern neighbour. In the last years of the QING DYNASTY, it was still something of a frontier society. The homeland of China's Manchu rulers, it was host to new migrants, new ways, new wealth – and considerable lawlessness.

Until 1860, it was also much larger. Jilin was a coastal province facing the Sea of Japan and, further north, the Sea of Okhotsk. It even included the island of Sakhalin. Its lands were little populated in the mid-nineteenth century, facilitating Russian penetration and eventual annexation of a wilderness whose loss, almost alone among those incurred during the late Qing, Beijing has not sought to recover. (See RUSSIA; SOVIET UNION.)

Han immigration intensified during the late nineteenth and early twentieth century, bringing much of Manchuria into the cultural orbit of China 'proper' south of the Great Wall. Political and economic integration with the rest of China proved more elusive. The presence of Russia and Japan set limits to Chinese authority in all three Manchurian provinces, and the local militarist Zhang Zuolin (1875–1928), the major warlord of the northeast, ruled the region as a semi-autonomous enclave.

His son and successor, ZHANG XUELIANG, chose a different path: in 1928 he pledged loyalty to Chiang Kai-shek's newly formed Nationalist government. It was a matter of tactics rather than a change of heart. But Japanese military officers, worried by growing resistance to their presence in Manchuria, decided on a pre-emptive strike. In 1931 the 'Mukden Incident' (an explosion on the railway in modern Shenyang staged by Japanese soldiers) enabled them to bring all of northeast China under control, and in 1932 Tokyo turned its new domains into the puppet state of MANCHUGUO. The 'country of the Manchus' was ruled, at least in name, by PU YI, the last Qing emperor. Its capital was Xinjing ('new capital'), modern Changchun, present capital of Liaoning. Manchuguo rapidly became the most industrialized part of China.

Japan's rule over northeast China ended with its defeat in the Second World War. Soviet troops brought the episode to a conclusion by entering the region under the terms of the YALTA CONFERENCE. When they withdrew almost a year later – after stripping Manchuria of much of its industrial equipment – the entire northeast became a vital battlefield in China's CIVIL WAR. Jilin was at the heart of the struggle.

Chiang was determined to assert authority over an economically dynamic region long denied him by warlord rule and foreign invasion. He went about it in almost entirely the wrong way. An example was his decision to divide the three Manchurian provinces into nine smaller provinces governed by outsiders. The aim was to weaken pro-Manchurian sentiment and facilitate central control. The result was to drive local forces – many of them still loyal to Zhang Xueliang, the 'Young Marshal' – into the arms of the Communists who, under LIN BIAO, had poured into the Manchurian countryside after Japan's defeat.

Government forces occupied most of Manchuria's key cities but failed to hold them. Defeat came in the form of sweeping raids and skilful manoeuvres by Lin's forces which isolated, besieged and, in the case of Changchun, starved the Nationalists into submission. A rare, candid account of the human costs of the siege of Changchun was published in the Mainland in 1988. *White Snow, Red Blood*, by Zhang Zhenglong (1947–), an officer in the People's Liberation Army, and based on previously unavailable documents, was soon withdrawn from sale.

Rapid immigration and industrialization were important themes in Jilin's development during the early years of Communist rule. Changchun, the capital after 1954, and Jilin city, the capital from 1945, were built into major centres of heavy industry. Siping, an important railway junction on the border with Liaoning, became a centre of the engineering industry. Liaoyuan, to the southwest, was turned into a 'coal city'.

Soviet aid and advice played an important role in some of these developments. Changchun Number One Autoworks, founded in 1956, became one of the best known fruits of Sino-Soviet cooperation. JIANG ZEMIN worked there for the best part of six years. Changchun Auto produces the 'Liberation' brand trucks which still rule China's highways at the start of the new era. It made the Red Flag limousines once beloved of top Beijing officials. Since the early 1990s it has turned out Audi saloons in a joint venture with Volkswagen.

In common with many other interior provinces, and in particular with its neighbours in the northeast, Jilin's reliance on state-owned industry has stood it in poor stead in the era of reform. By the late 1990s, almost twenty years after DENG XIAOPING introduced free market reforms and opened China's doors to the outside world, state enterprises accounted for 60 per cent of industrial output in Jilin. The province attracted one quarter of the foreign investment utilized by Liaoning, and only slightly more than half of that put to work in Heilongjiang. Jilin ranked an even poorer third among the Manchurian provinces in foreign trade.

Trade and investment with South Korea grew in importance during the 1990s, especially after Beijing and Seoul established diplomatic relations in 1992. Most of China's almost two million ethnic Koreans live in Jilin. Many of them reside in the Yanbian Korean Autonomous Prefecture in the southeast, along the borders with North Korea and Russia. A sense of cultural mission, coupled with the search for profits, propels thousands of South Korean businessmen, tourists and even Christian missionaries into a region from which Cold War politics have long excluded them.

There is much for the visitors to see. A chief attraction of south Jilin is the Changbaishan mountains and nature reserve, spiritual homeland of the Korean people, an area of great natural beauty, and a source of ginseng and other rare commodities. No less important is the border with troubled North Korea, many of whose people starved to death in the 1990s because of poor weather, disastrous agricultural policies and the general malfeasance and incompetence of the Korean Workers' Party led by Kim Jong-il.

South Korean companies have invested in Yanji, Tumen and Hunchun – the main cities in Jilin close to North Korea – with a view to securing better returns than they might enjoy at home or elsewhere overseas. But in the event of North Korea's collapse or unification with the South, investments along this northern fringe of the Korean cultural world may serve a broader strategic purpose. Much depends upon events in Pyongyang.

To some extent the same is true of plans by China, the two Koreas, Russia and MONGOLIA to develop the Tumen River Economic Zone, much of which falls within southeast Jilin. The potential of a new regional economic zone linking the mineral and energy resources of Siberia and Mongolia with the industry of Manchuria and the technology, investment and know-how of South Korea and Japan is enormous. So, in the absence of improved relations on the Korean peninsula, and a pressing but perhaps temporary lack of funds, are the obstacles.

Tumen is unlikely to be the source of rapid development in Jilin and neighbouring parts of northeast China until several years into the new century. Yet its promise cannot be discounted. Renewed access to the Sea of Japan would transform Manchuria's fortunes, ending its long sentence as a prisoner of geography, and casualty of the international politics of the twentieth century.

K

Kang Sheng (1898–1975)

A Moscow-trained expert in security and Marxist ideology, Kang was an influential member of the CHINESE COMMUNIST PARTY from the 1940s until his death. He combined refined artistic tastes with a gift for polemics; fondness for calligraphy with cruelty and cunning. He put all these attributes to work in the cause of the Party and in particular MAO ZEDONG, whose radical vision – and the terror often associated with it – he did much to realize. During the CULTURAL REVOLUTION, Kang was Mao's henchman and ideological warrior.

Kang left his native SHANDONG as a young man for SHANGHAI, but not before he had met JIANG QING, Mao's future wife. It was the start of a relationship that helped shape the course of Chinese Communism. After several years as a member of the Communist underground in Shanghai, Kang moved to Moscow where he studied MARXISM and learnt the techniques of struggle, criticism, and purge developed by the Soviet security apparatus to crush opposition. In 1937 he brought these talents to YANAN, headquarters of the Chinese Party, and placed them at the disposal of Mao, then struggling to gain the upper hand over rivals in the leadership. Kang also helped stifle criticism of the Chairman's romantic alliance with Jiang, who had also moved to the Communist's wartime headquarters.

As security chief, Kang became known as 'Mao's pistol' or 'dark shadow' for his part in organizing the great purges and rectifications of the early 1940s which established the Chairman's authority. He 'investigated' cadres, 'screened' them and, as the quasi-religious language of the Party put it, helped 'save' them from errors. These terms were euphemisms for terror: Kang, often dressed in leathers and riding a black horse followed by a fierce police dog, oversaw the persecution and humiliation of dissenters in the Party. One of the more famous among them was Wang Shiwei (1900–1947), a writer who criticized the privileges Party leaders enjoyed. He was branded a Trotskyite. Kang later had him shot.

Ill-health kept Kang out of the limelight during most of the 1950s. But he resumed his close relationship with Mao in the early 1960s as the Chairman developed his attack on the Soviet Union and, later, Party leaders in Beijing, both of whom he accused of betraying socialism. Paradoxically Kang's Moscow years again stood him in good stead: an expert on Marxism, he was used to exposing 'revisionists' and 'counter-revolutionaries'. He helped write the 'nine polemics' against Moscow, the texts at the heart of the Sino-Soviet split (see SOVIET UNION).

Kang's ideological views, mastery of the Party apparatus and closeness to Jiang Qing made him a natural ally for Mao during the Cultural Revolution. He helped arrange the exposure and humiliation of the Chairman's critics at the highest levels of the Party. He also took the lead in the attack on 'feudal culture' at the heart of the movement, even though the shelves in his Beijing residence are known to have contained thousands of ancient books, pictures and erotic prints. When LIN BIAO, the chairman's nominal successor, was exposed as a traitor in 1971, Kang sought to turn the campaign to discredit his former ally – the movement to 'criticize Lin Biao, criticize Confucius' – into an attack on ZHOU ENLAI, the more moderate premier.

Ill health closed in on Kang in the early 1970s at the same time as it did on Mao and Zhou. Aware that the Chairman was worried about the ambitions of Jiang Qing, Kang sought to discredit her by raking up details of her past. It was a desperate, final move in a life of manipulation. Within the space of 10 months in 1976, Kang, Zhou and Mao all died, and Jiang and the three other members of the 'GANG OF FOUR' were arrested. The Party, keen to put the Cultural Revolution behind it, yet avoid inflicting too much harm on Mao's reputation, exposed Kang as the movement's principal inquisitor and torturer. In 1980 he was posthumously expelled from the Party whose Chairman he had served so enthusiastically. His ashes were removed from the Babaoshan cemetery for revolutionary martyrs in Beijing.

Kang Youwei (1858–1927)

Kang, chief inspiration of the abortive '100 Days Reform' of 1898, an attempt to revive the ailing QING DYNASTY, was an intellectual of rare vision and considerable eccentricity. He combined utopianism with something close to idolatry of the ill-fated GUANGXU Emperor – an approach which placed him at odds with revolutionaries such as SUN YAT-SEN as well as LIANG QICHAO, his former student and occasional ally during the final, tempestuous years of imperial rule.

Almost alone among his generation, Kang grounded his argument for sweeping political change on a radical reinterpretation of Confucius' teachings (see CONFUCIANISM). He argued that, so far from being an essentially conservative figure, the Sage was a radical who had identified a dynamic at work in society and history. It was the duty of the imperial government to respond to the demands of change accordingly, and never more so than during the late 1890s, when defeat at the hands of JAPAN threatened the very existence of the Chinese nation.

While most officials were horrified by such ideas, the young Guangxu Emperor, temporarily out of the shadow of the EMPRESS DOWAGER, his overpowering aunt and true power behind the throne, granted Kang an audience. 'It is necessary to dismantle the building and build anew if we want something strong and dependable,' the scholar told his emperor in the summer of 1898. Guangxu responded with a flurry of imperial decrees which bore the imprint of Kang's ideas and promised to transform despotic Manchu rule into a constitutional monarchy. The experiment lasted 100 days before it was crushed by conservatives. In the ensuing crackdown several of the reformers were killed, Kang's younger brother among them. Guangxu spent the rest of his life under 'palace arrest' for his pains.

Kang fled into exile where he competed with Sun Yat-sen for the support of the OVERSEAS CHINESE communities in Japan, Southeast Asia, Europe and North America. While Sun advocated the violent overthrow of the Qing and the creation of a Chinese republic, Kang, founder of the 'Protect the Emperor Society', believed that if the Empress Dowager were only toppled, Guangxu would at last come into his own as the champion of reform. The battle for allegiance of the Chinese diaspora was as bitter as the struggles at Court. Kang lost: the death of Guangxu in 1909 and the REPUBLICAN REVOLUTION two years later all but ended his political influence.

Yet during his ceaseless wanderings across the world, usually in the company of a succession of young Chinese girlfriends, Kang developed a utopian scheme of world government known as the 'great community' – an idea he again traced back to Confucius. In this ideal world, the family would be replaced by state institutions, homosexuals could marry, and men and women would be equal.

Kang's earlier political aspirations flickered into life briefly in 1917 when General Zhang Xun (1854–1923), a Manchu loyalist, seized Beijing and allowed the young PU YI, the last Qing emperor, to reclaim his throne. But this second imperial revival was even less successful than that launched by YUAN SHIKAI a year earlier: Kang's desire to see an emperor rule China again was dashed. Still revered by some, but rejected by most of the new generation of revolutionaries, the great reformer died in Shanghai, a year after he had turned his attention to the possibility of intergalactic travel and formed the Academy of Travel Through the Heavens – a legacy of his sole aeroplane journey some years earlier.

Korea (North and South)

Principle and pragmatism meet in China's policy towards the Korean peninsula where Beijing has matched its longstanding, close relations with Communist North Korea with vigorous commercial ties and formal recognition of rival South Korea. This has given Beijing unusual, though far from decisive, leverage in one of the world's most volatile regions, and one which has a major bearing on China's own security.

lost tributary

Korea was a tributary of China for centuries until defeat in the war against Japan of 1894–5 forced the QING DYNASTY to acknowledge the kingdom of Korea's full independence. Successive governments in Beijing chose not to make a formal return to the status quo part of their policy towards the peninsula, even though China's grounds for exerting at least preponderant influence in the region seemed as strong (or as weak) as its claims to ownership of TIBET and MONGOLIA. In the event Korean independence was shortlived: Japan won control of the peninsula in the war against Russia of 1904–5; and in 1910 made it part of the Japanese empire. This facilitated Japan's penetration of Manchuria (northeast China) and, in 1932, its creation of the state of MANCHUGUO.

close allies: China and North Korea

Japan's defeat in the Second World War and Beijing's participation in the KOREAN WAR of 1950 re-established Chinese influence in the region. A chief expression of this is China's close, if not always comfortable, relationship with the Communist state in the North – the Democratic People's Republic of Korea. The Korean War united the governments of MAO ZEDONG and Kim Il-Sung while they were in their infancy. Their common, Marxist ideology and close ties to the Soviet Union reinforced the bond in the years that followed. Cultural affinities between Chinese and Koreans played a part, too. Together, these factors ensured that the relationship was, and according to Chinese propaganda remains, 'as close as lips and teeth'.

However these ties did not make Kim a twentieth-century equivalent of those traditional Korean kings who revelled in Chinese 'suzerainty'. Gratitude for China's support in the war, and much help afterwards, endured in Pyongyang. But the same was true of a determination that North Korea should be an independent Communist state, free of excessive Chinese *and* Soviet influence. For Kim, common opposition to the presence of American troops on the Korean peninsula, and a refusal to recognize what he regarded as the 'puppet' state in the South did not mean that he had to do things China's way in domestic policy. Neither did his reliance on Soviet and/or Chinese aid. In 1961, at a time of enmity between the two giant Communist powers, he signed treaties of friendship and mutual assistance with both Beijing and Moscow. The pact with Beijing, which provides for China's participation on North Korea's side in the event of a conflict, remains in effect at the start of the twenty-first century.

During the Sino-Soviet split of the 1960s and long thereafter, North Korea gently played off one Communist neighbour against the other. Hatred of the United States as the prime obstacle to both Korean *and* Chinese unification – by virtue of the American troop presence in TAIWAN and South Korea, and treaties binding their governments to Washington – kept Pyongyang and Beijing in the same camp. The fact that they sometimes practised similar economic policies, including the creation of agricultural communes and the pursuit of self-reliance, had a similar effect. This did not stop Red Guards attacking Kim as a 'fat revisionist' in the CULTURAL REVOLUTION, but the aid kept flowing despite the insults. China and the Soviet Union alternated as North Korea's main suppliers of weapons and economic assistance throughout the 1960s and 1970s. From the mid-1970s, China began to supply large quantities of oil to Pyongyang and emerged as its major trade partner.

balancing act: Beijing and Seoul

The nature of China's relationship with North Korea began to change in the late 1970s following Beijing's rapprochement with the UNITED STATES and its pursuit of free market reforms. Neither development went down well in Pyongyang, and Chinese leaders sought to paper over the gaps between 'lips and teeth' with frequent visits to North Korea and pledges of aid. They also politely declined to criticize Kim's plans to make Communist rule in North Korea a dynastic affair by designating Kim Jong-Il, his son, as successor. They even showed Kim senior round China's SPECIAL ECONOMIC ZONES in the hope he would adopt similar policies at home.

Sentiment aside, the imperatives of Chinese domestic development, and pursuit of unification with Taiwan required good relations with the United States, Japan and, it gradually became clear, with the previously despised government in Seoul, capital of the Republic of Korea. Preserving the status quo on the Korean peninsula began to seem more attractive to Beijing than sponsoring unification. If unity was attempted on the North's terms, that is, by invasion, then the US and South Korea would fight back. If, on the other hand, the government in the North collapsed as a result of internal problems, or invasion by the South, American power would once again extend to China's back door, the Yalu River. The value of North Korea to Beijing was – and remains – its ability to perform the role of buffer state.

The truly radical aspect of China's approach became apparent in the early 1990s. It concerned relations between China and South Korea. Unofficial contacts and indirect trade had mushroomed during the previous decade. In 1988, China took part in the Seoul Olympics. South Korean investors visited China in large numbers. Then, in 1992, China and South Korea established full diplomatic relations, one year after both Koreas joined the United Nations.

Sino-Korean trade and investment blossomed. SHANDONG, the Chinese province jutting into the Yellow Sea, quickly became a favoured destination for South Korean capital. Southern LIAONING, whose towns and cities are home for many of China's almost two million ethnic Koreans, was a prime target, too. Many Chinese Koreans live in that part of the province which falls within the TUMEN RIVER ECONOMIC ZONE, an ambitious co-operative development project involving China, both Koreas, Russia and Mongolia.

the search for security in Korea

Most of these developments were body blows for Kim Il-Sung, who repaid Beijing with new displays of recalcitrance, many of them sustained and developed after his death in 1994 by his son. Yet as far as China was concerned the gains easily outweighed the losses. Until 1992, Seoul had maintained diplomatic relations with Taiwan. Its recognition of Beijing deprived Taipei of its last major ally in Asia (see TAIWAN/ARMS ACROSS THE STRAITS).

Potentially, Beijing's recognition of Seoul has made China the most important power on the Korean peninsula. Unlike Japan and the United States it has a foot in both camps, North and South. However, exercising this power has not been easy. In 1994, when North Korea sparked alarm by threatening to develop nuclear weapons, Beijing pressured its old ally to sign up to the Geneva Accords of 1994. These required Pyongyang to halt its own, unmonitored nuclear programme in exchange for the supply of several light water reactors of overseas manufacture, and the provision of 500,000 tonnes of fuel oil a year until such time as the reactors became operational.

Beijing's 'good offices' achieved less during efforts to turn the 1953 armistice agreement ending the Korean War into a long overdue peace treaty. The issue became enmeshed with the desperate food shortages which afflicted North Korea at the close of the twentieth century. The result of bad weather and gross economic mismanagement, they were believed to have cost hundreds of thousands of lives. China began to worry about the possibility that thousands of starving North Koreans would flee north into its territory. Pyongyang seemed more put out by the flight, to the South Korean embassy in Beijing early in 1997, of Hwang Jang-yop, the 73-year-old architect of its *juche* ideology of self-sufficiency. Two months later, North Korea's most senior defector was spirited out of China to Seoul, where he lambasted the Communist government for letting its people starve.

Anxieties about the North's military intentions intensified as the century came to a close, creating a security environment in the region distinctly unfavourable to Beijing. In 1998, Pyongyang test-fired a missile which passed over Japan. In 1999, it threatened to test a longer-range version capable of reaching parts of the United States. These developments, coming after the nuclear scare of the mid-1990s, heightened fears in Seoul and Tokyo over their vulnerability to attack and encouraged both to seek closer military ties with the United States. One result of this was the approval of new defence guidelines agreed between Tokyo and Washington which allowed Japanese forces to play a larger role in unspecified 'surrounding areas' of Japan (see JAPAN). Another was renewed interest in a US-controlled theatre missile defence (TMD) system to protect South Korea and Japan from North Korean missiles. Beijing saw both developments as indirect attempts to contain its own military power, especially as Taiwan backed the US–Japan defence pact and sought inclusion in the TMD system. Thus, at the close of the twentieth century, North Korea's past role as an ideological soulmate and a buffer state seemed in danger of being over-shadowed by its capacity to generate hostile, potentially anti-Chinese alliances in the region. The meeting in Pyongyang in June 2000 of the leaders of North and South pointed to a new but equally uncertain future.

Korean War (1950–53)

A short but intensely savage conflict, the Korean War still defines the international security environment in East Asia. More than half a century after the fighting broke out, the Korean peninsula remains divided into two hostile camps separated by a highly militar-ized border. South Korea's closest ally is still the UNITED STATES, while China remains North Korea's best, if sometimes less than enthusiastic, friend. At the start of the new century, a peace treaty eludes the belligerents, the meeting in Pyongyang in June 2000 of the leaders of the two Koreas suggested it might not be far away.

The causes of the war are less clear than its consequences. There is little doubt – except in North Korea and among official circles in China – that in June 1950 Kim Il-Sung launched a devastating attack across the 38th parallel, where the peninsula was divided into Soviet- and American-influenced spheres after Japan's defeat in the Second World War. In Beijing and Pyongyang, where political imperatives rank higher than historical facts, South Korea is held to have attacked the North.

The UNITED NATIONS was quick to condemn the invasion and sent a US-led force to the aid of South Korea. It might not have been able to move so swiftly had the SOVIET UNION attended meetings of the Security Council and exercised its veto. Moscow's absence, a protest against the continued occupation of China's seat at the UN by representatives of the Nationalist government of TAIWAN, proved untimely (see UNITED NATIONS).

Within days of Kim's attack, the United States moved the Seventh Fleet into the Straits of Taiwan, making the island an American protectorate for the duration of the conflict and the next 30 years. Kim's forces were soon on the retreat after their rapid advance. In mid-October UN troops approached the Yalu River, the border between Korea and China's northeastern provinces, the country's indus-trial heartland (see LIAONING; JILIN). Despite warnings from Beijing that it would intervene, General MacArthur, the UN commander, indicated that he wanted to unify the entire peninsula, and perhaps take the fight into China as well. In 1951 President Truman dis-missed MacArthur for his impetuosity.

Exactly when MAO ZEDONG decided to com-mit Chinese 'volunteers' – so-called in order that China should avoid the formal status of belligerent – to aid North Korea is uncertain. In the late 1990s evidence emerged from Soviet archives that he had promised to do so before the war broke out. Another suggestion, again based on new materials, was that Stalin forced Mao to rescue Kim from defeat by UN forces on pain of losing aid. In any event, by the end of November 1950 about 300,000 Chinese soldiers had swept south across the Yalu and forced UN expeditionary forces into a long retreat beyond Seoul. The frontline shifted to and fro for several months as both sides attacked and counter-attacked. It had stabil-ized by the end of 1951, though a further two years passed before an armistice was signed at Panmunjon, since then one of the world's best-known border villages.

China's role in the war was decisive. Had the 'volunteers' not intervened, Kim Il Sung's regime might have perished and the Commu-nist regime in Beijing itself come under threat. The war proved decisive for China in other ways. The performance of its troops (the second time China dispatched 'expeditionary' forces in the twentieth century; the first was to BURMA) raised the country's international profile. The 'volunteers' demonstrated brav-ery and skill, until they were outgunned and worn down by a technologically superior enemy. China's participation also helped the Communist Party consolidate its rule at home. The war sharpened political tensions, facilitating mobilization for a nationalist cause in which the US was depicted as the enemy and North Korea and the Soviet Union as friends (see UNITED STATES; SOVIET UNION).

Yet there was a price to pay. China lost per-haps 900,000 men, among them one of Chair-man Mao's sons. Weapons supplied by the

Soviet Union during the conflict had to be paid for, a requirement some Chinese Communists felt showed a want of solidarity. At the same time, the war forced China into a closer alliance with Moscow than might otherwise have been the case. It also cemented a marriage between Beijing and Pyongyang which subsequently proved stormy, but remains in place at the start of the new century.

China's participation in the conflict scuppered the possibility of rapprochement with Washington and the West. Rapprochement had not seemed very likely before the war, but the effect of Beijing's participation in the conflict was to extend the Cold War to Asia in general and China in particular. The United Nations condemned Beijing as an 'aggressor'. For a while, a primary image of China in the West was that of a 'Red menace', a dangerous country of Communist fanatics given to cruelty and deception.

These were serious matters for Beijing. Isolation from the West, and later from the Soviet Union, provided an unhappy context for domestic development. It played its part in the fanaticism and violence of the GREAT LEAP FORWARD and the CULTURAL REVOLUTION. An equally serious consequence was the re-engagement of the United States in the Chinese CIVIL WAR as a result of the conflict in Korea. Early in 1950, Washington had made it clear that both Taiwan and Korea were beyond the American defence perimeter. In the spring, Mao was preparing to 'liberate' Taiwan by force. However, Kim Il Sung's impetuosity put a stop to that. The United States extended its defence frontiers in East Asia to include Taiwan and contain Communist China.

Kuomintang (KMT or Nationalist Party)

One of the two political parties that have dominated Chinese politics since the early 1920s (the other is the CHINESE COMMUNIST PARTY), the Kuomintang was driven to TAIWAN in 1949 where it finally shed its authoritarian past, conducted reforms and retained power in a series of elections. As it did so, its leaders claimed to have fulfilled the goals of SUN YAT-SEN, the party founder, and to have charted a democratic path for the Communist-ruled Mainland. There was an element of hyperbole in this, but an element of reality, too. First under Sun and then under CHIANG KAI-SHEK, the Nationalist Party tried, and failed, to bring peace, unity and modernization to China. In Taiwan it survived at first through recourse to military rule and support from the UNITED STATES.

Yet as Taiwan's economy took off in the 1960s and 1970s, and political reforms followed during the 1980s, democracy took root. This enabled the Kuomintang, under the leadership of LEE TENG-HUI, to win the kind of legitimacy denied its great rival across the Straits. However, legitimacy of this kind can be lost as well as gained; and in the presidential elections of March 2000 CHEN SHUI-BIAN of the DEMOCRATIC PROGRESSIVE PARTY (DPP) triumphed over a Kuomintang riven by faction and deprived of popular support. The KMT thus became the first political party in China to *lose* as well as retain power through genuine elections. Its defeat points to a thorough shake-up in the party during the early years of the new century, and the restructuring of Taiwan's political landscape.

birth and reorganization, 1912–24

The Kuomintang was formed in 1912 by core members of Sun's UNITED LEAGUE to fight the first parliamentary elections following the collapse of the QING DYNASTY (see DEMOCRACY/ELECTIONS). Under the leadership of SONG JIAOREN it triumphed at the polls and sought to curb the powers of President YUAN SHIKAI, China's new strongman. This move cost Song his life and the party much of its influence: Yuan had Song assassinated, crushed his military supporters in a campaign known as the 'Second Revolution' of 1913, and banned the Kuomintang altogether. Sun Yat-sen kept the flame alive, both in exile and in south China, where he sought support from sympathetic WARLORDS at odds with Yuan and his successors in Beijing. But the Kuomintang could make little headway in the highly militarized politics of the early Republic. To unify the country it required an army of its own, an ideology to provide clear goals, and the funds, advice and organizational discipline necessary to achieve them. The newly established SOVIET UNION helped provide all these wants.

The First World War and the Bolshevik Revolution transformed the international order, and the MAY FOURTH MOVEMENT of political and cultural renewal begun in 1919, extended the effects into China. All of them helped revolutionize China's political environment, paving the way for the appearance of mass revolutionary parties. One of them was the tiny Communist Party. Another was the larger, more influential and, from 1924, *reorganized* KMT.

revolutionary nationalism, 1924–7

Moscow's role in the party's rebirth was immense. Lenin and, later, Stalin wanted to protect and extend their revolution at home. They sought to do so by aiding 'bourgeois' political parties in colonies and the undeveloped world the better to defeat capitalism – and its latest manifestation, imperialism – worldwide. Weak, but keen to overthrow the warlords, unify China, curb foreign privileges, and modernize the country, the Kuomintang seemed a good candidate for assistance. Advisers from the Communist International (Comintern), among them Mikhail Borodin, found Sun and his colleagues susceptible to their overtures.

Soviet aid poured in to Sun's foothold in the south. Leninist techniques of party discipline and organization were applied and a revolutionary army formed loyal to the party. On Comintern instructions, members of the Communist Party, MAO ZEDONG included, joined the KMT to spread the revolution among workers and peasants. Two years later the Nationalist Party's fortunes had been transformed – fuelled by the surge of popular nationalism associated with events such as the May 30 Incident of 1925, in which British police in SHANGHAI killed striking protestors, and the Hong Kong strike-boycott which nearly paralysed the colony (see HONG KONG). With its new policies of revolutionary nationalism it was now ready to transform China.

Or it would have been had Sun not died suddenly in June 1925. His demise created the first succession crisis in China's revolutionary politics and, like most of those that followed, resulted in a change of policy as well as leader. Chiang Kai-shek lacked the political stature of many of his rivals within the KMT but he could count on his command of the best sections of its new army. Within months of Sun's death he was firmly in charge of the National Revolutionary government in Guangzhou, and in July 1926 launched the NORTHERN EXPEDITION to reunify the country, end imperialism and make China rich, strong and revolutionary.

revolution and reaction under Chiang

Just *how* revolutionary China should be was a matter of dispute between Chiang, Left-wingers in the KMT, the Communists and, ultimately, Stalin and Trotsky in distant Moscow. As the revolutionary armies forged northward from Guangzhou, firebrand activists won over peasants and workers to the cause of revolution and organized anti-imperialist protests. The foreign community was outraged and alarmed. There was talk of raising expeditionary forces to enforce treaty rights. Indeed, as Kuomintang armies approached Shanghai and local Communists rose up to greet 'liberation', BRITAIN and the UNITED STATES dispatched thousands of extra troops to the city.

The rebels, and ultimately the foreigners, reckoned without Chiang's determination to keep the national revolution within moderate bounds, avoid foreign intervention, and consolidate his personal hold over the KMT. Chiang and his allies in the party wanted to transform China, to make it strong, modern and powerful. But they saw no necessity to do so through violent social revolution of the kind that would dispossess landlords, check the growth of capitalism in the cities, and place power in the hands of a Communist 'mob' in league with Moscow. The Soviet Union and the Chinese Communist Party might claim to be pursuing the moderate 'national' stage of the revolution in their alliance with the KMT. But it was far too radical for Chiang.

Arguments over tactics within the revolutionary camp had intensified the further its armies marched from Guangzhou. By April 1927, most of China south of the Yangtze was under Nationalist control, but the party itself was split between senior military commanders and Right-wingers under Chiang in Nanjing; Left-wingers under WANG JINGWEI in Wuhan; Communists in charge of the workers' movement in Shanghai; and various half-hearted warlord converts in between. In the course of 1927, with the ruthlessness, cunning and skill which characterized his career, Chiang imposed a degree of unity on these forces. He crushed the Communists, slaughtering hundreds of them, outwitted recalcitrant warlords, and put an end to the rival government in Wuhan – a process helped by the discovery that, on orders from Moscow, Communists in the city planned to turn on the KMT as soon as conditions were ripe. The alliance with the Soviet Union was at an end. The era of Chiang Kai-shek had begun.

Fortified by this house cleaning, and comforted by tactical alliances with remaining rivals, notably FENG YUXIANG, chief warlord of north China, Chiang's armies continued northwards and reached Beijing in 1928. At least on paper, the Kuomintang had unified China. Barely four years after its 'reorganization', the party of revolution had become the party of government.

KMT rule: the first decade, 1928–37

The party itself changed after 1928 as well as its purpose. Chiang, alarmed how ripe for revolution China had proved to be in the course of his passage to power, purged the Kuomintang of its messianic teachings as well as its Marxist messengers. Commitment to revolution moderated into commitment to reform. Before long the KMT degenerated into an authoritarian party of the status quo. 'Democratic centralism', the legacy of reorganization along Leninist lines, ensured that individual party members remained subordinate to the organization, and rival leaders subordinate to Chiang. Party cells and branches kept the army in check and snuffed out dissent in the cities and universities. Rural China was generally beyond the party's reach, as the Communist Party soon discovered to its great advantage.

Sun's 'three principles' became the official ideology of the new National government, based in Nanjing. But they were to be implemented through legislation and reform, not the violent upheaval seen during the first phase of the Northern Expedition. Sun's 'three-stage theory' of party rule – in which Kuomintang China would pass through a period of military rule and political tutelage before entering the era of genuine constitutional government – guided such long-term plans for China's political development as the KMT possessed. Military rule was said to have come to an end with the Northern Expedition and reunification. After 1928 it was up to the Kuomintang to tutor the Chinese people in the ways of democracy.

Chiang's struggle to survive meant he and his fellow leaders had little time for political education. Not that the reforms carried out during the 'Nanjing Decade', the 10 years leading up to the SINO-JAPANESE WAR, were insignificant: attempts were made to provide China with the infrastructure, industry and modern systems of civil service and education it so badly needed. Britain and the United States recognized the new government in 1928, and rewarded the abandonment of revolution

by granting China TARIFF AUTONOMY, a novelty for a country which had lost it as long ago as 1842 with the Treaty of Nanjing.

Yet if these developments gave Kuomintang China a new start it was at best a halting one. Peace and unity proved elusive – partly because of the nature of the KMT regime, partly because of Communist insurrection, partly because of Japanese aggression. Worldwide depression aggravated China's difficulties, which were those of a huge, traditional agrarian economy in need of fundamental reform. Only a resolute, popular and highly motivated government could begin to tackle such problems. The KMT regime was none of these things. Throughout its years in power on the Mainland, the hollowness of the reunification it achieved was exposed by continued battles between rival militarists in the regions, and constant infighting among political cliques. Both undermined attempts at modernization, sapped the war effort against Japan and made the Communist victory in 1949 easier than it might have been.

suppression and resistance

Chiang devoted his best efforts to eradicating Communism. Although Japan was consolidating its hold over the northeast, notably with the creation of its puppet state of MANCHUGUO, and in 1932 staged a devastating attack on Shanghai, his priority was unity first, resistance later. Between 1930 and 1934, Nationalist troops mounted five 'annihilation campaigns' against Mao Zedong's Communist republic in JIANGXI province, the last of them a huge operation carried out on the advice of German military instructors. In 1934 the Communists were at last forced out of south China on their LONG MARCH. But their survival meant the KMT's victory proved hollow.

It was not very popular, either. By the mid-1930s calls were growing across China for resistance to Japan. Government military campaigns against fellow Chinese were seen as dangerous digressions at a time of national crisis. Various warlords, much of their former power intact despite 'unification', played on these sentiments in order to upstage Chiang, weaken his hold over the party, and prove their own loyalty to Sun Yat-sen's ideals. So, for obvious reasons of survival, did the Communists. All these developments meant that the KMT, which had dallied with fascism by forming a praetorian guard known as 'Blue Shirts', and launched a 'New Life Movement' designed to reinforce traditional moral values rather than tackle current political and economic problems, was at odds with the popular mood.

Part of the problem stemmed from the fact that many of the leading members of the Kuomintang (excluding military figures such as Chiang) were unrepresentative of the country they sought to rule. They tended to be intellectuals, a number of them Western-educated. They were drawn disproportionately from coastal areas and richer provinces. Given their background it was only natural many of them should lose touch with the backward, essentially rural nature of much of China and many of its problems.

Yet undeterred by Japanese aggression and popular disquiet, Chiang continued to pursue the Communists who had stopped marching in 1935 and created a new base in SHAANXI, in the north (see YANAN). His attempt to deliver a knock-out blow against his foes was thwarted by the XIAN INCIDENT of 1936. Local militarists kidnapped him, demanded that he call off the anti-Communist campaign and recruit the rebels into a broad front against Japan. It was a tense moment, and one that stunned China. But Chiang survived. He returned to Nanjing, the head of a government suddenly injected with purpose and unity. The Kuomintang renewed its tactical alliance with the Communist Party against a common, national foe. These extraordinary events were not lost on the Japanese army. Its commanders launched an attack on China at the Marco Polo Bridge near Beijing in July 1937, marking the start of the SINO-JAPANESE WAR.

Kuomintang China at war, 1937–45

Although a grim saga of crushing military defeats, the first stage of the Sino-Japanese War produced plenty of Chinese grit. It also showed a new level of popular support for the beleaguered Kuomintang government. Faced with overwhelming Japanese power, Chiang retreated to the mountain fastness of CHONGQING, where his regime withstood fierce bombing, economic hardship arising from the closure of the Burma Road (see BURMA), and the defection of WANG JINGWEI, a leading figure in the party. Chiang's resistance earned him support in the West, particularly the United States. His Kuomintang was seen to be leading 'Free China' – a title the party aspired to again after 1949 when the Mainland fell to the Communists and Chiang's government fled to Taiwan.

Allied support for the KMT increased after December 1941 when the Japanese attack on Pearl Harbor made the Sino-Japanese conflict part of the much bigger Pacific War. The United States provided lend-lease aid, assigned General JOSEPH STILWELL, one of its brightest soldiers, to Chongqing and, to British scorn, talked of China as a 'great Power'. In 1943, SOONG MEI-LING, Chiang's wife and China's 'first lady', visited the United States, where she was received with great acclaim. The culmination of these developments was Britain and America's relinquishment of EXTRATERRITORIALITY in 1943; Chiang's presence at the CAIRO CONFERENCE, the wartime summit of November the same year; and China's founding membership of the UNITED NATIONS. Under the Kuomintang, China managed to secure a degree of international prestige it had not known for at least a century.

Yet it was hard to square this with the consequences of Nationalist rule in China itself. As the war against Japan dragged on, the government sank into a mire of CORRUPTION, demoralization and infighting spiced with covert trading with the enemy. It lost the ability and the will to mobilize the population and generate loyalty, let alone challenge the invaders on the battlefield. Instead, Chiang resumed his struggle against old domestic enemies the better to deal with them once and for all when the United States had defeated Japan. This meant keeping crack government troops tied up in a military blockade of the Communists in the north, and ensuring that funds and US-supplied equipment were kept from Kuomintang armies loyal to regional leaders rather than Chongqing. In the light of these events the Allies tended to discount China as a theatre in which to defeat Japan, preferring to 'island hop' over the Pacific to reach the Japanese homeland. The post-war prospects for peace in China looked grim.

defeat and flight to Taiwan, 1945–50

So they proved. The glow of being on the winning side in the war boosted the Nationalists' prestige, and the US rapidly extended the government's physical reach by airlifting thousands of Kuomintang troops to key areas so that they could accept the surrender from the Japanese. This appeared to be the makings of a new start for Chiang and his regime.

But the Communists were on the move, too. This was particularly true in Manchuria (northeast China) where, under the terms of the YALTA CONFERENCE, Soviet troops had in 1945 launched a brief invasion of Japanese-occupied territory. On their retreat in 1946 they let power and weapons fall into Chinese Communist hands rather than wait for the Nationalists to arrive. The Chinese Communists consolidated their grip on this strategic heartland with land reform in the countryside, and experiments in large-scale urban administration in Harbin and other cities in HEILONGJIANG.

Further south, inflation and mismanagement rather than Communism impeded the Kuomintang's smooth recovery of territory lost in earlier stages of the war. Official corruption was particularly serious – especially that of the so-called 'four big families' of the Kuomintang: Song Tzu-wen (T. V. Soong, 1894–1971), Kung Hsiang-hsi (H. H. Kung, 1880–1967), Chen Kuo-fu (1892–1951) and Chen Li-fu (1900–). After the exhaustion of an 8-year war with Japan, such incompetence, coupled with the continued infighting characteristic of the Kuomintang, hardly seemed an acceptable price to pay for peace.

It was not paid for very long. Despite the popular demand for peace, the Kuomintang and the Communist Party refused to abandon their struggle for supremacy. Rivalry and distrust scuppered every attempt to broker a truce between them, including that mounted in 1946 by the US General George C. Marshall. Efforts to form a coalition government ran aground on the Communists' refusal to relinquish control of their armies, and Chiang's determination to ensure Nationalist – and particularly his *own* – dominance in any new government. Full-scale CIVIL WAR resumed in 1946. One of its first results was a spectacular defeat for Chiang who, against advice from some fellow leaders, and the United States, insisted on trying to take the three northeastern provinces of Manchuria from the Communists.

It was a reverse from which the Kuomintang never recovered. Yet the party's defeat in the Civil War was more than a military one. It was also a function of popular demoralization; of uncontrolled inflation; of bitter struggles between Chiang and his rivals, notably LI ZONGREN, the GUANGXI leader; and of the party's seeming lack of purpose. In the late 1940s, all the Kuomintang seemed to offer the Chinese people was the fact that it was not the Communist Party. In town and countryside, many began to wonder whether this was any kind of advantage at all.

Nevertheless, despite its floundering fortunes on the battlefield, the party pursued, somewhat half-heartedly, the goal of constitutional rule. A Constituent National Assembly was convened in November 1946 which adopted a new constitution. It came into effect in 1947. The same year elections were held for a new National Assembly whose members in 1948 elected Chiang as president and LI ZONGREN vice-president of the Republic.

Complex rivalries and machinations accompanied these experiments in limited democracy. They were swept into oblivion by the Nationalists' military collapse in the months which followed, and the flight in 1949 of the central government and its remaining troops – accompanied by many of China's art treasures and most of its gold – to Taiwan. A Kuomintang splinter group, the 'Revolutionary Committee of the Kuomintang', formed in Hong Kong by anti-Chiang activists, remained behind on the Mainland (see DEMOCRATIC PARTIES). By the end of 1949, the Communists controlled virtually the whole of Mainland China. The PEOPLE'S LIBERATION ARMY prepared to 'liberate' China's islands, Taiwan chief among them.

Taiwan years, repression and growth

In early 1950 there was little reason to imagine that a Communist conquest would take very long. True, Taiwan had the natural advantages of being an island. But so did HAINAN, which the People's Liberation Army occupied in just a few days in January 1950. Kuomintang rule in Taiwan was scarcely four years old in 1949. It had been imposed in 1945 after 50 years of Japanese colonialism. One of the chief consequences was the FEBRUARY 28TH INCIDENT of 1947, an island-wide protest against the new administration which ended in bloodshed. The United States, tired of involvement in China's Civil War, had all but washed its hands of Chiang and his Nationalist government. Washington hoped Taiwan would not fall to the Communists. But it was not prepared to do much to stop it. The last act of the Civil War seemed about to begin. Oblivion stalked the Kuomintang.

It was soon banished and five decades passed before it haunted the party again. The KOREAN WAR prevented the conquest of Taiwan by drawing the United States into the fight against Communist expansion in East Asia, a cause to which Washington remained committed for most of the following 30 years.

This gave Chiang a security guarantee, enabling his government to consolidate its rule in Taiwan, build up the island's defences and develop the economy. Within the relatively confined spaces of China's island province, the Kuomintang scored more successes in a few years than it had during the two decades it ruled the Mainland.

Few of these successes were distinctly political, other than in the sense that the party's authoritarian rule provided a degree of stability that may have facilitated economic development (see TAIWAN/ECONOMY). Chiang continued to dominate the Kuomintang, and the Kuomintang continued to dominate the by now much smaller state apparatus. Martial law, implemented before the central government's flight to Taiwan, remained in force, along with the suspension of constitutional freedoms that accompanied it. The party's Leninist structure, its organization of tightly controlled cells, enabled it to penetrate every level of society. A militant anti-Communism and a determination to nip all forms of opposition in the bud kept most of the population in check. The KMT's claim to rule and represent *all* of China, and its pledge to recover the Mainland by military force, were used to justify the dominance of Mainlanders and exclusion of Taiwanese at top levels of the administration. In its control over society, as in its intolerance of dissent, Kuomintang rule in Taiwan after 1949 at first resembled that of the Communists on the Mainland.

Yet it differed, too. In Taiwan, the KMT soon shed the anti-capitalist leanings it had displayed in the past. Private property was preserved and private business encouraged. Manufacturing expanded; exports surged. There were as yet few indications of the island's future economic power, but by the mid-1960s, Taiwan's economy had taken off. On the political front, elections, though sometimes subject to fraud and mostly confined to local government, were held regularly. The Kuomintang's official commitment to democracy – the second of Sun's 'three principles' – promised more polls in the future. Its ideological, diplomatic and strategic attachment to the Western world seemed to do the same.

At the same time the harshness of Kuomintang rule was tempered by a concern to develop and enhance traditional Chinese culture and values. This tended to be rather overpowering for local Taiwanese, whose traditions, often very different from those of the Mainland, were neglected and often suppressed. But the KMT had neither the power nor the inclination to engage in social upheavals and iconoclasm of the kind unleashed by the Communists across the Straits during the late 1950s and 1960s. If anything the party tried to make Taiwan and the Taiwanese more Chinese, not less.

Dramatic changes confronted the KMT during the 1970s. In 1975 the death of Chiang Kai-shek marked a real and symbolic break with the past. The United States' opening to Beijing, followed by that of other Western powers, left Taipei in the diplomatic lurch. Meanwhile, rapid economic growth had created an educated, affluent population increasingly unwilling to accept political controls. It was apparent in many parts of the world that old forms of authoritarianism had clearly had their day. They certainly had in Taiwan, where Kuomintang rule was grounded in the constitutional conceits of a bygone age and kept alive only by the politically dominant but rapidly ageing Mainlanders.

KMT and China's first democracy

The process of demolishing these obstacles to change was begun in the late 1980s by CHIANG CHING-KUO, son of Chiang Kai-shek, who in 1986 lifted martial law, tolerated the formation of opposition parties and removed controls on the media. The process was continued by Lee Teng-hui, his successor. Three processes were at work during the rule of the two men: 'Taiwanization'; democratization; and a cautious opening to the Mainland. They were often indistinguishable. Sometimes they were identical.

Lee's ascendancy was an example of all three. A Taiwanese with little emotional attachment to the Mainland, his succession to the party chairmanship and state presidency in 1988 made him a representative leader in ways his predecessors were not. In the same year, Taiwanese for the first time occupied a majority of seats in the Kuomintang's ruling Central Executive Committee. They soon dominated proceedings there, forming the so-called 'Mainstream Faction' which forced its rival 'non-Mainstream' faction, composed of those born on the Mainland and fiercely opposed to Taiwanese independence, into the wilderness. The process was completed in 1993, when some of Lee's opponents left the KMT to form the New Party, a vehicle for forging closer ties with the Mainland, though not at the expense of Taiwan's democracy.

This struggle within the Kuomintang coincided with, and was often caused by, the wider issue of political reform on the island. Democratization was the goal here, but it often amounted to 'Taiwanization', too. When the KMT lifted martial law and a long-standing ban on the formation of political parties, a principal beneficiary was the Democratic Progressive Party, founded to campaign for Taiwanese independence. In a series of constitutional changes during the early 1990s, the Kuomintang formally abandoned its quest to recover the Mainland; opened up all seats in the Legislative Yuan and National Assembly to elections in Taiwan (rather than reserving many for now mythical former Mainland constituencies – see TAIWAN/GOVERNANCE); redefined the area under its control as 'The Republic of China on Taiwan'; and allowed people to elect their president in direct elections. The first such polls took place in 1996. They resulted in a substantial victory for Lee.

After years of forcing Taiwan into a Mainland mould, Kuomintang policy was now, at least unofficially, one of 'Taiwan for the Taiwanese'. Reunification with the Mainland was still part of party agenda, but only as a distant, almost remote goal to be accomplished when the Communist Party gave up its monopoly of power. And if there was no question of the KMT pursuing formal independence for Taiwan, there was a strong desire to preserve its political separation from the Mainland – despite growing trade and financial ties, most of them indirect and conducted through Hong Kong. In policy terms this brought the Kuomintang much closer to the Democratic Progressive Party at the end of the century than had seemed possible a decade earlier.

Beijing viewed all these developments with alarm. Each made the prospects of cooperation between the Communist and Nationalist parties on the issue of reunification more difficult, despite high-level unofficial talks between representatives of the two sides in 1993 and, after a hiatus, in 1998. From the Communist's point of view, if Lee was not pursuing Taiwanese independence, he was creating 'One China, One Taiwan', a deviation they detested equally strongly, and one which they warned would have to be settled by force should it continue unchecked. The war games and missile tests that the People's Liberation Army staged close to Taiwan at the time of the 1996 elections were a

sign of Beijing's determination to curb independence sentiment, overt or covert. The strong, though largely verbal, reaction of Communist leaders to Lee's assertion in 1999 that contacts across the Straits should be conducted on the basis that they were special relations between 'two states' was a further sign of its concern.

None of these at times unnerving events slowed the Kuomintang's general disengagement from a society it had once controlled, and its transformation into just one – if still the main one – of several political parties competing for power in Taiwan during the 1990s. Not that this withdrawal was complete: the party retained control over a large business empire, including a newspaper and several television stations. And despite rapid democratization, it was dogged by allegations of corruption, vote-buying and links with organized crime during almost every poll.

Yet at the close of the twentieth century it was clear that the Kuomintang had presided over a fundamental change in Taiwanese politics with important implications for the Mainland. It had made the transition from dictatorship to democracy *and* – at least for a while – remained in power. This amounted to an admission that Taiwan was bigger than the KMT. The island was the home of what Lee in 1998 called 'New Taiwanese': those who belonged to the island, and who benefited from its prosperity and freedoms irrespective of their ancestral origins, and regardless of which political party they supported.

The implication of Lee's remarks – that Taiwan might at some point be ruled by a party other than the Kuomintang – was not immediately apparent. In March 2000 it suddenly became so. In the presidential elections of that year the KMT's support collapsed, enabling Chen Shui-bian of the Democratic Progressive Party to secure a narrow victory over Soong Chu-yu (James Soong, 1942–), a former Kuomintang stalwart whose decision to run as an independent was grounded in a feud with Lee Teng-hui over who in the KMT should be chosen to campaign for the presidency. On polling day, Chen won 39 per cent of the popular vote against Soong's 36 per cent. Lien Chan (1936–), the official Kuomintang candidate, secured just 23 per cent of votes cast.

This was an astonishing result for a host of reasons. Among them was the Taiwan people's defiance of Beijing whose leaders sustained a daily barrage of abuse and threats of military invasion in the run-up to the polls

Party Structure and Leadership

At the start of the twenty-first century the KMT has shed much of the Leninist organizational structure it acquired in 1923–4, but not all: it remains a centralized, disciplined organization whose 2.1 million members are grouped into cells, committees and congresses on an ascending scale from the district level. The apex of power in the party is the Central Committee. However, key decisions are taken by the 33 members of the Central Standing Committee, who meet once a week when the full committee is not in session. Members of the Central Committee are elected by the party's National Congress, which met every 4 years until 1993 when it was decided it would do so every two years. The National Congress determines party policy and elects the party chairman. The Kuomintang has had just 4 major leaders in its nearly 90-year-history: Sun Yat-sen, Chiang Kai-shek, Chiang Ching-kuo and Lee Teng-hui. The first three died in office. The fourth, Lee, was forced out of it following the party's humiliating defeat in the presidential elections of 2000. He was succeeded by Lien Chan, the defeated presidential candidate.

in an effort to weaken support for Chen, the independence candidate. Such tactics failed even more miserably than those adopted in 1996. They left Beijing facing a new leader in Taipei less committed to reunification than his predecessor.

The Kuomintang's humiliation was as obvious as that of the Chinese Communist Party, even though the election did not challenge the party's narrow majority in the Legislative Yuan and National Assembly (see TAIWAN/GOVERNANCE). During its 55-year-rule, the KMT brought economic prosperity to Taiwan, followed by political reforms that helped erase painful memories of an authoritarian past, facilitated trade and cultural exchanges with the Mainland, and turned the island into the first genuine Chinese democracy. Its reward in March 2000 was massive rejection at the polls and the retirement of Lee Teng-hui as Kuomintang chairman amid violent protests by disgruntled party members. Critics claimed the KMT had lost the Mainland in 1949 and Taiwan in 2000. Oblivion seemed to stalk Sun Yat-sen's party again.

Five days after the election, Lien Chan succeeded Lee as 'acting' KMT chairman with a mission to rescue the party. He announced an investigation into the cause of its defeat and promised far-reaching reforms to ensure it would never happen again. His task was handicapped by James Soong's announcement that he would form a new party – the *Ch'inmintang* or 'People First Party' – which he hoped would attract disillusioned KMT members. A fierce struggle for control over the Kuomintang's formidable assets seemed inevitable.

Disillusionment with the Kuomintang was widespread. During the election campaign the party had been unable to shed a reputation for corruption and money politics that, in the heat of the moment, mattered more to voters than the party's longstanding political accomplishments. Meanwhile, the split in the party, symbolized by James Soong's decision to stand as an independent, fatally divided the pro-KMT vote and allowed Chen Shui-bian, who subdued the pro-independence rhetoric of his own party, to capture the presidency. The fact that more than 75 per cent of the electorate voted against the official Kuomintang candidate was a clear sign that the people of Taiwan wanted change. And the fact that 83 per cent of eligible voters went to the polls showed they were determined to secure it.

The Kuomintang therefore begins the new century where its distant ancestor, Sun Yat-sen's 'Revive China Society', began the last: out of power and in disarray. Accustomed to the role of a ruling party, and to imposing its views, values and visions (to say nothing of the historical 'baggage' it has acquired during a long history on the Mainland as well as Taiwan) on those under its sway, it must take on the novel role of opposition. This calls for profound psychological as well as political changes within a party that, as recently as the later 1990s, exercised a seemingly unbreakable grip on Taiwan's political life

Yet if the Kuomintang is unlikely again to exercise the kind of authority it once enjoyed over all or part of China, reports of its demise seem premature. The work of repair and reform began well before Lee Teng-hui vacated the presidency in favour of Chen Shui-bian in May 2000. And even if the party's decline should indeed prove terminal, then at least its fall has not resulted in the collapse of Taiwan's political system, or the end of the newly acquired freedoms its people exercised so tellingly in March 2000. In the context of China's political culture and history, this, too, is a remarkable turn of events. The Kuomintang lost the election in 2000, but democracy, *Chinese* democracy, won.

L

labour camps

Rapid economic growth transformed the face of China in the 1990s, engulfing major cities in shiny office towers, development zones, expressways and shopping malls. It had less effect on the country's Communist political system and hardly any at all on its hand-maiden: a nationwide network of labour camps. China's 'gulag' – a system of forced labour designed to 'remould' inmates and turn a profit for the state – remains in place. The number of inmates is a state secret, but the system's existence is as powerful an indict-ment of China's HUMAN RIGHTS record as recent economic growth is an accolade.

Since the CHINESE COMMUNIST PARTY came to power, millions of people have endured the harsh regimes of prison farms, factories and other penal institutions scattered across the country. HARRY WU, a former inmate and later chief chronicler of China's labour camps, identified more than 990 labour camps in the 1990s with a high concentration in vast, remote areas of QINGHAI and XINJIANG. In the first 30 years of Communist rule, most inmates were real or imaginary political opponents of the regime. They included landlords, former members of the KUOMINTANG, 'counter-revolutionaries', 'Rightists' (see ONE HUNDRED FLOWERS MOVEMENT), and those generally not considered enthusiastic enough in their sup-port for the repeated political campaigns unleashed by MAO ZEDONG. Common crimi-nals mingled with these 'class enemies'.

The composition of inmates changed with the relaxation of political life following Mao's death. Thousands of 'Rightists' and other vic-tims of Mao's injustice were rehabilitated. A new generation of political prisoners soon took their place. They included WEI JING-SHENG and other leaders of the DEMOCRACY WALL MOVEMENT of 1979, and many of those arrested for their part in the 1989 TIANANMEN SQUARE DEMOCRACY MOVEMENT. Lesser-known DISSIDENTS were sent to labour camps in the late 1990s, though by that time ordinary criminals accounted for an estimated 90 per cent of their inhabitants. The camps were home for about 85 per cent of China's con-victed criminals. The remainder, mostly those found guilty of serious crimes, were sent to more conventional prisons.

Since the mid-1950s, those confined to the gulag have been subjected to 'reform through labour', 'education through labour' or 'forced job assignments'. Only the first category involves conviction through a formal judicial process. The second is an 'administrative pun-ishment' meted out by the police, initially for a maximum of three years and often to dissidents. The last, 'forced job assignments', which are determined by camp authorities in conjunction with the police, ensures that some inmates are *never* released: they are com-pelled to work in the camp even when they have completed their sentence.

The purpose of the camps is to remove government opponents and general miscre-ants from society and subject them to the transforming power of labour and ideological remoulding. The idea that 'bad' people can be 'saved' in this way is closely associated with Mao Zedong. It remains a cardinal belief of the Chairman's successors, though not to the exclusion of the view that widespread use of the death penalty is necessary to curb crime. Inmates of labour camps are subjected to military-style discipline and encouraged to remould their outlook by means of confession, self-criticism, political study and mutual supervision. Work is harsh and poorly rewarded. Mistreatment of prisoners is common. Torture and deaths are not unknown.

The economic role of the gulag is as important as the social and political. Labour camps are rarely identified as such in public. They operate under commercial names and engage in a wide range of business activities. Together they generate substantial tax revenues and profits for the government, though their exact contribution to the economy as a percentage of GDP is never revealed. In the mid-1990s, the discovery that goods made in labour camps were being exported – in violation of international trade laws – caused controversy in the United States. China denied charges that it was using prison labour to make its exports more competitive, but the complicated and secret nature of the gulag system made it hard for outsiders to be sure.

land reform

Overpopulation, underdevelopment, a shortage of fertile land and an abundance of natural disasters made life precarious for most people in China at the best of times. A grossly unequal system of land ownership, high rents and taxes made matters worse, ensuring that rebels nearly always demanded a change in property relations, that is, land reform, when they raised revolt (see AGRICULTURE). Only the CHINESE COMMUNIST PARTY accomplished this on any scale, with profound consequences.

SUN YAT-SEN, China's first 'modern' revolutionary, sought the equalization of land rights as part of his programme for change. 'Land to the tiller', was a key aim of the UNITED LEAGUE he helped form in 1905. However, the policy was not implemented on any scale until the mid-1920s, when the great tide of radicalism and nationalism launched by the NORTHERN EXPEDITION carried the KUOMINTANG to victory over its warlord foes. As part of the alliance between the Kuomintang and the Communist Party, activists organized revolts in the countryside along the path of the advancing National Revolutionary Army. Peasant associations were formed and protests launched to demand reductions in rent and tax. In many areas, land was taken from landlords and redistributed to the peasants – much to the concern of CHIANG KAI-SHEK and other Nationalist leaders who wanted China unified and modernized but not necessarily plunged into social revolution.

The Communists, of course, wanted just that. In his investigation of the peasant movement in Hunan of 1927, MAO ZEDONG identified the peasantry as the genuinely revolutionary class in China on whose backs the Party would ride to power. At Jinggangshan, the first of his rural bases in JIANGXI, and later at Ruijin, capital of the Central Soviet Republic, Mao and his comrades experimented with land reform. Landlords were stripped of their possessions and often killed. Rich peasants sometimes suffered the same fate – until the Party found mistreating them cost it support. At YANAN, north China, capital of the Party's main base during the SINO-JAPANESE WAR, land policy took a more moderate turn: the Communists were keen to form a United Front with those they otherwise regarded as 'class enemies' in the interests of defeating Japan. But the goal of rural revolution was postponed not abandoned; and land reform was conducted with considerable brutality during the CIVIL WAR as a means of destroying the social base of Nationalist rule and winning support from the peasantry.

Once their armies had triumphed in 1949, the Communists moved to carry out land reform in the newly 'liberated' areas. Since these amounted to about two-thirds of China's farmland, it was an enormous task. The agrarian reform law of June 1950 provided some guidance, but things acquired a momentum of their own. Once regular Communist forces had penetrated the countryside, work teams followed to organize peasant associations, and institute rent and tax reductions. Struggles were waged against 'local despots' and 'bullies'.

Progress was uneven until the KOREAN WAR. The conflict heightened tension at home and made those reluctant to engage in land reform appear potential enemies of the new regime. Class labels were affixed to the rural population and peasants encouraged to hold 'speak bitterness' meetings recalling past oppression. Landlords were humiliated at public trials and executed in the hundreds of thousands. At

China's Paramount Leaders in the Twentieth Century

1 The Empress Dowager (Ci Xi). Her belated sponsorship of reforms in the early years of the century helped sweep the Manchu Qing Dynasty into oblivion.

2 Yuan Shi-kai, military strongman of north China, was the dominant figure in the early Republic but failed to unite or modernize his country.

3 Sun Yat-sen. Most Chinese regard the quixotic, romantic revolutionary as the 'father of modern China' but his legacy remains in dispute.

4 Chiang Kai-shek, China's wartime leader. Communist rebellion, Japanese invasion and the desire to retain power sapped his reform drive and forced him to flee to Taiwan.

5 Mao Zedong, founder of the People's Republic, transformed the lives of millions, many of whom, unlike the Chairman's official reputation, are still suffering.

6 Deng Xiaoping set China on the road to power and prosperity, but at Tiananmen Square in 1989 crushed the largest anti-government demonstrations of the century.

China's Leaders at the Start
of the New Century

7 (*left*) Jiang Zemin, a man of modest attainments but much staying power, is expected to remain leader of the Communist Party, state president and commander in chief until at least 2002.

8 (*right*) Chen Shui-bian, whose victory in Taiwan's presidential elections in 2000 marked the first change of government by electoral means in Chinese history, and whose past support for Taiwanese independence alarms Beijing.

9 (*left*) Beijing chose Tung Chee-hwa, a local shipping magnate, as Hong Kong's first chief executive, or post-1997 'governor'.

10 (*right*) Edmund Ho Hau-wah, the Western-educated banker whom Beijing appointed chief executive of Macau, which was restored to Chinese rule in 1999.

11 China's seven most powerful men at the start of the century. The Politburo Standing Committee, *from left to right, and in order of rank*: Jiang Zemin, Li Peng, Zhu Rongji, Li Ruihuan, Hu Jintao, Wei Jianxing, Li Lanqing.

12 Rebellion and retribution. The suppression of the Boxer Rebellion in 1900 and the public execution of its leaders, demanded by the Western powers, humiliated Qing China.

13 Hunting down revolutionaries. An armed picket searches a man for revolutionary literature in March 1927 as conservatives and radicals struggle to gain control of Shanghai.

14 Japanese soldiers on the march in Hangzhou, capital of Zhejiang province, in December 1937, six months after the start of the Sino-Japanese War.

15 Mao in full flow. The Chairman addresses Party members in May 1938 at Yanan, his war-time head-quarters.

16 And again, this time on the rostrum of Tiananmen Square, Beijing, in October 1949, declaring the foundation of the People's Republic of China.

17 A Production Brigade, or militarized labour team, marches to work in an agricultural com-mune near Shanghai. Communes were founded in 1958 as part of Mao's ill-fated Great Leap Forward.

18 (*above*) An image of the Cultural Revolution (1966–76). The adoring masses hail Chairman Mao in a poster exhorting the Chinese people to 'Carry out the Great Proletarian Cultural Revolution to the Bitter End'

19 The reality of the Cultural Revolution: 'class enemies', defined and humiliated by dunce's caps, are paraded before the masses

20 In 1978–79 ordinary citizens placed posters demanding more democracy on walls in several cities, most prominently Beijing. Alarmed, the authorities closed the capital's Democracy Wall and arrested key supporters, notably Wei Jingsheng.

21 Religious life in Tibet revived during the 1980s. So did the determination of many Tibetans to end Chinese rule in their homeland, as the unrest of 1987 demonstrated.

22 Pro-democracy supporters fill Tiananmen Square, the symbolic heart of China, with demands for change in 1989 before troops crushed the movement with heavy loss of life.

23 A full square again – this time with hand-picked, regimented citizens marshalled in October 1999 to celebrate fifty years of Communist rule.

24 Despite two decades of rapid economic change, China remains primarily an agricultural country in which farming is conducted along traditional lines. A water buffalo ploughs a paddy field in Hainan while a farmer prepares to plant rice seedlings in the fertile soil.

25 China is the world's largest potential car market, and before long perhaps its largest car manufacturer. Shanghai Volkswagen is one of the country's pioneering modern car plants.

26 (*above*) Solemnity, scale and sterility: the National People's Congress in session in Beijing's Great Hall of the People. The set pieces of Chinese Communist political theatre have changed little despite upheavals in every other area of life.

27 The view cast along Nanjing Road, Shanghai's busiest shopping street, is crowned by the television tower in Pudong, the city's new financial centre.

28 History hovers over China however much it changes. A young couple out shopping in Beijing in 1997 pass an advert for an epic film on the war that resulted in Britain's occupation of Hong Kong, and which was made to celebrate its return 150 years later.

least 2 million were killed in the space of a few months. Those spared were allocated small portions of land, usually of poor quality, which they had to work themselves. The land-lord-gentry – sustainers of a rural tradition dating back to ancient times – were wiped out. So, almost, was the influence of other established sources of authority in the countryside: CLANS and SECRET SOCIETIES.

Between 1949 and 1952 about 50 per cent of all the arable land in China was redistributed. It was divided into tiny plots and worked by owner-occupiers, who now included WOMEN, previously denied such rights. The new rural order in China was composed of Party cadres and 'middle' peasants – the social group which tended to fare best during one of the most fundamental upheavals in China's social history.

During the early 1950s moves towards collective farming were made in some parts of the country even before land reform had been undertaken in others. The Party had not broken the power of landlords merely to create a new class of owners in the countryside, even if their holdings were tiny and generally equal in size or yield. The longer-term aim was to boost rural productivity and provide a surplus for industrialization – and to do so in a politically acceptable way, that is, through the establishment of rural collectives. Mutual Aid Teams, in which farmers pooled labour and tools, were set up first, followed by agricultural producers' cooperatives (APCs) and 'higher' (that is, larger) APCs. By 1956 Chinese agriculture had been collectivized nationwide. Apart from subsidiary private plots, private farming was a thing of the past. Land belonged to the state.

There was some resistance to collectivization, but far less than when similar steps were taken in the Soviet Union in the 1930s. There was none of the famine, and little of the physical cruelties which accompanied the Soviet experience, either. But neither was there much in the way of the expected boost in agricultural output. Partly for this reason, Mao grew anxious about the prospects for China's rapid industrialization. In 1958 he devised a new strategy – the GREAT LEAP FORWARD – to realize it.

The Leap brought two phenomena to the countryside: people's communes, in which collectives were merged and life in them subjected to almost military-style discipline; and mass famine, the consequence of ludicrous industrial policies and neglect of simple farming. In the end, the costs of politicizing the means of subsistence in China proved even greater than in Soviet Russia. By the early 1960s, with the country in ruin, the communes were scaled back in size and purpose. However, they continued to exist as administrative entities for 20 years, keeping agricultural growth in check throughout this period by stifling incentives.

The 'household responsibility system' – another form of land reform or reorganization, and the one still in force throughout much of China at the start of the new century – was introduced in 1978 to tap the enthusiasm of farmers for improving their lot and boosting production. It reduced the basic unit of production to that of the family, and let farmers retain for private sale what they grew in excess of that contracted to the state. Output soared, soon bringing problems of its own. Market forces returned to the countryside on a grand scale. So did private farming in most things but name, since families contracted to work the land for 15 years at first and then for a further 30. Land still belongs to the state in China: in legal terms there has been no return to the pre-cooperative situation of the mid-1950s, let alone conditions before 1949. But the right to use land is a commodity bought and sold across the country, and the dividing line between use and ownership is wearing thin.

law

Nearly a century after the ailing QING DYNASTY introduced a modern legal system, the rule of law has yet to be firmly established in Mainland China. Neither Republican nor KUOMINTANG governments were bound by law, and at the start of the new century it is the CHINESE COMMUNIST PARTY, not the legislature or the courts, which decides most important issues. Beijing's poor HUMAN RIGHTS record, its mistreatment of DISSIDENTS and its failure to develop DEMOCRACY all reflect the lack of an independent judiciary – the cornerstone of the rule of law – to enforce individual freedoms. A flurry of law-making at the close of the century has enhanced popular consciousness of law and strengthened the legal profession. It has not established the *primacy* of law in the People's Republic.

customs, codes and legal reform

China's failure to create an independent legal system owes much to tradition. In imperial times, the state used law to control society; individuals or society rarely used law to control the state. The purpose of law was to regulate rather than offer recourse. It was designed to maintain the supremacy of ruler over people. Punitive in nature, laws prescribed stiff penalties, including torture. Whenever possible people preferred to settle disputes without recourse to law. Custom and personal relationships mattered more than legal codes; leaders more than laws.

This was at odds with the legal theories of the West that China encountered in the nineteenth century. Precisely because of the inadequacies of China's legal system the powers insisted on EXTRATERRITORIALITY in China. And precisely because of the UNEQUAL TREATIES, which established this legal apartheid, and the TREATY PORTS, where it was practised most visibly, Chinese Nationalists pursued legal reform as a means of making their country modern and free. There was little progress until the final years of the Qing Dynasty when modern Western legal theories at last made some headway, often via Japan. In its dying days, the dynasty carried out sweeping political, administrative and legal reforms. A ministry of law was created along with an independent judiciary, new legal codes, and a modern court system.

Most of these measures survived the REPUBLICAN REVOLUTION of 1911. Leaders of the new Republic insisted that the judiciary remain independent of the executive and the legislature, and prohibited judges from joining political parties. The behaviour of Republican governments often belied this official fondness for legality but failed to erase it as an ideal. Much the same was true of the Kuomintang's years in power between 1927 and 1949: legal process hardly restrained Chiang Kai-shek's regime, but Nationalist officials stressed the importance of law and the need for legal reforms. Effective governance was one of the goals; an end to extraterritoriality, achieved in 1943, was another.

Yet the Nationalist government's attitude towards law was ambiguous. The provisional constitution provided for the separation of powers and called for the protection of individual rights. The Kuomintang, on the other hand, sought the politicization of the judiciary. It required judges and lawyers to be members of the Kuomintang and further the party's 'revolutionary' goals. The ambiguity arose from the context. Given China's weakness and division, many reformers favoured a legal system which facilitated the work of revolutionary government rather than checked it in the name of individual rights. China needed a strong executive, not one likely to be paralysed by conflict with the legislature or judiciary. In the context of national revolution there seemed little need to worry about friction between the interests of the state and the citizen.

in pursuit of 'socialist legality'

This view, solidified by Marxist dogma and strengthened by revolutionary mission, became orthodoxy when the Communist Party seized power in 1949. The language of law under the new regime was modern but its purpose owed something to the past. Law was an instrument of social control, a tool to be used against 'class enemies'. China was a 'people's state': the 'people' enjoyed democracy while their 'enemies' were subjected to dictatorship. Since the interests of the state and the people were deemed to be the same, there was no question of a fundamentally adversarial relationship between them, either in the courtroom or elsewhere. That kind of thing was reserved for disputes between the people and their enemies.

The dangers of this theory were exposed during the political campaigns of the 1950s. In the 'Anti-Rightist Movement' (see ONE HUNDRED FLOWERS MOVEMENT), even the semblance of legality was swept aside as Mao Zedong demanded the dismissal, disgrace and dispatch to LABOUR CAMPS of thousands of intellectuals considered politically unreliable. The legal profession also was swept into oblivion. It remained there during the CULTURAL REVOLUTION when the law was dismissed as 'bourgeois'. The 'will' of the Party, in the person of Chairman Mao, was supreme, even though it drove the country into chaos.

A determination to prevent such things happening again was behind demands for a new legal system after Mao's death. It was high on the agenda of the DEMOCRACY WALL MOVEMENT of 1978–9, several of whose leaders combined it with a call for an end to one-party rule. Deng Xiaoping and his fellow reformers were not prepared to go that far. But they, too, wanted legal reform. More and better laws would introduce an element of certainty, stability and predictability into national life. They would facilitate the move from a planned to a market economy. And they would help secure – and *control* – the foreign capital, technology and expertise China needed so badly.

These demands generated a stream of new legislation which began in 1979 with a revised Criminal Law and the People's Republic's first law on Sino-foreign joint ventures. After years of neglect the NATIONAL PEOPLE'S CONGRESS (NPC), the legislature, stirred into action. Under PENG ZHEN, Wan Li (1916–) and QIAO SHI, NPC chairmen in the 1980s and 1990s, it acquired a new importance, even if sometimes as a means of combating opponents in the Party rather than advancing the reformist agenda. 'Socialist legality' was the new orthodoxy; the NPC passed hundreds of laws governing almost every area of life. The number of lawyers grew, too, though at 150,000 by the turn of the century, it remained woefully inadequate. Nevertheless litigation was as common as legislation. The volume and variety of both speak of the growing complexity of China's society and economy, its closer contact with the outside world, and the increasing importance attached to the rule of law.

limits of law

Yet China's leaders, for all their emphasis on the rule of law, have never envisaged a legal system capable of challenging the Party's dominance of political life. Apart from anything else, the preamble to the Constitution precludes this. It mandates Party leadership, a socialist economy and Marxism-Leninism-Mao Zedong Thought as state ideology. This suggests there can be no significant change to China's legal system without prior political change. Until that happens, the Party's concern is to establish rule *by* law rather than the rule *of* law. In this scheme of things, laws are mainly rules for administration. They ensure bureaucratic regularity and an orderly state. They curb arbitrary behaviour by the authorities. They cannot be used to challenge Party rule, query socialism or undermine MARXISM.

Once this is understood, problems in the administration of justice in China become more intelligible, if no less reprehensible. The most serious of them arises from the fact that the Party is above the law. While the Constitution, amended in 1999 to emphasize the importance of the rule of law, suggests this is not the case, ordinary courts have no jurisdiction over the acts or the policies of the Communist Party. It is rare for senior Party figures to be charged with criminal offences. They are subjected to 'Party discipline' first and, if necessary, legal sanction later. Before that can happen, those accused are stripped of their Party membership, as was the case with CHEN XITONG, the former Party boss of Beijing convicted for corruption in 1998.

The PEOPLE'S LIBERATION ARMY is similarly beyond legal reach. Ordinary courts cannot enforce judgments against it or its commercial operations. The military is largely exempt from the jurisdiction of courts in HONG KONG, where the British-style system of justice survived the end of colonial rule, and MACAU, whose Portuguese-derived legal system remains largely intact after the transition in 1999. At every level, China's military is subordinate to the Communist Party, not the state or the courts.

This illustrates the weakness of law in the People's Republic and emphasizes the fact that the courts are merely one layer of administration within the Party-state. At the local level they are beholden to government and Party organizations whom they dare not offend. Judges, though nominally independent, are state functionaries, and often rather minor ones. This is one of the reasons why judgments in the Mainland are often hard to enforce, especially if they are made outside the area in which they apply. 'Local protectionism' obstructs their execution and exposes the inability of the law to cut across bureaucratic hierarchies. Bribery and corruption are equally common, particularly as judicial departments, like the military, the police and government at all levels, acquired extensive business operations during the 1990s which they were required to relinquish at the end of the decade (see CORRUPTION).

The Communist Party makes its presence felt in the legal system on a day-to-day basis through its 'political and legal committees' which determine the outcome of important cases before a trial takes place. Until 1997, when changes to the Criminal Procedure Law gave more weight to events in the courtroom, trials were conducted to educate the public rather than determine a defendant's guilt. It was a case of 'verdict first, trial second'. The role of defence lawyers was not to plead a client's innocence so much as stress the accused's regret and set out any mitigating circumstances.

The amendments of 1997 granted judges more power to decide and defendants earlier access to counsel. But they did not prohibit arbitrary arrest or ensure protection against unfair trial, torture or ill-treatment. Neither did they abolish the system of 'administrative punishments', applied without reference to the courts, which enable police to sentence dissidents and other undesirables to labour camps, sometimes indefinitely. Similarly, the abolition, again in 1997, of the crime of 'counter-revolution' in favour of 'endangering state security', did nothing to weaken the Party's power to silence critics. Early evidence suggested that Beijing's signing, in 1998, of the United Nations Covenant on the Protection of Civil and Political Rights did just as little for dissidents' rights.

towards rule by law

Yet these developments coincided with growing awareness among ordinary citizens of the importance of law as a means of enforcing rights. Political change might be required before China's laws can perform this function unhindered, but it would be a mistake to imagine nothing can change until everything does. Significant if piecemeal legal reforms during the last years of the century are slowly

acquiring a critical mass. Calls for the rule of law and an independent judiciary grow louder. In TAIWAN such demands played a part in the wider processes of democratization. They may augur similar change in the People's Republic.

Even if they do not, economic reforms at home and foreign investors abroad continue to generate momentum for legal reform in China. Hardly an item on Beijing's economic agenda at the start of the new century can be accomplished satisfactorily in the absence of a competent, efficient, transparent system of justice. In the Mainland's confused and confusing market economy, only the law can determine the vital questions of ownership and rights necessary for fundamental reform and economic rejuvenation. This requires more than rule *by* law, even though that is an improvement on earlier periods of China's modern history. It requires the rule *of* law – a genuinely independent, superior form of administration denied to most Chinese citizens during the last century but sought by a growing number at the start of this.

Lee, Martin Chu-ming (1938–)

A lawyer, legislator and leader of HONG KONG's Democratic Party, Lee has long been the liberal conscience of his homeland – both before and since its return to Chinese sovereignty. A thorn in the side of its colonial and current masters, he has pricked both with complaints that neither has given Hong Kong people what they deserve: full democracy. Lee's single-minded pursuit of this cause places him in a tradition which stretches back to LIANG QICHAO and SONG JIAOREN in the late Qing and early Republic and, in his own era, includes Mainland dissident WEI JINGSHENG, leaders of the TIANANMEN SQUARE DEMOCRACY MOVEMENT, and the founders of Taiwan's DEMOCRATIC PROGRESSIVE PARTY.

The son of a senior KUOMINTANG officer, Lee entered Hong Kong politics in the early 1980s as representative of the legal community in the Legislative Council (Legco). He took a close interest in the Sino-British negotiations on Hong Kong's future and was an enthusiastic supporter of the Joint Declaration handing the territory back to China. Beijing sought his advice and that of Szeto Wah (1931–), another leading liberal, who entered politics via the Hong Kong teachers' union. Both men were outspoken members of the China-

appointed committee set up to draft the Basic Law, Hong Kong's post-handover constitution.

Lee's support for the Tiananmen Square protests in 1989 changed his attitude towards Beijing – as it did Beijing's towards him. Already unhappy with the slow pace of democracy outlined in the draft of the Basic Law, Lee and Szeto were stunned by the suppression across the border. They publicly burnt sections of the document and resigned from the drafting committee. Later, Beijing formally expelled them. Later still, the *People's Daily* branded both men 'counter-revolutionaries' because of their support for democracy on the Mainland.

As an independent critic of Beijing – and, increasingly, BRITAIN – Lee achieved still greater prominence. He accused both countries of conspiring to restrict democracy in Hong Kong before and after the handover. Throughout the 1990s he spread this message far and wide during visits to Europe and North America, heightening international perceptions of what was going on in Hong Kong and the apparent risks to the territory's freedoms. Foreign leaders, including the president of the United States, met Lee on a one-to-one basis.

This infuriated Beijing, but heightened Lee's credentials as a genuine representative of Hong Kong people.

However, many in Hong Kong, particularly among the business community, regarded him as a nuisance. Senior British diplomats believed he threatened the good relations with China they held to be essential if Hong Kong was to enjoy a smooth transition. China-controlled newspapers in the territory attacked him as a 'pro-British', 'anti-China' element almost on a daily basis.

Yet supporters far outnumbered critics. In 1985 and 1988 Lee was (indirectly) elected to Legco. In 1991 he triumphed in the territory's first direct legislative elections as leader of the United Democrats, Hong Kong's first genuine political party. In the polls of 1995, conducted according to Governor CHRIS PATTEN's controversial reforms, Lee's party, by then known as the Democratic Party, captured 17 out of the 20 directly elected seats. Together with its allies, it enjoyed a narrow majority in the 60-seat chamber.

Though his party was a beneficiary of the Patten reforms, Lee frequently attacked Britain during its final years of rule. He was particularly critical of a Sino-British agreement setting up a Court of Final Appeal in Hong Kong. Lee said the Court's inability to hear cases involving 'acts of state' after the handover gave too much power to Beijing.

Precisely because it feared a repeat of 1995's election results under Chinese sovereignty, Beijing made clear it would scrap the Legislative Council on 1 July 1997, and replace it with a carefully selected 'provisional' body, pending the outcome of fresh elections conducted on a narrower franchise. China said the 1995 electoral arrangements had to be abandoned because they violated previous Sino-British accords. But its opposition stemmed largely from a desire to check the influence of Martin Lee and his allies.

This was accomplished on the transfer of sovereignty when a provisional legislature, minus the Democrats and their allies, who refused to participate, assumed office. During a midnight protest at the Legco building beforehand, Lee and other legislators vowed to return through elections scheduled the following year, 1998. Many, Lee included, duly did so. Led by the energetic, quietly spoken lawyer, they promptly resumed their demand for full democracy, including direct elections for the position of chief executive, occupied by TUNG CHEE-HWA, Hong Kong's postcolonial 'governor'.

Long after the handover, Lee was a symbol of how much Hong Kong remained at odds with its new sovereign. On security grounds the Communist authorities refused to allow the most popular and famous politician of China's new Special Administrative Region to cross the border and visit his 'Motherland'. Senior Mainland leaders likewise refused to meet him or have any contact with his party. The anomalous nature of this was apparent in June 1998 when President Bill Clinton of the United States went out of his way to meet Lee during his visit to Hong Kong. Jiang Zemin, president of Lee's own country, dared not do the same during his visits to the territory.

Lee Teng-hui (1923–)

The first Taiwanese to lead TAIWAN, the first Chinese leader to preside over a genuine democratic revolution, and the first to be directly elected by his people as a result – such achievements secure Lee Teng-hui, chairman of the KUOMINTANG, a place in the history of modern China, even though they occurred in the controversial, sometimes dangerous context of national division.

Lee was far from solely responsible for Taiwan's transformation: CHIANG CHING-KUO began the process of reform, which was itself the product of powerful social and economic forces as much as individual leaders. But Lee helped shape these processes, moving the island steadily towards full democracy in the 1990s despite the odds. In the presidential elections of March 2000 such changes finally got the better of Lee's own party: voters ended more than 55 years of Kuomintang rule, electing CHEN SHUI-BIAN of the DEMOCRATIC PROGRESSIVE PARTY (DPP) their president. Lee was forced to resign as party chairman, ending a remarkable political career on a surprisingly sour note.

Taiwanese first, Chinese second

Lee was a representative leader of Taiwan before his 1996 victory in the first direct presidential polls. Born in the rural suburbs of Taipei, he became part of the local elite that JAPAN, Taiwan's colonial master between 1895 and 1945, sought to acculturate and make its own. He studied at Kyoto Imperial University and, as he admitted in later life, regarded himself as Japanese until he was at least 21. Even in old age, his spoken Japanese was at least the equal of his Mandarin.

Lee was representative of many Taiwanese intellectuals, too, in that he added advanced education in the UNITED STATES to a Taiwanese-Japanese cultural upbringing. He studied agronomy at Iowa State University in the early 1950s and in 1968 obtained a PhD from Cornell University in the same field. This background, coupled with his devout Christian beliefs, meant he had little sentimental attachment to the Mainland and a natural antipathy towards Chinese Communism, even though he had been a member of the Party briefly as a youth. He was thus at odds with the Mainland origins and outlook of the Kuomintang, whose leaders regarded their flight to Taiwan during the CIVIL WAR as a temporary retreat pending a victorious homecoming. Lee said on one occasion that he regarded the Kuomintang as an 'outside force' that had occupied the island.

rise of a reformer

He rose through the party and government ranks regardless, thanks largely to the patronage of Chiang Ching-kuo, son of CHIANG KAI-SHEK. The younger Chiang, freed of his father's influence, and more personable and flexible by nature, sought to reconcile Kuomintang rule with Taiwanese realities and the sudden decline in the island's status arising from American recognition of Beijing. Promoting Taiwan-born leaders such as Lee, who became vice-president in 1984, was an example of this. But it provided few clues to the radical steps to come. In the months leading up to his death in January 1988, Chiang turned a blind eye to the creation of the Democratic Progressive Party, Taiwan's first opposition party, abolished Martial Law, and lifted a ban on travel to the Mainland for the many thousands of Taiwanese with relatives there. These moves undermined authoritarian Nationalist rule and exposed the constitutional fallacies on which it was based. They did not provide ready substitutes for either. This task fell to Lee Teng-hui, who succeeded Chiang as both president and chairman of the Kuomintang.

As he struggled to modernize a political structure created almost 50 years earlier on the Mainland, Lee faced three main sources of opposition. The first came from the old guard within the Kuomintang. The second took the form of repeated street protests, many of them led by the DPP, whose supporters wanted faster reforms and independence for Taiwan. The third was located in Beijing where Communist leaders loathed and feared what they saw as Lee's pursuit of independence in everything but name. All these constituencies had cause to complain. None succeeded in blowing Taiwan's democratization off course – at least they had not done so at the start of the new century.

towards a new Taiwan

The landmarks in Taiwan's democratic transformation included an amnesty for dissidents in 1990, the lifting in 1991 of repressive regulations dating back to the Civil War, and the forcible retirement at the start of 1992 of ageing Mainland deputies from their elected offices, which were subsequently opened to direct voting by Taiwanese. This political revolution required a redefinition of Taiwan's international status. It was no longer the temporary seat of the government of the Republic of China. It was the 'Republic of China on Taiwan', one of two separate political entities (the other being the 'People's Republic of China') that ruled a divided nation.

Here was a halfway house between Taiwanese independence and the 'one China' principle beloved of an earlier generation of Kuomintang leaders and their Communist counterparts then and since. As such it reflected Lee's own political and cultural ambiguity, as well as that of Taiwan generally – an island *of* China whose people lacked a clear desire to be *in* China, at least as it was then represented on the Mainland. However, the new formula displeased the by now minority Mainland faction within the Kuomintang, and the Communist leadership in Beijing, who warned it would still be necessary to reunify China by military means if pro-independence forces got out of hand.

democracy and diplomacy

As the Taiwanese people revelled in their new electoral freedoms, Lee proceeded with constitutional revision. 'Unofficial' talks were held with Mainland representatives, and although a loose agreement reached in 1993 was short on substance, it still represented a breakthrough in ties between the 'two Chinas'. Yet things did not always go Lee's way. Though the Kuomintang rapidly shed much of its historical baggage, many Taiwanese felt the party was corrupt and had been in power too long. In this sense, a vote for the DPP was not necessarily, if at all, a vote for independence: it was often simply a vote against the Kuomintang. Lee's response was to work with the DPP when necessary to counter foes in his own ranks while stealing that party's 'pro-Taiwanese' policies to weaken its public appeal. This was too much for some in the Kuomintang, who in 1993 left to form the New Party. They claimed to be the custodians of 'true' Kuomintang values, and firm foes of independence. Lee, meanwhile, succeeded in making the presidency subject to direct elections, the first of which was held in March 1996.

During the run-up to the polls, Lee tried to undermine the DPP's calls for formal independence with a series of overseas visits, and intensified campaigning for Taiwanese representation at the UNITED NATIONS. Many of his outings had to take the form of 'golf' or 'vacation' diplomacy because the countries which received him lacked formal ties with Taipei. Their leaders felt the diplomatic wrath of Beijing, despite the private nature of their meetings with the 'pariah' president.

This was nothing to Beijing's anger when Washington bowed to pressure from Congress and allowed Lee to attend a reunion at Cornell University in 1995. He had persisted with the trip, despite President JIANG ZEMIN's mildly conciliatory statement on unification earlier in the year. Moreover, he revelled in the occasion. This was a challenge that could hardly go unanswered in Beijing. The PEOPLE'S LIBERATION ARMY held manoeuvres opposite Taiwan, and the official press lambasted Lee in language redolent of the CULTURAL REVOLUTION.

The following year, Beijing matched Taiwan's first direct presidential elections with missile tests and prolonged war games designed to unsettle the island's inhabitants, and show the vulnerability of Taiwan's economy to Mainland mischief-making. These moves had unexpected consequences. One was a decision by the US to deploy two battle fleets in Taiwanese waters to calm fears of a Chinese invasion. The other was the patent determination of Taiwan voters not to be bowed by threats: they returned Lee to the presidency with 54 per cent of the vote against 21 per cent for the DPP's candidate, Peng Min-min (1923–). Taiwanese evidently approved of their president, despite Beijing's description of him as the 'scum of the nation'.

China's leaders resorted to abuse again and suspended high-level negotiations across the Straits in 1999 when Lee declared that talks between Beijing and Taipei should be conducted on the basis of 'special state-to-state relations'. This new cycle of Chinese threats, Taiwanese defiance and growing alarm in the region reached a climax in March 2000 during the island's second direct presidential elections. ZHU RONGJI was one of several Communist leaders who warned that China was ready to 'spill blood' if Taiwanese voted for independence forces, a none-too-oblique reference to Chen Shui-bian of the Democratic Progressive Party.

Lee was prevented from serving as president a third time by the constitution. However, long before the polls, he secured the selection of Lien Chan (1936–), his vice-president, as successor. This provoked a bitter split in the Kuomintang that cost the party the election. It was led by Soong Chu-yu (James Soong, 1942–), the popular former governor of Taiwan Province, who campaigned for the presidency as an independent. He secured 36 per cent of the vote. This was comfortably ahead of Lien Chan, who could manage only 23 per cent, but less than Chen Shui-bian, who won 39 per cent.

The humiliation of the Kuomintang, which had ruled Taiwan for more than half a century, was thus complete. As disgruntled KMT supporters waged street battles in Taipei, Lee was forced to resign as chairman. The party he had led for 12 years was forced into the unaccustomed role of opposition, its leading figures at each other's throats, its popularity waning further as the meaning of its defeat struck home. It remained for Lee Teng-hui – his position in the history of Chinese democracy secure, despite the eclipse of his own party – to serve the remaining two months of his presidency and hand over to Chen Shui-bian, the harbinger of a new, even less certain, period in Taiwan's tempestuous history.

Li Dazhao (1889–1927)

China's first major Marxist theorist and a teacher of MAO ZEDONG was captivated by the Bolshevik Revolution in RUSSIA and what it might mean for his own country. 'The bell is rung for humanitarianism! The day of freedom has arrived!' he wrote, extolling the revolution. 'See the world of tomorrow; it assuredly will belong to the Red Flag.' His attempt to raise the Red flag in China cost him his life.

Li was a key figure in the MAY FOURTH MOVEMENT of 1919 and friend of CHEN DUXIU, a fellow Marxist and pioneer of intellectual and political renewal. Both were on the opposite side to HU SHI in the controversy over whether '-isms' (complete ideological systems) or 'problems' (tackling specific ills in a gradual manner) was the best approach in redressing China's weakness. Li, first Librarian and then Professor of Political Science at Beijing University, helped 'isms' – particularly MARXISM – win the day. The young Mao was among many

who came under its influence. Li was not present at the founding conference of the CHINESE COMMUNIST PARTY in 1921, but Party historians regard him as one of its creators.

In 1924, he joined the upper ranks of SUN YAT-SEN's newly reorganized KUOMINTANG, which Moscow ordered China's Communists to join and radicalize from within. Li worked for the revolutionary cause in BEIJING. However, this cause, and Li's life, came to an end in the spring of 1927 when CHIANG KAI-SHEK purged the Nationalist party of its Communist allies in an attempt to keep the revolution within moderate bounds. A few days later the foreign diplomatic corps allowed police in Beijing to raid the Soviet embassy compound in search of incriminating materials on the grounds that Moscow was fomenting rebellion in China. Thousands of documents were found along with dozens of Chinese activists, Li among them. He and 19 others were arrested, tried and executed.

Li Lanqing (1932–)

Li Lanqing was appointed to the CHINESE COMMUNIST PARTY's seven-strong Politburo Standing Committee in 1997 and made senior vice-premier in charge of the economy the following year. His promotion reflects the importance for China's modernization drive of FOREIGN TRADE AND INVESTMENT, over which he had responsibility for much of the 1980s and 1990s. He was also in charge of China's long campaign to join the World Trade Organization (WTO), which began in 1986, when the trade body was known as the General Agreement on Tariffs and Trade (GATT), and which did not draw close to a successful conclusion until 2000.

Li was born in JIANGSU and graduated from Fudan University in SHANGHAI. He studied at a car plant in the SOVIET UNION for two years

in the mid-1950s before taking on the position of director of planning at the Changchun automobile works in JILIN. He remained in the automobile industry until the start of the reform era in 1978 when he was put in charge of foreign investment at the Ministry of Foreign Economic Relations and Trade (MOFERT). During the following 20 years, the only time Li was not directly involved in this vital sector of the economy was between 1983 and 1986, when he was deputy mayor of TIANJIN under LI RUIHUAN.

Li became minister of MOFERT in 1990 and joined the Politburo two years later. In 1993, he was made a vice-premier. His two promotions in 1997 and 1998 testify to his competence as an administrator and his expertise in trade and finance as well as science, technology and education.

Li Peng (1928–)

The long career in the CHINESE COMMUNIST PARTY of Li Peng, a dour, Soviet-trained bureaucrat, is testimony of Beijing's determination to combine rapid economic change with political rigidity. Li was the chief target

of the TIANANMEN SQUARE DEMOCRACY MOVEMENT and a main author of its suppression. Yet at the start of the new century he remains one of China's most powerful if least inspiring men, his continuing authority a symbol of the Communist political system's capacity to survive dramatic change in almost every area of Chinese life. Li Peng, Chairman of the NATIONAL PEOPLE'S CONGRESS, is not due to retire until 2003. Little significant political change can be expected until he does.

child of the Party

The roots of Li Peng's power lay in an unassailable revolutionary pedigree as the adopted son of ZHOU ENLAI; utter dedication to the Communist Party's cause; intense conservatism; and, when it mattered most during the 1980s and early 1990s, support from the small group of veteran revolutionaries who ruled from behind the scenes and saw in Li the best hope that their values would survive them. Mastery of a complex bureaucratic machine during ten years as premier, and a solicitous personal manner towards subordinates, were Li's own, more direct contributions to his extraordinary career.

He was born in Chengdu, capital of SICHUAN, the son of a Party member executed for his political activities. The young Li was one of several 'revolutionary orphans' adopted by Zhou and his wife, Deng Yingchao (1904–92), and educated at YANAN, the Party's wartime headquarters in north China. He studied at the Moscow Power Institute (1948–54), worked in power stations in Beijing, and rose through the municipal and then the national power bureaucracy to become minister in the early 1980s.

Neither the GREAT LEAP FORWARD nor the CULTURAL REVOLUTION interrupted the quiet progress of this technocrat with a penchant for discipline, loyalty and obedience. This was a surprise given that Li's specialist training in the Soviet Union and status as a professional bureaucrat made him a potential target of the last of these movements. Perhaps Li escaped trouble because of his relative unimportance. Perhaps he simply kept his head down. In any event, years later, he seemed to lack the visceral hatred for the mayhem of MAO ZEDONG's last years voiced by many of his fellow leaders. Always concerned about the standing of the Party, he appeared less ready than them to write off the Cultural Revolution in its entirety.

reluctant reformer

Under DENG XIAOPING he was usually less ready to embrace free market reforms, too. Economically there was no alternative: even the most hidebound Stalinist had to concede that continued public ownership, the planned economy and centralized control could not make China rich. But for CHEN YUN and others among the old guard who regarded Li as their man, free market reforms and contact with the outside world were as much a political challenge as an economic opportunity. Throughout the 1980s, Li – elected to the Central Committee in 1983, the Politburo in 1985 and the powerful Politburo Standing Committee in 1987 – opposed the radical reforms championed first by HU YAOBANG and then by ZHAO ZIYANG, with campaigns against 'bourgeois liberalization' and calls for Party discipline.

This innate conservatism, a stiffness in public and seeming inability to say anything without recourse to the ritualized phraseology of Party-speak made Li unpopular. Hu, a sparky, spontaneous character, had a following among intellectuals, whom he tried to accommodate within the narrow, permitted confines of freedom. Zhao, bold and imaginative, pioneered economic reforms that brought a taste of prosperity and a hunger for more. Li, premier from 1988, promised nothing but the old virtues of 'plain living and hard work'. Uninspired and *uninspiring*, he was particularly unpopular with students.

Just how unpopular became clear as the protests unfolded in Tiananmen Square in April 1989. High on the list of student demands was a direct dialogue with Li Peng on fighting corruption and extending democracy. Li refused, prompting taunts from the demonstrators of a kind unheard since the Cultural Revolution. 'Come out, Li Peng!' thousands of them shouted from the steps of the Great Hall of the People. Across the capital, China's premier was vilified in slogans, posters, cartoons and songs.

For almost a month the taunts continued and the tension mounted. The protestors made the centre of Beijing their own, defying stern warnings from the leadership, which had branded their movement 'counter-revolutionary', and half-hearted attempts to control them by the People's Armed Police (see PEOPLE'S LIBERATION ARMY). On 18 May, with Party leaders divided over how to handle the movement, and demoralized by the challenge to their authority, Li at last summoned the student leaders for a televised 'dialogue'.

It was a dispiriting experience for all concerned: the student leaders humiliated Li by re-stating their demands, while the premier warned that something would have to be done about the 'chaos' in Beijing. The Chinese people next heard Li's voice two days later when, opposed by Zhao Ziyang but backed by Deng and others among the old guard, he declared martial law in parts of Beijing. It was the end of Zhao's career as Party leader, and the beginning of the end for the democracy movement.

The end came on the night of 3–4 June, and Li was both an architect and a principal beneficiary of the military dénouement. Or at least he was in terms of domestic politics, for he was associated so closely with the suppression that any attempt to remove him, other than on the grounds of health and age, would inevitably invite speculation that the Party was changing its mind about Tiananmen.

China's grey man

Yet Li's role in the military crackdown scarred his career, both in the minds of many Chinese and in public opinion in the West. His persona, as 'grey', harsh and unforgiving as his politics, compounded the problem. Li Peng became the symbol of repression. The collapse of socialist governments in Eastern Europe in the face of their own pro-democracy movements reinforced his reputation as the 'butcher of Beijing'.

However, Li and his fellow architects of China's neo-Stalinist revival in the early 1990s, (who included an occasionally reluctant JIANG ZEMIN, the new Party leader), reckoned without Deng's determination to leave a happier mark on his country than the bloodshed of Tiananmen. The patriarch's calls in early 1992 for faster, bolder reforms caught the formal leadership off balance. It was a particular blow for Li: the premier's policy of re-centralization and slow growth was Deng's chief target. At that year's meeting of the National People's Congress (NPC), Li was forced to make an unprecedented number of changes to his annual policy speech. His days of undisputed control over economic policy were over.

He was more successful in securing approval for construction of the THREE GORGES DAM on the YANGTZE with which he had long been associated. Again there was strong opposition in the form of 'no' votes and abstentions at the NPC, but Li won the day. He subsequently made several visits to the construction site in HUBEI. The project's scale, huge demands on manpower and money and grand plan to transform nature were all close to Li's heart. For a Moscow-trained engineer fond of the grand public works beloved of Chinese emperors, the Three Gorges Dam had considerable appeal.

Jiang, Li and Zhu: China's troika

During the 1990s Jiang Zemin and Li Peng, respectively ranked numbers one and two in the Party, established a working relationship unusual in China's Communist politics for its stability. Whether the two men respected or were fond of each other was impossible to tell. That they were able to work together – at least without much in the way of open conflicts – was beyond doubt. The rise of ZHU RONGJI added a new dimension to the partnership. By far the most enterprising and charismatic of the three men, Zhu also had a better understanding of the economy. When Li suffered a heart attack in 1993, Zhu gained greater control over the economy and pushed for more radical reforms.

There was no question of Zhu upstaging Li politically. The latter's command of the State Council, and the support he enjoyed from the dwindling band of veterans, would not allow that. Moreover, Li was no worse for vacating the driving seat as far as the economy was concerned. As in the era of Zhao Ziyang, so in that of Zhu Rongji: Li was perfectly placed to profit from the errors of more ambitious and talented men. On the other hand, as number two in the Party and premier of the State Council, *their* successes were also his.

Li's importance to the regime in the 1990s rested mainly on his ability to bend a bureaucratic machine to the Party's purpose, and on the fact that he served as an ideological lodestone whose removal would raise unwelcome questions about Tiananmen and other matters. Perhaps the first of these functions could only be performed by a man whose lack of spontaneity and discomfort on the few occasions he was forced to face the Western press made Jiang, and more particularly Zhu, seem warm and human by comparison. The second function only sustained Li's dismal reputation overseas, particularly in the West. Much to his irritation, his few visits to Western Europe were dogged by demonstrations and criticism from his hosts of China's HUMAN RIGHTS record.

Elsewhere Li's diplomacy was more successful. A visit to INDIA in 1991 helped bring the two countries closer together than they had been for decades, though the process was interrupted by New Delhi's explosion of a nuclear device in 1998. In 1992 Li cemented the normalization of relations with VIETNAM during a visit to Hanoi. A 10-day tour of Central Asia in 1994 extracted promises from governments in the region that they would not aid ETHNIC MINORITIES opposed to Chinese rule in XINJIANG.

These foreign policy achievements had little impact on Li's reputation at home or outside the countries concerned. The wealth, aspirations and overall freedoms of the Chinese people expanded dramatically during the 1990s, but there was no apparent change in Li's views. These remained a quintessential expression of those of his Party. There could be no relaxation in the Party's domination of political life, control of the media and supremacy in law; Western-style political reforms were out of the question, their exponents not so much DISSIDENTS as criminals to be punished or banished into exile; and the handling of Tiananmen, though rarely referred to in public, was both necessary and justifiable.

from premier to parliament

Li Peng's two terms as premier ended in 1998. There had never been any doubt that Zhu Rongji would succeed him, but at first there was some uncertainty over Li's own future. It ended at the Party's 15th National Congress in 1997: QIAO SHI was ousted from the Central Committee, paving the way for Li to replace him as chairman of the National People's Congress the following year. The change reduced Li's exposure to the public but not his power. He retained his number two ranking in the Party, above Zhu.

As chairman of China's parliament Li has echoed his predecessor's desire to enhance the legislature's prestige. He has also spoken of the importance of the rule of law, a sentiment written into the constitution in 1999. But he has been less enthusiastic than Qiao Shi in establishing the absolute supremacy of the NPC. For Li, China's political situation admits of no ambiguities: the legislature, like other institutions, is the handmaiden of the Party. It exists to do the Party's bidding and transform its policies into law.

Li Ruihuan (1934–)

Li, the most 'liberal' member of China's Communist elite in the years following the suppression of the TIANANMEN SQUARE DEMOCRACY MOVEMENT in 1989, was made Politburo member in charge of ideology, and then chairman of the CHINESE PEOPLE'S POLITICAL CONSULTATIVE CONFERENCE (CPPCC), a position he was due to hold until 2003. Both appointments required him to put a human face on the reality of Party control, which he did with some success.

A former 'model worker', and leader of the Young Carpenters' Shock Brigade of Beijing, Li joined the CHINESE COMMUNIST PARTY in 1959. He placed his professional skills at the service of politics in 1977 when he was put in charge of the construction site for the MAO ZEDONG Memorial Hall in Tiananmen Square. In the early 1980s he abandoned carpentry for good to build a political career in TIANJIN, the city of his birth, where he rose to become mayor.

At the time, Tianjin was recovering slowly after the devastating earthquake of 1976 in nearby Tangshan. Li launched ambitious construction programmes which made him popular with some residents, even though the new buildings failed to change the generally run-

down appearance of north China's leading port city. However, his populist style of leadership, which saw him take part in live radio phone-in programmes, marked him out from other senior Communists.

The same was true of the way in which he defused student protests over campus living conditions and demands for more democracy which broke out in Tianjin and a score of other cities at the end of 1986 and beginning of 1987. Li is said to have told demonstrators they could not hope to overthrow the government unless they were prepared to shed as much blood as the Communists had during the CIVIL WAR. This endeared him to anxious veterans in Beijing, and especially to DENG XIAOPING. After the PEOPLE'S LIBERATION ARMY shed blood itself in Tiananmen Square in 1989, Deng elevated Li, who had joined the Central Committee in 1982 and the Politburo in 1987, to the then six-man Standing Committee of the Politburo and placed him in charge of ideology and propaganda.

It was an unusual job for a former woodworker whose formal education consisted of six years of part-time study at Beijing's Institute of Architectural Engineering. It was also an unusual time: Communism had become almost extinct outside China. It had also taken a battering *in* China. After the events of 1989 the country's sullen, suppressed intellectuals found even less reason to believe in MARXISM than before. However, that some of them escaped reprisals at the hands of the neo-Stalinists who regained control over the intellectual establishment owed something to Li Ruihuan's desire to promote a 'humane' form of Marxism that resolved rather than heightened social tensions.

In 1993, Li was made chairman of the CPPCC, the advisory body which gives expression to the Party's 'United Front' – its policy of alliance with members of the DEMOCRATIC PARTIES and those without any political affiliation. His task was to secure the façade, if not the reality, of political unanimity Communist parties everywhere seek for their policies.

In his capacity as CPPCC chairman, Li made a striking speech on the future of HONG KONG in 1995, two years before it was returned to China. There was much unease in the territory at the time because of China's determination to reverse the democratic reforms introduced by CHRIS PATTEN, the last British governor. Li sought to meet it with an analogy. It concerned an elderly lady who agreed to sell an ancient, valuable teapot. Unaware that the quality of the tea poured from it derived from the residue built up inside over many years, she cleaned the pot out, greatly reducing its value. Li's point, which was not lost in Hong Kong, was that a failure to understand what makes a thing valuable can result in its destruction. Li never enjoyed any direct responsibility for Hong Kong, but his message appeared to rub off on those in the Communist leadership who did: Beijing generally maintained a hands-off policy during the first year or so of the Special Administrative Region's existence.

Li Yuanhong (1864–1928)

Li Yuanhong was the military chief of the first independent local government set up in Wuhan, capital of HUBEI, following the REPUBLICAN REVOLUTION of 1911. He went on to serve two brief terms as state president, both of which ended in defeats at the hands of his opponents.

Born in Hubei and a colonel in one of the 'new armies' set up during the final years of the QING DYNASTY, Li was a decidedly reluctant revolutionary (see ARMIES). He had to be persuaded almost at knife point to cast in his lot with the rebels in Wuhan. It proved the route to a career that this man of integrity but little political talent could not have dreamed of. He became vice-president of the Provisional Republican government founded in 1912 and led by SUN YAT-SEN. A year later he served as vice-president to YUAN SHIKAI, whose campaign he supported to suppress the 'Second Revolution' launched by the KUOMINTANG in protest against Yuan's drift towards dictatorship. Li assumed the presidency himself following Yuan's abortive imperial restoration and death in 1916. However, he was soon driven out of Beijing by Zhang Xun (1854–1923), the 'pig-tailed general' whose loyalty to the Manchus caused him to retain his queue and organize another attempt at reviving the empire. This, too, failed. Li's second presidency, in 1922–3, ended when supporters of Cao Kun (1862–1938), leader of the 'Zhili Clique' (see WARLORDS; HEBEI), drove him out of office in another of the crude power struggles at the heart of Republican politics in Beijing. He sought safety first in TIANJIN and then SHANGHAI, where half-hearted attempts to revive his career came to naught.

Li Zongren (1891–1969)

Li Zongren was a talented, ambitious KUOMINTANG leader from GUANGXI who chafed under CHIANG KAI-SHEK's rule but could neither defeat him on the battlefield nor outsmart him in the complex world of warlord politics. Together with Bai Chongxi (1893–1966), his fellow Guangxi leader, he was at odds with Chiang from the completion of the first stage of the NORTHERN EXPEDITION in 1927 until the collapse of Nationalist power on the Mainland in 1949.

This enmity was at its most obvious during the war between Chiang and the 'Guangxi Clique' in 1929 and again during the 1930s, when Li, Bai and Huang Xuchu (1892–1975) – the third figure in the Guangxi triumvirate –

built up their province as a quasi-independent model of reform for the rest of the country. They put it on a war footing, partly to ward off the Japanese, but also to prevent 'encroachments' by the Central Government. Truce of a kind was established during the early months of the SINO-JAPANESE WAR, and in 1938 Li commanded the Nationalist troops in their first (and only) significant victory over the invaders at Taierzhuang in SHANDONG. But the rivalry between Li and Chiang resumed and bedevilled the Nationalist war effort.

It also undermined the government during the struggle against the Communists which followed (see CIVIL WAR). Li and Bai were skilled commanders whose Guangxi troops were among the Nationalists' best. Had Chiang been able to cooperate effectively with them and other regionalists in the late 1940s, MAO ZEDONG might have found it harder to seize power. But Chiang viewed the Guangxi leaders as WARLORDS whose power had to be broken if unity was to be assured. Li, and to a slightly lesser extent Bai, on the other hand, believed Chiang wanted to monopolize political power and deny them their rightful place in government. In this context, the armies and territory under their control were all that

stood between them and political oblivion.

Political oblivion, however, is what awaited them. Li was elected vice-president to Chiang in 1948; and when Chiang resigned in January 1949 following a string of government military reverses, the Guangxi leader became 'acting' president with full executive power. Li's moment of national prominence proved a tragedy. Real power still rested with Chiang, who retained the loyalty of key army commanders, and who soon moved his headquarters to Taiwan, leaving Li to do what he could to save Nationalist rule on the Mainland through a mixture of war and diplomacy with the Communists.

In the closing weeks of 1949, with Communist troops consolidating their hold over Guangxi, Li fell ill. Rather than flee to Taiwan, where Bai was to spend his final, powerless years, he travelled to the United States for medical treatment. Chiang was alarmed at the idea of having the 'acting' president so far beyond his reach. On 1 March 1950, he reassumed the presidency in Taipei – a day before Li met President Harry Truman at the White House. In 1966, Li returned to China, where the Communists found him a useful tool in their propaganda war against Taipei, and where he spent the final years of his life.

Liang Qichao (1873–1929)

Towards the end of a life in which he had proved one of the most influential scholars and champions of renewal of his age, Liang Qichao struck a positive note: 'I am completely optimistic in regard to the political future of China ... I feel that China, during the last fifty years, has been like a silkworm becoming a moth, or a snake removing his skin. How can they be accomplished easily?' This was a controversial stance to take in 1922, when the Republic had fallen prey to WARLORDS, and JAPAN had supplanted the West as China's biggest foe. Even darker days lay ahead. Yet throughout his career Liang, born in GUANGDONG, was a beacon of hope for a better China: one that was democratic, united, at peace with itself, and occupying its rightful place in the world.

Despair over China's defeat at the hands of JAPAN in 1894–5 first inspired Liang to pursue this cause, as it did his mentor, KANG YOUWEI. Both men played a leading role in the 100 Days Reforms of 1898, an attempt to establish constitutional government which ended

when the EMPRESS DOWAGER placed the movement's chief sponsor, the GUANGXU EMPEROR, under 'palace arrest' and ordered the execution or imprisonment of its leaders. Liang and Kang escaped into exile, the latter to pursue the cause of defending the emperor, Liang to champion the cause of DEMOCRACY and constitutional government, mostly among OVERSEAS CHINESE students in Japan. A voracious reader, gifted interpreter and accomplished journalist and pamphleteer, he introduced Rousseau, Montesquieu and other political philosophers to his growing number of admirers. Liang became a leading proponent of modern nationalism and democracy which he saw as keys to China's survival in a dangerous world. It was true that China's institutions needed to be overhauled, but it was even more true that the Chinese people themselves had to be rejuvenated before real change could be accomplished. In *The Renovation of the People* (1902), Liang argued that the state consisted of the assembly of its people, and that China would never stand up as a nation as long as its people were disorganized and confused. Calls for patriotism and popular participation of this kind were novel and influential.

In exile, Liang was often at odds with SUN YAT-SEN in the battle to win Overseas Chinese to the cause of change at home. This was because he advocated constitutional monarchy rather than republican revolution. It was also because his methods were different. Sun was a skilled conspirator and activist. Liang was a publicist in the grand tradition of literary scholarship. The two men returned to China following the REPUBLICAN REVOLUTION of 1911, but Liang was active in political parties opposed to Sun's KUOMINTANG.

As a professional politician, Liang was less effective than he had been as an educator and champion of reform. An association with YUAN SHIKAI, with whom he broke over the latter's attempt in 1916 to restore the monarchy, did little for his reputation, and he began to lose his early enthusiasm for the West as a source of inspiration for China. At the age of 50 he reviewed China's progress during his lifetime. Much had been achieved in a half century of upheaval, and there was hope even more could be in future. But he raised questions which stalk China still, and point to the incomplete nature of the national renewal he worked for. 'Let us ask our scientists, do we have one or two things which may be considered inventions of world importance? Ask our artists, do we have one or two productions which can be offered for world appreciation? And in our publication circles, do we have one or two books which are important works of the world?' The mainly negative answers to these questions echoed down the twentieth century.

Liaoning Province

The most southerly of the three Manchurian provinces – the two others are JILIN and HEILONGJIANG – was once China's industrial showcase. Before 1949 Russian and then Japanese investment made it the most industrialized and urbanized region in the country. Rapid development after 1949 reinforced this position. But the new priorities of the reform era and the poor performance of Liaoning's state sector have turned past glories into pressing burdens. Nowhere do Beijing's plans to revive its ailing state firms face so severe a test as in the strategic heartland of northeast China where, once again, the interests of China, RUSSIA, JAPAN and KOREA meet.

where empires meet

Until the 1870s, China's Manchu rulers sought to preserve their vast tribal homeland beyond the Great Wall as a retreat, hunting ground and source of precious commodities. Chinese immigration into the area was controlled. While it gathered pace throughout the nineteenth century it failed to populate the region fast enough to deter Russian military adventurers. Under the treaties of Aigun (1858) and Beijing (1860), the Tsar gained all of northeast Manchuria north of the Amur (in Chinese, the Heilong) and east of the Ussuri (in Chinese, the Wusuli). Heilongjiang and Jilin provinces lost their access to the Sea of Japan. Ever since, the whole of northeast China has had to look west, to the distant port of Dalian,

for maritime contact with the outside world.

Dalian is at the tip of the Liaodong peninsula in what, until 1929, was known as Fengtian province. It was the part of Manchuria in which Chinese migration, much of it from SHANDONG, was greatest, and its southern tip figured large in Russia's search for an ice-free port in the Far East.

Nevertheless Japan was the first to stake a claim to the Liaodong peninsula. It did so following the Sino-Japanese war of 1894–5. However, rival powers forced Tokyo to relinquish its gains in favour of Russia, which built the naval base of Port Arthur (modern Lushun), southwest of Dalian, and set about constructing a Southern Manchurian railway to link the region with Mukden (modern Shenyang), Fengtian's capital, and Harbin in the north. Harbin was the headquarters of the Russian-controlled Chinese Eastern Railway, built to provide a shorter route to Vladivostok from central Siberia (see HEILONGJIANG; RAILWAYS).

Japan returned to Liaoning after the Russo-Japanese War of 1905, a conflict fought in Manchuria and resolved in the United States under the Treaty of Portsmouth. China was not a party to the war but was its main theatre and principal casualty. In the years which followed Japan took control of the Southern Manchurian railway, built mines and industries along its route – notably at Anshan, Fushun and Benxi, still major industrial centres at the start of the twenty-first century – and founded the modern port-city of Dalian. Tokyo even formed a special military unit, the Guandong Army, to keep Southern Manchuria safe for Japan.

Manchuguo to Communist Manchuria

China's freedom of movement in the region, limited at the best of times, narrowed still further after the fall of the QING DYNASTY. Marshal Zhang Zuolin (1875–1928), warlord of Manchuria from the Republican Revolution until 1928, sought to turn the Japanese presence to advantage both at home and in his wider struggle for control of north China. He at first enjoyed some success. But in 1928 Japanese agents assassinated him, blowing up his train as he returned to Mukden after a brief period as head of a 'national' government in Beijing.

ZHANG XUELIANG, his son, known as the 'young marshal', took over at a time of growing anti-Japanese sentiment in China. Officers of the Guandong Army decided to bring things to a head. In the 'Mukden Incident' of 1931 they destroyed a section of the Southern Manchurian railway as a pretext for placing the entire region under their control. In 1932 Japan turned Manchuria into MANCHUGUO, a nominally independent state ruled from modern Changchun, capital of Jilin, by PU YI, the last Manchu emperor.

Manchuguo was founded to serve Tokyo's economic, political and strategic interests. Long an important source of raw materials, it was built up as a major, predominantly *Japanese*, centre of industry and transport. It was cut off from the rest of China until Tokyo's defeat in the Second World War.

Even then Manchuria's travails were not over. In accordance with decisions taken at the YALTA CONFERENCE, the Soviet Union entered the war against Japan and occupied the former puppet state. Soviet troops stripped the region of all the industrial facilities they could lay their hands on and shipped them back to European Russia. They also made good their rights, under the Sino-Soviet Treaty of 1945, to 'joint management' of the Chinese Eastern Railway, and access to Port Arthur and Dalian.

The Soviet presence had a more important consequence: it facilitated the takeover of much of the Manchurian countryside by Communist troops who raced to the region from north China via INNER MONGOLIA, and by junk across the Bohai Gulf from Shandong.

This set the scene for the bitter struggle for control over the northeast between the Communists and Chiang Kai-shek's Nationalists (see CIVIL WAR).

Chiang had never ruled Manchuria. Before the war, the 'old' and the 'young' marshals curbed his power in the region. After 1931, the creation of Manchuguo ended all forms of Chinese authority northeast of the Wall. Japan's defeat in 1945 at last held out the promise of government rule over an area rich in resources, thoroughly developed (despite Soviet depredations), and of immense strategic significance.

It was a fateful, if understandable, obsession. Chiang moved his best forces into south Manchuria and ordered them to fight their way north where the Communists were strongest. They occupied most cities in the region together with the main lines of communication. But in a series of brilliant campaigns directed by LIN BIAO, Communist troops gradually isolated, besieged and defeated their opponents. By November 1948 Shenyang had fallen and the Nationalist position in Manchuria had collapsed. Chiang's government never recovered; the following year it fled to Taiwan.

industrialization and revolution

Liaoning's new masters made the most of their province's industrial supremacy. With Soviet help, they invested heavily in the coal, iron and steel, and transport industries, all of which made major contributions to the PRC's *national* drive for industrialization. This was especially true during the First Five Year Plan (1953–7). Liaoning's role as a staging area for Chinese troops during the KOREAN WAR, and the fact that it was the object of occasional American bombing, had little lasting impact. Meanwhile, Moscow's transfer of the former Chinese Eastern Railway to exclusive Chinese ownership in 1952, and the final withdrawal of Soviet troops from Lushun in 1955, marked a symbolic end to almost a century of foreign control over all or part of Manchuria.

Nevertheless the position of northeast China in the national economy was sometimes a matter of controversy in Beijing. An example was the Gao Gang affair, named after the senior Party official (1895–1954) in the region who enjoyed close ties with Moscow. Promoted to Beijing in 1952, where he seemed destined for the very highest ranks of Party and government, he decided to speed the process up by plotting against those he believed

The Lie of the Land

At the centre of Liaoning is the Liao River plain, a large, fertile, rectangular-shaped strip of territory where most of the province's wheat, maize and soybeans are produced. It is the location of several grain 'production bases': large-scale, specialized, highly mechanized farms. The Liao rises in Inner Mongolia and meets the Yellow Sea in the Gulf of Liaodong. It is the longest river in Liaoning. To the southwest is the Liaodong peninsula, its southern tip barely 65 miles (104 kms) from the coast of Shandong across the Gulf of Bohai. It stretches from the Yalu, the border between China and North Korea, to the port of Yingkou in the west.

In west Liaoning, the Nuluerhu mountains set a limit to the central plain and rise to meet the Mongolian plateau. The Liaoxi corridor is a coastal plain to the south which skirts the Bohai Gulf. A key strategic region, it is the main land corridor between Manchuria and China proper. At the close of the 1990s Liaoning's 56,260 square miles (146,000 sq kms) were home for 41 million people, 95 per cent of them Han Chinese. The province contains one quarter of China's iron ores, and large quantities of oil. It is second only to SHANXI in coal reserves. Shenyang, the economic as well as the political heart of the province, is at the centre of a network of cities which produce iron and steel, coal, oil, chemicals, heavy machinery, electrical equipment and aircraft.

stood in his way: LIU SHAOQI and ZHOU ENLAI.

The activities of Gao and Rao Shushi (1903–75), the senior Party official in east China and a close ally, were soon exposed and condemned. The two men were purged. In August 1954 Gao committed suicide. Though there had been criticism of Gao's 'independent kingdom' in Manchuria, Liaoning and northeast China were only marginally involved in this first split in Party leadership since 1949. But there is no doubt that Gao's demise deprived the region of a powerful representative in Beijing.

Liaoning fell under a far more searching spotlight during the GREAT LEAP FORWARD. From Mao Zedong's point of view the province symbolized much that was wrong with the Soviet model of development. It relied heavily on food imports – a function of long years of neglect of agriculture and excessive concentration on industry; its strengths were in capital investment rather than intensive labour; it placed more faith in a professional bureaucracy than popular mobilization; and it tended to favour technical experts over politically sound generalists. All these phenomena were at odds with the stratagems and goals of the Great Leap.

Local officials struggled valiantly to correct the situation, – particularly on the farming front. A sign of their zeal was Liaoning's declaration, made even ahead of radical HENAN, that it was the first province to amalgamate its Agricultural Producers' Cooperatives into full communes. Delivering the promised record grain harvests proved much more difficult: famine and death stalked Liaoning in the early 1960s as they did other parts of the country.

The same was true of political radicalism. In 1960, during what is sometimes known as a 'second or mini-Leap', Mao devised a controversial new 'constitution' for the giant Anshan Iron and Steel Works southwest of Shenyang. It put politics in command rather than production targets, called on cadres to engage in labour, and required managers themselves to produce rather than simply supervise those who did so. Opposition to Mao's plans meant that the Constitution was not implemented until 1970. By that time the CULTURAL REVOLUTION was well under way, and Liaoning was at the forefront of Mao's last attempt at fundamental revolution.

One of its chief instruments in the province was Mao Yuanxin (c. 1943–), the Chairman's nephew, who exercised real power in Liaoning, and whose control extended throughout much of the northeast. His rule was based on an untouchable revolutionary lineage and close links with those later designated the 'GANG OF FOUR'. Neither asset survived the Chairman's death, the fall of the 'Gang' and the rise of DENG XIAOPING. In the later 1970s Mao Yuanxin's reign in Liaoning came to an end.

reforming the rust belt

And with the new emphasis on free market reforms and opening to the outside world, Liaoning's record ended as one of China's fastest-growing provinces. The persistence of 'Leftism'; the preponderance of industry over agriculture and, within that, of heavy industry over light industry; the dominance of the state sector; and the fact that so many of the province's goods were uncompetitive made Liaoning a laggard in the early 1980s. China's 'equipment department' – once a main source of the nation's producers' goods – acquired a new identity as China's rust belt.

After a slow start, and several local personnel changes, the province managed to get back on to a high growth track by developing township and village enterprises (TVEs). Unlike the situation elsewhere – notably in GUANGDONG, FUJIAN and ZHEJIANG – the state took the lead in founding rural industry in Liaoning. Individual entrepreneurs were thinner on the ground, as were private enterprises generally in the northeast. But the collectively owned sector of the economy developed rapidly, generating most of the growth which has enabled Liaoning to remain one of the big players among China's provinces, and driving down the state sector's share of industrial output.

FOREIGN TRADE AND INVESTMENT played an important role, too. Again, Liaoning lagged behind the southern provinces in making the most of its coastal location. Political changes in Beijing and local uncertainties made life difficult. Dalian was one of the 14 coastal cities opened to foreign trade and investment on favourable terms in 1984. But it was not until 1988, when much of the Liaodong peninsula was opened on similar terms, that parts of the province became engaged with the international economy on any scale.

Chief among them was – and remains – Dalian. In the words of mayor Bo Xilai (1949–), son of the veteran revolutionary Bo Yibo (1908–), Dalian has positioned itself as the 'Hong Kong of the north'. It is the centre for finance, business, trade, transport, and tourism for much of northeast China. Its aspirations are to perform the same role for a much larger Northeast Asian regional economy, including the two Koreas, Japan and the Russian Far East.

To some extent, the city has resumed the role it played during its long years of Japanese rule, though in the happier climate of peace and Chinese sovereignty. One of China's biggest ports, it is the main conduit linking the riches of the Manchurian hinterland with the investment and know-how of the wider world. And in another throwback to the past, much of this investment and know-how is coming from Japan, a four-hour flight from Dalian and not much more from Shenyang. Hong Kong was the largest investor in Liaoning during the 1990s, but the high-quality projects in Dalian were set up by Japanese companies such as Canon, Toshiba and Matsushita. Together with other firms they employ a disciplined, well-trained workforce of thousands.

The decentralization of decision-making *within* the province during the 1990s spurred economic growth in Liaoning as it did elsewhere. Shenyang, the location of American, Russian and North Korean consulates since the 1990s, competes for foreign investment with Yingkou (a port-city in the Gulf of Liaodong known to an earlier generation as the treaty port of Niuzhuang), and Dandong on the border with North Korea. None of these cities is as successful as Dalian. But all have gained from growing interest in the potential of northeast China in particular and northeast Asia in general.

state firms; socialism's future

At the start of the new era two major problems stand in the way of realizing this potential. One is the general economic slowdown in the region arising from the Asian financial crisis of 1997–9. Its effects have been profound but are not likely to be longlasting. The other, more fundamental, issue is the poor performance of China's state sector, whose problems are writ depressingly large in the northeast (see INDUSTRY).

Despite more than two decades of reform, Liaoning's large state enterprises remain the backbone of the local and, to some extent, even the national economy. Fundamental restructuring is required to revive such huge, inefficient, often highly polluting concerns. Carrying out this task without provoking major social unrest is proving difficult.

Shenyang has been trying to do so since 1986, when it became the first city in China to experiment with bankruptcy. In the years which followed several state firms were merged, restructured or closed. However nowhere near enough were subjected to this fate. The authorities found it even harder to provide new jobs for those who ought to be laid off than pay the hugely bloated local workforce. An indication of the seriousness of the problem came to light in 1994 when the mighty Anshan Iron and Steel Works had to stop production because it could not sell its products. Emergency loans were needed to pay the workforce, and massive investment sought to renovate the plant.

During the 1990s, resolving the kind of problems which plague state enterprises in Liaoning moved smartly up the national agenda. In 1992–3, ZHU RONGJI, then a vice-premier, was charged with settling state firms' huge domestic debts. In 1995, WU BANGGUO was made vice-premier with particular responsibility for state enterprise reform. Two years later, at its 15th National Congress, the Communist Party called for the conversion of many state factories into joint-stock companies, and the closure of others. In 1998, Zhu Rongji, by then premier, promised the completion of such measures within three years. Progress on the ground was less impressive than the rhetoric. In almost every major centre of heavy industry, strikes and protests were common in the 1990s. In Liaoning, and particularly Shenyang, the industrial capital of the northeast, reports of unrest were legion. It was no cause for surprise. The workers of south Manchuria belong to one of the oldest working-class communities in China. Many were nurtured on the belief that they were masters of the state and the vanguard of socialism. It is no wonder that they do not take kindly to the idea of redundancy. It is no wonder, either, that their fate is symbolic of the wider fortunes of Liaoning – a province whose achievements in the age of central planning and state control have cast a long cloud over the era of mixed ownership and the free market.

Lin Biao (1907–71)

Lin Biao, a brilliant Communist military commander whose victory in Manchuria presaged the KUOMINTANG's defeat in the CIVIL WAR, challenged MAO ZEDONG's supremacy in the CULTURAL REVOLUTION and died in a plane crash, allegedly after trying to assassinate the Chairman. His fate, like his enigmatic personality, remains one of the great mysteries of Chinese politics.

Lin was involved in many of the seminal events of Communist history before 1949. Born in HUBEI, he trained at the Whampoa Military Academy in Guangzhou, training school of the Kuomintang's National Revolutionary Army; took part in the NORTHERN EXPEDITION of 1926 and the LONG MARCH of 1934–5; and led Communist troops to victory in battles against the Japanese during the SINO-JAPANESE WAR. The high note of his military career was the capture of the northeastern provinces of Manchuria (modern LIAONING, JILIN and HEILONGJIANG) in 1947–8 from Nationalist troops vastly superior in numbers and equipment. His victory paved the way for the fall of Beijing and the Communist conquest of north China (see CIVIL WAR).

Illness, much of it apparent hypochondria, kept him on the sidelines during the early years of the People's Republic. But in 1959, when Mao purged PENG DEHUAI, the defence minister who defied him over the GREAT LEAP FORWARD, the Chairman turned to Lin as a replacement. Ambition and revolutionary idealism brought the two men together in a partnership that plunged China into disaster. Under Lin in the early 1960s, the PEOPLE'S LIBERATION ARMY (PLA) became the exemplar of revolutionary purity, and the advocate of 'people's war': the strategy of engulfing a technologically superior invader in a 'sea' of politically inspired defenders deep inside Chinese territory.

More importantly, the PLA proved the sole guarantor of Communist Party power in China as Red Guards swept across the country during the Cultural Revolution, seizing power from the established authorities. In the ensuing chaos, Mao ordered the PLA to intervene and 'support the Left'. Order of a kind gradually returned, but it was not much to Mao's liking. By 1969, Lin and the PLA had emerged as the chief political victors of the Cultural Revolution. Lin was even designated Mao's successor in the Party's new constitution: an elevation achieved by no other would-be leader in the history of Communism in China or elsewhere. The only question was when he might be inclined to claim his inheritance.

In the course of 1971 Lin, his wife, son and other close allies were said to have made plans to assassinate Mao, whom they believed to have turned against them, and whom they nicknamed 'B52', after the American bomber. Their plot, known as 'Engineering Outline 571' because the last three letters in Chinese are homonyms for the term 'armed uprising', allegedly involved the setting up of a rival regime in GUANGDONG. If all else failed, Lin was said to have laid plans to seek refuge in the SOVIET UNION.

All else did fail. On 13 September 1971 Lin, his wife and son were among all eight passengers killed when the Trident jetliner they were travelling in crashed in Mongolia. Mao had won the day. But he and other leaders were left to explain how a man who might have been the next leader of the CHINESE COMMUNIST PARTY had died while trying to flee into the arms of the then arch enemy, Moscow. Mao also had to find another suitable successor – an even more difficult task amid the maelstrom of revolutionary politics that marked the early 1970s.

Liu Shaoqi (1898–1969)

'China's Khrushchev'. 'The number one Party person in authority taking the capitalist road'. 'A renegade, traitor and scab'. The language used against the president of the People's Republic during the CULTURAL REVOLUTION was as gruesome as his end. Toppled and tortured, Liu died in prison, his medical ailments untreated, his white hair a foot long, his family unaware of his fate. Liu's fall was a symbol of the excesses of the Cultural Revolution, and the murderous forces at the heart of China's Communist politics.

Before he fell foul of MAO ZEDONG, Liu's political life appeared to embody the principles set out in his own influential pamphlet *How To Be A Good Communist* published in the 1960s. Born in HUNAN, he joined the CHINESE COMMUNIST PARTY in its very earliest days and was trained in the SOVIET UNION. Much of his early revolutionary life was devoted to organizing labour, often in KUOMINTANG controlled areas.

Experience and instinct made of Liu a very different Communist from Mao. He was an organization man and a disciplinarian, not a Marxist dreamer desperate to make a mark on history. For all this, he ranked second only to Mao in the Party after 1949, was at one with the Chairman on the need for a GREAT LEAP FORWARD in 1958, and did nothing to save PENG DEHUAI, the defence minister, whose criticism of the resulting famine and death resulted in dismissal.

State president from 1959 following Mao's decision to give up the day-to-day work of government in favour of revolutionary theorizing, Liu differed with the Chairman over how to recover from the effects of the Leap and the future direction of the Revolution. Liu, together with DENG XIAOPING, favoured the use of material incentives to boost production and the confinement of political movements to Party members and cadres – the political 'elect'. That there were errors and problems with the Chinese Revolution was undeniable. The exchange of polemics with Moscow in which Mao revelled made things more difficult. But if a CULTURAL REVOLUTION was necessary to save the Revolution from going down the Soviet path, as Mao and fellow radicals said, it should at least be kept within bounds. The age of class struggle was supposed to have passed in the 1950s with the socialization of the means of production.

These views, and Liu's attempts to confine the impact of the Cultural Revolution, soon fell victim to the Chairman's power, prestige and determination. The formal Party apparatus crumbled before the onslaught of a powerful Maoist coalition consisting of the army under LIN BIAO, the radicals gathered around JIANG QING, Mao's wife, and the Red Guards. Liu fell, too. In 1968, with the country in turmoil, he was dismissed from all his posts 'once and for all', and passed the remaining year of his life in even greater ignominy than Communists usually reserve for 'class enemies'.

Justice was dispensed posthumously. In 1980 Liu was fully rehabilitated, and his 'crimes' revealed as a monstrous frame-up by Lin Biao and the 'GANG OF FOUR'. Little was said of Mao's own role in toppling his would-be successor.

Long March (1934–5)

The epic flight of the CHINESE COMMUNIST PARTY from its scattered bases in south China to YANAN in the north nearly destroyed it as a fighting force. The fact that the Party survived – a triumph of will over almost overwhelming odds, including dissension within the marchers' ranks – turned the episode into one of the great victories and defining myths of the Communist movement. Partly as a result, Long March veterans dominated Chinese politics well into the 1990s.

The flight was caused by the success in 1934 of CHIANG KAI-SHEK's fifth 'bandit sup-

pression' campaign against the foes he had been trying to exterminate since 1927. Four earlier attempts to crush the Central Soviet, set up by MAO ZEDONG in JIANGXI to consolidate Communist power, failed because of faulty tactics, inferior troops and lack of political mobilization. The fifth campaign, assisted by German military advisers, rectified these errors: KUOMINTANG troops built a network of blockades and 'strategic hamlets' as they advanced into enemy-held territory. Squeezed mercilessly, the Communists were forced to break out.

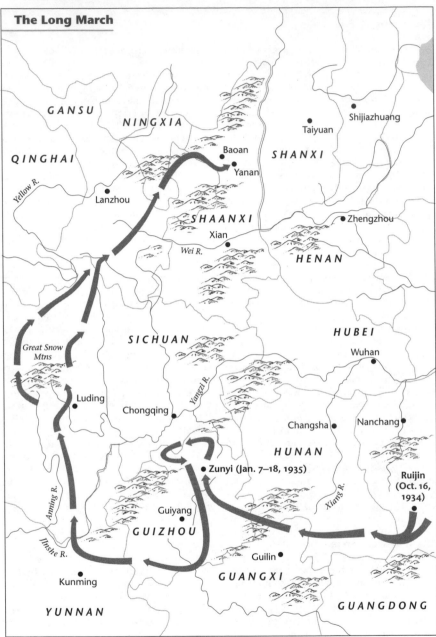

The Long March

GANSU

QINGHAI

NINGXIA

Baoan
Yanan

SHANXI

Taiyuan

Shijiazhuang

Yellow R.

Lanzhou

SHAANXI

Xian

Wei R.

Zhengzhou

HENAN

Great Snow
Mtns

SICHUAN

HUBEI

Wuhan

Luding

Chongqing

Yangzi R.

Changsha

Nanchang

Anning R.

Jinshe R.

Zunyi (Jan. 7–18, 1935)

HUNAN

Ruijin
(Oct. 16,
1934)

Guiyang

GUIZHOU

Xiang R.

Kunming

Guilin

GUANGXI

GUANGDONG

YUNNAN

Mao's First Front Army, joined en route by other Communist forces, spent the best part of the following year on the run, passing west and north through nine provinces. Under attack from local forces as well as the central government armies on their trail, they scaled mountain ranges, forded rivers and traversed bleak plateaux. There were episodes of real heroism, despite the crude exaggerations of later propaganda. Perhaps 10,000 of Mao's original force of 100,000 reached the sanctuary of Yanan in SHAANXI, home of another soviet base. The marchers covered the best part of 6,000 miles (9,600 kms).

Two foreigners travelled with them: Otto Braun, Soviet adviser to the Party, who completed the journey; and Alfred Bosshardt, an English missionary, whom the Communists captured en route but later released. Chiang lived to regret his failure to destroy his foes completely. But there was some consolation to be drawn from the fact that his policy of hot pursuit projected central government power deep into south and west China, previously almost immune to his authority.

Mao turned Communist military defeats to his political advantage at a Politburo meeting in Zunyi, a town in GUIZHOU, where the marchers rested for a few days in January 1935. He gained the upper hand over those in the Party, including Braun, whose opposition to Mao's often successful military tactics during earlier 'bandit suppression' campaigns in Jiangxi was now weakened by the circumstances of the flight, and lack of contact with Moscow, from whom they took their orders. Victory of another kind soon followed: warlord armies in northwest China destroyed Communist forces under Zhang Guotao (1897–1979), another rival in the Party with whom Mao fell out over political tactics and the most appropriate destination of the march.

At the time of their flight from Jiangxi, Communist leaders gave little thought to where they and their Party might end up. It became an issue only after several weeks on the road, when Mao and his allies settled on Yanan as the best base from which both to develop the Revolution and fight JAPAN, possibly in the form of a 'United Front' made up of all patriotic Chinese. Zhang Guotao preferred to head northwest, where his forces, and perhaps a government led by him, might be able to count on support from the SOVIET UNION. Mao and Zhang thus led their forces in different political as well as geographical directions. The division was settled, in Mao's favour, when Zhang's army was crushed by Muslim cavalry loyal to local, pro-Kuomintang militarists. Unable to get his way in the Party without military backing, Zhang defected to the Nationalists.

Yet it was the SINO-JAPANESE WAR that saved the Communist Party from defeat at the hands of Chiang's 'anti-bandit campaigns', rather than the Long March. Had it not been for the war – and the XIAN INCIDENT of 1936, in which Chiang was kidnapped and forced to work with the Communists in the interests of national resistance against Japan which preceded it – the extraordinary trek across much of the country might be remembered for delaying the Party's defeat, rather than avoiding it.

This does not deprive the event of its significance, either as a human feat or a key element in the iconography of the eventually victorious Communists. The Long March created a revolutionary pedigree without equal. In a political culture where seniority in almost every form counts for much, the Long March afforded its leading participants (almost) unassailable revolutionary credentials. Not until the death of DENG XIAOPING early in 1997 did Chinese politics genuinely emerge from the shadow of the Long March generation. And even then a Long Marcher remained in the highest councils of the Party. Liu Huaqing (1916–) retired from the Politburo Standing Committee at the Party's 15th National Congress in September 1997, aged 80.

Lu Xun (1881–1936)

Numerous intellectuals, reformers and revolutionaries strove to diagnose China's ills during the twentieth century. None did so in such a telling, searing, humane and often unwelcome fashion as Lu Xun, modern China's finest writer and most powerful social critic. His latter-day flirtation with MARXISM enabled the CHINESE COMMUNIST PARTY to canonize him after his death and claim him as one of its own. But the official cult of Lu excludes much of what he stands for. He subjected Chinese civilization to withering examination and sharp condemnation; and the questions he raised – about the 'tragedy' of being

Chinese, and the cruelty of Chinese society – haunt his country still.

Like many of his generation, Lu travelled to JAPAN during the final years of the QING DYNASTY to learn how China might follow its smaller Asian neighbour on the road to modernization. Also like many Chinese students overseas, he studied medicine, perhaps in the belief that curing individuals was the best way of healing a sick society. He abandoned medicine for literature, but soon displayed more forensic powers as a writer than he could ever have done as a surgeon.

He was less sure of his ground on the question of how best to revive the society he so painfully dissected. Pessimism and despair were always at hand. They set in after the collapse of a literary magazine he founded in Tokyo, and they accompanied him back to China where he taught and immersed himself in the classics. When asked to contribute to the magazine *New Youth*, a flagship of the MAY FOURTH MOVEMENT of 1919, written in the BAI HUA or vernacular style, Lu queried the optimism of its editors. In a powerful metaphor, he described his country as an iron house, devoid of windows, in which the people were fast asleep and destined to be suffocated. Since they would not know the pain of death, was it not cruel to wake the light sleepers among them? Lu reluctantly decided to do so in a series of short stories which changed the face of modern Chinese literature.

Lu's work was radical in form, style and content, but he was a captive of tradition as well as a revolutionary. One aspect of this was his combination of classical and vernacular styles which loaded his texts with meaning. The short story was a powerful new genre; but in the hands of Lu, its message was not always direct. This reflected a dilemma at the heart of his writing: he often seemed torn between remaining faithful to his personal, often pessimistic vision of reality, and meeting the demands for leadership and inspiration placed on him by younger writers desperate to revive their country. Reconciling these inner and outer worlds often proved impossible.

The collections of stories Lu published during the early 1920s explored the crowd and the fate of ordinary, insignificant individuals. Their inescapable message was that China was a diseased country whose people lived in sloth and servility, superstition and cruelty. In the *Diary of a Madman*, Lu described the Chinese as cannibalistic: the words 'eat people' could be found between the lines of the classical texts. The diary ends with a despairing 'save the children'. In the *True Story of Ah Q*, he used the grim life of a mediocrity to illustrate what he described as two of the worst characteristics of Chinese people: their tendency to make 'spiritual victories' out of severe setbacks and their 'slave mentality' which made them either oppressors or oppression's willing victims. Thus was born Ah Q-*ism*; a phrase which damned Chinese people in the first half of the century in the same way that Bo Yang's notion of *The Ugly Chinaman* did towards its end (see BO YANG).

The apparent hopelessness at the heart of Lu's work, the idea that only a spiritual revolution rather than a political or economic one could truly rescue China, placed him at odds with many of the young radicals of his day. For them Lu was China's Don Quixote, casting a bleary gaze at the landscape and tilting at windmills. They rejected his pessimism.

So, towards the end of his life, did Lu himself. In 1928, fearing persecution at the hands of CHIANG KAI-SHEK'S KUOMINTANG government, he moved to the relative safety of SHANGHAI'S international concession, home of most of China's radical intelligentsia. Partly as a result of translating the Marxist literary theories of Plekhanov and Lunacharsky, partly in response to the Nationalists' execution of radicals and Communists, Lu accepted the 'revolutionary mission' of literature. He was a prominent member of the League of Left-wing Writers, formed in 1930. For him, as for other members, all literature had a class background. The 'human nature' it depicted was class-based, not a universal or abstract concept. To imagine otherwise was a bourgeois deceit. Literature was a political weapon and it had a part to play in ending the rule of reactionaries.

Exactly *what* part and what it was that constituted revolutionary literature were questions that continued to divide Lu and some of the radicals. His Marxism aside, there was never any question in Lu's mind that writers could not be expected to dance to the changing tune of the Communist Party, which he declined to join. If they did, they would produce only 'eight-legged essays' – the stylized, vacuous literary form students had to master to pass the civil service examinations under imperial rule. All literature might be propaganda; not all propaganda was literature.

Lu spent the final years of his life engaged in polemics of this kind rather than genuine literary creation. He took particular exception to the sudden dissolution of the League in 1936 and of attempts, ordered by the Party, to foster a 'literature of national defence' in keeping with the United Front policy adopted on the eve of the SINO-JAPANESE WAR. He had come round to the Marxist view of literature through a long and painful process. Now he was being instructed to abandon it overnight in the interests of political expediency. Perhaps paradoxically, his refusal to do so placed him on the side of creative freedom in opposition to the Party's cultural tsars.

But Lu's resistance proved fleeting, and not just because of his death in 1936. At YANAN, where the Communists had founded a Lu Xun Academy of Literature and the Arts, MAO ZEDONG imposed control over writers and artists as part of his 'rectification campaign'. At the Yanan Forum on Literature and the Arts of 1942, Mao said the era of Lu Xun, the era of the biting, sarcastic essay that exposed the dark forces of society, was over. A new era had begun in Yanan and a new literature was required to extol it. It should be 'people's literature': writing that was bright and positive, and which advanced the Party's cause.

Posthumously, Lu – the scourge of commissars in later life as he was of all society during his prime – was made the patron saint of this monochrome vision of poetry and prose. Sixty years later, this title mocks him still, and the Communist version of letters mars most serious attempts at literary creativity in the People's Republic. It is an open question whether the nature of the Chinese people has changed much in the 80 years since Lu Xun penned the most excoriating and uncomfortable of his short stories. It is certain that the censors in Beijing are reluctant to let writers and readers try to find out.

Macau

The history of European settlement in China came to an end on 20 December 1999 when Macau, the first Chinese port to be occupied by a Western power, was the last to be returned. It was an occasion rich in symbolism for Beijing and for Portugal, which traces its settlement of the territory – a tiny peninsula and two islands in the Pearl River estuary – to the mid-1550s. Substantive change in Macau, an unusual, hybrid society under Portuguese rule, latterly better known for gaming and gangland crime, is bound to follow the resumption of Chinese control. Leaders of Beijing's second Special Administrative Region (after HONG KONG) will find it difficult to preserve Macau's distinct identity amid the stampede towards economic development and integration with GUANGDONG.

a colony eclipsed

Macau's once mighty role as the principal Western trading post and missionary base in China did not survive the arrival of the British in Chinese coastal waters during the early nineteenth century. With the foundation of Hong Kong, most of the China trade and nearly all the foreign community either moved across the estuary or relocated to newly opened TREATY PORTS. These developments reflected the power of other Western nations in the Pacific relative to Portugal, and exposed the insecure legal basis of Lisbon's presence in Macau itself. For more than 300 years, until a treaty with China was concluded in 1862, Portugal's occupation was a matter of Chinese sufferance. It became so again during the final decades of Portuguese rule.

Prior to the SINO-JAPANESE WAR of 1937–45, Macau was among the least important of the many foreign concessions, spheres of influence and possessions scattered across China. When that conflict became part of the Second World War, Portugal's neutrality made Macau the only such territory not subjected to Japanese occupation or control. Its significance soared accordingly. Refugees from the Mainland and Hong Kong flooded in, swelling the population to more than 600,000. Feeding so many people taxed the territory's resources. Espionage, evasion and escape operations mounted by all sides tested the tolerance of its rulers.

More refugees arrived during the late 1940s as a result of China's CIVIL WAR. But, as was the case with Hong Kong, the new Communist government in Beijing showed little interest in recovering sovereignty over Macau. The KOREAN WAR demonstrated the value of having foreign-ruled territories on China's periphery: Macau became the principal conduit for smuggling strategic goods into the People's Republic whose sale was banned under a UNITED NATIONS trade embargo. In the 1950s Portugal sold to China large quantities of gold, some of it originally confiscated by the Nazis and acquired by Lisbon in exchange for precious metals. All of it passed into the Mainland via Macau.

a colony out of control

India's forcible resumption of control over Goa, another Portuguese enclave, in 1961 raised questions about Lisbon's ability to hang on to Macau. Doubts increased five years later

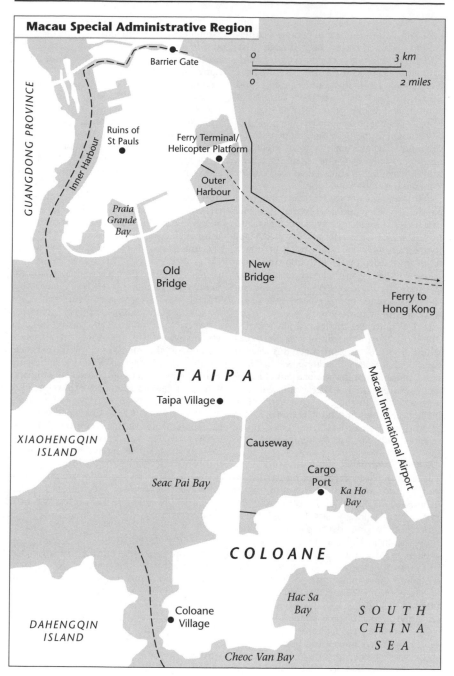

Macau Special Administrative Region

Barrier Gate

0   3 km

0   2 miles

GUANGDONG PROVINCE

Ruins of
St Pauls

Ferry Terminal/
Helicopter Platform

Inner Harbour

Outer
Harbour

*Praia
Grande
Bay*

Old
Bridge

New
Bridge

Ferry to
Hong Kong

T A I P A

Taipa Village

Macau International Airport

*XIAOHENGQIN
ISLAND*

Causeway

Cargo
Port

*Ka Ho
Bay*

Seac Pai Bay

C O L O A N E

*Hac Sa
Bay*

Coloane
Village

*S O U T H
C H I N A
S E A*

*DAHENGQIN
ISLAND*

Cheoc Van Bay

when the CULTURAL REVOLUTION spilled into the territory. In 1966, Macau became a battleground between local KUOMINTANG and CHINESE COMMUNIST PARTY activists; pro-Beijing groups and the Portuguese. At least eight people were killed during protests and riots which paralysed the territory. Lisbon lost control, despite the presence of Portuguese troops. Beijing then forced the colonial government to apologize and compensate the casualties of what amounted to an attempted uprising fostered by China's own supporters. It also demanded – and secured – an end to Kuomintang activity in Macau.

Yet China was not ready to assume formal control of the territory. When the demoralized colonial government offered to leave Macau, Beijing refused and called a halt to the street violence. It refused again in 1974 following the democratic revolution in Lisbon when Portugal again talked of abandoning the territory. Portugal's position in Macau, though weakened by the events of the 1960s, was not entirely powerless.

It had, however, changed fundamentally. The Macau Organic Statute of 1976, a new constitution for the territory, made this clear. It declared that Macau, though subject to Portuguese administration, was not a part of Portugal. The same principle was acknowledged in a secret clause to the 1979 agreement establishing diplomatic relations between Lisbon and Beijing: Macau was defined as Chinese territory under Portuguese administration.

economic integration, gambling, crime

The 1970s and 1980s were years of relative calm and rapid economic growth in Macau. Textile exports led the way; toys, artificial flowers and low-end electronic goods followed. Some aspects of economic development resembled those begun in Hong Kong 15 years earlier, though on a much smaller scale. The opening up of the Chinese economy in the early 1980s, including the establishment of the Zhuhai Special Economic Zone across the border, supplied fresh impetus for growth (see SPECIAL ECONOMIC ZONES). Some Macau investment moved north across the border; more Mainland investment moved south. By the mid-1990s PRC banks, property companies and other concerns had acquired a large, sometimes dominant influence in various sectors of Macau's economy, including the territory's new airport and airline.

The distinguishing feature of Macau's economy has long been its reliance on gambling and tourism to provide customers. A ban on gambling in the Mainland following the Communist Revolution, and strict rules against betting on anything save horses in Hong Kong, created new opportunities for the local gaming industry. *Sociedade de Turismo e Diversoes de Macau* (STDM or Macau Travel and Amusement Company), run by Stanley Ho, made the most of them. In exchange for a monopoly, the company modernized gambling in Macau. It also began to provide ferry services to and from Hong Kong, still the source of four-fifths of tourist arrivals at the close of the twentieth century despite growing numbers from Taiwan and the Mainland. In the late 1990s gambling accounted for at least 20 per cent of Macau's GDP and about one-third of all government revenue.

Gaming brought organized crime as well as cash to the enclave. The former has accompanied the latter almost everywhere, and for many years gambling-related crime in Macau, though a problem, seemed manageable. But beginning in the mid-1990s, rivalry intensified between loan syndicates and protection rackets, many of them linked to Triad societies, and potential competitors for a formal stake in the industry when STDM's monopoly expires in the year 2001. Scores of gangland killings, robberies and bomb explosions took place. The Macau police often seemed unable to cope. In 1998, China's patience with the situation wore thin. It announced that PEOPLE'S LIBERATION ARMY troops would be sent to Macau following its return to Chinese rule on 20 December 1999. Beijing was quick to say that the Macau police would remain responsible for law and order after the handover, but the message was no less plain for that.

the politics of transition

The troops issue was a rare departure from the consensus-based approach to Macau's transition Lisbon and Beijing maintained in public. This began in 1987 with the Sino-Portuguese Joint Declaration restoring Macau to Chinese rule. The declaration spoke of China recovering the exercise of *sovereignty* over Macau – even though Portugal had ceded sovereignty, as opposed to administration, to Beijing in the secret agreement of 1979.

As with Hong Kong, whose future had been decided three years earlier, China promised that Macau people, not Mainlanders, would rule Macau after 1999. In a reprise of Deng Xiaoping's 'one country, two systems' formula, the territory would become a 'Special Administrative Region'. Its freedoms and way of life would be preserved for 50 years. It would enjoy a high degree of autonomy in everything save defence and foreign affairs.

In 1993, Beijing promulgated a Basic Law for Macau, a post-1999 constitution. Again, it was closely modelled on that for Hong Kong except that it did not call for the stationing of troops in Macau after the transition – an absence remedied in fact, though not in the Basic Law.

Another, possibly more important, difference concerned the development of representative government in Macau. The Basic Law called only for a *majority* of members of the Legislative Assembly to be elected, not *all* members as in Hong Kong. Neither did it make universal suffrage the goal of elections for either the Legislative Assembly or the chief executive, Macau's post-1999 'governor'. While this removed much of the ground for disputes of the kind that marred the final years of British sovereignty in Hong Kong, Macau was never going to be an object of struggle between Lisbon and Beijing in the way Hong Kong was for Britain and China (see HONG KONG; CHRIS PATTEN). It was too small and Portugal too weak for that. The absence of ill-defined electoral promises in the Basic Law nevertheless made things easier for all parties concerned.

Whatever the future of democracy in Macau, it has a longer history there than in Hong Kong. Direct elections for the Legislative Assembly were introduced in 1976, albeit on a narrow franchise. This was enlarged in 1984 to include ethnic Chinese residents irrespective of the length of their stay in the territory. Local Chinese have dominated the Assembly ever since, a position once monopolized by expatriate Portuguese and Macanese, the offspring of mixed marriages in the territory.

The last legislature elected under Portuguese rule survived the handover and was due to serve until October 2001. Of its 23 members, 8 were directly elected, 8 were indirectly elected by business, labour and community associations, and 7 were appointed by the governor, General Vasco Rocha Vieira (in office 1991–9). During the first 10 years of Macau's life as a Special Administrative Region, the Basic Law provides for an increase in the number of directly elected seats to 12 and indirectly elected seats to 10. The number of appointed seats, now in the gift of Edmund Ho Hau-wah, the pro-Beijing banker whom a

The Lie of the Land

The city of Macau, located on a squat, hilly peninsula, and the two islands of Taipa and Coloane to the south, occupy 8 square miles (21 sq kms) and contained about 425,000 people at the turn of the century. Land is increasing in Macau more rapidly than people. Reclamation projects associated with the new airport and container terminal, the construction of a new city in the historic Praia Grande Bay, and landfills between Taipa and Coloane will add up to another 3 square miles between them. Macau is rapidly changing shape. This is not a new story even if it has become a more dramatic one. Macau has not been the 'sleepy enclave' of journalese since at least the early 1970s when the islands were woken from their slumbers by construction of the Nobre de Carvalho Bridge linking the peninsula with Taipa. A second bridge, even more dramatic in style than the first, was built to cater for airport traffic and opened in 1994.

carefully selected committee chose as Macau's first chief executive in 1999, remains the same. Changes in the make-up of the Legislative Council, as it is now known, are possible after 2009 only if two-thirds of legislators and the chief executive agree.

The middle years of Macau's transition were overshadowed by fiery arguments between Britain and China over Governor Chris Patten's political reforms in Hong Kong. While London and Beijing bickered over the construction of a new airport and other infrastructure projects, Macau quietly built an airport and container port of its own. Initial economic returns from both projects proved disappointing, partly because of Macau's small size, partly because of the Asian financial crisis.

It was not all sweetness and light between Lisbon and Beijing. Security concerns aside, China complained about Portugal's reluctance to promote the use of Chinese language and appoint Chinese to top positions in the civil service. These complaints were a reminder that, in some respects, Macau remained far more of a colonial society on the eve of its transition to Chinese rule than Hong Kong had been. Expatriate Portuguese held on to most of the senior government positions until the very end, conducting official business in a language understood by less than 2 per cent of Macau's 450,000 people.

parting shots

On the eve of their departure from the territory, the Portuguese laid plans to increase this percentage. Though late in the day, they sought to 'Lusify' their last major overseas territory. The aim was to preserve the influence of Portuguese culture in general, and the Macau variety – a unique mix of Portuguese, Macanese and Chinese elements – in particular. Clauses in the Basic Law, one of them stipulating that Portuguese would remain an official language after 1999, another calling for protection of the interests, customs and traditions of the Macanese, promised to help.

China agreed not to impose Chinese nationality after 1999 on the up to 10,000 Macanese of Macau, in some ways the most remarkable fruit of Portugal's long occupation of the territory. Yet the fate of this Cantonese- and Portuguese-speaking minority remained uncertain in the run-up to the transition. Like Macau Chinese born before 1982, to whom Lisbon granted Portuguese citizenship, Macanese could retain their Portuguese passports as travel documents after 1999 but at the cost of forswearing consular protection from the former occupying power when at home in Macau. This mattered less to ethnic Chinese who at least had the advantage of being able to rise to the top of the civil service, now reserved for Chinese citizens. As Eurasians, the Macanese were not entitled to Chinese citizenship and showed little interest in acquiring it if they had been. On the other hand, if they left Macau for Portugal, they faced the prospect of being regarded by society at large as Chinese, despite their Portuguese citizenship.

Portuguese officials, burdened psychologically by the bloody demise of their once mighty empire elsewhere in the world, sought to leave a mark on Macau by stressing that, unlike other European powers, Lisbon had never fought a war with China during its long occupation of the territory. Rather, over the centuries, Macau had become a vital meeting point between different races and cultures. There was no other place like it in the world.

It was a place of 'encounter'; a symbol of tolerance and understanding – one whose survival was in the interests of all concerned; one whose destruction would be a loss for China and the world.

If there was an element of romance to this there was an element of reality, too. They still meet in some of the densely packed streets of Macau where Christian churches rub shoulders with Chinese temples, where cobblestone courtyards give way to restored colonial buildings surrounded by narrow alleys and Chinese markets. The different communities meet in architecture, if not always in person. Macau's diverse cuisine and its ethnic and linguistic complexity are further testimony to an encounter between China and the West which endured far longer than elsewhere in the country.

Whether this means much to the local Chinese and, more to the point, Chinese on the other side of the border, is another matter. If the recovery of Macau is a matter of national pride for China there hardly seems much to be said for preserving Portuguese culture, other than as a museum piece. Moreover Macau is too small to be viable economically: integration and loss of identity seem inevitable. The process is already under way. Land reclamation and building projects begun in the last years of Portuguese rule are redefining the entire shape of the territory. High-speed road and rail lines will soon link it with the rest of Guangdong.

As a financial and service centre for west Guangdong, the least developed part of one of the Mainland's richest provinces, Macau has a modest role to play in China's modernization. But it may be at the cost of China failing to meet the standards of another kind of modernity: willingness to preserve and encourage political and cultural diversity – qualities which enrich a nation as well as the rest of the world.

Manchuguo (1932–45)

Alone among the powers which occupied parts of China in the twentieth century, JAPAN turned its most important piece of Chinese territory into an independent kingdom: 'Manchuguo' – the country of the Manchus.

Tokyo's interest in northeast China, rich in natural resources and contested by RUSSIA, dated from the late nineteenth century. The region was the cockpit of northeast Asia,

affording whoever gained possession of it control over the Korean peninsula, much of north China, eastern Mongolia and the Russian Far East (see HEILONGJIANG; JILIN; LIAONING).

In the early 1930s, Japan was battered by worldwide depression, worried by China's unification under CHIANG KAI-SHEK, and expecting war. Right-wing army officers secured domination over Manchuria despite

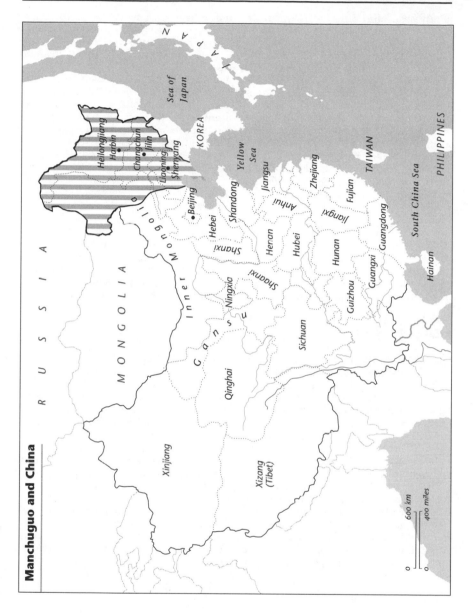

Manchuguo and China

dismay about their tactics in Tokyo. These included blowing up a section of the railway line near Mukden (modern Shenyang, in Liaoning) in September 1931 – the 'Mukden Incident' – and blaming it on Chinese troops. Japan's rapid occupation of the city was followed by the conquest of the rest of Manchuria and, in 1932, the founding of Manchuguo. ZHANG XUELIANG, warlord of Manchuria, and his troops sought refuge south of the Great Wall, in China 'proper', where in 1936 their presence proved decisive in China's domestic politics (see XIAN INCIDENT). Condemnation of Japan's aggression by the League of Nations succeeded only in persuading Tokyo to leave that ineffective world body.

To rule its new state, Japan turned to PU YI, the last Manchu emperor. To strengthen its presence on the ground it looked to immigrants from Korea, then a Japanese colony, and to Japan itself. Despite Manchuguo's supposed independence, Japan remained in control of its 'puppet state'. Among the major powers only Germany, Italy and, of course, Japan recognized the new state, which the Imperial army turned into an industrial war base for Japan's expansion elsewhere in Asia. At the end of the Second World War Manchuria was the most industrialized region in China. It remains the country's industrial heartland at the start of the twenty-first century, though one plagued by the preponderance of ailing state enterprises (see INDUSTRY).

Local Chinese resistance to Japanese rule in Manchuria continued throughout the war, but it took the brief invasion by Soviet troops in 1945, agreed among the Allies at the YALTA CONFERENCE, to topple Manchuguo. Soviet forces plundered the region of as much plant and equipment as their transport facilities could shift to European Russia. They also let Chinese Communist troops infiltrate the Manchurian countryside before KUOMINTANG forces could arrive to begin their abortive attempt to rule the region (see CIVIL WAR).

Mao Zedong (1893–1976)

Like Stalin and Hitler, Mao was a titan and tyrant of the twentieth century who transformed his country, sometimes through extraordinary feats of will and often at terrible cost. Like his fellow dictators he realized long-cherished dreams of national revival only to turn them into nightmares. His GREAT LEAP FORWARD and CULTURAL REVOLUTION cost millions of lives: they were disasters on an epic scale. He raised his people up as no other leader of modern China but left them broken, traumatized and scarred. Much of his long reign was a tragedy – the more so for the fact that it began with an extraordinary revolutionary victory which boosted China's international status, unified continental China and saw spirited attempts to make a new society.

the proper grounds of revolt

Mao was a Marxist from his early twenties, but his rise to power and that of the Party he came to lead say more about the force of the individual in history than any 'inevitable' revolution arising from blind social and economic forces. Will, whether his own or that he attributed to the 'masses', underpinned his philosophy and political career: it was the locomotive of change rather than the consequence. But it was manifested in the specific conditions of China: rural poverty, backwardness and national weakness that Mao, born of a peasant family in HUNAN, was particularly familiar with. He was also familiar with Western political theories, which he studied at school in Changsha, capital of Hunan, from which he graduated in 1918, and during a brief career as Librarian at Beijing University, where he worked alongside LI DAZHAO, a pioneer of Marxism in China. Yet almost alone among the revolutionaries exposed to the great debates of the MAY FOURTH MOVEMENT of 1919, Mao came to ground his revolt in the 'real' conditions of China, developing strategies and techniques which enabled the CHINESE COMMUNIST PARTY to triumph over enormous obstacles.

Mao was present at the formal founding of the Party in 1921 in SHANGHAI, where he represented Hunan. In the mid-1920s he participated enthusiastically in the cooperation between the infant Communist Party and the KUOMINTANG, newly reorganized and revolutionized on the recommendations of the SOVIET UNION and led by SUN YAT-SEN. Mao spent much of this period organizing peasant associations and exploring the revolutionary potential of poor farmers. The conclusions he drew, which can be dated to 1927 – the year CHIANG KAI-SHEK crushed his Communist allies during the first stage of the NORTHERN EXPEDITION in order to keep the national revolution within 'moderate' bounds – were profound. Chief among them was his identification of the peasantry as the main force of the Revolution. This was a controversial matter for a Party which, though shattered by Chiang's suppression and forced to flee into the countryside, nevertheless remained in thrall to a strategy devised in Moscow and wedded to the idea that only workers could make a worthwhile revolution.

In this context, several Party leaders, including Li Lisan (1899–1967) and Wang Ming (1904–47) regarded Mao's emphasis on land reform and the creation of rural bases or soviets (firstly in Jinggangshan and later in Ruijin, both of them remote areas in JIANGXI) as matters of tactics, to be abandoned when the time was ripe. For Mao, however, they were the keys to overthrowing a corrupt and oppressive social order symbolized by the landlord class. Equally important in his view, and that of ZHU DE, his close comrade in arms, was the formation of a Red Army to protect the bases from attack, extend their power and eventually topple the 'reactionary' Kuomintang. In accordance with Party orders, Mao committed his forces to attacks on cities designed to spark an imagined 'high tide' of urban revolt. But the failure of these attacks in Hunan – first in 1927 and again in 1930 – confirmed him in his views about the revolutionary role of the countryside and the errors of an urban-based revolutionary strategy in China.

It was some time before he won the Party over to these ideas or, what amounted to the same thing, gained control over its leadership himself. There were many reverses during the early 1930s as Chiang launched 'anti-bandit' campaigns against the Central Soviet Republic in Jiangxi, where Mao was at first the leading light. From 1932 he was sidelined in his own fief by the 'Bolshevik faction' of the Party whose leaders were close to Moscow and one of whose senior figures was ZHOU ENLAI. These men opposed Mao's tactics of luring Kuomintang forces into the soviet area in order to destroy them. Instead they ordered the Red Army to engage in positional warfare as a prelude to taking control of one or more provinces. The change of tactics proved costly; in 1934 the Party was forced to embark on the Long March.

However, with the Party's fortunes at low ebb and its leaders frequently out of contact with Moscow, Mao began to gain the upper hand over those he blamed for the military and political setbacks in south China. A celebrated Politburo meeting in January 1935 at Zunyi, an isolated town in GUIZHOU, at which Mao's tactics were vindicated by a majority, including Zhou Enlai, marked an important stage in this process.

the road to victory, 1935–49

In October 1935 what remained of Mao's First Front Army reached the relative safety of northern SHAANXI, home of another rural soviet. With the threat of Japanese aggression hanging over China, Mao tempered the Party's revolutionary zeal with stiff doses of patriotism and political moderation. This enabled the Communists to steal the political advantage over Chiang Kai-shek who wanted to crush the Communist 'bandits' first and deal with the Japanese later. The XIAN INCIDENT of 1936, in which Chiang was kidnapped by ZHANG XUELIANG and other generals sympathetic to the new Communist line, forced the government's hand. The Communists and Kuomintang renewed their alliance – this time against a foreign foe rather than domestic class enemies. The SINO-JAPANESE WAR provided Mao and his Party with breathing space of a different kind: it destroyed some of the Kuomintang's best armies and drove Chiang far into the interior, away from his traditional base of support.

China's darkest hours were Mao's most successful. From their new headquarters in bleak, poverty-stricken YANAN, the Communists expanded their area of control through guerrilla warfare and populist policies. Mao stamped his authority on the movement by dint of force of personality, strategic brilliance and cunning. He wrote a series of essays which became part of the canon of his 'Thought'. He launched campaigns to 're-educate' a Party and Red Army whose ranks were swollen by thousands of new adherents drawn to the Communist cause by patriotism and the desire for change. He removed opponents and silenced critics. He managed to inspire people with his revolutionary mission yet comfort them with his apparent moderation and patriotism. And, not least, he married JIANG QING – a union which began in a Yanan cave and yielded a bitter political harvest during the Cultural Revolution.

By 1945, Mao's victory over the Party was complete. As Chairman, a position he held until his death, he was undisputed leader and

Mao Zedong Thought

Mao was the philosopher-king of modern China, a man whose 'Thought' and political power were inseparable, particularly during the Cultural Revolution. But what was his philosophy? It was often as complicated as its author's personality. Mao set great store on will and revolution. Given will, given the proper revolutionary spirit, he believed men and women could conquer their material circumstances and remould reality in accordance with their ideals. Revolution had to be *made*. It was no good waiting for objective historical laws of the kind spoken of by Marx to run their course. And it was no good worrying – as did some Chinese Communists – about conditions for revolution not being ripe. The pace had to be forced; the new era ushered in by violent political action. Mao was a 'voluntarist', an impatient revolutionary determined to act and transform the minds as well as the material circumstances of his people.

Mao maintained that Chinese Communists and ordinary Chinese citizens required 'correct' ideological consciousness and thought. As the author of 'correct' ideology, this usually meant they had to subscribe to his views. For those who, despite Party control of the media and, for long periods, China's isolation from the rest of the world, found this difficult or chose another course, 're-education' and 're-moulding' were available in the form of study programmes, criticism and self-criticism and violent 'struggle sessions'. These political campaigns, common in the Party since Yanan times and a staple of life throughout China after 1949, 'saved' some. But they left far more broken, their lives ruined by ceaseless denunciations and fear. Mao believed the creation of such a climate was essential to attain his goals. A state of constant struggle obtained in the human and natural worlds: there could be no state of rest. Progress, especially revolutionary progress, depended on the existence of creative tension and ceaseless struggle.

The stigma of being declared a 'class enemy' in Mao's China was often deadly and always difficult to reverse. Yet the Chairman had an elastic definition of class. It often depended more on one's attitude towards the Revolution – as defined by Mao and the Party – than on one's economic position in society. Thus there were classes even in socialist society. So much so that, according to Mao, a Cultural Revolution had to be waged in China in the mid-1960s to purge the Party's highest ranks of representatives of the 'bourgeoisie' who were forcing the Revolution into reverse.

The temper of Mao's thought was populist and anti-bureaucratic. The 'mass line' he championed required local Party officials to maintain close contact with the people and transmit their views to the leadership for incorporation into policy. Once the policy was settled the 'mass line' would be evoked again to whip up popular support for the Party. The fear of local officials that the 'masses' would criticize their work, the mixture of paranoia and megalomania often at work in Mao, and the Party's control over most aspects of life – including the courts and the press – meant that in practice the 'mass line' was often a myth.

Mao was opposed to occupational specialization and had an anti-urban, anti-intellectual bias. He was in favour of economic development and modernization, but this line of thought was often submerged by a more impulsive, romantic strain. He was convinced of the innate goodness and revolutionary righteousness of the masses, particularly the Chinese peasant masses whose son he was. They became a metaphor for the *world proletariat*, the force which, correctly led, would topple capitalism across the globe.

He often had much less faith in either the Chinese or other Communist parties. In later life, he believed they had fallen prey to 'revisionism'. A new revolution had to be carried out within their ranks. Its consequences in China – ten years of chaos which ended only with Mao's death – tarnished the Chairman's reputation, drained the Party of its prestige, and even threatened its grip on power.

The post-Mao leadership sought to reverse all of these trends. In the *Historical Resolution on Certain Questions in the History of Our Party Since the Foundation of the People's Republic of China* of 1981, an evaluation of the Chairman and his works, the Party declared that not everything Mao Zedong thought was Mao Zedong Thought. The Great Leap Forward, and the Cultural Revolution in particular, were departures from the Chairman's own precepts of 'seeking truth from facts' and basing policy on experience and China's actual situation. The *Resolution* also claimed Mao Zedong Thought to be the work of other Party leaders apart from Mao. It was a collective enterprise. Nevertheless, Mao Zedong Thought, the 'integration of the universal principles of Marxism-Leninism with the concrete practice of the Chinese Revolution', was the Party's spiritual treasure. The treasure has since been refined by 'Deng Xiaoping Theory' (see DENG XIAOPING/DENG'S THEORIES).

chief theoretician. He still shared power with a circle of fellow revolutionaries, including Zhou Enlai with whom he formed an enduring if unequal partnership which lasted until Zhou's death in 1976. And, as later events, notably the Cultural Revolution, were to prove, he could not always get his own way within the Party – at least at first try. But he was the source of authority and, increasingly, the object of obedience. He was said to have

'sinified Marxism', making it the tool of a Party tempered by war and hardship, genuinely independent of Moscow, and above all *Chinese* (see MARXISM). On Japan's defeat in 1945, Mao's prestige was such that he could lay claim to be a national leader.

Just four years later, he was exactly that – thanks to the brilliance of his military commanders, the decrepitude of the Kuomintang, and a population worn down by years of war

Chinese on Chairman Mao

Most of Chairman Mao's policies were abandoned long ago, but his presence still hovers over China. It could hardly be otherwise given that Mao not only ruled China for decades, he *was* China. He transformed his country, touching the minds and hearts of hundreds of millions, often scarring their lives irreparably.

The Chairman is kept alive in another sense by the Communist Party, which derives its authority from him and is the guardian of his reputation. For all these reasons, Mao will continue to excite fear and fascination, anguish and admiration among Chinese in the future, as he has in the past. The diversity of Chinese verdicts on Chairman Mao is illustrated by the following:

'I think most people have had a pretty good idea about what type of man Mao really was for quite some time now. He cast virtually the whole of China into a state of violence, duplicity and poverty. He was indirectly responsible for more than 100 million people starving to death and for the destitution of a similar number who were forced to abandon their homes and become beggars. Another 100 million were subjected to direct or indirect political persecution and suffered years of spiritual and physical anguish. As a youth I too worshipped Mao Zedong. When I finally woke up to myself, I was overcome with remorse.'

[WEI JINGSHENG, China's most famous dissident of modern times, writing on Mao during his brief spell of freedom in 1993. G. Barmé, *Shades of Mao: The Posthumous Cult of the Great Leader* (M. E. Sharpe, Armonk, New York, 1996).]

'Comrade Mao Zedong was a great Marxist and a great proletarian revolutionary, strategist and theorist. It is true that he made gross mistakes during the Cultural Revolution, but if we judge his activities as a whole, his contributions to the Chinese revolution far outweigh his mistakes. His merits are primary and his errors secondary.'

[From the Communist Party's 'Resolution on Certain Historical Questions in the History of Our Party Since the Founding of the People's Republic' (1981). BBC, *Summary of World Broadcasts*, Part 3, The Far East (2 July 1981). This document, fiercely fought over within the Party, remains the official verdict on the Mao era at the start of the twenty-first century.]

'Hundreds of millions of people were turned into clones of Mao himself. They all believed they belonged to Mao, regardless of whether they were rebelling against the authorities or protecting the power-holders; regardless of whether they declared themselves to be revolutionaries or were branded counter-revolutionaries. It is a truism to say that you get the government you deserve. The collective stupidity of the Chinese meant that they got, and they deserved nothing more than to get, a ruler like Mao Zedong.'

[Li Jie, a Shanghai-based critic, writing in 1989 before the TIANANMEN SQUARE DEMOCRACY MOVEMENT. G. Barmé, *Shades of Mao: The Posthumous Cult of the Great Leader* (M. E. Sharpe, Armonk, New York, 1996).]

'He is undoubtedly an Historical Hero for the following three reasons: In the first place he was a Revolutionary Hero born into a lowly family who brought about a political miracle. Second, he was a Patriotic Hero who led the Chinese people to wipe clean the slate of national humiliations suffered over a century. Third, he was a World-Class Hero in the league of Stalin, Roosevelt and Churchill and, like them, he changed the international political and economic balance of power and had a massive influence on world history in the second half of the twentieth century.'

[He Xin, an outspoken pro-establishment intellectual, who in the early 1990s energetically defended the government's suppression of the Tiananmen Square protests. G. Barmé, *Shades of Mao: The Posthumous Cult of the Great Leader* (M. E. Sharpe, Armonk, New York, 1996).]

'Comrade Deng has resolutely criticized all tendencies to negate entirely Comrade Mao and Mao Thought on the basis of the mistakes he made in his old age. He has said that only by following Mao Thought did the Chinese revolution achieve success. We cannot abandon the banner of Mao Thought. If we do not pursue Mao Thought we will be guilty of a grave historical error . . . We will continue to hold high the banner of Mao Zedong Thought, not only today but in the future as well . . .'

[President JIANG ZEMIN, addressing the official meeting to commemorate the centenary of Mao's birth, December 1993.]

and yearning for change. On the rostrum of Tiananmen, the Gate of Heavenly Peace, in October 1949, Mao, then 55, declared the founding of the People's Republic.

restless revolutionary: Mao in power

It is a measure of Mao's mark on Chinese and indeed world history that, after 1949, China and its people often became mere agents of his thought and casualties of the conflicts, tension and contradictions within his own personality. His power was truly formidable. He sought to change the character of his

people, inspiring them, yet subjecting them to horrific ordeals in the quest to keep his Revolution alive.

This was not apparent during the first years of the People's Republic. Shunned by the West, Mao brought the 'new' China into alliance with the SOVIET UNION and adopted Soviet-style policies of state planning and central control. The era of 'new democracy' was hardly one of moderation for landlords, 'counter-revolutionaries' and other 'hostile elements' (see DEMOCRACY). But many supported the new regime. There was much to be proud of, few hints of the traumas to come, and many suggesting that the Party would stick to its course of rapid, yet rational, economic development and modernization.

The awakening came in the mid-1950s when Mao began to grow dissatisfied with the Soviet way of doing things, and what he came to regard as the bureaucratic, corrupt, elitist nature of China's own brand of Communism. These were not the characteristics that had brought the Party to power. Neither, in his view, were they what power had been won *for*. State building and modernization were important: Mao at his most radical did not deny that. But he believed they did not depend upon a centralized bureaucracy, a highly trained elite and Soviet experts. Rather, China's poor, revolutionary masses could be mobilized to transform their own fortunes and that of their country. Ideological fervour could accomplish more than material rewards; political zeal more than pedestrian planning. Such methods had worked in Yanan; they would do so again, this time throughout China.

The new line was apparent first in AGRICULTURE. In the early 1950s, cooperatives were formed and land collectivized in an effort to boost production and attain political goals of unity and equality. Arguments about the pace of these changes ended in 1956 when Mao intervened to say it must be stepped up. The same year saw the nationalization of INDUSTRY. Another departure concerned policy towards intellectuals, whom Mao encouraged to speak out, or 'bloom', in the ONE HUNDRED FLOWERS policy of 1956. He believed the intelligentsia were fundamentally loyal to the regime. They could be given a little slack; it would help keep the Party in check. He changed his mind when the criticism – slow at first but soon torrential – challenged the basis of Communist rule. Mao felt betrayed. He exacted revenge with a vicious 'Anti-Rightist Movement' which squandered the lives and careers of thousands of writers, scientists and technicians. They were denounced, humiliated and purged. Most of them spent the next 20 years in prison or LABOUR CAMP. Mao never again trusted intellectuals. Neither, fully, has his Party.

References to Mao's 'Thought' had been omitted from the new Communist Party Constitution drawn up in 1956, largely in response to Nikita Khrushchev's 'secret speech' in Moscow of the same year denouncing personality cults – in the Soviet Union's case, that of Joseph Stalin. In these circumstances, the Chinese Party thought it prudent to emphasize collective leadership. But any idea that this meant a weakening in Mao's power was scotched in 1958 when he launched the Great Leap Forward, a catastrophic exercise in utopianism which established his role as a powerful, though flawed, 'people's emperor'.

China was convulsed by zeal as people's communes were established and the country devoted its energy to making a 'leap' into Communism. Mao's idea was to short-circuit the long historical process required to realize socialism which Marx had envisaged, and which had been borne out by experience in the Soviet Union. This was another manifestation of his 'nationalism' or Chineseness. In China, the revolution would be different. The Chinese people were different. They were poor, backward and uneducated. Yet, properly motivated, they had the potential to accomplish revolutionary goals beyond the capacity of others and stand tall in the world.

But they did not have the capacity to live without food. The reverse of Mao's ability to command and motivate was the fear he induced in others when it came to pointing out the negative consequences of his policies. Criticism, even of the most constructive kind, was dangerous – as PENG DEHUAI discovered. With food supplies breaking down and starvation looming in many parts of the country, the defence minister took the Chairman to task over the Leap. The consequences were traumatic. Mao accepted the need for some adjustments, but insisted that the communes and policies associated with them remain. In 1959, Peng and his allies were purged as leaders of an 'anti-Party coup', and China began to starve on a scale she had never done before.

As death stalked the country, and the Leap into Communism quietly gave way to rehabilitation and famine relief, Mao made a modest retreat. In the early 1960s he became preoccupied with developing new theories about the revolution and building up a power base in the PEOPLE'S LIBERATION ARMY, now led by LIN BIAO, from which to project them. His main conclusion was that Communist revolutions could decay: they could fall prey to 'revisionism' as 'capitalist-roaders' rose to the top and pursued a 'bourgeois' line. This had happened in the Soviet Union since the death of Stalin. And it was happening in China under LIU SHAOQI, the number two in the Party and the Chairman's nominated successor. The Chinese Party had to be 're-

Mao in his Own Words

Mao justifies and explains violent peasant revolution in his home province.

'Revolution is not a dinner party, or literary composition or painting or embroidering. It cannot be done so delicately, so gentlemanly, and so gently, kindly, politely, plainly and modestly. Revolution is insurrection, the violent action of one class overthrowing the power of another.'
[Report on an Investigation of the Peasant Movement in Hunan, 1927. C. Brandt, B. Schartz and J. K. Fairbank, *A Documentary History of Chinese Communism* (Atheneum, New York, 1966).]

On the need for the infant Communist Party to develop armed forces of its own.

'From now on we ought to concentrate on the military problem. We must understand fully that political power grows out of the barrel of a gun.'
[Comments on the Report of the Comintern Representative, 1927. This was written following the failure of the 'August Harvest Uprisings': attacks on major cities in south China in 1927. T. Saich with a contribution by Benjamin Yang, *The Rise to Power of the Chinese Communist Party* (M. E. Sharpe, Armonk, New York, 1994).]

Mao explains that the revolution will succeed only if rural base areas, or soviets, are set up.

'The unquestionably correct policies are those of . . . establishing base areas and systematically setting up political power and expanding this power emphasizing the coordination and organization among the Red Army, the guerrilla force, and the broad peasant masses . . . This is the only way to build the confidence of the masses towards the nationwide revolution . . .'
['A Single Spark Can Start a Prairie Fire (1930)', T. Saich with a contribution by Benjamin Yang in *The Rise to Power of the Chinese Communist Party* (M. E. Sharpe, Armonk, New York, 1994).]

Mao believed the Chinese bourgeoisie was revolutionary because it was oppressed by foreign capital. It would therefore join with the proletariat to expel foreign influence and establish 'New Democracy': the 'joint dictatorship of all revolutionary classes'. In economic terms, this transitional stage leading to socialism called for state control of the commanding heights of the economy and a policy of land to the tillers.

'The first step is to change China from a colonial, semi-colonial, and semi-feudal society into an independent, democratic society. The second step is to continue the revolution and establish a socialist society. The first step or stage of this revolution will never – can never – establish a capitalist society under the dictatorship of the Chinese bourgeoisie, but will result in the establishment of a new democratic society under the joint dictatorship of all the revolutionary classes of China to complete the first stage.'
['New Democratic Politics and New Democratic Culture (1940)', T. Saich with a contribution by Benjamin Yang in *The Rise to Power of the Chinese Communist Party* (M. E. Sharpe, Armonk, New York, 1994).]

Mao describes the need for 'rectification' campaigns to remould the Party, a policy perfected in Yanan during the early 1940s and later extended to the rest of China.

'Past errors must be exposed with no thought of personal feelings or face. We must use a scientific attitude to analyse and criticize what has been undesirable in the past so that more care will be taken in later work, so that this will be performed better. Our object in exposing errors and criticizing shortcomings is like that of a doctor in curing a disease. If a person who commits an error, no matter how great, does not bring his disease to an incurable state by concealing it and persisting in the error, and if in addition he is genuinely and honestly willing to be cured, willing to make corrections, we will welcome him so that the disease may be cured and he can become a good comrade.'
['Correcting Unorthodox Tendencies in Learning in the Party and Literature and Art (1942)', C. Brandt, B. Schartz and J. K. Fairbank in *A Documentary History of Chinese Communism* (Atheneum, New York, 1996).]

Mao derides – and undermines – the independent status of artists and intellectuals in a speech whose message blights creativity in China to this day.

'Art for art's sake, art which transcends class or party, art which stands as a bystander to, or independent of, politics does not in actual fact exist. Since art is subordinate to class and party in a society which has classes and parties, it must undoubtedly follow the political demands of those classes and parties . . .'
['Speech at the Yanan Forum on Literature and Art' (1942). B. S. McDougall, *Mao Zedong's 'Talks at the Yan'an Conference on Literature and Art': A Translation of the 1943 text with Commentary* (Michigan Papers in Chinese Studies, No. 39, 1980).]

The Chairman, exalted, acquires his own personality cult.

'In the course of its struggle, the party has produced its own leader, Comrade Mao Zedong . . . Comrade Mao Zedong has creatively applied the scientific theory of Marxism-Leninism – the acme of human wisdom – to China . . . and he has brilliantly developed the theories of Lenin and Stalin . . .'
['Resolution of the CCP on Certain Historical Questions' (1945). T. Saich with a contribution by Benjamin Yang in *The Rise to Power of the Chinese Communist Party* (M. E. Sharpe, Armonk; New York, 1994).]

Mao spells out the new political order in China in 1949.

' "You are dictatorial." Dear Sirs, you are right: that is exactly what we are. The experience of several decades, amassed by the Chinese is: the right of reactionaries to voice their opinions must be abolished, and only the people are allowed to have the right to voice their opinions. Who are the "people"? At the present stage in China, they are the working class, the peasant class, the petty bourgeoisie, and the national bourgeoisie.'
['On the People's Democratic Dictatorship' (1949). C. Brandt, B. Schartz and J. K. Fairbank, *A Documentary History of Chinese Communism* (Atheneum, New York, 1996).]

Mao explains the difference between contradictions *between* the 'people' and *among* the 'people' – that is, those arising in capitalist, and those in socialist societies. He encouraged intellectuals to speak out during the One Hundred Flowers Movement of 1956–7, believing their views would not be 'antagonistic'. He soon changed his mind and launched the 'Anti-Rightist Movement'.

'Contradictions in socialist society are fundamentally different from those in the old societies, such as capitalist society. In capitalist society, contradictions find expression in acute antagonisms and conflicts, in sharp class struggle; they cannot be resolved by the capitalist system itself and can only be resolved by socialist revolution. The case is quite different with contradictions in socialist society; on the contrary they are not antagonistic and can be ceaselessly resolved by the socialist system itself.'

['On the Correct Handling of Contradictions Among the People' (February 1957). Mao, *Selected Works*, Vol. 5, p. 393. (Foreign Language Press, Beijing).]

In 1958, Mao developed the idea of permanent or uninterrupted revolution, of which the Great Leap Forward was but the latest manifestation.

'Our revolutions follow each other, one after another. Beginning with the seizure of power on a nationwide scale in 1949, there followed first the anti-feudal land reform; as soon as the land reform was completed, agricultural cooperativization was begun . . . We must now have a technical revolution, in order to catch up with and overtake England in fifteen years or a bit longer.'

[Cited by Stuart R. Schram, 'Mao Tse-tung and the Theory of the Permanent Revolution, 1958–1969', in *The China Quarterly*, No. 46 (April–June 1971) pp. 226–7.]

In March 1966, Mao urged people to attack the Communist Party and launch a Cultural Revolution. They should do so on the grounds that, in the phrase he coined in 1949, 'to rebel is justified'.

'The Propaganda Department of the Central Committee is the palace of the King of Hell. We must overthrow the palace of the King of Hell and set the little devils free. I have always advocated that whenever the central organs do bad things, it is necessary to call on the localities to rebel and attack the centre.'

[Cited in Roderick MacFarquhar and John K. Fairbank, eds. *The Cambridge History of China*, Vol. 15, Part 2, p. 82 (Cambridge University Press, 1991).]

revolutionized'. If it would take on this task voluntarily, so much the better. If not, its formal leadership and organization would have to be toppled and replaced – violently if necessary.

Mao turns on the Party, 1966–76

This is what happened as Mao turned on the men and the Party he had led to victory 15 years earlier, humbling them, and paving the way for iconoclasm, destruction and violence of a kind that marked a departure from the norms of human society. The early stages of the Cultural Revolution, which began in 1966, marked the apogee of Mao's political and personal power. Alone among twentieth-century dictators, his 'thought', contained in 'the little red book', or *Selected Quotations*, became the basis, not only for political conduct, but for the personal and collective behaviour of hundreds of millions of people. On several occasions in 1966, he reviewed millions of Red Guards in Tiananmen Square, basking in their fervent, adolescent adulation, chants of 'Long Live Chairman Mao!', and vigorous waving of millions of copies of his *Selected Quotations*. Mao was the 'Great Teacher, Great Leader, Great Commander and Great Helmsman'. He was the 'red, red sun' in the hearts of his people. He suffered no institutional curbs. Given China's feudal tradition of authority worship, the idea of absolute obedience came naturally to many of his subjects and was hard to challenge. And, fortified by his new, almost divine status, the Chairman believed his leadership and 'thought' were all that was required to guide the Chinese people in their revolution.

Yet as revolutionary fervour degenerated into factional violence and the threat of anarchy, the Chairman realized something more tangible was required to keep the revolution in line. This was the military. There had to be limits to the 'spontaneity of the masses', and they were to be set by a re-constituted, politically reliable Communist Party backed by a military itself subordinate to Party control. Establishing such arrangements across the country took time and proved costly. Competing rebels egged on by various factions in Beijing, including that led by Jiang Qing, Mao's wife, fought pitched battles that cost thousands of lives. Many government operations came to a halt. Chaos stalked industry. Liu Shaoqi was toppled, and the Chairman found a new successor in Lin Biao, the radically minded defence minister.

The real damage, however, was caused by the absence of restraint on the part of ordinary people as spurious political values governed almost every aspect of behaviour. Intellectuals were persecuted, foreign things condemned as counter-revolutionary, and tradition and custom assaulted at every turn, whether they found expression in museum artifacts, institutions or people. Throughout much of the mayhem of the late 1960s, the Chairman remained silent and sometimes unseen, content to manipulate a divided leadership from behind the scenes in time-honoured imperial fashion. He was surprised by the apparent defection and death in a plane crash of Lin Biao in September 1971, but if he felt anything about the fate of Liu Shaoqi and other revolutionary veterans, for whose death he was responsible, or the thousands of others who died violent deaths, he kept it to himself. In this sense, at least, he was truly above the people.

Mao was less ambiguous on the FOREIGN POLICY front. Serious border clashes between Chinese and Soviet troops in 1969, the product of years of polemical abuse between Beijing and Moscow and unresolved frontier disputes, exposed China's vulnerability to attack from its northern neighbour. Mao sought refuge in rapprochement with the UNITED STATES, JAPAN and Western Europe, a policy which culminated in President Richard Nixon's visit to Beijing in 1972. The Chairman did not live to see China's diplomatic and economic integration with the developed world that followed. Neither is it likely he would have approved of many of its consequences. But he began China's opening to the United States and, unlike the case with many of his other policies, his successors did not depart from it.

Mao the man and Mao the myth

The era of Mao Zedong came to an end, not so much with his own death in September 1976 as with the arrest a few weeks later of the 'GANG OF FOUR', led by his widow who sought to succeed him. Even then, HUA GUOFENG, whom the Chairman preferred to both radicals and moderates, clung to Cultural Revolution-style goals if not methods. It took DENG XIAOPING, purged twice by Mao, to fill the leadership and policy vacuums when he returned for good in 1977. He soon sidelined Hua and led China rapidly away from Mao's obsession with political zeal, into a new world of reform, economic modernization and engagement with the international community.

The 'Emperor's' Private Life

Mao's extraordinary political career was accompanied by personal privileges and excesses of the kind many traditional Chinese emperors enjoyed. This had long been known to a select few in China, but it only became public knowledge – outside China – in 1994 when Li Zhisui (1920–95), the Chairman's personal physician, published a memoir. Li's portrayal of Mao's court was utterly feudal. Almost all Party leaders, and especially Zhou Enlai, were cast as courtiers desperate to ingratiate themselves with a leader who delighted in creating an atmosphere of suspicion, rivalry and fear. Mao refused to be ruled by time: he frequently slept all day and worked at night. He spent many hours lolling around on a huge bed reading works of ancient Chinese statecraft.

When he was not reading he amused himself with peasant girls, subscribing to a traditional Chinese belief that making love to young women can prolong a man's life. In the process, Mao contracted venereal disease. He declined to have it treated, even though Li recommended that he did so to protect his sexual partners. 'If it's not hurting me, then it doesn't matter. Why are you getting so excited about it?' the Chairman asked his physician. Mao's favourite companion towards the end of his life was Zhang Yufeng, a train attendant whom he met in 1960. Power rather than anything else seems to have attracted women to Mao. He rarely bathed and never brushed his teeth, preferring to rinse his mouth with tea in true peasant fashion.

Mao's journeys around China were decidedly more regal. When he travelled by train, railway schedules across China were dislocated for up to a week. When he flew, which he did rarely, the entire nation's air traffic was grounded. Dr Li's revelations, kept from most Chinese people by strict censorship, but greatly enjoyed by many of those able to get hold of them, were bitterly attacked by Communist leaders. Rival 'memoirs', casting Mao in favourable light, were hastily published. Questions can be raised over the accuracy of some parts of Li's book because for the most part it consists of the recollections of its elderly author. But *The Private Life of Chairman Mao* provides a generally credible account of life around the Chairman, one that makes its subject more human and more terrifying.

Yet at the start of the new century, Mao's presence hovers over China still. Almost all his policies have been abandoned, but his Party remains in power. His reputation has been cut down to size, but he has been spared the posthumous disgrace that seems his due. An official verdict on his role, published after much argument within the Party in 1981, said Mao had made 'gross mistakes', but that they were secondary to his contributions. China is in many respects a different society from what it was in Mao's day, but his vast mausoleum, its ticket office often besieged by visitors, still lies in the middle of Tiananmen Square. His giant portrait hangs from the Gate of Heavenly Peace, and his 'thought' is still enshrined in both state and Communist Party constitutions. Mao remains the supreme icon of the Chinese Revolution: a symbol of its victory against overwhelming odds, and the architect of the achievements of the early years of the People's Republic. His status is secure as long as China's leaders need to draw on the Chairman to boost their own legitimacy.

More surprising, but no less true, is the fact that the Chairman's image remains a generally positive one in the minds of many of his countrymen. On several occasions during the 1980s and 1990s a 'cult of Mao' surfaced, apparently in reaction to the rise in crime, corruption, inflation and other problems associated with the free market reforms of his successors. Peculiarly, the era of Mao was seen as calm and stable by comparison. Even those who endured the Great Leap and the Cultural Revolution seemed to feel no need to destroy his official reputation.

Partly this is because Mao's crimes have not been exposed in the way those of Hitler and Stalin have. *Their* deeds have long been the subject of examination: they are widely regarded as negative examples, as leaders of a kind that must never be allowed to seize power in their countries again. There have been no such developments in China. There has been no reckoning; no thorough investigation of the Chairman's reign. Such an undertaking has not been permitted on the grounds that it might cause the Communist Party to be swept into oblivion along with the reputation of its former leader.

But, at least in the 1990s, there was also a popular feeling that such an exercise would not be worthwhile. Mao was still too close in time; his stature as the great, if terrifying, 'people's emperor' still overpowering, despite shocking revelations about his private life that circulated among intellectuals. Given these political, personal and psychological imperatives, many Chinese appeared to feel that selective amnesia was the best way of dealing with the historical burden of achievements and disasters, exhilaration and excesses bequeathed by Chairman Mao.

Marxism

Abandoned by most governments that embraced it during the course of the old century, Marxism remains the core ideology of the People's Republic of China at the start of the new, dominating the language if not the conduct of politics. This state of affairs would have astonished Karl Marx as much as it perplexes contemporary observers confronted by changes in the wider world and the capitalist-style reforms that transformed China's economy during the 1990s. In this context, Beijing's insistence that it remains a Marxist state suggests, again as Beijing insists, that Marxism has been enlarged and enriched by practice in China. Alternatively, it indicates that the CHINESE COMMUNIST PARTY has abandoned Marxism while cynically retaining Leninism to justify its dictatorship. Perhaps both statements are true; at the start of the century a conclusive answer seems elusive. The same cannot be said of the impact on China of Marxism, or what many Chinese chose to *call* Marxism, during the previous 100 years.

the appeal of Marxism

Early twentieth-century Chinese publications contained scattered references to Marx, but the meaning of his ideas did not become apparent to Chinese radicals until the Bolshevik Revolution of 1917 and the creation of the SOVIET UNION. Before Lenin's victory, ANARCHISM had more adherents among revolutionaries than socialism. After it, the appeal of socialism soared, largely because the Bolshevik leader actually *made* a revolution, turning a vast, agricultural country long ruled by autocrats into a new, revolutionary nation state. Marx and Lenin – 'Marxism-*Leninism*' – seemed a winning combination, particularly since liberal democratic ideas appeared to have died on the battlefields of the First World War. The Soviet Union's renunciation of most privileges seized from China under the UNEQUAL TREATIES of the nineteenth century confirmed the impression that a new era had begun.

These developments inspired LI DAZHAO, CHEN DUXIU and other leaders of the Nationalist intellectual upheaval known as the MAY FOURTH MOVEMENT of 1919. In study societies and in periodicals, Li and Chen pioneered the propagation of Marxism. Both men saw Lenin's adaptation of the creed as China's salvation from warlord rule, exploitation by the powers, poverty and backwardness.

So, naturally, did Lenin. In the early 1920s agents of the Comintern (the Communist International based in Moscow) travelled to China in an effort to extend the world revolution and protect its Russian heartland. Lenin said the proletariat must link up with the 'national bourgeoisie' in developing countries to overthrow foreign privilege and militarist rule. This would weaken the capitalist world whose governments had built empires overseas to escape the economic crises and political revolutions Marx had identified as their fate.

One consequence of Lenin's policy in China was the formation of a Communist Party in SHANGHAI in 1921, which included MAO ZEDONG among its founders. Another was the Party's tactical alliance with SUN YAT-SEN'S KUOMINTANG, newly reorganized along Leninist lines and now committed to national revolution. The KMT's flirtation with Marxist revolution did not last long, but it retained its Leninist structure for more than 60 years until, long after fleeing to TAIWAN, it at last yielded to demands for more democracy.

China's Communists, who numbered a few hundred in the early 1920s, were junior partners in the alliance with the Kuomintang. Most were bourgeois intellectuals active in major cities. Others, such as ZHOU ENLAI and DENG XIAOPING, who joined the Party in France, became Communists while studying or working overseas. For most of these men, as for Marx himself, politics mattered more than philosophy; changing the world more than understanding it. They valued Marxism for its *utility* not its beauty or consistency as an intellectual doctrine.

Not that the philosophy was unattractive. Marx identified universal laws: by adhering to them China would enter the mainstream of world development, a comforting thought in a country long used to thinking of itself as the centre of the civilized world. Yet if Marxism provided convincing explanations of China's predicament – that is, the country was exploited by domestic reactionaries in league with imperialists – it offered even more powerful solutions: the overthrow of both by the 'revolutionary masses' led by the Communist Party. For the most part, Marxism appealed because it promised to work. It substituted the notion of movement, progress and perpetual struggle for the stability and harmony cherished by CONFUCIANISM. And it placed the

goal and ideal of society in the future rather than, as the Sage had insisted, in the past.

Marx, Lenin and Mao

It did not do so without considerable doctrinal change, much of it the work of Mao. The route to the Chairman's supremacy led via his insistence that peasants, rather than workers, were the main revolutionary class in China; that LAND REFORM was needed to win them over; that rural soviets had to be created to administer the Revolution; and that a Red Army was necessary to protect it (see MAO ZEDONG; CHINESE COMMUNIST PARTY; ARMIES; PEOPLE'S LIBERATION ARMY). These ideas, many of which combined Marxism with the practice of China's traditional peasant rebellions, took shape during the Party's years in the wilderness – years of crushing defeats at the hands of CHIANG KAI-SHEK in the late 1920s, the perils of the LONG MARCH in 1933–4, and the hardship of life in YANAN during the late 1930s and 1940s. But by 1945, thanks largely to the SINO-JAPANESE WAR, the Communists controlled a larger area of China than ever before, Mao had become undisputed leader, and his vision of Marxism – Marxism-Leninism-*Mao Zedong-Thought* – was adopted as Party orthodoxy. With the Communist victory in the CIVIL WAR in 1949, this vision became the guiding ideology of the entire country.

Mao differed from Marx and Lenin in more than just revolutionary tactics. He was a nationalist leader as well as a Marxist revolutionary. The Chinese Revolution was about national independence and territorial integrity as well as overthrowing the traditional social order. The Party triumphed over its enemies at home in 1949 only to be beset by foes abroad, chiefly the UNITED STATES and, later, thanks to Mao's row with Moscow, the Soviet Union. In this context of Cold War abroad and Communist dictatorship at home, many found that simply being Chinese meant accepting Mao's leadership along with his version of Marxism. Some doubtless did so out of genuine admiration for both; some probably felt they had no choice. Ultimately the issue involved questions of patriotism and loyalty, and of national identity or 'Chineseness' – as the new regime never failed to point out.

For Mao the Marxist, correct consciousness was the key to action. This was acquired through familiarity with China's 'actual conditions', usually acquired by learning from the peasants, and Mao's own teachings, which were said to combine these conditions with the 'universal truths of Marxism-Leninism'. Those who, through 'errors' or ignorance, could understand neither had to be 're-educated' – often in LABOUR CAMPS.

Errors of this kind were first 'rectified' on any scale during the Party's years in Yanan when Mao attained his dominance. After 1949, Yanan-style political campaigns, denunciations, self-criticisms and 'struggle sessions' were waged regularly throughout the country in an attempt to enhance ideological uniformity, ensure political consensus and sustain revolutionary momentum. The destruction of Mao's opponents within the Party was an equally important goal.

Mao's Marxism differed from that prevalent in Moscow, the headquarters of the world Communist movement for most Marxists during the early 1950s. One aspect of this was the Chairman's emphasis on will and revolution. He believed that, once infused with revolutionary spirit and led correctly, men and women could triumph over their material circumstances, however unfavourable such circumstances might be. Will could re-shape reality. Mao was a 'voluntarist' who felt it was not always necessary for the historical 'laws' identified by Marx to work their course before change occurred. Those who waited until conditions were 'ripe' to wage revolution might wait for ever; in China, revolution had to be *made* to happen. The GREAT LEAP FORWARD of 1958–60, an attempt to realize Communism overnight, was a disastrous example of a 'forced' revolution.

The very failure of the Leap prompted Mao to devote more time to theoretical studies and these led, in turn, to a deeper rift with Moscow (see SOVIET UNION). By inclination, the Chairman opposed occupational specialization and nursed a suspicion of urban life in general and intellectuals in particular. His thinking was populist and anti-bureaucratic in nature. He favoured economic development and modernization, but was not prepared to countenance either if the cost was inequality or the creation of new political and professional elites.

This is exactly what he believed had happened in the Soviet Union under Khrushchev. And it was what he feared was happening in China during the 1960s under LIU SHAOQI, DENG XIAOPING, and others in the Party who opposed his more impulsive, charismatic approach to revolution. 'Bourgeois revisionists' had taken over the Chinese Party;

they and their ideas had to be struck down in a CULTURAL REVOLUTION to avoid regression. So far from being complete, the victory of revolution in China was still at issue: it depended on the outcome of a merciless 'two-line struggle' within the Party. Beginning in the mid-1960s China became a 'great school of Mao Zedong Thought' and a theatre of political conflict. The ensuing disruption, chaos and cruelty did much to destroy popular faith in Marxism, Chairman Mao and the Communist Party itself (see CULTURAL REVOLUTION).

Marxism in the era of reform

When Mao died in 1976 his successors declared the Cultural Revolution theoretically unjustified and a national disaster. A Party Resolution of 1981 stated that the Chairman had committed 'grave errors' towards the end of his life. He had become 'arrogant with power'. However, his mistakes were those of 'a great proletarian revolutionary': they were temporary aberrations from 'Mao Zedong Thought', which was found to be a fruit of the Party's 'collective wisdom' and its 'valuable spiritual asset'. Mao's thought, like his entire life, was inseparable from the triumphs and the tragedies of Communist Party rule. It could not be abandoned simply because of the mistakes or the death of its founder without the Party itself stepping down from power, and that was never contemplated.

However, Mao's thought could be reinterpreted. Under Deng Xiaoping it was in order to justify greater private ownership, free market reforms, and engagement with the international capitalist economy of the kind Mao had spent much of his career attacking. The pursuit of national rejuvenation – now defined as rapid economic modernization by almost any means available – gained the upper hand over class struggle and the search for ideological purity.

But it did not replace them, at least as far as the Party was concerned. Under Deng, as under his successor JIANG ZEMIN, there were limits to China's retreat from Marx and Mao. They took the form of the 'four principles' promulgated in 1979 and later incorporated into China's constitution. Still binding at the start of the new century, they provide for the Party's dictatorship, adherence to socialism and the ideological supremacy of Marxism-Leninism and Mao Zedong Thought.

The four principles accompanied 'new interpretations' of Marxist-Leninist and Mao Zedong Thought which emphasized that

Chinese Communists must 'seek truth from facts' (a phrase of Mao's that Deng commandeered in the 1970s) and understand that 'practice is the sole criterion of truth'. This pragmatic approach attempted, on the one hand, to protect reformers in the Party from those who insisted the correct way to develop socialism had already been laid down by Marx and his chief disciples, Lenin, Stalin and Mao. On the other, it provided for the rapid abandonment of policies perceived not to work – either because they failed to develop the economy, now the core task of Marxism and chief purpose of socialism – or because they weakened or challenged Party rule.

New slogans were devised to justify the economic transformation wrought by free market reforms and opening to the outside world. China was said to be pursuing 'socialism with Chinese characteristics'. It was building a 'socialist market economy'. The reality behind both was that the People's Republic of China was still in the 'initial stage' of socialism in which the chief task was that of developing the economy by a variety of means, and at various speeds, depending on local conditions. Though never abandoned, the goal of common prosperity was postponed indefinitely. Soon after Deng's death in 1997, these ideological novelties were defined as 'Deng Xiaoping Theory', and added to Marxism-Leninism and Mao Zedong Thought in the Party's charter. Party members were instructed to study them since Deng Xiaoping Theory was the 'Marxism of contemporary China'.

These ideological gymnastics did not occur in a vacuum. They took place against the background of leadership struggles (including the fall in 1987 and 1989 respectively of HU YAO-BANG and ZHAO ZIYANG, reforming Party leaders who fell foul of veteran hardliners), political unrest (notably the TIANANMEN SQUARE DEMOCRACY MOVEMENT of 1989), and the collapse of socialism outside China. China's ideologues had to contend with a moving target at home as well as overseas.

That they bothered to do so at a time when Marxism was being abandoned almost everywhere showed the importance still attached to doctrine in Chinese politics. Dominant yet not subject to popular election, the Communist Party's legitimacy was seen to depend on its mastery of a 'correct' body of theory. The idea that the politically virtuous should rule and that only the doctrinally adept could lead the country successfully dates back to traditional times when officials had to master

Confucianism. Similar principles, though a different doctrine, are still at work, long years after the collapse of imperial rule.

What is harder to determine at the start of the new century is whether Marxism in its various Chinese guises means much beyond providing a sanction for one-party rule. Certainly it seems shorn of its messianism: few Chinese appear to believe Marxism defines the destiny of all mankind. Indeed, few ordinary Chinese appear to believe in Marxism at all. Many prefer the consolation of RELIGIONS, much to the Party's concern.

Opponents of China's reforms, such as DENG LIQUN, based their critiques on Marxism, but so, in a different way, did reform's defenders. Beyond these polemics, and the obligatory doctrinal references in Communist Party documents, there is little evidence that Marxism is valued by intellectuals or ordinary people. It is an undeniable mercy that the Party no longer insists every Chinese believes in Marxism. It remains a considerable limit on individual freedom that the Party forbids anyone from openly challenging it, especially those parts of the doctrine used to justify the Party's monopoly of power and its current policies. Those who do so can expect to be punished (see DISSIDENTS).

Whatever meaning 'Marxism-Leninism, Mao Zedong Thought and Deng Xiaoping Theory' might have in terms of domestic politics, it appears to count for little in China's FOREIGN POLICY. At the start of the reform era, Beijing abandoned its revolutionary mission at home *and* abroad. Such fraternal ties with Communist parties overseas that survived the Cultural Revolution were not developed. Little was said of the world victory of the proletariat and, if the future did belong to socialism, as Chinese leaders occasionally said it did, the future seemed so far off that capitalists had nothing to worry about.

At the start of the new era, the success of China's entire reform programme depends upon accommodation with the international capitalist economy rather than its overthrow, as desired by Mao and his fellow radicals. In this context an economic downturn in the capitalist West or Asia would spell disaster for China; it would not be welcomed as the long-awaited international crisis of capitalism foretold by Marx. This is why Beijing was so quick to contribute to the financial aid package organized by the International Monetary Fund in 1997 to deal with the Asian financial crisis. It was striking to see a 'Marxist' government shell out foreign exchange to patch up the international financial order. But perhaps no more so than to see one recover sovereignty over HONG KONG the same year, and then seek to preserve the territory as an emblem and exponent of world capitalism.

May Fourth Movement (1919)

The May Fourth Movement of 1919, a culmination of two decades of intellectual ferment and desperation over China's weakness, gave birth to modern Chinese nationalism. Students took to the streets in the country's first example of mass urban protest. Intellectuals debated solutions to China's problems with a passion – and a freedom – they would not experience again during the century. It was a liberating experience for intellectuals who had traditionally been servants of the Confucian state. Rural China, and even many of those who lived in the cities, 'slept' through the movement: its appeal and 'modernity' could not easily overcome custom, tradition and rudimentary communications. But the May Fourth Movement was China's equivalent of Europe's Enlightenment. Its ideas and ideals echoed down the century and retain their appeal.

May 4 1919 was the day protests broke out in BEIJING at the decision of the Versailles Peace Conference, which concluded the First World War, to award Germany's pre-war privileges in SHANDONG to JAPAN rather than restore them to China. Tokyo, like Beijing, had joined the First World War on the Allied side. About 3,000 students, many of them from Beijing University, gathered at the Tiananmen Gate to show their disgust over a decision Chinese government delegates in Versailles seemed ready to comply with. The protestors beat up an official deemed to be pro-Japanese, and set fire to a cabinet minister's residence.

The government, led by Duan Qirui (1865–1936), broke up the protests and arrested hundreds of students. These measures were far milder than those adopted by the Communist government 70 years later when faced with much bigger protests in Beijing (see TIANANMEN SQUARE DEMOCRACY MOVEMENT). But they sparked further demonstrations which spread to scores of Chinese cities. Public indignation over the fate of the country ran high. The age of mass urban politics had arrived; and the government was forced to free the demonstrators it had detained, and refuse to sign the Versailles accord. In this sense alone, May Fourth marks a watershed in Chinese politics.

What makes the movement even more significant is the fact that the protests associated with it were an expression of intellectual upheaval during the early years of the century in which thinkers of all persuasions sought answers to their country's (and often their own personal) dilemmas at a time of national crisis and cultural decay. About the only thing they could agree on was China's parlous fortunes in a predatory world.

The country had cast off Manchu QING DYNASTY rule, but was still in the thrall of the CONFUCIANISM which hindered renewal. The republican ideals of 1911 (see REPUBLICAN REVOLUTION) had come to grief on the rocks of warlordism (see WARLORDS), and the lingering imperial pretensions of so-called presidents, notably the late YUAN SHIKAI. Many felt a new *culture* was required as much as a new politics if China was to survive in a fiercely competitive international environment. The young would have to take over from the old. Iconoclasm was a necessary prelude to rejuvenation.

Controversies raged in newspapers, journals and university classrooms across the country as debate about the future took an autonomous, unofficial form it had seldom known before and has not seen since. A leading figure in the ferment in academe was Cai Yuanpei (1868–1940), who as president of Beijing University hired some of the country's brightest, most radical intellectuals as lecturers. Revolution scored a speedy victory on the linguistic front: writers insisted on using BAI HUA – the vernacular, or 'plain speech' – for their discourse instead of confining 'high thoughts' to the arcane, ancient literary script. Almost overnight, China eradicated a mental gap that had existed since ancient times between what was *said* and what was *written*.

Consensus was not won so easily on political, ideological and philosophical solutions to the country's crisis. Western science and democracy – depicted in writings as 'Mr Sai' (science) and 'Mr De' (democracy) – carried enormous appeal, despite the fact that these attributes had propelled foreigners to China's shores and now threatened its survival. ANARCHISM also had its adherents. For HU SHI, a key May Fourth figure, the pragmatism involved in solving individual problems was a better way of remaking China than the wholesale adoption of 'isms' or 'systems'.

Yet this cautious, prosaic approach lacked the dynamic, romantic appeal of MARXISM which, shaped by Lenin, had just fashioned a revolution in Russia. LI DAZHAO, a future founder of the Chinese Communist Party, and CHEN DUXIU, the Party's first general secretary, found in Marxism a link between democracy and science. Here was the most 'modern' political creed of all, and one which had just triumphed in a large, backward agricultural country long subject to feudal rule. Marxism showed that external evils, rather than solely Chinese ones, were responsible for the country's fate. It combined a romantic appeal for action with the comforting view that history was 'on one's side'. The new creed was propagated by small discussion groups in various Chinese cities and, in July 1921, emissaries from the new SOVIET UNION helped found the CHINESE COMMUNIST PARTY in SHANGHAI.

Because the Party went on to defeat its enemies and capture power in 1949, it is easy to view the introduction and popularization of Marxism as the most significant legacy of May Fourth. Easy, but wrong. Marxism's appeal as an intellectual creed in early twentieth-century China was due partly to the fact that it addressed the problem of *political power* more effectively than its rivals. It was made more persuasive still by Soviet support for the Nationalist Revolution of the late 1920s; MAO ZEDONG'S refashioning of its tenets to suit China's conditions; and sweeping Communist victories in many parts of the world following the Second World War. But the May Fourth Movement was bigger than Marxism. It was a movement of criticism and national soul searching which flourished amid the breakdown of established values and institutions, and penetrated almost every area of intellectual and political life. It was a function of China's political weakness, which it sought to address. Principal protagonists sought ways to make the Chinese state strong and representative.

The fact that the movement led, eventually, to the triumph of Marxism accomplished the first goal, but only at the expense of the second. In a sense 'Mr Sai' triumphed at the expense of 'Mr De'. Almost ever since, intellectuals have been trying to find ways of making the Chinese state *weaker* so as to allow genuine individual freedoms, creativity, criticism and nationalism to emerge (see HUMAN RIGHTS; DEMOCRACY). The massive pro-democracy unrest of 1989 was one of the most spectacular examples. As in 1919, the protests were crushed. But they showed that, while the Communist Party has sought to monopolize the meaning of the May Fourth Movement, the ideals of freedom and democracy it spawned remain a powerful source of inspiration, and a formidable enemy of authoritarianism.

media

An instrument of change but also one of its principal casualties; a source of public enlightenment yet a far more powerful tool of government control – the fate of the media in China is a reflection of their importance in a culture where knowledge and information have always been keys to power. So much so that Communist Party rule is inseparable from control of the media. Press freedom in the Mainland of the kind enjoyed in TAIWAN and HONG KONG would end the Party's domination of political life. It might even sweep it into oblivion.

nationalism and the need to know

Mass media had a revolutionary effect the moment they appeared in China during the 1890s. Non-government newspapers, magazines and pamphlets of the era were media with a small audience that strained the adjective 'mass'. But they challenged the idea that politics was the business of a trained elite. They threatened the secrecy at the heart of decision-making. And they created 'public opinion' along with pressure groups to influence it. As such they constituted a powerful threat to Manchu rule.

The birth of modern communications in China, and thus of modern politics, arose from a need to know. In the 1890s China was in crisis. Defeat in the war against JAPAN of 1894–5 provoked national angst. The world was in flux, China's fate in the balance. What was going on? What was the government doing about it? More important, what *should* the government do about it?

A host of new publications met the need for description and prescription. Most were products of the reform movement led by LIANG QICHAO, KANG YOUWEI and other radicals. Modern newspapers pre-dated their activities: foreigners founded many titles in the TREATY PORTS earlier in the century. But whereas the treaty port press concentrated on local and commercial news and left politics alone, the new publications of the 1890s appeared in inland as well as coastal cities, covered national and international news, and made a deep impact among educated Chinese.

Liang was to the fore in spreading their message. He pioneered a revolution in style as well as content: modern punctuation and headlines made their debut in literary Chinese, increasing the impact of what was being conveyed. And what was conveyed – the need for a fundamental political overhaul, for constitutional rule and democracy – was powerful stuff.

Modern Chinese journalism was polemical from the start. Its purpose, like that of the new schools and study societies of the QING DYNASTY'S final years, was to *change* China. Its role was to mobilize and empower, to serve as a bridge between people and government of the kind reformers believed to be the hallmark of a modern nation.

The fate of the media fluctuated with the reformist cause. Many of their exponents were captured, executed or fled when the EMPRESS DOWAGER crushed the 100 Days Reform movement of 1898. Their enterprise revived with the foundation of the Republic in 1911, which saw a sharp rise in the number and variety of publications. The MAY FOURTH MOVEMENT of intellectual renewal which began in 1919 produced even more. The battle for the intellectual soul of China was waged in a host of new titles whose message, often conveyed in BAI HUA, or plain speech, gained immediacy for a readership thirsting for change. May Fourth was in essence an explosion of discourse, a dazzling, diverse, *public* discussion of issues and creeds. In this sense, as an airing of ideas, it was of greater significance than the reform movement of the 1890s.

rise of the Party press

Partly this was because of the rise of MARXISM in the Chinese mind. Partly it was because May Fourth paved the way for the media's first role in popular, rather than merely intellectual, mobilization. The KUOMINTANG was able to unify China during the NORTHERN EXPEDITION in the late 1920s because of its new sense of mission, a powerful army and Soviet aid and advice. But popular mobilization in the cause of revolutionary nationalism played a large part. And much of this was the work of the Party-controlled media: propaganda was inseparable from political power.

Both the Nationalists and the Communists – rivals following the bloody end of their alliance in 1927 – were aware of this. Primarily their struggle was a military one. But it was also one of ideas and, more importantly, of getting those ideas across. Both parties created and controlled media to achieve this purpose. And in both Kuomintang- and Communist-controlled areas censorship was customary, the penalties of defying it serious. From its infancy journalism was a risky profession in China.

Yet once in government the Nationalists proved only partially effective censors. For one thing they failed to crush the Communists and thus eliminate an alternative voice. For another their control over many parts of country was fragile: even during the SINO-JAPANESE WAR regional militarists allowed media under their control to criticize CHIANG KAI-SHEK. The same was true during the CIVIL WAR. Despite martial law, Chiang never quite stamped out dissent.

It was a different matter when the Nationalists fled to TAIWAN. From 1949 the island's media were obliged to speak with one voice – the government's. This remained the case for almost 40 years. The situation changed when Taiwan's politics did: almost immediately after martial law was abolished in 1987, scores of new newspapers appeared. Lively, free media have been a key feature of rapid democratization in Taiwan ever since.

mouth and ears of the Party

The Communist Party proved more adept at monopolizing and manipulating the media than the Kuomintang. The very phrase 'Party journalism' makes the issue plain: Party first, journalism second. MAO ZEDONG and others spelt out the role of the media on numerous occasions. Their successors continue to do so. Media are the Party's mouthpiece.

But not just the mouthpiece. If the first task of press and broadcasting is to transmit Party policies, the second is scarcely less important: providing intelligence for the leadership. Almost from the beginning of Party journalism, its practitioners have filed two kinds of report: one for publication; the other for circulation to the leadership on a restricted basis according to its sensitivity. This was the case as early as the 1930s in the JIANGXI Soviet when the Red China News Agency, forerunner of the Xinhua News Agency, was founded. It remains the case at the start of the new era, despite numerous shifts in Party policy and revolutionary changes in media technologies.

Under Communism all news is value-laden, avowedly and necessarily so. In fact it is rarely 'news' at all. Publishing the details of a Party or government report usually takes precedence over covering 'something that happened yesterday' – a common definition of 'news' outside China. 'Protocol news', such as a meeting between a Party leader and a foreign statesman, generally enjoys priority over an event with no direct relevance to domestic politics, however important it might be deemed outside China. Objectivity and impartiality are as impossible as they are undesirable. The media are instruments of a class – under Communist rule the proletariat or, rather, its representative, the Communist Party. The function of journalism is social engineering.

In this scheme of things there can be no question of independently owned newspapers or freedom of the press. Neither can there be anything beyond mild criticism of Party rule or Party policies. Both would place journalism before the Party, a grave political error, and a challenge to orthodoxy every bit as serious as the one Liang Qichao's new journalism posed to the Manchus.

toeing the line, testing the line
After 1949 the Party imposed its view of the media throughout China. Private newspapers and radio stations were closed, emasculated or taken over. All were required to adhere to the line set down in the *People's Daily*, the organ of the Central Committee, and take copy from the Xinhua News Agency, the chief supplier of domestic and international news.

Media organizations were converted into DANWEI – socialist work units where control was facilitated through the Party's monopoly over the supply of everything from editorial assignments to housing benefits. In these circumstances, and those created by the repeated political campaigns of the 1950s, self-censorship accomplished what state censorship could not. The media expanded under Communist rule but generally stayed in line.

The question was: whose line? The end of the ONE HUNDRED FLOWERS MOVEMENT ended attempts by more courageous journalists, such as Liu Binyan (1925–), to criticize the Party in print, but contributed to strains within the leadership over the nature of the Chinese Revolution. They came to the surface in the CULTURAL REVOLUTION whose opening shots were fired in a press which, though tightly controlled, was not monolithic. Shanghai papers took the lead in promoting Mao's revolution in the summer of 1966; Beijing's resisted but were forced to follow suit.

The end of the Cultural Revolution and the rise of DENG XIAOPING raised questions about reform of the press as well as the economy. Many believed an independent, or at least more critical, press was the best defence against a repetition of past errors. DEMOCRACY WALL advocates favoured the first option. They went some way towards realizing it with posters and unofficial magazines. Reformers in the leadership preferred the second. Deng appointed Hu Jiwei (1916–) editor of the *People's Daily* with a brief to champion reform and expose its opponents. Both campaigns fell foul of the leadership's fear that abandoning Party journalism would end their grip on power. The police crushed Democracy Wall. Conservatives led by DENG LIQUN ousted Hu and other 'liberals' at the *People's Daily*.

Yet the battle for more freedom raged throughout the 1980s as reformists and conservatives struggled for political control. Free market reforms made ever deeper inroads into daily life. News of the outside world increased. Once Deng placed political reform on the agenda, press reform seemed close behind.

Hu Jiwei championed the cause by drafting a press law setting limits to the Party's power. Liu Binyan and two other leading journalists, Wang Ruowang (1917–) and Wang Ruoshui (1926–), demanded that independent voices be heard. In Shanghai, editors of the *World Economic Herald* tested the frontiers more directly, covering sensitive topics with a candour that owed much to the patronage of ZHAO ZIYANG, the reformist Party leader.

The TIANANMEN SQUARE DEMOCRACY MOVEMENT marked the climax of this campaign for press and other freedoms. The demonstrations would have been less of a challenge had the Party not lost control of the media. Journalists not only took part, they demanded the right to tell the truth. Once the Party lost its 'voice', recourse to military force was almost inevitable. It was no coincidence that, after the tanks had moved into Tiananmen, Party 'work teams' entered editorial offices. Several journalists were jailed. Many more were purged. The media, like the Square itself, were 'cleansed'.

media and market in the 1990s

For almost three years after Tiananmen China's television, radio and newspapers spoke with one voice: that of opposition to 'bourgeois liberalization' and the West's campaign to change China through 'peaceful evolution' – the infiltration of capitalist values. Then, after a hesitant start due to conservative resistance, they trumpeted a new tune, that of faster, bolder reforms championed by Deng during his landmark tour of south China in 1992. It was the start of a period of rapid change in China – and the media world itself.

Commercialization was the new watchword. Advertising soared as news, like much else in China, became a commodity. Growing revenues and unrestrained enthusiasm for materialism led to a huge expansion in media of every kind: newspapers, magazines, television and radio. Since the Party could barely afford to subsidize its chief instruments of ideological control – Xinhua and the *People's Daily* – the expansion was welcome. It still wrote the tune: the Propaganda Department set the political 'line' while a strict registration system meant new media enterprises could not be founded without permission. The main difference was that the Party no longer had to pay so much to get the message across.

There were changes in form and content during the 1990s as well as in finance. Radio stations broadcast phone-ins, topical discussions, and foreign music. Specialist newspapers met the new need for information about finance, business, sport and entertainment. Once dour dailies published racy weekend supplements dealing with the lifestyles of the rich and famous, crime and sensations of almost every kind – save politics.

The changes were as real as they were welcomed by a public tired of Party journalism and hungry for 'infotainment' of the kind popular in the West. Yet the media were still pursuing the Party line. It was simply that the line had changed from class struggle to consumerism, a preferable but no less obligatory policy as far as journalists were concerned. Serious questioning of free market reforms and the Open Door was no more possible in the 1990s than critical examination of the Cultural Revolution had been during the late 1960s.

In some respects, the fact that Party journalism put itself at the service of business created more problems than it solved. Companies 'bought' good coverage by showering journalists with presents. Newspapers established commercial ventures unrelated to newsgathering. Staff journalists combined writing with more remunerative pursuits. These activities undermined such faith in the media as existed after more than 40 years of distortions, and even prompted the Party to step in and promote journalistic ethics.

These were striking developments whose legacy lives on in the new era. They have taken China's media in a very different direction from that followed under Mao. Editors have more latitude as well as more money. As a result, watching television, listening to the radio and reading newspapers and magazines are more interesting, pleasurable activities than they have been at any time in China since 1949.

Yet what has happened to the Mainland media constitutes a change of form rather than function. Ultimately mass communications remain the Party's servant. There is no editorial independence, no genuinely independent media ownership – and no constitutional guarantees of free speech of the kind needed to underpin them. In the sense that genuine journalism begins when the media can subject the authorities to critical questioning, there is little worthy of the name in the People's Republic – a shortcoming which mars national development.

Judging from Beijing's determination to control the Internet, and keep overseas providers of radio, television and other media at bay, this will remain the case for some time. (See TELECOMMUNICATIONS.) While China is changing fast, control of information – whether derived from home or abroad – and pliant media remain the lifeblood of the Communist regime. The occupational hazards of journalism in China, conceived as the free pursuit of critical inquiry, are considerable. They include jail as well as censorship.

The costs of all this for China's wellbeing have been enormous. It is difficult to imagine that the famine induced by the GREAT LEAP FORWARD of 1958 would have been possible had China's press been free to report the disaster. And it is hard to believe CORRUPTION would be so serious in the reform era were the media free to expose it. Yet, as China's Communist leaders are well aware, it is harder still to imagine their rule, at least in its present form, surviving a free flow of ideas. They have a vital interest in ensuring the media do not succumb to one.

missionaries

Merchants went to China to make money, diplomats to extend and defend their countries' interests. Alone among resident foreigners, missionaries sought a fundamental change in the spiritual lives of the Chinese people. In many cases, they succeeded: China's numerically small but flourishing brand of CHRISTIANITY is their legacy. So are controversies over the missionaries' apparent reluctance to allow the development of an indigenous Chinese church, and their links with 'imperialism' before 1949. The covert return of missionaries to China in the 1990s has proved equally sensitive.

The BOXER REBELLION of 1899–1900 was a milestone in the history of Christian missions in China, as it was in China's history generally. During the course of their violent, xenophobic revolt, the rebels slaughtered at least 200 missionaries and many thousands of Chinese Christians. It was the biggest setback for the Church in China since the persecution of Catholics in the eighteenth century. It was also the prelude to a period of growth, particularly on the part of Protestant missions.

In 1905 there were 3,445 Protestant missionaries in China, 300 Chinese ministers and about 100,000 Chinese Protestants. Fifteen years later, the number of missionaries – most of them subjects of the British Empire and North Americans – had almost doubled while the number of missionary societies reached 130. The largest of these by far was the China Inland Mission with 246 'stations' across the country. By 1949, the end of the 'formal' missionary era, the number of Protestant missionary personnel stood at just over 4,000. There were about one million Chinese Protestants.

Missionaries penetrated every province and hundreds of counties. Statistically they were a drop in the ocean given China's size and population, but their influence was disproportionate to their number. At one point they had even nurtured hopes of 'Christianizing' the Chinese government. Timothy Richard, a Welshman and Baptist, cultivated friendships with leading reformers KANG YOUWEI and LIANG QICHAO for whom some aspects of Christianity seemed to endorse their campaign to modernize China during the last years of the QING DYNASTY. At the same time, mission-controlled publishing houses dominated the diffusion of Western ideas. Christianity was a 'filter' through which modern knowledge passed into China. The failure of the reformers in 1898 and the Boxer Rebellion closed the first of these opportunities. Increased travel and study abroad by Chinese ended the second.

Neither development stopped the association of Christianity with political change. SUN YAT-SEN was baptized a Christian. So were other leading lights in the 'Revive China Society', his first revolutionary organization. But in the early twentieth century Protestantism made its mark in HEALTH and EDUCATION rather than politics.

Missionaries and mission stations were the main providers of modern medicine and care in China until the state began to take over the function in the late 1920s. Hardly a mission station did not have at least a dispensary and very probably a small hospital. Millions of Chinese were treated in them. Hundreds were given a medical training in Christian foundations such as Peking (Beijing) Union Medical College.

Missionaries were concerned to educate the Chinese people as well as make them healthy. They pioneered and developed education for WOMEN, just as they had lobbied for an end to the practice of footbinding, concubinage and infanticide. They also encouraged the teaching of the English language. By the 1940s there were 13 Christian Universities in China. Nine thousand students were studying in Protestant colleges and 3,600 in Catholic ones.

There were more Catholics than Protestants in China throughout the first half of the twentieth century, though there were far fewer Catholic missionaries. In 1900, 886 European (mostly French) and about 470 Chinese priests served 700,000 Catholics. In 1949, the numbers were 2,698, 2,090 and 3.2 million respectively. The Catholic missionary effort tended to focus on the countryside. It exercised little influence over intellectual life in China, finding adherents mostly among the poor and uneducated.

Most missionaries, Catholic and Protestant, were caught unawares by the tides of nationalism and revolution which swept through China from the mid-1920s. Some were attacked and hundreds temporarily left their stations to escape the anti-foreign sentiment at work in the KUOMINTANG'S NORTHERN EXPEDITION. However, one missionary saw the

Revolution at close quarters: in 1934 Communist troops captured Alfred Bosshardt, a Briton working for the China Inland Mission, and forced him to accompany them on part of their LONG MARCH. The overall missionary effort resumed once Chiang Kai-shek established his central government in Nanjing. It continued without further interruption until the SINO-JAPANESE WAR, when many missionaries were interned with other Allied nationals in China.

An even bigger challenge lay ahead: the triumph of a particularly nationalistic brand of Communism. In the late 1940s, most Protestant and almost every Catholic missionary believed the Chinese church was not ready to dispense with foreign leadership, finance and organization. Some Chinese Christians, many ordinary citizens and the CHINESE COMMUNIST PARTY thought differently. For them, the missionary presence was a reminder of the era of TREATY PORTS, UNEQUAL TREATIES and EXTRATERRITORIALITY. Such privileges had underpinned the missionary effort for more than a century. Now they had gone. The new government, determined to control every aspect of its citizens' lives, organized Christians into 'national' churches, shorn of foreign influence. The 'Three-Self Patriotic Movement' – self-support, self-government, self-propagation – was founded for Protestants. The Catholic Patriotic Association, designed to break the hold of the Vatican, was set up in 1957 for Catholics (see CHRISTIANITY). Any residual goodwill towards the missionaries that survived the first few months of Communist rule evaporated during the KOREAN WAR when some were persecuted and most expelled.

Many elderly missionaries returned to China as tourists in the 1980s to see how the work they had been forced to abandon 40 years earlier had fared. Most were pleasantly surprised to find churches flourishing, despite decades of persecution. A new generation of missionaries was less satisfied with the spread of the faith. As China opened up in the 1990s, many of them entered the country surreptitiously as teachers, aid workers and ordinary tourists to preach, dispense funds and deliver religious materials. Their number was small but large enough to worry the government. In 1994 Beijing promulgated regulations forbidding foreigners to proselytize in China or appoint Chinese as religious workers.

Mongolia (Formerly 'Outer Mongolia', Mongolian People's Republic)

Alone among the frontier peoples subjected to Manchu-Chinese rule, the Mongols of Outer Mongolia took advantage of the collapse of the QING DYNASTY in 1911 to found their own enduring state. Several Chinese governments sought to reverse this situation or declined to recognize it. And at the start of the twenty-first century, the government in TAIWAN still maintains that Outer Mongolia is part of China. But this aside, and thanks largely to Russian and Soviet sponsorship, Mongolia achieved independent legal status of the kind denied TIBET, a territory with which it otherwise has much in common.

Predominantly a pastoral people, the Mongols preserved their own religious beliefs, social and political organizations, and memories of the great empire they once ruled, despite long years of subjection to the Qing. They also declined to adopt the Chinese script. While they depended on China in some aspects of their economic life, their spiritual and cultural roots were in the Lamaist Buddhism of Tibet (see RELIGION).

Chinese attempts in the early 1900s to recentralize and reinvigorate the decaying Qing empire encountered resistance in Outer Mongolia. Nobles and military chiefs sought help from RUSSIA to throw off Manchu rule. They received it: Outer Mongolia declared independence during the REPUBLICAN REVOLUTION of 1911, and Jebtsundamba Khutuktu (1869–1924), the Living Buddha, was enthroned as leader of a new theocratic state. In 1913 Mongolia and Tibet signed a treaty recognizing each other's independence

Russia declined to back full statehood for Outer Mongolia. Neither did it support the pan-Mongol dreams of those who wanted a new Mongolian state to include Inner Mongolia. Given the changing balance of power in Central Asia, this would create too many hostages to fortune. Furthermore, many of the princes of Inner Mongolia had become sinicized: their desire for an independent Mongolia was weaker than that of their brethren to the north. In 1913, Russia and China agreed Outer Mongolia would enjoy autonomy under Chinese 'suzerainty'. BRITAIN sought the same status for Tibet, but YUAN

SHIKAI, leader of the new Republican government rejected it.

Yuan was not keen on autonomy for Mongolia, either, and managed to reverse it. With Russia in revolution and Outer Mongolia the apparent plaything of Baron Ungern-Sternberg, a White Russian general, Chinese troops forced the Mongolian leadership back into the fold: Outer Mongolia was incorporated in the Chinese Republic. It broke free again in 1921, this time with Soviet Russian assistance. The Mongolian People's Republic was established in 1924, the same year in which a Sino-Soviet Treaty again affirmed Chinese sovereignty/suzerainty over the region.

China was forced to abandon its claims to Mongolia in the 1940s as the price of bringing the SOVIET UNION into the war against Japan. This was one of the conditions of the YALTA CONFERENCE of 1945, whose results China had to respect, even though it had no hand in shaping them. Under the Sino-Soviet Treaty of 1945, China agreed to Mongolian independence as long as a plebiscite showed Mongols wanted it. A poll showed they did and CHIANG KAI-SHEK'S government reluctantly recognized the new state in 1946. But in 1953, by which time the Nationalists had fled to Taiwan, Chiang de-recognized Mongolia on the grounds that Moscow had violated its obligations under the Sino-Soviet Treaty by helping the Chinese Communists seize control of the Mainland. The Kuomintang government was no longer obliged to keep its side of the bargain. The People's Republic of China recognized Mongolian independence as part of the Sino-Soviet Treaty of Friendship, Alliance and Mutual Assistance of 1950.

Outer Mongolia's escape from Chinese rule – which deprived Mainland Chinese maps of a huge chunk of territory – gave way to subjection to a new master. The Mongolian People's Republic was not a colony of Moscow in the formal sense, but its entire history was dictated by developments in Soviet politics until the eve of the Soviet Union's collapse in 1991. Politics compounded the disadvantages of geography: landlocked Mongolia was deprived of contact with the outside world save for the Soviet bloc.

That meant it took Moscow's side in the Sino-Soviet split and the border clashes between Soviet and Chinese troops of 1969 (see SOVIET UNION). The former led to the expulsion of many Chinese from Ulan Bator, the Mongolian capital. The latter saw the arrival of the Soviet Red Army in large numbers under a defence agreement designed to counter possible Chinese aggression. Tension remained high until the withdrawal of Soviet forces from Mongolia in the 1980s, and Moscow's absorption, first with reforming the Soviet regime, and then replacing it.

By 1990, political change was also under way within Mongolia. The Mongolian People's Revolutionary Party was forced to reform, share power and, before long, step down. Mongols exhumed their past and condemned the Communist repression that had killed it. Freedom spawned a resurgence of nationalism.

It also threw into sharp relief the fact that while much of the *land* of the Mongols had escaped foreign rule with the founding of Mongolia, most Mongols had not. They continued to live in China. In 1947 Beijing made Inner Mongolia the first of its autonomous regions for ethnic minorities (see INNER MONGOLIA). This did not stop Chinese immigration: of the 23 million inhabitants of the region in the late 1990s, Mongols accounted for just 3.3 million. The population in the 249,000 square miles (645,000 sq kms) of independent Mongolia was 2.4 million.

Some Mongols wondered whether the imbalance between land and population in their country would tempt China to expand north again. Even after the Sino-Soviet Treaty of 1950, a few Chinese leaders seemed unreconciled to Mongolia's independence. And as late as the 1990s, a book published in China entitled *The Secret of Mongolia's Independence*, which cast doubt on Mongolian qualifications for statehood, caused a storm in Ulan Bator.

Some Mongols in China, on the other hand, were inspired by developments in the north and sought new freedoms themselves. On several occasions in the 1990s, Chinese security police broke up Mongolian 'study associations' and a human rights league founded to develop national consciousness among local Mongols. Repression has kept this cause in check, and economic difficulties have made Mongolia less of a lure than it might have been. However, Beijing cannot be sure that either of these developments will blunt the appeal of a free, genuinely independent Mongolia indefinitely in the minds of Chinese-ruled Mongols.

N

National People's Congress (NPC)

China's legislature – created in 1954 to exercise the functions previously performed by the CHINESE PEOPLE'S CONSULTATIVE CONFERENCE – is the highest organ of state power in the People's Republic. However, this power is largely illusory and NPC meetings, plenary or otherwise, usually a formality. Neither drama nor genuine debate are common. Delegates, selected every five years by members of provincial-level people's congresses (see DEMOCRACY/ELECTIONS), are not sent into Beijing's Great Hall of the People to deliberate so much as affirm, in public and on behalf of the people, the policies of the CHINESE COMMUNIST PARTY, to which most of them belong and all of them are beholden.

NPC plenary sessions are held every spring, when about three thousand delegates gather for what is usually a two- or three-week meeting. The occasion is a major ritual of Communist politics and, like all such rituals, is not allowed to go wrong. On the opening day the premier delivers a long 'work report' to the ranks of delegates who occasionally punctuate the successes declared from the podium with applause. On subsequent days, the finance minister, legal chiefs and other ministers repeat the performance. The remainder of the two weeks is given over to small group discussions in which delegates from the same provinces mull over the meaning of the issues of the day for their localities. Senior Party leaders drop in to listen and dispense wisdom. Policies and key government personnel changes – all of them decided in advance and in secret by the Communist Party – are voted on at the end of the session whose 'vic-

torious' closure is trumpeted in the official MEDIA.

On paper, the *powers* of the NPC are formidable. They include the right to amend the Constitution, decide issues of war and peace, and appoint and remove the president, premier and vice-premiers. Such powers are exercised only on government or Party initiative: individual delegates can initiate bills, but power rests not with them so much as with the NPC Standing Committee, whose more than 100 members, made up of the chairman, vice-chairmen and others, exercise the powers of the NPC for the 50 weeks of each year it is not in full session. The NPC has never voted down a government or Party bill.

The fact that the NPC neither lives up to its own standing in the Constitution nor behaves like a parliament in a democracy does not mean it is insignificant. Policies are aired during its sessions, even if they are not truly debated in public. Furthermore, the fact that it provides some of the *forms* if not the functions of a genuine parliament enables it to be used as a focal point for campaigns for more democracy and freedom.

An example occurred during the TIANANMEN SQUARE DEMOCRACY MOVEMENT when Hu Jiwei (1916–), a 'liberal' member of the Standing Committee, sought to convene the NPC to challenge the government's declaration of martial law in Beijing. The attempt failed, partly because the Party pressured Wan Li (1916–), then chairman of the NPC, into supporting a tough line against the protests. Nevertheless, throughout the 1990s, DISSIDENTS and others openly petitioned the NPC to re-examine the use of military force against civilians and release political prisoners – even though they were nearly always punished for their pains.

On a few occasions the NPC itself even managed to humble the government, albeit modestly. In the 1992 vote on the THREE GORGES DAM, 177 delegates opposed the controversial scheme while 664 abstained. This 'no' vote was almost one-third of the 2,633 ballots cast. In 1995, 1,006 out of 2,752 delegates either voted 'no' or abstained in the poll to appoint Jiang Chunyun (1930–), an unimpressive official from SHANDONG, vice-premier. Jiang won far more votes than he needed, but he failed to make an impression as vice-premier and was quietly moved sideways in 1998.

Between 1992 and 1998, under the chairmanship of QIAO SHI, a senior Party leader, the NPC acquired a higher profile and approved a large amount of legislation. It often did so after revising many bills. The government made sure such revisions were conducted by the Standing Committee at the drafting stage rather than risk a large number of 'no' votes during plenary sessions.

Qiao spoke often about the legislature's supremacy and how even the Communist Party had to obey its laws. In turn, some foreign observers spoke of Qiao, a former security chief, as a closet democrat. They tended to overlook the fact that he never challenged the Party's 'leadership' of the NPC, and that during his chairmanship, a National Defence Law was passed which specified that the PEOPLE'S LIBERATION ARMY was under the

leadership of the Communist Party rather than the 'highest organ of state power' which enjoys the authority to declare war.

Qiao's chairmanship was not an exercise in cynicism, but the emphasis he placed on the NPC stemmed partly from his desire to develop it as a power base. PENG ZHEN, a veteran revolutionary who was one of Qiao's predecessors as well as his mentor, was driven by similar motives during his chairmanship between 1983 and 1988. He did much to set the legislature to work again after the hiatus of the CULTURAL REVOLUTION and wanted Party policy expressed through law and legal codes rather than administrative fiat. But Peng also used his power within the NPC to defeat some of the radical policies of the reformers close to Party leader HU YAOBANG. In other words, parliament for both Qiao and Peng was often a weapon in the wider struggle for power in the Party.

While greater transparency, more debate and a higher profile were characteristics of the NPC during the 1990s, there were plenty of signs that some time would be required before the congress blossoms into a parliament worthy of the name. One was the replacement in 1998 of Qiao as NPC chairman by LI PENG, the conservative former premier who played a major role in the suppression of the Tiananmen Square Democracy Movement. Another was the fact that when, at the same session, JIANG ZEMIN was elected president, and ZHU RONGJI premier, there were no other candidates for the two posts. Delegates were not required to debate, still less challenge the candidates. Their job was simply to affirm.

Ningxia Hui Autonomous Region

China's smallest Mainland provincial unit is also one of its youngest: it was created in 1928 to cover part of the vast inner Asian territories once controlled by the Qing dynasty, only to disappear in 1954 when it was subsumed by neighbouring INNER MONGOLIA and GANSU. Ningxia reappeared in 1958, reduced in size and redesignated an Autonomous Region for the Hui Muslims, one of China's most numerous ETHNIC MINORITIES. These changes did much to facilitate central control over a traditionally restive region. They did less to transform its POVERTY relative to most other parts of the country.

In its first guise, Ningxia extended north to the frontier with newly independent MON-

GOLIA. However, the provincial government did not administer the territory northwest of the Helan mountains, which presently mark the western boundary of the autonomous region and Inner Mongolia. This was, and remains, steppeland: the home of Mongol pastoralists rather than the Chinese or Hui agriculturalists found to the south, along the Yellow River valley and site of the provincial capital, Yinchuan. In the KUOMINTANG era (1927–49), Ningxia's Mongols ruled themselves under the remote jurisdiction of the central government's Commission for Mongolian and Tibetan Affairs. The remainder of the province was in the grip of the powerful Ma family of Muslim WARLORDS whose chief representative in Ningxia was Ma Hongkui (1892–1970).

During the 1930s and 1940s Ma ruled the southern half of his province with an iron fist in an effort to keep CHIANG KAI-SHEK and the rapidly expanding CHINESE COMMUNIST PARTY at bay. Ma was a member of the Kuomintang and held important if honorary positions in the central government in Nanjing. This did not make him any less keen to retain exclusive control over his own fiefdom. Neither did it make Chiang any less determined to weaken it. Relations between Ma and Chiang were a typical example of the confrontation between region and centre which impaired central government authority in the Republican era.

The fact that about 25 per cent of Ningxia's inhabitants were Muslim added to a feeling that the province should not come under the domination of a Han Chinese government. Muslim identity made Ma and many of his senior officials oppose the Chinese Communists even more vehemently.

The Communists encroached on Ningxia before 1949. In the late 1920s, FENG YUXIANG, the dominant warlord of north China, controlled much of the province. Sympathetic to the Soviet Union as well as to Christianity, he allowed Left-wing activists a free hand in his domains until he formed an alliance with Chiang. In 1935, the Communists passed through the mountainous south of Ningxia on the final stage of their LONG MARCH. Soon afterwards they set up the Shaan–Gan–Ning Border Region government whose capital was YANAN, in neighbouring SHAANXI. As its name implies, the border region included Ningxia, though only a tiny part of what was then the southeast of the province.

Despite his fierce opposition to Communism and tight control over Ningxia, Ma could do little to delay the People's Liberation Army's conquest of the region during the CIVIL WAR. In 1949, as Nationalist power collapsed across northwest China, he fled to Taiwan.

Ningxia survived as an administrative unit for the first five years of Communist rule and then disappeared. When it reappeared in 1958 it was shorn of its Mongol territories, which became part of Inner Mongolia, and was redesignated the Ningxia Hui Autonomous Region, one of several province-level units Beijing created to curb resistance to Chinese rule among ethnic minorities in outlying regions. Since the Hui are Chinese in almost every-

The Lie of the Land

The richest, most densely populated part of Ningxia's 25,500 square miles (66,000 sq kms) is the plain in the north which is watered by the Yellow River. Elsewhere in China the Yellow River is known as 'China's sorrow' because of its propensity to flood. In the Autonomous Region it is 'Ningxia's delight' for it makes intensive agriculture possible in an otherwise arid, forlorn part of the country. Wheat, rice, millet and gaoliang (sorghum) are grown. The plain runs southwest-northeast and is bisected by a range of mountains; the Yellow River breaches them at Qingtong Gorge, the site of a major hydroelectric power station. The region is rich in coal – one of the reasons it was linked to the national railway network as early as 1958. The eastern corner of Ningxia, south of the Yellow River, forms part of China's loess plateau, while the Liupan mountains in the south divide the loess plateaux of northern Shaanxi and middle Gansu. The completion in the late 1990s of a rail link between Baoji in Shaanxi and Zhongwei on the Yellow River ended the isolation of Guyuan, the main city in poor, mountainous southern Ningxia.

thing save religion their resistance to Beijing's rule has usually fallen short of demands for national independence voiced by many Tibetans, Mongols and Uigurs in XINJIANG. Moreover, when the Ningxia Autonomous Region was set up, as remains the case at the start of the new century, more Hui lived beyond than within its frontiers. Most of China's 8.6 million Hui are scattered across north China and constitute only one-third of Ningxia's total population of 5.3 million. Nevertheless, in 1958 the concentration of Hui in Ningxia, and their traditional dominance of political life in the region, was enough to persuade Beijing to revive part of the province as an autonomous region. The fact that, at least in name, the Mongols had been granted autonomy in 1947, and the Uigurs in 1955, probably played a part in the decision.

Chinese relations with the Hui, while less fraught than those with other minorities, have not been trouble-free. The flashpoint has usually been religion, or rather, Chinese Communist attempts to eradicate it during periods of heightened radicalism. One of these, the GREAT LEAP FORWARD, brought disaster to Ningxia, though for reasons only partly concerned with Islam. The nationwide famine created by Mao Zedong's rapid communization of agriculture in 1958–60 struck the region hard, particularly the south where animal husbandry is a mainstay. Cannibalism was said to have been common; and Zhang

Xianliang (1936–), author of *Grass Soup*, a record of his days in a Ningxia labour camp, reported in 1960 that those inside the camp often ate better than those outside.

The CULTURAL REVOLUTION of 1966–76 caused havoc of a different kind: mosques were closed and Muslims humiliated and persecuted by Red Guards. The upheaval soured relations between the Chinese and the Hui, and made a mockery of Ningxia's 'autonomy'.

Some of this lost ground was recovered as China focused on economic development under DENG XIAOPING. In Ningxia as elsewhere, mosques reopened and the clergy re-emerged. Political life became more relaxed. However, more than 20 years later Beijing's relations with the Hui still depend on careful handling of religious issues. The government must square the revival of religion with its own materialistic outlook; Hui 'autonomy' with Chinese control; national moderniz-ation with the persistence of traditional social and cultural practices. And if ethnic Han dominance means the Autonomous Region is likely to remain under Chinese control, insensitive treatment of religious questions, whether in published, spoken or practical form, might easily provoke unrest among the devout Hui.

Developing Ningxia's economy has proved as difficult as ensuring harmony among its peoples, though for reasons of geographical isolation and lack of resources as much as politics. These factors, coupled with its modest size and small population, contributed to the fact that Ningxia had the lowest GDP of all of China's provinces in the late 1990s save TIBET and QINGHAI. Per capita GDP in the region was about one-sixth of that of Shanghai while rural incomes were two-thirds the national average. FOREIGN TRADE AND INVESTMENT made few inroads despite efforts by the authorities to attract funds from the Islamic world.

Northern Expedition (1926–8)

The military campaign which brought the KUOMINTANG to power in 1927 began in Guangzhou, capital of GUANGDONG, and ended in BEIJING with China's reunification. But it ground to a halt at the halfway point of the Yangtze where the revolutionary camp split into factions. Pitched battles and violent purges ensued before the Nationalist armies continued northwards, their ranks shorn of Communists, their leaders subordinate to CHIANG KAI-SHEK and his more moderate brand of revolution.

A Northern Expedition to reunite China had been the dream of SUN YAT-SEN from the moment he established a foothold in Guangzhou in 1917. It remained a dream as long as the great revolutionary had to rely on 'friendly' WARLORDS to help him carry it out. What made it a reality was aid and advice from the SOVIET UNION, a pact with the CHINESE COMMUNIST PARTY and the Kuomintang's reorganization into a mass revolutionary party with an army of its own. Sun died before the troops could set off. It was left to Chiang, his successor, to launch the expedition in July 1926.

Three great warlord coalitions stood in the way of the Nationalist armies: those of WU PEIFU, in HUNAN and HUBEI; Sun Zhuanfang (1885–1935), in the coastal provinces of the east; and Zhang Zuolin (1875–1928), who was based in the Manchurian provinces of the northeast. All were to crumble or concede in the face of a remarkable outburst of military resourcefulness and resolve.

Conventional battlefield victories only partly explain the Northern Expedition's early success. Equally important were the political campaigns waged by Communists and Kuomintang Left-wingers who organized strikes, boycotts, protests, trade unions and peasant associations in the wake, and sometimes even ahead of, the National Revolutionary armies. Revolution swept through the cities of south China as they fell into Nationalist hands.

Many of the protests, and some of the violence, were directed against foreign privilege, particularly that enjoyed by BRITAIN, the premier foreign power in China. First in the Hankou section of what is now known as Wuhan, capital of HUBEI, and then in Jiujiang, a TREATY PORT in JIANGXI further down the Yangtze, protestors stormed the British concessions. Britain subsequently ceded them – a barely disguised admission that, for the first time, privileges granted by treaty had been taken back by force. Hostility to foreigners was even more intense in Nanjing where several were murdered.

These developments mortified the foreign community in SHANGHAI. Thousands of British and American troops poured in to

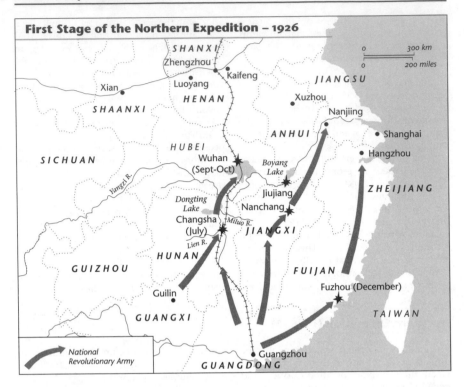

First Stage of the Northern Expedition – 1926

protect the bastion of imperial privilege in China. The city's Communists and labour activists made preparations of their own, organizing an uprising to shake off warlord rule and welcome the arrival of the revolutionary armies.

While they did so, Chiang battled with his rivals over the leadership and future direction of the Nationalist Revolution. There were two formal centres of power: Chiang's base in Nanchang, capital of Jiangxi, and that of WANG JINGWEI in Wuhan, where the Soviet advisers and their Left-wing allies were concentrated. Arguments raged over whether Beijing or Shanghai should be the next destination, and whether the social revolution, and thus the role of the Communist Party, should be intensified, wound down or eliminated.

The disputes acquired a Byzantine complexity. They were settled by Chiang's brutal purge of the Communist Party in April 1927 – first in Shanghai and then elsewhere within his domain; his battlefield superiority over rival militarists; and, soon, the crumbling of Wang Jingwei's forces in Wuhan. An alliance with FENG YUXIANG, warlord of north China, secured Chiang's northern flank, while extortion ensured businessmen in Shanghai kept his coffers full. By early 1928, Chiang had consolidated his hold over the Kuomintang, crushed or cowed its left wing, and severed all links with Moscow. He was ready to launch stage two of the Northern Expedition.

This proceeded along very different lines from that of the march on the Yangtze. The revolutionary drive was confined to the battlefield: there was little organization of the masses, and few protests or strikes. There was, however, a major clash with a foreign power, this time JAPAN. Tokyo sent an expeditionary force to Jinan, the capital of SHANDONG, because it was home for thousands of Japanese citizens and lay in the path of the Nationalist armies. Chiang sought to allay Japanese concerns, but Nationalist sentiment was running too high on both sides. Fighting broke out in May 1928 and thousands of Chinese soldiers and civilians were killed. Anti-Japanese sentiment intensified across the country. It was to increase still further three years later when Japan consolidated its hold over Manchuria (see MANCHUGUO).

The Manchurian issue cast a cloud over the final weeks of the Northern Expedition. Tokyo was worried about the fate of Zhang Zuolin (1875–1928), the Manchurian warlord, whose forces were then the only obstacle to the Nationalists' occupation of Beijing. It wanted Zhang to give up the capital peacefully and return home. Above all, Japan wanted the civil war kept out of its domain in northeast China. It got its way. Zhang and his armies vacated Beijing in favour of those of the northern warlord YAN XISHAN who had joined the National Revolution. However, things did not go according to plan for Zhang: Japanese officers blew up the train in which he was travelling as it approached Mukden (modern Shenyang), and he died almost immediately.

On 6 July 1928 Chiang declared the Northern Expedition accomplished and China reunified. It was time for reform and reconstruction. Attention switched to Nanjing in the south, where the new National Government established its capital and promised to lead its people into a new era.

Euphoria subsided as it became apparent that the Northern Expedition had spawned almost as many problems as it had solved. Chief among them was a chronic decentralization of power. Militarist converts to the Nationalist cause fell out with Chiang, and each other, over territorial spoils and political position. Unification remained a mirage as long as commanders retained control over their own troops and the provinces from which they were raised. Large parts of the country, especially the west, had been left untouched by the National Revolution. The Communists, weakened but not wiped out by Chiang's moves against them two years earlier, were in rebellion against the new government. Massive efforts would be required to deal with these problems, and carry out the economic, social and political reforms needed to create a modern nation state. They proved beyond Chiang's capacity.

O

One Hundred Flowers Movement 1956–7

'Let a hundred flowers bloom, let a hundred schools contend,' declared MAO ZEDONG in May 1956, encouraging intellectuals to voice their opinions about Communist rule. But when, after a slow start, they did so with a candour that questioned the leading role of the Party, Mao subjected the blooms to savage pruning. They were swept away in the 'Anti-Rightist Movement' of the following year – the start of a 20-year nightmare for many, and one that changed the course of Chinese politics.

In 1949, goodwill towards the new government persuaded many intellectuals to work for the Communist cause. Thousands who were overseas when the People's Republic was founded returned home. Since the government assumed responsibility for their living conditions, intellectuals usually enjoyed a more comfortable life than had been the case under the KUOMINTANG.

Creative freedom was in shorter supply and, by the mid-1950s, China's intellectuals were chafing under Party control. Almost all of them worked in a system of Party-controlled universities and institutes modelled on those of the Soviet Union. Pressures to substitute Soviet intellectual orthodoxies for those of the West, and to conform generally to the regime's priorities, created tension and trauma. The denunciation in 1955 of Hu Feng (1902–85), a writer whose calls for academic freedom resulted in his disgrace and imprisonment as a Kuomintang agent, demoralized the intelligentsia still further.

The Party had asserted its primacy over creative life while in YANAN, its wartime head-quarters, and after 1949 set out to discipline and control intellectuals, most of whom were not Communists. But it would be hard to modernize China without tapping the expertise and enthusiasm of its scientists, technicians, thinkers and writers. Thus in 1956 Mao and other Party leaders set about creating a freer intellectual atmosphere.

At first there was little response. The following year Mao took things a stage further, effectively soliciting criticism with a speech on 'contradictions' which maintained the Party had nothing to fear from the 'non-antagonistic' complaints of intellectuals. The 'antagonistic' contradictions between the 'people' and their 'enemies' were the ones to worry about (see MAO ZEDONG/MAO ZEDONG THOUGHT). The fact that neither this speech nor his earlier remarks about 'blooming and contending' were published at the time suggested that some Party leaders disagreed with the Chairman. Mao, however, believed that most intellectuals had been won over to socialism. Their criticism would be like a 'gentle breeze or mild rain'. It would be a way of keeping the Party in line. Uprisings in Hungary and Poland in 1956 had shown what happened when Communists lost touch with the people.

When it came, the criticism constituted a typhoon. There were complaints about the way Party bureaucracy was stifling creative life and attacks on prevailing dogmas – objections Mao might have been able to live with. But articles in learned journals and the main-stream press, essays and posters pasted up in universities, speeches by members of the democratic parties, and even street protests attacked the very foundations of Communist rule. Clearly, the intellectuals had not been won round to the new regime; drastic steps were needed to ensure that they were.

The change from encouraging criticism to punishing it took a matter of weeks and was the work of Mao himself. The intellectuals had let the Chairman down. They were 'Rightists' who endangered socialism. They were to be purged and subjected to the discipline of hard labour as undertaken by the peasantry, the class to whom Mao would turn to implement his utopian GREAT LEAP FORWARD in a few months' time.

The ranks of China's intelligentsia were decimated as its members denounced each other in a frenzied campaign of psychological terror. DENG XIAOPING, then the Party's general secretary, supervised the campaign. Officials were required to declare 5 per cent of the staff in their works units 'Rightists', a crude system which led to numerous injustices, nervous breakdowns and suicides. Exactly how many people ended up as political and social outcasts remains unclear. It is thought to be in excess of 500,000. Among them was ZHU RONGJI who, alone among the victims, managed to reach the top ranks of politics in the 1990s. Hundreds of thousands of intellectuals were sent to prison or labour camps where they either died, or rotted away for the next 20 years.

In the late 1970s, the Party ordered their release and, in some cases, quiet rehabilitation. Yet more than 50 years after it began, the Communist Party is far from conceding that the 'Anti-Rightist Movement' was a mistake. 'It was entirely correct and necessary . . .', said the official version of Party history published in 1981. It added: 'But the scope of this struggle was made far too broad, and a number of intellectuals, patriotic people and Party cadres were unjustifiably labelled "Rightists", with unfortunate consequences. '

Apart from its toll of numerous personal tragedies, the 'Anti-Rightist Movement' destroyed any possibility that a harmonious, genuinely cooperative relationship might be established between the Communist Party and China's intellectuals. Thinkers have never again been asked to speak out in public on any scale. Neither have they been entirely trusted by a Party which fears ideas above all. For Mao, the 'failure' of the One Hundred Flowers showed that the 'wisdom of the masses' and the collective counted for more than the role of intellectuals with their specialist skills and often pro-Western, pro-liberal outlook.

Overseas Chinese

Agents of political change, financiers of the 'economic miracle', custodians of traditional values and exponents of new – Overseas Chinese have performed all these functions and more for their homeland during its encounter with modernity. Whether located in HONG KONG, TAIWAN or MACAU, whose inhabitants might best be described as 'Offshore Chinese', or further afield in Southeast Asia, they have made contributions to China's modernization other countries of similar size but without such a loyal diaspora, notably India and Russia, greatly envy. The Mainland drove many of its own into exile. It often mistreated those who returned. But it has not been repaid in kind. Overseas Chinese (about 25 million of them in Taiwan, Hong Kong and Macau, 20 million in Southeast Asia, and perhaps five million elsewhere at the start of the new century) supplied much of the energy, capital and know-how that transformed China during the final two decades of the twentieth century.

the diaspora and domestic politics

Push and pull factors were at work in the emigration of Chinese as of other peoples. What was different about China was that under the QING DYNASTY emigration, though common, was technically illegal until the mid-nineteenth century; that for a further 100 years successive Chinese governments exerted a political claim over overseas emigrants, whom they regarded as Chinese citizens; and that this, coupled with their distinct identity, frequent success in business and apparent attachment to their homeland, often made Overseas Chinese the subject of resentment and suspicion, particularly in Southeast Asia where most of them settled.

These issues proved more troubling in the second half of the twentieth century than the first. In the final years of the Qing, the Chinese government worried more about the loyalty of its exiles than did the authorities in the European colonial empires and other parts of the world that received them. The Chinese diaspora, most of it drawn from the southern coastal provinces of GUANGDONG, FUJIAN, ZHE-JIANG and HAINAN, was fertile ground for the revolutionary teachings of SUN YAT-SEN and the less radical but still unwelcome notions of KANG YOUWEI. The battle of ideas over China's future was waged among Chinese in the Straits Settlements and Hong Kong, Hawaii and Vancouver, San Francisco and Tokyo.

From all these places, and others where large numbers of Chinese were found, money and munitions, pamphlets and political ideas – all of them instruments of revolutionary change – flowed back to the Mainland. In the event, the REPUBLICAN REVOLUTION of 1911 was the work of internal rather than external forces; but republicanism and constitutional government, ideas with many adherents among Overseas Chinese, *defined* political change in the Mainland even if they did not always determine it.

Despite its failures at home, the foundation of the Republic in 1912 provided a new focus of loyalty for many Overseas Chinese: it supplied a political identity to complement the traditional one based upon culture. Commitment to the nation intensified during the early 1920s as Sun's KUOMINTANG, newly reorganized, allied to the CHINESE COMMUNIST PARTY, and in league with the Soviet Union, sought to end warlord rule and foreign privilege. BRITAIN in particular began to take a closer interest in political activism among the many Chinese within its imperial domains, fearful of what it might mean for its position in China proper. Kuomintang agents got to work again in the late 1930s in an effort to turn growing resentment among Overseas Chinese at Japanese aggression in China into a steady flow of funds and supplies for the beleaguered Mainland.

The Second World War, and the political settlements that followed it, opened a new, more sensitive era for the Overseas Chinese in Southeast Asia. Leaders of newly independent INDONESIA, BURMA, Malaya as well as Thailand, which had never been colonized, sometimes looked askance at their Chinese minorities. Acumen and energy had made many of them rich and powerful: Chinese communities controlled disproportionate amounts of the wealth of their adopted countries. The creation of the People's Republic of China in 1949 (which prompted a new wave of emigration that included many rich businessmen), and local Chinese involvement

in Communist insurrections in Malaya and Singapore, raised new questions about Chinese loyalties. Whether Overseas Chinese were cast as arch capitalists or fanatical Communists, many in Southeast Asia's fragile new nations believed they were not to be trusted.

The fact that both the Communists in Beijing and the Nationalists in Taipei regarded emigrants and their descendants as Chinese nationals (as long as at least one parent was Chinese), and competed vigorously for their political allegiance as well as their financial remittances, made matters worse. Not only were Chinese communities disproportionately rich, they were seen as aliens under the protection of a foreign power. This situation continued until 1955 when Beijing changed its policy towards the Overseas Chinese in an effort to improve relations with governments in Southeast Asia. The Sino-Indonesian Dual Nationality Act of that year allowed Chinese in Indonesia to chose whether they wanted to be Indonesian or PRC nationals – a move that severed one of the ties between the emigrants and their homeland.

But only one. It did not end suspicions about the Overseas Chinese in Southeast Asia, and it did not stop Beijing acting on their behalf when it found it convenient to do so. Both tendencies reached an explosive climax in Indonesia. In 1959–60, the People's Republic transported more than 100,000 Indonesian Chinese home to escape persecution. Five years later, Beijing's support for the radical President Sukharno and the largely Chinese Indonesian Communist Party prompted a countercoup by Right-wing generals. In the weeks that followed more than 100,000 Indonesian Chinese were killed by mobs desperate for revenge and a final settling of accounts with the rich and 'traitorous' minority population. Jakarta suspended diplomatic relations with Beijing in 1967; they were not resumed until 1990 (see INDONESIA).

The Indonesian disaster, and the CULTURAL REVOLUTION which followed, soured relations between Beijing and almost every country in Southeast Asia with a significant Chinese minority. Even Singapore, an independent state from 1963, sought to downplay its predominantly ethnic Chinese identity, choosing Malay rather than Chinese as its national language. The attempts of Chinese diplomats to encourage Red Guard activities among younger members of the Overseas Chinese, and Beijing's support of insurrection across the region, marked the low point of PRC

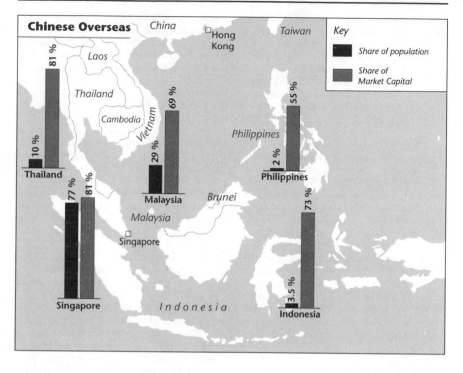

Chinese Overseas

Key
- Share of population
- Share of Market Capital

China
Laos
Thailand
Cambodia
Vietnam
Hong Kong
Taiwan
Philippines
Brunei
Malaysia
Singapore
Indonesia

Thailand — 10 %, 81 %
Malaysia — 29 %, 69 %
Philippines — 2 %, 55 %
Singapore — 77 %, 81 %
Indonesia — 3.5 %, 73 %

foreign policy and its ties to the diaspora. Neither improved until DENG XIAOPING returned to power in the late 1970s and opened China to the outside world.

financiers of reform

The economic success of the Offshore Chinese in Hong Kong, Taiwan and Southeast Asia was an important inspiration for the Mainland's reform-minded Communists. Almost everywhere, Overseas Chinese communities were rich and hard working. Only in Taiwan and Singapore were they political masters. Elsewhere they were either in the minority, preferred (or were obliged) to stay out of politics or, as in the case of Hong Kong until 1997, were colonial subjects. But everywhere in the region, they created prosperous family firms and far-reaching trading and financial networks which enabled their host countries to prosper as never before. Surely, given the chance, they could they do the same for their homeland?

During the following twenty years they did just that, pouring capital and expertise into China directly or via Hong Kong, the great meeting point of the internal and external Chinese worlds and the wider, international one beyond. Patriotism and profit, cultural affiliation and cruder acquisitiveness were all at work in what amounted to a 'homecoming' for a diaspora long cut off from its source by the murderous pursuit of revolution. By the late 1990s, Overseas Chinese had become the largest single source (though one drawn from many different countries and regions) of direct 'foreign' investment in the Mainland (see FOREIGN TRADE AND INVESTMENT). Perhaps this was not surprising in the light of an Australian government study of 1995 which estimated that Overseas Chinese generated a GDP equivalent of US$450 billion, then only US$50 billion short of that of the entire People's Republic. Figures of this kind fuelled talk of a 'Greater China' – an economic entity comprising the Mainland, Taiwan, Hong Kong, Macau and, according to some definitions, even the Chinese diaspora in Southeast Asia.

The idea of a 'homecoming' does not imply

that the Overseas Chinese found everything about China to their liking. Still less does it mean they identified with the regime in Beijing, forsook the identities they had acquired as Hong Kong Chinese, Taiwanese or ethnic Chinese citizens of Malaysia, Thailand, Singapore and elsewhere, and took up residence in China. It was more subtle than that. Cultural ties and associations with native places had always been strong among the diaspora. New opportunities for business and philanthropy in the homeland made them stronger still.

So, in turn, did the growing economic power of China which the Overseas Chinese contributed to. It generated a new pride in being Chinese, and it gave rise to a cultural effervescence and celebration of the allegedly unique, 'Chinese' way of doing things, whether in family life or politics, business or personal morality. One aspect of this was the vogue for ASIAN VALUES of the mid-1990s. It was also at work in the admiration many Mainland officials as well as ordinary people felt for SINGAPORE – the ethnic Chinese state whose social discipline, wealth, cleanliness and mild authoritarianism they hoped to replicate at home.

Chinese identities

China's economic reforms did not usher in an era of success for Overseas Chinese everywhere. VIETNAM expelled many of its ethnic Chinese inhabitants as relations with China soured in the late 1970s. Their fate was an issue in the Sino-Vietnamese war of 1979. In the 1980s and early 1990s many Hong Kong Chinese emigrated to North America, Australia or elsewhere rather than face the territory's return to China in 1997. Many returned before the handover, but they might not have done so had they not acquired an option on citizenship elsewhere. And in Southeast Asia, the surge of Overseas Chinese investment into the People's Republic raised fresh questions about the loyalty of the region's rich and powerful minority population. Anti-Chinese pogroms accompanied the riots and protests that toppled President Sukharno from power in Indonesia in 1998, prompting angry complaints from both Beijing and Taipei.

Yet the Overseas Chinese are not engaged in a zero-sum game. In an age of economic globalization, assimilation within their adopted homes and cultural and commercial affiliation to their ancestral homeland need not be incompatible even if, at least in the eyes of third parties, it might be difficult to strike the right balance. In any event, there can be no doubt of the importance of the Overseas Chinese to China's rejuvenation. For many Mainlanders, though not for all, Overseas Chinese present the acceptable face of modernization. They act as an interface, a comforting *Chinese* interface, between continental China, traditionally conservative and insular, and the wider, modern, yet foreign world beyond. Mercifully free of the experience of Communism, many of them combine traditional Chinese values, including religious beliefs, with modern Western ways – a marriage of values and ideas with considerable appeal in the People's Republic.

P

Pakistan

China's closest ally in Asia, with the possible exception of North Korea (see KOREA), derived this status first from its role as a buffer state between threatening areas of Soviet influence in INDIA, Afghanistan and the SOVIET UNION itself. The absence of ideological and territorial disputes between Beijing and Islamabad made relations even warmer – as, during the 1980s and 1990s, did Chinese aid for Pakistan's nuclear weapons programme and its sale of missiles to the Pakistani military. For all these reasons Sino-Pakistani ties have rarely faltered since their establishment in 1951. Continued economic and military aid, repaid by Pakistan's willingness to facilitate Chinese influence in South Asia and provide Beijing with a window on the Islamic world, are likely to keep things that way in future.

Beijing's attempts in the 1950s to befriend the Third World first brought China and Pakistan together (see BANDUNG CONFERENCE). Their relationship soon acquired a strategic dimension. From its foundation, Pakistan was in fear of India, its giant neighbour. China fell out with India, too, fighting a brief but victorious war against the country in 1962 over their disputed border (see INDIA). New Delhi drew closer to Moscow at a time when the Sino-Soviet split was driving the erstwhile Communist allies apart. This made good relations with Pakistan even more vital to Beijing. China's leaders extended financial assistance to the country and generally took its side on the question of the disputed territory of Kashmir. They also backed Pakistan in its wars with India.

For their part, Pakistani leaders helped facilitate China's landmark rapprochement with the UNITED STATES of the early 1970s. When President Richard Nixon visited Pakistan in 1969 he let his hosts know he wanted to open talks with Beijing. Pakistan was Henry Kissinger's supposed destination in 1971 when the US secretary of state made his secret visit to China.

Sino-Indian relations improved with the end of the Cold War and the waning of Moscow's influence in the subcontinent. Relations with Pakistan, however, grew even warmer. China saw in the Muslim state a useful means of keeping resurgent Indian nationalism in check. Islamabad tactfully refused to join international criticism of China's HUMAN RIGHTS record and adhered closely to Beijing's line on TAIWAN and other issues.

In the early 1980s, Beijing began to supply nuclear equipment and technology to Pakistan. It soon added intermediate-range missiles and other weapons to the sales list (see ARMS SALES). These transfers alarmed Washington as much as New Delhi: on several occasions during the 1990s, China's nuclear and missile sales to Pakistan were major sources of friction with the US.

China acceded to the nuclear non-proliferation treaty in 1991 and in 1996 promised not to transfer nuclear equipment to facilities anywhere in the world that were not open to inspection by the International Atomic Energy Agency. It also promised to abide by the terms of the Missile Technology Control Regime, forbidding the transfer of technology and equipment for missiles with a range of 300 kilometres and a payload of 500 kilograms. None of these moves quietened fears in the West and India that China was contributing to tension in South Asia by arming Pakistan.

In 1998, India made its views known in the most dramatic way possible. It carried out a series of nuclear tests, justifying them by reference to the security threat posed first by Beijing, and second by Islamabad. Within days, Pakistan responded with tests of its own. Reports referred to the birth of the 'Islamic bomb'. In fact it was a rebirth of the Chinese one: Beijing had supplied Pakistan with the design for a bomb, highly enriched uranium, and most of the key components for a nuclear

weapons complex. It was even believed to have carried out a nuclear test on behalf of Pakistan in China.

China condemned India's test and expressed 'grave concern' over Pakistan's. It called on both sides to exercise restraint and sign the Comprehensive Test Ban Treaty. Such statesmanlike behaviour failed to disguise Beijing's sympathies. The Cold War is long past, and Russian influence in India a shadow of that of the Soviet era. But a common desire to tie India down, and a strong Chinese one to secure its southwest flank – in particular, TIBET – make a compelling case for close ties between China and Pakistan.

Panchen Lama(s)

In the form of Buddhism practised in TIBET, the Panchen Lama is second only to the DALAI LAMA, the supreme religious leader. In the matter of preserving Tibet's unique way of life when faced with overweening Chinese influence, the role of the Panchens proved more controversial and sometimes tragic. Of the three who flourished in the twentieth century, China nurtured the 9th as a Pretender, used the 10th to control Tibet, and intervened in the selection of the 11th to extend its influence over Tibetan religious life into the twenty-first century. This did not make the Panchens 'chopsticks', as some Tibetan patriots alleged, but it often placed them in a difficult position with their own people.

Panchen Lamas and Dalai Lamas are heirs of the Gelugpa, or Yellow Hat, school of Tibetan Buddhism founded by Tsong Khapa (1357–1419). Whereas the Dalai is the incarnation of the Compassionate Buddha, known as Avalo-kiteswara, the Panchen is an incarnation of Amitabha, master of the meditative sphere. This gives him a 'spiritual edge' over the Dalai. In the neighbourhood of his traditional seat, the Tashilhunpo Monastery in Xigaze, the Panchen was revered as both feudal and spiritual master. In Tibet, as a whole, the Dalai was usually supreme.

Dalais and Panchens often combined spiritual respect for each other with political rivalry. Chinese governments played upon this, seeking to build up Panchens as compliant alternatives to the Dalai Lamas who ruled from Lhasa. The 9th Panchen, Chokyi Nyima (died 1937), spent the last 14 years of his life in China, where he fled in 1923 after a dispute with the Dalai over his monastery's

tax bill. Throughout his exile, he haunted the 13th Dalai – and Britain, which was keen to keep China out of Tibet – with the threat of return in the company of Chinese troops.

The 10th Panchen, Choekyi Gyaltsen (1938–89), was an even more controversial figure. Born in QINGHAI province, he went to Tashilhunpo to study after Communist troops entered Tibet under the 1951 agreement on 'peaceful liberation'. Eight years later, Tibet was in revolt and the Dalai Lama fled to India. The Panchen became the most senior Tibetan leader in his homeland.

His compliance in China's rule was soon exhausted. Young and idealistic, he was horrified by the effects of Chinese policies on his people. During the suppression of the rebellion, thousands of Tibetans were killed or sent to labour camps. Thousands more died of starvation as a result of the GREAT LEAP FORWARD. Monasteries were destroyed, and an entire way of life along with them. The very existence of the Tibetan people seemed at stake.

In 1962, the Panchen wrote a 70,000-word secret report to premier ZHOU ENLAI chronicling the 'sufferings of the masses' and suggesting how Beijing might relieve them. It did not challenge China's claims over Tibet or its suppression of the 'counter-revolutionary rebellion'. But it lambasted Communist policies with a candour rare even for a document written only for a restricted audience. The Panchen's report was the equivalent of PENG DEHUAI's celebrated, and similarly private, assault on MAO ZEDONG's Great Leap Forward of 1959. Like that attack, it had grave consequences for its author, turning him into the tragic hero of modern Tibet.

This was not apparent at first. The Panchen's candour was welcomed. Keen to show it could respond to criticism, the Communist Party adjusted its policies in what, by 1965, it had designated as the Tibetan Autonomous Region (TAR) (see TIBET). But high politics in Beijing was moving away from tolerance towards class struggle. Mao, preparing the assault that would soon develop into the CULTURAL REVOLUTION, branded the report a 'poisoned arrow aimed at the Party by reactionary feudal overlords'. The Panchen was asked to examine his mistakes. They were brought home in 1964 when he was branded an enemy of the Party, the people and socialism. He spent more than eight of the following 14 years in prison and the remainder under house arrest. His sole outings took the form of mass 'struggle sessions' in which he was publicly humiliated.

Freedom of a kind came in 1978, but it was not until 1982 that the Panchen returned to Tibet after an absence of 17 years. Beijing was in forgiving mood towards those who suffered during the Cultural Revolution. It looked to the Panchen to reconcile Tibetans to Chinese rule in exchange for the economic development of their homeland and a degree of autonomy manifest mainly in a revival of traditional Tibetan culture.

Both of these things were hard to deliver for the government in Lhasa, dominated by 'Leftists', and a central government ill-informed about developments in Tibet. The Panchen resumed treading his fine line: he attacked those who sought independence for Tibet, but criticized the neglect of Tibetan language and the denial of the region's promised autonomy. In his last speech, delivered a few days before his death, he declared that 'liberation' had brought development, but at too high a price. It was the last testament of a man who, compelled to accept China's occupation of Tibet, sought to preserve what he could of his people's way of life.

The search for the Panchen's successor sparked a bitter controversy between Beijing and the Dalai Lama. In 1995, the Dalai proclaimed that he had recognized Gedhun Choekyi Nyima, a six-year-old boy born in Tibet, as the 11th Panchen. This was also the choice of the official search committee, led by Chadrel Rimpoche (c 1944–), abbot of Tashilhunpo Monastery. Beijing was furious at being upstaged, and attacked Chadrel for 'colluding' with the Dalai. Like their imperial predecessors, China's Communist leaders insisted on the right to confirm the choice of reincarnation. They refused to recognize the Dalai's candidate, reorganized the search committee, and insisted on a drawing of lots – as used during past selection controversies – to decide which of three new candidates was the reincarnation.

There was resistance from some lamas but Beijing eventually got its way. In November 1995, Gyaincain Norbu, born in 1990 in Lhari, Nagqu prefecture, was declared the 11th Panchen Lama. China confirmed the choice, and the boy was enthroned at Tashilhunpo the following year. President JIANG ZEMIN, more Chinese than Marxist, in this as in other respects, sent a plaque to commemorate the occasion. It bore the inscription 'Protect the Country, Benefit the People.' China had its Panchen in place again.

The Tibetan people paid a high price for this development, too. Gedhun Choekyi Nyima, the Dalai's candidate, and his family disappeared from public view. The same was true of Chadrel Rimpoche, sentenced to six years in prison for 'splitting the nation'. Others who refused to recognize Beijing's choice were also arrested. Monasteries were subjected to 'patriotic education' campaigns to enforce allegiance to 'China's Panchen'. This has created a schism in Tibetan Buddhism whose consequences are unclear but which seem likely to help China 'divide and rule' the Tibetan people. It is symbolized at the start of the century by two Tibetan boys – one of them favoured by the exiled God King, but reared in obscurity somewhere in China, and the other brought up by lamas under the watchful eye of the Communist Party in the hope that he will grow up to do Beijing's bidding in its distant Himalayan outpost.

Patten, Chris (1944–)

The last British governor of HONG KONG was also the most controversial. His determination to extend democracy in the territory during the twilight years of British rule was bitterly opposed by Beijing, most of the local business community and even many in the British Foreign Office. He pressed on regardless, buoyed by support from ordinary people keen to have a greater say in their affairs as they prepared for the uncertainties of the handover. The governor's electoral reforms did not survive the change of sovereignty; the 'Patten effect' on Hong Kong's wider society lasted longer. It created expectations which the post-colonial government, confronted with the Asian financial crisis, found it hard to live up to.

When Patten assumed office in 1992, much of the script for Hong Kong's transition from Crown Colony to Special Administrative Region (SAR) of China had been written. The suppression of the TIANANMEN SQUARE DEMOCRACY MOVEMENT in 1989 blew things off course, but Sino-British diplomacy restored a sense of direction. While it was not clear who would succeed David Wilson when his retirement was announced at the end of 1991, it seemed likely that the next, and probably last, governor of Hong Kong would be preoccupied with quiet diplomacy rather than crusading democracy.

The appointment of Patten, a former Conservative Party cabinet minister who had lost his seat in the 1992 general election, defied these expectations. He brought to the job little familiarity with the Chinese world, a close friendship with prime minister John Major, the convictions and media skills of a democratic politician – and some of the vanity that often goes with them. His appointment, though the result of favouritism of the kind often criticized when conducted in Beijing, testified to concern in Britain that the departing sovereign had not done all it should for its last major colony given its imminent return to Beijing. For Patten, the concern became a conviction. It was late in the day, but he resolved to do something about it.

The occasion was arrangements for the legislative elections of 1995, the last to be held under British rule and the first in which every member of the council would be elected, if only indirectly in the case of many seats. Under British rule, democracy in Hong Kong had enjoyed a short, inglorious history. It was promised a slightly better future under the Basic Law, the constitution drafted by China to govern the territory after 1 July 1997. But the pace of reform was slow, and the franchise restricted – apparently to ensure the election of pro-China candidates.

Patten widened the franchise dramatically. He did not do so by increasing the number of directly elected seats in the Legislative Council, which he left at 20 (one-third of the total). Instead he opened up the functional constituencies – in which, traditionally, small elites voted according to their profession – to the entire working population. He also arranged for an electoral college charged with returning 10 seats in the legislature to be composed of people who had themselves been elected to serve in local government rather than appointees.

Beijing objected strongly to these measures, on which it had not been consulted. It claimed they violated the Joint Declaration on the future of Hong Kong, signed by Britain and China in 1984; the Basic Law; and previous secret accords between Britain and China. The first two charges were unconvincing. The last was harder to answer, especially as Patten did not discover the existence of the accords or 'seven letters', exchanged in early 1990, until after he put forward his plans.

At the very least, Beijing had cause to complain about Patten's departure from the past practice of quiet diplomacy on major issues concerning Hong Kong. At most, it had reason to feel the seven letters constituted some sort of agreement on aspects of the electoral arrangements. Chinese officials made known their objections during Patten's sole, uncomfortable, visit to Beijing as governor in 1992.

Questions of agreements aside, Beijing's real objection to the Patten reforms was that they seem designed to weaken Chinese control over Hong Kong after 1997. For China's suspicious leaders they were a plot to extend British influence beyond the handover by allowing 'anti-China' elements to dominate the legislature. This was a reference to people such as MARTIN LEE, leader of the Democratic Party, whose members had supported the demonstrations in Tiananmen Square and demanded more democracy in Hong Kong. Beijing wanted the 1995 elections organized along lines that curbed the influence of this group in favour of pro-China politicians and businessmen.

The standoff between Patten and Beijing cast Hong Kong into crisis but never quite despair. China's official media hurled insults at the governor. Many in the local business community deserted him. Previous Hong Kong governors and senior retired diplomats – notably Sir Percy Cradock, former ambassador to Beijing and adviser to prime minister Margaret Thatcher – attacked the Patten plans and accused their author of sacrificing the territory's interests for the sake of a career in British politics after the handover.

However, the governor's popularity generally held up among ordinary people, fascinated by a man who swapped an improbable gubernatorial uniform for a business suit or shirt sleeves, and who enjoyed kissing babies during visits to housing estates. Such spectacles infuriated Beijing all the more. It reminded China's leaders that they rarely risked spontaneous visits to the 'masses' they claimed to represent.

Patten's wit, eloquence and earnestness won admiration from many in the international media, whom the governor skilfully kept 'on side' during the dispute. These qualities made much less impact across the border: though China's leaders detested Chris Patten, they never really understood him. Patten returned the compliment: history, culture and sharp differences in personality made for a profound gulf between the principals during the last phase of Hong Kong's transition.

The 1995 polls produced the landslide for the Democrats Beijing feared. Chinese officials pledged to disband the Legislative Council on 1 July 1997 and replace it with a provisional body composed largely of their allies. As Chris Patten departed Hong Kong in the early hours of 1 July 1997, they did just that. His electoral reforms, the object of such controversy for so long, did not survive the change of sovereignty. The 1998 legislative elections, the first under Chinese rule, were conducted on a much narrower franchise and succeeded in reducing the number of Demo-cratic Party councillors. However, pro-democracy candidates still won 60 per cent of the popular vote.

In a way, this was testimony to the Patten years. If there was something absurd about a colonial governor, an appointee of the Queen, a foreigner who could not speak a word of Cantonese, giving voice to growing demands for democracy among Hong Kong Chinese, there was something real, too. He provided them with a taste of noisy, participatory politics that many found to their liking. Those who did not benefited from the fact that Patten made an already efficient Hong Kong government more open and less paternalistic, more accountable and less complacent. Senior civil servants often resented this as much as local businessmen and distant Beijing.

Whatever the fate of Britain's brief, latter-day experiment in extending democracy, the Patten approach to government left its mark on the post-handover administration. It set standards of approachability, even accountability, that TUNG CHEE-HWA, Hong Kong's first chief executive, and his senior officials felt compelled to live up to. And with the passage of time, it was only in Beijing, not Hong Kong, that Chris Patten was regarded a 'sinner for a thousand years', as a senior Communist official in the early 1990s predicted would be the case.

Peng Dehuai (1898–1974)

Alone among senior leaders of the CHINESE COMMUNIST PARTY, Peng, an uneducated, battle-hardened defence minister, took MAO ZEDONG to task over the disastrous GREAT LEAP FORWARD of 1958–60. He was purged for his pains and died years later in disgrace. His fall shattered the unity Communist leaders had managed to maintain since they came to power in 1949.

Peng, born in HUNAN, took up the military life shortly after the REPUBLICAN REVOLUTION in 1911. He fought with KUOMINTANG forces during the NORTHERN EXPEDITION to unify China but was purged in 1927 when CHIANG KAI-SHEK eliminated Communists from the revolutionary ranks. The following year he joined the Communist Party, by which time he had already linked forces with Mao and ZHU DE at Jinggangshan, the Party's revolutionary base area in JIANGXI.

In 1930, on instructions from the Party leadership, then wedded to an urban-based revolutionary strategy devised in Moscow rather than Mao's preference for rural revolt, Peng's forces twice attacked Changsha, the Hunanese capital, but failed to hold it. He withdrew to the Central Soviet Republic in Ruijin, Jiangxi, where he played a prominent role in resisting Chiang Kai-shek's 'bandit extermination' campaigns of the early 1930s. Peng undertook the LONG MARCH to north China in 1934–5 and, with the outbreak of the SINO-JAPANESE WAR in 1937, was made deputy to Zhu De, then commander-in-chief of all Communist forces. During the CIVIL WAR of 1946–9, he led the PEOPLE'S LIBERATION ARMY'S First Field Army in its conquest of northwest China. Peng continued his outstanding contributions to the Party's military cause after 1949 by leading the Chinese 'volunteers' in the KOREAN WAR.

These achievements secured Peng considerable influence and prestige in the post-1949 Party hierarchy. But his policy preferences and his fiery temperament often placed him at odds with Mao. Strains between the two men were apparent over the role and purpose of the People's Liberation Army. Peng wanted it turned into a modernized, professional fighting force, equipped with the latest weapons and functioning, like armies elsewhere, in accordance with a system of ranks. Mao and his radical allies placed emphasis on the PLA's political role. It was to serve as a beacon of ideological purity and immerse itself in economic construction and production as well as national defence.

However, it was over the consequences of the Great Leap Forward that Peng, by then a full marshal and defence minister, took issue with Mao publicly. He did so against the background of widespread hunger and distress arising from the overnight communization of agriculture that began in 1958. Official statistics spoke of soaring production. The reality, as Peng discovered during a series of visits to the provinces, was one of desperation and disaster. At the Lushan Conference of 1959, named after the hill resort in Jiangxi where it was held, he wrote a long letter to Mao about it.

Instead of regarding this as legitimate inner-Party criticism, the Chairman treated Peng's letter as a vicious attack on his policies and leadership. There were several reasons for this. The Leap had made the country, and thus the Party, tense. Relations with the SOVIET UNION were deteriorating. Peng had recently returned from Moscow. As he did so, Nikita Khrushchev cancelled an agreement under which the Soviet Union was to provide nuclear aid to China, and criticized the People's Communes established during the Leap. These developments, coupled with the fact that Mao was keen to appoint LIN BIAO, a favourite, as defence minister, encouraged the Chairman to take on Peng. He branded the astonished defence minister a 'Right opportunist' and dismissed him. Peng's supporters, most of them of second and third rank in the Party, were accused of forming a 'military clique'.

The nature and severity of this first major split at the top of the Party since the founding of the People's Republic meant that any criticism of Mao would in future court charges of betrayal. More immediately, the campaign against Peng and 'Right opportunism' intensified, prolonging the Leap long beyond the point at which it should have been abandoned and the country rescued. Peng passed the next few years in obscurity until 1965, when Mao assigned him a role in the creation of a 'Third Line' of defence industries deep in the interior capable of avoiding attack by either the United States or the Soviet Union (see INDUSTRY). Despite his pedigree as a Long Marcher, and his once heroic status as commander of Chinese forces in Korea, Peng was hounded and tortured during the CULTURAL REVOLUTION. Denied medical attention, he died in disgrace. He was posthumously rehabilitated in 1978 as China, under DENG XIAOPING, sought to correct Mao's excesses.

Peng Zhen (1902–97)

The first member of the CHINESE COMMUNIST PARTY's Politburo to be toppled in the CULTURAL REVOLUTION survived to champion legal reform in the 1970s and 1980s. But a liking for 'socialist legality' did not make Peng advocate a lesser role for the Party, or support many of the radical reforms championed by DENG XIAOPING and his allies. Instead, he resisted them in his capacity as chairman of a revived NATIONAL PEOPLE'S CONGRESS (NPC).

Already a Party veteran at the time of the Communist victory in 1949, Peng Zhen became a key figure in the new regime as mayor and Party secretary of BEIJING. His relationship with MAO ZEDONG was strained by the GREAT LEAP FORWARD but not sundered until 1965 when the Chairman again sought to radicalize the Chinese Revolution. Mayor and Chairman fell out over the meaning of a play written by Wu Han (1909–69), a deputy mayor of Beijing and leading historian. The *Dismissal of Hai Rui* was an oblique attack on Mao's dismissal in 1959 of PENG DEHUAI, the sole critic of the Leap among the top leadership. Peng Zhen defended his deputy but was no match for the radicals backing Mao's call for a 'cultural revolution'. Timidity on the part of moderates made the task even harder. Peng was sacked in 1966 and publicly humiliated at mass rallies organized by Red Guards. It was astonishing treatment for someone so senior in the hierarchy. Little was heard of him for the next 13 years.

He returned to public life in January 1979 – later than many of his fellow persecuted veterans, and after the key Central Committee meeting of December 1978 which inaugurated Deng's economic reforms. Peng did not oppose these policies so much as attack their consequences. He complained that they weakened the social, economic, ideological and, above all, political discipline essential to China's modernization drive. His position as head of the internal security apparatus, and chairman of parliament, provided platforms from which to fight back.

Peng, spritely throughout the 1980s despite advanced years and earlier political misfortunes, was most visible as chairman of the NPC's Standing Committee, its executive body. He trumpeted a new role for the legislature after years of neglect. Peng insisted that it 'examine and approve' Party policies rather than simply 'rubber stamp' them, as had previously been the case. China could not survive on policies alone; it needed a body of LAW if the country was to be run in an efficient, orderly way. Peng's vision of 'socialist legality' included close monitoring of the State Council, or cabinet, by the legislature, and in particular its Standing Committee.

New legal codes introduced an element of predictability and stability into life after the chaos of the Cultural Revolution. But it was less easy to secure an unambiguous role for the legislature in policy making. Peng's desire to boost the NPC's status stemmed more from his opposition to the policies of radical reformers such as HU YAOBANG, the Party leader, and ZHAO ZIYANG, the premier, than a fondness for parliamentarianism: he did not wish to see a formal separation of powers between legislature and executive. His concern was to check the influence of 'dangerous radicals' and prevent them from setting the agenda of modernization.

In large part he succeeded. Before he retired in 1988, Peng managed to delay or water down controversial legislation on bankruptcy, reform of state enterprises (see INDUSTRY) and the introduction of village-level elections (see DEMOCRACY). Yet though these moves might have been made for the 'wrong' reasons, they strengthened the idea that the NPC should have a bigger say in the life of the nation. A few reformers tried – and failed – to make a reality of this during the TIANANMEN SQUARE DEMOCRACY MOVEMENT by calling on the NPC to reverse the government's declaration of martial law in Beijing.

In common with that of other veterans in the 1980s, Peng's 'retirement' was largely illusory. He re-emerged in May 1989 to demand suppression of the pro-democracy protests. The veterans' call was heeded. Again like his fellow elders, Peng passed the final years of his life fêted by the younger, formal Party leaders but largely at odds with the aspirations of the society around him.

People's Liberation Army (PLA)

The People's Liberation Army brought the CHINESE COMMUNIST PARTY to power in 1949 and has kept it there ever since. In the process it defeated the KUOMINTANG and fought American-led United Nations troops in KOREA (1950–53). It engaged in border wars with INDIA (1962) and VIETNAM (1979). It launched battles with TAIWAN (1953–4 and 1958) for control of offshore islands, and dangerous skirmishes with the SOVIET UNION (1969). It aided North Vietnam in the fight against the United States (1964–5). And it clashed first with South Vietnam (1974) and then a united Vietnam (1988) over territories in the SOUTH CHINA SEA. Internally, the PLA crushed a rebellion in TIBET (1959), ruled much of the country during the CULTURAL REVOLUTION (1966–76), and suppressed the 1989 TIANANMEN SQUARE DEMOCRACY MOVEMENT. At the start of the new century, China's large but still poorly equipped military is grappling with the impli-

cations for national defence of the Gulf War of 1990–91, and NATO's 1999 campaign in Kosovo. Increased defence spending, military aggression towards Taiwan and the PLA's subordination to the Party all raise anxieties over China's growing military power.

rise of the Red Army

China's Communist military history dates from 1 August 1927, when Communist-led troops of the Kuomintang's National Revolutionary Army briefly seized Nanchang, capital of JIANGXI. 1 August has been Army Day in China since 1949. It marks the birth of a military unlike any other in China's modern history (see ARMIES).

Survivors of the Nanchang uprising led by ZHU DE joined MAO ZEDONG at his first revolutionary base, Jinggangshan. In the years that followed, the Party and its army learned the techniques of peasant revolution, guerrilla

China and the Bomb

Chairman Mao boasted in the 1950s that atomic weapons were 'paper tigers'. But he made sure China acquired one. The alternative was to be bullied in international politics. Without the bomb, China could never be a front-rank power, let alone a genuinely modern one.

In 1957 the Soviet Union promised to help China build an atomic weapon. It was the high summer of Sino-Soviet relations. In Moscow, Mao enthused over Soviet technological achievements. The launch of Sputniks I and II, and the testing of an intercontinental ballistic missile (ICBM), proved that 'The East Wind is prevailing over the West Wind.'

A few months later another remark of the Chairman's caused Khrushchev to question the wisdom of helping China build a bomb. Mao urged the socialist camp not to fear nuclear war with the United States since, even if 'half of mankind died, the other half would remain while imperialism would be razed to the ground and the whole world would become socialist'.

The implications of this became clear in 1958 when Mao launched a sudden assault on the Nationalist-held island of Quemoy (Jinmen). The American response was more vigorous than expected and there were even hints that Washington was prepared to use nuclear weapons to ensure the island did not fall. Soviet leaders, tied to the defence of China by the treaty of 1950, were alarmed. Publicly they supported Beijing. Privately, they reneged on the 1957 nuclear agreement. Worse, from China's point of view, Moscow began talks with the United States and Britain on ways to ban nuclear tests, and in 1963 signed a treaty to that effect. The Soviet Union was in league with 'imperialism' to deny China the bomb. Official US documents released in 1998 showed that Washington had considered, and then ruled out, a pre-emptive

military strike in early 1964 against China's infant nuclear installations.

The nuclear issue contributed to a growing gulf between Chinese and Soviet perceptions of how revolution should be conducted. Mao's Great Leap Forward, which coincided with the bombardment of Quemoy, was an expression of the divergence. In 1959 the Soviet Union withdrew all its advisers and the Sino-Soviet split was exposed.

Construction of nuclear facilities at Lop Nor in XIN-JIANG began before the Soviet exodus, and it is unclear how much Chinese scientists learned from their Russian comrades. The explosion of an atomic device in 1964 was a remarkable achievement all the same, and one that owed much to Marshal Nie Rongzhen (1899–1992), chairman of the Science and Technology Commission, and Qian Xuesen (1912–), an American-trained nuclear physicist. Just a few years earlier, China's accession to the nuclear club had seemed a remote possibility. In the event, it happened while the country was recovering from the disastrous famine caused by the Leap. Four years later, at the height of the Cultural Revolution, China detonated its first hydrogen bomb. Politics was in command of most areas of life under Mao, but on the question of nuclear weapons, science and expertise ruled the day.

The human, financial and environmental costs of China's nuclear programme are unclear. What is certain is that not one Chinese scientist or indeed any Chinese citizen is known to have publicly opposed their country's development of nuclear weapons on grounds of cost or morality. China is the only nuclear power without a tradition of nuclear dissent.

It is also alone in its 'no first use' policy and its call for the complete prohibition and destruction of nuclear weapons. China has made this last conditional on prior moves by others, that is, the United States

warfare and Nationalist mobilization that enabled Communism to survive CHIANG KAI-SHEK's extermination campaigns and the LONG MARCH of the 1930s; expand its reach during the SINO-JAPANESE WAR; and seize victory in the CIVIL WAR of 1946–9. It is a remarkable story in which a dedicated but dishevelled guerrilla army matured into a disciplined force and won the country in set-piece military battles involving hundreds of thousands of troops. During these 20-odd years Communist forces were known, in turn, as the 'Red Army', the 'Eighth Route Army' and, from June 1946 when the civil war started in earnest, the 'People's Liberation Army'. The term 'People's Liberation Army' refers to the Mainland's navy and airforce, as well as its ground forces.

conquest and controversy after 1949

After 1949 individual PLA 'Field Armies' garrisoned those areas of the country they conquered or 'liberated' during the civil war. On the surface, it looked as though this might make them local armies reminiscent of those controlled by WARLORDS before the Revolution. However, the PLA's loyalty to the Party, whose senior leaders exercised military command and insisted on controlling the gun, meant otherwise. Regional differences in China persisted after 1949, but under a strong new central government in Beijing they found little direct political or military expression. The exceptions were Tibet and other areas inhabited by large numbers of ETHNIC MINORI-TIES. Elsewhere, national unity was prized after 1949. More to the point, for the first time since the REPUBLICAN REVOLUTION of 1911, China had a government with the military power to enforce it.

Yet 'new' China had many weaknesses on the military front. 'Human wave' tactics of mass assault and high morale earned the 'Chinese People's Volunteers' a favourable military reputation during the early stages of and the Soviet Union. At first it said Washington and Moscow would have to make 50 per cent reductions before China's arsenal could be cut. But when, as a result of the thaw in the Cold War during the late 1980s, they began to do just that, China changed its mind. Other nuclear powers would have to reduce their armaments to China's levels before Beijing could act.

China's accession to regional treaties on the creation of nuclear-free zones in South America, the Antarctic and the South Pacific represented the 'softer' side of its nuclear policy. But this did not involve much in the way of constraints. Likewise, when China signed the Non-Proliferation Treaty (NPT) in 1991, its main interest appeared to be that of shedding the pariah status it acquired following suppression of the 1989 democracy protests. In 1994 China announced it would adhere to the terms of, but not formally accede to, the Missile Technology Control Regime (MTCR). The MTCR was devised by the world's four other nuclear powers to curb the export of equipment and technology used for the production of missiles with a range of 300 kms (187.5 miles) and a payload of 500 kgs (1,100 pounds) of the kind that would make them nuclear-capable (see ARMS SALES).

In 1996, after protracted negotiations, China joined the other nuclear powers in signing the Comprehensive Test Ban Treaty (CTBT). Beijing announced its decision to do so at the same time as it conducted a nuclear test, its 44th, which it promised would be the last. By this time the United States and Russia had carried out far more tests than China, providing them with data of the kind that could facilitate further development of their arsenals without recourse to detonations. China was anxious not to be frozen out as a second-rate nuclear power. On the other hand, signing the CTBT had advantages. At the time, it appeared likely to leave China the only nuclear power in Asia and decreased the possibility of proliferation on the Korean peninsula and in Japan. It also improved China's image as a responsible power with a clear stake in the status quo.

Yet the theory – advocated chiefly by Washington – that the NPT and the CTBT enhanced the security of *non-nuclear* as well as nuclear states was not accepted by all of them. In May 1998, first India and then Pakistan carried out nuclear tests. India found itself in the same position China had been in during the early 1960s. It refused to be excluded from the nuclear club by the five already paid-up members. And, to Beijing's concern, Delhi cited a security threat posed by China as the main reason for going nuclear. By the close of the century, China, in common with many other signatories, had yet to ratify the test ban treaty.

China's exact nuclear capabilities at the start of the new century are unclear. The test firing in 1995 of a first *mobile* intercontinental ballistic missile confirmed that development was under way. In 1999 Beijing announced it had mastered neutron-bomb technology. This followed allegations in Washington that China had, over several years, stolen America's most valuable nuclear secrets, including formulae for the production of miniaturized warheads. None of these developments pointed to a dramatic improvement in China's ability to fight a nuclear war. The largest estimate of the number of Chinese warheads is 450. The lowest 200. How many of these are deliverable is unclear. At most, China is thought to have 20 missiles capable of reaching the USA. The effectiveness of China's entire nuclear arsenal is impaired by the lack of a space-based early-warning system, and the command, control, communication and intelligence capabilities (C^3I) required to fight a 'limited' nuclear war.

the Korean War. But the lack of modern arms and poor logistics proved costly as the war dragged on. By the mid-1950s the PLA needed modernizing. Since China was following the Soviet model of national development and was tied to Moscow by treaty, Beijing turned to the same source for military reform.

During the 1950s, the Soviet Union provided aid, equipment and advice to the PLA. It also helped lay the foundations of a Chinese defence industry. China's army became more professional, and more like its Soviet counterpart. But if progress was conspicuous, so were problems – most of them of a political nature. The 'new look' PLA forsook much of its Maoist 'people's' past. The authority of commanders supplanted that of political commissars. An emphasis on ranks fostered elitism. Military life became divorced from civilian society. Emphasis was place on weapons and equipment at the expense of political indoctrination.

Mao believed these developments were alien to the Chinese Revolution. His objections, most of which amounted to implied criticism of PENG DEHUAI, the outspoken defence minister who supported Soviet-style military modernization, formed part of the Chairman's overall critique of Moscow's way of doing things. He abandoned the Soviet model in its entirety in 1958 in favour of a GREAT LEAP FORWARD.

people's war; political intervention

The Leap was a disaster for China and a political tragedy for Peng who was dismissed and disgraced for opposing it. The experiment in military modernization came to an end, too. LIN BIAO, Peng's successor, pursued Maoist values with gusto, turning the PLA into a 'great school of Mao Zedong Thought'. In 1965, he abolished ranks in the PLA – a striking example of the egalitarianism at the heart of Mao's thinking. The military was committed

Chinese Seapower

Naval expansion has accompanied the rise of almost every power in the modern era and China is no exception. Beijing's determination to assert control over offshore territory requires an ability to project power at sea. So does the defence of an enormous coastline. The Communists are not the first rulers of China to build a modern navy: wreckage of the first attempt lies at the bottom of the Yellow Sea, a casualty of the Sino-Japanese War of 1894–5. Republican governments lacked the resources to build a fleet and, during the first years of their rule, the Communists were too busy with revolution: China remained primarily a continental power.

The disappearance of the 'threat from the north' following the collapse of the Soviet Union focused attention on the southern maritime regions. The thrust of China's economic development – which has seen the maritime provinces prosper from their relationship with the international economy – has done the same. Growing power, and growing interests, have spawned calls for the transformation of the People's Liberation Army Navy (PLAN) from a coastal defence force into a 'blue water' navy capable of making China a seapower, something it has not been since the Ming dynasty (1368–1644), when fleets under the eunuch admiral Zheng He (1371–1433) patrolled the Indian Ocean.

China has made no secret of its plans: scholars and military chiefs have emphasized the need to secure the 'living space' provided by the oceans and their resources. Liu Huaqing (1916–), the most senior politician in uniform during the 1990s and a former PLAN commander, was one of many who spoke of the twenty-first century as 'the century of the sea'. He said China had 11,250 miles (18,000 kms) of coastline, more than 6,000 islands, and three million square miles (7.7 million sq kms) of territorial waters. It needed a modern navy to protect it.

The technology, training and equipment needed to move beyond coastal defence to amphibious warfare operations, replenishment at sea and submarine warfare cannot be acquired quickly. Money is required as well as time. Yet China is making progress. The first overseas visit (to Pakistan, Sri Lanka and Bangladesh) by a Chinese naval vessel occurred in 1985. In 1997, three PLAN ships berthed in San Diego, the first time Chinese naval vessels had reached mainland United States. For China's neighbours, the PLAN's growing power is apparent in the SOUTH CHINA SEA. Taiwan, long familiar with Communist military might, had a foretaste of its naval potential in 1996 when Beijing staged tri-service war games across the Straits to coincide with the island's presidential elections. It took the presence of United States warships in the area to bring Beijing's adventurism to a halt. Of more direct concern to Taiwan are Beijing's moves to upgrade its submarine fleet. China has launched its indigenously made *Song* class vessels and purchased four Kilo-class submarines from Russia. It has also unveiled a new class of frigate, the *Jiangwei*, complete with indigenously manufactured guided missiles.

These developments aside, China's naval build-up does not yet threaten the balance of power in East Asia. The navy lacks an aircraft carrier and large landing craft. The airforce has little in the way of in-flight refuelling capacity and has only recently begun to acquire airborne warning and command (AWAC) platforms. China's desire for an aircraft carrier is well known. The same goes for the problems involved in obtaining one, deploying it, and defending it. It seems unlikely that the navy will be able to muster the money, skills and associated frigates, submarines and aircraft necessary to support carrier operations before 2010.

to fighting a 'people's war' against invaders who, by the mid-1960s, were thought most likely to be Soviet armies attacking from the north or American forces extending their campaign against Communism in North Vietnam into China. In the event of war, PLA strategy was to lure these technologically superior foes deep into China and then overwhelm them using politically inspired defence forces.

To some extent this strategy reflected the fact that there was little money for the purchase of modern weapons because of the havoc wrought by the Leap. Such funds as were available were devoted to the drive to build an atomic bomb following Moscow's refusal to supply the one it had promised China in 1957. Beijing exploded its first atomic device in 1964.

Under Lin Biao, the PLA became a key actor in the second of Mao's two epic disasters: the Cultural Revolution. As the struggle over the scope and purpose of this movement intensi-

fied, the army sided with the radicals in Beijing associated with JIANG QING, Mao's wife. This tended to make the military a tool of a faction within the Party rather than the servant of the Central Committee. Once the Cultural Revolution began, and vicious struggles broke out across China between the Party establishment and warring Red Guards, the PLA had to step in and run the country. In theory its task, as spelt out by Mao and Lin in 1967, was to 'support the Left'. In practice it, too, fell prey to the divisions and conflicts that rent almost every sector of society.

The effects of this on PLA morale, discipline and combat ability – all of them put to the test in serious border clashes with the Soviet Union in 1969 – were grave. Moreover they long outlasted the mysterious demise in a plane crash of Lin Biao in 1971, allegedly after failing to carry out a plot to assassinate Mao. The military had to 'hold the ring' while Party and government organizations struggled to

The People's Armed Police: China's Paramilitary

A paramilitary force, close to 1-million strong, occupies the frontline in the fight against internal disorder across China. Simmering ethnic unrest, growing unemployment, sporadic protests and rising crime keep the People's Armed Police (PAP) busy. It was formed in 1983 to relieve the PLA of most of its internal security duties. Its ranks contain regular soldiers demobilized during the PLA's modernization programme. PAP troops guard China's borders, prisons, government and Party buildings, communications facilities, foreign embassies and diplomatic residences. They also form the country's fire brigade.

The PAP performed badly during the 1989 Tiananmen Square protests. The scale of the demonstrations caught the paramilitary by surprise. Units in Beijing lacked both equipment and experience to deal with massive civil unrest. They were rapidly overwhelmed, forcing the Communist Party to call in the regular army. After Tiananmen the PAP underwent a thorough reorganization.

Fighting conventional crime is the duty of China's 1 million regular police, or Public Security Bureau officers. But PAP units join them in campaigns against organized crime, particularly drug smuggling. They are also active curbing unrest in the countryside over taxes, corruption and the government's use of IOUs to pay farmers for grain; suppressing ethnic protests in Tibet, Xinjiang and Qinghai; and stamping out demonstrations by workers laid off during the reform of state-owned enterprises. Such duties have tested the PAP's resources, efficiency and discipline. A sensational incident in 1996 showed these were not all they should be. The PAP bodyguard assigned to Li Pei-yao (1933–96), a vice-chairman of the National People's Congress, murdered his charge during the course of an attempted robbery. Ba Zhongtan (1930–), PAP commander, and a protégé of Jiang Zemin, was dismissed as a result.

unite and reassert themselves during the Chairman's last days. The agony continued until October 1976, a month after Mao's death, when HUA GUOFENG, the Chairman's chosen successor, ordered PLA Unit 8341 to arrest Jiang Qing and the other members of the 'GANG OF FOUR' who were bent on seizing power. In 1977 DENG XIAOPING, twice disgraced during the Cultural Revolution, re-emerged to assume a senior position in Beijing. The following year he set China on a new course of economic reform and modernization.

modernization, intervention

Deng, whose long years as a political commissar with the PLA meant he could count on military backing for many of his policies, forced the army to withdraw from politics. He

demanded a reduction in troop numbers and rapid modernization of weapons, strategy and tactics. The importance of the military could not be denied. Neither could its role in the Revolution. But national defence was the last of the FOUR MODERNIZATIONS, the Party's new, post-Mao orthodoxy. The military budget was cut and new emphasis placed on quality and specialization rather than quantity and politicization. The poor performance of the PLA during the border war against Vietnam in 1979 showed how necessary this was (see VIETNAM); and during the 1980s China's military underwent significant change.

By the end of the decade, the three service arms between them had demobilized one million men, many of whom were absorbed into the newly formed People's Armed Police. This reduced overall PLA strength to about three and a half million. Ranks were reintroduced and military doctrine transformed. The new orthodoxy – 'People's War Under Modern Conditions' – called on the PLA to fight an enemy 'at the gates' rather than lure foes into Chinese territory.

Until the very end of the 1980s, the most likely invader was still felt to be the Soviet Union. China's gravest threat still came from the north, as it had in traditional times. To meet it, Beijing was forced to rely mainly on weapons manufactured at home. Its attempts to obtain defence technologies from the United States and Western Europe met with little success. The spectacle of PLA troops gunning down unarmed protestors on the streets of Beijing in June 1989 made the prospect of arms deals with the West more remote. Washington and the European Union imposed a ban on military sales to Beijing that endured for the remainder of the century.

The suppression of the Tiananmen Square Democracy Movement marked the second great military intervention in Chinese politics after 1949. However, it was quite different from the first. Since parts of Beijing were under martial law between May 1989 and January 1990, the PLA did assume a role in civil administration. But it differed from that taken on during the Cultural Revolution. In May 1989, the PLA was ordered to suppress a protest movement against the regime. It did so, remained on the streets until the emergency was deemed to be over, and then returned to barracks. There was no coup – disguised or otherwise – or military meddling in civilian politics.

Yet the exercise dealt an enormous blow to the prestige of the 'people's' army. No pre-

Formal Structure of PLA

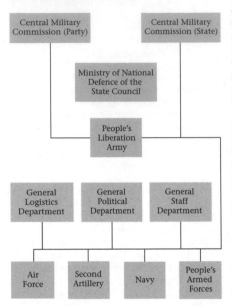

Central Military Commission (Party)

Central Military Commission (State)

Ministry of National Defence of the State Council

People's Liberation Army

General Logistics Department

General Political Department

General Staff Department

Air Force

Second Artillery

Navy

People's Armed Forces

Victory would go to the force that mastered computers and complex electronics rather than Mao Zedong 'Thought'. Wars would be won by elite forces – suddenly and without the need for lengthy fighting on land or even military occupation. Command, control, communications and intelligence (C³I) were essential. So were flexible operations in the air and at sea. These two elements had been neglected in traditional Chinese military thinking. Things would have to change.

The Gulf War coincided with a change of geographical focus in Chinese defence thinking, one that marked a break with the past and contained major implications for East Asian security. It was a shift in threat perceptions from north to south, from China's continental to its maritime provinces which had grown rich and strategically important on the back of economic reforms. The collapse of the Soviet Union, the establishment of good relations with the RUSSIAN FEDERATION, and the settlement of the disputed Sino-Russian border during the 1990s, meant that for the first time in centuries, China faced no serious military threat from the north. Far from threatening China's 'inner' frontiers, Moscow was keen to secure them. It has since become a valued source of modern arms for the PLA – notably of fighters and submarines. At the start of the new century, China is more secure along the entire length of its land frontiers than at any time since the Opium Wars of the 1840s.

The same cannot be said of China's long coastline or the oceans and islands beyond. While there is no immediate military threat in this vast region, China faces several challenges. Chief among them is the existence of a rival Chinese government in Taiwan, and the threat that it will seek independence, fall under foreign influence, or simply seek refuge inside an American Theater Missile Defense (TMD) to avoid a recurrence of the cross-Straits crisis of 1996 when Beijing test-fired missiles close to the island's two main harbours (see TAIWAN). Rivalry with JAPAN over the Diaoyutai Islands in the East China Sea is a minor matter by comparison. But the strengthening of Tokyo's defence ties with Washington in 1999 provides for a greater Japanese military role in the region with implications for Beijing's military ambitions towards Taiwan. In the South China Sea, a region of considerable economic and strategic importance, Beijing's claims to territory are contested by several ASEAN countries as well as Taiwan.

vious Chinese regime dared attempt what the Communists did in 1989: turn the army on unarmed citizens in the heart of the capital. The PLA, almost certainly out of loyalty to Deng Xiaoping and other members of the old guard, behaved professionally in the sense that it acted as ordered by the civilian power. Tiananmen therefore was not so much a failure of the military as a failure of a political system in which the Party, in the form of a handful of veteran revolutionaries, controlled the gun.

Nevertheless, some commanders hesitated before turning their troops on the people. And once the crisis was over, Yang Baibing (1920–), head of the PLA's Political Department and half brother of the then president, YANG SHANGKUN, weeded out 'unreliable elements' among the top brass and sought to re-politicize the military from top to bottom. It was a minor – and brief – retreat from the pre-Tiananmen goals of professionalism and modernization.

high-tech wars, maritime strategies

The Gulf War of 1990–91 helped check this campaign. It showed that future wars were likely to be local and high tech in nature.

China's Air Force: A Weak Link?

The Kuomintang and even several warlords possessed small air forces, but military aircraft made almost no impact in the battles Chinese fought against each other during the first half of the twentieth century. During the Civil War, the Nationalists failed to use their air superiority arising from the fact that they owned a few planes while the Communists had almost none. This did not spare Chinese the horrors of aerial bombardment: Japan's air force caused widespread fear and destruction during the Sino-Japanese War, subjecting first Shanghai and then Chongqing to sustained, deadly assault. Air battles played an important role in the Korean War, and formed part of the Communist assault on Quemoy during the Taiwan Straits crisis of 1958. But in China's conflict with India of 1962, the Soviet Union in 1969 and Vietnam 10 years later, air power was either non-existent or played a marginal role.

Perhaps this explains why, during China's military build-up of the 1980s and 1990s, the People's Liberation Army Air Force (PLAAF) was the weakest of the three service arms. The weakness is still apparent in terms of technology and personnel.

At the start of the new century most of the PLAAF's 4,000 or so fighters are of 1950s and 1960s Soviet vintage. Its bombers, though in some cases nuclear-capable, are equally old and vulnerable to attack from modern fighters. The air force is working on the development of in-flight re-fuelling capabilities; and Israel is among the governments willing to supply China with airborne warning and command (AWAC) facilities, possibly for installation in Ilyushin airframes.

China has boosted its air power by purchasing up to 100 Sukhoi-27 (SU-27s) fighter bombers from Russia, and securing the right to co-produce them at home. Agreements on the sale of superior SU-30s were pending as the twentieth century came to a close. These developments suggest that Taiwan's American-made F-16s and French-made Mirage fighters will soon face a more serious challenge in the skies over the Straits. Beijing is also at work on an indigenous fighter bomber, the *Jian 10*, in which Israel Aircraft Industries is believed to be involved. These new technologies call for intensive pilot training, and the small amount of flying time granted to Mainland pilots at the close of the century suggested the PLAAF enjoyed only limited all-weather and night-time navigation capacities. Thus several years are required before China's air force can shed its backwardness and project power very much further than the limits it had reached in the late 1990s.

For China, neutralizing these challenges is an essential – and natural – part of national rejuvenation. There can be no question of China becoming a major power if it cannot assert absolute control over its territory, however far offshore that territory might be and whoever might claim it. Economic imperatives complement questions of national pride:

overpopulated and hungry for ENERGY, China seeks control of the rich aquatic and mineral resources of the South China Sea to sustain rapid economic growth. In a highly competitive world, continental shelves and exclusive economic zones need military protection as much as the Mainland.

military spending and expansion

This requires military spending. Excessive secrecy surrounding China's military budget worries Beijing's neighbours and accounts for wide discrepancies in the estimates of overseas analysts. Beijing's publication of defence 'White Papers' has not shed much light. There is no doubt that military spending is on the rise, probably at a faster rate than official figures suggest. China is devoting more funds to the military at a time when it has never been so secure.

The PLA derives significant extra-budgetary revenue from ARMS SALES and, until the close of the century, a vast business empire. During the 1980s and 1990s, the military controlled thousands of companies. Many produced defence equipment, but many turned out civilian goods. Several owned luxury hotels, discos and nightclubs. Commercial activity on this scale fostered corruption and impaired military professionalism. In 1998 President JIANG ZEMIN tried to tackle both, and secure greater control over the military, by ordering the PLA to cease all its business operations by the end of that year. It was a brave move by a man whose position as Party leader made him commander-in-chief of the PLA but whose non-military background suggested the new policy entailed risks. A year after the order went out, the official media reported that the PLA had handed over control of its businesses to a civilian commission pending their sale, and that the defence budget would be increased to compensate the military for any losses. About the same time the Party confirmed that the demobilization of 500,000 men, announced in 1997, was under way to reduce the ranks of the PLA to approximately three million.

While China's military might is growing at the start of the new century, it is not disproportionate to the country's aspirations to become a major power – a status its rulers have dreamt of for the past 150 years. Since Beijing is determined to recover 'lost territories' in the seas to its south, it seeks to project its power in the form of a modern navy and air force. Since it is keen to catch up with the advanced world in material terms, it tries to keep pace with modern weapons technology, and spends more on buying or developing them. It starts the new century with a particularly formidable armoury of missiles, many of them targeted on Taiwan. This is not to say China's aspirations are justified, or that China presents no military threat to Taiwan or its other neighbours. The PLA could easily snatch a few outlying islands from the Nationalists, mount a naval blockade of the main island, or subject Taipei and other cities to sustained missile attack. Beijing is a menace to Taiwan and soon might be to those countries who dare assert their claims in the South China Sea.

Yet missiles aside, the PLA is far behind the state-of-the-art in weapons technology, and there is little question of it catching up before at least 2010, however big Beijing's defence budget. The chances of the PLA making up for lost ground by devising a telling new military strategy are no more encouraging, at least from China's point of view. NATO's air war against Yugoslavia in 1999 prompted a new round of strategic soul searching in Beijing made pertinent by the accidental bombing of the Chinese embassy in Belgrade. For if PLA chiefs could draw comfort from the ability of Yugoslavia's military machine to survive the war largely intact there was little cheer to be derived from Belgrade's loss of Kosovo and the fact that NATO achieved its objectives without the loss of so much as one serviceman in combat. This war of systems and technologies rather than generals and peoples pointed to the need for a another doctrinal shift in warfare – as well as better equipment and training – for the PLA.

controlling the gun

Outside China, uncertainty about the ambitions and capabilities of the PLA is compounded by concern over the army's relations with the Communist Party. The Party created the PLA and the PLA does its bidding. In organizational terms, it is subordinate to the Party's Central Military Commission, the high command, and controlled through a system of interlocking hierarchies, political commissars and committees that stretch down into the ranks within the seven great military regions into which the Mainland is divided. The Party, not the ministry of defence, controls the army (see GOVERNMENT AND ADMINISTRATION).

In the past, the PLA was under the personal control of senior political figures, notably Mao

Zedong and Deng Xiaoping, who rose to power with and, in some respects, *within* the military. Between 1949 and the 1990s these men, and a handful of others, such as Lin Biao, LIU SHAOQI and ZHOU ENLAI, combined in their persons power over the Party, the PLA and the state, all of whose interests were deemed to be the same.

This changed with the decline of Deng's health in the early 1990s and his death in 1997. Jiang Zemin became China's supreme leader – and the first since the EMPRESS DOWAGER to lack either a military background or even solid connections with the armed forces. Jiang sought to remedy this with frequent visits to barracks, well-publicized promotions of men he viewed as allies and increased defence spending. A new national defence law in 1997 made clear the Party's absolute control over the PLA. And Jiang frequently echoed Mao's remarks dating back to the late 1920s, that the Party must control the gun. But all this still left open the questions of whether the Party would – and whether it should.

The first question arose because the legacy of the Cultural Revolution and the suppression in Tiananmen Square, growing professionalization in the forces and, more recently, the demise of the Long March generation all suggested that the PLA might be reluctant to come to the defence of the Party in the event of civil unrest. Perhaps, in the worst of all worlds, *some* military units would obey orders to crush peaceful protests while others refused. In other words, the PLA's attempts to operate as both a professional and a Party army would generate divided loyalties.

The second question touched on the constitutional position of the PLA as the servant of the Chinese Communist Party rather than the state. In Communist China's occasional moments of relative intellectual freedom, there have been pleas for the army to be decoupled from the Party and 'nationalized'. Party dominance of the military has been seen as outdated, a sign of the Party's inability to shed its past as a rebel movement which swept to power on horseback. According to this view, since the Party has been in power for decades it should feel confident enough to relax its grip on the armed forces, as it has over many other areas of life.

However, the fact that such views have been heard but rarely, and then swiftly countered, testifies to the fact that, in an important respect, China still cannot be regarded as a 'modern' state. For it shows that the Commu-

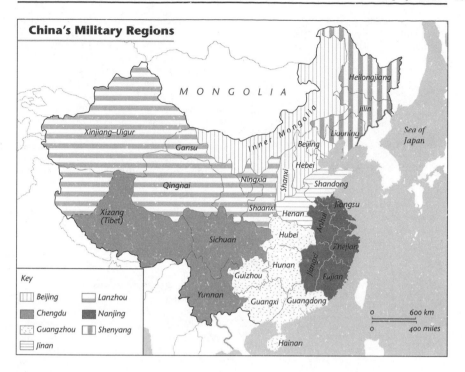

China's Military Regions

MONGOLIA

Heilongjiang

Jilin

Xinjiang–Uigur

Gansu

Inner Mongolia

Liaoning

Beijing

Sea of Japan

Hebei

Qinghai

Ningxia

Shanxi

Shandong

Shaanxi

Henan

Jiangsu

Anhui

Xizang (Tibet)

Sichuan

Hubei

Zhejiang

Hunan

Jiangxi

Fujian

Guizhou

Yunnan

Guangxi

Guangdong

Hainan

Key

- Beijing
- Chengdu
- Guangzhou
- Jinan
- Lanzhou
- Nanjing
- Shenyang

0   600 km
0   400 miles

nist Party feels, probably correctly, that it lacks both the legitimacy and the popularity needed to stay in power without the backing of the People's Liberation Army.

population

For centuries the world's most populous state, Mainland China at the start of the new millennium has a population just short of 1.3 billion (including HONG KONG and MACAU). No government has ever tried to rule so many people, let alone subject them to rapid modernization on the basis of fragile material resources. And if history provides few clues to the problems of governing on such a scale in such circumstances, the Communist government's demonization of demography for 30 years has made matters worse. So much so that when Beijing woke up to its population problem in the late 1970s it embarked on the most draconian birth control policy undertaken anywhere in the world. Many governments have imposed controls over the growth of their populations; only China's Communists have intervened directly, on a massive scale and using punitive means, to regulate reproduction itself. The consequences have been both dramatic and traumatic.

counting heads

A huge population has long been one of China's defining characteristics. So have official head counts to determine its size. But by the middle of the twentieth century, few had any clues as to the number of people who lived in China. Estimates, samples and assessments, some of them conducted by foreigners, none of them worthy of the name census, ranged from 350 million to 600 million. Republican governments, like the QING DYNASTY that preceded them, lacked the administrative muscle – to say nothing of the political control – required to enumerate their subjects. The first government to do so on a scientific basis was that of the People's Republic. Its census of 1953 fell short of the standards of

Eugenics

In 1994 China unveiled a draft law on Eugenics and Health. It was designed to prevent 'new births of inferior quality' in a country where 10 million people were mentally retarded and a further 10 million disabled from birth. Health minister Chen Minzhang (1931–) said such figures could be reduced by 'better controls'. The law provided them by requiring deferral of marriage, abortion or sterilization on the part of those likely to give birth to children with major congenital defects. It provoked outrage in the West because of its apparent similarity to Nazi-style eugenics. Beijing quietly renamed it. The Natal and Health Care Law, designed to 'upgrade the quality of the population', came into effect in June 1995. Under it, the state is obliged to provide pre-marriage or pre-natal health care, check-ups, consultation and guidance to citizens. Those found to be suffering from mental or contagious diseases must defer marriage, while pregnant women found to be carrying seriously abnormal babies are advised to have abortions. In various 'explanations' issued over subsequent years, and said to have the force of law, it was pointed out that sterilizations and abortions could take place only with the consent of the couple concerned or their guardians. It was unclear if this meant much given some of the abuses associated with the one-child policy.

Western demography but was a tribute to the purpose and organizational ability of the young Communist state. The same is true of its introduction of the HUKOU system of household registration.

The census revealed a Mainland population of 582.6 million. While this precise figure was new, the main reasons why China's population was so large were well understood. The engine of growth was – as it remains – the demand for sons. Sons are needed to work the land, still the primary occupation for about half the total workforce at the start of the new century. (See AGRICULTURE.) Sons are needed to carry on the family name, less important amid the rapid urbanization of the 1990s but still a factor among rural families. And sons are needed to provide for parents in old age, a vital form of social security given the absence of a national pension scheme and where, as again remains the case, daughters usually leave home on marriage to assume responsibility for their husband's family (see FAMILY; WOMEN).

The 1953 census provided statistical evidence of another feature of China's population that remains prominent half a century later: its extremely uneven distribution. Climate, terrain and communications have determined this, populating China densely in the east, sparsely in the west. Perhaps 70 per cent of China's people live on the plains, valleys and hills confined largely to the coastal provinces, and those of the east and south. Together these regions account for about one-third of the total land area. 'Outer' China – the inland provinces and homelands of the least assimilated of the ETHNIC MINORITIES – is inhabited by 10–15 per cent of the population yet constitutes just over half of China's total land area. The Communist government has tried to redress this imbalance by encouraging migration to the north and west. The aim has been to develop the economy in frontier regions and beef up the ethnic Chinese presence there to deter attempts at secession. To some extent both goals have been achieved, though at the cost of poor relations between Han and non-Han.

Mao on people: more means better

Despite some opposing views, the overriding assumption in China during the 1950s was that a large population was an asset not a hindrance to development. Among the ideological dispositions Beijing acquired from the Soviet Union was fierce opposition to the ideas of Thomas Malthus (1766–1834), the English economist who prophesied that mankind was doomed to poverty because of its tendency to multiply beyond the means of existence. The only solution was birth control; famine, war or disease would accomplish what late marriage and contraception did not.

Malthus's teachings did not square with those of Marx. More important, they were anathema to MAO ZEDONG for whom people, once infused with revolutionary will, were not subject to the constraints of the material environment. There were no population problems that ideology, revolution and production could not solve; poverty arose because of oppression not overpopulation.

The Chairman's view was characteristically liberating and characteristically wrong. Ma Yinchu (1882–1982), chancellor of Beijing University, found the courage to say as much in his paper *New Population Theory*. In 1960 he was condemned as a Malthusian and purged. Less than 10 years after it had taken power in the world's most populous country, the Communist Party denied China had a population problem and effectively outlawed demography. When, 20 years later and in a mood of thinly disguised panic, the Party changed its mind, one of the first things it did was rehabilitate Ma. He was then close to 100 years old. Since the publication of his *New Population Theory*, 22 years earlier, China's population had grown by 325 million.

For the most part the period of Ma's disgrace was a departure from science and rational behaviour of almost every kind. Certainly there was little interest in population control. In the late 1950s Mao was mobilizing the millions for the GREAT LEAP FORWARD. Since China's masses were going to propel their country into Communism overnight, the more people there were the better. Economic development aside, China needed a massive population for national defence. The Sino-Soviet split (see SOVIET UNION) of the early 1960s added Moscow to Beijing's already long list of ideological foes. War with the UNITED STATES or the Soviet bloc might break out at any moment. China's millions were the country's primary weapon against technologically superior enemies.

Tragically, within two years of the Leap, China's people became less numerous. Famine, much of it the result of the neglect of traditional farming techniques in favour of madcap planting schemes and 'backyard' industries, claimed millions of lives. The losses during 1958–63 only came to light outside China 20 years after they occurred when foreign demographers examined newly available statistics for the period. A 50 per cent fall in the birth rate, a 100 per cent increase in the death rate and a slip in overall population growth from 2 per cent per annum to 1.5 per cent meant there were up to 30 million premature deaths during and immediately after the Leap years.

Beijing conducted another census in 1964. Its results were kept secret for 15 years. They showed a population of 694.5 million. Hopes that this exercise might see a return of demography worth the name were dashed by the CULTURAL REVOLUTION. For much of the following 10 years the state was in crisis. For most of the first 3 it was in chaos. Population planning and control were as impossible as they were politically undesirable.

the 1970s: demography rediscovered

This began to change in the early 1970s. Beijing opened to the West and claimed China's seat at the UNITED NATIONS. It joined the world body at a time of global concern about overpopulation. Some in China shared the anxieties. Quietly, falteringly, demography was rediscovered. Specialists and, soon, some

Party leaders realized that, at the very least, the growth of China's population would have to be controlled if there was to be any hope of genuine material improvement for the people. This became even clearer in the late 1970s when the Party, then led by DENG XIAO-PING, abandoned Mao's pursuit of revolution in favour of higher living standards.

Although China's birth rate had come down compared with earlier periods, further increases in the population were inevitable because of the baby boom of the 1950s. A detailed picture would have to wait until the third census, conducted in 1982 (it showed a population of 1.008 billion, not far short of double the 1953 figure). But it was already clear that well over 100 million women were approaching marriageable age. The new Marriage Law of 1980 raised the minimum age for marriage to 22 for men from 20 and from 18 to 20 for women, but this was too little too late. A drop in infant mortality due to improved health care, and an increase in life expectancy partly for the same reason, fuelled population growth (see HEALTH).

Given the alarming new scenario, the Party maintained that child-bearing was not simply a matter for individuals or the family. It was a matter for the nation, the state and the future of socialism. And it was necessary not merely to *control* population growth but to *reduce* it. The Party had once denied China had a population problem. Since 1979, when the one-child policy was implemented, it has pursued the most comprehensive birth control policy in the world.

the era of the only child

The one-child-per-family policy marked the extension of Chinese state power into the most private realm of human behaviour. Like many Chinese Communist campaigns it pursued an ideal that was unattainable: one-child families became the rule in the cities, but in the countryside two or more was the norm. In principle, ethnic minorities were exempt from the policy. Yet the goal of reducing family size was pursued vigorously, almost throughout the country, with a mixture of incentives and harsh punishments. Abuses and cruelties accompanied the general indignity of state intervention in the reproductive process. One-child-per-family soon became the most hated of all the Party's policies. And opposition to it was not diminished by the fact that, thanks to Deng's capitalist-style reforms, living standards were improving and most

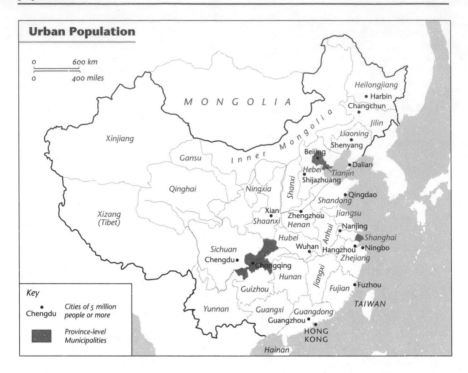

Urban Population

Key
- • Cities of 5 million people or more
- ▨ Province-level Municipalities

people were reclaiming their lives after years of Maoist tyranny.

On the incentive side, couples who pledged to have only one child were rewarded with bonuses, larger apartments, improved medical care and places at the best schools for their sole offspring. Those who refused, or agreed but then went ahead with a second birth, faced fines and discrimination in the distribution of everything their employers or DANWEI (work units) provided. Until the 1990s, and for most urban residents thereafter, the *danwei* supplied almost everything from apartments to holidays. They also conducted the monitoring of people's sex lives which was at the heart of the one-child policy, approving or refusing marriages, distributing contraceptives, keeping track of employees' menstrual cycles and trying to ensure that birth 'quotas' handed down by the government were not exceeded.

Control was looser in the countryside, where couples whose first child was a girl were often allowed to try again for a son. But cadres charged with reducing the number of births were sometimes feared more than in the cities. Far from major administrative centres, they were subject to less restraint and more open to corruption. If this benefited richer families it left those who were poor and without influence at the mercy of local officials in matters of pregnancy. In towns and villages, compulsory sterilization and abortion – sometimes conducted dangerously late – were common. Wherever it was practised, the one-child policy frequently crossed the line between persuasion and coercion, a difficult line to draw in China's authoritarian society. Birth control Chinese-style soon attracted international criticism on HUMAN RIGHTS grounds.

Baby girls were among the main casualties of the policy. Thirty years of Communism did much to improve the status of women but failed to overcome centuries of prejudice. If the desire for sons diminished in the cities, it remained as strong as ever in the countryside. Couples who failed to produce a son first or second time now faced the possibility of not being able to try their luck again. Some desperate parents resorted to female infanticide, an ancient, gruesomely well-attested practice in traditional China. More turned to technology, using ultrasound scanners, widely available in rural China from the late 1980s, to discover the sex of their unborn children. Female foetuses were often aborted in the

Urbanization: 'Floating Population'

Urbanization in China is a methodologist's minefield: complex criteria are used to measure the movement of people into the Mainland's towns, cities and megacities. But the confusion has not disguised the fact that an ever larger share of China's population lives and works in urban areas, and that new urban and peri-urban areas are transforming the landscape as the pace of industrialization intensifies.

During the nineteenth century the drift to the towns proceeded at the same rate as the overall increase in population. It picked up in the twentieth century: in 1938 an estimated 27 million people – 5–6 per cent of the total of around 500 million – lived in cities with a population of more than 50,000. Mainland cities grew rapidly after the Communist Revolution, luring people with the promise of a better life and providing work on giant construction projects. This was particularly the case during the Great Leap Forward: in 1958 alone the urban population swelled by at least 30 million and, according to some estimates, by more than twice that number. When famine struck, the Party tried to empty the cities to take the strain off grain stores. The outflow intensified during the Cultural Revolution when at least 14 million city residents were rusticated, mainly so they could 'learn' from the peasants.

Urbanization revived and accelerated during the reform era. For much of the 1980s the *hukou* system of household registration helped preserve the divide between city and countryside; it was difficult to change official domicile from village to town and enjoy the entitlements that followed. But at the end of the decade and throughout the 1990s, a vast 'floating population', perhaps 100 million strong and composed mostly of surplus farm workers – many of them from poor, overpopulated provinces such as ANHUI and SICHUAN – settled in, or on the outskirts of, almost every major Mainland city.

The new arrivals undertook low-paid, dirty jobs that most established urban residents shunned. There were complaints about the crime and prostitution *waidiren* ('outside people') allegedly brought with them. Certainly the quasi-shanty towns that housed them in Beijing and other cities were unsightly. There was also concern that, simply by virtue of their mobility, nearly all of the migrants had escaped controls imposed to restrict families to one child. It was less often acknowledged that the services they performed, whether as maids, construction workers, or stallholders in local markets made life in China's cities more comfortable than it might have been. Also important was the fact that migrants transferred billions of *renminbi* each year back to their families, from the towns to the countryside, from the coast to the interior. Given the widening gulf between rural and urban China, this redistributive function was welcome.

The 'floating population' has contributed to China's modernization in another sense: its members have forsaken their villages and the rhythms of agriculture for hard, but more sophisticated, lifestyles in the cities. They are often at the bottom of the social heap in cities such as Beijing, Shanghai and Shenzhen. But they are exposed to a whole new range of Chinese and international experiences. For many of them, life will never be the same.

In 1949 6 Mainland cities had more than 1 million people: SHANGHAI, TIANJIN, BEIJING, Nanjing, Guangzhou and Shenyang. At the start of the new century, 23 do. Beyond the Mainland, Hong Kong, Taipei and Kaohsiung (also in Taiwan) are in the same league. Urbanization is most advanced in the eastern provinces where an unofficial study in the late 1990s put it at 40 per cent compared with 20 per cent in the west of the country. The national level in the mid-1990s was 33 per cent, 3.1 per cent higher than that claimed in official estimates.

Though urbanization has inflicted grave harm on the environment, and many of China's cities lack redeeming features, in terms of either architecture or urban planning, their rapid expansion points to radical changes in the nature of Chinese society. Potentially they are seedbeds of a more independent, sophisticated political culture of the kind seen in the West and centres elsewhere in Asia. As China's urban residents grow wealthy and become better educated, the shoots of civil society are emerging.

hope that the next pregnancy might produce a son.

The government banned both practices but with mixed success. This was clear from statistics on the sex ratio obtained from the 1990 census. It showed a total population for the People's Republic of 1.13 billion and revealed that far more boys were being born than girls. Millions of baby girls had gone 'missing'. The birth of some, perhaps many, simply went unreported by parents keen to disguise the fact that their first child was a girl and they would try again for a son. But abortion, infanticide and the dumping of baby girls in orphanages, described by the Western media in the 1990s as 'Dying Rooms' (see HUMAN RIGHTS), must have accounted for many of the rest. In any event, the imbalance between the sexes created fears that in future an 'army of bachelors' would have to roam China in search of wives. This created business opportunities of its own: beginning in the early 1980s gangs abducted peasant girls and smuggled them to other parts of the country where they were sold as wives.

Anxiety was also expressed over the consequences for Chinese society of millions of single children. The 'little emperors' of the 1980s and 1990s were the sole subjects of parents' and grandparents' concern. They had no need to share anything with brothers, sisters, or multiple cousins, all of whom, along with aunts and uncles, are destined to be become rare in urban China.

Old people, on the other hand, will become more common. China's population – and that of TAIWAN, home of 22 million at the start of the century – is ageing rapidly with perhaps one quarter of the population likely to be elderly by 2030–2040. At the close of the twentieth century, questions were raised over the care of China's future pensioners. Pending the creation of a comprehensive welfare system, the government in 1996 passed a law on the protection of the rights and interests of the elderly. It was an enlightened measure. But in so far as it obliged children to provide economic and spiritual support for their parents, and warned of punishment for those who failed to do so, it pointed to the hardships faced by China's elderly, once provided for as a matter of course in keeping with the traditions of CONFUCIANISM.

a continuing burden

When the one-child policy was introduced, the aim was to restrict the population to 1.2 billion by the year 2000. That figure was reached in February 1995. In the late 1990s, 21 million babies were born in China each year, ensuring a net annual increase in population of 13 million. The government announced that the total should be kept to less than 1.3 billion by the turn of the century, 1.4 billion by the year 2010 and between 1.5–1.6 billion by the year 2030.

These figures may prove unattainable, despite the dramatic reduction in growth attributable to birth control and Beijing's

China's Ten Most Populous Provinces *(to the nearest million in 1997)*	
1. Henan	92m
2. Shandong	88m
3. Sichuan	84m
4. Jiangsu	71.4m
5. Guangdong	70.5m
6. Hebei	66m
7. Hunan	65m
8. Anhui	61m
9. Hubei	59m
10. Guangxi	46m

turn-of-century pledge to stick to such policies for a further 50 years. This is because economic reform is weakening the hold of the state over people's lives *and* making couples rich enough to bear the costs of fines imposed for having too many children.

Prosperity and improved levels of education have reduced family size in many parts of the world. As the century came to a close, they were doing so in parts of China, too – notably in SHANGHAI, one of China's most sophisticated cities. But only in parts. For at least the next 50 years, China's huge population will place a heavy strain on food supplies, the environment, the job market and the national budget. And however strong the performance of the economy, China's hundreds of millions will ensure that, on a per capita basis, the benefits remain modest.

poverty

Difficult to quantify but far harder to endure, poverty scarred millions of Chinese lives in the last century and haunts many at the start of this. Its roots lie in overpopulation, a weak agricultural base and a fragile environment – factors likely to keep China poor on a per capita basis for years to come (see POPULATION; AGRICULTURE; ENVIRONMENT). Prevailing political, social and economic arrangements ensure unequal distribution of such wealth as exists.

A desire to escape poverty, both personal and national, is the common denominator behind virtually every movement for political change in modern China. The search for wealth, as well as power, links LIANG QICHAO, the early twentieth-century reformer, with DENG XIAOPING, the Communist strongman

of the 1980s and early 1990s; it binds SUN YAT-SEN to MAO ZEDONG. Each of these leaders pursued different policies; all wanted to make China rich, as well as strong, and to secure fundamental improvements in the material lives of its people.

The CHINESE COMMUNIST PARTY was the first to do so on any scale, largely by redistributing wealth through LAND REFORM, and then trying to equalize it by establishing collectives and communes. The first of these measures raised the incomes of the poorest peasants. The second and third introduced the principle, if not always the practice, of egalitarianism – an ideal (though often only an ideal) that dominated urban and rural life in the Mainland under Mao. The gains delivered by redistribution and economic growth in the early years of Communism were checked by the disastrous GREAT LEAP FORWARD of 1958–60 and later the CULTURAL REVOLUTION (1966–76). Mao's experiments in revolution delivered political and economic misery on a massive scale, claiming the lives of millions and committing more to long-term poverty.

There was no significant improvement in the wealth of the Chinese people until Deng launched the reform and Open Door policy in 1978. The return to household farming at the heart of the new approach sparked a rapid rise in rural incomes. Reforms in the urban areas during the 1980s and the rapid growth of FOREIGN TRADE AND INVESTMENT boosted living standards in the cities. An estimated 200 million people were lifted out of absolute poverty between 1978 and 1995. Progress was uneven during this period, and poverty levels sometimes remained stubbornly high despite improvements in average per capita GDP. But, overall, it was an extraordinary exercise in poverty reduction. China's leaders speak of their efforts to banish poverty as a great achievement in improving the HUMAN RIGHTS of their people and a riposte to Western criticism of their record.

There is some uncertainty about the number of Chinese who remain poor at the start of the new century. In 1997, the government pledged to resolve by the end of the century the problem of food and clothing it said was still plaguing the lives of 'more than 50 million' people. Two years later it said about 42 million faced this plight. The official absolute poverty line is based on an intake of 2,150 calories a day, plus an approximation of the cost of non-food subsistence items based on their share of the budget in low-income households. The World Bank, on the other hand, estimated in the late 1990s that there were an additional 100 million 'near poor' who had to survive on an income of less than US$1.00 a day at 1985 prices, adjusted for purchasing power parity.

For many Chinese poverty is endemic. This is particularly true of those who live in remote uplands with few natural resources and poor land. They tend to be less healthy and educated than the average, and to have more dependants. Sustained rapid growth of the economy has done only so much to change their lives. Highly focused relief programmes are needed to end their misery.

To some extent poverty relief has been hampered by a sharp growth in inequalities. That this has occurred along traditional fault lines in Chinese society is a reminder that while two decades of rapid economic growth have changed much, much remains the same. The major divisions in income, employment and access to EDUCATION and HEALTH are still those between city and countryside, coast and interior, Chinese and ETHNIC MINORITIES, and men and WOMEN. The poor can be found in almost every province: even GUANGDONG, one of China's wealthiest regions, has its poor areas. Yet poverty remains most persistent in west China, particularly in TIBET, GANSU, QINGHAI, NINGXIA and, further south, in GUIZHOU. Attempts to relieve it have sometimes attracted controversy.

In 1999, the World Bank approved a scheme to alleviate poverty in Qinghai by moving thousands of mainly Han Chinese farmers from a poor part of the province to a more fertile one traditionally inhabited by Tibetans and Mongols. International pressure groups criticized the scheme as an attempt by Beijing to dilute the non-Chinese presence in the area. The World Bank said no funds would be disbursed until an independent inquiry had determined that the scheme did not present a threat to the way of life of the indigenous inhabitants.

The persistence of 'traditional', mainly rural, poverty has been accompanied by a growth in the number of urban poor. Most are casualties of the reform of state enterprises: the need of thousands of ailing state firms to shed labour in order to survive. (See INDUSTRY.) Estimated to number between 12 and 20 million at the close of the twentieth century, China's 'new poor' grew up in a system that provided housing, medical care and education as well as jobs for life. As a result of reform they have been deprived of almost all these benefits including, on occasion, even their pensions. Prospects for the swelling urban underclass will not improve until China establishes a comprehensive welfare system to cover those living in its towns and cities.

Pu Yi, Henry (1906–67)

Pathos alternated with tragedy during the long career of China's 'last emperor' who began his life as the favourite of the EMPRESS DOWAGER, the most powerful figure during the final years of the QING DYNASTY, and ended it as a gardener and product of the CHINESE COMMUNIST PARTY's 'thought reform' movement. During the interim, Pu Yi acceded to various thrones thrice and was deposed thrice – in less happy circumstances each time. Almost his entire life was spent in palaces or prisons.

A nephew of the GUANGXU EMPEROR, Pu Yi came to the throne in 1909 aged 3. The REPUBLICAN REVOLUTION of 1911 deprived him of his inheritance, but he was allowed to continue living in the Forbidden City on a grant provided by the new Republican government. Five years after he was deposed, history seemed to be moving back in Pu's direction: following YUAN SHIKAI's abortive attempt to restore a *Chinese* monarchy, General Zhang Xun (1854–1923), a Qing loyalist, captured Beijing and announced the restoration of Manchu rule with Pu Yi as emperor. The dream lasted less than a fortnight, and Pu Yi returned to boyish pursuits in the palace. These included tuition in English by Reginald Johnston, a British Foreign Office official well versed in Chinese ways from his days as an administrator in the leased territory of WEIHAIWEI.

Politics interrupted this idyll again in 1924, when troops of the warlord FENG YUXIANG put the imperial household to flight. Pu Yi sought refuge first in BEIJING's Legation Quarter, and then in the Japanese concession in TIANJIN. He engaged in intrigues with JAPAN with a view to restoring the dynasty, but can hardly have thought it would result in the return of Manchu rule over Manchuria (northeast China), the dynasty's homeland. Pu Yi was made 'chief executive' of the puppet state of MANCHUGUO in 1932 and 'emperor' two years later. He remained a powerless and pathetic figurehead until the defeat of Japan in 1945, when he was imprisoned by the Soviet Union, whose troops entered Manchuria in 1945, and then handed over to the new Communist regime in China.

Beijing regarded Pu Yi as a war criminal. He was jailed and subjected to an apparently mild version of the thought reform used to 'remould' the Party's less prestigious opponents and doubters of its wisdom. He was eventually granted an amnesty, freed, and employed as a gardener in Beijing, capital of the country he had been trained to rule.

Q

Qian Qichen (1928–)

Foreign minister from 1988 to 1998, Qian was instrumental in restoring China's international relations after the suppression of the TIANANMEN SQUARE DEMOCRACY MOVEMENT in 1989. His energy and skill in playing off one country against another prevented China's isolation even as its reputation sank to a low. These achievements, and his fund of experience, enabled him to retain the post of vice-premier in 1998, from which he was not due to retire until 2003.

Qian, born in SHANGHAI, joined the CHINESE COMMUNIST PARTY as a student and began his long career in foreign affairs in the early 1950s. He studied in the SOVIET UNION where he later became a senior diplomat. He was appointed vice-foreign minister in 1982 and a member of the Party's Central Committee the same year.

The use of force against unarmed protestors in Tiananmen Square caused a crisis in China's relations with the West which Qian fought hard to overcome. He had on his side China's growing economic and military power, its veto in the UNITED NATIONS Security Council and, particularly important for BRITAIN, the capacity to make life difficult for the transfer of power in HONG KONG. These were some of the reasons that inclined Western leaders, beginning with Britain's John Major in 1991, to travel to Beijing. Several of them hosted visits by LI PENG, the leader most closely associated with the killings in Beijing.

Qian also managed to improve relations with the Soviet Union, long Beijing's chief security concern and, in 1991, to transfer the new amity to ties with the Russian Republic under Boris Yeltsin. Good relations with the new republics of Central Asia, where China seeks ENERGY and hopes to curb the export to neighbouring XINJIANG of ethnic nationalism, also owe much to Qian.

Relations with the UNITED STATES took longer to repair. As ever TAIWAN complicated the issue. In 1995 President LEE TENG-HUI made a private visit to the United States. The following year, the US navy was deployed in the Taiwan Straits to counter exercises in the area by the People's Liberation Army which were designed to undermine support for Lee during the island's presidential elections. The crisis passed: President JIANG ZEMIN made a state visit to Washington in October 1997, and President Bill Clinton travelled to China the following year.

When Qian became foreign minister, China was reluctant to engage in diplomacy of a multilateral nature. Beijing preferred to maintain a low profile in international organizations unless it felt its immediate interests were at stake (see FOREIGN POLICY). When he relinquished the post, China's economic and military power made it a key player in Asia and beyond, and one whose voice acquired growing weight at the United Nations. During Qian's tenure, China signed key international conventions governing nuclear testing, child labour, WOMEN and HUMAN RIGHTS. Qian's diplomatic skills – and those of Tang Jiaxuan (1938–), his successor as foreign minister – were tested again in 1999 by the crisis in Sino-US relations caused by NATO's accidental bombing of the Chinese embassy in Belgrade.

Qiao Shi (1924–)

A solid background in security work and an ability to appeal to competing factions propelled Qiao to the top of CHINESE COMMUNIST PARTY politics in the mid-1980s. He stayed there until 1997 when age gave JIANG ZEMIN a chance to force him into retirement and remove a potential obstacle to his authority.

Qiao, from ZHEJIANG, joined the Party in 1940 and worked in its Shanghai underground organizations before 1949. After serving in technical and managerial positions in the 1950s he joined the Party's international liaison department, the body responsible for relations with Communist parties and other political organizations overseas. His involvement in the Party's organizational and security work, which he inherited from his mentor, PENG ZHEN, dates from the early 1980s. He was appointed to the Central Committee in 1982, the Politburo in 1985 and, in 1987, the Politburo Standing Committee.

As troops prepared to crush the TIANANMEN SQUARE DEMOCRACY MOVEMENT in May 1989, DENG XIAOPING is believed to have offered Qiao the job of general secretary of the Party in place of the disgraced ZHAO ZIYANG. Qiao declined; Jiang Zemin succeeded.

In 1993, the man who had built his career on management of the Party's files, organization and discipline work became chairman of the NATIONAL PEOPLE'S CONGRESS. He spoke up for the legislature's right to supervise the government and even keep the Party in check. And he encouraged his reformist deputy, Tian Jiyun (1929–), to do the same. There was no question of a constitutional crisis under Qiao's chairmanship: his power derived mainly from his membership of the Party's Politburo Standing Committee, not his position in parliament. But the *éminence grise* of Communist politics in the 1980s and 1990s made it clear that the NPC should not be a rubber stamp and persuaded some of his comrades to take both it, and the laws it passed, more seriously.

Qing Dynasty (1644–1911)

Imperial rule survived in China until 1911 when, after more than 250 years in power, a spirited attempt by reformers to turn the Manchu Qing Dynasty into a constitutional monarchy culminated in its rapid collapse. Imperial reform promoted imperial demise, ushering in an era of Republican government for which China was ill-prepared in almost every respect.

crisis management

In the early years of the twentieth century Qing officials were too concerned with the present to consider the long-term effects of their reforms. Bruised by the outcome of the BOXER REBELLION of 1899–1900, alarmed by the territorial inroads of JAPAN and RUSSIA, and vexed by growing anti-Manchu Chinese nationalism in the southern provinces, they did everything they could to preserve the dynastic rule. In the process, they implemented virtually all of the reforms championed by the GUANGXU emperor during the abortive '100 Days' of 1898, which had resulted in his virtual arrest and imprisonment at the hands of reactionaries led by the EMPRESS DOWAGER (see KANG YOUWEI; LIANG QICHAO). Conservative fears of a few years earlier were cast aside as the Court struggled to re-centralize power in an effort to weaken the wayward provinces, resist further foreign aggression, and modernize the machinery of government and national defence. At the same time, the Empress Dowager and her allies sought to concentrate power in the hands of the minority Manchus, the better to preserve the purity of the dynasty founded by their clansmen in the mid-seventeenth century.

These goals required a wholesale change in the running of the empire – vast and sprawling, but increasingly battered and fraying at the edges. In a series of moves which amount to the beginning of modern government in China, the Court abandoned the examination system for civil servants in 1905 which, for close to 1,500 years, had selected officials on the basis of their knowledge of the Confucian classics (see CONFUCIANISM). A ministry of education was set up and Western-type public schools founded (see EDUCATION). About the same time, other 'Boards' – the central administrative units traditionally responsible for different aspects of imperial government – were transformed into modern ministries, giving the country, among other things, its first ministry of foreign affairs, defence and trade. Often the *forms* of dynastic administration changed more than its operations or purpose, but the changes were no less significant for that.

Also important were the government's efforts to unify the currency, weights and measures, and centralize financial administration, all of which were in considerable disarray at the start of the century. In 1908, China adopted the metric system for weights and measures. Two years later, the silver dollar was made the standard coin which was to be issued only by the Central Mint. It was also decided that the main government bank alone would issue paper currency. In the same year, the government announced that no foreign loans could be contracted without the consent of the new ministry of finance. Permanently short of revenue, which the provinces preferred to keep to themselves, the central government in 1910 drew up China's first modern budget. It was for 1911, the year the empire came to an end, and it was in the red.

new polity, new armies

Most striking of all was the dynasty's commitment to constitutional rule – a novelty indeed for China, but one that appeared to be justified by, among other things, the victory of Japan (a constitutional monarchy since 1868) in 1905 over Russia (a feudal autocracy uncomfortably similar to China) in the Russo-Japanese War (see LIAONING). There was growing awareness that constitutionalism was the hallmark of modern nationhood. This did not settle the question of the form of constitutional rule most suited to China; and intellectuals such as SUN YAT-SEN and Kang, both of them *persona non grata* in Beijing at the time, argued respectively for the merits of republican or monarchical models until the REPUBLICAN REVOLUTION of 1911 settled the issue in favour of all but the most unrepentant monarchists. For the beleaguered Court, however, there was only one choice during the first decade of the twentieth century: the combination of constitutional government combined with the preservation, indeed the *restoration*, of imperial rule adopted by Japan almost 30 years earlier.

In 1908, the government announced a set of constitutional principles that owed much to Japanese experience (see DEMOCRACY/ELECTIONS). They did little to check the prerogatives of the throne and specified a 9 year introduction period in the interests of giving the central government time to adjust. However, in 1909, provincial assemblies, selected on the basis of a highly restricted, males-only suffrage, were set up. They quickly became vehicles for dissent and dissatisfaction with the government, which was forced to respond by restricting the powers of the throne, and speeding up the formation of a national parliament. To this end, a consultative national assembly met in Beijing – shortly before the Republican Revolution of October 1911 swept the dynasty into oblivion.

Significant military reforms accompanied these administrative and political changes (see ARMIES). At the start of the century, China lacked a modern national defence force worth the name and set about building one. The few trained, well-equipped armies that existed were controlled by powerful local officials such as YUAN SHIKAI in the north, and Zhang Zhidong (1837–1909) in central China. In 1904, the government reorganized the existing forces to create a new national army, close to half a million strong, whose future officers were sent to Japan's Central Military Academy.

Legal reforms and the abolition of antiquated customs completed the image of an archaic government belatedly trying to come to terms with the modern world. The criminal code was revised in 1905, eliminating the cruellest of punishments, including 'slicing' (death of a thousand cuts), public exhibition of severed heads, tattooing, collective punishment (in which relatives of the guilty were punished), flogging and torture (see LAW). The government publicly opposed footbinding (in which a girl child's toes would be strapped under the instep to produce in adult life the tiny, pointed feet favoured by men (see WOMEN), and prohibited opium smoking. Imports of the drug decreased sharply, though domestic production soon took up the slack.

In different circumstances, these reforms – as comprehensive as any undertaken by a Chinese government from the Opium Wars of the 1840s to the Communist Revolution a century later – might have saved the dynasty and ushered China into a constitutional age. In the conditions of the early 1900s, they helped strengthen an informal coalition of interests opposed to continued Manchu rule on racial, nationalistic, political and economic grounds, as well as those of simple, often local, self-interest.

road to oblivion

The Qing government was reforming from a position of weakness. The more avenues that were opened up for social mobility, individual improvement and political debate – as was the case, for example, resulting from dispatch of students overseas principally to Japan, the training of a new military elite, and the setting up of provincial assemblies – the more effective became the opposition to its rule. Republicans such as Sun Yat-sen and constitutionalists such as Liang Qichao, who had been forced to operate among Chinese communities overseas, found that late Qing liberalization created a market for their ideas at home. Their supporters staged numerous, mostly unsuccessful, rebellions which nevertheless sapped Qing power and prestige. Clubs and societies run by anarchists and socialists were active, too (see ANARCHISM). The revolutionaries, who cut off the queues, or pigtails, that Manchus made Chinese wear to demonstrate their loyalty to the dynasty, could rely on numerous allies in a rainbow coalition of anti-Manchu dissent which included members of SECRET SOCIETIES, merchants, modern-minded gentry, new army officers and provincial leaders keen to check interference from Beijing.

The clash between local and national interests was most apparent in the movement to recover railway rights that immediately preceded the dynasty's fall (see RAILWAYS). The government decided in the first decade of the century that China needed a *national* railway network, and that those built or planned by local interests should be nationalized to enhance efficiency and facilitate central control. However, a shortage of capital meant this required loans from overseas governments and banks, opening the government to criticism that it was selling the country's resources to foreigners – the most explosive accusation in the lexicon of political infamy.

Huge rallies were held in southern provinces, notably SICHUAN and HUBEI, to protest against Beijing's plans to buy up local lines. It was the beginning of the end. When revolutionaries accidentally exploded a bomb in Wuhan, capital of Hubei, in October 1911, they were forced to turn an error into an uprising. Local troops mutinied, and Wuhan was lost to the empire. Other provinces quickly declared their independence of the throne. Despite occasionally bitter resistance on the part of troops loyal to Beijing – weakened in several provinces by the mass slaughter of Manchus – more than two millennia of imperial rule came to an end in little more than two months. On 1 January 1912, the Republic of China was founded and first Sun Yat-sen (who headed the 'provisional' government), and then Yuan Shikai, became president.

The Court officially abdicated on 12 February 1912 under an agreement which allowed the Imperial Household to continue living quietly within the Forbidden City and enjoy a subsidy from the Republican government. PU YI, the last Qing emperor who was six years old when he abdicated, remained within the walls that had confined his illustrious ancestors. Outside, the new leaders of China fought each other and, on two occasions, briefly and abortively, sought to re-establish imperial rule. In 1916, Yuan Shikai declared himself emperor of a new *Chinese* dynasty. The following year, Zhang Xun (1854–1923), known as the 'the pigtailed general' because he continued to sport the symbol of allegiance to the Qing, occupied Beijing and declared Pu Yi's restoration. The revival of Manchu rule lasted less than a fortnight.

Yet there was another strange, unhappy postscript to Qing rule. In 1924, Pu Yi was evicted from the Forbidden City by FENG YU-XIANG, a powerful warlord, and sought Japanese protection in TIANJIN. Eight years later he was made 'chief executive', and then 'emperor' of MANCHUGUO, Japan's puppet state in northeast China. The last Qing ruler had returned to his ancestral home, courtesy of alien rulers, and in an alien era.

Qinghai Province

Qinghai is the historic meeting place of three cultures and peoples: the Chinese, the Hui or Chinese Muslims, and the Tibetans. Each has sought dominance within its part of Qinghai's vast, sparsely populated domains and has often come to blows over the issue. The Communist Revolution of 1949 established Chinese control over the entire area and the suppression of the Tibetan Revolt of 1959–60 reinforced it. Since then, Beijing has had good reasons to keep Qinghai on a tight leash: the province commands the best overland route to TIBET; serves as a dumping ground for prisoners who languish in its LABOUR CAMPS; and is a valuable source of raw materials.

Amdo

All but the river valleys in the eastern corner of Qinghai belong to the cultural and geographical world of Tibet. All but these river valleys are sparsely populated pastures, mountains and, in the far west, desert. Together they comprise a huge expanse of territory which forms the northern half of the Tibet–Qinghai plateau. This is historic Amdo, or northeast Tibet. It is the birthplace of the 13th Panchen Lama (1938–89) and the 14th Dalai Lama (1935–), the spiritual leaders of their people, and the location of Kumbum (*Taersi*), one of the four great monasteries of Tibetan Buddhism (see PANCHEN LAMA; DALAI LAMA).

Though a Tibetan area, Amdo rarely fell under the firm political control of Lhasa, the capital of 'Tibet proper'. Local Tibetans acknowledged the spiritual authority of the two great living Buddhas, and some paid taxes to the government in distant Lhasa. But until the arrival of Chinese Communist power in the region they tended to rule themselves.

A significant Han Chinese presence in the area dates from the nineteenth century when the QING DYNASTY encouraged settlement and colonization. Under the empire Qinghai was a superintendency of neighbouring GANSU; it did not become a regular provincial unit until the KUOMINTANG established their new central government in China in 1928. Xining, located in the valley of the Huangshui River, was made the provincial capital.

By this time Han Chinese outnumbered non-Chinese in Qinghai. They did not, however, control political life in the province. This was in the hands of the Ma clan of Hui Muslims, the third most numerous ethnic group after the Han and the Tibetans. Governor Ma Bufang (1902–75) dominated Qinghai between 1931 and 1949 thanks largely to his control over the Muslim cavalry, the most powerful military force in northwest China until the arrival of the PEOPLE'S LIBERATION ARMY (PLA).

In so far as Ma paid only lip service to the central government in Nanjing and resisted Chiang Kai-shek's attempts to interfere in his province, he was a warlord. In so far as he sought to modernize Qinghai by building modern schools, factories and roads, and imposing a disciplined, martial air within his domain, he was something of a reformer. In any event, his

political career came to an abrupt end in 1949: the People's Liberation Army defeated his military forces during the CIVIL WAR and occupied all of northwest China. Ma fled to Cairo and later moved to Saudi Arabia, where he served as ambassador of the Nationalist government, then confined to Taiwan.

reintegration and rebellion

The arrival of the Communists in Qinghai marked the end of Muslim political dominance and the beginning of a confrontation between the Han Chinese and the Tibetans. This did not start immediately. Neither was it the only significant development to occur during the first decade or so of Communist rule in Qinghai. Like other inland provinces, Qinghai, and in particular Xining, benefited from Beijing's policy of rapid development of the interior. The province was connected with the national rail network in 1958. Later the line was extended more than 500 miles (800 kms) west of Xining to Golmud (*Geermu*), the first leg of a planned (but, at the end of the century, still unbuilt) link to Lhasa. Roads were built. Industries were established, both during the GREAT LEAP FORWARD of 1958–60 and a few years later, when MAO ZEDONG ordered the construction of key factories along a 'third line', deep in the interior, away from possible air attack by the United States or the Soviet Union (see INDUSTRY). Qinghai remained poor and backward relative to most coastal provinces, but modernization made greater inroads than ever before.

So did Mao's vision of political revolution, and Qinghai's Tibetans were among its principal victims. Like Kham – historic southeastern Tibet, then divided between the two Chinese provinces of Xikang and SICHUAN – Amdo was regarded by Beijing as outside that part of Tibet governed by the 17-point agreement with the Dalai Lama (see TIBET). Under this accord of 1951 the Tibetan government acknowledged that central Tibet was part of China. In return, Beijing granted autonomy to the region so that its inhabitants could preserve their traditional way of life rather than go through LAND REFORM, collectivization and other forms of revolution. The Tibetan areas of Qinghai, Xikang, Gansu, Sichuan and YUNNAN, however, were not to be spared this fate; and in the mid-1950s they were subjected to the same revolutionary upheavals as other parts of China.

Many of their inhabitants resisted this assault on their traditional way of life. By 1956

The Lie of the Land

With an area of 278,000 square miles (720,000 sq kms), only Tibet, XINJIANG and INNER MONGOLIA are bigger than Qinghai. And with a mere 5 million people at the start of the new century, about 40 per cent of them ethnic minorities, only Tibet is less populated. Almost 80 per cent of the population, most of them Han Chinese and Hui, are concentrated in the Huangshui and Yellow River valleys in the eastern corner of the province. This is the location of Qinghai's best farmland and most important industries, and it is responsible for most of the province's output. In terms of size, however, the region is tiny compared with the predominantly pastoral areas of the Tibet–Qinghai plateau in the east of the province. This is where most of Qinghai's Tibetans live. It is also the home of Qinghai Lake, China's largest saltwater lake with an area of 1,770 square miles (4,584 sq kms), from which the province acquires its name; the Qaidam (*Chaidamu*) Basin; and the uplands to the south where both the Yangtze and the Yellow rivers rise.

Kham was in full-scale revolt against forced collectivization and so were parts of Amdo. The Geluo horsemen of southeast Qinghai put up particularly strong resistance. While the PLA brought both Kham and Amdo to heel, military suppression sparked the massive revolt in central Tibet of 1959–60 which culminated in the Dalai Lama's flight to India accompanied by thousands of his followers. Beijing abandoned its hands-off policy in the Tibetan heartland, subjecting it to the radical political and economic policies which had already engulfed other areas of the country.

These policies had particularly severe effects in the Tibetan areas of Qinghai. Tibetans and Han Chinese both suffered from the famine caused by Chairman Mao's disastrous Great Leap Forward. But Tibetans endured a double humiliation: mass starvation *and* 'foreign' rule. By 1960, hundreds of thousands of Tibetans in Qinghai were starving to death. The Panchen Lama, on a rare visit to his homeland, saw something of their plight at first hand. His secret, highly critical report on the situation was submitted to the Communist leadership in 1962, and shortly afterwards he was denounced and detained (see PANCHEN LAMA).

Among those who suffered during Qinghai's encounter with famine were inmates of the labour camps scattered across the province. In the early 1950s the Communist regime saw Qinghai's bleak, undeveloped wastes as an ideal destination for its opponents, critics and common criminals. In the years that followed thousands were sent to 'reform through labour' and 'education through labour' camps in the region where they engaged in production and underwent 'ideological remoulding'. WEI JINGSHENG was among the Qinghai's more famous prisoners during the 1980s. But his years in China's gulag seemed to reinforce rather than change his radical views.

The authorities kept details of the size of Qinghai's prison population secret. But there was no disguising the fact that many of those banished to the province had to remain there after release because neither homes nor jobs were available in their home towns. In the mid-1990s it was estimated that 1 in 10 of Qinghai's 4.5 million people were former convicts, a fact to which some local people attributed rising crime in the province.

limits of growth in the reform era

Free market reforms invigorated Qinghai's economy during the 1980s and 1990s, but the province's small population, limited amount of agricultural land and weak industrial base set limits to growth. Geographical remoteness, poor communications and low levels of education had the same effect. In common with its neighbours, Qinghai lagged far behind the developed provinces of the east. FOREIGN TRADE AND INVESTMENT were negligible compared with coastal regions, and POVERTY widespread. Half a million people, 10 per cent of the population, were below the official poverty line in 1997.

Moves to eradicate poverty in the province, though urgent, generated controversy in 1999. The World Bank approved a scheme to relocate thousands of mainly Han Chinese farmers from a poor part of Qinghai to a more fertile region further west. The destination area, Dulan county, is inhabited mainly by Tibetans, and the Dalai Lama and international pressure groups criticized the World Bank for financing a scheme they said would facilitate Beijing's desire to tip the ethnic balance in favour of Han Chinese. The Bank approved the West China Poverty Reduction Project, but said it would not dispense any funds for it until an independent inquiry had established that the way of life of the indigenous people would not suffer as a result of an influx of migrants. China promptly said it would finance the project from its own resources.

Another serious problem in Qinghai is

environmental degradation (see ENVIRON-MENT). Only about one-third of the province is suitable for the cultivation of trees, and much of the rest is subject to relentless desertification. Heavy rain in 1997 sent mud and rocks crashing into the Loyang Gorge, location of one of China's major hydropower stations. All four of the plant's generating units were damaged and unable to produce power for a month. Officials blamed the disaster on excessive logging in the region and poorly planned construction projects.

Despite its poverty and remoteness, Qinghai is a province of great strategic importance for Beijing. It enables China to maintain its military grip on Tibet to the south, and develop much-needed ENERGY and mineral resources throughout the region. The main overland route from China proper to Tibet runs via Xining by road and rail to Golmud (*Geermu*) in central Qinghai, and then by road south to Lhasa. This supply line acquired a new importance in the 1980s with the outbreak of anti-Chinese disturbances in Tibet. On the energy front, the Qaidam (*Chaidamu*) Basin in northwest Qinghai is the location of major oil and gas fields, some of whose output is piped north to Gansu and south to Tibet. Among other important reserves in one of China's most forbidding territories are lake salt, sylvites, lithium, natural sulphur and magnesite.

R

railways

The need to enhance national security and develop the economy fuelled a century of railway building in China. At the start of the new millennium, lines extend into every Mainland province save TIBET, and there is talk of a link to Lhasa to end an anomaly determined by terrain. Yet a century of effort still leaves the People's Republic ill-served: railways are concentrated in coastal regions, overburdened with staff as well as freight and passengers, and underfunded. They are poorly equipped to cope with the increase in freight traffic and surge in personal mobility unleashed by rapid economic growth.

railways and revolution

At first, considerations of sovereignty compelled QING DYNASTY officials to *oppose* railway construction. In 1877 they bought out the first, foreign-built line (in SHANGHAI), tore up the tracks and banned future projects on the grounds that railways would facilitate foreign invasion. It took a new round of imperialist encroachments in the 1890s to persuade the Court that railway lines could be used to transport *defenders* as well as invaders. This gave the green light for construction but left open the question of how it was to be financed. BRITAIN, RUSSIA, JAPAN, Germany and other powers stepped in with loans to build lines within and beyond their concessions or 'spheres of influence' (see TREATY PORTS).

More than finance was at stake. As creditors, the powers could appoint or control senior staff of the new railway companies, claim the right to deploy police or troops along their routes, and develop industrial or mining pro-

jects nearby to boost revenues. By the time of the REPUBLICAN REVOLUTION in 1911 most of China's approximately 6,000 miles (9,600 kms) of railway were under foreign control. They included the Chinese Eastern Railway and the South Manchurian Railway in northeast China, built by Russia and later controlled by Japan; the Jiaozhou–Jinan line in SHANDONG, built by Germany but also later controlled by Japan; and the Hanoi to Kunming line in YUNNAN, constructed by France.

Chinese involvement in all these projects was negligible; and the railway network in Manchuria, location of Harbin, China's first 'railway town', remained outside China's jurisdiction until 1952 when the Soviet Union at last relinquished its privileges in the region. The only line built and funded solely by Chinese prior to the fall of the dynasty was that linking Beijing with Kalgan (modern Zhangjiakou, in Hebei). It was one thing for China to have a railway network; it was quite another for it to be beyond the government's control.

Provincial leaders in the late Qing, many of them radical and nationalist in outlook, sought to reassert Chinese control on the ground. They raised funds to recover the rights to build or finance lines Beijing had granted to the powers. The economic consequences of their efforts were marginal. The political results were spectacular. Beijing's attempts in the first decade of the century to nationalize the railways and bring them under centralized control – even at the expense of contracting foreign loans to buy out Chinese shareholders – sparked a revolt in the provinces that helped bring the dynasty down (see SICHUAN).

railways in the republic

The end of Qing rule did not clear the way for the coordinated programme of railway building envisaged by SUN YAT-SEN. Warlord rule, Communist rebellion and Japanese invasion meant construction was patchy and the railway's influence on the national economy limited. In the first half of the Republic railways were instruments of war and objects of political control, as the career of warlord WU PEIFU demonstrated. In the second half, new lines were built, even after the start of the SINO-JAPANESE WAR, but their rationale was strategic. The only parts of China in which railways exerted an important economic effect was Manchuria (the modern provinces of LIAONING, JILIN and HEILONGJIANG), where Japanese-controlled lines facilitated exports from the resource-rich region, and TAIWAN, where Japanese efforts again ensured that there were almost 3,000 miles (4,800 kms) of railway in 1950 compared with approximately 14,000 miles (22,400 kms) for all of continental China on the eve of the Communist victory.

The small size of China's network was just one problem. Ninety per cent of it was either in the northeast or along the coast. One-third of inland provinces had no railway at all. The most westerly extension stopped a few miles beyond Xian, capital of SHAANXI. Even the 'grain basket' of Sichuan lacked a railway to link it with the provinces that traditionally relied on it for food. The Communist government remedied many of these weaknesses during the first Five Year Plan of 1953–7.

integration and internationalism

Concern to strengthen national security, as well as facilitate economic development, were again to the fore. Beijing needed to project its power into distant regions, many of them inhabited by ETHNIC MINORITIES, and establish rail links with friendly (for the moment) powers across its frontiers. These considerations were behind the construction of lines to XINJIANG, QINGHAI, NINGXIA, Sichuan, GANSU, and a link, via INNER MONGOLIA and the Mongolian People's Republic (see MONGOLIA), to Moscow. A new line, via GUANGXI, to the Communist-controlled north of Vietnam, showed socialist solidarity at work at the other end of the country. The construction of a first line into FUJIAN, on the other hand, spoke of the Communists' desire to move troops swiftly into the region in preparation for an attack on Taiwan.

In their first 25 years in power, the Communists doubled the size of China's railway network. They might have done more had it not been for the aftermath of the GREAT LEAP FORWARD in the early 1960s when construction stalled, and the CULTURAL REVOLUTION a few years later, when Red Guards briefly brought much of the network to a halt by commandeering trains the better to export their revolution to the provinces. This period none the less saw completion of one of the most difficult of all Chinese railway projects from an engineering point of view: the line from Chengdu in Sichuan to Kunming, capital of Yunnan. Beijing was so concerned with national security that word of the project did not leak out until well after the first services began in 1970. Work on a second north–south trunk line, west of the established Beijing–Guangzhou line, began in the same year. It was completed in 1979.

There is no doubt that China's railways, though late in reaching many parts of the country, and often built for other than economic reasons, had a profound impact on the national economy. In common with other forms of modern communications – notably CIVIL AVIATION and TELECOMMUNICATIONS – they have broken down natural boundaries created by geography, history and tradition, and made possible the flow of goods and ideas across otherwise formidable frontiers. The most visible aspect of this has been the growth of large industrial cities in north China. Many of them would be hard pressed to grow enough food to support themselves. They are supplied by north–south railways, much as in traditional times grain barges from the Yangtze supplied Beijing, either via the Grand Canal in JIANGSU and Shandong or by sea.

meagre mileage, low density

Yet at the start of the twenty-first century, it is the inadequacy of the Mainland's railway network that is most apparent. Firstly there is simply not enough of it. China has slightly more than 21 per cent of the world's population but only 4 per cent of the total mileage of world railways. A survey in 1996 found that on a per capita basis China's railway mileage was the eighth smallest in the world. Its railway density, per 100 square kms, was one-twentieth that of Japan, one-sixth that of the US, and one-quarter that of India. Less than a third of China's approximately 40,000 miles

(64,000 kms) of railway is double tracked. Only about one-quarter is electrified.

Secondly, the distribution of the network reflects the imbalance between east and west, coast and the interior, city and countryside which has long characterized China's development, and which has intensified in the reform era. At the end of the 1990s more than three-quarters of China's railways were still found east of the Beijing–Wuhan–Guangzhou line. Railways remain sparse in the west: only three lines run west of Kunming, Chengdu and Lanzhou, and they are rail links rather than the rail 'networks' of a modern system of transport.

New construction is easing some of these problems. A line between Beijing and Kowloon (Hong Kong), opened just before the territory's transition to Chinese rule, passes through nine provinces and many poor, once isolated parts of the country. A link between Nanning in Guangxi and Kunming, completed about the same time, provides southwest China with a new outlet to the sea. An east-coast line will link China's three key economic zones of the northeastern provinces, the Bohai Gulf (southern Liaoning, Beijing, Tianjin and Hebei) and the Yangtze valley. A 'bullet train' is planned to provide express services between Beijing and Shanghai. Beijing's target is to increase total mileage to 56,000 by the year 2010 and to raise running speeds throughout the country.

It will be a tall order. Customers are plenty, even though since 1995 more Chinese have travelled by road than rail on a passenger per kilometre basis. More freight and much more coal is still carried by rail compared with ROADS. Excessive demand has exhausted capacity on many routes. Yet rail travel is cheap by international standards and the industry employs far more people than it needs. In 1994 the network made its first loss in modern times. All these developments suggest that sweeping reforms in management, pricing and funding are necessary before China's railways can hope to penetrate further into the interior, or serve the burgeoning mega-cities created by rapid economic growth and urbanization (see POPULATION).

religion(s)

CONFUCIANISM, Daoism and Buddhism – the first a creed of state and all three cardinal features of the old order – came under attack during the course of China's Revolution. They were discredited, their institutions destroyed and, after 1949, their adherents at best tolerated, at worst persecuted. Yet as a source of personal belief and devotion, these and other creeds, including CHRISTIANITY, retain their hold over the popular mind. So much so that a religious revival is under way in the People's Republic. This is a sensitive matter for Beijing. Religions involve questions of authority. In the case of Islam and Lamaist Buddhism, they concern restless ETHNIC MINORITIES such as Tibetans, Mongols and Uigurs. And everywhere their presence speaks of the failure of MARXISM to provide meaning amid the maelstrom of modernization.

creeds and cults under the old order

The variety of religious experience in China is immense. It includes Confucianism, a humanism open to religious values, whose stress on social relationships, stability, moral improvement and an ideal past made it attractive to emperors, bureaucrats and ordinary people. It includes the mysterious, esoteric beliefs at the heart of Daoism, a pantheistic, individualistic counterpoint to Confucian rationalism. And it includes Buddhism, which in Chinese guise met a need for devotion and an interest in monasticism.

Each of these creeds spoke to different aspects of the Chinese psyche. All, on occasion, were at odds in the battle for patronage of Court and commoner. Yet none of them was exclusivist, at least at the level of practice. Many Chinese found no difficulty at all in being Confucian in action, Daoist in contemplation and Buddhist in devotion.

This was especially true at the level of popular or folk religion, the syncretic faith of the common people which provided meaning and morality in an often harsh material environment. In this world, where institutions and texts mattered less than temples and rituals, Confucianism, Daoism and Buddhism came together and were enriched by community-based cults and densely populated pantheons of local deities.

Eclectic, often idiosyncratic, beliefs and superstitions flourished around 'core' practices such as ancestor worship and observation of the lunar-based liturgical year. Divination and geomancy, particularly in the form of *fengshui*, the doctrine of finding auspicious locations for everything from office towers to family graves; witchcraft and prophecy; *qigong* breathing exercises; and the search for, and claims of, immortality and supernatural powers – these were just a few of the concerns of folk religion.

Many of them challenged the established social order. Heterodox beliefs found expression in SECRET SOCIETIES and fuelled rebellions against imperial rule. The Taiping Uprising of the mid-nineteenth century against the Qing was one example. The BOXER REBELLION of the late 1890s was another. Both testified to the state's interest in controlling religious 'excesses' when possible, and crushing them when necessary.

minority faiths

Islam and Lamaist or Tantric Buddhism presented challenges of a different kind for a government committed to ruling a multi-ethnic empire. These are the faiths, 'voluntary' or otherwise, of China's ethnic minorities – those for whom, originally, Han Chinese rule was the result of military defeats, subjugation or assimilation.

The largest single group of Muslims in China is the Hui, a widely scattered minority with a historic homeland in the northwest, location of the NINGXIA HUI AUTONOMOUS REGION. Centuries of acculturation and intermarriage have made the Hui 'Chinese' in almost everything but religion, and therefore dress and diet. But they are no less zealous defenders of their identity for that. Slights against Islam – real and imagined – and struggles between believers and non-believers for control of territory were behind the great Muslim uprisings of the nineteenth century in northwest China and YUNNAN.

Islam is no less important to the Uigurs, Kazakhs and Kirghiz of XINJIANG. These are Turkic-speaking peoples and thus even further removed from the world of Han Chinese culture than the Chinese-speaking Hui. Centuries of Chinese insensitivity and repression have made them (along with Tibetans) the least reconciled of all China's national minorities to rule by Beijing.

As Islam is to the Hui, so is Lamaist Buddhism to the Tibetans and Mongols (see TIBET; MONGOLIA; INNER MONGOLIA). Almost everything about this faith – from its elevation of the monastic life to its preference for theocracy and rule by the DALAI LAMA – marks its adherents out from Han Chinese. The fact that both Tibetans and Mongols occupy homelands of their own, on the fringes of the Chinese empire, reinforces the sense of separate identity that religion provides.

On occasion, diplomacy and dynastic intermarriage brought these Chinese and non-Chinese worlds together. On occasion, Chinese weakness allowed the Tibetans and the Mongols to go their own way. But for both groups, and particularly the Tibetans, this made for difficulties when China grew strong under Communist rule and Beijing reasserted Qing-era claims of empire. There was little contest as far as territory was concerned: Tibetan muskets were no match for the People's Liberation Army, in 1950 or 1959. But in Tibet, and to some extent in Inner Mongolia, the struggle for minds, and thus for religion, goes on. In Tibetan areas especially, secular and essentially sacred modes of existence remain in conflict.

Christianity provided yet another type of challenge. It was part of the great assault on traditional values arising from China's encounter with the West in the nineteenth century. In an earlier age, the Jesuits sought to accommodate Christianity with Confucianism. In a later one, some MISSIONARIES tried to 'contextualize' their faith in an effort to make it relevant to China's specific needs – usually defined as enlightenment, progress and radical reform. But none of these attempts overcame Christianity's exclusivist nature. And none of them disguised its potency as a solvent of the old order in China.

In the nationalistic China of the early twentieth century, Christianity's ability to win over educated minds suffered, not so much as a result of the faith's foreign origins, as its reputation as the handmaiden of imperialism. It is true that it offered solace and contained much of benefit for the reformist cause. But it is also true that, as part of the matrix of foreign exploitation, it did not necessarily seem more suited to the task of China's renewal than the established religions: Confucianism, Daoism and Buddhism. *All* would have to be jettisoned and replaced by the more promising creeds of science, democracy and Marxism.

modernization and materialism

The demolition of China's traditional intellectual foundations and popularization of alternatives was at the heart of the MAY FOURTH MOVEMENT of 1919. Confucianism was a principal casualty because of its political bankruptcy and reactionary social ideals.

Other religions had less of a hold over the state, and were not attacked in the same way. But the May Fourth Movement was secular, rational and positivist in temper. Religions of all kinds were seen as irrelevancies. China faced foreign aggression and warlord rule. The task was to save the state rather than the soul.

Of the many ways of doing this, revolutionary nationalism and Marxism proved the most dynamic. These creeds mobilized millions during the first stage of the NORTHERN EXPEDITION, the KUOMINTANG-led campaign to unite China during the mid-1920s. But they parted company in 1927; and once CHIANG KAI-SHEK had turned on his Communist allies, he ruled China as a secular and nationalist but certainly not Marxist state. Kuomintang ideology claimed to be all-inclusive but was not. Neither was it very pervasive. Chiang's government had neither the desire, nor the ability, to usurp the hold of traditional gods in the Chinese mind. The regime made few inroads into religious life.

It was a different matter under the CHINESE COMMUNIST PARTY. As early as 1927 MAO ZEDONG spoke of popular religion as one of the 'four bonds' enslaving China's peasants. The Party's atheism was as militant as its opposition to 'local tyrants and evil gentry'. Its determination to overturn the social order deemed responsible for both was greater still. Marxism, particularly in the form fashioned by Mao, would accomplish this. It promised to remake the state *and* the soul; to establish justice in this life and thus end the yearning for it in the next.

But not, of course, immediately. Under the 'new democracy' of the early years of Communist rule different social classes, forms of ownership, political parties and faiths were allowed to coexist (see DEMOCRACY; MAO ZEDONG/MAO ZEDONG THOUGHT). In the case of religion, this was deemed particularly important. Marxism holds religion to be a social phenomenon: it has a life of its own and dies along with the social need for it. While the triumph of Communism meant the death of religion in China was in prospect, it was not necessarily imminent. Pending its demise, the Party concentrated on controlling religious behaviour. It did so because religious belief touched on citizens' loyalty – an important matter for a revolutionary government with an all-encompassing creed, and a determination to see it accepted in a climate of international hostility.

The problem was that many Chinese believers could claim a 'higher' loyalty than that due to the Party. Worse, most Christians and some Muslims claimed it was due to foreigners. In the case of Catholics this loyalty was to the Pope. In the case of Protestants it was to overseas denominations. For their part, many Muslims felt attachment to the international Islamic community.

Beijing dealt with these problems by creating 'patriotic' associations for the main religions capable of taking institutional form – Buddhism, Daoism, Islam, and Christianity (divided into Protestantism and Catholicism). This 'nationalization' of religious life cut Chinese believers off from their overseas counterparts, and forced them to finance themselves and train their own successors. It also made them susceptible to manipulation by cadres of the Bureau of Religious Affairs, the body set up to administer religious life in the People's Republic.

The ban on foreign connections mattered less to China's Buddhists, Daoists and the millions who practised the various forms of popular religion that often encompassed both. What mattered more to them was the destruction of the old society. LAND REFORM eliminated the semi-private pools of wealth necessary to conduct many of the more elaborate religious rituals, and sequestered or divided ancestral property. And although the Party tolerated religion, it opposed 'superstition'. This was bad news for Daoists, with their traditions of alchemy, witchcraft and shamanism. There was little place for divination in the 'new' China, nor for religion of any kind. The prevailing intellectual climate was atheistic. Advocates of the religious life were given little quarter. They were prominent among those persecuted in the political campaigns of the 1950s, especially the 'Anti-Rightist Movement' (see ONE HUNDRED FLOWERS MOVEMENT).

They suffered again during the CULTURAL REVOLUTION when organized religious life came to a halt and worship was dangerous and generally conducted in secrecy. The religious life of China was confined to the 'offshore' Chinese of Taiwan, Hong Kong, Macau and OVERSEAS CHINESE communities further afield. These groups sustained and reinforced traditions temporarily wiped out in their homeland.

The Cultural Revolution's chief targets were the 'four olds' – old culture, beliefs, customs, and habits – each of which found expression in religious life. Many churches, temples, monasteries and mosques were destroyed, damaged or put to secular use. Religious materials were incinerated. The material emblems of spiritual life all but disappeared. Curiously, religious modes of thought and speech fared better. In many rural homes Chairman Mao replaced ancestors as an object of worship, while religious terminology was employed to denigrate 'class enemies': the 'ghosts, demons and monsters' of many a speech and editorial during the Cultural Revolution.

In the predominantly Han areas of China, the Cultural Revolution was a disaster that destroyed life and property on a huge scale and constituted a fundamental breach of HUMAN RIGHTS. In those parts of the country inhabited by ethnic minorities – especially Tibet, Inner Mongolia and the northwestern provinces – it took the form of a holocaust. The attack on the 'four olds' not only curbed the freedom of inhabitants, it threatened their identity and very existence, which derived from their religion. The wholesale destruction of Tibetan monasteries, prohibitions on the use of Arabic script, and forcing of Muslims to rear pigs and eat pork were just a few of the measures which set back relations between these groups and the Han, and drove some of them of them into armed opposition during Mao's final, tempestuous decade.

room to believe: the reform era

The reform era has created new 'space' for China's believers, as it has for people generally. Free market reforms and engagement with the outside world have undermined the Party's claims to sovereignty over people's lives, a development with profound implications for believers, who have taken advantage of the new, relatively liberal atmosphere.

To some extent the Party's new toleration of religion is tactical. At home, harmonious relations between Han and non-Han, and thus stability along China's frontiers, would be impossible without a measure of religious freedom. And even within Han areas the ideal of national unity around the goal of economic development would be no more than an idea if believers felt oppressed.

China's ability to attract FOREIGN TRADE AND INVESTMENT – an economic imperative and key foreign policy objective under DENG XIAOPING and since – is also at stake. Religious freedom is valued in the West, the main source of the capital and technology that Beijing needs. Religious persecution at home would

threaten China's agenda abroad. It might also drive visitors away from China's holy mountains and other religious sites, reopened and refurbished during the 1980s in pursuit of the tourist dollar.

Theoretical arguments underpin these practical concerns. Since the late 1980s the Party has deemed China to be in the 'initial stage' of socialism (see CHINESE COMMUNIST PARTY/ SOCIALISM). It is a period in which all sorts of phenomena alien to mature socialism, religion among them, can continue to exist. There can be no question of eradicating religious belief – that has been tried and has failed. The task is to rally believers to the cause of China's rejuvenation and coopt their leaders. The most important of them are fêted on a regular basis by Party leaders and have been given positions in the CHINESE PEOPLE'S POLITICAL CONSULTATIVE CONFERENCE, the country's main advisory body.

revival and repression in the 1990s

At the start of the new century all of China's main religions have experienced revival. Churches and mosques have reopened. Monasteries have been rebuilt. The Bible, the Koran and the Buddhist scriptures are widely available. Religious communities have resurrected once dangerous ties with believers overseas. Academics engage in canonical and textual studies. The government claims that there about 100 million believers in China, less than one-tenth of the population, but almost certainly more than a still militantly atheist Communist Party feels comfortable with. Buddhists and Daoists account for about 70 million, Christians 15 million, and Muslims the remainder.

Tensions between sacred and secular sources of authority remain. Thanks to the Cultural Revolution, every major faith lacks trained leaders and teachers. In many parts of the country disputes over confiscated property still poison relations between local authorities and religious communities. And religious practice still involves risk: constitutional promises of freedom of religious belief are still violated regularly, though on a smaller scale than under Mao.

Certainly there is no disguising the regime's continuing, if now more softly spoken, opposition to religion. The Party still views religion as 'false'. The constitutional right to belief does not extend to proselytization. And while believers are supposed to run their own affairs, the Party keeps a close eye on all senior appointments across every creed. In the case of Tibet, it insists on the right enjoyed by emperors of approving the selection of reincarnations of the Dalai Lama, the PAN-CHEN LAMA and lesser lights. Religion, particularly in Tibet, but also elsewhere in China, is too important to be left to the religious.

And its importance is growing. In the countryside, the new gods of Marx and Mao have been supplanted by the old. Ancestor worship has returned. So have Daoist and Buddhist deities, along with the temples, festivities and rituals required to celebrate and propitiate them. Cults abound, some of them Christian, such as the 'Lord God Sect' which flourished in HUNAN until the government arrested its leaders in 1999. Secret societies and clan activities are filling the void created by the withdrawal of the state (see CLANS). Parts of the countryside are once again a source of religious heterodoxy, and an object of concern for the government.

Educated urban Chinese are proving equally susceptible to religion's appeal. An example is the extraordinary interest in *qigong* breathing techniques and their alleged power to heal, empower and transform. In 1999, followers of *Fa Lun Gong*, a *qigong*-based cult founded by Li Hongzhi (c 1951–), whom the government forced into exile, flexed their muscles in a peculiarly physical way. Angered by the refusal of the authorities to afford them official recognition, thousands of them laid siege for a day to Zhongnanhai, the compound in central Beijing where China's leaders live and work. Two months later the government declared the group illegal and arrested its leaders.

None of this suggests that Mainland China greets the new millennium in the grip of religious frenzy – though examples of this do exist. Deep reserves of rationalism and pragmatism help keep spiritual ecstasy and the excesses of eschatology in check. But there is little doubt that in an era of rapid, unsettling change, religions, old and new, answer needs that Marxism and the Party cannot. For many Chinese, life is easier than ever before but the question of how it should be lived remains unanswered. The extent to which religion is able to answer it will have an important bearing on the future of Chinese tradition, and on the relationship between state and individual in the People's Republic.

Republican Revolution (October–December 1911)

On 9 October 1911, members of the Progressive Association, one of scores of small, revolutionary groups opposed to the QING DYNASTY, accidentally exploded a bomb in Wuhan, capital of HUBEI. The incident probably occurred because a comrade was careless while smoking. Police arrived on the scene to find lists of conspirators' names and other incriminating evidence. The revolutionaries realized they had to strike, or be crushed themselves. Within days, a series of mutinies and military revolts won Wuhan to the revolutionary cause. The revolt spread from Hubei to almost every other province, where local leaders promptly declared their independence of the throne. The Qing fought back, and, for a spell, fierce fighting ensued. But, on 1 January 1912, less than three months after the explosion in Wuhan, more than 2,000 years of dynastic rule came to an end and the Republic of China was founded.

If the initial explosion in Wuhan was an accident, the upheavals which followed were not. Despite the dynasty's attempts at political and constitutional reform, there was widespread resistance in the early 1900s to continued Manchu rule (see QING DYNASTY). Revolutionaries led by SUN YAT-SEN formed just one strand of this resistance. More important in the actual unfolding of the revolt were officers of the 'new armies' formed during the previous decade to boost the Manchu's ailing military power (see ARMIES); ambitious, enlightened merchants who dominated local chambers of commerce; provincial leaders angered by Beijing's attempts to curb their power; and SECRET SOCIETIES with their own, sometimes parochial but no less determined, reasons for wanting to overthrow the Qing.

What united these disparate groups was simple dissatisfaction with the dynasty and, in some cases, undying hatred of it. It was seen as inadequate to the tasks facing China – those of resisting further foreign encroachment, undertaking rapid political change and sponsoring economic reform and national revival. The very idea of imperial rule had lost its hold over much of the educated public, many of whose younger members had acquired a taste for change as a result of studying in JAPAN. In this context the Court's recourse in the 1900s to foreign loans to nationalize local railway construction projects in SICHUAN, Hubei and elsewhere, the better to control such regions, sparked huge resentment (see RAILWAYS). The idea that the 'racially alien' Manchus might be in league with foreigners to exploit China was intolerable.

For all of these reasons the fall of the Qing was sudden, swift, complete, and little lamented. News of the revolt in Wuhan spread quickly because of the development of the telegraph linking the provinces and Beijing. Technology thus made the collapse of dynastic rule swifter than it might otherwise have been. But the end of the Manchus had long been in sight and, though some military leaders threw in their lot with the Court during occasionally fierce battles against the rebels, the imperial cause was beyond saving.

The collapse of a 2,000-year-old political tradition and its replacement by the novelty, at least in the Chinese context, of republicanism ranks as a major event in world history. CONFUCIANISM, the creed of state exemplified by the rule of emperors, supposedly bound by ties of loyalty and obligation to their subjects, was formally abandoned. The revolutionaries could hardly be faulted for declaring the dawn of a new era and adopting a calendar which took the foundation of the Republic in 1912 as Year One – a system still used in all official documentation in TAIWAN.

The collapse of Manchu rule also had more immediate, practical consequences. At least for a while, the great ideological debates about China's future could take place inside the country rather than being confined to its foreign-ruled periphery or among OVERSEAS CHINESE communities further afield and free of Qing suppression. The departure of the Manchus also clarified the situation regarding Chinese nationalism. There need be no more talk about the country suffering under the 'Tartar yoke', as the revolutionaries' phrase had it. Nationalism could, and soon did, focus on opposition to the genuine foreign presence in China: that of RUSSIA, Japan, BRITAIN and the UNITED STATES. Sun Yat-sen – who was travelling in the United States when the revolt broke out – and his revolutionaries quickly dominated the language of debate about China's future after the Revolution. It was the language of republicanism and democracy, and how to implement both in a vast, undeveloped country that had only just broken free of its ancient shackles.

Yet at this point, the novelty of the events that began in Wuhan in 1911 comes to an end. For if political tradition had collapsed, society as a whole, particularly in the countryside, was changing less rapidly. The same was true of political behaviour, custom and even thought. There were no 'modern' political parties in China, and little understanding of how parliaments worked. The idea of a 'loyal opposition' was not only foreign, it was alien. This remains the case not much short of a century after the upheavals of 1911.

The energy and bravado many displayed in trying to implement republican government in China during the early twentieth century were striking. So were the failures as YUAN SHIKAI, chosen as president at the founding of the Republic in 1912, moved to crush parliamentary opposition in 1913, tried to centralize power in his own hands and, in 1916, declared himself emperor the better to extract loyalty and obedience from his people. Perhaps no less could be expected of a man whom the Court, in the immediate aftermath of the revolution, had entrusted with its defence. Republicanism survived Yuan's betrayal, but only to become the plaything of the various governments which came and went in Beijing after his death, and the various WARLORDS who backed them.

It proved easier to topple an established if decaying political order than build a new one. The Republican Revolution had its origins in a military revolt, and from the moment it broke out until at least the Communist victory in the CIVIL WAR almost 40 years later, Chinese politics remained in thrall to men with guns. Worse, since the collapse of imperial rule removed the established relationships between the centre and the provinces, and Republican governments proved unable to create either the institutions or an ideology capable of replacing them, China dissolved into various shifting regional and provincial blocs, most of them led by warlords backed by local armies. This meant that would-be rulers of China could accomplish little without the backing of a politically dedicated, disciplined army. The true legacy of 1911 therefore was not so much republicanism as the acute militarization of politics – a militarization that still marks aspects of China's political life at the start of the twenty-first century (see PEOPLE'S LIBERATION ARMY).

roads

For decades China's roads were the least developed form of surface transport. Successive governments have built them for the same purposes as RAILWAYS: to enhance political, administrative and economic integrity in a sprawling country haunted by fears of disintegration and determined to modernize. There is also the question of penetrating sensitive frontier regions the better to counter external and internal foes. By the end of the 1990s China's 800,000-mile (1.28 million kms) road network – all but a small proportion of it built after 1949 – had gone some way to meeting these needs. But the greatest challenge lies ahead: providing an efficient road system capable of serving a rapidly urbanizing population at minimal cost to the ENVIRONMENT.

One of the first modern roads in China was built in 1906. About 25 miles (40 kms) long, it linked the city of Longzhou, in GUANGXI Province, with the pass on the border with Vietnam then known as Zhennanguan but redesignated in 1949 'Friendship Pass'. When the Communists came to power 43 years later there were perhaps 50,000 miles (80,000 kms) of roads open to motorized traffic. About half were earth roads while the remainder had gravel surfaces. This hardly amounted to a road network, especially as some regions, notably TIBET, were not linked by road to neighbouring provinces let alone the national capital. There were no road bridges across the YANGTZE RIVER until 1957, and at numerous points in south China vehicles had to cross rivers by ferry. In the 1930s the KUOMINTANG government built a series of roads to link those provinces, mainly along the Yangtze, where it was strongest. However the most spectacular road-building effort of the pre-Communist era was the Burma Road: a 350-mile-long supply line hacked out of the jungles and mountains of southwest China by 200,000 labourers at the start of the SINO-JAPANESE WAR.

Strategic considerations conditioned road construction after 1949 as they had before. Roads often were precursors and auxiliaries to railway lines: they were built to project military and political power, secure access to valuable resources and generally knit the country together. This was the rationale behind the construction in the 1950s of all-weather roads into TIBET, YUNNAN, XINJIANG, LIAONING (to the border with North Korea) and FUJIAN (opposite Taiwan). Road-building

intensified during the GREAT LEAP FORWARD.

It intensified again in the very different circumstances of the reform era beginning in the late 1970s. By the close of the century, roads had reached every county save one: Medog, in Tibet. At township level, road penetration was 97 per cent. At the levels of the 'administrative village', it was about 80 per cent There were more than 20 motorways, or expressways, (*gaosugonglu* in Chinese – 'highspeed roads') with a total mileage in excess of 1,250. More were planned. China's most important international highway, the Karakorum Highway, linking Xinjiang with Pakistan, was opened in 1986.

At the close of the century roads accounted for about 14 per cent of freight transported in China and 54 per cent of passengers. Railways shifted more freight than road transport. But inland and coastal shipping, the traditional form of transport in China, moved as much freight as railways and roads combined.

Despite the flurry of road construction in the 1980s and 1990, many parts of the country remain poorly served, especially border areas and, what often amounts to the same thing, areas inhabited by ETHNIC MINORITIES. In the mid-1990s China's road density of 11 kms of road per 100 square kms was tiny compared with the 299 kms of Japan, the 67 kms of the United States, and the 65 kms of India. The poor quality of many roads – a consequence of lack of investment, poor planning and lack of maintenance – impaired the network's overall efficiency.

So did the rapid economic growth which generated traffic flows quite beyond the capacity of most roads, particularly those in the cities. During the 1990s, the number of vehicles increased at nearly twice the pace of road construction. At the close of the decade the total vehicle fleet was more than 12 million. Car ownership – at 24 per 1,000 people in Beijing, 21 in Guangzhou, 15 in Shanghai in the mid-1990s – was low by international standards, but increased rapidly as living standards soared. Motorcycle ownership is also growing, presenting a new challenge to the bicycle's dominance of city streets.

Acute congestion is one of the most obvious result of these developments as pedestrians, bicycles, slow-moving heavy lorries and light cars clog China's streets. Another is pollution (see ENVIRONMENT). Slow operating speeds, outdated vehicle design, and widespread use of leaded fuel, despite bans on the sale of such vehicles in several cities, make them a major source of emissions throughout the country.

The People's Republic is facing a crucial choice as far as urban transport is concerned. It can tolerate the growth of cities at the present rate in the almost certain knowledge that rising incomes and market forces will increase car ownership, boost fuel prices, add to congestion and smog, and raise demands for road construction. Or it can take advantage of the Mainland's still relatively low dependence on cars and the high density of its cities to plan future urban development around public transport systems. A chief element of this would be a modern road network, accompanied by better land-use planning and stricter fuel standards. As with many of the major problems facing China at the start of the new era, Beijing's approach to its urban transport dilemma will have an environmental impact far beyond its frontiers.

Russia (Imperial)

Tsarist Russia became the pre-eminent power in Manchuria (northeast China) during the nineteenth century – almost without firing a shot. Like the UNITED STATES, it secured its territorial gains as a result of China's defeats by other powers and Beijing's preoccupation with domestic rebellion rather than by waging war itself. Under Sino-Russian treaties of 1859 and 1860, the Qing lost all of northeast Manchuria to the Russians, depriving what later became one of China's richest, most developed regions of an outlet to the sea, other than the southern port of Dalian (see LIAONING; JILIN; HEILONGJIANG). A century later, the loss of so much territory still rankled with Chinese Nationalists. And during the Sino-Soviet split of the 1960s Mao Zedong hinted that he wanted to reopen the issue (see SOVIET UNION; RUSSIAN FEDERATION).

In 1900, the situation grew even more serious: Russians threatened to take over the whole of Manchuria. Tsarist troops moved into the area during the suppression of the BOXER REBELLION, nominally to protect newly acquired railway rights and the leased territories of Dalian and Port Arthur, the naval base at the tip of the Liaodong peninsula. This brought long-simmering Russo-Japanese rivalry in Manchuria and Korea to a head. China was not a combatant in the war of 1904–5 between the two powers but its predicament was no better for that: the conflict was waged on Chinese soil by foreign powers bent on extending their influence in China. Beijing could only look on helplessly, and hope that third countries would restrain Japan, the victor in the war and soon the dominant power in Manchuria. China was also powerless when, following the REPUBLICAN REVOLUTION of 1911, Russia supported a movement for autonomy in MONGOLIA with a view to increasing its own influence in the region.

The Bolsheviks renounced many of Imperial Russia's privileges in China when they came to power in 1919. This went down well among Chinese Nationalists during the MAY FOURTH MOVEMENT, even though Russia's new rulers declined to hand back northeast Manchuria, and insisted on holding on to the Chinese Eastern Railway, which crossed Manchuria to reach Vladivostok.

Russian Federation/Commonwealth of Independent States (CIS)

The collapse of the Soviet Union in 1991 presented more than ideological problems for Beijing. (See also SOVIET UNION; RUSSIA.) Relations had to be forged with a new, unpredictable political entity in Moscow and three new states along China's border – Kazakhstan, Kirghizstan and Tajikistan – whose people were fired up by independence and the Islamic revival that helped them win it. The situation presented China with a string of potential security headaches, especially in XINJIANG, whose non-Chinese population has long looked west rather than east to Beijing for inspiration. However, deft diplomacy and a crackdown in Xinjiang eased the situation. By the close of the 1990s, a desire to counter United States influence, reinforced by China's need for Russian arms, oil and gas, enabled Beijing and Moscow to forge a 'strategic partnership'. Both parties are keen to maintain close relations in the new century.

Relations between China's leaders and

President Boris Yeltsin proved better than expected given the circumstances under which the Russian leader came to power. Yeltsin's early image in the West as an anti-Communist crusader determined to entrench capitalism and democracy in Russia found no echo in Beijing. In the Chinese capital, he was the international statesman who enjoyed good personal relations with JIANG ZEMIN and LI PENG based partly on the fact that both Chinese leaders had studied in the Soviet Union. China needed a good relationship with the new Russia to settle the border dispute inherited from the Soviet era. Both countries needed one to show Washington they were powers to be reckoned with (see UNITED STATES).

The boundary dispute, whose origins lay in the eastward expansion of Muscovy in the eighteenth century, was tackled in two accords. The first, in 1996, was between China, Russia and the three Central Asian successor states – the 'Shanghai Five'. The second, the following year, was between Moscow and Beijing. This last did not resolve the matter completely: the exact alignment of the Sino-Russian border in two small areas along the Amur (Heilongjiang) River in the east awaited settlement. But the border was neutralized as an issue in bilateral ties. Two accords signed in 1999 settled China's boundaries with Kirghizstan and Kazakhstan, leaving only the frontier between China and Tajikistan to be demarcated.

Boundary issues aside, the new republics of Central Asia pose a threat to China by virtue of the cultural affinities between their peoples and those in Xinjiang. Uigurs, Kirghiz and others in China's most western, and most restive, region draw inspiration – and sometimes support – for their struggle against Chinese rule from the newly independent 'stans'. Some activists smuggle weapons across the borders and use them against their Han masters. Beijing has sought to neutralize the threat in three ways. At a series of Central Asian summits, attended by the 'Shanghai Five' – China, Russia, Kirghizstan, Kazakhstan and Tajikistan – it extracted promises from participating governments that they would not aid or abet independence movements in Xinjiang. It has increased investment in the region to show local inhabitants that the best hope for a better life lay in continued Chinese rule. And it has tried to suppress, often with considerable ferocity, those who seek independence.

The Sino-Russian Joint Declaration of 1996 was the first to speak of relations between Moscow and Beijing in terms of a 'strategic partnership'. Beijing used this phrase several times during the 1990s to describe its ties with foreign states. To some extent it was an attempt by China to insulate diplomatic relations from possible domestic changes within the 'partner' countries. The Sino-Russian statement spoke of a trend towards a 'multi-polar world' but one in which 'hegemonism' and 'power politics' were still at large. These barbs were directed at Washington. In 1996 Russia was unhappy over the eastward expansion of NATO while China was incensed at what it saw as US support for TAIWAN and Western criticism of its HUMAN RIGHTS record.

Three years later NATO's war against Serbia provided China and Russia with a powerful new common cause. Both countries, prey to ethnic disputes of their own, expressed alarm at the implications of NATO's new doctrine of 'humanitarian interventionism' on behalf of a national minority. Both felt a sense of weakness and helplessness in the face of NATO's military campaign, which was conducted without the specific approval of the United Nations. Both countries also opposed American plans to build missile defence systems of the kind that threatened to weaken Russian and Chinese strike capabilities.

Another aspect of the post-Cold War, reconfigured strategic triangle formed by Russia, China and the United States concerns arms. The US and the European Community banned weapons sales to Beijing following the suppression of the TIANANMEN SQUARE DEMOCRACY MOVEMENT in 1989. This made Russia a valuable source of modern weapons for Beijing. During the 1990s China bought several dozen Sukhoi-27 fighters and secured the rights to produce a version of its own. In 1999 it agreed to buy up to 60 SU-30 fighters, a multi-purpose aircraft designed to compete with the American F-15s. Beijing also purchased a small number of Kilo-class Russian submarines during the 1990s which made a modest contribution to the expansion of its navy (see PEOPLE'S LIBERATION ARMY/SEAPOWER). These developments worried defence planners in Taiwan, who saw the island's days of air supremacy coming to an end.

By the close of the twentieth century China had become Russia's second-biggest arms customer after India. Weapons sales accounted for about one quarter of trade between the two countries. However, the modest growth of bilateral trade in commodities other than weapons disappointed both parties, despite vigorous local trade between China's HEI-LONGJIANG and the Russian Far East.

China's growing demand for ENERGY will help correct this in the new era, and provide a further impetus to Sino-Russian relations, as well as those between Beijing and the new states of Central Asia. An agreement to use Russian equipment at China's third nuclear power station, under construction at Lian-

yungang in JIANGSU, is one example of this. Others include a plan to pipe gas from Lake Baikal, just north of Mongolia, to east China, and another to transport gas from Siberia to Xinjiang. In 1997 China agreed to develop two oil fields in Kazakhstan and build a pipeline to transport it east into Xinjiang. This, the largest of China's overseas joint ventures, has given Beijing another reason to insist on tight control over its remote Western borders – and maintain a close interest in the affairs of Russia and Central Asia beyond them.

secret societies

Reformers, republicans and revolutionaries have stolen the limelight in China's quest for change. Their activities over more than a century suggest China's progressive 'enlightenment'. Yet 'darker' but equally dynamic forces were also at work. Until well into the twentieth century the most powerful opponents of the old order were secret societies not political parties. Communism curbed their power in 1949, by then often manifest in organized crime, which remains a staple activity still in TAIWAN, HONG KONG and MACAU. But they have since re-emerged in the Mainland. In some parts of China, the 'old' world of secret societies, CLANS and BANDITS is very much part of the 'new'.

roots of rebellion under the Qing

China's numerous secret societies traditionally fall into two categories: predominantly religious organizations of the north; and more political, southern groups, generically known as Triads. Northern societies date back to the White Lotus rebellion of the fourteenth century. The origins of the Triads lie in resistance to the Manchu conquest of China in the mid-seventeenth century.

History, rituals, allegiances and doctrine divided the societies, but they were similar in function and purpose. At their most exalted, they sought to reverse injustice and establish utopia. At a minimum, they offered protection in a predatory, precarious world. In an age of imperial decay, foreign intrusion and the first, disruptive stirrings of modernization, this counted for much. Heterodox beliefs and elaborate initiation ceremonies provided a sense of hope, belonging and community which established institutions and ideas could not.

In the absence of formal political opposition, secret societies were the chief opponents of the traditional order. The QING DYNASTY treated them as such. It condemned their heretical religious views; recognized their role in almost every great rebellion; and sought to crush them at every turn. An exception was the Boxers, whose fierce xenophobia, reinforced by alleged immunity to bullets, the Court unleashed against the foreign powers. In 1900 the eight-power army crushed the myth of Boxer immunity and the dynasty's hopes along with it (see BOXER REBELLION).

There was no repeat of this alliance between secret societies and government under the Qing. Instead, most secret societies were fiercely anti-dynastic. Some, such as the Elder Brother Society, the predominant group in the Yangtze valley, still yearned for an end to the Manchu dynasty and the restoration of Chinese rule. The Red Beards, founders of the Republic of Zeltuga, a primitive Communist society in northern HEILONGJIANG that the Qing crushed in the early 1900s, were almost alone in having clear political ideas of their own. Other groups fought to preserve local gentry and merchant interests in the face of government attempts to centralize power. All had something to gain from the collapse of Qing rule.

In this they were at one with the republicans, many of whom recruited among and learned from secret societies. SUN YAT-SEN and ZHU DE, both of them members of societies, were just two examples. The conspiratorial activities and secretive nature of Sun's UNITED LEAGUE also owed much to the societies' world. So did the entire course of the REPUBLICAN REVOLUTION: imperial rule was brought down by an informal alliance between reforming merchants and gentry, new army officers and republicans, but in many parts of the country secret societies provided the organization and manpower of the revolt.

They were less adept when it came to providing goals for the new order. In the Republic this task fell to political parties, their leaders and the new, revolutionary ideas of nationalism, DEMOCRACY and MARXISM. The distinctly *political* role of the secret societies seemed to die with Manchu rule.

from compromise to control

The societies' power and influence remained considerable all the same. In the cities, they often controlled labour unions and organized crime. Little could be achieved without their cooperation. SHANGHAI was a case in point. When in 1927 CHIANG KAI-SHEK decided to break the power of the organized Left in the city he turned to Du Yuesheng (1887–1951) and Huang Jinrong (1868–1953), leaders of the underworld Green Gang. Elsewhere, KUOMINTANG rule often depended upon the acquiescence of secret societies; a direct challenge to their hold over society would have been costly.

A similar pattern was apparent in the countryside where the CHINESE COMMUNIST PARTY focused its efforts during the late 1920s and 1930s. The Party made overtures to the Red Spears – so called because of the small red flags members attached to their spears – who fought a peasant war in HENAN; and, later, to the Elder Brother Society, whom MAO ZEDONG envisaged as allies in the fight against JAPAN and the old rural order.

Yet secret societies could be only occasional, informal partners of a genuinely revolutionary party. It is true that they were often concerned to protect the weak and the poor. But it is also true that they engaged in banditry as well as resisted it; that they often sought to defend a particular, localized version of an ideal rural order rather than challenge it. Their *revolutionary* potential, in other words, was slim.

Sometimes it was non-existent. This was the case with the *Yi Guan Dao*, the 'Way of Basic Unity', which came to prominence in the 1930s and 1940s, notably in Japanese-occupied regions. This society provided comfort of a more spiritual kind (see RELIGION(S)). Its title reflected its eclecticism: the 'Way of Basic Unity' encapsulated elements of CONFUCIANISM, Daoism, Buddhism and even CHRISTIANITY in an apparent attempt to appeal to as many people as possible. It promised members happiness based on improved conduct and adherence to rituals; and deliverance from a cosmic calamity that was expected at almost any time.

This was a powerful message amid the tribulations of the SINO-JAPANESE WAR. It was also a compromised one given the context of Chinese politics. Leaders of the cult were closely associated with the 'puppet government' of WANG JINGWEI in Nanjing. The nature and provenance of *Yi Guan Dao* doctrine made it particularly suspect when the Communists came to power in 1949.

The same was true of all secret societies as far as the new regime was concerned. They were 'feudal', predatory and inimical to the Party's goals. Worse, they gave succour to its enemies: landlords, 'reactionaries' and the Kuomintang. LAND REFORM broke the power of the societies, and the old order, in the countryside; the 'Campaign Against Counterrevolutionaries' of 1951 crushed *Yi Guan Dao* and other sects in the cities. The government took over the societies' organizational functions by forming peasant associations and trade unions, neighbourhood committees and professional bodies. It replaced their ideological aspirations with the sole permitted creed: Marxism-Leninism-Mao Zedong Thought (see MARXISM; MAO ZEDONG). Other than as vehicles for organized crime, chiefly among OVERSEAS CHINESE outside the frontiers of the People's Republic, the age of – and the need for – secret societies appeared to be over.

revival: societies in the reform era

The obituaries proved premature. It was no surprise that Triads continued to trouble the authorities in HONG KONG and MACAU, and the Bamboo Union Gang the police in TAIWAN: rapid economic growth made for rich pickings in all three territories, particularly in the construction and entertainment businesses. The prevalence of official CORRUPTION made business even better. In Macau especially, rival Triad gangs struggled to control the gaming industry in the late 1990s, provoking gun battles and defeating the best efforts of the Portuguese-controlled police.

The post-handover government promised the violence would end with colonial rule.

The revival of secret society activity on the Mainland during the 1980s and 1990s was more of a surprise, especially to the Communist Party. It followed the break-up of communes, the return to family farming and the general relaxation of government control arising from DENG XIAOPING's reforms. The withdrawal of the state from so many areas of life allowed older organizations, and even older ideas, to come back to life.

One aspect of this was the revival of clans. Another was a resurgence of interest in religion, both Chinese and foreign. Renewed stirrings by secret societies were part of the same picture: they have contributed to the resurrection of an older social matrix in town and countryside that the first decades of Communist rule failed to destroy.

Organized crime has staged a comeback, too. Triad activity has even received a guarded official welcome. Beijing's top policeman astonished many in 1993 by describing certain Triad groups as 'patriotic' because they had provided protection for a Chinese leader during an overseas visit. He said nothing of the reported involvement of Hong Kong Triads in smuggling dissidents out of the Mainland after the suppression of the TIANANMEN SQUARE DEMOCRACY MOVEMENT.

The apparent benevolence changed towards the close of the decade. In 1997 the *People's Daily* condemned Triad involvement in entertainment centres run by Overseas Chinese on the Mainland, and the Penal Code was amended to include prohibitions against Triad-type crime.

The government was quicker to condemn other secret society-style organizations. Reports of the activities of 'gangs', many of them with exotic names such as the 'Green Dragons' of GUANGXI, the 'Sea Spring Gang' of SHANDONG and the 'Butterfly Gang' of ZHE-JIANG, formed part of a wider critique about the collapse of socialist values in the era of free market reform.

Some of these groups were organizations of criminals. Most were small. Yet, as ever, their very secrecy makes it hard to determine the extent of their influence – a worrying matter for the authorities.

What is clear is that some of these groups champion eschatological beliefs that seek to answer deeper needs in a new era of change and uncertainty, corruption and decay, rather as certain secret societies did in pre-Communist days. An example is the *Fa Lun Gong*, the mystical Buddhist sect whose adherents staged mass protests in Beijing and elsewhere in 1999 against the authorities' refusal to grant them official recognition. Alarmed by the appeal of the group, the government banned it and arrested its leaders.

Still other clandestine organizations appear to be manifestations of societies once thought to have been crushed. Groups advocating teachings almost identical to *Yi Guan Dao*, which has many adherents in Taiwan and among Overseas Chinese, have appeared in the northeast and elsewhere in the People's Republic. All of them, 'criminal' or otherwise, are a reminder of the persistence of the past, and the vibrancy of old forms and ideas in China, despite decades of political, scientific and technical advance.

Shaanxi Province

The central dictum of DENG XIAOPING's free market reforms – that some parts of China should be allowed to get rich before others – has condemned Shaanxi to a long wait. Deng's strategy favoured the coast rather than inland regions. It called for the development of light industry, not heavy industries of the kind set up in Shaanxi during the era of state control, central planning and egalitarianism. And it required an ability to tap FOREIGN TRADE AND INVESTMENT, relative strangers in Shaanxi prior to the 1980s. The province whose arid northern region of YANAN was the proving ground for Communist doctrines and policies imposed on the rest of China in 1949

has had its work cut out in the age of reform.

For centuries central Shaanxi was the seat of successive Chinese states. For centuries, one of them, Changan (modern Xian), capital of the Tang Dynasty (613–907), was the most prosperous, sophisticated and cosmopolitan city in the world. Then, and for just as long, the centre of Chinese power shifted east, alternating between the north China plain around Beijing and the great commercial cities of the Yangtze valley. This was where the great dramas of China's modern encounter with the West were played out in the nineteenth century, not remote, isolated, conservative Shaanxi.

Indeed foreigners made such little impact in the province that the EMPRESS DOWAGER and the demoralized Qing Court chose to flee there in 1900 to escape retribution for the BOXER REBELLION. Shaanxi was a traditional refuge for rebels. At the start of the twentieth century, its capital, Xian, the most important trading centre in China *not* to have been opened as a treaty port, became a temporary sanctuary for China's beleaguered rulers.

The Republican era brought a veneer of modernization to the region but no more than that. Neither local warlords, the most prominent of whom was FENG YUXIANG, nor CHIANG KAI-SHEK's central government, brought much change to Shaanxi. Development was confined to Xian and the Guanzhong, or Wei valley area, east and west of the capital, home for most of the population. South and north Shaanxi remained poor, remote and untouched. The north in particular was plagued by harsh weather conditions, poor soil, banditry – and, from the early 1930s, Communism.

This might not have amounted to much had MAO ZEDONG not chosen north Shaanxi as the final destination of the LONG MARCH, the Communists' epic retreat from south to north China. But the poor, isolated, loess region offered the rebels shelter from the troops pursuing them, a chance to build on an existing soviet base, and improved communications with the SOVIET UNION. Each might prove decisive at a time when Japan seemed ready to launch a full-scale invasion of China with unpredictable consequences for Chiang's shaky regime.

Demoralized and much reduced in numbers, Mao's armies reached their goal at the end of 1935. A year later Chiang's generals rebelled against the idea of resuming the fight against them at a time of growing menace from Japan. In the XIAN INCIDENT they kidnapped their commander to make their point. Chastened but unharmed by his ordeal, Chiang agreed to forsake 'anti-bandit' suppression for national resistance. In the space of a few days, events in Shaanxi had transformed China's domestic politics.

Different but even more profound developments followed. The SINO-JAPANESE WAR gave Mao and his Party a chance to adjust their policies to the new demands of national resistance and social revolution; perfect techniques of mass mobilization, ideological control and Party discipline; build new political and military institutions; and expand their power

> ### *The Lie of the Land*
>
> Geography divides Shaanxi's 77,200 square miles (200,000 sq kms) into three distinct regions. Northern Shaanxi is part of of the loess plateau – predominantly 'yellow' country bleached and scarred by centuries of bad weather and soil erosion. Generally undeveloped and sparsely populated, it is the spiritual homeland of Chinese Communism. The Guanzhong plain in the centre of the province extends from Tongguan in the east, close to where the Wei joins the Yellow River at its great bend, to Baoji, a major industrial city in the west. This region is home for 60 per cent of the population – who numbered 36 million at the close of the century – and about two-thirds of its output. South Shaanxi nestles between the Qingling mountains, watershed of the Yellow and Yangtze river systems, and the Daba range, just north of the border with SICHUAN. Its principal river is the Han, whose valley is intensively cultivated and which flows south to join the Yangtze at Wuhan. Shaanxi's main crop is grain, chiefly wheat and maize. Some rice is grown in the south. Animal husbandry is generally confined to the north, close to the Great Wall.

across large tracts of north China. All of these things they did first and most intensively in territory controlled by the Shaanxi–Gansu–Ningxia (Shaan–Gan–Ning) Border Region government whose headquarters were at Yanan. The cradle of the Chinese Revolution, Yanan was the centre of a remarkable political experiment that, by the end of the war, had turned the Communists into a major force and, in 1949, made them a victorious one (see CHINESE COMMUNIST PARTY; YANAN).

The brooding presence of China's 'Camelot' partly explains why Shaanxi's leaders were so zealous in implementing Chairman Mao's policies after 1949. Living up to the 'Yanan spirit' required absolute loyalty to its embodiment in Beijing. There was also the question of the gains Mao's strategy brought to the province. The GREAT LEAP FORWARD and the CULTURAL REVOLUTION were two very obvious exceptions, but the post-1949 emphasis on heavy industry, self-reliance and development of poor inland regions brought rapid change after decades of stagnation.

Shaanxi was home for 24 of the 156 major projects undertaken with Soviet assistance under China's first five-year plan (1953–7). It was also a beneficiary of Mao's decision in the early 1960s to build a 'third line' of industry deep in the interior. Industry spread throughout the Guanzhong region. The province became a centre for engineering, the production of high voltage transmission equipment, metallurgy, and the manufacture of aircraft, heavy equipment and machinery. Xian acquired a national reputation for its scientific, technological and educational institutions as well as manufacturing (see INDUSTRY).

These developments improved Shaanxi's position relative to other, traditionally more prosperous, provinces in the south and east. But they brought with them many of the hallmarks of China's encounter with state control and central planning: waste, inefficiency and irrational investment. Transport and communications were neglected. So was agriculture. Light industry was overlooked, too, save for textiles. Host to a large number of defence-related industries and hundreds of ailing state firms, Shaanxi was almost wholly dependent on handouts from Beijing.

In the reform era the province's past successes and failures both turned out to be handicaps. Shaanxi had the 'wrong' industrial mix. It was ill-placed by geography and tradition to develop trade and attract new sources of capital. And it had to rely more on local revenues and less on subsidies from Beijing. The prices of its raw materials, notably potentially valuable supplies of coal and oil, were kept low to suit manufacturing centres in the east. Perhaps worst of all there was no question of preferential policies for Shaanxi of the kind that enabled coastal provinces to forge ahead. For all these reasons, local Party leaders – almost all of them Shaanxi men and conservative in outlook – were often slow to bring their province into line with Deng's harsh new world.

None of this is to say that Shaanxi's economy failed to grow during the 1980s and 1990s. It often did so rapidly. Living standards improved in absolute terms even though the province lost ground in the league table of provincial economies across a range of indices. Furthermore, Shaanxi has by far the most developed industrial base among the four other northwestern provinces it is usually grouped with: GANSU, XINJIANG, QINGHAI and NINGXIA. In the late 1990s it regularly attracted more foreign investment than all of these other provinces put together. These developments suggest that while Shaanxi may have to wait a long time before it can catch up with the richer parts of China to its south and east, the provinces to its west must wait longer still.

Shandong Province

The modern history of Shandong is a cocktail of imperial rivalry, xenophobic unrest, poverty, natural disasters – and belated but rapid development. JAPAN's occupation of the province during the First World War gave birth to modern Chinese nationalism while in the 1940s the CHINESE COMMUNIST PARTY found Shandong fertile ground for its brand of agrarian revolution. In 1949 Communist rule brought change but little development of Shandong's potential as a coastal province naturally oriented towards northeast Asia. This remained the case until the 1990s when Shandong made up for a slow start in reform by opening up to the international economy, in particular to South Korea. China's most populous coastal province has since become one of its star performers.

rebellion and rivalry in the Qing

As the birthplace of Confucius and Mencius, Shandong has perhaps the best claim to be considered China's spiritual homeland. As a province whose densely populated, fertile lowlands have for centuries been at the mercy of the unpredictable Yellow River, it gained an equally strong reputation as a land of natural disasters, BANDITS, SECRET SOCIETIES and popular uprisings. Governing Shandong was a vexatious matter at the best of times. For long periods during the QING DYNASTY it was impossible: the White Lotus, Nian and Taiping were merely the better-known rebel bands who had the run of the province in the mid-nineteenth century. Attempts to suppress them subjected Shandong to constant civil war.

Many people sought refuge in emigration to Manchuria, the Manchu homeland now divided into the three northeastern provinces of LIAONING, JILIN and HEILONGJIANG. The Court at first prohibited Chinese movement into this region, but Russian and Japanese encroachments soon showed the folly of doing so. Partly in order to strengthen their claims to the territory and, if necessary, defend them by force, the Manchus encouraged Chinese settlement in the region. Emigration from Shandong into Manchuria continued well into the Republican era: hundreds of thousands of people in northeast China trace their origin to the province.

At the close of the nineteenth century the growing foreign presence in Shandong led to new outbreaks of popular unrest. Imperial Germany, a latecomer on the scene in China, took advantage of the murder of two of its missionaries in Shandong in 1897 to stake a claim to the province. German troops landed at Jiaozhou Bay and in 1898 signed a 100-year lease with the Qing government that gave Germany exclusive rights inside almost 200 square miles (518 sq kms) of territory centred on the then small fishing village of Qingdao (see TREATY PORTS). They also secured the right to build a railway to Jinan, Shandong's capital, and exploit mineral rights within several miles either side of it (see RAILWAYS). In the same year Britain leased WEIHAIWEI, more than 280 square miles (725 sq kms) of territory surrounding a fine natural harbour on the opposite side of the Shandong peninsula.

These local encroachments were an extreme example of the general malaise facing China. The Qing government was weak and unable to resist foreign aggression. Several attempts at reform seemed to have achieved little. The country was being divided up by foreign adversaries. It was also being misgoverned, as repeated natural disasters and a general breakdown in law made clear. These problems were writ large in Shandong. And so, at least in the minds of some, was a solution to them.

It took the form of the BOXER REBELLION, an uprising of members of the 'society of righteous and harmonious fists'. Boxer attacks on foreigners and Chinese Christians enjoyed the protection of Yu Xian (d. 1901), Shandong's xenophobic governor. Partly due to foreign pressure Yu was replaced by YUAN SHIKAI, the future strongman of China. Yuan suppressed the Boxers in Shandong but was powerless to stop Court patronage of their cause and the disastrous siege of the foreign legations in Beijing that followed. As part of the heavy punishment imposed by the powers once the crisis was over, civil service examinations were suspended in the areas of Shandong where the Boxers had been most active.

nationalism, occupation, Communism

Just as Shandong was the origin of China's last great traditional peasant uprising, so the fate of the province became the object of the modern nationalism that emerged in the aftermath of the REPUBLICAN REVOLUTION. The occasion was the Versailles Peace Conference of May 1919 where the victors of the First World War sought to remake the inter-national order on the basis of national self-determination.

China had declared war on Germany in 1917. For the most part Beijing remained on the sidelines of the conflict, though thousands of Shandong people got rather closer. They did so as members of the Chinese Labour Force, a 'civilian' army of some 150,000 men, mostly from Shandong, who were recruited by Britain and France to serve behind the lines in Europe. The experience of these men was a minor but unique episode in China's modern encounter with the outside world.

The Labour Force aside, China hoped its involvement in the war on the Allies' side would be rewarded at the peace congress. At the very least, Germany's former possessions in Shandong, taken over by Japan in 1914, would be restored. When that failed to happen, and Japan was allowed to keep its gains, protests erupted in Beijing and other Chinese cities, sparking the MAY FOURTH MOVEMENT of political and cultural renewal.

Japan did not agree to give up its possessions in Shandong until forced to do so at the WASHINGTON CONFERENCE of 1921–2. Britain agreed to relinquish Weihaiwei at the same time, but did so only in 1930. By that time the anti-Japanese roots of modern Chinese nationalism were well established.

They grew stronger thanks to a clash between Japanese and Chinese troops in Jinan in 1928 during the course of the NORTHERN EXPEDITION to reunify China. Tokyo had sent soldiers to the city to protect about 2,000 Japanese citizens who lived there. The ill-will created by the foreign military presence proved too much for local diplomacy to cope with. Atrocities on both sides and severe losses inflicted by the Japanese soured relations between the two countries, reinforcing the sense that they were on the path to war.

As indeed they were. Shortly after the outbreak of the SINO-JAPANESE WAR in 1937, Japanese troops moved south along the railway line from Tianjin to Jinan hoping to persuade Han Fuqu (1890–1938), Shandong governor, to give up his province without a fight. He obliged, moving his administration, and the province's gold reserves, south where he was arrested by Chiang, tried and executed for treason.

Japanese troops swiftly occupied the strategic centres of Shandong but then suffered their first and only large-scale defeat at Nationalist hands. It occurred in 1938 at Taierzhuang, on the border with JIANGSU. Forces

The Lie of the Land

One of only three provinces with a peninsula – the others are Guangdong and Liaoning – Shandong also contains an extensive hinterland that extends west of the Grand Canal and north of the Yellow River. This region of the province forms part of the north China plain. Much of it is highly fertile and densely populated. Shandong has two main mountainous regions. One is found in the southern central part of the province, home of the sacred Mount Tai, and the second in the interior of the peninsula. A marshy plain formed by the Jiaolai River separates the peninsula from the interior. At the close of the century more than 88 million people lived in Shandong's 58,000 square miles (150,000 sq kms), making it the second-most populous province after Henan. The province contains China's best gold reserves and ranks second in terms of diamonds. The Shengli oil field in the northwest is the second-largest in the country after Daqing in Heilongjiang. There are extensive coal reserves in the Zibo region, west of Jinan. Shandong is one of China's grain baskets. The main crops are wheat, potatoes and maize, cotton, tobacco, peanuts and fruit.

under LI ZONGREN halted the Japanese advance on Xuzhou, a strategic railway junction to the south, and inflicted heavy losses on the invaders. It was a brief moment of glory in an otherwise sorry Nationalist war effort.

As Nationalist power crumbled in Shandong and the Japanese swept south, Communist guerrillas moved in to fill the gaps. By the early 1940s they controlled large areas of the province. Major towns and the two main railway lines were often denied them by Japanese and Nationalist troops, but their mobility and support in the villages enabled them to survive and expand. As elsewhere in north China, the Communist presence in Shandong was substantial by the end of the war. Parts of the province changed hands during the early stages of the CIVIL WAR as a result of fierce, large-scale battles. But by the middle of 1947, all but a few enclaves were in Communist hands. The Nationalists' loss of Shandong opened the way for the Communist conquest of east and south China.

after 1949: radicalism to reform

Shandong experienced many excesses of the Maoist years in full. The first post-1949 leader of the province was KANG SHENG, a Shandong man and former security chief, who ensured that LAND REFORM was conducted with rigour and brutality within his domain. The GREAT LEAP FORWARD brought horrific famine to parts of the province, particularly the north-

west where peasants tend to produce cotton and non-staple products rather than grain.

Hundreds of thousands fled south of the Yellow River where they tried to barter their possessions for food. As many as 7.5 million Shandong people may have died during the early 1960s. Finally, Shandong was second only to Heilongjiang in answering Mao's call to topple established forms of government at the provincial level and set up revolutionary committees during the CULTURAL REVOLUTION.

Local leaders were slower off the mark when it came to carrying out the de-collectivization of agriculture, free market reforms and opening to the outside world championed by DENG XIAOPING in the late 1970s. They preferred caution to innovation, perhaps aware that they were much closer physically and politically to Beijing than their more adventurist counterparts in distant GUANGDONG and FUJIAN. Despite the inclusion of both Yantai (the former treaty port known as Chefoo) and Qingdao in the list of 14 coastal cities opened to FOREIGN TRADE AND INVESTMENT on favourable terms in 1984, it was not until the late 1980s that Shandong entered the front ranks of reform.

Several factors made this possible. One was the coastal development strategy advocated by ZHAO ZIYANG, the reform-minded premier and later Party leader. This gave the green light for the maximization of Shandong's geographical advantages as a coastal province with a history of maritime trade and foreign contact. It was particularly advantageous for Qingdao, one of China's major international ports. Many other parts of the province benefited from a decentralization of decision-making in foreign trade.

Another factor was China's rapprochement with South Korea (see KOREA). This had been under way for some time before 1987 when Beijing quietly allowed Shandong to start a ferry service from Weihai (the final *wei*, meaning to 'guard' or 'defend', having been dropped) to Inchon, and issue visas to South Korean businessmen visiting the province. Beijing kept quiet on the issue to avoid offending its longstanding ally North Korea.

The impact of South Korea was immediate and large. It became even more so in 1992 when Seoul switched diplomatic relations from Taiwan to the People's Republic, delighting Beijing and depriving Taipei of its last major ally in Asia. South Korean investment flooded into Shandong in search of cheap land and labour rather as HONG KONG money had poured into Guangdong and Taiwanese into Fujian.

To some extent, this enabled the Mainland to benefit from the Chinese diaspora again: about 90 per cent of South Korea's 20,000-strong Chinese community have links to Shandong (see OVERSEAS CHINESE). But economic forces, not ethnicity, have been the most powerful forces at work. They are driving South Korean companies, including several of the biggest, to seek comparative advantage by manufacturing in Shandong. By 1995, South Korea had become the second-largest buyer of Shandong exports after Japan, and the second-biggest source of foreign direct investment after Hong Kong.

China's handling of relations with South Korea is an example of the pragmatism and sometimes almost brazen self-interest at the heart of its FOREIGN POLICY. Beijing's ties with Pyongyang are friendly and firm: China values North Korea as a buffer state protecting it from the United States' major ally to the south. But it is not prepared to subsidize the unpredictable socialist north in the way the Soviet Union did. Neither is it prepared to forgo substantial investment from South Korea. If closer ties with Seoul bring both capital and diplomatic discomfort for Taiwan, so much the better.

Deng Xiaoping's tour of south China in 1992 boosted the cause of reform and opening up in Shandong. So did an influx of investment from Taiwan about the same time. An estimated 800,000 Taiwanese have affiliations with Shandong. Many have turned their connections to good account.

Jiang Chunyun (1930–), governor of Shandong from 1987 to 1988, and local Party leader from 1988 to 1994, made the most of these conditions. Under his leadership new roads and rail links were built, and the less developed regions of the interior encouraged to learn from the go-ahead cities of the peninsula. His efforts won him promotion to the Politburo in 1992 and to Beijing as vice-premier in charge of agriculture in 1995, despite an unusual display of opposition from delegates to the NATIONAL PEOPLE'S CONGRESS apparently concerned over his wife's alleged involvement in corruption.

Shandong and Northeast Asia

Shandong prospered in the 1990s by making the most of its external linkages, particularly with South Korea. But there could be limits to this in the new century. The analogy with Hong Kong and Guangdong, and Taiwan and Fujian cannot be pressed too far. All the actors in these linkages are Chinese. Many Chinese, in Shandong and elsewhere in the country, on the other hand, welcome South Korean capital with greater enthusiasm than they do South Koreans. Complaints over the sharp business practices, hedonistic lifestyles and alleged haughtiness of South Korean investors are common.

Moreover, Shandong's future depends to some extent on the broader issue of peace on the Korean peninsula and China's relations with Japan. The province forms a natural part of the Bohai Gulf economic zone, bounded by HEBEI, TIANJIN and Liaoning, all of them Chinese territories. But it will only really come into its own when the international and security situation in northeast Asia facilitates the emergence of a wider Yellow Sea economic zone consisting of northeast and east China, the entire Korean peninsula and Japan.

Shanghai

Nowhere are the great issues of twentieth-century China spelt out more clearly, more tellingly or more traumatically than in the history of modern Shanghai. The mighty city at the mouth of the YANGTZE has been both locus and focus of the struggle between tradition and modernity, reform and revolution, and the vexed question of China's relationship with the outside world. To a large extent, the outcome of these debates still hinges on the fate of the metropolis as, engulfed by reconstruction and the ambition of its leaders, it enters the twenty-first century.

foreign city, Chinese soil

Modern Shanghai was built by and largely for foreigners and was the first truly cosmopolitan city to emerge on Chinese soil. Largely because of the way in which this occurred, most Chinese nationalists regarded the city and what it stood for as, at best, an irritant. For many, it was a national disgrace.

Yet reformers, rebels and revolutionaries of every stamp benefited from the fact that Shanghai was under foreign control. For one thing they could meet, discuss and publish their ideas in the International Settlement or the French Concession free of interference from their government. Virtually all the important challenges to orthodoxy in almost every field of Chinese life during the first decades of the century could be found in speeches, books, journals and newspapers published in foreign Shanghai. And almost everything about the city – from its efficient, modern police force to its humming textile factories; from its retail fashions to its modern roads, buildings, power supplies and telephone network – was an indictment of Chinese rule beyond its boundaries.

But if Shanghai aspired to point the way for the rest of China, it was a flawed emblem of modernity. While it gave China its first real taste of modern INDUSTRY and banking, it also gave the country its first proletariat, a Communist Party dedicated to serving it, and provided the occasion for strikes, protests and a violent anti-imperialist movement that swept across the country and threatened to drive foreigners from China's shores.

Early twentieth-century Shanghai consisted of three parts which, nearly 100 years later, can still (just about) be distinguished by their different architectural styles. The oldest was the 'Chinese City', bounded until 1911 by high walls that subsequently became the site of an early ring road. Separating the Chinese City from the Bund, and enclosing it from the north and the west, was the French Concession. Further north still was the International Settlement, formed by a merger of the original British and American settlements during the previous century. From 1899 until it was overrun by the Japanese in 1941, the International Settlement covered an area of just over 8 square miles (20 sq kms) that extended foreign control inland from the Bund, along the south bank of the Suzhou Creek, and north and east along the bank of the Huangpu (Whangpoo) River.

There were minor differences in legal standing between the French Concession and the International Settlement, and larger ones arising from the fact that different powers were at work seeking to transplant themselves on an alien shore. But together they formed *foreign Shanghai*: an area in the heart of a Chinese city where, thanks to EXTRATERRITORIALITY, the host country's sovereignty had been extinguished in everything but name, and where some of the best, most modern assets in China, both foreign- and Chinese-owned, were beyond the reach of the national government.

Apologists, most of them foreign, argued that this was precisely why the city was so successful: foreign control enabled Shanghai to escape the crises of imperial collapse, civil war and Communist insurrection that afflicted most other parts of the country. The Shanghai Municipal Council and the *Conseil Municipal* that ruled the International Settlement and the French Concession respectively provided standards of modern civic administration that the Chinese authorities would have done well to learn from. When they showed signs of doing so, when the Chinese agreed to stop fighting each other over their political future, *then* would have been the time to discuss retrocession of the foreign enclaves.

The fact that during the 1920s Shanghai became a magnet for domestic as well as foreign refugees, that it lured to seeming safety those who wanted to escape the world as well as those who wanted to change it, appeared to support this argument. The architecture and ruling culture of the settlements might be European, but its teeming streets and crowded tenements, its luxurious villas and magnificent banks, its numerous nightspots and gaudy pleasure houses played host to a polyglot community without equal in Asia. Russian exiles rubbed shoulders with Ashkenazi and Sephardic Jews. European and American businessmen mingled with their Chinese counterparts from almost every province. Beggars and prostitutes, MISSIONARIES and failed mandarins, gangsters and adventurers, writers, artists and professional revolutionaries – they all made Shanghai truly Bohemian.

Shanghai under siege: the 1920s

Yet Shanghai was still China. The International Settlement was a quasi-autonomous enclave of uncertain legal standing. Strictly speaking, it grew up outside the formal network of UNEQUAL TREATIES China signed with foreign governments. And its rulers, most of them British, were frequently at odds with their own consuls as well as their distant government at home. The Shanghai Municipal Council made a good job of administering foreigners in the Settlement, but the much more numerous Chinese, deprived of a government of their own, were vulnerable to rule by SECRET SOCIETIES. Foreign Shanghai existed under Chinese sufferance. It was both a consequence and a cause of China's national weakness.

Until the mid-1920s, the main physical

threat to Shanghai stemmed from the collapse of central authority beyond its narrow confines. On several occasions, feuding rebels and warlords threatened to engulf the city, spread their internecine struggle along its tree-lined streets, and snuff out foreign privilege and the modernization associated with it. Fear of international reaction, and a feeling on the part of many of those engaged in China's complicated struggle for power that they had something to gain from leaving Shanghai intact, helped the city survive.

But this did not last. New forces emerged in China during the 1920s, many of which took shape in Shanghai itself. One of them was the CHINESE COMMUNIST PARTY, founded in a house in the French Concession in July 1921. Four years later, Shanghai and many other parts of southern China were caught up in the NORTHERN EXPEDITION, the revolutionary movement that briefly threatened to turn the established order upside down before it ran aground on the rocks of factionalism and the ambitions of CHIANG KAI-SHEK.

Although the National Revolutionary government was established first in Guangzhou, capital of GUANGDONG, events in Shanghai showed many the rightness of its cause. On 30 May 1925 (later enshrined in China's revolutionary history as the 'May 30th Incident'), police who were unable to break up a protest over the death of a Chinese worker at a Japanese textile factory opened fire on the crowd, killing 11 people and wounding many others. Shanghai promptly went on strike, and workers throughout much of south China responded with protests and anti-foreign boycotts, most of them directed at Britain. The violence intensified a month later, when British and French troops on Shamian Island, the foreign concession in Guangzhou, opened fire on Chinese protestors, killing more than 50. Anger swept through Guangzhou and plunged HONG KONG into a year-long strike/boycott that crippled the colony. Shanghai, the source of this new kind of unrest, escaped lightly by comparison. But with the approach towards the city of the National Revolutionary armies in early 1927, Shanghai's days as a generally peaceful, foreign enclave seemed to be over.

Two factors saved the city: massive reinforcement by British and American troops; and an anti-Communist purge by Chiang Kai-shek, carried out in league with Du Yuesheng (1887–1951), Shanghai's leading gangster, and conducted with the connivance of authorities in the International Settlement. In April 1927, Chiang and his allies crushed Shanghai's Communist-controlled workers' movement, moving troops and plainclothes vigilantes through the Settlement to do so. Hundreds of Left-wingers were killed or arrested. The purge in Shanghai spread rapidly to other cities occupied by the National Revolutionary army, and the Communist movement was driven into the countryside, from which it did not emerge for almost two decades. The Party's Central Committee continued to operate on a clandestine basis in Shanghai until 1932, but was eventually forced to flee to JIANGXI, where Mao had established a revolutionary base. The city that gave birth to the revolutionary workers' movement had, at least temporarily, also proved its graveyard.

Yet if foreign Shanghai survived the Nationalist storm, it rested on ever more shaky foundations. Chinese control was regarded as inevitable, but it was unclear, certainly to the foreign community, how this could be reconciled with the continued protection of their substantial interests in the city. Symbolic changes – such as introducing Chinese representation on the Municipal Council and allowing Chinese to enter the Settlement's parks (from which most of them had been banned under regulations which included a prohibition on dogs, but which did *not* say, as the Communists later alleged, 'No dogs or Chinese') – did little to address the issue. The problem was thrown into sharper relief by the growth of Chinese business in the city during the 1930s.

Shanghai at war

In the event, war wrought changes that diplomacy could not. The outbreak of the SINO-JAPANESE WAR in July 1937 brought catastrophic defeats for the Nationalists, who lost control over Shanghai, Nanjing and Wuhan in rapid succession. The International Settlement, now a shadow of its pre-war self, survived until December 1941 when, following Pearl Harbor, the Japanese, and the Chinese puppet administration led by WANG JINGWEI, assumed control. Little over a year later, Britain and the United States abandoned extraterritoriality out of respect for their occupied wartime ally. Shanghai, a TREATY PORT for the previous century, would never be the same again.

But what kind of place would it be? There were few clues to this during the five years the Nationalist government controlled the city before they were driven out by the Communists. In the late 1940s, Shanghai became a microcosm of much that was wrong with China as its chief contenders for power fought each other. CORRUPTION, inflation and incompetence within the city, combined with crushing military defeats beyond, rapidly exhausted the prestige Chiang had earned from his government's victory over Japan. Refugees and defeated Nationalist soldiers poured into Shanghai. Foreign and domestic businesses faltered, and many of their owners and managers poured out, many of them to Hong Kong. Students and Left-wing intellectuals staged anti-war protests. Ordinary people, their resilience tested beyond endurance by the twin scourges of Japanese occupation and, now, civil war, yearned for change. And that, once Communist armies marched into the city in May 1949, rapidly overcoming token Nationalist resistance, is what they got.

Shanghai strangled: 1950s and 1960s

The hope that Shanghai would exert greater influence over Mao's peasant armies and the newly established Communist government than Communism would over Shanghai quickly evaporated. Shanghai's 'Liberation' entailed a reckoning. Two worlds came into conflict in the city in 1949. One was that of an outward-looking, entrepreneurial anything-goes version of Chinese modernization whose nationalism was seen as dangerously unfocused politically and tainted by foreign contacts and privilege. The other was the world of peasant 'simplicity' and revolutionary ardour which, fuelled by a desire for revenge, was committed to the overthrow of an unjust economic order, and the exclusion of 'corrupting' foreign influence.

The mainstream Communist view of Shanghai was that it was parasitic. It was a city of consumption and corruption. It was the centre of 'bourgeois influence' in China whose century of foreign control merely confirmed the need for thoroughgoing 'purification'. Repeated, often vicious, mass movements targeted those deemed to oppose the new order, and the nationalization of private, as well as what remained of foreign, capital quickly asphyxiated 'old' Shanghai. Hong Kong assumed – and grew fat on – Shanghai's former role as a key centre where Chinese and Western values, customs and commerce met.

China's new rulers had other things in mind for Shanghai. They built it up as a mighty industrial city whose products, at least for a while, became bywords for quality throughout the country, and whose revenues made a major contribution to the national budget. Together with BEIJING and TIANJIN, Shanghai was made a province-level municipality directly under the central government. However, the fact that it was squeezed mercilessly by the centre for taxes tended to undermine this exalted status. Shanghai became an industrial powerhouse, but its general fabric sank into slow decline. Those who ran the city did so for Beijing rather than Shanghai.

The city was more of a pace-setter on the political front, particularly during the CULTURAL REVOLUTION. One of the opening shots of Mao's campaign to re-radicalize his Revolution was fired in the Shanghai press. In 1965, Yao Wenyuan (1931–), then a literary critic, published an oblique but telling attack on the Party leadership in Beijing. Together with JIANG QING, Zhang Chunqiao (1917–91), and Wang Hongwen (1934–92), Yao would later be known as one of the 'GANG OF FOUR', the group held responsible for all the ills of the Cultural Revolution. All four had a close association with Shanghai. Yao and Wang made their careers there. Zhang worked in Shanghai for many years before he became involved in high politics in Beijing. Jiang lived in Shanghai in the 1930s when she was a minor film star. These connections helped them build a power base in the city during the Cultural Revolution.

At the close of 1966, Shanghai was in the grip of strikes, protests and infighting of the kind it had not seen since the mid-1920s. Rebel factions struggled to win control of the municipal government. In January 1967, a 'People's Commune' was set up in a seizure of power that radicals in Beijing extolled as a model for the rest of China. In fact, Mao soon curtailed the Shanghai experiment, preferring to set up 'revolutionary committees', with strong army participation, rather than potentially anarchic 'communes'. But Shanghai, under the urgings of Wang, Yao and the formidable militia they controlled, remained a bastion of Leftism until the death of Mao and the sudden arrest of the 'Gang of Four' in October 1976. Had the 'Gang' spent more time in Shanghai after Mao's death rather than plotting in Beijing, their opponents might have found it harder to oust them.

reform in search of former glory

Shanghai at first found it difficult to adapt to the new demands of the reform era. Throughout the 1980s, the city laboured under its heavy tax burden and tight political control by Beijing. Its ageing industries sapped what funds were available, and forced the proud inhabitants of China's mightiest city to watch as their compatriots in 'upstart' provinces such as Guangdong and FUJIAN grew rich on the back of FOREIGN TRADE AND INVESTMENT and the rapid development of rural industry. Even the announcement in 1990 of plans to build a new Shanghai in Pudong, the relatively undeveloped flatlands on the east bank of the Huangpu River, failed to shake the city out of its torpor.

Shanghai woke up two years later when DENG XIAOPING made his celebrated tour of southern China. During a stopover in the city, Deng said it had been a mistake not to develop Shanghai earlier as the 'head of the Yangtze dragon', a vast economic zone containing close to one-third of China's population. His remarks galvanized the local leadership. They were also endorsed in Beijing, where central government leaders – several of whom, such as JIANG ZEMIN and ZHU RONGJI, had made their careers in Shanghai – viewed rapid development of the city as a necessary counterweight to the growth of the southern provinces.

During the mid-1990s, domestic and foreign investment poured into a Shanghai bent on recovering its former glory as Asia's leading financial centre. Scores of new shares were listed on an infant stock market which in 1997 moved into new, purpose-built premises. A frenzy of construction gripped the city. It took China's version of capitalism little more than four years to accomplish what more than 40 years of socialism had not: the transformation of the face of a city whose main lines had been laid down by foreigners almost a century earlier. Amid all the new glass and concrete, and the spread of the city east, across the river into Pudong, Shanghai at last began to lose the architectural identity of the concessions era. The city added property speculation to its established ship building, petro-chemical, iron and steel, vehicle, electronics and (flagging) textile industries.

Shanghai's spectacular development in the late 1990s prompted the kind of exaggerated predictions from domestic and foreign observers often associated with new trends in China. As Hong Kong approached its transition to Chinese rule in 1997, some prophesied the territory's gradual demise as a leading financial centre in favour of a newly resurgent Shanghai. With its industrial base and vast population, both in the city itself and the hinterland, Shanghai seemed destined to become a key metropolis of the twenty-first century. Hong Kong would remain an important centre for south China, but not, perhaps, much else.

Such views owed more to the imagination than to careful analysis. By the close of the twentieth century, Shanghai, a city of 15 million people, had laid down much of the infrastructure required of a modern city. It had also built a museum, opera house and library worthy of many of its counterparts in the developed world. What was lacking was a clear, predictable legal system, and a transparent process of political decision-making of the kind that makes foreign investors – to say nothing of ordinary citizens – feel at ease. Moreover, Shanghai was so far from being a financial centre that it was often at odds with neighbouring JIANGSU over project financing and control. Foreign banks were only grudgingly allowed to engage in business in local currency, which remained unconvertible on the capital account (see FINANCE). Clearly there was a long way to go. The obstacles are related to China's political culture as much as to Shanghai itself. If Shanghai is to realize its full promise and live up to its ambitions, *China*, not just its leading city, must change.

Shanxi Province

Geographically Shanxi is the most distinctive of the core provinces of north-central China. Its recent history is no less unique. Yet neither geography nor history has shielded it from the broader changes sweeping across China. Instead, events within its relatively isolated confines have often had an impact on the rest of the country. In YAN XISHAN Shanxi produced one of the most prominent of China's WARLORDS. During the SINO-JAPANESE WAR it was the site of major Communist Party base areas, foundations for the Party's national victory in 1949. And, though built up as an industrial and mining centre under Communist rule, it gave birth to an icon of Maoist agriculture in the form of Dazhai Production Brigade, whose productivity was first the subject of legend and later dismissed as lies. Burdened with a large state sector at a time of national economic slowdown, Shanxi is finding it harder to make a mark at the start of the new era.

bankers, bandits, Boxers

Elevated above and secluded from the north China plain, Shanxi has always been something of a strategic enclave, despite its relative proximity to Beijing. The same features have made it prone to drought, famine and POVERTY. Its unforgiving yellow earth is scarred by jagged peaks and deep defiles. Agriculture is particularly precarious. Communications, traditionally prey to underdevelopment and banditry, have often been difficult.

Yet in the nineteenth century Shanxi's position astride key trade routes made it the unlikely centre of a flourishing private banking network. The province's bankers exercised a near monopoly over the supply of commercial credit during the late QING DYNASTY. They financed much of China's domestic trade and, with the coming of the Western powers, funded the trade in tea, silk and opium, too.

These activities did little to mitigate the harshness of life for ordinary Shanxi people. Conditions in the province spurred MISSIONARIES to broaden their vision of saving souls into relief work, medicine and EDUCATION. Prominent among them was Timothy Richard of the English Baptist Missionary Society. Richard combined efforts to relieve the destitute in Shanxi with attempts to change China at the top through association with LIANG QICHAO, KANG YOUWEI and other leaders of the Qing reform movement.

Both campaigns suffered setbacks. The 100 Days Reform Movement ended in repression while the BOXER REBELLION took a particularly heavy toll on Christians in Shanxi. This was partly due to Yu Xian (d. 1901), the virulently anti-foreign governor of the province who had patronized the Boxers in his previous post as governor of SHANDONG. Yu presided over the massacre of about 2,000 Chinese Christians and more than 40 missionaries – women and children among them – in Taiyuan, the provincial capital.

rebuilding: the era of Yan Xishan

The REPUBLICAN REVOLUTION of 1911 ushered in a long period of faltering yet remarkable change in the province under Yan Xishan, the 'model' governor and China's most enduring warlord. A former military student in Japan, Yan played an important part in the army revolt that ended Manchu rule in Shanxi. For most of the following 40 years he treated the province as his private domain, seeking to exclude outsiders of every kind, Nationalist and Communist Chinese as well as Japanese. He did not always succeed: during the Sino-Japanese War most of Shanxi was occupied by Japanese invaders and the Communist Eighth Route Army. But until the late 1930s, Yan's skilful political manoeuvring enabled Shanxi to avoid the worst warlord conflicts and concentrate on economic development.

Rapid industrialization, the construction of ROADS and RAILWAYS, and political indoctrination were some of the most striking consequences. Much of Shanxi is coal country; it accounts for about one-third of China's reserves. Yan's Northwest Industrial Company, a government monopoly theoretically owned by the public, tapped local energy and other resources to produce iron and steel, cement, weapons and textiles. By the standards of the day he built a fairly large industrial base, most of it located around Taiyuan. New railway lines and roads facilitated the shipment of Shanxi products to other parts of the country.

Yan paid less attention to agriculture. His main concern was to raise men for the Shanxi army, the bastion of his rule. Schemes to pool land and work the fields efficiently and fairly freed farmers to join the ranks. They did little to improve rural livelihoods or break the power of landlords. Despite years of intensive anti-Communist propaganda, Party activists received an enthusiastic welcome from many Shanxi peasants when they entered the province.

Communist base areas

They began to do so in strength following the outbreak of the Sino-Japanese War in July 1937. (See CHINESE COMMUNIST PARTY.) Nominally incorporated into the Nationalist armies led by CHIANG KAI-SHEK, the Eighth Route Army moved east from its base in YANAN into Shanxi to meet the Japanese advance. Yan at first cautiously welcomed the intruders, believing them less of a threat to his rule than central government troops. He soon changed his mind. Although Communist and Shanxi troops managed to inflict heavy losses on the Japanese at the Battle of Pingxingguan, close to the border with HEBEI, Taiyuan fell to the invaders in November 1939 along with other key provincial centres. By the end of the year Yan was beaten back into southwest Shanxi while the Communists melted into rural 'base areas' from which, in some cases, they were never evicted. The pact between Yan and the Communists fell apart.

Different parts of Shanxi were incorporated into different base areas or border regions. The northwest of the province fell within the Shanxi–Suiyuan (now part of INNER MONGOLIA) base area, theatre of the Eighth Route Army's 120th division, commanded by He Long (1896–1969). Northeast Shanxi was part of the Shanxi–Chahaer (also now part of Inner Mongolia)–Hebei border region, locale of the 115th division led first by LIN BIAO and then by Nie Rongzhen (1899–1992). Southeast Shanxi formed part – usually the most solid part – of the Shanxi–Hebei–Shandong–Henan base area, headquarters of the 129th division. Liu Bocheng (1892–1986) commanded the 129th division. Its political commissar was DENG XIAOPING.

The north China base areas were not as secure as the Shaanxi–Gansu–Ningxia (Shaan–Gan–Ning) Border Region government centred on Yanan to the west. Neither were they theatres of political and military experiment in the way Yanan was. They were behind enemy lines, and their frontiers expanded and contracted with the fortunes of war. The Eighth Route Army's 'Hundred Regiments Offensive' of 1940 challenged Japanese power throughout north China but was followed by retaliation in the form of the 'three-all' campaign: 'kill all, burn all, loot all'. This inflicted misery on ordinary Chinese and drove the Communists underground, particularly in Hebei. Even in the mountainous Taihang region separating Hebei from Shanxi, the Communists were often under pressure.

Yet their dedication, determination and discipline, and their willingness to experiment when building political and military institutions in the shifting areas under their control, gradually paid off. Sometimes the Communists incorporated local bandit organizations into their military ranks. Sometimes they cooperated with SECRET SOCIETIES. Often they pursued low tax policies or conducted only moderate versions of LAND REFORM in an effort to build strategic alliances with rich peasants and 'progressive' landlords. Invariably they propagated a compelling mix of nationalism and revolution that obliged would-be opponents to fend off charges of treason as well as 'feudalism'. Always the presence of the Japanese menace heightened the drama and urgency of the situation. Neither

The Lie of the Land

Shanxi's 60,230 square miles (156,000 sq kms) are bound by the Great Wall to the north, the Yellow River to the west and southwest, and the Taihang mountain range in the east. Much of the province takes the form of a plateau about 3,000 feet above sea level and high above the north China plain to the east. The central Shanxi basin extends from Datong, the major mining and industrial city in the north, in a series of valleys all the way south to Yuncheng, close to the borders with Shaanxi and Henan. Watered by the Sanggan and Fen rivers it contains some of the province's best agricultural land. Two of China's most sacred mountains, Wu Tai Shan and Heng Shan, are located in northeast Shanxi. Further south the Taihang range encloses flat, productive basins, particularly around the cities of Pingding and Changzhi. Much of western Shanxi, running up to the Yellow River, is mountainous land which towers over the central Shanxi basin. At the end of the century Shanxi's population was 31 million. Wheat, maize, millet and sorghum are the main crops. Cotton is grown in the south.

Yan Xishan nor other Nationalist forces could match these policies – in Shanxi or elsewhere.

For much of the war, the Eighth Route Army headquarters was located in the Taihang section of the Shanxi–Hebei–Shandong–Henan base area. This region, though often overshadowed by others under Communist control, proved a training ground for many of those who ran China after 1949, and particularly after 1978. Among those who worked in the Taihang area during the 1940s, apart from Deng himself, were Bo Yibo (1908–), YANG SHANGKUN, ZHAO ZIYANG and Wan Li (1916–), each of them Deng's allies (to different degrees) in the struggle to change China in the years following the death of MAO ZEDONG.

In 1948, the Shanxi–Hebei–Shandong–Henan border region merged with the Shanxi–Chahaer–Hebei base to the north to form the North China's People's government, the immediate precursor of the government of the People's Republic of China. By 1948, too, the 129th division, led by Liu and Deng, had been renamed the Second Field Army of the PEOPLE'S LIBERATION ARMY and was undertaking the conquest of central China.

Yan Xishan's hold over Shanxi soon disintegrated during the CIVIL WAR. Following Japan's surrender he had reoccupied the key cities and communications lines of his province. But he began to lose them as Nationalist fortunes ebbed across north China. At one point Yan hinted at a fight to the finish for Taiyuan, where his troops – many of them led, at his request, by Japanese officers – were besieged by Communists. In the event, the 'model' governor fled to Nanjing and then Taiwan, taking Shanxi's reserves with him. Yan's troops slogged it out in bitter fighting against a superior foe. Taiyuan was 'liberated' in April 1949.

the rise and fall of Dazhai

The new Communist government was quick to build on the industrial foundation Yan had laid down in Shanxi. Heavy investment in mining and railway construction placed one of the country's most important energy bases at the service of China's wider industrialization drive.

But if Shanxi's economic importance to the rest of China was usually defined in terms of coal, it acquired a different kind of fame from the mid-1960s as the home of Dazhai Production Brigade where farmers were said to have combined staggering productivity with exemplary class attitudes. Thanks to enthusiastic backing from Mao Zedong, peasants in the rest of China were urged to 'learn from Dazhai' in much the same way that workers were encouraged to 'learn from Daqing', the model oil enterprise in HEILONGJIANG.

Dazhai was located in Xieyang county, close to the border with Hebei. In the late 1950s local farmers in the region tilled 50 or so hectares of poor, loess soil dispersed over a series of gullies, ridges and slopes. At issue was the question of whether the escape from poverty lay in state aid or cooperativization and political mobilization. Chen Yonggui (1914–86), the local Party leader, opted for the latter. Despite resistance and setbacks, local harvests soon exceeded those of other brigades.

More to the point, Dazhai peasants rewarded themselves with 'work points' based as much on their political attitudes as their physical output. At a time of national debate over the nature and purpose of the Revolution, Dazhai became a powerful cause célèbre for Mao and his fellow radicals.

The political fortunes of Chen Yonggui, usually pictured wearing his trademark head towel, rose along with those of his Brigade. In 1964 he appeared beside Mao in the *People's Daily*. In 1969, with the CULTURAL REVOLUTION in full swing, he entered the Central Committee. In 1973, still a favourite with the radicals in their struggle against ZHOU ENLAI and Deng Xiaoping, he joined the Politburo.

Meanwhile Dazhai had become a byword for economic self-reliance, social solidarity and political awareness. Its achievements testified to the merits of Mao's 'eight-point charter' which stressed soil improvement, use of fertilizers, water conservancy, close planting, high-yield seed strains, plant protection, innovation in farm tools and field management. Millions of Chinese and hundreds of foreigners – many of them 'friends of China' (see 'FOREIGN EXPERTS AND FOREIGN FRIENDS') – flocked to remote Dazhai to pay homage.

Or at least they did until it was exposed as a fraud shortly after the Chairman's death. Neither Dazhai nor Chen Yonggui survived the return to family farming introduced by Deng Xiaoping. Dazhai disappeared from the political vocabulary, and in 1980 the *People's Daily* dealt a deathblow to everything it stood for. So far from a beacon of self-reliance, the brigade was found to have relied on a massive injection of state funds and conscript military labour. As for Chen Yonggui, he was discovered to have persecuted more than 100 people to death during the Cultural Revolution while his relatives habitually abused their positions. Dazhai and Chen were heard of no more.

reform challenge and coal crisis

Shanxi's traditional reliance on mining and heavy industry, and the strong presence of the state in both these sectors of the economy, have made it hard for the province to respond to the challenges of the reform era. Taiyuan has found it difficult to break its financial dependence on Beijing for the same reason. Internationalizing the local economy is hardly an option: FOREIGN TRADE AND INVESTMENT have made less impact in Shanxi than in neighbouring provinces – with the exception of Inner Mongolia, itself something of a special case.

The provincial government has tried to maximize Shanxi's value as an energy base by improving local transport links, marketizing the mining and distributing of coal, and securing the best possible price for its most valuable commodity. The results have been mixed at best. At one stage during the 1990s, the authorities became so frustrated at the low price of coal that they established a checkpoint at Ningzi Pass, on the main rail and road route to Hebei, to stop its export from the province. Hebei retaliated with a ban on grain, oil and vegetable exports to Shanxi. Taiyuan soon relented.

China's economic slowdown at the end of

the century created new problems, plunging the coal industry into deeper crisis. In Shanxi and elsewhere, large collieries produce stockpiles of unwanted coal. Many are owed billions of dollars by state-owned firms unable to pay for their fuel. To protect the larger mines, the government is closing hundreds of local 'unofficial' mines. While these are often unsafe, and the cause of most of China's mining accidents, many have managed to build market share at the expense of their bigger, less efficient competitors. The outcome of China's decision to shake up its coal industry is uncertain, but given Shanxi's significance as an energy base it is bound to have a major impact on the province.

Shenzhen Special Economic Zone

The most flamboyant and successful of China's SPECIAL ECONOMIC ZONES (SEZs) created a buffer of wealth and innovation between HONG KONG and the interior that helped facilitate the former colony's return to China. This was one of the roles DENG XIAO-PING had in mind in 1980 when he founded the zone. It was not the only one: like its fellow first-generation SEZs, Shenzhen was set up to pioneer capitalist-style experiments in FOREIGN TRADE AND INVESTMENT, FINANCE, ownership and management that could later be applied elsewhere. It fulfilled many of these goals – sometimes with considerable success, but rarely without controversy.

Once a market town famous only as the point at which most visitors entered 'Red China' from Hong Kong, Shenzhen SEZ occupies 126 square miles (327 sq kms) of territory between the Mainland and the former British colony. A larger municipal area to the north separates the zone from the rest of GUANG-DONG province, reinforcing the feeling that the SEZ is a place apart.

The zone's transformation was rapid. Heavy investment during the early 1980s turned a once sleepy border crossing into a building site. It remained so until the end of the decade when towering office blocks, hotels and bank buildings suggested to the casual observer that Shenzhen had become another Hong Kong.

Many in Beijing thought so, too, and some of them disapproved. Almost alone among Communist Party leaders, CHEN YUN, head of the Party's conservative wing until his death in 1995, refused to visit the city that, for most in the outside world and many at home, symbolized China's commitment to radical free market reforms. For Chen, Shenzhen went too far, too fast. It provided a new base for capitalism within the People's Republic, one that might overrun the entire country.

In some respects his fears were realized. Foreign investment flowed in, much of it from Hong Kong and OVERSEAS CHINESE communities rather than from Japan and the West as Beijing originally hoped. Factories were set up to process textiles, foodstuffs and electronics for export using cheap labour, much of it supplied by WOMEN. The Party's hold over political life was never abandoned in Shenzhen; but the zone's proximity to Hong Kong, to which most local people turned for information, including radio and television broadcasts, and its reform experiments fostered a liberal atmosphere quite unlike that in other parts of the People's Republic. Party leaders, including Deng himself, described some of the manifestations of this as 'flies and insects' that were bound to enter China through the Open Door along with the more desirable capital, technology and expertise. However, Shenzhen was a key destination during his celebrated tour of south China in early 1992 that reinvigorated the country's reform drive. In the same year the zone acquired its own legislative powers, formerly invested in the provincial administration based in Guangzhou.

In August 1992 the zone was in the news for a different reason. Hundreds of thousands of people went to Shenzhen to buy lottery tickets that would entitle them to purchase shares of companies due to list on the zone's infant stock exchange, one of only two in the country (the other was in SHANGHAI). As the queues formed, it became clear there would not be enough tickets to go round, largely because officials had got their hands on them first. Protests erupted, the largest of their kind since the TIANANMEN SQUARE DEMOCRACY MOVEMENT, and police had to use tear gas and water cannon to restore order.

Shenzhen was at the centre of a new controversy during the mid-1990s. As foreign investment spread north, further into Guangdong, and factories left the zone in search of cheaper labour and land in the interior, questions were raised over the tax and other privileges enjoyed by Shenzhen and its fellow SEZs.

There were complaints of too much low-end export processing and not enough investment in high tech; of too much trading in foreign exchange and not enough earning it; of too many budgetary exemptions and insufficient contributions.

These arguments were framed in the context of national concern over growing inequalities between the zones and the interior, and Beijing's desire to curb financial auton-omy in the regions. This is not to say there was no room for improvement in Shenzhen: in 1996 Beijing endorsed the idea that it and the other zones should remain 'special', but encouraged them to pursue new reforms in the service sector, particularly finance. Progress was slower than anticipated, but this did not challenge the role Shenzhen in particular played as a source and symbol of China's modernization drive.

Sichuan Province

A vast, fertile basin ringed by mountains, the province known as 'heaven's granary', is a key political, economic and military region of China. Governments that have failed to control Sichuan have usually failed to control the country. The QING DYNASTY discovered this in 1911: anti-government unrest in Sichuan preceded the REPUBLICAN REVOLUTION in neighbouring HUBEI. The Japanese discovered it, too: during the SINO-JAPANESE WAR they occupied virtually all of south China *except* Sichuan, where CHIANG KAI-SHEK'S Nationalist government sought refuge. As a result Japan failed to subdue China. These and subsequent developments show that firm control and good management of Sichuan's abundant resources are vital to China's overall well-being.

towards an independent kingdom

Sichuan's role in the end of imperial rule centred on the development of RAILWAYS. Local merchants and gentry planned to end their province's isolation by building a line from Chengdu, the capital, to Wuhan, capital of Hubei. The Court's decision to buy out this and other proposed lines with foreign loans to strengthen central control sparked fierce opposition. It began with complaints by Sichuan businessmen over inadequate compensation. It ended in a province-wide revolt against 'undemocratic and traitorous' Qing rule. Manchu authority in Sichuan evaporated several months before the Republican Revolution was declared in October 1911. Effective central control was not restored until the Communist conquest nearly 40 years later.

The first of several intermediate stages was one of anarchy: for more than a decade after 1911 infighting between various WARLORDS kept Sichuan in turmoil. The second saw the rise of Liu Xiang (1889–1938) who ruled the province as his private domain. He ensured that neither the revolutionary upsurge of the NORTHERN EXPEDITION of 1926–8, nor the national government Chiang Kai-shek set up after its completion, had much impact. This remained the case until 1935 when Communist troops passed through west Sichuan on their LONG MARCH. Endurance and heroism allowed the Red Army to evade the central government troops pursuing them, but the presence of Chiang's forces in Sichuan spelt the end of Liu's autonomy.

In Liu's heyday Sichuan covered a smaller area than it did once the Communists had consolidated their rule. The western half of the modern province of Sichuan, geographically and culturally part of TIBET, was known first as the 'Sichuan Border Region' and, from 1939, the 'province of Xikang'. It stretched west to within about 100 miles (160 kms) of Lhasa, the Tibetan capital.

Xikang was created to strengthen China's claims to Tibet and weaken the power of the Sichuan militarists. From its creation until the Communist takeover 10 years later it was ruled as a private kingdom by Liu Wenhui (1895–1976). However, Chinese control over this vast area, most of it mountains, pasture and plateau, was nominal before 1949: all but its eastern edge, and the provincial capital of Kangding, was sparsely populated and inhabited by Tibetans. It was abolished as a province in 1955: eastern Xikang was absorbed into Sichuan and the west incorporated in what later became the Tibetan Autonomous Region. Liu, who turned his troops over to the Communists in 1949, was rewarded with high but largely honorary positions first in the southwest then Beijing.

war and reintegration

As with much of southwest China, the Sino-Japanese war brought Sichuan into the mainstream of national and even international life.

This was particularly true of CHONGQING, the city perched on a promontory above the confluence of the Yangtze and Jialing rivers, which became China's wartime capital. Industry and investment flooded into the region along with officials, government organizations and troops desperate to escape the Japanese advance. Chongqing was bombed and subjected to other privations of war: rationing, inflation and CORRUPTION. But, safe from overland attack and protected by the Three Gorges from an advance along the Yangtze, it survived – and the Nationalist government along with it.

The province became something of a backwater again with the defeat of Japan in 1945 and the government's return to Nanjing. It also became semi-autonomous once more. Sichuan's post-war leaders did not defy Chiang with the kind of vigour Liu Xiang had displayed, but they tried to avoid fighting on his side during the CIVIL WAR. In the closing weeks of 1949, the Sichuan authorities surrendered to the advancing PEOPLE'S LIBERATION ARMY, allowing the Communists to capture one of the most strategic parts of the country with a minimum of fighting. The province was 'liberated' by the PLA's Second Field Army. Its military commander, Liu Bocheng (1892–1986), was a Sichuanese. So was its political commissar, DENG XIAOPING.

The new government was quick to consolidate authority over Sichuan which became the headquarters of a powerful regional administration designed to integrate all of southwest China into the national polity. The Communists were concerned to build on the province's economic strengths, too. Improving communications, heavily reliant on water transport, was a priority. Sichuan's first passenger railway began service in 1952. It linked Chengdu and Chongqing, the two most important urban centres. The province was connected to the national network in 1956 via SHAANXI. Other lines followed but forbidding terrain and low population densities meant Sichuan's railway-builders had to confine their activities to the east of the province

The rapid development of industry saw Chongqing become a major centre for the production of iron and steel, chemicals and other major products. Chengdu focused on energy – it is close to major coal fields – aircraft manufacturing and light industry. Several other cities across the province were turned into industrial centres as a result of MAO ZEDONG's policy of constructing strategic bases deep in

> ### The Lie of the Land
>
> The 'si chuan' ('four streams') that give Sichuan its name all feed into the Yangtze, which enters the province from Qinghai; forms the border between Sichuan and Tibet; dips into Yunnan; and then drains the fertile east of the province before entering Hubei from Chongqing. The streams are, from west to east: the Min, the Tuo, the Jialing and, entering from the south, the Wu. Sichuan covers an area of 180,000 square miles (466,200 sq kms) and had a population at the close of the century of 85 million. The overwhelming majority of its people live in the Sichuan basin and Chengdu plain in the east of the province. Fertile and well watered it is home to some of the most productive farmland in China.
>
> Since Chongqing became a separate entity, Sichuan is no longer equally divided between a fertile densely populated east and a mountainous, largely inaccessible west. The high terrain of the Qinghai–Tibet plateau now accounts for most of Sichuan's territory but less than 10 per cent of its people. There is some fertile agricultural land in the extreme southwest, in the Anning valley, but most of the land to the north is formed of towering peaks and deep gullies. It leads to the grasslands of Tibet – a land of yaks and barley, and a world away from 'Chinese' Sichuan in the east.

the interior, the so-called 'third line'. Most were run by the military. Nearly all proved difficult to reform in the new climate of the 1980s and 1990s (see INDUSTRY).

suppression, starvation, reform

These economic changes paled alongside the upheavals inflicted on Sichuan as a result of Mao's radicalization of politics in the 1950s. The first to feel the effects in a big way were the Khampas of east Tibet, or what, following the abolition of Xikang province in 1955, became west Sichuan. A fiercely independent people, the Khampas rose up against Han Chinese attempts to collectivize their animals, curb the power of the monasteries and generally undermine their way of life. Communist troops suppressed the revolt, but at the cost of driving thousands of Khampas west, into Tibet proper, where a much bigger uprising against Chinese rule occurred in 1959–60 (see TIBET).

The GREAT LEAP FORWARD took a huge toll on the entire province. The tragedy was that it did so in a part of China that, though densely populated, often produced more grain than it needed. In good years Sichuan supplied neighbouring provinces, and produced up to 11 per cent of China's total output of grain and soybeans. Two years after the communization of agriculture and creation of backyard industries, 'heaven's granary' was empty. Millions suffered from starvation. Accurate figures of the number of those who died in Sichuan are as elusive as for other parts of the country but it may have been higher than 1 in 10 of the province's 70 million population.

The CULTURAL REVOLUTION was waged in the province with similar intensity to the Leap. In Chengdu and Chongqing rival factions of Red Guards attacked each other with military weapons. Glimpses of the chaos, cruelty and confusion in Sichuan during the late 1960s have been provided by personal testimonies published in the West. They describe scenes of civil war that were among the worst in China.

Restoring political and economic order in Sichuan fell to ZHAO ZIYANG, who emerged from a period of political disgrace in 1975 to become governor and first Communist Party secretary of the province. His methods were so successful that they were implemented throughout the country, and Deng Xiaoping, by 1978 paramount leader in Beijing, promoted him to premier. They became known as the 'household responsibility system': farmers were allowed to produce as much as they wanted on land contracted to them on a household basis, provided they agreed to sell a fixed portion to the state. The contracts allowed private *use* of land rather than private ownership, but the effects were the same: soaring harvests, vigorous local markets and the beginnings of rural prosperity. Wan Li (1916–) pursued similar policies in the much poorer province of ANHUI. The results were identical and Wan, too, was promoted to Beijing to join the growing band of economic reformers in the capital (see AGRICULTURE).

Zhao also helped revive some of Sichuan's lumbering industries by giving factory managers a freer hand when it came to sourcing their materials and selling their products. This was another foretaste of policies pursued throughout the country.

Yet compared with the coastal provinces of the south and east, Sichuan was poorly placed to benefit from the first phase of economic reform in the 1980s. Far from the coast, its communications remained undeveloped. Though poor on a per capita basis it was too important to be granted the kind of decentralization Beijing had allowed other parts of the country. Its large population ensured that Sichuanese formed the largest contingent among the 'floating population', the millions of migrants who left the countryside to work in towns and cities across China during the 1990s (see POPULATION/URBANIZATION).

The opening of the Yangtze valley to FOREIGN TRADE AND INVESTMENT in 1992 improved the situation; investors from TAIWAN, many of whom had connections with the province from pre-Communist times, established a presence in Chongqing, Chengdu and other cities. But the legacy of past policies and the thrust of the new reforms made it difficult for a huge, landlocked province to make as much headway as those in the east. The reform of ailing state-owned factories in Sichuan proved particularly problematic (see INDUSTRY).

taxes and democracy in the 1990s

On some occasions managing the traditional economy has been as troublesome as developing the modern one. As China's granary, Sichuan's fortunes are tied to the quality of the harvest, rural productivity and the government's administration of the rural economy. During the 1990s the last left much to be desired. Local officials levied taxes and fees on farmers for construction projects that often failed to materialize. They also paid peasants for grain in IOUs rather than cash. These phenomena were common throughout China but particularly serious in Sichuan. In Renshou, a county south of Chengdu, thousands of farmers attacked officials and government buildings in a series of protests over illegal levies during the summer of 1993. Paramilitary police resorted to tear gas to restore order. The unrest in Renshou was rare only in the sense that reports about it appeared in the international media: small-scale rural protests were common in Sichuan, and other key agricultural areas, elsewhere during the 1990s.

Controversy of a different kind erupted in the province on the eve of the new century. Buyun, a township in Suining city, about 80 miles (128 kms) southeast of Chengdu, held the first direct elections in the history of Communist China for the post of head of a township government. Under the constitution, direct elections are held only at village level, an administrative rank below townships. Elections at all other levels are indirect. Buyun authorities tried to conceal news of the poll, which was held in December 1998 and resulted in a narrow victory for the government's candidate, but one of China's more daring local newspapers publicized it. Beijing praised the smoothness of the proceedings but warned that the election was illegal and therefore not to be repeated.

shrinking Sichuan

What was once China's most populous province enters the new century shorn of its southeast corner. Chongqing and nine of its surrounding counties, extending to the borders of GUIZHOU, HUNAN, Hubei and Shaanxi, were combined in 1997 into the new municipality of Chongqing which, like SHANGHAI, TIANJIN and BEIJING, reports directly to the Central Government. Chengdu no longer has much say over developments in what was once Sichuan's most important city. Neither does it have to worry about resettling up to 1 million people whose homes will be flooded as a result of the THREE GORGES DAM project, hundreds of miles downstream in Hubei. That is Chongqing's responsibility, a burden Beijing agreed to soften by granting the city greater status and power.

Singapore

Most Chinese Communist leaders since MAO ZEDONG, and many leaders in TAIWAN and HONG KONG, have expressed admiration for the ethnic Chinese city state of Singapore. They have viewed the urban planning, public housing, technological success, financial power and stable, mildly authoritarian politics of the island republic as models for China's own modernization.

During the 1990s TUNG CHEE-HWA of Hong Kong, LEE TENG-HUI of Taiwan and most of the leadership in Beijing either publicly extolled or privately sought the advice of Lee Kuan Yew, the founder of modern Singapore. For many he symbolized the success of ASIAN VALUES – the supposedly distinct, communitarian way of building a society allegedly more appropriate for Asians than the individualism of the West. The Asian financial crisis swept away some of these illusions, but they did not diminish Lee's 'Chinese' credentials or his political accomplishments. Both secured him a ready audience in Beijing.

Relations between Singapore and the People's Republic were not always so harmonious. During Mao's years in power, foreign policy served the Revolution: Beijing supported Communist movements in Southeast Asia as part of its struggle against both the UNITED STATES and the SOVIET UNION. It did not do so consistently, but the fact that Communism in Southeast Asia was associated with the region's Chinese communities meant non-Communist Chinese such as Lee Kuan Yew resolved to keep Beijing, and its local agents, at bay.

Singapore, a founding member of the ASSOCIATION OF SOUTHEAST ASIAN NATIONS (ASEAN), quietly sent its troops to Taiwan for training and maintained close, though unofficial, relations with the Nationalist government in Taipei. It did not establish diplomatic relations with Beijing until 1990, after which Lee sought to engage China in regional cooperation and encourage its entry to the international community. Beijing responded warmly but cautiously. It was much more enthusiastic about the large flow of investment from Singapore into the Mainland. One of the most conspicuous (though not particularly successful) of these investment projects was Suzhou Industrial Park in JIANGSU. In 1993 Singapore hosted the first high-level (though unofficial) talks between representatives of China and Taiwan (see TAIWAN/ARMS ACROSS THE STRAITS).

Sino-Japanese War (1937–45)

China's bitter struggle with JAPAN was no ordinary military conflict. It exerted a profound effect on China's domestic politics, fatally weakening CHIANG KAI-SHEK'S KUOMINTANG government and strengthening his Communist opponents. It transformed China's international position, providing a premature glimpse of its potential as a great power. It brought UNITED STATES involvement deep into Chinese affairs and helped make the SOVIET UNION a Pacific power. And it did all these things at a terrible cost in Chinese lives and property. In China's modern history, as well as that of East Asia, the Sino-Japanese War was a transforming experience.

national resistance, 1936–40

Japan's designs on China had been clear from the late nineteenth century. The seizure of SHANDONG in 1914; the occupation of Man-

The Marco Polo Bridge Incident

The details and motives behind the incident that started the Sino-Japanese War are less clear than its consequences. On the night of 7 July 1937 Japanese troops conducted exercises near the Marco Polo Bridge, about 15 miles (24 kms) southwest of Beijing. They claimed Chinese troops fired on them. When they demanded entry to the nearby garrison town of Wan Ping to look for one of their number who had gone missing, the Chinese defenders resisted. Neither the Nationalist government nor Tokyo could leave matters there. Chinese patience, strained by years of Japanese aggression, snapped. Japan believed the emperor had been slighted. Just over two weeks after the 'incident', the two sides were locked into a war that lasted eight years.

churia (northeast China) in 1931; the creation of MANCHUGUO in 1932; and the attack on Shanghai the same year all confirmed that Japan had become the chief external threat to China's security. As a result, Tokyo became the primary target of Chinese nationalism. By 1936, the Japanese menace loomed so large that – thanks partly to the XIAN INCIDENT – China's Nationalists, Communists and warlords subordinated their regional rivalry to national resistance. The term 'United Front' was a Communist one used at that time to rally different forces in the fight against Fascism. It accurately described the political situation in China in July 1937 when Japan manufactured the incident at Beijing's Marco Polo Bridge that started the war.

The ensuing military struggle passed through distinct phases, each accompanied by different political moods within China and varying patterns of international relations beyond. The first, from 1937–40, was that of resistance.

The Japanese attack centred first on SHANGHAI. Nationalist armies fought valiantly, holding up the invaders for weeks despite Japan's mastery of the sea and air, cruelly witnessed in the bombing of civilian targets. Chiang Kai-shek's forces fell back on Nanjing, but soon left the capital to suffer one of the most gruesome outrages ever inflicted by an invading force.

A rare military victory in 1938 at Taierzhuang in SHANDONG, where government troops under LI ZONGREN checked the Japanese advance on Xuzhou, failed to stem the Nationalist collapse. Ousted in turn from Wuhan and Guangzhou, the government retreated to CHONGQING, safely beyond the Japanese armies, though not their bombs.

Hundreds of thousands of civilians fled west, too, taking factory equipment, libraries and other valuable assets with them in order to work for the enemy's defeat from the 'great rear area'. Many, attracted by the patriotism and plain living championed by the Communists, moved northwest to YANAN.

National adversity kept relations between the Nationalists and the Communists cordial at first. But Communist forces – now designated the Eighth Route Army in the north, and the New Fourth Army in the south – expanded their operations behind Japanese lines, to the consternation of Chongqing. By 1939, Japan controlled most of north China and every key port and industrial centre in the south and southeast. Its grip on Manchuria remained firm. Chiang's government was in a terrible predicament. Holed up in Sichuan, far from its traditional base of support, it was isolated diplomatically as well as geographically. The Soviet Union supplied some matériel until 1942, when Moscow signed a non-aggression pact with Japan; and aid trickled along the Burma Road as long as Britain was brave enough to defy Japan and keep it open. But 'Free China', though the subject of sympathy in the West, essentially fought alone.

defeat and demoralization

By 1940 the front line, though not static, had stabilized, and the war became one of attrition. Demoralization set in, especially in Nationalist-controlled areas. Japan created a

The Rape of Nanjing

Japanese troops slaughtered up to 350,000 Chinese soldiers and civilians, women and children when they occupied China's capital in December 1937. The exact number killed is in dispute, though not the methods. Groups were made to dig trenches and machine-gunned into them. Others were doused with petrol and set on fire. Japanese troops carried out thousands of beheadings, bayonetings and rapes during a six-week-long exercise in blood-letting that was grim even by the standards of the Second World War. Corpses were burnt, thrown into the Yangtze or buried by relief organizations. Senior Japanese officers did nothing to halt the carnage which appeared to be an attempt to terrorize the Chinese government into submission. In fact, it incensed people so much that it made it impossible for Chiang Kai-shek to come to terms with Japan. Events in Nanjing dog Sino-Japanese relations still, with some historians and politicians in Tokyo reluctant even to acknowledge that a massacre took place.

number of puppet regimes in the areas controlled by its troops, the most important of which was led by WANG JINGWEI, a Kuomintang 'elder' and long-time rival of Chiang. Its talk of a 'Greater East Asia Co-prosperity Sphere', in which Asian people supposedly would look to Japan for leadership even as the Imperial Army occupied their lands, pointed to prolonged slavery. Corruption and inflation added to the miseries of war. So did shortages and crop failures. Famine in HENAN in 1943 claimed hundreds of thousands of lives. Forced conscription into the Nationalist armies, and the brutality of life in the ranks, undid the reputation that Chiang's armies earned in the first months of heroic resistance. Phenomena of this kind were less apparent in Communist areas. But a rare offensive by Mao's troops, the '100 regiments battle' of 1940, brought devastating Japanese reprisals in the form of a 'three-alls' policy: 'kill all, burn all, loot all'.

The struggle against the invader became as complex as it was tragic. On the surface, China's armies were pitted against those of the Japanese. In fact, China was not fighting the war as a modern nation at all but as a constellation of military and political forces as much at odds with each other as they were with the Japanese. In this sense, Japan and China were hopelessly ill-matched. Japan was a modernized, unified, industrial power with an army to match. China was backward by comparison: a weak, poor, divided nation whose size alone saved it from total occupation.

The Nationalists and Communists fought pitched battles in south China in early 1941, the so-called 'Anhui' or 'New Fourth Army Incident'. (See ANHUI.) The New Fourth Army, badly mauled in the clash, moved north of the Yangtze. Conflict between Chiang and the regional militarists allied to his regime was no less bitter – even though actual fighting was rare. Rivalry and skirmishes took place between Nationalists and puppet troops of whose loyalty nobody could be sure. As the overall military stalemate endured, none of the principal actors in China dared take the initiative against the Japanese without first considering the implications for their own position.

War in Europe at first worsened China's fortunes: Japan moved into French Indochina, tightening the noose around Chongqing. But direct American assistance, mostly channelled along the reopened Burma Road, was

not far behind. One aspect of it was less earthbound: a 'volunteer' air force, the 'Flying Tigers' founded by Colonel Claire Chennault, a retired US Army Air Corps officer. The Japanese attack on Pearl Harbor in 1941 transformed the international situation. There was little immediate change in the military situation in China – although the Japanese soon occupied HONG KONG – but the Sino-Japanese War became part of the Second World War, and Chiang's China an ally of BRITAIN, the SOVIET UNION and, particularly, the UNITED STATES. Sooner or later, the defeat of Japan seemed certain.

US aid and the 'great power' myth

Washington assigned Colonel JOSEPH STILWELL to Chongqing as Chiang's chief of staff. His job, which the blunt, Chinese-speaking Stilwell turned into an intense personal mission, was to boost China's military capabilities. He became convinced that, properly trained, led and equipped, the Chinese soldier was the equal of any. He set about proving it. An early obstacle was the Japanese thrust into Burma in 1942 which meant China had to be supplied via the 'hump', the air route over the Himalayas. Another was the determination of Chiang to retain control of the military and conserve the best forces for the struggle he and MAO ZEDONG knew was coming between the government and the Communists. However, Stilwell's faith was justified, at least outside China. In 1944, Chinese forces trained and equipped in India (the so-called 'X-force') drove the Japanese out of much of north Burma (see BURMA).

Within China it was a different story. Chiang would not allow a foreigner operational control over his armies. Neither would he tolerate American aid being given to Communist troops. He also ruled out the possibility of a coordinated attack with them against Japan. Chiang had a different agenda from Washington: post-war survival. The war against Japan was often an adjunct to this wider struggle for dominance at home. (See CHIANG KAI-SHEK.)

The Americans found him an increasingly intractable ally. Even while they treated China as a Great Power – notably by relinquishing EXTRATERRITORIALITY in 1943 and bringing Chiang, Roosevelt and Churchill together at the CAIRO CONFERENCE the same year – the Americans all but abandoned hopes that Chinese forces might play a major role in the defeat of Japan. Stilwell still argued for an offensive by ground troops. Chennault believed aerial strikes on Japan from the new air bases strung across south China would bring Tokyo to its knees. Japan's *Ichigo* ('Number One'), offensive of 1944 dashed the hopes of both men. Designed to provide an overland link between the occupation forces in Manchuria and Southeast Asia, it brought Japanese troops deep into the heart of southwest China. Most of Chennault's airfields were knocked out. There was panic in Chongqing as the Japanese – still distant, but much closer than before – advanced on the city. Yet even at the height of the crisis, Chiang refused an American request to give Stilwell command over all military forces in China. On the contrary, he successfully demanded his withdrawal.

After almost 8 years in which they had borne the brunt of the war, the *Ichigo* offensive dealt a devastating blow to the Nationalists. It weakened Chiang's position relative to the Communists whose forces had been expanding rapidly across north China despite a government blockade. Expansion was accompanied by consolidation: Mao established his personal and ideological ascendancy within the Party with a series of 'rectification campaigns', study sessions and purges. Land reform, rent reduction and a cooperative movement enabled the Communists to penetrate society in the areas they controlled. By 1945, the Party had a membership of more than 1 million and a regular army of about the same size. It was an infinitely more powerful – and popular – force than it had been at the start of the war (see CHINESE COMMUNIST PARTY).

bitter victory: the end of KMT China

Despite Stilwell's best endeavours it became clear well before *Ichigo* that the best the Allies could hope from Chiang was that his armies would tie Japanese troops down in China. While they did so, American forces could 'island hop' across the Pacific towards Japan. What was unclear was how long this would take. With the atomic bomb an uncertain prospect, the Americans urged the Soviet Union to enter the war against Japan. Stalin agreed in exchange for certain rights in China which he secured at the Yalta meeting of the Allied leaders (see YALTA CONFERENCE). The Americans kept Chiang in the dark about the deal until it was struck, then persuaded him to accept it. On 9 August 1945, the day Nagasaki became the target of the world's second

---

China's Losses

The human cost of the Sino-Japanese War is easily lost amid discussion of the conflict's broader historical significance. Apart from the horror of the Nanjing Massacre, Japan employed biological warfare in China. It was the only country to do so on any scale anywhere during the Second World War. Unit 731 was set up in Manchuguo in the modern province of HEILONGJIANG in 1936. It developed a porcelain bomb to deliver fleas to a target, and the Ha bomb to disseminate anthrax or tetanus on the battlefield. In the course of developing these weapons, a large but unknown number of Chinese petty criminals and prisoners-of-war were subjected to fatal experiments. In the 1990s, Japanese scientists were still searching northeast China for dangerous chemicals developed by Unit 731 and buried in the surrounding countryside. In 1942, Japan deployed anthrax, cholera, dysentery, typhoid and plague germs against Chinese troops in the southern provinces of Zhejiang and Jiangxi. The number of casualties is unknown, but 10,000 Japanese troops were accidentally infected during the operation. The exact human cost of the Sino-Japanese War on the Chinese side can only be imagined: figures, official or otherwise, are incomplete and unreliable. But the order of magnitude is clear from remarks made in 1995 on the 50th anniversary of VE Day by President JIANG ZEMIN. In Moscow to join the celebrations with other leaders of the former Allied powers, he put the number of Chinese dead and injured at 35 million.

---

atomic bomb, Soviet troops poured into Manchuria. Emperor Hirohito announced Japan's surrender on 15 August. The conflict in China, which had endured far longer than in any other country caught up in the Second World War, was over.

Fresh misery and renewed fighting were not far behind. With American help, Chiang's government sought to impose its authority in areas long controlled by the Japanese and to thwart the ambitions of the Communists. Both attempts failed. As post-war euphoria succumbed to pre-war rivalries, US-led attempts to broker peace failed. Bottled up in the southwest for so long, the Nationalists were strangers in many parts of the country to which they returned. The only familiar thing about them was their corruption and inefficiency. Chiang could muster neither the military muscle, political purpose nor popular support necessary to lead his country in the task of reconstruction. Within two years of Japan's defeat, China was at war again – this time with itself. Two years later, Chiang's government had collapsed and what remained of his armies fled to Taiwan. (See CIVIL WAR.)

Snow, Edgar (1905–72)

Edgar Snow, an American journalist, wrote the first systematic, detailed account of the CHINESE COMMUNIST PARTY to appear in English. *Red Star Over China*, published in 1937, provided a thorough and generally accurate account of the Party, its history, policies, hopes for the future and personalities of its leaders, MAO ZEDONG and ZHOU ENLAI among them. It was a bestseller and ranks among the most remarkable pieces of reportage of the twentieth century.

In 1936, Snow spent four months in Communist-controlled northwest China gathering materials and interviewing his subjects. At that time, information about the Chinese Communists was fragmentary and frequently unreliable – a casualty of Nationalist censorship, prejudice, poor communications and the generally conspiratorial business of waging revolution. Snow's triumph was made possible by the Party's willingness to talk: Mao and his comrades had recovered from the LONG MARCH and, as the threat of Japanese invasion loomed, were keen to stress their Nationalist credentials in line with Moscow's new United Front policy of resistance against Fascism. At the same time, they were not averse to the world knowing that the Chinese Party was independent of Moscow and frequently at odds with the Com-

intern, the Communist International, over tactics.

Red Star told the outside world – and, through covert translations, many in China – about these things for the first time. It did so in lively, often gripping prose. Snow's wife, Helen, who wrote under the name Nym Wales, proved similarly adventurous and committed to the Left-wing cause in China. If anything, some of her many books on the Chinese Communist movement, though they did not contain scoops of the kind provided by *Red Star*, were even better written and have proved of equal historical value.

Edgar Snow's inquisitive journalistic instincts proved less reliable in his *Red China Today: The Other Side of the River*, an account of his five months in China in 1960, ten years after the Party seized power. China was in the grip of famine induced by the GREAT LEAP FORWARD. It claimed millions of lives, but Snow categorically denied that mass starvation could take place in China under Communism as it had under previous governments. When he visited China in 1970, Mao and Zhou invited him to the rostrum of Tiananmen to review the National Day Parade. It was an attempt to signal their interest in improving relations with the UNITED STATES.

Song Jiaoren (1883–1913)

Song Jiaoren occupies an unusual place in Chinese political history. He was a leading advocate of Western-style democracy; secured national prominence in one of the closest things to a genuine election seen on the Mainland; and was assassinated a few weeks later for trying to exercise his new-found power.

Born in HUNAN, Song studied law in JAPAN and was a key member of SUN YAT-SEN'S UNITED LEAGUE. He took part in several of the abortive uprisings against Manchu rule which preceded – and paved the way for – the REPUBLICAN REVOLUTION of 1911. In common with other revolutionaries, Song reluctantly conceded that YUAN SHIKAI, military strongman of north China, should serve as president of the new Republic. But he argued that real power should rest with the premier and a cabinet formed by elected members of the largest political party. In 1912 the United League

renamed itself the KUOMINTANG, or Nationalist party, in order to fight the Republic's first parliamentary elections on this platform.

Song led the election campaign. Voting, which took place in 1913, was indirect and conducted according to a highly restricted franchise. Between 4 and 6 per cent of the population registered to vote (see DEMOCRACY/ELECTIONS). The Kuomintang won a majority in both houses of parliament. Flushed with victory Song demanded the creation of a cabinet formed of Nationalist party members. He also called for limits on presidential power of the kind that threatened to reduce Yuan Shikai to a figurehead beholden to the cabinet and parliament.

This attempt to gain power through the ballot box – the only one of its kind in the history of the Mainland during the twentieth century – failed. In March 1913 Song was assassinated by Yuan's agents at Shanghai station while waiting for a train to take him north in order to assume his new parliamentary duties. Under Sun Yat-sen the Kuomintang turned to rebellion, linking up with provincial militarists who shared the party's dislike of Yuan.

However, the president, still in command of China's most formidable armies, crushed this so-called Second Revolution and drove the Kuomintang into exile. His actions helped ensure that political parties could not hope to come to power in China unless they had powerful military forces of their own.

Song Qingling (1893–1981)

The widow of SUN YAT-SEN was the most prominent woman in the Chinese Communist government until the rise in the early 1960s of JIANG QING, Mao Zedong's wife. She was also the second most prominent of the three Song sisters, the youngest of whom, SOONG MEI-LING, married CHIANG KAI-SHEK, and the oldest of whom, Ai-ling, married Kung Hsiang-hsi (1880–1967), a KUOMINTANG finance minister. As such, Song Qingling was one of a handful of Chinese women to enjoy an international reputation during the twentieth century.

While her husband was alive, Song, born into a wealthy Christian family and educated in the UNITED STATES, played little part in politics. When he died in 1925 she became conscious of her role as wife of the founder of the Republic and sought to preserve his legacy at a time of acute factionalism within the Kuomintang.

In her view this meant pursuing Left-wing policies and cooperating with the CHINESE COMMUNIST PARTY. Both moves placed her at odds with Chiang and (from 1927) his new wife Mei-ling, Qingling's sister. Dismayed at Chiang's suppression in 1927 of the Communists and the Kuomintang Left wing, she left China in 1927 and spent the following two years in the SOVIET UNION.

The new spirit of unity in China that greeted the outbreak of the SINO-JAPANESE WAR prompted a public reconciliation between Song and Chiang. It did not last long. As the war dragged on, and Chiang's dictatorship intensified, she moved to HONG KONG where she associated with pro-Communist dissidents. In 1948 they formed the Revolutionary Committee of the Kuomintang, an organization designed to sustain Sun's revolutionary ideals (see DEMOCRATIC PARTIES).

Song's revolutionary lineage made her a major political asset for the Communist Party, then on the point of forming a new national government in Beijing. In 1949 she was made a vice-chairman of the Central People's Government of the People's Republic of China. There were two other vice-chairmen. None of the three was a Communist, enabling the Party to claim that the new government was representative.

Song held a string of positions in the new regime, all of which testified to her potency as a political symbol but none of which allowed her to exercise real power. During the 1950s and 1960s she travelled widely in the Soviet bloc and the Third World as an ambassador of Communist China.

Years after her death in 1981, reports circulated that Song had been highly critical of Party policy from the late 1950s onwards but that she had confined her complaints to close friends and comrades. Perhaps it was in recognition of this, coupled with their desire to make her one of their own at last, that China's leaders had inducted her into Communist Party membership while she was on her deathbed, and made her honorary chairman of the People's Republic of China.

Soong Mei-ling, (1897–)

Four Chinese women – the EMPRESS DOWAGER, Soong Mei-ling, SONG QINGLING and JIANG QING – established an international reputation during the course of their country's struggle for modernity. None did so with such glamour and style as Soong Mei-ling, wife of CHIANG KAI-SHEK. She was a guest of the White House, addressed a joint session of the UNITED STATES' Congress and, for a spell, won the hearts of the American people.

The occasion of Soong's triumph was the SINO-JAPANESE WAR. American popular sentiment towards China had been warm for years. The spectacle of Chiang's Nationalist regime

– the government of 'Free China' – holding out in CHONGQING in the face of overwhelming odds brought a new intensity to the romance. With the Japanese attack on Pearl Harbor in December 1941, the United States and China became allies.

These were ideal circumstances for China's 'first lady' to use her skills in the cause of her husband's government. They included excellent English, learnt during her predominantly American education, much of it at Wellesley College in Massachusetts; familiarity with Western ways of looking at things; and a physical presence that, in the American imagination, epitomized the dignity of the Chinese nation under threat. Rarely has a Chinese government had so effective an ambassador.

For his part, Chiang derived political advantage from his relationship with Soong long before the outbreak of war. It made him a member of a prestigious dynasty. Soong Mei-ling was the daughter of Charlie Soong (1866–1918), an American-educated missionary turned merchant. One of her two older sisters, Qingling, was the widow of SUN YAT-SEN. Chiang's marriage to one of the late Sun's sisters-in-law in 1927 strengthened his claim to be the great revolutionary's successor. At the Soong family's request, he agreed to become a Christian. He did so formally in 1930, shortly after the United States and Britain recognized his KUOMINTANG administration as the legitimate government of China.

Soong Mei-ling was a visible and active supporter of the new central government. In December 1936 she flew to Xian in an effort to secure her husband's release following his kidnapping by rebellious generals opposed to his attempts to crush the Chinese Communist movement rather than resist Japan. (See XIAN INCIDENT.) But it was in her dealings with foreigners that she excelled, acting as Chiang's interpreter, and his personal window on the outside world.

Soong's tour of the United States in 1943, when she was a guest of the Roosevelts, addressed Congress and appealed to thousands of ordinary Americans to support Free China, was an extraordinary success. She took America by storm, leaving most people blissfully unaware of the corruption, demoralization and defeatism undermining the Nationalist war effort at home, and her own imperious behaviour in private. Soong's insistence on the dignity of her person was at least as great as that she demanded for her nation and its government.

Unfortunately for her, the American government tired of both. In 1948, with Communist troops gaining the upper hand in the CIVIL WAR, Soong visited the United States again. She was received politely but failed to persuade Washington to intervene militarily on behalf of her husband's beleaguered regime. She rejoined him in early 1950 in Taiwan, by then the 'temporary' seat of the Nationalist government. Song Qingling, at odds with Chiang since he turned on his Communist allies in 1927, remained on the Mainland and became a vice-chairman of the new Communist government.

Soong Mei-ling remained an influential figure in the Nationalist government until her husband's death in 1975. He was succeeded by CHIANG CHING-KUO, Chiang's son by his first wife, Mao Fumei. Relations between Soong and the younger Chiang were proper but not warm. Relations between Soong and LEE TENG-HUI, the Taiwanese-born vice-president who succeeded Ching-kuo in 1988, were cooler still. Her attempts to interfere in the succession process came to nothing: authoritarianism was dying rapidly in Taiwan and the power of the Chiang family with it (see TAIWAN). Soong moved to New York, where, at the start of the new century, she still lived in seclusion though not quite obscurity.

South China Sea

Beijing's attempts to exert longstanding claims over the islands and waters of the South China Sea have done more than any other single issue to raise fears about Chinese expansionism in East and Southeast Asia. It has brought China into real or potential conflict with VIETNAM, the Philippines, Malaysia and Brunei, each of whom claim all or part of the area; and it has fuelled traditional rivalry with TAIWAN which, as a rival Chinese government, claims it all. It also has sparked concern in JAPAN and the UNITED STATES over the security of vital shipping lanes.

Maps produced in China claim as Chinese territory a huge swathe of ocean (often depicted on a different scale from the land-

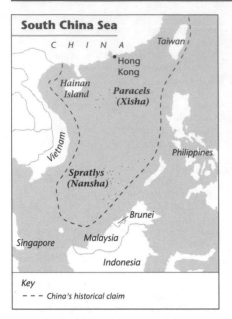

South China Sea

C H I N A   Taiwan

• Hong Kong

Hainan Island   Paracels (Xisha)

Vietnam

Philippines

Spratlys (Nansha)

Brunei

Singapore   Malaysia

Indonesia

Key
– – – China's historical claim

mass because it is so large) south of HAINAN ISLAND. It includes two main island chains: the Paracels (*Xisha* in Chinese), some 130 largely barren islands about 165 miles (264 kms) southeast of Hainan; and the Spratlys (*Nansha*), close to 400 islets, reefs and atolls further south. The Spratlys stretch 500 miles (800 kms) from north to south and lie more than 800 miles (1,300 kms) off the Chinese Mainland. Both groups of islands fall within the administrative remit of Hainan, and are patrolled by vessels from naval bases in Hainan.

Vietnam claims both groups of islands and their surrounding oceans, as does Taiwan. The Philippines, Malaysia and Brunei claim sovereignty either over some of the rocks, reefs and atolls that make up the Spratly Islands, or over the nearby waters. None of the islands is inhabited, save for military personnel and itinerant fishermen. Many are submerged at high tide. Some are permanently awash in a metre or so of water.

Questions of the legality of ownership have taken second place to an ability to assert it. Here China has made the running. Nationalist troops occupied some of the Paracels shortly after the Second World War and Communist China was quick to claim the inheritance in 1949. But it was not until 1974 that Beijing

was able to evict troops of the government of South Vietnam from the Paracels. A further 14 years passed before China's second big move south: the capture of 6 islands in the Spratly group from the government of united Vietnam. During this conflict several lives (most of them Vietnamese) were lost in a brief naval battle.

Beijing's growing influence in the region alarmed its neighbours. Were China to make good all of the claims made in its definition of territorial waters, Chinese power would be brought into the heart of Southeast Asia. In 1992, members of the ASSOCIATION OF SOUTH-EAST ASIAN NATIONS (ASEAN) issued a Declaration of the South China Sea. It called on all parties to settle their territorial disputes in the region peacefully. Taiwan, in possession of Tai Ping Island in the Spratlys, was not consulted since no ASEAN state formally recognized Taipei. Vietnam, then outside ASEAN, welcomed the move. China merely noted it. Both China and Vietnam continued their war of words over the area. Both allowed foreign oil companies to conduct exploration in the region, reinforcing their claims through third parties.

The belief that the South China Sea is rich in gas, oil and other resources injected urgency into the competition. It has proved a particularly strong magnet for China, whose rapid growth during the 1990s has placed a huge strain on ENERGY supplies. The region's rich stocks of fish have provided another lure. So also, though it is rarely stated, has the importance of the Spratly Islands from a strategic point of view. The islands straddle the shipping lanes between the Indian and Pacific oceans – the 'lifelines' of the Japanese economy through which much of its oil, as well as that bound for Taiwan, passes. The possibility of a strong Chinese presence at this 'choke point' is of concern to Tokyo, Taipei and Washington.

Anxiety over China's creeping assertiveness intensified throughout the region in 1995. Personnel in Chinese 'fishing boats' penetrated as far south as Mischief Reef, about 135 miles (216 kms) west of the Philippines island of Palawan, where they erected 'shelters'. Photographs of the reef showed military-type structures, complete with gun emplacements, satellite dishes and China's national flag. To many, Beijing seemed bent on conquest. The United States put on record that it regarded continued freedom of navigation in the Spratlys as essential.

These expressions of concern neither prompted an evacuation of Mischief Reef nor stopped China from ratifying the United Nations Law of the Sea in a way that consolidated its claims over the northern part of the South China Sea. It did so by defining its waters as if it was an archipelagic rather than a continental state.

China sought to defuse tension at the end of 1997, signing a Joint Declaration with ASEAN that renounced the use of force to settle disputes in the region. But by that time, Southeast Asia was in the grip of the financial crisis that began in Thailand that summer. China emerged as the region's 'responsible' power, contributing to International Monetary Fund rescue packages for stricken economies and declining to devalue the *renminbi*. These developments strengthened Beijing's hand vis-à-vis ASEAN and removed the international spotlight from the South China Sea. Yet events of the previous few years had already suggested that diplomacy could only accomplish so much in this strategic, sensitive region. Settlement of territorial disputes seemed to depend on the speed with which China could develop its seapower and reinforce its claims with gunboats. It was largely with this in mind that the Philippines in 1999 approved the Visiting Forces Agreement, providing for a resumption of large-scale joint military operations between United States and Philippines armed forces, and visits by American warships.

Soviet Union

MARXISM, revolutionary aims, a common border and a hostile international environment brought China and the Soviet Union together in the 1920s. (See also RUSSIA; RUSSIAN FEDERATION.) Disputes over the same issues in the different circumstances of the 1960s led them to the brink of war. Relations improved after the death of MAO ZEDONG, but not much; Moscow and Beijing pursued different roads to socialism and competed for international influence as part of a 'strategic triangle' with the UNITED STATES. These later developments cannot disguise the fact that the Soviet Union exercised a profound influence on China. Marxism-Leninism (complemented by 'Mao Zedong Thought' and 'Deng Xiaoping Theory') remains China's official ideology. Leninism even managed to keep capitalist TAIWAN in an organizational straitjacket until the late 1980s, when the KUOMINTANG finally shed its Soviet-era past. Soviet-style organizations still provide the dominant framework for political life on the Mainland. And JIANG ZEMIN and LI PENG, the two highest-ranking Chinese leaders, were educated in the Soviet Union.

mission and method in China, 1919–27

Little of this could be foreseen in 1919, when the victory of Bolshevism in Russia inspired the young intellectuals of China's MAY FOURTH MOVEMENT. LI DAZHAO and CHEN DUXIU welcomed it as the dawn of a new era. It showed that Marxism – until then one of several '-isms' circulating in China – worked. Bolshevism was transforming Imperial Russia, like China an enormous, backward, feudal country, into a modern revolutionary state. One of its first acts of diplomacy was to renounce, in the Karakhan Declaration of 1919, many of the territorial rights Tsarist Russia had won from China under the UNEQUAL TREATIES.

For idealists, the birth of the Soviet Union pointed to the end of global exploitation, imperialism and war. For Lenin and his Russian comrades it meant a bitter fight for survival against domestic and foreign foes. Fortunately, the Revolution had friends on its flanks: the 'bourgeois nationalist' parties in underdeveloped and colonized countries. They were revolutionary because they wanted to overthrow foreign rule. Should they succeed, the crisis of world capitalism would intensify and revolution break out in its heartland, the West. Lenin's logic dictated that Moscow aid such parties. At some point 'bourgeois nationalists' might come into conflict with proletariat and peasantry in their own countries, but that could be dealt with at the time. The important thing was to stoke up the anti-feudal, anti-foreign fires – in China as elsewhere.

Comintern (the Communist International based in Moscow) agents spread the Marxist word and in 1921 helped create the CHINESE COMMUNIST PARTY. They also presented SUN YAT-SEN, leader of the ineffectual Kuomintang, with a plan to turn his party, then dependent on unstable alliances with southern militarists, into a fighting machine capable of ending warlord rule, uniting China and expelling the imperialists. Sun liked the idea.

With Soviet assistance and arms, the Kuomintang was reorganized and members of the young Communist Party admitted. A national revolutionary army was formed, controlled by political commissars. 'Mass' policies were used to mobilize workers and peasants in the cause of revolution. The entire enterprise, based first in Guangzhou, was guided by Soviet 'advisers', led by Mikhail Borodin.

Moscow was not so committed to Sun that it refused to deal with the warlord governments then occupying Beijing. Under a treaty of 1924, it secured joint Sino-Soviet management of the Chinese Eastern Railway in Manchuria, (northeast China) and acknowledged Chinese sovereignty in MONGOLIA. Chinese troops later fought, but failed, to reverse the first of these agreements. The second meant little even when it was signed, for Moscow had already agreed secretly to support the formation of the Mongolian People's Republic.

In south China, Soviet influence increased with the rapid progress of the NORTHERN EXPEDITION, led by CHIANG KAI-SHEK, Sun's successor. It declined just as quickly when Chiang turned on his Communist and Left-wing allies. In April 1927 he sent Soviet advisers packing and drove those Communists lucky enough to survive his purges into the countryside where they remained for the next 20 years. A rival, Left-wing Nationalist government in Wuhan survived a few months longer. Its demise was hastened by the discovery of a telegram from Stalin instructing local Communists to seize power. By mid-1927, Soviet attempts to foster revolution through the Nationalist Party were at an end.

rise of a Chinese Communist Party

The cause of Communism in China, however, was not ended – at least not quite. Moscow's problem now was to guide a revolutionary movement whose main forces, such as they were, had scattered to the countryside. Logistical difficulties were compounded by those of ideology. While MAO ZEDONG and other Chinese leaders sought to develop strategies of their own, the nature of the Revolution in China became entangled in the bitter dispute in Moscow between Stalin and Trotsky. The Chinese Party oscillated between attacking cities and developing rural bases, adopting different 'lines' and leaders as it did so (see CHINESE COMMUNIST PARTY). In the early 1930s a pro-Moscow 'Bolshevik' faction, whose members, including ZHOU ENLAI, gained the upper hand at the expense of Mao. But

Nationalist campaigns drove the Party out of its main base in JIANGXI in 1934 and on to the LONG MARCH, beyond the reach of Stalin or his rivals.

Mao regained lost ground during the epic flight north and cemented his authority during the Party's years in YANAN. The Comintern kept in touch with Chinese leaders, who saw their Party as part of the international Communist movement which took its lead from Moscow. The difference was that, by the early 1940s, Mao was in charge of a strong, independent, *Chinese* party – one that owed its success to skill in adapting to local conditions. The chief of these, indeed a primary reason for the Party's survival and success, was the SINO-JAPANESE WAR.

At the start of this conflict, the Soviet Union and the Nationalist government entered into a non-aggression pact. As the Japanese drove Chiang's forces inland to isolated CHONG-QING, Moscow, almost alone among the powers at this stage, sent military aid to the Nationalists. This ran dry after April 1941 when the Soviet Union and Japan, keen to concentrate on their immediate foes, pledged neutrality towards each other. Though technically on the side of China, soon one of the 'big four' Allied powers, the Soviet Union played no part in Chiang's subsequent struggle against Japan until the closing weeks of the war.

When it did become involved, the consequences were momentous. At the YALTA CONFERENCE, Moscow agreed to enter the Pacific War in exchange for rights in China of the kind renounced by the Karakhan Declaration. Chiang's 'reward' was the Sino-Soviet Treaty of 1945 in which Moscow recognized the Nationalist regime as the sole legitimate Chinese government and pledged to aid neither rival nor rebel. The Chinese Communists, now stronger than ever, kept their dismay to themselves.

Indirectly, Moscow soon helped them grow stronger still. Soviet troops swept into Manchuria in August 1945 and destroyed Japan's Kwantung army. This brief but intense battle almost did as much to persuade Tokyo the war was over as the two atomic bombs dropped by the United States a few days earlier. Russian troops handed over to local Communist forces many of the weapons they captured from the Japanese. They also proved unwilling to allow Chiang's armies, still largely confined to south China where they awaited a US airlift, to move into Manchuria. They pulled out only after stripping China's most developed region of almost all its industrial plant and machinery, and shipping it home as war booty.

Soviet intervention in the Far East gave the Communists a head start in the CIVIL WAR, but there were few indications of how rapid and complete their victory over the Nationalists would be. Stalin urged caution throughout the conflict. So reluctant was he to believe Mao could win, that staff of the Soviet embassy in Nanjing were instructed to follow Chiang's government to Guangzhou in the spring of 1949 when Communist troops forced the Nationalists out of their capital. Yet six months later, Mao proclaimed the founding of the People's Republic. A few weeks after that he arrived in Moscow to establish a new partnership with Stalin. The Chairman sought to make good his pledge that in foreign as in domestic policy, the 'new' China would 'lean to one side' – the side of the Soviet Union.

the Soviet model, 1950–58

Mao's first overseas visit lasted longer than expected. Chinese and Soviet leaders had trouble reaching agreement on the terms of a treaty, partly because of Moscow's reluctance to abandon claims in Manchuria of the kind that had dogged relations since Tsarist times (see RUSSIA). However, when it was finally signed, the Sino-Soviet Treaty of Friendship, Alliance and Mutual Assistance of 1950 spoke, at least to the West, of a brotherly relationship between the two socialist states. The fact that Mao saw it as something less became clear only later. Under the treaty, Moscow and Beijing pledged to come to each other's aid if attacked by a third party. China was obliged to concede the independence of (Outer) Mongolia (see MONGOLIA) and allow Sino-Soviet joint-stock companies to exploit mineral resources in XINJIANG.

Sino-Soviet friendship was soon put to the test. China's participation in the KOREAN WAR demonstrated the bravery and skill of its soldiers and helped the young Communist regime consolidate its rule at home. But Beijing's losses in men, matériel and money were huge. The UNITED NATIONS branded China an 'aggressor' and the People's Republic was excluded from the world body for the following 20 years. Equally important, China lost an opportunity to 'liberate' Taiwan because of the US decision to send the Seventh Fleet to the Taiwan Straits in response to the crisis. These were large sacrifices to make for stand-ing in the 'front-line of the defence of socialism' – especially since the Korean War was of Soviet and North Korean rather than Chinese making.

Sino-Soviet relations warmed after the death of Stalin in 1953. More Soviet aid and advisers were assigned to China. Thousands of Chinese studied in the Soviet Union. Soviet economic strategies, institutions, and intellectual orthodoxy made deep inroads into Chinese life. The clearest sign of this was the first Five Year Plan (1953–7). It called for high rates of investment, emphasized capital-intensive projects and the development of heavy industry financed by a surplus from agriculture (see INDUSTRY). Similar policies had enabled the Soviet Union to industrialize in the 1930s.

China's 'transition to socialism' – the nationalization of industry and creation of agricultural cooperatives – was accompanied by the establishment of new institutions. The NATIONAL PEOPLE'S CONGRESS (NPC) was modelled on the Soviet Union's Congress of Deputies. The constitution passed in 1954 bore a strong resemblance to its Soviet counterpart of 1936 (see GOVERNMENT AND ADMINISTRATION/CONSTITUTIONS). Large ministries and commissions were set up to manage an increasingly centrally planned, state-owned economy.

At every level of administration and in almost every area of life, Party institutions paralleled those of the state and controlled them. Intellectuals were organized in Soviet-style academies where everything from houses to holidays were provided by the state, and were just as easily withdrawn from those whose cast of mind proved too independent for the regime's comfort. Soviet orthodoxy exercised a stranglehold over Chinese intellectual life. In the arts, the sciences, politics and the economy, Moscow's theories held sway. Both 'modern' and Marxist, they were deemed fruits of a superior social and economic order destined to spread all over the world. 'Today's Soviet Union,' as the Chinese expression had it, 'is China's tomorrow.'

Unfortunately for those who looked forward to a lasting partnership between Moscow and Beijing, tomorrow never came. Ghosts of the past and arguments over contemporary policies combined to create a profound rift that began to heal only in the final years of the Soviet Union's existence.

The Sino-Soviet Split, 1958–64

In July 1964, the *People's Daily* published the ninth in a series of polemical articles. 'Khrushchev's phoney communism and its historical lessons for the world' referred to 'the revisionist Khrushchev Clique' whose members were said to be 'the political representatives of the Soviet bourgeoisie and particularly of its privileged stratum, which had gained control of the Party, government and other important organizations'. The article marked the triumph of scurrility over solidarity in Sino-Soviet relations.

The split was caused by ideological arguments *and* disputes in bilateral relations. The very different personalities of Mao Zedong and Nikita Khrushchev also played a part. So, at a further remove, did the equally distinct historical experience of the Chinese Communist Party which, unlike its counterparts in Eastern Europe, came to power largely unaided by Moscow and was of independent outlook.

There were straws in the wind before the formal outbreak of the dispute in 1958. Khrushchev's denunciation of Stalin in 1956 and his condemnation of the personality cult raised uncomfortable questions of authority for the Communist movement. Attempts at liberalization were crushed in Hungary in 1956, and in China the following year with the 'Anti-Rightist Movement' (see ONE HUNDRED FLOWERS MOVEMENT). Broader issues concerning the development of socialist society remained unsettled.

In 1958, Mao sought to resolve them, at least for China, with his GREAT LEAP FORWARD, a radical new strategy that reflected his unhappiness with the Soviet model of development. China would pursue self-sufficiency rather than rely on its 'elder brother'. This was necessary because Khrushchev's talk of peaceful coexistence with the United States pointed to a dangerous compromise with 'imperialism'. Doubts grew as to the Soviet leader's commitment to Marxism-Leninism and his qualifications to lead the socialist camp. Was he a reliable friend of China?

A critical outburst from Khrushchev about China's new communes suggested he was not and his decision to renege on a promise to help China build an atomic bomb confirmed it (see PEOPLE'S LIBERATION ARMY/CHINA AND THE BOMB). The Soviet leader had been alarmed by Mao's decision in 1958 to bombard the Nationalist-held island of Quemoy (Jinmen) without advising him. Doubtless he also recalled the Chairman's remarks in Moscow the year before to the effect that a nuclear war would destroy imperialism completely, but allow socialism to be rebuilt and conquer the world.

These issues, fuelled by Moscow's neutrality in the Sino-Indian border dispute (see INDIA), generated fierce ideological polemics between the erstwhile comrades. By 1960 Khrushchev's patience had worn thin. He withdrew all Soviet advisers from China and stopped aid, adding to the economic disaster caused by Mao's 'Leap'. He struck another blow in 1963, signing the Test Ban Treaty, which China saw as an attempt to stop it becoming an independent nuclear power.

It failed to do so: Beijing exploded a device of its own in 1964. But by then the damage had been done and the Sino-Soviet split had widened beyond repair. Beijing accused Moscow of demanding military facilities in China and conducting border incursions. Mao declared that Russian gains at China's expense in the Far East during Tsarist times had yet to be dealt with. The Soviet Union disputed China's territorial claims along the border with India and mocked its tolerance of foreign rule in Hong Kong and Macau.

The polemics intensified as Moscow and Beijing struggled for the allegiance of the Communist world. A bizarre aspect of this was a series of fierce verbal attacks by Beijing on Yugoslavia, and equally vicious assaults by Moscow on Albania. Both European countries were proxies in the dispute. Yugoslavia was newly reconciled with Moscow, while Albania, at odds with the Soviet Union for reasons of its own, was China's sole ally in Eastern Europe.

The battle for influence extended to the non-aligned world, including Africa, where Zhou Enlai made two unusual, but only partly successful, diplomatic forays in 1964 and 1965. Closer to home, the rift presented serious security problems for China when the United States stepped up its military involvement in Vietnam. With Moscow and Beijing so clearly at odds, there was no guarantee that Washington would refrain from invading North Vietnam. It might even launch air strikes over Chinese territory to prevent military supplies reaching Hanoi.

For all its importance in terms of diplomacy, it was Mao's extension of the principles behind the Sino-Soviet dispute to Chinese domestic politics that made it damaging. After the failure of the Leap, the Chairman decided that Khrushchev was not the only 'phoney Communist'. 'Revisionists', notably LIU SHAOQI and DENG XIAOPING, had taken control of the Party in China and were following the 'capitalist road'. A CULTURAL REVOLUTION was necessary to overthrow this 'bourgeois' leadership, and set the Chinese Revolution on the right path.

'revisionism' to rapprochement

The Sino-Soviet split and the Cultural Revolution reduced China's relations with Moscow to a series of verbal harangues laced with Red Guard protests and attacks on Soviet diplomats in China. If there was a single thread running through the movement it was that Moscow was the centre of heresy, an allegation that made the Soviet Union an even greater danger than American 'imperialism'. The danger intensified following the Soviet invasion of Czechoslovakia in 1968 when Brezhnev enunciated the doctrine of 'limited sovereignty'. This seemed to provide *carte blanche* for Soviet intervention wherever socialism was seen to be threatened. Beijing began to revile the Soviet Union as a 'social-imperialist' state: socialist in name but imperialist in nature – and

The Collapse of Communism and the Soviet Coup

Relief among China's leaders in 1989 that they had crushed a major challenge to their rule in Tiananmen Square soon gave way to concern over the collapse of Communism in Eastern Europe. Beijing's relations with the Soviet satellite states had improved in pace with those with Moscow. In the new climate of mutual non-interference and equality between socialist states, ideological affinities were played down. But this did not mean China's leaders could not recognize a setback to their cause when they saw one.

And see one they did as, first in Poland and then elsewhere, Communist parties gave up their monopoly of power or were forced to do so. China's official media reported such developments little and late; 'internal' analyses for Party leaders were quicker off the mark and more candid. The real blow came in Romania, where the fall from power in December 1989 of Nicolae Ceausescu, a frequent visitor to Beijing, was as sudden as it was violent. The execution of this 'old friend of the Chinese people' warranted a few lines buried inside the *People's Daily* but a vast increase in security in Beijing in case anyone felt China's leaders deserved the same fate. The bad news continued in February 1990: the Soviet Communist Party, the first to claim a monopoly of power in Communist history, became the latest to give it up.

China's leaders rarely commented directly and in public on these worrying changes. This was because they could not agree on their meaning and preferred to keep their differences to themselves. Where they could agree was that China would fall apart if the Chinese Communist Party stepped down or shared power. The only beneficiary would be the United States which was bent on eradicating socialism and asserting its dominance throughout the world.

As the last major bastion of socialism, China was in the front line of the fight against what the Party called 'peaceful evolution' – the alleged attempt of the West to destroy socialism peacefully by disseminating its values of freedom, democracy and the rule of law. By definition these values were difficult to combat. Anti-Western ideological campaigns reminiscent of earlier years were waged in the aftermath of Tiananmen. They achieved little among a sullen, resentful population in a country that seemed to have lost both energy and direction. The sense of ennui and faltering economic growth endured throughout 1990 and much of 1991.

For a few days in August 1991 it looked as though relief was at hand for the cause of socialism. The arrest of Gorbachev and the formation of a new leadership in Moscow was reported almost instantly in China. The Chinese Politburo was understood to be jubilant. Joy evaporated with Boris Yeltsin's triumph amid loud acclaim from the West.

For two and a half years after Tiananmen, the Chinese leadership floundered while socialism collapsed abroad. Not until early 1992, and then only with difficulty, did Deng Xiaoping break the mood of defeat and despair that had settled over Beijing. He did so with his *nanxun*, his 'imperial tour' of the south, in which he called for faster, bolder reforms and opposition to hardline Marxists who wanted to turn the clock back. Poverty was not socialism, Deng declared. Communist rule could survive only if it made people richer, which was its main purpose. The Chinese people needed to liberate their thinking. Debates about whether policies were 'socialist' or 'capitalist' were pointless. What mattered was whether such policies promised to make the people and the country strong. If they did, they were quite 'socialist' enough and should be implemented. Deng's remarks galvanized the formal leadership in Beijing as well as much of the country. Chinese politics at last broke out of the stupor induced by the collapse of Communism abroad and, at least for while, ensured the survival of Communist Party rule at home.

stepped up efforts to make peace with Washington.

The process was aided by a series of military clashes along the Sino-Soviet frontier. For reasons that remain unclear, one of the most serious battles, at Zhenbao Island in March 1969 on the Ussuri (Heilongjiang) River in HEI-LONGJIANG, was provoked by China. Sporadic fighting broke out in several other places, including Xinjiang and Mongolia. A massive Soviet military build-up along the border was seen in Beijing as the prelude to a nuclear strike. Underground tunnels and nuclear shelters were rapidly built in several Chinese cities. The apparent flight to the Soviet Union in 1971 of LIN BIAO, Mao's designated successor, sharpened the perception that Moscow was a menace which China could counter only by improving relations with Washington. There is little evidence Lin was pro-Soviet, but some that, because it might have weakened his position in domestic politics, he was opposed to closer ties with the West.

Formal rapprochement with Washington relieved China of a two-front-war fear. It also weakened ties between the United States and Taiwan. While these were considerable gains, fear of Soviet ambitions remained. From the mid-1970s until the late 1980s Beijing sought to compensate for America's perceived appeasement of Moscow by strengthening ties with Western Europe and calling for vigilance on the part of NATO. Soviet advances in Southeast Asia were a problem, particularly in VIETNAM. In 1978, Hanoi sought protection from the growing friendship between the US and China by signing a treaty of friendship with the Soviet Union. It then invaded Cambodia, ruled by the Chinese-backed Khmer

Rouge, to crush a two-front-war fear of its own. China's response, a brief and only partly successful strike across Vietnam's northern border, checked Hanoi's influence in Indochina, but at the expense of driving Vietnam still closer to Moscow (see CAMBODIA).

The Soviet invasion of Afghanistan in December 1978 added to the anxieties in Beijing. During the 1980s China regarded it as one of 'three obstacles' in the way of better ties. The other two were the presence of large numbers of Soviet troops along the frontier with China, and Vietnam's occupation of Cambodia. However, all three concerned matters of territory and realpolitik rather than ideology. This did not mean they were less important, but at least Sino-Soviet differences were tangible rather than theoretical. The fact that by the later 1980s both countries were pursuing socialist reform – 'restructuring', in the case of the Soviet Union under Mikhail

Gorbachev; free market economics in China under Deng – seemed to provide new grounds for mutual understanding.

Such grounds proved flimsy and fleeting. The historic reconciliation between the Soviet and Chinese Communist parties occurred in May 1989 with a visit by Gorbachev to Beijing. But the occasion was eclipsed by the TIANANMEN SQUARE DEMOCRACY MOVEMENT. This popular movement for change was crushed in China but similar mass protests triumphed in the different circumstances of Eastern Europe and, later, the Soviet Union itself. Thus the Sino-Soviet summit proved less a 'normalization' of ties between two great Communist parties than a valediction for one of them. China would soon have to deal with different leaders and a different political entity when trying to settle outstanding differences with its giant neighbour to the north (see RUSSIAN FEDERATION).

Special Economic Zones (SEZs)

China's Special Economic Zones – coastal laboratories for capitalist experiment and windows on the global economy – sparked controversy from their inception in the early 1980s, but were soon flattered by imitations in almost every province. Arguments over their political significance could not disguise their importance as catalysts of reform and symbols of China's hunger for development.

The experiment began in 1980 in SHENZHEN, just across the border from HONG KONG; Zhuhai, adjacent to MACAU; Shantou, home of a particularly industrious group of OVERSEAS CHINESE; and Xiamen, a major port in FUJIAN opposite TAIWAN. DENG XIAOPING was the main force behind their creation.

The location of the zones was crucial. They were chosen to access the world economy and tap the wealth and experience of prosperous Chinese areas south of their frontiers. They also contributed to the reunification of Hong Kong and Macau by creating reform-minded, rich communities at the points where these territories came into contact with the People's Republic.

Yet the zones were designed to be a bridge to the entire world, not just the Chinese part of it beyond the Mainland's borders. They were founded to attract foreign investment and earn foreign exchange through exports. A key aim was to attract capital from the

West and Japan to seed a first generation of high-tech industries. They were encouraged to make mixed-ownership enterprise the mainstay of their economies. And they were urged to conduct experiments in finance, foreign trade and industry of the kind economically impossible and politically difficult elsewhere in the Mainland. Accordingly, the zones were given special policies ranging from tax exemptions to the freedom of managers to hire and fire staff. In the still ideologically unsettled era of the early 1980s such policies made them true flagships of reform.

It made them controversial, too. Conservatives in Beijing saw the zones, and the 14 open coastal cities granted similar powers in 1984, as sources of spiritual pollution as much as economic experiment. Their similarity to the TREATY PORTS – special enclaves subject to different rules from the rest of the country – was remarked upon. There were complaints that the CHINESE COMMUNIST PARTY was encouraging the return of capitalism and demolishing socialist ideals built up during three decades of struggle. Surely the Party had not triumphed over its foes merely to see first Shenzhen, then GUANGDONG PROVINCE, (home of three of the zones), and finally the rest of China become like Hong Kong?

Perhaps not, but that is what happened, at least in coastal China. Progress was most remarkable in Shenzhen, a muddy, border market town in the late 1970s, and a modern city of skyscrapers a decade later. Foreign capital, mostly from the OVERSEAS CHINESE rather than Japan or the West, know-how and technology combined with cheap labour and local initiative transformed Zhuhai, Shantou and Xiamen, too. As inland residents flooded into them – despite strict regulations and, in the case of Shenzhen, a high security fence designed to keep them out – the SEZs became the People's Republic's first pinpricks of prosperity and rapid growth. So much so that in 1988 Beijing turned HAINAN ISLAND into a province in its own right *and* an SEZ, making it the biggest in the country. Comforted by the island's geographical isolation, the central government told local leaders to carry out free market policies considered too daring even for Shenzhen.

The suppression of the TIANANMEN SQUARE DEMOCRACY MOVEMENT in 1989 cast a new cloud over the zones, as it did China's reforms generally. Economic growth dipped at home. Communism collapsed abroad. Demoralized and disunited, Party leaders seemed unsure what to do. Deng Xiaoping ended the impasse in early 1992 with his landmark tour of south China calling for faster, bolder reforms. He visited both Shenzhen and Zhuhai, praising them in terms that encouraged hundreds of cities, many of them far inland, to set up zones of their own, lure foreign capital and conduct experiments in management and ownership supposedly prohibited beyond their boundaries. There were 9,000 zones nationwide by the end of 1993, by which time Beijing banned the creation of new ones and tried to subject the provinces to financial discipline.

During the mid-1990s the original zones faced a new, more sophisticated challenge. It stemmed from concern that they were aggravating regional inequalities – a source of anger in the interior and anxiety in Beijing. Hu Angang, an outspoken social scientist, said the age of tax exemptions and other privileges was over; it was time for the market to rule *all* of China, not just parts of it. Otherwise the market could not be said to rule at all. He also complained that the zones were not paying their way: in the boom years of the mid-1990s the five SEZs accounted for about 15 per cent of all foreign investment and about one-fifth of foreign trade yet, proportionately, paid a fraction in taxes to Beijing. The zones were not so much 'special' as privileged, right down to their limited legislative autonomy.

Zone officials fought back, though not very convincingly. Their case for the retention of privileges was undermined by the fact that during the 1990s investment poured into areas outside their frontiers, turning large tracts of the Pearl River delta into a vast SEZ of its own. The original zones were losing their status as primary destinations of overseas capital, technology and know-how, partly because they charged too much for land and labour.

Beijing considered the complaints and pondered the effect that too many 'special' policies in the regions might have on its campaign to join the World Trade Organization. But, again, neither the name nor the 'special' reality of the Zones changed. Instead they remained special by pioneering new reforms, this time in finance and banking, designed to lead the way for the rest of the country.

Stilwell, Joseph (1883–1946)

Gifted, well versed in Chinese, yet of acerbic disposition, 'Vinegar' Joe Stilwell in the 1940s came close to being the first foreigner to command China's national armed forces – a move that would have jeopardized the wartime rule of CHIANG KAI-SHEK, had he allowed it to happen. Instead, Chiang secured the American general's recall from China, where he had been based for almost three years, ensuring that US aid for his regime continued free of 'unacceptable conditions' for the remainder of the SINO-JAPANESE WAR and far beyond.

The plan to impose Stilwell on Chiang as 'Field Chief of Staff' commanding all of China's disparate troops, Communist forces

included, dated from mid-1944. It stemmed from UNITED STATES disappointment with Chinese military performance during the war against Japan. Chiang's armies had crumbled before Japan's *Ichigo* (Number One) offensive. As a result, Japanese forces established an overland link from Manchuria (northeast China) right across China to Indochina in the southwest. They also briefly threatened CHONGQING, Chiang's capital. Washington feared China would be knocked out of the war, making the 'island-hopping' strategy in the Pacific designed to bring Tokyo to its knees much more difficult. China still had potential to resist: it was a question of exerting proper leadership, training and supply of her armies, something that seemed impossible as long as Chiang retained direct control. President Roosevelt was persuaded that Stilwell, who had long argued this case, was the man for the job.

Militarily, the American case was sound. Politically, it reflected Washington's naive view about the nature of Chiang's regime and the possibility of reforming it from the outside. Stilwell's personal animosity towards Chiang, to whom he was chief of staff and whom he nicknamed 'Peanut', rendered the task even harder.

The relationship between the two men was a case study in Sino-Western misunderstanding, even though the principals were fighting a common foe. Combative and intolerant of form and pettifogging, Stilwell wanted to turn Chiang's armies into the superior fighting forces he felt sure they could be, given adequate command and supplies. He went some way towards proving this point in BURMA, where Nationalist troops successfully 'walked out' to India in 1942 and, under his command, walked in again in 1944. Stilwell wanted Chiang to release further divisions for

US training, leadership and supply, and advocated unleashing Communist troops against the Japanese.

Such moves would have spelt disaster for Chiang, whose regime depended for its survival on his personal control over the armed forces, and the blockading of the Communists in their north China redoubt. Stilwell's presence was necessary as a symbol of China's status as an ally, and the US money and matériel that went with it. But operational control of China's armed forces was a domestic matter: Chiang would not cede it to another Chinese, let alone a foreigner.

While it was necessary to defeat Japan, Chiang's main concern was to marshal his resources for the forthcoming struggle against rivals in the Nationalist government and the Communists. He branded Roosevelt's attempt to make Stilwell Field Chief of Staff an infringement of China's sovereignty and a return to imperialism. In October 1944, despite the apparent weakness of his, and China's, position *vis-à-vis* the United States, he secured his tormentor's recall, and the defeat of external attempts to weaken his rule.

Sun Yat-sen (1866–1925)

The leading figure among China's first generation of professional revolutionaries, Sun Yat-sen remains a potent symbol to many Chinese of their country's desire for revival, unity and national power. He is regarded as the 'founder of modern China' in the Mainland and revered as 'father of the nation' in TAIWAN. Both 'Chinas' claim to have built on Sun's legacy. Both agree – as did Sun himself – that China must be united. Yet there the consensus breaks down. Sun has long been hostage to the historical forces he helped shape: currently respected as a non-partisan advocate of nationalism, his death led to the split between the KUOMINTANG and the CHINESE COMMUNIST PARTY of 1927 from which China's current division derives.

making of a revolutionary

Sun's political career was as complex – and in some ways as peculiar – as his legacy. A farmer's son, born near MACAU and educated in HONG KONG and Hawaii, he spent years at a time outside the country he worked so tirelessly to transform. He was quite removed from the great tradition of reform represented by the classically trained mandarin Li

Hongzhang (1823–1901), or the reformist intellectuals KANG YOUWEI and LIANG QICHAO, both of whom shared his yearning for change, though not his republicanism.

Sun operated in the 'fringe world' of the Chinese diaspora. He spoke fluent English and converted to CHRISTIANITY. A student of medicine, he was active in Hong Kong – until banished from the colony in 1896 as an irritant to Britain's relations with the QING DYNASTY – as well as in Southeast Asia, the UNITED STATES and particularly JAPAN, where his views were welcomed by radical Chinese students sent overseas by the Qing to learn modern ways (see JAPAN; OVERSEAS CHINESE). In this climate, Sun developed his skills as an orator, fundraiser for the revolutionary cause and publicist for the vision of a new China, free of decrepit Manchu rule, and committed to reform, modernization and equality with the powers. He became something of an international celebrity in 1896 when he was kidnapped in the Chinese embassy in London and managed to avoid deportation through the intervention of influential British friends.

Two years earlier, Sun had founded the 'Revive China Society', his first revolutionary organization. It staged an uprising near Guangzhou, capital of GUANGDONG, the following year – the first of a series of failures that pointed to the group's poor organization and lack of support in China proper, despite growing popular dissatisfaction with the Manchus. In 1905, Sun created the UNITED LEAGUE which brought together disparate revolutionary groups among overseas Chinese, and secured the services of Huang Xing (1874–1916), a gifted organizer and political tactician.

Sun's was not the only vision of change or source of opposition to the Qing in the early years of the twentieth century, either inside China or among Chinese overseas. He was engaged in a constant battle to win the hearts, minds and money of the diaspora in the face of similar appeals by Kang Youwei, leader of the 'Protect the Emperor Society', and Liang Qichao, the leading advocate of constitutional monarchy. Sun's principal asset in this battle, as in those that followed, was his personality as a supremely flexible leader ready to enlist help from any quarter, be it SECRET SOCIETIES, Western governments or, later, the SOVIET UNION to realize his goal of changing China. This proved more important than his somewhat vague ideological programme, which came to be known as the 'Three Principles of the People': nationalism, democracy and people's livelihood, a poorly defined form of socialism. In the early years, the first principle – that Chinese not Manchus should rule China – was by far the most important to Sun.

For Sun and many other revolutionaries, nationalism at first meant ending alien Manchu rule, which they believed had made it impossible for China to treat other modern countries as equals and undertake much-needed reforms. Anti-imperialism meant freeing China of the 'Tartar yoke', an event Sun hoped would benefit the West as well as his homeland. He sought help from the West and Japan to achieve this before 1911, and turned to them again after the Revolution to rid China of President YUAN SHIKAI, and the Beijing warlord governments whom Sun accused of usurping the Revolution. It was not until the early 1920s that Sun despaired of Western governments, and brought his Kuomintang, or Nationalist Party, into alliance with Soviet Russia. From then on, the mainstream of Chinese nationalism focused on 'external' targets: in particular the need to resist Western and, later, Japanese imperialism in China.

revolutionary optimism

Sun's approach to China's transformation foreshadowed that of MAO ZEDONG in that he believed sweeping change could be introduced almost overnight, despite apparently often insurmountable obstacles. Sun held that it was merely a question of marshalling sufficient will and energy, and harnessing it to a correctly motivated, properly led political machine. This revolutionary optimism and belief in the ability of political power to overhaul society informed the various reconstruction programmes he drew up, which called for, among other things, rapid industrialization, the construction of a comprehensive railway network and the damming of the Yangtze at the Three Gorges (see THREE GORGES DAM).

These schemes were as divorced from the reality of China in the early years of the century as Sun and his Revolutionary League were from the events of 1911 which brought down the Qing (see REPUBLICAN REVOLUTION). In most provinces, republican revolutionaries of Sun's stamp were minor actors in the collapse of Manchu power. Sun himself was in the United States when the Revolution broke out, and the key forces behind the upheavals at home were local coalitions of disaffected gentry and foreign-educated army officers, leaders of chambers of commerce and secret societies. Members of the League were almost everywhere in the minority. What Sun and his revolutionaries did was to help define the massive anti-Qing revolt as a republican revolution and supply the goals and ideals of the movement: the creation of a republican government. In this regard, Sun Yat-sen's credentials and pedigree were impeccable. Shortly after he returned to China at the end of 1911, he was made president of the provisional Republican government based in Nanjing, capital of JIANGSU.

Though Sun symbolized the Revolution, he was in no position to play the role of strongman China needed as the country disintegrated into chaos and civil war. That role fell to Yuan Shikai, whom the ailing dynasty turned to for salvation, but who believed the best thing he could do for his country was to engineer the demise of the Qing and draw the sting of republicanism by becoming leader himself. He secured the abdication of the Manchus, the agreement of the Republicans that he should succeed Sun (then 'provisional' president), and their approval to move the government to his stronghold of Beijing.

Little more than a year after Sun ceded the presidency to Yuan, he was at war with him. The 'Second Revolution' of 1913, a battle over the extent to which Yuan should be subject to parliament, and how far Beijing's power should extend into the provinces, was quickly suppressed. Sun and his allies were driven into exile again. When Yuan attempted to revive the monarchy in 1916, the Republican cause – and Sun's with it – seemed lost.

Yet, dreamer though he was, Sun was indefatigable. Three times between 1917 and 1922 he established toeholds in Guangzhou, courtesy of alliances with the local militarists who had their own grievances against Yuan Shikai. In January 1923 he returned again and helped turn the city into the bastion of the Nationalist Revolution whose armies went on to conquer most of China and, in 1927, establish the Nationalist Government in Nanjing (see NORTHERN EXPEDITION). In this brief, final stage of his career, Sun emerged as the leader of a far more formidable revolutionary movement than had appeared either before or immediately after 1911. The difference was due to the situation in China, where years of warlord misrule had led to new demands for change, and to the role of the Soviet Union, whose leaders saw in Sun's movement a chance of advancing their own revolutionary cause.

alliance with the Communists

Through the agency of the Comintern (the Communist International, set up by Moscow to foster revolution overseas), the Soviet Union helped Sun turn the amorphous military and political support he enjoyed in the south into a genuine, revolutionary force of a kind China had not seen before. Lenin believed it was necessary to attack capitalism through its colonies, and Sun's movement, while deemed 'bourgeois-democratic' rather than 'proletarian', could be used to carry out the fight in China. For his part, Sun was willing to cooperate with Moscow. He was not a Marxist himself, and his revolutionary horizons did not extend far beyond China. But, as ever, he was willing to use whatever forces were available to attain his ends.

Soviet money, military equipment, expertise and advice – the latter in the form of Mikhail Borodin, Moscow's chief adviser to China – were used to rejuvenate the Kuomintang and provide it with its own disciplined, politically loyal army. To this end, the Whampoa Military Academy was set up in Guangzhou to train officers and political commissars for the new army. Sun agreed that members of the Chinese Communist Party, founded in 1921, should join the KMT. The Kuomintang would take on a 'mass' nature and foster revolution among workers and peasants. One of its main programmes was 'land to the tiller' to be preceded by sharp tax and rent reductions for farmers. It would also actively oppose imperialism and seek an end to foreign privileges in China. A National Military Revolutionary government was established in Guangzhou – Sun was named 'Generalissimo' – which was committed to crushing the WARLORDS and reunifying China.

These moves transformed the political situation in south China and, soon, far beyond. Revolutionary sentiment intensified, to the consternation of many of the more conservative elements within the Kuomintang and the Western powers. Sun, whose authority was unchallenged even if some of the consequences of his cooperation with Moscow came under fire, was able to hold this explosive social and political movement together. But when he died in March 1925, the divisions came out into the open.

A struggle for control of the Nationalist Revolution ensued amid growing strikes, boycotts and protests occasioned by the May 30th Incident in Shanghai, and the Shamian Massacre in Guangzhou a few days later, during both of which foreign police or troops opened fire on Chinese demonstrators (see SHANGHAI; NORTHERN EXPEDITION). CHIANG KAI-SHEK emerged supreme among this tumult and in July 1926 embarked on the NORTHERN EXPEDITION which extended the National Revolution to the Yangtze and eventually as far as BEIJING. But an even greater split in the revolutionary camp was in store. In April 1927, Chiang turned on his Communist and Left-wing allies in the Kuomintang on the grounds that they had hijacked the Revolution. He established a government in Nanjing that, while it continued to claim Sun's mantle, was shorn of many of the policies and personnel brought together by the founding revolutionary.

Sun's legacy

Sun's 'Three Principles of the People', and the three-stage theory of political rule he had proposed whereby China would pass from military government to a period of 'political tutelage' before finally enjoying constitutional rule, were at the heart of the Nationalist government's ideology under Chiang. Sun was the icon of the regime, and a huge tomb was built for him in the outskirts of Nanjing. The Communist Party, by now forced into the countryside, had less use for him, though it insisted Chiang had betrayed Sun's Revolution. This has remained the Party's line ever since, largely in order to undermine Taiwan's claims to have fulfilled Sun's dream by instituting democracy in the Republic of China.

The fact that, until her death in 1981, SONG QINGLING, Sun's widow, sided with the Communists and lived in Beijing provided useful propaganda in this regard.

Arguments over Sun's legacy reflect his importance as a symbol of modern China. He called for revolution and national revival and his appeal echoed down the century. It is likely to inspire Chinese in future, despite his shortcomings as a political thinker and leader.

T

Taiwan

Japanese colony, Chinese province, temporary seat of a rival central government, home of the 'Republic of China on Taiwan' – the island of Taiwan was all these things during the twentieth century. Long an object of feuding between the CHINESE COMMUNIST PARTY and the KUOMINTANG, its fate remains one of the principal issues in East Asian security at the start of the twenty-first century. The electoral victory in 2000 of CHEN SHUI-BIAN, presidential candidate of the pro-independence DEMOCRATIC PROGRESSIVE PARTY (DPP), is likely to keep it that way. Should Beijing come to blows with the outside world during the next few years, and in particular with the UNITED STATES, it is most likely to do so over Taiwan, which it covets not because it is the first Chinese democracy but because it regards it as a mere province, and an inseparable part of the People's Republic of China.

Japanese Taiwan, 1895–1945

Japanese rule in Taiwan began with the Treaty of Shimonoseki of 1895 – a shameful accord for Chinese Nationalists that ended a disastrous war with Japan and marked the start of a new phase in the search for national rejuvenation. Tokyo gained control of most of KOREA, southern Manchuria (see MANCHUGUO), and all of Taiwan (including the Pescadores, or Penghu Islands), a province of the QING DYNASTY since 1885, but under effective Manchu control from the late seventeenth century.

Effective, but not always welcome: anti-Qing sentiment was an enduring theme of Taiwanese political life. The idea of rule by JAPAN was even more unpopular. Shortly before Japanese troops arrived in 1895, local Taiwanese leaders proclaimed their island the 'Democratic Nation of Taiwan'. Their revolt lasted 10 days before petering out into sporadic guerrilla resistance.

Japan rapidly set about transforming its new, underpopulated colony. It modernized agricultural production and introduced new crops, notably sugar and new varieties of rice. It built harbours, roads, railways and industry. It developed a modern bureaucracy, education system and police force. There were even local elections in the 1940s that allowed Taiwanese some say in running affairs. As time went by, Japan energetically imposed its own cultural values on the island, encouraging people to adopt a Japanese identity and think of themselves as children of the emperor in Tokyo.

Some of these moves encountered resistance. Early in the colonial experience members of the Taiwan elite were not willing to sever their intellectual and cultural ties to China. Throughout the period of Japanese rule Taiwanese chafed at discriminatory policies that kept them out of top positions in the administration. There were campaigns for more autonomy. And there was a persistent, if sometimes remote, attachment to Chinese traditions.

But there was also widespread appreciation of Japanese methods and what they had done for Taiwan. By the late 1930s the island's average standard of living was twice that of the Mainland. Before the start of the SINO-JAPANESE WAR, a new generation emerged whose members had assimilated Japanese

The Lie of the Land

The 13,900 square miles (36,000 sq kms) of the Republic of China on Taiwan include the island of Taiwan, named *Formosa*, 'beautiful isle', by the Portuguese; the *Pescadores* or Penghu Islands, to the southwest; Green and Orchid Islands to the southeast; and the Kinmen (*Quemoy*) and Matsu Islands close to the Mainland. In common with Beijing, Taiwan claims the Diaoyutai Islands (see JAPAN) in the East China Sea, and the Spratly and Paracel Islands in the SOUTH CHINA SEA. It actually controls Taiping Island, the largest in the Spratly archipelago, and a few reefs in the Tungsha group to the east. At the widest point, 138 miles (220 kms) of ocean separate Taiwan from the Mainland and at the narrowest 81 miles (130 kms). The island's central mountain range slopes gently to the west where it meets a fertile plain. About one-quarter of Taiwan is arable. Some of the island's rivers can generate electric power. All are too short for navigation. At the start of the new century Taiwan has a population of 22 million, all but 380,000 of them ethnic Chinese and the remainder aboriginal peoples.

values and been educated in Japan. An example was the young LEE TENG-HUI, Taiwan's future leader. Another was Peng Min-min (1923–), who in 1996 was the Democratic Progressive Party (DPP) candidate in Taiwan's first direct presidential elections. Typically, members of this generation held to Chinese traditions in family life and other aspects of social behaviour, but otherwise embraced 'Japaneseness' with an enthusiasm not seen among Chinese in MANCHUGUO or other foreigners subjected to Japanese rule. Many of them even adopted Japanese surnames.

There were very few incidents of violent resistance to Japanese rule in Taiwan, and apparently no examples of atrocities committed by the colonial power. In the eyes of many Taiwanese, the Japanese approach to modernization had something to teach all of China.

Japan's occupation of much of Mainland China after 1937 strained the colonial relationship in Taiwan but did not break it. If it was emotionally hard for many Taiwanese to celebrate Tokyo's victories over the government of CHIANG KAI-SHEK, it was even more difficult to understand the new Chinese nationalism fostered by Japanese aggression and cruelties. Taiwan's experience of imperialism was quite different from that of the Mainland.

It was not so different that Japan's defeat was not welcome in the island. The CAIRO CONFERENCE of 1943 had provided for the return of Taiwan to Chinese rule. Japan's sur-render meant the end of war and deprivation. It also promised a new era of peace, construction and prosperity as part of the Republic of China built on what the Japanese left behind. Many Taiwanese greeted the arrival of Nationalist troops on the island in late 1945 with euphoria. The rapid replacement of that euphoria with disillusionment, hatred and fear is one of the saddest chapters in Taiwanese history.

false start: Chinese Taiwan 1945–7

Victors soon became the vanquished in Taiwan. Mainlanders moved in, dominated the new provincial administration, reduced its ranks and yet insisted on retaining Japanese technicians and specialists to keep the economy going. They sequestered Japanese property but made it difficult for Taiwanese to regain what had once been theirs. The new government intervened directly in the economy in the interests of ensuring benefits for all, but the Monopoly Bureau set up to control the supply of essential commodities squeezed private merchants out of business and lined bureaucrats' pockets. Taiwan's resources were shipped to the Mainland in ever larger quantities – an unhappy demonstration of the island's new identity as a Chinese province, and a fairly unimportant province at that.

Nationalist troops, ill-equipped and ill-disciplined compared with their Japanese predecessors, preyed on the population. Mainland bureaucrats, including Chen Yi (1883–1950), the new governor, made no concessions to local cultural and linguistic mores. They insisted on conversing in Mandarin rather than the southern Fujianese (*minnan-hua*) widely spoken on the island. Food shortages, inflation and demoralization gripped the island, as they did other parts of China during the final years of Nationalist rule. So far from being respected for what they had achieved under Japanese rule and, perhaps, could teach the Mainland, Taiwanese found themselves detested and shunned because of their contamination by the 'enemy'. In early 1947 these factors sparked a massive upheaval.

The FEBRUARY 28TH INCIDENT lasted little more than a week but left wounds that took more than 40 years to heal. The trouble began when police beat up a Taiwanese woman selling untaxed cigarettes in Taipei. It culminated in an island-wide revolt against Nationalist rule. Confronted with demands for political and economic reform in Taiwan and firm action from Nanjing, Chen Yi played for time.

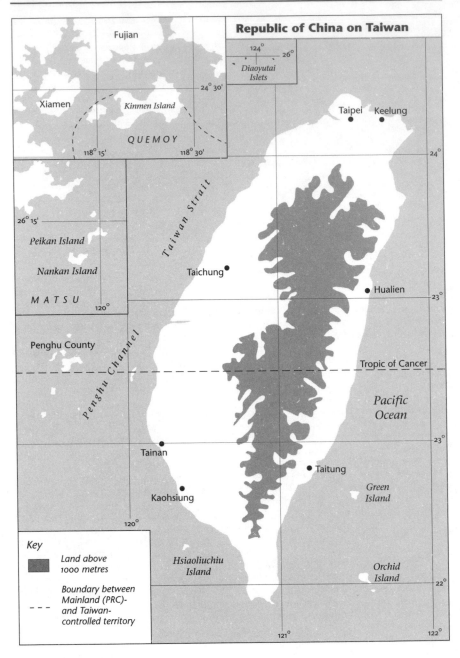

Republic of China on Taiwan

Fujian

Xiamen

Kinmen Island

QUEMOY

118° 15'   118° 30'

124°   26°
*Diaoyutai
Islets*

24° 30'

Taipei   Keelung

24°

Taiwan Strait

26° 15'

Peikan Island

Nankan Island

MATSU

120°

Penghu County

Penghu Channel

Taichung

Hualien

23°

Tropic of Cancer

*Pacific
Ocean*

23°

Tainan

Taitung

*Green
Island*

Kaohsiung

120°

*Hsiaoliuchiu
Island*

*Orchid
Island*

22°

Key

Land above
1000 metres

Boundary between
Mainland (PRC)-
and Taiwan-
controlled territory

121°   122°

The clock stopped ticking when 10,000 troops arrived from the Mainland and suppressed the rebellion. Perhaps as many as 30,000 people, Taiwanese and Mainlanders, were killed. The local urban intelligentsia were devastated. It was the prelude for the Mainland domination of Taiwan that began in earnest in 1949 with the arrival of Chiang Kai-shek's forces following their defeat in the CIVIL WAR. It also hardened the fundamental divide between Mainlanders and Taiwanese that disfigured life in the island until the final years of the twentieth century.

refuge of the defeated; US protection

The Nationalist regime was on its last legs when Chiang led thousands of its functionaries, 800,000 troops, all of China's gold reserves and most of its arts treasures to Taiwan. Taipei was the last stop in a flight that had already passed through Guangzhou, CHONGQING and Chengdu following the abandonment, in April, of Nanjing. By the end of 1949, the PEOPLE'S LIBERATION ARMY (PLA) had wiped out organized resistance to Communist rule on the Mainland. Early in 1950 it took HAINAN ISLAND. The United States had tired of its involvement in China's Civil War and was unwilling to save Taiwan from imminent 'liberation'. Chiang seemed likely to last a year at most.

Kim Il-Sung's invasion of South Korea in June 1950 spared the Nationalist leader this ignominy. Washington decided that the Soviet-backed invasion raised the stakes in East Asia so high that Taiwan had to be defended against Communism: the Seventh Fleet was ordered into the Taiwan Straits to thwart an invasion (see KOREAN WAR). Within a few months, US-led United Nations forces were fighting Chinese Communist 'volunteers' in Korea. Taipei and Washington were at one in their opposition to Beijing. In 1954 they made it plainer still by signing a Mutual Defence Treaty. For the next 25 years Taiwan was a protectorate of the United States, sparing the island from Communist attack, building up its military capability and freeing its government to concentrate on reconstruction, modernization and, eventually, political reform.

In fact, Chiang had more than the Americans on his side in the 1950s. Although Taiwan's economy had been disrupted by the Sino-Japanese War, the restoration of Chinese rule and the effects of the Civil War, the Japanese left behind a modest industrial base, roads, railways and power stations. The Taiwanese were well educated and industrious. The two million or so Mainland refugees who fled to the island between 1948 and 1950 included the cream of China's economists, scientists, educators and administrators, many of them trained in the West. Their arrival not only spared them persecution, as the history of Chinese Communism was to prove, it made Taiwan's small population of 7.3 million 'top heavy' in terms of its skills profile. Government policies designed to facilitate economic growth rather than dominate the economy and substantial US financial aid added to the favourable conditions for rapid development.

AGRICULTURE was rejuvenated first. Land reform turned Taiwan into an island of highly efficient owner-occupiers. Farming provided exports, government revenue and capital for industrialization. Infrastructure construction allowed private entrepreneurs to start up import-substitution businesses and, beginning in the early 1960s, process imported materials for export. Foreign trade, much of it conducted in a hospitable American market, became the mainstay of the economy. A cheap and well-educated labour force, a high savings rate and a growing domestic market lured foreign investment in such quantities that worries over the cessation of US aid in 1965 were soon forgotten. Between 1952 and 1966 Taiwan doubled its per capita GDP. Despite hiccups due to the oil crisis, rapid growth continued during the 1970s and 1980s.

Society changed as rapidly as the economy. Urbanization transformed living patterns on the island. Taiwanese flocked to the cities, not to escape rural poverty as they did elsewhere in the developing world, but simply because cities offered even more wealth and opportunity. A yearning for better education was met by the rapid development of schools and colleges. Thousands of Taiwanese studied in universities in the United States, some to return on graduation, others to wait until Taiwan had more to offer the highly skilled. Returnees contributed to the growing international orientation of Taiwan – a marked contrast to the situation on the Mainland. Local society and culture developed into an amalgam of Japanese, indigenous, Mainland Chinese and American influences. Its most lively representatives were members of a burgeoning middle class. By the early 1980s, newly educated, and newly rich, many Taiwanese were determined to shape their political as well as their economic lives.

one party, one China?

There was a large obstacle to this in the shape of the government. During their first three decades in Taiwan, the Nationalists allowed little political freedom and less political change. Chiang, aided by martial law, ran the island as a dictatorship. Life was nowhere near as oppressive as on the Mainland, but most forms of opposition, and virtually all criticism of the government, were banned. Those who opposed and criticized regardless found themselves in jail.

The structure of the central government had hardly changed since its days on the Mainland. Two of its main 'elected' organs, the National Assembly and the Legislative Yuan, were still occupied by those voted into office in 1947–8 in nationwide polling (save the areas under Communist control). When these deputies died, those who had come second in the original polls often took their place. A desire to increase representation from Taiwan itself meant there was a need for occasional, small-scale 'supplementary elections'. But these challenged neither the structure nor the rationale of Chiang's regime, which claimed to represent all of China, and to be located in Taipei temporarily, pending military re-conquest of the Mainland. Until 1971, when Taiwan was ejected from China's seat at the UNITED NATIONS, and most countries in the West 'de-recognized' Taipei, much of the non-Communist world appeared to subscribe to the same view.

The government's claim to represent all of China while controlling a tiny portion of it was a licence for continued Mainland domination of Taiwan politics. Independent candidates, most of them Taiwanese, won local elections in the 1950s and even captured the mayoralty of Taipei. But too great a role for Taiwanese at senior levels would undermine the credibility of China's exiled 'Central Government'. The island was locked in a political straitjacket. Liberalization would mean 'Taiwanization'; the Republic of China would become the 'Republic of Taiwan'. Hardliners in the Nationalist Party hated this idea as much as their Communist foes. They were determined to stop it.

For a while, their control of the Kuomintang helped them do so. The Party's Leninist structure survived defeat on the Mainland and the emergence of a very different kind of society in Taiwan (see KUOMINTANG). Until the mid-1980s and in some cases beyond, it controlled the media, the military and the police. Its tentacles extended into universities, schools, trades unions, big business and parts of the underworld. And its agents could be brutal as well as authoritarian.

But, at least in principle, the Party's ideology sometimes tempered its harsh rule. One of SUN YAT-SEN's 'Three Principles of the People' was democracy, which the Party was committed to implementing – when conditions were ripe. This enabled opponents to claim that, in suppressing freedoms and freezing the political structure, the government was not living up to Sun's ideals, let alone those of the 'free world' Nationalist leaders said they admired.

As a one-party state, political reform in Taiwan had to begin within the ruling Party or follow from its overthrow. Discontent, though sometimes widespread, was rarely strong enough to encourage the latter, which in any event hardly seemed possible: Chiang's grip on the military and security apparatus was firm. The prospects for inner-Party reform, on the other hand, improved with a change of leadership, a dramatic shift in the international environment and growing demands for democracy on the streets. Coping with these dynamic forces would be difficult enough for any developing society. In the case of Taiwan there was an added complication: the attitude towards political change in Taipei of a Chinese Communist government that, militarily, seemed too close for comfort, and a wider world that, in diplomatic terms, was too far away.

defeats and victories

Until the start of the 1970s, Taiwan managed to hold on to its diplomatic status as the seat of the legitimate Chinese government led by Chiang Kai-shek, and a partially convincing international identity as 'Free China'. By the end of the decade, Chiang had died and been replaced by his son, CHIANG CHING-KUO; Taiwan had lost its United Nations seat to Beijing; and third-country diplomats had staged a rapid exodus from Taipei, including, in 1979, the United States. (See below.) The West's desire to improve relations with the People's Republic required the diplomatic desertion of Taiwan. And while the Taiwan Relations Act of 1979 (see below) meant the US had not entirely abandoned its former ally, there was no doubt that Nationalist political pretensions had been punctured. The KMT's authoritarian rule came under closer, more critical, scrutiny at home and abroad.

Chiang Ching-kuo, no liberal, but more tolerant and less aloof than his father, was among those who did not like some of what he saw. He began to change things by making room for Taiwanese at the top of the Party, promoting, among others, Lee Teng-hui. He even seemed ready to tolerate the growth of an opposition – until he deemed it too serious a challenge. For many in the Kuomintang, the Kaohsiung, or 'Formosa Incident', of December 1979 showed this was the case. The incident began as a rally associated with the magazine *Formosa*, the voice of and a synonym for the *dangwai* – those 'outside the Party', or the opposition. It ended in a riot and the jailing on charges of sedition of almost 50 opposition leaders. Among them was Shi Ming-teh (1941–). He had already spent almost 10 years in prison and was to endure 10 more, making him Taiwan's longest-serving political prisoner.

Yet this proved the tail-end of repression, not a new beginning. Opposition voices, nearly all of them Taiwanese chafing at domination by Mainlanders, insisted on being heard. They continued to push at the frontiers of freedom. Some of their representatives won the limited elections the system allowed. Environmental and consumer protection groups, labour leaders and students, women and indigenous peoples – all of them representatives of Taiwan's burgeoning civil society – made their presence felt, often through demonstrations, even though they were illegal under martial law.

There was much to protest about. The murder in the United States in 1984 of Henry Liu, an American citizen who had angered Taipei by writing a critical biography of Chiang Ching-kuo, was found to be the work of Kuomintang intelligence agents in league with the underworld Bamboo Union gang. American opinion was incensed. Washington spoke of cutting off the supply of weapons to Taiwan. The Nationalist government was in disgrace.

Loans scandals and corruption in companies owned by Party members added to the complaints. So did unhappiness over the lack of planning and general degradation of urban life in increasingly prosperous Taiwan. Pressures were growing from every quarter, including Beijing, where Communist leaders began a new peace offensive towards Taipei in 1981. Few of these demands for change could be accommodated by a political system in which the formation of new

parties was banned, the press censored, parliamentary life frozen by the presence of ageing deputies elected on the Mainland, and where the government insisted that it represented *all* of China. Something would have to give or the entire regime could be swept away.

Much did give, and in very little time. In the 18 months leading up to his death in 1988, Chiang Ching-kuo tolerated the formation of the Democratic Progressive Party, Taiwan's first opposition, lifted Martial Law, allowed the registration of new newspapers, and paved the way for Taiwanese to visit relatives on the Mainland. This was a radical break with the past but not necessarily an irreversible one. While the smooth succession of Lee Teng-hui suggested reform would continue, it was unclear whether the first Taiwanese to lead the government and the Kuomintang would be able to overcome opposition from hardline Mainlanders or command the loyalty of the military and security services. The future was decidedly uncertain.

In the space of a further six years, Lee delivered much more than he had seemed to promise. Sometimes responding to an explosion of street demonstrations, sometimes pre-empting them; sometimes defying the opposition, sometimes subjecting the Kuomintang to so much pressure that it split into open factions, one of which eventually broke away to form the rival New Party; and always testing the patience of Communist leaders on the Mainland who saw in his reforms the spectre of Taiwanese independence, Lee presided over a transformation of Taiwan politics.

In 1990, he announced an amnesty for dissidents such as Shi Ming-teh. In 1991, he authorized an investigation of the February 28th Incident, and later apologized for its excesses and compensated its victims. Also in 1991, he lifted measures introduced during the Civil War that suspended parts of the Constitution (see GOVERNMENT AND ADMINISTRATION/CONSTITUTIONS). By the end of that year, he had forced the retirement of elderly Mainlanders from all elected offices and opened them to elections in Taiwan alone. In 1992, the Taiwan Garrison Headquarters, a feared institution in charge of security, was disbanded. In 1994, the governor of Taiwan province and the mayors of Taipei and Kaohsiung were chosen by direct elections. Four years later, Lee won 54 per cent of the vote in the first direct elections for the presidency – the first time so many Chinese

Arms Across the Straits

For the best part of 50 years, Chinese governments on either side of the Taiwan Straits were intensely hostile to each other. Both spoke of their desire for peaceful reunification, but while the Kuomintang abandoned its always unrealistic commitment to recover the Mainland by force, the Chinese Communist Party has yet to rule out military conquest as a means of incorporating Taiwan into the People's Republic. Until the end of 1999 Beijing threatened to do so under any one of three conditions: a declaration of independence by the island's leaders; 'foreign interference' in Taiwan; and social chaos on the island. In February 2000 it added a fourth: indefinite delay on the Taiwan side towards unification talks. This attempt to shape the outcome of Taiwan's presidential elections in March 2000 failed. Chen Shui-bian of the Democratic Progressive Party, which has less interest in reunification than the other major parties, won the presidency.

From 1949 until the late 1970s, the Communists' sole policy towards Taiwan was to 'liberate' it through military conquest. To prevent this, and signal its determination to resist North Korea's invasion of the South, the United States in 1950 moved the Seventh Fleet into the Taiwan Straits. Four years later it signed a mutual defence treaty with Taipei. However, Washington was also keen to stop Chiang Kai-shek trying to recover the Mainland. The islands of Kinmen (*Quemoy*) and Matsu, just off FUJIAN, and the Tachens, near ZHEJIANG, all of them under Chiang's control and possible springboards for re-conquest, were therefore excluded from the defence treaty. On the other hand, Washington did not want Chiang to lose the islands, which might hamper the defence of Taiwan proper. Before the 1954 treaty was signed, Communist forces subjected Kinmen to heavy bombardment. The following year they captured the Tachens. In response to this first 'Straits Crisis', Congress passed a resolution allowing American troops to defend regions outside Penghu and Taiwan Island deemed to be 'in friendly hands'.

The second Straits Crisis was more serious than the first. In August 1958 Mao Zedong decided to test the US commitment to Taiwan by launching a fierce artillery attack and blockade of Kinmen, the largest of the Nationalists' 'outer islands' and the closest to Mainland shores. As Nationalist and Communist planes struggled for supremacy, 80,000 KMT troops and 40,000 civilians on the island ran short of supplies. They were reinforced courtesy of the Seventh Fleet whose vessels transported soldiers from Taiwan to within three miles (4.8 kms) of Quemoy, where they completed the journey in Nationalist ships. Mao was surprised by the obstinacy of the defenders, and angered by weak verbal support from the Kremlin. He abandoned the blockade in October, and confined the shelling to alternate days. Some years later, explosive shells were replaced by those bearing Communist propaganda leaflets. Shelling of every kind stopped when the United States and the People's Republic established diplomatic relations in 1979. Formal ties between Washington and Beijing were predicated upon termination of the 1954 defence treaty, *and* an informal understanding that the Communists would pursue peaceful reunification with Taiwan rather than invade it.

In 1981, Marshal Ye Jianying (1897–1986) in Beijing suggested Communist and Nationalist Party leaders open talks on Taiwan's future. The island was promised a glorious future as a Special Administrative Region of the People's Republic with a high degree of autonomy. This was an early outing of the formula under which HONG KONG returned to Chinese sovereignty in 1997. It differed in that Taiwan was to be granted the right to maintain its own military forces, and that positions in the central government would be reserved for Taiwan's leaders. It differed, too, in that President Chiang Ching-kuo rejected it outright. He re-stated the Nationalists' determination to have no dealings with the Communists. The timing of China's peace initiative – which did not include the renunciation of force – partly reflected concern in Beijing that the Kuomintang old guard was dying off, like their counterparts in the Communist Party. If there was one thing these old foes agreed on it was that there was one China and that Taiwan was part of it. There was no certainty that the next generation, particularly in Taiwan, would think the same.

Another factor in Beijing was the feeling that the Nationalists, now isolated diplomatically and deprived of US military support, might be amenable to talks on reunification. Also important was China's desire, under the leadership of DENG XIAOPING, to tap Taiwan's wealth and know-how for its own newly declared modernization drive. All of these motives reinforced, but were not substitutes for, the great nationalist impulse: Beijing's desire to see China united again. There was altogether less urgency about this cause in Taipei. The adherence of new Nationalist leaders to the 'one China' principle was not so great that they were ready to see their administration turned into a local government. And while the Taiwanese people were indisputably Chinese, many felt they had more to lose than gain from reunification under a Communist government, however loose Beijing's embrace promised to be.

However, there was a desire in Taiwan to re-explore the Mainland culturally, economically and, particularly on the part of old soldiers, personally. After almost 40 years in Taiwan, the exiles wanted to see their towns, villages and relatives again. They began to do so in the late 1980s as part of a thaw that soon saw Taiwanese of all ages make millions of journeys each year. Most did so via Hong Kong and Macau since Taipei refused to countenance direct transport links across the Taiwan Straits on security grounds. Many of the travellers discovered that the Mainland was not home at all. The first returnees were often horrified by the poverty they saw in some parts of the country and saddened by the grasping attitude of many of their compatriots, relatives included. There had been dark days in Taiwan, but the Nationalists had neither broken the spirit of those they ruled, nor destroyed China's traditional culture, customs and manners as the Communists evidently had.

Yet China's poverty – and the Communist Party's commitment to shed it – meant there were business opportunities on the Mainland for Taiwanese firms.

By the mid-1990s two-way trade, again conducted indirectly, exceeded US$20 billion a year. The Mainland soon became Taiwan's largest trade partner after Japan and the United States. Taiwanese investment on the Mainland was worth even more. It was thought to exceed US$40 billion by the end of the century. Problems accumulated as well as profits. Taiwanese investors complained about the lack of legal protection on the Mainland. Beijing did not quite regard them as domestic investors but, clearly, they were not foreigners either. For the most part, they were on their own. The kidnapping and murder of Taiwanese businessmen became common. A low point was reached in 1994 when 24 Taiwanese tourists were robbed and murdered while taking a pleasure cruise on Qiandao Lake in Zhejiang. The brusque way in which Beijing dealt with the tragedy did nothing to foster mutual understanding, and provoked harsh words from President Lee Teng-hui.

Still, Taiwanese businesses found the economic lure of the Mainland as irresistible as many of their counterparts in the West. So much so that Taipei soon began to fear that the island's economy would grow too dependent on the People's Republic. If this was the case it might prove difficult to resist political reunification on Beijing's terms. The Nationalist government moved to restrict investment to projects requiring a maximum investment of US$50 million, and specifically forbade involvement in infrastructure development that might build up the PRC's national power. A 'go south' policy encouraging Taiwanese investment in Southeast Asia was also designed to reduce dependency on the Mainland.

These personal, cultural and commercial contacts formed part of a great encounter between Chinese on both sides of the Taiwan Straits after decades of estrangement. It was a welcome development, and a further sign that the Cold War was a thing of the past in East Asia as well as Europe. But the thaw did little to bring the two Chinas together politically, and not much to reduce the threat of war across the Taiwan Straits. This was because the entire thrust of nearly a decade of political liberalization was to turn Taiwan into a *de facto* state rather than the resting place of a rival Chinese government. Taipei made this plain in 1991. It declared that China was divided into two separate political entities: the People's Republic, and the Republic of China *on Taiwan*. President Lee said the governments of each side should recognize each other, work together in international organizations and, eventually, bring the whole of China under unified rule.

This final goal was decades away. Lee's aim, summed up in his phrase 'Don't rush, be patient', was to 'normalize' relations with Beijing, not unite Taiwan with the Mainland under a Communist administration. 'One country, two systems' was not an option. It would make Taipei subordinate to Beijing and require Taiwan to work within a Communist political system, even if it could preserve its capitalist freedoms at home. Reunification could take place only after democracy and freedom had appeared on the Mainland, and Taiwan had secured its rightful place in the international community, including membership of the United Nations. In 1993, Taipei began to campaign for UN membership without challenging the PRC's right to a seat in the world body. The main result was to annoy Beijing without bringing the prospect of membership for Taiwan nearer. Still, Taipei persisted (see UNITED NATIONS).

Lee also pursued negotiations with Beijing. They were formal but 'unofficial'; neither the People's Republic nor the ROC was ready to recognize the political legitimacy of the other. In 1990 Taiwan formed the Straits Exchange Foundation (SEF) to handle relations with the Mainland authorities. Beijing responded by creating an 'unofficial' body of its own: the Association for Relations Across the Taiwan Straits (ARATS). They conducted a dialogue, largely by phone and fax, in which thinly veiled insults often got the better of courtesy and, usually, substance. The 'two Chinas', though talking, were still at cross purposes; goodwill was in short supply. A high point of a kind was reached in April 1993: SEF and ARATS leaders met in Singapore and signed an accord on the authentication of documents, and compensation for the loss of registered mail destined for either the Mainland or Taiwan.

The symbolism of the so-called Koo–Tang talks, named after Koo Chen-fu (1917–), chairman of the SEF, and Tang Shubei (1931–), chairman of ARATS, was greater than the substance, but at least it was a start.

The Qiandao Lake affair marred cross-Straits relations. So did other incidents, including a rash of hijackings of Mainland planes to Taipei by PRC citizens who imagined financial rewards and personal freedom awaited them in Taiwan. Prison and return to the Mainland more often did. But what really ruptured ties between the two sides was Taiwan's continued pursuit of a formal international identity distinct from that of the People's Republic. It was reinforced by a feeling that the United States, despite its pledge to reduce weapons sales to Taiwan, could still be counted on to defend Taipei. President George Bush's decision in 1992 to sell 150 F-16s to Taiwan seemed proof of this. A move by France, later the same year, to supply 60 Mirage jets gave another boost to Taiwanese confidence.

In Beijing, all of these developments, including strong showings in local polls by the opposition Democratic Progressive Party, were signs that Taiwan was moving towards formal independence rather than reunification. An eight-point statement on reunification issued by JIANG ZEMIN in 1995 elicited a slightly encouraging response from President Lee, but the two leaders were still at odds over the question of Beijing's refusal to renounce the use of force against Taiwan. A few months later, the Communists' worst fears were realized when Washington allowed President Lee to make a 'private visit' to Cornell University, his *alma mater*. Exulting in his diplomatic breakthrough, the Taiwanese president made an inflammatory speech. Hardliners in the PEOPLE'S LIBERATION ARMY (PLA), decided tough measures were needed to bring the 'rebel province' to heel.

The opening salvo took the form of a stream of articles in the official media denouncing Lee in the most vituperative terms. Round two, in July and August 1995, involved missile tests and military manoeuvres opposite Taiwan in an attempt to destabilize the island's economy and weaken Lee's standing. Neither objective was achieved, leading Beijing to increase the pressure – and the risks – during the island's presidential elections in March the following year. The third Straits Crisis was different, and in some ways more dramatic than its predecessors. It took place during a fierce contest for political supremacy in Taiwan between Lee, two rival former-Kuomintang candidates who took a moderate line towards the Mainland, and Peng Min-min, leader of the pro-independence DPP. When the PLA test-fired missiles into the sea close to Keelung and Kaohsiung harbours, the stock market shuddered, there was a flight of capital and popular unease in Taipei. Protracted military manoeuvres in the sea and airspace close to Taiwan and the beaches across the Straits kept the pressure on – up to and beyond polling day.

Yet the results confounded Beijing's expectations. Lee won the election by a landslide, Peng came a poor second, and the allegedly pro-Mainland independent candidates were humiliated. Worse, Mainland sabre-rattling drew the United States directly into the drama, reminding both parties of its continuing involvement, even if sometimes at arm's length, in China's unfinished civil war. Two US naval task forces, one led by the *Nimitz*, the other by the *Independence*, moved into waters close to Taiwan to deter PLA adventurism. The point made and the polls over, tension soon subsided. Replacing it with trust proved much harder. Taipei and Beijing hardly spoke to each other in the years immediately following the elections. Trade and tourism continued, but Taiwan refused to set up direct transport links. Beijing repeated its 'one country, two systems' formula for reunification, yet declined to renounce the use of force. Both sides continued a military build-up designed to provide the PLA with a capacity to conquer the island, and Taiwan's 400,000-strong forces an ability to resist it. Both sides still locked horns in the diplomatic arena where things continued to go Beijing's way.

Beijing's greatest gain concerned relations with the United States, which improved rapidly after the dangerous days of March 1996. It soon dawned on Taiwan that while the island had relied on the US to stop military intimidation during the election, it might not be able to do so in future. American officials made this clear to Taipei privately. In particular they warned against any moves towards formal Taiwanese independence, a message not lost on the DPP whose ardour for the cause was fading rapidly following its election defeat. President Bill Clinton made Washington's position clear during his visit to China in 1998. In a somewhat gratuitous re-statement of Beijing's own formula, he said the United States opposed the idea of 'two Chinas'; opposed the idea of 'One China, One Taiwan'; and would not support Taiwan's efforts to gain membership of international bodies reserved for sovereign states. America wanted to see representatives of Taiwan and China talking to each other again. The Taiwan Relations Act remained in force: just as Taipei could not count on US military intervention in future, Beijing could not *discount* it. But in dealing with its giant neighbour, the Republic of China on Taiwan would have to rely increasingly on its own resources and political skills.

This did not deter Lee Teng-hui. Cross-Straits talks resumed in 1998 when Koo travelled to Beijing and met President Jiang Zemin. Yet the following year Lee declared that all future contacts between the two sides should be regarded as those between two states, undermining the 'one China' policy Beijing insisted was the only basis for discussion. Angered by Lee's declaration but mistakenly comforted by the fact that his leadership of Taiwan was coming to an end, China postponed a visit to Taiwan by Tang Shubei (1931–) scheduled for late 1999 and debated the merits of military action as a means of achieving national unity compared with the frustrations of cross-Straits diplomacy. The debate continues in the early twenty-first century, its terms brought into even sharper relief by Chen Shui-bian's election victory and the formation of the first Chinese government in Taiwan not controlled by the Kuomintang.

people had voted so freely for their principal leader.

None of this was the work of just one man. Social and economic change, the bravery of dissidents and changes in the international environment all played their part. But Lee's role, though often the subject of controversy, was instrumental. In any event, without the violence that accompanied similar political change in South Korea or the Philippines (though with repeated fisticuffs and regular mayhem in parliament) Taiwan underwent rapid democratization. Given the KMT's continuing grip on some of the media, its control of a huge business empire, persistent vote-buying and links between election candidates and organized crime, democracy was hardly complete. But by the mid-1990s, Taiwan, long the richest part of China ruled by Chinese, had become the most free, too.

security in China's shadow

Yet by this time was Taiwan part of China at all? If so, what part? Almost 40 years of authoritarian Kuomintang rule had suppressed discussion about Taiwan's identity, as it had the island's people, the vast majority of whom were Taiwanese. Now that one-party rule was a thing of the past, the issue of Taiwan's place in the world – a world in which democracy and self-determination seemed everywhere on the advance – acquired new significance. Even children of Mainland 'exiles', born and bred on the island after 1949, saw themselves as Taiwanese. So, from the early 1990s, did most leaders of the Kuomintang. Lee's 'mainstream' or Taiwanese faction triumphed over its Mainland or 'non-mainstream' opponents, some of whom left to form the New Party in protest against what

Taiwan Relations Act

This Act of the United States Congress, passed in March 1979, provided a new basis for ties with Taiwan following Washington's diplomatic recognition of the government of the People's Republic of China in Beijing on 1 January that year. A skilful exercise in ambiguity, it left both parties in China's unfinished Civil War unsure as to whether, and under what circumstances, the US would intervene in their dispute. The Act declares that attempts to solve Taiwan's political future by anything other than peaceful means would be of 'grave concern' to the US. It requires the US to provide arms 'of a defensive nature' to the island so that it can 'maintain a self-sufficient defence capacity'. And it pledges the US to maintain the capacity to resist the use of force to jeopardize the social system of Taiwan. A further clause created a mechanism to handle 'unofficial' ties between Washington and Taipei – the 'American Institute in Taiwan' (AIT), a *de facto* embassy. Beijing objected strongly to the Act. In a Sino-US Joint Communiqué of 1982 it extracted a promise from Washington to reduce the sale of arms to Taiwan. However, President George Bush's decision in 1992 to sell 150 F-16 fighters to Taiwan suggested that the United States gave precedence to the Taiwan Relations Act. The deployment of US warships close to Taiwan in March 1996 while Beijing was seeking to intimidate the island with missile tests and war games confirmed it (see UNITED STATES).

they saw as the KMT's compromise with the DPP on the issue of independence.

Political liberalization and the discovery of 'Taiwaneseness' that flowed from it acquired a celebratory feel. Enthusiasm for Taiwan studies gripped schools and universities. Books, newspapers, conferences, television programmes and films examined what it meant to be Taiwanese and how this differed from being Mainland Chinese, Hong Kong Chinese, OVERSEAS CHINESE and non-Chinese. Democracy and academic freedom encouraged debate of what, just a few years earlier, had been the most sensitive of subjects.

Important and potentially dangerous implications for the island's political future arose from these developments. For the DPP, Taiwan's distinct historical experience and identity justified the pursuit of full independence. Until defeat in the presidential elections of 1996, it campaigned to create a Republic of Taiwan. The Kuomintang under Lee Teng-hui pursued a compromise. It sought to meet Taiwanese needs yet ease anxieties in Beijing where worries over Taiwan's drift towards independence were growing rapidly. In 1991, the government described the territory under

its control as the 'Republic of China on Taiwan'. It declined to scrap the ROC Constitution of 1947 but amended it on several occasions during the 1990s to reflect the fact that China was administered by two separate political entities. The New Party held fast to an older 'one China' ideal, though it remained a bitter foe of Communism.

These and other issues were slogged out at the polls, and during high-level, though unofficial, talks between representatives of the Mainland and Taiwan which began in Singapore in 1993. During the 1990s the election results varied according to the levels of government being elected. Generally, the DPP fared well at the local level where voters seemed to feel it was safe to show their satisfaction with the Kuomintang by electing pro-independence opposition candidates. In 1994, DPP candidate Chen Shui-bian triumphed in elections for mayor of Taipei. The Kuomintang remained the largest single party during voting for the National Assembly and the Legislative Yuan, even though its majority in the latter was sometimes wafer thin thanks to the presence of deputies from the New Party and a handful of independents.

The Nationalists' clearest triumph came in 1996 with Taiwan's first direct elections for the presidency. Beijing, its patience with Lee exhausted by his 'private' visit to the United States the year before and dogged pursuit of international living space for Taiwan, halted further high-level talks and staged war games to coincide with the polls. The aim was to humiliate Lee, weaken support for the DPP and generally remind Taiwan and the rest of the world that it had the decisive say in the island's political future.

The last point was made at the expense of the first. Lee won 54 per cent of the vote, Peng Min-min of the DPP 21 per cent, and the two remaining candidates 25 per cent between them. But though the interposition of US warships sent a clear message to Beijing, it was unclear whether Taiwan really was its own master – even after nearly a decade of radical political reforms. Most of the world recognized this state of affairs by *not* recognizing Taipei as the seat of an independent government. And at home, while it was true Taiwan was no longer ruled by Mainlanders *for* Mainlanders, their counterparts on the other side of the Straits remained determined to set the parameters of Taiwanese politics.

Yet they, too, had their work cut out constraining the island's dynamic democracy. In mid-1999, in the final months of his second and last term as president, Lee Teng-hui sought to create more elbow room for the island, both in the context of 'unofficial' talks with Beijing (resumed at last in 1998), and in relation to the rest of the world. He declared that talks between the 'two Chinas' should be seen in the context of 'special state-to-state relations'. Beijing saw the hand of separatism at work again: it subjected Lee to another round of abuse and re-emphasized its determination to counter Taiwanese independence by military conquest. Senior US officials, alarmed by Beijing's reaction, hinted publicly that Lee had unnecessarily raised tensions across the Taiwan Straits.

In fact, he had done little more than state the obvious. Though few countries recognized the island, Taiwan *was* a sovereign state in the obvious sense that it enjoyed unchallenged jurisdiction over its own territory. Moreover, Lee's declaration was made with Taiwanese voters in mind as much as Communist officials. The presidential elections of 2000 loomed. Lee was concerned to undermine support for Chen Shui-bian, the DPP candidate, by taking the Kuomintang almost as far as the opposition on the question of Taiwanese independence, *and* make life difficult for James Soong Chu-yu (1942–), the former provincial governor of Taiwan, who ran as an independent candidate and favoured closer, but poorly defined, ties with the Mainland. Another consideration was to make it all but impossible for Lien Chan (1936–), Lee's preferred successor and the official Kuomintang

An Economic Powerhouse

High costs and unstable relations with the Mainland had taken the gloss off Taiwan's economic performance before the Asian financial crisis struck in 1997–8. Yet growth continued during the downturn, albeit at a slower pace, even as it disappeared elsewhere in the region. And the end-of-century slowdown did not challenge Taiwan's reputation, established during the previous four decades, as an economic powerhouse. The real GNP growth rate in the 1950s was 7.5 per cent. In the 1960s it was 9.7 per cent, and in the 1970s 9.6 per cent. The average growth rate of 8.8 per cent for the period 1952–90 was among the highest in the world. It was achieved despite the sudden increase in population caused by the arrival of exiles from the Mainland in 1948–9, and heavy military expenditure that, in the late 1990s, still accounted for at least 7 per cent of GDP and made Taiwan one of the world's largest buyer of arms.

In the 1950s, agriculture's share of output was 29 per cent, industry's 24 per cent and services' 47 per cent. Almost half a century later, agriculture contributed just 3 per cent, industry about 35 per cent and services 62 per cent. Land reform, cheap labour, compulsory education, government incentives – and open markets in the United States – had all by the 1980s helped make Taiwan one of the region's four 'tiger' economies alongside Singapore, Hong Kong and South Korea.

Taiwanese trade and investment have helped fuel growth throughout Southeast Asia. They have made major contributions to the economy of Mainland China as well as Hong Kong, through which virtually all Taiwanese business has to pass in the absence of direct trade and transport links across the Straits. Coastal Fujian in particular owes much of its wealth to Taiwanese enterprise and capital. By the early 1990s the island had become one of the world's top 15 trading nations and built up massive foreign exchange reserves.

The backbone of Taiwan's economy is made up of thousands of small and medium-sized enterprises (SMEs) rather than the conglomerates characteristic of many developing countries. They employ 80 per cent of the workforce and account for half the value of all exports. In the 1990s the service sector's contribution to GDP continued to outpace that of industry, but growth in the information technology industry was particularly rapid. By the middle of the decade, more computer hardware products were made in Taiwan than anywhere outside Japan and the United States. Hardware exports became the island's biggest source of foreign exchange. So much so that in 1997 the International Monetary Fund reclassified Taiwan as an 'advanced' economy on the basis of its huge output of computer goods, and the fact that it held the third-largest foreign exchange reserves in the world. Taipei rejected the label. It said the island's per capita GDP of US$12,838 (the 1996 figure) was still too low for such exalted status.

If wealth has come more rapidly to Taiwan than many other parts of the world, it has also spread more evenly among the population. Income differentials are low compared with those in many developing countries. In the 1980s the emergence of a middle class was the most striking development in Taiwanese society. But prosperity was not limited to this group. It was dispersed so widely that some surveys found that half the population saw themselves as members of the middle class, even though, in terms of their profession, they did not warrant such status.

In an attempt to extend economic growth well into the new century, the government announced it would turn Taiwan into an 'Asia-Pacific Regional Operations Centre'. Multi-national corporations were encouraged to locate their headquarters in the island the better to manage operations throughout the region. It was an imaginative move but not necessarily a practical one, at least in the short term. Among other things, it requires a substantial improvement in Taiwan's infrastructure and an even bigger one in relations with the Mainland so that trade, communications and people can travel between the two parts of China directly rather than through the Special Administrative Regions of Hong Kong or Macau.

Governance in Taiwan

Martial Law, a 40-year-long 'temporary' suspension of constitutional freedoms, a ban on the creation of new political parties, and the Kuomintang's penetration and control of almost every area of life, deprived the Taiwan people of a genuine voice in government for more than 40 years. In the final decade of the twentieth century they at last spoke out. Every major level of government was opened up to genuine elections. And since 1996, the president of the Republic of China on Taiwan has been chosen through direct elections held every four years.

The president is the highest representative of state and commander-in-chief of the armed forces. He appoints the president of the Executive Yuan, or premier, and has the power to dissolve the Legislative Yuan, the principal legislative organ. Some legislative functions were performed by the National Assembly. Its chief powers were those of amending the Constitution, electing the vice-president (should the office fall vacant) and impeaching the president or vice-president. In 1996 Assembly members were directly elected to serve 4-year terms. However in 1999, amid controversy, they voted to extend their term by two years to 2002 by which time elections for the Legislative Yuan were due to take place. The idea was to synchronize elections for national-level legislative bodies, and change the voting method for the National Assembly so that delegates were selected by proportional representation according to the number of votes the parties received during elections for the Legislative Yuan. The move was seen as a prelude to revising the Constitution in such a way as to abolish the National Assembly and concentrate its remaining powers in the Legislative Yuan. However, in March 2000 the Council of Grand Justices, Taiwan's supreme court, declared the extension to the 4-year term to be invalid, whereupon the major parties agreed the Assembly would meet only when necessary. Its abolition seems inevitable.

The Legislative Yuan is one of five *yuan* or branches of government beneath the presidency and the National Assembly. The Executive Yuan, headed by a president or premier, is the equivalent of a cabinet. It supervises the various ministries, among them the Mainland Affairs Council, which handles relations with the People's Republic.

The Legislative Yuan is the highest legislative organ. Its 200-odd members are directly elected, save for 50 who represent Overseas Chinese and the 'nationwide community' – the ROC's continued, but increasingly understated, claim to represent a larger China than Taiwan. Deputies serve 3-year terms. The Judicial Yuan exercises supervision over Taiwan's legal system and interprets the Constitution. The Examination Yuan is responsible for the employment and management of civil servants. The Control Yuan is a quasi-judicial body in charge of the impeachment, audit and censure of public officials.

Until 1998, the most important administrative organ below central government level was the Taiwan provincial government. For many years the premier nominated and the president appointed the provincial governor. But in 1994 the post was opened to direct elections. They produced an overwhelming victory for the Kuomintang candidate, James Soong Chu-yu (1942–). Four years later, amid much controversy, Soong's position and the government he led were abolished as part of an exercise in administrative streamlining. This caused a rupture in personal relations between Soong and Lee Teng-hui which culminated in Soong's decision to contest the 2000 presidential elections as an independent, and which fatally divided the KMT vote in favour of Chen Shui-bian of the DPP.

Since 1994, the mayors of the two special municipalities of Taipei and Kaohsiung have also been chosen by direct elections. Similarly, mayors of lesser cities and county magistrates are elected by popular vote every 4 years.

candidate, to back-down on the question of the island's status.

These stratagems reckoned without the capacity of Taiwan's rumbustious democracy to surprise. During the presidential elections, issues of Taiwan's status took a back seat to concern over corruption, fatigue with a ruling Party riven with faction following Soong's departure, and a general desire, particularly on the part of the young, for change. The result was a victory for Chen, who won 39 per cent of the vote, narrowly ahead of Soong with 36 per cent but far in front of Lien, who managed only 23 per cent. The short but remarkable history of democracy in Taiwan notched up another triumph: it secured the peaceful downfall of the Party that had ruled the island for 55 years and led it, at last, into the constitutional era. Nowhere else in the Chinese world – including Singapore – had people secured a transfer of power from one party to another through elections. Taiwan was indeed the first Chinese democracy.

Chen's victory opened new vistas of change for Taiwan, many of them laden with anxieties. Chief among the latter was Beijing's attitude towards a DPP administration – even one formed of those with political affiliations to parties other than the DPP as well as those with none. There was also the related question of Taiwan's identity. On his inauguration as president, Chen said there would be no change to Taiwan's constitution, national flag or designation as the 'Republic of China on Taiwan'. He also launched new peace initiatives towards the Mainland, including the opening of direct trade, transport and postal links, the so-called *san tong*, or 'three links', long sought by Beijing. This pointed to a fundamental change in relations across the

Wars of Diplomatic Recognition

For more than 50 years Taipei and Beijing have fought a zero-sum battle for diplomatic recognition from the international community. For most of this time, the rivals deprived third countries of the option of dual recognition. Their claims were mutually exclusive: diplomatic recognition of one ruled out the possibility of official dealings with the other. An exception was BRITAIN. It recognized the People's Republic of China in 1950 yet maintained consular representation in Taiwan until 1972. For 20 years the wars of recognition went Taipei's way, thanks to its alliance with the United States. For many governments, American backing, Taiwan's membership of the United Nations and staunch anti-communism made the ROC the more attractive Chinese diplomatic partner. By 1970, 67 countries maintained diplomatic ties with Taipei and 54 with Beijing. One year later, as a result of Taiwan's expulsion from the UN and its replacement by Beijing, the proportions were almost exactly reversed.

The United States opening to the People's Republic accelerated the diplomatic flight from Taipei. In 1979, when Washington switched recognition from Taipei to Beijing, only 22 countries recognized Taiwan compared with 117 for the Mainland. The ROC'S diplomatic allies never numbered so few again during the twentieth century. Yet neither did they number many more. In 1990, Saudi Arabia deserted Taipei for Beijing. In 1992 South Korea did. In 1998, after some personal anguish on the part of President Nelson Mandela, who fondly recalled Taiwan's support for the African National Congress, South Africa followed suit, as did Tonga, the Central African Republic and Guinea Bissau. This left Taipei with just under 30 diplomatic partners, many of them in Central or South America, and none of them of much weight. At the start of the twenty-first century, no state in Asia recognizes the ROC and only two in Europe do so: the Vatican, a longstanding ally, and Macedonia, a newer one, which established diplomatic ties with Taipei in 1999. Neither genuine aid from Taiwan nor cruder recourse to 'dollar diplomacy' seems likely to add to the list in the near future.

Communist leaders in Beijing, relentless in their campaign to squeeze Taiwan out of the diplomatic arena, take comfort from this. But their obsession with symbolism sometimes overlooks the fact that scores of countries – including all the important ones – maintain unofficial but substantive relations with Taipei. They do so through 'cultural', 'trade' or 'representative' offices that perform many of the functions of embassies. Indeed, much of the work of diplomacy has been found not to depend on formal diplomatic relations at all.

Nevertheless, Taipei still covets formal ties with other countries. In the early 1990s it gave up insisting that prospective partners first abandon Beijing. The Mainland's refusal to adopt the same approach continued to rule out dual recognition. Taiwan's forced exit from international organizations in favour of Beijing has proved a main cause of its diplomatic demise on the bilateral front. The campaign for representation in the UN that began in 1993 was designed to reverse this, but has encountered insurmountable Mainland-led opposition. The ROC is a member of the International Olympic Committee, the Asian Development Bank and the ASIA-PACIFIC ECONOMIC COOPERATION (APEC) council among other international bodies. It was expected to join the World Trade Organization in 2000, shortly after the People's Republic. However, in none of these organizations can it use the name 'Republic of China', and must appear instead under the designation 'Chinese Taipei' or a similar, politically neutral, formula.

Straits, particularly on the economic front. It also posed a threat to Hong Kong, which had grown rich virtually monopolizing trade and transport between the Mainland and Taiwan.

The effect of the DPP victory on Taiwan's domestic politics promised to be equally profound. After the elections James Soong announced he would form a new political party – the *Ch'inmintang* or 'People First Party'. The strong support he enjoyed at the polls suggested it would be a force to be reckoned with. The Kuomintang's prospects looked less rosy. Lee Teng-hui resigned as chairman five days after the elections, leaving Lien Chan to revive a Party whose aura of invincibility had been shattered at the polls. Incredibly, the KMT appeared to face extinction as a major force in Taiwanese politics unless drastic reforms were introduced.

And what of the implications of these extraordinary developments for Beijing's determination to negotiate or, failing that, *impose* national unification on Taiwan? In March 2000 the people of Taiwan spoke, electing as their leader the man least likely to lead them into unification with the People's Republic of China. Such a challenge could hardly go unanswered in Beijing, however prudent Chen Shui-bian might be on the question of Taiwanese independence. The question, ultimately, is whether China's leaders will be able to come to terms with Taiwan's determination to retain an independent identity for an indefinite period of time, or whether the great centralizing, unifying impulses to which they, like most Chinese governments before them, are hostage, will force them into some form of action. The fate of the first Chinese democracy hinges on this question. So does security in Asia-Pacific.

tariff autonomy

From the Sino-British Treaty of Nanjing of 1842 until the final stage of the Nationalist Revolution in 1928, China's tariff rates were set by agreement with the foreign powers. This deprived Beijing of direct control over a major source of revenue. For the capital's cash-strapped governments, as for generations of Nationalist reformers, it was an unacceptable manifestation of China's loss of sovereignty arising from the UNEQUAL TREATIES.

More than imperialist greed was at work here. Dishonesty in Chinese customs houses in the mid-nineteenth century meant that domestic and foreign merchants were cheated and the central government shortchanged. The powers made it their business to include what they called 'fair and reasonable' tariffs in any treaties they signed with China. In 1854 they imposed a foreign inspectorate on China's maritime customs which, particularly under Robert Hart, the long-serving inspector general, kept revenues flowing to Beijing.

But foreign control of the customs – including pilotage in most harbours, the management of lighthouses and the entire Post Office – infringed upon China's sovereignty still further. The wound deepened in the early twentieth century when the powers made customs receipts hostage to the repayment of loans and indemnities by the Chinese government (see FINANCE).

The unwillingness of the powers to grant China tariff autonomy was part of their reluctance to abandon other treaty privileges such as the TREATY PORTS and EXTRATERRITORI-ALITY. Their argument was that China was plagued by anarchy. Its changing, rival governments seemed incapable of guaranteeing what foreign governments believed to be their lawful rights.

This perception did not change until the completion of the NORTHERN EXPEDITION to reunify China in 1928, by which time the KUO-MINTANG government had abandoned most of the radical anti-imperialist policies of its early years. Even then tariff autonomy was ceded reluctantly. The UNITED STATES did so first by recognizing the new Nationalist government in July 1928. BRITAIN followed suit.

As a result government revenues increased and Chinese industry enjoyed greater protection. Foreigners, most of them Britons, continued to work in the customs administration until the early 1950s, but it, too, was restored to Chinese control in 1928.

telecommunications

Longstanding tensions between national sovereignty and foreign participation, state monopoly and privatization, government control and individual liberty meet in China's rapidly growing telecommunications industry. In one form or another they have dogged China's modernization drive since the late nineteenth century. But in the information industry, where the forces of globalization, privatization and personal freedom challenge the CHINESE COMMUNIST PARTY's efforts to free the economy yet retain political control, they are particularly sensitive. An example is the internet, an unstable new frontier in the long battle between 'Chinese' and Western values.

Foreigners pioneered the development of telecommunications in China as they did RAILWAYS. Western companies provided China's first telegraphic links with the outside world and its first telephone network, set up in SHANGHAI in 1881. QING DYNASTY officials fought to free China's international communications of foreign control; in 1906 they created a ministry of posts and transportation to strengthen Beijing's control over the small but strategically important modern system of communications and transport. The very attempt hastened the dynasty's demise (see REPUBLICAN REVOLUTION). It was Republicans, not the Manchus, who nationalized China's fledgling telecommunications sector.

The KUOMINTANG did as much to develop modern communications as civil wars and foreign invasion allowed. During the 1930s, the government ended the foreign monopoly of China's international communications, built a modest network of short-wave radio stations and linked most of the eastern provinces by telephone. This was a start but no more. When the Communists came to power in 1949, China's telephone penetration rate was 0.05 per cent of the population and the network was concentrated in developed areas.

The Party's determination to unify the country and build a socialist economy made for the rapid development of communications and modern, official media based on associated technological advances (see MEDIA). In 1950 Beijing established a telephone link with the SOVIET UNION, its most important ally. Two years later every province was connected to Beijing save TIBET and NINGXIA. Yet the public network remained small, and the military together with several ministries established communications networks of their own, some of which they retain at the start of the new century. During the first three decades of Communist rule, the telephone was primarily a means of government administration, not citizens' convenience. Rare and costly, telephone lines were for officials rather than the general public. This remained the case until the reform era.

The effects on China's telecommunications industry of rapid economic growth and opening to the outside world were dramatic. In 1978 there was 1 telephone for every 300 people. Eighteen years later the ratio was 1 for every 22 with an average of 1 phone for every 4 people in major cities. There were fewer than 15 million telephone lines at the end of 1991 but something like 120 million at the close of the decade. In the 5 years ending in 1997, China installed 73 million lines – more than the rest of the developing world put together. Telephone traffic between the Mainland and HONG KONG, and the Mainland and TAIWAN (routed through third countries at the insistence of Taipei) soared. Growth across the board, in traffic, fixed lines, mobile phones and pagers, far outstripped that of GDP. Yet a relatively low telephone penetration rate of 10 per cent at the end of the century pointed to the potential that remained. Foreign and domestic companies battled for access to the Chinese market at a time when competition, liberalization, privatization and globalization made telecommunications a driving force of world growth.

Beijing was less than enthusiastic about some of these vital new forces. Like their counterparts in the late Qing, Communist leaders insisted on state control over telecommunications, which they regarded as a strategic industry. To do otherwise would be to cede sovereignty *and* lose revenue. Rapid growth in the industry was welcome; it promised to enlarge the reach of the state through rapid transmission of information. It

was also necessary for maintaining the surveillance, censorship and control over society crucial to Party rule. With these political and economic goals in mind, the ministry of information industries was slow to tolerate domestic competition in the late 1990s and banned foreign companies from running telecoms networks.

A major question at the start of the new era is how quickly demands for more capital and better service will force the ministry to change its mind, and open the market to local and foreign competition. Pressure to do so will increase as a result of China's membership of the World Trade Organization. The Sino-American accord of November 1999, paving the way for Chinese entry, allowed foreigners to acquire a stake of up to 50 per cent in telecoms joint ventures, including the internet. However, Beijing's compliance was expected to be gradual and modest. In such an important, dynamic sector of the economy as telecommunications, phantoms of the past and the need for revenues in the present cloud the prospects for rapid liberalization.

China's initial encounter with the internet did much to expose the conflicts in its policy of development without democracy, information without liberty, economic pluralism combined with one-party rule. After a rapid growth in subscribers during 1995, Beijing forced all internet users to register with the police and undertake not to access or disseminate materials deemed harmful to the state. Many of these materials concerned DISSIDENTS, the TIANANMEN SQUARE DEMOCRACY MOVEMENT, democracy in Taiwan and criticism of China's rule in TIBET. Government censors got to work blocking off sensitive sites on the worldwide web, at times rendering the internet almost useless when accessed within China.

Alarmed that a growing number of Chinese have access to news and information other than that supplied by the official media, Beijing has set up new providers to act as 'intranets': government-controlled gateways to the world of information beyond China's frontiers. This amounts to a 'filtering' operation of the kind long familiar to Chinese officialdom but on this occasion conducted by internet companies, many of them involving prestige foreign partners and some of them registered on overseas stock exchanges where they have attracted huge investor interest.

At the start of the new era, just as during the past one, China wants and needs access to the outside world. In particular Beijing recognizes the importance of e-commerce and believes it can help reform the economy. But it wants to develop information industries on its own terms, which means preventing them from challenging the authority of the government or the ideology of the state.

Evidence from other parts of the world suggests this is not possible. Modern information services are cheap, widely available and usually accessed in private – even in the People's Republic of China. The way they operate, indeed, their very ethos, makes them typical products of liberal, democratic societies. It is easy to assume they will swiftly undermine authoritarianism wherever they encounter it.

Easy, but in China's case, not necessarily correct. The information industry is a *fruit* of liberal capitalism. It has yet to prove it is the root of such. In the absence of a *political* will to change – and in China that probably means an unambiguous initiative from the top – a rapid expansion in telecommunications is unlikely, of itself, to challenge the Communist Party's monopoly on power. Moreover, the number of internet users, though increasing rapidly, remains tiny in proportion to the total population because of limited access to personal computers. The pace of 'informatiz-ation' cannot exceed that of industrialization, in China or elsewhere.

Yet a growing number of China's brightest and youngest people do have access to the internet. Perhaps 7 million did so by the end of the twentieth century, among them members of the quasi-religious sect the *Fa Lun Gong* who used it to spread their message, until the government cracked down on the movement (see RELIGION(S)). It was estimated that by 2003, 33 million people would enjoy internet access. Controlling what these people read and write will prove increasingly difficult. However, it will not be impossible. On the threshold of the 'information century', Lin Hai, a dissident who supplied exiled democracy activists with e-mail addresses in China, which were then deluged with anti-government propaganda, was jailed for two years for subversion. Police in SHANGHAI formed a special unit to patrol the internet and track down the source and destination of 'hostile' materials.

These developments suggest that, at least for the time being, the information industry in China, along with the telecommunications market that serves it, is less a vehicle for political transformation than a new battleground on which to fight an old war over old issues. It is a war whose ultimate outcome remains uncertain.

Three Gorges Dam

Rarely has there been a battle between man and nature on the scale of that under way in the Three Gorges, where the waters of the YANGTZE, China's longest river, are being diverted and forced to flow through a network of power turbines. Construction of the Three Gorges Dam, in the scenic area of the river around the borders of HUBEI and CHONGQING, is an example of unparalleled hubris or a spectacular feat of Chinese engineering, depending upon one's point of view. Certainly it is a departure from tradition in a country many of whose philosophers emphasized man's unity with nature rather than the need to conquer it. Just as certainly, the project, a totem of China's modernization since the days of SUN YAT-SEN, raises fundamental questions about ENERGY, the ENVIRONMENT and the relationship between the Chinese government and its people, more than a million of whom will lose their homes as a result of the scheme.

The Three Gorges – from east to west, Xiling, Wuling and Qutang – form a 150-mile-long corridor where the 'Long River' narrows in some places to a width of about 350 feet. Its staggering peaks, deep defiles and dangerous rapids inspired poets and artists for centuries. Nationalist reformers looked upon the scene with different eyes. In the mighty rush of waters they saw power to be harnessed for China's modernization drive. They saw the Gorges as 'choke points' for controlling disastrous floods. And in the age of steamships along the upper river, they dreamt of improving navigation and opening up inland ports, particularly Chongqing, to bulk, ocean-going trade.

Sun Yat-sen's plans to dam the Gorges date to 1919. The government of CHIANG KAI-SHEK, his successor, conducted feasibility studies in the late 1940s, and the Communist government embraced the idea soon after it came to power. But a lack of resources and Mao Zedong's pursuit of revolutionary purity got in the way. So did the split with the Soviet

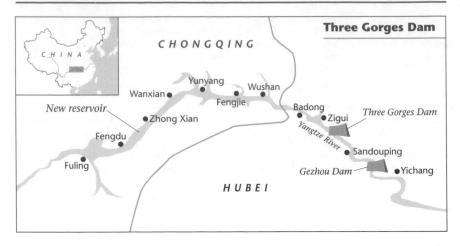

Union, whose experts China relied on – until they abruptly left for home. Meanwhile, the Yangtze continued to flood regularly, claiming hundreds of lives and millions of acres of farmland each year.

In 1970 work on the smaller, but still significant, Gezhouba dam began near the city of Ichang, 25 miles (40 kms) downstream from the nearest of the gorges. Phase One was completed in 1980, Phase Two in 1987. Construction took more time and money than expected, but it provided valuable experience for the 'real' thing: a dam at Sandouping, about halfway between Ichang and Xiling Gorge. Rapid economic growth in the early 1980s placed a huge strain on China's energy resources. The Three Gorges project was seen as a valuable alternative to reliance on coal-fired, oil-fired and, in future, nuclear power stations. It would also demonstrate the power of the CHINESE COMMUNIST PARTY to accomplish a public works project on a truly imperial scale: the Three Gorges Dam would be a physical monument to the Communist 'dynasty'.

Controversy soon dogged these ambitions, and for good reason. The project calls for the construction, over a period of 15 years, of a dam 185 metres high and more than 2,300 metres long that will raise the water level in the gorges by up to 175 metres and create an inland lake stretching hundreds of miles up river. Ship locks will be installed together with turbines capable of generating 18,200 megawatts of power. New homes must be found for more than 1 million people whose land will be submerged or in other ways threat-ened by the dramatic rise in water levels. The cost, estimated at US$25 billion in 1998, and destined to keep growing, easily exceeds that of other infrastructure projects in the world.

Objections have been raised to the Three Gorges scheme on grounds of cost, safety, potential damage to the environment and, later, human rights. Criticism came first from members of the DEMOCRATIC PARTIES, whose ranks included elderly scientists and engineers. Another prominent opponent was Dai Qing (1943–), a campaigning journalist and author of *Yangtze! Yangtze!*, a collection of articles questioning the safety and soundness of the scheme. Foreign experts also spoke out.

Critics warned that interrupting the flow of the Yangtze would create a risk of earthquakes and landslides, cause sedimentation and wipe out rare flora and fauna peculiar to the area. They held that a dam at the Three Gorges would not necessarily control flooding and drew attention to the fact that, outside China, large-scale hydroelectric schemes have fallen out of favour because of the damage they caused the environment. Some objected on the grounds that those forced to leave their homes were not consulted about the project and poorly compensated. Others worried that the dam would present too obvious a target should China come under military attack. Yet others based their opposition on the disas-trous collapse – hushed up at the time – of two dams in HENAN in 1975 at the cost of thousands of lives.

In the relatively open atmosphere of the late 1980s these complaints grew loud. It was a different matter after the suppression of the TIANANMEN SQUARE DEMOCRACY MOVEMENT in 1989. Dai Qing was one of hundreds of outspoken intellectuals sent to jail for her part in the protests. In the new climate of repression, objecting to *any* government policy was a risky business. This was particularly true of the Three Gorges Dam, a project close to the heart of LI PENG, then premier, and a Soviet-trained electrical engineer with a penchant for power projects.

Delegates to the NATIONAL PEOPLE'S CONGRESS (NPC) mounted some resistance. At their annual meeting in 1992, 177 of the 2,633 votes cast were opposed to the scheme while a further 664 delegates abstained – a 'negative' total of less than one-third, but still a rare example of dissent by NPC standards. Grassroots opposition in the vicinity of the dam site was quickly stamped out. Human Rights Watch Asia, an international human rights organization, said that in 1992–3, 179 members of the 'Democratic Youth Party' had been charged with 'counter-revolutionary activities' whose purpose was to sabotage construction of the dam.

Arguments in favour of the dam dominated the official media. The government insisted that safety was not an issue; that sedimentation could be solved; that few historical artifacts would be submerged and many removed and restored; that Chongqing would benefit because ships up to 10,000 tonnes would be able to reach the city; and that rare species, such as the Yangtze dolphin, would be protected. It also warned of the consequences of *not* building the dam. They included continued, uncontrolled flooding of the Yangtze, and severe atmospheric pollution as a result of trying to meet China's energy needs by constructing scores of coal-burning power stations.

In 1992, Beijing declared the entire Yangtze valley open to FOREIGN TRADE AND INVESTMENT in an attempt to invigorate one of the most important economic areas in the country. The Three Gorges Dam was part of this plan and work began on the project amid official fanfare in 1994. From the start, completion was deemed to be a matter of national pride and testimony to the vitality of the Chinese people under the leadership of the Communist Party. The propaganda reached new heights when the main flow of the Yangtze was diverted in November 1997. But it failed to drown out news that the evacuation of residents – much of it handled by the new municipality of Chongqing – was proving bitterly unpopular, or remove fears that the risks of the project remained at least as great as the benefits.

Costs were a constant worry, too, particularly when the Asian financial crisis appeared to rule out the possibility of raising funds for the project overseas. Several foreign banks and investment houses, anxious to avoid criticism, stayed away from Sandouping. In 1999 the official media raised questions over finance for the dam and the quality of construction work. But if doubts seemed to be growing in some quarters in Beijing, work continued. The true costs of taming the Yangtze will be known only after the project is complete, and borne by future generations of Chinese who live and work along the Long River.

Tian Jiyun (1929–)

How Tian Jiyun, then a member of the CHINESE COMMUNIST PARTY's Politburo and a vice-premier, survived his close association with ZHAO ZIYANG following the suppression of the TIANANMEN SQUARE DEMOCRACY MOVEMENT in 1989 was something of a mystery. But that veteran revolutionaries and younger 'Leftists' in the leadership came to regret they had not removed this vigorous reformer from power soon became clear.

The most dramatic sign of this occurred in early 1992, when reformers and conservatives within the Party were at loggerheads over China's future. Tian joined the debate with an extraordinary speech at the Central Party School in Beijing, the training ground for the elite. If hardliners were convinced economic reforms would lead to the revival of capitalism and economic disaster they should set up a SPECIAL ECONOMIC ZONE of their own, Tian said. They could run it on Maoist lines and let its inhabitants return to the glory days of food rationing, shortages and hardships. The speech provoked laughter within the audience and support across the country, particularly among intellectuals and reforming officials chafing under the post-Tiananmen conservative revival. The official media refused to publish its contents but bootleg videos of the address circulated widely.

Tian's mockery of a cause championed by, among others, DENG LIQUN, helped the reformists seal victory at the Party's 14th National Congress later in 1992. The following year he relinquished his post of vice-premier to become first vice-chairman of the NATIONAL PEOPLE'S CONGRESS (NPC) under QIAO SHI. Without overtly challenging the rule of the Party, of which both men were senior members, Qiao and Tian called for greater emphasis on the rule of law, genuine elections and more youthful, better informed deputies.

Tian, a SHANDONG man with a long career in finance and agriculture behind him, was particularly outspoken. In 1995, in another controversial address, this time to the NPC, he said it was wrong that there tended to be the same number of candidates as positions during elections for ministerial and other posts. In other countries candidates defeated in elections regarded their participation as a matter of honour. They did not look upon defeat as a matter of shame. Those in China should do the same.

Tian also complained that when he looked down from his position on the rostrum of the NPC he saw too many bald heads in front of him and not enough dark hair – a reference to the fact that there were many retirees and time servers on the NPC's Standing Committee, the legislature's executive body. This call to arms was kept out of the Mainland media, too, though it was reported by a Communist-controlled newspaper in HONG KONG.

Tian's outspokenness, his closeness to Zhao Ziyang during the reforming days of the 1980s and his affiliation with Qiao Shi, raised questions about his future when LI PENG succeeded Qiao Shi as NPC chairman in 1998. Li had been a key antagonist of Zhao's and seemed less enthusiastic than either Qiao and Tian about the merits of democracy and the primacy of law. In the event Tian kept his job, perhaps as a concession to Qiao. But there were few reasons to believe that he would be able to work happily with a man he was at odds with for much of his career.

Tiananmen Square Democracy Movement (15 April–4 June 1989)

The rise and violent suppression of the largest urban protest movement in Chinese history, much of it conducted in front of an international television audience, provided graphic testimony of the limits of DENG XIAO-PING's reforms. Rarely had so many Chinese people demanded change in such a spontaneous yet concentrated fashion. Never had the CHINESE COMMUNIST PARTY faced such a direct challenge to its rule. And never, at least in the twentieth century, had a Chinese government been forced to take such drastic steps to remain in power. The armoured assault on Tiananmen Square on the night of 3–4 June 1989 saved Party rule, defined as the domination of China by a handful of veteran revolutionaries led by Deng. But it cost hundreds of lives, crushed the hopes of millions, and damaged China's international reputation. It also set back the cause of genuine modernization, blocking the road to political reform and creating huge historical and psychological burdens for the Party. Tiananmen dogs Chinese politics still: no significant political change can occur in China without a rehabilitation of the protest movement synonymous with its name.

hallowed ground

The location defined the movement in more ways than one. A vast open space in the centre of BEIJING, just south of the Forbidden City, Tiananmen Square has been the most potent political site in China since the start of the twentieth century. It is where official power – emanating from the Forbidden City under the emperors, and from a different location within the same complex under the Communists – meets the world of ordinary people. No other single location is so redolent of the triumphs and tragedies of China's modern history. There were demonstrations in Tiananmen Square during the MAY FOURTH MOVE-MENT of 1919, the birth of modern protest in China. In October 1949, MAO ZEDONG proclaimed the founding of the People's Republic of China from Tiananmen, which properly refers to the gate overlooking the Square. And in 1966, he occupied the same vantage point as hundreds of thousands of Red Guards gathered in the Square at the start of the CULTURAL REVOLUTION. Ten years later, crowds gathered there to commemorate the death of ZHOU ENLAI and criticize the 'GANG OF FOUR'. Flanked by the imposing yet grim bulk of the

Great Hall of the People on one side and the Museum of Revolutionary History on the other, the open space of the Square is infringed only by the monument to the martyrs of the Revolution and the much larger Mao Zedong Memorial Hall. Physically and symbolically it is the dead centre of Chinese political life.

What made it come alive in 1989 was the death on 15 April of HU YAOBANG, the disgraced former leader of the Communist Party. Many students, intellectuals and ordinary people looked upon Hu as a martyr. He had overseen the rehabilitation of thousands of those persecuted in the 'Anti-Rightist Movement' (see ONE HUNDRED FLOWERS MOVEMENT) and the Cultural Revolution. He had refused to take a tough line against pro-democracy student protests in 1986. The following year the old guard rewarded him with dismissal. When his death was announced, thousands of people marched into Tiananmen Square to commemorate the former leader, complain about his mistreatment and criticize his opponents. Their mourning took the form of demands for more democracy, less corruption and a dialogue with LI PENG, the unpopular, Soviet-educated premier. Li became the students' main personal target during almost seven weeks of protest that touched nearly every major city in China.

the call for change

Hu's death was the catalyst rather than the source of the unrest. Its roots lay in the previous decade of political, social and economic change ushered in by Deng's free market reforms. These had removed many of the political restrictions affecting everyday life, but left China's Leninist political structure intact. They had improved living standards, yet ushered in record inflation. They had enabled people to develop their talents and skills, but opened the door to official CORRUPTION on a scale not seen since 1949. They had allowed intellectuals more freedom than at any time since the early 1950s while subjecting them to occasional crackdowns that sometimes lasted just a few months. Above all, they had shown that at least some in the leadership were ready to countenance *fundamental* change of the kind that might make the government more open, responsive and representative. Perhaps this process could be helped along?

Students, first in Beijing, then almost everywhere in China where there were major institutes of higher education, spearheaded the protests. Full of idealism and energy, they took seriously their historical obligation to act as the conscience of the Chinese nation and point out the government's errors. They boycotted classes and formed new student unions to replace the official bodies whose role was to discipline rather than demonstrate. Gifted, articulate leaders emerged, such as Wang Dan (1965–), a history student, Wuer Kaixi (1968–), a student of education management, and Chai Ling (1966–), a psychology major.

While students made the running, other social groups joined in as the movement developed. Among them were workers whose low wages were eroded by inflation. The Federation of Autonomous Workers, the first independent workers' body set up since the Communist Revolution, was founded by Han Dongfang (1962–), a railway electrician. It set up a temporary headquarters in the northwest corner of Tiananmen Square, closest to the Great Hall of the People. As the government moved to suppress the protests, the Federation called on workers in Beijing to strike.

Private entrepreneurs also joined the ranks. Prominent among them was Wan Runnan (1946–) of Stone Corporation, an electronics company, which supplied the demonstrators with communications and printing equipment. China's infant capitalists were troubled by corruption and lack of legal protection for their activities.

Then there were the intellectuals. As the weeks went by, many of those who had been working from within the regime for change sided with the protestors. They gave up on Deng Xiaoping and the Party and joined the marchers, addressed crowds and wrote petitions. However, these 'establishment intellectuals' exercised little control over what remained a student-led movement. They often sought, unsuccessfully, to persuade the students to abandon their protests and avoid endangering the reformers in the Party led by ZHAO ZIYANG, Hu's successor as general secretary.

Another smaller group of independent, better organized intellectuals exerted more influence. Wang Juntao (1959–) and Chen Ziming (1952–), later punished heavily for their part in the protests, were never the 'black hands' behind Tiananmen as the Party alleged. The movement was far too large and diverse to be manipulated by any particular force. These two men certainly could not have done so – however experienced they might have been as a result of their participation in the DEMOCRACY WALL MOVEMENT of the late 1970s and other protests. Yet the independent nature of their activities, facilitated by the successful consultancy services and publications they had developed during the 1980s, made them something of a novelty in the context of Chinese politics – and a particularly dangerous one as far as the Party was concerned.

This coalition of forces might never have taken shape had the Party maintained its grip over the MEDIA. Journalists from virtually all major print and broadcast media took to the streets. Their participation, and the refusal of many editors to obey the Party and keep news of the demonstrations off the front pages, did much to link the protestors with ordinary people.

the Party strikes back

Deng insisted on a tough line against the protestors from the start. An editorial in the *People's Daily* on 26 April reflected his sentiments and those of the old guard. It described the movement as a planned conspiracy to overthrow the government. The effect was electric. Even more people poured on to the streets and into the Square to register their disgust. A dialogue between Party officials and student leaders achieved nothing. The rhythms of protest quickened to mark the anniversary of the May Fourth Movement, slowed, and then intensified again as the students began a hunger strike in support of their demands. Tiananmen became a vast, scruffy, but riotously colourful encampment. At its heart, surrounded by tents and plastered with posters, was the monument to the revolutionary martyrs, the kidnapped symbol of the Communist regime transformed into the headquarters of a massive opposition movement.

The demonstrators did not always behave democratically. Their demands were diverse, sometimes unfocused, often naive. Yet those who took to the streets of Beijing, Shanghai, Wuhan, Chengdu and scores of other cities in the spring of 1989 were united in their hatred of official corruption and inflation. They were at one in their demand for change in a system that not only bred such phenomena but denied ordinary people a meaningful say in determining their own lives and that of the nation. They wanted to choose their own leaders and monitor their performance rather than let a handful of veteran Marxists monopolize power. They wanted the freedom to

think, organize and publish – rights stipulated in the Chinese Constitution but denied to all but a tiny Communist elite; rights at the heart of any meaningful definition of democracy.

In this sense they presented a fundamental challenge to the handful of LONG MARCH veterans who ruled China from 'behind the screen', much as the EMPRESS DOWAGER had done in the dying days of the Qing Dynasty. Now that the protestors were attacking Deng and other members of the old guard personally, it was a challenge that could not go unanswered. For the veteran revolutionaries, the protests and insults were all too reminiscent of the Cultural Revolution when many of them had been physically abused and humiliated.

Yet meeting the challenge with force, the option they favoured from the first, was not easy. Mikhail Gorbachev, the Soviet leader, was due in Beijing for a historic visit on 15 May, bringing the international media with him. There was also a deep split within the formal Party leadership over how to handle the protests. Zhao opposed the use of force and, to the fury of the old guard, praised the students' patriotism in public. He broke with convention again during his talks with Gorbachev, revealing to the Soviet leader that the Chinese Politburo had passed a resolution requiring it to seek Deng's advice on all important issues. The challenge from the Square, and the threat from within the Party, were too much for the hardliners and their younger allies led by Li Peng and CHEN XITONG, mayor of Beijing. It was time to strike back.

martial law, military suppression

The old guard, meeting in secret, made the running and the formal Party apparatus fell into line. The only major dissenter in the leadership was Zhao who, isolated and exhausted by the struggle, was shoved aside. On 18 May, the Party decided to introduce martial law in parts of Beijing, making it the second city in China to suffer that indignity. Lhasa, capital of TIBET, was under military rule at the same time because of violent anti-Chinese unrest. The next day, a tearful Zhao appeared in the Square to urge the students to go home. It was his last public appearance before he was formally sacked, disgraced and confined to his house in Beijing.

The declaration of martial law on 20 May heightened tensions throughout the capital and stiffened the protestors' resolve. Citizens erected barricades at every major road junction leading to the Square. Hu Jiwei (1916–), a liberal-minded member of the NATIONAL PEOPLE'S CONGRESS (NPC), tried to persuade the legislature to examine the legality of Li Peng's declaration of martial law. The Party put a stop to that, just as it killed any hopes that Wan Li (1916–), the reformist chairman of the NPC, might support Hu's cause when he returned to China from a visit to North America. A few days after he arrived home (his flight conveniently diverted to Shanghai), Wan came out in support of martial law. The democracy movement's last major act of defiance was to erect the 'Goddess of Democracy', a striking replica of the Statue of Liberty, in the very Square that had been expanded to flatter the Communist leadership.

At first, the military assault on Tiananmen Square seemed to have failed: on the night of 2 June, troops rushed towards it from the east and the west but were soon surrounded, abused, humiliated and sometimes beaten up by protestors. Twenty-four hours later the People's Liberation Army launched a coordinated attack on the centre of Beijing with tanks, armoured cars and infantry drawn from several of China's armies so that none of them could ever claim not to have taken part in the attack on unarmed civilians. The resistance continued even as troops smashed their way through the barricades and gunned down those in their way. But by dawn the army had occupied the Square, destroyed the tented city and felled the Goddess of Democracy. Liu Xiaobo (c. 1958–), Hou Dejian (c. 1960–), Gao Xin (c. 1958–) and Zhou Duo (c. 1948–) – four prominent intellectuals who had staged a hunger strike near the monument – acted as intermediaries between the troops and the students allowing a coordinated exit of the remaining protestors. The government claimed to have put down a 'counter-revolutionary rebellion'. The old guard had been avenged.

Beijing under military occupation

However, the killings continued as protestors taunted the troops and rushed the defensive lines soldiers had formed near the Square. They were shot down. Elsewhere, bystanders were killed or wounded as troops in lorries opened fire while their drivers picked their way through the wreckage of barricades and other obstacles strewn across the road. Beijing

---

How Many Died?

When it sought to put over its version of events to a stunned world the government was quick to seize on the fact that no one – protestor, soldier or bystander – appears to have been killed *in* Tiananmen Square during the crackdown. The lack of fatalities in the sacrosanct heart of the capital has clouded the general issue of casualties ever since. In the hours after the military assault, a source at the Chinese Red Cross said 2,600 people had died. The Chinese government dismissed the figure as a fabrication. Amnesty International said in a thorough report on the movement published in 1990 that 'at least a thousand' had died. By the government's own admission on 6 June 1989, 300 people had died and 400 were still missing. Just over three weeks later the figures were adjusted. The official *Report on Checking the Turmoil and Quelling the Counter-revolutionary Rebellion* delivered by Chen Xitong, said: 'According to the information we have so far gathered, more than 3,000 civilians were wounded and over 200, including 36 college students, died during the riot. Among the non-military casualties were rioters who deserved the punishment, people accidentally injured, and doctors and other people who were carrying out various duties on the spot. The government will do its best to deal with the problems arising from the deaths of the latter two kinds of people.'

More than 10 years later it had yet to deal with such problems and hounded those who have tried to do so. Ding Zilin (c. 1939–), a former professor of philosophy in Beijing whose son was killed during the protests, spent much of the 1990s trying to contact others who had lost loved ones and friends during the crackdown. By the time of Deng Xiaoping's death in 1997, she had been in touch with 150 such families. Ms Ding also called publicly for punishment for those responsible for the killings, compensation and a formal apology. As a result, police were stationed outside her Beijing apartment twenty-four hours a day and her telephone was bugged. On at least one occasion, she and her husband were forced to leave the capital and live in the south.

---

gave every appearance of a city at war. The mood of shock gave way to terror – precisely what the government intended in order to show it was in charge and that defiance on such a scale would never be tolerated again. There was fury and fresh demonstrations in many provinces as news of the events in Beijing became known. But fear and resignation soon set in, and within a few days of the military occupation of Tiananmen Square popular resistance to the government throughout China was at an end.

Overseas, resistance and anger were just beginning. The West was stunned by Tianan-

Arrests, Executions, Purges and Trials

Thousands of 'rioters' were arrested all over China in the weeks following the crackdown. Some, particularly if they were workers accused of being involved in attacks on the army, were given summary trials and executed. The new independent student unions were declared illegal. A list, including photographs, of 21 most-wanted student leaders was publicized in newspapers and broadcast on television. The public were encouraged to report the whereabouts of the ringleaders by calling specially designated hotlines. Of the top four – Wang Dan, Wuer Kaixi, Liu Gang (c. 1961–) and Chai Ling – the first and third were caught while the second and fourth escaped to the West. They and many others fled by means of an 'underground railroad' organized by supporters. For more than a year after the suppression it continued to spirit dissidents out of China via Hong Kong or Macau.

Fang Lizhi, whose calls for more democracy earlier in the 1980s angered Deng Xiaoping and resulted in his expulsion from the Party, fled with his wife, Li Shuxian (1934–), to the United States embassy in Beijing. The couple spent a year in the American ambassador's residence until China agreed they could leave for exile to the US. The four intellectuals on hunger strike in the Square at the time of the assault spent brief periods in prison, as did other prominent activists, including Dai Qing (1943–), the controversial journalist and environmentalist. Most of them were not tried and soon released. There were exceptions: three protestors from Hunan arrested in May after they had thrown paint over Chairman Mao's portrait in Tiananmen Square were sentenced to 16 years, 20 years and life respectively. Not until early 1991 was the government ready to try those it regarded as the instigators of the unrest.

Well before then – in fact immediately after the bloodshed – the authorities had moved to stamp out the sources of the protests. Troops occupied key universities and research institutes in Beijing. A year's military training was made compulsory for new students attending elite universities in Beijing and Shanghai. Liberal academics were disciplined and some sacked. 'Work teams' were assigned to newspapers to bring them back under Party control. Army officers who had been reluctant to enforce martial law were

weeded out. Communist Party members were required to give an account of their participation in the democracy movement and their attitude towards its suppression. Political study classes were stepped up across the country.

These moves were accompanied by nationwide campaigns against the 'bourgeois liberalism' said to be behind the unrest, and 'peaceful evolution', the alleged attempt by the West to subvert China's socialist system. Purges of this kind were troublesome, but soon petered out in the face of widespread passive resistance. In China's half-reformed, half-open society, they showed the weakness of the Party rather than its strength.

The state revealed a stronger side when it brought those it had arrested before the courts. In set-piece, closed-door trials at which the verdicts, and probably the sentences, were decided beforehand, student leaders were jailed for between 2 and 6 years. Wang Dan was sentenced to 4 years in prison while Liu Gang, an older, politically astute and therefore more 'dangerous' student leader, received 6 years. Ren Wanding (1947–) a veteran human rights activist who played little part in the Tiananmen Square movement, was given 7 years, presumably because he had refused to change his views during an earlier spell in prison.

The longest sentences were imposed on Wang Juntao and Chen Ziming, the independent intellectuals whom the government regarded as the 'black hands' behind the movement. They were each sentenced to 13 years. Neither served their full term. Both were maltreated and became seriously ill while in jail. The same is true of the most senior Communist official tried for his part in the unrest. Bao Tong (1933–), a member of the Central Committee, was Zhao Ziyang's private secretary. He was detained immediately before the crackdown, and in 1992 was sentenced to 7 years in prison (including the two and a half years he had already spent in detention) for 'leaking state secrets' and 'counter-revolutionary propaganda and incitement'. His crime was to have let students in the Square know that the government was about to introduce martial law. On the tenth anniversary of Tiananmen, human rights groups in the West said at least 250 people were still serving prison sentences for their part in the protests.

---

men. The suppression was reported live on television and covered extensively by the print media, many of whose representatives had arrived in Beijing with Gorbachev and decided to stay on. The Chinese government was too preoccupied with the crisis to disrupt international telephone traffic or stop journalists arriving in the country immediately after the crackdown. The UNITED STATES and several European countries registered their dismay over the killings, and announced economic sanctions. However, none broke off diplomatic relations with Beijing over the

incident. The response in HONG KONG, a major source of moral and material support for the democracy movement, was more dramatic. More than 1 million people took to the streets to show their anger and sorrow at what had happened. Tiananmen poisoned relations between Britain and China for most of the territory's remaining years as a colony.

The failure of a single major leader to appear in the immediate aftermath of the bloodshed added to the widespread fear that China had no effective government and might fall prey to civil war. This anxiety lasted until 9 June when Deng was shown on television offering his condolences to the generals over the losses their troops sustained while 'suppressing the rebellion'. Though he looked frail, his appearance and, even more, what he said, marked the first genuine political initiative by the Communist Party since the death of Hu, seven long, hot weeks earlier. He said that this storm was 'bound to happen'. It was the result of domestic and international forces whose aim was to overthrow the Party, defeat socialism and plunge China into chaos. Fortunately, there were still some veteran Communists such as himself around to deal with a crisis that had clearly proved too much for the younger generation of leaders. Ultimately, the PEOPLE'S LIBERATION ARMY had demonstrated its loyalty. Just over two weeks after Deng's appearance, Zhao was formally dismissed from all his posts and replaced by JIANG ZEMIN. Hu Qili (1929–), Zhao's ally in the Politburo Standing Committee, was also sacked.

The Party's propaganda machine sprang back into life soon after troops secured Beijing. An official version of the rise and suppression of the 'counter-revolutionary rebellion' was delivered by Chen Xitong for consumption at home and abroad. A 'tiny handful of people' had exploited the student unrest to plot rebellion. Prominent intellectuals, including the dissident astrophysicist Fang Lizhi (1936–) who championed 'bourgeois liberalism', were the chief culprits (see DISSIDENTS). Their work had been aided by Zhao who had 'split the Party' and 'aided the turmoil'. Thanks to the veteran revolutionaries led by Deng and the heroism of the army, a major victory had been won. The 'turmoil' had been checked, the 'counter-revolutionary rebellion' quelled.

The police and state security apparatus resumed their normal duties, too. Virtually all the student leaders and others prominent in the movement who failed to flee the country were arrested. Repression was extended deep into universities, the media and other areas of life from which the democracy movement had sprung. A mood of obedience overshadowed by sullen resentment emerged. Not until January 1990 did the government feel secure enough to lift martial law and allow people unrestricted access into Tiananmen Square again.

Time and Tiananmen

Time has helped still the terror of Tiananmen. As early as 1992, the third anniversary of the bloodshed, the face of Beijing had changed thanks to a new burst of economic growth. Buildings sprayed with bullet holes during the assault were repaired and the sole physical signs of the assault on the Square were occasional faint tank tracks on the roads leading to it. Attitudes changed, too: for many, Tiananmen showed there was no future in politics. In Beijing and elsewhere it seemed wiser to concentrate on 'getting rich'. Yet, as one of the more literary slogans of 1989, scrawled in English on a subway wall, put it: 'All these things are to be answered for.' That is what the Party fears, and that is why every anniversary of the crackdown is the occasion of tension and heightened security in the Square and university district. Tiananmen cannot be confined to history. The idea that it was a 'counter-revolutionary rebellion', whose gravity warranted the rape of the capital by the military, and whose followers deserved death and long prison sentences, will have to be re-examined.

Throughout the 1990s, a handful of dissidents regularly called on the Party to do just that. They were usually hounded by the police for their pains, but they spoke for many more who lacked their courage. At the Communist Party's 15th National Congress in 1997, a letter by Zhao Ziyang demanding the same thing circulated unofficially among the delegates. In 1998 Bao Tong, Zhao's former secretary, emerged from prison and called for 4 June to be declared a 'national day of shame'. There are precedents, both in China and elsewhere, for the belated rehabilitation of a people's movement suppressed by the military. It happened in Taiwan, where the government apologized for the FEBRUARY 28TH INCIDENT of 1947 and compensated its victims. The process took more than 40 years to accomplish thoroughly. The island's Kaohsiung Incident of 1979 was redressed with greater speed (see TAIWAN).

In 1996, one former South Korean president was sentenced to death and another to 22 years in jail for, among other things, ordering the military suppression of the Kwangju Uprising of 1980 in which at least 200 pro-democracy protestors lost their lives. Much closer to home was the Chinese Communist Party's own reassessment of an earlier 'incident' in Tiananmen Square: the movement of April 1976 to commemorate the death of Zhou Enlai and protest against the 'Gang of Four' which paramilitary police suppressed. In 1978, what had been condemned at the time as a 'counter-revolutionary rebellion' was redesignated a 'patriotic revolutionary movement'. This was part of a sea change in Chinese politics occasioned by the death of Mao and the arrest of the 'Gang'. And it was a consequence rather than the cause of this change. At the start of the new century, the possibility of similar political upheavals in Beijing seemed remote: there were few prospects that the 1989 democracy movement would be re-examined in the immediate future.

Tianjin

For decades the second great commercial and industrial centre in China after SHANGHAI, Tianjin's importance has been obscured by proximity to BEIJING; the apparent conservatism of its inhabitants; and, in Communist times, years of neglect. City leaders tried to overcome all these obstacles during the reform era. Their efforts to recapture past glories met with some success. But the economic rebirth of Tianjin has made less impact than the revival of Shanghai or the rise of other commercial centres along the YANGTZE and further south. This hardly squares with the city's potential as the leading port and industrial centre of north China.

cosmopolitan enclave of the north

Foreign powers were under no illusions about the significance of Beijing's gateway to the sea. Sixty miles (96 kms) southeast of the capital, barely 20 miles inland from the Bohai Gulf, and located at the junction of the Hai River and the Grand Canal which kept Beijing supplied with vital grains from the south, Tianjin was the strategic crossroads of north China. It became a TREATY PORT and acquired all the trappings of a cosmopolitan enclave in Qing Dynasty China: foreign concessions, foreign buildings, foreign businesses, and the municipal councils, clubs, churches, newspapers and a racecourse that usually went with them. The arrival of the railway in the early years of the twentieth century made Tianjin even more important; it was the junction of the Beijing–Shanghai and Beijing–Harbin lines.

In terms of foreign presence (Britain, the United States, Japan, Russia, France, Germany, Belgium, Italy and Austria-Hungary each at one time owned concessions in the city) as in economic importance, Tianjin deserved the accolade 'Shanghai of the north'. Where it differed from the great metropolis to the south was in its history as a flourishing commercial centre long before the arrival of foreigners in the nineteenth century, and its closeness to the centre of political power in China. If the first was a cause of pride, the second made for a sensitivity towards China's national fortunes that constrained Tianjin but rarely troubled distant Shanghai. (See SHANGHAI.)

North China's fortunes in the early twentieth century turned on the outcome of a struggle for influence between Tsarist RUSSIA and JAPAN. Japan's victory in the Russo-Japanese War of 1904–5, much of it fought in northeast China, established Tokyo's primacy in the region and boosted its presence in Tianjin. Japanese influence of another kind was at work in the city in the shape of the constitutional reforms undertaken by YUAN SHIKAI, a leading official during the final years of the Qing. The military strongman of north China was determined to bring order to the region following the chaos of the BOXER REBELLION. His method, following that adopted in Japan, was to establish a modern police force and hold limited elections for a local assembly. The Tianjin Council, an attempt to establish bureaucratic control over an important urban centre, was elected in 1907.

Political novelties of this and other kinds were rare in Tianjin during the Republican era. Local students took part in the MAY FOURTH MOVEMENT of 1919, and were to the fore again in the December 1935 demonstrations against Japanese advances in north China in the run-up to the SINO-JAPANESE WAR. The presence of several prestigious colleges and universities in Tianjin ensured the city a high profile in such unrest (see EDUCATION). But there was no similar tradition of radicalism among workers in Tianjin, even though they constituted one of the largest concentrations of urban labourers in China. Unlike their brothers and sisters in Shanghai, the Tianjin proletariat did not rise to meet the troops of the National Revolutionary Army when they entered the city in 1928 at the closing stage of the NORTHERN EXPEDITION; and many were just as passive when the PEOPLE'S LIBERATION ARMY marched in just over 20 years later during the CIVIL WAR. On occasion Tianjin seemed aloof from the great dramas going on around it.

commercial centre

This was not the case as far as the economy was concerned. Before 1949 Tianjin was the financial, industrial and trade centre of north China – a vast region that stretched north into LIAONING and INNER MONGOLIA, and west across the north China plain. It was, and remains, the most convenient outlet to the sea for the northwestern provinces of SHAANXI, NINGXIA, GANSU, QINGHAI and even remote XINJIANG. This huge market was served by Tianjin's numerous foreign and domestic banks, a stock market, prosperous textile, concrete, chemical and carpet-making industries, and, of course, its port. Since this, located close to the heart of the city, became prone to silting and, in the north China winter, ice, the Japanese began work on a new one when they occupied the city during the Sino-Japanese War. Located at Tanggu, about 20 miles (32 kms) from the city centre, at the point where the Hai River meets the Bo Hai Gulf, it is still known as *Xingang*, 'new port', and is one of the largest in China.

Tianjin's industry grew rapidly under Communist rule as the new regime launched a programme of industrialization along Soviet lines. Investment was concentrated in capital-intensive plant for the production of machinery, iron and steel, electrical goods and petrochemicals. The city's significance as a major centre of production was reflected in its status as a province-level municipality directly under the central government in Beijing. At the start of the new century, the municipality of Tianjin covers an area of just over 4,365 square miles (11,305 sq kms) with a population of almost 10 million, more than half of whom live in the city proper and the remainder in suburban districts and counties.

too close to the capital

Industrialization, administrative change and rapid growth in population turned Tianjin into a major metropolis. They did less for the fabric of the city, which became shabby as local leaders turned their backs on Tianjin's traditional strengths as a centre of finance and light industry. The need for urban renewal become even more pressing following the 1976 earthquake in Tangshan, about 60 miles (96 kms) northeast of Tianjin. About 240,000 people died and a further 164,000 were injured in this calamity which took a heavy toll on the city. Rehabilitation work was still high on the agenda of LI RUIHUAN when he became mayor of Tianjin in 1981.

By that time, the city was keen to take advantage of China's new commitment to economic reform and opening to the outside world. On the face of it, it was well suited to do so: Tianjin had been north China's window on the outside world in the past and was eager to perform the same role again. Yet there were obstacles in the way other than those arising from three decades of lop-sided industrial development and urban neglect. Beijing was keen to let the south, comfortably removed from the centre of political power, experiment

with the new reforms first. The SPECIAL ECONOMIC ZONES had the advantages of proximity to Hong Kong and Taiwan, and a ready source of funds in the Overseas Chinese, most of whom hailed from the area. Tianjin was too close to Beijing to enjoy the benefits of decentralization and was denied the chance of going its own way.

The outlook improved in 1984. Tianjin was included in a list of 14 'Open Cities' which were granted greater autonomy in order to attract FOREIGN TRADE AND INVESTMENT. A Tianjin Economic Development Area (TEDA) was set up between the city and the port of Tanggu. It soon attracted high-quality investment and became one of the most successful zones of its kind. By the close of the century TEDA had grown rich and ambitious enough to purchase a stake in a development zone in Egypt, in the Gulf of Suez. A high-speed road, one of China's first, linked Tianjin municipality with Beijing. The development of the Dagang oil fields, onshore, just south of the city, and the offshore fields in the Gulf of Bohai, added to Tianjin's importance.

City officials pushed for greater attention and autonomy in the early 1990s in response to DENG XIAOPING's calls for faster, bolder reforms. The decaying foreign bank buildings that formed the heart of Tianjin's once vibrant financial district were refurbished and restored. Local newspapers revived memories of the district's past as the 'Wall Street' of north China. And the government appealed openly for Tianjin to be the location of China's third stock market following the successful, if sometimes controversial, establishment of exchanges in Shanghai and SHENZHEN. Beijing resisted, presumably on the grounds that had so often frustrated ambitions in Tianjin: the city's closeness to the capital.

rise and fall of Daqiuzhuang

Indeed, around the same time, Tianjin provided an unwelcome example of how much trouble it could cause Beijing – and itself – in the new get-rich-quick climate. The problem centred on Daqiuzhuang, a rural community south of the city. By 1990 the local Communist Party secretary, Yu Zuomin, had turned this poor village into the wealthiest in China by abandoning farming in favour of industry. Coverage in the official media was generally ecstatic. The entire village was turned into a corporation producing electronics, machinery and other goods, sometimes in co-operation with foreign partners. Real estate, both in Tianjin and further afield, was another source of the wealth that enabled many inhabitants to live in villas equipped with the latest household gadgets.

Yu was the richest of all and ran Daqiu-zhuang as his personal kingdom. This was clear when he detained and tortured those he believed to be guilty of corruption. One of them died as a result of mistreatment, but when Tianjin police arrived to investigate the matter, Yu had them detained. At one point paramilitary police advanced on Daqiu-zhuang only to be confronted by barricades and residents bearing makeshift weapons determined to defend their village. Conflict was avoided but Yu had overplayed his hand. He was arrested in 1993 and jailed for 20 years. The media said no more about 'China's richest village' other than to attack Yu's arrogance and flouting of the law.

There was little evidence that the drama at Daqiuzhuang harmed Tianjin's attempts to assert itself as the great commercial centre of north China. Rather, it was an example of the problems created by the decentralization at the heart of China's reforms, and the ease with which Party secretaries could become local chieftains. Tianjin's future was a separate, more important matter, even if local leaders often found securing it hard work.

Under the Ninth Five-Year Plan (1996–2000) and the long-term development programme for the period to 2010, the city is being developed as the hub of the Bohai Gulf Economic Zone, an area stretching from the Liaodong peninsula of southern Liaoning to the Jiaodong peninsula of eastern SHANDONG, and including the two municipalities of Beijing and Tianjin and the province of HEBEI that surrounds them. The area's heavy concentration of industry, advanced communications and abundant resources of minerals and energy have the potential to make it – and Tianjin – one of the richest regions in China.

Tibet

The fate of Tibet in the twentieth century offers a peculiarly intense example of the tumult and tragedy at the heart of China's modern history. The very fact that Tibet became an 'internal' part of that history, after long periods on the fringes of the Chinese world, had much to do with this. Unlike MONGOLIA, Tibet lacked a powerful foreign sponsor to nurture its independence at a time of Chinese weakness. It paid for this when China was strong. At the start of the twentieth century, most Tibetans did not wish to come to terms with the outside world. Neither did they want to be ruled by China. They managed to keep the world at bay for the best part of 50 years, but at the expense of raising questions about Tibet's international status that a militantly nationalist Communist China settled by force of arms in the 1950s.

Beijing has subjected Tibet's theistic culture to Communist revolution and rapid development. The costs have not necessarily been greater than elsewhere in China, but they are more visible. The partial destruction of a unique way of life has ensured that. So have the activities of the DALAI LAMA, the exiled religious leader. Both have made China's position in Tibet controversial, raising questions over HUMAN RIGHTS and the ENVIRONMENT, and casting a shadow over Beijing's relations with the West.

old Tibet and the end of isolation

As with China proper 60 years earlier, it was BRITAIN that first woke Tibet from its slumbers. The defence of INDIA required a secure northern frontier. That meant knowledge of what lay beyond the Himalayas, and a policy to guarantee its neutrality in the face of expansion by RUSSIA. Colonel Francis Younghusband's expedition to Lhasa of 1903–4 established a British interest in Tibet at the cost of a few skirmishes and several hundred Tibetan lives. During the upheaval, the 13th Dalai Lama (1876–1933) fled to Mongolia – one of several spells in exile he and his more celebrated successor endured in times of difficulty at home.

Younghusband penetrated an isolated society fashioned and favoured by the mountain ranges that protected it on all sides save that of China, from where access was slightly easier. Within these confines, noble and peasant, monk and official, lama and herdsman inhabited a feudal world united by adherence to the Tibetan variety of Buddhism and devotion to its chief representatives: the Dalai Lama and the PANCHEN LAMA. Both 'God Kings' reconciled temporal and spiritual power in their person, but the Dalai usually took precedence.

Land in Tibet belonged to the state and the

monasteries. Almost every family sought to send a son to the monastery, significantly reducing the working population. Sera, Dreprung and Ganden near Lhasa; Tashilhunpo close to Xigaze; Kumbum in QINGHAI; and Labrang in GANSU were the great monastic institutions and centres of learning.

Over the centuries Tibet was influenced by India, Nepal and China. It tasted both Mongol and Manchu-Chinese rule. But for long periods Tibetans – culturally and ethnically as unlike the Chinese as their lofty homeland is distinct from the rest of China – were left to themselves. Whether gathered in cities or scattered elsewhere across their vast homeland, they pursued the spiritual life and maintained a primitive rural economy free of the notions of progress and technological change transforming the world around them, China included. Neither the Shangri-La of Western myth, nor the 'feudal hell' of later Communist propaganda, Tibet simply wanted to be left alone.

the quest for autonomy, 1911–49

Britain's intrusion excited hopes that Tibet might be able to turn its *de facto* independence of China into *de jure* autonomy. This would suit Britain because it would make the Himalayan kingdom a more effective buffer against Russia. It would suit Lhasa because it would tie China's hands. Perhaps it would even be acceptable to distant Beijing? In exchange for genuine autonomy, Britain and Tibet were willing to recognize China's 'suzerainty' over the area, despite the fact that Tibetans had expelled Chinese troops during the REPUBLICAN REVOLUTION.

At the Simla Conference of 1913–14 representatives of Britain, Tibet and China agreed on the division of Tibetan territory into Inner (eastern) and Outer (western) Tibet, with full autonomy for the latter. Beijing quickly disowned the accord. Though weak and preoccupied with troubles closer to home, the new Republican government of YUAN SHIKAI refused to give up China's historic claims over all Tibet. Successive governments, Nationalist or Communist, weak or strong, took the same line, keeping the door to formal Tibetan independence closed and, before long, bolting it by means of military occupation.

This proved impossible before the Communist victory in the CIVIL WAR. During the 25 years leading up to it China relied on its small mission in Lhasa, and occasional military feints along the border, to try and bring Tibet

---

Who 'Owns' Tibet?

China bases its claim to sovereignty over Tibet on history – a complex, flexible tool that could be used to substantiate claims to present-day Vietnam and Korea with scarcely more imagination than that required to assert ownership over Tibet. Tibetan assertions of independence have been based on experience: for long periods of time, Tibet was *not* ruled by China, or by anyone save Tibetans. Yet even then, Tibetans often acknowledged China's importance. They sought the approval of Chinese emperors and, later, republican leaders, for their choice of spiritual leaders. Whatever the meaning of distant Sino-Tibetan dynastic marriages, meetings between Chinese emperors and Tibetan Dalais, and religious niceties, one fact stands out: Tibet fell under Chinese sway whenever a strong dynasty was in power. When China was weak, as it was from the late Qing until the foundation of the People's Republic, Tibet was free. As Chinese Communist troops entered its territory in 1950, Tibet met the international standards required for statehood. Lhasa even had a bureau for foreign affairs. But its government lacked the time, resources and diplomatic skills required to capitalize on the situation. The rest of the world was not very interested. The 1951 'Agreement on Peaceful Liberation' weakened any say the international community might have had in determining the status of Tibet. At the close of the twentieth century, the only route to Tibetan independence lay via a collapse of Chinese power – either in the region itself or China proper – or a formal concession by Beijing of the kind that would mark a major break with China's political past.

---

to heel. It also played on the rivalry that often existed in Tibetan politics between the Dalai Lama and the Panchen Lama. In 1923, the 9th Panchen (by Chinese count) fled to China, where he was nurtured as a Pretender. Until his death in 1937, he haunted his countrymen and the 13th Dalai Lama with the prospect that he would return to Tibet with a Chinese escort.

The SINO-JAPANESE WAR and the conflict between the KUOMINTANG and the CHINESE COMMUNIST PARTY postponed 'settlement' of the Tibet question. British policy towards the region, half-heartedly continued after 1947 by the government of independent India, failed to establish Tibet's autonomy. Everything depended on the military power and intentions of the Chinese government. By 1949 that government was the nationalist, revolutionary one of the People's Republic. And in 1950 it backed up its claim to Tibet by invading much of the territory.

revolt and repression

Tibetan military resistance soon crumbled, weakened by the defection of the Khampas in the east who resented rule from Lhasa. A Tibetan appeal to the UNITED NATIONS also failed. Negotiation with Beijing was the only option. In May 1951, Chinese and Tibetan officials signed an 'Agreement on the Peaceful Liberation of Tibet'. This 'Seventeen Point Agreement' granted autonomy to Tibet as part of China and pledged to leave the territory's traditional government, religion and society in place. Chinese troops were to enter the region. A military committee based in Lhasa would implement the accord, which applied to the domains administered by the government headed by the young Dalai Lama (the 14th, 1935–), not the much larger entity many Tibetans claimed as their homeland, but which had been incorporated into the provinces of SICHUAN, QINGHAI, GANSU and YUNNAN. The chief signatory on the Tibetan side was Ngabo Ngawang Jigme (1910–), who was to prove China's most trusted Tibetan.

The agreement formalized a longstanding *de facto* division of Tibetan territory, and subjected Tibetans either side of it to different experiences. Within the heartland controlled by the Dalai, Tibet's traditional way of life endured, though somewhat uneasily, alongside the powerful new Chinese presence. China brought ROADS, electricity, new buildings and other symbols of modernization to a region untouched by such novelties.

Tibetans further afield were subjected to the traumas of LAND REFORM, collectivization and communization that engulfed the rest of China. In the mid-1950s they rose up against this destruction of their traditional way of life. Beijing promised to delay reforms in Tibet proper on the grounds that the region was not ready, but Tibetans elsewhere stepped up their resistance to Communism and extended the fight closer to Lhasa. Pitched battles took place. There were many casualties. The CIA, whose masters sought every opportunity to weaken the Communist regime, supplied the rebels with arms and money.

By 1959 Tibet was in turmoil. In Lhasa much depended on the attitude of the Dalai Lama. Both rebels and Chinese had an interest in claiming him as their own and, perhaps, kidnapping him should he prove uncompliant. In early March thousands of Tibetans surrounded the Norbulingka, the Dalai's palace, to protect their God King. They disregarded Chinese orders to disperse. Tension in the city, and elsewhere in Tibet, was high. On 17 March, the Dalai and his entourage fled in secret to India, a remarkable escape that took them across some of the world's most forbidding terrain.

Dalai Lamas and Panchen Lamas had fled Tibet before, in some cases never to return. But the flight of the 14th Dalai marked a true departure in Tibetan history. Not only had the symbol of the Tibetan state fled abroad, but the government, economic system and religious way of life left behind were swiftly destroyed: Tibet was brought fully into the fold of Chinese Communism. Destruction of a distinct culture made the consequences of revolution in Tibet seem even more calamitous than its effects elsewhere.

With the Dalai, most of his cabinet and thousands of his followers in exile, opposition to Chinese policies in Tibet lost its most influential voice. A United Nations resolution of 1959 condemned China's violation of human rights in Tibet, but remained silent on the question of Tibet's international status. Yet not everyone was silenced. In 1962 the Panchen Lama, then the most senior Tibetan leader in the country, wrote a 70,000-word petition to ZHOU ENLAI, attacking the way China suppressed the rebellion. Thousands of Tibetans had been killed, thousands more died as a result of the famine caused by the GREAT LEAP FORWARD, and many had been sent to LABOUR CAMPS. Monasteries had been closed or destroyed. The Tibetan nationality faced extinction – something only Chinese Communism had been able to achieve.

What was regarded as valuable criticism in 1962 became, in the words of MAO ZEDONG, a 'poisoned arrow' during the run-up to the CULTURAL REVOLUTION. In 1964 the Panchen was criticized as an 'anti-Party element'. He spent the following 14 years in prison or under house arrest. This was little compared to the suffering endured by his homeland, defined from 1965 as the Tibet Autonomous Region (TAR) (see ETHNIC MINORITIES). Chinese and Tibetan Red Guards extended Mao's pursuit of revolutionary purity to the region, destroying what remained of an ancient way of life.

the 1980s: relaxation to repression

With the death of Mao and the arrest of the 'GANG OF FOUR', Beijing abandoned revolution in Tibet, as it did elsewhere. It began to justify its position in the territory solely in terms of the prosperity it had brought the inhabitants. Emissaries of the Dalai Lama were not impressed when they returned home in 1979 and 1980. They saw at least as much poverty as existed before 'peaceful liberation' and more devotion to the Dalai than any of them had expected. In extraordinary scenes that embarrassed the authorities, they were engulfed by demonstrations of affection – a negative but powerful expression of Tibetans' hatred of Chinese rule.

Beijing was sensitive to the problem and, within limits, sought to make amends. In 1980, HU YAOBANG, newly appointed general secretary of the Communist Party, visited Tibet. He delivered the closest thing to a *mea culpa* Chinese Communism allowed. Tibetans were still poor. The Party had let them down. In future, they would run their own affairs. Tibetan culture and language would be revived. There would be new emphasis on economic development and more aid from the central government. It was a new start for Tibet, though still one that required Tibetans' unconditional acceptance of Chinese sovereignty.

As elsewhere in China, the early 1980s was a period of political relaxation in Tibet. The economy began to stir. Some monasteries were rebuilt. Religious life revived. Perhaps it would be possible after all for a distinct Tibetan identity to re-emerge and survive under Chinese rule?

Yet what kind of identity would it be? Who would define it? Would it be Beijing? Would Tibetans inside Tibet be allowed to do so? And what of the Dalai Lama and his exiled government in Dharamsala, northwest India? The Western world, newly (and belatedly) sensitized to the horrors of Mao's rule, took an interest. Almost alone among the diverse lands Beijing insisted on calling 'China', Tibet was becoming an international issue again. Not only did it engage the attention of foreign governments, Tibet also caught the popular imagination in the West. The cost to China of reform and opening up was closer monitoring and frequent criticism of its policies in Tibet.

Regular, if surreptitious, contact between Tibetans and their exiled leader was another consequence of China's new approach. The Dalai launched an international campaign for his homeland which took him round the world and brought him into contact with world leaders, despite fierce objections from Beijing.

His words did not fall on deaf ears at home. In 1987, he unveiled a Five Point Peace Plan. China rejected it, sparking riots and demonstrations in Lhasa. There were more protests, and deaths, in 1988. In the same year the Dalai called on Beijing to grant Tibet the kind of autonomy promised HONG KONG: self-government in everything save foreign affairs and defence. Tibet would be 'de-militarized' as part of the deal. Its fragile environment would be protected. There was talk about talks between the two sides, but nothing came of it.

In January 1989, the Panchen Lama died, shortly after making a speech critical of Chinese policy towards Tibet. The Dalai declined China's invitation to attend the funeral in Beijing. He believed more could be achieved abroad. In March serious unrest broke out in Lhasa, forcing China to declare martial law in the city. About 200 protestors were killed and thousands arrested. Martial law remained until May 1990, by which time China was still being ostracized for its suppression of the TIANANMEN SQUARE DEMOCRACY MOVEMENT. Beijing seemed everywhere on the defensive. The time for talks with the Dalai, by then holder of the Nobel Peace Prize, again seemed ripe.

dealing with the Dalai

Contacts were fitful in the early 1990s and abandoned in 1993. The stumbling block was Beijing's insistence that Tibet was an 'inalienable' part of China. China's main aim was to entice the Dalai home. Its position hardened as the Chinese economy grew stronger and Western criticism of its human rights record abated. It seemed wiser to solve the problem of Tibet by transforming the region from within rather than negotiating with its exiled leader. Revolution had not tamed Tibet. Perhaps rapid development would?

Certainly development was needed. At the end of the twentieth century, Tibet was the only province without a railway. Medog, one of its counties, was the only one in China without a road. The region's gross domestic product was minuscule by comparison with every other province. Nearly half a million of its 2.4 million people lived below the poverty line. Access to HEALTH and EDUCATION was poor compared with other parts of China. By mid-1997, Tibet had attracted a meagre US$237 million in foreign investment. Even the hotel chain Holiday Inn withdrew from Lhasa.

Beijing adopted a multi-pronged strategy to deal with these problems and reconcile Tibet to Chinese rule. First it cracked down hard on all manifestations of separatism, even whisking defiant monks and nuns off to prison. Several hundred activists remain in detention at the start of the new era. Second, it worked

Tibet

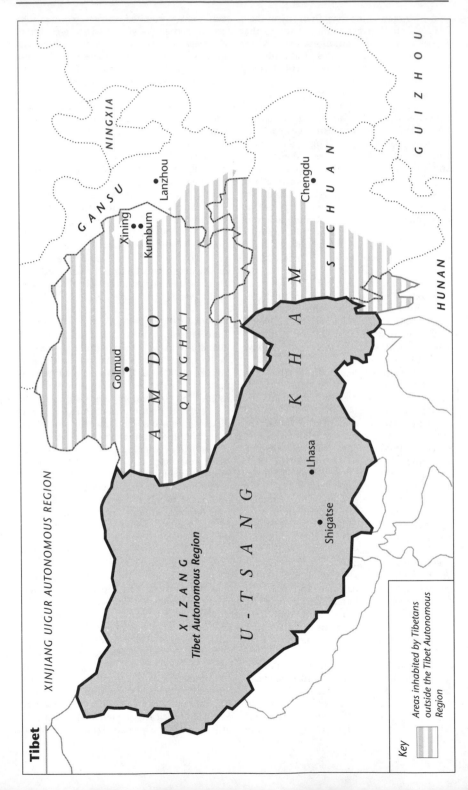

XINJIANG UIGUR AUTONOMOUS REGION

NINGXIA

GANSU

Lanzhou

Xining Kumbum

SICHUAN

Chengdu

GUIZHOU

HUNAN

AMDO

QINGHAI

Golmud

KHAM

Lhasa

XIZANG
Tibet Autonomous Region

U - TSANG

Shigatse

Key

Areas inhabited by Tibetans
outside the Tibet Autonomous
Region

Land and People

Many Tibetans are at odds with China over the size of their homeland as well as its history. The Tibetan government in exile maintains that Tibet is much bigger than the present Autonomous Region, and includes the traditional Tibetan areas of Amdo and Kham in the east. This 'Greater Tibet' is more than twice the size of the present one. By the late 1990s there were more than 4.5 million Tibetans in China, 2.4 million of whom lived in the TAR. Those who lived outside, in what was east Tibet before it was divided up into the provinces of GANSU, QINGHAI, SICHUAN and YUNNAN, were long ago outnumbered by Chinese who moved into the area in large numbers after the Communist Revolution. Within the TAR, the least populated of all of China's provinces or autonomous regions, more than 97 per cent of the population were said to be Tibetan. Few Chinese live in rural areas of the TAR, but thousands moved into Lhasa.

In the late 1990s, the Tibetan capital began to look and feel like many other cities in China. There was also a strong military presence in the region, almost all of it Chinese. Little about Tibet's geography is 'Chinese'. The Tibetan plateau offers some the most stunning scenery in the world, all of it entirely different from that in other parts of the country Beijing says it belongs to. The average height of the plateau is 4,000 metres yet it is still surrounded by towering mountain ranges. The Himalayas protect Tibet from India, Nepal and Bhutan in the south. In the west the Karakoram range divides Tibet from Pakistan. The Kunlun mountains to the north separate XINJIANG and Tibet, while in the east, the traditional boundary between Tibet and China is situated in the Hengduan range. Some of Asia's mightiest rivers rise within these confines, including the Yangzte, the Yellow River, the Salween, the Indus and the Brahmaputra.

for the economic and ethnic integration of Tibet with the rest of China. This meant allocating huge subsidies to the region and allowing an influx of Chinese to use the funds for development and modernization. The effects were rapid and conspicuous. In the late 1990s, at least half of Lhasa's population were Han Chinese. In terms of architecture as well as demography, the capital of Tibet was becoming a Chinese city.

The new forward policy extended to religion. Restoration of monasteries, and the complete refurbishment of the Dalai's Potala Palace, were undertaken. There was a minor revival in religious life. Beijing undertook this work partly with international tourism in mind. But it was more concerned to win hearts and minds in Tibet by appearing as the patron of traditional culture. The price was tighter control over the conduct of religious life. An

example was a campaign in the monasteries to denigrate the Dalai Lama as a heretic and charlatan as well as the 'splittist' propaganda had always held him to be. Monks and nuns were subjected to these views during 'patriotic re-education' campaigns.

The most remarkable episode in this war of ideas between the atheistic government and the followers of the living Buddha concerned the search for the 11th Panchen Lama. Teams of Tibetans started combing the scriptures and the countryside for portents of the child almost immediately after the 10th Panchen's death. The Dalai was kept informed of progress and, in May 1995, suddenly announced that he had recognized a six-year-old, Gedhun Choekyi Nyima, as the next reincarnation. The God King was determined to assert his authority ahead of any official announcement from Beijing.

The gamble did not pay off. China's leaders were furious. They could not accept the prior, apparently unilateral, choice from outside the country, of the Dalai Lama. In keeping with their imperial predecessors, they insisted on exercising the power to confirm any reincarnation.

New candidates, excluding the Dalai's, were selected and leading lamas instructed to make a choice. After customary rituals, Gyaincain Norbu, a five-year-old from Nagqu prefecture, was chosen as the 11th Panchen. He was enthroned at Tashilhunpo Monastery in Xigaze in 1996. President JIANG ZEMIN, again emulating emperors of old, sent a plaque bearing the inscription 'Protect the Country, Benefit the People.'

The fate of the 'Dalai's Panchen' was unknown. He became an object of concern for human rights groups overseas. So did Chadrel Rimpoche (1944–), abbot of Tashilhunpo, who had kept in contact with the Dalai during the search and supported his choice of Gedhun Choekyi Nyima. He was jailed for 6 years in 1996 for 'splitting the nation'. Work teams were sent to the monasteries to extract declarations of loyalty to 'China's Panchen' and further condemnation of the Dalai, whose influence the authorities were determined to eradicate.

The exiled leader, still tireless in his campaign and apparently ready to talk to Beijing, seemed to have been left out in the cold by these developments. Time was not on his side. His death presumably will allow the Chinese to control the search for *his* next reincarnation, as they did that of the Panchen.

Beijing would then be in control of both 'God Kings', and, indirectly, in control of Tibet, too.

However, at the close of 1999, China's attempts to control the process of recognizing, installing and educating major reincarnated lamas suffered a setback. The 14-year-old Karmapa Lama, ranked third in Tibetan Buddhism after the Dalai and the Panchen, fled Tibet for India. In the absence of convincing alternative explanations, there was little doubt that the boy, Ugyen Trinley Dorje, whom both the Dalai Lama and Beijing recognized as a living Buddha, left his homeland to escape curbs on his activities and further his religious studies. He and his advisers believed both goals could be accomplished best by joining the Tibetan community in exile.

The dramatic flight of the Karmapa confirmed that decades of Chinese control over Tibet had failed to command the allegiance even of those whom Beijing had nurtured most intensively. At the same time it was a reminder that such allegiance, though desirable, has never been Beijing's ultimate goal. China retains its hold over Tibet, not so much for its own sake, but because it believes the region has always belonged to the Chinese world. A Chinese government unable to rule Tibet would be weak. It would be a pale imitation of the great empire established in the eighteenth century by the Qing Dynasty, and therefore to be despised. The fact that control of Tibet offers strategic advantages relative to India, and valuable mineral resources, is important but, ultimately, secondary. A desire to demonstrate power is foremost. Respect for, and even interest in, Tibet's unusual history and culture is a decidedly minority pursuit among Chinese. And support for Tibetan independence is rare even among Chinese DISSIDENTS.

In all these respects, Tibetans under Chinese rule are peculiarly alone. They are outnumbered and outgunned. Their essentially spiritual culture is overwhelmed by that of the militantly materialistic Chinese. Given such odds it is hard for them to maintain a true Tibetan identity.

That does not stop them from trying. They remain peculiarly tenacious in the defence of their way of life and in their adherence to the Dalai, despite his long absence. In the course of 50 years the Communist Party transformed Tibet as violently as it had the rest of the country. Beginning in the early 1980s, it sought to make up for it by making Tibetans rich. Many have become better off. Even more have enjoyed the return of limited religious freedoms and other glimpses of a past life that had been taken from them. But this hardly amounts to gratitude, still less allegiance to China. Much has changed in Tibet. But at the start of the new century, as during the 1950s, the region's Communist newspapers are still preoccupied with the threats posed by the 'splittists', and minor protests against Chinese rule still occur as do sporadic outbreaks of pro-nationalist terrorism. The Tibetans' desire to be left alone is still alive.

treaty ports

The fruit of China's encounter with the West in the nineteenth century, treaty ports remained sources of modernization and, for Chinese nationalists, symbols of humiliation in the twentieth – until BRITAIN and the UNITED STATES finally relinquished the rights on which they were based during the Second World War. Their disappearance, along with EXTRATERRITORIALITY, under which they flourished, marked the end of a chapter in China's encounter with the outside world.

ports, concessions and leaseholds

Many 'treaty ports' were not opened by treaty and some were not so much ports as remote inland towns whose value was political rather than commercial. The term 'treaty port' is used here to describe all of them, as well as other areas of China subject to foreign control or preponderant influence. Exceptions include Britain's *possessions* (granted in perpetuity) of Hong Kong Island and Kowloon (see HONG KONG), the Portuguese-administered territory of MACAU, and Japan's 'puppet state' of MANCHUGUO.

SHANGHAI in the 1920s was the classic example of the treaty port: a mighty commercial centre built and run by foreigners who replicated much of the wealth and power of home – including social class and other conventions – in a distant, foreign clime. The Chinese government 'opened' Shanghai under duress, in this case the 1842 Sino-British Treaty of Nanjing which ended the Opium Wars, and was forced to open scores more ports later in the century following defeats

Treaty Ports and Foreign Territories

Key

- Ports opened by 1900
- Ports opened 1900–1920
- Major cities that never became treaty ports
- Foreign Leased Areas, 1898

  Port Arthur and Liaotung Peninsula (Kwantung) *(Russian)*
  Weihaiwei *(British)*
  Kiaochow *(German)*
  Kowloon New Territories *(British)*
  Kwang-chow-wan *(French)*

- Neutral zones

0   500 km
0   300 miles

RUSSIA

Russian influence

Aigun

Manzhouli

Qiqihaer

MONGOLIA   MANCHURIA

Harbin

Suifenhe

Changchun   Jilin

Hunchun

Japanese influence

Shenyang

Niuchuan

BEIJING

Dongdan
Dadongkou

Tianjin

Dalian

Longkou   *Weihaiwei (Br.)*

Taiyuan

Yantai

KOREA

Lanzhou

Jinan

German influence

Qingdao

Yellow R.

Haizhou

Xian

Zhenjiang

JAPAN

Chengdu

Wanxian

Nanjing   Suzhou
Wusong

British influence   Shanghai

Chongqing

Ichang

Wuhu   Hangzhou

Shashi

Ningbo

Yangtze R.

Changde

Jiujiang

Yuezhou

Nanchang

Guiyang

Changsha

Wenzhou

Kunming

Fuzhou

Dengyue

French influence

British influence

Xiamen   Tamsui

Simao

Mengzi

Japanese influence

Wuzhou

Guangzhou   Shantou

TAIWAN

Longzhou

Nanning

Sanshui

Hong Kong (Br.)

Tainan

Macao

Beihai

FRENCH INDO-CHINA

GUANGZHOUWAN
French influence

Qiongzhou

Hainan

PHILIPPINES

at the hands of the powers. It opened some centres of its own volition to avoid having to do so on unfavourable terms. Nanning in GUANGXI was an example. It was opened to foreign trade and residence in 1901. Though commercially and politically insignificant, Nanning, like Shanghai, was a treaty port.

In the major treaty ports, foreigners lived in concessions or settlements set aside for their residence. They formed municipal councils, raised taxes, established police forces and built hotels, offices, churches and clubs. Many of their buildings, put to new purpose long ago, survive in Shanghai, TIANJIN, Wuhan and elsewhere at the start of the new century. In the lesser ports there were no concessions: foreigners lived among the Chinese community and tried to survive on such pleasures as their work and limited social life could provide.

In none of the treaty ports (as opposed to the leaseholds) was China's sovereignty explicitly extinguished. It still owned the land, which was leased either to foreign governments or foreign nationals. This was a technical matter. In every treaty port foreigners, their schools, businesses and mission stations were exempt from Chinese law and taxes. Extraterritoriality gave them the right to be tried in China according to the laws of their own country in courts set up for the purpose.

By early 1900, hardly an important city in China had not been 'opened' for trade and residence. Worse, the embattled QING DYNASTY had to contend with powers 'lopping off' parts of the country and turning them into 'leaseholds' (see opposite.) The 'scramble for concessions' of the late 1890s spurred the development of modern nationalism. KANG YOUWEI, an early exponent, believed his country was being sliced up 'like a melon'. He was right: in the leased territories, unlike the treaty ports, Chinese sovereignty was alienated by the lessees for the duration of the lease.

'Spheres of influence' were another manifestation of the treaty port phenomenon. Fluid and less well defined than ports or leased territories, they were areas, sometimes occupying two or more provinces, where foreign powers claimed preponderant interests. Sometimes they did this by agreement among themselves; sometimes by agreement with the Chinese government, which promised not to let third parties make their presence felt. Within their 'spheres of influence', foreign governments and companies sought to dominate the construction of railways, mining and other major projects.

models of modernization

The influence of treaty ports on Chinese society, broadly defined, was immense. Minor inland ports were an exception: some were closed as of little value soon after they opened. MISSIONARIES, in direct contact with the local population, often in remote stations, proved of more lasting influence. However, the emergence of major cosmopolitan centres such as Shanghai and, to a lesser extent, Tianjin, Wuhan, Dalian and Guangzhou was another matter. It was not that these cities became racial melting pots: mixed marriages were relatively rare, and social intercourse between foreigners and Chinese was frequently confined. Most foreign residents lived as if they were at home in everything from their tastes in food to their leisure pursuits. Few took an interest in the Chinese world beyond the boundaries of the Settlement – other than in the sense that it concerned life in the treaty port itself or the prospects for their business. In outlook and behaviour, most of those who lived in the Settlement could hardly claim to be bearers of a superior or sophisticated civilization.

Yet the foreign and Chinese communities interacted in a host of ways. Treaty ports were sources of ideas and instruments of cultural transmission. For some Chinese, the paved roads, motor cars, manicured lawns, modern police forces of the foreign concessions, though reminders of the gap between their country and the powers, also acted as a spur to reform. If foreigners could do this, why should Chinese not be able to do so? This idea of the treaty ports as an inspiration was apparent in the writings of Kang Youwei and SUN YAT-SEN at the turn of the century.

It also occurred to Kang, Sun and other Nationalists that the treaty ports were *obstacles* to China's reform and rejuvenation. The insistence of foreigners on their treaty rights, including the ports, extraterritoriality and control over import tariffs (see TARIFF AUTONOMY) pending significant Chinese reforms, was exactly what made such reforms impossible. Few foreigners in China in the early decades of the century seemed able to grasp the point that the treaty ports brought more blight than benefit as far as Nationalists were concerned.

However, that the foreign enclaves (again, particularly Shanghai), were useful as well as instructive was beyond doubt. For one thing, as islands in the storm of early twentieth-century politics they provided havens for

Leased Territories

Area	Country	From	Restored
Jiaozhou Bay in Shandong (193 sq miles/500 sq kms)	Germany	March 1898 (for 99 years)	Occupied by Japan 1914–22, when restored
Liaodong peninsula, including Dalian and Port Arthur (1,438 sq miles/3,724 sq kms)	Russia	March 1898 (for 25 years)	Occupied by Japan 1905–1945, when restored
New Territories, Hong Kong (306 sq miles/793 sq kms)	Britain	June 1898 (for 99 years)	1997, under 1984 Sino-British Joint Declaration
Weihaiwei, Shandong (552 sq miles/1,430 sq kms)	Britain	July 1898 (for as long as Russia holds Port Arthur)	By agreement in 1930
Guangzhou Bay, port opposite Hainan Island (325 sq miles/842 sq kms)	France	May 1898 (for 99 years)	1945

Chinese radicals to escape arrest and organize. Shanghai boasted a lively press and modern publishing industry free of China's censorship laws. Revolutionary ideas circulated in the city. Some of them, such as nationalism and MARXISM, fed on treaty port practice: racism and capitalist exploitation of China.

treaty ports under attack

An end to the imperial privileges that made this possible was a primary goal of the reorganized KUOMINTANG in the mid-1920s. As its armies swept north during the NORTHERN EXPEDITION, opposition to the foreign presence intensified. In the treaty ports, missionaries, merchants, even diplomatic staff were attacked and sometimes killed. Britain sought to stem the tide with salvoes from gunboats, but it restored the concessions in Hankou (modern Wuhan) and Jiujiang to China after they were attacked by angry protestors. These were Britain's most conspicuous defeats in China since the days of the Opium Wars (see BRITAIN). It was followed by the voluntary rendition of concessions in Zhenjiang, Xiamen and, in 1930, the leased territory of Weihaiwei.

The ascendancy of CHIANG KAI-SHEK in the later 1920s marked an end to popular antiforeign movement. Instead, Chiang made recovery of lost territories, the end of extraterritoriality and tariff autonomy principal aims of his diplomacy. He secured the latter in 1928, the year in which things even

began to change in foreign-ruled Shanghai: the municipal council opened its doors to Chinese representatives, and well-dressed Chinese were allowed into the city's parks. However, the treaty ports and extraterritoriality endured for a further 15 years. They were abolished by agreements with Britain and the United States in 1943, by which time China was regarded as one of the 'big four' Allied powers in the fight against Japan. It no longer seemed appropriate to maintain a century-old system of imperial privilege in China.

The agreements of 1943, implemented at the conclusion of the SINO-JAPANESE WAR in 1945, did not imply an end to the foreign presence in China. Shanghai and other cities might have remained cosmopolitan centres under Chinese rule. The Communist victory in 1949 put a stop to that. The treaty port past and the presence of so many foreigners were incompatible with the goals and ethos of the new regime. China's involvement in the KOREAN WAR made things even more difficult. Foreigners of all professions – businessmen, missionaries and diplomats – were slowly squeezed out of the cities over which their predecessors had long held sway and in some cases even founded. Treaty ports and their many iniquities became lightning rods of the new nationalism: some of it redolent of earlier forms of xenophobia dressed up in the modern language of class struggle and hatred of capitalism.

Tumen River Economic Zone

This trade and development zone, located along the river where the borders of China, Russia and North KOREA meet, is designed to realize the advantages of economic cooperation in an area riven with historic rivalries. Described by some of its protagonists

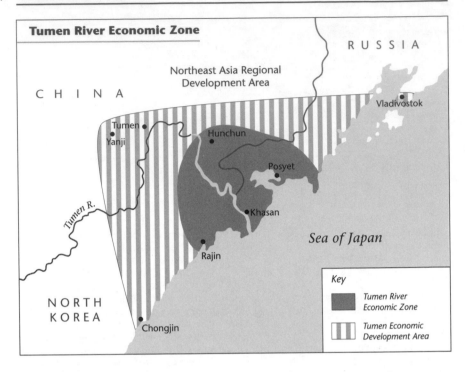

Tumen River Economic Zone

Northeast Asia Regional Development Area

RUSSIA

CHINA

Vladivostok

Tumen
Yanji

Hunchun

Posyet

Tumen R.

Khasan

Sea of Japan

Rajin

NORTH
KOREA

Chongjin

Key

Tumen River
Economic Zone

Tumen Economic
Development Area

as the 'Rotterdam of the East', it is the heart of a potential Northeast Asian trade area encompassing MONGOLIA, northeast China, the Russian Far East, JAPAN and the two Koreas. A main advantage for Beijing is that it promises a new outlet to the sea for HEILONG-JIANG and JILIN, the two provinces of northeast Manchuria, whose products must pass through Dalian, the major port in LIAONING, hundreds of miles to the south.

North and South Korea, China, Russia and MONGOLIA adopted an action plan for the project in 1992 under the auspices of the United Nations Development Programme (UNDP). They envisaged an investment of US$30 billion over 20 years.

The zone itself is a 625-square-mile (1619 sq kms) triangle of territory bounded in the north by the Chinese city of Hunchun, Russia's Posyet in the northeast, and Rajin, North Korea's first special economic zone, to the southwest. Russia and North Korea meet

in a ribbon of territory along the coast, depriving China of direct access to the Sea of Japan by a mere 2 or 3 miles. This is a galling matter for Beijing: China enjoyed access to the Sea of Japan, further north, until Tsarist Russia seized northeast Manchuria in 1860.

The zone is envisaged as the core of a powerful new regional economy built on cheap Chinese and North Korean labour, the untapped natural resources of Mongolia and Siberia, and the financial and technological power of Japan and South Korea. Its location offers the prospect of faster sailing times across the Pacific for goods bound to and from north China, and a quicker rail route across Central Asia to Europe. These advantages have drawn the potential beneficiaries into discussions about cooperation. They have yet to overcome the mutual wariness, historic suspicions, and shortage of investment which stand in the way of carrying it out.

Tung Chee-hwa (1937–)

The first chief executive of the HONG KONG Special Administrative Region (SAR) – and thus the first Chinese 'governor' of Hong Kong – was a Shanghai-born businessman whose political conservatism appealed to both Beijing and the local commercial elite. His decent, avuncular nature also made him acceptable to a cross-section of Hong Kong people. But his low profile, tendency to deliver homilies when candour and initiative were required, and apparent distaste for politics made it hard for him to become genuinely popular. So did his stress on the 'Chinese' values of community and responsibility rather than the personal freedoms valued, if not always articulated, by many in Hong Kong.

Tung's father, C. Y. Tung, founder of the family's Orient Overseas shipping business, fled Shanghai for Hong Kong to escape Communism. Tung junior, 'C. H.' to his friends in the international community, was educated in Britain and spent several years in the UNITED STATES. In the 1980s China's economic reforms helped close the gulf between the family and its homeland. Mainland business ties proved particularly valuable when the family faced heavy debt: local pro-China figures and the Bank of China provided a US$120 million bail-out.

Tung Chee-hwa was selected chief executive in December 1996 by a 400-strong committee made up of Beijing's allies in the territory. He won 320 votes against 42 for Sir T. L. Yang, who gave up his position as chief justice to stand, and 36 for Peter Woo, another prominent businessman. It was clear long before the election that Tung would be chief executive. He was 'anointed' almost a year earlier by President JIANG ZEMIN who surprised those attending a gathering of Hong Kong worthies in Beijing by singling Tung out for a particularly warm handshake.

Tung's 'election' was a more democratic process than that surrounding the selection of British governors of Hong Kong, who were appointed by the Queen on the recommendation of the prime minister. But it left much to be desired. The Basic Law, Hong Kong's mini-constitution, does not provide for the selection of the chief executive by universal suffrage before the year 2007.

After his selection, Tung – a member of

CHRIS PATTEN's executive council throughout the long battle with Beijing over the pace of democracy in Hong Kong – distanced himself from British rule. Hong Kong's outgoing and incoming 'governors' met rarely during the last six months of British rule. But they sparred frequently over the fate of the territory's legislature and its freedoms, adding a new element of tension to the final stages of the transition.

Tung lacked the personal touch that made Patten popular, inviting unfavourable comparisons with Hong Kong's last British governor. He compensated for this by enjoying the trust of Beijing, whose leaders left Hong Kong alone immediately after the handover on 1 July 1997. Tung emphasized the 'one country' element of the 'one country, two systems' formula China had devised for the recovery of Hong Kong. This did not please everyone, but it went down well in Beijing.

Partly as a result, Tung and his team of executive councillors, many of whom had pro-China business backgrounds, ran the territory unhindered, and the civil service, a thoroughly British institution, functioned with little change. The post-handover legislature – a 'provisional' body set up by Beijing to replace that elected under British rule – offered little challenge to executive rule. The legislature elected in May 1998 proved more lively thanks to strong support at the polls for Democratic Party candidates and their allies, even though the voting method was stacked against them.

C. H. Tung faced his first serious crisis in 1999. The Hong Kong court of final appeal ruled against the government, and indirectly against Beijing, by opposing the attempts of both to stop Mainlanders born of one parent or more in Hong Kong emigrating to the territory. The court declared that, even if the parent(s) themselves were not permanent residents of Hong Kong, such moves violated the Basic Law. Tung warned that the territory would be swamped by immigrants as a result of the ruling, and asked the NATIONAL PEOPLE'S CONGRESS (NPC) in Beijing to overturn it. The NPC, offended by the court's presumption, did so. Critics saw the move as the beginning of the end for Hong Kong's judicial independence. Others were gratified that there would be no influx of immigrants at a time of economic recession.

Twenty-one Demands (January 1915)

To Chinese minds, JAPAN's demands that the government of the young Chinese Republic grant Tokyo more territory and privileges than most other powers had won through war and treaty occupies a special place in the infamies of imperialism. Most of the demands were not met, but those that were helped spark the modern sense of nationalism behind the MAY FOURTH MOVEMENT of 1919.

The demands arose out of Japan's declaration of war on Germany shortly after the start of the First World War. Japanese troops occupied Germany's leased territory in SHANDONG and much of the rest of the province. With the powers locked in war in Europe, Tokyo pressed home its advantage. It presented President YUAN SHIKAI with a memor-andum demanding new rights for Japan in Manchuria (northeast China), INNER MONGOLIA and the Yangtze valley, as well as confirmation of those just obtained in Shandong. Another set of demands called for the placement of Japanese officials in key departments of the Chinese government. If implemented, the overall effect of the Twenty-one Demands would have been to reduce China to semi-colonial status.

Japan's memoranda were leaked to the other powers, and Tokyo quietly backed away. However, it retained its hold over Shandong for the best part of a decade – to the fury and frustration of China's first generation of modern Nationalists.

unequal treaties

The unequal treaties forcibly opened China in the nineteenth century to trade and diplomacy on unfavourable terms. Typically, they ceded to foreign governments, territory (see TREATY PORTS), EXTRATERRITORIALITY and the right to set China's tariffs (see TARIFF AUTONOMY). Many of them, including the Treaty of Shimonosheki (1895) (see JAPAN), and the Boxer Protocol (1901) (see BOXER REBELLION), obliged China to pay huge indemnities for losses sustained by foreigners during wars with China or caused by other domestic incidents. These and other treaties permitted the stationing of foreign troops on Chinese soil and allowed gunboats to sail on China's rivers and merchants and MISSIONARIES to take up residence in the interior. Principal signatories were BRITAIN (which signed the first, the Treaty of Nanjing, in 1842), France, RUSSIA, the UNITED STATES and JAPAN. Thanks to the 'most-favoured-nation' clause, all these (and other) powers benefited when any one of them signed a new treaty with Beijing in an attempt to curb rivalry between them.

Chinese nationalists deemed these treaties 'unequal' because were signed under duress and their terms were not reciprocal. As such, they offended justice and patriotism. In this context, the fact that international law does not accept a treaty to be invalid simply because it is classified as 'unequal' was, and remains, besides the point.

Many Chinese were impressed in 1919 when the SOVIET UNION abandoned most (but not all) of the treaty privileges the new revolutionary state had inherited in China from the Tsars. The Nationalist government of CHIANG KAI-SHEK fought hard to revise the treaties in the late 1920s and 1930s. It won tariff autonomy in 1928, but the unequal treaties themselves endured until 1943, when China's status as an ally of the United States and Britain in the SINO-JAPANESE WAR made the maintenance of imperial privileges politically inappropriate and impractical. They were relinquished under the terms of Sino-US and Sino-British treaties of that year.

However, Britain held on to its colony of HONG KONG, all three parts of which – Hong Kong Island, Kowloon and the New Territories – were ceded by separate 'unequal territories' in 1842, 1860 and 1898. Argument over the territory therefore seemed likely when the CHINESE COMMUNIST PARTY came to power in 1949 and declared that it reserved the right to examine, abrogate, revise and renegotiate all treaties signed in the pre-Communist era.

In fact, Beijing declined to challenge Britain's position in Hong Kong other than to deny the legal validity of its occupation of Chinese territory. There was an exception during the CULTURAL REVOLUTION: Left-wingers in Hong Kong tested the determination of the colonial authorities to hold on to their colony by staging riots and terrorist bombings. The police and public backed the government, which was more than Beijing did for the rebels. In 1982 Britain and China agreed to discuss Hong Kong's rendition. On 1 July 1997, when rendition occurred, China insisted it had recovered the *exercise* of sovereignty over Hong Kong – sovereignty itself never having been lost because the treaties ceding the territory to Britain were 'unequal' and invalid.

United League (*Tongmeng Hui*)

SUN YAT-SEN founded the United League, China's first important modern revolutionary organization, in Tokyo in 1905. It brought together various strands of anti-Manchu radicalism, and launched several unsuccessful uprisings against the QING DYNASTY. More than any other political group, the United League put revolutionary republicanism on the map of modern China.

Most League members were drawn from the OVERSEAS CHINESE community whose political allegiance was divided between the revolutionary republicanism championed by Sun, and the constitutional monarchy favoured by LIANG QICHAO. Still other members supported KANG YOUWEI's 'Protect the Emperor Society' whose aim was to restore the GUANGXU EMPEROR and unseat the EMPRESS DOWAGER. The formation of the League did not end these divisions. But it gave the revolutionaries the upper hand in terms of organization, power and influence, both overseas and on the Mainland.

Much of this was due to Sun's prestige and skill as a leader, and the determination of hardened revolutionaries such as Huang Xing (1874–1916) and SONG JIAOREN, both of them from HUNAN, who joined him. Most members were drawn from GUANGDONG with Hunan a close second. Three-quarters were students studying in JAPAN.

The League's ideology was eclectic and reflected Sun's aim of uniting as many people as possible behind the cause of ending Manchu rule. His 'Three Principles of the People' – nationalism, democracy and people's livelihood or socialism – were the most prominent of several theories espoused by the organization, some of whose members were influenced by ANARCHISM. All agreed that China needed to establish unity and national sovereignty and to enhance national strength. Many, Sun among them, believed that there was little Chinese revolutionaries could not achieve when properly motivated and led.

Their record of actually making revolution often suggested otherwise. When staging uprisings the League relied heavily on SECRET SOCIETIES. Operating from exile to avoid capture, Sun and other leaders were often too distant, ideologically and socially as well as geographically, from their target. All the League's attempts to foment rebellion failed; and when the REPUBLICAN REVOLUTION eventually broke out in Wuhan in 1911, Sun was in the United States and members of his group, who numbered 10,000 in total, just one of several social forces behind the upheaval.

However, Sun and the League played a much larger role in *defining* the revolt. They supplied much of the language and meaning of political life in the young Republic. In 1912 the United League disbanded and formed the KUOMINTANG to fight the first parliamentary elections under the new order and sustain the revolutionary cause (see SONG JIAOREN).

United Nations

The inhabitants of China *in their entirety* enjoyed representation in the United Nations for only the first 4 years of the international body's existence. From 1949 to 1971, the People's Republic of China, the world's most populous state, was excluded, rendering the very idea of the UN something of a farce. From 1971, the Republic of China on TAIWAN, a rich, democratic state by the close of the century, was excluded, impairing the UN in a lesser, but still unfortunate, way. Unlike the case with East and West Germany and North and South Korea, each of whom became members, divisions between the 'two Chinas' have proved too great for both to find a home in the United Nations at the same time.

founder and outcast, 1945–71

China was a founder of the United Nations. The KUOMINTANG government signed the United Nations Charter at the San Francisco Conference in 1945. One of its delegates was Dong Biwu (1886–1975), a senior member of the CHINESE COMMUNIST PARTY. Four years later, the Nationalists lost the CIVIL WAR and fled to Taiwan. UNITED STATES opposition to the new Communist government in Beijing meant that the Kuomintang retained China's seat at the UN, despite the fact that it controlled only a small part of the country. At least in name, CHIANG KAI-SHEK's government represented China at the world body for the following 22 years, during which time the

People's Republic was an angry outcast and fierce critic of the UN.

Beijing's exclusion might have lasted a matter of months had it not been for the KOREAN WAR of 1950–53. And the war itself might have taken a different course had the People's Republic been represented at the UN. The conflict broke out at a time when the SOVIET UNION had refused to take its seat in the UN Security Council in protest at the presence of Taiwan and absence of China. This made it hard for Moscow to counter American diplomatic efforts to condemn North Korea's invasion of the South and raise an international army to reverse it. By November 1950, Chinese 'volunteers' were fighting US-led United Nations' forces on the Korean peninsula. The following year, the UN branded China an 'aggressor nation' and imposed an embargo on the sale of strategic goods to the People's Republic. In 1959 it condemned China again – this time for human rights violations in TIBET.

The Cold War, and in particular Washington's determination to contain Communism in East Asia, blocked Beijing's entry into the United Nations for the rest of the 1950s and the 1960s. Taiwan was one of Washington's closest allies in the Far East, and its UN representatives almost always voted with those of the US. They were amply rewarded: in the 1960s the US secured passage of a resolution that required two-thirds of UN members rather than a simple majority to approve any measure that would unseat Taiwan in favour of Beijing.

American efforts to keep Beijing out of the international community were aided by the twists and turns of MAO ZEDONG's Revolution and its consequences for China's FOREIGN POLICY. The moderate line associated with the BANDUNG CONFERENCE of 1955 soon gave way to adventurism; diplomacy became an extension of the Revolution at home. This was particularly the case after the Sino-Soviet split of the early 1960s (see SOVIET UNION), and during the CULTURAL REVOLUTION that followed. Determined to oppose what it called 'revisionism' abroad as well as at home, Beijing supported Marxist insurgents in several Asian and African countries – much to the alarm of their governments, several of whom maintained diplomatic relations with the People's Republic and looked to it for leadership of the Third World. China's Communists had a different world order in mind from that of either the West or many of the developing countries. In the mid-1960s Beijing supported Indonesia's sudden withdrawal from the United Nations and the creation of a 'revolutionary' alternative, the 'Conference of New Emerging Forces'.

changing seats: the watershed of 1971

In the end the conventional organization proved good enough for China's leaders. When Beijing began to seek rapprochement with the United States in the late 1960s, Washington dropped its opposition to the Mainland's entry to the UN. In 1970, a majority of members voted for the first time to expel Taiwan and allow Beijing in. The following year, under resolution 2758 of 25 October, the General Assembly decided to recognize the People's Republic as the only legitimate representative of China, *including* Taiwan. Taiwan's representatives walked out of the assembly and were expelled from all UN-related organizations. The resolution, submitted by Albania and Algeria, was adopted by 76 votes to 35 with 17 abstentions. It was a long-sought triumph for Beijing which, as a nuclear power, acquired a permanent seat on the Security Council. For the Nationalist government in Taipei it was a disaster: the island has been the Chinese outcast in international diplomacy ever since.

If entry into the UN indicated China was *in* the world, there were few signs that it was yet *of* it. At home the Cultural Revolution dragged on. The economy stagnated. So did Chinese diplomacy. The 'GANG OF FOUR' manoeuvred for position in readiness for Mao's death. China was absorbed in its own struggles.

It was in this context that DENG XIAOPING, temporarily between purges, addressed the General Assembly of the United Nations in 1974. He spoke on Mao's 'three worlds' theory of international relations. The United States and the Soviet Union made up the First World; developing countries in Asia, Africa and Latin America constituted the Third World. Developed countries between the first two, most of them in Europe, were the Second World. Deng said that as a socialist, developing country, China belonged to the Third World.

Four years and another purge later, Deng was the most powerful man in China. Elbowing opponents aside, he committed China to reopening its doors to trade and investment, and introducing free market reforms. The implications for almost every aspect of Chinese life were immense. This was particularly true of China's relations with the outside world. Deng's reforms set in train a process of integration with the international community which, though it has not always moved in a logical, or even linear, way, has proved unstoppable. Changes in China's relations with the UN and its related organizations provide abundant evidence of this.

seeking room for manoeuvre

In 1978, after years of refusing UN aid, China unexpectedly requested it. Within 4 years it was the single largest recipient of assistance from the United Nations Development Programme. In 1980, Beijing joined the World Bank and the International Monetary Fund (IMF) (see FINANCE). Both organizations have assisted China's modernization, reform and rapid economic growth by providing pools of cheap capital, expertise and advice. World Bank loans to China were frozen for 18 months following the suppression of the TIANANMEN SQUARE DEMOCRACY MOVEMENT in 1989 but resumed on an even larger scale. By mid-1995, the Bank had committed US$22 billion to China, confirming its position as the largest borrower. Two years later, Beijing was in a financial position – and a political frame of mind – to *lend* money to the IMF so it could rescue countries hit by the Asian financial crisis. The world was presented with the spectacle of a 'Communist' government staving off the crisis of international capitalism with billions of dollars rather than welcoming it as the potential dawn of socialism.

Such developments could not be foreseen in 1979 when China provided the UN with a detailed breakdown of its national income together with a request that its contributions to the organization be scaled down. To the chagrin of some Third World countries, the request was granted. This enabled China to extricate itself from a financial dilemma which threatened to curb its political influence in the UN. It concerned the financing of UN peacekeeping operations, a particularly heavy burden for the 5 permanent members of the Security Council. China's refusal to contribute meant that it faced the prospect of losing the right to vote in the General Assembly. The reduction in its overall contributions enabled Beijing to pay its way and retain its vote.

Paying for peacekeeping was one thing. Taking part in such operations, or going along with the UN policies which seemed to place less emphasis on national sovereignty than on ending civil wars, relieving famine and improving HUMAN RIGHTS, was another. China looked upon the UN primarily as a means of protecting its sovereignty. As the foundation of the world order, nation states brooked no interference, especially from 'hegemonistic' powers such as the United States. In a world dominated first by the superpower rivalry of the Cold War era, and then by a single superpower, China sought maximum room for manoeuvre. Sometimes it resurrected its claims to lead, or at least represent, the Third World at the 'top table' of diplomacy. Sometimes it simply appeared to revel in its status as one of the 'big five'. But always and increasingly, Beijing relished its growing role in international affairs and took heart from the fact that little could be accomplished of significance within the UN without, at the very least, its acquiescence.

The diplomatic run-up to the Gulf War of 1990 was an example. China went along with various sanctions directed against Iraq, but managed to exclude from a crucial resolution on the crisis any specific reference to the use of military force against Baghdad. The final version threatened to evict Iraqi troops from Kuwait by 'all necessary means'. China abstained when the resolution was put to the vote. It chose not to antagonize the West by using its veto, yet preferred not to lose all its credibility among the Arab world by voting in favour. Beijing's tactics produced direct benefits. The fact that it chose not to scupper American efforts to liberate Kuwait enabled it to shed some of the obloquy it had earned in the West by crushing the 1989 democracy movement – even though Washington had tried to persuade China to support the resolution.

On the question of CAMBODIA, another major issue at the UN in the early 1990s, China took a more proactive stance. It voted in favour of setting up the UN Transitional Authority that ran the country pending the outcome of elections. Beijing even sent a peacekeeping force to Cambodia, the first time its troops had engaged on such a mission in substantial numbers. Earlier a smaller number of Chinese soldiers had taken part in peacekeeping operations in the Sinai peninsula.

A landmark of a different kind was established in 1995. China hosted its first full UN conference, the international women's conference and an associated meeting of non-governmental organizations which gathered in Beijing (see WOMEN). The first taxed the

Taiwan and the United Nations: Abortive Re-entry

In 1997, China exercised its veto in the Security Council for the first time in years. The issue was the apparently obscure one of sending UN observers to monitor a peace pact in Guatemala, where three decades of civil war were coming to an end. The problem for Beijing was that Guatemala maintained diplomatic ties with Taiwan and had supported the island's attempts to join the UN. It was resolved when the Central American state agreed not to back such moves in future. In 1999 China exercised its veto again, this time to prevent renewal of a mandate governing UN peacekeepers in the new Republic of Macedonia. Beijing was angry at Skopje's decision earlier the same year to establish diplomatic relations with Taipei. Both incidents showed how far China was prepared to go to crush Taiwan's search for international recognition.

Taipei's attempt to re-enter the UN began in 1993, when several of its few allies lent their weight to what became an annual campaign. The Nationalist government sought 'parallel representation' for the Republic of China on Taiwan along with the People's Republic of China rather than the ejection of Beijing. It argued that the People's Republic could not – as both Beijing and the UN claimed – represent the people of Taiwan since the Communist government had never controlled the island. The Republic of China sought admission to the UN on the same terms as those attained by the governments of East and West Germany and, later, North and South Korea – that is, that their nations were, temporarily, divided.

Taiwan also insisted that it was unjust for its 21 million people to be excluded from the UN, especially when they were citizens of one of the world's largest trading nations whose foreign exchange reserves ranked (in 1993) second only to those of Japan. It was also self-defeating for, given formal status, the ROC would be able to play a positive role in the international community. The kind of role Taiwan had in mind became clear in 1995 when it offered the UN US$1 billion in development aid.

The main result of Taiwan's efforts was to anger China, whose status as a permanent member of the Security Council meant it could veto all attempts by the UN even to consider the matter of Taipei joining the body. For Beijing, Taiwan's pursuit of UN membership was proof of its determination to seek independence. President LEE TENG-HUI might talk about his desire for unification, but his actions, often supported by the opposition, the pro-independence DEMOCRATIC PROGRESSIVE PARTY, showed otherwise.

When Lee visited the United States in 1995 and sought a higher international profile for Taiwan, China vilified him as a traitor. Relations between Beijing and Washington suffered. They deteriorated still further in early 1996 when China staged missile tests and war games opposite Taiwan during the island's first direct presidential elections. Beijing wanted to deter Taiwanese from voting for pro-independence candidates. Washington moved naval forces into the area to deter a possible Chinese attack on Taiwan (see TAIWAN/ARMS ACROSS THE STRAITS; UNITED STATES). Partly as a result of this crisis, the United States and China decided to try to improve their relationship. At Sino-US summits in the United States in 1997 and China the following year, leaders of the two sides sought to establish a 'strategic partnership'. An unspoken aspect of this was quiet American pressure on Taiwan not to pursue independence, and a specific, public commitment by Washington that it would not support the island's attempts to enter organizations of sovereign states. Taiwan's campaign to enter the United Nations continued, but seemed doomed. It had run into the same obstacle that kept Beijing out of the organization for 22 years: an informal alliance between the United States and the Chinese incumbent – this time, the much more formidable one of the People's Republic.

government's organizational skills, the second its political tolerance. Both passed off without major incident.

national sovereignty and its enemies

Within the United Nations as outside it during the 1990s, China remained a staunch defender of the sovereignty of the nation state. This has been a core value of Chinese Communism since 1949. It is set to remain one well into the twenty-first century, even as globalization tends to weaken the theory and practice of sovereignty almost everywhere. At the same time China showed some acceptance of the idea that the conduct of governments, including its own, should be governed by international norms. Its accession to numerous UN covenants was a symbol of this.

China was a signatory to treaties banning nuclear proliferation and nuclear testing (see PEOPLE'S LIBERATION ARMY), protecting the ENVIRONMENT, developing science and technology and much else. It acceded to conventions outlawing chemical and biological weapons.

Neither did it shy away from covenants dealing with human rights, the most sensitive of topics. By the mid-1990s, China had acceded to 15 international conventions governing this area of life. In 1997, largely in an attempt to thwart annual, American-led attempts to censure it at the UN Commission on Human Rights, Beijing signed the International Covenant on Economic, Social and Cultural Rights. The following year it signed the International Covenant on Civil and Political Rights. These moves promised to bring China within the fold of the 'international bill of rights', as the two covenants, together with the UN Charter of 1945, are known.

At the dawn of the new century it was unclear when this might happen: Beijing had yet to ratify the covenants let alone implement them. A desire to decrease international pressure over human rights often appeared greater than Beijing's commitment to an overhaul of the relationship between the individual and the state. Similar sentiments were probably at work in its adherence to other UN norms, covenants and treaties. Nevertheless, China ended the century embracing many UN ideas and ideals it had explicitly rejected during its long years of exclusion from the organization – and for several years after it rejoined in 1971. This was true across a range of policy issues in different areas of Chinese national and international life.

Yet there were limits to China's tolerance of 'global values'. And they were breached, fundamentally and unacceptably in Beijing's view, by NATO's war of 1999 against Yugoslavia to protect the Albanian Kosovars. China's objections stemmed from the fact that a regional military alliance had intervened in the affairs of a sovereign state without consulting the UN. Equally important, the episode legitimized such intervention by seeming to place humanitarianism above national sovereignty (see FOREIGN POLICY). Even Kofi Annan, the UN General Secretary, called for a new definition of state sovereignty in order that the international community could intervene in other countries to prevent unacceptable death and human suffering.

These developments were unwelcome in China – a country with a substantial number of ETHNIC MINORITIES, many of them unreconciled to Chinese rule; a human rights record under constant criticism in the West; and military designs on Taiwan likely to be criticized – and perhaps even physically opposed – by several countries, including the United States. Events in Kosovo spawned an interventionist doctrine in the UN which threatened the Communist Party's freedom of action at home and reminded China's leaders that they had much to fear as well as gain from their country's participation in the international community.

United States of America

Sentiment and self-interest, rivalry and respect, mission and menace all meet in the relationship between China and the United States. They form the ingredients of a powerful, emotional dynamic that has done much to shape the modern history of East Asia. Few major bilateral relationships have demonstrated so much capacity for misunderstanding. None will prove more crucial in determining the pattern of international relations during the new century. In the 1990s, arguments over HUMAN RIGHTS, trade, ARMS SALES and Beijing's belligerence towards TAIWAN resulted in repeated diplomatic skirmishes and the occasional military stand-off. They can be expected to do so again in the new century as the world's sole established superpower rubs shoulders with its chief regional rival in East Asia, the Pacific and beyond.

moral imperative, material advantage

America began its twentieth-century relationship with China by insisting that its interests were different from those of the other powers. As foreign rivals divided China into concessions and spheres of influence, secretary of state John Hay in 1900 issued the second of his 'Open Door Notes'. Like the first of a year earlier they called for the preservation of China as a 'territorial and administrative entity'. It was a timely move given that the powers were bound to seek new gains once they had crushed the BOXER REBELLION of 1899–1900.

It was also in America's interests as much as China's. While the United States had not fought a war against China, it owed its position there to the military victories and UNEQUAL TREATIES secured chiefly by BRITAIN. With the pace of imperialism quickening, the US was in danger of being squeezed out. The 'open door' would secure material advantage *and* meet the moral imperative of supporting a rapidly decaying state at the mercy of imperialism. There was less charity towards China at home, where Congress renewed the exclusion laws designed to keep Chinese immigrants out of the United States. The 'open door' apparently allowed only one-way traffic – an injustice that drove Chinese merchants to boycott US goods in 1905 in one of the earliest expressions of modern Chinese nationalism.

Yet idealism *was* at work in America's relations with China, though events sometimes suggested otherwise. For many Americans, China was less a country than a symbol of hope. Weak and bullied, it attracted strong sympathy and generated powerful sentiments. Despite obvious cultural differences, some Americans imagined they enjoyed a natural affinity with the Chinese, and that a basis for understanding existed of the kind denied other powers and peoples. As empire gave way to republic, and republic to chaos, China was felt to be undergoing a unique process of transition. The United States sought to help by missionary effort, philanthropy, and medical and educational work, much of it financed by remission of the American share of the Boxer indemnity. (See EDUCATION; HEALTH; MISSIONARIES.) The expectations this kind of thinking generated were unfulfilled; eventually they were dashed by the Communist Revolution and a bitter inquisition in the United States over who 'lost' China. But while the debate subsided, the tendency towards idealism, towards alternately demonizing and romanticizing China, lingered on. It is still at work in America's approach to China.

US China mission in the Republic

In the first few decades of the twentieth century, American efforts to change China by converting, educating and training its citizens made more impact than formal diplomacy. During the First World War, Washington's advocacy of the 'open door' was not enough to prevent JAPAN from occupying Germany's possessions in SHANDONG, or blunt the TWENTY-ONE DEMANDS of 1915 which Tokyo imposed on the government of YUAN SHIKAI. When the Versailles peace conference of 1919 also failed to evict Japan from its new possessions – despite President Woodrow Wilson's emphasis on national self-determination as the basis of a new, post-war order – protests broke out across China that marked the start of the MAY FOURTH MOVEMENT.

The United States played a more proactive role at the WASHINGTON CONFERENCE of 1921–2. Japan finally agreed to return Shandong, and entered into a naval pact with Britain and America. But despite US goodwill, the other goals of Chinese nationalism – TARIFF AUTONOMY and revision of EXTRATERRITORIALITY – were not met until 1928 and 1943 respectively.

American popular sympathy for China grew with Japan's aggression in Manchuria, northeast China, in 1931. It did so again when Japan launched full-scale war in 1937 (see SINO-

JAPANESE WAR). Washington began to think about abandoning isolation in favour of becoming the 'arsenal of democracy'. It agreed to aid Britain against Nazi Germany, and 'Free China' against imperial Japan. As the war unfolded, the United States woke up to the growing *international* threat to security. It was thinking globally, a precondition of superpower status.

US aid to China at first took the form of government loans and the development of a 'semi-official' air force: the American Volunteer Group, or 'Flying Tigers', led by Claire Chennault, a retired US Army Air Corps colonel. But with the Japanese attack on Pearl Harbor in December 1941, America became an enemy of Japan and an ally of CHIANG KAI-SHEK. Fatefully, the nature of the American interest in China changed. It was now wedded to a particular government, the particularly corrupt and inefficient one of the KUOMINTANG, which was unable to contribute much to the war or win the support of the majority of its citizens.

This was not apparent at first. The image of 'Free China' – a poor nation of freedom-loving farmers, merchants and officials valiantly fighting off cruel attack by a technologically superior militarist power – was a forceful one. It was reinforced by Chiang's austere, determined personality, and the much more colourful figure of SOONG MEI-LING, his wife, who in 1943 made a spectacularly successful visit to the United States. The romance between America and China reached its height. China was already a valued ally and friend. It only remained to turn the country into a 'great power'. This was achieved, at least on paper, at the CAIRO CONFERENCE of December 1943, when Chiang met Roosevelt and Churchill for the first Sino-Western summit.

disillusionment and defeat: the KMT's fall

Yet beneath the glamour lurked numerous uncomfortable truths about Nationalist China, and America's relationship with it. JOSEPH STILWELL, the US general appointed Chiang's chief of staff as part of the war effort, was familiar with many of them. He loathed Chiang personally and hated the corruption and inefficiency of his regime. The Generalissimo was far more interested in pursuing a policy of divide and rule within the Nationalist camp than fighting the Japanese. He insisted on controlling the government's best forces personally, both to defeat his rivals in the Kuomintang and to keep Communist forces bottled up in YANAN, the Party's wartime headquarters. A master at outsmarting his foes, even if they were emissaries of the most powerful country in the world, Chiang forced Stilwell's resignation in 1944 over plans by Roosevelt to place him in charge of all of China's armed forces, Communists included.

Propaganda aside, China was of little military value in the struggle against Japan. Naval and air power based outside the Chinese Mainland brought Tokyo to its knees. In combat terms, Nationalist China was a sideshow. As the war went on, the government alienated ever larger numbers of people. It seemed incapable of reform. Renewed civil war with the Communists appeared inevitable. Yet having created the fiction of Chiang's China as a 'great power', the United States was forced to try and sustain it. It did so by means of diplomacy, military intervention and mediation.

At the YALTA CONFERENCE, the Americans persuaded Stalin to enter a treaty of friendship and alliance with Chiang. The unspoken trade-off, kept from Chiang until it had been agreed, was the granting to Stalin of rights in Manchuria of the kind once exercised by the Tsar (see RUSSIA). In the military field, the US airlifted thousands of Nationalist troops into north and east China so they could accept the surrender of Japanese ground forces and secure the area against Communist infiltration. When conflict between the Nationalists and Communists intensified, President Truman sent General George Marshall to mediate.

Marshall's efforts soon fell foul of the combatants' determination to gain supremacy. Washington sought to play midwife to a strong, united, democratic and friendly China – an infant that has yet to emerge more than half a century later, despite the best efforts of the US. The problem in the late 1940s was that the US sought to mediate *and* maintain the supremacy of a government that could not bring its own people round to the view that it should remain in power. The Communists defeated the Nationalists on the battlefield (see CIVIL WAR). Away from the battle, the Nationalists defeated themselves by mishandling the economy, failing to curb corruption, and appearing to have little purpose and even fewer policies.

This explanation for the collapse of Chiang's regime found little favour in the United States. The Communist conquest was a spectacular defeat for American efforts to guide and change China. Indeed, it was a defeat for *Western* attempts to transform the country that began with the Opium Wars of the 1840s. By 1949 'Free China' had become Communist China. In the context of Soviet expansion and the Cold War, this was a very serious matter. With the outbreak of the KOREAN WAR a few months later, it was more serious still. China turned from friend to menace, ally to enemy. The search for scapegoats began. They were found, courtesy of Senator Joseph McCarthy and others, in the form of the Communists and fellow travellers said to be working in the State Department and other areas of American life. The idea that China had its own dynamic; that external influences, while important, were nothing compared with the indigenous forces at work in the country, seemed lost on all but a few American sinologists and those with long experience of the country.

containing Communism: 1950–71

From 1950 until 1971, America's sole significant source of contact with the Chinese people centred on Taiwan, the former Japanese colony where the defeated Nationalist government and armies regrouped at the end of 1949, ready to ward off Communist invasion and, perhaps, reconquer the Mainland. Washington was not ready to sponsor Chiang's dreams of conquest. But neither was it willing to see the Communists take Taiwan. When North Korea attacked South Korea in 1950, Truman moved the Seventh Fleet into the Taiwan Straits. It saved Chiang from almost certain defeat. His regime also survived the Straits Crises of 1954 and 1958 (see TAIWAN/ARMS ACROSS THE STRAITS) in which the Communists, with varying degrees of enthusiasm, sought to take over Taiwan's outlying islands.

Nationalist-ruled Taiwan grew rich and strong under American protection. It was a beneficiary of the principal aims of US policy in Asia which were to ensure the diplomatic isolation of Beijing, including blocking its accession to the UNITED NATIONS; encircle and contain the People's Republic with a network of alliances and military bases; and intervene forcefully in those countries – principally VIETNAM – where Communism threatened to advance.

By the late 1960s, these policies were in trouble. America was bogged down in Vietnam. The administration was keen to begin a dialogue with Beijing and put pressure on the 'real' enemy: Moscow. Rapprochement with the West suited Beijing, too. China had long been at ideological odds with the Kremlin, and in 1969 engaged in military skirmishes with Soviet troops along the disputed Sino-Soviet frontier. (See SOVIET UNION; HEILONG-JIANG.) At first dialogue between Washington and Beijing took the form of 'ping-pong diplomacy': the visit to China in April 1971 of a US table tennis team. A few weeks later, Henry Kissinger, President Richard Nixon's national security adviser, made a secret trip to Beijing. A decidedly public one by President Richard Nixon followed in 1972. The fruit of that visit, the 'Shanghai Communiqué', marked a new start in Sino-American relations. Two decades of estrangement between the world's most prosperous nation and its most populous were at an end.

strategy, sentiment, strife

It was less clear – to both sides – exactly what they had been replaced with. For China, rapprochement was a strategic anchor. It had been lowered by MAO ZEDONG and ZHOU ENLAI to warn off Moscow, but also, especially in the case of Zhou, to provide a much needed opening for China's economy to trade and investment with the West. This became the primary function of rapprochement after the death of Mao, throughout the rule of DENG XIAOPING and beyond. However, it generated heated arguments within the CHINESE COMMUNIST PARTY over the extent to which China should be exposed and dependent on the capitalist West and the US in particular.

For at least some in the United States, rapprochement seemed to point to a return to the close, 'sympathetic' relations of the first half of the century. Perhaps the 'natural affinities' between the two peoples would reassert themselves as China turned outwards and shed at least some of its obsession with ideology? In any event, it was clear from their growing zeal for economic reform that the Chinese Communists were preferable partners compared with their comrades in the Soviet Union and Eastern Europe.

Common antipathy towards Moscow and its satellites generated enough impetus to keep Sino-American ties on track despite constant arguments over Taiwan. By 1979, Washington had put enough distance between itself and its erstwhile Chinese ally to shift diplomatic recognition from Taipei to Beijing. Yet both Washington and Beijing found it difficult to manage their new relationship. Their

---

Sino-US Summits

(Formal summits between the most powerful American and Chinese leaders, as opposed to meetings at the sidelines of other international gatherings)

1. Cairo, November 1943: Chiang Kai-shek met President Roosevelt and Prime Minister Churchill.

2. Taipei, June 1960: Chiang Kai-shek met President Eisenhower.

3. Beijing, February 1972: Mao Zedong met President Nixon.

4. Beijing, December 1975: Deng Xiaoping met President Ford.

5. Washington, January–February 1979: President Carter met Deng Xiaoping.

6. Beijing, April 1984: Deng met President Reagan.

7. Washington, July 1985: President Reagan met President Li Xiannian.

8. Beijing, February 1989: Deng met President Bush.

9. Washington, October 1997: President Clinton met President Jiang Zemin.

10. Beijing, June 1998: President Jiang met President Clinton.

---

tacit alliance against Soviet Communism, reinforced by cooperation in intelligence matters and US arms sales to the People's Republic, could not disguise the fact that, while the two countries might share certain interests, their political and social values could hardly be more different.

The most dramatic illustration of this was Beijing's suppression of the TIANANMEN SQUARE DEMOCRACY MOVEMENT in 1989. This revealed a different China from the one many Americans thought they had become familiar with. Secret diplomacy managed to stop Sino-US relations running completely off the rails, but only just. The collapse of the Soviet Union in 1991 created fresh difficulties by removing the strategic imperative from the US–China relationship. What was the purpose of relations with Beijing, it began to be asked in Congress and elsewhere during the mid-1990s, if there was no common foe to justify them? Perhaps, in the post-Cold War world, China itself was the foe?

China's one-child policy (see POPULATION); its treatment of DISSIDENTS and religious believers; its behaviour in TIBET; and its use of prison labour and organ transplants from executed prisoners all suggested this might be the case. So did the huge trade surpluses China ran with the US, its unwillingness to open its markets to more American products and its piracy of intellectual goods and services. The US business community was often ecstatic about China's rapid economic growth, but Beijing's weapons sales to regimes the US disliked, and its willingness to supply nuclear technology to PAKISTAN, Iran and elsewhere, only added to the burdens of diplomacy for Washington (see ARMS SALES). Some Americans, responding to domestic political rhythms as much as to developments in China itself, began to call for the containment rather than the encouragement of Beijing. China's forward policy in the SOUTH CHINA SEA hinted at a 'coming conflict with China', which was the title of an influential book published in the US in 1996. In this context, the decision by President Bill Clinton in 1994 to decouple human rights issues from the annual renewal of Most Favoured Nation (MFN) status for Beijing, and pursue a policy of 'engagement' with the People's Republic, largely in order to change it, did not go down well in Washington.

Neither was it very popular in a Beijing angry about negative perceptions in the United States and keen to seek closer ties with Russia. Moscow proved a useful source of military equipment no longer available from the West because of post-Tiananmen sanctions. Russia also had complaints of its own about America's 'overweening' foreign policy. From China's point of view, the US was forever intervening in domestic Chinese politics, trying to weaken the country, split it up, or erode Communist Party rule. Washington seemed determined to preserve its world supremacy in the face of an increasingly powerful China.

'two China' troubles

Nowhere were American aims more evident, or more feared in Beijing, than in its policy towards Taiwan, the 'tinder box' in Sino-US relations since the Civil War. Despite the Shanghai Communiqué of 1972 and two succeeding declarations (see right), Washington remained – and *remains* – involved in the unfinished conflict between the 'two Chinas'. This involvement takes the form of the Taiwan Relations Act of 1979, and continuing arms sales to the island which, in 1992, included an agreement to supply 150 F-16 fighters.

Beijing declared in 1981 that it sought peaceful unification with Taiwan, but has never

Ties that Bind: Four Accords between the USA and China

1. In the *Shanghai Communiqué*, signed on 27 February 1972 during President Nixon's visit to China, the US acknowledged that Chinese on both sides of the Straits of Taiwan maintain there is but one China of which Taiwan is a part. Washington did not challenge this position and affirmed its interest in a peaceful settlement of the Taiwan issue by the Chinese themselves. It declared its ultimate objective of withdrawing all its forces and military installations from Taiwan, and pledged to do so on a progressive basis as tension in the area diminished.

2. On 16 December 1978 Washington and Beijing issued a *Communiqué on the Establishment of Diplomatic Relations Between China and the USA*. It stated that diplomatic relations between the US and the People's Republic of China would be established on 1 January 1979, and that those between the US and Taiwan would be broken. The Mutual Defense Treaty between the US and Taiwan would also be terminated within one year and US military personnel withdrawn from the island. The US recognized the government of the People's Republic as the sole legal government of China, and acknowledged that Taiwan is part of China. However, it pledged to maintain cultural, commercial and other unofficial relations with the people of Taiwan. And in the course of negotiations leading up to the communiqué, the US said it would continue to supply arms to Taiwan for defensive purposes – something China objected to strongly.

3. On 16 March 1979 the US Congress passed the *Taiwan Relations Act* which established a new basis for American relations with China following recognition of the People's Republic. Its key elements were: to make clear that the establishment of diplomatic relations with the People's Republic rested upon the expectation that the future of Taiwan would be settled peacefully; to declare that attempts to settle Taiwan's future by non-peaceful means, including boycotts and embargoes, would threaten the peace of the Western Pacific and be 'of grave concern to the United States'; to provide Taiwan with arms 'of a defensive nature' – such as to enable the island to 'maintain a self-sufficient defense capacity'; to maintain the capacity of the United States to resist any resort to force or coercion that would 'jeopardize the security, or the social or economic system, of the people on Taiwan'. China objected strongly to the Act.

4. On 17 August 1982, Washington and Beijing signed a *Joint Communiqué on the Question of Arms Sales to Taiwan*. They did so against the background of peace overtures towards Taipei by Beijing which allowed the US to soften its policy on arms sales to Taiwan. The US said it would not carry out a long-term policy of arms sales to the island; arms would not exceed in quantity or quality the levels of recent years; and they would be reduced gradually over time.

abandoned the use of force against the island to protect what it regards as China's national integrity. It has threatened to intervene militarily if Taiwan declares independence, foreign powers forcibly intervene, or the island falls into social chaos. Washington's response has been one of 'strategic ambiguity': a carefully nurtured lack of clarity as to US willingness to defend Taiwan should the occasion arise. The strategy is designed to keep Beijing in check without giving a blank cheque to Taipei. Up to a point it has achieved both, though at the cost of ill will in Beijing. But it has depended upon studied indifference in Washington both to Taipei's desire for greater international recognition and to fundamental political change within the island itself. By the second half of the 1990s, neither of these conditions obtained.

In 1995, with Sino-US relations mired in rows over human rights, trade and the protection of intellectual copyright, the Clinton administration dropped its objections to an 'unofficial' visit to the US by Taiwanese president LEE TENG-HUI. It was a major diplomatic triumph for the island. In response China cancelled scheduled ministerial visits of its own and arrested the exiled dissident HARRY WU while he conducted an undercover operation in the country on behalf of the Western media and human rights groups. He was convicted of spying and sentenced to 15 years in prison – only to be expelled to the US on the understanding that Hillary Clinton, wife of the US president, would attend the United Nations Women's Conference in Beijing later that year.

Six months later, America and China engaged in their most serious military stand-off for almost 30 years. In March 1996 President Bill Clinton ordered two carrier battle fleets to approach Taiwan just as the island became the target of huge military exercises on the Mainland timed to coincide with its first direct presidential elections. The polls were conducted peacefully and were a triumph for Lee, whom Beijing had branded a traitor for his alleged pursuit of Taiwanese independence. Sino-US tension over the island subsided.

Yet the calm proved shortlived as political change in Taiwan accelerated. In elections during the late 1990s, the Kuomintang's control over local government and the legislature passed briefly to the DEMOCRATIC PROGRESS-IVE PARTY (DPP), the pro-independence opposition. In March 2000, CHEN SHUI-BIAN, the DPP candidate, won the presidential elec-

tions, driving the Kuomintang out of power for the first time. These developments alarmed Beijing, despite the DPP's announcement that it would neither declare Taiwan independent nor change the island's constitution. Washington urged restraint on both the new administration in Taipei and the Communist regime in Beijing.

US impact: rival or role model?

Partly, but not solely, because of the Taiwan issue, moods of mutual hostility were common among sections of the Chinese and American public during the late 1990s. US media coverage of China was often negative – a reflection of the fact that there was often a lot that was negative to report, but also of an ill-defined feeling that 'bad news' was generally what the American public expected from China. A book entitled *China Can Say No*, a paranoid, frustrated outburst against America's economic power and the 'cultural imperialism' of Hollywood, became popular in China. Beijing banned the book when it feared it might damage Sino-American relations.

In some ways it need not have bothered. The inroads made into urban China by American cultural icons from baseball stars to Coca-Cola, pop music to hamburgers demonstrated long ago that many Chinese neither could nor wanted to say 'No'. The problem for China's few genuine xenophobes was that both the government and many ordinary people defined their own importance by reference not to a Third World country in a similar condition to China, such as India, but to America, the world's most powerful country. The United States might, in many respects, be hostile towards China, but it was – and remains – a point of reference. The logic of this form of Chinese nationalism is that once Americans respect China, China can respect itself. This partly explains why Beijing insisted President Jiang Zemin receive *full* honours at the White House when he made his state visit to the United States in October 1997.

None of this is to suggest that American popular culture is shaping China in the way that an earlier generation of Americans imagined their missionaries and educators could. Large gaps exist between hamburgers and genuine elections; Michael Jackson and a free press. Yet the influence of the United States is formidable and growing. An example concerns the training of China's future elite. If Republican China went to school in JAPAN, as has been said of the young Chinese national-ists who studied in Tokyo at the end of the Qing Dynasty, then China of the twenty-first century went to school in the United States. Between 1978 and 1996, 250,000 Chinese stu-dents entered American universities, the larg-est body of foreign students in the United States. Among them were sons and daughters of the Communist elite, including Deng Xiao-ping and JIANG ZEMIN. Many did not return. But far more did. Technocrats educated in the Soviet Union during the 1950s played a major role in Chinese politics during the 1990s. Their US-educated equivalents stand a chance of doing so in future.

Again, this is neither a guarantee of future American political influence in China, nor an assurance that relations between Washington and Beijing will prove any more stable in future than they were during the second half of the twentieth century. In a world without the Soviet Union, both sides are still searching for acceptable grounds for their relationship. Shared goals include peace on the Korean peninsula, nuclear non-proliferation and environmental protection. Yet each of these issues is at the mercy of renewed argu-ments over trade, where China runs a huge surplus with the US; human rights, where improvement remains negligible despite exhaustive American efforts; China's military build-up, which continues to exercise the Pen-tagon; and the fate of Taiwan, where the Nationalist government insists on its own terms for reunification with the Mainland and maintains close, if unofficial, ties with the United States.

tensions at the turn of the century

A series of events in the final months of the twentieth century exposed the volatile nature of Sino-American relations. The exposure was more striking for the fact that it followed the visits of President Jiang to the US in 1997 and President Clinton to China the following year, during which both men affirmed that their countries had formed a 'strategic partnership'.

The first issue concerned allegations that China had secretly funded the Democratic Party during the 1996 presidential elections. The second stemmed from claims that China had for years stolen military secrets from the United States, enabling Beijing to develop advanced nuclear weapons of a kind other-wise beyond its capability to produce. Mutual trust, painstakingly nurtured during the Jiang–Clinton summits, drained away. In

Beijing, Washington's suggestion that Chinese weapons specialists were better at spying than science fuelled nationalist resentment.

The United States' strengthening of security ties with Japan was another cause of concern (see JAPAN). The two countries' agreement to consider developing a theatre missile defence, ostensibly to counter the missile threat from North Korea, added to fears in Beijing that China was again being hemmed in by US-led military alliances of the kind built to contain it in the 1950s. Taiwan's eagerness to partici-pate in the missile defence scheme rubbed the message in.

Yet it was events far from China, in the Balkans during NATO's war in Yugoslavia over Kosovo, which revealed the flimsy nature of official Sino-American friendship. From the first Beijing opposed the war against Serbia on the grounds that it set a dangerous precedent: a regional alliance had attacked a sovereign state on 'humanitarian grounds' to protect an ethnic minority without the approval of the United Nations. When NATO forces accident-ally bombed the Chinese embassy in Belgrade in May 1999, killing two diplomats, injuring many more and destroying the building, China's leaders could not believe it was an accident. Neither could many Chinese citi-zens. Their protests outside American and British diplomatic missions in China turned violent, exposing the government's com-pliance in the demonstrations, and the readiness of even urban China's most cosmopolitan urban youth to identify the United States as their country's principal enemy. NATO's masterplan, according to the Chinese media, was 'Kosovo today; China tomorrow'.

Beijing froze military and other contacts with the United States, including negotiations on China's entry into the World Trade Organ-ization (WTO), pending an explanation of the bombing, compensation for its victims and the punishment of those responsible. At the close of the century it had to settle for some-thing less: China needed improved relations with Washington to counter Lee Teng-hui's assertion in July that relations between Beijing and Taiwan must be conducted on the basis of ties between 'two states'; and because the window for entry to the WTO was narrowing. A Sino-American accord in November paving the way for China's entry into the world trade body improved the atmosphere.

But it failed to revive hopes that the vision of a 'strategic partnership' would amount to much in the new century. Instead, past and present conflicts; mutual misunderstandings arising from political and cultural differences; and the fact that an established superpower and an aspiring one must come to terms with each other in an unsettled part of the world are likely to ensure Sino-American relations remain volatile for years to come.

V

Vietnam

Historical enmity, revolutionary solidarity and regional rivalry have made for volatile relations between China and Vietnam. Vietnamese and Chinese troops fought alongside each other against the UNITED STATES during the first stages of the Vietnam War, but against each other over regional influence in 1979, and disputed territory in 1988. Rival claims over the SOUTH CHINA SEA have kept mutual suspicions – and even the possibility of renewed war – alive ever since.

Vietnam was the subject of Communist China's first significant diplomatic foray in the international community. At the GENEVA CONFERENCE ON KOREA AND INDOCHINA of 1954, Vietnam was divided along the 17th parallel pending elections to determine the country's future. This was more to China's liking than that of Ho Chi Minh, the Vietnamese Communist leader. Beijing was anxious not to draw American influence into the region, while Ho wanted to capitalize on his recent military victories over the French and expand south. Neither got his way: Ho's attempts to extend the revolution resulted in a massive commitment of American troops and firepower, much of it subsequently loosed on North Vietnam in the form of aerial bombing.

MAO ZEDONG regarded the cause of Communism in Vietnam as vital to China's future. This tied in with his campaign during the mid-1960s against opponents at home, who feared another military involvement along the lines of the KOREAN WAR, and the bitter ideological row with the SOVIET UNION. The Chairman believed 'reactionaries' were plotting war against China, the new headquarters of world revolution now that Beijing had declared the Soviet Union 'revisionist'. China would fight back, promoting revolutionary struggles in the Third World (the world's 'countryside') and capture the capitalist West (the world's 'cities'). In other words it would be a repeat, on a grand scale, of Communism's victory in China during the CIVIL WAR.

In line with these theories, Beijing gave substantial military aid to North Vietnam, including artillery, trucks, planes and naval vessels. Between 1964 and 1969 it also supplied military engineers for the construction of defence works, railways and roads, and 150,000 anti-aircraft troops to defend strategic targets. There is no evidence that Chinese forces engaged in operations south of Hanoi or along the Ho Chi Minh trail, but they did claim to have shot down 1,707 American planes and damaged a further 1,608.

China's desire for rapprochement with the UNITED STATES, as a means of both avoiding war with the Soviet Union and weakening Washington's ties with TAIWAN, got the better of its commitment to a rapid, outright Communist victory in Vietnam. By the late 1960s the United States and its South Vietnamese ally seemed all but beaten. Subtly, though much to Hanoi's annoyance, China urged North Vietnam to seek reconciliation with the 'puppet government' in Saigon.

Yet in this, Beijing had more in mind than securing advantages over Moscow and Taipei. It was growing apprehensive about the prospects of a united Vietnamese state and perhaps a Vietnamese-dominated Indochina. China disliked the fiercely independent nature of the

Vietnamese Communist Party. Paradoxically, it also feared that Hanoi was subservient to Moscow. China's behaviour did much to make the last fear a reality.

The triumph of Communism in Indochina in 1975, first in CAMBODIA, then in Vietnam and finally in Laos, made the region a focus of rivalry between Moscow and Beijing. In November 1978, Hanoi sought security against its vast neighbour to the north in a treaty of peace and friendship with the Soviet Union. The following month it invaded Cambodia, toppling the government of the Khmer Rouge, China's main ally in the region. DENG XIAO-PING, just back from the tour of the United States that celebrated the resumption of diplomatic relations between Washington and Beijing, decided to teach the region's 'small hegemonist' a lesson and punish it for mistreating its ethnic Chinese, many of whom fled across the border to China (see OVERSEAS CHINESE). In February 1979, Chinese troops launched a punitive war across the border into North Vietnam.

Militarily, the Sino-Vietnamese war was a mixed success at best. Chinese losses were high, sparking new calls for modernization of the PEOPLE'S LIBERATION ARMY. There was little obvious effect on Vietnamese operations in Cambodia, whose government remained subservient to Hanoi for a further 10 years. China secured Vietnam's diplomatic isolation – but at the cost of bringing the enmity between the erstwhile allies into the open: they exchanged accusations of betrayal and perfidy dating back to the 1950s.

The bitterness faded during the 1980s, but rivalry over the islands and oceans of the South China Sea kept the mistrust alive long after Hanoi and Beijing 'normalized' their relations at the end of 1991. Neither the collapse of the Soviet Union, which might have brought two of the world's remaining Communist parties closer together, nor the fact that Vietnam had begun to pursue free market reforms along Chinese lines, took the heat out of the territorial issue. Growing trade and traffic across the Sino-Vietnamese land border – itself the subject of dispute and discussions during the late 1990s – improved the overall atmosphere, but not the prospects for agreement in the South China Sea.

China's forward policy in the waters south of HAINAN ISLAND dated from 1974, when it seized the Paracel (Xisha) Islands from troops of the then government of South Vietnam. (See SOUTH CHINA SEA.) In 1988 it occupied several islands in the Spratly (Nansha) chain, further south, and fired on Vietnamese naval vessels that tried to resist. Hanoi said many of its sailors were killed or went missing in the clash. Similar incidents did not recur during the 1990s, but they might have done at any moment. Both sides persisted in their claims, sometimes reinforcing them by granting foreign oil companies exploration rights in the resource-rich region.

Vietnam is China's principal disputant in the South China Sea, but not the only one. Taiwan aside, the Philippines, Malaysia and Brunei all claim some of the thousands of islands and/or the waters surrounding them. Their membership of the ASSOCIATION OF SOUTHEAST ASIAN STATES (ASEAN) gives them a locus in which to discuss the issue and try to check Chinese expansion. Vietnam's admission to the group in 1995 strengthened their hand at a time when personnel from Chinese 'fishing vessels' were building defence structures on Mischief Reef, close to the Philippines. A Joint China–ASEAN Declaration of 1997, in which both sides renounced the use of force to settle their disputes in the South China Sea, demonstrated a desire to avoid further clashes. However, it has not guaranteed that. Neither has it removed a threat to peace in East Asia and a major obstacle in China's relations with Vietnam.

Wang Jingwei (1883–1944)

Republican revolutionary, attempted assassin, leader of the KUOMINTANG's Left wing and, finally, head of a Japanese 'puppet regime' – Wang Jingwei lost his moorings in the choppy waters of Chinese politics during the first half of the twentieth century and ended up reviled by all as a traitor. His imposing tomb in Nanjing was blown up immediately after the SINO-JAPANESE WAR and time has not lessened his infamy – on either side of the Taiwan Straits.

Wang's career began and ended in JAPAN, and was an extreme example of the complex hold that country exerted over many Chinese minds in the early decades of the century. For most, Japan was a source of inspiration *and* hatred; admiration *and* fear. For Wang, Japan was a natural, if unasked for, ally against 'foreign' (that is, Western) cultural influences and control in his homeland.

Wang's radicalism was born in Tokyo. While a law student there, he became a leading member of SUN YAT-SEN'S UNITED LEAGUE. His attempt in 1910 to assassinate the Manchu Prince Regent (the father of PU YI, the 'last emperor') made him a national figure, especially when he was released from jail after the QING DYNASTY collapsed the following year.

Wang went abroad as the young Republic descended into warlordism, but returned to China in the early 1920s to play a major part in the development of the Nationalist Revolution and the NORTHERN EXPEDITION to reunify China. He did so first as an ally of Sun and then as a rival of CHIANG KAI-SHEK, Sun's successor. In 1927, Wang was head of the Left-wing Kuomintang government in Wuhan, HUBEI province. Dismayed by Communist attempts at subversion, he eventually purged the radicals from his administration and was forced to yield to Chiang's leadership of the new Nationalist government based in Nanjing.

Wang and Chiang were never really reconciled. As prime minister and acting foreign minister, Wang faced the problem of dealing with Japanese aggression. His solution was appeasement. It was a policy that made him deeply unpopular, and in 1935 led to an assassination attempt which left a bullet lodged in his body for the rest of his life.

Wang believed resisting Japan was futile and that China had more to gain through cooperation with Tokyo than confrontation. In October 1938, 15 months after the start of the Sino-Japanese War, he flew to Hanoi, then occupied by Japan. He cabled Chiang, urging him to give up the fight. It was a blow for the Nationalist government, then isolated in CHONGQING and facing a powerful enemy almost alone.

Two years later, Wang was appointed head of a puppet Chinese national government based in Nanjing. It was a fleeting and frustrating moment of prominence, for Tokyo allowed neither it nor Wang much autonomy. In 1944 he went to Japan for medical treatment and died there, 40 years after he had first arrived in the country as an idealistic student.

warlords

From 1916 until 1928, and in some parts of China until 1949, regional militarists or warlords held sway. Their power testified to the drift towards national disintegration and the militarization of politics that scarred the country during the first half of the twentieth century. Both phenomena had antecedents in traditional times. Both were a function of China's size, regional diversity and weak central government. In these circumstances, the complex business of managing relations between the centre and the provinces broke down. Regions went their own way under local leaders and the cliques and armies they controlled.

The term 'warlord' is a pejorative one. It was, and is, a byword for local, selfish interests pursued by violence and accompanied by oppression. Official history in Beijing and Taiwan presents the warlord era as a uniformly dark age. The description is accurate for many, but not for all, of the scores of warlords who ruled parts of China following the death in 1916 of YUAN SHIKAI, the military strongman of the early Republic. There were patriots and reformers among them as well as those whose concern was mainly to loot and terrorize those under their control.

What warlords had in common was control over a 'personal' army whose officers and ranks were bound by ties of loyalty deriving from common geographical origins, schools or, perhaps, political aspiration. They also enjoyed control over a locality, province or series of provinces which could be used to raise men and money – without which warlord rule would be impossible. For much of the population this meant heavy taxation and brutal conscription, the twin scourges of life during the Republican era. It also meant war: warlords fought each other for territory and the economic and political spoils that went with it. Notionally, most of them hoped for an end to warlord rule and sought national unification, but they were interested in unity only on their own terms.

Unity on any terms proved impossible during the years immediately following Yuan's death and long thereafter. The president's attempt to restore the monarchy in 1916 and his own death removed the façade of national unity that had existed since the REPUBLICAN REVOLUTION of 1911. His successors in Beijing lacked the personal power needed to stamp

their authority on the rest of the country. They were also quite unable to fill the void arising from the collapse of traditional institutions. Republicanism was powerful, but only as an ideal. National unity existed only in name. Military power was what counted and nothing could be accomplished without it. Those who possessed it fought to retain and extend it. China disintegrated into regional military blocs.

Warlordism on this scale lasted a dozen years. It came to an end in 1928 with the completion of the NORTHERN EXPEDITION when CHIANG KAI-SHEK unified the country under the KUOMINTANG. Most warlords were either defeated on the battlefield or submitted to central authority on pain of being crushed by its superior troops. However, many 'submissions' fell far short of such. Militarists such as YAN XISHAN in SHANXI, LI ZONGREN in GUANGXI and Long Yun (1884–1962) in YUNNAN were often at odds with Chiang during the 1930s and 1940s. At best they could only be described as his allies. They undertook social and economic reforms in the areas they controlled in an attempt to steal a political march on the Nationalist leader. For years, the central government in Nanjing could not control the military forces these men commanded or make lasting inroads in the territories they occupied. 'Residual warlordism' of this kind hampered the government's military campaigns during the SINO-JAPANESE WAR, and contributed to its rapid collapse in the CIVIL WAR of 1946–9 against the Communists. After 1949, the new central government in Beijing, backed by superior military resources, made a point of breaking the power of the remaining regionalists.

The warlord era was a graphic example of the new relationship between military and political power in modern China following the fall of the QING DYNASTY in 1911. Politics were determined on the battlefield, or at least by the threat of a battlefield encounter. In traditional China, pursuit of the military life was regarded as the least prestigious calling. In the early twentieth century, it began to acquire a grim glory stemming from necessity. Civilian politics seemed to lead nowhere.

Yet the *ideal* of civilian government was never overturned. Neither was the notion that military force should be the servant of govern-

Principal Warlords, 1916–49

Names	Dates	Principal Areas of Rule
Li Zongren, Bai Chongxi, Huang Shaohong, Huaung Xuchu (the 'New Guangxi Clique')	1925–49	Guangxi, Anhui
Zhang Zuolin, the 'Old Marshal', leader of the 'Fengtian (Liaoning) Clique'	1916–28	Manchuria, occasionally parts of north China, including Beijing
Zhang Xueliang, the 'Young Marshal'	1928–31	Manchuria
Wu Peifu (the 'Zhili Clique')	1920–26	Central and parts of north China
Yan Xishan	1916–49	Shanxi
Feng Yuxiang (the 'Guominjun Clique')	1916–30	Shaanxi, parts of north China

ment rather than its master. The CHINESE COMMUNIST PARTY's triumph in 1949 grew out of the barrel of a gun. But the gun, though used to rescue the regime during the CULTURAL REVOLUTION in the 1960s and again by crushing the TIANANMEN SQUARE DEMOCRACY MOVEMENT in 1989, remained subservient to the Party, if not the government (see PEOPLE'S LIBERATION ARMY).

At the same time, the experience of warlordism did little to foster the idea that, because of its size and diversity, China might be ruled best as a series of independent or quasi-independent political units. Even the most narrow-minded warlord of the 1920s did not seek to turn the *de facto* independence of his region into a genuinely independent state. And a strong impulse towards unity among ethnic Chinese helped bring the warlord period to an end.

Washington Conference (November 1921–February 1922)

A concerted attempt by the powers to grant China a new diplomatic start occurred at the Washington Conference, during which JAPAN agreed to restore territory it had taken over in SHANDONG, settling one of the most sensitive issues for Beijing (see MAY FOURTH MOVEMENT). BRITAIN offered to return the leased territory of WEIHAIWEI, and France Guangzhou Bay, in GUANGDONG, about 250 miles (400 kms) west of HONG KONG. Other attempts to improve China's international standing included pledges, notably from the UNITED STATES, to respect her territorial integrity, encourage equal opportunity for foreign commerce, and ban the pursuit of new rights and privileges. China's representatives at the conference demanded the abolition of EXTRA-TERRITORIALITY and TARIFF AUTONOMY. They won neither. But it was agreed that subsequent commissions would discuss judicial reforms of the kind needed to secure them.

China was not the main subject at the conference, which was called to curb a naval race in the Pacific. This, in turn, was part of the attempt in the 1920s to find lasting international security arrangements of the kind that might avoid another world war. A spirit of goodwill towards China was apparent, possibly stemming from some of the participants' unease over past policy towards the country, and a feeling that the Republican government in Beijing should be given every chance to undertake reform.

The goodwill remained little more than that. Lack of sanctions against Japan, where militarism was on the rise, meant that the conference resolutions on naval armaments broke down. At the same time warlordism in China and battles between rival governments in Beijing and Guangzhou threatened to dissolve into anarchy of the kind that made the powers think twice about giving up their extraterritoriality (see WARLORDS). The case for restoring full sovereignty to China seemed less compelling when Chinese themselves could not agree who among them should exercise it.

Wei Jianxing (1931–)

Wei Jianxing's promotion to the CHINESE COMMUNIST PARTY's Politburo Standing Committee in 1997 was a sign of how serious the problem of CORRUPTION had become and an indication of the Party's determination to wipe it out. His long career in disciplinary, security and organization work made him the hammer of official corruption – or rather the next best thing to it, given the Mainland's lack of democracy, transparency and independent media. Wei held another position of importance in the context of the reform agenda in Beijing: president of the All-China Federation of Trade Unions whose members bore the brunt of the controversial reforms in state-owned enterprises (see INDUSTRY/SAVING SOCIALISM).

But it was as an organization man and a graft-buster that Wei, born in ZHEJIANG, a graduate in engineering from Dalian Engineering Institute, and a former student in the SOVIET UNION, rose to prominence. In this he owed something to the patronage of QIAO SHI, the former security chief turned parliamentary chairman. Qiao, forced to retire in 1997 from the Politburo, and thus from all his senior positions, agreed to go quietly on the understanding that Wei would join the top ranks of the Party.

Two years earlier, Wei had played an important role in securing the downfall of CHEN XITONG, the former Party boss of Beijing, who combined a taste for the fast life and corrupt business practices with political opposition to JIANG ZEMIN, the Party leader. He paid for these errors with a 16-year jail sentence. For a while, Wei succeeded Chen as Beijing Party secretary.

At the start of the new century Wei combines his position in the Politburo Standing Committee – where he is ranked sixth after Jiang Zemin, LI PENG, ZHU RONGJI, LI RUIHUAN and HU JINTAO, and before LI LANQING – with that of secretary of the Party's Central Commission for Discipline Inspection. This body is charged with purifying the Party's ranks of corruption at all levels.

Wei Jingsheng (1950–)

'The people should have democracy. When they call for democracy they are demanding nothing more than that which is inherently theirs. Whoever refuses to return democracy to them is a shameless thief more despicable than any capitalist who robs the workers of wealth earned with their own sweat and blood.'

A clearer – or more acerbic – assertion of the right to DEMOCRACY than this extract from Wei Jingsheng's poster 'The Fifth Modernization' had not been made public in Communist China before it appeared on Beijing's 'Democracy Wall' in December 1978. Its sentiments were as inflexible as its author, a former Red Guard who became a democracy activist while working as an electrician at Beijing Zoo. Both proved too much for the CHINESE COMMUNIST PARTY and, in particular, DENG XIAOPING. In 1979 Wei was arrested.

Wei's 'fifth modernization' – democracy – was an unofficial addition to the FOUR MODERNIZATIONS championed by the Party after the death of MAO ZEDONG in 1976 as a means of recovering from the political and economic chaos of the CULTURAL REVOLUTION. Wei said the four would be 'new lies' without the fifth. The fifth implied a much-reduced role for the Party, and for leaders such as Deng, whom Wei branded a dictator for closing down the DEMOCRACY WALL MOVEMENT, a remarkable outburst of dissent that erupted in Beijing and other cities in 1978–9.

Wei was accused of conducting 'counter-revolutionary propaganda' and leaking state secrets. The last charge referred to his discussion with foreign reporters of China's widely known military losses during the 1979 war with VIETNAM. Both charges showed the limits of tolerance in post-Mao China. Wei, sentenced to 15 years, disappeared into the gulag but refused to recant despite harsh treatment, including beatings and long spells in solitary confinement (see LABOUR CAMPS).

Human rights groups overseas kept Wei's name alive at a time when the West was keen to court a reforming China as a strategic counterweight to the SOVIET UNION. For most of the 1980s, neither the United States nor Western Europe took Beijing to task over HUMAN RIGHTS with the enthusiasm they showed when dealing with Moscow. The suppression of the TIANANMEN SQUARE DEMOCRACY MOVEMENT in 1989 changed that. So did

Wei's personal courage: already China's leading dissident, he became one of the best-known political prisoners in the world.

This irked Deng. He felt a strong personal animus towards a man who, so far from being grateful to the Party for the more relaxed life it ushered in by carrying out economic reforms, publicly challenged its supremacy and that of its paramount leader. However, in 1993, he approved Wei's release in an attempt to persuade the International Olympic Committee to let Beijing stage the Games in the year 2000.

The plan failed on two counts: Sydney won the Games and Wei immediately began speaking out for the cause he had championed in the 1970s. He disappeared into police custody again in March 1994 and the following year was sentenced to a further 14 years in jail. Eventually he became such an obstacle to China's relations with the West that in November 1997, 9 months after Deng's death, he was sent into exile to the UNITED STATES, where he promptly attacked American politicians and businessmen for going 'soft' on human rights in China.

Courage and resilience were just two of Wei's remarkable qualities. He lacked much in the way of formal education yet was as well read as many of the intellectuals among China's dissident community. His incarceration meant he had never been abroad, spoke no foreign languages and was by custom and habit typically Chinese. Yet, intellectually, he was a true internationalist, arguing for a form of democracy that made no concessions to race, culture or class.

Wei was contrary by nature, dismissing almost as an irrelevance the economic growth that transformed the lives of millions of his countrymen while he was in prison, and insisting that nothing would change in China without immediate, genuine democracy. Before his arrest in 1979, during his brief period of freedom in 1993–4, and while in exile in the United States, he put these views forward with passion and humour, usually while smoking endlessly. While in prison, he argued the same cause in numerous letters to his jailers and Communist leaders, Deng Xiaoping included.

Together with other exiles, Wei pledged to work from the United States for the introduction of democracy in China. His ability to accomplish much in this regard was uncertain. But there can be no question of Wei returning to his homeland in the absence of fundamental political change in Beijing.

Weihaiwei

Weihaiwei, an enclave in SHANDONG, north China, administered for three decades along traditional Chinese lines by BRITAIN, provides more than just a curious footnote to imperial history. Its voluntary restoration to China in 1930 by a country otherwise reluctant to abandon treaty privileges assures it a place in the history of colonial retreat as well as of Chinese nationalism.

Britain acquired a lease on 288 square miles (746 sq kms) of northeast Shandong, around the walled city of Weihai, in 1898. In the same year it extended its possession of HONG KONG, extracting from the feeble QING DYNASTY a 99-year lease on the New Territories.

There, the similarities between the territories ceased: Weihaiwei was designed to be a coaling station for the Royal Navy, not the defensive perimeter of an established colony. It was a means of countering German and particularly Russian influence in north China. Under the terms of the lease, Britain was to hold Weihaiwei, not for 99 years, but for as long as RUSSIA held Port Arthur (modern Lushun), the naval base across the Bohai Gulf at the tip of the Liaodong peninsula in Manchuria, the Tsar's 'sphere of influence' in northeast China (see LIAONING).

In fact, Britain occupied it for much longer. The victory of JAPAN in its war of 1904–5 with Russia broke the latter's hold over southern Manchuria. The First World War and the Bolshevik Revolution removed Russia and Germany from the Chinese scene completely as far as threats to British interests were concerned. Under the new, post-war order, Japan was dominant in north China, and Japan was an ally of Britain.

In 1916, Britain formed the Chinese Labour Corps, a non-combatant army founded to build railways, roads and factories in France and free regular troops for the front line in the battle against Imperial Germany. Weihaiwei was a chief recruiting station of the Corps, many of whose almost 200,000 men came from Shandong (see OVERSEAS CHINESE).

Tokyo's occupation during the First World War of territory leased to Germany in Shan-

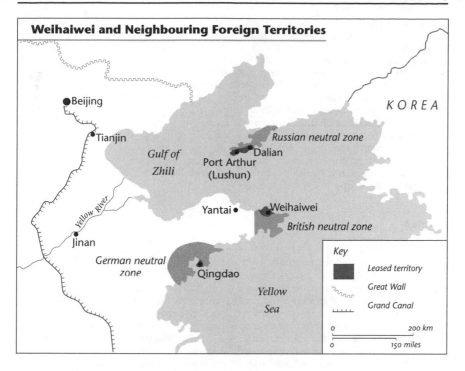

Weihaiwei and Neighbouring Foreign Territories

KOREA

Beijing

Tianjin

Gulf of
Zhili

Russian neutral zone

Dalian

Port Arthur
(Lushun)

Yellow River

Jinan

Yantai

Weihaiwei

British neutral zone

German neutral
zone

Qingdao

Yellow
Sea

Key

Leased territory

Great Wall

Grand Canal

| 0 | 200 km |
| 0 | 150 miles |

dong sparked the new breed of Chinese nationalism at the heart of the MAY FOURTH MOVEMENT of 1919. At the WASHINGTON CONFERENCE of 1921–2, the powers persuaded Japan to restore its Shandong territories to China, and Britain offered to do the same regarding Weihaiwei. A further 8 years passed before London honoured its pledge: with China convulsed by struggles between WARLORDS and the upheaval of the NORTHERN EXPEDITION to reunify China, it was hard to find a stable, national government to whom

the territory could be rescinded. This changed in 1928 when CHIANG KAI-SHEK founded the KUOMINTANG government in Nanjing.

The rendition of Weihaiwei, in October 1930, reflected British recognition of the heightened sense of nationalism in the 'new' China of the early 1930s; a realization that its continued presence in the territory served no purpose; and a willingness – precisely on those grounds – to give it up. It was the first time that the imperial 'last post' was sounded voluntarily in China on any scale.

Wen Jiabao (1942–)

A geologist turned specialist in AGRICULTURE, FINANCE and the ENVIRONMENT, Wen was a close, though unobtrusive, aide to ZHAO ZIYANG in the 1980s and JIANG ZEMIN in the 1990s. Both of these very different leaders of the CHINESE COMMUNIST PARTY found his expertise and mastery of administrative machinery invaluable. Both qualities make Wen a candidate for even higher office in future than he had attained at the close of the

twentieth century: membership of the Politburo (from 1997); secretary general of the Party's 'leading group' on finance and the economy; and vice-premier (from 1998).

Wen was born in TIANJIN and graduated from Beijing Geological Institute. He joined the Party in 1965 and worked in the GANSU provincial geological bureau for more than 10 years. In the early 1980s he moved to Beijing and became deputy director and then director of the General Office of the Party's Central Committee, a backstage position of considerable power.

During the late 1980s Wen worked closely with Zhao Ziyang. He accompanied the reformist Party leader on his fateful visit to the hunger strikers in Tiananmen Square in May 1989 (see TIANANMEN SQUARE DEMOCRACY MOVEMENT). It was Zhao's last public appearance as general secretary of the Party.

Wen was demoted after Zhao's fall, but his competence and expertise enabled him to escape disgrace. He adapted quickly to political life under Jiang Zemin. In 1992 he was made an alternate (that is, non-voting) member of the Politburo and often accompanied the new general secretary on his travels around the country. His promotions in 1997 and 1998 saw him add responsibility for poverty relief to his portfolio (see POVERTY).

Wen will have relative youthfulness on his side in the contest for key leadership positions in Beijing during the first years of the new century. But his apparent preference for working behind the scenes suggests he will not challenge the likes of HU JINTAO or WU BANG-GUO for the very highest posts in the Party or government.

women

Of all the evidence of China's backwardness at the start of the twentieth century – the inability of its ideology, politics, economy and social institutions to cope with the challenges of the modern world – the inferior status of Chinese women was among the most shaming. It was not just that women were defined solely in terms of their relationship to men. It was that they were subordinated absolutely by beliefs, customs, practice and legal codes which seemed to deprive them of much of their humanity, save that arising from their roles as producers, hopefully, of sons. No wonder women participated at every stage of the struggle to remake China. No wonder, either, that though their status improved in the process, sexual equality eludes them still at the start of the new century.

subordination under the old order

By the late QING DYNASTY women were heirs to centuries of discrimination that deprived most of them of meaningful work, property rights, EDUCATION, save in the art of 'becoming conduct', and choice of marriage partner (see FAMILY). Parents might not despise their daughters, but they treasured them less than sons. Sons engaged in farm work, inherited the family business, looked after parents in old age and sustained the male line. Daughters left home on marriage and joined their husband's family whom they served, ideally by producing sons and obeying their mother-in-law. Concubines often ousted wives in their husband's affections. Divorce was next to impossible. Widowhood was for life. A wife who produced one or more sons might gain prestige in her new family but not legal protection. The authorities rarely intervened when a husband physically mistreated his wife. CONFUCIANISM reinforced and justified this patriarchal society.

In some respects, Chinese women did not suffer more than their sisters in agrarian societies elsewhere. In others they did. An example was the high rate of female infanticide in traditional China. Parents sometimes preferred to drown or expose a new-born girl – a potential burden for the family until she could be married off, usually at a price – in the hope that the next born would be a son, a 'real' investment for the future. The same thinking was behind less common, but still *too* common, incidents of female infanticide in the 1990s (see POPULATION).

Another grim example of female subordination was the practice of footbinding. The toes of girls, usually aged between seven and eight, were bound under their insteps until the arches of their feet were broken. A crippling experience, it left women with short, pointed feet that Chinese men found erotic. In so far as women could walk at all, they were forced to do so in a slow, measured gait that men said resembled the swaying of willows in the wind. Bound feet, more common in north China than the south, were regarded as 'golden lilies' and celebrated in sensuous poems and songs. More prosaically, they confined women to their homes or at least their villages, and were a potent symbol of sexual inferiority.

liberating feet, liberating minds

Abolition of footbinding was an early target of campaigns to improve the position of Chinese women in the late Qing. MISSIONARIES were among the leaders of the movement along with reformers such as KANG YOUWEI and LIANG QICHAO. In a Court edict of 1902, the EMPRESS DOWAGER – a rare example of a politically powerful Chinese woman – urged abolition of the custom. Regulations drawn up a few years later forbade it. Yet these strictures made little impact beyond the cities and not always much there.

Missionaries and reformers tried to unbind female minds as well as feet. They founded girls' schools, overturning established conventions which said educating women was a waste of time, indecorous, dangerous and possibly all three. Again the Court followed the reformers' lead, creating government schools for the education of women during last-gasp reforms before imperial collapse in 1911. Such moves often encouraged protest and dissent: in 1907, troops were dispatched to put down a rebellion in ZHEJIANG led by Qiu Jin (1875–1907), an early feminist who had studied in Japan and returned to China to overthrow Manchu rule. Her revolt, based on a local girls' school in the city of Shaoxing, was crushed. Qiu was tortured and beheaded.

Women played a part in, and were beneficiaries of, the growth in revolutionary consciousness associated with the REPUBLICAN REVOLUTION of 1911, the MAY FOURTH MOVEMENT of 1919, the foundation of the CHINESE COMMUNIST PARTY in 1921 and the reorganization of the KUOMINTANG in 1923–4. They, too, were humiliated by China's weakness in the face of the outside world. They, too, were influenced by the ideas of science and DEMOCRACY, the doctrines of ANARCHISM, nationalism, and MARXISM that inspired men to fight for the future of their country. And, just as urban women widened their horizons through formal education, so rural women learned lessons of a different, but no less important, kind by moving to cities and working in factories.

Yet China's small but growing band of politically active women had more specific tasks on their agenda than most of their male counterparts. They were those of ending the tyranny of sexual discrimination at home, in the workplace and in society at large. This, for them, was the true revolution. Both the Communists and the Kuomintang, operating in alliance in the mid-1920s, were committed to equality of the sexes. Both promised a new deal for women. But they would have to seize power first. That involved years of struggle, division and war. Female emancipation, a sub-

sidiary of the wider Revolution, would have to wait.

The cause of sexual equality advanced at a different pace and sometimes in different directions during the 1930s and 1940s. The Civil Code passed by CHIANG KAI-SHEK'S Nationalist government in 1930 specified that women could inherit and own property. It also provided for equal rights in the workplace. Yet this long-awaited legal emancipation was really no more than that: implementation was patchy, and few people in the rural areas seem to have heard about it. Chiang's 'New Life' movement, designed to counter Communist influence, encouraged women to pursue virtue rather than learning, family responsibilities rather than future careers (see CONFUCIANISM). Few women entered politics in Kuomintang China, and SOONG MEI-LING, Chiang's wife and China's 'first lady', owed her importance during the war against Japan to her ability to win support for China in the West.

In Communist-controlled areas, particularly YANAN, women experienced a genuine, if limited, form of liberation. Its chief expression was female involvement in war, politics and production. Chinese Communism involved the mobilization of all sectors of society for the Revolution. The task of the Party's Women's Federation was to rally women to the cause in their own interests and those of the Party's survival and victory. Women were encouraged to work, both to end their own economic dependency and to develop the backward economy of 'base areas' during the SINO-JAPANESE WAR. That this meant *extra* burdens rather than emancipation for many women, who were still required to perform traditional duties at home, was made clear by Ding Ling (1904–85), a Left-wing novelist who had moved to Yanan. She was purged for her heretical view that socialism did not necessarily deliver sexual equality, and that feminism had to be pursued as a 'higher', separate goal.

socialism and feminism after 1949

Following their victory in the CIVIL WAR the Communists introduced two measures which exerted a profound effect on women's lives. The marriage law of 1950 abolished concubinage, bridal 'gifts' or dowries, and arranged marriages. It also provided for the dissolution of forced unions, sparking a wave of divorces across the country instigated by unhappy women. Marriages had to be registered, one of several moves during the 1950s that brought the state into direct contact with ordinary people. LAND REFORM, the second measure, empowered women economically. Not only could they own property, they were *granted* it in the course of a massive exercise in redistribution. The effects were tempered by the fact that property was usually vested with households, and households were still run largely by men. But in terms of women's rights, land reform was a genuine legal and conceptual breakthrough.

Yet if women in China no longer depended solely on men to determine their lives, they still could not do so entirely by themselves. The opportunity – and soon the obligation – to work, to engage in production was not a small matter, but 'New' China was a man's world. Despite the prominence of SONG QING-LING, women were under-represented in politics and most professions. Often they were paid less than men in comparable positions. A preference for sons easily survived the Revolution in the villages. And while the Women's Federation gave women a voice, feminism had to take a back seat to socialism, the struggle between the sexes to that between classes. National solidarity and Party dominance always came first.

This remained the case during the violent policy swings of Mao Zedong's years in power beginning with the ONE HUNDRED FLOWERS MOVEMENT of 1956–7, continuing with the GREAT LEAP FORWARD of 1958–60 and culminating in the CULTURAL REVOLUTION (1966–76). These cataclysms changed women's lives just as they did men's. The creation of communes during the Leap, and the communal eating in canteens that often went with them, tended to free women of the household chores they usually had to undertake in addition to their paid work. But these were modest, probably illusory, gains given the disruption with which the Leap began and the chaos and famine with which it ended. And, once the Cultural Revolution was over in the late 1970s, there were no signs that Chinese women dissented from the general view that the movement had been a catastrophe. In particular there was relief that the reign of JIANG QING, Mao's widow, and easily the most powerful woman in Chinese politics since the Empress Dowager, was over.

women in the reform era

Free market reforms and the opening of China's economy in the late 1970s to the out-side world promised a new start for all Chinese, male and female. This was welcome after years of political struggle in which living standards had hardly improved at all. But it did not address specific problems facing women. Their economic status had improved but they were still subject to prejudices that made life much less comfortable than it was for men. Once again, the Party said such issues could be solved only in a piecemeal fashion in the course of China's development. Meanwhile, everything had to be subordinated to the Party's new central task: economic construction.

During the 1980s it became clear that the new policies might mean more rather than less hardship for women. One reason for this was the sudden introduction of birth control measures designed to restrict urban families to one child, and reduce births among families in rural areas (see POPULATION). Traditional prejudices against baby girls revived. Female infanticide and a high incidence of female abortion were among the causes of a sharp imbalance between the sexes of China's newborn. Among the consequences was a lively trade in the abduction and sale of women to men increasingly desperate to find wives.

Women were involved, often intimately, in many aspects of the commercialization of life that characterized China during the 1990s. Whether they were always casualties is more difficult to determine. Females often formed the majority of the workforce in the thousands of factories set up in the SPECIAL ECONOMIC ZONES and other coastal cities. Usually country girls, they helped produce the exports that did so much to turn China into a trade giant at the close of the century. Women workers undoubtedly earned more than they might have done had they stayed on the farm. But their long hours, vulnerability to physical and sexual abuse and often grim living conditions were reminders that industrial revolutions are not particularly pleasant for many of those caught up in them.

Less ambiguous were the effects on women of the commercialization of sex in many Chinese cities. Prostitution, some of it backed by the police and even the People's Liberation Army, survived numerous campaigns to eradicate it. The preference of men from Hong Kong and Taiwan for keeping mistresses on the Mainland – sometimes, though not always, in some style – proved equally enduring.

If industry and willingness to work for relatively low pay sometimes made women attractive as employees, such qualities did not always keep them in employment once state enterprises and other businesses sought to shed labour as a result of reforms. Women were over-represented among the urban unemployed at the close of the twentieth century, just as they were among the illiterates and school drop-outs of the rural areas, where their status remained worse than in the cities.

These and other developments were apparent when the UNITED NATIONS held its international women's conference in Beijing in 1995. The Communist Party welcomed the formal conference proceedings, presenting the fact that they took place in Beijing as a tribute to China's progress and importance. But the associated gathering of non-governmental organizations, some of whose members pursued radical causes at odds with the Party's semi-stated position of 'socialism first, feminism second', was another matter. It was confined to Huairou, a small township 30 miles (48 kms) north of Beijing, where many of the participants were closely monitored.

At the start of the new century, women in China are handicapped by the same factors that make life less free and agreeable than it might be for men. Chiefly these have to do with the absence of DEMOCRACY and HUMAN RIGHTS. But they also face a special set of problems arising from the persistence of traditional forms of discrimination. Eradication of these prejudices is not high on the Party's agenda. Indeed, many are beyond the capacity of the Communist Party in its current form to do much about. This is not just because the past half century has shown that traditions cannot easily be rooted out. It is because there are very few women in politics powerful enough to make an issue of them. Part, but by no means all, of the indictment against the Party's treatment of women arises from the fact that in the year 2000 only one woman, trade minister Wu Yi (1938–), was a member of the Politburo, and she was an 'alternate' member without voting rights.

Wu Bangguo (1941–)

Ability, relative youthfulness, and perhaps above all close association with JIANG ZEMIN, leader of the CHINESE COMMUNIST PARTY, accounted for Wu Bangguo's rise during the 1990s to the position of Party boss in SHANGHAI and then transfer to Beijing as vice-premier in charge of industry. The same factors may propel him even higher in the new century, making him a contender to succeed ZHU RONGJI as premier.

Wu became secretary of the Shanghai Party Committee in 1991, in succession to Zhu. Jiang, Zhu and Wu had worked together in the city for several years, and the two older men valued the younger for his long experience in Shanghai's electrical and electronic industries. Born in ANHUI, a graduate in radio engineering from Beijing's Qinghua University, and a member of the Communist Party since 1964, Wu spent almost 30 years in Shanghai until Jiang moved him to Beijing in 1995.

In Wu's case the prestige of promotion was sullied by the portfolio: rescuing, closing or merging hundreds of state-owned industries burdened with excessive debt, unwanted employees, outdated production methods and, often, unmarketable products (see INDUSTRY/SAVING SOCIALISM). The ideological objections to such treatment of what had once been a pillar of socialism were not removed until the Party's 15th National Congress in 1997. It was decided that shareholding was justified while China was still in the 'initial stage' of socialism, and that many of those enterprises which could not flourish under government ownership might sell their assets to other entities, including private individuals and even foreigners (see CHINESE COMMUNIST PARTY/SOCIALISM.)

Ideological 'breakthroughs' of this kind have not made Wu Bangguo's work much easier. He still has to revive or retire hundreds of firms employing millions of people, many of whom find it difficult to secure new jobs. The Asian financial crisis of 1997–9 made things worse by curbing growth throughout the region, China included. Fresh challenges arise from China's membership of the World Trade Organization. If there was little evidence that these problems were about to frustrate Wu's promising career there was no disguising their seriousness either.

At the close of the century another potential difficulty stood in his way, one that had proved a major source of strength earlier in his career: Wu's Shanghai connection. The perception that he was part of a 'Shanghai Gang', and too close to Jiang, played a part in his failure to win election to the 7-man Politburo Standing Committee in 1997. It was not a terminal setback to Wu's chances of reaching the very top. But it was a consider-able one. He will have to perform well in a sensitive area and during difficult times to recover lost ground.

Wu, Harry Hongda (1937–)

Harry Wu did more than any other single Chinese in the 1990s to publicize China's HUMAN RIGHTS abuses in the West. He did so on the basis of experience, having spent 19 years in various kinds of LABOUR CAMPS after his condemnation in 1960 as a 'Rightist'.

Wu left China in 1985 and became an American citizen. He began to document China's labour camps, and said at least 50 million people had passed through them between 1949 and 1996. His memoir *Bitter Winds: A Memoir of My Years in China's Gulag* was published in 1994.

Wu helped expose China's export of goods made by forced labour, and the sale and trans-plant of organs from executed Chinese prisoners. Much of his information he gathered during secret trips to China. He was arrested while on one of them in 1995, a period of tension in relations between China and the UNITED STATES. Wu was convicted of spying, sentenced to 15 years in prison but promptly expelled to the US to prevent a further deterio-ration in ties with Washington. He continued to campaign for an end to China's labour camps, and warned American companies and international lending agencies that some of their investments in China risked strengthening the gulag system by employing its victims in the form of cheap labour.

Wu Peifu (1874–1939)

Military skill and political cunning helped Wu Peifu become the dominant warlord of north-central China during the early 1920s. Equally important was his control of the Beijing–Hankou railway: a key north–south artery that ran through the provinces of Zhili (modern HEBEI), HENAN and HUBEI at the heart of his domain.

The railway line provided a valuable source of revenue for Wu and a means of rushing troops to trouble spots within the often vast but always unstable empire run by the 'Zhili Clique', of which he was the most powerful figure (see WARLORDS). Wu, born in SHAN-DONG, was a Confucian in his outlook but one who believed in reinforcing the moral code with military training. He cracked down hard when workers threatened his grip on the railway line in 1923. His troops opened fire on strikers, killing many of them and dealing a crushing blow to the labour movement within the area he controlled.

This shrank dramatically in 1924 when FENG YUXIANG, another leading militarist and his nominal ally, deserted him for arch rival Zhang Zuolin (1875–1928), leader of the Fengtian Clique based in Manchuria, northeast China. Wu made a partial recovery and re-established control over Hubei and Hunan whose resources he pledged to the struggle against the armies of the newly reorganized KUOMINTANG under SUN YAT-SEN and CHIANG KAI-SHEK based in GUANGDONG. He fought the revolutionary armies hard but did not prevail: in 1926 Kuomintang troops defeated his forces during the first stage of the NORTHERN EXPEDITION to unify China. Wu fled to SICHUAN where his career came to an end but where he enjoyed personal protection from a local warlord.

X

Xian Incident, 12 December 1936

The ancient capital of SHAANXI was the setting for a tense, defining moment in China's modern history when some of CHIANG KAI-SHEK's generals kidnapped their leader and forced him to abandon attempts to suppress the CHINESE COMMUNIST PARTY in favour of resisting JAPAN. The Xian Incident almost certainly saved the Communists from further, possibly devastating, setbacks. It also boosted Chiang's own prestige, bringing him into line with a popular determination to resist Japanese encroachments. The KUOMINTANG leader remained committed to 'bandit-suppression' – as he styled his anti-Communist campaign – throughout the SINO-JAPANESE WAR. But in the immediate aftermath of events in Xian, China appeared more united than at any time since the REPUBLICAN REVOLUTION of 1911.

The key protagonist in the Xian Incident was ZHANG XUELIANG, whose personal fate symbolized China's crisis. In 1932, the 'Young Marshal' was driven from the Manchurian domain he had inherited from his father, Zhang Zuolin (1875–1928), by Japan's creation of the puppet state of MANCHUGUO. Chiang promptly deployed Zhang and his troops against the Communists who, having completed their LONG MARCH, had established a new headquarters at YANAN in northern Shaanxi.

Given the growing Japanese menace to China this was an unpopular move. Anti-Japanese protests erupted in many cities. Even various WARLORDS pledged to use their forces against Japan. And the Communists, under the guidance of the Communist International

in Moscow, promised to put patriotism before revolution. From their redoubt in Yanan they echoed the SOVIET UNION's appeal for a 'United Front' of all Chinese forces against the international menace of Fascism.

Zhang, cut off from his home base, and his troops soon blooded from their involvement in the anti-Communist campaign, proved increasingly susceptible to this nationalist sentiment. After meeting privately with the Communist leader ZHOU ENLAI he warmed still further to the United Front idea. Together with his senior officers he decided to force Chiang to abandon his planned 'final push' against the Communists during a scheduled meeting of the military command in Xian.

The drama began at dawn on 12 December 1936. Zhang's forces stormed Chiang's headquarters outside the city, forcing the Nationalist leader to flee into the hills. He was quickly captured and presented with 8 demands. Chief among them was an end to civil war and the reorganization of the central government along more representative lines.

These developments stunned China. Forces loyal to Chiang went on the alert and prepared to move on Xian. Most warlords preferred to wait and see. The Communists sought advice from Moscow and learned that Joseph Stalin preferred Chiang kept alive in order to lead China against Japan. After tense negotiations, in which Chiang agreed verbally to the demands, he was released and returned to Nanjing where he received a hero's welcome.

Zhang, who returned with him, was jailed for his treachery and became a prisoner for all but the final few years of his life. Seven months after the Xian Incident had injected a new spirit of resistance into the Chinese government, Japan launched full-scale war against China, beginning with the Marco Polo Bridge Incident (see SINO-JAPANESE WAR).

Xinjiang Uigur Autonomous Region

History hardly substantiates China's claim to the remote region of Central Asia it calls Xinjiang ('new frontier'): during the first 2 millennia of the Christian era it was free of Chinese control for longer periods than it was subjected to it. Neither does culture: the relatively small part of the region that supports habitation is the homeland of Uigurs, Kazakhs and Kirghiz, Turkic-speaking Muslims who look west, not east to Beijing, for inspiration. But the imperatives of national security, access to natural resources and a desire to be at least the equal of past dynasties give Beijing a vital stake in an area it refuses to relinquish – even at the price of constant racial tension, frequent outbreaks of anti-Chinese terrorism and occasional large-scale revolts. At the start of the new century Xinjiang is the least secure part of the People's Republic. If its secession is unlikely, so is the prospect of harmony within its frontiers.

rivalry, secession, conquest

The current period of Chinese control dates from the 1870s when QING DYNASTY generals suppressed a Muslim rebellion led by Yakub Beg (c 1820–77). Yakub was an adventurer who represented the demands of local people for greater freedom. But he was also an agent of BRITAIN, which was concerned to counter the influence of RUSSIA in the region and protect British India. Chinese Turkestan, as it was known to many at the time and long thereafter, was a cockpit of ethnic and imperial conflict; its indigenous inhabitants were pawns in a triangular struggle between the Qing Dynasty, the British and the Russian empires.

Despite victory over Yakub, an influx of Han Chinese settlers, and the incorporation of Xinjiang into the empire as a province in 1884, Chinese control proved elusive. From the Republican Revolution of 1911 to 1944, Chinese warlords ruled Xinjiang as a semi-independent kingdom. Neither Beijing, nor Nanjing, when it became the capital in 1928, could exert much influence. Within Xinjiang itself the dramas of the nineteenth century were repeated on a smaller scale: the SOVIET UNION inherited imperial Russia's interests in the region, and the local Uigurs, Kazakhs and Kirghiz resisted the weak Chinese presence. On two occasions, 1933 and 1944, they declared a Republic of East Turkestan in territory they controlled.

The second of these republics lasted the longest. It was set up after the departure from the province of Sheng Shicai (1896–1961), Xinjiang's most formidable warlord, whose pro-Soviet sympathies and general insensitivity towards non-Han peoples made him feared in Nanjing and loathed at home. Moscow's influence in Xinjiang during the 1930s and early 1940s was immense. Sheng signed over to his giant neighbour the right to exploit the region's valuable mineral resources. He accepted Soviet arms for his troops and advisers in his government. He even joined the Soviet Communist Party. And, with the outbreak of the SINO-JAPANESE WAR in 1937, he allowed Soviet troops to garrison part of the province. Moscow was as surprised as the rest of the world when Sheng suddenly threw in his lot with CHIANG KAI-SHEK in 1942, purged Xinjiang of Chinese and Soviet Communist influence and, two years later, left to become a minister in the Nationalist government. For the first time since 1911, the Chinese central government was able to impose some form of control over its most distant region.

But only some form. Moscow was quick to recoup its losses by backing the Uigur-led revolt in the Ili valley, northwest Xinjiang, that founded the second Republic of East Turkestan. The new Chinese authorities in Dihua, Xinjiang's capital until it was renamed Urumqi (*Wulumuqi*), tried but failed to come to terms with the rebels. With the advance of Communist troops into the province in 1949 during the closing stages of the CIVIL WAR, the Nationalists faced enemies to the east and the west. The civil administration and most of Chiang's troops surrendered to the PEOPLE'S LIBERATION ARMY (PLA).

So did the leaders of the Republic of Eastern Turkestan – or rather, those who remained. Most were killed in a plane crash en route to Beijing to take part in a meeting of the CHINESE PEOPLE'S POLITICAL CONSULTATIVE CONFERENCE (CPPCC), the Communist-controlled forum that declared the foundation of the People's Republic in October 1949. The remaining rebels, their Soviet backers drawing closer to MAO ZEDONG as he led the Communists to victory, dissolved their republic and agreed to work with the new Chinese regime.

integration and immigration

If these developments pointed to a new start for Xinjiang, the persistence of older problems soon prevented it. Chief among them was the racial question. When the PLA entered Xinjiang, Han Chinese numbered about 250,000, or approximately 6 per cent of the total population of 4 million. Uigurs, farming people scattered throughout Xinjiang but concentrated in the southwest, particularly around Kashgar, were the largest group, constituting perhaps 75 per cent of the population. Kazakhs were the second largest with 10 per cent. A nomadic people, their homeland is in the northwest of the province. The third-largest non-Han group was the Kirghiz.

Beijing's determination to integrate Xinjiang with the rest of China and develop it necessitated a huge influx of Chinese settlers. This upset the existing population ratios and altered the political and cultural complexion of the province. Worse, at least from Xinjiang's point of view, Beijing's determination during the GREAT LEAP FORWARD and the CULTURAL REVOLUTION to *revolutionize* the region along with other, predominantly Chinese, provinces provoked racial hostility and widespread disturbances. None of these developments threatened Communist Chinese control of Xinjiang. But each of them made it harder – at the time and for years after – to exercise it.

The main vehicle of integration, development and Han settlement in the region was the Xinjiang Production and Construction Corps. It was formed in 1954 from Communist troops of the First Field Army that 'liberated' Xinjiang, and former Nationalist soldiers in the region. Its leader was Wang Zhen (1908–93), at this stage in his career perhaps the closest any Communist military leader came to becoming a warlord. In later life, Wang dedicated his career to fighting 'bourgeois liberalization', or the popular demand for political liberty, that accompanied Deng Xiaoping's economic reforms. A third element of the corps was at least as important as the first two: ethnic Chinese recruits from all over the country who volunteered to develop one of the poorest, most backward areas of the

People's Republic. From Beijing's point of view, the merit of the scheme was that work in a frontier region promised to transform the ideological outlook of those who undertook it. From the point of view of the authorities in Urumqi, nationwide recruiting provided a stream of Chinese settlers to tip the balance of population away from the non-Han.

The corps reclaimed land, managed state farms, ran prisons, operated businesses, defended the borders and generally maintained security in China's most unruly province. It also helped build the railway that, by 1961, connected Urumqi with Lanzhou, capital of neighbouring GANSU (see RAILWAYS). At the start of the twenty-first century, the corps – renamed the China Xinjiang Construction Company – is the largest business conglomerate in the country and one of the best examples of China's variety of state capitalism.

The first decade of Communist rule saw significant industrial development, much of it aided by the partnership between Moscow and Beijing (see SOVIET UNION; INDUSTRY). Iron and steel works, petrochemical plant, cement and textile factories were built in a region almost devoid of industry before 1949. In the late 1950s, facilities were set up at Lop Nor, the remote, dried-up lake in the west of the province, where in 1964 China exploded its first atomic device (see PEOPLE'S LIBERATION ARMY/CHINA AND THE BOMB).

revolution and racial tension

In 1955, Xinjiang was redesignated the Xinjiang Uigur Autonomous Region. Ever since, a succession of non-Han leaders – Seypidin Azizi (1915–), Ismail Aymat (1935–), Tomur Dawamat (1927–) and, at the start of the new century, Ablait Abdurexit (1942–) – have chaired the regional government. However, real power has remained with the Han-controlled Communist Party and military, as has been the case in China's other 'autonomous regions' (see ETHNIC MINORITIES).

On the surface the creation of the Xinjiang Autonomous Region was a concession to local opinion that suggested a certain confidence on the part of the Han-dominated political and military establishment. If so, it soon proved misplaced. Tensions in the region increased with the radicalization of national politics in China during the late 1950s. Mao's Great Leap Forward was designed to eliminate ethnic as well as class differences: leading members of non-Han groups who stressed

The Lie of the Land

Xinjiang's 615,000 square miles (1.6 million sq kms) make it the largest provincial unit in China, yet, with just over 17 million people at the close of the century, among the least populated. Terrain, climate and the region's traditional remoteness account for its relative dearth of people. Xinjiang consists of two giant basins, both of them surrounded by mountains and divided by the mighty Tianshan range which runs east–west. The Jung-gar Basin is the northerly and smaller of the two. It is bounded to the north by the Altay mountains. Karamay, the oil town, is in the southwest of the basin. Urumqi is located on its southern edge. To the north and west are the predominantly Kazakh areas, and the Ili valley, inhabited by Kazakhs, Kirghiz and Uigurs, which is one of Xinjiang's most fertile areas. At the heart of the Tarim basin in the south is the Taklimakan Desert which covers over half of Xinjiang's total area and is also believed to be rich in oil and gas. The oasis cities along its southern and western edges permit some agriculture and are mainly Uigur areas. The same is true of Turfan, halfway between Urumqi and Hami on the road and railway line heading east towards Gansu. The greatest concentration of non-sinicized Uigurs are found in and around the historic trading city of Kashgar, close to the border with Kirghizstan and Tajikistan.

Xinjiang's differences from the rest of China were condemned as 'local nationalists'. Non-Chinese were told to abandon Arabic for a more 'modern' Latin script that would have the advantage, at least for Beijing, of weakening ties with their brothers and sisters across the border in the Soviet republics. Religious customs deemed 'superstitious' were banned.

While these moves damaged Han–non-Han relations, the economic policies of the era proved even more harmful. First Xinjiang's agricultural land, and then the grazing pastures in the north, were communized, leading to shortages and starvation of the kind that struck many parts of China during the early 1960s. In 1962 up to 80,000 people, most of them Kazakhs, fled across the border into Soviet Kazakhstan in search of food and shelter. Soviet authorities, embroiled in the polemics of the Sino-Soviet Split (see SOVIET UNION/SINO-SOVIET SPLIT), encouraged an exodus that renewed fears in Beijing about Russian territorial ambitions in the region.

The Cultural Revolution led to chaos of a different but even more intense kind. It was mainly a Chinese affair: the post-1949 Han establishment waged a bitter struggle for power with Chinese Red Guards and other radicals who arrived in the region during the mid-1960s to revolutionize it. The latter won, toppling Wang Enmao (1913–), the region's longstanding Party boss. But if the non-Han population was less involved in the infighting, it was no less affected by the instability and neglect of economic development and construction which characterized the era. Attempts to preserve national identity were politically impossible. Some Muslims were ordered to tend pig farms. And the arrival of thousands more Chinese settlers – whether 'volunteers' or subjects of Chairman Mao's rustication campaigns – diluted the non-Han population still further.

Once again, the Soviet Union played on these fears with a string of appeals to the 'oppressed peoples' of Xinjiang. In 1969 and 1974, Soviet troops provoked border clashes with the PLA in the Ili region. As elsewhere in China, order did not return to Xinjiang's borders or the rest of the region until the death of Mao in 1976 and the rise of DENG XIAOPING as paramount leader two years later.

rebellion and reform

Yet 'order' has always been a relative term in the troubled context of Xinjiang. Ethnic issues complicated the bitter legacy of the Cultural Revolution. One aspect of this was the desire of many Han Chinese, mostly those who arrived in the 1960s and 1970s, to return home. When the authorities in their home towns failed to provide either work or accommodation, effectively marooning them in the northwest, they protested. In the early 1980s, Urumqi had to order fresh Han troops in to quell the unrest. This ignited demonstrations by non-Han angry over Chinese dominance of political life, attempts to enforce the new one-child policy on the indigenous population (see POPULATION) and, on occasion, the use of Xinjiang to conduct nuclear tests. Intercommunal violence claimed hundreds of lives. Sometimes, as in Baren, south of Kashgar, in 1990, anti-Chinese protests spilled into open revolt. Troops had to be deployed and many lives lost before order was restored.

Racial unrest coincided with rapid economic growth during the 1980s and 1990s as Xinjiang, in keeping with the rest of the country, implemented free market reforms and opened to the outside world. Both were striking developments given the two decades of stagnation and isolation that preceded them. The farmers of the oases and the Ili valley resumed family farming while the nomads of the north tended their herds as of old, free of interference from collective or commune. Many abandoned the pastoral life altogether in pursuit of riches in the region's valleys and towns. Much of Shanghai's cotton industry relocated to the region. Beijing poured money as well as people into Xinjiang. At the close of the century Xinjiang's per capita GDP was about one-third that of Beijing and less than a quarter of Shanghai's. But it was much higher than that of other northwestern provinces.

The opening of Xinjiang – once China's 'back door' and then, under Communism, a closed one – was equally remarkable. The completion of the Karakorum Highway in 1986 allowed access to PAKISTAN. Improved relations with the Soviet Union in 1990 enabled completion of the rail link between Urumqi and Alma Ata, capital of Kazakhstan. A new line from Korla, in the centre of Xinjiang, to Kashgar, in the southwest corner, suggested the possibility of a rail link with Kirghizstan and on to Tashkent, capital of Uzbekistan. At the close of the century international bus routes and flights linked Urumqi with all of its neighbours and some cities, such as Istanbul, much further afield.

These reforms exerted a profound effect on Xinjiang's economy but a less obvious one on the region's fundamental contradiction: Han dominance of a non-Han majority. Race relations were not uniformly bad at the close of the century, as they had been when Xinjiang's rulers sought to eradicate the difference between Chinese and non-Chinese. Some nationalities, and some parts of the region, were either reconciled to Chinese rule or 'sinified' sufficiently to support it. A master of divide-and-rule tactics, Beijing exploited differences between and among non-Han groups.

Population trends in the region improved in favour of the Chinese each year. In the late 1990s, Uigurs constituted about 40 per cent of the population, other non-Han groups a further 22 per cent, and Han the remainder. At this rate of increase, an ethnic Chinese

majority in Xinjiang is likely some time during the second decade of the twenty-first century.

This promises to do little for racial harmony. In the late 1990s bombings, assassinations and other acts of terror were common. The region's leaders, as well as those in distant Beijing, called for constant vigilance and regular crackdowns against 'splittists'. Official media made no secret of the seriousness of the situation; and in 1999 Amnesty International recorded cases of nearly 200 political prisoners and drew attention to the high incidence of executions in the region, mostly of Uigurs.

Xinjiang's new links with its neighbours have made it difficult for the authorities to curb ethnic separatism. Following the collapse of the Soviet Union the region shares borders with newly independent states composed of Kazakhs, Kirghiz and Tajiks, all of whom are found in substantial numbers on China's side of the border. Uigurs, alone among the major nationalities in Central Asia, remain a nation without a state. They must make do with an 'autonomous region' within China. To make sure they do Beijing has reached agreements with all three successor states to the Soviet Union in which each party pledges not to let its territory be used for secessionist purposes. It was not clear whether this diplomatic coup will mean much on the ground, particularly given the length and remoteness of Xinjiang's frontiers (see RUSSIAN FEDERATION/CIS).

What is not in doubt is China's determination to retain control over Xinjiang. It is necessary to secure the region's enormous oil reserves, particularly if, as planned, a pipeline is to pass through the region en route from Kazakhstan to China proper (see ENERGY). It is essential to maintain the nuclear testing facilities at Lop Nor. And it is vital to control an area whose loss in the distant past has been the prelude to a massive attack on China proper, and might prove so again. These are the tangible, strategic imperatives at the heart of Beijing's insistence – inherited from the Qing and earlier dynasties – that China was, is, and must remain a multi-national state.

Yalta Conference 4–11 February 1945

At the CAIRO CONFERENCE of 1943, the UNITED STATES had cast China, its wartime ally, as a great power. Yet two years later CHIANG KAI-SHEK was not invited to the Yalta Conference between President Roosevelt, Joseph Stalin, the Soviet leader, and Prime Minister Winston Churchill of Britain; and China's territory and sovereignty were compromised during the proceedings in order to bring Moscow into the war against JAPAN. This was to hamper Chiang in his post-war military struggle against the Communists (see CIVIL WAR).

The United States and BRITAIN agreed that, in return for Stalin's declaration of war against Japan, which at the time still seemed far from defeat, the SOVIET UNION would regain some of the privileges it lost in northeast China during the Russo-Japanese War of 1904–5. They included use of the naval port just south of Dalian in LIAONING, formerly known as Port Arthur (modern Lushun); rights in Dalian itself, which would be declared an 'open port'; joint control with China of the Chinese Eastern and Southern Manchurian Railways; and China's acceptance of the status quo in MONGOLIA – that is, its independence. For its part, the Soviet Union said it was ready to conclude a pact of friendship and alliance with Chiang's KUOMINTANG government.

Chiang was unhappy about this secret diplomacy, but powerless to do much about it. The promised Sino-Soviet Treaty of Friendship and Alliance was signed in August 1945. Moscow softened the blow of Yalta by promising to confine its physical and moral support to the Nationalist government at the expense of the CHINESE COMMUNIST PARTY. China's acceptance of the status quo in Mongolia was made subject to a plebiscite showing that was what Mongolians wanted.

By the time the treaty was signed Soviet troops had poured into northeast China and destroyed Japan's 'puppet state' of MANCHUGUO. They disarmed Japanese forces and handed over much of their military equipment to the Chinese Communist armies which had raced into the area under LIN BIAO. The Soviet army then stripped Manchuria of most of its industrial equipment, and shipped it back to the Soviet Union as war booty. These developments made it hard for Chiang to re-establish authority over northeast China, something he was determined to do. When Soviet troops finally left in 1946, Nationalist armies exercised a brief hold over the region's major cities before they were surrounded, isolated and destroyed by the Communists.

Yan Fu (1853–1921)

'I think the greatest difference between China and the West, which can never be made up, is that the Chinese are fond of antiquity but neglect the present. The Westerners are struggling in the present in order to supersede the past.'

The idea of progress was a revolutionary and troubling one for Chinese society during the final years of the QING DYNASTY. Yan Fu, a brilliant scholar and champion of reform, played a key role in introducing and advocating it.

Yan's intellectual roots were in the West, where he had studied. He made the ideas of Herbert Spencer, Thomas Huxley, John Stuart Mill and Adam Smith available to his countrymen in lucid, influential translations. Many of these thinkers spoke of social and national development in terms of a struggle in which only the fittest would survive. It was gloomy reading for the Chinese during the late nineteenth and early twentieth centuries who saw their country imprisoned by the past and assaulted by foreigners.

Yan's prescription was *wholesale* if gradual reform: it was not enough to adopt the old nineteenth-century formula of 'Chinese learning for substance, Western learning for use' in which modern, mainly Western, technology would be grafted on to a core of culture, ethics and politics that remained stubbornly Chinese or Confucian in nature (see CONFUCIANISM). New patterns of thought and knowledge were required, not just new weapons and technology.

Yan, like LIANG QICHAO, another great reformer and intellectual pioneer, lost something of his enthusiasm for the West as a result of the carnage of the First World War. In later life he began to wonder whether 'Chinese ways' might not be best for his country after all. Also like Liang, he embarked on a more partisan political career – one that saw him become a councillor of YUAN SHIKAI, the strongman of the early Republic and a supporter of his imperial pretensions. The great reformer thus ended his life a conservative and a critic of the new culture of the MAY FOURTH MOVEMENT of 1919, which in earlier days he might have welcomed and championed.

This placed Yan at odds with China's younger generation of nationalists and reformers, many of whom preferred revolution to evolution. However, it did not diminish his importance in the overall context of China's modern intellectual awakening. Yan alerted his countrymen to the dynamic of struggle at work in human history and warned them that their country faced a bleak future unless it shaped its policies accordingly.

Yan Xishan (1883–1960)

Alone among China's WARLORDS, Yan Xishan based his power on the control of a single province – SHANXI – virtually throughout the entire Republican period. His authority was often challenged: Japan occupied much of the province during the SINO-JAPANESE WAR and Communist troops established base areas along its borders. But Yan was the dominant figure in Shanxi for the best part of 40 years, during which he tried to turn his isolated, traditionally poor homeland into a model of reform for the rest of the country.

Yan's adroit manoeuvring in the choppy waters of warlord politics enabled Shanxi to avoid many of the military conflicts that afflicted other parts of China during the 1920s. A graduate of the Tokyo Military Academy, where he joined the UNITED LEAGUE, China's first modern revolutionary organization, he played a leading role in the military revolt of 1911 that ended QING DYNASTY rule in Shanxi. Thereafter he sided with whichever faction or coalition in China seemed least likely to threaten his position in the province.

There was a setback in 1930 when an alliance with FENG YUXIANG, another important northern warlord, against CHIANG KAI-SHEK's newly established national government in Nanjing, collapsed, forcing Yan out of Shanxi. He soon returned. His relations with Chiang were correct but distant. The two men were allies but no more than that. Yan even formed his own political party, the Democratic Revolutionary Comrades' Association – to rival KUOMINTANG activities in Shanxi.

Yan's reforms involved the development of INDUSTRY, AGRICULTURE and trade, the building of ROADS, RAILWAYS and schools (see EDUCATION), and improved rights for WOMEN. To all of these issues, as to the entire business of government, he brought an eclectic ideology that contained elements of Communism and CONFUCIANISM. Campaigns of political indoctrination were designed to inculcate the same views among the general population. Such 'modern' methods could not disguise the fact that Yan held the traditional view that the morally upright should rule, and that they should do so with few restrictions.

The 'model governor's' reforms brought significant changes to Shanxi. Factories were set up around Taiyuan, the provincial capital, to produce iron and steel, cement, weapons and textiles. Coal, one of Shanxi's most abundant and valuable resources, was mined intensively and transported to other parts of the country via the province's relatively developed railway network. However, Yan insisted that Shanxi's railways continue to use a 1-metre rather than standard gauge in order to make it difficult for enemies to move troops into the province by rail.

Yan's commitment to social reform fell far short of support for the CHINESE COMMUNIST PARTY, whose headquarters, from the mid-1930s, were located at YANAN in neighbouring SHAANXI. However, during the opening stages of the war against Japan he welcomed the Communists' Eighth Route Army into his province to join the fight against the invaders. When the Japanese advance forced him and his demoralized forces into southwestern Shanxi, and the Communists built up base areas deep in the countryside, he had second thoughts. Yan spent the rest of the war trying to curb further Communist inroads into his province rather than defeat the Japanese.

His efforts met with little success. Yan regained Taiyuan and other strategic centres on Japan's surrender in 1945, but failed to re-establish his former dominance over the province. Shortly before Taiyuan fell to the Communists in April 1949 he emptied the provincial treasury, and flew first to Nanjing and then to TAIWAN, where he spent the remainder of his life.

Yanan

In and around this isolated, poverty-stricken township of SHAANXI during the late 1930s and early 1940s the CHINESE COMMUNIST PARTY transformed itself from a group of demoralized, disorganized revolutionaries into a powerful, disciplined fighting force. MAO ZEDONG rose to supremacy in Yanan, and the Communist Border Region government, of which Yanan was the capital, became the proving ground for many of the techniques that enabled the Party to seize power in the rest of China in 1949.

The earthen yellow caves of Yanan became the headquarters of the Communist movement shortly after the XIAN INCIDENT of 1936, which brought the Party and the KUOMINTANG government into a new alliance of resistance against JAPAN. CHIANG KAI-SHEK, concerned that he had not been able to crush the Communists during or immediately after their LONG MARCH, maintained a military blockade of the area throughout the SINO-JAPANESE WAR. But neither his troops nor those of Japan were able to bring the region to heel. The Communists consolidated their grip and expanded control behind enemy lines. Between 1934 and 1945, Party membership grew from 20,000 to 1.2 million. The ranks of the Red Army expanded from 22,000 to 800,000.

In the eyes of many Chinese and some foreigners – notably EDGAR SNOW, whose visit to the region in 1936 was described in *Red Star Over China* (1937) – Yanan made a refreshing contrast with CHONGQING, the Nationalists' wartime capital. Propaganda boasted, and many believed, that in Yanan men and women could be born again through ideological struggle; poverty could be overcome by communal efforts and adherence to Mao's 'mass line'; and human will, properly motivated and directed by Mao's 'Thought' and the methods of his Party, could transform the environment.

During its Yanan years the Party abandoned some of its more revolutionary goals, including radical LAND REFORM, in favour of building a United Front of all Chinese against the Japanese invaders. Non-Communists were allowed to take part in local elections, as long as there was no danger of them gaining control. Plain living and patriotism – part of the 'Yanan Way', a key myth of Chinese Communism at the time and since – drew thousands of pilgrims from all over the country.

The fact that the 'way' involved the suppression of all forms of criticism, the subordination of intellectual life to the Party and vicious purges and 'struggle sessions', many of them the work of KANG SHENG, Mao's security chief, does not detract from its importance as a reality and symbol in China's modern history. Neither do discoveries by Western scholars in the 1990s that the Communists used profits from the sale and production of opium to develop their base area. Rather, they help form a true picture.

They are of a piece with what Yanan stands for: the Party's emergence as a truly indigenous force – one that, with energy, enthusiasm and cruelty, grafted modern techniques of control and mobilization on to a traditional society in the throes of change wrought by national and economic crisis. At Yanan, the Chinese Communist Party emerged from the shadow of Moscow's largely unsuccessful attempts to lead it. At Yanan, it shed much of its remaining attachment to its cosmopolitan, urban intellectual roots in the MAY FOURTH MOVEMENT of 1919 and became a thoroughly Chinese party, oriented towards the countryside and controlled by Mao Zedong.

Yang Shangkun (1907–98)

Yang was president of China during the TIAN-ANMEN SQUARE DEMOCRACY MOVEMENT of 1989, which he played a key role in quelling in his capacity as a member of the revolutionary old guard and vice-chairman of the PEOPLE'S LIBERATION ARMY's Central Military Commission, the high command. The sword-bearer for DENG XIAOPING – until the latter ousted him in 1992 for pursuing factionalism – Yang helped swing the army behind the Communist leadership during the crisis, persuading it to crush the protests.

Yang was born in SICHUAN and joined the CHINESE COMMUNIST PARTY in 1926. Between 1927 and 1931 he studied in the SOVIET UNION. He was one of the pro-Moscow 'returned student faction' whose members were critical of what they regarded as MAO ZEDONG's conciliatory approach towards rich peasants during the early 1930s. They also decried his emphasis on promoting rural revolution at the expense of urban insurrection. Yang took part in the LONG MARCH of 1934–5, and in YANAN, the Party's headquarters during the SINO-JAPANESE WAR, began the involvement in military organization and intelligence work that was to make him a powerful figure after 1949. However he was dismissed and disgraced during the CULTURAL REVOLUTION, when his crimes were said to have included bugging Chairman Mao's quarters.

Yang's rehabilitation began with military and political appointments in the southern province of GUANGDONG in the late 1970s, but he was soon transferred to Beijing where he joined the Politburo. A confidant of Deng Xiaoping, he played an important role in modernizing and streamlining the PEOPLE'S LIBERATION ARMY following its poor performance in the 1979 war against VIETNAM. His long revolutionary pedigree and his senior position in the Central Military Commission made him one of the most powerful men in China during the 1980s. His appointment as president (1988–93) provided him with a more public but largely ceremonial role.

Despite Yang's role in crushing the democracy protests in 1989, Deng shunted both him and Yang Baibing (1920–), his half brother and head of the army's political department, aside when it appeared they were becoming too ambitious. The two men were believed to be enlarging their power base within the military in preparation for Deng's death. Yang Shangkun bore his last dismissal with good grace. He enjoyed much better health than his peers among the rapidly dwindling band of veteran revolutionaries and, long after he retired, continued to speak out in favour of Deng's polices of economic reform during frequent 'inspection tours' of the provinces.

Yangtze River

The 'Long River' (changjiang), as it is known in Chinese, has been the setting for many of the great dramas of China's modern history. This stems from the fact that most contenders for power in China have been required to control the river coursing through much of central China. The 'Heavenly Kingdom of the Taipings', the rebels who nearly toppled the QING DYNASTY in the 1850s, established their capital in Nanjing, the first major city upstream after SHANGHAI. The REPUBLICAN REVOLUTION of 1911 was made and won in Wuhan, capital of HUBEI, on the middle Yangtze. In 1927, CHIANG KAI-SHEK established

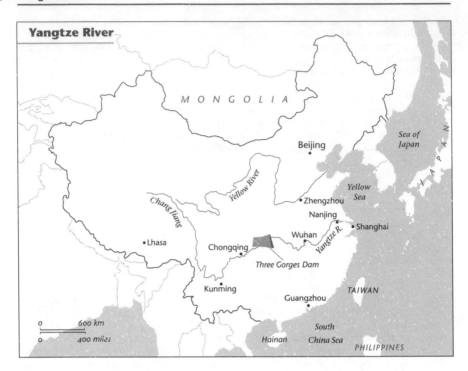

Yangtze River

the capital of his new KUOMINTANG government in Nanjing. It survived until the Japanese attack at the start of the SINO-JAPANESE WAR. Chiang returned to the city in 1945, only to be ejected again in April 1949 when the PEOPLE'S LIBERATION ARMY crossed the Yangtze during the CIVIL WAR. In the current era, problems vie with potential, opportunities with obstacles along the Yangtze, China's largest economic development zone.

China's lifeline

Like most of China's major rivers, the Yangtze flows from west to east, and most of its tributaries from north to south. Like several of Asia's major rivers, it rises on the Tibet–Qinghai plateau. Unlike any of them it is navigable for about 1,500 miles (2,400 kms), as far inland as the city of Yibin in SICHUAN, approximately 300 miles (480 kms) upstream from CHONGQING. At that point the Yangtze has already traversed more than half of its total length of 3,900 miles (6,240 kms). Yet the important section still lies ahead; that between Chongqing and Shanghai, the two largest cities in China. Both owe their size,

significance, indeed their very existence, to the river.

The Yangtze links these two vast commercial centres with the scarcely less important cities of Wuhan and Nanjing, dozens of smaller towns, much of China's most fertile farmland, and a good deal of its modern industry. Some of China's richest provinces are found along the Yangtze, notably JIANGSU and metropolitan Shanghai in the Delta. The Yangtze valley economic region includes all or parts of the population in metropolitan Shanghai, Jiangsu, ANHUI, JIANGXI, HUBEI, HUNAN and Sichuan – a total of close to 350 million people. Small wonder that the Long River is the economic spine of China. It is a vital commercial and strategic axis whose waters sometimes meander, sometimes rush, across the middle of the country.

foreigners, Three Gorges, revolution

BRITAIN opened the Yangtze to foreign trade in the mid-nineteenth century by means of wars and UNEQUAL TREATIES. At one time there were ten TREATY PORTS along its banks, stretching upstream as far as Chongqing.

Foreign shipping, much of it British, dominated the river. By the start of the twentieth century, almost all foreign, and most domestic trade was conducted by 'foreign-style' vessels, nearly all of them owned by foreigners.

However, the commercial potential of the upper Yangtze remained unexploited until the first decade of the twentieth century. Largely this was due to the lie of the land between Ichang and Chongqing. The Three Gorges might have stirred poets and artists into life, but they spelt destruction for many of the ships that tried to negotiate the rapids and shallows lurking between them. Passage was possible only with the assistance of 'trackers' – scores of men, often wearing nothing more than loin cloths – who struggled along the river banks hauling the ships upriver by means of hawsers.

Large junks would carry as many as 80 trackers to ensure their journey upstream. In some areas, and in certain weather, even more manpower was needed. It was hired locally. Descriptions and photographs of trackers, their bodies bent double by the strain of defying the mighty power of the Yangtze, are common in Western accounts of China during the late Qing and Republican periods. They symbolized the ingenuity of the Chinese *and* their primitive technology; the country's abundant labour as well as the almost cosmic forces of nature it was up against. Trackers were a common sight in the Three Gorges area until the early years of Communist rule.

In the first decade of the twentieth century steam broke the stranglehold that the Gorges and trackers exercised over shipping on the upper river. The first steamship to reach Chongqing – the *Leechuan*, commanded by the Briton Archibald Little – arrived in 1898. It did not do so unaided: trackers had to help the vessel over difficult stretches of the river. Two British gunboats made the passage in 1900, but again required aid. It was not until 1909, when the *Shutung*, a powerful, 115-foot tugboat designed and commanded by Cornell Plant, another Briton, berthed in Chongqing that China's greatest inland city started to enjoy a regular, commercial service by steamship. Even then, there were restrictions on the size of vessels able to make the journey beyond Ichang. Every voyage called for skill on the part of pilot and crew.

Until the Communist Revolution, foreign navies, notably those of Britain and the UNITED STATES, 'policed' the Yangtze, enforcing treaty rights and protecting their nationals. The Royal Navy was particularly active, sometimes with dramatic results. In 1926, during the anti-foreign movement that was part of the NORTHERN EXPEDITION to re-unify China, a steamer belonging to the British company Butterfield & Swire collided with a ship carrying Chinese troops near Wanxian in Sichuan. About 65 Chinese soldiers drowned. The authorities in Wanxian detained a Butterfield & Swire vessel in retaliation and demanded compensation. A Royal Navy gunboat responded by bombarding the town for three hours, killing or wounding 1,000 people and destroying property. The Royal Navy's reign along the Yangtze came to an end with the Sino-Japanese War and Britain's relinquishment of treaty privileges. But it took the AMETHYST INCIDENT of 1949 to make the point that the river had new masters.

dams, bridges, development strategies

It was one thing to traverse the Three Gorges, quite another to tame them. Bringing the Yangtze to heel was in the minds of all those, beginning with SUN YAT-SEN, who supported construction of a giant dam in the area (see THREE GORGES DAM). Work finally began on the project in 1994 with the aim of generating cheap power, controlling the floods that cause so much damage downstream almost every year, and allowing ships of up to 10,000 tonnes to reach Chongqing. Years of intensive construction have yet to silence controversy over the scheme, which is due to be completed in 2009. Anxiety remains over the effects on the Long River of so blatant an interference in nature.

Building bridges over the Yangtze has proved a more benign though still difficult business. None was erected until well into the Communist era. The first road bridge was built at Wuhan in 1957. It is 1,826 yards (1,670 metres) long. A bridge was built at Nanjing between 1960 and 1968. Work on the city's second bridge began in 1997 by which time a second had also been constructed in Wuhan. At the start of the new century a total of 15 bridges span the turbulent waters of the Yangtze between Chongqing and Shanghai.

Before work on the Three Gorges project began, Beijing unveiled its Yangtze Valley Development Strategy, a master plan to open the entire river up to foreign trade and investment on terms similar to those enjoyed by the SPECIAL ECONOMIC ZONES of the south coast.

The policy was one of the fruits of DENG XIAO-PING's tour of south China early in 1992 during which he called for faster, bolder reforms. Still supreme, despite formal retirement, Deng took himself to task for not developing Shanghai and the Yangtze valley earlier. His new vision called for Shanghai, and in particular its new financial centre of Pudong, to be the 'head of the dragon' (see SHANGHAI). The dragon's neck, back and tail stretched upriver, all the way to Chongqing.

The effects of Deng's announcement were dramatic. Shanghai's economy, tied down for decades by its obligation to subsidize the central government, soared along with the high rises that soon dwarfed the old city. Municipal leaders spoke of recapturing Shanghai's glorious past as China's – and Asia's – financial centre. Foreign banks and investors responded enthusiastically, lured by Shanghai itself, and the unimaginable riches of a revitalized Yangtze valley beyond. Even once sleepy port-cities, hundreds of miles upriver, stirred. In 1996 alone, the Yangtze valley attracted US$15.5 billion in foreign investment – 30 per cent of China's total (see FOREIGN TRADE AND INVESTMENT).

For foreign and Chinese observers, the Yangtze region seemed to have a brighter future than the Pearl River Delta in GUANG-DONG, which grew rich in the 1980s on the back of investment from HONG KONG, or FUJIAN, whose impressive performance owed much to investment from TAIWAN. Shanghai was an *industrial* centre, one whose people were known for their superior education, resourcefulness and commercial acumen. Unlike the situation in the south, Shanghai and the scores of cities beyond the heart of China's *domestic* economy. The largest consumer market in the world appeared to be opening for business.

Much of the euphoria was misplaced, as is often the case in China. And if the potential of Shanghai and the Yangtze was undeniable, so were the problems involved in tapping it. In the late 1990s they ranged from official corruption to poor communications; from a determination to protect local business to a lack of adequate property laws. There was also the fact that enormous sums of capital were required to rejuvenate so vast an area whose huge population placed heavy strains on the natural environment. Evidence of the fragility of the environment was legion. It included the silting up of the Dongting and Poyang lakes in the middle Yangtze, thanks in part to uncontrolled reclamation, and the floods in 1998 and 1999 triggered by intensive logging in the upper reaches of the river (see ENVIRONMENT).

The serious nature of these problems is not in doubt. Neither is the fundamental importance of the Yangtze to China. In future, development of the region might be fast or it might be slow. But it is essential if China is to realize its potential as an economic power.

Yuan Shikai (1859–1916)

Orthodoxy has cast Yuan Shikai as the villain of China's modern history. The military strongman of north China is accused of betraying the GUANGXU EMPEROR's daring reforms in 1898 and the QING DYNASTY itself in 1911 before sabotaging the REPUBLICAN REVOLUTION, selling out China to JAPAN, and trying – but failing – to restore the monarchy in 1916. There is something in all these charges. But Yuan is better understood as a man of his times than a villain. One of the towering figures of modern China, he grappled with the problems faced by those who succeeded him as ruler: how to bind China together in the face of foreign threats, national disintegration and the collapse of traditional institutions and values at home.

Yuan owed his power to control over the Beiyang Army, the most formidable military unit in China during the early twentieth century. One of several 'new armies' formed in the late Qing to defend the dynasty from foreign and domestic foes, the Beiyang force was among the best trained and equipped (see ARMIES). It was also completely loyal to its commander, a reforming, resourceful imperial official keen to extend his influence. Yuan began to do so at the turn of the century by siding with hardliners at the Court, including the EMPRESS DOWAGER, rather than supporting the '100 Days' reforms championed by the Guangxu emperor and devised, among others, by KANG YOUWEI and LIANG QICHAO, the country's leading reformers. Yuan saw no benefit in attempting to enforce constitutional rule on an unwilling, and militarily powerful, largely Manchu elite. It would only result in chaos.

In the years that followed, Yuan grew strong while the dynasty grew weak; and when a desperate government turned to him to defeat the revolutionaries in 1911, he came into his own (see REPUBLICAN REVOLUTION). Yuan engineered the abdication of the Manchu Court, and secured an agreement with the revolutionaries that allowed him, rather than SUN YAT-SEN, to become president of a new Republican government based in Beijing. Republicans, Sun included, considered Yuan too powerful and important not to have on the side of the Revolution. He was also likely to be more acceptable to the foreign powers.

Yet this was an extraordinary development, for Yuan was neither a republican nor a revolutionary – as events would soon show. When the KUOMINTANG emerged as the strongest party in parliamentary elections in 1913 and sought to constrain the president's power, Yuan had SONG JIAOREN, its leader, assassinated, and his party banned.

In the midst of these attempts to extend his authority, Yuan grappled with another key problem: securing finance for his impoverished regime (see FINANCE). The central government was poor as well as weak, and the president had to pay the armies to whom he owed his power. He did so by signing the Reorganization Loan of April 1913 with the foreign powers. A 5-power banking consortium lent Yuan £25 million secured against the salt revenues. Much of the money was used to finance the Beiyang Army.

This infuriated the revolutionaries and gave impetus to the 'Second Revolution' of 1913, a provincial revolt against Yuan's attempts to centralize power. The rebellion failed, forcing Sun and many of his fellow Republicans into exile again, less than two years after they had formed a government and handed power to Yuan.

In January 1915, Yuan signed what Chinese Nationalists then and since have regarded as an even more objectionable agreement, this time with JAPAN. The TWENTY-ONE DEMANDS arose from Tokyo's participation in the First World War on the side of the Allies, and its acquisition of Germany's interests in SHANDONG. In their fullest form, the Demands threatened to turn China into a Japanese protectorate. They provoked uproar. Deft diplomatic footwork by Beijing and resistance from other powers resulted in their modification. But Yuan was still forced to accede to some of them, earning him fresh opprobrium.

Yet the greatest source of his infamy still lay ahead. By the end of 1915 Yuan had consolidated power, and enjoyed the backing of the powers who had come to regard him as an indispensable strongman at a time when chaos threatened. What he lacked was *authority*. He felt, probably correctly, that republicanism exerted little hold over the minds of most of his people, and that its institutions were unsuited to the task of preserving unity and building up national power. Yuan's solution, unveiled in 1916, was to restore the monarchy with himself as a new, Chinese, emperor. He took on the reign title *hong xian*: abundant constitutionality.

Yuan's monarchical experiment lasted a matter of months before it was broken by resistance on the part of the would-be emperor's fellow Beiyang Army leaders, and opposition from the provinces. China might not be ready for republicanism, but it was certainly not prepared to return to dynastic rule, especially under someone with Yuan's record. Yuan died in June 1916, his 'dynasty' in ruins and his country in as much ferment as when he had become president four years earlier.

Yuan's death led to a leadership vacuum that was not filled until CHIANG KAI-SHEK rose to power in 1927 as a result of the NORTHERN EXPEDITION. In the meantime, China succumbed to rule by WARLORDS and civil war as the Kuomintang, under first Sun and then Chiang, extended its rule north from its revolutionary stronghold in GUANGDONG.

In some respects Yuan Shikai was a warlord himself. He relied on military power, as did all of China's leaders during the twentieth century – a time when political institutions were in flux, weak or non-existent. In these circumstances, most politics, inevitably, were military in nature. Yet Yuan aspired to be a national leader, not a regional one. And though his military base was in the north, he attempted to create a modern army, free of local ties of the kind that characterized traditional warlord forces. He also sought to extend the power of the central government and preserve China's national unity, including distant regions such as TIBET and MONGOLIA. He would not concede the independence of the former in negotiations with BRITAIN, and agreed (temporarily) to the secession of the latter only under overwhelming Russian military pressure.

The problem was that Yuan lacked the resources, physical, ideological and administrative, to accomplish his goals. His often corrupt, violent rule generated fierce opposition from powerful provincial leaders and their armies. He failed to centralize power, and his death inaugurated a prolonged crisis of central authority that Chiang could not remedy and which endured until the establishment of Communist rule in 1949.

Yunnan Province

National security, political integration and economic development have long been primary concerns in Yunnan, as they have in China's other border provinces. Little progress was made in any of these areas until the CHINESE COMMUNIST PARTY seized power in 1949; and some of that which followed was undermined by the political upheavals of Maoist times. The reform era provided new opportunities for change but not a panacea for Yunnan's traditional problems: remoteness, ethnic complexity and forbidding terrain. All have made development difficult. All have contributed to a wave of drug-related crime and associated health problems.

a law unto itself

The area now known as Yunnan was among the last parts of 'China Proper' (as opposed to regions inhabited mainly by non-Chinese) to be incorporated into the formal administrative structure of empire. Several centuries later, and despite intensive Han immigration, it remains the least like other parts of China Proper in its ethnic composition. At the start of the new century, ETHNIC MINORITIES constitute one-third of Yunnan's population of 40 million and occupy about two-thirds of its territory. The province is home for more than 20 different minority groups, many of them quite different from each other.

A mosaic of peoples, scattered across a sensitive frontier composed of inhospitable terrain, made central government control over Yunnan difficult at the best of times. At the worst of times, they made it impossible. Almost throughout the Republican period, Yunnan was a law unto itself. On one occasion it tried to impose its law on the rest of the country: in 1915–16 the province's military leaders rebelled against YUAN SHIKAI's attempt to abandon republicanism and declare himself emperor. Cai E (1882–1916), local military commander, renamed his provincial forces the National Protection Army, and marched them into SICHUAN, then held by troops loyal to Yuan. Among the rebels was ZHU DE, later a co-founder of the Communist Party's Red Army. Regional commanders elsewhere in China rallied to the Yunnan cause, forcing Yuan to abandon his imperial pretensions.

For most of the following two decades Yunnan and its leaders kept themselves to themselves. BRITAIN and France remained interested in the province: the former with a view to protecting BURMA; the latter because of French Indochina to the south. Both powers maintained a presence in Yunnan in the form of TREATY PORTS, and the French built a railway from Hanoi to Kunming, Yunnan's capital. Service began on the line in 1910.

Though generally poor, Yunnan has always been rich in minerals, particularly tin and copper. It was also a primary source of opium: taxes on its sale provided a major source of government revenue. Yet French efforts aside, poor communications made access to Yunnan's resources difficult for locals and foreigners alike.

regionalism during the Republic

Among the 'foreigners', in the minds of many Yunnanese, were troops and officials of CHIANG KAI-SHEK's government in Nanjing. Long Yun (1884–1962), a sinicized member of the Yi nationality who was governor and chief warlord of Yunnan, paid lip service to Nanjing but kept its emissaries and influence at bay. Like local militarists elsewhere he retained firm control over his own troops and hung on to all provincial revenues. Under his rule Yunnan was autonomous. Nominally a part of the Chinese Republic, it was Long's personal kingdom, which he ruled in cooperation with the hereditary chiefs who still held sway over many of the minority groups.

The passage of Communist troops through the province in 1935 in the course of their LONG MARCH heralded a threat to Long's position. But it arrived in the form of the central government troops pursuing them rather than the revolutionaries themselves. Chiang failed to crush his old foes during their flight, but he was able to impose his will in many of the areas they passed through, Yunnan, to some extent, among them.

However it was the SINO-JAPANESE WAR of 1937–45 that truly exposed the province to outside influence. With the flight of the central government from the eastern seaboard to CHONGQING, its wartime capital, Yunnan became part of the 'rear area' for the Nationalist war effort and China's principal access to the outside world. At first this took the form of the Burma Road, hastily constructed in 1938, but later closed as a result of the Japanese conquest of BURMA. By that time the Japanese presence in Indochina had rendered the rail line to Hanoi useless. Southern China was completely isolated save for the 'hump' airlift from western Burma and India. The eastern terminus of the hump was Kunming, then the headquarters of the United States 14th Air Force in China.

This military presence, together with the arrival of thousands of immigrants from east China, including businessmen, members of the professions, entire academic communities and government officials, led to unprecedented economic and political activity in Yunnan. Roads were built and factories constructed. Makeshift universities, composed of staff and student bodies from coastal China, were set up. Chief among them was Southwest Associated University (*Lianda*), which brought together personnel from Beijing University, Qinghua University (also in Beijing) and Nankai University in TIANJIN (see EDUCATION). Scores of newspapers were published in the province and associations of artists and intellectuals founded. Kunming, then at the centre of China's struggle to survive, and prey to the corruption and inflation that stalked the entire war effort, became an unlikely centre of liberal, critical opinion, and of hope for a better China after the defeat of Japan.

Many of these developments suited Long Yun. Though at one with Chiang on the need to defeat Japan, he had no intention of giving up control over Yunnan, either during or after the war. The presence of a powerful anti-central government sentiment in the province promised to help keep Chiang at bay.

It did not do so for long. Following the defeat of Japan, Chiang ordered Long's armies south to Indochina to accept the surrender of Japanese troops there. Long himself was left in Kunming where Chiang arrested him, moved him to Nanjing, and placed him under house arrest. Chiang chose Lu Han (1896–1974), one of Long's military subordinates and a distant relative of his erstwhile superior, as the next governor of Yunnan. He was careful to send the province's best troops to northeast China

to fight the Communists in the CIVIL WAR. Yunnan appeared to have succumbed to the central government.

It was an illusion. Lu Han lacked Long Yun's battalions but not his determination to keep Yunnan for the Yunnanese. Neither heavy-handed attempts by Chiang to snuff out anti-KUOMINTANG dissent in Kunming nor menacing central government troop movements managed to bring the province to heel for long. By late 1949, with the Nationalist position crumbling throughout southwest China, Lu turned his troops over to the Communists. As a result, the PEOPLE'S LIBERATION ARMY was able to 'liberate' much of Yunnan peacefully.

taming the borders

Yet it was only peace up to a point in Yunnan during the first years of the People's Republic. Nationalist power in China collapsed last in the southwest. Thousands of Kuomintang troops fled through Yunnan into Burma, Thailand, Laos and Indochina from where they harried the new Communist authorities with cross-border raids. The armies based in Burma under General Li Mi (1902–73) proved the most troublesome. Supplied by air from Taiwan, the new home of the Nationalist government, they staged incursions deep into western Yunnan and appeared to enjoy support from the local hill tribes. Not until the late 1950s did the Communists manage to secure Yunnan's long international frontiers. By that time, most exiled Nationalist troops had become more interested in growing opium than opposing Communism.

By that time, too, the new government had set up 'autonomous' regions in which Yunnan's leading ethnic minorities were supposedly allowed to govern themselves. In Yunnan, as elsewhere in China, the new administrative structures were designed to replace traditional patterns of political authority among non-Han people and preserve local languages and customs rather than devolve political power (see ETHNIC MINORITIES). Neither Long Yun, who in 1948 had escaped from Nanjing and joined up with the Communists, nor Lu Han were given positions of power under the new order in Yunnan. Communist Han Chinese were in charge. They were determined to bring Yunnan into the national body politic rather than let it remain a semi-autonomous enclave on the frontiers of the Chinese world.

Also as elsewhere, policy towards ethnic

The Lie of the Land

The Yuan Jiang (Yuan River) divides Yunnan's 150,600 square miles (390,000 sq kms) into two roughly equal halves. To the east is the Yunnan-Guizhou plateau. To the west and north are the uplands and mountain ranges which form part of the Qinghai–Tibet plateau and through which some of Asia's mightiest rivers run: the Salween, the Mekong and the Yangtze. Most of the province's population, and nearly all its best farmland, are located in the east where karst formations and depressions define the topography. The largest of these is the Dianchi basin, location of the Dianchi lake, south of Kunming. Han Chinese dominate this region, and the tin mining cities of Kaiyuan and Gejiu in the far south. The Yi people, the most numerous of Yunnan's minorities and often the most sinified, also inhabit this half of the province. The land west of the Yuan River is home for most of the remaining 20 or so ethnic minorities, including the Bai and the Hani, the second- and third-most numerous respectively. The former farm the valleys around Dali and the Erhai lake, the best agricultural land in northwest Yunnan. The latter inhabit the region along the border with Laos to the south.

minorities in Yunnan was a casualty of politics in Beijing as MAO ZEDONG pursued his GREAT LEAP FORWARD in 1958–60 and, beginning in 1966, the CULTURAL REVOLUTION. Both wrought havoc in Yunnan. The first brought starvation; in the early 1960s many Dai people in the Dehong region, close to Burma, fled across the frontier in search of food. The frontier with Vietnam was tense during America's Vietnam War and became a war zone itself with the outbreak of the Sino-Vietnamese conflict of 1979. The provincial government had to provide food and accommodation for about 30,000 Vietnamese Chinese whom the authorities in Hanoi summarily expelled. Chinese and Vietnamese troops exchanged artillery fire and border incursions for most of the following decade until relations between the Communist neighbours gradually improved towards the end of the Cold War (see VIETNAM).

These episodes aside, the government's nationality policy eventually afforded it greater control over Yunnan's international frontiers than previous Chinese regimes had enjoyed. Border areas were not trouble-free; neither were relations between the Han and non-Han. But, though the costs often proved high, by the 1980s, both were better than they had been.

development and drugs: the reform era

Development proved harder to deliver than security. Before 1949 the modern sector of the economy was tiny. Afterwards, it developed only slowly: conditions in Yunnan did not favour the rapid construction of heavy industry that occurred elsewhere in the country under the first Five Year Plan (1953–7). Neither, as a frontier region, did Yunnan benefit from Mao's call to build heavy industries along a 'third line', deep in the interior (see INDUSTRY). Attention focused instead on developing the extractive industries and light manufacturing, building on the province's traditional strengths as a producer of cigarettes, liquor and tea, and improving communications.

This last was a slow process. Yunnan was linked to the national railway network after 1949 with lines to GUIZHOU and Sichuan. But it was not until the late 1990s that a line penetrated the west of the province in the form of a spur from Kunming to Xiaguan, close to the historic city of Dali. About the same time, work on a line from Kunming to Nanning, capital of GUANGXI, was completed. This improved communications in southeast Yunnan and gave the province a valuable outlet to the sea via the Guangxi port of Qinzhou.

As in communications, so in FOREIGN TRADE AND INVESTMENT: Yunnan was slow to benefit from the reforms which made provinces in the south and east rich during the 1980s and 1990s. Not until the early 1990s were its borders opened to trade with Burma, Laos and Vietnam. Business with Burma was particularly brisk, fuelled by Beijing's good relations with Rangoon (see BURMA). Wanding, and particularly Ruili, two towns on the Chinese side of the border, rapidly became major entrepôts handling everything from betel nuts to gems. Chinese manufactured goods, including arms, poured into Burma in exchange for raw materials and rare, high-cost items (see ARMS SALES).

Among the latter were large quantities of heroin. The opening of China's interior borders sparked a revival of drug-taking and drug-smuggling that caught the authorities by surprise. It was not confined to Yunnan: Kashgar in XINJIANG, Lanzhou, capital of GANSU, Xian, capital of SHAANXI, and SHANGHAI formed a network for the entry, transhipment and exit of substances produced in Afghanistan or Pakistan. But China's drug trade was concentrated in Yunnan because of its proximity to the Golden Triangle, a major centre of heroin production.

Most heroin passed through the province and found its way to the outside world via Guangzhou or Hong Kong. But much was consumed in Yunnan, as a rise in the registered number of the addicts showed. Many users tended to be members of ethnic minorities. Poor and poorly educated, they sought consolation in the needle, ensuring that these groups featured prominently among those who contracted the HIV virus in China. At the close of the twentieth century the government said up to 300,000 people had been infected, and warned that the number could rise to more than one million by the early years of the new era.

The Yunnan authorities waged a fierce battle against the drug trade. Dealers were dragged before public 'sentencing rallies' before being taken away for execution. Large quantities of opium and other drugs were consigned to the flames in sports stadia and other public venues. The official media resurrected China's shame during the Opium Wars of the nineteenth century in order to renew the struggle against an old menace. That this was not just talk was clear from events in 1992: paramilitary forces had to be mobilized to break up a drugs and arms smuggling ring based in Pingyuan, southeast Yunnan. The region had become a private domain of smugglers and criminals.

Yunnan and Southeast Asia

Yunnan's opening to the outside world towards the close of the century also had more positive consequences. One of them was a rise in tourist revenues. The tropical enclave of Xishuang Banna in the south, home of many of Yunnan's Dai people, is among the best-known holiday destinations in China. Dali, the predominantly Bai city, in the west, and Lijiang, home of the Naxi, further north, have become popular with foreigners for their outstanding natural beauty and local inhabitants, many of them very different in outlook and background from the Han. An earthquake struck Lijiang in February 1996, claiming more than 200 lives and razing much of the city.

The growth in trade and tourism aside, Yunnan's per capita GDP at the close of the twentieth century was the sixth-lowest among China's provinces and autonomous regions. In terms of utilized foreign capital it ranked higher only than NINGXIA, QINGHAI and TIBET. The provincial economy grew rapidly during the first two decades of the reform era, but Yunnan remained poor by comparison with all but China's poorest regions.

At the start of the new century, governments in Beijing and Kunming, Thailand, Burma, Laos, Cambodia and Vietnam are pursuing growth in the region by developing the entire Mekong basin. The river rises in Tibet and flows through Yunnan before entering Laos, skirting Burma and Thailand, bisecting Cambodia and meeting the sea in Vietnam. More than 230 million people live either side of its meandering course from the Tibetan uplands to the South China Sea. There have been disagreements over how best to exploit the region. And several governments have expressed concern over the downstream consequences of China's plans to tap the hydropower potential of its stretch of the river, known in Chinese as the Lancang. But the very fact that these countries are able to discuss such projects is a sign of how much Yunnan has changed from its not-so-distant days as a remote province, isolated from both the mainstream Chinese world and that of Southeast Asia on the other side of its long frontiers.

Zhang Xueliang (1898–)

Zhang Xueliang played a key role in the kidnapping of CHIANG KAI-SHEK at Xian in December 1936 which forced the KUOMINTANG leader to fight the Japanese rather than concentrate on exterminating the CHINESE COMMUNIST PARTY (see XIAN INCIDENT). This move, made amid growing national crisis, secured the man known as the 'Young Marshal' – to distinguish him from his father, Zhang Zuolin (1875–1928), the former warlord of Manchuria whom the Japanese blew up in his train – a unique place in the history of Chinese nationalism, at least as it is written in Beijing.

Zhang's rebellion occurred 4 years after he and his forces were ejected from northeast China by Japan's decision to create the 'puppet state' of MANCHUGUO. Chiang deployed these formidable exiled forces in SHAANXI where he planned to deliver a knockout blow against the Chinese Communist Party. However, Zhang's troops preferred the idea of fighting the Japanese and returning home. Their commander staged the kidnap drama at Xian partly to achieve this end. He released Chiang on condition that the Chinese leader abandon civil war in favour of national resistance. Chiang's agreement to do so forged a new sense of unity and purpose in the country which played a part in hastening Japan's military strike (see SINO-JAPANESE WAR).

Zhang Xueliang's actions endeared him to patriotic opinion but not to Chiang. During the following 50 years the Kuomintang leader kept his rebellious subordinate under close surveillance, firstly in the Mainland and later in TAIWAN. He did not grant him complete liberty until 1988, by which time Zhang had reached the age of 90, and become one of the world's longest-serving political prisoners.

During the 1990s, which for the most part he spent in Hawaii, Chinese Communist leaders sought to entice Zhang back to the Mainland. They refurbished his former home in Shenyang (once known as 'Mukden'), the capital of LIAONING, and promised him a welcome worthy of a man who had changed the course of history. Ill health, and an apparent desire not to embarrass the government in Taipei, dissuaded him from making the trip and made the possibility of doing so in future highly unlikely.

Zhao Ziyang (1919–)

'*Comrade Zhao Ziyang committed the serious mistake of supporting the turmoil and splitting the Party. He had the unshirkable responsibility for the shaping up and development of the turmoil.*' These words, taken from the government's report on the rise and fall of the 1989 TIANANMEN SQUARE DEMOCRACY MOVEMENT, remain China's official verdict on Zhao Ziyang – former premier, leader of the CHINESE COMMUNIST PARTY and champion of economic reform – more than a decade after the suppression of the protests which ended his career. He has passed the years since 1989 under house arrest in Beijing, a fallen symbol of how things might have been had his hard-line veteran opponents not sacked him for opposing the use of troops against the pro-testors. Zhao's fate, decided by the Party rather than the courts, remains an emblem of the 'illegality' at the heart of China's Communist politics.

Zhao was born in HENAN, joined the Party in 1938 and held leading positions in a number of provinces before and after the CULTURAL REVOLUTION. He rose to national power at the start of the reform era after an outstanding performance as Party secretary of SICHUAN. While there he pioneered reforms in AGRICUL-TURE at the same time as Wan Li (1916–) in ANHUI. They amounted to the return of house-hold farming after years in which production had been carried out in communes. Zhao was made premier in 1980, and brought his zeal for change to Beijing, where he at first enjoyed strong backing from DENG XIAOPING.

The main force behind the reform of INDUS-TRY during the mid-1980s, Zhao was also a leading advocate of the Open Door policy. He championed the SPECIAL ECONOMIC ZONES, and Open Coastal Cities, centres for FOREIGN TRADE AND INVESTMENT and capitalist experi-ment. The economic success of GUANGDONG and FUJIAN during the 1980s; the transforma-tion of HAINAN ISLAND into a province and special economic zone; and the 'coastal devel-opment strategy' in which China's maritime provinces were linked with the international economy in an attempt to spur national devel-opment, all owed much to Zhao.

The same is true of some of the problems these policies generated. They included inflation, CORRUPTION, loss of central control and a weakening in the Party's hold over national life. Conservatives among the old guard complained and fought hard to clip Zhao's wings, as well as those of HU YAOBANG, the Party leader. Zhao shared some of Hu's desire for political change but not his methods of achieving it, which he felt jeopardized economic reform. In late 1986 he sided with the conservatives when, amid student protests in several cities for more democracy, they sacked Hu on the grounds that he was too soft on dissent. Reluctantly Zhao took over the reins as Party general secretary and fought off conservative attempts to turn the clock back on economic reform. With Deng's backing, he managed to build a consensus around a programme of further economic and political reform, and the partial retirement of the revolutionary elders. Both measures were endorsed at the Party's 13th National Congress in 1987. Reformers seemed in the ascendant.

No sooner had the Party committed itself to change, than the economy began to go badly wrong. As the 1980s came to a close, inflation, overheating and uncontrolled growth in investment tore at the fabric of society and politics, frightening the government into a partial retreat into state planning and central control. Zhao was forced to relinquish decision-making power over the economy, which passed to the conservative premier LI PENG. Reformist idealism gave way to econ-omic austerity; vision and boldness to plod-ding caution. By early 1989 liberal intellectuals were complaining publicly about the betrayal of reform, and chafed anew at the Party's monopoly of political power and the lack of individual freedoms. Seeds of dissent began to sprout which, between April and June 1989, overran much of the country and snuffed out Zhao's career.

Zhao's exact role in the complex, behind-the-scenes manoeuvring in Beijing as the democracy movement unfolded in Tianan-men Square may never be known: the Party guards its secrets zealously, especially when they touch upon crises and failures. But it is clear that the struggle over how to deal with the demonstrations almost tore the Party apart, took a heavy toll on Zhao's health and resulted in one of the most spectacular inci-dents in China's modern history. A rare glimpse of Zhao's *personal* involvement in the drama came on 19 May 1989, the day before a desperate, divided leadership declared martial law in central Beijing. Looking tired and worn, he made a surprise visit to the Square where he urged the students to abandon their protests and go home before it was too late. It was his last public appearance as Party leader. The fol-lowing month he was sacked and disgraced. JIANG ZEMIN, then Communist Party secretary in SHANGHAI, and a much more cautious figure, was the surprising choice as Zhao's successor.

The 'error' attributed to Zhao in the official report on the events of 1989 was to have opposed the use of force to crush the student-led demonstrations and to downplay their seriousness. This was said to have been the culmination of his longstanding reluctance to oppose 'bourgeois liberalization' – the grow-ing tendency of intellectuals and many ordi-nary people during the 1980s to question the Party's monopoly of power. In fact, Zhao's real crime was to have opposed the veteran hardliners, including Deng, his mentor, who had formally retired from politics but refused to hand over power, and who, correctly, saw the protests as a direct challenge to their rule. Like his predecessor Hu Yaobang, whose death in April 1989 sparked the demonstrations, Zhao was a victim of China's political gerontocracy and a casualty of the crisis of succession that has haunted Communist politics almost everywhere they have been practised, especially China.

The possibility that Zhao would make a comeback was one of a number of spectres that haunted Chinese politics in the aftermath of Tiananmen. However, it was a minor one, for a purge of his allies and supporters in the Party rendered it unlikely. The conservatives' grip on power was strong enough to override any pressure to 'reverse verdicts' – either on Zhao or the events of Tiananmen. Meanwhile, the resurgence of economic reform triggered by Deng Xiaoping's trip to the south in 1992 indirectly deprived Zhao of his legitimacy as the sole champion of change.

Yet though confined to his quarters in Beijing during the 1990s, save for the occasional trip to one of the city's golf courses, Zhao occasionally made his presence felt in political life. On the eve of the Party's 15th National Congress in 1997, and again during the visit to China of US President Bill Clinton the following year, he wrote to the Party calling for a reappraisal of Tiananmen. On both occasions the appeal went unpublished; on both it went unanswered.

Zhejiang Province

Together with JIANGSU, Zhejiang has been a centre of Chinese political, economic and cultural power for centuries. Proximity to SHANGHAI and the Yangtze Delta, fertile northern plains, and good communications account for this. They provided ideal conditions for the development of AGRICULTURE banking and the handicraft industry that made Zhejiang rich. Yet these traditional strengths counted for little after 1949 when much of what Zhejiang stood for was at odds with the goals of the Communist regime. During the reform era the province exacted 'revenge' in a particularly ironic form: private and collectively owned industries grew so fast that they weakened the state's hold over the local economy and generated controversies about the nature of Chinese socialism.

rich and rebellious

For successive central governments, Zhejiang was a vital source of revenue and a key object of political control. Western powers were attracted to it for the same reasons. In the nineteenth century they forced Beijing to open three of the province's major coastal cities – Ningbo, Wenzhou and Hangzhou (the provincial capital) – as TREATY PORTS. Each became the site of consulates, foreign banks, trading houses and Christian missions. Each was the source of foreign ideas that spread far into the interior.

These developments made life difficult for QING DYNASTY authorities in the province. Zhejiang's urban centres were rich, but they were also exposed to the outside world and relatively cosmopolitan. They were well endowed with libraries and schools but many of those associated with them had studied in JAPAN and returned home to champion nationalism, democracy and republicanism. As elsewhere in China, Zhejiang's radicals teamed up with SECRET SOCIETIES as well as reform-minded gentry and military officers. Also as elsewhere, their efforts to overthrow the Manchus came to naught until the REPUBLICAN REVOLUTION of 1911 broke out in Wuhan.

Yet the Zhejiang revolutionary movement had characteristics of its own, thanks largely to the role of the woman revolutionary and feminist QIU JIN (1875–1907). Qiu broke all Chinese conventions save that requiring national heroes (and heroines) to sacrifice themselves for their cause. In 1907 she led the students of her Shaoxing girls' school (really a thinly disguised military training camp) in revolt. Captured, tortured and beheaded, Qiu became one of the most compelling martyrs of the Republican cause.

The collapse of the empire in Zhejiang brought first the rule of the 'Anhui Clique' of warlords associated with national statesman Duan Qirui (1865–1936), and then domination by the opposing 'Zhili Clique' (named after the areas around Beijing now known as HEBEI), in the person of Sun Chuanfang (1885–1935) (see WARLORDS). Sun controlled Shanghai and all of southeast China until the NORTHERN EXPEDITION to reunify China sent him into political oblivion in 1926. For most of the following 25 years, Zhejiang remained a bastion of support for the often beleaguered KUOMIN-TANG regime of CHIANG KAI-SHEK.

The fact that Chiang was a Ningbo man probably had something to do with this. The fact that the capital of his government was located in nearby Nanjing probably had rather more. Control over many parts of China eluded Chiang; they were either too far away or too different in their ethnic, cultural or political make-up from the Yangtze valley, where his power was strongest. Zhejiang, on the other hand, was close at hand. Hangzhou was linked to Shanghai by rail even before the collapse of the Qing, and the line was extended west to Nanchang in the years that followed. For the most part Zhejiang's leaders were Chiang loyalists. It was no surprise that the rich revenues of their province, reinforced by remittances from the many Zhejiangese overseas, were a vital source of funds for the impoverished government (see OVERSEAS CHINESE).

rich but rejected

It was no surprise either that many of these factors stood the province in poor stead after the Communist Revolution in 1949. Zhejiang specialized in light industry and the production of consumer goods at a time when Beijing's priorities centred on developing heavy industry. The province's tradition of openness to foreign trade and investment was at odds with the new emphasis on economic autarky and opposition to foreign capitalism. And, finally, Zhejiang was too close for comfort to the exiled, rival Nationalist regime in TAIWAN. It was deemed neither safe nor suitable for large-scale state investment.

This did not stop those in charge, most of them 'outsiders', from pursuing Beijing's national agenda in the province with enthusiasm under Communist rule. Their insistence on building heavy industry in Hangzhou, and further west along the Qiantang valley, sparked a frantic search for the coal and other ores needed to supply it. Many years of fruitless prospecting passed before it was finally accepted that even Maoist political zeal could not overcome Zhejiang's poor resource endowment, and that inputs would have to be brought in from elsewhere.

In the meantime, the southeastern part of the province, with its fine harbours at Wenzhou and Ningbo, was starved of funds and attention. The same was true of agriculture, rural industry and transport generally. They had once made Zhejiang rich, powerful and important but were neglected during the first three decades of Communist rule. Fortunately this did not stop these sectors of the economy from generating enough revenue to make Zhejiang one of the most important sources of central government finance throughout the Maoist era.

capitalism Wenzhou-style

Deng Xiaoping's free market reforms allowed Zhejiang to return to type. However, there was no question of the province pioneering change in the way GUANGDONG and, to a lesser extent, FUJIAN did during the early 1980s. Zhejiang's leaders were conservatives rather than trail blazers, and Zhejiang people lacked the sense of local identity that Cantonese and Fujianese derived from their dialects and subcultures. The province did not have a foundation from which to take on the central government.

On the other hand since Zhejiang quickly became a powerhouse of reform there was little need for one. Local people ignored the caution of their leaders and made the most of the new policies granted them by Beijing. The most striking consequence of this was the rapid movement of the provincial workforce out of agriculture into rural INDUSTRY in the form of township and village enterprises.

Across China these operations – many of them processing farm products, but many others turning out light-industrial goods unconnected with agriculture – were responsible for most of the country's rapid growth during the 1980s and 1990s. The majority chose to describe themselves as 'collectively owned', but in fact were private businesses seeking protection from political ostracism and economic discrimination in a socialist-sounding name. Township and village enterprises boosted incomes and changed local patterns of life wherever they appeared in China. In Zhejiang, they did both on a massive – and often controversial – scale.

Much of the controversy centred on Wenzhou, the once prosperous port-city that had been almost forgotten for much of the Maoist period. Despite its position on the coast, Wenzhou has long been isolated from other parts of China. Its people speak a unique dialect and, again uniquely, have managed their own affairs for decades. Local Communists even 'liberated' the area before regular units of the PEOPLE'S LIBERATION ARMY arrived in the summer of 1949.

Developments in Wenzhou often bore only

The Lie of the Land

Zhejiang's richest and flattest land is in the north of the province around Hangzhou Bay. Densely populated, and bisected by numerous waterways, including the Grand Canal, it has been cultivated continuously for at least 2,000 years. South of the plain, rugged mountains and hilly uplands dominate the province's 39,000 square miles (101,000 sq kms), which contained 44 million people at the close of the century. The main range in the northwest is the Tianmu. It runs northwest–southeast, parallel to the Qiantang or Fuchun River, Zhejiang's longest. The upper basin of the Qiantang, in the southwest of the province, is intensively cultivated. Zhejiang's coastline is extremely rugged and dotted with hundreds of islands. Many of them, such as the Zhou Shan group, are fairly large. They contribute to the province's rich fishing resources. Zhejiang is known for its silk, tea, oranges and other specialized products. Since 1990 it has acquired fame of a different kind: Qinshan, in Hangzhou Bay, is home of China's first, mainly domestically equipped, nuclear power station (see ENERGY).

superficial resemblance to the usually disastrous exercises in collectivization, communization and ideological soul-searching conducted elsewhere. Even during the CULTURAL REVOLUTION the city failed to cut off the 'tails of capitalism', as private enterprise was then known. When Beijing began to encourage diversified forms of ownership in the early 1980s, it became the first city in the People's Republic in which the private sector dominated the economy. 'Underground' banks offered credit at floating interest rates, and peasants transferred their landholdings in order to leave the soil and go into business.

These developments attracted the attention of reformers in Beijing, particularly as Wenzhou became one of the wealthiest as well as one of the most unusual enclaves in the country. Capitalism was frowned upon, even in the early years of the reform era, but in Wenzhou it was flourishing. Should this be affirmed, attacked or ignored?

The reformers decided on the first of these options. ZHAO ZIYANG, premier and later Party leader, was among those who visited the city in the mid-1980s and championed it as a model other parts of the country might learn from in their pursuit of development and reform. Conservatives were outraged at what they saw as the beatification of capitalist phenomena. Even provincial leaders, accustomed to regular visits to Hangzhou by senior or nominally retired revolutionaries such as CHEN YUN, were far from overjoyed.

As a national 'model', Wenzhou did not survive Zhao's political demise which followed suppression of the TIANANMEN SQUARE DEMOCRACY MOVEMENT in 1989. But as an enclave of unbridled capitalism, some of it conducted in grim factories by an overworked labour force, it overcame the chill political winds from the north. On one level Wenzhou is famous as the centre of China's button and low-voltage switch industries. On a more profound one, it is the only important area of Communist China where the state has next to no stake in the economy and where even the government and Party bureaucracies are relatively lean and efficient.

the end of socialism?

Wenzhou is not representative of the whole of Zhejiang: it is the product of a distinct geographical, historical and political environment. Yet the issues raised by its experience have been reinforced by developments elsewhere in the province. They concern the extent to which the decline of state control over the economy can be tolerated and accommodated in Communist-ruled China.

The scale and the significance of this decline are striking. In 1978, state enterprises produced 61 per cent of Zhejiang's industrial output. In 1995, collectively and/or privately owned township industries did so, and the state's share fell to 16 per cent. In 1998 private enterprises generated 43 per cent of provincial GDP. At the start of the new century planning plays little role in Zhejiang's economy, leaving the market to determine almost every major decision from allocating investment to setting prices. The mixed economy and the market have both made profound inroads in Zhejiang.

At the close of the 1990s, Beijing belatedly recognized these developments – in Zhejiang and elsewhere – by amending the constitution in favour of private enterprise. This followed a similar, more modest, move in 1988 when private enterprise was defined as a 'complement' to public ownership. The 1999 amendment described it as an 'important component of the socialist market economy', and promised to protect the lawful interests of entrepreneurs (see GOVERNMENT AND ADMINISTRATION/CONSTITUTIONS). More specific legislation followed, providing a full legal identity for private business.

These changes flowed from the Communist Party's various redefinitions of socialism during the course of the 1980s and 1990s (see

CHINESE COMMUNIST PARTY/SOCIALISM). The most significant concerned the proposition that China was at the 'primary stage' of socialism and that the country's main task was to develop productive forces rather than focus on questions of ownership. At the Party's 15th National Congress in 1997 this notion was expanded to legitimize the conversion of state enterprises into joint stock and even private corporations.

The extent to which, as certain orthodox Marxists in Beijing feared, socialist political values might come under attack as the private and collective sectors of the economy attained dominance was unclear at the close of the century. However, there were hints that this was indeed the case in Zhejiang. While the province depended less on foreign trade and investment for its growth than on the domestic market, it was exposed to international influence. A sharp influx of foreign capital followed Deng's tour of south China in 1992, and Zhejiang's developed communications, wealth of scenic spots and historical associations made it a primary destination for foreign tourists. Hangzhou and other centres regained something of the cosmopolitan, liberal, experimental feel they displayed earlier in the century.

An unusual exercise in political openness occurred in the city in 1993 when Ge Hongsheng (1931–), the unpopular governor, was voted out of office and a new man, Wan Xueyan (1941–), was elected without Beijing's prior approval. Delegates to the provincial people's congress considered Ge too 'conservative'. In particular they disapproved of his enthusiasm for developing heavy industry at the expense of collective and private concerns.

Radicalism of a more profound nature emerged at the end of the decade. A group of DISSIDENTS in Hangzhou, chief among them Wang Youcai (1966–), a former Tiananmen activist, tried to form a branch of the China Democratic Party, Communist China's first opposition party. Wang was arrested in 1998 and sentenced to 11 years in jail for trying to overthrow the government. It was not the end of the matter: Hangzhou police broke up a gathering of about 50 Democratic Party activists the following year.

These developments do not suggest that political change is under way in Zhejiang, or that the Communist Party faces a genuine challenge in the province. Neither is it clear that such modest departures from political orthodoxy as occurred in the 1990s were a function of broader social and economic change. Yet the proposition that rapid free market economic reforms are bound to give rise to a more liberal, democratic form of politics in China is unlikely to be put to a better test than in that part of the country where private enterprise and the market economy have made the greatest progress.

Zhou Enlai (1898–1976)

Zhou was the most popular of China's first generation of Communist leaders at home, and the most widely admired abroad. To many Chinese he stood for reason and moderation in a world often deprived of both by the excesses of MAO ZEDONG. Foreign leaders, obliged after 1949 to deal with a mysterious, possibly dangerous China, found him a particularly welcome presence: his charm and pragmatism made him the 'human face' of Chinese Communism.

the enigma of Zhou

Yet to say Premier Zhou had more of a personal touch than Chairman Mao and his fellow revolutionaries is not saying much. Neither is the assertion that he stood for saner policies. These are slender grounds for canonization – even by a country understandably keen to find at least one saint among its Communist leadership. Zhou's image as an unwilling accomplice in the CULTURAL REVOLUTION who saved many from persecution is dissolving under scholarly investigation in the West. It can only be preserved in China by selective handling of the archives.

Three things can be said about Zhou Enlai with certainty: his career was inextricably bound up with that of Mao, whom he rarely openly opposed as Party leader; his knowledge of the world beyond the Party and China enabled him to become the sole successful statesman of Chinese Communism; and he stood for the reform and economic modernization of China – as long as Mao did not set another agenda. Unfortunately for Zhou, and for China, the Chairman often did.

Zhou and Mao formed an extraordinarily successful political partnership which, almost alone among those between senior Chinese

Communist leaders, lasted from the 1930s until their deaths in 1976. Mao was the peasant leader turned emperor; the revolutionary strategist whose messianic teachings and almost mystic power commanded the obedience of millions – particularly during the GREAT LEAP FORWARD and the Cultural Revolution. He was earthy and often had little time for formal education or those who acquired it. He was as uninterested in detailed problems of administration as he was sometimes ignorant of developments in the outside world, which he visited twice, on both occasions confining his travels to the SOVIET UNION.

Zhou was suave and sophisticated by comparison. He was born of a JIANGSU gentry family. He studied in JAPAN and France. His cast of mind was practical and given to statecraft rather than reshaping the world. Such a background made him the natural link between the CHINESE COMMUNIST PARTY and the wider Chinese world, and between China and an international community often at a loss as to what to think about his country. The perfect foil to Mao, Zhou played the supreme courtier; one whose loyalty to the Party took the form of absolute obedience to its often mercurial leader.

from Moscow's man to Mao's

However, there was friction between the two men at the start of their relationship, which began when Zhou fled SHANGHAI in 1931 for the revolutionary base in JIANGXI where Mao and ZHU DE were in charge. Zhou had by this time acquired a significant revolutionary pedigree of his own. He had joined the Communist Party in 1922 while in France; worked with CHIANG KAI-SHEK during the mid-1920s at the Whampoa Military Academy, founded in Guangzhou to train the KUOMINTANG army; helped organize the workers' uprising in Shanghai of 1927 – during which he was arrested and narrowly escaped execution – at the time of the NORTH-ERN EXPEDITION; and participated in the Nan-chang uprising of the same year which marked the founding of the Red Army.

He had also been in Moscow in 1928 for a Congress of the Chinese Party whose participants looked askance at Mao's methods of rural revolution, particularly his military tactics and reluctance to eradicate the rich peasants as a class. As a result, Mao was sidelined in his own fiefdom from 1932, his strategy of mobile, fluid warfare to counteract Chiang Kai-shek's 'anti-bandit' campaigns modified in favour of defensive positional warfare, and

Zhou, one of several senior newcomers to the soviet, promoted above him.

The LONG MARCH changed this state of affairs as it did much else. At a Politburo meeting in January 1935 in Zunyi, GUIZHOU province, Zhou 'apologized' for supporting the incorrect strategy that had eventually cost the Party its base in south China, and backed Mao against his pro-Soviet rivals among the leadership. This was an early glimpse of the Zhou 'style'. Admirers described it as 'frank'; critics, such as Li Zhisui (1920–95), Mao's personal physician, thought it 'slavish'.

While the Party turned in on itself in YANAN – its headquarters after the Long March and for much of the SINO-JAPANESE WAR – and submitted to Mao's 'rectification' campaigns, Zhou developed the role of Communist diplomat that would make him famous. In 1936 he took part in negotiations with ZHANG XUE-LIANG, the Manchurian warlord who kidnapped Chiang Kai-shek in Xian in an attempt to persuade him to abandon suppression of the Communist movement in favour of resisting Japan (see XIAN INCIDENT). Zhou subsequently became the most visible Communist advocate of a United Front with the Kuomintang against the common foe. In CHONGQING, the Nationalists' capital where he spent some of the war years, diplomats and the foreign press were taken with his candour and commitment to China's cause. His image as a statesman grew as the UNITED STATES stepped up its efforts to end the CIVIL WAR that cast a cloud over China's future following the defeat of Japan. At the time, Zhou was the Communist Party's chief spokesman and negotiator.

He also won sympathy – and sometimes more – for the Communist cause among Chinese intellectuals, patriots and those without party affiliation. Zhou was a masterful exponent of United Front tactics: the art of strengthening one's own political position and weakening that of the enemy by winning over 'middle' or 'wavering' elements. Zhou and his wife Deng Yingchao (1904–92) were childless, but helped nurture 'revolutionary orphans': infants whose parents were killed for the Communist cause. Among them was LI PENG, a future premier.

'beloved' premier, foreign minister

With the foundation of the People's Republic in 1949, Zhou acquired a larger canvas on which to practise his arts. As premier, he headed a government whose tentacles extended further into Chinese society than any of its predecessors. Ranked third in the leadership after Mao and LIU SHAOQI, he was a powerful and indispensable figure in the new regime. As foreign minister, a post he held concurrently until 1958, he was no less important, sustaining his role as the charming, civilized envoy of Chinese Communism to the outside world. He engineered diplomatic successes at the GENEVA CONFERENCE ON KOREA AND INDOCHINA of 1954, and the BANDUNG CONFERENCE the following year, where China made its mark among the Third World. Zhou's visits to Africa in 1963–4 and 1965 were less successful. Local leaders were quick to observe that Beijing was concerned mainly to counter Moscow's influence in the continent. They were even more put out by the fact that while Zhou was cultivating them, China was training insurgents bent on overthrowing them.

Zhou's record at home during the turmoil of the late 1950s and 1960s was less impressive than his diplomacy. He was one of the few top leaders to oppose (privately) the Great Leap Forward, possibly because he believed it would mean a greater role for the Party and a diminished one for the government of which he was head. But he backed Mao when PENG DEHUAI challenged the strategy behind the Leap. He also supported the Chairman during the crucial run-up to the Cultural Revolution. Perhaps alone among the leadership, Zhou might have kept Mao in check. But there are few, if any, signs that he tried to do so during the meetings that launched the movement and then helped turn it into a catastrophe. Instead, he contributed to the process, writing a savage attack on the Party bureaucracy, criticizing PENG ZHEN, mayor of Beijing and the first member of the Politburo to be toppled in the movement, and helping the radicals publicize their views.

As the turmoil intensified during the later 1960s, Zhou tried to prevent key departments falling victim to the 'seizures of power' which paralysed most government operations. He also protected officials from attack and was occasionally protected himself – sometimes by Mao. But recent scholarship has shown that Zhou was associated closely with the investigation of alleged 'counter-revolutionaries', and that he may have helped persecute more people than he saved. While his role in the Cultural Revolution remains poorly understood, there are few signs Zhou departed from the practice he adopted throughout much of his career: always to side with Mao, and then

seek to modify the consequences of the Chairman's policies should they prove disastrous.

Yet there was more to Zhou's career than blind obedience to his master. He played a key role in China's reopening to the UNITED STATES, and was one of the earliest advocates of the FOUR MODERNIZATIONS, a programme of fundamental economic modernization. Both policies have been at the heart of Beijing's development strategy since the late 1970s.

last years: détente, crisis and Deng

By the late 1960s, common fear of the Soviet Union provided grounds for an end to the 20-year estrangement between Beijing and Washington. Mao sought rapprochement; Zhou, the statesman, did the leg work. First, in 1971, came 'ping-pong diplomacy' when the American table tennis team played in China. Then came secret diplomacy with the visit to Beijing of Henry Kissinger, US national security adviser. President Richard Nixon's arrival in China in February 1972 set the seal on a process largely facilitated by Zhou, sometimes in the face of opposition and uncertainty at home.

The premier did not live to see the resumption of diplomatic relations with the US in 1979. But in 1971–2 he presided over an extraordinary turnaround in his country's international fortunes. Beijing regained China's seat in the UNITED NATIONS; relations with the US were better than at any time since 1949; Washington conceded that TAIWAN was a part of China; the Soviet Union posed less of a threat along the border; and the visit to Beijing of Kakuei Tanaka, Japanese prime minister, pointed to a new start in ties with Tokyo.

The period was no less eventful in domestic politics. In September 1971, LIN BIAO, defence minister and Mao's most likely successor, died in a plane crash in Mongolia, allegedly while fleeing to the Soviet Union after an unsuccessful attempt to assassinate the Chairman. Lin's demise enabled the civilian administration to get the upper hand over the military but it failed to break the hold of the radicals led by JIANG QING, Mao's wife, and the three other members of the 'GANG OF FOUR'. Increasingly incapacitated by cancer, Zhou spent the last few years of his life battling with the 'Gang' over policy and personnel issues. Mao, also dying, mainly looked on. But in 1974 he stirred, sanctioning a bizarre campaign to 'criticize Lin Biao and criticize Confucius' (see CONFUCIANISM). The movement was targeted at Zhou, whose call for the rehabilitation of cadres toppled in the Cultural Revolution threatened the 'Gang'.

Another target of the 'Gang' was DENG XIAO-PING, whom Mao had brought back from the wilderness in 1973. Deng was an advocate of the Four Modernizations, and was viewed – with apprehension by the 'Gang' – as Zhou's most likely successor. In fact, when the premier died in January 1976, Mao replaced him with HUA GUOFENG, a less well-known figure whose appointment pleased no one, perhaps as had been intended. But it was the end neither of Deng nor the Four Moderniz-ations.

This was largely the result of an extraordi-nary postscript to Zhou's career. If, in life, simple humanity was enough to elevate Zhou above other Communist leaders in the eyes of many, in death his policies and personality were publicly commemorated as a means of criticizing the 'Gang', the Cultural Revolution and even Mao himself. The commemoration began in Tiananmen Square in April 1976, on the occasion of the *Qing Ming* festival, when ancestors are remembered and graves swept. The public laid wreaths in the Square along with poems extolling the late premier and attacking Jiang Qing and other members of the 'Gang of Four'. Leftists, in a move which foreshadowed that taken to quell the much more serious protests in Tiananmen Square in 1989, defined the outpouring of grief as 'coun-ter-revolutionary' and ordered the wreaths cleared. Huge crowds gathered and the com-memoration of Zhou rapidly turned into thorough-going criticism of the 'Gang'.

Troops and police had to be brought in to protect the Square from 'rioters'. The 'Gang's' victory was shortlived. It ended with their arrest in October 1976, a month after the death of Mao. In 1978, with Deng in charge, the 'coun-ter-revolutionary riot' was officially redefined as a 'revolutionary struggle' to mourn Zhou and oppose the Cultural Revolution.

Zhu De (1886–1976)

Zhu, one of the founders of the Red Army, was an architect of the CHINESE COMMUNIST PARTY's military survival in the 1930s and stun-ning victory in 1949. This helped spare him some of the twists and turns of MAO ZEDONG's China, but did not prevent him being branded a 'black general and 'warlord' during the CUL-TURAL REVOLUTION. He might have fared worse were it not for the fact that his career was perceived to be over.

The 'warlord' accusation had some sub-stance: Zhu began his military career in YUN-NAN, where he served in the armies of various local militarists following the REPUBLICAN REVOLUTION of 1911. He also shared another of the province's vices: addiction to opium. But Zhu's military ambitions were matched by political ideals. He offered his services to SUN YAT-SEN in the early 1920s and went to study in Europe where he met ZHOU ENLAI and joined the Chinese Communist Party. He returned to China to take part in the NORTH-ERN EXPEDITION of 1926–8 and spread Commu-nist ideas among his troops.

Zhu was a key figure in the Nanchang Upris-ing of 1 August 1927, which the Communist Party celebrates as the foundation of the Red Army, ancestor of the PEOPLE'S LIBERATION ARMY. The Party's fortunes were then at low ebb. CHIANG KAI-SHEK had just purged the KUOMONTANG of its radical allies, and the breakaway Left-wing Nationalist government in Wuhan did the same. The Communists responded with military revolts and the 'Autumn Harvest Uprisings' – peasant upris-ings timed to coincide with the most impor-tant time in the agricultural year. They were all spectacular failures.

Far more successful was the partnership Zhu established with Mao in 1928, when their small, disorganized forces met at Jinggang-shan, in JIANGXI, one of the Party's early rural bases. The fame, and for the Kuomintang the infamy, of 'Zhu Mao' – many believed them to be one man – spread as the two leaders struggled to perfect the political and military techniques that would enable the Red Army to survive government attempts to crush it. Though often weak and ill-equipped, the Com-munist forces were disciplined and commit-ted. They waged guerrilla war. And they were the servant of a political cause rather than its master. They were the seed of revolutionary change out of which grew political power.

Zhu was commander-in-chief during the first stages of the LONG MARCH. But he was not at one with Mao throughout the epic flight. In 1935 he supported the decision of Zhang Guotao (1897–1979), another key Communist military leader and rival of Mao, to make remote northwest China rather than the YANAN region of SHAANXI the destination of the march. Zhu survived the dispute that saw the two main Communist armies march in different directions; Zhang did not. When the armies met up again in Shaanxi, Zhu retained his supreme military role while Zhang – still at odds with Mao and now a spent force militarily thanks to the defeat of his troops in the northwest by local government forces – defected to the Nationalists.

From the mid-1930s until 1954, Zhu was in operational command of all Communist armed forces. It was the period of the Party's greatest military and political success, culminating in victory during the CIVIL WAR of 1946–9. He remained commander-in-chief when a Chinese 'volunteer' army fought US-led United Nations forces to a standstill in Korea (see KOREAN WAR).

Zhu's precise role in these various battlefield triumphs has been obscured by the Party's insistence that politics counts for more than military tactics in explaining its success, and the dominant personalities of Mao, LIU SHAOQI and other civilian leaders. Certain Communist commanders, including LIN BIAO and PENG DEHUAI, also enjoyed much of the limelight. All these men were prominent during the tempestuous early years of the People's Republic while Zhu, though revered, occupied mostly symbolic positions. Among them was the chairmanship of the NATIONAL PEOPLE'S CONGRESS, the legislature. In the final years of his life he suffered the indignity of being attacked in wall posters, but escaped the fate – persecution and premature death – of Liu and Peng.

Zhu Rongji (1928–)

Reforming zeal, determination and a grasp of economics enabled Zhu Rongji to overcome political 'errors' earlier in his career, reach the top ranks of Communist politics, and in the 1990s become the most popular Chinese leader in the West since ZHOU ENLAI. His authority, warmth and frankness met Western leaders' need for a senior figure in Beijing they could 'do business with' – something that seemed impossible with the dour LI PENG and unpredictable JIANG ZEMIN. However, Zhu's position as the senior official in charge of the economy has rarely been better than precarious. His reform policies promise to transform China's economy and society. That is why the man appointed to serve as premier until 2003 has one of the most difficult – and dangerous – jobs in Chinese politics.

rise of an economic 'tsar'

Alone among senior leaders of the CHINESE COMMUNIST PARTY at the start of the twenty-first century, Zhu Rongji's political career was interrupted in 1957 by the 'Anti-Rightist Movement', the nationwide anti-liberal purge that followed the ONE HUNDRED FLOWERS MOVEMENT of political relaxation. He passed most of the following two decades in semi-disgrace, a victim of the crude labelling at the heart of MAO ZEDONG's approach to revolution. This denied China the services of a talented young official. Born in HUNAN, Zhu had studied electrical engineering at Beijing's elite Qinghua University and worked as an economic planner in the northeast before moving back to Beijing.

Though the circumstances of his fall are unclear there is no doubt about its duration: not until the late 1970s was he able to shed completely the stigma of being branded an 'anti-Party Rightist element'. He spent most of the 1980s working in the State Economic Commission, Beijing's economics 'super' ministry, where he was responsible for the upgrading of China's technology and for management reform.

It was not long before Zhu's knowledge of economics and commitment to reform brought him to the attention of DENG XIAOPING, and foreign businessmen keen to take advantage of China's Open Door. He made an impression on both while working in SHANGHAI, of which he was first mayor (from 1988) and then both mayor and Party secretary (1989–91). The man known as 'one-chop Zhu' waged war on a city bureaucracy whose procedures for approving business deals during the 1980s required scores of 'chops' or seals. He simplified the process and formed a council of foreign businessmen to advise the municipal government. It was also in Shanghai that Zhu began a working relationship with Jiang Zemin, a more cautious bureaucrat and his senior in both Party and government. The two made an effective team; in the early 1990s they resumed their partnership – this time on the national stage in Beijing.

Their transfer to the capital owed much to the effect on national politics of the 1989 TIANANMEN SQUARE DEMOCRACY MOVEMENT, and something to the way the two men handled the associated demonstrations in Shanghai.

The two men managed to support the military crackdown in Beijing while avoiding the need for it in Shanghai. Police and workers' pickets restored order in the city, ensuring that the protests ended with little bloodshed.

In the midst of the crisis, Deng and his fellow veterans picked Jiang to succeed the disgraced ZHAO ZIYANG as leader of the Communist Party. Two years later, in 1991, they plucked Zhu from Shanghai – where he had presided over the launch of the Pudong Economic Development Zone, the 'new' Shanghai east of the Huangpu River – and made him a vice-premier in Beijing (see SHANGHAI). The following year he entered the then 6-man Politburo Standing Committee and was given responsibility for reforming the economy.

Zhu the 'rectifier'

As far as the West was concerned, Zhu's appointment as China's 'economic tsar' pierced the post-Tiananmen pall that had engulfed politics in Beijing. The presence of this hard-talking, fast-moving reformer, who placed emphasis on results rather than ideology, struck a chord with Western politicians and business leaders keen to find a 'good' Communist who understood the world economy. Since Zhu also understood that China must open up further and become part of the international economy, he enjoyed even greater appeal. A bluff manner, colourful turn of phrase, and talent for self-deprecation placed him in a league of his own.

Domestically he cut a different figure. It was that of Zhu the 'rectifier': the scourge of CORRUPTION, ailing state enterprises and the provincial autonomy that had sent inflation spiralling and made a mockery of central government attempts to control the economy and levy taxes (see INDUSTRY/SAVING SOCIALISM; FINANCE). Most of these problems stemmed from Deng Xiaoping's call in early 1992 for radical reform and faster growth. Zhu's attempts to deal with the consequences of these policies encountered powerful opposition, especially from provincial leaders keen to make their regions rich as quickly as possible. Deals had to be struck with vested interests at all levels of the administration. Neither the ministries in Beijing nor Zhu personally managed to get things all their own way.

Yet by 1996, after three difficult years, Zhu had made a mark. Inflation had all but disappeared. The go-ahead coastal provinces, though resentful, had been reined in. And economic growth, if not efficiency, continued

to surge, inviting some Westerners to make exaggerated projections about China's economic future beloved of China Watchers of every generation. Zhu, whose power over the economy had increased in 1993 as a result of premier Li Peng's long absence from work due to ill health, appeared to have ended the stop-go cycles characteristic of China's era of growth. The China of Zhu Rongji seemed very different from that of the immediate post-Tiananmen era five or six years earlier.

It had been clear long before the Communist Party's 15th National Congress in August 1997 that Zhu would succeed Li Peng as premier the following spring. He was lined up accordingly but was careful to play a role in the Congress that made it plain he was subordinate both to Jiang – the Party leader and thus China's principal ideologue – and Li, who retained his number two position in the Party hierarchy. Zhu ranked three in the 7-strong Politburo Standing Committee formed at the close of the Congress.

economic reform and world trade

The era of Zhu Rongji proper began in 1998 when he was made premier. 'Made' is the appropriate word for, despite his popularity with some of the delegates to China's parliament, and his image abroad as an enlightened leader, Zhu was the only choice for premier. The Party was not ready to let its candidate be subjected to a genuine free vote.

Yet that Zhu's appointment made a difference was clear almost immediately. For one thing, his performance at the press conference that traditionally closes annual sessions of the legislature placed him several leagues above the wooden Li Peng. He sustained the bluntness and humour year after year, as he did when meeting the press on other occasions, especially overseas. For another, the reform programme he announced to the legislature that appointed him pointed to a new future for the Chinese economy.

In essence Zhu's measures promised to redefine the economic relationship between the citizen and the state by ending the promise of a job for life; abandoning government ownership over all but the 'strategic heights' of the economy; reforming the banks; and replacing subsidized housing and health care with commercial property and welfare markets. He also announced a 50 per cent reduction in the government bureaucracy.

Implementing these policies would have been difficult at the best of times. The economic slowdown caused by the Asian financial crisis of 1997–8 made a hard task even more formidable. Zhu's reforms, though necessary for China's overall economic health, have caused economic hardship for many, at least in the short term. Workers and civil servants are destined to lose their jobs. Many of those who do not will lose their welfare benefits. This will happen at a time when slower rates of growth mean there are few new employment opportunities. It is no surprise, therefore, that Zhu faces powerful, if occasionally ill-defined, opposition from provincial leaders anxious about unemployment and conservative ideologues in Beijing angered by the apparent restoration of capitalism in the People's Republic. There is no certainty that his strong-arm tactics will win the day, or even that, politically, he will survive to apply them.

Zhu's efforts at the close of the 1990s to end the anomaly whereby China was a major trading nation yet not a member of the World Trade Organization (WTO) provided some indications of this. In common with other pro-reform leaders in Beijing, Zhu pursued WTO membership on the grounds that it would add weight to efforts to restructure the economy in the face of bureaucratic resistance and conservative ideological opposition. Membership would mean a painful shake-up in AGRICULTURE, FINANCE and especially state-owned INDUSTRY. But, after the passage of time, it would deliver benefits in the form of increased FOREIGN TRADE AND INVESTMENT, less corruption and greater efficiency.

Yet securing membership required agreement with the UNITED STATES, and that meant separating trade issues from HUMAN RIGHTS, TAIWAN, TIBET and other questions fuelling the general climate of rivalry and suspicion between the two powers. An agreement seemed close in early 1999 when Zhu made his first visit to Washington as premier and offered significant concessions opening the Chinese market to foreign investors. However, President Bill Clinton spurned them because he believed they were not generous enough to secure Congressional approval. Plans to continue negotiations were interrupted by NATO's accidental bombing of the Chinese embassy in Belgrade during the war against Serbia. Amid a resurgence of ultra-nationalism in several Chinese cities, evident in government-sanctioned student protests

and attacks on US diplomatic missions, Zhu's concessions of a few weeks earlier seemed almost treasonable. The reformist premier lost much of his personal authority and there was a hiatus in Sino-US relations.

His fortunes did not improve until November 1999 when China and the United States at last resumed talks on trade. At one point the discussions seemed about to break down – until Zhu intervened personally and secured a deal on China's entry into the WTO.

Zhu and the limits of renewal

Zhu's willingness and ability to secure a fundamental overhaul of his country remain uncertain at the start of the new century, less than halfway through his five-year term as premier. There is no doubt that he provided much of the drive for reform that, on the whole, made the 1990s a successful decade economically for the People's Republic. Less would have been accomplished without him. There is no doubt, either, that his achievements and personal qualities refreshed the jaded image of China's Communist leaders – at home and abroad. In the West in particular he exerted the kind of hold over the imagination once exercised by premier Zhou Enlai. Zhu, like Zhou, seemed more a man of the world than a Chinese Marxist; Zhu, like Zhou, seemed an expert, a pragmatist, a doer rather than an ideological dreamer or dull Stalinist. His reforms, still on the agenda in the new era, promise to change China's economic and social landscape.

But none of these characteristics make Zhu Rongji a closet liberal or democrat. The Communist Party might have ruined his career when he was young but it made it in later life. His calls for change have never extended to the political system itself, a principal obstacle to genuine national rejuvenation. And, as different as he is from Li Peng in terms of personality and, to some extent, policy, there is no evidence that he is at odds with his predecessor as premier on the need of the Party to retain its dominance over political life. Even if there were, there are few signs to suggest he would be able to overcome opposition within the Party on such an important issue. These observations suggest that the capacity of China's most impressive Communist leader of the 1990s to carry out fundamental change in his country in future is limited.

Chronology[1]

1900   BOXER REBELLION; siege of legations in Beijing; eight-power relief force occupies the capital; flight of EMPRESS DOWAGER to Xian

The UNITED STATES reiterates its new 'Open Door' policy designed to protect China's territorial integrity and administrative independence

RUSSIA invades Manchuria (northeast China)

1901   Boxer Protocol signed, imposing harsh conditions; officials punished for supporting the rebels

QING DYNASTY upgrades the 'Office for Handling General Affairs' into the ministry of foreign affairs

1902   The Court urges abolition of footbinding (see WOMEN)

1904   Russo-Japanese War, fought largely on Chinese soil; Beijing declares neutrality

British troops under Francis Younghusband occupy Lhasa, capital of TIBET

1905   Abolition of traditional examination system; ministry of education formed (see EDUCATION)

SUN YAT-SEN forms the UNITED LEAGUE in Tokyo

Japanese troops occupy southern Manchuria; Treaty of Portsmouth (New Hampshire) ends war, restoring Manchuria to China

Chinese merchants boycott US goods to protest American discrimination against Chinese labourers

1906   The Court overhauls government structure, creating modern ministries and declaring its intention to draft a constitution (see QING DYNASTY)

1907   Revolutionary uprisings, led by Sun and others, shake but fail to topple Qing power in south China

The Court orders the establishment of a national and local assemblies (see DEMOCRACY)

---

1 Events within each year are listed in order of significance rather than chronological sequence. The use of small capitals indicates that a full discussion of the topic may be found in the text.

1908   Death of GUANGXU EMPEROR and EMPRESS DOWAGER; accession of PU YI, the 'last emperor'

The Court announces an eight-year programme of constitutional reform

1909   Provincial Assemblies meet

1910   National Assembly meets

1911   REPUBLICAN REVOLUTION ends Manchu and imperial rule

1912   Republic of China proclaimed; emperor abdicates; provisional government established in Nanjing with SUN YAT-SEN as president; government moves to Beijing; YUAN SHIKAI becomes president

Elections for China's first regular parliament (see DEMOCRACY/ELECTIONS); KUOMIN-TANG, formed to fight them, emerges as largest party

1913   YUAN SHIKAI has SONG JIAOREN, Kuomintang leader, assassinated; bans the party; and crushes provincial resistance (the 'Second Revolution') to his rule; Sun Yat-sen returns to exile

China forced to recognize autonomy of Outer MONGOLIA in accord with RUSSIA

1914   China declares neutrality in First World War, but JAPAN declares war on Germany and seizes its possessions in SHANDONG

Bandit leader 'White Wolf' and his forces crushed in HENAN (see BANDITS)

The Simla Convention establishes autonomy for TIBET but China refuses to ratify it

1915   Japan presents, and Yuan Shikai accepts, the TWENTY-ONE DEMANDS

Yuan decides to re-establish the monarchy; YUNNAN declares independence in protest

1916   Provincial opposition forces YUAN SHIKAI to abandon plans for monarchy; Yuan dies and is succeeded as president by LI YUANHONG

1917   SUN YAT-SEN establishes a military government in Guangzhou, capital of Guangdong

Beginning of the 'New Culture' movement, known later as the MAY FOURTH MOVEMENT

The Bolshevik Revolution inspires Chinese intellectuals but plunges Russia into chaos, allowing Japan to be dominant power in Manchuria

China declares war on Germany

Zhang Xun's abortive attempt to restore Qing rule

1919   MAY FOURTH MOVEMENT: popular uproar in Beijing and elsewhere over the Allies' decision to award Germany's rights in SHANDONG to JAPAN

The SOVIET UNION renounces claims to territory seized from China in Tsarist times, save for northeast Manchuria's access to the Sea of Japan

1920   Socialist groups formed in several major cities

1921   First Congress of the CHINESE COMMUNIST PARTY; SUN YAT-SEN and Marin, Soviet representative, discuss cooperation between Communist Party and KUOMINTANG in unifying China

1922   At the WASHINGTON CONFERENCE, JAPAN agrees to restore former German possessions in SHANDONG to China, and BRITAIN the leased territory of WEIHAIWEI

1923   SUN YAT-SEN and Soviet representatives agree that Moscow will aid China's unification

        WU PEIFU crushes the Beijing–Hankou railway workers' strike

        BANDITS hijack a luxury express in the Lincheng Incident

1924   The first national congress of the KUOMINTANG pledges to cooperate with the CHINESE COMMUNIST PARTY and seek aid and advice from the SOVIET UNION in the reunification of China; National Revolutionary Army formed; SUN YAT-SEN appoints CHIANG KAI-SHEK chief of staff.

        MONGOLIA (Outer) declares full independence; China refuses to recognize it

1925   SUN YAT-SEN dies; National Revolutionary government consolidates its hold over GUANGDONG; May Thirtieth Incident in SHANGHAI and Shamian Incident of June in Guangzhou provoke anti-foreign unrest; HONG KONG–Guangzhou strike-boycott paralyses the British colony

1926   CHIANG KAI-SHEK launches NORTHERN EXPEDITION against the WARLORDS; Nationalist forces swiftly take major cities south of the YANGTZE RIVER; continued labour unrest against foreign privileges; organized peasant uprisings.

1927   The revolutionary camp splits: CHIANG KAI-SHEK crushes the CHINESE COMMUNIST PARTY in Shanghai and other areas under his control and, thanks to alliance with FENG YUXIANG, overcomes the Kuomintang Left in Wuhan (HUBEI)

        The Communists opt for military insurrection; MAO ZEDONG 'discovers' the revolutionary power of the HUNAN peasantry; Communist attempts to take cities – Nanchang (JIANGXI), Changsha (HUNAN) and Guangzhou (GUANGDONG) – fail but give birth to the Red Army, later the PEOPLE'S LIBERATION ARMY; the Communists are driven into the countryside

1928   Completion of the NORTHERN EXPEDITION and foundation of the Nationalist government in Nanjing led by Chiang Kai-shek

        China secures TARIFF AUTONOMY

        ZHANG XUELIANG succeeds his father as strongman of Manchuria

1929   Mao Zedong's Fourth Red Army moves from Jinggangshan on the HUNAN–JIANGXI border to Ruijin, south central Jiangxi, home of the future Central Soviet

        Chiang Kai-shek defeats the GUANGXI warlords

        The Nationalist government unifies China's weights and measures according to the metric system

1930   CHIANG KAI-SHEK defeats the armies of FENG YUXIANG and YAN XISHAN

        Communist forces seize but then lose Changsha, capital of HUNAN; Nationalist armies stage the First Extermination Campaign against the Communists

        BRITAIN restores WEIHAIWEI to China

1931   JAPAN seizes Manchuria following the 'Mukden (Shenyang) Incident'

        Chinese Soviet Republic founded in Ruijin with MAO ZEDONG as Chairman; government's Second Extermination Campaign fails; Third Campaign begins

1932   Japan creates MANCHUGUO with PU YI as head of state

        Chinese and Japanese troops clash in Shanghai

MAO ZEDONG loses influence in CHINESE COMMUNIST PARTY dispute over military tactics; Third Extermination Campaign fails; Fourth begins

1933　Communist Party's Central Committee moves from Shanghai to Ruijin, JIANGXI; defeat of Fourth Extermination Campaign; start of Fifth using German military advisers and blockade tactics

Japan creates Federated Autonomous Government of MONGOLIA; China and Japan sign the Tanggu Truce eliminating Chinese control north of the Great Wall

Kuomintang rebels form a rival 'People's Government' in FUJIAN

1934　The government's Fifth Extermination Campaign ejects the Communists from south China, forcing them on the LONG MARCH; Chiang Kai-shek launches 'New Life Movement' (See KUOMINTANG; CONFUCIANISM)

1935　Mao Zedong regains lost ground at the Zunyi Conference in GUIZHOU; LONG MARCH ends with arrival of Communist forces in north SHAANXI

Students in Beijing and elsewhere protest government inaction against Japanese aggression

1936　XIAN INCIDENT ends government military campaigns against Communists and leads to a United Front between the Nationalists and the Communists against Japan

1937　Start of SINO-JAPANESE WAR; government loses control of Yangtze Delta; Rape of Nanjing; Communist forces reorganized under government control

1938　Rare Nationalist military victory in Taierzhuang, SHANDONG, and bursting of Yellow River dykes in HENAN fail to stem Japanese advance; government loses control of coast and relocates to CHONGQING; WANG JINGWEI defects to Japan

1939　War in Europe; opening of the Burma Road (see SINO-JAPANESE WAR; BURMA; ROADS)

1940　Japanese 'puppet government' set up in Nanjing led by WANG JINGWEI; Communist Eighth Route Army's '100 Regiments Offensive'

1941　War in the Pacific; Japan occupies HONG KONG; Chinese Expeditionary Force enters BURMA

Nationalist and Communist troops clash in the 'New Fourth Army Incident' (see ANHUI)

1942　MAO ZEDONG launches 'rectification movement' in YANAN

1943　BRITAIN and the UNITED STATES sign treaties with China abrogating EXTRATERRITORIALITY; CHIANG KAI-SHEK attends CAIRO CONFERENCE

Famine in HUNAN

1944　Japan's *Ichigo* offensive opens an overland route from Korea to Vietnam; Chiang Kai-shek demands the recall of JOSEPH STILWELL, his American chief of staff

1945　YALTA CONFERENCE; China signs UNITED NATIONS Charter; SOVIET UNION declares war on Japan and occupies Manchurian provinces, sparking contest between Nationalist and Communist troops in the area; end of Second World War

MAO ZEDONG emerges supreme at Communists' 7th National Congress

Mao and Chiang Kai-shek talk peace in CHONGQING

China recovers TAIWAN

Rebels in XINJIANG form the 'East Turkestan Republic'

1946   American mediation attempts fail to prevent full-scale CIVIL WAR

Government promulgates the five-power constitution (see GOVERNMENT AND ADMINISTRATION)

China recognizes the independence of (Outer) MONGOLIA

1947   Early Nationalist victories in the CIVIL WAR melt away as Communists go on offensive; soaring inflation feeds urban protest; government suspends constitutional freedoms

FEBRUARY 28TH INCIDENT in TAIWAN

Communists establish INNER MONGOLIA AUTONOMOUS REGION

1948   Communist military victories in northeast, north and central China pave the way for Nationalist collapse

Government convenes National Assembly which elects Chiang Kai-shek president, LI ZONGREN vice-president

1949   People's Republic of China founded in Beijing

Nationalist government flees to TAIWAN

1950   KOREAN WAR; United States orders Seventh Fleet to protect TAIWAN; China enters war

China signs Treaty of Friendship with SOVIET UNION

Communist troops invade TIBET

Marriage and Agrarian Laws passed (see WOMEN; LAND REFORM)

1951   The UNITED NATIONS condemns the People's Republic of China as an aggressor in Korea

Agreement on the 'Peaceful Liberation of TIBET'

Campaign against 'Counter-revolutionaries'

1952   'Three Antis- Movement' (against corruption, waste and bureaucracy) ends; 'Five Antis-Movement' (against bribery, tax evasion, theft of state property, shoddy work and theft of economic information) begins

1953   KOREAN WAR armistice

PRC's first census (see POPULATION)

First Five Year Plan begins

1954   PRC Constitution approved; NATIONAL PEOPLE'S CONGRESS meets

Purge of regional Party leaders Gao Gang and Rao Shushi (See CHINESE COMMUNIST PARTY)

GENEVA CONFERENCE ON KOREA AND INDOCHINA

First TAIWAN Straits Crisis

UNITED STATES and ROC sign Mutual Defence Treaty

1955   BANDUNG CONFERENCE of non-aligned nations

Agricultural cooperatives set up (see AGRICULTURE)

1956   ONE HUNDRED FLOWERS MOVEMENT

Socialist 'transformation': nationalization of INDUSTRY

1957	'Anti-Rightist Movement' (see ONE HUNDRED FLOWERS MOVEMENT)
	Mao Zedong visits the SOVIET UNION
1958	GREAT LEAP FORWARD
	Second TAIWAN Straits Crisis
1959	PENG DEHUAI criticized and dismissed; rise of LIN BIAO
	Rebellion in TIBET; flight of DALAI LAMA
1960	Famine and deaths caused by GREAT LEAP FORWARD
	Sino-Soviet split becomes public (see SOVIET UNION)
	President Eisenhower of the United States visits TAIWAN
1961	Sino-Soviet polemics intensify
1962	War with INDIA
	Mainland refugees pour into HONG KONG; ETHNIC MINORITIES flee XINJIANG for the Soviet Union
	Socialist Education Movement (see EDUCATION)
1963	JIANG QING criticizes cultural establishment
1964	PRC explodes atomic device (see PEOPLE'S LIBERATION ARMY)
	'Learn from the PLA' Movement (see CULTURAL REVOLUTION)
1965	Battle lines drawn in struggle between 'old' and 'proletarian' culture
	Beijing aids VIETNAM in military struggle against United States
	United States phases out economic aid to Taiwan
1966	CULTURAL REVOLUTION begins; Red Guard rallies; LIU SHAOQI and DENG XIAOPING criticized; riots in MACAU
1967	Revolutionary 'seizures of power'; military intervenes to restore order; armed clashes in many parts of the country; burning of Britain's mission in Beijing; riots in HONG KONG
1968	Armed clashes between factions continue
	PRC explodes hydrogen device
1969	Military clashes along Sino-Soviet frontier in HEILONGJIANG and XINJIANG
1970	Mao Zedong begins to doubt loyalty of LIN BIAO
1971	PRC replaces the ROC as China's representative in the UNITED NATIONS
	Henry Kissinger, national security adviser to US President Nixon, visits China secretly
	LIN BIAO dies in a plane crash
1972	President Nixon of the United States visits Beijing; Japan recognizes PRC, severs ties with Taiwan
1973	China provides official version of Lin Biao's alleged conspiracy
	DENG XIAOPING reappears in public

1974   Campaign to criticize Lin Biao and Confucius

1975   Mao Zedong expresses concern over 'GANG OF FOUR'

CHIANG KAI-SHEK dies; Yan Chia-kan succeeds him as president and CHIANG CHING-KUO succeeds him as chairman of the KUOMINTANG

1976   MAO ZEDONG, ZHOU ENLAI, ZHU DE die; HUA GUOFENG succeeds Mao

Tangshan earthquake (in HEBEI) kills 240,000

'GANG OF FOUR' suppress mourning for Zhou in Tiananmen Square; DENG XIAOPING purged again

Arrest of 'GANG OF FOUR'

1977   Denunciation of the 'Gang of Four'; Deng Xiaoping returns to power

HUA GUOFENG champions the FOUR MODERNIZATIONS

1978   DENG XIAOPING launches free market reforms and Open Door policy

CHIANG CHING-KUO becomes president in TAIWAN

1979   The UNITED STATES switches diplomatic relations from Taiwan to China; US Congress passes the Taiwan Relations Act governing unofficial ties with Taipei

Sino-Vietnamese war (see VIETNAM); Vietnamese 'boat people' begin to arrive in Hong Kong

DEMOCRACY WALL MOVEMENT

1980   HU YAOBANG appointed general secretary of the Communist Party; ZHAO ZIYANG appointed premier

Hu visits TIBET and apologizes for years of misrule

Trial of 'GANG OF FOUR'

SPECIAL ECONOMIC ZONES founded

1981   'GANG OF FOUR' sentenced

Communist Party formally denounces CULTURAL REVOLUTION and reappraises MAO ZEDONG

Beijing makes peace overture to TAIWAN which is rejected

1982   BRITAIN and China agree to open talks on future of HONG KONG

Census reveals Mainland POPULATION in excess of one billion

1983   Thousands executed in anti-crime campaign; campaign against 'spiritual pollution'

Sino-British talks begin on future of HONG KONG; crisis of confidence in the colony; Hong Kong dollar pegged to US dollar

1984   China extends free market reforms to INDUSTRY; fourteen coastal cities opened to FOREIGN TRADE AND INVESTMENT

BRITAIN and China agree HONG KONG will return to China on 1 July 1997

1985   DENG XIAOPING says the PEOPLE'S LIBERATION ARMY to be reduced by one million

CHEN YUN insists on socialist nature of reforms and calls for emphasis on grain production

Car smuggling scandal in HAINAN ISLAND

1986   DENG XIAOPING calls for political reform

Students protest against CORRUPTION and for democracy

Taiwan's first opposition party, the DEMOCRATIC PROGRESSIVE PARTY, is allowed to meet

1987   HU YAOBANG sacked and succeeded by ZHAO ZIYANG; campaign against 'bourgeois liberalization'; LI PENG made 'acting' premier

Martial law lifted in TAIWAN; Taiwanese allowed to visit relatives on Mainland

Communist Party says China in 'initial stage' of socialism and calls for faster reforms

Anti-Chinese protests in TIBET

China and Portugal agree MACAU will return to China on 20 December 1999

1988   LI PENG confirmed as premier

Inflation and corruption spark controversy over price reforms

HAINAN ISLAND designated a province and SPECIAL ECONOMIC ZONE

Anti-Chinese protests continue in TIBET

CHIANG CHING-KUO dies; LEE TENG-HUI succeeds him as president and chairman of the KUOMINTANG

1989   TIANANMEN SQUARE DEMOCRACY MOVEMENT; ZHAO ZIYANG replaced as leader of the Communist Party by JIANG ZEMIN

Mass protests in Hong Kong and Taiwan against military suppression in Beijing

Martial law imposed in Lhasa, capital of TIBET, to curb nationalist unrest

Mikhail Gorbachev visits Beijing; Sino-Soviet relations 'normalized' (see SOVIET UNION)

1990   Curbs on economic growth, heightened political control

Martial law lifted in Beijing (January) and Lhasa, capital of Tibet (May)

Go-ahead for SHANGHAI's Pudong Development Zone

Basic Law, Hong Kong's post-1997 Constitution, promulgated (see HONG KONG)

1991   Collapse of SOVIET UNION alarms China's Communist leaders

Constitutional changes in TAIWAN break hold of ageing Mainlanders over law-making and redesignate the island the 'Republic of China on Taiwan'

First (partial) direct legislative elections in HONG KONG

1992   DENG XIAOPING calls for faster economic growth; Communist Party falls into line, championing the 'socialist market economy'

The NATIONAL PEOPLE'S CONGRESS approves the THREE GORGES DAM project

Rioting in SHENZHEN over irregularities in share-buying

UNITED STATES announces sale of F-16 fighters to TAIWAN

CHRIS PATTEN unveils plans for more democracy in HONG KONG

Beijing establishes diplomatic relations with South Korea (see KOREA)

Emperor Akihito of Japan visits China

1993   Beijing gripped by inflation and loss of economic control over provinces

Beijing releases WEI JINGSHENG but loses bid to stage year 2000 Olympics

'Unofficial' representatives from China and TAIWAN hold discussions in Singapore

1994   ZHU RONGJI battles to rein in wayward economy

Work formally begins on THREE GORGES DAM

CHRIS PATTEN's electoral reforms become law in HONG KONG

Direct elections in TAIWAN for the mayors of Taipei and Kaohsiung

1995   CHEN YUN dies

CHEN XITONG, mayor of Beijing, arrested for CORRUPTION

President LEE TENG-HUI makes unofficial visit to the United States, souring ties with Beijing

Legislative elections in HONG KONG

Beijing hosts United Nations Women's Conference (see WOMEN)

Beijing rejects DALAI LAMA's candidate as the next PANCHEN LAMA and approves its own

1996   Crisis in the TAIWAN Straits as Beijing stages war games to coincide with island's first direct presidential polls; LEE TENG-HUI wins elections

TUNG CHEE-HWA selected first chief executive of HONG KONG

Taiwan government apologizes to and compensates victims of FEBRUARY 28TH INCIDENT

1997   DENG XIAOPING dies

HONG KONG restored to Chinese rule

JIANG ZEMIN visits UNITED STATES

1998   Asian financial crisis slows growth on Mainland, Hong Kong and Taiwan

President Bill Clinton of the United States visits China

China and TAIWAN resume high-level 'unofficial' contacts

1999   NATO's accidental bombing of the Chinese embassy in Belgrade sparks crisis in Sino-US relations

Deflation takes its toll on the Mainland and in Hong Kong

LEE TENG-HUI declares relations between China and TAIWAN are those between 'two states'

Fiftieth anniversary of the founding of the People's Republic of China

China and the United States reach accord on terms of China's entry into the WTO

China recovers sovereignty over MACAU

2000   CHEN SHUI-BIAN of the DEMOCRATIC PROGRESSIVE PARTY elected president of Taiwan

Lee Teng-hui resigns as chairman of the Kuomintang

Selected Recommended Reading

Reference

Hook, Brian, ed. *The Cambridge Encyclopedia of China* (Cambridge University Press, 1991)

Hsieh Chiao-min and Hsieh Jean-kan, *China: A Provincial Atlas* (Prentice Hall, London, 1995)

Mackerras, Colin with McMillen, Donald H. and Watson, Andrew, *Dictionary of the Politics of the People's Republic of China* (Routledge, London, 1998)

O'Neill, Hugh B., *Companion to Chinese History* (Facts on File, Oxford, 1987)

Pan, Lynn, ed. *The Encyclopedia of the Chinese Overseas* (Curzon, Surrey, 1998)

General Histories

Cheng Pei-kai, Lestz, Michael with Spence, Jonathan D., *The Search for Modern China: A Documentary Collection* (Norton, London, 1999). A companion to Jonathan D. Spence, *The Search for Modern China*, below

Fairbank, John K., ed. *The Cambridge History of China Vol. 10: Late Ch'ing, 1800–1911, Part 1* (Cambridge University Press, 1978)

Fairbank, John K. and Liu, Kwang-Ching, eds. *The Cambridge History of China Vol. 11: Late Ch'ing, 1800–1911 Part 2* (Cambridge University Press, 1980)

Fairbank, John K. ed. *The Cambridge History of China Vol. 12: Republican China 1912–1949, Part 1* (Cambridge University Press, 1983)

Fairbank, John K. and Feuerwerker, Albert, eds. *The Cambridge History of China Vol. 13: Republican China, 1912–1949, Part 2* (Cambridge University Press, 1986)

Fairbank, John K., *China: A New History* (Harvard University Press, Cambridge, Mass., 1992)

Jenner, W. J. F., *The Tyranny of History: The Roots of China's Crisis* (Penguin, London, 1992)

MacFarquhar, Roderick and Fairbank, John K., eds. *The Cambridge History of China, Vol. 14: The People's Republic, Part 1: The Emergence of Revolutionary China, 1949–1965* (Cambridge University Press, 1987)

MacFarquhar, Roderick and Fairbank, John K., *The Cambridge History of China, Vol. 15: The People's Republic, Part 2: Revolutions within the Chinese Revolution, 1966–1982* (Cambridge University Press, 1991)

Spence, Jonathan D., *The Gate of Heavenly Peace: The Chinese and Their Revolution* (Faber and Faber, London, 1982)

Spence, Jonathan D., *The Search for Modern China* (Norton, New York, 1990). See documentary companion, eds. Cheng *et al.*, above

Personal Accounts

Chang, Jung, *Wild Swans: Three Daughters of China* (HarperCollins, London, 1991)

Chang, Nien, *Life and Death in Shanghai* (Grove Press, New York, 1986)

Cradock, Percy, *Experiences of China* (John Murray, London, 1994)

Liang Heng and Shapiro, Judith, *Son of the Revolution* (Knopf, New York, 1983)

Tyson, James and Tyson, Ann, *Chinese Awakenings: Life Stories from the Unofficial China* (Westview Press, Boulder, Colorado, 1995)

Wu, Harry and Wakeman, Carolyn, *Bitter Winds: A Memoir of My Years in China's Gulag* (John Wiley & Sons, New York, 1994)

Wu Ningkun, *A Single Tear: A Family's Persecution, Love and Endurance in Communist China* (Hodder and Stoughton, London, 1993)

Zhang Xinxin and Sang Ye, eds. W. J. F. Jenner and Delia Davin *Chinese Lives: An Oral History of Contemporary China* (Macmillan, London, 1987)

Close-of-century Overviews

Gittings, John, *Real China: From Cannibalism to Karaoke* (Pocket Books, London, 1997)

Goodman, David G. and Segal, Gerald, eds. *China Deconstructs: Politics, Trade and Regionalism* (Routledge, London, 1994)

Kristof, Nicholas D. and WuDunn, Sheryl, *China Wakes: The Struggle for the Soul of a Rising Power* (Nicholas Brealey, London, 1994)

Miles, James, *The Legacy of Tiananmen: China In Disarray* (University of Michigan, Ann Arbor, 1996)

Overholt, William, *China: The Next Economic Superpower* (Weidenfeld and Nicolson, London, 1993)

Schell, Orville, *Mandate of Heaven: A New Generation of Entrepreneurs, Dissidents, Bohemians and Technocrats Lays Claim to China's Future* (Simon and Schuster, New York, 1994)

Segal, Gerald, *China Changes Shape: Regionalism and Foreign Policy* (International Institute for Strategic Studies, Adelphi Papers, London, 1994)

van Kemenade, Willem, *China, Hong Kong, Taiwan Inc.: The Dynamics of a New Empire* (Knopf, New York, 1997)

Wilson, Dick, *China the Big Tiger: A Nation Awakes* (Abacus, London, 1997)

People, Politics and Political Economy

Barmé, Geremie, R., *Shades of Mao: The Posthumous Cult of the Great Leader* (M. E. Sharpe, Armonk, New York, 1996)

Baum, Richard, *Burying Mao: Chinese Politics in the Age of Deng Xiaoping* (Princeton University Press, Princeton, NJ, 1994)

Becker, Jasper, *Hungry Ghosts: China's Secret Famine* (John Murray, London, 1996)

Brook, Timothy, *Quelling the People: The Military Suppression of the Beijing Democracy Movement* (Stanford University Press, Stanford, Cal., 1998)

Byron, John and Pack, Robert, *The Claws of the Dragon: Kang Sheng, the Evil Genius behind Mao and his Legacy of Terror in People's China* (Simon and Schuster, New York, 1992)

Davin, Delia, *Mao Zedong* (Sutton Publishing, Stroud, 1997)

Evans, Richard, *Deng Xiaoping and the Making of Modern China* (Hamish Hamilton, London, 1993)

Friedman, Edward, Pickowicz, Paul G. and Selden, Mark, *Chinese Village, Socialist State* (Yale University Press, New Haven, Conn., 1991)

Gilley, Bruce, *Tiger on the Brink: Jiang Zemin and China's New Elite* (University of California Press, Berkeley, Cal., 1998)

Goldman, Merle, *Sowing the Seeds of Democracy in China: Political Reform in the Deng Xiaoping Era* (Harvard University Press, Cambridge, Mass., 1994)

Goldman, Merle and MacFarquhar, Roderick, eds. *The Paradox of China's Post-Mao Reforms* (Harvard University Press, Cambridge, Mass., 1999)

Goodman, David S. G., *Deng Xiaoping and the Chinese Revolution: A Political Biography* (Routledge, London, 1994)

Ladany, Laszlo, *The Communist Party of China and Marxism, 1921–1985: A Self-Portrait* (Hurst & Co., London, 1988)

Lam, Willy Wo-Lap, *The Era of Jiang Zemin* (Prentice Hall, Singapore, 1998)

Li Zhisui with Thurston, Anne F., *The Private Life of Chairman Mao* (Random House, New York, 1994)

Liberthal, Kenneth, *Governing China: From Revolution Through Reform* (W. W. Norton, New York, 1995)

Nathan, Andrew J. *Chinese Democracy: The Individual and the State in Twentieth-Century China* (I. B. Tauris, London, 1986)

Nathan, Andrew J., *China's Transition* (Columbia University Press, New York, 1998)

Saich, Tony and Van de Ven, Hans, eds. *New Perspectives on the Chinese Communist Revolution* (M. E. Sharpe, Armonk, New York, 1995)

Saich, Tony, ed. with a contribution from Benjamin Yang, *The Rise to Power of the Chinese Communist Party: Documents and Analysis* (M. E. Sharpe, Armonk, New York, 1996)

Salisbury, Harrison E., *The New Emperors: Mao and Deng, a Dual Biography* (HarperCollins, London, 1992)

Schell, Orville and Shambaugh, David, eds. *The China Reader: The Reform Era* (Vintage Books, New York, 1999)

Schoenhals, Michael, ed. *China's Cultural Revolution, 1966–1969: Not a Dinner Party* (M. E. Sharpe, Armonk, New York, 1996)

Shirk, Susan L., *The Political Logic of Economic Reform in China* (University of California Press, Berkeley, Cal., 1993)

The Military

Dreyer, Edward L., *China At War, 1901–1949* (Longman, London, 1995)

Joffe, Ellis, *The Chinese Army after Mao* (Weidenfeld and Nicolson, London, 1987)

Lewis, John Wilson and Xue Litai, *China's Strategic Seapower: The Politics of Force Modernization in the Nuclear Age* (Stanford University Press, Stanford, Cal., 1994)

Nathan, Andrew J. and Ross, Robert J., *The Great Wall and the Empty Fortress: China's Search for Security* (W. W. Norton, New York, 1997)

Shambaugh David and Yang, Richard, eds. *China's Military in Transition* (Clarendon Press, Oxford, 1997)

The Economy

Kueh, Y. Y. and Ash, Robert F., *Economic Trends in Agriculture: The Impact of Post-Mao Reforms* (Oxford University Press, Oxford, 1993)

Lardy, Nicholas R., *Foreign Trade and Economic Reform in China, 1978–1990* (Cambridge University Press, Cambridge, 1992)

Lardy, Nicholas, *China in the World Economy* (Institute for International Economics, Washington, 1994)

Lardy, Nicholas, *China's Unfinished Economic Revolution* (Brookings Institution Press, Washington, 1998)

Linge, Godfrey, ed. *China's New Spatial Economy: Heading Towards 2020* (Oxford University Press, Hong Kong, 1997)

Liou, Kuotsai Tom, *Managing Economic Reforms in Post-Mao China* (Praeger, Westport, Conn., 1998)

Maddison, Angus, *Chinese Economic Performance in the Long Run* (OECD, Paris, 1998)

Naughton, Barry, *Growing Out of the Plan: Chinese Economic Reform, 1978–1993* (Cambridge University Press, Cambridge, 1995)

Steinfeld, Edward S., *Forging Reform in China: The Fate of State-Owned Industry* (Cambridge University Press, Cambridge, 1998)

World Bank, *China 2020: Development Challenges in the New Century* (World Bank, Washington, 1997)

Society and Popular Culture (including women, population, the family)

Aird, John S., *Slaughter of the Innocents: Coercive Birth Control in China* (University Press of America, Lanham, Maryland, 1990)

Banister, Judith, *China's Changing Population* (Stanford University Press, Stanford, Cal., 1987)

Barmé, Geremie R. *In the Red: On Contemporary Chinese Culture* (Columbia University Press, New York, 1999)

Brook, Timothy and Frolic, Michael B., *Civil Society in China* (M. E. Sharpe, Armonk, New York 1997)

Croll, Elisabeth, *From Heaven to Earth: Images and Experiences of Development in China* (Routledge, London, 1994)

Davis, Deborah and Harrell, Steven, *Chinese Families in the Post-Mao Era* (University of California Press, Berkeley, 1993)

Davis, Deborah, Kraus, Richard, Naughton, Barry and Perry, Elizabeth, eds. *Urban Spaces in Contemporary China: The Potential for Autonomy and Community in Post-Mao China* (Cambridge University Press, Cambridge, 1995)

Dikötter, Frank, *Imperfect Conceptions: Medical Knowledge, Birth Defects and Eugenics in China* (Hurst & Co., London, 1998)

Dutton, Michael, *Streetlife China: Transforming Culture, Rights and Markets* (Cambridge University Press, Cambridge, 1998)

Evans, Harriet, *Women and Sexuality in China: Dominant Discourses of Female Sexuality and Gender Since 1949* (Polity Press, Cambridge, 1997)

Hoe, Susanna, *Chinese Footprints: Exploring Women's History in China, Hong Kong and Macau* (Roundhouse, Hong Kong, 1996)

Poston, Dudley L. and Yaukey, David, eds. *The Population of Modern China* (Plenum Press, New York, 1992)

West, Jackie, Zhao, Minghua, Chang Xiangqun, Yuan, Cheng, eds. *Women of China: Economic and Social Transformation* (Macmillan, London, 1999)

Zha, Jianying, *China Pop: How Soap Operas, Tabloids and Bestsellers are Transforming a Culture* (The New Press, New York, 1995)

The Regions (including ethnic minorities)

Barnett, Doak A., *China's Far West: Four Decades of Change* (Westview Press, Boulder, Colorado, 1993)

Dreyer, June T., *China's Forty Millions* (Harvard University Press, Cambridge, Mass., 1976)

Hook, Brian, ed. *Guangdong: China's Promised Land* (Oxford University Press, Hong Kong, 1996)

Hook, Brian, ed. *Fujian: Gateway to Taiwan* (Oxford University Press, Hong Kong, 1996)

Hook, Brian, ed. *Shanghai and the Yangtze Delta: A City Reborn* (Oxford University Press, Hong Kong, 1998)

Hook, Brian, ed. *Beijing and Tianjin: Towards a Millennial Megalopolis* (Oxford University Press, Hong Kong, 1998)

Mackerras, Colin, *China's Minority Cultures: Identities and Integration Since 1912* (St Martin's Press, New York, 1995)

Pan, Lynn, *Sons of the Yellow Emperor: The Story of the Overseas Chinese* (Secker & Warburg, London, 1990)

Pan, Lynn, *Tracing It Home: Journeys Around a Chinese Family* (Secker & Warburg, London, 1992)

Rossabi, Morris, *China and Inner Asia: From 1368 to the Present Day* (Thames & Hudson, London, 1975)

Van Slyke, Lyman P., *Yangtze: Nature, History and the River* (Addison Wesley, New York, 1988)

Winchester, Simon, *The River at the Centre of the World: A Journey up the Yangtze, and Back in Chinese Time* (Penguin, London, 1996)

Ideas (Including law and human rights)

Alford, William P., *To Steal a Book is an Elegant Offense: Intellectual Property Law in Chinese Civilization* (Stanford University Press, Stanford, Cal., 1995)

Amnesty International, *China: No One is Safe: Political Repression and Abuse of Power in the 1990s* (Amnesty International, London, 1996)

Bo Yang, trans. and ed. Don J. Cohn and Jing Qing, *The Ugly Chinaman and the Crisis of Chinese Culture* (Allen & Unwin, St Leonards, New South Wales, 1992)

Ching, Julia, *Chinese Religions* (Macmillan, London, 1993)

Davis, Michael C., ed. *Human Rights and Chinese Values: Legal, Philosophical and Political Perspectives* (Oxford University Press, Hong Kong, 1995)

De Bary, William Theodore and Tu Weiming, eds. *Confucianism and Human Rights* (Columbia University Press, New York, 1997)

Feuchtwang, Stephen, *The Imperial Metaphor: Popular Religion in China* (Routledge, London, 1992)

Hayhoe, Ruth, *China's Universities 1895–1995: A Century of Cultural Conflict* (Garland, New York, 1996)

Kent, Ann, *Between Freedom and Subsistence: China and Human Rights* (Oxford University Press, Hong Kong, 1993)

Link, Perry, *Evening Chats in Beijing: Probing China's Predicament* (Norton, New York, 1992)

Seymour, James D. and Anderson, Richard, *New Ghosts, Old Ghosts: Prisons and Labour Camps in China* (M. E. Sharpe, Armonk, New York, 1998)

Whyte, Bob, *Unfinished Encounter: China and Christianity* (William Collins, Glasgow, 1988)

Foreign Policy

Dittmer, Lowell and Kim, Samuel S., eds. *China's Quest for National Identity* (Cornell University Press, Ithaca, New York, 1993)

Garver, John W., *Foreign Relations of the People's Republic of China* (University of California Press, Berkeley, 1992)

Goodman, David S. G. and Segal, Gerald, eds. *China Rising: Nationalism and Interdependence* (Routledge, London, 1997)

Kim, Samuel S., *China and the World: Chinese Foreign Policy Faces the New Millennium* (Westview Press, Boulder, Colorado, 1998)

Madsen, Richard, *China and the American Dream: A Moral Inquiry* (University of California Press, Berkeley, Cal., 1995)

Mann, James, *About Face: A History of America's Curious Troubled Relationship with China from Nixon to Clinton* (Alfred A. Knopf, New York, 1999)

Robinson, Thomas W. and Shambaugh, David, eds. *Chinese Foreign Policy: Theory and Practice* (Clarendon Press, Oxford, 1994)

Westad, Odd Arne, ed. *Brothers in Arms: The Rise and Fall of the Sino-Soviet Alliance, 1945–1963* (Woodrow Wilson Center and Stanford University Press, Washington, 1998)

The Environment

Barber, Margaret and Ryder, Gráinne, eds. *Damming the Three Gorges: What the Dam Builders Don't Want You to Know* (second edn, Earthscan, London, 1993)

Cannon, Terry and Jenkins, Alan, *The Geography of Contemporary China: The Impact of Deng Xiaoping's Reforms* (Routledge, London, 1990)

China Quarterly, The, No. 156, December 1998 Special Issue: The Environment (School of Oriental and African Studies, University of London)

Dai Qing, trans. N. Liu, *Yangtze!, Yangtze! Debate Over the Three Gorges* (Probe International, Earthscan Publications, London, 1994)

Dai Qing (compiler) eds. John G. Thibodeau and Philip B. Williams, *The River Dragon Has Come!
The Three Gorges Dam and the Fate of China's Yangtze River and its People* (M. E. Sharpe, Armonk,
New York, 1998)

Edmonds, Richard Louis, *Patterns of China's Lost Harmony: A Survey of the Country's Environmental
Degradation and Protection* (Routledge, London, 1994)

Zhao Songqiao, *Geography of China: Environment, Resources, Population and Development* (John
Wiley & Sons, New York, 1994)

Hong Kong

Brown, Judith M. and Foot, Rosemary, eds. *Hong Kong's Transitions, 1842–1997* (St Anthony's
Series, Macmillan, London, 1997)

Chan, Ming K., ed. *Precarious Balance: Hong Kong Between China and Britain, 1842–1992* (M. E.
Sharpe, Armonk, New York, 1994)

Cottrell, Robert, *The End of Hong Kong: The Secret Diplomacy of Imperial Retreat* (John Murray,
London, 1993)

Patten, Chris, *East and West: The Last Governor of Hong Kong on Power, Freedom and the Future*
(Macmillan, London, 1998)

Roberti, Mark, *The Fall of Hong Kong: China's Triumph and Britain's Betrayal* (John Wiley & Sons,
New York, 1994)

Tsang, Steve, *Hong Kong: An Appointment with China* (I. B. Tauris, London, 1997)

Vines, Stephen, *Hong Kong: China's New Colony* (Aurum Press, London, 1998)

Yahuda, Michael, *Hong Kong: China's Challenge* (Routledge, London, 1996)

Taiwan

China Quarterly, The, No. 148, December 1996, Special Issue – Contemporary Taiwan (School of
Oriental and African Studies, University of London)

Lai Tse-Han, Myers, Ramon H. and Wei Wou, *A Tragic Beginning: The Taiwan Uprising of February
28, 1947* (Stanford University Press, Stanford, Cal., 1991)

Long, Simon, *Taiwan: China's Last Frontier* (Macmillan, London, 1991)

Tsang, Steve, ed. *In The Shadow of China: Political Development in Taiwan Since 1949* (Hong Kong
University Press, Hong Kong, 1993)

Tsang, Steve and Tien Hung-mao, eds. *Democratization in Taiwan: Implications for China*
(St Martin's Press, New York, 1998)

Tucker, Nancy Bernkopf, *Taiwan, Hong Kong and the United States, 1945–1992: Uncertain Friendships* (Twayne, London, 1994)

Wu, Jaushieh Joseph, *Taiwan's Democratisation: Forces Behind the New Momentum* (Oxford
University Press, Hong Kong, 1995)

Tibet

Barnett, Robert and Akiner, Shirin, eds. *Resistance and Reform in Tibet* (Hurst & Co., London,
1994)

Dalai Lama, *Freedom in Exile: The Autobiography of the Dalai Lama* (Hodder and Stoughton,
London, 1990)

Goldstein, Melvyn C., *China, Tibet and the Dalai Lama* (University of California Press, Berkeley,
Cal., 1997)

Hilton, Isabel, *The Search for the Panchen Lama* (Viking, London, 1999)

Shakya, Tsering, *The Dragon in the Land of Snows: A History of Modern Tibet Since 1947* (Pimlico,
London, 1999)

Macau

Cremer, R. D., ed. *Macau: City of Commerce and Culture* (UEA Press, Hong Kong, 1987)
Porter, Jonathan, *Macau, the Imaginary City* (Westview Press, Boulder, Colorado, 1996)
Shipp, Steve, *Macau, China: A Political History of the Portuguese Colony's Transition to Chinese Rule* (McFarland, Jefferson, Ky, 1997)

Index

Page references in **bold** indicate main entries
Page references in *italics* indicate maps and
    figures

Abdurexit, Ablait 471
Afghanistan, Soviet invasion 398
agricultural producers's cooperatives (APCs)
    265, 280
agriculture **25–8**, *26*
  clan activities 85
  collectivization 164, 265, 298
  Dazhai Production Brigade 27, 377, 380
  family production 133
  household responsibility system 134, 265,
      384
  production responsibility system 31
Ah Q-ism 286
AIDS 183
air force, military 81, 337
air travel, civil aviation **80–82**, 152
Alley, Rewi 140
Amdo 351–2
Amethyst Incident (1949) **29**, 50, 244, 479
Amoy *see* Xiamen
anarchism **29–30**, 302, 350
'Anhui Clique' 30, 184, 488
Anhui Incident (New Fourth Army) 30, 387
Anhui Province **30–32**
Annan, Kofi 448
Anshan Iron & Steel Works 281
Anti-Rightist Movement 11, 108, 113, 212, 298,
    320–21, 358, 495
April Fifth Forum 103, 113
armies **32–6**, 349
    see also Beiyang Army; National
      Revolutionary Army; People's Liberation
      Army (PLA)

arms sales **36–7**, 325–6, 338, 364, 452
Army of the Green Standard 33
Asia-Europe Land Bridge 245
Asia-Pacific Economic Cooperation (APEC)
    37
Asian financial crisis 149
'Asian values' 17, **38–9**, 87, 100, 215, 324,
    385
Association for Relations Across the Taiwan
      Straits (ARATS) 411
Association of Southeast Asian Nations
      (ASEAN) **37–8**, 53, 144, 385, 392–3,
      457
atomic bomb 142, 332–3
authoritarianism, fragmented 159
'autonomous regions' 129
Autumn Harvest Uprisings 246
Aymat, Ismail 471
Azizi, Seypidin 471

Ba Zhongtan 335
Bai Chongxi 30, 172, 276–7, 460
Bai Hua 114
bai hua (plain speech) 6, **40–41**, 56, 205, 286,
    306
Bai Lang (White Wolf) 41, 189
Baitou 249
Bamboo Union Gang 367, 409
bandits **41–2**, 189–90, 246, 370
Bandung Conference (1955) 38, **42**, 142
Bangkok Declaration 38, 215
banks 139
Banner Forces 33
Bao Tong 426, 427
Baotou 230
Beidaihe 186
Beihai 174

Beijing **42–6**
  Boxer rebellion 47–8
  see also Hebei Province; Tiananmen Square
    Democracy Movement
Beijing University (*Beida*) 116, 117, 120
Beiyang Army 33, 184, 480
Belgrade, Chinese embassy bombing (1999)
  17, 52, 75, 145, 242, 338, 347, 454, 497
biological weapons, Sino-Japanese War 388
'birdcage theory' 59
Blue Shirts 257
Bo Gu (aka Qin Bangxian) 66, 68
Bo Xilai 75, 281
Bo Yang **46–7**
Bo Yibo 379
Bohai Gulf Economic Zone 186, 430
Borodin, Mikhail 209, 394, 402
Bosshardt, Alfred 285, 312
Boxer Rebellion (1899–1900) 3, 43, **47–9**, 122,
    141, 366
  Shandong Province 47, 371
  Shanxi Province 378
Braun, Otto 285
Britain
  extraterritoriality 131–2, 436, 439
  Hong Kong 110, 193–202, 327–9
  protests against 317
  relations with China 29, **49–52**, 54
  treaty ports 436, 439
  unequal treaties 443
  Weihaiwei occupation 371, 460, 462–3
  Yangtze River 479
Brown, Lester 28
Buddhism 94, 326, 356, 357
Buhe 231
Burchett, Wilfred 140
bureaucracy, reforms 161–3
Burma
  ASEAN membership 39
  relations with China **52–3**, 223, 483, 484
Burma Road 362, 387, 483
Bush, George 413
Butterfield & Swire 49, 479
Butterfly Gang 368
Buyi ethnic minority 175
Buyun, election (1998) 384–5

Cai E 482
Cai Tingkai 151
Cai Yuanpei 117, 306
Cairo Conference (1943) 9, **54**, 142, 387, 405,
    449
Cambodia 38, **55**, 446
cannibalism 91, 173, 316
Canton *see* Guangzhou
Cao Kun 184, 276
car production, Changchun 249

cars 362–3
Catholic Patriotic Association 79, 80, 312
Ceausescu, Nicolae 398
censuses 339–40, 341
Chadrel Rimpoche 327, 435
Chai Ling 423, 426
Changbaishan mountains 249
Changchun 248–9
Changsha 217, 220
Changsha reform experiment 217
chemical weapons 187
Chen Boda 90
Chen Duxiu **56**, 66, 209, 272, 307
Chen Jiageng (Tan Kah Kee) 151
Chen Jitang 167
Chen Kuo-fu 87, 259
Chen Li-fu 87, 259
Chen Minzhang 340
Chen Shaoyu *see* Wang Ming
Chen Shui-bian **56–8**
  Democratic Progressive Party and 104–6
  elected Taiwan president 16, 106, 255,
    261–2, 404, 415
  Lee Teng-hui and 414
  relations with Mainland 203, 241, 271,
    415–16
Chen Xitong **58–9**
  corruption 46, 89, 240, 267, 461
  Tiananmen Square Democracy Movement
    and 46, 58, 425, 427
Chen Yi 135, 405
Chen Yonggui 380
Chen Yun **59**, 110, 273, 381
Chen Zaidao 91, 210
Chen Ziming 101, 114, 423–4, 426
Cheng Qian 218–19
Chengdu 77, 383–5
Chennault, Claire 81, 387, 388, 449
Chiang Ching-kuo **60–61**, 64, 105, 260, 270,
    408–9
Chiang Kai-shek 7–10, 34–5, **61–4**, 256–60
  Anhui Province 30
  Cairo Conference 54, 142
  character of 63
  in Chongqing 77, 258
  Civil War 62, 83–5, 244, 277
  foreign policy 141–2
  government of 158–9, 243, 402–3
  Guangxi Province 172, 276–7
  Manchuria 248
  Ningxia Province 316
  Northern Expedition 317–19
  purge of Communists 34, 65–6, 190, 246–7,
    257–8, 295, 329, 375
  Sino-Japanese War 34–5, 190, 243, 258,
    387–8, 399–400
  Soong Mei-ling and **390–91**

in Taiwan 63–4, 259–60, 407–8
United States and 399–400, 449–50
Xian Incident 469, 486
Zhejiang Province 488–9
children
abuse of 214
see also one-child policy
China Association for Promoting Democracy
103
China Democratic League 103
China Democratic National Construction
Association 103
China Democratic Party 115, 240, 491
China International Trust and Investment
Corporation (CITIC) 147
China Xinjiang Construction Company 471
Chinese Communist Party **64–75**
accounts of 389
Anhui Province 30–31
capitalism relationship 19–20
Chiang Kai-shek and 61–2, 257
Civil War 83–4
constitution 163
corruption 58–9, 88–9, 461
democracy and 99–100
dissidents and 112–15
economic policies 273
family policies 134
financial policies 138–40
foreign policy 142–3
foreign trade and investment 146–8
founding (1921) 6, 56, 65, 272, 303, 375
government by 159–63, *160*
Great Chinese Revolution 9–10
Guizhou Province 175–6
Harbin 187–8
health campaigns 182
history rewritten 72
Jiangxi Province 246–7
Kuomintang and 62, 65, 83–4, 402
land reform 26–7, 69, 264–5
leaders of 66, 74–5
legal system 266–8
media control 308–10
membership 70
organizational structure 70
PLA relationship 338–9
policies 68–9, 98–9
private enterprises and 227
religion and 358–9
rural rebirth 8, 62, 66–7, 246
secret societies and 367
Sino-Japanese War 67–8
socialism and 73, 490–91
Soviet Union influence 393–5
Taiwan relationship 410–12
women's position 465–7

Yanan headquarters 68, 156, 369, 476
see also Cultural Revolution; Deng
Xiaoping; Great Leap Forward; Hu
Yaobang; Hua Guofeng; Jiang Zemin;
Long March; Mao Zedong; National
People's Congress (NPC); One Hundred
Flowers Movement; Zhao Ziyang
Chinese Labour Force 371, 462
Chinese Peasants and Workers Democratic
Party 103
Chinese People's Political Consultative
Conference (CPPCC) **75–6**, 104, 159,
275–6
Chinese Socialist Party 30
Choekyi Gyaltsen 326–7
Chokyi Nyima 326
Chongqing **76–8**, 383–5, 387, 421, 478–9
Christianity **78–80**, 192, 311–12, 357
Churchill, Winston 9, 54, 142, 474
Ci Xi *see* Empress Dowager
civil aviation **80–82**, 152
Civil War (1946–9) 9, **83–5**
aircraft 81
Anhui Province 31
armies 35
Beijing 44
Chiang Kai-shek's role 62, 83–5, 244, 277
Deng Xiaoping 108
Fujian Province 151–2
Guangdong Province 167
Guangxi Province 172
Hainan Island 178–9
Hebei Province 185
Henan Province 190
Hong Kong 195
Jiangsu Province 244
Kuomintang 259
land reform 264
Liaoning Province 279
People's Liberation Army 35
Qinghai Province 351
Sichuan Province 383
Soviet intervention 395
clans **85–6**, 133, 246, 368
climate 2
Clinton, Bill 105–6, 241, 269, 347, 452, 453, 497
coal resources 123, 186, 381
coastal development strategy 152, 168,
179–80, 372, 487
Cold War 10, 142, 167–8, 332–3, 450–51
collective farming 164, 265, 298
commercialization, media 310
communes 27, 134, 165, 466
communications *see* civil aviation; railways;
roads; telecommunications
Communist International (Comintern) 256,
302–3, 393, 394

Communist Party *see* Chinese Communist
Party
Comprehensive Test Ban Treaty (CTBT) 326,
333
Confucianism **86–7**, 116, 251, 356, 357
Conscience Society 30
constitutions 163
corruption 58–9, **87–9**, 163, 179, 240, 267,
461
CPPCC *see* Chinese People's Political
Consultative Conference
Cradock, Sir Percy 328
criminals, secret societies 367–8
crops *26*
Cultural Revolution (1966–76) 11–12, 71,
90–93, 300–301
army role 36, 334
Beijing 45
Confucianism and 86
dissidents 113
education system 119
family impacts 134
foreign relations breakdown 51
Guangxi Province 173
Kang Sheng 250–51
Macau 290
religious persecution 79, 358–9
Shanghai 376
Wuhan 210–11
Xinjiang Province 472
see also Gang of Four

Dagang Oil Fields 429
Dai Qing 114, 420–21, 426
Dai Xianglong 139
Dalai Lama **94–6**, 129, 221, 326–7, 351
13th 431
14th (Tenzin Gyatso) 432–6
Dalian 278, 281, 474
dangan (personal dossiers) 69, **96**
danwei (work unit) **97**, 309, 342
Daoism 356, 358
Daqing 188, 226
Daqiuzhuang 429–30
Dawamat, Tomur 471
Dazhai Production Brigade 27, 377, 380
De Wang 230
defence spending 337–8
see also arms sales
democracy **97–102**, 389, 461
Taiwan 415–16
Democracy Wall Movement (1978–9) 13–14,
102–4, 461
demands of 266
Deng Xiaoping and 45, 99, 109, 208
leaders of 113–14
press reform 309

Democratic Progressive Party (DPP) 56–8,
104–6, 136, 241, 255, 270–71, 413–16
Democratic Revolutionary Comrades'
Association 475
Democratic Youth Party 421
Deng Liqun ('Little Deng') **106–7**, 305,
309
Deng Xiaoping 11, 12–15, 45, **107–12**
agricultural policy 27
army role 335, 379
Chen Yun and 59
Communist Party leadership 72–3, 92–3,
109–12, 304–5, 397
corruption and 88
democracy and 99–100, 102–3, 110–11,
461–2
exiled 71, 91, 92, 247
family policies 134
financial policies 138
foreign policies 143
Hu Yaobang and 109, 110, 161, 206–7
Hua Guofeng and 207–8
industrialization 226–7
Jiang Zemin and 238–9, 241
Mao Zedong and 108–9
Open Door policy 13, 147, 168, 345
personal image 109
reforms of 161
'southern journey' (1992) 88, 112, 138, 169,
180–81, 211, 239, 373, 377, 399, 480
'theories' of 73, 111, 305
Tiananmen Square Democracy Movement
424, 426–7
United Nations membership 445–6
Yang Shangkun and 477
Deng Yingchao 273, 492
Diaoyutai Islands 236, 336, 405
Ding Ling 68, 99, 113, 465
Ding Zilin 425
diplomatic relations, Taiwan 416
dissidents 99–100, **112–15**
Deng Xiaoping and 72
Hefei 31–2
imprisonment 213, 263
Inner Mongolia 232
Wei Jingsheng 72, 109, 113, **461–2**
divorce 134–5
Dong Biwu 444
Dong ethnic minority 217
DPP *see* Democratic Progressive Party
drug trade 484–5
Du Yuesheng 367, 375
Dual Nationality Treaty, Sino-Indonesian
(1955) 223–4
Duan Qirui 30, 184, 306, 488
Dulles, John Foster 157
'dying rooms' 214, 343

earthquake, Tangshan (1976) 124, 185–6, 429
East Turkestan, Republic of 470–71
economy
    deflation 16–17
    development of 20–21
    Taiwan 414
    Zhejiang Province 489–90
    Zhu Rongji's policies 496–7
education **116–21**
    Cultural Revolution 90, 91, 119
    ethnic minorities 130
    future of 120–21
    missionary role 311, 464–5
    reform 4, 117
    women 45, 311, 465
Eighth Route Army 108, 378–9, 476
Elder Brother Society 366, 367
elderly population 344
elections 101, 389
    Buyun (1998) 384–5
    Taiwan 105, 409, 413
    Taiwan presidential (2000) 56, 58, 106,
        261–2, 271, 414–16
emigration
    Fujian Province 150–51
    Qing dynasty 321–2
    see also migration; Overseas Chinese
employment, women 466–7
Empress Dowager (Ci Xi) **121–2**, 174–5, 251,
    348, 369
energy **122–4**, 186, 353, 365
environment **124–7**, 352–3
Epstein, Israel 140
er erba see February Twenty-Eighth Incident
ethnic minorities **127–31**, *128*, 340
    Guangxi Province 171, 172–3
    Guizhou Province 175
    religion 357
    Xinjiang Province 471, 473
    Yunnan Province 482, 484
    see also under names of individual ethnic
        groups
eugenics 340
exceptionalism 22
executions 216
Explorations (tansuo) 102
extraterritoriality **131–2**, 146, 193, 374, 436–9,
    460

Fa Lun Gong 75, 242, 419
Fairfax-Cholmeley, Elsie 140
family **133–5**
famine (1943) 190, 387
famine (1959–62) 164, 165–6
    Anhui Province 31
    causes 27, 125, 298
    Gansu Province 157

Guizhou Province 176
Henan Province 191
Ningxia Province 316–17
population figures 341
Qinghai Province 352
Shandong Province 372
Fang Lizhi 31–2, 110, 114, 207, 426, 427
February Twenty-Eighth Incident (1947) 64,
    135–6, 259, 405–7
Federation of Autonomous Workers 423
Feng Guozhang 184
Feng Yuxiang **136–7**, 460
    Chiang Kai-shek and 316, 318
    Pu Yi and 346, 350
    Wu Peifu and 190
    Yan Xishan and 475
    'Zhili Clique' 184
'Fengtian Clique' 184, 460
Fengyang 31
Fernandes, George 223
finance **137–40**
First World War 234, 371
'five principles of peaceful coexistence' 42,
    142
Five Year Plan
    First (1953–7) 59, 226, 279, 369, 395
    Ninth (1996–2000) 430
floods 124
Flying Tigers 81, 387, 449
food security 27–8
footbinding 349, 464–5
Forbidden City 43, 45, 346, 350
foreign direct investment (FDI) 147, 323
'foreign experts and foreign friends' **140**,
    380
foreign policy **140–46**, 305–6
foreign trade and investment **146–50**, 179,
    227
    Jiangsu Province 245
    tariff autonomy 137, 257, **417**
    Three Gorges Dam 421
    Tianjin 429
    Yunnan Province 484
Formosa 104
'Formosa Incident' 57, 409
Four Modernizations 119–20, **150**
    fifth modernization 102, 461
    Hua Guofeng and 208
    industry 226
    military 335
    Zhou Enlai and 493, 494
Fu Zuoyi 44
Fujian Province **150–53**
Fuzhou 150

gambling, Macau 290
Gan River 245

Gang of Four 12, 45, 71–2, **154–5**
  Confucianism and 86
  Deng Xiaoping and 108–9, 155, 301
  Hua Guofeng and 72, 92, 207, 301
  Jiang Qing 237
  rise of 91, 376
  Zhou Enlai and 493–4
Gansu Province **155–7**
Gao Gang 70, 188, 279–80
Gao Xin 425
Ge Hongsheng 491
Gedhun Choekyi Nyima 327, 435
Geneva Conference on Korea and Indochina
  (1954) 42, 143, **157–8**, 456, 493
geographical features 2
Germany, Shandong occupation 371
girls
  undesirability of 340, 342–3
  see also women
globalization 19–20
Gong Pinmei 79
Gorbachev, Mikhail 111, 397, 424
government and administration **158–63**,
  160
Grand Canal 243
Great Hall of the People 45, 423
Great Leap Forward (1958–60) 11, 70–71,
  164–6, 298
  agricultural impacts 27
  Anhui Province 31
  education impacts 118–19
  environmental impacts 125
  family impacts 134
  Guizhou Province 176
  Henan Province 191
  Hunan Province 219
  industrialization 226
  Inner Mongolia 230–31
  land reform 265
  Liaoning Province 280
  opposition to 71, 108, 113, 330
  Sichuan Province 383–4
  Soviet opposition 396
  Xinjiang Province 41–2
  Yunnan Province 484
  Zhou Enlai and 493
Green Dragons 368
Green Gang 367
Grey, Anthony 51
Guangdong International Trust and
  Investment Corporation (GITIC) 139,
  149, 171
Guangdong Province **166–71**
  see also Hainan Island
'Guangxi Clique' 172, 276–7, 460
Guangxi Zhuang Autonomous Region 91,
  129, **171–4**

Guangxu Emperor 121–2, **174–5**, 194, 251
Guangzhou (Canton) 166–7, 401, 402
Guilin 172, 174
Guizhou Province **175–7**
Gulf War 336, 446
Guling 245
Gyaincain Norbu 327, 435

Hainan Island **178–81**
  corruption 88, 179
  Special Economic Zone 169, 179–81, 399
Hakka ethnic minority 166, 246
Han Dongfang 423
Han population 129–31
  Qinghai Province 351
  Xinjiang Provicne 472
Hankou 208, 209
Hanyeping iron and steel works 208, 209
Harbin 187, 278
Harcourt, Admiral 195
Hart, Robert 417
Hatem, George 140
Hay, John 448
He Jian 218
He Long 219, 379
He Xin 297
He Zhen 29–30
health **181–3**, 311
Heath, Edward 140
Hebei Province **184–6**
  see also Beijing
Hefei, dissidents 31–2
Heihe 189
Heilongjiang Province **186–9**
Henan Province **189–92**, 420
Ho Chi Minh 456
Ho Hau-wah, Edmund 291
Ho, Stanley 290
Hong Kong **193–204**
  APEC membership 37
  Basic Law 199, 202, 203
  Democratic Party 269
  economic development 196–7
  elections 269
  foundation of 193–4
  geography of 196
  governance of 199–202, 327–9, 441
  handover to China 15, 51–2, 110, 198–202,
    241, 268–9, 276, 327–9, 441
  immigrants 196–7
  investment in Mainland 147–8, 168–70,
    200, 323–4
  Joint Declaration (1984) 51–2, 199, 200, 328
  occupation by Britain 49, 193
  Overseas Chinese 323–4
  Special Administrative Region (SAR) 195,
    199, 200, 441

unequal treaties 443
see also Lee, Martin Chu-ming; Patten,
  Chris
Hong Xiuquan 78–9
Hou Dejian 425
household responsibility system 134, 265, 384
Hu Angang 138, 177, 399
Hu Feng 113, 320
Hu Jintao 23, 30, 74, 161, **204–5**
Hu Jiwei 309, 314, 425
Hu Ping 101
Hu Qili 427
Hu Shi 40, **205**, 306–7
Hu Yaobang 66, **206–7**, 487
  death of 14, 239, 423
  democracy and 100, 114, 273, 423
  Deng Xiaoping and 72, 109, 110, 161, 206–7
Hua Guofeng **207–8**
  Communist Party leader 66, 72, 92, 161
  Deng Xiaoping and 109
  Gang of Four and 72, 92, 154, 237, 301, 335
  Hunan Province 219
Huai-Hai, battle of 31, 84, 108, 244
Huang Jinrong 367
Huang Ju 75
Huang Shaohong 460
Huang Shaoxing 172
Huang Xing 217–18, 401, 444
Huang Xuchu 172, 276, 460
Hubei Province **208–12**, 360
Hui ethnic minority 128, 155, 315–17, 350–51,
  357
hukou system (household registration) 27,
  212
human rights **212–16**, 468
  'Bangkok Declaration' 38
  labour camps 263–4
  one-child-policy 342
  policy on 144, 447–8
Hunan Province **217–20**
hutongs 46
Hwang Jang-yop 253
hydro-power 124

Ichang 208
India **221–3**
  border disputes 221, 222
  China's relations with 274–5, 325
  nuclear weapons 325, 332
Indonesia **223–5**
  Overseas Chinese 322, 324
Indonesian Communist Party (PKI) 224
industry **225–9**
  Gansu Province 157
  Hebei Province 186
  Henan Province 190–91
  Hubei Province 210

Jilin Province 249
Liaoning Province 278–9
Pearl River Delta 170
Shaanxi Province 369–70
Shanxi Province 378, 380–81
Tianjin 428–30
Wuhan 208, 209, 210
Xinjiang Province 471
Yunnan Province 484
infant mortality 181
infanticide 214, 343, 464
Inner Mongolia Autonomous Region 129,
  130–31, **229–32**
see also Mongolia
intellectuals
  persecution of 11, 113, 298, 320–21
  protests by 306–7, 423–4
International Monetary Fund 149, 305–6, 446
international trade and investment
  corporations (ITICS) 139, 149
Internet 418–19
Iran, arms sales to 36
Islam 155, 156, 316–17, 357

Japan **233–6**
  Liaoning Province 278–9
  Mongolia 230
  Northern Expedition clashes 318–19
  Second World War 142
  Shandong occupation 141, 234, 318, 371–2,
    449, 460
  Taiwan occupation 135, 151, 404–5
  Twenty-one Demands 141, 234, **442**, 449,
    481
  see also Manchuguo; Sino-Japanese War
Jardine Matheson 49
Jebtsundamba Khutuktu 312
Jiang Chunyun 315, 373
Jiang Kanghu 30
Jiang Qing **237**
  Cultural Revolution 11, 71, 90
  Gang of Four 154–5, 376, 493–4
  Kang Sheng and 250–51
  Mao Zedong and 237, 295
Jiang Zemin 15, 66, 73–4, **238–42**
  army and 338
  leadership of 161
  Li Peng and 274
  on Mao Zedong 297
  United States and 37, 453–4
  Zhu Rongji and 495–6
Jiangsu Province 227, **242–5**
  see also Shanghai
Jiangxi Province **245–8**
  Communist Party activities 67, 246–7,
    283–5
Jilin Province **248–9**

Jinmen Islands 151
Jiu San (Nine-Three) Society 103, 104
Jiujiang 245, 317
Johnston, Reginald 346
Joint Declaration on Hong Kong (1984) 51–2, 199, 200, 328

Kaiping, coal mining 184
Kang Sheng 68, 237, **250–51**, 372, 476–7
Kang Youwei 166, 194, **251**, 401, 444
  and Christianity 311
  Confucianism 86
  One Hundred Days Reform 3, 43, 116, 122, 174–5, 233, 277
Kaohsiung Incident (1979) 60
Karakorum Highway 362, 473
Karmapa Lama 223, 436
Kazakh ethnic minority 357, 470, 471, 472
Kazakhstan 123, 363–4, 365
Kerans, John 29
Kham 351–2
Khampa ethnic minority 383
Khmer Rouge 55
Khrushchev, Nikita 298, 330, 332, 396
Kim Il-Sung 252–3, 254, 407
Kirgiz ethnic minority 357, 364, 470, 471
Kirgizstan, boundary dispute 363–4
Kissinger, Henry 143, 325, 451, 493
Koo Chen-fu 411
Korea **252–4**
  see also North Korea; South Korea
Korean War 10, 84–5, 142, 195, 235, **254–5**, 333, 395, 407, 445, 450
Kumbum 351
Kung Hsiang-hsi 87–8, 259
Kunming 483
Kuomintang **255–62**
  Chiang Kai-shek's leadership 61–3, 158–9, 256–60
  Chinese Communist Party and 62, 65, 83–4, 402
  Civil War 83–5, 259
  corruption 87, 259
  election defeat (2000) 261–2, 271
  government of 158–9
  land reform 264
  Leninist structure 303, 393–4, 408
  media coverage 308
  policies 98
  Revolutionary Committee 103
  rural revolution 25
  'Southern Anhui Incident' 30
  Sun Yat-sen's leadership 65, 393–4, 401–3
  in Taiwan 16, 56–8, 104–6, 135–6, 259–62, 269–71, 408
  taxation 137
  United Nations membership 44

Wang Jingwei and 458
  see also Nationalist Government; Northern Expedition

labour camps 213, **263–4**, 321, 352
land reform 26–7, 69, 134, **264–5**, 344–5
language 118
  bai hua (plain speech) **40–41**
Lanzhou 156–7
law **265–8**
  foreign investments 148
Lee Kuan Yew 385
Lee, Martin Chu-ming 201, 202, **268–9**, 328
Lee Teng-hui 16, **269–71**, 409–16
  Democratic Progressive Party (DPP) 105
  February 28th Incident 136, 409
  Kuomintang leader 255, 260–61
  United States relationship 240–41, 347, 447, 453
Legation Quarter, of Beijing 44, 47–8
Lei Yu 179
Lenin, V.I. 302–3, 393
Li Changchun 75, 171
Li Dazhao **272**, 307
Li Hongzhang 184, 225, 400
Li Hongzhi 360
Li Jie 297
Li Ka-shing 197
Li Lanqing 74, **272**
Li Lisan 66, 295
Li Mi 483
Li Peiyao 335
Li Peng 59, **272–5**
  NPC chairman 315, 422
  policies of 239
  Politburo Standing Committee 73–4, 496
  Tiananmen Square Democracy Movement 273–4, 423
  Zhou Enlai and 273, 492
Li Ruihuan 74, 75, **275–6**, 429
Li Shuxian 426
Li-Yi-Zhe poster 113
Li Yuanhong **276**
Li Zhisui 492
Li Zongren 30, 34, 64, 84, 172, 259, **276–7**, 459
Liang Heng 101, 219–20
Liang Qichao 3, 97–8, 175, 217, 234, **277–8**, 311, 350, 401
Liang Shuming 86
Liang Xiang 179–80
Liao Yaoxiang 52
Liaoning Province **278–82**
Lien Chan 56, 106, 261–2, 271, 414–15
life expectancy 181
Lijiang 485
Lin Biao 91–2, **282**, 397
  army leader 333–4, 379

Civil War 84, 187–8
criticism of 250–51
Cultural Revolution 11, 71
death of 12, 71, 92, 143, 154, 301, 493
Gang of Four and 86
Manchuria 248
Lin Hai 419
Lin Yi-hsiung 105
Lincheng Incident (1923) 41
Little, Archibald 479
Liu Binyan 114, 207, 309
Liu Bocheng 108, 185, 379, 383
Liu Gang 426
Liu, Henry 60, 409
Liu Huaqing 285, 334
Liu Qing 103
Liu Shaoqi 11, 71, 91, 108, 219, **283**, 298, 301
Liu Shifu 29–30
Liu Wenhui 382
Liu Xiang 77, 382
Liu Xiaobo 425
Long March 8, 34, **283–5**, *284*
    Chiang Kai-shek and 62
    Jiangxi Province 247
    Shaanxi Province 67–8, 369, 495
    Zhu De and 494–5
Long Yun 459, 482–3
Loyang Gorge 353
Lu Han 483
Lu Hsiu-lian, Annette 57, 106
Lu Ruihua 171
Lu Xun 40, 118, **285–7**
Lushan 247

Ma Bufang 155, 351
Ma clan 155–6, 315–16
Ma Hongkui 155, 316
Ma Yinchu 164, 340–41
Ma Ying-jeou 57
MacArthur, General Douglas 254
Macau 15, **288–92**, *289*
    Triads 367–8
Major, John 347
Malthus, Thomas 125, 340
Manchu ethnic minority 128
Manchu rule 3–5
Manchukuo 141, 187, 225, 248, 279, **292–4**, *293*, 346, 474
Manchuria
    Civil War 84
    immigration from Shandong 370
    railways 354, 355
    Russian occupation 363
    see also Heilongjiang Province; Jilin Province; Liaoning Province
Mandela, Nelson 416
Mao Yuanxin 280

Mao Zedong **294–302**
    agricultural policy 27, 298, 380
    Communist Party leader 8, 67–8, 303–4
    corruption and 88
    cult of 71, 302
    Dazhai Production Brigade 27, 377, 380
    democracy and 99
    Deng Xiaoping and 108–9
    education policies 118–19
    foreign policy 301
    Hunan Province 218, 295
    Jiang Qing and 237, 295
    Jiangxi Province 246–7
    Kang Sheng and 250–51
    Khrushchev and 396
    Lin Biao and 282
    Marxism of 303–4
    mausoleum 45, 301
    Peng Dehuai and 71, 108, 113, 165, 247, 298, 329–30
    Peng Zhen and 330
    population policy 340–41
    private life 301
    rule of 10–12, 67–71, 161, 297–301
    Soviet Union and 395–6
    swim in Yangtze (1966) 210
    Thoughts of 296, 298, 304
    Vietnam and 456
    Zhou Enlai and 296, 491–2
    Zhu De and 494–5
    see also Cultural Revolution; Great Leap Forward; Long March; One Hundred Flowers Movement
Mao Zhiyong 219
Marco Polo Bridge Incident (1937) 185, 234, 386
Marriage Law (1950) 134, 465–6
Marriage Law (1980) 341
Marshall, George 450
Marxism 6, 98, 141, **302–6**
mass media *see* media
May Fourth Movement (1919) 6, **306–7**
    aims of 44, 98, 141
    bai hua 40, 306
    Chen Duxiu 56, 302
    Confucianism 86
    family reform 133
    Hu Shi 205
    Japanese relations 141, 234
    Li Dazhao 272, 302
    media 308
    religion and 357–8
May Thirtieth Incident (1925) 50, 167, 194, 256, 375
media **307–10**
Mekong basin 485
Miao ethnic minority 172, 175, 217

migration
  rural–urban 28, 32
  see also emigration; Overseas Chinese
military spending 337–8
Ministry of Foreign Economic Relations and
  Trade (MOFERT) 272
Mischief Reef 392–3, 457
Missile Technology Control Regime (MTCR)
  36, 325, 333
missionaries 49, 78–9, **311–12**, 357
  Fujian Province 151
  Henan Province 192
  liberation of women 464–5
  persecution of 47, 217, 311
  Shanxi Province 378
Mongol ethnic minority 229, 312–13
Mongolia 127, 229–30, **312–13**, 394
  see also Inner Mongolia Autonomous
    Region
Mukden Incident (1931) 234, 248, 279, 294
Muslims *see* Islam
Mutual Aid Teams 265

Nanchang Uprising (1927) 246, 331, 494
Nanjie 192
Nanjing
  massacre (1937) 243–4, 386
  Nationalist capital 167, 402–3, 458, 477–8
  Treaty of (1842) 131, 242, 436, 443
Nankai University 117
Nanning 438
National Environmental Protection Agency
  125
National People's Congress (NPC) 76, 100,
  104, 159, 267, 275, **314–15**, 331, 348, 421,
  422
National Revolutionary Army 33–4, 43, 61,
  65, 331, 378–9
National Revolutionary Government 167,
  375–6
Nationalist Government 257
  constitution 163
  legal system 266
  see also Kuomintang
Nationalist Revolution 6–7
NATO
  China's relationship with 364
  Chinese Embassy bombing (1999) 17, 52,
    74, 145, 242, 338, 347, 454, 497
navy 334
'New Democracy' 99, 104, 159
New Fourth Army 30, 387
New Youth magazine 56, 286
newspapers 308–10
Ngabo Ngawang Jigme 432
Nian 370
Nie Rongzhen 185, 332, 379

Ningxia Hui Autonomous Region 129,
  315–17, 357
Nixon, Richard 51, 140, 143, 325, 451, 493
North China's People's Government 379
North Korea 235–6, 249, 252–4
Northern Expedition (1926–8) 256–7, **317–19**,
  318
  Beijing 43, 137
  Chiang Kai-shek and 61, 136–7
  Guangdong Province 167
  Henan Province 190
  Hunan Province 218
  Jiangsu Province 243
  National Revolutionary Army 34, 43, 65
Northern Industries Corporation
  (NORINCO) 37
NPC *see* National People's Congress
Nuclear Non-proliferation Treaty 36, 325, 333
nuclear power 124, 365
nuclear weapons 326, 332–3, 396

oil resources 123, 186, 188, 365
one-child policy 12, 125, 134, 341–3
One Hundred Days Reform (1898) 3, 21, 43,
  116, 122, 174, 251, 277, 348, 480
One Hundred Flowers Movement (1956–7) 11,
  70, 99, 108, 113, 164, **320–21**
One Million Heroes 210
Open Door policy 13, 147, 168, 345, 487
opium 349
Opium Wars 141, 193
orphans 214
Outer Mongolia *see* Mongolia
Overseas Chinese **321–4**, *323*
  Indonesian 223–5, 322
  investments by 147, 323
  South Korea 373

Pakistan 36, 221, 223, **325–6**
Panchen Lama 94, 96, 131, **326–7**, 351, 352,
  430–36
Pao, Y.K. 197
Paracel Islands 16, 392, 405, 457
Patten, Chris 15, 52, 201–2, 269, **327–9**, 441
Pearl River Delta, industrialization 170
peasants, Communist Party and 67
Peng Dehuai **329–30**
  army commander 156, 218, 219
  Great Leap Forward opposition 70–71, 108,
    113, 165, 247, 298, 333
Peng Min-min 105, 271, 405, 412
Peng Pai 67, 167
Peng Zhen 45, 91, 185, 267, 315, **330–31**, 493
People First Party, Taiwan 416
People's Armed Police (PAP) 335
People's Bank of China 139
People's Daily 309

People's Liberation Army Air Force (PLAAF) 337
People's Liberation Army (PLA) 35–6, **331–9**, *336*
  Civil War tactics 84
  corruption 89
  Cultural Revolution 282
  legal immunity 267
  military spending 337–8
  Peng Dehuai 156, 329–30
  power of 160
  Tiananmen Square suppression 14, 36, 46, 112
  Wuhan 210
People's Liberation Army Navy (PLAN) 334
People's Republic of China
  constitution of 163
  foundation of 9, 69, 76
  government of 159–63, *160*
Philippines, relations with 38, 39
Pingxingguan, Battle of 378
pinyin romanization 118
PKI *see* Indonesian Communist Party
PLA *see* People's Liberation Army
Plant, Cornell 479
Pol Pot 55
police 89, 335
Politburo Standing Committee 58–9, 73–4, 461, 463–4, 496
political parties 75–6, *76*, 103–4
political prisoners 213, 263–4, 461–2
pollution 126, 170, 183
Polytechnologies Incorporated 37
population **339–44**, *342*
Portugal, Macau occupation 288–92
poverty **344–5**
  Guizhou Province 176–7
  Qinghai Province 345, 352
power supplies 123
prisoners, political 213, 263–4, 461–2
private enterprise 227, 490
production responsibility system 31
property rights, land 28
Pu Yi **346**
  Forbidden City isolation 5, 43, 136, 251, 350
  Manchuguo puppet ruler 248, 279, 294
putonghua (common speech) 118

Qian Qichen **347**
Qian Xuesen 332
Qiandao Lake affair (1994) 411
Qiao Shi 241, 267, 275, 315, **348**, 422, 461
qigong 357, 360
Qin Bangxian *see* Bo Gu
Qing dynasty 3–5, **348–50**
  communications 417

  education 116, 348
  emigration 321–2
  foreign influences 436–8
  Hong Kong 194
  legal system 265–6, 349
  overthrow of 346, 360–61, 480–81
  railways 184, 350, 354
  secret societies 366–7
  Shanxi Province 378
  trade 146
  see also Boxer rebellion; Empress Dowager; Guangxu Emperor
Qingdao 371, 372
Qinghai Province 345, **350–53**
Qinghua University 117
Qinhuangdao 184, 186
Qinshan 490
Qiu Jin 465, 488
Qu Qiubai 66, 67
Quemoy (Jinmen) 85, 332
Qufu 87

railways **354–6**
  Asia-Europe Land Bridge 245
  Hebei Province 184
  Heilongjiang Province 187
  Henan Province 190
  Hubei Province 209
  Hunan Province 219
  Jiangsu Province 242–3, 245
  Jiangxi Province 247–8
  Mongolia 230
  nationalization 350
  Qing dynasty 184, 350, 354
  Sichuan Province 383
  warlord control 468
  Yunnan Province 484
Rao Shushi 70, 280
realpolitik 144–5
Red Army 34, 295, 332, 494
Red Beards 366
Red China News Agency 309
Red Flag Canal 191–2
Red Guards 45, 71, 90–91, 119, 282, 300, 384
Red Spears 190, 367
Red Star Over China 389, 476
regional administration 162
regional autonomy 18–19
religion **356–60**
  Buddhism 94, 326, 356
  Christianity **78–80**, 192, 311–12, 357
  ethnic minorities 131, 357
  Islam 155, 156, 316–17, 357
  popular 192, 356–7, 367
  see also missionaries
Ren Wanding 103, 113, 426

Republican Revolution (1911) 5, **360–61**
  anarchism 30
  democracy and 98
  education reform 117
  foreign policy 141
  Overseas Chinese role 322
  Qing Dynasty overthrow 346, 350
  secret societies 367
  Sun Yat-sen and 401
  Wuhan 209–10, 276, 350, 360–61
  Yangtze 243
  Yuan Shikai and 480–81
Revive China Society 311, 400–401
rice production 217
Richard, Timothy 311, 378
Rittenberg, Sidney 140
roads **362–3**
Rong Yiren 70, 147
Roosevelt, Franklin 9, 54, 142, 474
rural areas, industrialization 226–7
rural revolution 25–6, 67
Russia (Imperial) **363**
  Heilongjiang Province 186–7
Russian Federation **363–5**
  arms sales to China 364–5
  Heilongjiang Province 189
  relations with China 336
  see also Soviet Union
Russo-Japanese War (1904–5) 233

schistosomiasis (snail fever) 182
Sea Spring Gang 368
Second World War 9, 54, 142, 322, 387–8
secret societies 246, **366–8**
Shaan–Gan–Ning Border Region 67–8, 156,
    316, 369, 379
Shaanxi Province **368–70**
Shamian Island 375
Shandong Province **370–73**
  Boxer Rebellion 47, 371
  Japanese occupation 141, 234, 318, 371–2,
    449, 460
  Weihaiwei 371, 460, **462–3**, 463
Shanghai **373–7**, 478, 480
  British presence 50, 51, 317, 436
  foreign control 373–4, 436–9
  growth of 242
  Northern Expedition 317–18
  occupation by Kuomintang 61
  Pudong Development Zone 245, 377, 480
  secret societies 367, 374
  Wu Bangguo 467–8
  Zhu Rongji 495–6
Shanghai Communiqué 451, 452
Shanghai Shanda University 120
Shantou, Special Economic Zone 168
Shanxi Province **377–81**

Communist Party 68
  industry 225
  Yan Xishan 475–6
Shaoshan 219
Shapiro, Sidney 140
Shashi 208
Sheng Shicai 470
Shenyang 280, 281
  see also Mukden Incident
Shenzhen, Special Economic Zone 168,
    381–2, 398–9
Shi Ming-teh 104, 409
Shijazhuang 184, 185
Shimonosheki, Treaty of (1895) 233, 404, 443
Sichuan Province **382–5**
Sihanouk, King Norodom 55
Simla Conference (1913–14) 431
Singapore **385**
Sino-Japanese War (1937–45) 8–9, 34–5,
    234–5, **385–8**
  air combat 81
  Anhui Province 30, 387
  biological weapons 388
  Chiang Kai-shek's role 62
  Communist bases 67–8, 379
  Gansu Province 156
  Guangxi Province 172
  Guizhou Province 176
  Hainan Island 178
  Hebei Province 185
  Heliongjiang Province 187
  Hong Kong 194–5
  Hunan Province 218
  international interests 142
  Jiangsu Province 243–4
  Kuomintang 258
  Shandong Province 371–2
  Shanghai 375
  Shanxi Province 68, 378–9, 476
  Sichuan Province 382–3
  Soviet intervention 156, 394–5
  United States intervention 258, 387–8,
    399–400, 449–50
  Wuhan 209–10
  Yunnan Province 482–3
Sino-Russian joint declaration (1996) 364
Sino-Soviet split (1958–64) 396, 472
Sino-Soviet Treaty (1945) 394, 474
Sino-Soviet Treaty of Friendship, Alliance
    and Mutual Assistance (1950) 313, 395
Sino-US summits 451
Sino-Vietnamese war (1979) 457, 484
smoking 183
Snow, Edgar **389**, 476
socialism 73, 490–91
Socialist Education Movement 119
Song Jiaoren 5, 98, 255, **389–90**, 444, 481

Song Ping 59
Song Qingling **390**, 391, 403, 466
Song Tzu-wen 87–8, 259
Soong Chu-yu, James 56, 106, 261–2, 271, 414–16
Soong Mei-Ling 63, 258, **390–91**, 449, 465
South China Sea, territorial claims 16, 38–9, 123–4, 144, 180, 336, **391–3**, 392, 457
South East Asian Treaty Organization (SEATO) 55
South Korea 249, 253, 372–3
Southeast Asia, Overseas Chinese 321–4
Soviet Union **393–8**
 border clashes with China 188–9, 397
 collapse of 143, 398
 formation of 141
 industrial model 226
 Kuomintang support 256, 393–4, 402
 Manchuria occupation 279
 military aid from 333
 Mongolia relationship 313
 nuclear weapons 332–3
 relations with China 11, 12, 20, 61, 71, 83, 142, 165
 Sino-Japanese War 156, 394–5
 Sino-Soviet split (1958–64) 396, 472
 Xinjiang influence 470, 472
 Yalta Conference (1945) 474
 see also Russia (Imperial); Russian Federation
space programme 81
Special Administrative Regions (SARs)
 Hong Kong 195, 199, 200, 441
 Macau 288, 289, 291
Special Economic Zones (SEZ) 109–10, 138, 168, **398–9**
 corruption 88
 Hainan 169, 179–81, 399
 Shenzhen **381–2**, 398–9
 Xiamen 152–3
Spratly Islands 16, 39, 144, 392, 405, 457
Stalin, Joseph 298, 450, 469, 474
state-owned enterprises (SOEs) 228, 281–2
Stilwell, Joseph 9, 35, 52, 62, 258, 387–8, **399–400**, 449–50
Straits Crises 410, 412, 450
Straits Exchange Foundation (SEF) 411
students, protests by 207, 219–20, 239, 306, 423, 428
suicide 183
Sukarno, President 223, 224
Sun Chuanfang 317, 488
Sun Liren 52
Sun Yat-sen 4–5, 251, 278, **400–403**
 army and 33
 Christianity 311, 400
 Communist Party and 65, 393–4

 in Guangzhou 166–7
 in Hong Kong 194, 400
 Kuomintang 255–6, 408
 land reform 25, 264
 Northern Expedition 317
 Republican Revolution 360–61, 480–81
 United League 444
 widow of 390, 403
sustainable development 126–7
Suzhou, treaty port 242
Suzhou Industrial Park 245, 385
Szeto Wah 201, 268

Taiping 370
Taiping Rebellion (1850–64) 78–9, 171–2, 357
Taiwan **404–16**, 406
 Confucianism 87
 democracy 415–16
 Democratic Progressive Party (DPP) 56–8, **104–6**, 136, 241, 255, 270–71, 413–16
 diplomatic recognition 416
 divorce 134–5
 economy 414
 elections 105, 409, 413
 energy resources 124
 February Twenty-Eighth Incident (1947) 64, **135–6**, 259, 405–7
 governance 415
 Hong Kong relationship 203–4
 investments in Mainland 148, 152, 323–4
 Japanese occupation 135, 151, 404–5
 Jiang Zemin and 240–41
 Kuomintang 16, 56–8, 104–6, 135–6, 255, 259–62, 269–71, 408
 language 118
 Mainland relationship 15–16, 19, 60–61, 84–5, 144, 152–3, 261, 338, 410–12
 Overseas Chinese 323–4
 People First Party 416
 presidential elections (2000) 56, 58, 106, 261–2, 271, 414–16
 South China Sea claims 391–2, 405
 Straits Crises 410, 412, 450
 United Nations membership 416, 445, 447
 United States relations 10, 64, 105–6, 240–41, 407, 447, 450, 452–3
 see also Lee Teng-hui
Taiwan Democratic Self-Government League 103
Taiwan Independence Party 105
Taiyuan 378, 379–80, 476
Tajikistan, boundary dispute 363–4
Tanaka, Kakuei 493
Tang Fei 57, 106
Tang Jiaxuan 347
Tang Shubei 411
Tangshan, earthquake (1976) 124, 185–6, 429

Tao Sen 101, 219–20
Tao Siju 89
Tao Zhu 219
tariff autonomy 137, 257, **417**
taxation 137
telecommunications **417–19**
telephones 417–18
Tenzin Gyatso (14th Dalai Lama) **94–6**,
    432–6
theatre missile defence (TMD) 145, 236,
    253–4, 336
'Third Line' policy 157, 176, 226
Three Gorges Dam 78, 211–12, 274, 385,
    419–21, *420*, 479
  opposition to 104, 114, 315, 420–21
'Three Self Patriotic Movement' (TSPM) 79,
    312
Tian Jiyun 348, **421–2**
Tiananmen Square 45, **422–3**
Tiananmen Square Democracy Movement
    14, 100, 120, **422–7**
  after effects 427
  casualty figures 425
  causes of 110, 207, 423
  Chen Xitong and 46, 58, 425, 427
  Deng Xiaoping and 110–12, 424, 426–7
  Hong Kong impact 201, 426
  international reactions 347, 426, 451
  Jiang Zemin and 238–9
  Li Peng and 273–4, 423
  media coverage 309, 424, 426
  suppression of 36, 46, 161, 214, 335–6,
    425–6, 477
  Zhao Ziyang and 424, 427, 464, 486–8
Tianjin 184, 186, 275, **428–30**
Tibet 18, 205, **430–36**, *434*
  Dalai Lama **94–6**, 129, 221, 326–7, 351,
    430–36
  ethnic minorities 129, 130–31
  Panchen Lama 94, 96, 131, **326–7**, 351, 352,
    430–36
  religion 357, 360
  Sino-Indian relations 221, 223
  see also Qinghai Province
Tibet Autonomous Region 129
Tong Zhi Emperor 121
topography 2
tourism 485
township and village enterprises (TVEs) 27,
    226–7, 244–5, 280–81, 489
trackers, Yangtze 479
trade
  foreign trade and investment **146–50**, 179,
    227
  tariff autonomy 137, 257, **417**
  unequal treaties 8, 9, 33, 50, 54, 233, 417,
    443

transplants, organs from executions 216
transport *see* civil aviation; railways; roads
treaties, unequal treaties 8, 9, 33, 50, 54, 233,
    417, **443**
treaty ports **436–9**, *437*
  Chongqing 77
  Fujian Province 150
  Hebei Province 184
  industry 225
  Jiangsu Province 242
  Shanghai 436, 438–9
  Tianjin 428
  Yangtze River 208, 478–9
  Zhejiang Province 488
Triads 366, 367–8
Trudeau, Pierre 140
Truman, President 450
Tsong Khapa 326
Tujia ethnic minority 217
Tumen River Economic Zone 249, 253,
    439–40, *440*
Tung Chee-hwa 15, 37, 202, 241, 329, **441**
Tung, C. Y. 197, 441
Twenty-one Demands 141, 234, **442**, 449, 481

Ugyen Trinley Dorje 436
Uigur ethnic minority 128, 130, 131, 357, 364,
    470, 471, 473
Ulanhu (Wulanfu) 230–31
unequal treaties 8, 9, 33, 50, 54, 233, 417, **443**
Ungern-Sternberg, Baron 313
United League (Tongmeng Hui) 4, 25, 166–7,
    255, 367, 389, 401, **444**
United Nations **444–8**
  China's membership 9, 125, 142, 143, 444–8
  human rights concerns 215–16, 268, 447–8
  international women's conference (1995)
    446–7, 467
  Taiwan membership 416, 445, 447
United Nations Development Programme
    (UNDP) 440, 446
United States **448–55**
  arms sales concerns 36–7
  Cairo Conference (1943) 54, 387
  Chinese Civil War 83
  Korean War 84–5, 254–5
  nuclear weapons 332–3
  Open Door policy 448–9
  relations with China 9, 17, 37, 63–4, 143,
    145, 241–2, 347, 448–55, 493, 497
  relations with Taiwan 10, 64, 105–6,
    240–41, 407, 416, 447, 450, 452–3
  Sino-Japanese War 258, 387–8, 399–400,
    449–50
  Taiwan Relations Act (1979) 58, 408, 413,
    452
  trade with China 148

Yalta Conference (1945) 474
universities 117, 483
urban areas
    population 342, *342*, 343
    poverty 344–5
    transport 362–3

Versailles Peace Conference (1919) 141, 306,
    371
Vietnam
    Overseas Chinese 324
    relations with China 158, 174, 398, **456–7**
    Sino-Vietnamese war (1979) 457, 484
    South China Sea claims 391–2, 457
Vietnam War 55
'voluntarism' 67

Wade-Giles romanization 118
Wales, Nym 389
Wan Li 31, 267, 314, 379, 384, 425
Wan Runnan 423
Wan Xueyan 491
Wang Baosen 46, 58
Wang Dan 114–15, 215, 423, 426
Wang Daohan 240
Wang Enmao 472
Wang Hongwen 92, 154–5, 376
Wang Jialie 175
Wang Jingwei 34, 172, 209, 234, 318, 367, **458**
Wang Juntao 114, 115, 423–4, 426
Wang Ming (aka Chen Shaoyu) 66, 68, 295
Wang Ruoshui 309
Wang Ruowang 114, 207, 309
Wang Shan 28
Wang Shaoguang 138
Wang Shiwei 68, 99, 113, 250
Wang Xiaofeng 181
Wang Youcai 491
Wang Yungching 153
Wang Zhen 219, 471
Wanxian 479
warlords 6, 33, **459–60**
    Chongqing 77
    Guangxi Province 172
    Hebei Province 184
    Henan Province 189–90
    Ningxia Province 315–16
    Northern Expedition 317
    Shanxi Province 378, 475–6
    see also 'Anhui Clique'; 'Fengtian Clique';
        'Zhili Clique'
Washington Conference (1921–2) 132, 141,
    234, 371, 449, **460**, 463
Wei Guoqing 173
Wei Jianxing 74, **461**
Wei Jingsheng 13, 72, 102–3, 113, **461–2**
    fifth modernization 45, 99, 150, 461

on Mao Zedong 297
    treatment of 109, 114–15, 215, 263, 352
Wei Tao-ming 136
Weihaiwei 371, 460, **462–3**, *463*
Wen Jiabao **463–4**
wenyan 40
Wenzhou 489–90
'Western' values 38
Whampoa Military Academy 61, 492
White Lotus 370
White Wolf *see* Bai Lang
Wilson, David 201, 328
Winnington, Alan 140
Witke, Roxanne 237
women **464–7**
    education of 45, 311, 465
    employment 466–7
    political activity 465
    position in the family 133
    United Nations conference (1995) 446–7,
        467
Woo, Peter 441
work units *see danwei*
World Bank, Chinese membership 149, 446
World Trade Organization, China's
        membership 17, 139, 145, 149, 228, 242,
        272, 418, 454, 497
Wu, Harry 216, 263, 453, **468**
Wu Bangguo **467–8**
Wu Han 91, 154, 330
Wu Jiaxiang 100
Wu Jie 231
Wu Peifu 136, 184, 190, 209, 218, 317, 460, **468**
Wu Shu-jen 57
Wu Yi 467
Wu Zhifu 191
Wuer Kaixi 423, 426
Wuhan
    Cultural Revolution 210–11
    Hubei Province capital 208–12
    Republican Revolution 209–10, 276, 350,
        360–61

Xiamen
    Special Economic Zone 152–3, 168
    treaty port 150
Xiamen Airlines 152
Xiamen University 151
Xian 368, 369
Xian Feng Emperor 121
Xian Incident (1936) 8, 34, 258, 285, 295, 369,
        469–70, 486
Xiang Zhongfa 66
Xidan, Democracy Wall Movement 45, 102
Xie Fei 171
Xikang Province 382
Xinhua News Agency 309

Xinjiang Production and Construction
Corps 471
Xinjiang Uigur Autonomous Region 129,
143–4, **470–73**
ethnic minorities 127, 128, 129, 130–31, 357,
470
Russian influence 363–4
xitongs 159
Xu Jiatun 201
Xu Kuangdi 75
Xu Wenli 103, 113, 115
Xu Xiangqian 190

Yakub Beg 470
Yalta Conference (1945) 187, 279, 313, 394,
450, **474**
Yan Fu 3, **475**
Yan Xishan 225, 319, 378–80, 459, 460, **475–6**
Yanan **476–7**
Communist Party 68, 156, 369, 476
Shaan–Gan–Ning Border Region 156, 316,
369
Yang Baibing 240, 336, 477
Yang Shangkun 240, 336, 379, **477**
Yang, Sir T.L. 441
Yangpu Economic Development Area 180,
181
Yangtze River **477–80**, *478*
Amethyst Incident (1940) **29**, 50, 244,
479
Anhui Province **30–32**
bridges 362, 479
gorges 210
Hubei Province 208
Hunan Province 220
Jiangsu Province 242
Jiangxi Province 245
Mao's swim in 210
Republican Revolution 243
see also Three Gorges Dam
Yantai (Chefoo) 372
Yao ethnic minority 172
Yao Wenyuan 154–5, 376
Yao Yilin 59
Ye Jianying 410
Yellow River
Henan Province 189, 190, 191
Ningxia Province 316
Yeltsin, Boris 364, 398
Yen Chia-kan 60
Yi Guan Dao 367
Young, Mark 199
Younghusband, Francis 430
Yu Xian 371, 378
Yu Zuomin 429–30
Yuan Shikai 5–6, 43, 243, 371, 401–2, **480–82**
Beiyang Army commander 33, 184, 480

finances of 137
imperial restoration attempt 276, 278, 346,
350, 361, 481
Kuomintang and 255
Mongolia 312–13
Song Jiaoren and 389–90
Tianjin reforms 428
Yunnan Province **482–5**

Zeltuga, Republic of 366
Zeng Guofan 217, 225
Zeng Qinghong 75
Zhang Chunqiao 154–5, 376
Zhang Guotao 156, 190, 285, 494–5
Zhang Wentian 66
Zhang Xianliang 316–17
Zhang Xueliang 8, 34, 62, 248, 279, 294, 460,
469, **486**
Zhang Xun 43, 251, 276, 346, 350
Zhang Zhenglong 248
Zhang Zhidong 208–9, 217, 225
Zhang Zuolin 136, 248, 279, 317, 319, 460
Zhangjiagang 245
Zhao Ziyang 66, **486–8**
coastal development strategy 152, 168, 179,
372, 487
Deng Xiaoping and 72, 109, 110, 161, 239,
487–8
Li Peng and 273, 274
production responsibility system 31
Sichuan governor 384, 487
Tiananmen Square Democracy Movement
14, 424, 427, 464, 486–8
Zhejiang Province 227, **488–91**
Zhenbao Island 188, 397
Zheng He 334
Zheng Yi 173
Zhengzhou 190
Zhenjiang 242
Zhi Gong Dang (Public Interest Party) 103
Zhili 184
'Zhili Clique' 30, 184, 276, 460, 468, 488
Zhou Beifang 89
Zhou Duo 425
Zhou Enlai 42, 71, 86, 92, 142, **491–4**
Geneva Conference (1954) 157–8
Li Peng adoption 273, 492
Mao Zedong and 296, 491–2
Zhou Guanwu 89
Zhou Nan 201
Zhu De 246, 329, 482, **494–5**
Zhu Rongji 102, 139, 170–71, 274, **495–7**
Zhu Senlin 171
Zhuang ethnic minority 128, 171, 172–3
Zhuhai, Special Economic Zone 168
Zunyi, Chinese Communist Party 176
Zuo Zongtang 155